C000205680

The Combat History of the

23RD PANZER DIVISION

IN WORLD WAR II

0 11557 01086 2

The Combat History of the
23RD PANZER DIVISION
IN WORLD WAR II

+ ERNST REBENTISCH +

STACKPOLE
BOOKS

Published in paperback in 2012 by
STACKPOLE BOOKS
5067 Ritter Road
Mechanicsburg, PA 17055
www.stackpolebooks.com

Cover design by Wendy A. Reynolds

Printed in the United States of America

10 9 8 7 6 5 4 3 2 1

Library of Congress Cataloging-in-Publication Data

Rebentisch, Ernst.
The combat history of the 23rd Panzer Division in World War II / Ernst Rebentisch.
p. cm.
Originally published: To the Caucasus and the Austrian Alps. J. J. Fedorowicz Pub., 2009
Includes bibliographical references.
ISBN 978-0-8117-1086-2
1. Germany. Heer. Panzer-Division, 23. 2. World War, 1939–1945—Campaigns—Eastern Front. 3. World War, 1939–1945—Tank warfare. 4. World War, 1939–1945—Regimental histories—Germany. I. Title. II. Title: To the Caucasus and the Austrian Alps.
D757.5623rd .R42 2012
940.54'1343—dc23

2011052611

Contents

APPENDICES

Foreword

The author over the war years: As a Hauptmann in March 1943 and as a Major in August 1944. Note the numbered tank assault badge that the experienced armor commander wears in the latter image.

As I present this history of the *23. Panzer-Division* to my former comrades and to the public, I do so after having examined all of the sources available to me up to the time of publication. Among those sources were daily logs and fragments of the same for elements of the entire division, as well as the division itself. In addition, there were statistical documents from the federal Archives in Koblenz, the casualty lists prepared by the German Red Cross and the federal government, after-action reports concerning the fighting and personal reminiscences. A number of details were clarified as the result of inquiries. An overview of the development of the "big picture" was provided by works already published concerning the Second World War. The photographic portions of the book were made possible by the use of numerous photographs coming from the private possession of former members of the division and, for the English edition, additional images provided by private individuals in Germany.

The objective of my work was and is to portray the formation, the history and the end of one of the "young" armored divisions of the German Army in World War 2, based on well-researched military history, and to demonstrate how the division performed its duty, in both good times and bad.

I am well aware that there can never be a complete portrayal of all of the events, especially the experiences and deeds of the smaller units and the individual men. No unit daily logs keep a record of such things. Many individual details have been lost to memory over the years or can only be reconstructed in outline form. Names have been forgotten by those who have survived, so that it was difficult to decide how the names of individuals who became identified should be handled and to what extent. In the desire to reawaken sleeping memories, I have named men who stepped into the spotlight as the result of special events or through the nature or significance of their missions as part of a larger whole.

The majority of the daily logs of the division and its individual troop elements, together with their valuable individual notations and map entries, remained unavailable to me, since they were destroyed at the end of the war or—in the case of the volumes already archived during the war—were removed by the victors as spoils of war and have not yet been returned.

The opportunity to properly praise the rear-area services and logistics personnel of the division, whose performance of duty was perforce overshadowed by the combat operations, has been especially hampered by a lack of documentation. No combat-arms soldier can ever forget, however, that he owes the maintenance of his ability to resist to just those duty-conscious and brave men who performed their duties quietly, with never-ending industriousness and frequently with weapon in hand. The field cook, the rations runner, the driver of a fuel or ammunition truck, the medic with whom the front-line soldier had direct daily contact; the maintenance teams, the medical companies, the ambulance platoons, the logistics columns, the maintenance companies, the bakery and butcher company—they all kept alive the thought in the soldier in the main line of resistance that he was only that part of a large entity that happened to be in direct contact with the enemy.

The field post of the division may not be forgotten either. It always ensured that contact with the homeland was never broken. The field post always let the soldiers know and recognize exactly why they had to undergo the difficult and deprivation-filled struggles along the Eastern Front.

If the thoughts of the reader turn to past times, experiences and thoughts of former comrades, then this book will have served its purpose.

At this point, I would like to thank all of the comrades who provided me or the *23. Panzer-Division* organization with accounts, maps and pictures and who helped clarify individual events and close gaps in narratives. In particular, I would like to thank *Generalmajor a.D.* Werner-Ehrenfeucht, the former commander of *Panzer-Regiment 201*, who helped me considerably in his tireless support in assembling documents, so that this book could appear. Finally, my thanks are extended to the veterans' organization of the *23. Panzer-Division*, the design team at Herzog and the printer, Harald Boldt, who enabled the printing and production of the commemorative work.

Ernst Rebentisch
Garmisch-Partenkirchen, Easter 1963

Publishers' Acknowledgments

Thanks to Mike Olive for his laying out of the book and to Bob Edwards for his usual precise translation. This was their last project together for J.J. Fedorowicz Publishing, and it certainly allows them to leave on a high note.

I also wish to thank Generalleutnant a.D. Dr. Ernst Rebentisch for writing one of the best divisional histories to come out of the German side of World War II. Beside agreeing to our many requests for additionl information and details, he also provided personal photographs not available in the German edition and proofed the English text for accuracy.

One again, Shawn Biettner has provided a tremendous service in fact-checking the book as well.

I am also indebted to you, the reader, for purchasing this book and all of you who have written me with kind words of praise and encouragement. It gives me the impetus to continue translating the best available German-language books and produce original titles. Our listing of books published is on the page iii and can be viewed on our web site at *www.jjfpub.mb.ca.* Many of these are due to your helpful proposals.

I look forward to your continued comments and constructive criticism.

John Fedorowicz

Editors' Remarks

When translating German military terminology, modern American Army terminology is generally used wherever an equivalent term is applicable. In cases where there may be nuances where we think the reader might enjoy learning the German term, we have included it parenthetically.

In cases where the German term is commonly understood or there is no good, direct English equivalent, we have tended to retain the German term, e.g., Schwerpunkt (point of main effort), Auftragstaktik (mission-type orders) etc. We have also retained German practise in unit designations, e.g., the 8./SS-Panzer-Regiment 1 means the Eighth Company of the 1st SS Armored Regiment. Arabic numerals indicate companies or company-sized units (e.g., batteries or troops) and Roman numerals represent battalions (or battalion-equivalents) within a brigade or regiment.

In an attempt to highlight the specific German terminology, we have italicized German-language terms and expressions. Since most of the terms are repeated several times, we have not included a glossary. Since we assume the reader will already have a basic understanding of German terminology used for vehicles, we have likewise not included any separate annexes to the book to explain them.

The History of the 23. Panzer-Division

The Establishment of the 23. Panzer-Division

The campaigns in Poland, France and the Balkans had captured the attention of the world. In lightning campaigns, the field armies of those states had been overrun and forced into capitulation. A new type of breakthrough strategy had tossed the traditional fundamentals of warfare, inherited from the 1st World War, overboard and made armored formations the lead agents of an attack, which captured terrain and demoralized the enemy.

These successes served to justify a few far-sighted officers, who had recognized the opportunities early on within the technical arena and in the properties of the German soldier and who had defended their ideas against the resistance of a conservative-thinking military. Finally, in 1939 and 1940, they were afforded the opportunity in the operations conducted then to turn their theories into practice. The armored force—the *Panzertruppe*—along with the motorized and mechanized infantry, as well as the other branches of service that fought with them, initiated a chain of victories that seemed unstoppable. In the end, the *Panzertruppe* formed an impression of the entire war for both sides.

As the prospects of a rapid end to hostilities dwindled, the German armed forces received new missions, especially after the signs of an impending conflict with Bolshevism became ever clearer. Those missions could only be accomplished by increasing the number of combat formations, primarily armored and motorized formations.

The original 3 armored, 3 light and 4 motorized divisions that had been created in 1936 increased to 10 armored and 5 motorized infantry division by the time of the Campaign in the West in 1940. In the years of warfare that followed, their number increased considerably. The army reorganized several battle-tested formations—for example, the conversion of the *1. Kavallerie-Division* to the *24. Panzer-Division*—or it assembled troop elements from far and wide into divisions, such as what occurred with the *22. Panzer-Division*, the *23. Panzer-Division* and the *25. Panzer-Division*.

The 1st of October 1941 is the "birthday" for the *23. Panzer-Division*. It activation was started in the area around Paris under the auspices of the Commander-in-Chief West.

The troop elements, companies, cadres and individual soldiers came from practically all of the military districts and regions of the *Reich* to form the new division. A large contingent of cadre personnel came from elements stationed in the region of Baden-Wurttemberg. That, coupled with the fact that most of the later recruiting for the division came from replacement detachments in Military District V (Stuttgart), led to the division being known in the history of the German armed forces of the Second World War as the

23. württembergisch-badische Panzer-Division.[1]

The first commander of the division was *Generalmajor* Hans *Freiherr* von Boineburg-Lengsfeld,[2] an experienced officer, who had previously commanded *Schützen-Regiment 1* of the *1. Panzer-Division* and *Schützen-Brigade 7* of the *7. Panzer-Division*. Assigned to his headquarters, which was formed from the former *Panzer-Brigade 101*, were the following troop elements:[3]

Panzer-Regiment 201[4]
Headquarters, *Schützen-Brigade 23*
Schützen-Regiment 126
Schützen-Regiment 128
Panzer-Artillerie-Regiment 128
Kradschützen-Bataillon 23
Panzer-Pionier-Bataillon 51
Panzerjäger-Abteilung 128
Panzer-Nachrichten-Abteilung 128
Division Support:
Divisions-Nachschubtruppen 128
Sanitätstruppen 128
Werkstatt-Kompanie 128
Bäckerei-Kompanie 128
Schlächterei-Kompanie 128
Divisions-Verpflegungsamt 128
Feldpostamt 128
Divisionskartenstelle 128
Feldgendarmerietrupp 128[5]

Complete troop elements with peacetime training but with differing frontline experience formed the backbone of the division. A few of the formations had already had combat experience in Russia and came directly from frontline operations to the newly forming division. The division was then filled with personnel detailed from a wide variety of formations from within the replacement army. That was especially true in the case of the motorized rifle regiments, where small cadres from battle-tested rifle companies had to be formed into a cohesive whole of battle-ready combat forces with infantry units and combat-inexperienced personnel from the replacement army.

General von Boineburg's mission was to bring together the newly created elements within the shortest time possible and then, in the short time remaining, to forge them into a powerful large-scale formation together with the other forces of the division. It would only be after that had been accomplished that the *23. Panzer-Division* would be in a position to manage its growing combat missions on the Eastern Front.

The German Army High Command had dictated that the division was to be ready for combat employment by the beginning of March 1942.

Formation and Training in France

While the personnel cadres assembled in the area around Paris, major items of equipment began to be issued. The heavy weapons and the majority of the hand-held weapons were of German manufacture, as were the armored vehicles. The wheeled vehicles—motorcycles, staff cars, light and heavy trucks and special-purpose vehicles—primarily came from French firms. Names such as Gnome-Rhone, Laffly, Peugeot, Citroen, Renault and Berliet were encountered and became etched into the memories of all of the soldiers of the division, since they were far inferior to the German

1 Translator's Note: The 23rd Armored Division of Baden-Wurttemberg.

2 Translator's Note: *Freiherr* is a title of nobility, equating to baron.

3 Additional information on the individual formations is provided in the appendices.

4 Translator's Note: Hereafter referred to as *PR201*; the infantry regiments as *SR126* and *SR128*; the divisional artillery as *PAR128*; the motorcycle battalion as *KB23*; the engineers as *PPB51*; the antitank battalion as *PJA128*; and the signals battalion as *PNA128*, except when confusion would result.

5 Translator's Note: The support elements, in order: Division Support Command 128; Medical Detachment 128; Maintenance Company 128; Bakery Company 128; Butcher Company 128; Division Rations Section 128; Field Post Office 128; Division map Section 128; and Military Police Detachment 128.

Panzer-Abteilung 301, which was one of several battalions that eventually provided much of the cadre for the formation of the division's *Panzer-Regiment 201*, started forming in 15 January 1941. Like all of the armored formations activated in France at the time, it was initially equipped with captured French tanks and other armored fighting vehicles. The initial picture of this series shows the first unit formation of the battalion. None of the vehicles had radios, so hand and arm signals had to be used for movement and control. Opposite page top: The comany commander's tank and the tanks of the platoon leaders were all Somua 35's, while the remaining tanks were Hotchkiss 38's.

The first field trials with the French tanks, in this instance Hotchkiss model 39. The main gun is a 37mm L/33.

On 11 February of that year, *Generalfeldmarschall* von Brauchitsch, the Commander-in-Chief of the German Army, visited the battalion to check on its status. Reporting to the field marshall is the battalion commander, *Major* Mildebrath. Behind him is *Oberst* Werner-Ehrenfeucht, the commander of *Panzer-Regiment 201*, which would soon consolidate this battalion into its ranks. Also present are *Hauptmann* Stiewe, the commander of the *2./Panzer-Abteilung 301*, and *Leutnant* Reinicke.

Caserne Mortier (Paris), the garrison for the fledgling *PR 201*.

One of the Hotchkiss issued to the regiment.

Panzer-Regiment 201 started forming in 1941 in the *Caserne Mortier* near Paris and Versailles. It was originally equipped with stocks of captured French equipment, wheeled vehicles and armored fighting vehicles, such as this Somua S-35. *Generalfeldmarschall* von Brauchitsch, the Commander-in-Chief of the German Army visited the *II./PR 201* during this period, while the regiment was still practising for the planned invasion of Gibraltar. This series of photographs within the walls of the garrison show differing aspects of the Commander-in-Chief's visit.

Officers and noncommissioned officers prepared to brief the high-ranking visitor.

It would appear that some sort of marksmanship training, perhaps with tank machine guns, was conducted for the benefit of the Field Marshall.

Prior to joining the division, the regiment was assigned to *Panzer-Brigade 100*, which it officially joined on 5 March 1941. These images mark the occasion of the change of senior command. The regimental commander, *Oberst* Werner-Ehrenfeucht, is seen entering the gates of the former French garrison, flanked by *Oberleutnant* Lossen, his adjutant, and the regimental liaison officer, *Leutnant* Rebentisch. The commander of the *I./PR 201*, *Major* von Heydebreck, reports to the regimental commander and discusses matters with him in front of his assembled battalion.

Leutnant Grahn of the *3./PR 201*.

Major von Heydebreck addresses the assembled *I./PR 201*. With him is *Leutnant* Krämer.

Leutnant Grahn makes his way out of the Officers' Club.

Members of the regimental headquarters (from left to right): *Oberleutnant* Lossen, *Major* Rothbarth (the regimental engineer), *Leutnant* Rebentisch and *Leutnant* Hensel (regimental weapons officers).

Other officers enjoying their meal:(left to right): *Leutnant* Andersen and *Zahlmeister* Panthen .

Departing thee Officers' Club after a luncheon is *Leutnant* Rebentisch, smiling and carrying his evening provisions.

Oberleutnant Ott shares a laugh with his comrades. *Leutnant* Reuther and *Leutnant* Grahn are on the right.

The brigade commander conducts a pass-in-review with the regimental and battalion commanders.

Leutnant Rebentisch, *Hauptmann* Pfaff and *Leutnant* Grahn do some sightseeing in Versailles.

The *7./PR 201* of *Oberleutnant* Ott conducted gunnery training. The S-35 was an excellent vehicle in its day and was a very good training vehicle. By 1942, however, its combat capabilities were totally inadequate.

111

The gunnery training receives its share of visitors.

More visitors, of the higher ranking variety, at gunnery training.

Commander's Call before a company exercise. (May 1941)

Two views of Mailly le Camp in the summer of 1941, when the fledgling *23. Panzer-Division* started formation training there.

Oberstleutnant Kelpe served as the commander of the *II./PR 201* for a while.

Oberleutnant Tritschler and *Oberleutnant* Stiewe of the *6./PR 201.*

Oberleutnant Fechner, the commander of the *3./Panzer-Abteilung 301* and, upon consolidation, the *5./PR 201.*

Leutnant Schewe and Tritschler.

Tritschler and Stiewe with *Luftwaffe* personnel.

The regiment's light platoon undergoes training at Mailly Le Camp in June 1941.

Leutnant Rebentisch in conversation with *Oberleutnant* Burmester, the regiment's Signals Officer and the commander of the Headquarters Company, along with the company First Sergeant, *Hauptfeldwebel* Meiners.

Oberfeldwebel Schmitdinger, *Leutnant* Rebentisch's Platoon Sergeant.

Leutnant Rebentisch gives *Gefreiter* Schid some instructions.

A French Somua pulls duty as a regimental command and control tank.

Gunnery training continued through much of the summer at Mailly Le Camp.

The light platoon of the regiment being briefed.

Preparations for gunnery training.

Leutnant Rebentisch's tank.

Another image of the range firing.

The range safety officer issues instructions.

The officer corps of *Panzer-Regiment 201* in Paris in April 1941.

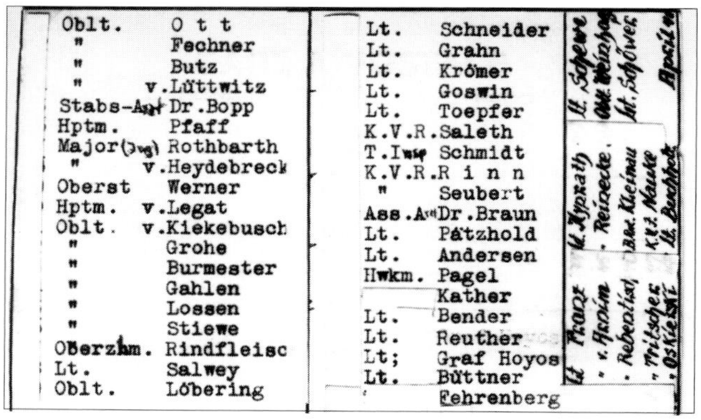

Oblt.	O t t	Lt.	Schneider
"	Fechner	Lt.	Grahn
"	Butz	Lt.	Krömer
"	v. Lüttwitz	Lt.	Goswin
Stabs-Arzt	Dr. Bopp	Lt.	Toepfer
Hptm.	Pfaff	K.V.R.	Saleth
Major(Ing)	Rothbarth	T.Insp	Schmidt
"	v. Heydebreck	K.V.R.	R i n n
Oberst	Werner	"	Seubert
Hptm.	v. Legat	Ass.Arzt	Dr. Braun
Oblt.	v. Kiekebusch	Lt.	Pätzhold
"	Grohe	Lt.	Andersen
"	Burmester	Hwkm.	Pagel
"	Gahlen		Kather
"	Lossen	Lt.	Bender
"	Stiewe	Lt.	Reuther
Oberzhm.	Rindfleisc	Lt;	Graf Hoyos
Lt.	Salwey	Lt.	Büttner
Oblt.	Löbering		Ehrenberg

Oberstleutnant Kelpe and *Leutnant* Grahn pay a courtesy call on naval personnel while the division was assigned security duties in the Quimyer area of the Bretagne.

The regiment finally gets issued German tanks. The regiment commander's tank and crew (from the right): *Oberleutnant* Burmester, *Oberst* Werner-Ehrenfeucht, *Unteroffizier* Meyer, *Oberfunkmeister* Schündel and *Unteroffizier* Schuh.

After the regiment was issued German tanks, it departed for the Jura Mountains in February 1942 for training.

Finally, some up-to-date equipment for the *Panzer III Ausf. J* with the L/60 50 mm main gun, capable of knocking out a T34 - at close range.

Oberleutnant Ott, who was killed on 30 June 1942, can be seen on the skis.

The winter training at Le Valdehon.

The officer corps of *Panzer-Regiment 201* in March 1942.

Oberst Werner-Ehrenfeucht, the "father" of the tank regiment.

Awaiting the train to Kharkov.

The headquarters building of *PAR 128* in Paris.

Personnel of *PAR 128* start boarding trains for the journey east.

Oberst von Buch, the Divisional Artillery Officer and Commander of *PAR 128*, talks to his officers prior to their rail transport to Kharkow.

Elements of the regiment move out to Kharkov at the beginning of March 1942.

Bad luck during the load out. An incident like this normally required a crane to be brought in to lift the entire tank and reposition it.

The endless stream of troop trains to the insatiable Eastern Front.

The railhead at Kharkov: *A Panzer III* detrains.

Kharkov's famous "Red Square".

Kharkov was one of of the Soviet Union's major cities, an important industrial center and transport hub. It changed hands several times, finally being re-captured for the final time by the Soviets in August 1943.

"Under new management."

The calm before the storm...the division enjoys a few days of quiet in Kharkov before it begins its initial operations.

These party functionaries have been decapitated by angry Ukrainians, if only in the form of statues.

The impressive Kharkov Tractor Works, the temporary home of the regiment.

A reminder of the "good old days" and the eating area for the companies. Antiarmor training is conducted for infantry and the place of much business for the *1./ PR 201*, conveniently separated by rank.

Providing antitank training for the infantry.

Peasant hut in the Ukraine.

equipment in the Soviet Union and the procurement of any and all spare parts became a big problem for the division. Only a small portion of the tactical vehicles were of German production; these included Mercedes and Steyr, as well as the special-purpose vehicles of the division's signals battalion. But it took weeks and months before the final items of equipment arrived; this was especially true in the case of the artillery pieces and the motor vehicles. In order to conduct training, it was often necessary to rotate equipment among the troop elements.

In spite of the difficulties associated with becoming trained on the equipment, training made progress. While the rifle regiments saw squad and platoon training transition to company-level exercises, other elements of the division were already conducting large-scale exercises in the Champagne region, in the Ile de France, south of the Loire near Tours and in the French Jura Range.

Movement training alternated with live-fire exercises. In the Sissonne area, rifle battalions, the 3rd Battalion of the tank regiment and the artillery regiment's 2nd Battalion conducted combined-arms exercises. In La Valdahon, the tank regiment (minus its 3rd Battalion) and the artillery regiment's 3rd (Heavy) Battalion conducted combined live-fire exercises. The snow, which was almost a meter deep, provided a foretaste of what was to come in Russia. At the same time, a winter-fighting course was conducted by the division at Le Valdahon. The engineer battalion's bridging column practiced with its new equipment. The division signals battalion conducted radio exercises, while the rear-area services practiced loading plans and standard operating procedures. The antitank battalion and the motorcycle battalion conducted gunnery and battalion-level exercises, which were concluded at the training areas in the Champagne region.

Map and staff exercises of combined-arm formations required the commanders and officers to become acquainted with one another and practiced command and control. The 1st Battalion of *SR126*, which was outfitted with *Schützenpanzerwagen*,[6] and the 1st Battalion of the artillery regiment were schooled in working closely with the division's tank regiment.

The months of January and February 1942 flew past. Logistical difficulties with regard to ammunition and fuel caused delays in training, but they were overcome with all sorts of improvisation. The training of the division was brought to a close to a acceptable standard in accordance with its orders.

At the beginning of March 1942, the warning orders concerning the movement of the division to the Eastern Front arrived. A few days later, the advance parties and billeting personnel were already *en route* via rail. The division's soldiers did not know where this journey at the start of spring would lead. They only knew that they would experience the ebb of a Russian winter on the Eastern Front. Apparently, the enemy knew more about the division's area of operations than its own personnel: The rail transports were greeted with flybills in the Vinnitza area, announcing the railhead as Kharkov.

The Battle for Kharkov 12-29 May 1942

The winter of 1941/1942 was coming to an end. The reversals at Moscow and Rostov had followed the impetuous German advance of the summer and fall months of the previous year. Winter was spent by the German and allied forces defending the areas that had been taken. The frontage of *Heeresgruppe Süd* ran from Taganrog to the north along the west bank of the Mius, where it ran into the Donez. It then continued along its southern and western banks as far as Belgorod, where it ran into the friendly forces to the north, *Heeresgruppe Mitte*, north of Kursk. German infantry held a large bridgehead across the Donez to the East in the bend of the river between Balakleja and Tschugujew, although Soviet forces had succeeded in making a deep penetration as far as Losowaja, further to the south, in January 1942.

Hitler's intent was to bring final victory over the Red Army in 1942. The Soviet command, for its part, mobilized all available forces to brace itself against the German armed forces while, at the same time, sought good jumping-off points for offensive operations.

The pivot point on the southern front for the operational thinking on both sides was the city of Kharkov. The good lines of communication to the west and southwest made it easier for the German command to prepare its offensive, secure its supply lines and bring up new forces and materiel. For the Red Army, the possession of Kharkov was not only important psychologically, it provided the Soviets with a jumping-off point, from which a thrust to the southwest would bring the entire German front in the Donez Basin to collapse.

In the area around Kharkov in March 1942, the Soviet forces of Marshal Timoschenko faced off against the *6. Armee* of *General der Infanterie* Paulus, which consisted of the *VIII. Armee-Korps*, the *LI. Armee-Korps* and the *XVII. Armee-Korps*. Under the protection offered by the infantry divisions, which had been in uninterrupted combat in the front lines for months on end and had been severely weakened—not to mention that they also had large sections of frontage to defend—the armored and motorized infantry divisions began their approach march. In March and April 1942, the *23. Panzer-Division* was moved in by rail from its areas of activation around Paris.

The division headquarters, the headquarters of the motorized rifle brigade, elements of the divisional artillery, the 3rd (*SPW*) Company of the divisional engineers, the bridging column, the signals battalion and the divisional logistics elements were billeted in Kharkov and its suburbs. The tank regiment was billeted in the tractor works at Lossewo. *SR126* was dispatched to Merefa and Ostro-Werchowka, while *SR128* was temporarily housed in the Lossewo tractor works and at Roganj. The latter regiment was later moved to Besljudowka. Elements of the divisional artillery were in both Besljudowka and Nowo-Bavaria.[7] The antitank battalion was initially billeted in Gawrilowka, 18 kilometers west of Kharkov, only to be moved later to Wyssokij. The motorcycle battalion set up operations west of Kharkov.

Individual battalions of both *SR126* (*Oberst* Kieler) and *SR128* (*Oberstleutnant* Bachmann) were soon detailed to front-line divisions and employed to relieve the fought-out and overextended infantry. The *I./SR126* relieved elements of the *71. Infanterie-Division* in the Wiknina area, to the east of Kharkov. A few days later, the regiment's 2nd battalion relieved other elements of the *71. Infanterie-Division* in the front lines at Kupjewacha. The nighttime cold and the onset of soupy mud during the day gave the riflemen a foretaste of their coming operations in Russia. Training was continued right next to the enemy positions but, with the arrival of the first casualties, the fact was brought home that the enemy in the trenches facing the German positions was always on alert. On 17 April, the *II./SR128* returned to division control; it was followed by the 1st Battalion on 30 April. The regiment's troops were billeted in Besljudowka, while the 1st battalion was in Wassischtschewo and the 2nd Battalion in Lisoglubowka, Ternowoje and Schmarowka.

At the beginning of April, the 3rd (Heavy) Battalion of the divisional artillery (*Oberst* Büscher) was employed in the front east of Kharkov to reinforce the artillery in position there. While there, the guns of the 3rd Battalion found ample opportunity to make up for the gunnery exercises they missed in France that they did not have time to complete after their re-equipping.

6 *Schützenpanzerwagen* = armored personnel carriers, hereafter referred to in its standard German abbreviation of *SPW*.

7 Nowo Bavaria ("New Bavaria") was an ethnic German enclave in the Soviet Union.

The remaining elements of the division were designated as a ready reserve for *Heeresgruppe Süd* and continued the training that had been started in France to shape the formations into cohesive wholes. An antitank course, sponsored by the engineers and supported by the tank regiment's 1st Company, was held, as were gunnery exercises, field training and map exercises. The 2nd Medical Company established the *Ortslazarett West* ("Local Military Hospital—West"), which was primarily founded to care for the wounded and sick of the division, but it also provided services to another division. Some soldiers will recall with a debt of gratitude the help and care they received there from the Russian nurses. The division post office, under Postmaster Weiß, ensured that contact was quickly established with the field-army's postal system.

The formations that arrived until the end of March 1942 were placed under temporary alert conditions, but that status was quickly lifted, since the anticipated Soviet offensive did not materialize. The Russian plans also appeared to be disrupted by the weather. The spring thaw started practically overnight; the seemingly bottomless mud of the Ukraine prohibited any and all troop movements. Everything sank in the soupy mud. It was only possible to move on the few improved roads; but they were to be found only in the vicinity of the larger cities.

Even the all-wheel-drive vehicles, the light *Volkswagen* staff cars and the *SPW's* with their half-track drive had great difficulties. Not a few tanks and prime movers got stuck. During the night, the temperature dropped to well below freezing. The soupy mud turned into a crust of ice, which covered the unprotected tracks and wheels so thoroughly that it had to be broken free with blowtorches and bars the next day.

At the end of April, the mud yielded to the rays of the sun. The front started to become unsettled. Soviet fighters and ground-support aircraft—above all, *IL-2's* and American Airacobras—appeared above Kharkov and dove on anything that moved on the ground. While the *Luftwaffe* held back or was not even present, the enemy attacks increased daily. The tension among both leadership and forces on the ground increased.

At the start of 12 May 1942, the Russian offensive broke loose at first light. From the very beginning, two main efforts could be identified, which attempted to envelop and take Kharkov. The northern pincers came from the Woltschansk area and moved directly to the west and the northern part of the city. The southern arm moved out of the area of the bend in the Donez and south of Merefa. It headed northwest to initially interdict the Kharkov—Dnjepropetrowsk rail line and then the Kharkov—Poltava rail line.

To the north, the enemy forced the German infantry back across the Babka and committed masses of armor and infantry in the gaps in the front that were growing ever larger.

Baptism of Fire Northeast of Kharkov

At 0730 hours on 12 May, the division was alerted by the headquarters of the *6. Armee* and placed under the command and control of the *LI. Armee-Korps* of *Generalleutnant* von Seydlitz. In the hours that followed, enemy intelligence was received and the division received orders. Its mission:

No later than the afternoon of 12 May, the main body [of the division] is to reach the Kamenaja-Jaruga — Saroshnoje area and prepare to launch an attack to the northeast on 13 May by means of a massed thrust into the flank of the enemy advancing west and throw him back over the Donez.

Kradschützen-Bataillon 23 screened the assembly area of the division in a general line Saroshnoje — 206.2 — collective farm 3 kilometers northeast of Priwolje.

Schützen-Regiment 128 initially remains at the disposal of the *6. Armee* in the Besljudkowka area.

Panzerjäger-Abteilung 128 is attached to the *VIII. Armee-Korps* for operations in the Merefa area; in its place, *Panzerjäger-Abteilung 171* [*71. Infanterie-Division*] is attached to the *23. Panzer-Division*.

The division moved out from the tractor works at Lossewo at 1430 hours. In spite of continuous enemy aerial attacks, the designated assembly area was reached by all troop elements. The first vehicular losses were suffered. That same night, elements of the tank regiment crossed the creek bottom land northwest of Saroshnoje and established a valuable bridgehead for the upcoming attack.

The rear-area services and trains elements of the division that remained behind were placed under the command and control of line officers who were part of the unassigned officer manpower pool and combined under the central leadership of *Major Dr.* Korte. Later on, security elements were formed from this force, which were employed in the local defensive planning due to the direct threat to Kharkov posed by the Russians.

During the night of 12/13 May, the enemy entered the northern part of Bolschaja Babka, located in front of the division's assembly area. He attacked with two battalions towards the southwest from west of the village. The left wing of the *297. Infanterie-Division*, which was positioned around the village, held it and also bent its line back to the south as far as Point 191, establishing an orientation toward the northwest.

At first light, the division's motorcycle battalion was attacked by strong infantry and armored formations between Point 218.4 and the collective farm. It was overrun on its left wing by armor. These tanks then advanced without infantry support and fell victim to the guns of Jartzow's battery (*Artillerie-Regiment 171* of the *71. Infanterie-Division*)—firing over open sights—and a company from *Panzerjäger-Abteilung 171*, which forced the enemy armor to turn back. At 0800 hours, the 10th Company of the tank regiment joined the fray in the vicinity of Hill 211.1. Eleven enemy armored vehicles were eliminated. The motorcycle battalion maintained an outpost line running along Point 187.4 — 211.1 — Priwolje.

At 0945 hours, the division moved out from its assembly area with the mission of initially capturing Pestschanoje. Advancing on the right: *Kampfgruppe von Heydebrand und der Lasa* with the tank regiment (minus its 3rd Battalion), the *I./SR126* and the *I./PAR128*. On the left was *Kampfgruppe Kieler*, consisting of *SR126* (minus the *I./SR126*), the *9./PR201*, a 105cm howitzer battery and a single 10cm cannon (for direct-fire purposes against enemy armor). The motorcycle battalion and the *III./PR201* (minus the *9./PR201*) attacked directly to the left of *Kampfgruppe Kieler*. The latter grouping was to take back the line 218.4 — spit of woods 2 kilometers east of Tscherwona Roganka, which had been lost in the morning.

In the vicinity of Point 206.2, the right wing of the division encountered massed Soviet infantry advancing to the southwest. Working closely together, the tanks and riflemen scattered them. Even the Russian tanks could no longer help their infantry and had to turn back in the face of fire from the *8./PR201*, which was advancing toward them. A broad band of marshy terrain 1,500 meters outside of Pestschanoje stopped the division's continued advance to the north.

Under fire from Soviet artillery, tanks and antitank guns, as well as under constant aerial attack, *Kampfgruppe von Heydebrand* bypassed the marshy terrain to the west. Exploiting the aggressively mounted attack of *Major* Cunze's *II./SR126*, which had taken the patches of woods southwest of Pestschanoje at 1400 hours, it moved against the village again.

At 1700 hours, *Hauptmann* von Kunow's motorcycle battalion and the *III./PR201* reported: "Attack objective in the line 218.4 — collective farm achieved". A strongpoint in the collective farm that had been manned by six men from *KB23* was liberated.

Pestschanoje was not reached until evening twilight; it was defended by a tough enemy force defending in a resourceful manner. It was taken

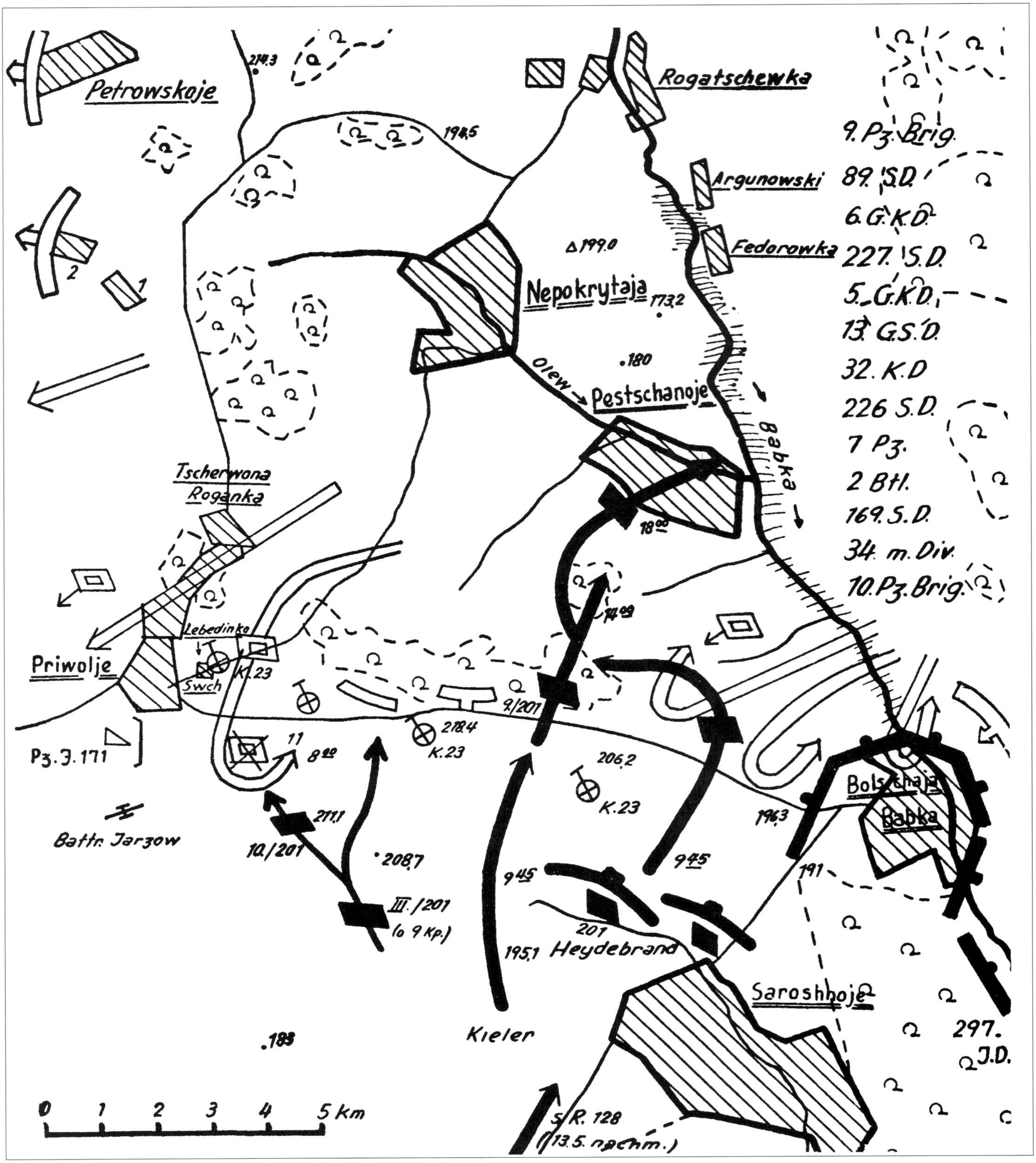

Map 1: Counterattack of the *23. Panzer-Division* on 13 May 1942.

by the tank regiment's 1st Battalion (*Oberstleutnant* von Heydebreck) and the *I./SR126* of *Hauptmann* Neubeck.

The new division had attacked for the first time and been successful.

During the afternoon of 13 May, *SR128* (*Oberstleutnant* Bachmann) was returned to division control. Attacking the gap between Bolschaja Babka and Pestschanoje, it reached the Babka River by first light of 14 May.

In Kharkov, the medical personnel of the division had to master the first occurrences of large-scale casualties. In uninterrupted work, both day and night, the surgeons and their assistants fought to save the lives of the wounded.

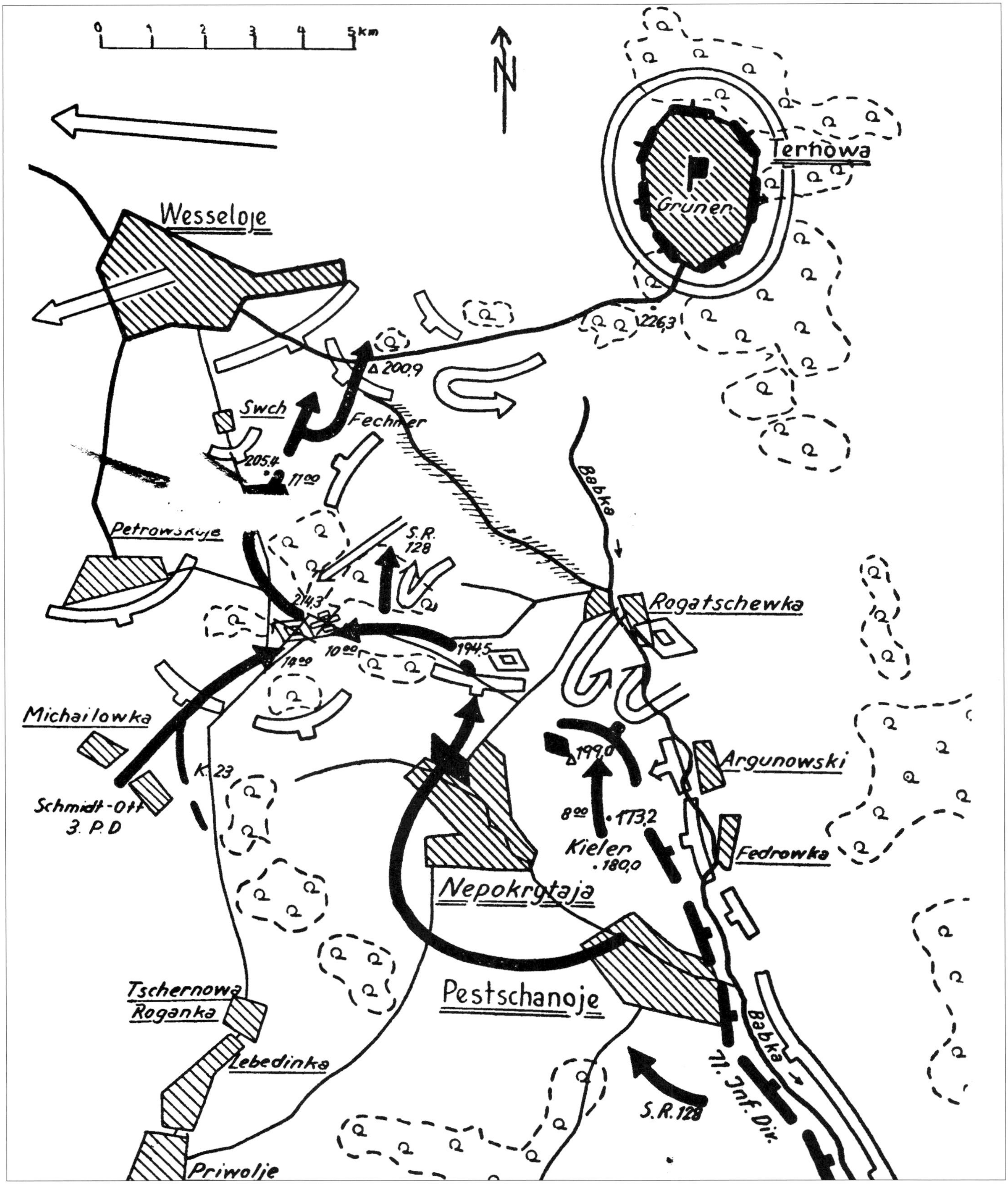

Map 2: Attack of the *23. Panzer-Division* on 15 May 1942.

On 14 May, the *Kampfgruppen* attacked north, with the right wing anchored on the Babka. It was intended for the division to obtain jumping-off points for the continued attack to the northeast on Star. Ssaltow. The enemy's stubborn resistance and several immediate counterattacks did not allow the *II./SR126* to take Point 180, a key terrain feature, until late in the morning. Russian infantry and tanks attacked again and again from the north and east. They finally forced the division over to the defensive, especially since *Kampfgruppe Schmidt-Ott* of the *3. Panzer-Division*, attacking from the west out of Nepokrytaja, was only making slow progress.

The oppressive enemy air superiority continued. Every 5 to 10 minutes, fighters, ground-support aircraft and bombers dove on the *Kampfgruppen* of the division and in the depths of the fighting area.

At 1430 hours, an order arrived:

Strong enemy forces at Wesseloje. *23. Panzer-Division* is attached to *Korpsgruppe Breith* and is to attack, right wing anchored on the Babka, to the north to destroy these enemy forces.

Kampfgruppe von Heydebrand moved out and took Point 173.2 against extremely heavy resistance. Around 1730 hours, the hotly contested Nepokrytaja was in the hands of the *3. Panzer-Division*.

The left wing of the division—*KB23* and the *III./PR201*—cleared areas of the enemy further to the south in the area around Lebedinka and the extended, narrow woods to its east. This was practically in the rear of the fighting around Nepokrytaja. After completing this mission, *KB23* was attached to *Kampfgruppe Schmidt-Ott* of the *3. Panzer-Division*, while the *III./PR201* returned to the tank regiment. The regimental commander, *Oberst* Werner-Ehrenfeucht, was wounded and evacuated; temporary command was assumed by *Oberstleutnant* Soltmann.

During the night of 14/15 May, it was intended to relieve *SR128* in its newly held lines along the Babka north of Bolschaja Babka by elements of the *71. Infanterie-Division*, which were being brought forward. Strong enemy counterattacks led to several penetrations, which had to be sealed off and eliminated by the formations in the midst of the relief-in-place. At first light on 15 May, the last elements of the regiment were finally able to disengage from the enemy, although they suffered heavy casualties.

The mission of *Korpsgruppe Breith* on 15 May was to attack the enemy forces that had advanced far to the west in the Wesseloje area. Attacking to the north to the right of the *3. Panzer-Division*, the *23. Panzer-Division* was to take the Ternowaja—Wesseloje road at Point 200.9 (3 kilometers east of Wesseloje).

To that end, the main body of the division moved out from the Babka River line to the west and then headed north via Nepokrytaja. It launched its attack north toward Point 199.0 starting at 0800 hours.

Kampfgruppe von Heydebrand had barely moved beyond Nepokrytaja, when its lead armored elements encountered Soviet tanks, which were holding the ridgeline on both sides of Hill 194.5 with strong infantry. Hill 194.5 was assaulted and, after heavy fighting, the Russians were forced back with heavy casualties to the north and east. Deep defiles with marshy bottom ground and small patches of woods blocked a straight approach to the north and provided the bitterly defending enemy with support for his defense. The *I./PR201* and the *I.(gep.)/SR126*, which was following, turned on their own initiative to the northwest while on the ridgeline and surfaced—much to the surprise of the enemy—in the rear of massed enemy tanks and artillery around Hill 214.3. The enemy was scattered in a rapid one-two punch. The enemy lost 16 guns and 11 antitank guns; 14 tanks were "gutted" and one aircraft from the Red Air Force, which continued to attack ground targets unabated, was shot down by machine-gun fire.

The attack was rapidly continued, moving around the patches of woods and headed north. By 1100 hours, forward elements had reached Point 205.4 south of Wesseloje. The friendly forces to the left, *Kampfgruppe Schmidt-Ott* of the *3. Panzer-Division*, had encountered considerable resistance when it had moved out of the Michailowka area and was unable to establish contact with *PR201* at Point 214.3 until around 1400 hours.

The resurgence of Soviet resistance between Points 194.5 and 214.3 prevented the artillery regiment's 2nd Battalion (under *Major* Sänger) from following the tanks. As a result, the armored task force initiated its attack against Hill 204.5 at 1600 hours without artillery support. Fired on from three sides—from the left from the collective farm 1 kilometer northwest of Hill 205.4, from the front from the heavily built-up enemy field fortifications at Hill 200.9 and from the right from the enemy forces positioned further to the east—the attack did not make progress. Casualties were taken. *Oberleutnant* Gördeler and his entire crew (*6./PR201*) were killed in close combat after they dismounted from their tank, when it got bogged down in a tank ditch.

On his own initiative, realizing the decisive importance of Hill 200.9, *Oberleutnant* Fechner, the acting commander of the *II./PR201*, attacked the hill again. His tanks, coupled with elements of the *I./SR126* that were following, overran the strongpoint, captured all of the emplaced weapons there and knocked out three T-34's. Defending in the space of 300 square meters were 5 7.62cm antitank guns, 5 4.5cm antitank guns, 4 infantry guns, 12 antitank rifles and 15 mortars. An immediate counterattack by Soviet tanks and infantry was turned back, and the area that had been taken was defended during the night by all-round defensive positions.

Together with the *9./PR201* of *Oberleutnant* Schinner, the *II./SR126* of *Kampfgruppe Kieler* had assaulted Hill 199.0. It transitioned to the defense in order to act as a flank guard for the rest of the division and to cover the advance of *Infanterie-Regiment 211* of the *71. Infanterie-Division* along the ridgeline. The *Kampfgruppe* was subjected to heavy attacks by Russian infantry from the east during the entire day, as well as taking fire from artillery, "Stalin Organs" and ground-support aircraft. The destruction of 17 enemy tanks, scattered across the terrain, offered proof of the exemplary bravery of the men of the battle group over the previous two days. The brave commander of the *II./SR126*, *Major* Cunze, was awarded the Iron Cross, First Class on the battlefield. A short while later, an impacting Soviet artillery round ended his life.

The division's 1st Medical Company established its first main clearing station at Tscherwona-Roganka.

A heavy blow for the division was the loss of the headquarters of *Schützen-Brigade 23*. Killed in Nepokrytaja as the result of a direct hit by artillery were *Oberst* von Heydebrand und der Lasa, his adjutant, *Hauptmann* von Schierbrandt, and his liaison officer, *Leutnant* von Knoblauch. *Oberstleutnant* Bachmann assumed acting command of the brigade, which was serving as the left-hand *Kampfgruppe* of the division.

As terrible as those losses were to the division during its first three days of combat operations, so too, were the importance of its successes. The enemy had lost 45 tanks and his other heavy losses had robbed him of his strength in his advance to the west. The left flank of the enemy's attack wedge had been torn open.

The Fighting for Ternowaja

On the morning of 16 May 1942, the division was in a line running Hill 194.5 (north of Nepokrytaja) — the eastern edge of the patches of woods northwest of Nepokrytaja — Hill 200.9. *Schützen-Regiment 126* (minus its 1st Battalion) had been attached to the *71. Infanterie-Division* and was engaged in defensive operations east of Nepokrytaja at Hill 199.0.

The division's mission that day was to turn east from its previous direction of attack to the north and reach a line running Hill 189.0 (northwest of Peremoga) — Hill 226.3 (south of Ternowaja). At the same time, *Kampfgruppe Gruner* of the *294. Infanterie-Division*, which had been encircled in Ternowaja since 13 May, was to be relieved.

In spite of constant Russian artillery fire received early in the morning, the combat trains of the *II./PR201*, under the direction of *Hauptmann* Paetzold and *Oberleutnant* Schewe, succeeded in bringing fuel and ammunition to the all-round defensive positions of the battalion on Hill 200.9 and resupplying all elements. As a result, the advance on Ternowaja, which had been directed by the *Führer* Headquarters, which was slated for the evening of 15 May, could take place.

At 0600 hours, the division's armored group, consisting of the *II./PR201* and the *I.(SPW)/SR126*, moved out to the east. The ridgeline running from Hills 226.3 to 218.6 was taken in fighting with tanks, antitank guns, antiaircraft guns and artillery. Concentrated Soviet artillery fires were being constantly placed on the tanks and *SPW's*. Mortars, antitank guns and antitank-rifle positions had to be eliminated individually. The 30cm high-explosive and napalm rounds from the frame launchers on the *SPW's* of the engineer battalion cut a swath through the Russian lines. As a result of the lack of infantry, however, the attack was not successful in clearing the patches of woods, criss-crossed by deep defiles, around Hill 226.3 and pushing the enemy back. Disregarding the threat, the *Kampfgruppe* nonetheless continued its advance into Ternowaja, where it established contact with *Oberst* Gruner and was enthusiastically greeted by its defenders. Without hesitation, the tanks and riflemen joined the fray against the Soviets, who had penetrated into the eastern part of the village, and ejected them, despite enemy artillery and mortar support. Once again, the village was completely in German hands.

After the armored group had broken through, the enemy was able to reorganize on Hill 226.3. He interrupted the lines of communications between Hill 200.9 and Ternowaja by fires from numerous antitank guns and heavy weapons from the patches of woods on both sides of the hill. Towards evening, the light platoon of the *II./PR201* succeeded in escorting the commander of the *I./PAR128*, *Oberstleutnant* Schlutius, from Ternowaja to Hill 200.9. The light platoon's mission—to lead the resupply elements into the village on its way back—could not be executed because of the Russian front, which had closed behind it again. This meant that divisional elements—the headquarters of *PR201*, the *II./PR201*, the *I./SR126* and the forward observers of the *I./PAR128*—were then encircled in Ternowaja with *Oberst* Gruner. The *I./PR201*, to which the 9th Tank Company had been attached, along with a company-sized element from *Korps-Pionier-Bataillon 652*, held the "hedgehog" position around Hill 200.9.

During the attack of the armored group on Ternowaja, *SR128* (*Oberstleutnant* Bachmann) moved out toward Hill 207.2 from the line Hill 194.5 — edge of the wood line northwest of Hill 194.5. At the same time, strong Russian forces attacked from the east from the bottomland along the Babka and from Peremoga. The enemy penetrated in places within the sector of *Infanterie-Regiment 131* (*44. Infanterie-Division*) on the right, which was attached to the *71. Infanterie-Division*. The infantry fell back to the west in places. *Oberstleutnant* Bachmann stopped the attack of his riflemen and pulled them back to defend along their jumping-off positions. In the sector of *Infanterie-Regiment 131*, the heavy guns of the artillery regiment's 3rd Battalion pulled up in the open. *Oberst* Büscher's artillerymen then proceeded to scatter the attacking Russian infantry, and the German retrograde movements came to a halt. One company from the *III./PR201* launched an immediate counterattack, together with the riflemen and infantry, and threw the Soviets, who sustained considerable casualties, back to their start points. By the evening of 16 May, the German main line of resistance was firmly under control; on the other hand, the armored group remained in its pocket-like encirclement in the ridgeline-surrounded Ternowaja, 5 kilometers to the east of Hill 200.9

The Red Air Force no longer intervened on the massive scale it had previously, and *Stukas* attacked Russian batteries at Werchne Ssaltow and Warwarowka. Prisoners later stated that 27 guns had been destroyed.

During the night of 16/17 May 1942, the division had to pull the *I./PR201* out of its all-round defense around Hill 200.9 and expedite *Oberstleutnant* von Heydebreck and his men to the *VII. Armee-Korps* of *General der Artillerie* Heitz, which was involved in difficult fighting with the enemy that had advanced on Merefa, south of Kharkov.

The mission of von Heydebreck's battalion—to secure the key position at Hill 200.9—was assumed by 11 tanks, 6 of which were battle damaged. The stay-behind force was commanded by *Oberleutnant* Schinner, the commander of the *9./PR201*.

Schützen-Regiment 128, on the right wing of the division, was relieved by elements of the *71. Infanterie-Division* in the course of the night, so that it could be brought up closer to Hill 200.9. *Schützen-Regiment 126* (minus its 1st Battalion) continued to be employed with the *71. Infanterie-Division* east of Nepokrytaja.

Irrespective of the strong enemy attacks in the area north of Nepokrytaja on 16 May, it was intended to complete the cutting off of the Soviet attack group north of Kharkov on 17 May. To that end, *Panzerkampfgruppe Soltmann* received orders to move out at 0700 hours and, advancing north from Ternowaja, to clear the Murom Valley of the enemy, in conjunction with *Panzergruppe Schmidt-Ott* of the *3. Panzer-Division*, which was attacking 4 kilometers further west. It was also to relieve an encircled *Kampfgruppe* from the *79. Infanterie-Division* in the village of Murom.

Schützen-Regiment 128, released from attachment to the *71. Infanterie-Division*, assembled during the morning at Petrowskoje, 9 kilometers south of Wesseloje.

Around 0500 hours, in a cleverly led operation, three tanks from the regiment's 9th Company, under the direction of *Oberleutnant* Walther, succeeded in retrieving an armored observation vehicle of the artillery regiment's 1st Battalion that had become immobilized as a result of engine problems the previous day. The vehicle was evacuated from the middle of Soviet infantry positions in front of the patch of woods southwest of Hill 226.3. The signals instructions that were on board were also recovered.

The tanks had barely returned to Hill 200.9, when the Russians attacked the division's strongpoints there on a broad sector. Advancing from Bairak, the tanks and infantry were supported by artillery fires. At 0720 hours, there were 50 enemy tanks on the ridgeline between Hills 226.3 and 200.9. The tanks, mostly T 34's, were joined by three battalions of infantry, all attacking west. The strongpoint element at Hill 200.9 proper had no direct connections to friendly forces to either flank. A *Luftwaffe* observer also reported that some 70 additional tanks—moving in two waves—were advancing from Bair, following the first attack wave. The air-ground controller assigned by the *Luftwaffe* to the division was able to call in *Stuka* sorties from *Sturzkampfgeschwader 77*.

Schinner's tank company was engaged in a firefight with the vastly superior enemy. The crews of the six immobilized tanks, who were unable to avoid the fire of the enemy tanks, provided an inspirational example to the remaining defenders by their sticking it out. At 0750 hours, *Oberleutnant* Schinner reported: "Three enemy tanks on fire. I have expended all ammunition. Enemy approaching closer; I'm remaining here."

Schützen-Regiment 128 was moved out of Petrowskoje in an expedited manner and given the mission to move as far as the line Hill 205.4 — Hill 200.9. At the same time, a tank reserve group, formed near the division command post, was sent from Hill 214.3 to the north. It was under the command of *Hauptmann* Stiewe, the acting commander of the *III./PR201*, and consisted of the 10th and 12th Companies from that battalion, as well as tanks that had returned from repair.

Without being able to establish contact with *Korpsgruppe Breith*, *Generalmajor* von Boineburg decided to have *Panzergruppe Soltmann* move from Ternowaja to the southwest, which was against the original orders. It was intended for Soltmann's force to attack and take Hill 226.3 and hit the enemy armor attacking there in the flank.

The *II./PR201* was only able to deploy with difficulty while moving out of the depression at Ternowaja. It was under fire from the Russian howitzers, antitank guns and tanks grouped on the high ground around the village. Its employment was unavoidable, however, given the threat to the weakly manned Hill 200.9. The loss of 200.9 would have freed the

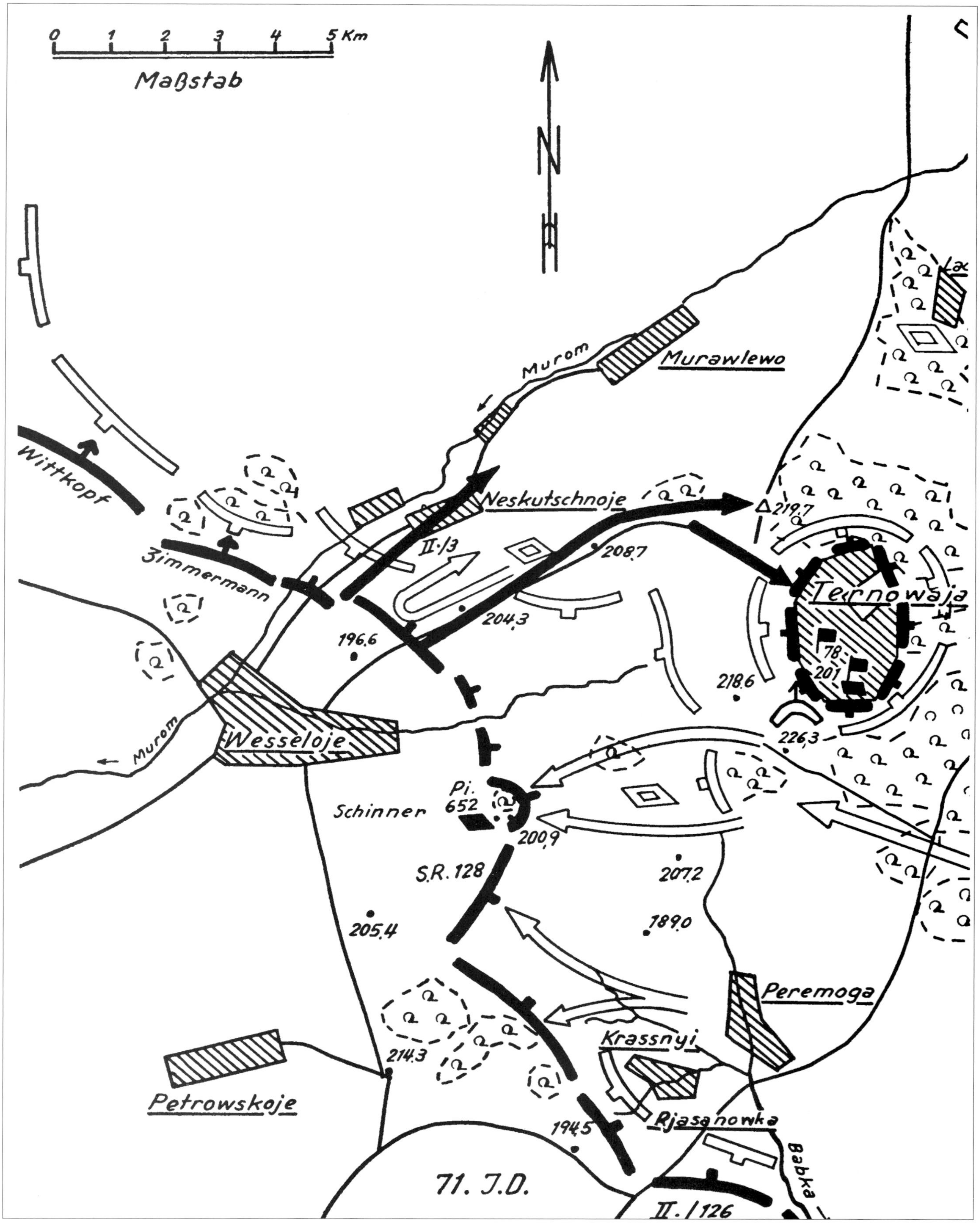

Map 3: Defensive Operations Around Hill 200.9 (17-22 May) and the Relief of Ternowaja on 21 May.

way for the enemy to Wesseloje and then to Kharkov. At the same time, it would have separated the defenders of Ternowaja even further from the German main lines.

In light of the unmistakable Soviet main effort in front of Hill 200.9, the division repeatedly and with great urgency requested *Korpsgruppe Breith* to stop the attack of *Gruppe Schmidt-Ott* in the Murom Valley and redirected that force to Hill 200.9.

While screening its flank to the southeast, the *II./PR201,* with its 36 operational tanks, took up the fight against the superior T 34's on the ridgeline running from Hills 218.6 to 226.3. In bitter tank versus tank engagements, the battalion lost 13 of its own as total losses. It is certain that at least 8 enemy tanks were set alight; other "kills" were possible, but they could not be verified, since the German tanks had run out of ammunition and had to pull back to Ternowaja after having lost a third of their number.

Even though the loses sustained by the tank battalion were painful, the flank attack into the enemy tanks had a decisive influence. The Russians had also been badly battered, and they pulled back to the southeast. The defenders of Hill 200.9 won a short but critical break in the action. Schinner's tank company was resupplied with ammunition; the *I./PAR128* were in firing positions in the open to the south and southwest of the hill. The artillery screened the approach of *SR128* into a line running Hill 205.4 — Hill 200.9. The *Luftwaffe* also promised additional *Stuka* support.

At 1100 hours, numerous T-34's with infantry moved against Hill 200.9. The enemy was turned back in a hail of fire from all available weapons, without being able to reach the German lines. The Russians attempted several times to renew their attack. The subsequent attacks showed less resolve than the first one, however. The Soviet tanks were also holding back more in the face of the powerful defensive fires that had been augmented in the afternoon by two 8.8cm *Flak.*

Due to terrain difficulties, *Gruppe Schmidt-Ott* of the *3. Panzer-Division* was only able to approach to within 4 kilometers of Hill 200.9 from the northeast. It then had to move via Wesseloje, only arriving at the hill in the afternoon hours. *Korpsgruppe Breith* had ordered this battle group to attack in the wake of *SR128*, but the attack could not be carried out due to the onset of darkness.

On that day, despite the considerable losses and the exhaustion that had arisen as a result of the fighting of the previous few days, the division was able to shatter the heaviest tank and infantry attack of the battle so far with its own forces. The enemy had sacrificed nine infantry battalions and numerous tanks on the battlefield in front of Hill 200.9.

After a short break during the night of 17/18 May, the next day started with deliberate counterbattery fire on the part of the divisional artillery. Continued over the next few days, the counterbattery fire had claimed 39 enemy guns out of 10 batteries by 21 May. In addition, the German guns also silenced an additional 16 batteries for short periods, as was confirmed by prisoner statements and aerial reconnaissance.

A planned attack to relieve Ternowaja had to be postponed due to the reduced combat power of *SR128*. No other infantry forces were available, since the *SPW* battalion was encircled in Ternowaja, the *II./SR126* had been attached to the *71. Infanterie-Division*, the division's motorcycle battalion was still being brought forward and the division's engineer battalion was not yet available.

In spite of the heavy losses sustained by the enemy at the hands of the division in the previous few days, he had still not abandoned his offensive intentions. He attacked again and again out of the woods south of Ternowaja with massed infantry forces supported by armor and placed the defenders of Hill 200.9 under intense pressure.

During the morning of 18 May, 10 enemy tanks and a battalion's worth of infantry assaulted across Hill 226.3 to the west. The enemy force had barely reached the ridgeline when it was taken under barrage fire by the divisional artillery, that was primarily being directed by the forward observers of the regiment's 1st Battalion in encircled Ternowaja. Two T-34's were knocked out, and the infantry forced back after taking heavy losses.

Toward 1500 hours, the enemy tried again to reach his objective, albeit in a different manner than previously attempted. Without any artillery preparation, 10 enemy tanks suddenly raced toward Hill 200.9. They were followed by at least three battalion's worth of infantry. Once again, there were hard-fought tank engagements. Two 8.8cm *Flak* and nine howitzers, which advanced and set up in the open, joined in. They were personally led by the 66-year-old commander of the artillery regiment, *Oberst* Buch. Three enemy tanks were eliminated and the rest turned back, battered. The Russian infantry took very heavy losses and became bogged down, but the Soviet command committed new armored elements to the fray.

At 1700 hours, the tanks of *Oberleutnant* Schinner and the two 8.8cm *Flak* had expended all of their ammunition. Coming to the aid of the defenders of Hill 200.9, who were again being hard pressed, were the motorcycle battalion and a group of six repaired tanks from *PR201*, which were led by an Assistant Operations Officer, *Oberleutnant* Puttkammer. *Panzergruppe Stiewe* (*III./PR201*) and the armored reconnaissance company of *KB23* supported the defensive efforts, the latter with their 2cm automatic cannon.

In all, some 40 enemy tanks and vastly superior infantry forces attacked. As on the preceding day, they placed extremely heavy pressure on the exhausted riflemen.

The division also continued to receive effective support from the *Stukas* of *Sturzkampfgeschwader 77*, which were launching sorties from the airstrip at Roganj, 20 kilometers away. Fighters, which also belonged to the *IV. Flieger-Korps*, and *Flak* formations kept the skies clear of the Soviets.

Hard pressed by the Soviet attackers, the German forces were faced with a difficult crisis when a *Stuka* attack shortly after 1700 hours threatened the friendly lines as a result of the uncertain situation. The acting commander of *SR128*, *Major* von Unger, had no other choice when the *Stukas* attacked several times than to have the main body of his riflemen pull back. Despite a wound to the upper thigh, he remained behind on Hill 200.9, where the remaining riflemen and the engineers of *Korps-Pionier-Bataillon 652* formed an all-round defense. The non-immobilized elements of *Oberleutnant* Schinner's tank company were also pulled back. *Leutnant* Schmiedel, with the division's support command, succeeded in resupplying the tanks, *Flak* and artillery with ammunition.

At the end of evening twilight, the rifle and tank elements that had been pulled back were able to reoccupy their positions. At 1945 hours, however, they had to fight back another Soviet attack, until the Russians decided to give up for the day and pulled their forces back to their start points. Twenty more knocked-out enemy tanks were scattered in front of the division's positions by the end of the day.

All day long, the tanks and riflemen, who had made it through to *Oberst* Gruner, were subjected to artillery and mortar fire. At evening twilight, the Russians attacked again and forced an entry into the eastern part of the village. The enemy could not be ejected until tanks were employed. The infantry, who had been encircled since 13 May, were so exhausted at that point that the tanks had to be split up even further among them so as to provide stays in the corset. Correspondingly, the ability of the *II./PR201* to be employed as an entire formation decreased considerably. Because of the supply situation, the issuance of rations had to be strictly controlled. Each individual tanker and rifleman received only 125 grams of hard tack and 200 grams of canned vegetables daily. Twice a day, the *Luftwaffe* air dropped fuel and ammunition. As a result of the location of the village, some of the containers landed among the Russians or could only be retrieved during the fighting for the village itself.

During the night, *General* Breith's headquarters was redirected to the southern sector of the Kharkov Front. The *23. Panzer-Division* was then attached to the *LI. Armee-Korps*. The division, in turn, received command and control of all of the forces of the *3. Panzer-Division* that were engaged in the Wesseloje area, including *Stab Westhoven* (*Schützen-Brigade 3*) and *Gruppe Schmidt-Ott* (reinforced *Panzer-Regiment 6*). The main lines of the division and its attached forces ran from Hill 205.4 (3 kilometers south of Wesseloje) — Hill 200.9 — Hill 204.3 (3 kilometers northeast of Wesseloje).

The Russians continued to launch attacks with tanks and infantry on 19 May. It was determined via prisoner interrogations that fresh Guards tank formations had been introduced. The main effort of the enemy's attacks had shifted more to the friendly forces on the right, the *71. Infanterie-Division*. However, it, in turn, was attacking the enemy forces from the depressions west of Peremoga. One of the larger attacks, conducted with 20 tanks and 2 battalions of infantry, aimed for Hill 205.4. In coordinated fires between the tanks and the heavy weapons, the enemy assault collapsed in front of the friendly lines with heavy losses. Once again, some of the artillery had to fire from open firing positions. Nine enemy tanks were eliminated.

Contributing greatly to the successful defensive efforts of the division was its own artillery, supported by general headquarters artillery formations. The fundamental dictum of *Oberst* von Buch—that every enemy tank attack was to be engaged by *every* battery—had proven its worth. Even the heavy howitzers, which really only had a psychological effect on the tanks, forced the Soviets to turn back prematurely. Not a single enemy tank penetrated into the division's lines during this round of fighting. The divisional artillery was credited with the destruction of 50 enemy tanks in the first week of the fighting around Kharkov.

By order of the corps, the line running Hill 205.4 — Hill 200.9 was to continue to be defended on 20 May. At the same time, on the division's left wing, *Gruppe Westhoven* was to attack toward the northeast from the area northeast of Wesseloje. Advancing via the ridgeline Hill 204.3 — Hill 208.7, it was to take Hill 219.7 northwest of Ternowaja. To that end, *Gruppe Westhoven* was reinforced with the light *SPW* company of *KB23*, two 8cm *Flak* and the *II./PAR128*.

In the midst of preparations for this attack, the Soviets launched a tank and infantry attack at 0300 hours after a short but intense artillery preparation. The main effort of the enemy attack was to the northwest of Hill 200.9, where the enemy committed numerous tanks but little infantry against the German positions between Hills 205.4 and 196.6.

Three Soviet tanks—two T-34's and one KV-I—succeeded in overrunning the positions of the riflemen in front of Hill 200.9. Under the leadership of the wounded *Major* von Unger, the riflemen, engineers and motorcycle infantry held fast in their positions and pinned down the infantry following the tanks. Tanks, artillery and *Flak* then blew the three tanks apart.

The enemy attack against *Gruppe Westhoven* also bogged down. The enemy was turned back and the *Kampfgruppe* moved out to attack at 1055 hours after reorganizing its forces. Tank-versus-tank engagements flared up at Hill 208.7, which ended with *Panzer-Regiment 6* being victorious. By noon on 20 May, the *II./Schützen-Regiment 3* (of the *3. Panzer-Division*) succeeded in entering Neskutschnoje and taking complete control of it.

Heavy artillery and *Stuka* support was necessary for the *Panzergruppe* from the *3. Panzer-Division* to succeed in overcoming the stubborn resistance of the Soviets in the patch of woods west of Hill 219.7 and take the hill itself by evening. The *SPW* Company of the motorcycle battalion cleared the area of Soviet infantry during this attack and safeguarded the resupply of the *Kampfgruppe* during the night. Two 8.8cm *Flak* provided cover for the advance of *Gruppe Schmidt-Ott* from positions between Hills 204.3 and 208.7. From there, it then joined the fray around Hill 200.9.

It was no longer possible that evening to establish contact with the forces surrounded in Ternowaja. However, the ongoing sorties flown by *Stukas* and other ground-support aircraft brought palpable relief to those encircled there. The besieged *Kampfgruppe*, which had a broad frontage and was not sufficiently resupplied by air, was unable to launch its own advance toward Hill 219.7 to break out of its encirclement.

In the evening, a concentration of 80 enemy tanks was reported in the patch of woods west of Ladyzkoje (6 kilometers north of Hill 219.7). The danger of an enemy attack into the flank of *Gruppe Schmidt-Ott* was matched by a severe threat to the division. As a precaution, Hill 219.7 was evacuated when it turned dark, and *Gruppe Schmidt-Ott* was pulled back to the patch of woods to the west of it.

That same night, the line running from Hills 205.4 to 200.9 was reinforced with elements from *PPB51* that had just arrived from Germany. Numerous mines were laid. The *IV. (Flak)/PAR128*, which was how the former *Heeres-Flak-Abteilung 278* was redesignated and reorganized, arrived in Kharkov.

The division sector was extended to the north during the night of 20/21 May as a result of the attachment of *Kampfgruppe Wittkopf* and *Kampfgruppe Zimmermann*—both of the *3. Panzer-Division*. They were employed between the Murom Valley and Lipzy, where they attacked to the northeast. The division then placed these two *Kampfgruppen* under the command of *Brigade-Stab Westhoven* (*Schützen-Brigade 3*).

On 20 May, the division recorded an additional 21 enemy tanks destroyed in its sector.

While the division made its preparations for the coming day during the night and into the morning hours of 21 May, the first reports of retrograde movements by the enemy filtered in. It was determined that the enemy tanks west of Ladyzkoje were pulling back to the east. The enemy forces surrounding Ternowaja continued to hold their positions, however.

The elimination of the flank threat from Ladyzkoje allowed *Gruppe Schmidt-Ott* to advance on Ternowaja via Hill 219.7 at 0930 hours. The *Kampfgruppe* overcame slight resistance and established contact with Gruner's and Soltmann's forces. The first supply column arrived for the relieved forces at 1120 hours; it brought rations, ammunition and fuel. Then the evacuation of the 350 German soldiers, who had been wounded in Ternowaja, was started. Up to that point, they had only been treated with the bare necessities.

To that end, 60 field ambulances rolled toward Ternowaja under the protection of the *SPW* Company of *KB23*. They initially took the wounded to Wesseloje. The division's entire 1st Medical Company, with all three platoons, was set up there and administered to the wounded in huts and under tentage. Picked up by the division's ambulances again, the wounded were then further transported to the division's 2nd Medical Company in Kharkov, where the onward transportation of the badly wounded to Germany was done via *Ju-52* transport aircraft of the *Luftwaffe*.

All day long, Soviet patrols and smaller elements attacked the village. In addition, the Russians attempted to disrupt events by constantly firing artillery.

In the evening, the complete evacuation of the village—including all personnel, weapons and equipment—was initiated by order of the corps. Protected by the light *SPW's* of the motorcycle battalion, these efforts were concluded by first light the next day, despite continuous efforts at disruption on the part of the Soviets. After the conclusion of this operation, when the tanks of Schmidt-Ott's group were already turning back to the west, the leader of the recovery platoon of the *II./PR201*, *Oberleutnant*

Salwey, arrived in Ternowaja with four prime movers. They brought back three German 10cm cannon that could not be previously recovered.

On 21 May, 19 enemy tanks fell to the fighting efforts of the division and the formations attached to it.

The retrograde actions of the Russians continued throughout 21 May and on 22 May as well. That led to the conclusion that the Soviets considered their large-scale offensive to break through north of Kharkov as a failure. On the other hand, the intense pressure south of the city continued unabated; the enemy's attack was gaining ground.

On 22 May, the *23. Panzer-Division* was relieved by the *71. Infanterie-Division* and the *294. Infanterie-Division*, which was approaching from the west. Smaller-scale Soviet attacks were turned back, with the enemy losing 7 tanks.

By noon, all of the formations of the division had been relieved and were *en route* to Kharkov. Expedited efforts were made to prepare for combat to the south of Kharkov.

***

By cutting through and scattering the Russian attack group northeast of Kharkov, the division had halted the northern arm of the pincers, which had been intended to envelop the city from that direction, in its initial stages. After initial success, the massed employment of 10 rifle divisions, 8 tank brigades, 1 motorized rifle brigade and a cavalry corps was crushed by a main-effort counterattack of the *23. Panzer-Division*, in conjunction with the *3. Panzer-Division*, the *71. Infanterie-Division* and the *Luftwaffe*.

In addition to the thousands of enemy dead left on the battlefield, the division also captured 4,470 prisoners. Captured or destroyed spoils of war by elements of the division totaled:

136 tanks
110 artillery pieces
66 antitank guns
92 antitank rifles
2 aircraft
12 infantry guns and
87 mortars.

The division's losses:

32 officers and 346 noncommissioned officers and enlisted personnel were killed

45 officers and 1,038 noncommissioned officers and enlisted personnel were wounded

2 officers and 70 noncommissioned officers and enlisted personnel were reported as missing

30 tanks were written off as total losses due to enemy action

21 other tanks could be repaired after sustaining battle damage.

Panzerjäger-Abteilung 128 and the I./Panzer-Regiment 201 in the Fighting South of Kharkov

While the main body of the division was involved in heavy fighting with the enemy advancing on Kharkov from the northeast, the division's antitank battalion and the 1st Battalion of the tank regiment—the latter starting on 17 May—were fighting south of Merefa as part of the *VIII. Armee-Korps* of *General der Artillerie* Heitz.

Shortly after the division arrived in the Kharkov area, its antitank battalion under *Major Dr.* Maus was attached to the *VIII. Armee-Korps* in expectation of a large-scale Soviet offensive south of Kharkov. From 30 April to 10 May 1942, the battalion was prepared for combat in the sector of the *62. Infanterie-Division* in Taranowka and Guliaje Pole. The Soviet attack did not materialize, since the mud period had started unexpectedly. As a result, the men of the antitank battalion returned to the division and took up billets in Wyssokij (12 kilometers south of Kharkov).

But just two days later, the Soviet offensive started on both sides of Kharkov. *Panzerjäger-Abteilung 128* was sent back to the sector of the *62. Infanterie-Division* and attached to it. It initially moved to Rjabuchino. Three infantry regiments—208, 515, and 179—were already under extreme pressure along the main line of resistance running along the line Chutor — Perwomaiskij — Hill 160.5 — Werchni Bischkin — Ssuchaja — Gomoljscha. The Hungarian 108th Light Division was also involved in the fighting. Enemy tank concentrations had been reported at Alexejewka and Kisselij.

Major Maus received orders to defend against the enemy tanks in the line Lichatschewo — collective farm east of Gruschino. When the battalion arrived in Taranowka at noon, enemy tanks had already broken through the infantry positions. An element of *Infanterie-Regiment 515* (parent formation: *294. Infanterie-Division*) of *Oberstleutnant* Dorow was defending in Bereka. The *1./PJA128* (minus its 3rd Platoon) of *Oberleutnant* Brünn went into position there. The *2./PJA128*, to which the 3rd Platoon of the 1st Company was attached, occupied positions in the open on both sides of the Taranowka — Alexejewka rail line. The 2nd Company was led by *Oberleutnant Graf* Asseburg.

The brave resistance of the German infantry was able to withstand the onslaught of the Soviet attack until 12 May. The 1st Platoon of the *1./PJA128* went into position on Hill 189.2. At a distance of 600 meters, the platoon engaged oncoming Soviet tanks, knocking out one T-34 and one KV-I, whereupon the rest turned back. One more T-34 was destroyed during a nighttime attack.

On 13 May, two infantry regiments—*515* and 179—moved out to counterattack. They were supported by *PJA128*. Several Soviet tanks and heavy weapons were destroyed. Employing high-explosive rounds, the antitank soldiers broke up battalion-sized enemy attacks, but they also suffered losses at the hands of Soviet artillery. Despite the strongest of resistance on the part of the defenders, they could only hold up under the pressure of the enemy tanks and the masses of infantry for a limited time, however.

In the course of the morning, the Russians went around Bereka and encircled it. A short while later, more than 50 Soviet tanks and escorting infantry overran the weak defensive lines on both sides of the rail line. Without any infantry protection, the 5cm antitank guns took up the fight against the T-34's, KV-1's and KV-2's, which were far superior in both numbers and firepower. The antitank crewmembers waited until the Soviets had approached to within a few meters, since that was the only way they had any chance of penetrating the Soviet armor plating. One gun after the other was crushed beneath the tracks of the enemy. Only a few guns were able to pull back in time.

One antitank gun was forced back into a patch of woods by the Soviet tanks and was caught there by German barrage fire, which forced the seven antitank gun crewmembers to take cover. They barely had opportunity to catch their breath, when they had to get their gun into position. Two enemy tanks and armored personnel carriers were eliminated. After the prime mover was lost and the last round was fired, the men fought their way back to the German main lines.

The antitank battalion suffered heavy casualties. *Leutnant* Schilling, 2 noncommissioned officers and 10 enlisted personnel were killed; 2 officers, 13 noncommissioned officers and 43 men were wounded. One noncommissioned officer and two enlisted men were reported as missing.

On 16 May 1942, *Kampfgruppe Durow* fought its way back to the German lines. Part of the *Kampfgruppe* was *Oberleutnant* Brünn and elements of the *1./PJA128*.

The losses in men and materiel were heavy. There were only 5 5cm *Pak 38's* left out of the original 18 that the battalion had taken to the field

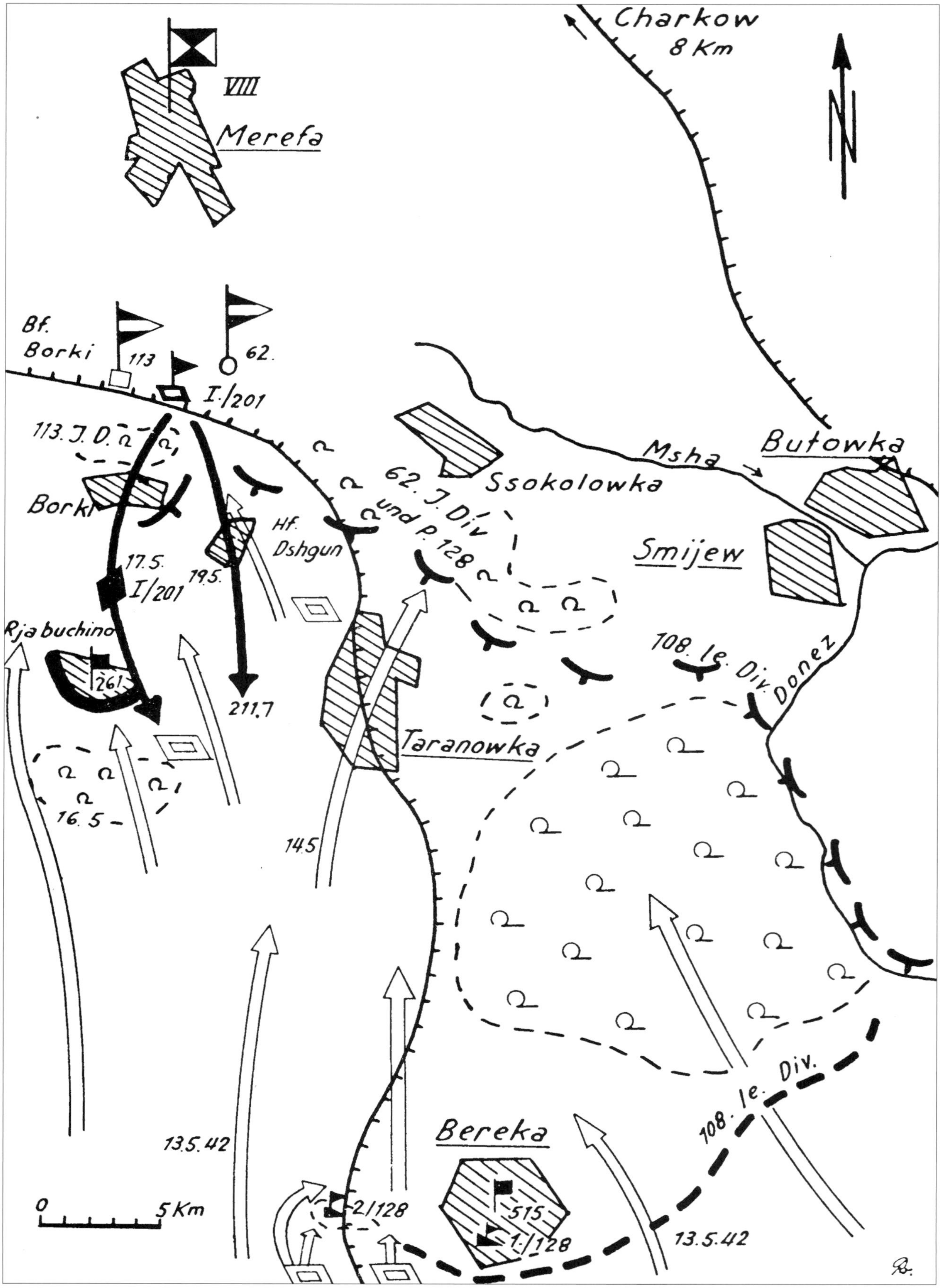

Map 4: Employment of *Panzerjäger-Abteilung 128* and the *I./Panzer-Regiment 201* in the sector of the *VIII. Armee-Korps*.

with three days earlier. Despite that, the remaining guns continued to provide the infantry with invaluable support. A rifle company was formed out of scattered elements from the infantry division and the headquarters of *PJA128*.

By 20 May 1942, the division's antitank battalion had destroyed 58 enemy tanks on its own. Among them were 3 KV-1's and 27 T-34's. Thanks to the tough defensive effort, the situation in the sector of the *62. Infanterie-Division* had cleared up enough to allow the antitank battalion to be pulled out of its lines and returned to the *23. Panzer-Division*.

During the critical juncture of the fighting in what was to become known as the Double Battle of Kharkov, *Oberstleutnant* von Heydebreck's *I./PR201* was pulled out of the line around the hotly contested Hill 200.9 east of Wesseloje during the evening of 16 may and rushed south, where it was attached to the *VIII. Armee-Korps*. After a short maintenance halt at Kharkov-Lossewo, the battalion reached the sector of the corps around noon on 17 May. After being briefed by the corps, the battalion commander established contact with the divisions fighting southeast of Merefa. *General der Artillerie* Heitz, the Commanding General, told *Oberstleutnant* von Heydebreck upon leaving the corps headquarters: "Act like a battleship and destroy every enemy tank that surfaces!"

Ever since 12 May, the *113. Infanterie-Division* and the *62. Infanterie-Division* were involved in extremely difficult defensive operations. The two divisions had been forced back north from the line Jefremowka — Bereka. At Rjabuchino and Taranowka, strongpoints south of Borki, *Kampfgruppen* from the infantry were offering desperate resistance. The enemy had not yet succeeded in breaking through, but the gaps between the strongpoints were growing ever larger. Neither of the two divisions had any reserves left.

Oberstleutnant Heydebreck's mission encompassed a lot: From an assembly area east of the rail station at Borki, his battalion was supposed to be ready to turn back all enemy armored attacks.

The dangerous situation soon made the employment of the tank battalion necessary. Elements of *Infanterie-Regiment 261* of the *113. Infanterie-Division* had been encircled in the village of Rjabuchino and were threatened with destruction. The *I./PR201* moved out in the afternoon. The Russians, who had already entered the extended village, defended against the German tanks with tanks, antitank guns and antitank rifles. Whoever was knocked out fought on as an infantryman. *Leutnant* Schellenberg, the platoon leader of the battalion's light platoon, distinguished himself by his bravery, when he smashed a Russian strongpoint. In the end, the Russians pulled back to the east in the direction of Taranowka. The men of the infantry regiment felt a palpable sense of relief. The tank battalion remained in Rjabuchino for the night, and left a few tanks there the following day.

On 18 May, enemy tanks attacked north on both sides of Dschgun, 6 kilometers northeast of Rjabuchino, and threatened elements of the *62. Infanterie-Division*. The tank battalion attacked and knocked out six enemy tanks. The Russians did not renew their attacks there.

At first light on 19 May, *Oberstleutnant* von Heydebreck's tanks, together with attached infantry from the *62. Infanterie-Division* and the *I./PJA128*, took back the village of Dschgun, pushing the enemy in front of them toward the south. Despite constant flare-ups of resistance and immediate counterattacks by Russian tanks, the objective, Hill 211.7 (2 kilometers east of Rjabuchino), was reached and German infantry went into position. The German defenses were further strengthened by this; contact was established between the *113. Infanterie-Division* and the *62. Infanterie-Division*. Eleven enemy tanks and larger enemy formations had been eliminated.

On 20 May, Russian combat power in this sector of the front also noticeably abated. The enemy's losses of the past few days, coupled with the German counterattack from the southeast from the area around Barwenkowo, began to take their toll. The *62. Infanterie-Division* pursued the enemy pulling back from Taranowka.

That same day, the *I./PR201* left the command and control of the *VIII. Armee-Korps*. The Commander-in-Chief of the *6. Armee*, *General der Infanterie* von Paulus, and the Commanding General of the *VIII. Armee-Korps*, *General der Artillerie* Heitz, sought out the battalion and expressed special praise, both in person and in writing, for its achievements. Numerous Iron Crosses, 1st and 2nd Class, were made available to the battalion commander for awarding to his men.

The antitank battalion also returned to the division. Its exemplary performance was praised in the following correspondence received from *General der Artillerie* Heitz:

> The Commanding General
> of the *VIII. Armee-Korps*
>
> Corps Headquarters, 21 May 1942
>
> TO: *Panzerjäger-Abteilung 128*
> THRU: *23. Panzer-Division*
>
> In the hard days of fighting from 12-20 May, *Panzerjäger-Abteilung 128* stood side-by-side with the forces of the *VIII. Armee-Korps* in turning back the onslaught of vastly numerically superior Russian divisions and tank brigades. During that period, it destroyed 52 enemy tanks.
>
> As the result of their brave fighting, the officers, noncommissioned officers and enlisted personnel of the battalion contributed significantly at the most threatened sector of the corps front in preventing the breakthrough of the enemy to Kharkov.
>
> I extend my gratitude and my special recognition to *Panzerjäger-Abteilung 128* for its magnificent performance and wish it continued success and good fortune.
>
> /signed/ Heitz, *General der Artillerie*

The Fighting to Eliminate the Enemy Southeast of Kharkov

Moving east of the Donez via Ssokolowo and Smijew, the *I./PR201* reached the area around Andrejewka on 22 May 1942. It was there that the *44. Infanterie-Division*, together with *Infanterie-Regiment 190*, which was attached to it, had established and held a narrow bridgehead south of the Donez. The intent was to expand it, using the tank battalion. The expanded bridgehead was to serve as the starting point for the *23. Panzer-Division*, arriving from the north, for the final encirclement and elimination of the Russian field armies positioned south of the Donez.

On 23 May, the *I./PR201* moved out with *Infanterie-Regiment 190* and captured Hill 208.5, 5 kilometers east of Schebelinka, after overcoming numerous minefields and considerable enemy resistance. The German tankers and infantry on the hill were happy to see German tanks approaching them from the south. Those were the lead elements of *Panzer-Regiment 2* of *Oberst Lt. Graf* Strachwitz of the *16. Panzer-Division*, which was fighting as part of the *III. Armee-Korps (mot.)* and had moved out toward the north on 15 May from Barwenkowo. When those forces established contact with von Heydebreck's battalion, they had succeeded in completing the encirclement of the Soviet forces that were fighting further to the west.

The *16. Panzer-Division* defended from a line running Hill 208.5 — "1 May" Collective Farm — Losowenka, oriented toward the west and the encircled Soviet forces, the main body of which was assumed to be along the Merefa in the Alexejewka area. The *14. Panzer-Division*, which was advancing with the *16. Panzer-Division*, turned to the east and screened the area that had been reached against possible enemy relief attacks from that direction.

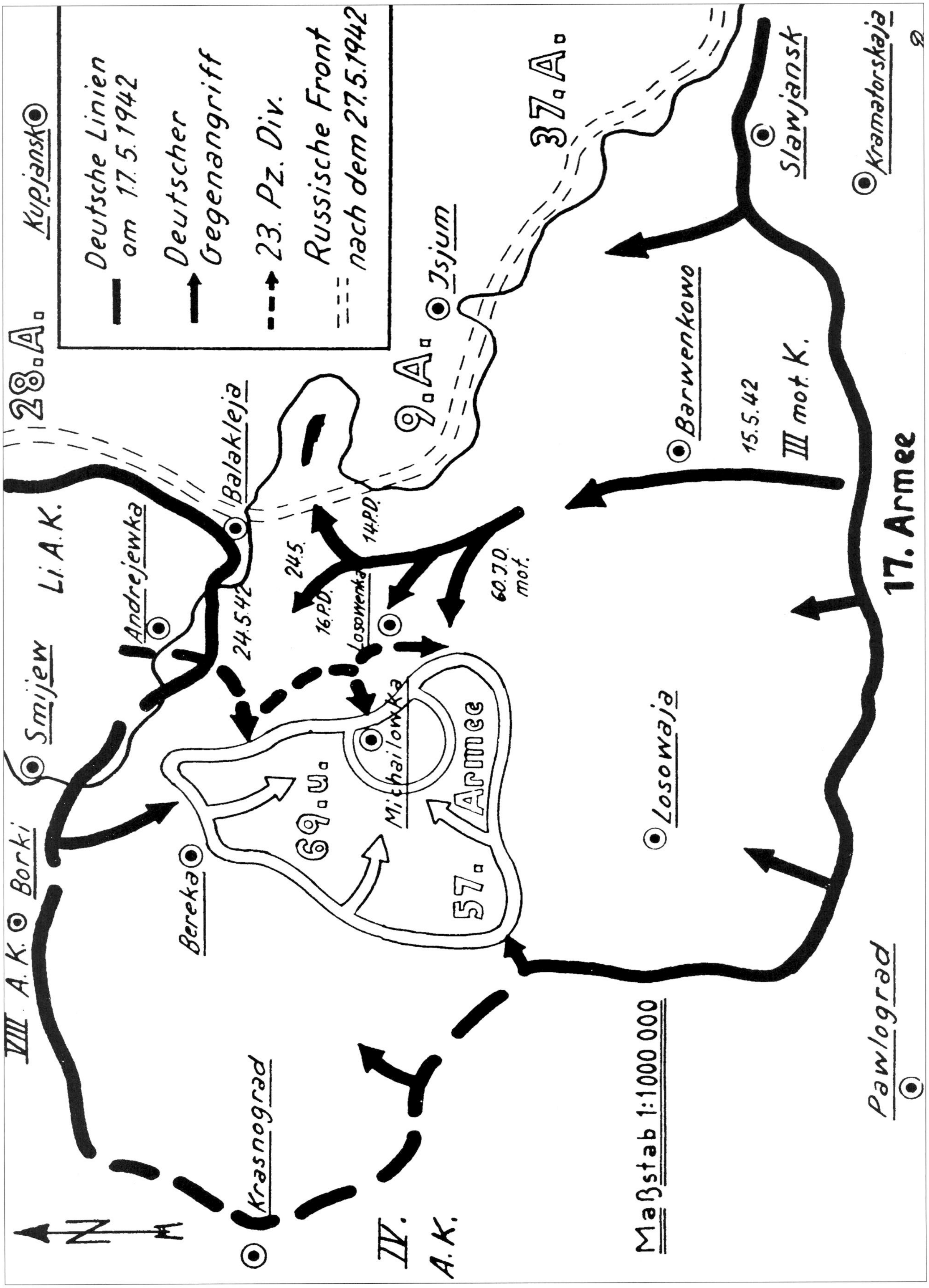

Map 5: The German Counterattack South of Kharkov from 15-27 May 1942.

An attack by the *I./PR201* against the high ground west of Schebelinka failed in the face of the massed Russian defenses. Five German tanks were lost.

After it was relieved in the Wesseloje area, the *23. Panzer-Division* reached the Kharkov area during the evening of 22 May.

The division commander, *General* Boineburg, released the following order-of-the-day upon conclusion of this first phase of combat for the division:

23. Panzer-Division

Division Headquarters, 22 May 1942

Division Order!

I extend my complete praise to the *23. Panzer-Division*, which fought together with elements of the *3. Panzer-Division* in heroic combat against strong enemy superiority.

The division demonstrated in this fighting that it possesses true "tanker" spirit, and it has proved itself equal to the reputation of our glorious, longer-standing divisions.

With your commanders at the front, all of you have mastered the missions assigned to you.

The proud results of these eventful days:

Total:		Of those, from the *I./PR201* and *PJA128* while with the *VIII. Armee-Korps*
Prisoners and deserters	4,970	500
Captured or destroyed:		
Tanks	198	62
Artillery pieces	101	3
Antitank guns	69	15
Mortars	102	20
Antitank rifles	112	—
Antitank / antiaircraft guns	2	—

Among the destroyed enemy tanks were: 15 KV-1's, 116 T-34's, 2 T-60's and 6 Mark II's.

Numerous trucks, including 2 trucks with signals equipment; large quantities of small arms and automatic weapons.

We bow our flags and standards in honor to our dead. They will remain a brilliant example of the highest form of devotion to duty for us.

Forward for *Führer* and Fatherland!

/signed/ *Freiherr* von Boineburg

The attack of the *III. Armee-Korps (mot.)* of *General der Kavallerie* von Mackensen from the area around Barwenkowo to the north had cut the rearward lines of communications of the Soviet attack armies in the area around Losowenka. The ring around the enemy grew ever tighter. The enemy attempted to escape his destruction by means of violent attempts to break out to the east and relief attacks from west of Isjum. The ring of encirclement established by the corps was subjected to extreme pressure, with the result that additional forces had to be inserted into the area around Losowenka. These forces consisted primarily of the *23. Panzer-Division*.

The division moved out again at 1400 hours on 23 May, moving through Tschugujew, to reach the bridgehead at Andrejewka. From this area, the division was to attack west as part of *Korpsgruppe Breith*. It was to attack through Kisselij to reach the high ground east of Alexejewka. *Major Dr.* Maus, the commander of the antitank battalion, was designated as the route commander for the approach march.

In the lead was the group that would form the main effort—*Kampfgruppe Soltmann*: *PR201* (minus the 1st battalion); *I./SR126*; *I./PAR128*; *10.(Flak)/PAR128*; *1./PJA128*; *3./PPB51* and a medical clearing station. That march serial was followed by *KB23*, *PAR128* (minus its 1st Battalion), *SR126* (minus its 1st Battalion), *PPB51* (minus its 3rd Company) and, bringing up the rear, *SR128*.

The approach march of the division was considerably delayed by roads that had become slippery on account of rain and the bottleneck in front of the bridgehead proper at Andrejewka. It was not until the morning of 28 May that the designated assembly area could be reached. The German air superiority in this area contributed greatly to taking the pressure off the ground forces; at the beginning of the battle for Kharkov in the north, it was completely missing and its absence caused a number of losses. In this sector, the German fighters were not allowing any Soviet aircraft to approach friendly forces on the ground.

At 1200 hours on 24 May, the division moved out to attack after the divisional engineers of *Major* Zeydlick had cleared both friendly and Soviet minefields. In all, some 1,200 mines were detonated. In the division sector, *Kampfgruppe* von Heydebreck moved on the right, abutting the *44. Infanterie-Division*. He had with him the remaining 9 tanks of his battalion and the reinforced *II./SR126*. *Kampfgruppe Soltmann* was in the middle; *Kampfgruppe Bachmann* (*SR128*) was on the left. Two hours after taking the formerly bitterly defended Schebelinka, *Kampfgruppe von Heydebreck* was supported by *Stukas*. Combat reconnaissance dispatched to the west determined that there were weak enemy forces in and around Kisselij. The continued attack to the west was stopped by *Korpsgruppe Breith*, however.

At 1610 hours, the following order was received:

Strong enemy attack from Michailowka against the *16. Panzer-Division*. *23. Panzer-Division* is to immediately move southeast of the Kisselij River and eliminate the enemy. Screen at Kisselij.

The *9./PR201* and *KB23* immediately started screening along a line running Hill 200.0 — Eastern outskirts of Kisselij. *Kampfgruppe Soltmann*, which was also joined by *Kampfgruppe von Heydebreck*, turned and attacked to the south toward Melowoj Jar by enveloping out to the east and moving across Hill 179.4. At the same time, *Kampfgruppe Bachmann* moved on Lipki through Sserafimowka and Nikolajewka. On both sides of Melowoj Jar, fires from the divisional artillery scattered enemy forces streaming from the west to the east. For the first time, the *IV. (Flak)/PAR128* of *Major* Draffehn engaged tanks and other ground targets with its 8.8cm *Flak*. Another portion of the *Flak* battalion was employed in providing air defense for the division, and it shot down several aircraft. The 1st and 2nd Battalions of the tank regiment encountered a strong antitank-gun belt north of Melowoj Jar. The onset of darkness made it impossible to compete the defeat of the enemy on this day. The *Kampfgruppe* set up all-round defenses at Hill 170.0. Further to the east, *Kampfgruppe Bachmann* was able to take possession of the weakly manned Nikolajewka. The 1st Company of the antitank battalion screened into the Kisselij Valley for the *Kampfgruppe*.

At first light on 25 May, the *II./PR201* took Melowoj Jar. Marshy terrain and the destruction of the only bridge in the village forced *Kampfgruppe Soltmann* to continue the attack to the south, swinging out through Nikoljewka. To the south and west, one could see Soviet columns and scattered forces moving back and forth, often proving to be lucrative targets for both tanks and artillery. At 0930, Hill 176.2, southwest of Terny, was taken. *Kampfgruppe Bachmann* entered Terny proper. From that point on, however, the division experienced great difficulties through considerable enemy resistance offered by tanks, antitank guns and infantry. Those forces were supported by flanking fires from antitank guns, artillery and rocket launchers from the area around the Petropawlowski estate. Additional reinforcements for the Soviets were approaching from the south and west.

While *Kampfgruppe Bachmann* continued its attack on Lipki, the armored *Kampfgruppe* swung out to the east from Hill 176.2, after leaving behind outposts. It advanced through Ploskojarski to the south, scattered large enemy forces and reached Hill 175.3, east of Michailowka. A Soviet attack conducted by KV-1's and T-34's bogged down in the face

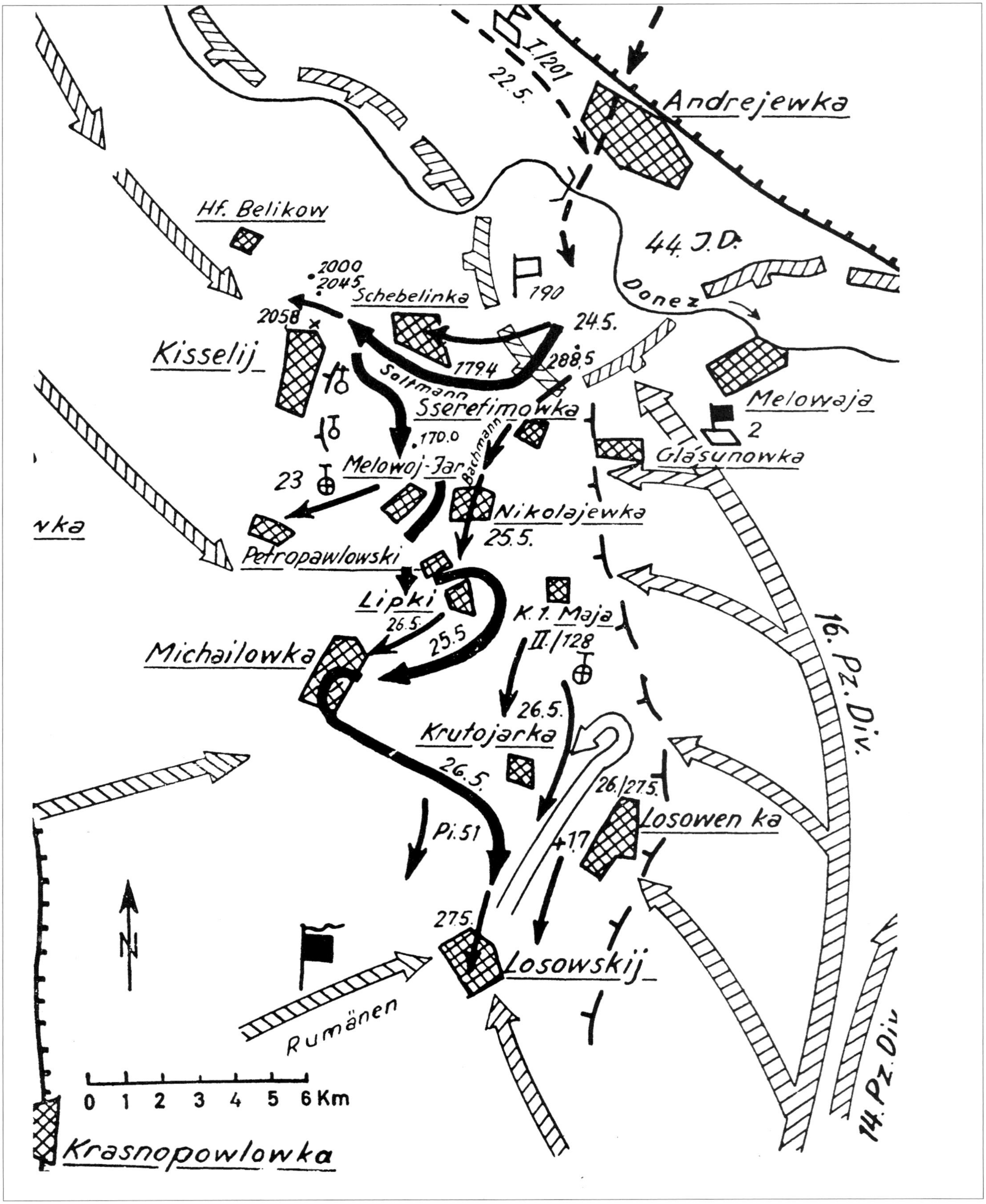

Map 6: Operations of the Division in the Elimination of the Soviet 57th and 69th Armies South of Kharkov from 24-27 May 1942.

of concentrated fires by the *II./PR201* of *Hauptmann* Fechner. Eight enemy tanks, of which five were KV-1's, were destroyed. Three German tanks were slightly damaged, and three men were wounded. The armored *Kampfgruppe* then blocked the Michailowka — Losowenka road and prevented all further attempts by the Russians to advance to the east by this route.

In contrast, the attack by *Kampfgruppe Bachmann* made no progress. A Soviet counterattack, launched from Lipki and conducted by tanks and infantry, overran a portion of the *II./SR128* and caused heavy casualties. Lipki was not taken on this day.

While the divisional artillery continued to engage enemy batteries along the patches of woods west of the Petropawlowski estate, the motorcycle battalion established contact at the estate around 1830 hours with the advance guard of the *113. Infanterie-Division*, which had broken through. Along the north wing of the motorcycle battalion, the light *SPW* company of *Kradschützen-Bataillon 3* of the *3. Panzer-Division* was employed at Hill 204.5. The light *SPW* company cleared the area around Belikow until the following day and took in some 600 prisoners, as well as numerous weapons, as spoils of war.

During the early morning hours of 26 May, massed Soviet infantry forces sought to take advantage of the darkness and break through in the sector of *Kampfgruppe Soltmann*. The attack collapsed in the face of concentrated tank fire. Four Russian tanks were destroyed.

From Hill 175.3, the *3./PPB51*, the *1./PJA128* and two 8.8cm *Flak* blocked the retreat route of the Soviets from Michailowka to Krutojarka.

The *Kampfgruppe* moved out at 0800 hours, entered Michailowka and took the village. Two-thousand five-hundred prisoners were taken; several guns, including two German heavy field howitzers, three tanks and a large quantity of equipment were captured. The Russian forces showed increasing signs of uncertainty. After their march columns were battered and scattered, they usually pulled back to the west, northwest and south, where they once again ran into the concentric fires of the attacking German divisions. German infantry arrived at Michailowka from the west and assumed responsibility for the village.

At the same time that the armored *Kampfgruppe* had moved out, *Kampfgruppe Bachmann* continued its attack on Lipki. Enemy resistance collapsed. The village was taken. In a rapid advance to the southwest, the Kisselij River and the northern edge of Michailowka were reached around 1000 hours.

An urgent order from *Korpsgruppe Breith* was received at 0940 hours:

> Strong enemy forces threaten to break through the sector of the *16. Panzer-Division* at Losowenka and to the south. Shift everything toward Losowenka and advance from there into the Bereka — Losowenka river fork.

That meant that the *Kampfgruppen* of the division had to turn 180 degrees. *Kampfgruppe Soltmann* moved out expeditiously to advance on Losowenka through Krutojarka. The motorcycle battalion, freed up from its mission at the Petropawlowski estate, was sent though Schopenka in the direction of Hill 186.0, to the north of Losowenka. It was closely followed by the *II./SR126* and the division's antitank battalion. An armored reconnaissance patrol reported from south of Hill 186: "Masses of Russians in front of me!"

At 1105 hours, the *I./PR201* entered Krutojarka. In spite of the heavy and well-directed fires by Soviet artillery, as well as the constant antitank-rifle fire on the German armored vehicles, the majority of the enemy forces was becoming increasingly leaderless. The earth-brown masses of Russian infantry approached the German tanks in densely packed groups in order to surrender. Mercilessly, the Soviet artillery fired among them and cut broad swaths though the ranks of their soldiers, who had no weapons and were only thinking of their own salvation by being taken prisoner. The barren meadows and farmlands were covered in the dead, in whimpering Red Army soldiers crawling forward, in weapons and in equipment. Somewhat offset from the masses were numerous dead officers and commissars who had committed suicide. In the middle of this chaos were the division's tanks and armored personnel carriers; Russian doctors, male and female, worked ceaselessly at a clearing station in Krutojarka.

The high ground outside of Losowenka was reached on a broad front. The motorcycle battalion, positioned on Hill 186, screened. The stream of surrendering Soviets continued unabated. Suddenly, however, three T -34's showed up amongst them, supported by Soviet artillery and antitank guns. Reacting quickly, the *II./PR201* knocked out one of the T-34's, whereupon the other two turned away.

West of Krutojarka, other enemy tanks attempted to break out to the northeast. At the last moment, the advance was terminated by the guns of the *III./PAR128*, especially those of the 7th Battery with its 10cm cannon, which set up in the open in the face of the advancing Soviet armor.

As it turned dusk, *Kampfgruppe Soltmann* moved out once again. Its objective was to throw the enemy south of Krutojarka back to Losowskij. The enemy resistance in the area of Point 154.1 was so strong, however, that no further advance was possible at the onset of night. The *Kampfgruppe* set up all-round defenses 1.5 kilometers southeast of Krutojarka, while the engineer battalion and the antitank battalion screened in front of the village. On the right, *Kampfgruppe Bachmann* closed up to the engineers at the northern part of Michailowka, while the *II./SR126* and the motorcycle battalion positioned themselves at Point +1.7, west of Losowenka.

Soon after the onset of darkness, there was a crisis on the left wing of the division. The strongpoints established by the *II./SR126* and *KB23* became the focal point of a desperate breakout attempt on the part of the Soviets. Dense masses of Soviet infantry, yelling their battle cry of "Uräh!", assaulted the ridgeline west of Losowenka and the defile adjoining it to the west. Some of them had been fired up with alcohol and were without weapons.

They were mown down in rows, but they kept on coming and were soon at the strongpoints, overrunning them or encircling them. Sixteen men of the motorcycle battalion were captured by the Soviets, disarmed and then clubbed to death in the most brutal manner possible with spades. The fury of their comrades, who discovered them the next day, was boundless. As the motorcycle infantry were increasingly pushed back from their positions, and they found themselves fighting their way clear to the north more with entrenching tools than rifles, the men of the light *SPW* company, who had been separated from their vehicles, held their positions and set up an all-round defense on Hill 186.0 for the rest of the night. The only assistance that could be rendered to the hard-pressed battalions was an advance of the tanks from their defensive position south of Krutojarka. They headed south and placed heavy fires against the Soviets advancing north further to the east, but in the pitch-black night the enemy was difficult to make out. The defensive positions of *Kampfgruppe Soltmann* were also subjected to attacks by Soviet forces, and two officers were wounded in their tanks.

The main clearing station manned by the 1st Medical Company in Nikolajewka was overflowing with the sudden increase in casualties.

Soviet forces pressed northward on both sides of Hill 186.0 in the sector of *Hauptmann* von Kunow's *Kradschützen-Bataillon 23*. Around 0200 hours, they reached the outpost line of the division headquarters 2 kilometers south of the "1 May" Collective Farm. The outposts were successful in turning back the enemy. Other Soviet forces pressed against the frontage of the *16. Panzer-Division* east of Schopenka and Losowenka. During the night, Soviet aircraft dropped numerous parachutes with rations and ammunition for the encircled forces. Most of them landed among the German forces, however.

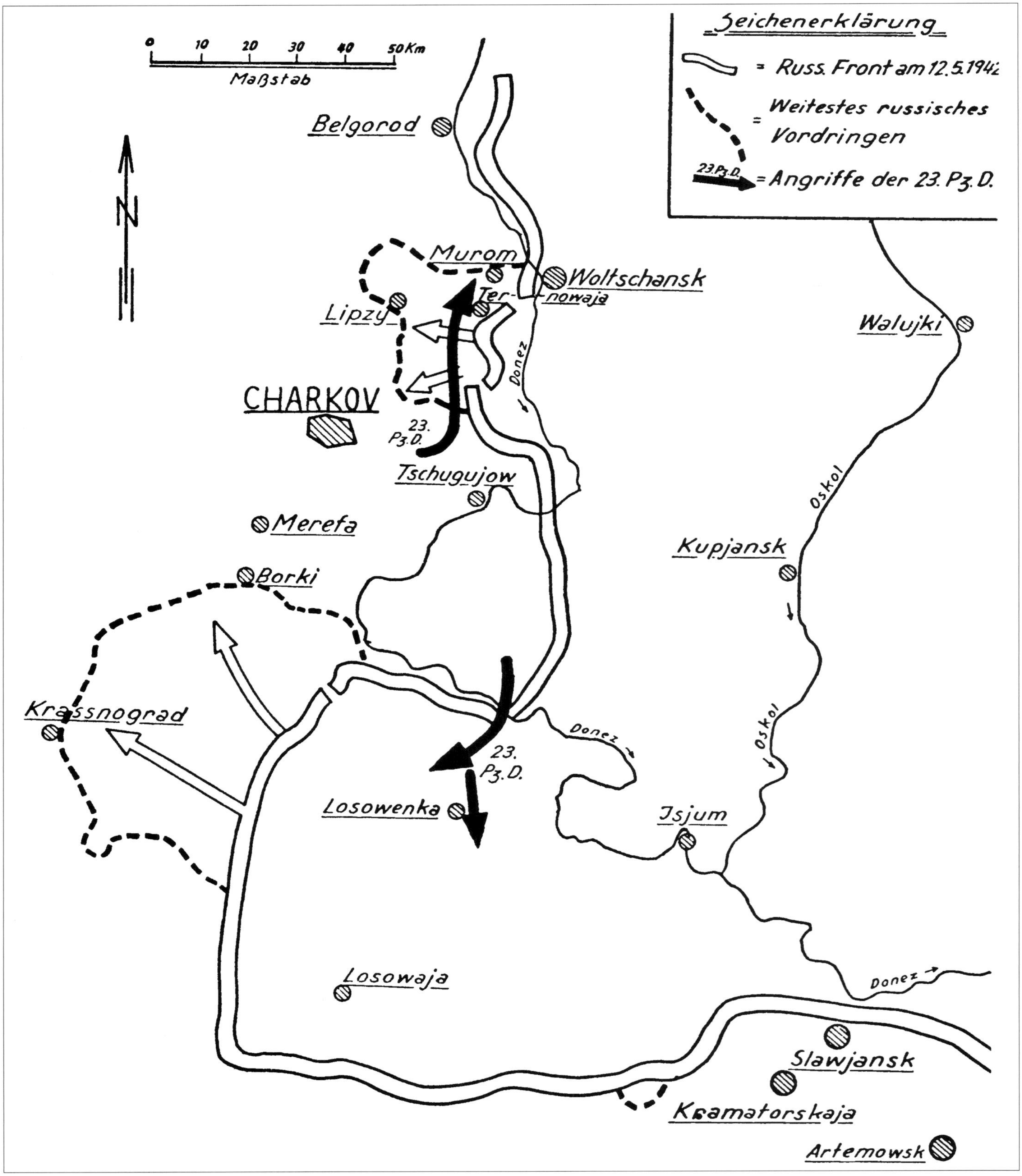

Map 7: The *23. Panzer-Division* in the Battle of Kharkov from 12-27 May 1942..

At first light on 27 May, elements of *Kampfgruppe Soltmann* reestablished the situation west of Losowenka. Two rifle companies from the *3. Panzer-Division*, as well as military police and motorcycle infantry, conducted a deliberate clearing action in the area of the fighting of the previous night. In the process, more than 1,000 prisoners were taken.

At 0600 hours on 27 May, *Kampfgruppe Soltmann* moved out to the south toward Losowenka. The *I./PR201* moved via Hill 171.8 and the *II./PR201* via Hill 163.7. The division engineers and the *I./SR126* followed. There was hardly any firing. The Russian will to resist had finally been broken. Prisoner upon prisoner was taken. But in the midst of this joyful occasion, there was a tragic occurrence. In the rapidly changing situation, a flight of *Stukas* mistakenly attacked the *II./SR126* of *Hauptmann* von Eisenhardt-Rothe. As a sobering result of this mistake, there were 18 dead and 21 wounded.

The 1st Battalion of the tank regiment entered Losowskij at the same time as lead infantry columns from the west. Romanian cavalry arrived from the south. Thousands of Soviets awaited their capture. Untold quantities of weapons, equipment, vehicles, tanks and horses filled the area. Numerous pieces of German equipment were recaptured. One tank company alone took in 4,000 prisoners and counted 39 guns in a sector measuring 1 kilometer wide and 5 kilometers deep.

Small groups combed the area the next day for scattered Soviet elements. The rifle regiments evacuated the prisoners and took them to *Infanterie-Regiment 190*, which was assigned the mission of guarding them. Engineers and the *I./PR201* cleared the Glasunowka — Melowaja area of individual Russians on 29 May. Eighty-five prisoners were taken in that effort. The division had accomplished its mission. During the night of 29/30 March, the division set out for Kharkov to reoccupy its former billets and rest.

***

The Battle of Kharkov was over. The major threat to the city and the German formations fighting in this area had been eliminated. At the same time, the Russian successes obtained in the February offensive were negated. The German front lines ran as far as the Donez again, which provided good starting points for the summer offensive. It had been the aim of the Soviet offensive to deny the Germans these jumping-off points.

The Soviet 57th and 69th Armies had been effectively destroyed. Elements of the two field armies included the 14th Guards, 41st, 47th, 99th, 103rd, 160th, 210th, 248th, 253rd, 260th, 270th, 317th, 333rd, 335th, 337th, 341st, 349th, 351st, 393rd and 411th Rifle Divisions. Other elements included the 23rd Motorized brigade, the 26th, 28th, 34th, 38th, 49th, 60th, 62nd, 64th and 70th Cavalry Division and the 5th Guards, 37th, 38th, 48th, 64th, 67th, 121st, 131st, 198th and 199th Tank Brigades.

The destruction of these enemy forces south of Kharkov was thanks in large measure to the *23. Panzer-Division*. The division captured or destroyed:

95 tanks	4 aircraft
402 guns	11 infantry guns
175 antitank guns	30 antiaircraft/antitank guns
172 mortars	10 "Stalin Organs"
200 antitank rifles	120 tractors and prime movers
2,100 vehicles of all types	30 field kitchens
2,000 horses	800 horse-drawn vehicles
350 machine guns	

47,000 prisoners were taken.

German losses:

	Officers	Noncommissioned officers and enlisted
Dead	10	146
Wounded	23	350
Missing	1	5

Five German tanks were total write-offs; nine could be repaired.

As impressive as the spoils of war from the fighting south of Kharkov were, even greater was the successful employment of the division northeast of Kharkov. According to statements made by the commander of the 226th Rifle Division, Colonel Towanzew, the largest massing of forces had occurred there. The advance on Kharkov was to have primarily taken place from the north.

The self-sacrificing employment in the attack along the Babka to the north in terrain that was completely ill-suited for an armored division—all the while threatened from the air by superior enemy air forces—justified a review of the recent events that was filled with pride. That the operations south of Kharkov then led to successes that were innumerable, was the reward for the combat morale of all of the formations.

The performance of the division was singled out for praise in the *Wehrmacht* Daily Report.

Start of the Summer Offensive 30 June to 7 July 1942

After the exertions of the recent fighting, the time that remained to the division for refitting was short. Replacements for the officers, noncommissioned officers and enlisted personnel, who had been lost, arrived and had to be integrated into the formations by means of training exercises. The experiences freshly gained in combat with the Soviets had to be evaluated. Weapons and equipment also had to be brought back up to authorized levels. The antitank battalion and the tank regiment benefitted the most, being brought back up to nearly full strength. All the better was the fact that the remaining 5cm antitank guns of *PJA128* were supplemented by 7.5cm guns. In the case of the tank regiment, *Panzer III's* with the long-barreled 5cm main gun (L 60) arrived, as did *Panzer IV's* with 7.5cm long-barreled main guns (L 48). The rifle regiments each received antiaircraft companies, which were designated as the regiments' 10th Companies. The *10.(Flak)/SR126* was formed from the *2./FlaMG-Btl. 48*, while the *10.(Flak)/SR128* was formed from the *5./FlaMGBtl. 52*.[8] Two experienced combat leaders were assigned to the division in the form of *Oberst Dr.* Müller and *Oberst* Pochat. The former assumed command of *Schützen-Regiment 126* and the latter of *Panzer-Regiment 201*. Both colonels were Knight's Cross recipients. *Oberst* von Bodenhausen became the commander of *Schützen-Brigade 23*.

The German summer offensive was just around the corner. Its objectives were to destroy the southern portion of the Soviet Front, reaching the lower Don and the Volga on both sides of Stalingrad. On the expressed desires of Hitler, it was also to take possession of the Caucasian oil region. Despite the misgivings of the Army's General Staff, which feared an excessive widening of the front and the corresponding weakening of the German forces, Hitler held obstinately to his idea.

In June 1942, five German and three allied field armies assembled in the area between the Asovian Sea and Kursk. It was intended for the *1. Panzer-Armee* and the *4. Panzer-Armee* to advance out of the areas of Isjum and Tschugujew, forming the main effort and breaking through the Soviet frontages. These were to be followed by the *6. Armee* and the *2. Armee* on a broad front. Later on, those two field armies were to be joined by the *17. Armee*, which was positioned, echeloned to the southeast, along the Mius and Donez. The Rumanian 3rd, the Italian 8th and the Hungarian 2nd Armies, which had closed up behind the German field armies, were intended to fill the gaps that were expected to develop between the German forces as they advanced eastward and, above all, to hold the areas that had been reached.

The *23. Panzer-Division*, together with the *3. Panzer-Division* and the *29. Infanterie-Division (mot.)*, which were all under the command of the *XXXX. Panzer-Korps* of *General der Panzertruppen* Stumme, were to advance to the northeast and the Don south of Woronesch as the armored fist of the *6. Armee* of *General der Infanterie* Paulus. The *XXXXVIII. Panzer-Korps* of the *2. Armee* was to attack at the same time, forming the northern arm of the pincers. The intent was to encircle the Soviet forces

8 Editor's Note: *FlaMGBtl. = Flugabwehr-Maschinen-Gewehr-Bataillon =* Antiaircraft Machine Gun Battalion.

The division underwent its baptism of fire in May 1942, during the fighting around Kharkov, where it acquitted itself well. *Leutnant* Jantzer and *Unteroffizier* Baumann confer during a break in the action.

Maintenance was a never-ending struggle.

Leutnant Reuther, exhausted from the fighting, catches some sleep.

Signal and recognition flares, as well as tracer rounds, illuminate the night-time skies.

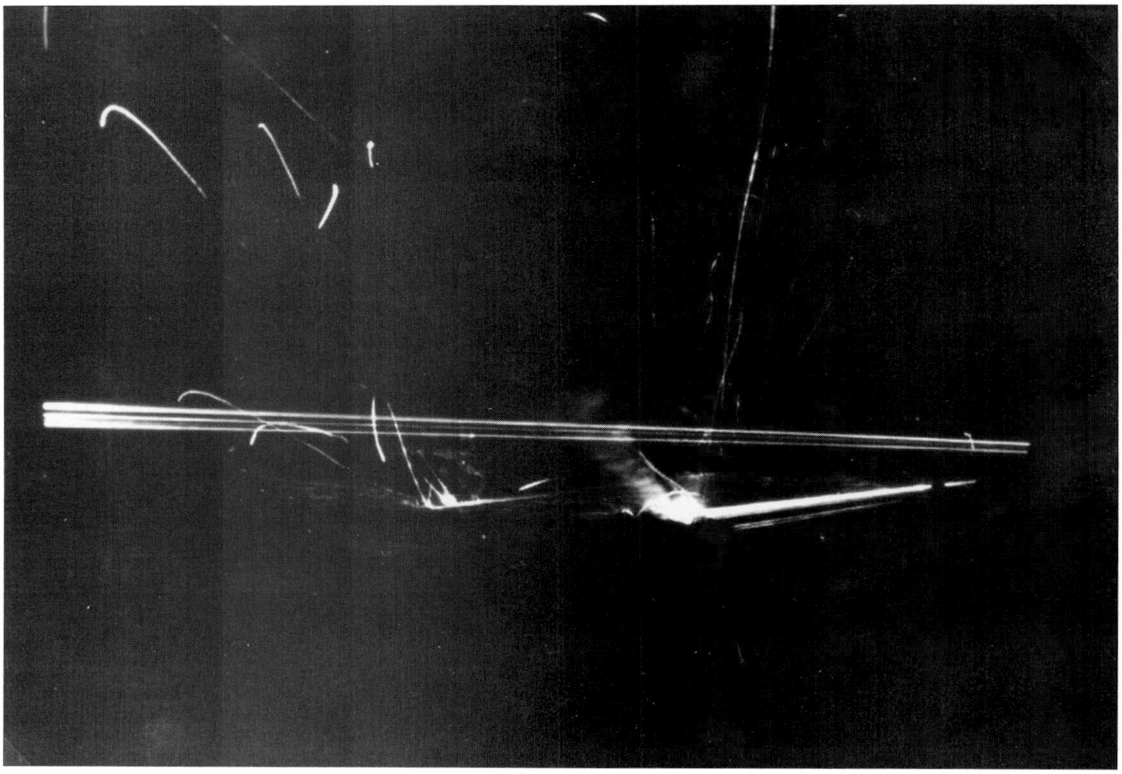

It pays to know your enemy. Examining a captured T-34.

Oberleutnant Grahn's brother pays a visit in May 1942.

One of the newly issued long-barreled *Panzer III's* armed with a 5cm main gun.

This *Panzer III* of the *6./PR201* ran off a road during a night march on 21 June 1942.

A Soviet "road".

This 1-ton prime mover fell victim to a Soviet wooden mine.

A break in the action.

A Soviet gun crew surrenders to the divisional antitank battalion.

The command post of *Oberleutnant* Butz, the commander of the *4./PR 201*. Notice how shelter halves have been draped around the running gear, probably added to protect the men of the command post from the elements and also to keep light from getting out during hours of limited visibility. *Oberleutnant* Butz was later killed in action.

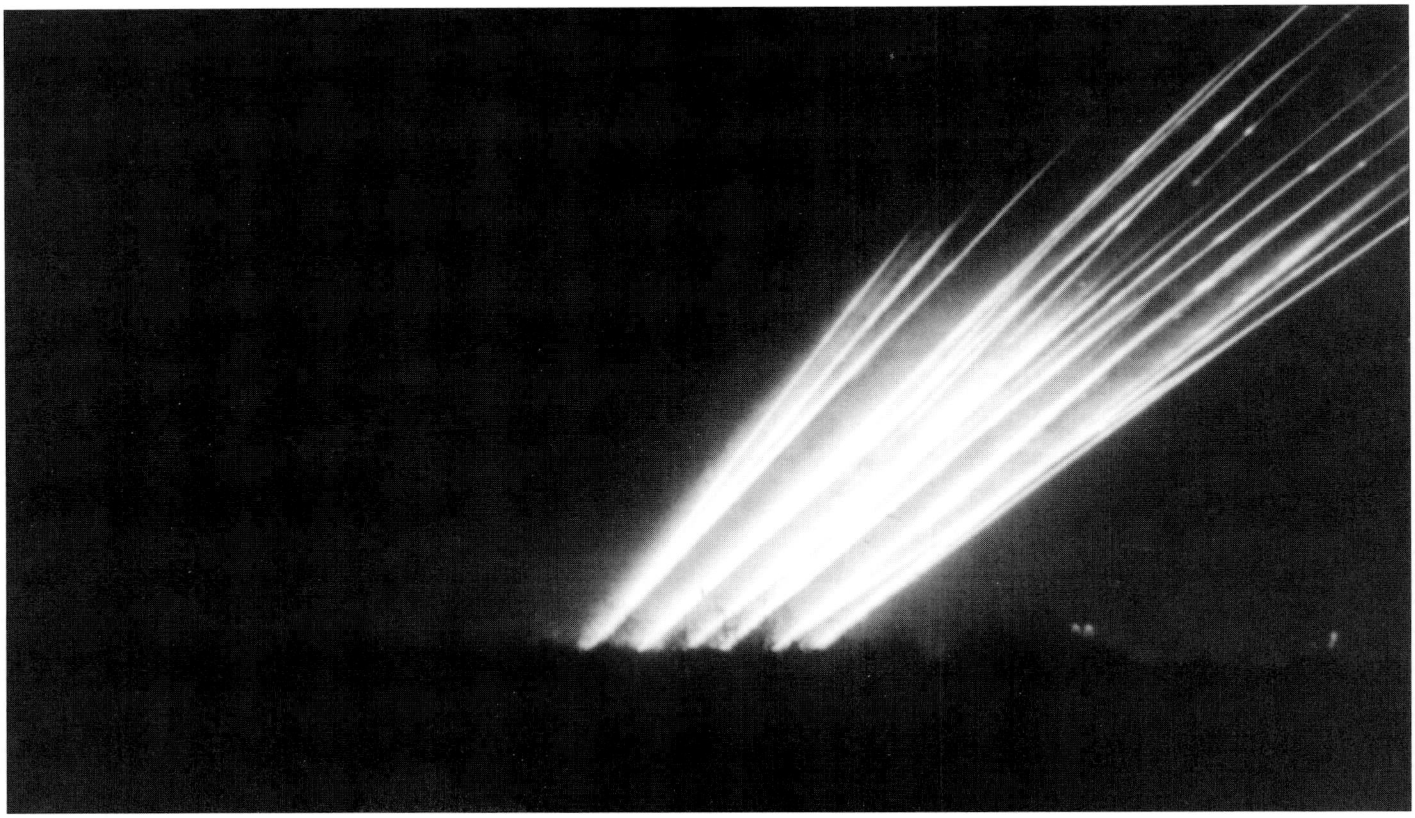

Nighttime fireworks provided courtesy of a "Stalin Organ".

A knocked-out KV-1. This vehicle was almost impossible for a *Panzer III* to knock-out at any range.

Panzer-Regiment 201 forms up for operations.

Knocked-out BT-7.

An abandoned Soviet 4.7cm light antitank gun.

Curious sheep check out a Mercedes truck undergoing repairs and maintenance.

Peasant huts, an open well and the seemingly endless land of the Soviet Union.

The tanks attack with artillery support.

The regiment moves on. The *Panzer II* would have been used as a reconnaisance vehicle.

The platoon leader of the scout platoon, *Leutnant* Oskierski, gets information from *Oberleutnant* Rüdt von Collenberg and *Oberfeldwebel* Wirwa (turret).

This *Panzer IV* of the *6./PR 201* fell victim to a mine.

These two tank crews had to take cover in a former Soviet trench after losing their vehicles to mines.

The Pocket Battle of Kharkov is over.

German soldiers check out a dug-in T-34.

June 1942: The road leads on to Woltschansk.

The *1./PR 201* lines up to wash its vehicles. The high pressure hose is used to dislodge the persistent Russian mud.

The regimental band also has a chance to practise one more time...

The 1./PR 201 in an assembly area west of Woltschansk in June 1942. Company noncommissioned officers catch up on paperwork.

The company's maintenance section

The Maintenance Sergeant with the leader of the maintenance section.

Camouflaged tank...

A *Panzer IV* takes up a covered and concealed position prior to the start of operations.

Oberstleutnant von Heydebreck and his liaison officer, *Leutnant* Ewerhard, who was later killed in action.

Officer conference with *Inspekteur* Kather, Major Illig, *Oberst* Pochat and *Hauptmann* Päzold. Both *Major* Illig and *Oberst* Pochat later paid the ultimate sacrifice.

Tanks form up for operations with the *1./PR 201* in the lead.

Just outside of Nesternoje. In the tank on the right (*RL 1*) was Schmidtinger, who was later killed.

The tanks form up again after passing Nesternoje.

The deadly accurate *Stukas* provide much needed support.

The air-ground coordination functioned well at this stage of the campaign. A dramatic image of a *Ju 87 Stuka* engaged in a low level attack.

Breakthrough at Nesteroje. *Oberleutnant* Ott's tank is on fire on the right (30 June 1942)

An attack against prepared Soviet positions on 30 June 1942: Tank-versus-tank.

The distinctive shape of the Soviet T34.

Grave site of a crew killed at Nesternoje (30 June 1942).

The knocked-out tank of *Oberleutnant* Ott.

Captured T-34.

The Company Motor Sergeant hard at work updating records.

The maintenance section goes for the bald look. One way to combat the discomfort of lice.

To the east of Nesternoje. The crew of *Feldwebel* Achternosch after being knocked out. One man is missing.

Oberst Pochat shortly before his death.

The advance continues.

A famous image...

A T-34 burns after being hit by *Leutnant* Rebentisch's gunner, *Unteroffizier* Pfleiderer.

Mechanized infantry work with the tanks...

Another famous image from this campaign.

The advance continues through the dust and heat.

July 1942: The *II./PR 201* advances toward Oskol.

Oberst Burmeister, the tank regiment commnder, and *Hauptmann* Rüdt von Collenberg.

A Gnome-Rhone Motorcycle moves past a burning T-34.

Oskol is in sight...

Infantry advancing the old-fashioned way...

This *Messerschmitt Bf 109E* of *II./SchG 1,* a ground attack unit, crashed near a supply route.

The first large masses of prisoners come streaming to the rear.

Although not of the highest quality, an interesting photo of a captured T-34 with *Leutnant* Eichler commanding. Considerable effort has been made to mark the vechicle as being in German hands.

A *Panzer III Ausf. J* with the 50 mm L/42 main gun. The crew obviously had some concerns about the 50 mm front hull armor.

This Kübelwagen from the divisional artillery takes a break to fill up.

The lead elements outside of Nowyi Put.

A *Panzer II—II L 4*—has suffered mine damage.

Impacting artillery on 4 July 1942 at Repjewka.

An unsung hero: A battalion physician at work.

A shot-down IL-2 at Ostrogoshsk.

Generalfeldmarschall von Manstein visits the divison.

Both the Germans and their allies—in this case, on the left, a Croatian—relied heavily on the horse for much of their supplies.

Oberst Burmeister, the commander of *Panzer-Regiment 201*.

Oberleutnant Hans-Harald Grahn, the commander of the *6./PR 201.*

Orders conference on 4 July 1942: *Oberstleutnant* Soltmann (Acting Commander, *PR 201*), *Leutnant* Krömer (Signals officer), *Oberleutnant* Grahn (Commander, *6./PR 201*), *Leutnant* Oskierski (Scout Platoon Leader), *Oberleutnant* Rüdt von Collenberg (Regimental Adjutant) and *Oberleutnant* Rebentisch (Acting Commander, *I./PR 201*).

The aftermath of the failed Soviet breakout attempt at Tschertowo on 14 July 1942.

The burial of Knight's Cross recipient *Major* Behr, the commander of the *I./PR 201*, on 23 July 1942.

This page and next: The victory of the *II./PR 201* at Tscherkowo.

Leutnant Streb, the platoon leader of the motorcycle scout platoon of the *II./PR 201*.

A catastrophic internal explosion has completely destroyed this T-34. The passing *Panzer III* was most unlikely to have been the cause.

The spoils of war are counted and individual prisoners continued to be taken.

A cannibalized *Tiger*. When parts were not available or in short supply, the battalion maintenance officers would often select a "hangar queen" to provide replacement items for other tanks that could be made operational.

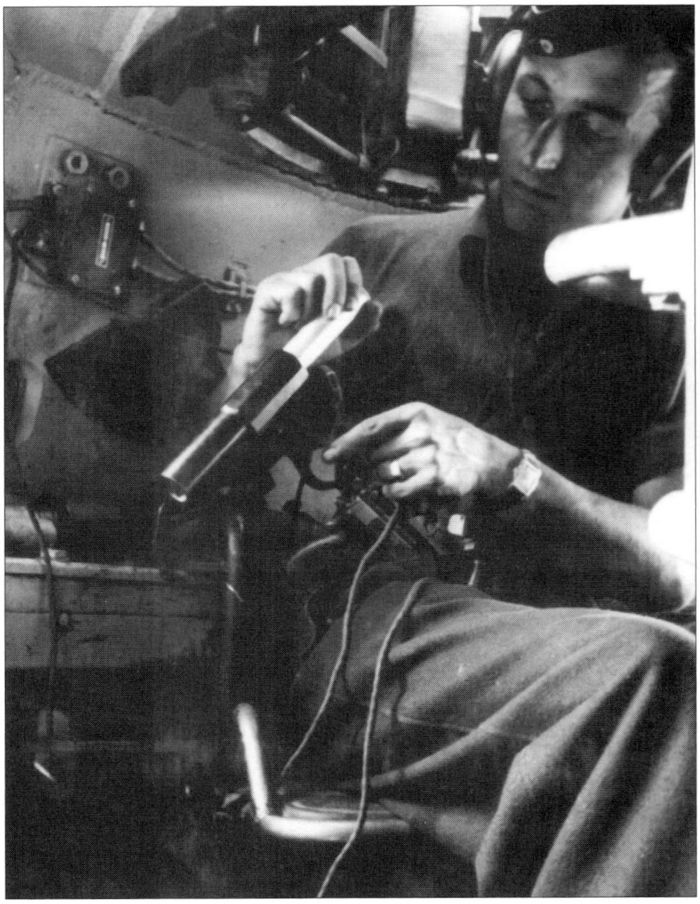

Leutnant Pietsch, the regimental Signals Officer, loads a flare pistol in the turret of command tank 201.

A view down the hatch of the commander's cupola.

Driver

Radio operator

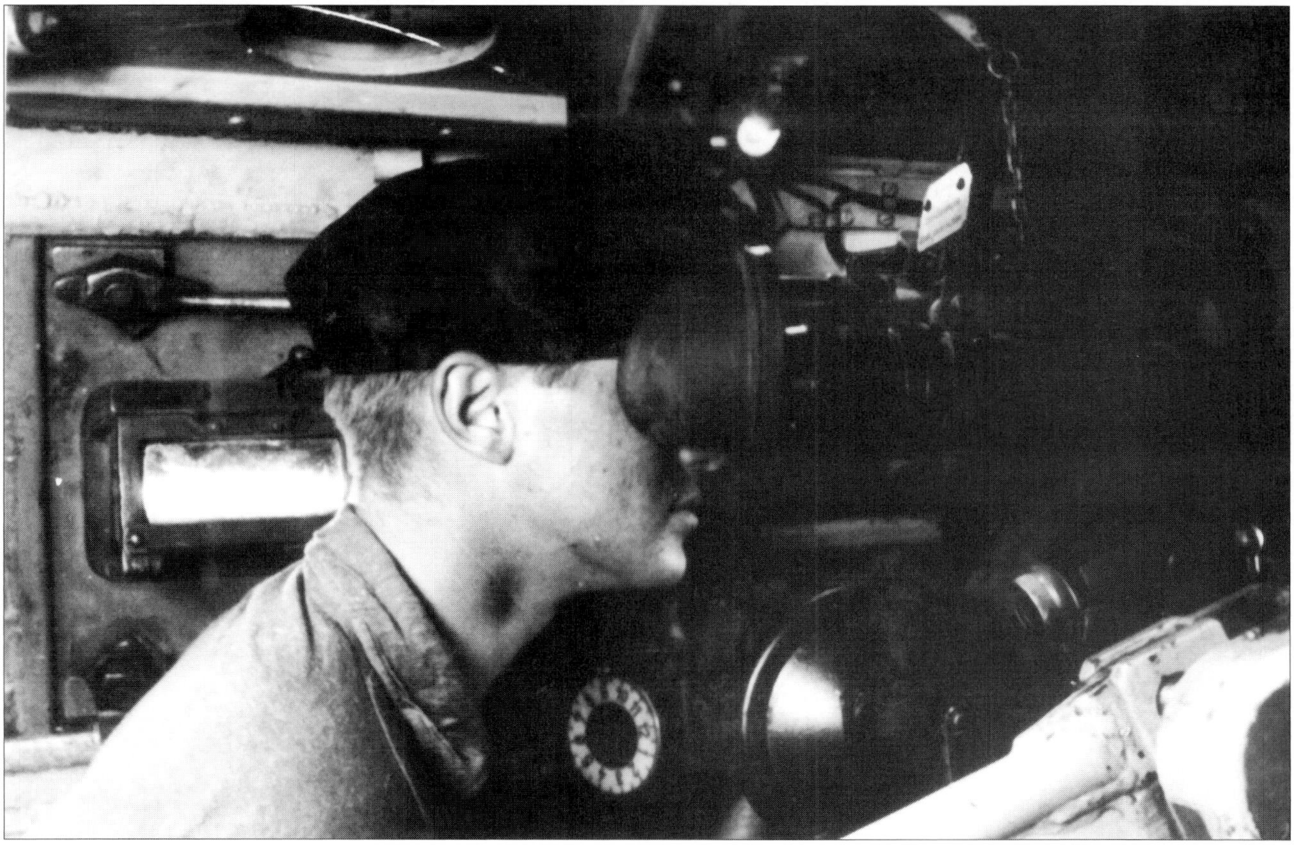

Gunner

Loader

Map 8: The Attack Route of the *23. Panzer-Division* from 30 June to 1 November 1942.

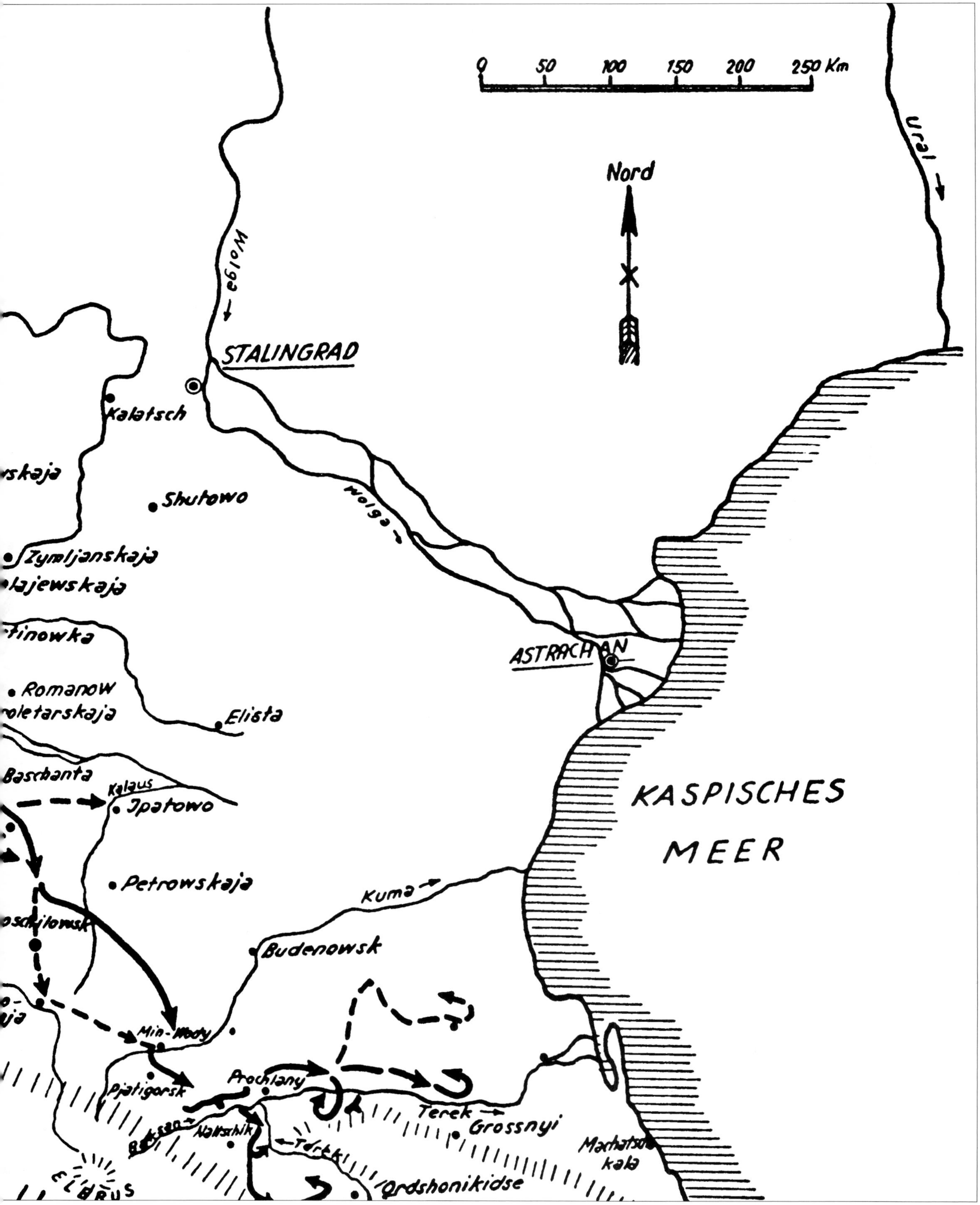
0 50 100 150 200 250 Km
Nord
Ural
Wolga
STALINGRAD
Kalatsch
Shutowo
Zymljanskaja
Wolga
ASTRACHAN
Romanow
Elista
Baschanta
Kalaus
Jpatowo
Petrowskaja
KASPISCHES
MEER
Kuma
Budenowsk
Min-Wody
Pjatigorsk
Prochlany
Terek
Grossnyi
Naltschik
Terek
Machatschkala
Ordshonikidse
ELBRUS

west of Woronesch, adding on to the successes of the earlier part of the year.

In the meantime, the German preparations for the offensive, which were interrupted by the Soviet offensive of 12 May, were continued. Armored formations moved out in the areas of Tschugujew, Starij Saltow and Woltschansk on 10 June and threw the Soviets back across the Donez and advanced the German front lines in several offensive operations as far as the southern branch of the Oskol. By dong so, good jumping-off points were created for the summer offensive.

In expectation of Soviet countermeasures, the *III./PR201* of *Major* Illig was attached to the *VIII. Armee-Korps* on 11 June and awaited employment in Murawlewo, north of Wesseloje. On 25 June, it returned to Kharkov without having been employed.

At that point, the division was handed an unfortunate twist of fate. After a situation briefing among the division commanders at the headquarters of the *XXXX. Panzer-Korps* and the distribution of the preparatory orders, the operations officer of the division, *Major i.G.* Reichel,[9] received orders to conduct a leader's reconnaissance of the intended division sector. He was given a *Fieseler Storch* light utility aircraft to fly as far as Woltschansk, in order to save time due to the continuing rain, which made ground movement difficult. Contrary to orders—and despite rain, fog and poor visibility—he decided to fly close to the front. He took the march orders for the division—classified secret—with him.[10]

The aircraft flew over no-man's-land by mistake due to the poor visibility. Infantry weapons were more than sufficient to bring down the low- and slow-flying aircraft. *Major* Reichel and his pilot were killed; with them, just in front of the Soviet lines, were the approach routes and attack plans of the division.

It was not until evening, when the orders were supposed to be issued and *Major* Reichel had not returned, that it was determined what had occurred. Patrols and two attacks by battalions from the *336. Infanterie-Division* led to the discovery of the remains, but the important papers were missing. The enemy had been quicker! He promptly reacted by regrouping his formations, bringing armor forward into the sector and emplacing extended minefields.

The *XXXX. Panzer-Korps* and the *336. Infanterie-Division* requested that the attack plans be changed—all in vain. Hitler ordered that the *23. Panzer-Division* was to move out in its designated attack sector. To add insult to injury, he directed that the Commanding General of the *XXXX. Panzer-Korps, General der Panzertruppen* Stumme, his Chief-of-Staff, *Oberst i.G.* Franz and the Division Commander, *Generalmajor* von Boineburg be relieved and be tried by a court-martial. Although von Boineburg was cleared of all charges in the court-martial proceedings chaired by *Reichsmarschall* Göring in August, the division itself had lost its commander and operations officer just before the attack.

In any event, the movement orders issued on 21 June released the built-up tension. During the night, the armored and wheeled vehicles of the division moved across the terrain they had first fought upon and into the area around and west of Woltschansk. A great deal of difficulties were caused by the rain-softened roads and the pitch-black night. The final preparations for the operation were conducted in the densely vegetated oak-populated woods along the Donez, which offered good concealment.

During the night of 25/26 June, the troop formations crossed the Donez and occupied their assembly areas in the woods southwest of Krassnjanskoje. Despite the pending court-martial charges, *Generalmajor* von Boineburg led these movements, since his replacement had not arrived. Soviet harassment aircraft looked for the columns and covered them with bombs and strafed them. Frequently, between 6 and 7 "sewing machines"[11] plied their trade above the division. The command and control vehicle of the division commander was hit and his enlisted aide was killed.

On the following morning, the new division operations officer, *Major i.G.* Freyer, arrived.

The start of the offensive—planned for the morning of 27 June—had to be postponed due to the heavy rainfall, which caused the ground surface to become seemingly bottomless. The divisional artillery occupied its positions to support the attack.

The Soviets remained very quiet; they wanted reassurance concerning the German intentions after the expected attack on 27 June did not materialize. Soviet reconnaissance aircraft were constantly over the approach march of the division: At night, it was the so-called "sewing machines"; by day, it was fighter aircraft and ground-support aircraft such as the *IL-2*.

During the morning of 28 June, Soviet tanks and infantry attacked from Pestschanoje. The barrage fires conducted by the divisional artillery and *Artillerie-Regiment 336* of the *336. Infanterie-Division* effectively stopped the attack in front of the infantry positions. The *I./PJA128* was attached to *Infanterie-Regiment 687* of the latter division at Derewenskoje.

In the morning, *Generalmajor Freiherr* von Boineburg-Lengsfeld left the division, which he had formed and led to its initial great success in the Battle for Kharkov. His successor was *Generalmajor* Mack. On the same day, *General der Panzertruppen* Stumme, the Commanding General, was replaced by Geyr von Schweppenburg, who held the same rank.

The opening chord of the summer offensive was sounded on this day when the *XXXXVIII. Panzer-Korps* moved out from the area around Kursk and advanced some 50 kilometers deep into enemy territory in the direction of Woronesch.

Within the *XXXX. Panzer-Korps*, codeword "Aachen" was issued during the evening of 28 June. The codeword signaled that the attack was to proceed "on the day after tomorrow in accordance with issued orders." The mission for the first day of attack:

> *XXXX. Panzer-Korps* is to advance with massed forces to the northeast as far as the Oskol and establishes a broad bridgehead in the area southwest of Nowji Oskol on the east bank of the river.

The orders for the division:

> The *23. Panzer-Division* is to attack across the 233.1 — 232.1 ridgeline to the northeast, advance through Tscherwonnji and reach the Oskol at Sslonowka, where it crosses.

Infanterie-Regiment 687 of the *336. Infanterie-Division*, which was the friendly force on the left, was attached to the division for the attack.

On 29 June, troop elements occupied attack positions upon receiving the codeword "Dinkelsbühl". *Kampfgruppe von Bodenhausen*, which formed the main effort, consisted of *PR201* (minus the 3rd Battalion) and the reinforced *SR128*. It took up positions along the ridgeline northeast of Oktjabriskoje. *Kampfgruppe Müller*, consisting of the reinforced *SR126* and the *III./PR201*, took up positions around Schabelnoje on the left. The divisional antitank battalion supported *Kampfgruppe von Bodenhausen* with its 1st Company; the 2nd Company was directed to support *Kampfgruppe Müller. Fla-Kompanie 633* supported the *Kampfgruppen* by platoon. The divisional engineers stood by to clear minefields and obstacles, while the *Flak* battalion provided general air defense for the division. The divisional signals battalion had signals elements standing by to establish communications behind the advancing forces.

9 Editor's Note: *i.G.* = *im Generalstab* = General Staff officer. A German division at the time did not have a chief-of-staff. The 1st General Staff Officer performed the duties of operations officer, while the 2nd General Staff Officer was the division logistics officer. Both were normally general staff officers and entitled to append *i.G.* to their ranks.

10 Editor's Note: The author refers to the orders as *geheime Kommandosachen,* which is roughly equivalent to the US military's "secret" classification.

11 Editor's Note: German foot soldiers referred to these aircraft as *Nähmaschinen*, which has been literally translated here. Usually, this was the Po-2, a rugged, single-engine biplane.

At 0215 hours,[12] the first *Stukas* flew over the attack positions in the dim morning light and dropped their bombs on Nesternoje, Krugloje and Pestschanoje. At the same time, the preparatory fires of the artillery and mortars started along the entire front. The engines of the fighting vehicles warmed up. At 0230 hours, the attack started, with the *I./PR201* leading the way. The tanks of *Kampfgruppe von Bodenhausen* encountered mines outside of Nesternoje. At the same time, they received heavy fires from antitank guns and tank fires from rear-slope positions and earthen fortifications. The first few tanks of both the *1.* and *2./PR201* were engulfed in flames, but the attack did not bog down. The tanks moved through Nesternoje. *Oberleutnant* Ott of the *8./PR201* and *Oberleutnant* von Cossel of the *2./PR201* were killed.

Weak enemy infantry forces in Nesternoje allowed the grenadiers of *Infanterie-Regiment 687* to swiftly enter the village. In contrast, the tanks had to defend against T-34's and KV-1's that were firing from the flank, often from hull-down positions. It was the hardest and bloodiest fight the tank regiment underwent in its entire history. Many comrades were lost in front of the enemy; the Soviet tankers fought bravely and with determination. Even though on fire, many attempted to escape from the Germans and did not evacuate their positions until they had been bypassed. *Balkas*[13] made their flight easier, even though they were followed tirelessly by diving *Stukas*.

Only two hours into the fight, the *I./PR201* had expended all of its ammunition, a sign of the harshness of the fighting. While that battalion was resupplied on the battlefield, the *II./PR201* of *Hauptmann* Fechner advanced on Degtjarnoje, swinging to the right. *Oberst* Pochat, always with the lead attack elements, rallied the attack forward. The attack only made progress with difficulty. It was flanked on the right from the patches of woods south of Krugloje and on the left from the depressions around Teresowka (Kuraljunoff).

Soviet artillery and mortars fired into the assembled tanks. One such artillery salvo landed on the regimental staff. *Oberst* Pochat collapsed in the cupola of his tank, hit in the heart by shrapnel. Next to him, the leader of the regiment's light platoon, *Oberfeldwebel* Schmitdinger, was also killed. An "old hand" at armor operations, Schmitdinger had first learned his craft in the fighting in Spain. *Oberstleutnant* von Heydebreck assumed acting command of the regiment, while the commander of his 1st Company assumed command of the battalion.

The 1st Medical Company's clearing station in Russki-Tischki had its hands full with massive amounts of casualties; wounded Soviet soldiers were also treated there.

While the main effort *Kampfgruppe* fought its way forward, meter-by-meter, *Kampfgruppe Müller* also had a difficult time of it. The enemy also put up a tough defense in front of it by means of antitank guns, tanks and mines. The *III./PR201* took considerable casualties. *Hauptmann* Neubeck's 1st Battalion of *SR126*, which was the regiment's *SPW* battalion, was unable to exploit its speed and mobility in the face of the massed enemy armor-defeating weapons. During the morning, these elements were gradually able to link up with the main body of the tank regiment on the left, with the result that both *Kampfgruppen* were then able to advance together after reaching Ssawin.

Before that could occur, however, the *II./PR201* had a difficult engagement against a strong anti-armor defensive belt consisting of antitank guns and tanks along the northwest edge of Degtjarnoje. While combating the enemy, some of the elements also ran into minefields. It was not until further losses had been sustained that the enemy was subjugated. At the same time, *Infanterie-Regiment 687* entered the village proper and German artillery targeted identified Soviet battery positions and armor.

Stuka-Geschwader 77 supported the attack by dive bombing and strafing, and it provided the air-ground coordination officer of the division with constant reports on enemy defensive positions and the enemy's actions. The *élan* of the aviators was something to behold.

Towards noon, the tanks started to run out of fuel; once again, all of the ammunition had been expended. The number of operational tanks in each company had sunk to almost exactly 50%. The trucks of the combat trains moved forward into hastily established hedgehog positions. While the tanks were being resupplied, Russian artillery and mortars fired into their ranks. There were numerous casualties, including *Oberstleutnant* von Heydebreck. There was no possibility of seeking cover along the broad, barren high ground.

The corps temporarily halted the attack and did not resume it until the evening hours, when Ssirotino was to be attacked. As evening approached and night rapidly descended, *Major* Illig moved out with the consolidated tank regiment and the *SPW* battalion. Shortly outside the village, however, the attack, which was conducted on both sides of the road, ran into concentric fires from antitank and antiaircraft guns and tanks in reverse-slope ambush positions. The *9./PR201* lost two experienced platoon leaders. Other tanks and *SPW's* were hit and immobilized. The attack was called off.

Infanterie-Regiment 687 returned to its parent division, which was advancing to the right of the *23. Panzer-Division*, south of the Woltschja. It was encountering little resistance and capturing considerable terrain.

In a night attack, the *II./SR126* of *Hauptmann* von Eisenhardt-Rothe advanced through the western edge of Ssawin and Ssirotino as far as Hill 233.1. It was supported by antitank elements and the *I. (SPW)/SR126*.

After a short night in a hedgehog position, the tank-versus-tank engagements flared up again at first light on 1 July. It was impossible to advance frontally against the Soviet's anti-armor blocking position, even though the antitank elements knocked out several tanks in their positions at first light. Once again, casualties were taken.

At 1000 hours, the tank regiment moved out to attack as part of *Kampfgruppe Müller*, swinging out to the left. At the same time, the riflemen, supported by the *2./PJA128*, moved out along both sides of the main route. *Stukas* and artillery supported the attack. The enemy tanks were attacked in the flank in their reverse-slope positions east of Ssirotino. They no longer had the benefit of built-up fighting positions. Four T-34's were set alight; the remaining tankers panicked and soon 25-30 enemy tanks were pulling back at high speed to the northeast. Unfortunately, the Russians had too great of a head start, despite the immediate pursuit, and they succeeded in establishing reverse-slope firing positions north of Perwomaiskji. The Russian infantry pulled back deliberately in waves, protected by their tanks. It was becoming obvious that the Soviet intention was to hold up the German armor for as long as possible and thus escape an encirclement. Another movement, swinging out to the left again, brought the German tanks into the deep right flank of the enemy. A KV-1 and a T-34 were knocked out. New enemy tanks approaching from the north turned back smoking after receiving numerous hits. Two more T-34's and a KV-1 went up in smoke west of Lomowka. There were no friendly losses.

Croatian infantry of the *100. Jäger-Division* approached from the left and, exploiting the armor attack, quickly gained ground without enemy resistance. The tank regiment swung back to the road again, advanced through Lomowka and then reached Point 236.0. Another T-34 was destroyed. Tschemerkin was captured, and a Russian field position with wooden bunkers on both sides of the village was overcome. Continuing to advance rapidly, *Kampfgruppe Müller* moved along the ridgeline road to the northeast. The enemy no longer offered any resistance.

12 Editor's Note: Times given in official records were adjusted to central European time, which meant that the actual local time was two hours later.

13 Editor's Note: A *balka* was a defile or washout. German forces in the east frequently used the Russian term when discussing them.

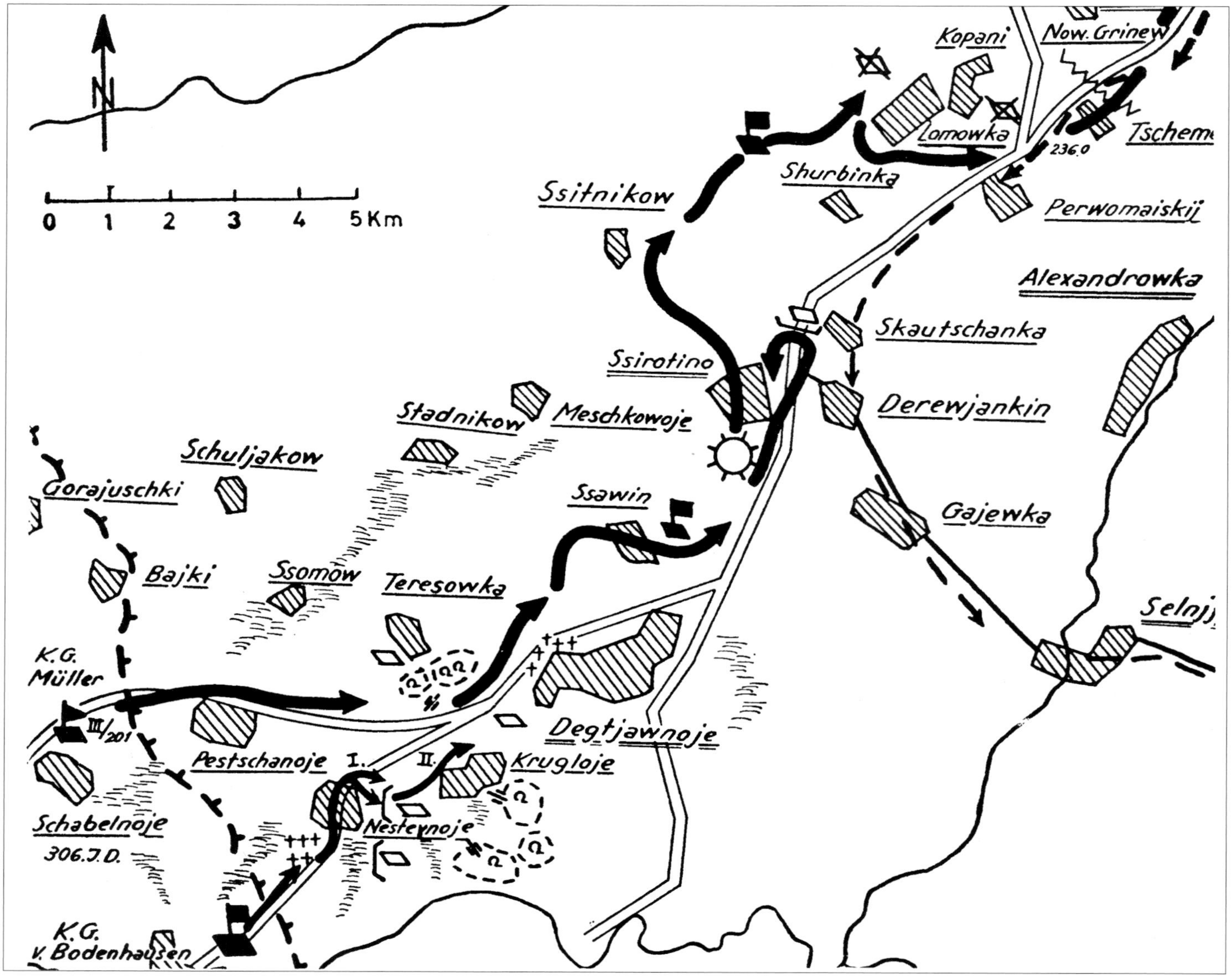

Map 9: The Attack of the *23. Panzer-Division* on 30 June and 1 July 1942.

The advance was stopped in the vicinity of Nowji Grinew at 1430 hours by order of the corps. Together with the *1./PJA128*, the tanks established an all-round defense. The motorcycle battalion immediately continued reconnaissance activities that determined there were enemy tanks and infantry abut 2-3 kilometers away that were pulling back to the northeast.

At 2130 hours, the division was pulled out of its attack sector to cross the Oskol on the bridge at Wolokonowka that was captured by the *336. Infanterie-Division*. From there, it was to take the retrograding enemy in his deep flank. The regret at not being able to exploit the complete breakthrough of the Russian lines in the original attack sector, which had initially been so difficult to obtain, gave way to an understanding of the intentions of the orders from the higher command.

The reinforced *SR128* of *Oberstleutnant* Bachmann remained in Tschemerkin. The regiment was attached to the *100. Jäger-Division* and formed an advance guard for the division on 2 July, which moved out at first light and was able to establish a bridgehead over the Oskol at Sslonowka by 0600 hours as the result of an aggressive advance.

The *1./PJA128* of *Oberleutnant* Brünn was attached to the *3. Panzer-Division* and screened the high ground against enemy armor at Pogromez, together with a tank and rifle company. In the evening, the company returned to the division.

The main body of the division marched west under a bright moon to Chutorischtsche, moving via Ssirotino, Derewjanken and Selenyi-Klin. Resupply had barely taken place there, when the tank regiment was alerted, because enemy tanks at Werchne Lubjanka were threatening the bridgehead at Wolokonowka from the southwest. The *II./PR201* determined there were eight T-34's at Ssret. Lubjanky. At the same time, four T-34's entered Werchne Lubjanka to the rear of the battalion. Tanks from all three battalions of the regiment became involved and eliminated the enemy in short order. The *I./PAR128* was also attacked by enemy tanks while on a road march. The howitzers were immediately unlimbered and opened fire on the Soviets, who turned away expeditiously. The continued advance was stopped at the bridgehead , since a German tank that had broken through the bridge had made it impassable. Under constant fire from Russian artillery and "Stalin Organs", as well as ground-support aircraft, the engineers of *PPB51* constructed a new bridge. The division's *Flak* battalion assumed point defense at the bridge site.

During the morning of 3 July, the *Kampfgruppen* crossed the Oskol at Jutanowka, just north of Wolokonowka and moved out along the Wolokonowka — Gruschtschenka road. The advance guard was formed by the motorcycle battalion and the 1st Company of the antitank battalion. *Kampfgruppe von Bodenhausen*, the headquarters of the rifle brigade, followed. It consisted of *PR201* (minus the 3rd Battalion), a platoon from

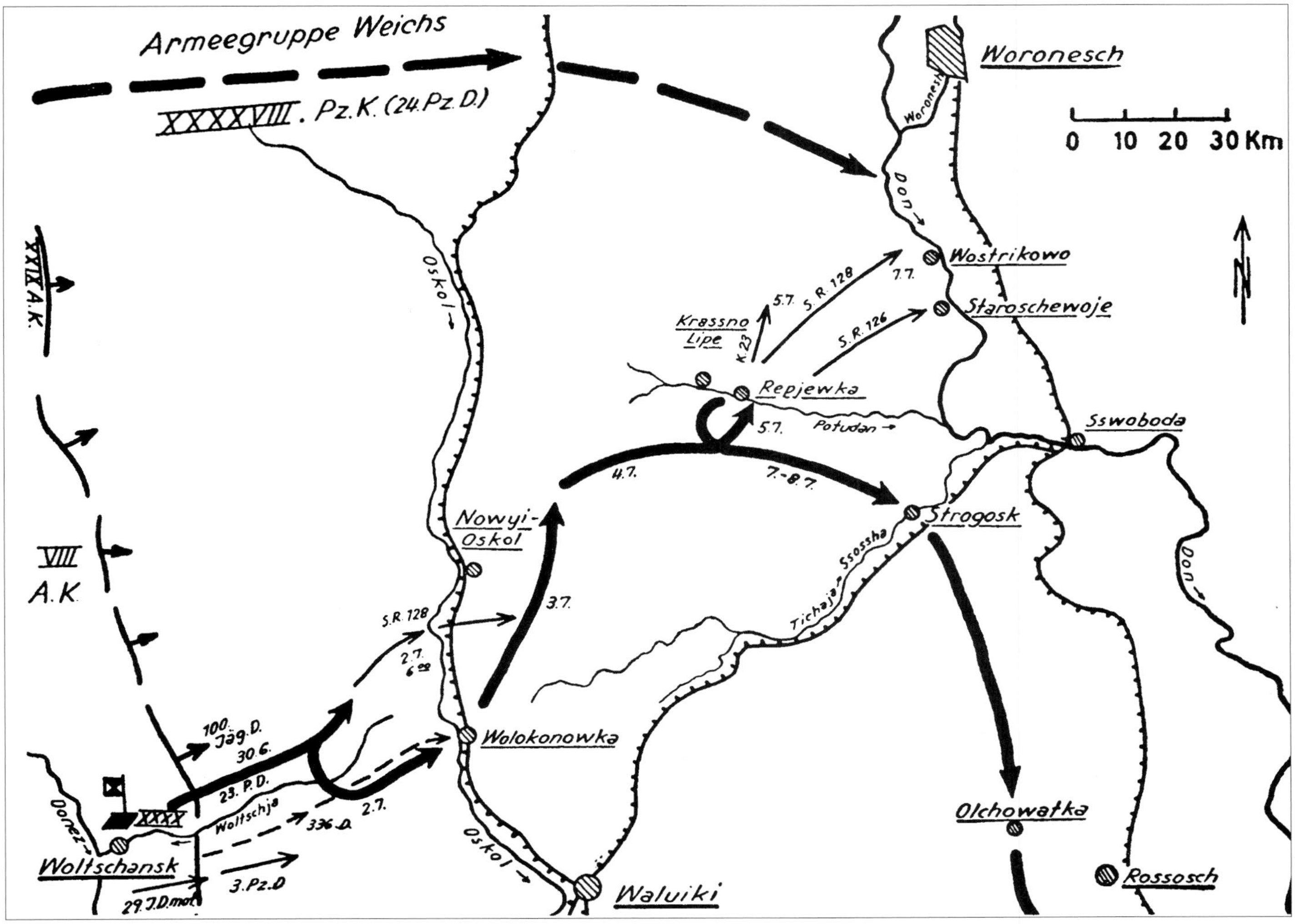

Map 10: The Advance of the *23. Panzer-Division* to the Don.

the *3.(SPW)PPB51*, the *7./PAR128*, the *I./SR126,* the *I./PAR128* and *leichte Flak-Abteilung 77* (minus its 1st Battery). That battle group was followed by *Kampfgruppe Müller*, consisting of the *III./PR201*, *SR126* (minus its 1st Battalion), one battery from the *II./PAR128*, one battery from *leichte Flak-Abteilung 77* and *PPB51* (minus one engineer platoon). Bringing up the rear was *Kampfgruppe Büscher* with the *III./PAR128* (minus its 7th Battery), the *II./PAR128* (minus one battery) and *PJA128* (minus its 1st Company). Temporarily leading *PR201* was *Oberstleutnant* Soltmann, the commander of the 2nd Battalion.

The advance encountered no serious enemy resistance. Only a handful of scattered Soviets were fished out of the vegetation along the sides of the road. The Nowyj Oskol road was crossed toward the southeast. It was at the road that the lead elements encountered the riflemen of *SR128*, who had advanced from the bridgehead at Sslonowka and, moving through Wassili—Pole and Kossizino, reached Jakowlewka. They had captured an important bridge there intact and were returning to the fold of the division.

At 0300 hours on 4 July, the division moved out again. Its mission was to establish a bridgehead at Tichaja Sosna (near Korotojak) within the framework of the *XXXX. Panzer-Korps*. Accompanied by the motorcycle battalion, the *Kampfgruppen* moved north through Papassnaja, Wesselyi and the Sarija Sozialisma Estate, since a blown-up bridge at Nowaja Besginka forced the formations to swing further out. Turning to the east, Wolotowo was crossed in the morning. Despite numerous minefields, which caused three tanks to become immobilized with slight damage, more than 70 kilometers had been covered by noon without encountering any enemy resistance.

Southeast of Nowyi Put, the lead armored elements encountered a tank ditch that had already been reported by aerial reconnaissance. The ditch was guarded by heavily manned fortifications with bunkers. A few antitank guns and bunkers were silenced. The attempt of the *I./PR201* to bypass the 5-kilometer long obstacle system failed when it was discovered to be skillfully anchored against marshy terrain and defiles. The dismounted riflemen of the *SPW* battalion attacked the defensive network under covering fire from the *II./PR201.* They breached the tank ditch and advanced on Krugloje. *Hauptmann* Fechner, together with some of his tank crews, blew up the sides of the tank ditch to even it out, so that the battalion's tanks could follow the riflemen. Working together closely, they shattered the Soviet resistance and took Krugloje by evening twilight.

During the night of 4/5 July, the division was attached to the *XXXXVIII. Panzer-Korps* of the *2. Armee*, which was advancing on Woronesh from the west. That corps had already crossed the Don south of Woronesh and was fighting for the city. Deviating from its previous line of advance, the division received orders to attack north, reach the Don south of Woronesh and, together with the *24. Panzer-Division*, block the retreat route to the east for the Soviet forces fighting west of the city.

After *Generalmajor* Mack issued oral orders, the division moved out to attack Repjewka and the high ground to its north. The formation moved through Sitischtsche. Just before Serdjuki, the *III./PR201* and *KB23* encountered stubborn Russian resistance coming from earthen bunkers and numerous antitank guns. Despite the reinforcement of the 1st Battalion of the tank regiment, the attack came to a standstill, sustaining considerable casualties. It was not until the motorcycle infantry attacked on foot—supported by the *I./PR201*—that Serdjuki could be taken and the advance continued on Butyrki. Just outside of the village, the enemy set off demolitions, establishing a brand new tank ditch. That only afforded him a short respite, however, since the *I./PR201* and a company from the *II./SR126* attacked Butyrki from the west after moving across Point 170.7. Despite heavy defensive fires from the high ground north of Repjewka, this force soon entered Butyrki. The divisional artillery and the heavy weapons of the motorized rifle regiments successfully engaged the enemy positions around Repjewka and made it easier for *KB23* to cross the Potudan. Repjewka was taken in the course of the afternoon. Despite the bridge over the Potudan having been blown up, the motorcycle infantry were able to get their light vehicles across the river with the help of the divisional engineers. The attack was continued north, until the important high ground (Hill 225.2), west of Krassno Lipe, was captured around 2200 hours.

On 6 July, *SR128* crossed the Potudan to the north, followed later by *SR126*. The regiments relieved *KB23* at Krassno Lipe and prepared to attack east, all the while providing security for one another to the west and north. The tank regiment was not able to cross the marshy bottom land of the Potudan and remained on the southern bank. From there, it screened to both the east and west. All of *Oberst* Buch's artillery regiment occupied firing positions in such a manner that it could prevent breakout attempts from the west as well as relief attacks from the east. However, there was no large-scale fighting.

The rifle regiments continued their attack on 7 July. The *I./SR128* turned back an enemy tank attack in the morning at 0550 hours. Soon thereafter, the *II./SR128* had to break resistance offered by enemy tanks at Boldyrewka. The 1st Battalion then gained ground and reached the Don at Wostrikowo at 1030 hours. A short while later, the regiment's 2nd Battalion was at the Don at Nowo Uspenska. It destroyed several enemy tanks that had not succeeded in getting back to the east bank of the Don in time. Both of the battalions set up defensive positions along a broad frontage.

A *Kampfgruppe* led by *Oberleutnant* Brünn, consisting of the *1./PJA128*, the *3./SR128* and a platoon of 2cm *Flak*, moved out at noon on 7 July to attempt to take the bridge over the Don at Uryw (Jaryw) in a *coup de main*, thus cutting off the retreat route over the Don for the enemy tanks. The *Kampfgruppe* moved stealthfully through depressions to approach Uryw. In the meantime, aviators reported that the bridge had been damaged but that Soviet vehicles remained jammed up at the crossing point. In advancing against the bridge, the 1st Antitank Company's 3rd Platoon knocked out five enemy tanks, and the accompanying *Flak* took a considerable toll in personnel and vehicles among the enemy. The 1st Platoon of the 1st Antitank Company knocked out a KV-1 and a T-34. Further to the right, the remaining platoon, the 2nd, eliminated pockets of enemy resistance.

That same morning, *SR126*, to the right of *SR128*, fought its way forward. It then set up defensively along the Don between Archangelskoje — Staroshewoje. The division's 2nd Medical Company established its clearing station in Krassno Lipe, and a forward clearing station was operating in Oktino.

The tank regiment had reconnoitered a crossing point over the Potudan at Rossoschi. But it had to swing out some 35 kilometers to the south from Butyrki in order to bypass the extended marshlands. Its initial elements did not reach the crossing point until around 1430 hours. Further movements were halted by orders received via radio, since the division was being returned to the command and control of the *XXXX. Panzer-Korps*.

Schützen-Regiment 128 remained attached to the *XXXXVIII. Panzer-Korps*, however, and it was instructed to leave outposts at the main crossing points, which were to be relieved later by Hungarian forces.

The *XXXX. Panzer-Korps* of *General der Panzertruppen* Geyr von Schweppenburg issued orders:

> Turn south and pursue the enemy via Ostrogoshsk to Olchowatka, where the arrival of the lead elements is expected by the evening of 7 July.

An advance guard was hastily formed from the motorcycle battalion and the *2./PJA128*, which moved out at 1830 hours in the direction of Ostrogoshsk from Repjewka. Elements of the divisional artillery followed, while the tank regiment moved out from Staro-Ukolowo to initially reach Sitischtsche, moving via Nowyj Put.

As it dawned on 8 July, the advance guard arrived in Ostrogoshsk at 0430 hours without encountering any enemy resistance. The main body of the division moved out from Sitischtsche shortly before that occurred. It intended to reach Olchowatka, moving via Ukolowo-Lesnoje — Kubarewka — Ostrogoshsk — Petrenkowo — Karpenkowo. The division's march took place under extreme heat. The hot, black dust penetrated into every hatch, into the uniforms, into the weapons and into the equipment. It was frequently the case in the thick dust that one could not see the person or vehicle ahead of him. For the enemy, it was a good warning.

In retrospect, the first week of the German summer offensive had taken a lot of ground, but it had only limited success. The *XXXX. Panzer-Korps* took in 8,000 prisoners. The pocket that was expected to be formed west of Woronesch between the pincers of the *XXXXVIII. Panzer-Korps* and the *XXXX. Panzer-Korps* could only be formed around enemy formations of a smaller size that had hung back. A large victory proved elusive.

For the logistical elements of the division, it was a time of heavy demands. The lines of communication quickly became extended. While the division's 2nd Maintenance Company was still in Kharkov repairing vehicles from the battle fought there, the two other maintenance companies leapfrogged behind the advance. Repair parts could only be had in Kharkov, however. It soon became evident that replacement parts for the French-built vehicles were especially difficult to procure.

The supply columns of the division's support command were often fired upon by the Russians during their lonely marches—Russians who were attempting to flee to the east from the ring of encirclement that was showing signs of forming.

The Advance to the South Through the Great Bend in the Don
8 to 29 July 1942

With its advance guard, the division closed up to the other two motorized divisions of the *XXXX. Panzer-Korps*—the *3. Panzer-Division* and the *29. Infanterie-Division (mot.)*—at Olchowatka on 8 July. Those two divisions had not participated in the attack toward the Don south of Woronesh and were advancing, in the meantime, from the Olchowatka — Rossosch area toward the southeast.

The objective of the armored corps—after the first two efforts at encirclement had failed—was to cut off the rearward lines of communication for the Soviet field armies positioned in front of the *17. Armee*. Following that, the corps was to cross the lower course of the Don to the south.

The main body of the *23. Panzer-Division* reached the area around Kriwonossowka on 9 July, after moving through KoscharnuyKoscharnyu, Jeremenkow, the Kalinowaja *Balka* and Point 231.4. For a short while there was enemy resistance at Legkodimow; *Kampfgruppe Müller* crushed it and captured two T-34's and one antitank gun. Large concentrations of the enemy were reported at Nowo Belaja, based on reconnaissance conducted by *KB23*. At 1100 hours, the *III./PR201* and *SR126* moved

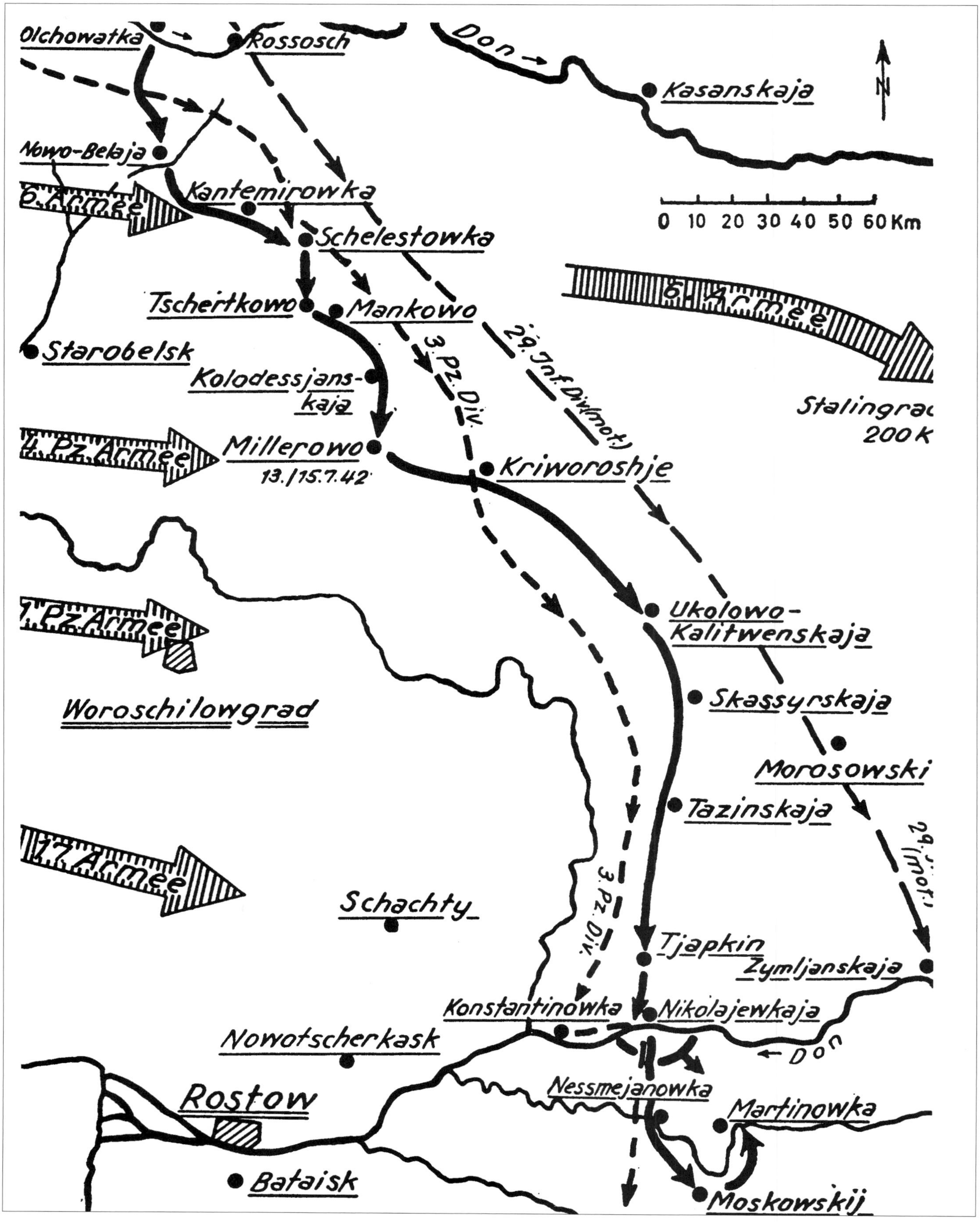

Map 11: The Advance Through the Bend in the Don to the South.

out to attack. The 9th Company of the tank regiment moved through Nowo Belaja and moved right into columns of fleeing enemy forces. *Leutnant* Hyprath of the *12./PR201* knocked out a KV-1 positioned on the bridge over the Belaja with his *Panzer IV*. The bridge, which had been prepared for demolition, was taken, and the charges removed by engineers. That established the primary prerequisite for the continued attack. Countless trains vehicles and guns were taken from the Soviets. The motorcycle battalion, elements of *SR126* and the *III./PR201* concentrated their forces and continued the advance further to the southeast, reaching the attack objective for the day, Hill 206.1, north of Ganusowka, at 1400 hours.

The main body of the division stopped in Nowo Belaja and just north of it. From there, it screened to the west, south and east. Enemy trains elements, which were pulling back south along the high ground west of Nowo Belaja, were taken under fire.

Kampfgruppe Müller, consisting of the reinforced *SR126* and the *II./PR201*, moved out of Nowo Belaja at first light on 10 July and reached Kantemirowka by 0900 hours, moving through Ganussowka and Markowka. Individual bands of scattered Soviet forces continued to surface across the path of the advancing German forces, but they generally avoided fighting. Only at Markowka did a single KV-1 attack a few wheeled vehicles following *Kampfgruppe Müller*, crushing them. The tank then disappeared to the northeast. While *Kampfgruppe Müller* left behind weak elements at Kantemirowka, so as to interdict the important crossroads 30 kilometers southeast of the village, the main body of the division was held up at Nowo Belaja and south of it. For the first time, the insidiousness surfaced with which the division would have to struggle again and again and which would cause many a victory believed certain to prove elusive: Lack of fuel.

It was not until around noon that the supply columns arrived, allowing *Kampfgruppe von Bodenhausen* and the main body of the tank regiment to move out. A cloudburst lasting a half hour then arrived, transforming the unimproved earthen roads to become a "blanket of soft soap". For a period of time, it nailed all wheeled vehicles west of Ganussowka to their then current location. Only the tanks could move out.

By then, *Kampfgruppe Müller* had linked up with the antitank battalion of the *29. Infanterie-Division (mot)* west of Kolessnikowa. The antitank personnel had been employed there since the previous day and had turned back a large Soviet tank attack in the morning, suffering considerable friendly losses. Elements of *SR126* and the *II./PR201*, which were following, moved out at 1400 hours to attack the crossroads. They encountered no resistance and advanced on to Bani, where the riflemen and the tanks established a blocking position.

Kampfgruppe von Bodenhausen remained in Kantemirowka, which it reached around 1900 hours, and secured the Moshki — Kantemirowka area.

The medical companies followed the advance by leapfrogging their clearing station platoons, with the result that a clearing station was usually some 6-10 kilometers behind the leading combat elements, ready to receive patients. An additional burden on the medical personnel was the essential requirement for security to be posted against the Soviet elements attempting to infiltrate through to the east from the west.

The division's signals battalion also had significant obstacles to overcome. Its landlines were not only constantly being cut by the tanks but by the Soviets as well. Line repair teams were on the go day and night.

On 11 July, *Kampfgruppe Müller* remained in the Bani — Schelestowka Rail Station — Prossjanij area to screen to both east and west. *Kampfgruppe von Bodenhausen* continued the advance to the south. Following behind the reconnaissance veil provided by *KB23*, the *III./PR201* attacked Tschertkowo and Melowoje. Early in the morning, *Oberleutnant* Koppe's light *SPW* company entered the village of Tschertkowo and the weak enemy resistance collapsed. Three abandoned T-34's were captured at the edge of the village and 24 Russian "Fords" were found inside the village. In a large icehouse, there were some 100,000 eggs and countless chickens stored, which was a very welcome addition to the menus of the foot soldiers.

Before *Kampfgruppe von Bodenhausen* could follow to Tschertkowo, it had to break the resistance of an enemy force that had marched to the north of the village in the meantime. At the same time, the motorcycle battalion conducted reconnaissance in all cardinal directions and determined that there were large-sized armored formations west and south of Tschertkowo.

In the sector of *Kampfgruppe Müller*, 15 T-34's attacked the rail station at Schelestowka around noon, which had to be temporarily evacuated by the riflemen. The enemy tanks continued rolling north. In the evening twilight, another 10 T-34's arrived from the northwest, of which the divisional artillery's 1st battalion destroyed four. The remaining tanks escaped the attack of the *II./PR201* as night descended. Unfortunately, the Germans knocked out a *Panzer IV* in the process. The enemy tanks, assisted by dismounted infantry, were able to block the main supply route and were also able to crush several wheeled vehicles that were there. All night long, the sound of Soviet armored and motorized vehicles could be heard west and east of the German outposts. As was later determined, these sounds were in connection with the deliberate attack on Tschertkowo by three Soviet tank brigades and a rifle brigade.

In Prossianny, the 2nd Medical Company's clearing station had to erect tents for the first time, since there was no room in the buildings there. In the evening, a few T-34's suddenly rolled through the village and just past the tents. Everyone took cover until an artillery battery that happened to be there eliminated 15 enemy tanks.

The combat outposts of *KB23* in Tschertkowo were kept busy all night; there were constant exchanges of fire. At 0330 hours, 12 enemy tanks, accompanied by infantry, entered the village, preceded by artillery and mortar fire. The light *SPW* Company of the motorcycle battalion was ejected from its positions on the edge of the village. In an engagement that was hard for both sides, the motorcycle infantry succeeded in eliminating the enemy or pushing him back, despite high losses. But newly brought forward enemy tanks and infantry continued to attack without a pause from the west and also from the east. Tanks engaged one another at pointblank range. The 2nd Battalion of the divisional artillery accounted for eight enemy tanks. It was not until the enemy had lost 28 tanks that he stopped his offensive activities around noon and started pulling back to the southeast. He had not been able to accomplish his mission—keeping open the retreat route for the Soviets to the east. In addition to suffering many killed, the Soviets also lost a number of personnel as captured, including the commander of the 86th Rifle Division. The division's formations lost 62 killed and suffered numerous wounded.

The new commander of the tank regiment, *Oberst* Burmeister, arrived with the main body of the regiment in Tschertkowo at 130 hours on 12 July. The tank regiment was followed by *Oberstleutnant* Bachmann's *SR128*, which rejoined the division after being relieved from its positions along the Don. In the Tschertkowo area, it assumed the screening mission to the west. The regiment's 2nd Battalion (*Major* von Unger) was still held up north of the Potudan, however.

Moving into the evening twilight, *Kampfgruppe Müller* (*KB23*, *SR126* and attached artillery) advanced through Mankowo and Kalitwenskaja to establish a bridgehead at Kolodessjanskaja.

On orders from the division, the tank regiment was reorganized. The operational tanks were consolidated into three companies under the command of *Major* Illig. The remaining battalions remained in the Tschertkowo — Mankowo area, where they were to be replenished with repaired vehicles.

On 13 July, Müller's advance guard first had to overcome resistance by four tanks and infantry at Kolodessjanskaja, before the advance could be continued through Maltschewskaja and Ssuchinowka and on to Millerowo. The strongly fortified Millerowo could not be attacked that night, however.

In the clearing station at Prossianny, the operating groups worked day and night on two tables. In the middle of operating, the clearing station was alerted: Soviet cavalry! Fortunately, the enemy passed by the village at some distance.

The attack on Millerowo started early in the morning of 14 July. The *I./SR126* eliminated three enemy tanks and captured another one. The *Luftwaffe* provided ground support. Unfortunately, German forces at the very front were also hit and the proven commander of the *I./SR126*, *Hauptmann* Neubeck, was badly wounded. The German attack slowly gained ground, but it was not possible to take the fortified village. Again and again, the elements attacking had to defend against Soviet forces counterattacking frontally or from the west. *Oberst Dr.* Müller was killed in his *SPW* by an antitank-rifle round. *Major* Zejdlik, the commander of the divisional engineers, assumed acting command of *SR126* and *Hauptmann* Bucher assumed acting command of the *I./SR126*. As a result of the pressure of the German attack, Russian columns started to pull back to the southeast in the afternoon.

On 15 July, the engineers of *PPB51* entered Millerowo and cleared the village of the enemy, together with *SR126*. The division took 1,400 prisoners. At the same time, the attack east of Millerowo gained ground. *Kampfgruppe von Bodenhausen* had closed up to the left of *SR126*, and it reached Ljutkowka and Salesskij. Further to the southeast, the *3. Panzer-Division* had already reached Nisowki, 40 kilometers southeast of Millerowo. There, however, it had to defend against enemy attempting to break through from the west to the east. To assist in cleaning up the situation, *KB23* was temporarily attached to the *3. Panzer-Division*.

On 15 July, the *XXXX. Panzer-Korps*, along with its three divisions, was attached to the *4. Panzer-Armee* of *Generaloberst* Hoth. Hoth's forces were advancing east of the Donez to the Don. In the course of the day, the *71. Infanterie-Division*, which was following the *23. Panzer-Division*, relieved *SR126* in Millerowo, which then assumed a defensive posture along a line running Maiskij — Salesskij, oriented to the southwest. The regiment's mission was to block the way to the east for larger enemy forces that had been cut off by the *XXXX. Panzer-Korps*.

Kampfgruppe Dr. Maus (*PJA128*) screened in a line running Salesskij — Antowka immediately to the left of *SR126*. *Maus'* forces consisted of the *3./SR126*, one platoon each from the *9. (sIG)* and *10. (Fla)/SR126*, the *1./SR128*, the *1./PJA128* and the *1./PAR128*.

Despite the constant attempts on the part of the Soviets to break through to the east, the division's blocking position held. On 16 July alone, *SR126* took in 2,000 prisoners. In all in this area, more than 12,000 prisoners were taken up through 18 July. On that date, Rumanian forces closed up from the west and made the employment of the division in its previous sector superfluous. The last battalion that had been employed along the Don south of Woronesh to return to the fold of the division was the *I./SR128*, which was relieved by Hungarian forces.

Kampfgruppe Dr. Maus, which had been reorganized with the *1./PJA128*, the *4./SR126*, the *7./PR201*, the *1./PAR128* and a platoon from the *9.(sIG)/SR126*, defended the Timaschewka — Antonowka sector on 16 July, in order to close off the crossing over the Kalitwa at Jakaterinowka. During a reconnaissance-in-force, two 7.62cm antitank guns were captured and 26 prisoners taken.

On 20 July 1942, the corps issued the following order:

The *23. Panzer-Division* is to cross the southern Don at Nikolajewskaja with an advance guard. *Leichte Flak-Abteilung 77* is detached [from support of the division].

Major Zejdlik was designated the leader of the advance guard, consisting of the headquarters of *SR126*, the *9.(sIG)/SR126*, *KB23*, the *III./PAR128* (minus the 8th and 9th batteries), the *I./PAR128*, the *1./PJA128*, the *1./PPB51*, elements of the light engineering column (with pontoons) and a landline section from *PNA128*.

At 0600 hours on 20 July, the advance guard moved out, led by an armored reconnaissance element from the *1.* and the *2.(SPW)/KB23*. This was followed by the advance guard headquarters and then the remaining element.

The rapid advance without enemy resistance through the hilly terrain was suddenly interrupted by a cloudburst. The wheels of the heavy vehicles of the artillery and engineers could not get any traction. With difficulty, the light halftracks towed the vehicles through a valley depression. A considerable amount of time was lost, which had to be made up by a more rapid tempo once the roads had dried out somewhat. The armored reconnaissance element reported village after village as clear of the enemy. The advance guard moved through Bolshinka, Skassyrskaja, Tazinskaja and Lissitschanski. The Don at Nikolajewskaja was reached at 1830 hours in the evening twilight.

Weak Soviet elements in the village did not have a clue as to the German advance. A line of bunkers 400 meters north of the village was unoccupied. Soviet soldiers walked through the village as if peace had been declared. At the ferry point, innumerable vehicles had gathered, as well as individual heavy weapons.

Without any artillery preparation, Koppe's light *SPW* company attacked the village along a broad front, although there was only short fighting along the left wing. A *Panje* outbuilding, which had caught on fire, was the only visible signs of a struggle for as far as the eye could see.

Twenty minutes after taking the village, the dismounted 1st Platoon of *Leutnant* Duday of the *SPW* Company crossed over to the southern bank of the Don. Eight light halftracks gave the platoon covering fire. Another platoon, which likewise did not have any *SPW's*, was transported to the other side by the combat engineers. The motorcycle infantry established a bridgehead with a depth of 2 kilometers in the heavily vegetated terrain. One patrol conducted reconnaissance to the south as far as Dubenskowskaja, where about a platoon's worth of the enemy was identified. Other patrols dispatched along the Don to the east and west up to 10 kilometers away did not find any Soviets.

In the meantime, the artillery set up its firing positions and the engineers built pontoon ferries in preparation for the continued crossings. An all-round defense protected the rear of the advance guard.

On 21 July, the engineers crossed the entire *2./KB23* over the river. The company had received orders to advance southward in its *SPW's* and take Dubenskowskaja. After a short while, the enemy was ejected from there. During the night of 21/22 July, the Soviets tried no less than seven times to cross the Don to the north on both sides of the bridgehead. They were turned back each time by the outposts manned by the engineers, the antitank personnel and the artillerymen.

Combat patrols dispatched by the antitank battalion brought in 24 prisoners. One antitank platoon secured a mill and a grain silo with large amounts of grain and oil fruits 3 kilometers southwest of Nikolajewskaja. Several enemy attacks with the mill and grain silo as their objective were turned back.

The next attack of the *SPW* Company—on Piroshok to the west and Morosoff to the east of Dubenskowskaja—failed on 22 July, because the Soviets had already been alerted. In response, a Soviet battalion then attacked the motorcycle infantry, using the concealment afforded by the early morning ground fog along the Don. Leaving behind some 250 dead, the enemy had to give up his intentions, however, even though he had been able to penetrate as far as the first few buildings of Dubenskowskaja.

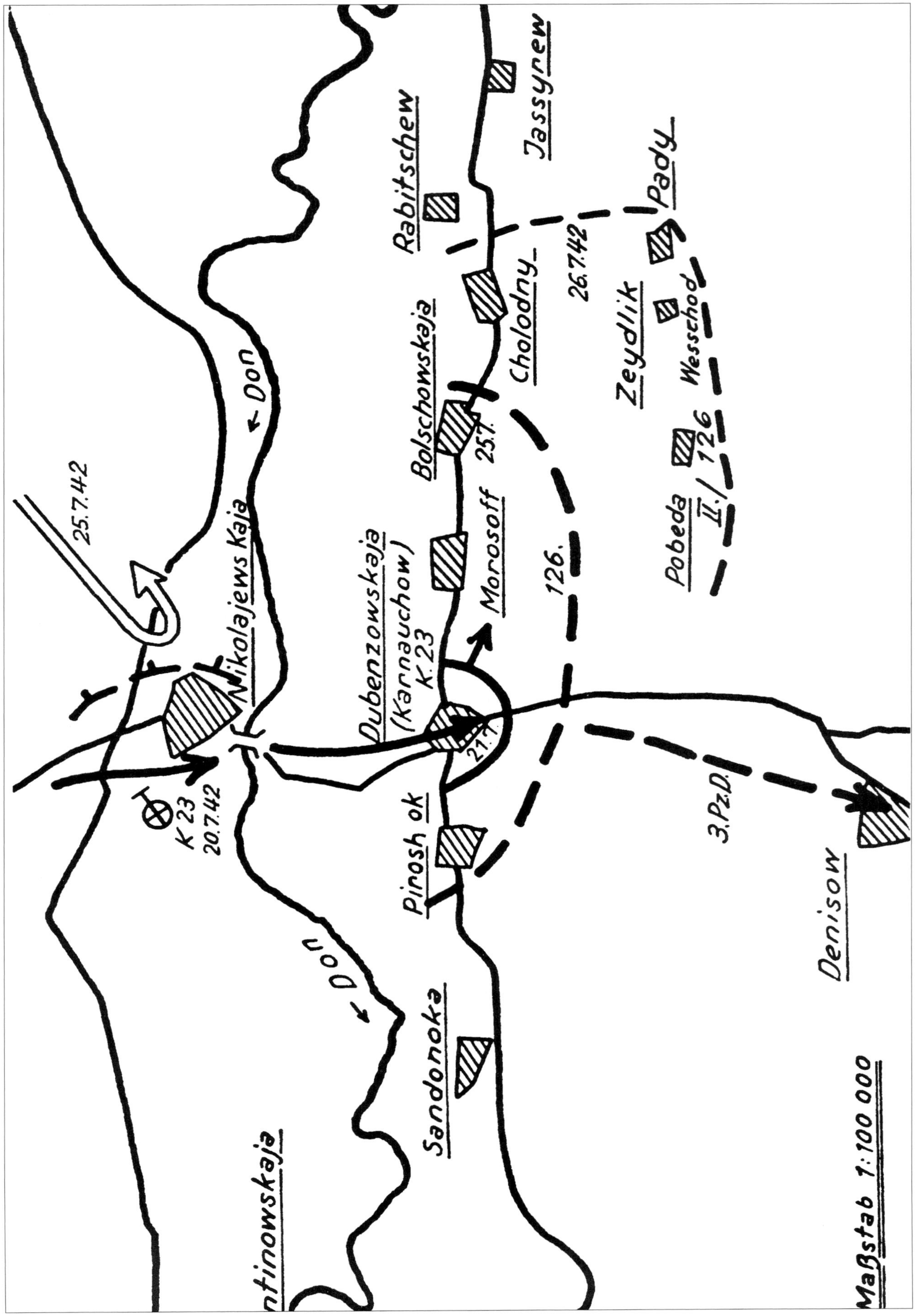

Map 12: Fighting Around the Nikolajewskaja Bridgehead from 20-27 July 1942.

The establishment of a bridgehead over the Don was an extraordinary achievement for the *23. Panzer-Division* and *Kampfgruppe Zejdlik*. Neither the *3. Panzer-Division* at Konstantinowka nor the *29. Infanterie-Division (mot)* at Zymljanskaja had a similar success.

Unfortunately, however, the poor fuel situation within the *23. Panzer-Division* did not allow any opportunity to crown this success with a continued advance. The better supplied *3. Panzer-Division* was pulled out of the line at Konstantinowka and assumed control of the crossing point at Nikolajewskaja. A platoon of the *1./PJA128* was ferried across the river on 22 July to reinforce the *SPW Company*. A pontoon bridge that was hastily erected by all combat engineer assets available allowed the initial elements of the *3. Panzer-Division* to roll into the bridgehead during the afternoon of 22 July.

Kampfgruppe Zejdlik was attached to the *3. Panzer-Division*, whereby the *III./PAR128* was directed to support *Panzer-Artillerie-Regiment 75* of the *3. Panzer-Division*. The newly arrived elements of the *3. Panzer-Division* provided relief to the motorcycle infantry of *Oberleutnant* Koppe, who had been hard pressed on two sides at Dubenskowskaja in the meantime.

The *3. Panzer-Division* accepted the recommendation of the *2./KB23* and allowed it to attack Morosoff. At 0430 hours on 23 July, the *SPW's* moved out, accompanied by forward observers from the artillery. Despite strong resistance, Morosoff was taken; numerous prisoners and artillery pieces of all types were among the spoils of war for the Germans. The entire *1./PJA128* was sent to Morosoff to support the motorcycle infantry.

In the meantime, the Soviet air force was constantly attacking the bridge site. On 25 July, it succeeded in hitting the bridge and destroying it. It was quickly repaired, however. The *IV.(Flak)/PAR128*, which had been brought forward in the meantime, suffered considerable casualties defending against the Red Air force attacks.

The main body of the division gradually moved forward from Millerowo—still struggling with a constant shortage of fuel—and set up in the Tazinskaja area as the field army's reserve. *Schützen-Regiment 128* continued to screen to the west at Kolodessjanskaja and, later on, along the hills of Olchowi-Rog. The 2nd and 3rd Battalions of the tank regiment once again had enough tanks, so they were brought forward to Alexandrowka on 21 and 22 July. The tanks that had been attached to *Major* Illig's *ad hoc* battalion were sent back to their parent battalions. Only the *I./PR201* remained behind in Millerowo, because it had no tanks. It was the last battalion to get its repaired vehicles back from the armor maintenance company of the regiment.

On 25 July, the *I.(SPW)/SR126* marched to Konstantinowka to assume a security mission along the Don.

On the same day, around 1100 hours, *Kampfgruppe Zejdlik* was subjected to a strong enemy attack from the east at Morosoff. Of the attacking enemy tanks, 13 T-60's were knocked out. The Russians pulled back. The motorcycle infantry immediately pursued and quickly took Bolchowskaja and Cholodnyj in aggressive attacks. Five hundred Soviets were captured by the considerably numerically inferior German forces.

Along the northern bank of the Don, the elements of *Kampfgruppe Zejdlik* that had remained behind there had to turn back smaller-size Soviet units coming from the northeast that attempted to force the Don crossings to the south at Nikolajewskaja.

During the course of 25 July, the *II./SR126* of *Major* Koenig, the *5.(schwere)/KB23*, the *10.(8.8cm Flak)/PAR128*, elements of the *12.(le. Flak)/PAR128* and *PPB51* (minus the 1st Company and the divisional bridging column) crossed the Don on the pontoon bridge. In the Tazinskaja area, the elements that had been held up due to a lack of fuel were finally able to receive it in order to take up the continued march. The 1st Medical Company established its clearing station in Nikolajewskaja.

The *3. Panzer-Division* moved out for the attack south from the bridgehead on 26 July. To cover its left flank, *Kampfgruppe Zejdlik* attacked to the southeast and advanced as far as the line running Pobeda — Wosschod. The riflemen, engineers and antitank personnel broke the resistance of a Russian infantry regiment in Pady. With the Russian infantry were nine tanks, of which two T-60's were knocked out. Pady was taken. During the night of 26/27 July, the *Kampfgruppe* succeeded in taking Kopani.

The main body of the *23. Panzer-Division* reached Tjapkin, 15 kilometers north of the Don, on 27 July and prepared to cross the river. Another enemy attempt to force a crossing over the Don to the south at Nikolajewskaja failed under the defensive fires of the division's forces positioned there.

The orders originally issued this day for *Kampfgruppe Zejdlik*—to attack east and open the bridgehead to the south that had been achieved with great difficulty by the *29. Infanterie-Division (mot.)* at Zymljanskaja—could not be carried out with the weak forces available. In addition, *Kampfgruppe Zejdlik* was being subjected to constant enemy attacks, which reached a new level of intensity on 28 July, especially in the area around Pady. Excellently placed fires by the divisional artillery caused heavy casualties among the Soviet infantry, especially ricochet fire. Despite that, the enemy succeeded in entering the village, and it could not be cleared out until an immediate counterattack had been launched. The clearing station established by the 2nd Medical Company in Morosoff worked ceaselessly in order to tend to the many wounded.

At first light on 28 July, the tank regiment (minus its 1st battalion) and *SR128* crossed the Don.

Since the enemy was pulling back in front of the *XXXX. Panzer-Korps* from the Ssal River at Kalininskij to the south and southeast but was stubbornly defending in front of the *29. Infanterie-Division (mot.)* at Zymljanskaja, it was intended for the division to attack to the south and southeast, all the while guarding the left flank of the *3. Panzer-Division*, which was making good progress.

At first light on 28 July, a Soviet battalion attacked the outposts at Cholodny, consisting of the *2./PPB51* and an antitank platoon from the *1./PJA128*. After the enemy enjoyed initial success, he started to exert such pressure on the village that a platoon from the *3.(Fla)/PJA128*, the *3./SR126* and a battery from the divisional artillery had to be sent in to provide relief. *Oberleutnant* Brünn led the task force. In the course of the day, he and his *Kampfgruppe* turned back an additional three enemy attacks in battalion strength.

Kampfgruppe Bachmann, the reinforced *SR128*, reached Denisoff at 0530 hours on 28 July without encountering any enemy resistance. Around 0800 hours, it reached the bridge over the Ssal at Nessmejanowka. At 0930 hours, the *II./SR128* had to move out to the east north of the Ssal. It ran right into an enemy attack launched from Martinowka and tossed the Soviets back. The motorcycle battalion relieved the riflemen posted as security on the bridge at Nessmejanowka and then reconnoitered to the sough and east. Batlajewskij and Moskowskij were reported as heavily manned by the enemy. By 1530 hours, the tank regiment, minus its 1st Battalion and the 8th Company, prepared for operations south of the Ssal and moved out against Moskowskij from Kropjanka, together with *SR126*, at 1600 hours. Just before the attack got started, five enemy tanks advanced. The *6./PAR128* knocked out three of them, causing the rest to flee. The German attack made good progress. By the onset of evening twilight, the riflemen had captured Batlajewskij and Moskowskij. Four enemy tanks—T-34's and T-70's—were destroyed. The tank regiment screened the day's attack objective, the crossroads between Batlajewskij and Moskowskij.

Throughout the day, *Kampfgruppe Zejdlik*, the reinforced *SR126*, had to beat back several strong enemy attacks on Pady and Cholodnyj.

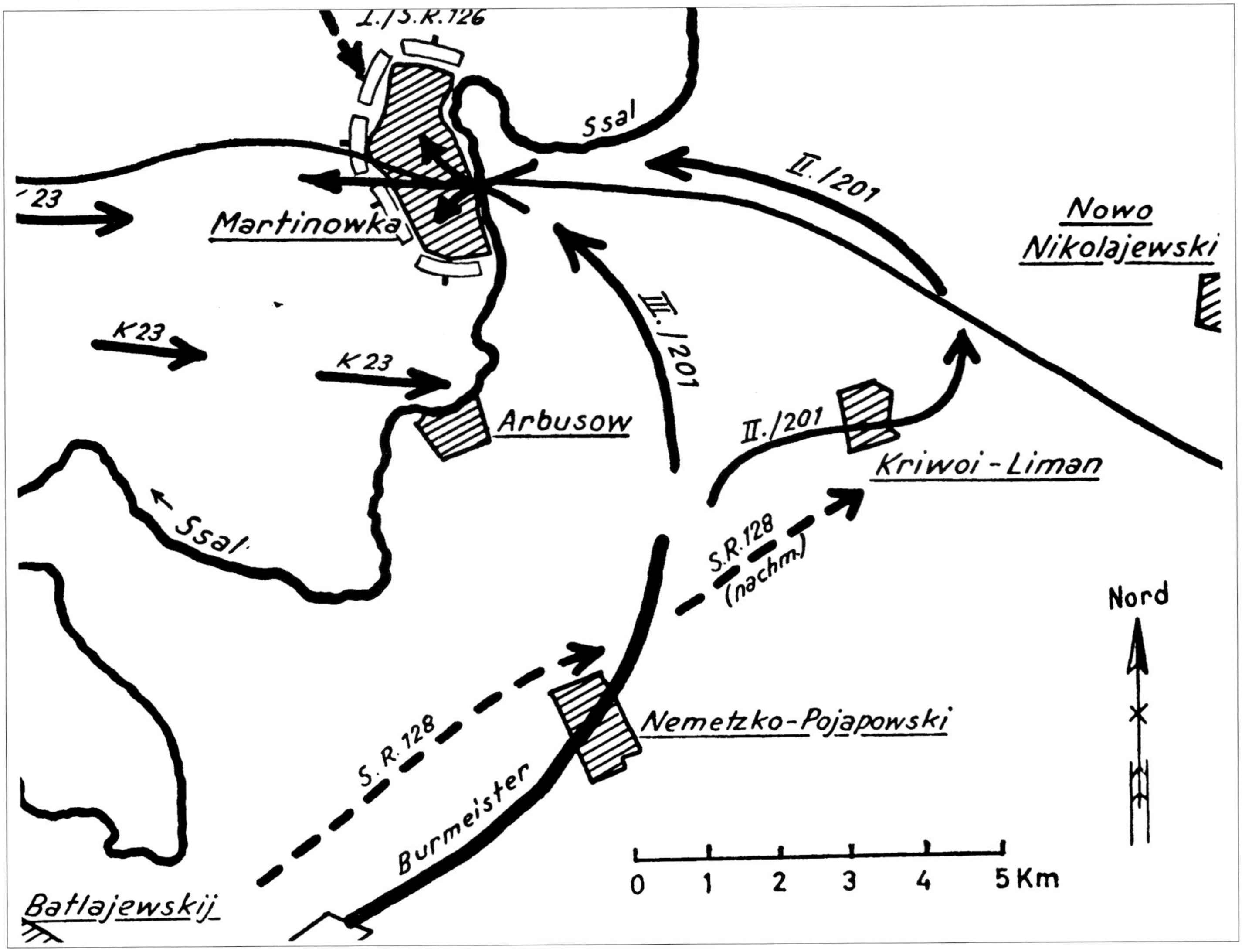

Map 13: Martinowka, 29 July 1942.

The *8./PR201* was sent to reinforce it. Well-placed fires by both the *1.* and *8./PAR128* inflicted heavy casualties upon the enemy and forced him to pull back. The riflemen and the *8./PR201* moved out from Cholodnyj to the east at 1745 hours. This force broke through the enemy frontage and 200 prisoners were taken. What remained of the enemy fled to the east. During the night, at 0245 hours, the *Kampfgruppe* turned back an enemy attack on Pady, along its southern wing.

Ground and aerial reconnaissance on 28 July identified weak enemy forces in Martinowka. To eliminate a possible threat to the division from there, *Kampfgruppe Burmeister—PR201* (minus the 1st Battalion and the 8th Company), the *II./PAR128* and the *3./SR126*—was to move out from Batajewskij to the northeast, while the motorcycle battalion, supported by the *5./PAR128*, attacked the village proper from the west simultaneously.

Kampfgruppe Burmeister moved out at 0430 hours. The *II./PR201*, which initially took the lead, ran into enemy columns northwest of Nemetzko, which were coming from the northwest and southwest. They attempted to pull back to the east by moving through Kriwoi Liman and Nowo Nikolajewskaja. The enemy was completely surprised by the German tanks arriving from the south. One T-70 was knocked out at Nemetzko; another one was captured. The *II./PR201* swung out to the east in order to block the escape route of the enemy, while the 3rd Battalion advanced on Martinowka proper. *Unteroffizier* Hoffmann of the *II./PR201* advanced in his tank by himself on a fleeing battery of antiaircraft/antitank guns and several heavy infantry guns, attacked into their midst and destroyed them. The 5th Tank Company destroyed two T-34's. In the meantime, the *III./PR201* had reached the east bank of the Ssal outside of Martinowka.

Prisoner statements indicated large masses of armor in the village, where a corps headquarters was also supposed to be located. The entire battalion set up a fire trap on the village, which was soon reinforced by the arrival of the 2nd Battalion, preventing any attempt by the enemy to leave the village. Four T-34's, appearing one after the other, were knocked out. The *III./PR201* then crossed the bridge over the Ssal and entered the village. Enemy tanks came from all directions—almost all of them T-34's—and attempted to get off a round. They only succeeded in doing that infrequently, since the German tankers fired more quickly and accurately. The tank engagements took place only meters apart. *Hauptmann* Fechner, the acting commander of the *II./PR201*, destroyed a T-34 by individually attacking it with a shaped charge.

The *9./PR201* was the first tank company into Martinowka. It bore the main burden of battle and destroyed 12 T-34's, 6 T-70's, 3 antitank guns and 2 infantry guns. Thanks to the superior German command and control, friendly loses were minimal. Three tanks from the company were knocked out from the rear, however, when they headed out of the village to the west. As was determined later, the enemy had expected the attack from the north and west and had larded these edges of the village with infantry, antitank guns and dug-in tanks.

In all, the 2nd and 3rd Battalions of the tank regiment eliminated 77 enemy tanks. *Leutnant* Neinhaus, three noncommissioned officers and seven men of the 3rd Battalion paid for the taking of the village with their lives.

During the hard armored fighting, the motorcycle battalion was also attacking from the west. It encountered stiff enemy resistance and only made slow progress, all the while sustaining heavy casualties. One company commander was killed; another was badly wounded. At noon, the Ssal was reached at Arbusow. Two enemy tanks were eliminated; *SR128*, which had reached Kriwoi Liman, east of Martinowka, knocked out an additional three.

At Pady, *Kampfgruppe Zejdlik* exploited the enemy's uncertainty in his positions at Martinowka to attack south. The enemy's resistance on the high ground south of Pady collapsed; numerous deserters were captured. Elements of the *94. Infanterie-Division* relieved the *I./SR126* at Cholodnyj. That battalion moved south through Konai and established contact with *Kampfgruppe Burmeister* at Martinowka. Weaker pockets of enemy resistance were broken; two enemy tanks were destroyed and 1,000 prisoners captured. Approximately 4,000 Russians fled to the east. South of Kriwoi Liman, four more enemy tanks fell victim to the *I./SR128*.

It was not until evening that the division was able to begin to appreciate the extent of its success. A Soviet motorized/mechanized corps had been surprised in Martinowka. It would have represented a serious threat to the German forces attacking south, and it had previously skillfully eluded being detected by German reconnaissance. The victory for the division, which held importance for the continued offensive into the Caucasus and which was mainly borne by the division on that day, was praised in the *Wehrmacht* Daily Report.

To the Caucasus
30 July to 26 August 1942

The forces in the field only had a few hours of night rest after the victory at Martinowka. The *23. Panzer-Division* received orders on 30 July to protect the eastern flank of the *XXXX. Panzer-Korps* while attacking south. Its initial objective was Beketny, 40 kilometers south of Martinowka.

Kampfgruppe Burmeister moved out at 0530 hours from Martinowka. The lead elements had barely reached the east bank of the Ssal, when they reported spotting a Russian march column heading northwest, 3 kilometers northwest of Nowo-Nikolajewskaja. The *II./PR201* attacked from its line of march, advanced into the dismounted Russian infantry and shattered them. It was not possible to advance further and destroy what remained of the enemy force because of a broad stretch of marshland that could not be bypassed and which was also covered by enemy tanks.

The *Kampfgruppe* received orders toward noon to move south, irrespective of the enemy at Nowo Nikolajewskaja, and get as far as the initially ordered objective. The weak German forces, which had been given the mission of rapidly advancing to the Caucasus, were simply not in the position to actually occupy and guard the areas that had been taken. Naturally, this led to the combat formations continuing the attack south, while the trains and logistics elements found themselves constantly fending off attacks by smaller groups of Russians. Individual vehicles were fired at. Whoever had mechanical problems became stuck and had to fend for himself against Russian ambushes.

The enemy, however, was in a complete state of disarray. The higher commands no longer had firm control over their forces. They kept on coming from the west, attempting to get through to the east: Smaller and larger groups; some motorized, some riding on horseback, but mostly on foot and completely exhausted; some armed, some without weapons, but always prepared to conduct desperate attacks or ambushes. A few individual groups with some combat power—such as the one at Nowo Nikolajewskaja—tried to hold ground or conduct local attacks so as to hold open the way east for their comrades coming from the west.

While *Generalleutnant* Breith's *3. Panzer-Division* stormed the important city of Proletarskaja on 30 July 1942 and forced the crossing of the Karytscheplak, a tributary of the Manytsch, the main body of the *23. Panzer-Division* reached the Beketny — Malaja Burgusta — Priwolnyj area. The divisional artillery was reinforced with the attachment of the *I./Werfer-Regiment 3. Kampfgruppe Maus*, consisting of Maus' *PJA128* and a company from the divisional engineers, screened at Beketny and the tank regiment (minus the 1st Battalion) at Malaja-Burgusta. Both forces oriented east. For the time being, both *KB23* and elements of *SR128* screened from the Moskowskij — Arbusow — Martinowka area, oriented east. Both the *II./SR126* and the *III./PAR128* were held back as corps reserve in the Komarow — Nowo Ssadkowskij area, where they guarded the open right flank of the corps to the west.

On 31 July, the tank regiment (minus its 1st Battalion) was brought forward to Nowo Rebritschanski. That same evening, the *III./PR201* reached Proletarskaja, moving via Donskoj. The division formed an advance guard at Proletarskaja, consisting of the *II./SR128*, the *2./PJA128*, elements of the divisional engineers, the *leichte Flak-Abteilung 699* and the *I./PAR128*. The advance guard was under the command of *Oberstleutnant* Schlutius, the commander of the *I./PAR128*. It was intended for the advance guard to move to the left of the *3. Panzer-Division*, which was advancing further to the south, after crossing the Manytsch at Proletarskaja.

With the crossing of the Manytsch, the lead elements of the *23. Panzer-Division* entered the Soviet portion of Asia in the gray light of dawn on 1 August 1942. The geographical border between Europe and Asia was formed by this river. At Schablijewka, a Soviet battle group consisting of infantry, antitank guns and mortars blocked the path of the *3. Panzer-Division*. Schlutius' advance guard attacked and scattered the enemy. His forces then turned east to forge their own path. The headquarters of the tank regiment and its 3rd Battalion closed up with the advance guard. *Oberst* Burmeister assumed command of the *Kampfgruppe*, with the *9./PR201* taking the lead. Moving through Nowo Manytschewskoje, the thrust was then directed at Nowo Jegorlyk. The lead elements ran into stronger enemy forces there that were trying to pull back to the south. The tanks and riflemen transitioned to the attack and eliminated in hard fighting the bravely defending rearguards of the enemy. At 1600 hours, the village was firmly in German hands, and the enemy continued to flee south. The nearly exhausted fuel supplies forced the German forces to come to a hasty halt. The enemy was able to save himself and gather his strength.

During the movement of the advance guard, Proletarskaja was threatened by strong enemy formations. Coming from the northeast, they wanted to open the Manytsch crossings for themselves. Under the command of *Oberst* von Bodenhausen's *Schützen-Brigade 23, SR128* (minus its 2nd Battalion), the *II./PAR128*, the *2./PPB51*, the *1./PJA128* and *KB23*, kept the area up to 20 kilometers east of Proletarskaja clear of the enemy and screened along a line running Romanow — Nowo Rebritschanski. To reinforce this element, the *II./PR201* was temporarily halted in Proletarskaja and dispatched to Romanow. An advance conducted by the tank battalion and elements of *SR128* 10 kilometers to the east did not turn up any strong enemy resistance, since the enemy pulled back to the east and southeast whenever German formations appeared.

In the meantime, however, the *II./SR126*, which had been employed along the west flank of the *XXXX. Panzer-Korps*, underwent heavy fighting. It attacked to the south from the Nowo Ssadkowskij area and took the villages of Ssuchoi and Dalni, all the while supported by the *III./PAR128*

Advance to the Don. This abandoned T-34 no longer poses a threat.

This tanker seems to be missing his normal mode of transportation.

These tankers seem to have commandeered a motorcycle/sidecar combination.

The Millerowo area. Desptite the nearby fighting, many areas remained virtually unaffected.

Prisoners at Millerowo in July 1942.

A crew prepares its dinner.

8 July 1942: This shot-down IL-2 at Ostogosk is inspected out by curious Croatian soldiers.

Leutnant Rebentisch after a "nature call".

Quiet flows the Don...

Scenes from the advance...

Soviet spoils of war along the Don.

Leutnant Rebentisch takes an official duty flight on an *He 111* back to Germany.

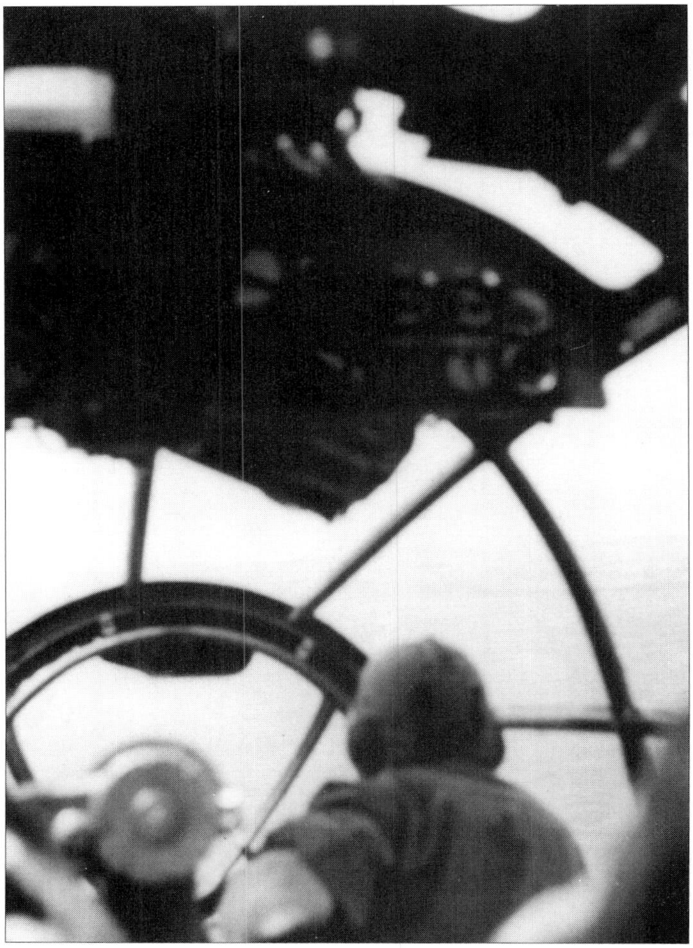

The view from the cockpit on the flight home.

Camp life at Millerowo

Mail call.

A proxy wedding takes place at Mankowo on 17 July 1942 with *Leutnant* Rebentisch officiating. In the first image, *Leutnant* Grahn can be seen sprucing up the makeshift altar, while *Feldwebel* Schubert looks on. In the second image, future Knight's Cross recipient, *Leutnant* Kujacinski, can be seen to the right of *Leutnant* Rebentisch.

More images of the proxy wedding.

A knocked out KV-I that has obviously taken quite a battering from numerous anti-tank rounds.

Knocked-out "Stalin Organ". A fearsome, but not particularly accurate, weapon.

Captured and destroyed US M3A3 Lee and M3A1 Stuart Lend-Lease tanks are the object of much curiosity. The Soviets regarded these vehicles as markedly inferior to the T-34 - which they were. However, at this stage of the war, the Soviets needed all the tanks they could get.

While Russian crews complained bitterly about the combat performance of the M3, American tanks crews in Tunisia were just as critical of their vehicles when faced with Panzer IV F2s and Gs with the long 75mm main gun.

Some of these vehicles will be shipped back to Germany for evaluation.

Shipping instructions painted on the hull.

The rear of a destroyed KV 1.

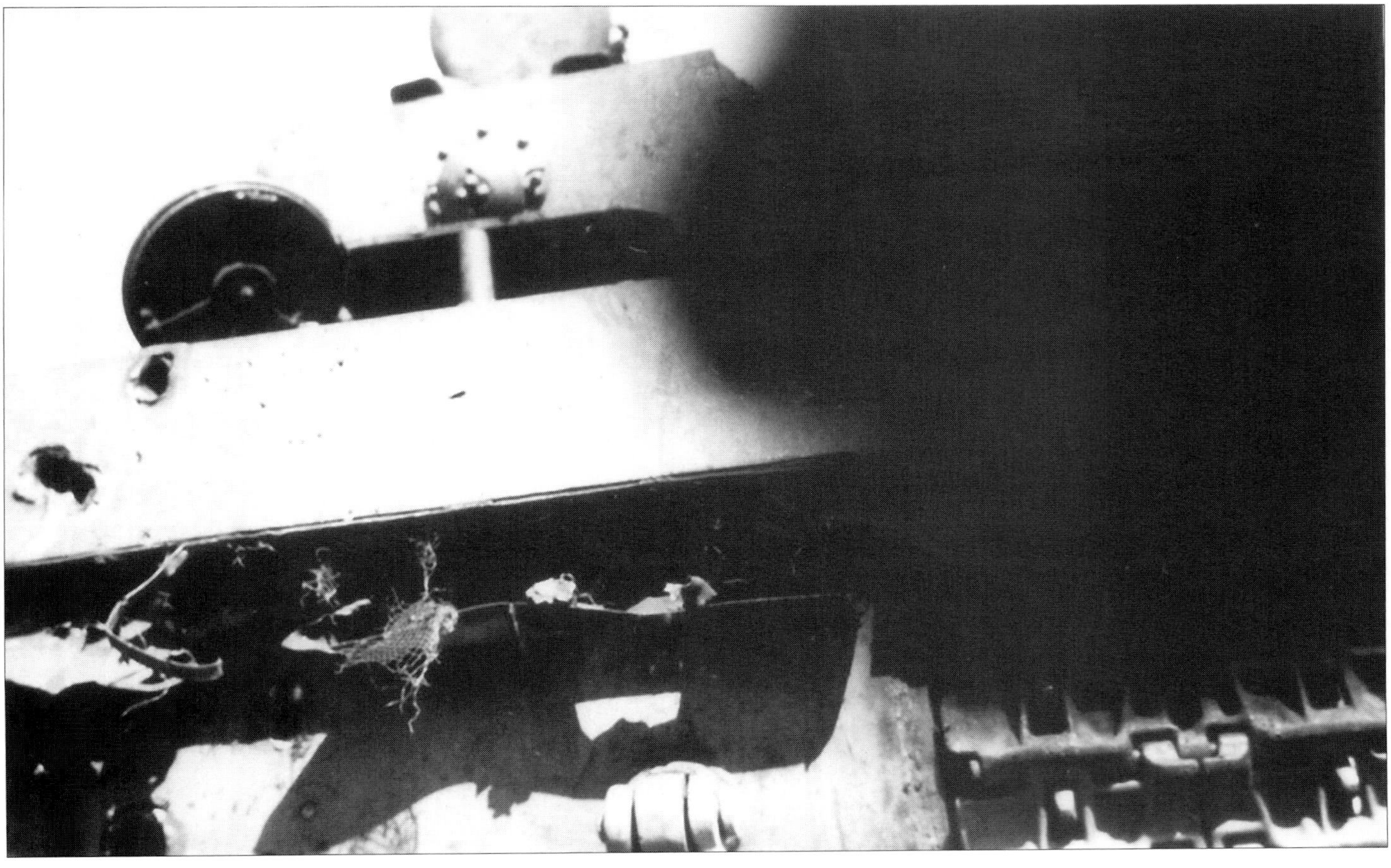

A German tank graveyard. Some vehicles will be repaired in the field or, if this is not possible, sent to rear area repair facilities. Others will be cannibalized for parts and then sent back to Germany for rebuilding/conversion or to be scrapped. If possible, nothing would be wasted.

A march seemingly without end...

The *1./PR 201* continues its advance and encounters an abandoned Soviet IL-2 along the way.

The vast and featureless Steppe.

A Mercedes-Benz heavy cross country car leads the *Panzer* regiment.

The Ukrainian peasants were often friendly to the German forces. At least in the initial phase of the campaign.

This crossing over the Manytsch Embankment marked the separation point between Europe and Asia.

For the time being, the dust posed no obstacle to the relentless advance.

More views of the division on the move. Note the additional fuel containers on the turret roof.

132

Although the tanks of the regimetnt had been switched to those of German manufacture, the wheeled vehicles were still a mixed bag. This staff car is a Citroen.

During this period, the division personnel spotted their first dromedaries, an indicator of how far east it had advanced.

Leutnant Rebentisch enjoys a quiet moment during a break in the advance.

The *I./PR 201* crosses the Don.

The noncommissioned officer corps of the *1./PR 201*.

Leutnant Rebentisch promotes members of the *1./PR 201*. On the left is the *Spieß, Oberfeldwebel* Klauke. Being promoted is *Unteroffizier* Gutschmiedl. In addition, awards were also presented.

An operational pause allows bathing along the Don, some fishing and an evening campfire in front of 101 (next page).

A shot-down I-16 Rata fighter. Still in front-line service at this stage of the war they were easy prey for marauding 109s.

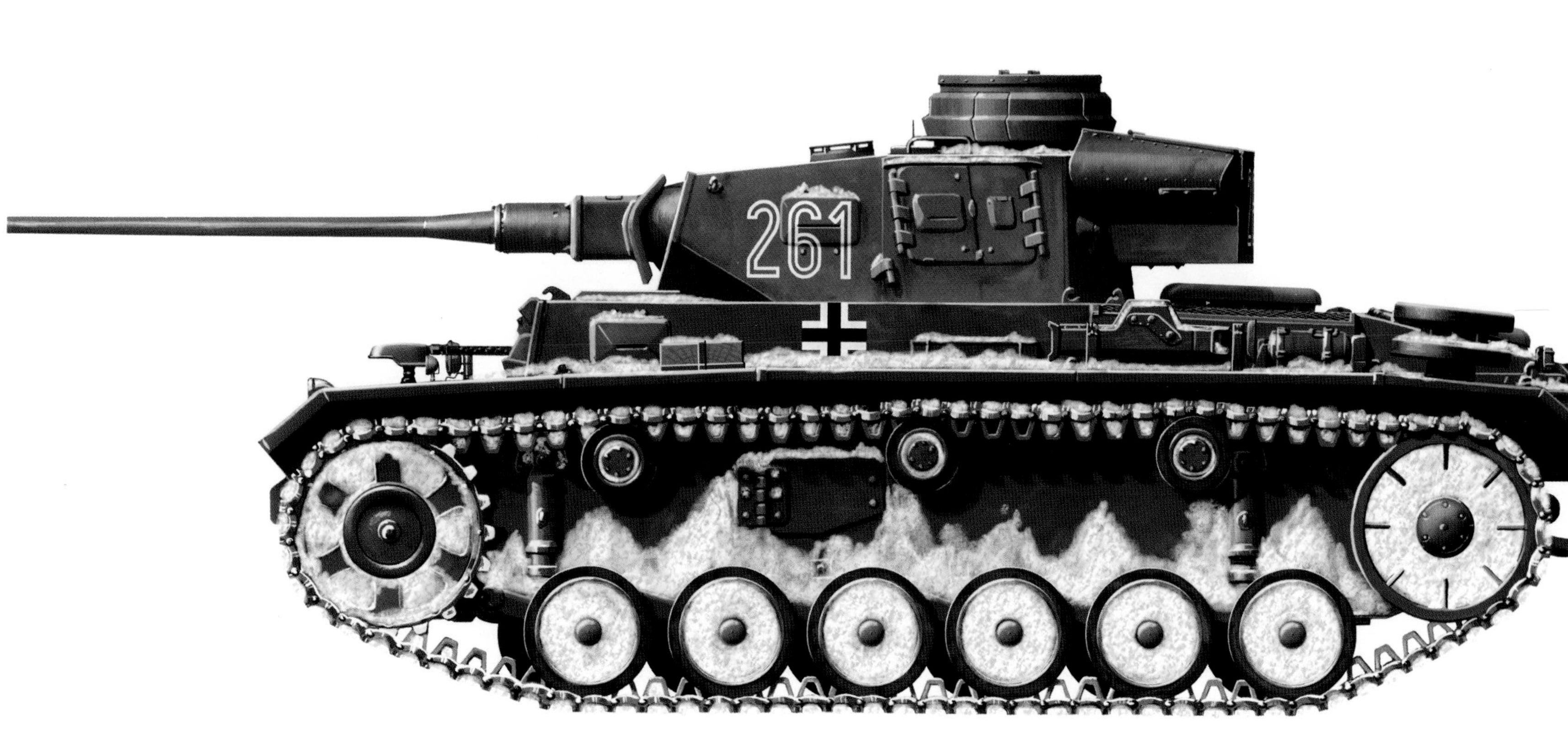

Pz.Kpfw. III Ausf. J, Pz.Rgt. 201, February, 1942.

Kolacha 2009 Zawiercie

Pz.Kpfw. III Ausf. L, Pz.Rgt. 201, Caucasus, Soviet Union, 1942.

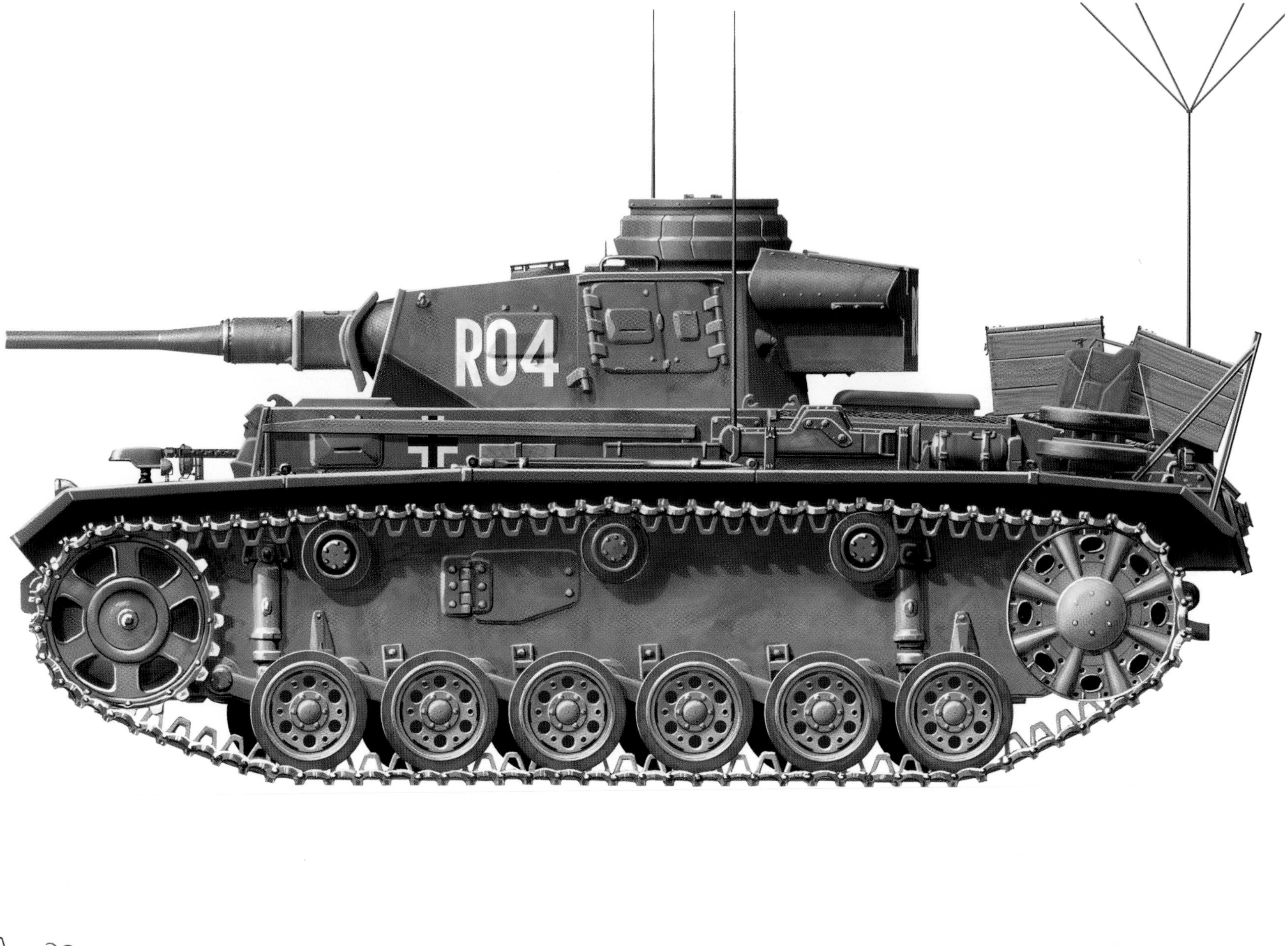

Pz.Bef.Wg. III Ausf. H, Pz.Rgt. 201, Caucasus, Soviet Union, 1942.

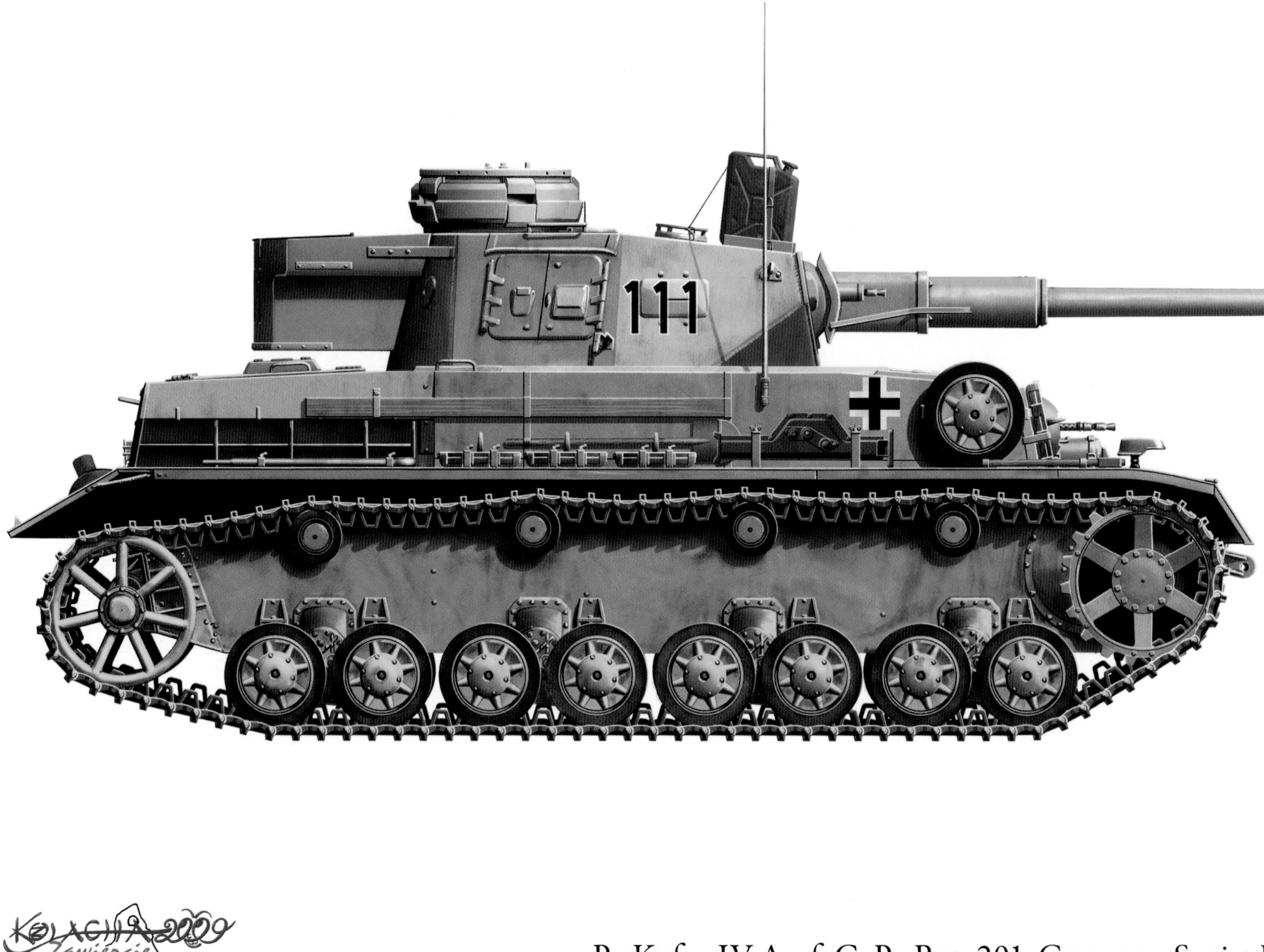

Pz.Kpfw. IV Ausf. G, Pz.Rgt. 201, Caucasus, Soviet Union, 1942.

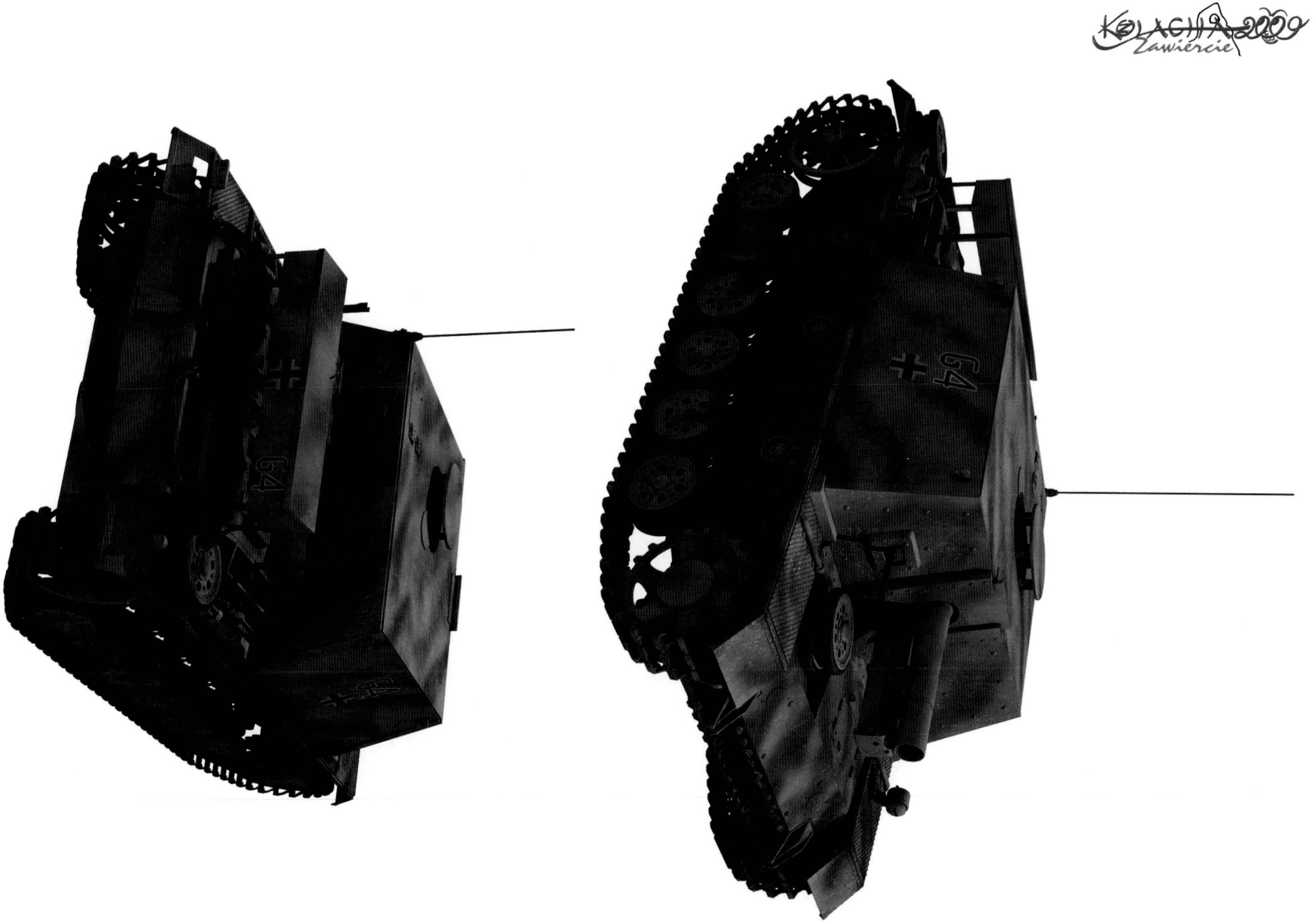

15 cm Sturm-Infanteriegeschütz, Pz.Rgt. 201, Operation Zitadelle, the area of Kursk, Soviet Union, July, 1943.

Pz.Kpfw. IV Ausf. -H, Pz.Rgt. 23, the area of Krosno - Jaslo, Poland, July, 1944.

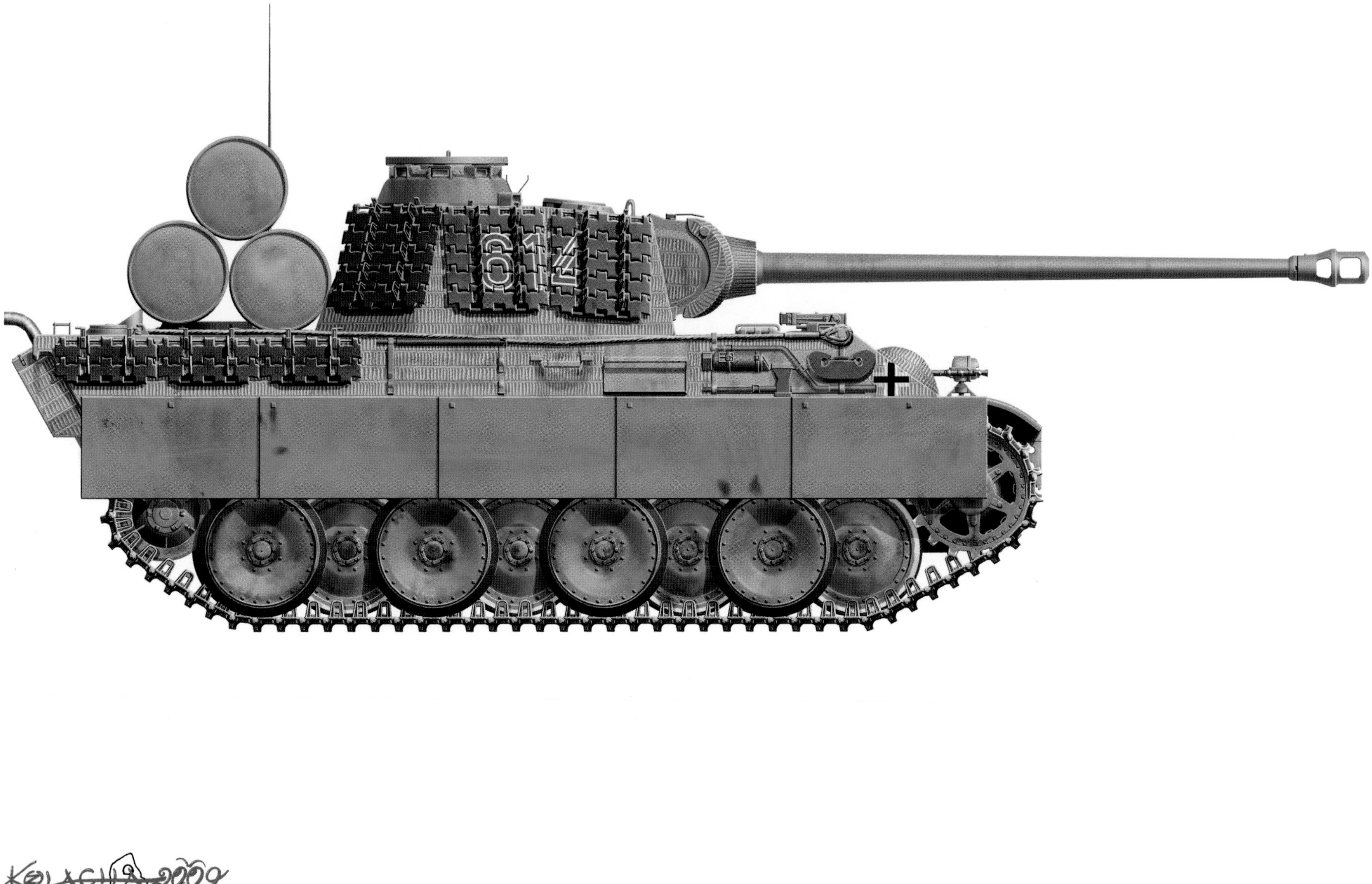

Panther Ausf. G, Pz.Rgt. 23, the area of Krosno - Jaslo, Poland, July, 1944.

Pz.Bef.Wg. Panther Ausf. A, Pz.Rgt. 23, Hungary, December, 1944.

The Headquarters Staff of the *I./PR 201*: *Unterarzt* Dr. Faltus, *Leutnant* Jantzen, *Hauptmann* Pfaff, *Leutnant* Pietsch, *Leutnant* Ewerhard and *Leutnant* Reinicke. Of those listed, only *Hauptmann* Pfaff and *Leutnant* Pietsch would survive the war.

The aftermath of the fighting at Martynowskoje on the Ssal on 14 July 1942.

Scenes from the advance in August 1942.

Along the Kuban at Newinnomyskaja.

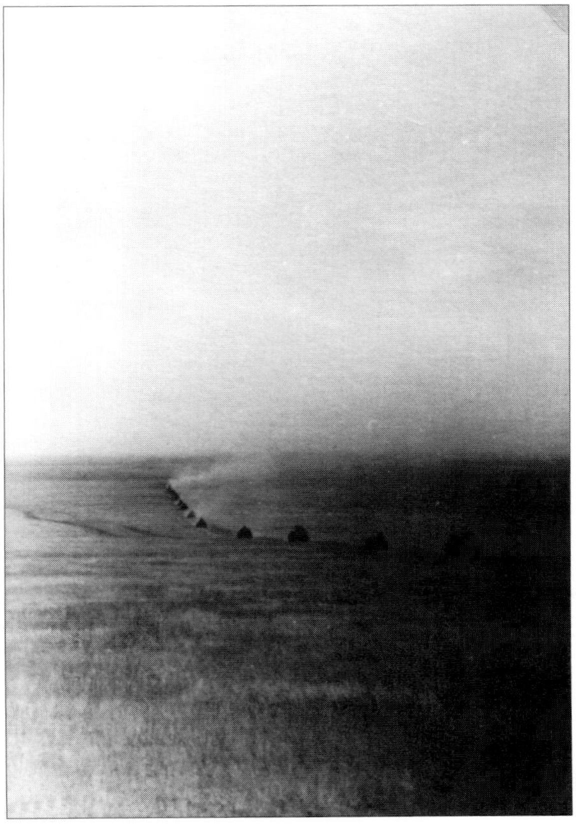

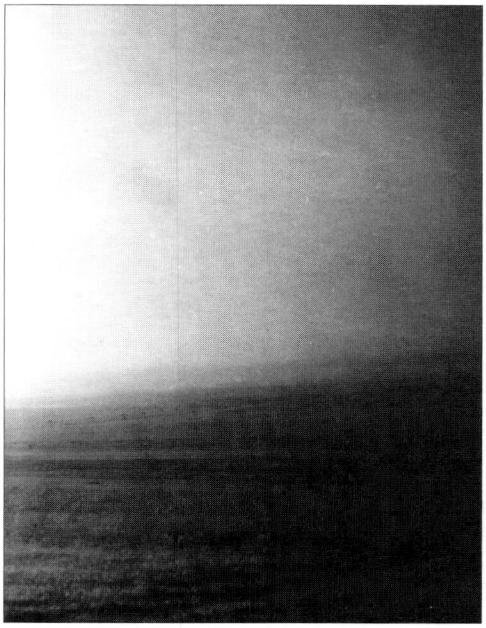

A Soviet Tupolev TB-3 "Maxim Gorki" Bomber has met its fate. These four-engine bombers were among the best in service in the 1930s. However, by 1942 they were flying museum pieces that lumbered along at 120 mph.

Pjatigorsk.

The *I./PR 201* advances through the Caucasus in August 1942.

A road sign for the advance ("Tank Trail K - East").

Kitschi-Balyk (2,000 meters)

Kisslowodsk

Pjatigorsk.

The unique, and fiercely independent, inhabitants of the Caucasus.

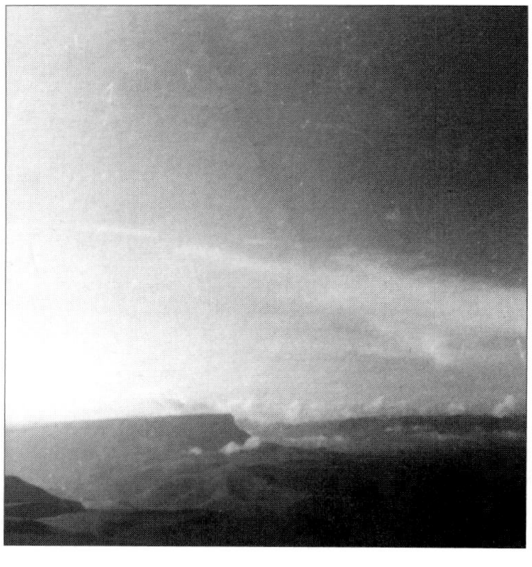

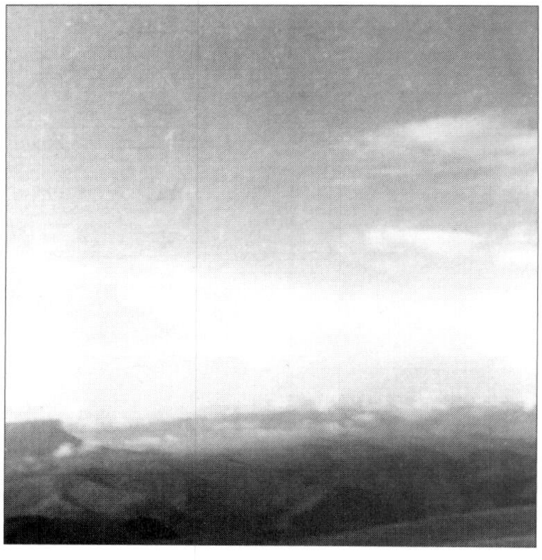

Scenes from the Causcausus: Beschtau Mountain (1,400 meters)

More views of Mount Elbrus.

Taken from 2,400 meters, this is the central range of mountains.

August 1942...excursion in the direction of Mount Elbrus.

A bemused and curious tank crew feed a new "friend".

Camels in the service of the German Army.

A Christian burial in a village populated by ethnic Germans.

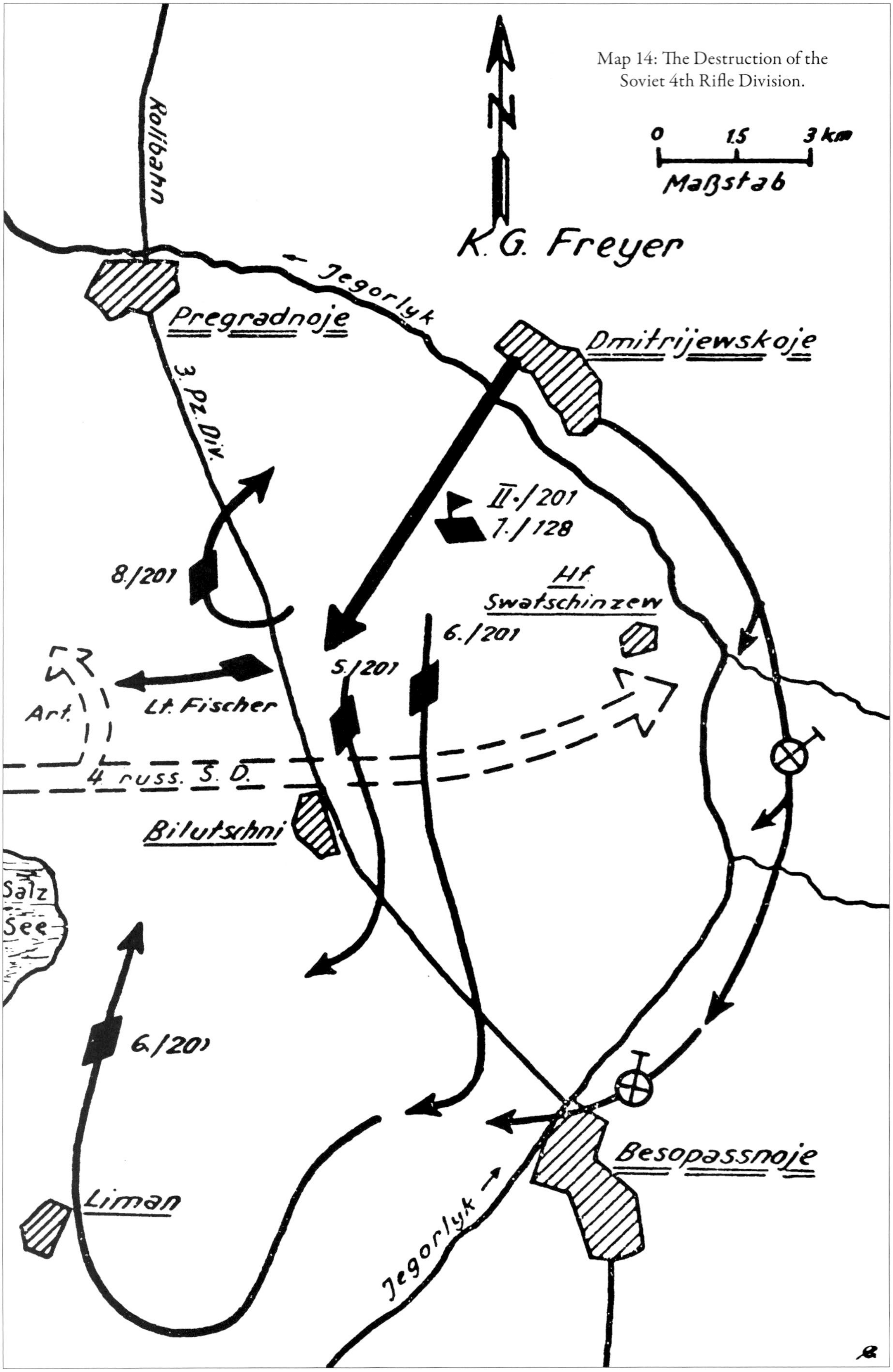

Map 14: The Destruction of the Soviet 4th Rifle Division.

of *Hauptmann* Hamann. During the course of the day, the regimental headquarters and the regiment's 1st Battalion also arrived and formed a new *Kampfgruppe Zejdlik* out of the elements already engaged. The mission of the *Kampfgruppe* was to destroy the enemy elements withdrawing to the south and southeast and to prevent their continued withdrawal over the Manytsch. Nowo Sutowski was cleared of the enemy. Numerous Soviet personnel were killed and 1,200 prisoners were taken at a loss of only 15 German dead and 25 wounded.

The lead elements of Burmeister's advance guard, the *9./PR201*, moved out under the command of *Rittmeister* Borchardt,[14] the commander of the *II./SR128*, from Nowo Jegorlyk at 0500 hours on 2 August. Proletarski (Zoros) and Baschanta were taken in the early afternoon hours against limited enemy resistance. The advance bogged down in the evening hours outside of Radykowskoje, since the heavy defensive fires prevented a crossing of the Bolschoi-Gok, which ran in front of the village. The *Kampfgruppe* established an all-round defense in front of the enemy positions, while elements of the *PJA128* under *Major Dr.* Maus screened 20 kilometers to the east, in order to secure the area around Nowo Jegorlyk.

General der Panzertruppen Geyr von Schweppenburg's *XXXX. Panzer-Korps*, with the *3. Panzer-Division* and the *23. Panzer-Division*, was allocated to *Generaloberst* von Kleist's *1. Panzer-Armee* on that day, thus leaving the advance on Stalingrad for good. The advance to Stalingrad was continued by the *4. Panzer-Armee*, the *6. Armee* and allied field armies.

Kampfgruppe Zejdlik was freed up by the approach of *Infanterie-Division (mot.) "Großdeutschland"* along the western flank of the corps, whereupon it relieved *Kampfgruppe von Bodenhausen* northeast of Proletarskaja. Von Bodenhausen's men marched south through Proletarsakja and Ssalsk. A lack of fuel forced the *II./PR201* to remain in Proletarskaja, however.

During the night of 2/3 August, a Soviet unit ambushed a supply column of the division northwest of Proletarskaja and scattered it. The *8./PR201* and a rifle company under the command of *Hauptmann* Fechner (*II./PR201*) were dispatched to deal with this enemy force north of Budennowskaja. The terrain as far as Bolgarski was swept, but nothing more could be found of the enemy group. On the next day, 4 August, only isolated groups of scattered Soviets could be found as far as Ssuchoi. Three trucks were also captured.

In the meantime, the division's advance guard entered Radykowskoje, which had been evacuated by the enemy, at 0500 hours on 3 August. Dmitrijewskoje was bypassed to the east and Besopassnoje was reached in a rapid advance by 0830 hours. It ran into the advance route of the *3. Panzer-Division* there, which was moving on Moskowskaja via Pregradnoje. Moving further to the southeast, the advance guard occupied Trunowskoje at 1100 hours, where the lack of fuel on this day forced a halt.

Major Maus' security group, consisting of the *1./PJA128*, the *3.(Fla)/PJA128*, a few motorcycle infantry squads and the *6./PAR128*, screened south and east of Dmitrijewskoje.

Kampfgruppe von Bodenhausen screened the route of advance between Nowo Jegorlyk and Dmitrijewskoje with the *I./SR128*. The reinforced *SR126* was still north of the Manytsch.

Disregarding the rearward lines of communications, which were becoming ever thinner, and only outfitted with the barest essential amount of fuel, Burmeister's advance guard moved out again on 4 August, taking Tuguluk that same morning. While the main body of the advance guard stopped there, the *9./PR201* was cross-attached to *Sperrgruppe Möllmann* of the *2./Regiment z.b.V. 800 "Brandenburg"*,[15] which was attached to the division.

At the same time, the *II./PR201* was able to receive fuel at Proletarskaja. Marching together with *KB23*, elements of *SR128* and the *II./PAR128*, it moved through Ssandata on 5 August and reached Dmitrijewskoje at 1530 hours.

Moving from the Kugulta area, *Sperrgruppe Möllmann* attacked Malaja Kugulta, 20 kilometers to the north, on 5 August. Moving further to the northeast, it ran into enemy columns attempting to withdraw to the east at Dobrowolje and Solotarewka. The enemy's rearguards defended against the attacking German forces with antitank guns and mortars. During the night, the *9./PR201*, together with half a company from the Brandenburg Regiment, secured the area around Solotarewka.

During that time, both German and Russian forces found themselves colorfully intermixed in the areas of operations. The German strongpoints, usually weakly manned, and the individual vehicles that had broken down found themselves to be attacked again and again by small units of the Soviets. The German soldiers had to prove themselves in a number of ways, and many an individual brave deed was done that was never recognized. The friendly attitude by the local Caucasians helped some get through a few difficult situations and gave the German foot soldier the feeling that he was fighting for a good cause.

On 5 August, the *1./PJA128* caught a relatively strong enemy force attempting to break out to the east at Mamonteff. Five trucks and a 7.62cm gun were destroyed, while four trucks, a 7.62cm gun and a motorcycle were captured.

At first light on 6 August, the *II./PR201* was alerted as the result of the sound of heavy fighting southeast and southwest of Dmitrijewskoje. The battalion moved out at 0400 hours. It was augmented by a motorcycle infantry company and motorized riflemen of the *1./SR128*, who mounted the tanks. The force was placed under the command of the division operations officer, *Major i.G.* Freyer. German outposts reported that a strong group of enemy forces had ambushed the light *Flak* column of the *I./Flak-Regiment 7* in Brilutschni and destroyed it. They had attacked from the west at 0315 hours. Blocking the main routes of advance for both the *3. Panzer-Division* and the *23. Panzer-Division*, the lead enemy elements had reached the Swatschinzew Estate, four kilometers south of Dmitrijewskoje. German artillery initiated the counterattack. The enemy responded and caused casualties among the riflemen. The *II./PR201*, together with the "tank riders", moved to the southwest, while the motorcycle infantry advanced in the direction of Besopassnoje to block the way east for the enemy force, which consisted of infantry and artillery. After a short delay, during which the tanks had to cross some badly muddied bottom ground, in some cases with the assistance of tow cable, the attack got underway.

The artillery fire and the tanks that suddenly appeared made the Soviets lose their composure. They attempted to flee to the north, west and south to escape the German grasp. The *6./PR201* of *Oberleutnant* Grahn, together with the motorcycle infantry company, pursued the enemy groups fleeing south. Two Soviet artillery columns attempted to withdraw west; only the battalion's light platoon with a single *Panzer III* and a single *Panzer II* was still available. *Leutnant* Fischer and *Feldwebel* Elsner immediately hunted down the columns and brought the enemy formation to a halt by firing from all weapons and employing hand grenades when they had closed to within a few meters. The Soviets surrendered to the two tanks, who had moved some 7 kilometers west in the course of their dashing attack.

The attack of the *6./PR201* and the *5./PR201* of *Oberleutnant* Krämer, which was following behind, soon gained ground in the direc-

14 *Rittmeister* = *Hauptmann* = Captain. It was a rank usually reserved for officers of the cavalry or reconnaissance forces. In this case, Borchardt was probably originally a cavalry officer before assuming acting battalion command within the rifle regiment.

15 Editor's Note: The "Brandenburgers" were the equivalent of special forces. A *Sperrgruppe* was a blocking force. The tank company was assigned to link up with these covert forces.

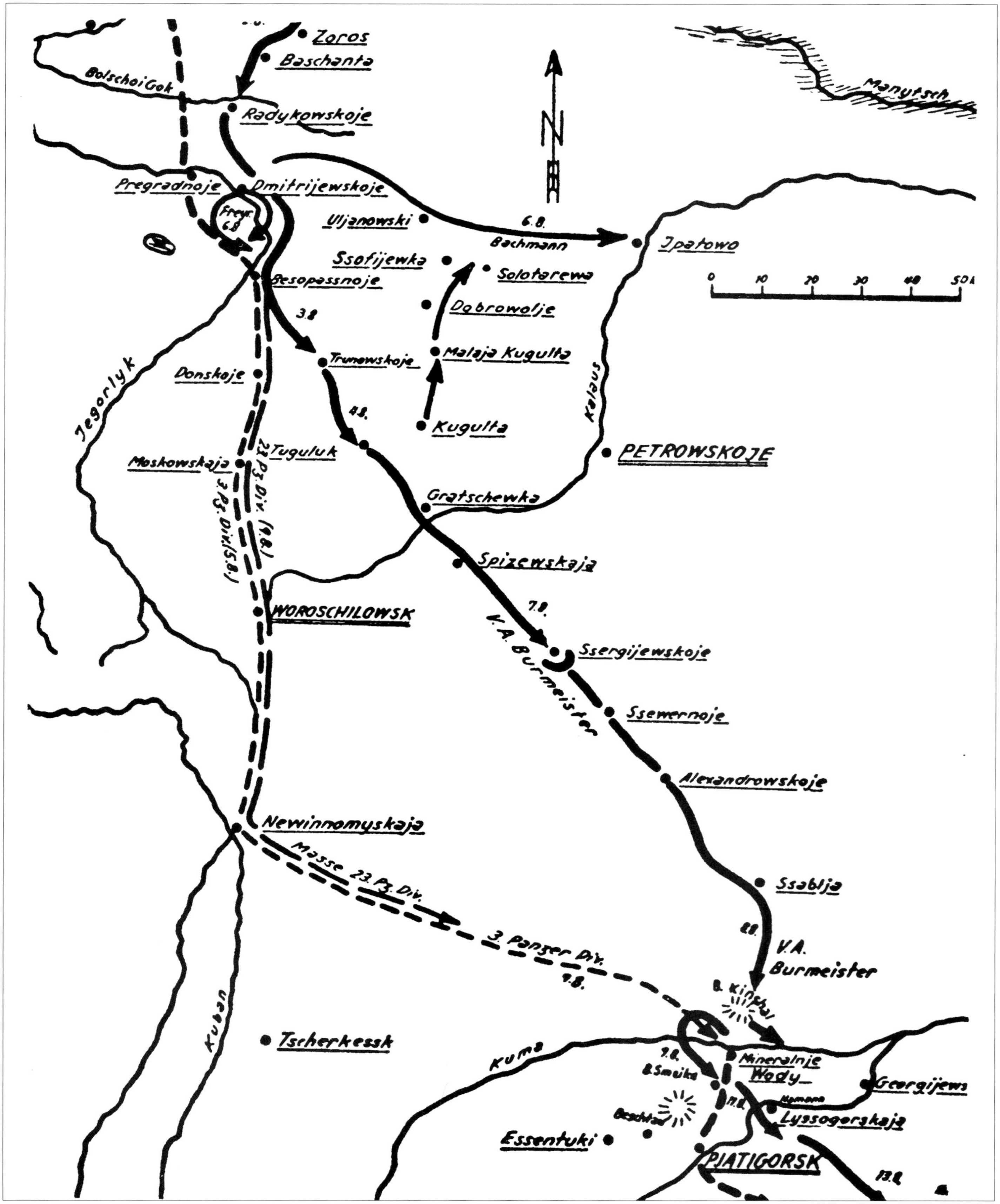

Map 15: The Situation Between 2 and 8 August 1942.

tion of Besopassnoje. Motorcycle infantry and riflemen combed through the area under the cover afforded by the tanks and took a lot of prisoners. The *6./PR201* continued to follow the enemy south, captured two 17.2cm guns and took the Liman farmstead after destroying an antitank gun.

During the fighting, large trains columns from the *3. Panzer-Division* assembled along the route of advance. Assault detachments were formed from their personnel and used to comb through the area with the tanks. In the meantime, the *8./PR201* of *Oberleutnant* Schewe pursued a Soviet motorized column fleeing to the north. The company caught up with the column and captured it, including all of its drivers. Eight hundred Russians being chased by the *8./PR201* ran into the arms of the German forces in Dmitrijewskoja. About 1,000 more prisoners were taken by the riflemen and motorcycle infantry. The success was overwhelming. It was determined that *Kampfgruppe Freyer* had spoiled the deliberate attempt of the Soviet 4th Rifle Division to break out. Among the spoils of war:

9 10.5cm artillery pieces	3 15cm guns
2 17.2cm cannon	7 21cm guns
1 28cm gun	4 guns of unknown caliber
3 heavy infantry guns	7 antitank guns (3.7 and 4.7cm)
23 tractors	5 field kitchens
100 horses	50 Panje carts with equipment and ammunition
2,240 prisoners	

Untold quantities of small arms remained behind on the battlefield and could only be gathered together after special collection details were employed.

The fighting was over by noon. The main supply route was clear again. The *II./PR201* and the other elements assembled in Dmitrijewskoja.

On 6 August, Burmeister's advance guard, consisting of the Headquarters and *II./PR201*, the *II./SR128* and attached elements, screened around Trunowskoje and Tuguluk. At the same time, the *9./PR201* of *Oberleutnant* Walther undertook armed reconnaissance in the Ssofijewka — Nowo Wassiljewka — Trunowskoje — Kugulta area as part of *Sperrgruppe Möllmann*. To the north of Möllmann's forces, elements of *SR128* and the *8./PR201*, all under the command of *Oberstleutnant* Bachmann, conducted a reconnaissance-in-force in the direction of Ipatowo, 70 kilometers east of Dmitrijewskoja.

Moving through Tachta, the Kalaus River line was reached on both sides of Ipatowo. The enemy was so stunned by the German advance that he did not occupy the defensive positions that had been prepared along the river. Instead, he continued to pull back to the south and southeast.

The persistent shortage of fuel did not allow the advance guard to move out until 1600 hours on 7 August. Moving through Spizewskoje, Achwerdowka was reached in the evening without encountering enemy resistance.

The reinforced *SR126* was returned back to division control. After being relieved by infantry of the *LII. Armee-Korps*, *SR126* followed the division north of the Manytsch along the main supply route. The 8th of August saw Burmeister's advance guard cover a lot of ground. It moved out from a bridgehead over the Kalaus at Ssergijewskoje that had been established the previous day by forward elements. Encountering no enemy resistance, it moved through Ssewernoje and Alexandrowskoje to Ssablja. At 1845 hours, the lead elements were on top of Kinshal Mountain (497.1 meters), 15 kilometers north of Mineralnyje Wody.

Moving along the main supply route—*Panzerstraße K-Ost*[16]—the main body of the artillery and the riflemen reached Woroschilowsk, which had been taken by the *3. Panzer-Division* on 5 August, at least those that did not have to remain behind for security duties in Tuguluk. The *5./Heeres-Artillerie-Abteilung 771* was placed in general support of the divisional artillery.

Stepping in for the commander of *Schützen-Brigade 23*, *Oberst* von Bodenhausen, was the new commander of *SR126*, *Oberst* Brückner. Acting command of *SR126* was assumed by *Oberstleutnant* Wellmann of the *3. Panzer-Division*. *Major* Zejdlik returned to his *PPB51*.

The formations of the *17. Armee* and the *1. Panzer-Armee* had reached the North Caucasian rail line on a broad front and saw the snow-capped peaks of the High Caucasus in front of them. The next operational objective of the *1. Panzer-Armee* was the passes through the ranges south of Ordshonikidse and the oilfields around Grosny, while the friendly force on the right, the *17. Armee*, sought to take the western foothills of the Caucasus as far as the Black Sea.

While the combat elements quickly took ground and destroyed any flicker of resistance on the part of the enemy, the trains and the logistical services of the division had to put in a peak performance. After all, they were informed to "never lose contact with the forces in the field and always maintain their combat readiness."

Ammunition, rations and every drop of fuel had to be brought forward over great distances and under the constant threat posed by scattered Soviet forces. At the same time, the bakers, the butchers, the rations personnel, and the maintenance companies worked in small villages along the main supply route and had to post their own men to guard against enemy ambushes. Field ambulances had to pick up wounded soldiers from the field, usually moving on their own, and deliver them to the clearing stations, where they then had to take them far to the north to the field hospitals. Not only was driving and mechanical skill required, but a good sense of direction—both day and night—was needed. In addition, they had to take care of the wounded while they were being transported, especially if they broke down or were close to the enemy. There were frequently backlogs of wounded at the main clearing stations before they could be evacuated. But everyone helped where he could. Empty convoys were loaded with wounded for moving to the next hospital; other vehicles brought medical supplies forward.

The radio and telephone operators of the divisional signals battalion ensured that communications with the individual elements of the division were never interrupted.

It was in that manner that the common will and the comradeship of all of the soldiers of the division helped overcome all obstacles.

Burmeister's advance guard moved out at 0445 hours on 9 August to attack Mineralnyje Wody from Hill 497.1. The Kuma River, between the latter village and Georgijewsk, was reached. All the while, there was fierce street fighting raging in Mineralnyje Wody between the *3. Panzer-Division*, advancing from the west, and the Soviets, who were attempting to keep their withdrawal route to the east open. Extensive minefields along the bridge over the Kuma forced *Kampfgruppe Burmeister* to swing around the village to the west. Moving through Klangli, the rail line to the south between Smeika Mountain (994 meters) and Mineralnyje Wody was reached and interdicted. Chelesnowodsk, south of the mountain, was taken, and the mountain itself was finally cleared of the enemy, whereby tank crews employed as infantry attacked and took 60 prisoners and captured 11 mortars, 2 heavy machine guns, 1 twin-barreled machine gun, 3 trucks and 20 cubic meters of fuel.

On 10 August, *Kampfgruppe Richter—KB23*, the *II./PR201* and the *1./PAR128*—relieved *Kampfgruppe Zimmermann—Schützen-Regiment 3* of the *3. Panzer-Division*—in Newinnomyskaja on the Kuban River. The *II./PR201* stopped in Barssukowskaja and established a strongpoint there, for which it was temporarily attached a motorcycle infantry platoon.

While Burmeister's advance guard had to remain in the Mineralnyje Wody — Pjatigorsk area as the result of a lack of fuel, *General* Mack or-

16 Editor's Note: = Armor Route K (East)

dered a *Kampfgruppe Hamann* to be formed on 11 August. Hamann, the commander of the *III./PAR128*, had the *6./SR126*, the *III./PAR128* and two platoons of light *Flak* at his disposal. The mission for *Kampfgruppe Hamann* was to advance via Mineralnyje Wody and take Lyssogorskaja, 15 kilometers south of the village. There it was to establish a bridgehead over the Lyssogorsk. By the onset of darkness, the mission had been accomplished. That same day, the division headquarters and *PNA128* reached Mineralnyje Wody.

On 12 August, *Kampfgruppe Hamann* undertook reconnaissance to the east and north. Nesslobnaja, northeast of Lyssogorskaja, was found to be occupied by the enemy. After short artillery fires, however, the Russians pulled back. Georgijewsk, on the other hand, was heavily occupied and energetically defended.

The main body of the division closed up from the Woroschilowsk — Newinnomyskaja area. *Kampfgruppe Bachmann*, the reinforced *SR128*, prepared to continue the attack east in the Lyssogorskaja Bridgehead.

Major Dr. Maus was transferred back to Germany and his position as commander of *PJA128* was assumed by *Hauptmann* Eisenhardt-Rothe.

Kampfgruppe Bachmann moved out at 0515 hours on 13 August. It crossed the Solka against gradually increasing enemy resistance at 0715 hours and cleared the enemy out of Marinskaja by 0945 hours. Moving rapidly, the riflemen of the *II./SR128* crossed the raging Malka and entered the village of Kuba on the south bank. The enemy did not abandon the village until after a fight, and he pulled back to the south after the onset of darkness. The tough opponent was strikingly well armed with mortars and antitank rifles and exploited the terrain excellently: Numerous grain and sunflower fields and Acacian hedges, with numerous *Balkas* in between. The friendly forces to the right, the *3. Panzer-Division*, made only slow progress in its attack along the Pjatigorsk — Naltschik road.

The divisional engineers built a military bridge over the Malka at Marinskaja. The *3./PPB51* launched a patrol far to the north, reached the Georgijewsk — Prochlady railway line at Apollonskaja and blew it up. An empty train was captured.

During the evening of 13 August, heavy Soviet combat aircraft launched a surprise raid on Mineralnyje Wody. The headquarters of the divisional artillery was hit. Two officers, *Hauptmann* Böckler and *Oberleutnant* Mehne, and five men were killed; the regimental commander, *Oberst* von Buch, was wounded. *Oberstleutnant* Schlutius assumed acting command of the divisional artillery. Later on the same night, additional enemy aircraft attacked within the area of the division. The enemy seemed prepared to put up a tough defense. Fortunately, the main clearing station of the 2nd Medical Company was spared during these attacks.

In the western sector of the division, however, elements encountered only demoralized Soviet forces For instance, the *II./PR201* took 100 prisoners in Newinnomyskaja.

Exploiting the bridgehead over the Malka that had been wrested from the enemy in Kuba by the *II./SR128*, the *I./SR128* advanced during the morning of 14 August. Mounted on its vehicles, it headed southeast. It drove weak enemy forces before it and took the village of Bakssanenok, after crossing the Tokay and the Psaryscha. There, together with the *III./PR201*, it established security to the north, east, south and even the west, since it was so far ahead of all other German formations. The strength of the Soviet air force, particularly noticeable the previous few days, increased steadily. It primarily concentrated on *Kampfgruppe Bachmann*, which had advanced so far.

The *III./PR201*, which had had to halt in Pjatigorsk due to a lack of fuel, was temporarily moved forward to Lyssogorskaja, since enemy forces coming from the north were threatening the deep left flank of the division. The danger was averted without the tanks having to be employed, however. One company was used to clear Georgijewsk, which had been taken in the meantime.

During the early morning hours of 15 August, a battery from *Flak-Regiment 7* shot to pieces a surprise attack at Kuba—deep to the rear of *SR128*—conducted by a Soviet cavalry squadron. *SR128* continued its attack south; the *III./PAR128*, with the 3rd, 4th and 7th Batteries, supported. It was only possible to enter Kischpek at 1900 hours in the face of strong enemy resistance, which was designed to cover the retreat of his columns fleeing Naltschik to the east. Elements of the *5.* and *7./SR128*, consisting of *Oberleutnant* Pöllmann and eight enlisted personnel, crossed the Bakssan to the south and were able to reach the eastern part of the village. In the hours that followed, those men were subjected to continuous enemy advances. The fighting turned dramatic when a tidal wave rushed down the mountain during the night after the Soviets had blown up a reservoir. The nine men of the east bank were suddenly cut off, with the rainfall making the river rise even more. No more men could be brought across the river to reinforce them.

Moving from Newinnomyskaja, the *II./PR201* reached Marinskaja and was attached to *Kampfgruppe Burmeister* (Headquarters and the *II./PR201* and the *I. (SPW)/SR126)*, where it prepared to attack Naltschik.

The situation of the men cut off in Kischpek grew ever more critical during the morning of 16 August. The order to evacuate the bridgehead could not be carried out, since the men could no longer get back across the river.

Kampfgruppe Bachmann was employed along the Bakssan toward the west. It was to take Bakssan and force the river crossing at Kysburun. Bakssan itself was taken in a rapid move. The strong resistance on the part of numerically superior Soviet forces prevented a crossing at Kysburun, however. During the afternoon, the lead elements of the *3. Panzer-Division*, coming from the northwest, linked up with *Kampfgruppe Bachmann* in Bakssan and relieved it. A 21cm heavy howitzer battery from *Heeres-Artillerie-Regiment 777* was placed in general support of the divisional artillery.

Kampfgruppe Burmeister was unable to move out on Naltschik as a result of the high waters in the river. It was turned instead toward the east and attacked in the direction of Maiskij. While 20 Soviet bombers and fighter-bombers attacked, the *Kampfgruppe* moved out. At 1430 hours, the *8./PR201* and the 2nd Battalion's motorcycle reconnaissance platoon were along the Tschegem at Nowo Poltawskoje. The steeply sloped river bed, over which there were no bridges, prevented any further advance. The *Kampfgruppe* spent the night of 16/17 August with the 8th Tank Company in Altud and the main body of the force in a linear village[17] 6 kilometers to the north. Reconnaissance conducted in the Geduko area also revealed no opportunities for crossing the river.

After *Kampfgruppe Bachmann* was relieved by the *3. Panzer-Division*, it attempted to cross the Bakssan at Kischpek one more time. It wanted to close up with the elements of the *II./SR128* that were cut off there. Unfortunately, the divisional engineers were not in a position to erect a bridge, since they did not have suitable equipment. The operation had to be called off after the only effort that succeeded was the ferrying of some limited rations over to the cut-off soldiers. The men were directed to look for a river crossing downstream and, if necessary, march as far as the German forces at Nowo Poltawskoje. Unfortunately, none of these soldiers reached friendly lines later on, so that they had to be reported as missing. On 29 August, a Soviet aircraft dropped a flybill over the sector of the division with a picture of *Oberleutnant* Xaver Pöllmann, the commander of the *7./SR128*, and a supposed exhortation by him to give up the struggle. No one believed this type of propaganda, however, since every soldier in the east had already had some experience with the Russians.

The formations of the division spent 17 August waiting in their positions. The enemy constantly attacked the German columns and strong-

17 Editor's Note: The original German term is *Straßendorf*, which denotes a village that extends along a road but has no real depth.

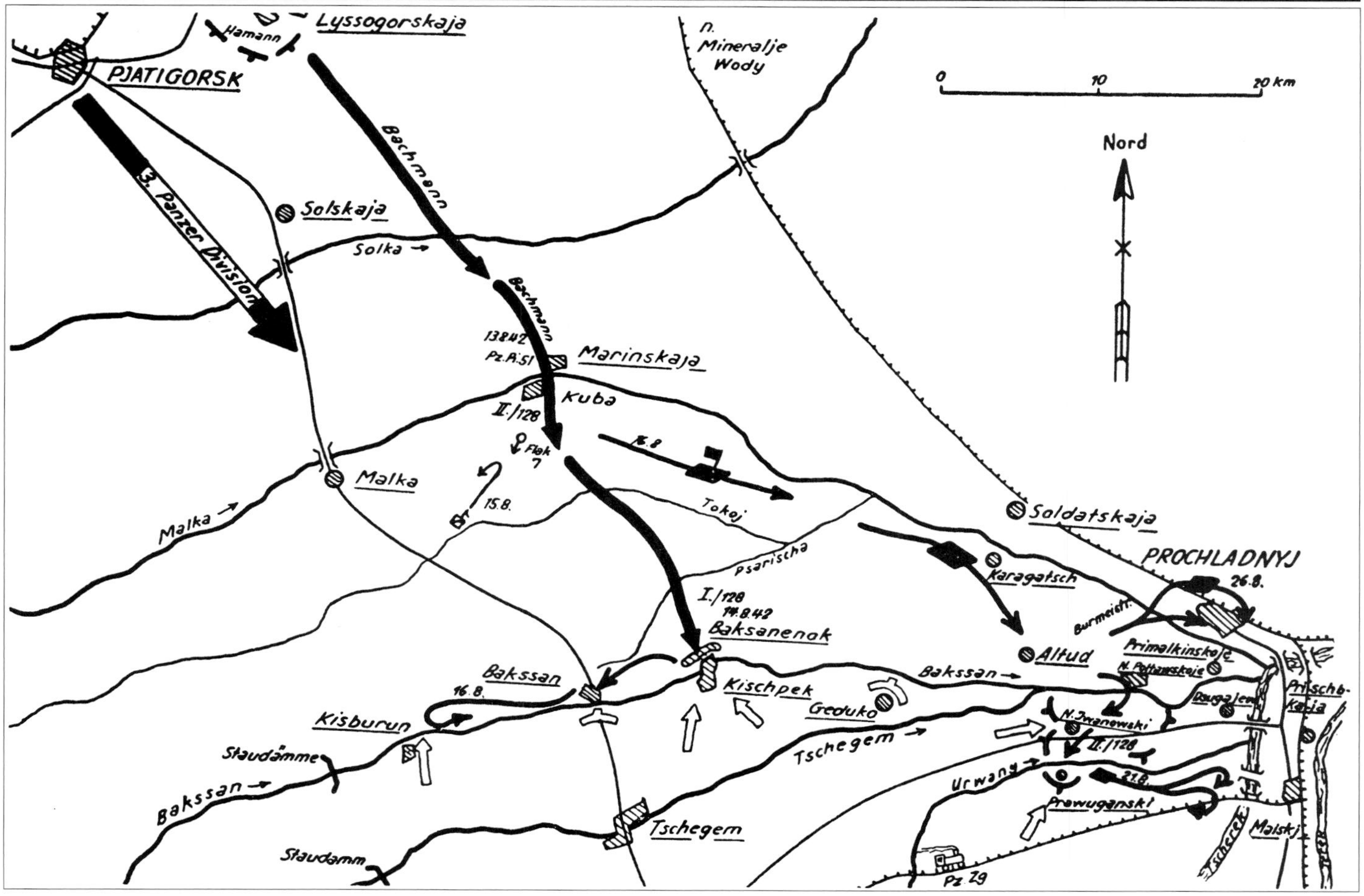

Map 16: The Advance to the Bakssan and on Prochladnyi.

points with his air force. No friendly air support was available. Also causing a considerable disturbance was well-placed Russian artillery fire of all calibers. Casualties were incurred, especially in the Altud — Soldatskoje — Karagatsch area.

During the night of 17/18 August, the *6./SR126* and the *1./PJA128* advanced on Gnadenfeld[18] via Karagatsch.

While *Panzergruppe Burmeister* remained in Altud on 18 August, the *I./SR128*, together with the *7.* and *9./PAR128*, was moved forward to Nowo Poltawskoje via Bakssanenok and Altud. Later on, the battalion was joined by the rest of the regiment. The first elements of the regiment immediately set about crossing the river and were able to establish a small bridgehead. Exploiting this success, the *I./SR128* crossed the river and attacked south from the bridgehead. The enemy was ejected, sometimes in bitter close combat. Nowo Iwanowskij was taken and held against several Russian immediate counterattacks.

Just in the Altud — Nowo Poltawskoje area alone, the enemy air force conducted 47 attacks on this day.

On this day as well, the *I./PR201*, which had remained behind in Millerowo in order to have its strength built up after the initial heavy fighting, finally headed out for the division. Outfitted with a sufficient number of operational tanks, it moved out under the leadership of its new commander, *Hauptmann* von Bülow. A number of days would pass, however, before the battalion would overcome the perpetual shortages of fuel and could rejoin the division.

On 19 August, the *II./SR128* was active at Nowo Iwanowskij and struggled for a small bridgehead over the Urwany. The small village of Prawurganski became the focal point of the fighting. The divisional artillery, which had been brought forward from the Bakssanenok area in the meantime, magnificently supported the fight and contributed in no small manner to the fact that several counterattacks launched by the numerically vastly superior enemy forces were turned back. Some of them collapsed before reaching the German lines, all the while sustaining heavy casualties.

Kampfgruppe Burmeister crossed the Tschegem in the course of 20 August and prepared to attack east—toward its original objective, Maiskij—just northeast of Nowo Iwanowskij. Meanwhile, *Schützen-Regiment 128* successfully defended against Soviets who charged again and again from the west along the northern bank of the Urwany and from the south in the Prawurganski Bridgehead.

Enemy artillery and air forces attempted to disrupt the German attack preparations through fires, strafing and bombing runs. A Soviet armored train injected itself into the fighting again and again along the Maiskij — Naltschik rail line.

The *II./PR201* moved out in the gray light of dawn on 21 August. It advanced through Nowo Iwanowskij and crossed the Urwany. At 0515 hours, enemy combat outposts were ejected from the collective farm south of Prawurganski and some of them were taken prisoner. The tank battalion reached the Maiskij — Naltschik rail line around 0800 hours and forced the locomotives of two freight trains coming from Naltschik to come to a halt when they were fired upon. The engineers accompanying the tanks blew up the rail line at several spots, whereupon the tank battalion returned to the collective farm in accordance with its orders. Once there, it prepared to attack the road bridge at Maiskij as part of *Kampfgruppe Burmeister.*

The *Kampfgruppe* moved out at 1000 hours, and the 1st and 3rd Artillery Battalions supported the attack. The tanks were able to fight their

18 Editor's Note: Most likely another originally ethnic German enclave along the lines previously noted.

way forward to within 600 meters of the bridge despite heavy defensive fires from Soviet artillery. Four antitank guns were knocked out in two separate antitank-gun belts. The Soviet artillery fired final protective fires in front of the bridge, and the enemy blew up the bridge at 1600 hours. The attack was called off.

At 1745 hours, the *II./PR201* moved out again. The objective that time was the railway bridge over the Tscherek further to the south. *Kradschützen-Bataillon 23* followed the tanks. The attack approached to within 500 meters of the bridge with artillery and rocket-launcher support. Against tough enemy resistance, as well as massive antitank-gun and artillery fires, the bridge was then approached to within 100 meters, when it was blown up. The attack was called off and *Kampfgruppe Burmeister* returned to its original attack positions.

During the morning of 22 August, the *8./PR201*, together with elements from *KB23*, was able to approach the road bridge at Maiskij, despite heavy Soviet artillery fire. These elements advanced from the bridgehead at Prawurganski, which was being threatened by the Soviets, especially from the west. The 12-ton bridge turned out to be destroyed and a crossing over the steeply sloping banks of the Tschegem was impossible. Constantly repeated attacks on the collective farm west of Prawurganski placed considerable pressure on the half company of Brandenburgers employed there. It was not until the *5./PR201* was employed, coupled with support from a rocket-launcher battery and the *I./PAR128*, that the infantry felt some relief. An armored train, which supported the fighting of the Soviets from Naltschik, was set alight by the *III./PAR128* around noon, so that it had to roll back.

On 23 August, the *5./PR201*, together with riflemen and combat engineers, advanced south. It tossed the enemy back from the rail line and disrupted it at two places through demolitions. The Russians, for their part, continued their efforts to reduce the bridgehead at Prawurganski. *Oberst* von Buch reassumed command of the artillery regiment after convalescing from his wounds.

A blocking formation was established on the left wing of the division under *Oberst* Brückner, consisting of *Kampfgruppe von Unger* (the *I./SR128*) and *Kampfgruppe von Eisenhardt-Rothe* (*PJA128*). The former oriented south, while the latter to the east. The 2cm *Flak* and the antitank guns of *PJA128* were integrated into the lines with weak elements of infantry.

The 24th of August was also marked by defensive efforts on the part of the formations of the division, with the exception of a few local immediate counterattacks. The enemy was unable to take any terrain at any location.

In view of the terrain difficulties, there was scarcely any hope of successfully continuing the attack south from the area that had been reached. In realization of that, the *3. Panzer-Division* had already been pulled back from the Pjatigorsk — Naltschik road and directed east after moving behind the sector of the *23. Panzer-Division*. Bypassing Prochladny, the attack of the *3. Panzer-Division* made good forward progress to the east. The *XXXX. Panzer-Korps* directed the *23. Panzer-Division* to pull its lines back to the northern bank of the Bakssan and to detach *PR201* (minus the 3rd Battalion) and *SR126* to support the *3. Panzer-Division*.

The headquarters of the *XXXX. Panzer-Korps* moved with the reinforced *3. Panzer-Division* along the north bank of the Terek toward the east, while the *23. Panzer-Division*, minus the two aforementioned regiments, and together with the Rumanian 2nd Mountain Division of Lieutenant General Dumitrache, was attached to the *III. Panzer-Korps* of *General der Kavallerie* von Mackensen, which had been brought forward into the area.

During the night of 24/25 August, the headquarters and the *II./PR201* moved back across the Bakssan. They were followed by the *III./PR201* and additional heavy weapons. On 25 August, the riflemen of *SR128* disengaged from the enemy and transitioned to the defense along a wide frontage on the northern bank of the Bakssan. The divisional artillery organized to support the riflemen and *Panzer-Beobachtungs-Batterie 128*[19] established a broad system of sound and flash ranging which would perform admirably over the next few days in enabling the engagement and destruction of enemy artillery positions.

The enemy attempted on 25 and 26 August to disrupt the establishment of defensive strongpoints by constantly shelling with artillery and mortars. While visiting *SR128* at 1000 hours on 26 August, the division commander and his battle staff found themselves in one such mortar attack. *Generalmajor* Mack, *Major* von Unger (commander of the *I./SR128*), *Hauptmann* von Hagen and *Leutnant* von Puttkammer were killed. In *Generalmajor* Mack, the division lost an exemplary and courageous commander. He was always to be found in his *SPW* among the forward-most attack elements. The magnificent victories achieved by the division under his leadership at Tschertkowo, Nikolajewskaja, Martinowka, Dmitrijewskoje and in the Caucasus will never allow his name to be forgotten among the division's soldiers.

Oberst von Buch assumed acting command of the division, which was later passed to *Oberst* Brückner, whose regiment was taken over by *Oberstleutnant* Wellmann. The divisional artillery was taken over by *Oberstleutnant* Schlutius.

The rear-area services of the division attempted to follow the *Kampfgruppen* as closely as possible. The lack of fuel, which was both dangerous and paralyzing for command and control of all of the formations, could not be overcome by the supply columns of division's support command. The Soviets had made the oil fields at Maikop unusable for the most part, so that nothing could be taken from the refineries there. The single-tracked railway supply line running Rostow — Woroschilowsk — Pjatigorsk did not allow the bringing forward of large quantities of fuel.

The division's 2nd Maintenance Company moved to Soldatskaja via Millerowo — Woroschilowsk — Pjatigorsk, where it arrived at the beginning of September. The division's replacement battalion, *Feldersatz-Bataillon 128*, was moved from Kharkov to Proletarskaja.

On 26 August, *Kampfgruppe Burmeister*, consisting of the headquarters and *II./PR201*, as well as *SR126*, received the mission to take the bulwark of the Soviet front, Prochladny. Then, advancing further east, it was to establish contact with the *3. Panzer-Division*. The *Kampfgruppe* attacked the locality with two forces starting at 0730 hours. Coming from the north was the *II./PR201* and the *I.(SPW)/SR126*, while the remainder of *SR126* attacked from the west. The attack from the west by the riflemen did not make good progress against the defenders, who were dug in along the outskirts. In contrast, the tanks and infantry attacking from the north entered the locality at 0930 hours and initially occupied its eastern portion. In the process, the railway line was reached and interdicted. The northern force then turned around and attacked the defenders from the rear. At noon, both forces linked up in the western portion of the village and conducted deliberate clearing operations against the Soviet defenses. Extensive minefields laid claim to a few vehicles, until the engineer platoons of both the rifle and tank regiments cleared the roads. Three hundred prisoners were taken, mostly students and pupils of a Stalinist academy. Numerous weapons, both heavy and light, were captured.

19 Editor's Note: = 128th Flash and Sound Ranging Battery (Armor), which was part of the divisional artillery regiment.

The flat plains are being left behind and the rugged mountains are ahead. The warlike hill tribes literally make their homes on the side of the mountains.

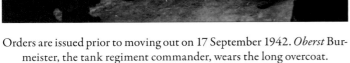

Orders are issued prior to moving out on 17 September 1942. *Oberst* Burmeister, the tank regiment commander, wears the long overcoat.

Oberleutnant Grahn, the company commander of the *6./PR 201*, and the regimental Signals Officer, *Oberleutnant* Krämer, talk to a Caucasian farmer.

An inconvenient position for the motorcycle combination rider as he follows the dust cloud of a tank.

Cow and camel manure was used as both a building material and a heating source.

A shepherd watches over his flock.

A break after the unsuccessful attack on Tscherskaja (Terek) on 17 September 1942.

This guard uses a unique form of transportation to watch over his prisoners.

Leutnant Gnielka, who was killed in action, was the regimental Signals Officer.

Personnel of *PAR 128* in Mineralnje Wody.

On 13 August 1942, Soviet bombers hit elements of the divisional artillery, killing two officers and many enlisted. This grave site marks their final resting place.

Additional views of the imposing terrain of the High Caucasus.

Generalmajor Werner-Ehrenfeucht. As an *Oberst*, he was a long-time commander of *Panzer-Regiment 201*.

Abandoned agricultural equipment, possibly horse drawn ploughs.

Generaloberst von Kleist, the Commander-in-Chief of the *4. Panzer-Armee* in the Caucasus.

A 10cm cannon of the *III./PAR 128* in a grain field south of Prochladny.

The divisional artillery command post in Altud.

Oberwachtmeister Hoyer oversees the paying of his soldiers in Altud.

Officers of the divisional artillery at an awards formation.

The Fighting in the Caucasus 27 August to 27 November 1942

Schützen-Regiment 126 and Panzer-Regiment 201 Along the Terek and in the Steppes

After taking Prochladny on 26 August, *Kampfgruppe Burmeister* left outposts in the city and moved out with its main body at 1100 hours on 27 August to head east, north of the Terek. It was to follow the *3. Panzer-Division*. Heavy enemy aerial activity did not succeed in slowing down the march. Soviet forces south of Dementjewski in the villages along the northern bank of the Terek kept quiet and were left to the lead elements of the *370. Infanterie-Division* of *Generalmajor* Becker, approaching from the northwest. *Schützen-Regiment 126* closed up to the lead attack elements of the *3. Panzer-Division* on 29 August, which were already far to the east of Mosdok and advancing along the railway line toward Machatsch-Kala on the Caspian Sea.

The *II./PR201*, with its 6th Company in the lead, moved out at the same time with the same mission, however, it was held up in Russkij II, northwest of Mosdok. The tank battalion was directed to reconnoiter for fording sites and bridges over the Terek west of Mosdok. It proved impossible to find suitable crossing points over the raging mountain river. It was anywhere from three to five meters deep, on either 30 August or 31 August.

Oberstleutnant Wellmann's *SR126*, together with an advance guard from the *13. Panzer-Division*, reached the furthest point southeast that German forces would reach in the war on 31 August. Operating under the command and control of the *3. Panzer-Division*, they interdicted the operationally important railway fork east of Stary Jurt by advancing through the surprised enemy. By doing so, they were 25 kilometers northeast of Grossny. The constantly stiffening enemy resistance and the chronic logistical difficulties paralyzed any further advance, however. Later on, the formations were pulled back to the west to the area around Ischerskaja.

On 2 September, the *II./PR201* was attached to *Generalleutnant* Recknagel's *111. Infanterie-Division*. It was given the mission of crossing the Terek south of Mosdok and expanding south the bridgehead established by four battalions of the infantry division through offensive operations. Despite extremely difficult circumstances, it was possible to ferry elements of the 5th Tank Company across the river during the night of 2/3 September. The rest were not able to follow until first light the following morning. Without waiting for the other companies, *Oberleutnant* Crämer moved out with his tanks and took the high ground 1,500 meters south of Predmostni (*Fischerdorf*[20]), together with an infantry battalion from *Infanterie-Regiment 117*. The *6./PR201* moved out from the ferry landing point and closed up on the right of the 5th Tank Company. Working closely with the infantry, the bridgehead was expanded to the southwest. By doing so, the prerequisites were created for building a pontoon bridge over the Terek.

On 4 September, the *II./PR201* moved out to the south with 23 operational tanks. Mounted on the vehicles were infantry from the *III./Infanterie-Regiment 117*. It was to take the ridgeline around Wosnessenskaja and Malgobek, which jutted steeply from the bottomland of the Terek, some 15 meters below sea level. Enemy resistance soon forced the infantry to dismount. In hard fighting, the tank battalion broke through an enemy line of resistance and eliminated 3 7.62cm antitank guns, 7 4.5cm antitank guns and 20 antitank rifles in the process. The infantry took 65 prisoners, but it also sustained heavy casualties. A shortage of ammunition and fuel forced the attack to be halted. Toward noon, the enemy brought armor forward. A concentration of 18 T-34's along the eastern flank of the *Kampfgruppe* did not move out to attack; instead, 7 T-34's with mounted infantry launched a surprise attack from the southwest. Without suffering any losses, the tanks of the battalion headquarters section and the *6./PR201* knocked out all of the Soviet vehicles, with the Russian infantry subsequently pulling back to the south.

Combat reconnaissance by tanks and infantry on the following day confirmed the impression that the enemy had identified the German intent of advancing from the north of Ordshonikidse and had correspondingly established a strong, deeply echeloned defensive front along both sides of the Mosdok — Wosnessenskaja road.

The higher levels of the German command remained committed to the plan of attack, however. The *111. Infanterie-Division* was reinforced with the *II./Panzer-Regiment 4* of the *13. Panzer-Division*, the *I./Panzer-Artillerie-Regiment 13* of the *13. Panzer-Division* and general headquarters antitank forces. A strong attack group was formed under the command of *Oberst* Herfurth (Commander, *Infanterie-Regiment 117*) on 6 September. With the exception of the infantry regiment, all of the other forces of the *Kampfgruppe* were armored. The first wave, consisting of the *II./Panzer-Regiment 4* and the *II./Infanterie-Regiment 117*, moved out at 0400 hours. It was followed by the *II./PR201*, with the *III./Infanterie-Regiment 117* mounted up on the rear decks of the tanks. Despite good support by the concentrated German artillery forces, the attack made only slow progress and took heavy casualties in the face of the massed Soviet defenses.

The *II./PR201*, moving left of the first wave, was able to wrest a slight rise from the enemy after turning east. The enemy then placed the battalion under barrage fire with artillery, "Stalin Organs" and antitank guns. Soviet ground-attack aircraft swarmed in incessantly. The fighting strength of the *III./Infanterie-Regiment 117* sank to 80 men. Aided by the terrain, the enemy held practically impregnable positions. The Russian artillery could not be engaged by the German artillery since they were unable to be targeted in their elevated and well-concealed positions.

Another attempt by the *II./PR4* to break through got it as far as a hill southeast of Wosnessenskaja and a hill west of the same village, however, it did not have any infantry accompanying it. As a result of numerous mines and a strong antitank-gun belt, the battalion had to pull back, suffering considerable casualties. The terrain south of Wosnessenskaja, which could be observed from those temporarily occupied hills, did not look promising for the continuation of the attack. The limit of advance was held, however. Late in the afternoon, a Soviet attack force with tanks and infantry conducted a surprise attack from the east along the southern bank of the Terek with the intent of reaching the bridge and cutting off the forces of *Kampfgruppe Herfurth* fighting far to the south. The *II./PR201* immediately moved back north, hit the enemy in his left flank and forced him to pull back after a short fight.

The days that followed were marked by constantly repeated enemy attacks against the bridgehead at Mosdok. *Infanterie-Regiment 117* and *Infanterie-Regiment 50* were subjected to constant fires from the numerically superior Russian artillery and heavy infantry weapons. Advances conducted by enemy armor were countered by immediate counterattacks of German tanks.

On 8 September, *Leutnant* Fischer suddenly found himself facing four T-34's in his short-barreled 5cm *Panzer III*. He had been left with the infantry as an observer after a successful advance of the *II./PR201*. The enemy tanks broke out of a row of thick vegetation and drove a weak infantry battalion in front of them. Despite the inferiority of his main gun, *Leutnant* Fischer took up the fight with the Russians. Firing at pointblank range, he set the lead Soviet tank alight. At that point, the remaining tanks took flight.

20 Editor's Note: = Fisherman's Village. Many settlements populated by ethnic Germans were referred to in two languages, Russian and German, and also entered on Soviet maps that way, as was the case here.

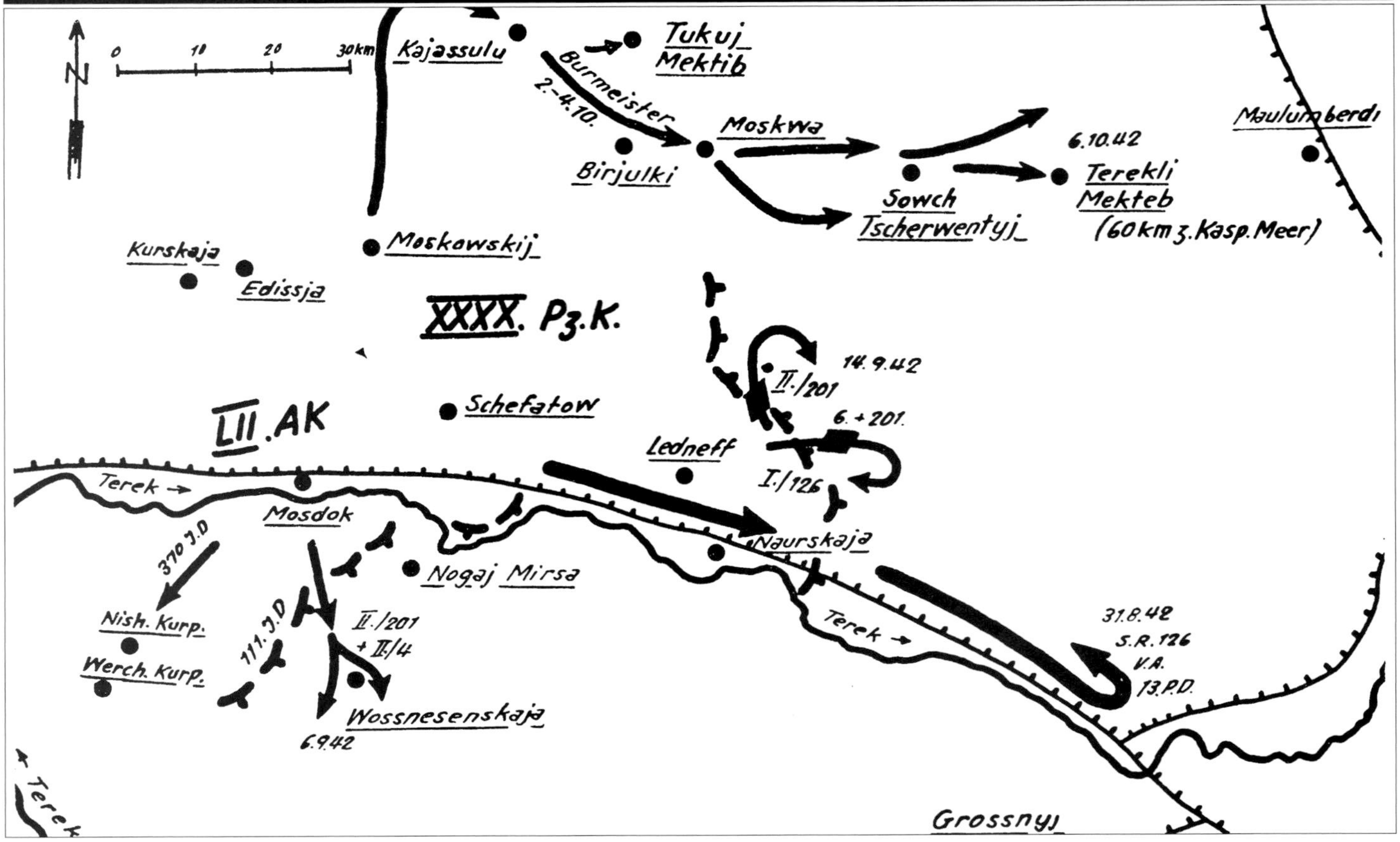

Map 17: The Fighting at Mosdok and in the Steppes.

To reinforce the bridgehead, a strong battalion from *Panzer-Regiment 6* of the *3. Panzer-Division*, as well as a *SPW* battalion, arrived on 10 September. Together, they attacked along the left wing of the *Kampfgruppe* on the southern bank of the Terek to the east. The bridgehead was expanded and the main line of resistance was pushed forward as far as the village of Terek. The *II./PR201* was attached to the *Kampfgruppe* from the *3. Panzer-Division*, which was under the command of *Oberst* von Liebenstein, the commander of *Panzer-Regiment 6*. On 12 September, the *II./PR201* participated in an attack in front of the eastern portion of the bridgehead, in which it was one arm of the pincers. Numerous Soviet field fortifications with heavy infantry weapons were cleared and approximately 200 prisoners were taken. That operations signaled the end of the employment of the *II./PR201* in the Mosdok Bridgehead.

On 13 September, the battalion crossed the Terek in the morning and reached *Kampfgruppe Westhoven* (headquarters of the *3. Schützen-Brigade*) at 1500 hours after an 85-kilometer march. The *Kampfgruppe* was guarding the left flank of the *XXXX. Panzer-Korps* in a line running Naurskaja — Alpatowo — Star. Ledneff — Naidonowskoje, after the lead elements of the corps had advanced almost 50 kilometers further east and then had to be pulled back. In the meantime, the enemy had brought forward the X Guards Rifle Corps, with its 4th, 6th and 7th Guards Rifle Brigades, as well as the 92nd Artillery regiment, in order to protect the oil fields at Grossnyj. The Soviet corps apparently had the mission to attack around what was perceived to be the weak German forces of only regimental strength and eliminate them.

The *II./PR201* was ordered to attack from the march at Naurskaja. Trailing clouds of dust and under constant artillery fire, the battalion headed east, followed by an *SPW* company from the *I./SR126*. After moving 4 kilometers, it turned south, where it encountered relatively strong enemy formations. Some of the enemy forces were eliminated and some driven south, where they ran into the rifles of *Kradschützen-Bataillon 3* of the *3. Panzer-Division*.

While this successful advance to the east took place, the Soviets went around the German outposts deep in the steppes and advanced far to the west. As a result, *Generalmajor* Westhoven pulled back his forces some 20 kilometers during the night.

The enemy pursued the German formations and continued his advances and envelopment maneuvers on 14 September. The *II./PR201* was alerted and moved out with a *SPW* company from the *I./SR126* around noon. That force ran into a Soviet tank destroyer battalion. The enemy defended bitterly and attempted to approach the tanks again and again. Foxhole after foxhole had to be smoked out. In some cases, tank crews dismounted and assisted the riflemen. Using Molotov Cocktails, the enemy set several of the battalion's tanks on fire, but the crews were able to extinguish the flames and continue the fight. Only one tank suffered casualties. Two crewmembers from a tank of the *8./PR201* were lost, and the tank could only be recovered—still on fire—by the exemplary performance of the platoon leader, *Oberfeldwebel* Lauterbach.

After completing its mission, the tank battalion moved on Naidonowskoje, where it scattered enemy resistance and prevented him from conducting additional envelopment attempts against the left flank of the *Kampfgruppe.*

An order-of-the-day from the *3. Panzer-Division* singled out the *II./PR201* for praise for its decisive success.

The enemy attacked again on 15 September. Once again, *Hauptmann* Fechner's *II./PR201* advanced into his ranks and defeated him. Numerous prisoners were taken and infantry weapons and antitank rifles captured.

During the afternoon, *Kampfgruppe von Liebenstein*, consisting of *Panzer-Regiment 6* and an *SPW* battalion, arrived in the area of operations. At the same time, the *I./PR201* of *Hauptmann* von Bülow, which had been refitted, arrived at the area north of Mosdok at full combat strength.

The *II./PR201* was attached to *Kampfgruppe von Liebenstein* on 16 September. Attacking from Naidonowskoje to the south, the *Kampfgruppe* soon found itself embroiled in difficult fighting with strong infantry and tank-destroyer forces of the enemy. The *II./PR201* moved in an echelon left formation behind *Panzer-Regiment 6*. Together with a company of combat engineers, it cleared Soviet positions on a ridgeline. One *Panzer III* from the 6th Tank Company was lost through an antitank-gun round. The village of Sponyj was captured, with 70 prisoners being taken and numerous infantry weapons captured. *Oberleutnant* Schewe, the commander of the 8th Tank Company, was badly wounded.

Turning to the west, the *Kampfgruppe* cleared out the Soviet positions that had been cut off by the attack up to that point. As in the previous days, they fought extremely bravely and with great determination. Without regard for their own personnel, the enemy artillery fired on the tanks and armored vehicles moving back and forth between the enemy field positions. After 1200 hours, the tanks of *Kampfgruppe von Liebenstein* linked up with the vehicles of *Kampfgruppe Burmeister*, which were arriving from the northwest from the direction of Schefatoff, after the *I./PR201* of the latter *Kampfgruppe* had moved out to attack from the march. The enemy was caught between the two battle groups and was wiped out. During the night, the two armored forces were positioned behind the combat-outpost line established by *Schützen-Regiment 394* (*3. Panzer-Division*) and *SR126*.

A unique concentration of armor found itself on the steppes on 17 September. Under the command of *Oberst* von Liebenstein, both *Panzer-Regiment 6* and *Panzer-Regiment 201* moved out to clear the area in front of the German positions of Soviet forces that had been badly battered the previous days. Moving in the lead was the *I./PR201*, which was followed by the regimental headquarters and then the *II./PR201*. *Panzer-Regiment 6* followed this force with two battalions. The two regiments swung out to the east and south in a 6-kilometer arc. The clouds of dust could be seen far away in the steppes. The Russians defended with infantry and antitank guns. Once again, the large issuance of antitank rifle among the Soviet forces was striking. Snipers used these rifles to fire into the vision ports on the tank cupolas. They had frequent success in aiming at those points, especially when a tank commander opened the port longer than was absolutely necessary. *Leutnant* von Viereck was killed in that fashion; *Leutnant* von Wiese was badly wounded. Two German tanks, including the tank used by the battalion physician of the *I./PR201,* were lost. The Russians were deliberately wiped out by the tanks moving back and forth among the foxholes. The enemy's weapons were destroyed. The armored force then returned to friendly lines, constantly fighting Russian infantry along the way.

The enemy was so badly battered by this round of fighting that he gave up his offensive intentions north of the Lenin Canal. It would not be until November 1942 that he would attempt to attack west again from a line running Alpatowo — Staro Ledneff — Kasputin — Point 107.

During the afternoon of 17 September, *Generalmajor* Breith, the commander of the *3. Panzer-Division*, extended his praise to *Hauptmann* Fechner's *II./PR201* for its magnificent and tireless operations during the period of 13-17 September. In the period of 2-17 September, the battalion destroyed or captured the following spoils of war:

650 Prisoners (partly in conjunction with other forces)
16 Tanks (Mark III's and T-34's)
45 Antitank rifles
21 Machine guns
8 7.62m Antitank guns
9 4.5cm Antitank guns
2 Artillery Pieces
Several light and medium mortars

Panzer-Regiment 201 remained at the disposal of the *3. Panzer-Division* in the Besorukin and Konsowod Stud Farm areas, where the soldiers initiated maintenance on the tanks and other vehicles.

On 20 September, the *1.* and *4./PR201* were moved into the bridgehead south of Mosdok and attached to *Schützen-Regiment 3* (*3. Panzer-Division*) at Terskaja. The rifle regiment was employed along the left wing of the *111. Infanterie-Division*. The *13. Panzer-Division* had moved out from the bridgehead to the west and southwest and had been able to make progress in the direction of Maiskij. The two tank companies from the *I./PR201* were used as the armored ready reserve for the bridgehead.

On 23 September, *SR126*, recently having come under the command of *Oberst* Brückner, relieved *Schützen-Regiment 3* in the bridgehead, with the result that the *1.* and *4./PR201* came back under the command and control of a battle group of the division. That evening, 200 Armenian deserters surrendered to the combat outposts. Among them were six officers and three commissars.

Two alpine companies composed of Georgians that were employed in the regimental sector successfully repulsed an attack by the enemy, inflicting heavy losses on him and taking approximately 50 prisoners.

To support an offensive operation of the *LII. Armee-Korps*—consisting of the *111. Infanterie-Division*, the *370. Infanterie-Division* and elements of the recently introduced *SS- Division "Wiking"*—the *I./PR201* of *Oberleutnant* Rebentisch and two *SPW* platoons of the *I./SR126*, under the commander of *Hauptmann* Enneper, the new battalion commander, conducted an attack against extended Soviet field fortifications, which were eliminated without taking any friendly losses. Thirty-five prisoners were taken. The German infantry, which followed up from the west, did not encounter any enemy resistance.

Until 1 October, most of the tank regiment did not see any combat operations. On 2 October, a mixed *Kampfgruppe* under *Oberst* Burmeister was established. It consisted of

Kosakenregiment von Jungschulz[21]
1 Engineer company
1.5 platoons of riflemen with *SPW's*
1 Section of field artillery
6./PR201 (*Oberleutnant* Grahn)
Light platoon of the *II./PR201* (*Leutnant* Dittmann)
1 Military police company
Motorcycle reconnaissance platoon of the *II./PR201*

The mission of the battle group was to eliminate an enemy force consisting of two regiments that had established positions in the Moskwa area. It was to advance to the northeast and east to accomplish that mission.

Moving through Kajassulu and then turning southeast, the *Kampfgruppe* moved on Moskwa, which was occupied without resistance by the assault group on the left. The right-hand assault group, led by the Cossack regiment, encountered weaker enemy resistance at Birjulkin. The riflemen and engineers advanced southeast from Moskwa, while the tanks moved east. They then concentrically attacked Collective Farm No. 8, where the enemy had established defensive positions (in front of it). After hard fighting, the enemy resistance was broken: 200 prisoners were taken and the rest of the enemy force scattered. A reconnaissance in force advanced on Terekli-Mekteb, Kirelin and Collective Farm No. II on 6 October. That marked the furthest point east that German tanks advanced during the war.

Up to that point in time, medical personnel operating under the protection of the Red Cross had only suffered casualties as a result of air attacks on the roads and villages. During this advance, however, the battalion physician of the *I./PR201*, *Assistenz-Arzt Dr.* Faltus, and his men

21 Editor's Note: = Cossack Regiment "von Jungschulz"

fell under the blows of sabers wielded by Soviet cavalry while they were tending to the wounded.

The enemy reassembled in the neighboring collective farm and could not be driven from there. The operation was called off on corps order on 8 October , and the battle group pulled back to the Konsowod Stud Farm.

After his release from the hospital, *Oberst* Werner-Ehrenfeldt returned to the division and relieved *Oberst* Burmeister in command of *PR201. Oberst* Burmeister was reassigned to the division headquarters and assumed command of *Schützen-Brigade 23* later on.

After a few days of rest, during which the vehicles were maintained and preparations were made for the coming winter, movement orders came as a surprise. The tank regiment, minus its 3rd Battalion and the 1st and 5th Tank Companies, assembled west of Mosdok. The 1st Tank Company remained in the Mosdok Bridgehead; on 20 October, the 5th Tank Company and the light tank platoon of the regiment's 2nd Battalion were also sent there. On 21 October, both of the companies attacked to the south of Terskaja in support of the *SPW* battalion. The attack was designed to reduce a Soviet salient jutting into the sector of *Infanterie-Regiment 117.*

Effective 24 October, the tank regiment and *SR126* returned to the command and control of the division. They moved into a new billeting area at Prischibskaja, where the last large-scale offensive operation in the Caucasus would be launched.

Defensive and Offensive Operations Between Bakssan and Tscherek

Ever since 26 August, the greatly weakened *23. Panzer-Division* had been fighting without the *PR201* (minus the 3rd Battalion) and *SR126*, which had been employed elsewhere (as previously described). The division was temporarily under the command of *Oberst* Brückner until a replacement for *Generalmajor* Mack could be designated. Those elements were positioned along a broad frontage along the north banks of the Bakssan and the Tschegem. The right wing of the division was at Baksonenok and the left wing, secured by outposts of *KB23*, was at Prochladny. Vastly numerically superior enemy forces, who appeared not to be familiar with any personnel shortages and who enjoyed artillery support heretofore not previously experienced, constantly attempted to break through the positions of the riflemen, motorcycle infantry and engineers. While there were only two German fighters available to protect the air space above the German positions, the Soviets attacked day-in and day-out with strong bomber, fighter-bomber and fighter formations.

The Soviet attacks were especially focused on the small bridgehead across the Bakssan at Nowo-Poltawskoje, which had been established by *SR128*. On 29 August, the artillery's 3rd Battalion had to lay down final protective fires and ricochet shots to scatter enemy larger-scale attacks in front of the German lines. Using flash ranging techniques, an additional three enemy batteries were silenced.

The days that followed were marked by considerable reconnaissance and combat patrol activity by both sides. On 2 September, an enemy patrol consisting of 40 men was scattered, with 15 men being taken prisoner. A task force consisting of the *1./PJA128,* a platoon from the *2./PPB51* and a platoon from the *3.(Flak)/PJA128*, cleared the villages of Petropawlowskij, Nowo Osetinskij and Minskij of Soviet partisans, scattered forces and the constantly appearing patrols. The Soviet artillery constantly increased in strength. With the help of an armored flash- and range-finding battery, the divisional artillery successfully engaged Soviet artillery posi-

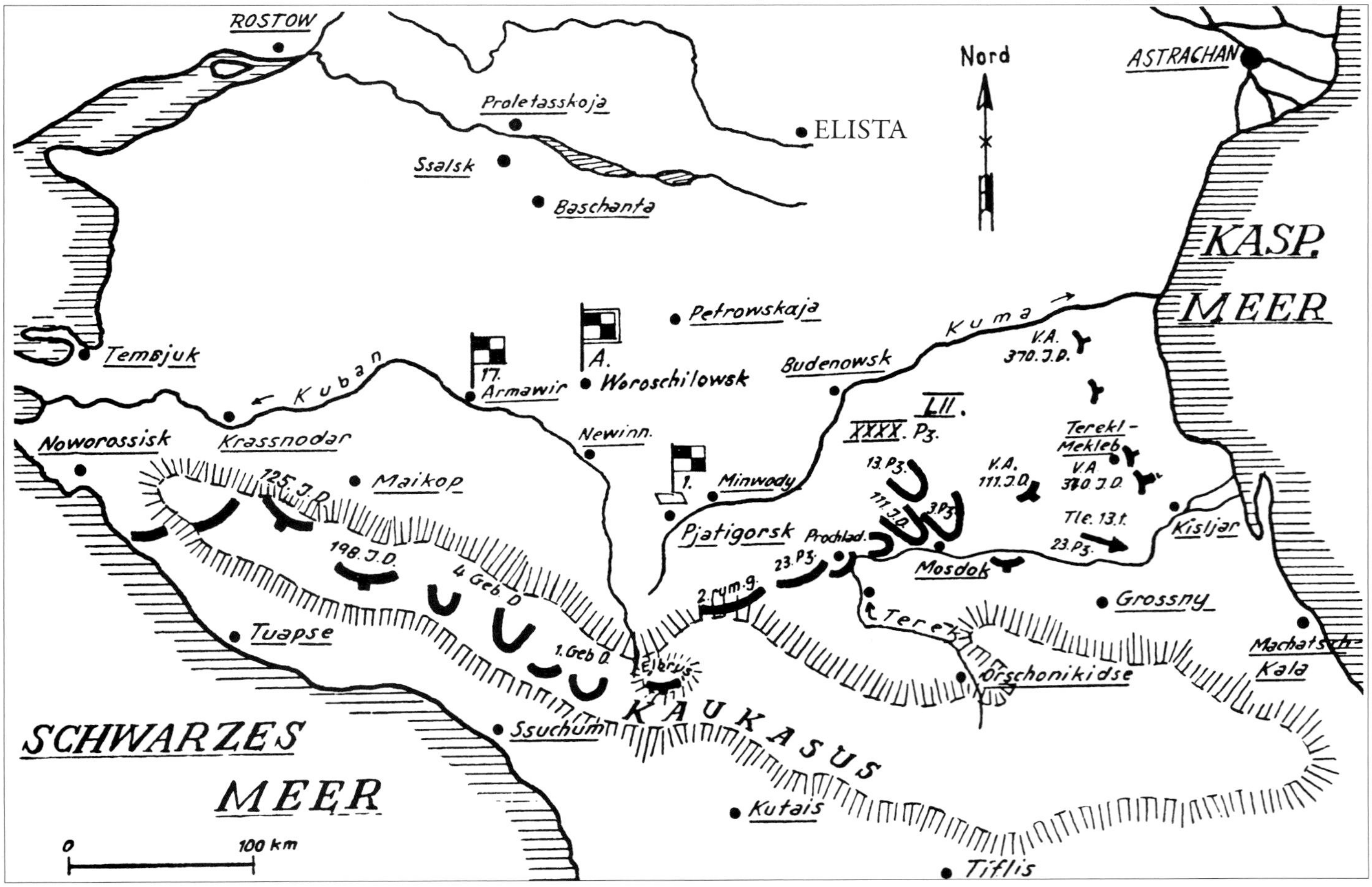

Map 18: The Over-all Situation in the Caucasus on 29 August 1942.

tions, whereby 11 enemy batteries were silenced during the period from 30 August to 5 September.

A weak enemy attack against the positions of *KB23* west of Nowo-Poltawskoje was turned back without difficulty.

At 0430 hours on 6 September, however, the enemy attacked *SR128* at Nowo-Poltawskoje with considerable artillery preparation. Weak enemy forces succeeded in crossing the Bakssan to the north and establishing a bridgehead there. The German artillery inflicted heavy casualties on the enemy force, and the immediate counterattack by the riflemen cleared up the situation once and for all. All of the Russian force was wiped out: 50 dead Russians were counted in front of the German lines and 300 prisoners were taken. As the result of additional counterattacks by the riflemen, another 200 prisoners were brought in on 7 September.

The enemy also continued to attack on the left wing of the division, especially at Prochladny. The weak outposts of *KB23* were relieved by the *II./Infanterie-Regiment 668* of the *370. Infanterie-Division*. That battalion, which then continued the fight in that sector, had been brought forward on orders of the *LII. Armee-Korps* after a difficult foot march through the Kalmuck Steppes. On 8 September, the enemy succeeded in taking the village of Primalkinskoje, to the southwest of Prochladny, which then threatened the deep left flank of the division. On 9 September, the Soviets entered Prochladny proper, thus expanding their area of penetration to the north. *Major* Zejdlik's reinforced *PPB51* counterattacked from the southwest, while the *II./Infanterie-Regiment 668*, which had been attached to the division, attacked Prochladny from the north at the same time. By the evening of 9 September, Primalkinskoje was firmly back under German control; the attack on Prochladny bogged down in heavy enemy defensive fires, however.

A Soviet armored train, which continued to advance up to the destroyed bridge over the Tscherek, caused a lot of problems for the German forces. Although artillery caused it to pull back rather quickly, it was never able to decisively hit the train.

Between 10 and 14 September, the Russians withdrew some of their artillery. They appeared to want to shift their defensive main effort into the area around Prochladny and further east, in the area around Mosdok, where the attack of the reinforced *3. Panzer-Division* and *General der Infanterie* Ott's *LII. Armee-Korps* had gained ground.

On 14 September, *Hauptman Dr.* Drescher's *II./SR128* moved out to conduct a reconnaissance-in-force with a limited objective. The operation, which was supported by the *III./PAR128*, encountered bitter resistance from an enemy equipped with heavy weapons along the southern bank of the Bakssan. Considerable casualties were taken, and the attack had to be called off. It was only with difficulty that the wounded could be evacuated. A similar advance by elements of *Major* Zejdlik's *PPB51* encountered a similar situation, and the major himself was wounded.

During the course of 14 September, the former commander of the division, *Generalmajor Freiherr* von Boineburg-Lengsfeld, returned to the division, where he was greeted enthusiastically, and reassumed command.

On 15 September, the enemy no longer attacked from Prochladny; instead; he transitioned to the defense. At that point, the *II./Infanterie-Regiment 668* moved out and attacked from the north and northeast, getting close to the two bridges over the Tscherek southeast of the village. At the last moment, the enemy blew them up.

A squadron of Cossacks was attached to the division to assist in clearing the rear area of enemy groups.

After being separated from the division for more than two months, the *I./PR201*, which had remained in Millerowo to undergo a battlefield reconstitution, returned to the front. It was immediately sent *en route* to *Kampfgruppe Burmeister*, which was attached to the *3. Panzer-Division*. The *III./PR201* of *Hauptmann* Stiewe, which also returned to operational readiness at the same time, was brought forward from Pjatigorsk and positioned at Soldatskaja. *Infanterie-Bataillon 795*, composed of Georgians, was attached to the division and brought forward to right behind the front lines at Krupsko —Uljankowski. In a short span of time, 2,100 replacements arrived from Germany for the division.

As a result of little combat activity, the divisional artillery conducted deliberate counterbattery operations, where the fires, directed by radio from the air from an observation aircraft, proved increasingly effective. Concentrations of enemy vehicles and field positions at Ssarski were covered with well-placed fires.

On 20 September, *KB23* attacked across the Bakssan to the south, supported by concentrated fires from the divisional artillery. The motorcycle battalion took Geduko and brought in one officer and 103 men from the 295th Grusinian Rifle Division as prisoners. By 0800 hours, the attack objective had been taken and was firmly under German control.

The *13. Panzer-Division* of *Generalmajor* Herr moved out of the Mosdok Bridgehead and attacked in the direction of Maiskij. It was able to take the road and railway bridge over the Terek southeast of Maiskij intact. The enemy, in the face of a possible encirclement, pulled back out the area between Malka and Terek in the area south of Prochladnyj, where he had held out stubbornly up to that point.

Attached to the division at the time, in addition to the 2nd Company of Brandenburgers, was *Technisches Bataillon 8* (in Prochladny), the *3./Brückenbau-Bataillon 699* and *Feldzeug-Bataillon 23*.[22]

Heavy Russian artillery placed harassing fires on Bakssanenok during the afternoon of 20 September. Ever since it was captured by *KB23*, Geduko was under constant artillery and mortar fire. That afternoon, at 1600 hours, it was evacuated by German forces, since it was of no importance to the division for the conduct of the fighting.

The division reorganized for attack, placing its main effort on the left with *SR128*. The motorcycle battalion and the *III./PR201* became part of *Kampfgruppe Bachmann*. *Kampfgruppe von Bodenhausen* (headquarters of *Schützen-Brigade 23*) was relieved of its duties by *Baustab Vierow*,[23] whereupon it assumed command and control of the sector of the reinforced *II./SR128*.

The main clearing stations of the 2nd medical Company in Altud and the 1st Medical Company in Prochladnyj had their hands full over those few weeks. Their operating rooms were often under direct threat from the enemy. In Altud, the threat was from Soviet patrols that appeared on the outskirts of the village several times; in Prochladnyj, it was from Soviet air attacks that laid waste to the village and blew all of the windows out of the building housing the clearing station. *Oberstarzt Dr.* Holstein left the division during this time period. His replacement as Division Surgeon was *Oberstabarzt Dr.* Becker.

On 21 September, *Kampfgruppe Bachmann* crossed the Bakssan, attacking east. It then swung south and moved on Maiskij, where the Russians put up a stubborn defense. Prischibskaja was taken on 22 September; Maiskij fell the next day. The *I./SR128* of *Hauptmann* Fanselau continued to advance south and ejected the enemy from his positions along the railway line south of the village. Advancing west of the Tscherek, the 2nd Company of the "Brandenburgers" wrested control of the embankment west of the railway bridge from the enemy. In the effort to cross the Tscherek south of Maiskij, so as to eliminate the threat to the western flank of the *Kampfgruppe*, *KB23* suffered heavy casualties. One motorcycle platoon was practically wiped out. *Leutnant* Ulrich and 12 men were

22 Editor's Note: The 8th Technical Battalion (most likely some sort of maintenance formation), the 3rd Company of the 699th Bridge Construction Battalion and the 23rd Equipment Battalion.

23 Editor's Note: = Construction Staff (Headquarters) "Vierow", presumably a construction engineer command and control element.

killed. *Major* Richter, the battalion commander, was badly wounded. Five assault rafts were shot up. The attack had to be called off.

Feldzeug-Bataillon 23 left its command and control relationship with the division; in its place came *Pionier-Bataillon 73* and *Straßenbau-Bataillon 563*.[24]

On 24 September, *Kampfgruppe Bachmann* renewed its attack south between Tscherek and Terek. Closely supported by the *12./PR201* and magnificently supported by the *2.* And *9./PAR128*, the battle group took Kotljarewskaja. Some 550 prisoners, mostly from the Soviet 790th Infantry Regiment, were taken. Contact was established at Arik with the *13. Panzer-Division*, which was on the eastern bank of the Terek.

While the attack of *Kampfgruppe Bachmann* over the previous few days was able to make good progress, *Kampfgruppe von Bodenhausen* succeeded in gaining very little ground against stiff enemy resistance. The enemy south of the Bakssan was literally clinging to the ground. Every German attack was followed by a Soviet counterattack. On top of all that, the Soviets were receiving excellent artillery support. With the village of Dsugajew serving as a defensive focal point, the elements of the enemy's 392nd Rifle Division were stubbornly holding out along the Bakssan and the Tscherek.

On 26 September, *Kampfgruppe von Bodenhausen* succeeded in establishing a bridgehead across the Bakssan east of Nowo-Poltawskoje, receiving support from the *III./PAR128* (the 7th and 8th Batteries, as well as the 1st Battery from the 1st Battalion). Dsugajew finally fell on 29 September to the battle group's attack. At almost the same time, it also reached the bridge over the Tscherek northwest of Prischibskaja and eliminated the remnants of the bitterly fighting enemy.

Oberst Schlutius received a posting to the German Army Mission in Rumania. His replacement in command of the divisional artillery was *Oberst* von Buch, who had since recovered and returned to the division. *Hauptmann* Hesse was designated as the new commander of *PPB51*. *Kosakenschwadron Eichele*[25] left the command and control of the division. The Georgian *Infanterie-Bataillon 795* took up positions along the Bakssan west of Nowo-Poltawskoje.

To the east of Nowo-Poltawskoje, in the Bakssan Bridgehead, *Kampfgruppe von Bodenhausen* was subjected to constant Soviet attacks from the west.

On 5 October 1942, the *III./PR201*, together with a rifle company, formed *Kampfgruppe Stiewe*. Supported by the *1.* and *8./PAR128*, the battle group moved west from Maiskij to conduct a clearing action between Urwanj and Tscherek. Despite marshy terrain along the southern bank of the Urwanj, the attack made good progress. The enemy was surprised and was unable to concentrate artillery fires on the attack sector for some time. The villages of Ssowjetskij and Wladimirski were taken. By reducing the large Soviet salient into the German sector, the division's frontage was considerably reduced.

Enemy concentrations in Krassnaja Poljana were engaged by German artillery. Following the operations by *Kampfgruppe Stiewe*, there were initially no offensive operations along the Bakssan and Terek river lines for some time. The forces in that sector transitioned to the defense. Moreover, winter positions were prepared as a result of lessons learned from the early onset of winter the previous year. Stockpiles of supplies were established. Only the divisional artillery remained active, supported by its flash- and sound-ranging battery and aerial observers. The artillery engaged enemy gun positions, observation posts and enemy concentrations. A Soviet railway gun that was employed near Naltschik caused considerable difficulties in locating and engaging it, however.

24 Editor's Note: = 563rd Construction Battalion (Road). Both battalions were general headquarters forces.

25 Editor's Note: = Cossack Squadron "Eichele".

On 10 October, a Soviet infantry attack of company strength against the bridge at Nowo-Poltawskoje ran aground.

To exploit the exceptional observation possibilities offered, the divisional artillery's armored flash- and sound-ranging battery was moved to the east bank of the Terek, where it established extensive measuring sites along the ridgelines, which later came to play an important role in future operations. The Soviet artillery positions could be identified well into the mountain ranges from those positions.

Cutting into the combat power of the forces in the field at the time was a rapid increase in the number of illnesses. *Kampfgruppe von Bodenhausen* alone reported 198 new cases from 27 September to 7 October, especially epidemic hepatitis (jaundice), malaria, and stomach and bladder disorders. Fortunately, a good number of the sick personnel could recover close to the front in the well-equipped military hospitals at Kisslowodsk and Essentuki, so that they were not lost permanently to the forces in the field.

On 8 October, the *1. Panzer-Armee* issued orders for "Training During the Winter of 1942/1943". All signs indicated that the offensive operations of the German formations for the year were coming to a close. Another order received at the time directed the redesignation of the rifle regiments into "mechanized infantry" regiments—*Panzergrenadier-Regimenter*. Thus, *SR126* became *Panzergrenadier-Regiment 126*; the same held true for *SR128*.[26] The redesignation was not only an honorific, it also indicated the uniqueness of the type of fighting these formations engaged in.[27]

Soviet deserters reported that elements of the Georgian *Infanterie-Bataillon 795* wanted to desert to the Soviets. The division ordered the battalion to be pulled out of the front lines immediately. Despite that, a few of the Georgians attempted to desert around 2345 hours. Most of them were caught and taken prisoner. Elements of *PJA128* engaged in a firefight with some of the Georgians. On 10 October, the Georgian battalion was disarmed and transported out of sector.

On 13 October, *Oberst* von Bodenhausen left the division due to an illness. *Oberst* Burmeister, who had become available after *Oberst* Werner-Ehrenfeucht returned to command *PR201*, initially became commander of *Panzergrenadier-Brigade 23*.

At 0615 hours on 15 October, a Soviet battalion attacked the positions of the *5./PGR128* along the southern edge of Kotljarewskaja after a preparation by artillery and "Stalin Organs". An equally strong attack was directed against the dairy west of the village. Despite heavy casualties inflicted by barrage fires of the division artillery, smaller groups succeeded in infiltrating between the village and the dairy. They were eliminated in immediate counterattacks conducted by the infantry.

Enemy artillery placed barrage fires on Kotljarewskaja, Maiskij and Prischibskaja, while German artillery attacked enemy artillery positions, troop concentrations and fortification work being conducted at Nowo-Iwanowka, the bulwark of the Soviet defensive system.

26 Editor's Note: The redesignations did not bring about substantive changes within the organizations. Most of the former "riflemen" were still transported to the battlefield in trucks, where they dismounted prior to fighting. For ease of identification, the division's mechanized infantry regiments will be referred to as *PGR126* and *PGR128* in the text. When referred to generically, the term used will generally be grenadiers or infantry, since "mechanized infantry" or *Panzergrenadiere* is misleading when only the *I./PGR126* was actually mechanized. The term "motorized infantry" is also somewhat problematic, since more and more soldiers of the two regiments became "foot soldiers" as the fighting wore on. In cases where it is obvious that the infantry in question were actually "mechanized" or "motorized" they will be referred to as such.

27 Author's Note: For ease of understanding, the armored personnel carriers will continue to be referred to as *SPW's* (*Schützenpanzerwagen*) instead of the term that was then introduced and often encountered: *GPW* (*Grenadierpanzerwagen*).

The artillery activities of the enemy continued to increase in intensity in the days that followed and expanded to include Dsugajew and Nowo-Poltawskoje. Soviet air activity also intensified. In addition to the constant presence at night of the "visitors"—harassment aircraft such as the *U2*—bombers and fighters began to appear over the area of operations again. At the same time, there was intense propaganda activity with the use of loudspeakers and fly bills, which were, in turn, answered by the German side. The German soldiers proved to be completely deaf to the Soviet slogans; even fly bills with supposed letters from German prisoners made no impression. Increasingly, the formations had been forged into organic wholes as a result of the fighting they had experienced together. Nothing could shake them.

Soviet patrols and raids continued to infiltrate through the thinly held strongpoint-type positions and raid the German rear area, ambushing individual vehicles. German raiding parties were often able to put an end to their activities.

From Kharkov, the division had a portion of the supply point brought forward that had been left there at the start of the offensive; it needed to do that in order to facilitate urgently needed repairs.

The preparations for the winter campaign were unexpectedly interrupted. The German Army High Command decided after all to continue the attack of the *1. Panzer-Armee* before the onset of winter. The objective was to interdict the two most important passes through the Caucasus, the Ossetian military road at Alagir and the Grusinian military road at Ordshonikidse, and take firm control of them.

Directly responsible for executing the attack was the *III. Panzer-Korps* of *General der Kavallerie* von Mackensen, to which the *13. Panzer-Division* and the *23. Panzer-Division* had been allocated. In addition, the corps had the *I./Gebirgsjäger-Regiment 99*, the Rumanian reinforced 2nd Mountain Division of Lieutenant General Dumitrache, and general headquarters artillery, rocket launchers and *Flak* at its disposal.

The *3. Panzer-Division* and the *111. Infanterie-Division* relieved *PGR126* and *PR201*. Those two regiments were dispatched to rejoin the division. On 22 October, *PGR126* reached the area north of Malgobek — Nish. Kurp and Nish. Bekowitsch. The tank regiment marched north of the Terek to Prischibskaja. The *1./PPB51* arrived from the rear area.

The enemy's industriousness in conducting artillery and aerial operations continued unabated; the *Luftwaffe* was not to be seen.

Heavy enemy vehicular traffic and convoys along the Naltschik — Nowo Iwanowski road, which had been observed over the previous few days, continued. The enemy was apparently bringing forward reinforcements and materials for the construction of field fortifications.

On 24 October, the *23. Panzer-Division* finished concentrating in its staging area of Kotljarewskaja — Maiskij — Prischibskaja. *Panzergrenadier-Brigade 23* turned over the command and control of its sector to the headquarters of *Werfer-Regiment 52* and *KB23* relinquished its sector to the *13. Panzer-Division*. The *2./PPB51* erected a 20-ton bridge and established a fording site for tanks over Argudan creek south of Maiskij.

During the night of 24/25 October, *Generalmajor* Herr's *13. Panzer-Division* approached from the east, crossed the Terek and moved through Maiskij, thus crossing through the sector of the *23. Panzer-Division*. Thanks to a full moon, the movements of that division could not remain hidden from the Russians. The first air attack on Maiskij—dropping high-explosive and incendiary bombs—took place at 1930 hours; other aerial attacks were directed against Prischibskaja. The *I./PGR126* and *PR201* took a few casualties. The motorcycle battalion and the *II./PR201*, which was coming from the Mosdok area, were able to enter Prischibskaja.

Oberst Werner-Ehrenfeucht took ill and his command of *PR201* was temporarily assumed by *Major* Illig. Assuming temporary command of *PGR128* for *Oberst* Bachmann was *Oberstleutnant* Stegmann.

The Attack on Ordshonikidse

Artillery fires of all calibers, rocket-launcher attacks and aerial sorties by combat formations of the *Luftwaffe* initiated the attack of the *III. Panzer-Korps* at first light on 26 October, which headed southeast and south from a line running Tschegem (northwest of Naltschik) — Maiskij. The main effort was formed by the deeply echeloned attack groups of the *13. Panzer-Division* and the *23. Panzer-Division* west of Maiskij and south of Kotljarewskaja. At the same time, the alpine troopers attacked Naltschik along a broad front.

The tanks and infantry moved out at 0430 hours. In the middle of the division was *Kampfgruppe Burmeister*, consisting of the headquarters of *Panzergrenadier-Brigade 23*, with *PR201* (minus its 1st Battalion), the *I.(SPW)/PGR126, PPB51 and the* 1./PJA128. To the right was *Kampfgruppe Brückner*, consisting of *PGR126* (minus its 1st Battalion), *KB23* and the *I./PR201*. Finally, on the left, was *Kampfgruppe Stegmann*, composed of *PGR128* and the *2./PJA128*.

Some 1,500 meters south of Kotljarewskaja, the *III./PR201* of *Hauptmann* Stiewe encountered an extensive minefield and two tanks were immobilized. *Oberleutnant* Fischer of the antitank battalion was killed shortly after the start of the attack. Utilizing covering fire from the remaining tanks, *PPB51* cleared a wide lane through the deep minefield in 45 minutes. A Soviet antitank-gun belt was eliminated by the *9./PR201*, although *Oberleutnant* Schinner, the tried and true commander of the company, was killed standing in his turret. Shortly thereafter, the commander of the *12./PR201* was wounded, but nothing could seemingly stop the breakthrough of the tanks at that point.

The armored vehicles rolled southwest toward Argudan across flat pasture land that was only broken up by occasional stands of vegetation. Eighty kilometers to the south in front of the attacking formations, the chain of mountains forming the High Caucasus between Elbrus and Kasbek could be seen in the sunlight of a clear, brilliant fall day. Argudan was reached after a short while; Soviet trains taken by surprise fell into German hands.

It was an attack of maneuver warfare on a grand scale with tanks and *SPW's* in the lead, with motorcycle reconnaissance platoons, motorcycle messengers and the tirelessly working radio relay stations of *PNA128* in between. Following behind were the mechanized and motorized infantry, mounted on their combat vehicles, the divisional artillery and the antitank elements. Bringing up the rear were the trains vehicles, always prepared to render assistance with ammunition and fuel.

Special mention should be made of the men of the radio company of the divisional signals battalion, who were detailed to support the regimental and battalion staffs of the line formations and who performed their duties, heavy with responsibility, day and night. The signals *SPW's* were the doctrinal connection between the armored elements, but their numbers gradually sank, with the result that the radio operators unhesitatingly went back to their boxy radio trucks and accompanied the armor and infantry commanders in them.

The enemy west of Argudan was cut off. Around noon, the attack against those forces commenced with the alpine infantry and the *13. Panzer-Division*, which only reached Argudan after the *23. Panzer-Division*, due to strong enemy forces in front of it in its attack sector. From Argudan, the *13. Panzer-Division* turned west.

The *23. Panzer-Division* established a blocking position, oriented to the southwest, and also moved out to the south against Staryj Tscherek and Staryj Lesken with *Kampfgruppe Brückner* and to the east in the direction of Osrek with *Kampfgruppe Burmeister*. At 1300 hours, the *II./PR201* took Osrek, eliminating a number of antitank and antiaircraft guns. The headquarters of the Soviet 257th Rifle Division and numerous supply elements were destroyed. In an advance on Stary Uruch, the *1./*

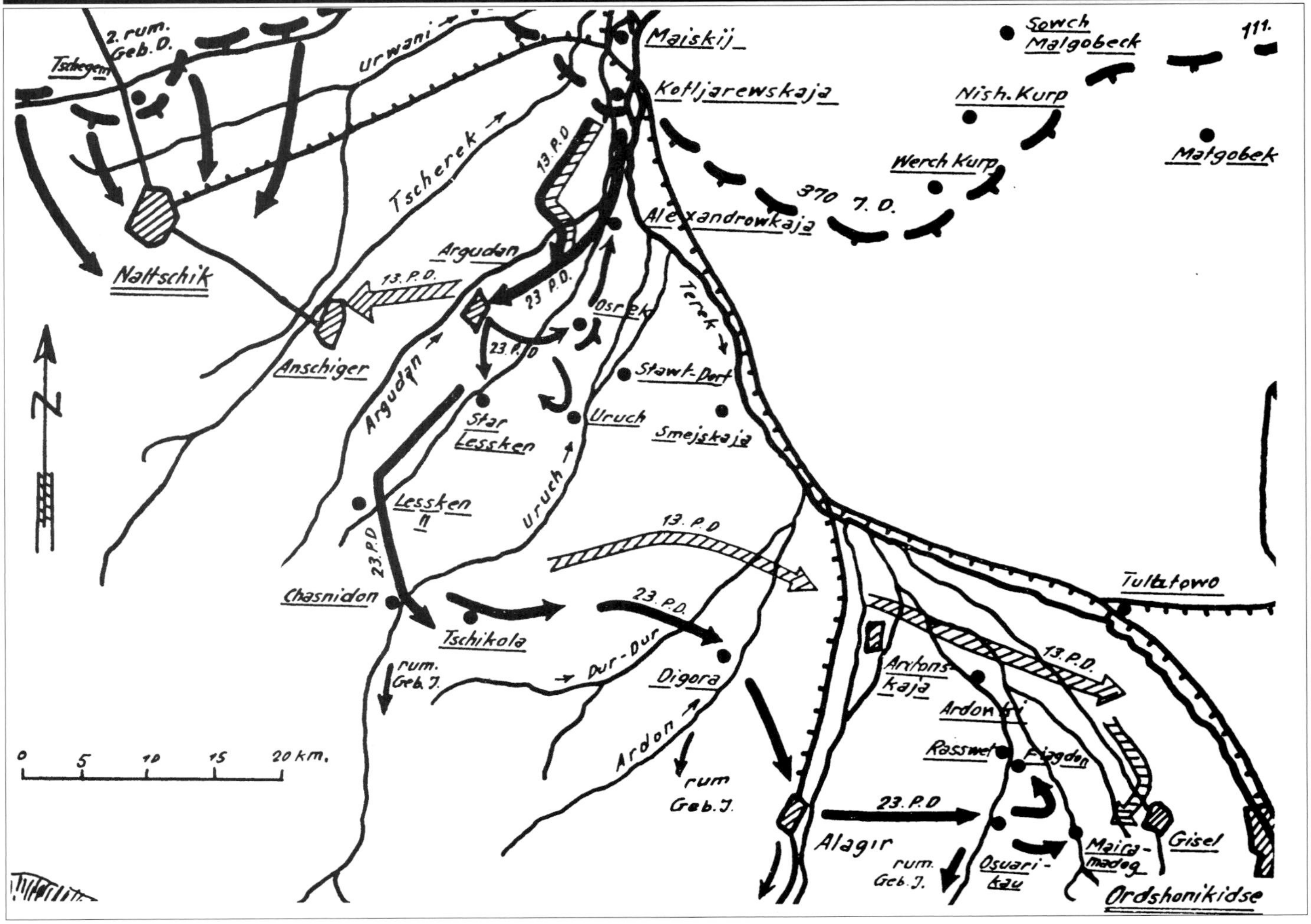

Map 19: Attack of the *III. Panzer-Korps* on Ordshonikidse.

PJA128 knocked out three enemy tanks. The *III./PR201*, together with *Oberleutnant* Seyring's *3./PPB51* and an *SPW* company, screened to the southeast from Osrek, while the main body of *Kampfgruppe Burmeister* attacked, later turning north. The intent was to hit the enemy, who was still stubbornly opposing the attack of *PGR128* south of Kotljarewskaja, in the rear. Enemy artillery was eliminated, and German tanks moved through Alexandrowskaja at 1700 hours. The *I./PGR126* dismounted and cleared one pocket of resistance after the other in the village, which had been heavily fortified to near fortress-like proportions. The close combat lasted until the night forced the fighting to cease.

At 2030 hours, Soviet battalions attempted to break through from the west to the east. In an engagement lasting two hours, they were defeated by tanks and infantry, during which there was frequent and bitter close-in combat. *Oberleutnant* Gleim of the *6./PR201* was killed in this fighting.

On 27 October, Alexandrowskaja was completely cleared of the enemy. To the north of the village, the enemy had pulled back to the east bank of the Terek during the night, but he was forced to pull back there as well in the face of an attack by the *370. Infanterie-Division*. *Panzergrenadier-Regiment 128* closed up to *Kampfgruppe Burmeister*.

In the western part of the area of operations, German and Rumanian alpine forces assaulted Naltschik.

Kampfgruppe Stegmann attacked further south on 28 October and cleared the area along the banks of the Terek with its left wing. The *12./PR201* was attached to the battle group to assist in that operation.

The *II./PR201* dispatched its 5th Tank Company—eight *Panzer III's* under *Oberleutnant* Crämer—to *Kampfgruppe Brückner*; the rest of the battalion was attached to support *Major* von Einem's *PJA128*. In Alexandrowskaja, those forces screened to the east.

On that same afternoon of 28 October, *Kampfgruppe Brückner* also took the villages of Lesken and Dargan by advancing rapidly south with the *5./PR201* as the lead element. The lead tank elements reached Chasnidon at 1630 hours after crossing an 800-meter-high pass. Without waiting for the arrival of the infantry, *Oberleutnant* Crämer moved through the village with his tanks and up to the steep banks of the wildly raging Uruch, which dug 40 meters deep into the cliffs. An intact wooden bridge crossed the dirty river. The tanks moved down steep serpentines and, while other tanks provided cover from above, they crossed to the east bank and ascended the equally steep banks. It was a deed that was decisive for the future of the entire attack.

The tanks then cleared Soviet field positions on the east bank of the river and advanced to within 2 kilometers of Tschikola. Elements of *Oberleutnant* Noever's *1./PPB51*, who were attempting to assist the tanks in their struggle against the enemy field positions, were taken by surprise and fired on by a Soviet position far behind the advancing tanks. *Feldwebel* Wilhelm, one of the tried and true "old hand" noncommissioned officers of the battalion, was killed by the Soviet fire. The last remaining non-wounded man of his platoon succeeded in clearing out the Soviet position. When the *II./PGR128* arrived, the village itself was attacked. The attackers were placed under heavy defensive fires from the heavily fortified village and from the high ground to its north, and the attack bogged down. Three tanks, including the company commander's tank, were knocked out by flanking fires from antitank guns and dug-in tanks. *Oberleutnant* Crämer and his entire crew were killed.

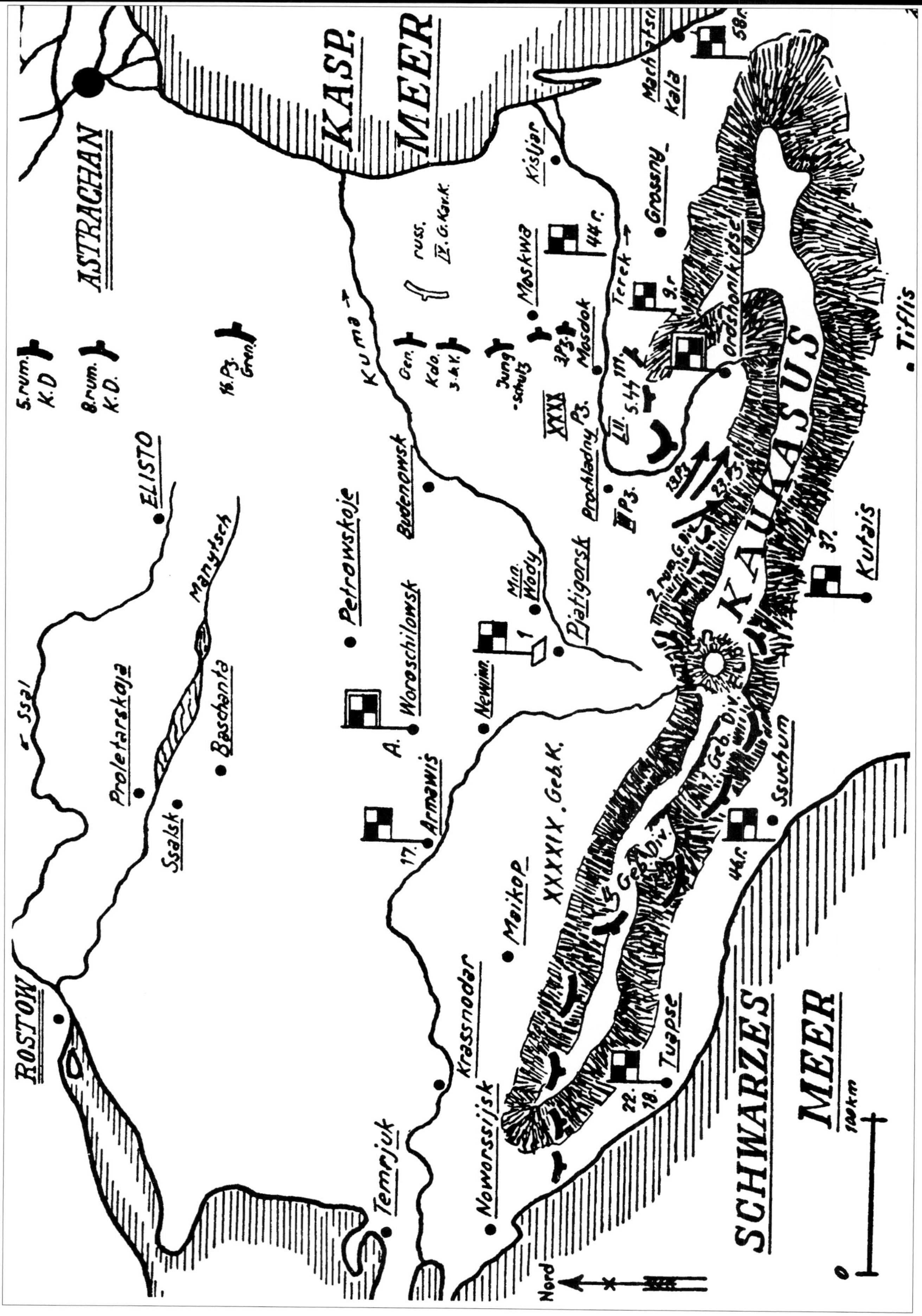

Map 20: The Over-All Situation in the Caucasus on 1 November 1942.

9 October 1942: The 6./PR 201 holds a common meal at Konsawod. The company commander, Oberleutnant Grahn, also delivered a few remarks.

September, 1942 at Mosdok: *General Mjr. der Panzertruppen* Breith confers with *Oberst* Burmeister.

The weather started to change in October.

Cossacks in the service of the Germans.

A "Gulaschkanone", as the field kitschen was known in soldier slang, moves forward with the help of Cossacks and camels.

Preparations for the crossing of the Terek...

...and the finished product.

Sturmgeschütz 106 of the *1./PR 23* took a hit in the area of its loader's hatch on 2 October 1943. Note the concrete reinforcement of the armor.

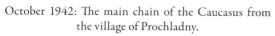

October 1942: The main chain of the Caucasus from the village of Prochladny.

A mine detonates.

Enemy mines being exploded to prevent endangerment of German personnel.

Mechanized infantry in the attack east while north of the Terek River.

With dash and daring, the *5./PR 201* crosses the wooden bridge over the turbulant Urach.

The attack on Orshonikidse on 24 October 1942.

Break through across a flame and oil obstacle.

Advancing through the seemingly endless sunflower fields.

This bridge could not support the weight of the tank. Normally marginal stuctures such as this one were reinforced by the engineeres prior to the crossing of heavy vehicles.

Obergefreiter Lohren hard at work on the staff car of his company commander, *Oberleutnant* Rebentisch.

Gravesite for fallen comrades of the *1./PR 201*.

A *Panzer IVG* is ready to move out. Note the additional fuel cans and the muzzle cover on the main gun. The tankers appreciated the hitting power of the long 75mm L/48 that could deal with the T-34 at most combat ranges.

The command post of the *4./PR201.*

Oberleutnant Kujacinski helps in the construction of a field oven.

Taking it easy under the mild autmun sun. An ingenious solution to hanging a hammock.

Signalmen laying wire.

The company commander's tank of the *5./PR 201* (*Oberleutnant* Krämer and crew).

Village elders.

Camels in service of the German Armed Forces.

A German military cemetary.

A Road through the rugged terrain.

Caucasians in the service of the German Army. (Note the swastika recognition flag.)

Men of steel: The company commander's tank of the 5./PR 201 (Oberleutnant Krämer and crew have switched from the Panzer III seen previously.).

Hauptmann Fechner's tank was responsible for knocking out this Soviet armored train.

Islamic memorials and grave markers.

Lesken 2.

Views of Kisslowodsk. *Oberleutnnt* Rebentisch spent November 1942 in the military hospital there, suffering from hepatitis.

Stalin's villa at Kisslodwodsk.

Soviet fighter-bombers were engaged by German antiaircraft fires at Chasnidon, and an *IL-2* was shot down.

The attack by *Kampfgruppe Stegmann* south of Osrek at Staryj Uruch bogged down, despite support by elements of *Kampfgruppe Burmeister* and the *III./PAR128*, due to the numerically superior enemy defending there. On the other hand, an immediate counterattack conducted by two Soviet companies from Stawt-Dorp was shot to pieces. Based on the successful advance of *Kampfgruppe Brückner*, the attack on Staryj Uruch was not continued. *Kampfgruppe Burmeister* assembled at Staryj Lesken during the afternoon, so as to be able to cross the Uruch at Chasnidon behind *Kampfgruppe Brückner*. It moved into the bridgehead until 1400 hours on 29 October and prepared to attack Tschikola. The deep defile gave little opportunity to the enemy to disrupt the river crossing.

Despite all that, there were no more attacks on that day. The corps wanted to bring up *Panzergrenadier-Regiment 66* of the *13. Panzer-Division* and *Werfer-Regiment 52* first. The Imperial Rumanian 10th Mountain Battalion was attached to the division to screen its right flank.

During the period from 26-28 October, the division captured or destroyed:

1,800 prisoners
15 Tanks
11 Guns
22 Antitank Guns
5 Antiaircraft guns
25 Antitank rifles

The main clearing station of the 2nd medical Company in Chasnidon received a hit from a "Stalin Organ" in the wall of its operating room, but the medical personnel continued to operate.

After a short preparation by artillery and rocket launchers, as well as several *Stuka* sorties, the enemy partially evacuated Tschikola at noon on 30 October. Without waiting for the arrival of the infantry from the *13. Panzer-Division*, *Kampfgruppen Burmeister* and *Brückner* moved out, crossed through the village with armored vehicles and penetrated into the well-fortified field positions of the Soviets, which were packed with antitank rifles and antitank guns. Two *Luftwaffe* destroyer aircraft—*Bf 110's*—also contributed to the fight in an exemplary manner. *Kampfgruppe Brückner* completely cleared Tschikola of the enemy. As darkness fell, the tanks and *SPW's* established a hedgehog position in the middle of the enemy's fortifications, which were still being hotly contested.

Coming from Alexandrowskoje, the *II./PR201* (minus its 5th Tank Company) closed up with *Kampfgruppe Burmeister* on the hills east of Tschikola on 31 October. Disregarding individual Soviet bunkers that were still being bitterly defended, the advance was continued east and heavily-manned infantry positions were rolled up. The enemy, consisting of officer candidates and railway personnel from Baku, as well as a special tank-destroyer battalion with 12 antitank guns and 72 antitank rifles, put up a brave fight. In all, 280 Soviets were taken prisoner and a large number killed. Despite the obstinate defense of the enemy, German losses were low.

The deep, pear-shaped earthen dugouts of the Soviets were so-well camouflaged that they often could not be indentified until within one or two meters. The mechanized infantry on the *SPW's* fought from their vehicles, even though the enemy's antitank rounds penetrated the light armor many times. The clicking noise of the antitank-rifle rounds could be heard again and again against the armored sides of the vehicles. Temporary confusion reigned when the armored group found itself in an extensive flame and oil obstacle. With a large bang, a wide area was set on fire and camouflage materials, personal effects and a few front tires on the *SPW's* caught on fire. A rapid advance forward was the way out of the situation.

The attack rolled towards the Dur-Dur Creek between the steeply climbing mountains of the Caucasus and the hills of Smeiskaja. To the east of the creek, the ground widened and the enemy had positioned tanks and artillery there. While the tanks and the *SPW's* of the *13. Panzer-Division* closed up on the left, the observers from the *I.* and *III./PAR128* directed fires against those positions. The *II./PR201* took the bridge over the Dur-Dur intact and advanced into the southern flank of the enemy's tanks, together with the tank regiment's 3rd Battalion, which was following closely behind. Not unlike a sea battle, the rolling tank formations initiated a firefight from all barrels at high speed. It was in such instances that the German technical superiority became manifest. Without incurring any losses, two T-34's and a *Panzer III*, which had been captured by the Soviets from the *13. Panzer-Division* previously, were knocked out. Two additional enemy tanks were immobilized by tank fires.

November started with radiant, warming sunshine. Digora, which had been abandoned by the enemy, was occupied during the early morning hours of 1 November. After sustaining a few losses due to well-concealed mines, Ssaberdon Creek was crossed. Turning southeast, *Kampfgruppe Burmeister* quickly advanced to within 1 kilometer north of Alagir. Enemy resistance with artillery, antitank guns and tanks picked up. Suddenly, an armored train advanced out of Alagir, firing rapidly from its numerous 7.62cm cannon. The *SPW's* pulled back, clearing the field for the tanks of the *II./PR201* to fire. After taking numerous hits and smoking, the train attempted to escape by moving at full steam toward Ardon. At Ardon, it ran into the barrels of 8.8cm *Flak*. *Stukas* administered the *coup de grâce*.

The *II./PR201* advanced into Alagir from the north, eliminated seven enemy tanks and then joined up with the *III./PR201*, which was attacking the southern part of the village. The bridge over the Ardon had not been blown up. Despite heavy enemy fires from the high ground east of the village, *Hauptmann* Bucher's *I./PGR126* succeeded in establishing a bridgehead and removing the demolitions that had been placed on the bridge. At the southern edge of the village, the *8./PR201*, along with antitank elements, blocked the Ossetian military road, which ran into the mountains from the Ardon Valley. The reaching of this first important objective was singled out for special mention in the *Wehrmacht* Daily Report.

At 1030 hours, *Kampfgruppe Brückner*, just north of Alagir, moved into the village. At 1220 hours, *Oberstleutnant* Stegmann's *PGR128* also arrived. The regiment employed *Hauptmann d.R.*[28] Drescher's 2nd Battalion to complete the interdiction of the Ossetian military road.

The successes of the division between 30 October and 1 November can be measured by the following:

500 Prisoners
17 Tanks
1 Damaged armored train
7 Artillery pieces
26 Antitank guns
20 Antitank rifles
10 heavy machine guns
15 Mortars

The division's losses during the period from 26 October to 1 November:

Personnel	Officers	Noncommissioned officers and enlisted personnel
Killed	7	22
Wounded	13	162
Missing	1	32

Twelve tanks were total losses.

28 Editor's Note: = *der Reserve* = reserve captain. It might be considered unusual not only for a captain to have a command billet normally reserved for a lieutenant colonel but also for one who was a captain of the reserves.

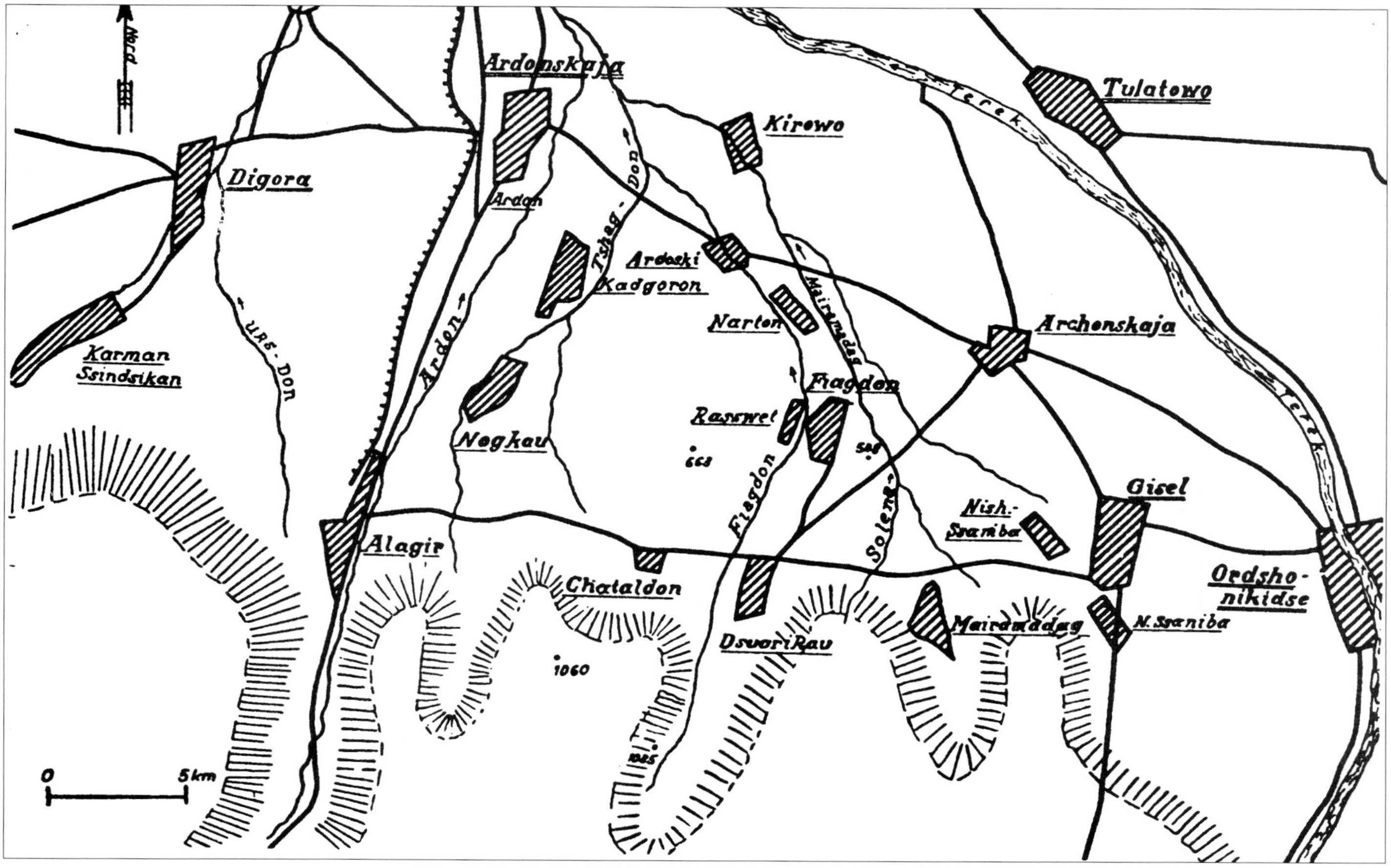

Map 21: Overview of the Ordshonikidse Area of Operations.

The Imperial Rumanian 16th Mountain Battalion was attached to the division and was used to block the Uruch Valley at Achsarissar to the south.

During the night of 1/2 November, *Hauptmann* Hesse's divisional engineers reinforced the bridge at Alagir for tank crossings.

On 2 November, elements of *Kampfgruppe Brückner* remained in Alagir to provide security. *Kampfgruppe Burmeister* moved out at 0630 hours to cross the Fiagdon and take Dsuarikau. The *II./PR201* took the lead with motorized infantry from the *II./PGR126* mounted on their vehicles. Smaller enemy formations were defeated and a battery was captured after being engaged. Just outside of Chataldon, bridge demolitions and minefields slowed down the advance. The *I./PR201* attacked north and ejected Soviet infantry from Tschurkau. *Oberleutnant* Butz, the commander of the 4th Tank Company, was killed. The combat engineers of *Oberleutnant* Stege cleared one mine obstacle after the other. In all, *PPB51*, which only had an effective strength of two companies, cleared some 1,040 mines in this sector up until 3 November.

Outside of Dsuarikau, enemy infantry, well supported by artillery, put up tough resistance to the attack. The 6th Tank Company broke through the enemy positions and took intact the bridge over the Fiagdon in a *coup de main*. The enemy continued to hold the village, however. *Hauptmann* Fechner, the commander of the *II./PR201*, was wounded by mortar fire; *Hauptmann* Wolf assumed acting command of the battalion. The *III./PAR128*, following closely behind the tanks, went into position at Chataldon and placed well-directed fires on the enemy, causing him to pull back to the north and east. The *I./PGR126* screened at the crossroads east of Dsuarikau.

The *13. Panzer-Division* broke through the Soviet positions on this day and advanced through Ardonski and Archonskaja as far as Gisel.

The spoils of war on that day:

200 Prisoners
5 Tanks
20 Antitank rifles
2 Antitank guns
5 Heavy machine guns

Eleven men of the division were killed that day.

At Ardonski and Archonskaja, at 0430 hours on 3 November, enemy tanks attacked the supply routes of the *13. Panzer-Division* from the north. They reached Fiagdon Creek and the village of Fiagdon proper. That meant that the *13. Panzer-Division* was cut off in the Gisel area. In the rain, *PGR128* moved out from Ardon toward Ardonski, but its attack bogged down in the defensive fires of numerically superior enemy forces in the village.

That same morning, tanks and infantry cleared the area east of Dsuarikau of the enemy. The morning fog allowed the enemy to pull back with most of his forces to the north in the direction of Fiagdon. Since it only appeared possible to continue the attack east by first eliminating the flank threat at Fiagdon and Rasswet, it was deiced to first clear those areas. At the same time, *Kampfgruppe Brückner* attacked the village of Dsuarikau and took it in the course of the morning.

With the *III./PR201* in the lead, *Kampfgruppe Burmeister* moved out at 0930 in the direction of Archonskaja. The 3rd Battalion was followed by the 2nd Tank Battalion, the *I./PGR126* and *PJA128*. After covering 2 kilometers, the attack bogged down in the face of increasing resistance from tanks and antitank guns, with the result that it had to be called off. The attack was renewed at 1100 hours. It advanced further to the east, swinging out as far as the banks of Mairamadag Creek. It hit enemy positions in the flank, overran them and destroyed a Soviet howitzer battery and several antitank guns.

At 1430 hours, *Kampfgruppe Burmeister*, with the *II./PR201* in the lead, moved out again from the area east of Fiagdon so as to advance to the northeast as far as the Ardonski — Archonskaja road and open up the rear of the *13. Panzer-Division*. The *II./PR201* soon received extremely heavy fires from enemy tanks, antitank guns and artillery and had to pull back to the east. As it turned dark, the tanks and antitank elements formed an all-round defense between the Kiselka and Burtschak Creeks. The Rumanian Imperial 16th Mountain Regiment relieved *KB23* in the blocking position along both sides of the Ossetian military road.

On 3 November, the division lost 20 men killed in action.

The division's spoils of war on that same day:

1 Tank
4 Artillery pieces
1 Infantry gun
6 Antitank guns
4 Antitank rifles
2 Antitank/antiaircraft guns
2 Mortars
2 Heavy machine guns

The gap in the front that had been torn open between the Terek and the *23. Panzer-Division* as a result of the advance of the Soviets into the deep left flank and rear of the *13. Panzer-Division* was covered by a *Kampfgruppe* formed under the command of *Oberst* Kampfhenkel, the corps artillery commander of the *III. Panzer-Korps*. The battle group consisted of *Pionier-Bataillon 73*, an infantry battalion from the *370. Infanterie-Division*, a battalion of Cossacks, three artillery battalions and an artillery sound- and flash-ranging battalion, which was primarily employed as infantry. It also had the only 24cm cannon battalion of the German Armed Forces, which was used to engage long-range targets around Ordshonikidse.

After increasing enemy pressure on 4 November again allowed no opportunity to continue the attack, the division received orders to transition to the defense, orienting to the northeast, to hold the limit of advance against newly introduced enemy forces and, at the same time, hold open the road for the elements of the *13. Panzer-Division*, which were fighting outside of Ordshonikidse. *Kampfgruppe Brückner* was employed on the right, supported by *Artillerie-Gruppe Hamann*, which consisted of the *I.* and *III./PAR128* and a battery of *Luftwaffe Flak*. On the left was *Kampfgruppe Burmeister*, to which the *I./PR201* was reattached. At the same time, the *II./PR201* turned over its remaining 10 tanks and was pulled out of the line to undergo battlefield reconstitution.

Kampfgruppe Burmeister took Rasswet in an attack, but the attack outside of Fiagdon bogged down.

Hauptmann d.R. Dr. Dreschler, the commander of the *II./PGR128*, and 42 men were killed on that day. *Oberst* Burmeister, the commander of *Panzergrenadier-Brigade 23*, *Oberleutnant* Berger and 203 men were wounded. One hundred prisoners were taken and two artillery pieces and four heavy machine guns were captured.

To the east and south of Dsuarikau, Rumanian alpine troops took over the positions of *PGR126* and attacked east toward Mairamadag, supported by *PAR128*.

On 6 November, the enemy attacked *Kampfgruppe Brückner* with strong infantry forces and 30 tanks, taking Hill 549.6, which could not be retaken until the following day. At the same time, Soviet forces advanced north from the Mairamadag Valley and eliminated a large portion of the trains of the *13. Panzer-Division* north of Mairamadag. *Major i.G.* Freyer, the operations officer of the *23. Panzer-Division*, formed an alert unit out of personnel from the trains of the *13. Panzer-Division*—some 800 men—and used them to occupy a bridgehead position east of Dsuarikau. *Generalmajor* von Boineburg directed the *I./PR201* to counterattack the enemy at Hill 549.6, but it was not able to obtain the objective due to the onset of darkness.

Panzer-Regiment 201 and *PGR128* formed alert units as well, which screened at Chataldon and Ardonski. In addition, the Rumanian Imperial 7th and 8th Mountain Battalions, as well as the Imperial 4th Cannon Battalion, were attached to the division with the mission of holding open the bridge north of Dsuarikau.

One hundred prisoners were brought in on that day; one officer and 31 enlisted personnel of the division were killed.

The demands placed on the logistical elements at the time were enormous. The heavy downpours caused the few supply routes to quickly become torrents of water and mud. There was no more differentiation between fuel and ammunition columns. Every one drove whatever was necessary to get to the front. Among the French-built trucks, such as the Panhard and the Berliet, virtual extinction set in.

On 7 November *Kampfgruppe Illig* moved out to the east from Dsuarikau to take the village of Mairamadag and Hill 549.6. This was to allow the establishment of a defensive line running Mairamadag—Confluence of the Mairamadag and Solena Creeks — Rasswet — Narton — Ardonskij. Contact was supposed to be established with the *13. Panzer-Division* at the latter village. At the same time, the Rumanian alpine forces moved south of the road to take the southern portion of Mairamadag and cover the right flank of *Kampfgruppe Illig*, orienting to the southeast. The attempt to establish contact with the *13. Panzer-Division* north of Mairamadag succeeded, but it could not be maintained since strong enemy formations forced the German forces back later on.

A surprise advance by a large enemy combat patrol against an observation post of the *III./PAR128* was turned back. In the subsequent German immediate counterattack, the entire patrol, minus its officer, was captured.

The division's infantry battalions had been reduced to the size of companies. The *II./PGR128* had a sector of some 4 kilometers to cover near the northern portion of Rasswet with a trench strength of only 64 men! *Hauptmann* Stetting was transferred into *PGR128* from the *13. Panzer-Division*. *Oberstleutnant* Stegmann reassumed command of his *II./PGR128*. Due to a shortage of officers, *Oberst* Bachmann had to appoint *Musikmeister* Reiter[29] as the adjutant of the 2nd Battalion.

The attack by the Rumanians against Mairamadag on the previous day, which had not quite reached the village, was continued on 8 November. Artillery support was inadequate due to the sharply broken-up and steep terrain. While the Imperial Rumanian 8th Mountain battalion was able to push the Russians back to the road cut east of Hill 1035 in a spirited attack, the Imperial Rumanian 7th Mountain Battalion was able to continue its advance on Mairamadag and get within 1 kilometer of it. The crossroads north of that locality was firmly under the control of *Kampfgruppe Illig*.

On 9 November, the enemy charged the division's positions in all sectors, but he was turned back everywhere. The *1./PJA128* knocked out three enemy tanks. At 2300 hours, under the protection afforded by the darkness, the enemy attempted to overrun the German lines. Once again, he was turned back by the infantry. The 1st Platoon of the *1./PJA128* eliminated two 7.62cm antitank guns.

The weakness of the infantry elements of the division forced the combing out of the trains elements in order to boost trench strength. The logistics personnel also formed an infantry platoon under the command of *Leutnant* Schlösser. Unfortunately, the losses—as was to be expected

29 Editor's Note: = "Music Master". Reiter was the leader of the regimental band! Although he held the equivalent of an officer's rank, it must be considered highly unusual and truly indicative of the dearth of officers to see a bandsman placed in a billet traditionally reserved for one of the "up and coming" officers of a line battalion.

when employing units unfamiliar with infantry fighting—were very high.

On 10 November, the first elements of *SS-Panzer-Grenadier-Division "Wiking"* arrived and were attached to the *23. Panzer-Division*. *Kampfgruppe Illig* fought east of Mairamadag Valley. Tanks from the *13. Panzer-Division*, which were returning from the east, reached German lines. They were supported by the *III./PAR128*.

On 11 November, remaining elements of the *13. Panzer-Division* moved back to the west from the Gisel area with tracked vehicles and reached German lines. The wheeled vehicles had to be left behind due to the completely muddied roads and lack of fuel.

The attempt to move both of the division's clearing stations forward to Dsuarikau and Ardonskaja because of the high losses sustained by both the *13. Panzer-Division* and the *23. Panzer-Division* had to be quickly abandoned. Soviet artillery immediately opened directed fires, whereby the medical companies suffered several dead and wounded among their own ranks.

Combat operations on the days that followed were minor and were primarily limited to counterbattery fires. Visibility was poor; it rained frequently.

On 13 November, the following forces were brought into the division's sector and attached: *SS-Panzer-Grenadier-Regiment "Germania"* (with its 1st Battalion); the *II.* and *III./SS-Panzer-Grenadier-Regiment "Nordland"*; *SS-Panzer-Abteilung 5*; *SS-Artillerie-Regiment 5* (minus its 1st Battery); the *I./schwere Werfer-Regiment 1* (minus its 3rd Battery); a company from *SS-Panzer-Jäger-Abteilung 5*; and the *II./Werfer-Regiment 52*. The formations were employed in the right-hand side of the division sector east of Dsuarikau.

Weaker enemy attacks were scattered by the divisional artillery. There were some eight attacks in *Kampfgruppe Burmeister's* sector alone on 16 November. Small penetrations were cleared up by *Panzerkampfgruppe Illig* and *SS-Panzer-Abteilung 5*.

On 20 November, orders were issued to establish defensive fortifications. On that day, *Oberst* Burmeister was reassigned from the division to the unassigned officer manpower pool of the German Army High Command.

The headquarters of *SS-Panzer-Grenadier-Division "Wiking"*, under the command of *SS-Gruppenführer und Generalmajor der Waffen-SS* Steiner, arrived and assumed command of its forces east of Dsuarikau, which were detached from the division's command and control.

At this time, *General der Kavallerie* von Mackensen was designated as the Commander-in-Chief of the *1. Panzer-Armee* in addition to being the Commanding General of the *III. Panzer-Korps; Generalleutnant* Breith (*3. Panzer-Division)* assumed command of the *III. Panzer-Korps* in January 1943.

Effective 24 November, the division's employment in the Caucasus came to a close. *SS-Panzer-Grenadier-Division "Wiking"* and the *13. Panzer-Division* assumed the defensive sectors of the division, which was pulled out of the line in the days that followed. From the Prochladny — Naltschik area, the division was moved to a new assembly area around Remontnaja on the Ssal, in same cases by road march, in others by rail. *Major i.G.* Liese assumed the duties of division operations officer from *Major i.G.* Freyer, who went on leave.

In view of the losses sustained by the division during its recent heavy fighting and the urgency of the new mission, which did not allow even a battlefield reconstitution, the division was reorganized as follows:

> *Kradschützen-Bataillon 23* is disbanded. The remaining elements of the 1st (Armored Car) Reconnaissance Company will be consolidated with *Panzer-Nachrichten-Abteilung 128* and report directly to the division. The 3rd and 4th Companies will be used to form one motorcycle infantry company, which will be consolidated with *Panzergrenadier-Regiment 128* as a separate unit. The company commander is *Oberleutnant Graf* Finkenstein. All remaining elements of the battalion will be distributed among the infantry battalions. *Hauptmann* von Kunow, the last commander of *Kradschützen-Bataillon 23*, will be reassigned to the [division headquarters] as an adjutant [for officer management].
>
> The two battalions of *Panzergrenadier-Regiment 128* will be consolidated into the 1st Battalion [*Hauptmann* Stetting]. The *II./Panzergrenadier-Regiment 126* will be redesignated as the *II./Panzergrenadier-Regiment 128* [*Hauptmann* Döring]. The *I.(SPW)/Panzergrenadier-Regiment 126* will become a separate *SPW* battalion for the division [reporting directly to the division headquarters].
>
> The headquarters of *Panzergrenadier-Brigade 23* will be disbanded. The headquarters of *Panzergrenadier-Regiment 126* will remain intact as an *Arbeitsstab z.b.V.*[30], minus its commander. *Oberst* Brückner is being reassigned from the division; with him, it loses one of its best infantry commanders.
>
> The *1./Panzerjäger-Abteilung 128* is to turn in its towed 7.5cm antitank guns and receive 12 self-propelled antitank guns (7.5cm) in their place.
>
> The hitherto used designation of *Divisions-Nachschubführer* is changed to *Kommandeur der Divisions-Nachschubtruppen*.[31]

The time of the large-scale offensive had passed. The successes of the division were large; but its casualties had also been high. In the period from 30 May to 30 November 1942, the division had lost 61 officers and 1,459 noncommissioned officers and enlisted personnel on the battlefield.

On the occasion of the detachment of the *23. Panzer-Division* from the *III. Panzer-Korps* and the *1. Panzer-Armee, General der Kavallerie* von Mackensen issued the following order-of-the-day:

> The *23. Panzer-Division* is being detached from the *III. Panzer-Korps* and the *1. Panzer-Armee*. I view its departure with great regret. Despite the great difficulties that the young armored division had to undergo anew on a daily basis, it had stormed forward in a spirited pursuit from the Manytsch to the Terek and it had proven itself in sometimes difficult fighting along the Bakssan for weeks on end. Finally, it contributed successfully and greatly to the victorious operations of the *III. Panzer-Korps* in decisive areas.
>
> The rapid advance of the division through Argudan and as far as the Uruch and beyond, the taking of Tschikola and Alagir, which blocked the Ossetian military road, are laurels of which the division can justly be proud. I would like to express my recognition and warmest thanks to the Division Commander in my capacity as Commanding General and as the Acting Commander-in-Chief of the *1. Panzer-Armee*. The division is headed off for new events. My best wishes go with it onto its new fields of battle.
>
> /signed/ von Mackensen
> *General der Kavallerie*

The division commander thereupon issued the following order-of-the-day:

> *23. Panzer-Division* Division Command Post, 14 November 1942
>
> Division Order-of-the-Day No. 85/42
>
> At the conclusion of the current operations, I would like to express my thanks and recognition to all officers, noncommissioned officers and enlisted personnel for their heroic performance of duty. Alagir, frequently mentioned in the *Wehrmacht* Daily Report and in the press, will forever remain a laurel for the division, as can be said for the difficult fighting of our hard-pressed neighboring division.
>
> Prisoners and spoils of war from 26 October to 13 November 1942:

30 Editor's Note: = *Arbeitstab zur besonderen Verwendung* = Special-Purpose Headquarters. In other words, it was a command and control entity without subordinate forces.

31 Editor's Note: The "Division Logistics Leader" became the "Commander of the Division Logistics Elements", a change perhaps to reflect the increased importance attached to the position, since *Führer*, in this context, did not connote the same status as *Kommandeur*.

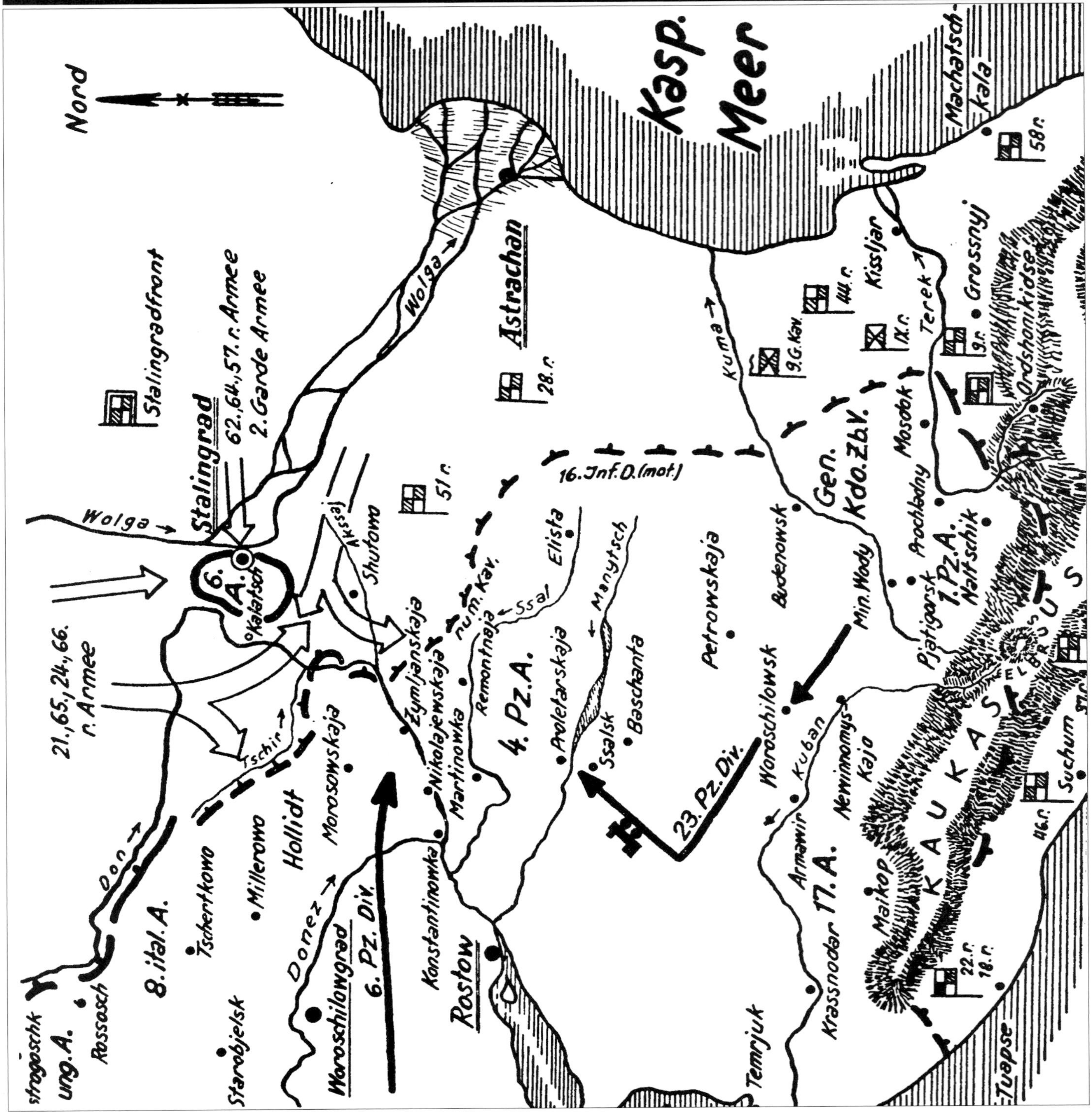

Map 22: General Situation on 26 November 1942.

4,333 Prisoners
1 Armored train
32 Guns
65 Antitank guns
168 Deserters
53 Tanks
70 Antitank rifles

In addition, there was a large number of mortars, antiaircraft guns, heavy machine guns, motorized and non-motorized vehicles, automatic weapons and small arms.

The division will continue to perform its duty with a proud and stalwart heart in the future and fasten victory to its banners.

Long live the *Führer* and Germany!

/signed/ *Freiherr* von Boineburg

Operation "Wintergewitter"

The Attack to Free the 6. Armee 28 November to 31 December 1942

While the *23. Panzer-Division* was setting up a defense outside of Ordshonikidse and starting to prepare its defensive fighting positions for the winter, one of the most important battles of the Second World War was taking place at Stalingrad, 500 kilometers to the north. On 19

November, strong Soviet armored, cavalry and rifle formations moved out 100 kilometers northwest of Stalingrad at Kleskaja on the Don. They overran the Imperial Rumanian 3rd Army in the first attack and then poured into the Don Basin to the southwest, the south and the southeast. To the south of Stalingrad, the enemy started his large offensive on 20 November. Using armored and cavalry forces, he broke through the positions of the Imperial Rumanian 4th Army and advanced to the Don. By 21 November, the lead elements of both assault groups linked up at Kalatsch. The *6. Armee* and elements of the *4. Panzer-Armee*—comprising five corps headquarters, the main body of 15 infantry divisions, three motorized infantry divisions, three armored divisions, a *Flak* division, a Rumanian cavalry division, a Rumanian infantry division, a Croatian infantry regiment, numerous general headquarters elements—were encircled in and around Stalingrad.

Along the western bank of the Tschir, *Heeresgruppe B* of *Generalfeldmarschall Freiherr* von Weichs attempted to establish a defensive front in order to prevent the enemy attack deep into the Don Basin, especially the supply bases of Morosowskaja and Tazinskaja. But only weak formations, rear-area services and scattered elements, as well as a Rumanian cavalry corps, were available to the German command. Despite that, the enemy was held back as a result of an elastic defense and counterattacks. These forces even succeeded initially in maintaining a bridgehead over the Don at Nishne-Tschirkaja.

Elements of *Generaloberst* Hoth's *4. Panzer-Armee*, principally the *29. Infanterie-Division (mot.)*, were pushed into the Stalingrad pocket by the southern attack wedge of Soviet forces. As a result Hoth's field army had only a few forces scattered widely across the Kalmuck Steppes: The *16. Infanterie-Division (mot.)*, a few *Flak* units and several weak formations of the Imperial Rumanian 4th Army with what remained of its VI and VII Army Corps.

The Headquarters of the *11. Armee* of *Generalfeldmarschall* von Manstein, which had been hastily withdrawn from its area of operations in the northern sector of the front at Leningrad, assumed command of the following forces as the Headquarters of *"Heeresgruppe Don"*: the *6. Armee*, the *4. Panzer-Armee* (with the attached Imperial Rumanian 4th Army) and the Imperial Rumanian 3rd Army. The German Army High Command planned to conduct a relief attack on Stalingrad from the southwest under the command of Manstein. At the same time, the *XXXXVIII. Panzer-Korps*, to which the *11. Panzer-Division* was also being attached, was to advance east in the Don Bend and re-establish contact with the *6. Armee*. Hitler remained adamant that the *6. Armee* was to remain in Stalingrad. The intent of the counterattack was simply to restore the situation.

The Headquarters of the *LVII. Panzer-Korps* of *General der Panzertruppen* Kirchner was allocated to the *4. Panzer-Armee*. The *6. Panzer-Division* and the *23. Panzer-Division* were expeditiously attached to the corps. It was intended for the *17. Panzer-Division* to follow later on, but, for the time being, it was being held behind the left wing of *Heeresgruppe B*.

Using this armored corps as the assault wedge of the *4. Panzer-Armee*, it was intended for it to attack along the Kotelnikowo — Stalingrad rail line and break open the ring of encirclement.

On 24 November, the first elements of the *23. Panzer-Division* left the area of operations around Dsuarikau to reach their railheads at Prischibskaja, Prochladnyj and Naltschik. Leading the division was its *SPW* Battalion, which, as detailed above, consisted of the former *I.(SPW)/PGR126*. The combat elements of the battalion arrived in Remontnaja on the Ssal through 1 December. There it made preparations, depending on the situation, to either move against Kotelnikowo or follow behind the right wing of the Imperial Rumanian VI Army Corps in the Atamanskaja — Schabilin area as a ready reserve.

In Ssalsk, the *II./PR201* was issued 22 *Panzer IV's* with long-bareled 7.5cm main guns (L48). Under its new commander, *Hauptmann* Tilemann, it took up quarters in Uljanowski, south of Remontnaja. *Major i.G.* Liese took ill; he was replaced as operations officer for the division by *Major i.G. Graf* Bernsdorff.

Corps Order No. 1 designated the Ssal River line between Atamanskaja and Remontnaja as a staging area and directed coordination with elements of *Flak-Regiment 7*, which were employed there.

Reconnaissance-in-force operations by the *SPW* Battalion, together with *leichte Flak-Abteilung 861*, screened the area between the Imperial Rumanian VII and VI Corps from advanced enemy elements. On 5 December, the battalion was temporarily attached to the *6. Panzer-Division*.

The approach of the main body of the *23. Panzer-Division* was considerably delayed due to transportation difficulties. As a result, the attack was postponed. The approach area was screened by two *Kampfgruppen* under the commands of *Major* Sänger and *Major* Illig (*III./PR201*). At the same time, they held open the crossings over the Ssal, while the *SPW* Battalion blocked the Karassal River line north-northeast and west of Kryloff.

In the meantime, the enemy attacked the positions of the *6. Panzer-Division* in its assembly area to the left of the *23. Panzer-Division*. Heavy fighting ensued, which did not end until 7 December.

On that day, the *II./PR201* was moved to Ssirotskij. *Oberst* von Buch, the commander of the divisional artillery, assumed command of the Gurejewskaja — Kudinoff sector.

The *SPW* Battalion, once again under the wing of the division, reconnoitered in the direction of Poperetschnyj — Krainjaja *Balka*. The *II./PR201* was sent to Kryloff, while the main body of the tank regiment was dispatched to Ssirotskij. Both snowfall and black ice hindered movements. The tanks had to swing out 20 kilometers to the west in order to cross the Ssal at Andrejewskaja. At the same time, the wheeled vehicles were towed across at Ssirotskij. A defensive blocking position was established at Kryloff by the headquarters of the *II./PR201*, consisting of the battalion's 6th Company, the Rumanian 85th Infantry Battalion, two Rumanian batteries and a German light *Flak* battery. There was no enemy contact.

At Krainjaja *Balka*, the *SPW* Battalion established contact with Colonel Korne's Rumanian 8th Cavalry Division, whereupon it had enemy contact with infantry, antitank guns and antitank rifles. The bad weather conditions, consisting of a slushy snow and rain, forced the delay of the attack planned for 10 December toward Pimen-Tscherni — Nebykoff. For the time being, a defense of the Kryloff — Krainjaja *Balka* — Ssolenka sector was ordered. The division's tank regiment reorganized so that each of its three battalions had 36 operational tanks.

Patrols sent out by the *SPW* Battalion brought back four prisoners, who had been assigned to the Russian 91st Rifle Division, which had newly arrived in the division's sector from the Volga area.

The weather situation improved during the evening of 10 December, with the advent of freezing temperatures that improved road conditions. The attack was ordered for 12 December. On 11 December, the reinforced *I./PGR128*—with the *1./PJA128*, the *9.(sIG)./PGR128*, the *10.(Fla)/PGR128*, and the *2.* and *3./Flak-Regiment 25*—moved to Budarka. The *III/PAR128* pulled forward to Poperetschnij. During the morning hours of 11 December, *Generalleutnant* von Boineburg and *Oberstleutnant* von Heydebreck (*PR201*) received the attack order from *Generaloberst* Hoth at the command post of the *6. Panzer-Division* in Ssemitschnaja. The mission of the *23. Panzer-Division* was to take Nebykoff, advancing from the Pimen-Tscherni area, and guard the flank of *6. Panzer-Division* to the east and north west of the Darganoff — Tschilekoff line. The attack objective was to break the encirclement of Stalingrad.

Generaloberst Hoth issued the following order-of-the-day to his forces:

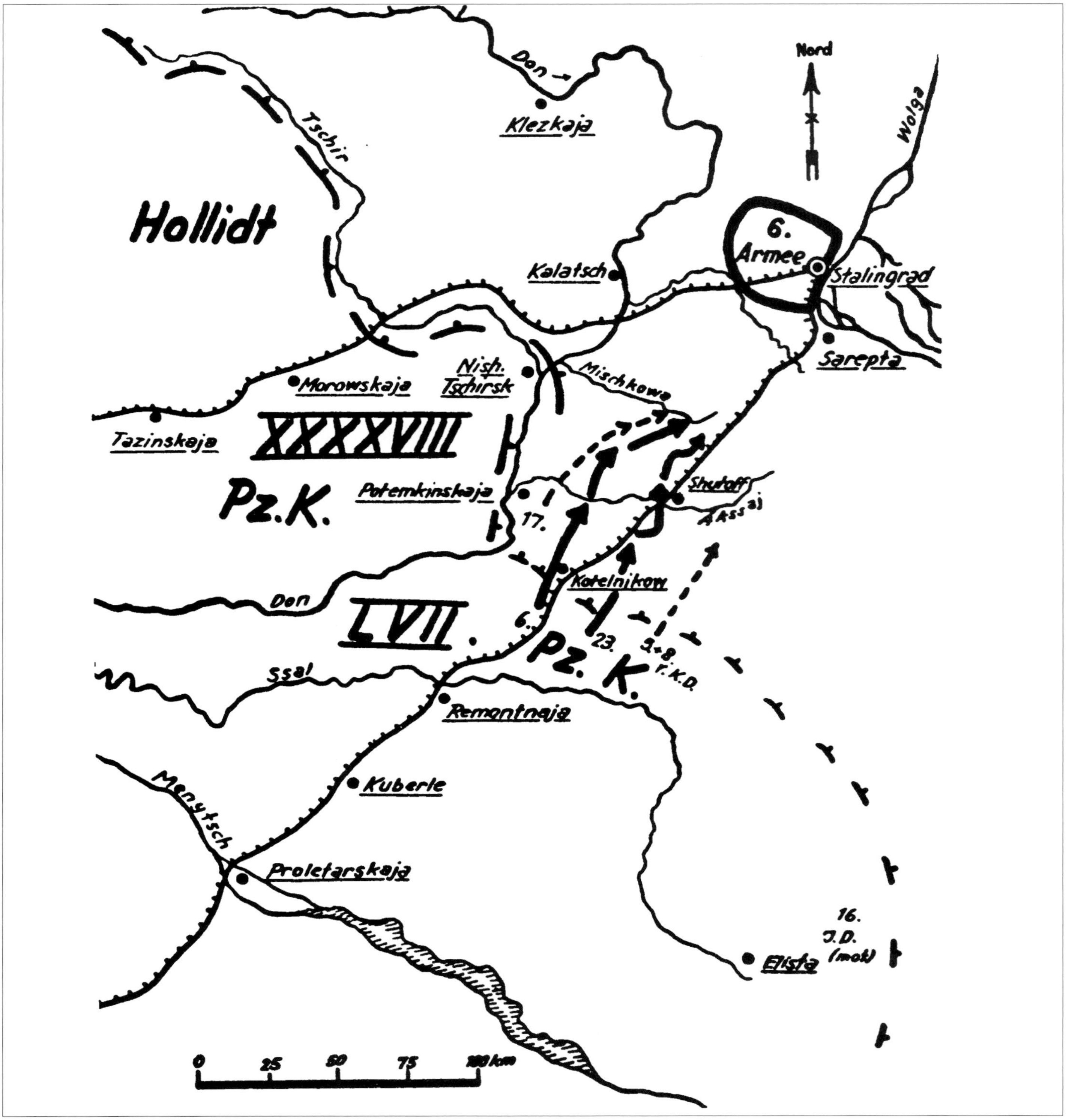

Map 23: Direction of Attack for the *LVII. Panzer-Korps* from 12 to 23 December 1942.

Soldiers of the *4. Panzer-Armee* and the Imperial Rumanian 4th Army!

The hour for the attack has arrived. To the west of Stalingrad, German and Rumanian forces have held their positions for weeks, encircled by the Reds. They are waiting for us. We will not leave them in the lurch. Once again, the power of German tanks will open a path for grenadiers and infantry into the rear of the enemy. Whoever stands in our way will be attacked and destroyed. There can be no hesitation when it concerns your comrades. They are placing their trust in your bravery and will break the ring of encirclement with you.

Forward to victory!

/sign/ Hoth

***

Under the command of *Hauptmann* Bucher, the *SPW* Battalion (minus two companies) departed at noon from Krainjaja *Balka* along with a battery of 8.8cm *Flak* and a battery of 2cm *Flak*. Its mission was to relieve elements of *Gruppe von Pannwitz*—Cossacks, Rumanians and Germans—screening in Pimen-Tscherni. The remaining elements of the

SPW Battalion, as well as the other *Flak* batteries, remained in Krainjaja *Balka*.

During the night of 11/12 December, the Russians attacked Pimen-Tscherni and entered the village in company strength. It was not until the *SPW* Battalion and the Rumanians launched an immediate counterattack that the enemy was ejected from the village, suffering heavy casualties.

The formations of the division moved into their staging areas. In the first march serial was the tank regiment, with the *III./PAR128* and the remainder of the *SPW* Battalion. It was followed by the reinforced *I./PGR128*, the remaining elements of *PGR128*, the divisional artillery (minus the 2nd and 3rd Battalions) and the division reserve, consisting of *PJA128*, *PPB51* and *Brüko K 151*.

At 0600 hours on 12 December, the friendly forces to the left, the *6. Panzer-Division* of *Generalleutnant* Raus, moved out to attack.

At 0950 hours, *Kampfgruppe Illig*—the *III./PR201* and the reinforced *I./PGR128*—attacked Nebykoff. To the right, the *SPW* Battalion advanced on Koschara 2. At 1335 hours, Nebykoff was firmly in German hands. Surprised, the enemy fled to the northeast with 3,000 men. He left behind 250 prisoners, just as many dead, 15 7.62cm cannon, 2 12.2cm cannon, 30 mortars, 7 antitank rifles and numerous small arms. Koschara 2 was occupied at 1445 hours after the enemy's resistance was destroyed. Despite temperatures reaching 10 below zero (14 degrees Fahrenheit), the tanks tore up the few still muddy crossings over Karaitschewo Creek to such an extent that the motorized infantry of the *I./PGR128* could not follow mounted. The *3./PPB51* of *Oberleutnant* Seyring had to be employed to create crossing points.

At 1400 hours, *Kampfgruppe Illig* reached its day's objective, the line running Point 148.5 to Tschilekoff, and established contact with the motorcycle battalion of the *6. Panzer-Division* on the left. The *SPW* Battalion screened from its limit of advance, Point 133.4 to Koschara 2.

The division reorganized for 13 December. The tank regiment and the *I./PGR128*, together with the *1./PJA128*, *PPB51* and supporting artillery, formed *Kampfgruppe von Heydebreck*. The *SPW* Battalion remained in the line it had reached the previous day around Koschara 2 and was supported by the *III./PAR128*. The *IV.(Flak)/PAR128* provided area defense for the air space over the division. *Oberst* Bachmann, the commander of *PGR128*, was designated as the commander of the division's reserve, consisting of all of the remaining elements, and was initially tasked to relieve the screening forces of the *I./PGR128* at Darganoff with a reinforced company. The *3./PPB51* established fords at Pimen-Tscherni and south of Nebykoff.

Two Soviet companies, accompanied by five tanks, appeared in front of the *SPW* Battalion. In front of *Kampfgruppe von Heydebreck*, the enemy pulled back. While pursuing, one *Panzer III* was lost.

At 1000 hours, the division received orders to move out against Tschilekoff and Klykoff and, abutting the *6. Panzer-Division*, which had crossed the Akssaj at Ssaliwskij in the meantime, to take the high ground north of the river. At 1020 hours, however, *Generaloberst* Hoth personally appeared at the division command post and held up the attack based on the interception of a Russian radio message that indicated a Soviet tank brigade was moving on Nebykoff. He ordered *PR201* to prepare to defend.

At 1225 hours, 12 enemy tanks appeared at Koschara 1 and six more at Koschara 2. The tank regiment attacked and forced the enemy to turn back after a short engagement. At Ternowyj, the tank regiment shattered an enemy attack in regiment strength, which had been supported by artillery. As it started to turn dusk, around 1430 hours,[32] the enemy in front of Koschara 2 turned back to the northeast.

On 14 December, the division moved out to attack with its main body again. Its mission: Advancing rapidly through Ssamochin, take Krugljakoff, Schestakoff and the bridges over the Akssaj, in particular the railway bridge; eliminate the enemy in the Tschilekoff Defile; and take the high ground north of Klykoff.

At first light, *Kampfgruppe von Heydebreck* ran into an armored enemy force by surprise after advancing 3 kilometers. Two German tanks were knocked out. In an immediate counterattack, five enemy tanks were knocked out, including two KV I's, without suffering any additional friendly casualties. The *1./PJA128*, which was following the tanks along with the combat engineers and the supporting artillery, knocked out an additional seven enemy tanks, of which five burned out completely. A self-propelled antitank gun, which was accompanying the *SPW* Battalion, received a direct hit, which killed two of the crew and wounded the remaining three. The remaining Soviet tanks—some 20 to 25, according to prisoner statements—pulled back to the north and northwest.

Advancing further, Ssamochin was taken at 1125 hours against minimal Russian resistance, with 236 soldiers from the 126th Rifle Division being taken prisoner. The reinforced *SPW* Battalion, which had been temporarily attached to *Oberstleutnant* von Heydebreck, was detached from the *Kampfgruppe* and assumed security in the village, along with attached self-propelled antitank guns and the aforementioned 8.8cm and 2cm *Flak* batteries in support. The *SPW* Battalion oriented its defenses to the east.

Kampfgruppe Bachmann, the reinforced *PGR128* minus its 2nd Battalion, moved out at the same time as the *Panzerkampfgruppe* and attacked in the direction of Ternowyj, moving on both sides of the Nebykoff— Point 148.5 road. Slight enemy resistance flared up at Point 148.5, but it became increasingly stronger and slowed down the attack south of Ternowyj.

The *II./PGR128* was brought forward to Nebykoff.

At 1245 hours, the tank regiment moved out against Krugljakoff from Ssamochin, crossed the Ternowaja and Ssuchaja Defiles and reached the edge of Krugljakoff at 1430 hours. Several tanks turned off in the direction of the railway bridge and took it intact from the surprised enemy. *Hauptmann* Behr and *Oberleutnant* Cornelius of the tank regiment distinguished themselves in particular, when they disregarded the enemy's defensive fires, dismounted and rendered the charges on the bridge ineffective. *Oberleutnant* Cornelius was wounded.

The remaining tanks of the regiment moved into Krugljakoff proper in the meantime, turned back strong enemy forces and took firm control of the village by 1530 hours. As night fell, the limit of advance was secured, while a section of tanks was able to take the road bridge intact as well.

The *I./PPB51* of *Oberleutnant* Noever, given personal instructions from *Generalleutnant* von Boineburg, drove back a Soviet patrol around 1830 hours, which was in the process of placing demolition charges on the railway bridge. The engineers took up positions within the 5-meter-tall vegetation along the embankment. During the night, enemy tanks and infantry advanced on the bridge in vain. In the meantime, a thin coat of snow covered the landscape.

While the fighting was going on for Krugljakoff, *Kampfgruppe Bachmann* was also making slow progress. At 1506 hours, the battle group reported the capture of Koschara 1. There was no further success outside of Ternowyj, however, since the Russians were covering that area with 17 T-34's. A nighttime reconnaissance conducted by two enemy tanks and infantry collapsed in the face of fires from three self-propelled antitank guns.

In order to continue the fight the next day, the tank regiment was in dire need of infantry support. *Generalleutnant* von Boineburg decided to pull *Kampfgruppe Bachmann* out of the line, despite the presence of

32 Editor's Note: The reader is again reminded that the Germans used Central European Time as the basis for official reports, irrespective of the actual local time. Thus, it was actually 1630 hours when it started to turn dark in that sector of the front.

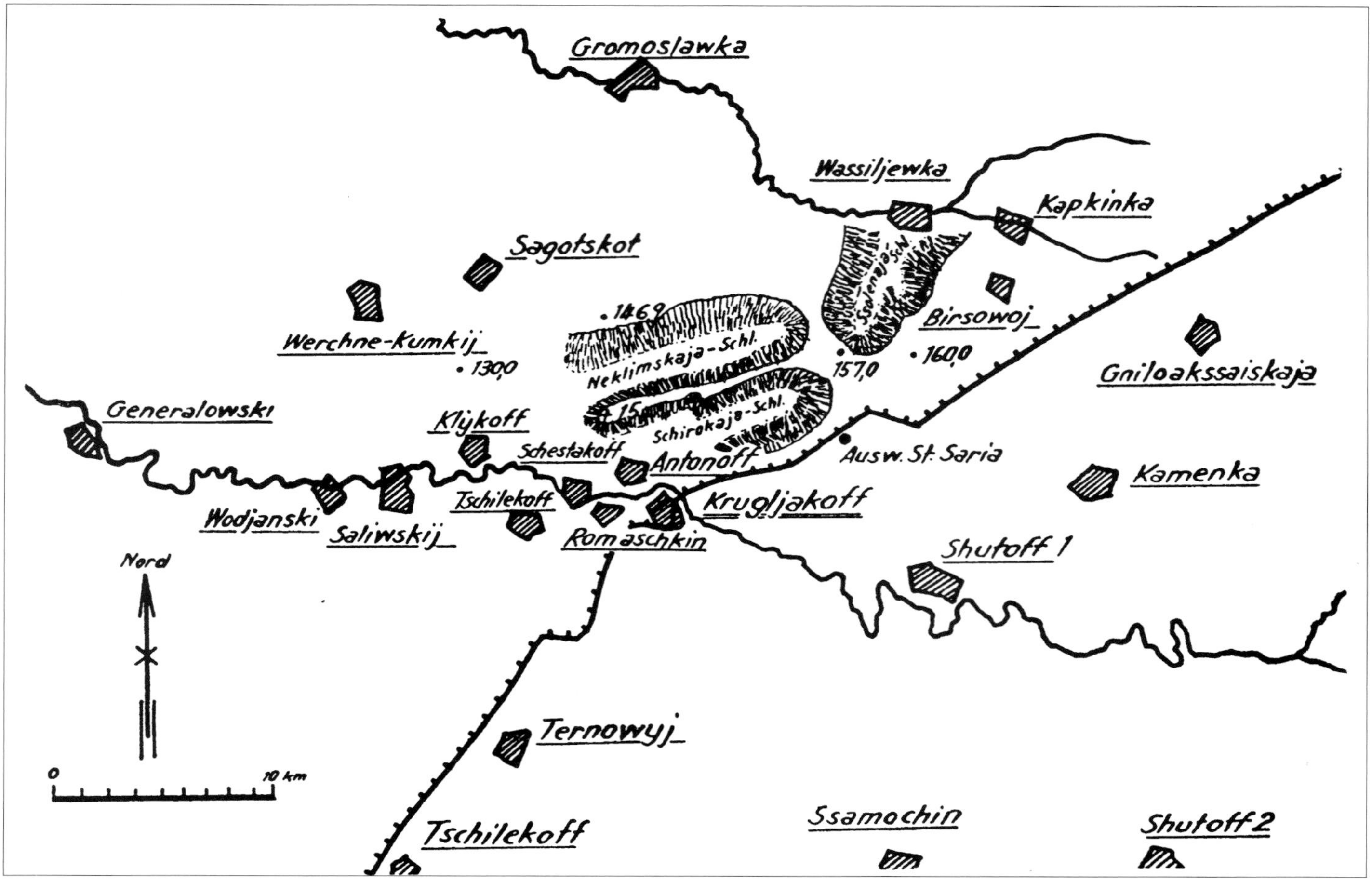

Map 24: Overview of the Fighting Along the Akssaj.

strong enemy forces outside of Ternowyj, and to bring them forward to Krugljakoff and place them in the attack sector of the *Panzerkampfgruppe*. *Hauptmann* Meerstein, the commander of the *I./Flak-Regiment 25*, took over screening Koschara. He had with him the *2./PJA128*, a battery of 8.8cm *Flak* and a battery of 2cm *Flak*.

Weak enemy advances on Ssamochin at dusk were turned back.

To all appearances, the division had run into a Russian tank attack on Nebykoff on 14 December. The Russian attack was aimed at the deep flank of the attacking German forces. The counterblow delivered by the German tanks took the wind out of the sails of the enemy force and kept it from pursuing its attack.

During the night of 14/15 December, German tanks and *SPW* outposts at the bridges at Krugljakoff turned back the enemy's attempt to place charges on the bridges with demolition parties. The enemy forces were eliminated.

Kampfgruppe Meerstein was involved in constant fighting in its positions northwest of Koschara against numerically superior enemy infantry and armor forces. Two enemy tanks were knocked out, but the German forces suffered the loss of two 8.8cm *Flak* and three 2cm *Flak*. Around 0700 hours on 15 December, additional Russian tanks and infantry mounted on 30 trucks advanced and threatened to encircle the battle group. Based on the critical situation, the division commander ordered *Kampfgruppe Bachmann*, which was still assembling in the Ssamochin area, to move out into the rear of the enemy from the east. One infantry company and one 2cm *Flak* battery were sent to Koschara as reinforcements. At the same time, the *6. Panzer-Division* had its motorcycle battalion move out on Ternowyj from the northwest. In the middle of the division's measures, the infantry and *PR201* reported that strong enemy forces were pulling back from Ternowyj to the northeast. *Panzergrenadier-Regiment 128* was rapidly sent after the enemy and caught him in his flank along the Ternowyj Defile. Three enemy tanks were destroyed, and many enemy dead were left on the battlefield. The enemy fled in the direction of Shutoff 1.

Strong reconnaissance elements employed by the tank regiment took intact the bridge over the Akssaj and found Romaschkin clear of the enemy. Advancing through Ternowyj, Bachmann's and Meerstein's battle groups closed up to Krugljakoff. These were followed by the *II./PGR128*, which rejoined its parent regiment. *Kampfgruppe von Heydebreck* conducted preparations for operations in Romaschkin.

The *6. Panzer-Division* was involved in difficult seesaw fighting against numerically superior enemy armored forces at Werchne-Kumski (10 kilometers north of Ssaliwskij).

On that day, the *23. Panzer-Division* succeeded in surprising the enemy with its advance on Krugljakoff. Employing very skillfully conducted counterattacks, the enemy pulled back east from Ternowyj — Kowalenko. In the process, however, he also had to take heavy losses. Among the captured or destroyed were 210 prisoners, 10 T-34's, 2 T-60's, 4 infantry guns, one 12.2cm howitzer, 3 7.62cm guns and 3 4.7cm antitank guns.

On 16 December, *PR201* was directed to work with *Oberst* von Hünersdorff's *Panzer-Regiment 11* of the *6. Panzer-Division*. It closed with the latter regiment at Ssaliwskij and prepared for operations. It was not employed, however.

A combat patrol conducted by the motorcycle company of *PGR128* identified enemy tanks and antitank guns south of Shutoff 1 along the right flank of the division. A *Panzer IV* from the tank regiment, which was accompanying the patrol, knocked out a T-34.

The rains of the previous few days, coupled with the increasing freezing temperatures, covered the steppes with a thick coating of ice. Both friend and foe slid more than they drove, especially with tracked vehicles. After a predominantly quiet period, which was used to push the frontage in the bridgehead further to the north, fairly strong infantry elements, together with two groups of seven to eight T-34's, attacked out of the depression in the ground between the 1st and 2nd Battalions of *PGR128*. They quickly advanced close to the bridges at Krugljakoff, destroying two antitank guns and three light field howitzers on the way. Several vehicles and some equipment fell victim to the Russian tanks that were sliding around on the ice until the defenders succeeded in stabilizing the situation. The *9.(sIG)/PGR128* had to temporarily abandon its guns and vehicles due to the surprise attack by the Russians. A short while later, after the Soviet tanks had pulled back, all of the equipment was recovered intact. The division commander personally became involved. In the end, the enemy was turned back. According to a *Führer* order, the bridges were of strategically decisive importance and had to be held under all circumstances.

In order to continue the attack north on 17 December, the division had to free up the *SPW* Battalion at Ssamochin. To that end, *Hauptmann* Löw's *Pionier-Lehr-Bataillon 1*[33] was attached to the battalion. The engineers, in turn, were reinforced by the attachment of the *1./PJA128*. The tank regiment was attached to *Panzer-Regiment 11*, leaving behind four tanks at the bridgehead position at Krugljakoff.

Russian combat aircraft bombed the bridgehead several times during the night. Again and again, Soviet tanks advanced aggressively against the German positions, with infantry assault detachments following them. The German infantry and tankers did not get a chance to rest. At 0530 hours of the morning of 17 December, enemy tanks were positioned right next to the contested bridge. An 8.8cm *Flak* destroyed a T-34; the remaining ones pulled back. Twenty Russian tanks appeared in front of *Kampfgruppe Bachmann*; 40 in front of Schestakoff, which was defended by the engineers and the *SPW* Battalion, which had just arrived. The enemy was sending out a massive greeting on this morning. One report followed the other.

At 0600 hours, *Kampfgruppe von Heydebreck* moved out to the north from the Klykoff area as part of *Panzer-Regiment 11*. Ten minutes later, numerous enemy tanks, accompanied by weak enemy infantry forces mounted on them, appeared in front of Schestakoff and entered the village by crossing over the frozen Akssaj. The enemy infantry was turned back in close combat, and six T-34's fell victim to antitank guns firing at pointblank range, despite the fact that the tanks were maneuvering skillfully. When the six tanks were knocked out, the enemy force pulled back. *Kampfgruppe von Heydebreck*, which had quickly been summoned to the rescue, arrived, but it could not be completely employed. It then rejoined the attack of *Kampfgruppe von Hünersdorff*. South of Sagotskot, an extensively fortified antitank gun and antitank rifle position of the enemy was destroyed. A firefight developed between Russian and German tanks around Hill 130.6. *Hauptmann* Bucher's *I./PR126* closed up to the tanks at 1140 hours.

It was quiet in the morning around the bridgehead at Krugljakoff. For the first time, *Stuka* formations participated in the fighting and brought palpable relief to the ground forces by their effective attacks on concentrations of infantry and tanks at Shutoff 1 and Kamenka, as well as "BW", 3.5 kilometers northeast of the railway bridge. The enemy turned back and allowed the infantry to reoccupy the outpost line of the previous day. The air-ground coordination officer from the *Luftwaffe*, who was posted to the division headquarters, distinguished himself several times through his effective direction of the air strikes.

Southwest of Shutoff 2, a Rumanian cavalry group—referred to in German as *Kavalleriegruppe Popescu*—which had arrived from the southwest, prepared to attack on 18 December.

After this day, the enemy only had weak forces with a few tanks in the area south of the Akssaj from Shutoff 2 to Kowalenko. North of the river, however, were the main forces of the Soviets. They were located in the Shutoff 1 — Kamenka — Rail Spur St. Saria area with strong armored elements. It was anticipated that additional attacks on the Krugljakoff Bridgehead would be launched from that area.

The tank regiment returned to division control. In addition, the *I./Flak-Regiment 61*, consisting of two 8.8cm *Flak* and one 2cm *Flak* battery, as well as *Oberst* Dietrich's *Werfer-Regiment 54* was directed to support the division.

An enemy attack against the positions of *PGR128* with tanks and drunk infantry was conducted as darkness fell. It was turned back with heavy losses to the enemy as the result of well-placed artillery fire and an immediate counterattack. The spoils of war on this day for the division: 260 prisoners; 10 T-34's; 6 T-70's; 2 IL-2 aircraft; 7 trucks with mortars; heavy machine guns; and 50 antitank rifles.

The logistic services of the division had a difficult time of it. The road running parallel to the Kotelnikowo — Krugljakoff rail line was the only supply route, and it was constantly under aerial attack from the Soviets. First it was the mud, then it was the flattened snow and ice that made every depression and *balka* an obstacle that could only be overcome with difficulty.

The few villages along the railway line were overcrowded. In addition to the numerous German and Rumanian trains elements and supply points, there were larger depots with rations and uniform items for the *6. Armee* that were supposed to be taken to the encircled forces as soon as contact was established.

The main clearing stations at Nebykoff and Pimentscherni were scenes of great activity. A forward clearing station was established in Tschilekoff. The evacuation of wounded was a constant cause for concern, since the field ambulances were never without work.

The 18th of December saw the division attacking northeast again. The *SPW* Battalion remained in Schestakoff as the corps reserve. The tank regiment, with its 13 remaining operational tanks, was in Klykoff. On the right wing of the division, the Rumanian Popescu Group, with the Rumanian 5th and 8th Cavalry Divisions, as well as *Pionier-Lehr-Bataillon 1*, took the village of Shutoff 2. The engineers were relieved by the Rumanians in Ssamochin and also placed in corps reserve status along with a 2cm *Flak* battery. The *I.(Sfl)/PJA128* remained attached to the Rumanian 8th Cavalry Division, under the command of Knight's Cross recipient, Colonel Korne. The antitank battery supported the taking of a bridgehead over the Akssaj.

The division's tank regiment reestablished contact with *Panzer-Regiment 11* at Hill 146.9.

Heavy concentrations of the enemy in the defiles near Shutoff 1 and Kamenka were attacked by *Stuka* formations. The enemy abandoned the Wodjanaja Defile and pulled back to the northeast.

During the night, the Red Air Force attacked in ever broader scope.

On 19 December, the enemy concentrated more forces in front of the division and its neighbors. At night, one could see Soviet columns with headlights on approaching the front and both sides of the *LVII. Panzer-Korps* along the broad ridgelines, bringing with them new forces.

At 1000 hours, the *6. Panzer-Division* took Werchne-Kumskij and continued its attack further to the northeast. An enemy tank brigade was reported on the march in the Schirokaja Defile. *Panzer-Regiment 201* rolled out against this force and soon encountered the rapidly approaching Soviets (24 T-34's and 16 T-70's). Following the enemy tanks were approximately three regiments of infantry. German artillery and *Stuka*

33 Editor's Note: This battalion was composed of personnel from the instructional elements at the engineer school. It was generally German Army policy to periodically send the instructional battalions (and larger formations) to the front to renew and sharpen combat skills so that the training base was qualified to instruct new personnel attending specialty courses or returning personnel from front-line units.

attacked, but the enemy also had bombers, fighters and ground-attack aircraft. Taking heavy losses, the enemy succeeded in penetrating the front lines with three tanks in the area of the Wodjanaja Defile. He was ejected in an immediate counterattack. In addition, some ground was gained to the north. The tank regiment knocked out two T-34's and a T-70 on Hill 81.8, while *Flak* accounted for another three T-34's. A *Stuka* attack at this phase of the fighting completely broke the will to fight on the part of the enemy, and he beat a hasty retreat. As was later determined, that signaled the end of the attack by the freshly introduced 87th Rifle Division of the 139th Tank Regiment of the 13th Tank Brigade. The enemy suffered heavy losses.

The enemy moved out against the German lines again at 1400 hours. This time it was a rifle regiment with 15 tanks that advanced against Hill 81.8. In the face of heavy defensive fires, it turned away toward the rail line and, finally, under the impact of the resistance of the German forces, it moved back to the northeast. Pursuing elements of *Kampfgruppe Bachmann* entered the Wodjanaja Defile and screened there. Tanks of the *II./PR201* felt their way forward as far as "BW", 3 kilometers southeast of St. Saria, until it turned dark.

Despite the inferiority of its weapons as a consequence of the loss, through battle damage or mechanical problems, of all long-barreled *Panzer IV's*, the tank regiment moved out at 0630 hours on 20 December from west of the Schirokaja Defile to attack north and, later on, east. An intercepted radio message from the Soviet 87th Rifle Division indicated that it was pulling back to the north and was reassembling around Gniloakssaiskaja.

At 0700 hours, *PGR128* moved out. The enemy defended stubbornly with antitank guns, antitank rifles and heavy weapons at "BW" and west of it. In difficult, casualty-intensive fighting, the infantry assaulted the strongpoint at 1000 hours. While the divisional artillery placed fires on enemy concentrations at Shutoff 1 and Kamenka and conducted counterbattery fire against mortar positions, the tank regiment reached the northeast end of the Schirokaja Defile in a light snowfall, where it destroyed an antitank rifle position and continued advancing in the direction of Point 141.5. Due to the enemy's superiority in weaponry, the fight was broken off, and the regiment turned south to cross the rail line and reach its objective of Kamenka. At the same time, *Hauptmann* Döring's *II./PGR128* entered the Antonowa Defile and *Hauptmann* Stetting's *I./PGR128* approached to within 300 meters of the spur line at St. Saria. Its attack then bogged down in the face of enemy tanks.

The tank regiment fought its way south against a deeply echelonned series of pockets of resistance consisting of tanks, antitank guns and antitank rifles. Attacking from the north, it joined the fighting around St. Saria. It could not cross the railway line, however, since it proved to be an impregnable armor obstacle.

Heavy mortar fires from Shutoff 1 impacted among the motorized infantry of the *6.* and *7./PGR128*, who were advancing as far as Hill 106. When five enemy tanks then advanced into the companies, they suffered extremely heavy casualties in the barren landscape and had to pull back to Hill 110.

Pionier-Lehr-Bataillon 1 was released from the corps and employed protecting the bridges at Krugljakoff and Schestakoff. The *SPW* Battalion, together with a battery each of 8.8cm and 2cm *Flak*, was moved into the area Quelle — northern edge of the Wodnajaja Defile to screen the left flank of the division. *Panzer-Pionier-Bataillon 51*, held as a corps reserve, was moved up behind *PGR128*. The tank regiment had 17 operational tanks.

The bloody losses sustained by the division during this time period were high. For instance, *PGR128*, with a numerically weak headcount, lost 24 dead, 106 wounded and 4 missing. Even if the losses of the enemy were many fold higher, they were replaced by the constant bringing forward of new formations. In the case of the *23. Panzer-Division*, every lost man left behind a gap that could no longer be closed.

At first light on 21 December, the tanks of the regiment, under the command of *Hauptmann* Stiewe (commander of the *I./PR201*), moved out against Point 162.7, advancing over Point 157.0 (8 kilometers west of Gniloakssaiskaja). A Russian battalion in field fortifications was overrun. Sixty soldiers were taken prisoner; five heavy machine guns, four mortars and numerous light machine guns and small arms were captured. The *SPW* Battalion and the tanks secured the area that had been captured.

Leutnant Borbonus, a patrol leader in the armored reconnaissance company of the division, brought back valuable information during a patrol to Birsowoj that moved through Gniloakssaiskaja and the rail stop at Kapkinskij. According to the patrol, the Russians had established a continuous defensive position along the line Kapkinskij — Shutoff 1. Combat reconnaissance conducted by the tank regiment also determined enemy positions and concentrations of tanks on both sides of Gniloakssaiskaja.

While the *SPW* Battalion assumed a screening mission at Point 162.7, along with the *Flak* elements in support, the tank regiment prepared to move out for operations at 1150 hours at Hill 157.5. The *SPW* Battalion was placed under the command of *Kampfgruppe Hesse*, which was formed primarily from *PPB51*. The battle group was being inserted into the line in this sector.

As dusk fell, five T-34's with mounted infantry attacked the infantry at St. Saria and pushed them back to the southwest. The situation was not restored until midnight, when St. Saria was taken back in a counterattack conducted by the *I./PGR128*, which was magnificently supported by artillery.

The tank regiment had 18 operational tanks at its disposal.

On this day, *Oberst* von Buch, who had originally established the divisional artillery regiment, relinquished his command and was transferred back to Germany. *Major* Hamann, the commander of the *III./PAR128*, assumed temporary command of the artillery regiment.

At 0500 hours on 22 December, a Russian battalion ejected the outposts of the *SPW* Battalion from Hill 162.7. The enemy was beaten back in an immediate counterattack and pursued as far as the edge of the well-fortified Gniloakssaiskaja.

St. Saria was lost one more time. It had been captured by four T-34's and strong infantry elements that had moved on it in the open during the seesaw fighting.

A radio message from the Commanding General at 0910 hours ordered the immediate attack of the tank regiment along the Gniloakssaiskaja — Wassiljewka road. The regiment was to attack the Soviet forces that were concentrically attacking the *6. Panzer-Division* in the rear.

Antitank guns and tanks in Birsowoj made it impregnable for German tanks. The effort to go around the village to the east failed on account of the deeply broken-up terrain. The regiment returned to its starting positions via the Beresowaja Defile.

On 23 December, *Kampfgruppe von Heydebreck* was employed to capture Birsowoj. The battle group consisted of the tank regiment, *Kradschützen-Bataillon 17* (*17. Panzer-Division*) and the *SPW* Battalion. The divisional artillery of the *6. Panzer-Division* was placed in general support. The attack rolled south and southwest from the Ssolenaja Defile and Kapkinka toward Birsowoj at 0800 hours. Despite the appearance of 11 enemy tanks and heavy infantry forces at Point 162.7, the attack was not interrupted. The divisional artillery, along with *Flak* and rocket launchers, scattered the enemy through barrage fires. In the meantime, the tank regiment overcame an antitank-rifle position and took Birsowoj and Hill 106.8 to its north at 0940 hours. A Russian rifle regiment was wiped out and 500 prisoners taken. In addition, 1 antitank gun, 3 mortars, 30 antitank rifles, several heavy machine guns and numerous small arms were captured.

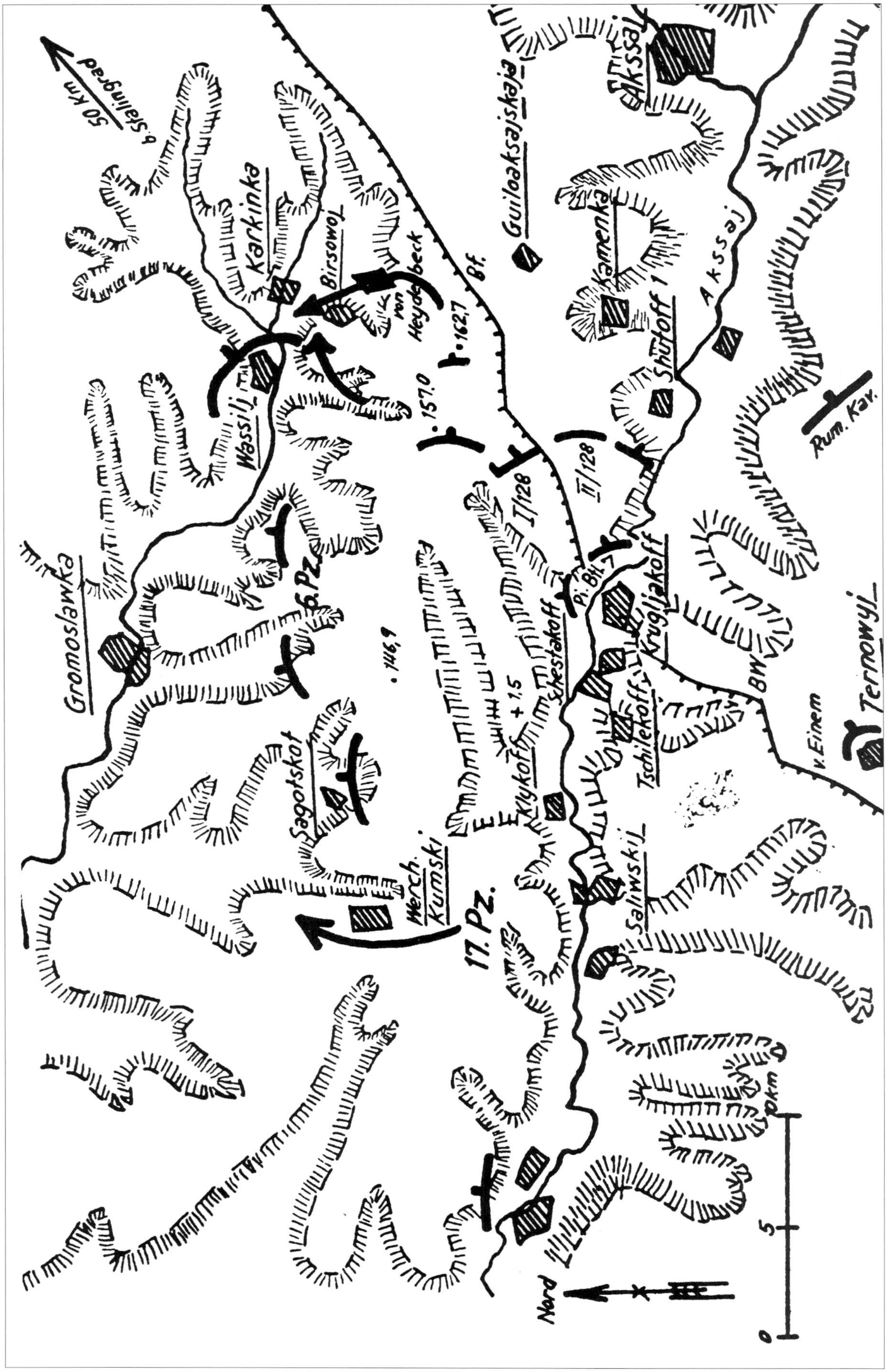

Map 25: The Situation on 23 December.

After completing the mission, *Oberstleutnant* von Heydebreck turned over the securing of the village to the *6. Panzer-Division*, which had defeated strong enemy forces north of Wassiljewka at the same time. The latter division saw a breakthrough to Stalingrad, which was only 48 kilometers away, palpably near. *Kampfgruppe von Heydebreck* immediately moved out across Point 162.7 to Gniloakssaiskaja, which was its next objective.

At 1030 hours, however, the division received orders to call off its attack to the northeast and transition to the defense of the Akssaj Bridgehead, since the *6. Panzer-Division* was being detached from the *LVII. Panzer-Korps* and moved to another location for a different mission. The division's main line of resistance ran Point 110.8 — Point 97.4 — rail spur at St. Saria — Point 157.0 — Point 146.9. The *17. Panzer-Division* of *Generalmajor* von Senger und Etterlin closed up on the left. It had been in an intense defensive struggle against a Russian armor corps around Werchne-Kumskij ever since the morning hours.

Even though the preceding successes had come at a high cost, they led the German formations close to the ring of encirclement around Stalingrad. Considerable enemy forces, numerically vastly superior, had been defeated again and again. At night, the soldiers of the *LVII. Panzer-Korps* saw the glimmer of fires around Stalingrad and heard the report of artillery. At that point, however, an event occurred on a faraway front that shattered the confidence that contact could be made with the *6. Armee*. On 16 December, the Russians exploited the weaker German allies and had moved out against the frontage of the Italian 8th Army of Colonel General Gariboldi in the area on both sides of Bogutschar on the Don. By bypassing the brave alpine corps, they had completely collapsed that front in advancing to the southwest. Not only were the forces in the Don Bend and the area to its south threatened by this advance from the north toward Rostov. In case that city were captured, all of *Heeresgruppe A*, still in the Caucasus, would have been cut off from its rearward lines of communications. At the same time, strong Soviet formations in the Don Bend had attacked and pushed back *Armee-Abteilung Hollidt*.[34]

All countermeasures initiated by *Generalfeldmarschall* Manstein's *Heeresgruppe Don* over the previous few days had not been able to bring the Soviet advance to a halt, with the result that the attack of the *LVII. Panzer-Korps* had to be stopped and the *6. Panzer-Division* pulled out of the front north of the Akssaj in order to be employed in the greater Don Bend. The last hopes of freeing the comrades encircled in Stalingrad had to be abandoned, especially since *Generaloberst* Paulus, the Commander-in-Chief of the *6. Armee*, could not decide whether to act in contravention of the *Führer's* orders by ordering his forces to break out to the southwest or at least to ignore it. On the morning of 23 December, there was still a possibility of linking up with the *4. Panzer-Armee*.

During the night of 23/24 December, the two divisions, the *17. Panzer-Division* and the *23. Panzer-Division*, reorganized in accordance with their new missions. The enemy only followed hesitantly. It was not until 0900 hours on 24 December that T-34's showed up in front of the positions of *PGR128*. Moving rapidly, they broke through the front lines and advanced as far as the positions of a rocket-launcher battalion, where they were engaged over open sights and forced back. At 1035 hours, eight T-34's, accompanied by strong infantry elements, hit *PPB51* at Hill 157.0. The *III./PR201* launched a counterattack with six tanks. At the same time, combat reconnaissance indicated enemy movements of tanks and infantry around Parishka and Komuna.

Strong enemy pressure ejected the *I./Panzergrenadier-Regiment 40* of the *17. Panzer-Division* from its positions at noon. That battalion was the left-hand neighbor of the division. The battalion pulled back to the southern edge of the Neklinkskaja Defile, with the result that the left wing of the division was hanging in the air. At 1445 hours, the *SPW* Battalion was also in the middle of an enemy attack conducted from the north and east. Despite the onset of darkness, the strong enemy pressure continued. The Russians wanted to reduce the northeastern bulwark of the German defensive front under all circumstances. The divisional engineers had to defend against attacks from two sides the entire day. The hard-frozen ground did not allow the construction of positions; the engineers were only able to dig a half meter into the ground over the course of the entire day. Finally, the corps ordered a shortening of the front as evening fell. A few enemy tanks were already operating in the rear area, causing unrest and disrupting the supply elements on their way to the front. Despite all that, rations and mail still made it forward.

Around 2200 hours, the effort succeeded in bringing the 4 8.8cm *Flak*, which were attached to *PPB51*, into the new positions, even though there were only two prime movers available. The engineer companies, which only had a trench strength of 30 men each, were the last to displace. When they reached the new main line of resistance, the exhausted men fell to the ground in the snow and immediately fell asleep.

The *I./Panzergrenadier-Regiment 40* was once again placed under heavy enemy pressure. *Pionier-Lehr-Bataillon 1*, still attached to the division, had to send a company to help out. The division's tank regiment stood by at Antonoff.

The soldiers of the *LVII. Panzer-Korps* spent Christmas Eve behind their weapons in a defensive struggle. Only a few Christmas trees could spread some candle light that evening. Despite all of the difficulties, the division's postal services was able to get a great deal of the Christmas mail to the front. The division's inventive postmaster always found new ways to get outgoing mail in the direction of home as fast as possible, whether it was via the means of air mail, which was introduced in June 1942, or by giving mail bags to flight crews of machines destined for Germany at airstrips near the front. It was always possible to get one more mailbag on board.

At midnight on 24/25 December, the main line of resistance ran from the Krugljakoff Bridgehead through Point 105.0 to the northeast outskirts of the Schirotaja Defile (*PGR128*); from there to the northeast outskirts of the Neklinskaja Defile (*PPB51*); and along the southern edge of the defile to the west (*SPW* Battalion). At 0100 hours, strong Soviet infantry forces attacked along the boundary between the *17. Panzer-Division* and the *23. Panzer-Division* along the Gromoslawka Schestakoff road. The *I./Panzergrenadier-Regiment 40* was bypassed from the west. *Pionier-Lehr-Bataillon 1* reported 200 Russians with 6 tanks on coordination point +1.5, 4 kilometers west of the Gromoslawka Schestakoff road, that is, deep in the rear of the *I./Panzergrenadier-Regiment 40*.

While the *17. Panzer-Division* attempted to clean up the situation with what remained of its tanks and *Kradschützen-Bataillon 17*, the divisional artillery of the *23. Panzer-Division* was pulled back to the area around Krugljakoff.

At 0305 hours, an attack by 100 Russians on St. Saria was turned back with bloody losses for the enemy.

Around 0400 hours, a Russian rifle regiment, supported by tanks, attacked the weakened *PPB51* and forced it to pull back to the south. While 12 tanks of *PR201* were already on their way to the left wing of the division to determine what the situation was with regard to the *I./Panzergrenadier-Regiment 40*, *Major* Illig moved out with the remaining 6 operational tanks and the motorcycle company of *PGR128* to restore the situation in the sector of *PPB51*. While awaiting the tanks, the engineers pulled back further along the Schirokaja Defile, since they were unable to hold their positions, despite the support of an 8.8cm *Flak*. That gun fired from its limber with the only type of ammunition it had left—antitank rounds—into the dense masses of the approaching enemy infantry. The enemy was pushed back once the tanks arrived, but then the Soviets

34 Editor's Note: An *Armee-Abteilung* was essentially an *ad hoc* formation larger than a corps and smaller than a field army.

pressed forward with armored reinforcements and drove the weak German elements back again. Two heavy artillery pieces of the *III./PAR128* had to be abandoned due to a lack of prime movers. The engineers suffered heavy losses.

The Soviet counterattack continued on a broad front. In the sector of the *17. Panzer-Division*, a Soviet attack group broke through as far as Klykoff and encircled the tanks and motorcycle infantry that had assembled there. The *SPW* Battalion of the *23. Panzer-Division* was attacked west of the Schirokaja Defile by strong enemy forces.

In the sector of the *23. Panzer-Division*, the bridgehead positions at Krugljakoff and Schestakoff were placed under the command of *Oberstleutnant* von Heydebreck. To conduct the defense, he was given *Pionier-Lehr-Bataillon 1* (minus its 1st Company) and the division reserve, which consisted of two companies composed of soldiers from trains elements.

To protect the deep right flank of the division, a strongpoint was established in Ternowyj under the command of *Major* von Einem, the commander of *PJA128*. His forces consisted of his battalion headquarters and trains elements from *PR201*.

At 0800 hours, *Major* Illig moved out with *PPB51*, which had been attached to him, and his tanks to counterattack along both sides of the Schirokaja Defile. He ejected the enemy, who was already confident of victory, and inflicted heavy losses among his forces. He then reoccupied the former main line of resistance. The two heavy howitzers, which had been abandoned there earlier that day, were recovered. *Kampfgruppe Illig* then organized for the defense.

At 0850 hours on that eventful Christmas Day, the division received orders to clarify the situation on the right wing of the *17. Panzer-Division*. To that end, the following elements were attached to the *23. Panzer-Division*: The headquarters of *Panzergrenadier-Regiment 40*, along with its 1st Battalion, and *Artilleriegruppe Dietrich*, with a battalion from *Werfer-Regiment 54* and the *I./Panzer-Artillerie-Regiment 40* (the latter battalion belonging to the divisional artillery of the *17. Panzer-Division*). At the same time, an additional *Führer* order was received:

> Hold the railway and vehicle bridges at Krugljakoff at all costs.
>
> Bridges of decisive importance for the outcome of the war.

Strong infantry attacks and envelopment maneuvers on the right wing of the division were broken up by *PGR128*, in close cooperation with the divisional artillery. Despite that, enemy elements continued to hold out in defiles and depressions right in front of the German lines.

The *I./Panzergrenadier-Regiment 40* was caught up in a large Russian attack at 1100 hours, which hit it from the front with a rifle regiment and from the right flank with two additional battalions. Enemy tanks attacked at the same time. In the nick of time, *PR201* and elements of the *17. Panzer-Division* arrived. The latter forces had fought their way clear of Klykoff and had been able to essentially scatter the enemy forces that had advanced that far. The *I./Panzergrenadier-Regiment 40* was able to catch its breath, especially after additional strong enemy forces in its rear were wiped out.

The *SPW* Battalion, on the right, reported the approach of Russian infantry, accompanied by two groups of tanks, one with 20 vehicles, the other with 30. The division no longer had any tank or antitank reserves, with the result that the battalion was unable to effectively defend against the enemy attack that followed. There were numerous losses. *Kampfgruppe Illig* and the *I./PGR128* were likewise pressed by the numerically superior enemy forces, but they were able to maintain their positions.

Under constant enemy pressure, the division ordered the *I./Panzergrenadier-Regiment 40* to pull back to Point +1.5. Twelve tanks from *PR201* advanced north as far as the Neklinskaja Defile to make the disengagement of the infantry easier. There, however, they ran into an enemy attack of 30 T-34's with massed infantry that had just started. Four of the tank regiment's tanks were knocked out; the number of enemy tanks knocked out could not be determined with certainty due to the pace of events. The withdrawing *I./Panzergrenadier-Regiment 40* was caught by the T-34's advancing south at a high rate of speed. It was overrun and further decimated. The grenadiers were on the verge of exhaustion.

Disregarding the German tanks, the Soviet tanks—by all accounts, expertly led—continued advancing south in a closed formation. Everything was moving so quickly that the German tanks under *Hauptmann* Tilemann, commander of the *II./PR201*, were only able to move back with them. Shortly before the north bank of the Akssaj, the German tanks swung west, turned around and established a firing line against the Soviet tanks advancing on Schestakoff. The Soviet tanks then came under defensive fires from the edge of the village, which consisted of antitank guns, 8.8cm *Flak* from the *II./Flak-Regiment 241* and individual immobilized tanks from *PR201*, which had been towed into position in the village to reinforce its defenses. Ten enemy tanks, including six T-34's, were burning in short order. Those that survived turned north and left. The Russian infantry had only followed the tanks halfway down the slope to the village when they were caught by German artillery and rocket launchers in massed fires. They also suffered such casualties that they likewise turned north and fled.

Orders were received from *Heeresgruppe Don*: "The railway bridge at Krugljakoff may not be blown up unless there is immediate danger."

The *4. Panzer-Armee* ordered: "Hold unconditionally. Defend the localities in the valley."

Based on the situation, the division recommended to the corps that *Kampfgruppe Bachmann* be pulled back to the hills north of Antonoff. In response, the division received the warning order that the *17. Panzer-Division* was being pulled out of the line in order to be employed elsewhere in the corps sector. The *23. Panzer-Division* would thereupon be responsible for the sector along the Akssaj River from Krugljakoff to Ssaliwskij. Its mission would be to defend along the Akssaj, incorporating the neighboring built-up areas into its defense, and hold the bridges firmly in its hands.

Through a liaison officer, the division commander expressly informed the corps that it would be impossible to hold the position in the new sector, if there were more attacks of the size that had been experienced that day.

The *I./Panzergrenadier-Regiment 40* and one company from the *Pionier-Lehr-Bataillon 1* were scattered and could not be accounted for. Strong tank and infantry forces attacked *Kampfgruppe Illig* and the attached *SPW* Battalion at 1430 hours and enveloped them on both sides. In the end, the *Kampfgruppe* had to fall back and was only able to reach the bridgehead by conducting a fighting withdrawal. The *SPW* Battalion had been reduced to a trench strength of 70 noncommissioned officers and enlisted personnel.

Oberst Bachmann, the commander of *PGR128*, had to personally give his word that the bridge at Krugljakoff would be held and only be blown up in the most dire of circumstances.

Under the concealment afforded by darkness, Russian tanks and infantry attacked Schestakoff. Three hundred meters in front of the first buildings, the Soviet attack bogged down in the face of the defensive fires. On the other hand, another group succeeded in entering the western part of Antonoff.

During the night of 25/26 December, the incremental movement of the formations to the left to relieve the *17. Panzer-Division* took place. As a result of the extension of the division sector by some 15 kilometers, its battle groups were no longer in a position to conduct a cohesive defense of their positions. For instance, to relieve the already weak *SPW* Battalion, only 20 men from *PGR128* were available. The 10 remaining operational tanks of *PR201* were positioned in Krugljakoff. *Hauptmann* Bucher, the commander of the *SPW* Battalion, was wounded. Assuming acting command of the remaining *SPW's* was *Oberleutnant* Kappauf.

Statements by deserters and reports from *Kradschützen-Bataillon 17* concerning Russian attack intentions were still being evaluated when the enemy came at first light on the second day of Christmas. A soldier who witnessed the attack stated:

The Russians came in waves of infantry, the likes of which nobody had ever seen before. At first, they were only accompanied by 5 or 6 tanks. They approached Schestakoff in dense groups, which you could compare to regular march formations, across the barren slope that was lightly covered with snow. Additional Soviet tanks rolled through the gaps. It was a terrific, unique target for the artillery and rocket launchers, which did not give the Russians much time to wait before placing barrage fires on them, which tore great gaps in the Soviet [ranks]. But the throng pressed forward inexorably. The enemy was soon outside of Schestakoff.

It was only then that efforts to separate the infantry from the tanks succeeded. The enemy infantry was bled white on the iced-over, barren terrain. Weak remaining elements could not be controlled by their leaders any more, and they fled up the slope to get away to the north. Six enemy tanks were set alight by the defensive fires of the *II./Flak-Regiment 241* and the immobilized tanks; the tanks that remained followed their fleeing infantry.

But the enemy repeated his attack at 0730 hours. That time, it was two rifle divisions, accompanied by 30 tanks, that assaulted Schestakoff on the narrowest of frontages. The defense force facing the Soviets: One platoon of motorcycle infantry; two squads of infantry; 50 men from the trains elements of *PR201* under the command of *Oberleutnant* Korte; *3* 2cm *Flak*; 2 5cm antitank guns; and 2 7.5cm self-propelled antitank guns. Once again, the Russian infantry suffered extremely heavy losses from the artillery and rocket-launcher fires, but the oppressive superiority in numbers made it possible to force an entry into Schestakoff. The enemy tanks held back from the village after losing several T-34's. The two self-propelled antitank guns, the three 2cm *Flak* and a 5cm antitank gun were put out of commission by antitank rifles. *Oberleutnant* Korte was killed. Schestakoff had to be abandoned; its bridge blown up.

The three self-propelled guns of *Oberleutnant* Sattler attempted to cross the frozen-over Akssaj, since the bridge was no longer negotiable. All three guns broke through the ice and had to be blown up.

Enemy infantry crossed the Akksaj west of the village and forced the divisional headquarters to pull back from Tschilekoff. They then gained another 4 kilometers of terrain to the south, until they were stopped in front of the battery positions of *PAR128*. The division sent its tanks from Romaschkin against this force. Under the command of *Hauptmann* Tilemann, the tanks swung out to the south and hit the enemy in the flank and forced him back across the Akssaj without sustaining any friendly losses.

A Soviet battalion was positioned outside of Ssaliwkij. Klykoff fell without a fight into enemy hands, since *Kradschützen-Bataillon 17* abandoned it prematurely, and *Kampfgruppe von Heydebreck* was unable to reoccupy it in time.

At 1130 hours, the Rumanian formations on the right fell back to the southwest, even though they were not under pressure from the Russians up to that point.

The self-propelled antitank guns of *Oberleutnant* Väth of the *1./PJA128* suddenly found themselves all alone in Ssamochin early in the morning and facing an enemy attacking with massed infantry and tanks. High-explosive and antitank rounds inflicted heavy casualties on the enemy. *Unteroffizier* Schulze knocked out 4 of 10 attacking Soviet tanks with his self-propelled gun. The Soviet tanks had inflicted heavy losses on the Rumanian infantry when they had attacked Ssamochin from Shutoff 2. It was not until all of the self-propelled antitank guns had sustained battle damage from antitank rifle and machine gun fire and the enemy had surrounded the Germans on three sides, that *Oberleutnant* Väth issued orders to break out to the west, where he established contact with the division at the Krugljakoff bridgehead. The combat trains of the antitank unit could not be evacuated from Ssamochin in time and fell into enemy hands.

With the retreat of the Rumanians, the *23. Panzer-Division* presented a salient far into the enemy lines along the Akssaj. The division was on the verge of exhaustion, had been considerably weakened and no longer had the combat power to strike back at the continuous attacks of the Russians, which were conducted with considerable numerical superiority. The only point of light were the brave operations of the weakened *Luftwaffe*. It saved a few apparently hopeless situations, primarily by means of *Stuka* attacks. The *Luftwaffe* allowed the numerically superior but less effective Red Air Force to be forgotten about.

The bridgehead position at Krugljakoff was initially not party to the Soviet attacks. Two of the self-propelled antitank guns positioned there assisted in the fighting for Schestakoff from the flank. *Hauptmann* Hesse was wounded and had to be evacuated; *Oberleutnant* Seyring assumed temporary command of *PPB51*.

While the tanks ejected the enemy at Tschilekoff, a Soviet battalion entered Romaschkin, south of the Akssaj. It forced the artillery and *Flak* there to change positions. *Hauptmann* Claussen's *II./PGR128* counterattacked and restored the situation there.

Five enemy tanks appeared in the deep left flank of the division at Werch. Jablotschnyj. *Sturmgeschütz-Abteilung 203*[35], the friendly forces to the left in Generalowskij, was involved in heavy fighting with enemy tanks and infantry.

From the east, five enemy T-34's soon attacked the Ternowyj strongpoint, just east of the railway line and the main supply route of the division. Since no armor-defeating weaponry was available, *Major* von Einem ordered the evacuation of the strongpoint and fell back to Nebykoff.

At 1340 hours, the enemy flanked Krugljakoff from the east, but he was soon pushed back.

In view of the critical situation, which offered absolutely no chance for a resumption of the efforts to relieve Stalingrad, higher headquarters decided to shorten the front. The *23. Panzer-Division* was to disengage from the enemy during the night of 26/27 December and pull back to a line running Darganoff — Pimen-Tscherni — Grjemjatschi (with the *17. Panzer-Division* to the left). The rearguards were to remain in contact with the enemy until first light.

Major i.G. Freyer resumed his duties as the division operations officer.

In the meantime, *Kampfgruppe von Heydebreck* turned back an enemy attack at Ssaliwskij that was conducted by eight T-34's and a rifle regiment. The battle group destroyed three of the enemy's attacking tanks. Bitter fighting continued in the area around Romaschkin.

At 1440 hours, *Kampfgruppe Bachmann* received orders to blow up the railway and road bridges at Krugljakoff.

At 1700 hours, *Kampfgruppe von Heydebreck* disengaged from the enemy; *Kampfgruppe Bachmann* followed at 2000 hours. The enemy remained quiet. The rearguard, commanded by *Hauptmann* Tilemann, consisted of the remaining operational tanks of *PR201*, the motorcycle infantry company of *PGR128*, a light battery from *Flak-Abteilung 261* and two self-propelled antitank guns. At midnight, the rearguard left Krugljakoff and moved to the rail spur at Birjukowskij and, later on, Tschilekoff. The enemy only felt his way hesitantly forward early in the morning.

Kampfgruppe Bachmann set up security at Ssowch. Wypassnoj at 0730 hours on 27 December with its 1st Battalion. The 2nd Battalion remained in Pimen-Tscherni. *Kampfgruppe von Heydebreck* closed up on the left. Individual Rumanians were in Ssowch. Wypassnoj, where they were to assume the screening mission, but they soon left the group of buildings to the Russians feeling their way forward. As a result, the enemy was again in the deep right flank of the division.

35 Editor's Note: = 203rd Assault Gun Battalion.

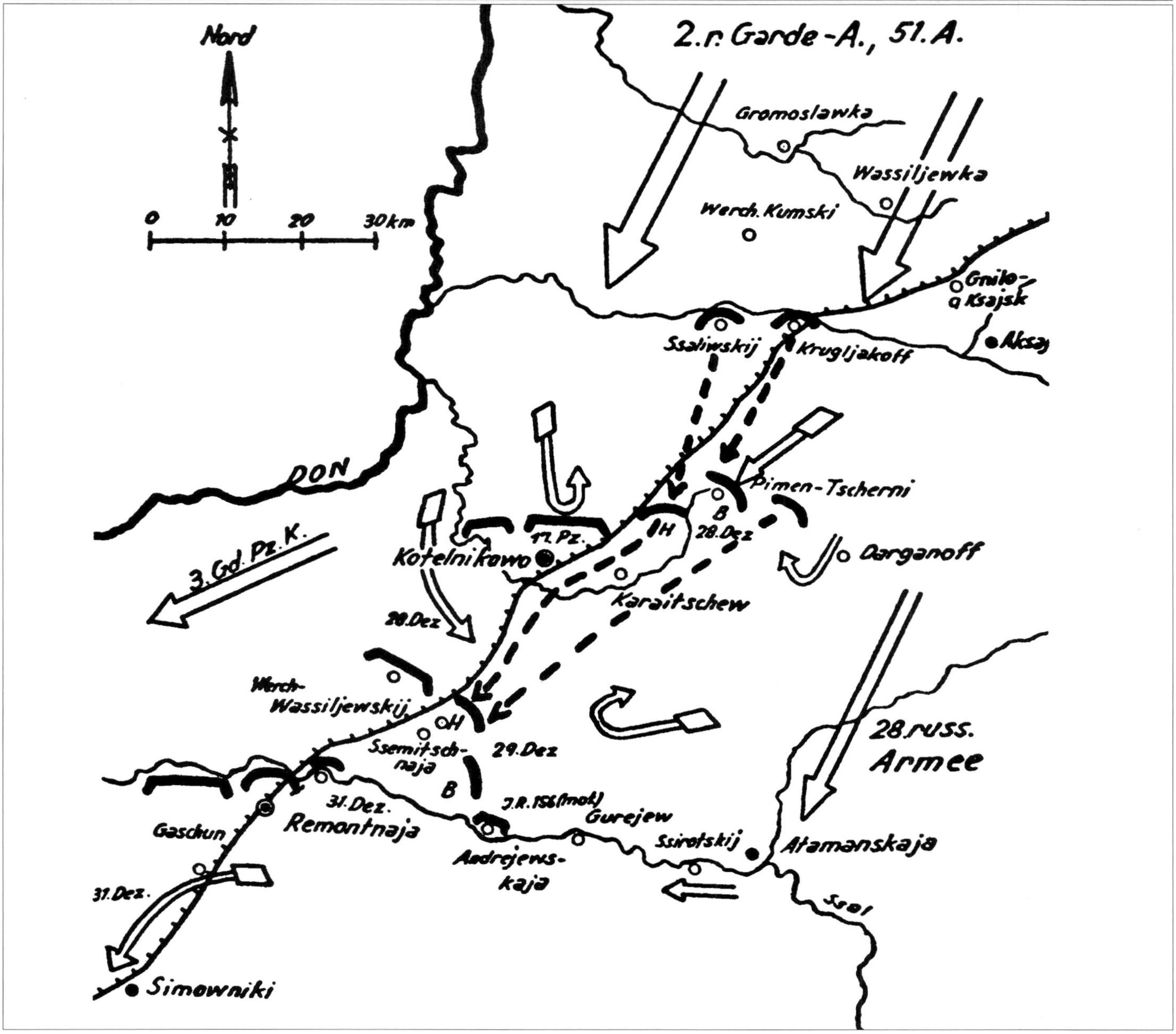

Map 26: Withdrawal Movements of the *LVII. Panzer-Korps* from 26-31 December 1942. (*H = Kampfgruppe von Heydebreck*; *B = Kampfgruppe Bachmann*)

PR201 had only five operational tanks left. It was reinforced by an additional eight tanks, which came from *Panzer-Kompanie Wohlleben* of *Panzer-Regiment 36* of the *14. Panzer-Division*, which had been formed from repaired tanks that had been outside the Stalingrad Pocket. A march unit composed of 300 men returning from leave was attached for employment as infantry. The headquarters of *PGR126*—with neither a command and control mission nor a commander at the time—was sent to Gurejew, 30 kilometers south of Kotelnikowo, to act as a movement- and straggler-control element for the division.

At 1250 hours, eight Russian tanks attacked Pimen-Tscherni. Three T-34's were destroyed there; two other ones continued advancing to Nish. Tscherni, where they were destroyed. The remaining three tanks withdrew.

A short time later, 20 enemy tanks with a company of infantry rolled against Pimen-Tscherni again. The decimated *Flak* element could barely offer any further resistance. The enemy overran the remnants of the *II./PGR128* and encircled a company with 22 men. Only a few individuals from that company were later able to break free to the south. The *III./PAR128* lost all of its guns, with the exception of a single 10cm cannon and a heavy field howitzer. *Hauptmann Dr.* Pickart's *I./PAR128* was able to fight its way through to *Kampfgruppe von Heydebreck* from north of the village.

The *I./PGR128* was forced back by enemy tanks and infantry and, moving past Ssowch. Wypassnoj, went into position in the vicinity of the stockyards, 10 kilometers east of Karaitschew.

Kampfgruppe von Heydebreck was able to hold its outpost line, turn back repeated enemy advances and destroy three T-34's. However, six other enemy tanks, accompanied by infantry, felt their way forward in the rear of the battle group from the southeast.

The divisional engineers were caught in concentric fires at the Ssamochina Defile and had to pull back to the south side of the Karaitschewo Defile, taking heavy casualties.

Despite the recommendation of the division to fall back to the Ssal River, the field army ordered Karaitschew to be held in strongpoint fashion. A fall-back line was established running Nagolnyj — Kotelnikowo.

In the sector of the *17. Panzer-Division*, the enemy conducted a strong attack on Kotelnikowo at 0120 hours on 28 December. The withdrawal movements of the *23. Panzer-Division* were not disrupted. On the other hand, extensive reconnoitering on the part of the Soviets along the right-hand (eastern) flank of the division became noticeable. The reconnaissance activities, conducted by small groups of tanks and infantry, were conducted in a skillful and imaginative manner and caused considerable unrest. The straggler control point established by the headquarters of *PGR126* in Gurejew had to pull back to the west.

At 0650 hours, an assault gun battery from *Sturmgeschütz-Abteilung 203* arrived in the sector of *Kampfgruppe Bachmann* and was attached to it. A lack of fuel prevented *Kampfgruppe Tilemann* from moving toward Budarka, where it had been intended to establish contact with the *16. Infanterie-Division (mot.)*, which was gradually approaching from the Kalmuck Steppes.

Generalleutnant Freiherr von Boineburg was transferred back to Germany as part of the unassigned officer manpower pool. *Oberst* Rossmann, the commander of *Arko 121*, was given acting command of the division until a new commander could be designated.

The widespread outposts of the division could barely be manned with personnel any longer. In a sector 4 kilometers wide, *Kampfgruppe von Heydebreck* had only 100 riflemen available. The division no longer had any reserves.

Along the right wing of the division, the enemy advanced to the south. Six T-34's with infantry in front of the sector of *PGR128* were driven back by rocket launchers. *Oberleutnant* Seyring was wounded; *Oberleutnant* Schlingmann stepped into his place as acting commander of *PPB51*. In the division's rear area, two enemy tanks appeared along the Pogoshka — Kalinin road. They destroyed several trucks and a light field howitzer and succeeded in blocking the road. The division's trains moved to the area south of Remontnaja.

Reconnaissance indicated a Soviet column on the march on the north bank of the Ssal from Atamanskaja. It was headed west.

The withdrawal movements planned for by the corps for the divisions to pull back to the Ssal on both sides of Remontnaja were quickly initiated when enemy tanks coming from the west (!) blocked the main road running parallel to the rail line south of Kotelnikowo. For the time being, however, the division screened in a line running Jablotschnaja — Kommissarewskij — Werch. Wassiljewskij. The assault guns returned to the command and control of the *17. Panzer-Division* from *Kampfgruppe Bachmann*. Higher headquarters attempted to improve the morale of the forces in the field by authorizing double rations.

At first light on 29 December, *Hauptmann* Tilemann's rearguard force reached the area around "Bw", 10 kilometers south of Kotelnikowo, while engaging antitank guns, antitank rifles and infantry. Seven self-propelled antitank guns were operational again, although the loss of the trains at Ssamochin could scarcely be replaced.

Aerial reconnaissance reported enemy movements south of the Ssal in the area around Ssirotskij, 30 kilometers southeast of Remontnaja.

Two Soviet rifle regiments, supported by tanks, made preparation for the attack in front of the division to the north of Ssemitschnaja and Kommissarewskij. At 1200 hours, they moved out in massed formation to attack. Of six attacking T-34's, the gunners of the antitank battalion knocked out two completely and damaged another two. Within an hour, *Stukas* and German fighters joined the fight and inflicted such heavy casualties in the narrow defiles through bombing runs and strafing that the enemy pulled back.

On 30 December, the division relieved *SS-Panzer-Grenadier-Regiment "Nordland"* of *SS-Panzer-Grenadier-Division "Wiking"* in the Remontnaja Bridgehead. The *SS* division had come from the *1. Panzer-Armee* in the Caucasus and had been allocated to the *4. Panzer-Armee*. The *SS* regiment thereupon moved to Simowniki. At that point, the following additional forces were attached to the division: *Radfahr-Wachbataillon 326*;[36] a battery from *Sturmgeschütz-Abteilung 203* and one each 3.7cm and 2cm batteries from *Flak-Regiment 25*. *Hauptmann* Beck-Broichsitter, who has been attached to the division as part of his general-staff training, had to take command of this battle group.

At 0930 hours, the division received a mission:

Guard Remontnaja and the railway line. Enemy advancing west and southwest from the area around Ssawetnoje. Set up outposts at Ilinka [10 kilometers east of Remontnaja]. The new friendly forces to the right is the reinforced *Grenadier-Regiment 156 (mot.)* of the *16. Infanterie-Division (mot.)*, located in the Andrejewskaja — Jerketinskaja area.

Enemy attacks at Kommissarewskij were turned back, with five tanks being destroyed.

At 1045 hours, six enemy tanks drove the remnants of the *I./PGR128* from Lenina — Jablotschnaja and into the Bulgatschkina Defile. Two T-34's fell victim to German armor in the subsequent immediate counterattack, with two other tanks being damaged. The infantry got to catch their breath.

Around noon, larger Soviet infantry formations prepared for operations in the Ssemitschnaja Defile. Two German tanks were lost in the attempt to further reconnoiter the enemy forces. The divisional engineers were pulled back to Ssemitschnaja.

The *17. Panzer-Division* forced back enemy forces at Wassiljewskij in a counterattack. In the sector of the friendly forces on the right, however, the enemy entered the northern portion of Andrejewskaja.

Soviet deserters reported that the Soviet 63rd Rifle Brigade, supported by armor, would attack at 0500 hours on 31 December. Heavy Russian artillery, mortar and rocket-launcher fires initiated the attack on Ssemitschnaja at 0540 hours. German rocket launcher elements suffered numerous losses. Despite that, the enemy infantry was unable to reach the village in the face of the concentrated fires from the heavy weapons. After suffering heavy casualties, the enemy broke off the attack. Twenty T-34's then attempted to rally the enemy forces forward, but their number was reduced to five by the fires from the tanks, the *Flak* and the antitank guns. The remaining tanks pulled back.

Besides artillery barrages, additional ground attacks—up to battalion strength—were launched the entire day, but they were unable to achieve any success.

At the same time, enemy tanks and infantry appeared by surprise to the east along the road at Gaschun, 20 kilometers southwest of Remontnaja. Attacking southwest, they entered Simowniki, the location of the division's quartermaster. Panic broke out among the massed trains elements there, and numerous vehicles were lost. It was not until later in the day that elements of *SS-Panzer-Grenadier-Division "Wiking"* succeeded in stabilizing the situation in the village. The *SS* elements were supported by the *4./PAR128*. A main clearing station of the 1st Medical Company of *Oberstabsarzt Dr.* Ostmann treated *SS* wounded in Ilinka.

The *LVII. Panzer-Korps* issued orders for 1 January 1943 to pull back to the line Andrianoff — St. Pestschanyj on the south bank of the Bolshoj Kuberle. The reinforced *Grenadier-Regiment (mot.) 156*, which had been attached to the division, was to assume responsibility for securing the Remontnaja Bridgehead.

In the meantime, on New year's Eve, enemy tanks with infantry attacked Komissarewskij. An 8.8cm *Flak* knocked out several T-34's; two more were eliminated in direct fire at pointblank range by rocket launch-

36 Editor's Note: = 326th Guard Battalion (Bicycle).

ers. As the enemy infantry pulled back, *Stukas* attacked and dropped bombs, completely scattering the enemy force.

Strong enemy attacks forced the *17. Panzer-Division* to pull back at 1315 hours. A *Kampfgruppe* from the division's *Panzergrenadier-Regiment 63* became encircled in Wassiljewskij. *Panzer-Regiment 201* advanced on the village and enabled elements of the battle group to pull back. The enemy attempted again and again to envelop the German positions to the east and west.

Major Draffehn (commander of the *IV./PAR128*), *Hauptmann* David (Division Movement Officer) and *Major* Görlach (commander of the division's military police) were given the mission of shunting the division through the bottleneck at the Remontnaja Bridgehead. The difficult assignment was flawlessly executed.

The trains were sent far to the rear to an area 30 kilometers west of Proletarskaja, south of the Manytsch. *Major* von Einem, the commander of *PJA128*, assumed command of those elements.

At 1910 hours, the *Kampfgruppen* moved into their new defensive sectors. *Hauptmann* Tilemann's rearguards followed them. The latter's march route was illuminated for a long time due to the explosions and fires in the large Rumanian ammunition depot in Remontnaja. It was blown up before the enemy could get to it. As a result, a unique form of fireworks ushered in the New Year of 1943.

Defensive Fighting Along the Manytsch and Southeast of Rostov 1 January to 4 February 1943

Numerically superior Soviet field armies pushed the thin lines of the *4. Panzer-Armee* further and further from the Akssdaj to the southwest, but Hitler did not want to hear anything of abandoning the Caucasus Front. It was not until 29 December that the *1. Panzer-Armee* was allowed to pull back from the Terek to the Kuma River line between Pjatigorsk and Preskowaja. It was there that the field army was to establish contact with the *4. Panzer-Armee*, oriented to the east.

Before these movements could be undertaken, a group of Soviet forces advanced to the south from the Ssawetnoje area, some 50 kilometers southwest of Elista. By doing so, it threatened the deep left flank of the *1. Panzer-Armee*. The *16. Infanterie-Division (mot.)* was employed against these forces as expeditiously as possible. The division succeeded in fixing the enemy forces south of the Manytsch and eliminating the threat to the *1. Panzer-Armee*. That meant, however, that the division was no longer available for employment by the *4. Panzer-Armee* north of the Manytsch.

The weak forces that *Generaloberst* Hoth had at his disposal had to master a dual mission in the meantime. They had to hold open the rear of the *1. Panzer-Armee* along the Manytsch and secure the withdrawal movement of *Heeresgruppe A* out of the Caucasus. On their left wing, they had to prevent the threatened breakthrough of Soviet forces along the southern bank of the Don to the west and Rostov. If the enemy were to succeed in his intentions, that would mean that not only *Heeresgruppe A* but also the *4. Panzer-Armee* would be cut of from its rearward lines of communications.

Opposing the *4. Panzer-Armee*, which only had the *LVII. Panzer-Korps* with the *17. Panzer-Division* and the *23. Panzer-Division* at its disposal—both of which had been bled white—were the 28th, 51st and 2nd Armies (the latter a Guards Army). The likewise weak *SS-Panzer-Grenadier-Division "Wiking"* was on its way, and there were also a few general headquarters and *Flak* elements available to the German field army. Both the 51st Army and the 2nd Guards Army had one tank corps, three motorized/mechanized corps and one cavalry corps each.

Generalfeldmarschall von Manstein, the Commander-in-Chief of *Heeresgruppe Don*, decided to initially focus the defensive main effort on the right wing of the *4. Panzer-Armee* and secure contact with the *1. Panzer-Armee*. For defending the area between the Ssal and the Don, no additional forces could be made available, a situation the Soviets would soon take advantage of.

On New Year's 1943, the *23. Panzer-Division* and the *17. Panzer-Division* set up defensive positions along the west bank of the Bolschoi Kuberle. The *23. Panzer-Division* was between Adrianoff and St. Pestschanyj. To the division's right were weak elements from *SS-Panzer-Grenadier-Division "Wiking"*.

Kampfgruppe Beck-Broichsitter, reinforced by *Panzer-Kompanie Crömer* of the tank regiment and a company from *Grenadier-Regiment (mot.) 156*, was still screening around Remontnaja. To the south of the city, *Grenadier-Regiment (mot.) 156* (minus the one company) had set up a passage point for the *Kampfgruppe*.

The new commander of the divisional artillery, *Oberst Dr.* Born, arrived in the division sector.

Kampfgruppe Beck-Broichsitter defeated two advances by enemy infantry, supported by antitank guns and armored cars, in the morning. In an immediate counterattack, *Panzer-Kompanie Crömer* destroyed five trucks, one armored car and one antitank gun. At 1015 hours, the battle group evacuated Remontnaja in the face of large Russian concentrations. The *I./Panzergrenadier-Regiment 40* and *Sturmgeschütz-Abteilung 203* returned to the control of the *17. Panzer-Division*.

While *PAR128* encountered and destroyed a T-34 during its movement through Simowniki, *Kampfgruppe von Heydebreck* set up positions to the right along the Kuberle, while *Kampfgruppe Bachmann* defended in the left-hand sector. The *SPW* Battalion had only 4 operational half-tracks left; the tank regiment, including *Panzer-Kompanie Crömer*, had 19 operational tanks.

Several patrols maintained contact with the enemy, who initially only followed hesitantly. On 3 January, the division's sector was extended to the south as far as, and including, Ostrowjanskij.

All non-essential personnel of the trains, which were located in the Sselem — Bratskaja — Kalinina — Bagodatnaja — Plodorotnaja area, were formed into combat elements under the command and control of *Major* von Einem and were used to screen along the banks of the Manytsch. *Oberleutnant* Schlingmann from *PPB51* formed an alert company out of elements from his battalion and the trains.

The enemy approached the right wing of the division. Twenty enemy tanks, accompanied by 300 men, occupied Orechow, 20 kilometers to the north of the large salt lake. Aerial reconnaissance indicated cavalry and infantry elements marching west from there. Three enemy tanks advanced as far as 3 kilometers east of Ostrowjanskij. When Russian columns reached Imeni Lenina with 200 vehicles and tanks, the signs of the enemy's intent—to break through to Proletarskaja—became clear.

SS-Panzer-Grenadier-Regiment "Germania", which was located south of the division, was supported by the divisional artillery. *Kampfgruppe Bachmann* was pulled out of its former sector and positioned south of Kurmojarskij for mobile operations. At the same time, the corps brought *Oberstleutnant* Post's *schwere Panzer-Abteilung 503*, the first *Tiger* battalion capable of being deployed at the front, forward to Stepnoje, 30 kilometers east of Proletarskaja.

The enemy continued to move up. Soviet columns drove with headlights turned on south of Andrianoff. Three hundred Russian soldiers dismounted from trucks 3 kilometers east of Ostrowjanskij. Most of the enemy came from the north and turned west at the southern wing of the division.

Ninety replacements for the *SPW* Battalion arrived at the rail station in Kuberle. They were sent to their battalion on foot because of a shortage of transport capacity. The division was instructed to release *Pionier-Lehr-Bataillon 1* to work on embankments along the Manytsch. Succeeding

Departing the Caucasus in November 1942 to participate in the relief effort for Stalingrad.

Tigers are seen for the first time.

Repainting vehicles at Proletarskaya.

Leutnant Danzer, regimental liaison officer, during the relief effort.

German infantry in former Soviet trenches.

Supply elements of *PGR 126* on its way to the Mius on 10 February 1943.

Peasantry in the Bataisk area.

21cm howitzer positioned along the Aksaj. This is a corps artillery asset.

Despite the fighting, this peasant continues with his business.

Under Soviet artillery fire.

What appears to be a 10.5cm battery firing at Sowchose I.

The *II./PAR 128*, with their 10.5cm howitzers, in open firing positions on the Kalmuck Steppes, south of Aksaj.

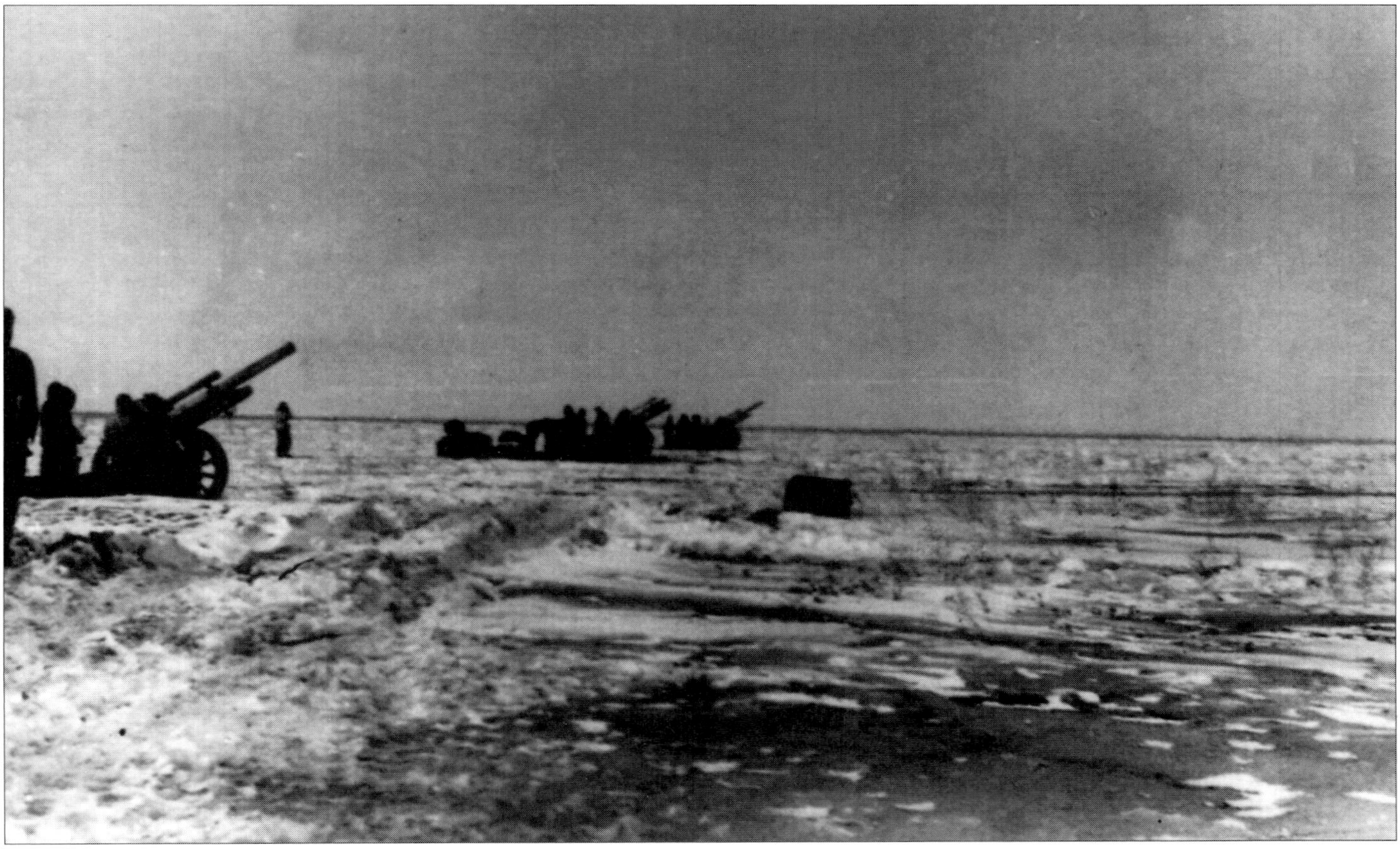

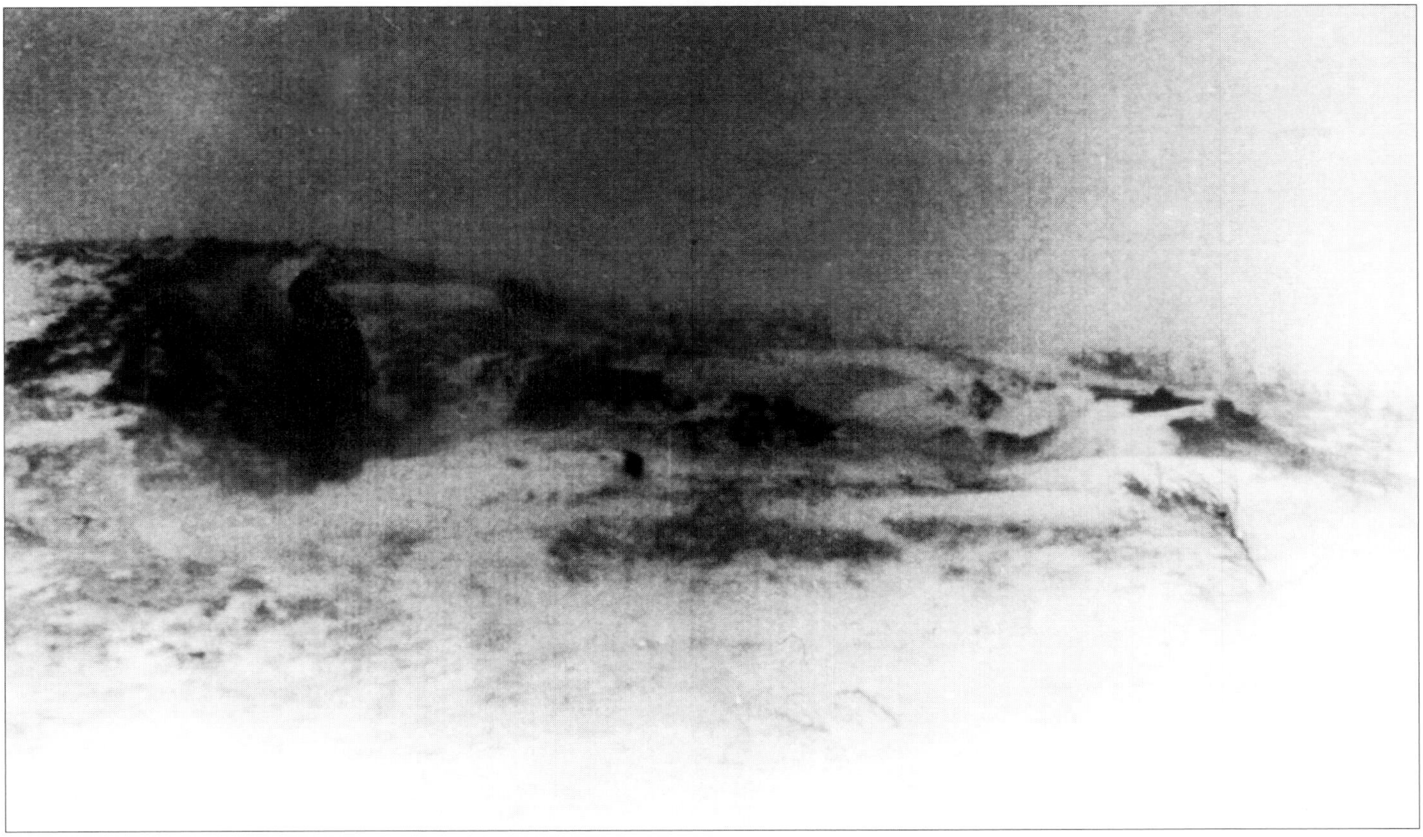

An artillery observation post in the middle of a snowstorm.

Due to the loss of guns, a company of artillerymen was formed that served as infantry.

An artilleryman stands guard at the command post, while an armored engagement rages in the background.

The retreat at Kotelnikowo.

Oberleutnant Rebentisch helps prepare the division's daily logs in his capacity as the Assistant Operations Officer (Rostov, January 1943).

Bitterly cold at Rostov. While the German army was now better able to cope with its second winter in Russia, it was still not what you could call elaborately supplied with cold weather equipment.

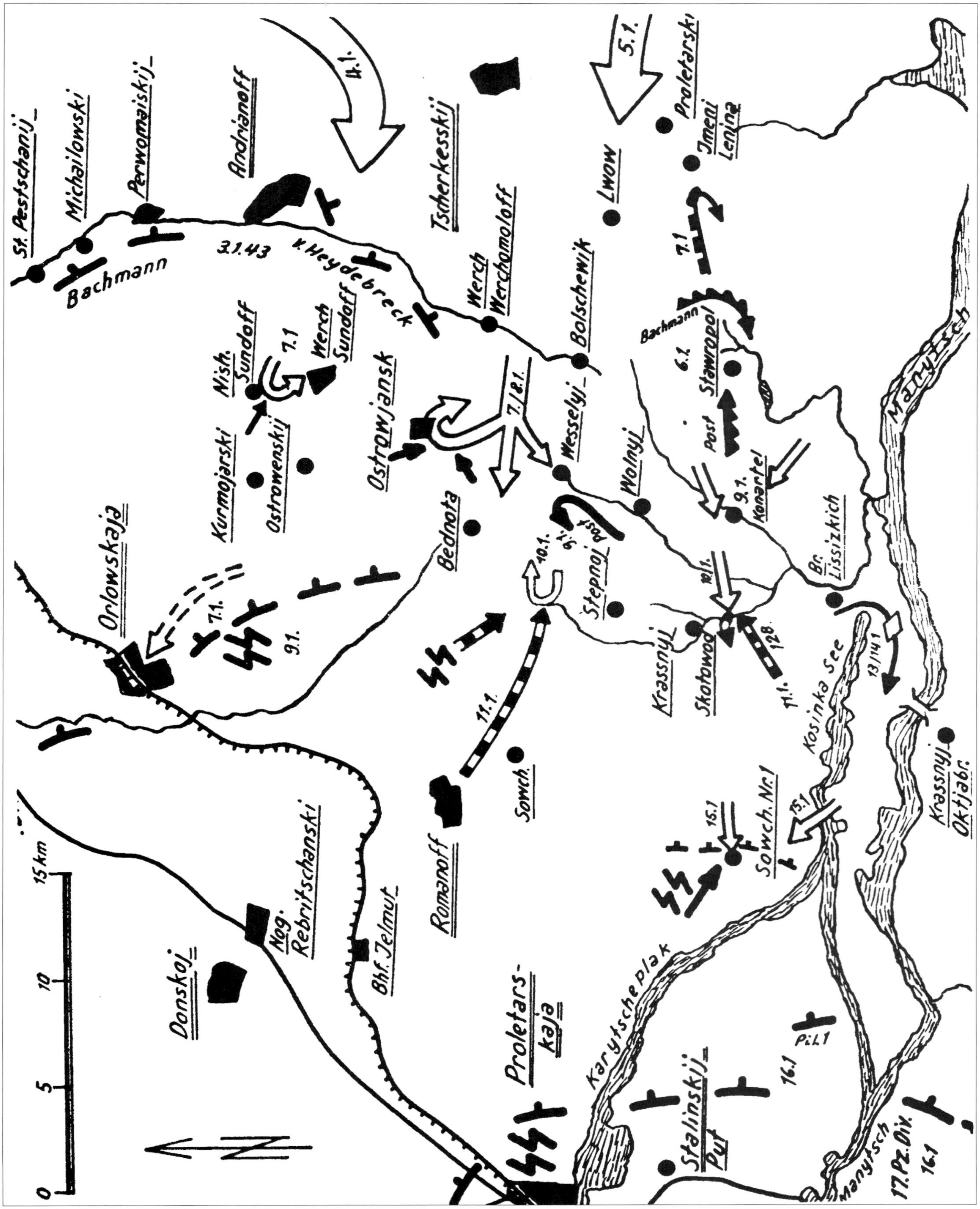

Map 27: Defensive Fighting Between the Kuberle and the Manytsch.

Hauptmann Stiewe in acting command of the *I./PR201* was *Hauptmann* Behr. *Hauptmann* Stiewe was sent to a commander's course.

At 0625 hours on 5 January, aerial reconnaissance reported a 3000-man, mixed-arms column moving west southeast of Nowo-Sselowka. Three enemy tanks were in Stawropol, and enemy infantry was following them. Other enemy infantry forces were caught by *Stukas* while dismounting from trucks south of Andrianoff; the forces was scattered with considerable casualties. Tscherkesskij was occupied by the enemy.

At 0920 hours, a Soviet battalion went around *Kampfgruppe von Heydebreck* to the south and advanced to the west at Werchne Werchomoloff. *Kampfgruppe Bachmann* (minus the *II./PGR128*), reinforced by *Panzer-Abteilung Tilemann*, counterattacked. In addition, artillery and rocket launchers inflicted heavy losses on the enemy force.

At Stawropol, *schwere Panzer-Abteilung 503*[37] encountered enemy tanks and antitank guns. The *Tigers* pulled back to Krassnyj Skotowod. The *II./PGR128* was sent there, temporarily motorized through the assistance of *SS-Panzer-Grenadier-Regiment "Germania"*. After overcoming heavy enemy resistance in the form of antitank guns and infantry, *Kampfgruppe Bachmann* took Andrianoff and pushed the enemy back to the southeast. At the same time, the enemy in front of *Kampfgruppe von Heydebreck* pulled back.

In accordance with the corps order, it was the division's intention to attack with its battle groups from the area around Ostrowjanskij during the morning of 6 January and eliminate the enemy around Stawropol.

The *1./PJA128* was attached to *SS-Panzer-Grenadier-Regiment "Germania"* and went into position at Kuberle.

At 0545 hours on 6 January, *Kampfgruppe Bachmann*, together with *Panzer-Abteilung Tilemann*, moved out to the south and reached the high ground west of Lwow while encountering only weak enemy resistance. *Kampfgruppe Post*, consisting of the *Tigers* and the *II./PGR128*, moved out from Krassnyj Skotowod at the same time, but it encountered strong resistance from enemy tanks after a short period. In heavy snow squalls, *Panzer-Abteilung Tilemann* advanced as far as 5 kilometers east of Stawropol, while the *Tiger* battalion fought its way to Stawropol from the west, knocking out 13 enemy tanks in the process. *Hauptmann* Claussen's *II./PGR128* suffered considerable casualties; the battalion commander was wounded but stayed with his men. *Kampfgruppe Bachmann* turned to the west and caught the enemy in the rear at Stawropol. The village was taken, and several antitank guns and artillery pieces, as well as several trucks, were destroyed. The enemy fled south.

At Konartel, west of Stawropol, the *Tigers* knocked out another five enemy tanks At 1335 hours, the battle groups linked up. *Kampfgruppe Post* was attached to *Oberst* Bachmann. While assault detachments from *Hauptmann* Stetting's *I./PGR128* followed the enemy south as far as the Manytsch, *Stukas* and fighter-bombers attacked the fleeing enemy columns with good success.

The spoils of war counted from the fighting around Stawropol: 60 prisoners, 18 knocked-out enemy tanks, 3 antitank guns, 1 artillery piece, 3 antitank rifles, 6 horse-drawn carriages and 2 trucks.

In the meantime, the enemy became stronger in front of *Kampfgruppe von Heydebreck*. Andrianoff had to be left to an attacking enemy battalion.

On 7 January, *Kampfgruppe Bachmann* advanced from Stawropol against Imeni Lenina and Lwow. Well supported by infantry and rocket launchers, the effort succeeded in dislodging the Red infantry from Lenina. Enemy tanks were in the village, however, and prevented any further advance by the artillery. The enemy was supported by heavy weapons to the south and southeast. The advance of *Panzer-Abteilung Tilemann* on Lenina got bogged down along the edge of the village along a deeply cut *Balka*. The battalion was only able to disengage from the enemy after losing a *Panzer III*. One enemy antitank gun was destroyed.

At the same time, *schwere Panzer-Abteilung 503* advanced across Lake Goloje as far as the Manytsch. Its employment against Lenina from the south was stopped by a corps order, which ordered the battalion back to Proletarskaja.

The enemy continuously brought reinforcements forward. Infantry reoccupied Lenina. In addition, infantry, supported by tanks and antitank guns, occupied the villages of Michailowskij and Proletarski as well. *Kampfgruppe Bachmann* held positions with its 2nd Battalion , reinforced by a rocket launcher battalion and a light field artillery battalion, to the west of Lenina and blocked the Nowosselowka — Stawropol road along the Chorewaja Defile. The *I./PGR128* was ordered to Stawropol; *PPB51* to Wesselyl, where *Panzer-Abteilung Tilemann* was also assembling. *Oberst* Dietrich, the commander of *Werfer-Regiment 54*, assumed command of the former *Kampfgruppe von Heydebreck*, with the headquarters of *PR201* being pulled out of the line.

Based on the enemy's massing of forces around Lenina, the division anticipated the Soviet attack moving through Bolschewik and on to either Wesselyj or Stawropol. Dense snow began to fall at the onset of darkness.

At 2300 hours, the Russians attacked the *SPW* Battalion and entered Nischne Sundoff, despite stiff resistance. Far to the west, at 0300 hours on 8 January, a line repair party sent out by the corps signals battalion ran into a Russian column of 70 *Panje* carts and a few motorized vehicles. Exploiting the snowstorm, they had bypassed the German strongpoints and had soon occupied Orlowskaja. Other than logistics elements, there were no German forces in the village. The main clearing station of the division's 1st Medical Company was attacked by Soviet riflemen at first light. The medical personnel had to grab weapons to defend themselves and the wounded. They succeeded in pushing back the Soviets, allowing all 58 badly wounded and the clearing station platoon to leave the village to the southwest in the direction of Proletarskaja. One medical soldier was killed by a head wound.

At the same time, the *SPW* Battalion, supported by elements of *Pionier-Lehr-Bataillon 1*, succeeded in its immediate counterattack on Nish. Sundoff. By 0500 hours, the village was again in German hands, and the enemy was pursued to the east.

At 0400 hours, the local security for the division headquarters in Wesselyj caught a Russian soldier, who stated that 500 men were approaching the village. Three hundred Russians massed in a collective farm south of Ostrowjanskij; further west, they blocked the Wesselyj — Ostrowjanskij road and attacked the latter village from the south. The enemy entered the southern edge of the village with tanks. At the same time, additional enemy forces infiltrated further west in company-sized elements, concealed by the snowstorm. A Russian battalion, supported by an armored car and several trucks, suddenly attacked Wesselyj. The armored car and three trucks were set alight by 2cm *Flak* and riflemen; two more trucks were captured.

The division ordered a counterattack by *Kampfgruppe Dietrich* in Ostrowjanskij and, at the same time, *Panzer-Abteilung Tilemann*, together with *PPB51*, against the southern edge of Ostrowjanskij. A corps-planned operation by *Panzergruppe Dietrich* at Orlowskaja had to be cancelled, especially since the battle group was being attacked from the front.

Panzer-Abteilung Tilemann, together with engineers, ejected a Soviet battalion supported by three tanks from the shores farm 2 kilometers south of Ostrowjanskij. In the village proper, however, the enemy attack against the *ad hoc* rifle company composed of artillerymen from *PAR128* and a few *Flak* was making progress. *Panzergruppe Tilemann*, arriving at the village at 1100 hours, received heavy tank and antitank-gun fires from the south side of the village.

37 Editor's Note: This was one of the first *Tiger* battalions, a general headquarters formation.

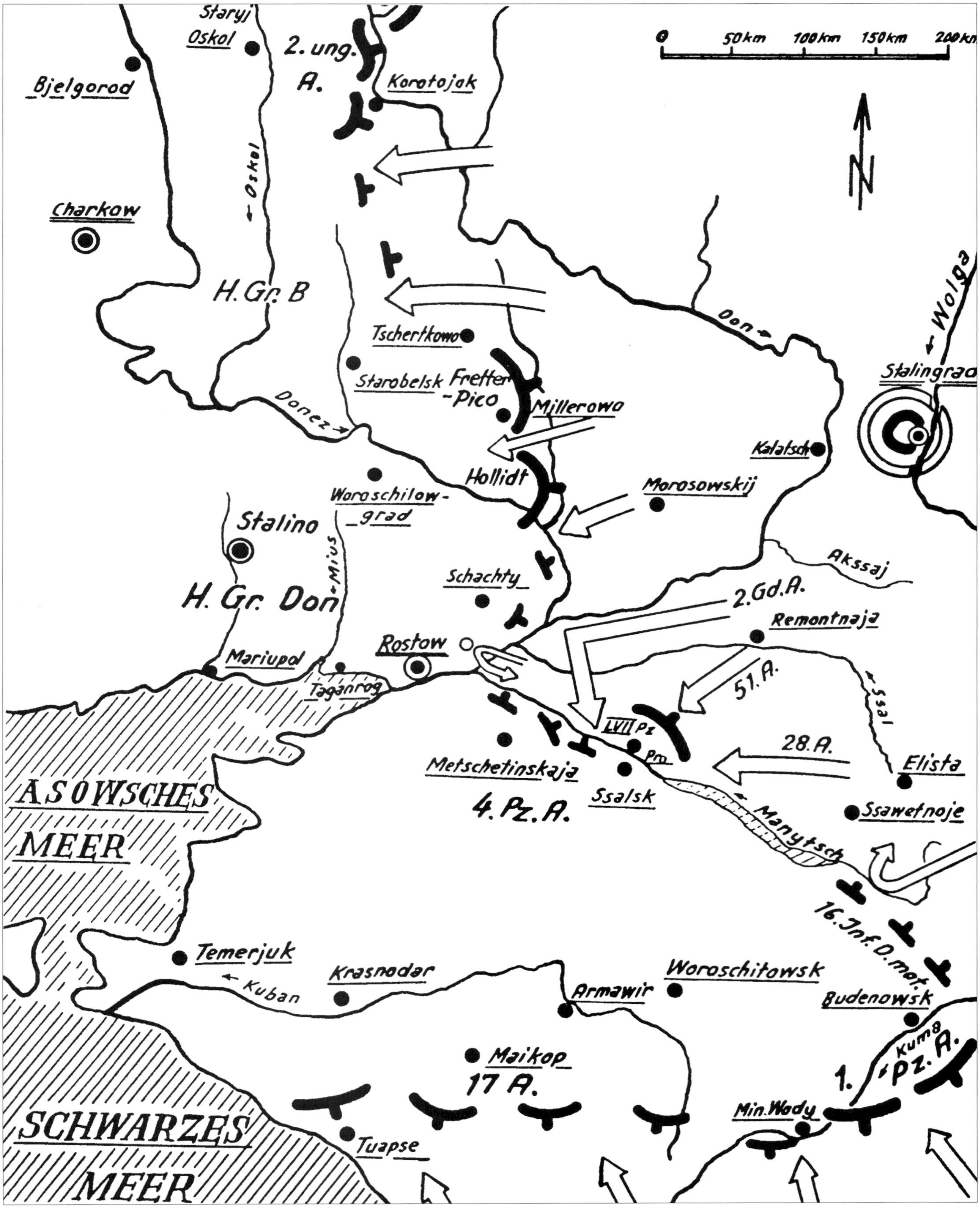

Map 28: The Over-All Situation on 9 January 1943.

Wesselyj, which was only being held by the division headquarters and weak artillery elements, was attacked by a Soviet regiment at 1130 hours. While the command and control section moved back to Krassnyj Skotowod, the acting division commander succeeded in leading the *II./PGR128*, which was arriving in the snowstorm, into Wesselyj and launching an immediate counterattack. The enemy was pushed back to the hill 1 kilometer east of Wesselyj, where three enemy tanks brought the German advance to a standstill. Enemy infantry soon started to go around the village to the south. The constant efforts to bypass resistance indicated that the enemy was placing a great deal of value on moving as rapidly to the west as possible.

Late in the afternoon, as it started to turn dusk, a Russian infantry regiment once again attacked the weak *II./PGR128* in Wesselyj. The Russians were supported by tanks. Without armor-defeating weapons, the battalion was unable to hold and pulled back to Nikolajewskij at 1550 hours. Pursued by tanks and motorized infantry, the battalion was unable to gain a foothold there and had to pull back further to Romanoff.

Kampfgruppe Bachmann, which had not been attacked in its positions around Stawropol and Wolnyj during this time, screened toward the northeast at Wolnyj. The enemy continued to march in front of the battle group to the northwest.

The *SPW* Battalion joined the continued fighting for Ostrowjanskij, by moving in from the north at 1620 hours. At the same time, *Panzergruppe Tilemann* attacked again from the south. Building after building was torn from the enemy, and Ostrowjanskij was cleared by 1900 hours.

The supply situation for *Panzergruppe Tilemann* was extremely critical. There were only 40 armor-piercing rounds left, along with 10% of the authorized basic load of machine-gun ammunition. There was only enough fuel for moving 40 kilometers.

SS-Panzer-Grenadier-Division "Wiking" was able to master the situation in Orlowskaja with the forces it had available in the course of the day. Five self-propelled antitank guns from the *1./PJA128* attacked with *SS-Pionier-Bataillon 5* and ejected the Russians from the village to the east and south, inflicting heavy losses on them. More than 800 enemy dead were counted.

The deep penetration in the middle of the division's sector forced it to pull back *Kampfgruppe Bachmann* during the night of 8/9 January. It occupied new positions on both sides of Konartel.

Just as the situation within the *23. Panzer-Division* was extremely tense on 8 and 9 January, so too was the situation within the areas of operation of *Heeresgruppe A*, *Heeresgruppe Don* and *Heeresgruppe B*. In the course of its withdrawal movements, the *1. Panzer-Armee* still had not reached the Kuma. The Soviet intention of enveloping the *4. Panzer-Armee* on both sides through attacks by three field armies was becoming increasingly clearer. While the Soviet 28th Army was attacking west along the Manytsch, the III Guards Tank Corps had reached Konstantinowka on the Don and was turning south in order to move past the German formations and on to Proletarskaja. Weaker enemy formations were already crossing the Don northeast of Nowotscherkassk. *Armee-Abteilung Hollidt*, in the great bend of the Don, was pulling back to the Kagelnik. *Armee-Abteilung Fretter-Pico*, with its weak forces, was fighting for Millerowo in the gap created in the front by the collapse of the Rumanians and the Italian 8th Army. By order of Hitler, the *6. Armee* in Stalingrad turned down the Russian capitulation offer.

At the time, the *4. Panzer-Armee* had orders to hold its lines under all conditions northeast of Proletarskaja. The mission assigned to the division by the *LVII. Panzer-Korps* on 9 January was the recapture of Wesselyj with *Kampfgruppe Post* (*schwere Panzer-Abteilung 503* and the *II./PGR128*) and defensive operations by *Kampfgruppe Bachmann* and *Kampfgruppe Dietrich* in the positions they were then holding.

The *II./PGR128* was ordered to move from Romanoff through Nikolajewskij to Krassnyj Skotowod. In the meantime, the enemy reinforced his elements around Wesselyj and placed harassing fires on Stawropol.

At 0630 hours, the new acting commander of the division, *Oberst d.G.*[38] Nikolaus von Vormann, arrived at the division command post. *Oberst* Roßmann returned to the corps in his previous capacity as the corps artillery commander *Arko 121*.

At 0645 hours, *Kampfgruppe Post* initiated its attack with11 *Tigers* and 12 *Panzer III's*. The *II./PGR128*, supported by a light artillery battery, followed the attack on the trails. *Schwere Panzer-Abteilung 503* was soon 2 kilometers west of Wesselyj; a Russian immediate counterattack was turned back. At 0935 hours, tanks and infantry attacked Wesselyj. Numerous T-34's, and probably also some KV-I's, as well as concentrations of antitank and antiaircraft guns, brought the German attack to a standstill. The acting division commander personally ordered the battle group to attack again. A third attack did not bring success, despite considerable sacrifice. Eight T-34's were destroyed. The Russians fought bitterly. A recklessly maneuvering T-34 was damaged. Although its turret was jammed, it broke through the German tank lines and made it to the artillery position, where it overran a gun and damaged a second one, before a third artillery piece knocked it out. At the end of the day, the *Tiger* battalion only had two operational *Tigers* at its disposal[39]. The infantry had taken heavy losses; in addition, they suffered terribly from the clear and cold snowy weather. *Oberstleutnant* Post pulled his battle group back to Bednota.

In the sector of *Kampfgruppe Bachmann*, the enemy attacked at 1015 hours. One enemy regiment reached the area south of Stawropol and, at the same time, a battalion attacked Konartel from the north.

A Russian attack conducted by two battalions outside of Ostrowjanskij collapsed as it turned dusk. The defender's ability to resist was dwindling, however. Only seven tanks of Tilemann's battalion were operational. Of those, only three were *Panzer IV's* with long barrels. The divisional engineers reported a trench strength of 6 officers, 14 noncommissioned officers and 96 enlisted men. Ammunition stocks had been consumed, for the most part.

While the division was involved in heavy fighting east of the important crossing over the Manytsch at Proletarskaja, the enemy forces operating between the Ssal and the Don had turned south. Ever since 5 January, security groups formed from the trains and local militias that were familiar with the area routes had been covering the area as far as the Manytsch and to the north of it. After many Russian patrols had felt their way forward, a *Panzerschützen-Bataillon* was formed on 8 January, consisting of two companies of trains personnel and tankless crews from *PR201*. Logistics for this *ad hoc* battalion was the responsibility of *Hauptmann* Burmester; its tactical command and control was by *Major* von Einem, who also had a company formed from the trains personnel of *PGR128* at his disposal.

On the same day, Soviet forces crossed over to the southern bank of the Manytsch, using the intact bridge at Wesselyj Chutor. A rail transport of replacement tanks for the *23. Panzer-Division*, which by chance happened to arrive and detrain in Ssalsk on that same 8 January, was ordered by the field army headquarters to report to *Major* von Einem. Under the command of *Hauptmann* Behr, the new tanks attacked the enemy on 9 January, along with the infantry companies composed of tank crews. They took Wesselyj Chutor and threw the Soviets back across the Manytsch to

38 Editor's Note: = *des Generalstabes* = of the General Staff. This designation applied to officers who had been on the General Staff but who had been released back to troop duty.

39 Editor's Note: It should be noted that *schwere Panzer-Abteilung 503* had been rushed to the front. It only had two of its three companies, and these companies still had the original "mixed" organization with both short-barreled *Panzer III's* and *Tiger I's*. Thus, the *Tiger* battalion really only had the strength of one full-sized *Tiger* company.

the north. The bridge was then blown up, and a combat outpost line was established along the river. The newly arrived tanks then marched to the division at Proletarskaja.

What remained of the division's field-replacement battalion was distributed among the two infantry regiments. The trains then returned to the command of the division logistics officer.

In the sector east of Proletarskaja, the enemy continued to exert pressure on a broad front, with his main effort directed at Wesselyj. The division ordered *Panzer-Abteilung Tilemann* and the engineer battalion to move from Ostrowjansk, even those formations were in the process of fending off an enemy attack that was taking place at the time. One tank was lost.

Starting at 1445 hours, between one or two Soviet regiments started attacking *Kampfgruppe Bachmann* in Konartel. It was only the magnificent support rendered by a rocket-launcher battalion and 2cm *Flak* that made it possible for the weak *I./PGR128* to fend off the enemy. The ammunition stockpiles of the rocket launchers soon diminished, however, and the Russians entered Konartel from the north. *Kampfgruppe Bachmann* pulled back 4 kilometers to the west to a blocking position along the Krjukowskaja Defile.

In accordance with its orders, *Panzer-Abteilung Tilemann* departed Ostrowjanskij; those remaining behind were subjected to enemy attacks that were becoming increasingly stronger. Under the cover of darkness, the Russians entered the village. At 2135 hours, *Oberst* Dietrich reported that half of the village had been lost. Contact was lost with the strongpoint at Nish. Sundoff. Friendly losses were considerable; the enemy, on the other hand, was constantly introducing new forces. Under the heavy pressure exerted by the enemy, the forces of *Oberst* Dietrich had to pull back more and more into the northern part of the village. Infantry, engineers from the instructional battalion, cannoneers, and crewmembers from *Flak* and rocket launchers clung to the last remaining houses of the village, both defending and conducting immediate counterattacks. The acting commander of the *SPW* Battalion, *Oberleutnant* Kappauf, and two of his company commanders were killed in the selfless performance of their duties. *Oberst* Dietrich, fighting with his men at the very front, served to rally them again and again. In the end, however, the village was lost. The battle group occupied a new position on both sides of Kundrjutschenskij, abutting the right wing of *SS-Panzer-Grenadier-Division "Wiking"*.

At 0100 hours on 10 January, the division ordered *Kampfgruppe Bachmann* to pull back to the line Krassnyj Skotowod and to the south of it. Combat outposts were to remain in contact with the enemy.

In Nikolajewskij, the enemy attacked the *II./PGR128* from the south. *Panzer-Abteilung Tilemann* was ordered to move forward expeditiously from Orlowskaja, where it had arrived at 0330 hours to be resupplied. However, at 0445 hours, the *II./PGR128* withdrew from Nikolajewskij, losing one Model 18 light artillery piece in the process. Pursued by tanks, the fought-out, decimated battalion pulled back through Romanoff to the southwest. It then received orders by radio: "Hold Romanoff to the last man. Tilemann approaching from Orlowskaja." The battalion turned around and took possession of Romanoff again.

During the morning hours of 10 January, the *LVII. Panzer-Korps* ordered *Kampfgruppe Dietrich* to be relieved by *SS-Panzer-Grenadier-Division "Wiking"*. The battle group was moved to Romanoff. The acting division commander expected the enemy's main attack effort to be in the area of Krassnyj Skotowod. The combat power of the division, especially that of *PGR128*, had sunk to alarming levels as a result of the fighting of the past few days.

At 0950 hours, the new commander of *PGR126*, *Oberstleutnant* Winning, arrived. He was given command of the former *Kampfgruppe Dietrich*, when *Oberst* Dietrich and his headquarters for *Werfer-Regiment 54* were pulled out of the line. In the recent fighting, *Oberst* Dietrich and his headquarters had proven themselves time and again. A battery from *Sturmgeschütz-Abteilung 203* and other elements of the division that were in Romanoff were also attached to *Oberstleutnant* Winning. He was given the mission of taking back Nikolajewskij in a counterattack.

Stukas shattered Russian concentrations in the Jelmuta Defile and, in a sortie that followed, they caught Soviet infantry between Konartel and Krassnyj Skotowod. The enemy pulled back in disarray.

As it started to turn dark, the enemy again moved against Krassnyj Skotowod, this time with heavy infantry elements and three tanks. The attack collapsed in the face of concentrated fires from all weapons in front of the sectors of the *1.* and *5./PGR128*. There was another attack wave at 1620 hours, however. The weakened *PGR128*, with its many inexperienced replacement personnel, personnel impressed into service when returning from leave and convalescents, was unable to hold the Russians. The lack of cohesiveness in the ranks of the infantry, increasingly thinned and insufficiently replaced, as well as the increasing lack of experienced officers and noncommissioned officers, had allowed its combat effectiveness to sink too low.

Entering Krassnyj Skotowod from three sides, the enemy wrested control of it, house by house. The *I./PGR128* pulled back. Officers of the regiment rallied it 1.5 kilometers west of the village. *Oberst* von Vormann ordered the village to be immediately retaken by all available means. To assist in the command and control of the battalion, *Major i.G.* Freyer, *Hauptmann* Beck-Broichsitter and *Oberleutnant* Senk, the division's assistance intelligence officer, were sent forward. The counterattack started at 1830 hours. Moving at the head of the companies, the officers broke into the Soviet lines. *Major i.G.* Freyer entered the southern part of the village. *Oberleutnant* Senk was killed. *Hauptmann* Beck-Broichsitter, *Oberst* Bachmann and Bachmann's adjutant were wounded. The western part of the village was cleared, but the Russians stayed put in the eastern half. The fighting raged back and forth, with no decision reached.

The 11th of January started with the sudden advance of Russian tanks with mounted infantry into the assembly area of *Kampfgruppe von Winning* around Romanoff. Three T-34's were knocked out in front of the village; one T-34 entered the village. From a distance of 10 meters, an artillery piece set it alight. The enemy infantry set up in a trench, where they were eliminated to the last man in close combat with personnel from *Pionier-Lehr-Bataillon 1*.

Eleven tanks under the command of *Hauptmann* Behr arrived and were immediately sent forward to Krassnyj Skotowod.

The acting division commander personally participated in the attack by *Kampfgruppe von Winning*. *Schwere Panzer-Abteilung 503* was reattached to the division and further attached to *Oberstleutnant* von Winning, whose forces moved out at 1000 hours. At the same time, a *Kampfgruppe* from *SS-Panzer-Grenadier-Regiment "Germania"* moved out from Kundrjutschenskij on Nikolajewskij. The enemy in front of *Kampfgruppe von Winning* defended bitterly. The *Tigers* eliminated an armored car, two 6-gun batteries of 7.62cm cannon, a 7.62cm antitank gun, three 4.7cm antitank guns, as well as several prime movers. Forty prisoners were brought in; the number of enemy dead was strikingly high.

The *SS* encountered less resistance and reached the area west of Nikolajewskij, while *Kampfgruppe von Wining* continued to be engaged in heavy fighting in the deeply cut Jelmuta Defile.

The renewed attack by the *I./PGR128* in Krassnyj Skotowod, also at 1000 hours, did not lead to the expansion of the penetration in the western part of the village until after several attempts. *Major i.G.* Freyer, fighting once again with the troops, was wounded. It was primarily thanks to him that the penetration had succeeded in the first place.

At 1330 hours, *Kampfgruppe von Winning* advanced to Nikolajewskij and linked up with the *SS*. *Oberst* von Vormann employed the *Tiger* battalion from Nikolajewskij to the east with the intent of shattering an enemy counterattack. He ordered the rest of *Kampfgruppe von Winning* to Romanoff, where it was to prepare for operations at Krassnyj Skotowod. The struggle there for each building continued.

A massed Soviet counterattack shortly after the onset of darkness inflicted heavy casualties on the *I./PGR128*. Finally, at 1645 hours, the entire village had to be abandoned, after even the tanks of *Hauptmann* Behr were no longer able to hold it in the face of enemy antitank gun reinforcements. *Hauptmann* Stetting, the commander of the *I./PGR128*, was wounded. The last 50 infantrymen of the battalion returned to their initial jumping-off points west of the village.

It was quiet in the area of the trains south of the Manytsch. Patrols established contact with elements of the *16. Infanterie-Division (mot.)*, which was covering the area north of the river between the *17. Panzer-Division* and the Don.

At 0500 hours on 12 January, *Kampfgruppe von Winning—PR201*, one each assault-gun battery from *Sturmgeschütz-Abteilung 203* and *Sturmgeschütz-Abteilung 243*, the *SPW* Battalion, *PPB51* and *Pionier-Lehr-Bataillon 1*—moved from Romanoff, crossed through Jelmut and Collective Farm No. 1 and attacked Krassnyj Skotowod. Its attack was supported by the entire divisional artillery and the *II./Werfer-regiment 54*.

The *II./PGR128* was sent to Proletarskaja to undergo a battlefield reconstitution. For the first time since December, a field element from the division was thus able be taken out of the front lines temporarily. *Hauptmann i.G.* Litterscheid, previously a staff officer with the *4. Panzer-Armee*, arrived and assumed the duties of the wounded division operations officer.

While *Kampfgruppe von Winning* only made slow progress in difficult terrain, two ground-attack aircraft and assault guns shattered a Russian infantry attack directed against the *I./PGR128*.

At 1400 hours, *Kampfgruppe von Winning* attacked Krassnyj Skotowod from the south. The rapid onset of darkness, the bitterly cold temperature and the difficulty of the terrain did not allow the attack to develop a full head of steam. In addition, a salvo of rockets from German launchers also landed in the midst of the infantry. *Pionier-Lehr-Bataillon 1* alone suffered 75 casualties. The acting division commander broke off the attack and ordered that defensive positions be established west of the village. *Pionier-Lehr-Bataillon 1* became the division reserve.

The tank regiment commander, *Oberst* von Heydebreck, a multifaceted, highly respected and tried-and-true officer, was transferred to the *17. Panzer-Division* at the request of the *4. Panzer-Armee* and that armored division. He was to become the commander of that division's *Panzer-Regiment 39*. Assuming command of *PR201* in his place was *Oberstleutnant* Sander. *Hauptmann* Tilemann, the commander of the *II./PR201* became the commander of the rear-area services of the tank regiment by order of the division commander. *Hauptmann* Behr, the commander of the *I./PR201*, assumed command of the remaining operational tanks of the regiment.

At 0500 hours on 13 January, five German tanks and two assault guns moved south to clear the spit of land south of Lake Kosinka of the enemy. A weak enemy force was completely wiped out; several motorized vehicles and horse-drawn wagons, as well as two antitank guns, fell victim to the German armored force. To the north of Krassnyj Oktjabr, the enemy fled from a farm, but then the armored element encountered a strong infantry and antitank-gun position blocking the bridge over the Manytsch. *Stukas* attacked the friendly forces, with one tank catching fire and the remaining armored vehicles all receiving battle damage. At that point, the leader of the element called off the advance.

Over the division sector, *Flak* shot down an IL-2.

During the night of 13/14 January, the *II./PGR128* relieved its sister 1st Battalion.

A single T-60, which advanced as far as the farm 7 kilometers southwest of Krassnyj Skotowod in the morning at 0500 hours was destroyed and its crew captured.

At 0600 hours, *Hauptmann* Behr moved out with 12 tanks and 2 assault guns against the eastern tip of Lake Kosinka. On the road near Br. Lissizkich, four enemy trucks loaded with riflemen were shot to pieces, an 7.62cm antitank gun was run over and an armored vehicle was forced to stop. Its crew, including a liaison officer from the Soviet 28th Army, was captured. An operations order for the 28th Army was captured, which only listed the enemy forces in front of it as being the *23. Panzer-Division*. The Russian intent was to attack with its main effort on both sides of the Krassnyj Skotowod — Proletarskaja road with freshly introduced forces and advance with a southern group across the spit of land south of Lake Kosinka, through Krassnyj Oktjaber and on to Ssalsk.

Pionier-Lehr-Bataillon 1 was employed south of Collective farm No. 1 to screen between the two arms of the Manytsch.

Panzergruppe Behr, while advancing west, encountered the antitank-gun belt that had been identified the previous day south of Lake Kosinka. Behr's tanks bypassed this defensive obstacle to the south, reached the area 2 kilometers north of Krassnyj Oktjabr and eliminated 30 *panje* carts at the bridge crossing. Further to the west, relatively strong Soviet infantry formations, supported by tanks, were concentrating along the spit of land.

Strong enemy forces approached the division's front. From Nikolajewskij alone, some 14-18 company-sized elements were observed marching out. A regimentally sized formation turned south when it was west of Nikolajewskij and attacked the *SPW* Battalion 5 kilometers northwest of Krassnyj Skotowod. Shortly thereafter, five T-34's with infantry on them advanced out of Krassnyj Skotowod. Two assault guns knocked out one of the T-34's and damaged another three. The enemy attack collapsed, as did the one against the *SPW* Battalion. Weak enemy forces were able to infiltrate in the gap between the *SPW* Battalion and the artillery positions, however. The gun section of the *1./PAR128* ran into Soviet infantry in the middle of a position change. It was not until after close combat that breathing room was created to continue the march to the new position.

A separate submachine-gun battalion appeared in front of the positions of *Pionier-Lehr-Bataillon 1*. According to statements made by deserters, the battalion was supposed to take Collective farm No. 1 from the south during the night of 14/15 January.

Given the situation, the acting division commander recommended to the corps that the division frontage be shortened by pulling it back to a new screening line. The corps' initial orders were to move all non-essential trains elements back behind the Manytsch and to have the division pull back to a line on both sides of Collective Farm No. 1. Before the orders could be carried out, the enemy attacked the *II./PGR128* with strong forces and ejected it from its positions. Assault guns knocked out one enemy tank and damaged another. The artillery had to change positions in the middle of the Russian infantry attack. As a result, one Model 18 light field howitzer and one 8.8cm *Flak* were lost. Further to the north, the *SPW* Battalion had to fight its way back through the Russian forces advancing past it to the south. The battalion had only two operational *SPW's*, which were used to cover the movement and support the fighting.

The division engineers reported a trench strength of 4 officers, 8 noncommissioned officers and 58 enlisted personnel.

On the morning of 15 January, at 0700 hours, 8-10 Soviet tanks with a strong infantry contingent suddenly advanced against Collective Farm No. 1. In the immediate counterattack launched by the tanks and assault guns, three T-34's and a T-60 were knocked out. The enemy infantry kept its composure, however, and continued to attack, while the German tanks and assault guns kept the eastern side of the farm clear of any further enemy. The *II./PGR128* was brought forward again to the collective farm;

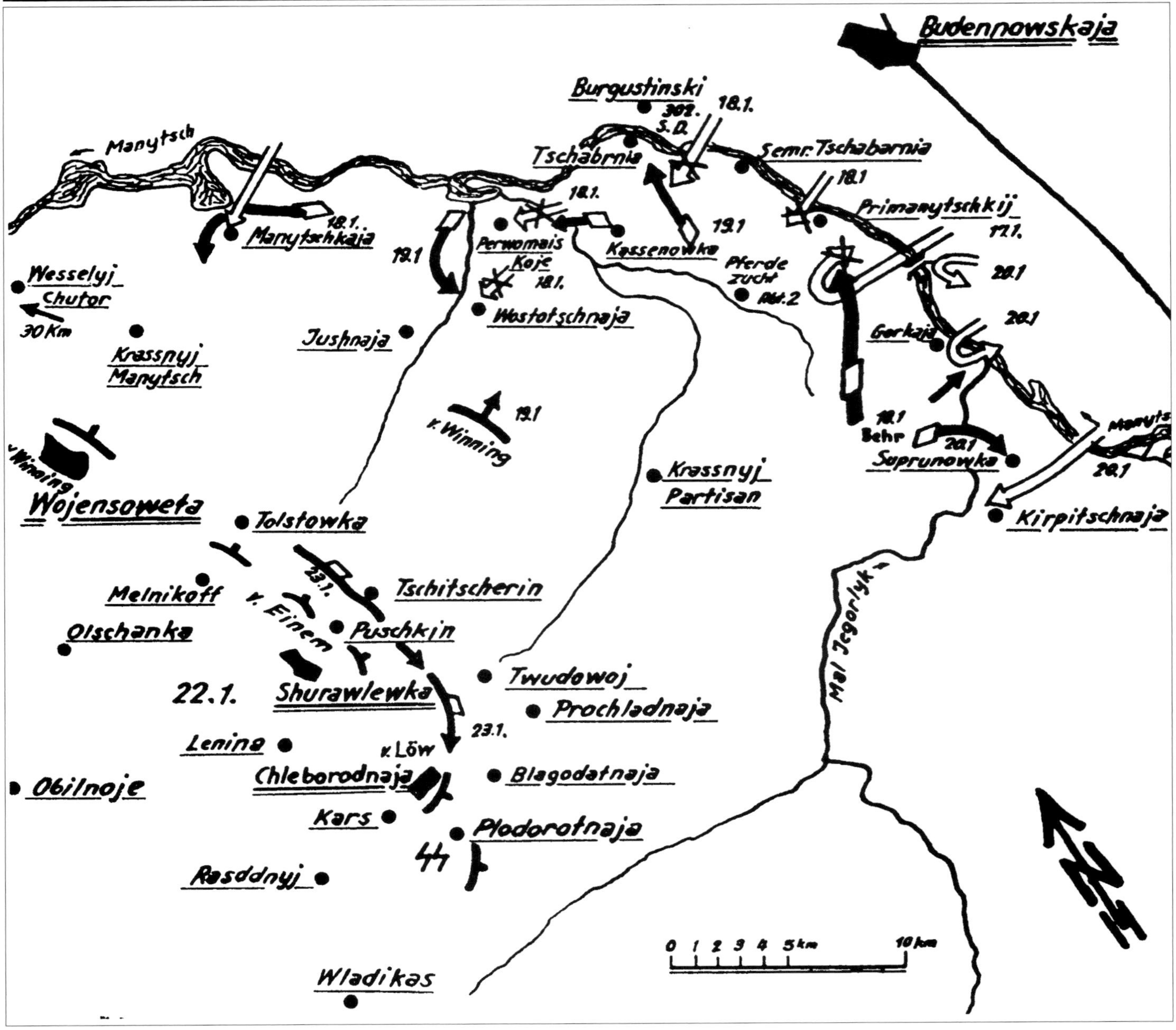

Map 29: Offensive and Defensive Operations Along the Manytsch, 18-22 January 1943.

the divisional engineers were holding their positions in the southern part of the farm and the western part was being held by the *SPW* battalion, on its own commander's initiative. The *LVII. Panzer-Korps* ordered the employment of a *Kampfgruppe* from *SS-Panzer-Grenadier-Division "Wiking"* and *schwere Panzer-Abteilung 503* to retake all of the collective farm.

In the meantime, the withdrawal movements of the *1. Panzer-Armee* were proceeding according to plan. The *4. Panzer-Armee* was able to pull the *LVII. Panzer-Korps* back behind the Manytsch. This meant that the first of the two missions for the field army had been fulfilled. The *17. Panzer-Division* reached the area around Jekaterinowka, south of the Manytsch, to screen the east flank of the corps. The *23. Panzer-Division* covered the area east of Stalinskij Put and oriented east. *SS-Panzer-Grenadier-Division "Wiking"* and *schwere Panzer-Abteilung 503* formed a new bridgehead around Proletarskaja.

All the while, the fighting for Collective farm No. 1 continued. The divisional engineers, together with the tanks, held the southern part of the farm. At 1130 hours, *SS* elements joined the fighting. Together, those forces succeeded in reclaiming a large portion of the fruit orchards on the eastern side of the collective farm. The enemy no longer attacked.

In the new division sector east of Stalinskij Put, *Kampfgruppe Sander*—consisting of the *I./PGR128*, the newly attached *Kradschützen-Bataillon 17* from the *17. Panzer-Division* and the attached *2./schwere Panzer-Abteilung 503*—set up positions. For the time being, *Pionier-Lehr-Bataillon 1* remained echelonned forward to the southeast. *Panzergruppe Behr* and the assault guns were designated as the division reserve and positioned in Stalinskij Put. To the west of the village was the entire divisional artillery of *Major* Hamann, as well as the *III./Werfer-Regiment 54*.

At 1830 hours, the defenders evacuated the collective farm without interference from the enemy. The *II./PGR128*, the *SPW* Battalion and *PPB51* crossed the Manytsch at Proletarskaja. During the morning of 16 January, the engineers and the *II./PGR128* were sent forward again in order to relieve *Kradschützen-Bataillon 17*, which was being returned to the *17. Panzer-Division*.

At 1000 hours on 16 January, *SS-Panzer-Grenadier-Division "Wiking"* relieved the committed elements of the division in the Proletarskaja

Bridgehead in the course of the evacuation. The *Tigers* remained with the *SS* division. The *23. Panzer-Division* moved out immediately, crossed the dams over the Manytsch, swung out to the south and reached the former area of the division's trains that same evening. The division's mission was to cover the south bank of the Manytsch and hold it.

The division's march from Proletarskaja through Schablijewka to the area between Suprunowka and Manytschkaja along the southern banks of the Manytsch took place under the severe conditions imposed by the harsh winter of the Russian steppe. Snowdrifts caused by the brisk winds forced everyone to become involved. The bitterly cold temperatures brought about a number of cases of frostbite.

Protected by *Sicherungsgruppe von Einem*[40], the other forces of the division entered their new sectors. Due to a shortage of fuel, the tanks and artillery remained in the horse farm Im. Budennogo, 2 kilometers west of Schablijewka, and the *ad hoc* motorcycle rifle company of *Oberleutnant Graf* Finkenstein was at Ssalsk. The *1./Sturmgeschütz-Abteilung 243* was not prepared to conduct any operations. The trains, except for those elements that had been formed as security units and were still employed, were sent off to the north, where they assembled though 26 January at Awdejewka, north of Stalino, under the command of *Major* Draffehn, the commander of the *IV.(Flak)/PAR128*.

The difficult fighting of the previous weeks had not only decimated the personnel of the division, but also its vehicles. Additional, difficult losses in vehicles were sustained during the evacuations of Proletarskaja and Ssalsk, because the maintenance companies were unable to repair numerous vehicles in time due to a lack of spare parts. Additional vehicles—already loaded on rail cars—were lost since the stretch of track was blocked, no locomotives were available and everything in the form of equipment had to be blown up prior to the arrival of the Soviets.

At 1030 hours on 17 January, combat reconnaissance conducted by the *ad hoc* infantry company composed of artillerymen revealed enemy forces in battalion strength with three tanks at the bridge 14 kilometers east of Krassnyj Partisan. The enemy attacked and forced the evacuation of the strongpoint after the loss of the only heavy weapon, a 2cm *Flak*. An immediate counterattack was launched by the sector commander, *Major* Sänger, with the divisional engineers and two assault guns from *Sturmgeschütz-Abteilung 203*. They pushed back the enemy forces, which had advanced as far as Stud Farm No. 2, far back to the east. The attacking force destroyed two T-70's, an armored car and two trucks. According to aerial reconnaissance, the Russian force had consisted of 1,500 men, three tanks and three armored cars.

Both of the *ad hoc* infantry companies composed of tankers were attached to *Oberstleutnant* von Winning's *Kampfgruppe*.

For 18 January, the division planned to eliminate the enemy forces grouped east of the stud farm. To that end, *Kampfgruppe Sander* was formed with the "majority of the combat forces", which consisted of *PR201*, the *SPW* Battalion, *Pionier-Lehr-Bataillon 1*, the rifle company formed from the trains elements of *PGR126*, two assault guns, elements of *PJA128*, elements of the rifle company formed from the artillery regiment and all available artillery. To the left of *Oberstleutnant* Sander's battle group was *Kampfgruppe Bachmann*, which maintained its previous combat outposts along the Manytsch and, to the left of Bachmann, Kampfgruppe von Winning, which had its combat outposts along the Manytsch, as well as the two rifle companies composed of tankers and elements of the divisional engineers. The route-poor terrain delayed the approach march considerably, with the result that the enemy was able to repeat his attack on the stud farm twice, albeit without taking any ground.

At 0715 hours, *Panzergruppe Behr* moved out. With just enough supplies, ammunition and fuel and without any accompanying infantry, it pushed through to the bridge along the Manytsch. The Russians fled across the river. Behr's men took in a great deal of weapons and trains vehicles: 11 7.62cm antitank guns; 3 3.7cm antiaircraft guns; 2 3.7cm antitank guns; 5 antiaircraft machine guns; 5 heavy machine guns; 10 heavy mortars; 10 antitank rifles; 1 infantry gun; 15 trucks; 2 staff cars; 2 field kitchens; several *panje* carts; and 150 prisoners. Numerous enemy dead were counted. The German riflemen, who arrived from the west in the meantime, cleared the area of scattered Soviet elements and set up along the Manytsch for the defense.

While that attack was taking place, 400 Soviets crossed the Manytsch between Semenowa Tschabarnia and Tschabarnia in the sector of *Kampfgruppe von Winning*. They headed in the direction of Wostotschnaja and Perwomaiskij. Toward noon, additional enemy groups forces attacked the artillerymen being employed as infantry at Primanystchkij. At 1320 hours, larger-sized Soviet forces attacked the stud farm from the northeast. At the same time, a company-sized enemy force infiltrated the Gorkaja Defile. *Kampfgruppe von Winning* evacuated Tschabarnia, Perwomaiskij and Manytschskaja. The four weak companies of the battle group, which had no heavy weapons at all, finally set up an all-round defense at the command post of the battle group 10 kilometers northeast of Tschitscherin.

A group of 700 replacements from the *Luftwaffe* that had been earmarked for the division was not sent, since the division could not move them on vehicles. At the same time, the division had to report that it was incapable of moving all of its combat elements at the same time by motor vehicle. The reason for that report was the inquiry from *Heeresgruppe Don* with regard to the new threat posed to the entire southern front by numerically greatly superior Soviet forces. On 18 January, they had defeated the Hungarian 2nd Army south of Woronesch and, together with the forces in the great bend of the Don bend, were only being held up by isolated German resistance in strongpoints as they advanced rapidly to the west and southwest.

The loss of vehicles affected not only the infantry, the engineers and the other combat elements. To an even greater extent, the loss of vehicles forced the division's logistics elements to pay tribute to the peculiarities of Soviet Russia. *Panje* vehicles, manned by Soviet volunteers[41], increasingly formed the image of the *23. Panzer-Division*. In April 1942, the division's field-replacement battalion had seven horse-drawn vehicles authorized for its trains. In the course of the year, those seven wagons grew to become *Fahrkolonne Lang*. Under the supervision of *Hauptwachtmeister* Lang, the horse-drawn supply column grew to become an indispensible crutch for the division's logistics officer. The need for prime movers during this period could not even be covered by the use of *panje* carts, however. Even teams of oxen were incorporated into the trains.

On 19 January, *Panzer-Abteilung Behr* moved out from the stud farm at 0600 hours. It took Kassenowka and shattered a Soviet regiment there, as well as another battalion. Several field pieces, numerous weapons and 150 prisoners were left behind by the enemy, along with many dead. Moving along the Manytsch in the direction of Tschabarnia, the tanks, accompanied by motorcycle infantry that had linked up with them, threw the Russians back. At the same time von Winning's and Bachmann's battle groups moved out from the southwest and retook the banks of the Manytsch. At 1000 hours, most of the Soviet 302nd Rifle Division was caught trying to cross the river at Tschabarnia. The enemy suffered extremely heavy losses on the barren terrain. Turning to the southeast from the area around Wostotschnaja, the armored force cleared the Ssolenaja Defile, turned around and advanced into other Soviet concentrations at Perwomaiskij. In that village alone, the enemy left behind more than 300 dead. Manytschkaja was reached at 1330 hours; by 1400 hours, the entire

40 Editor's Note: = (roughly) "Covering Force von Einem".

41 Editor's Note: These volunteers were referred to officially as *Hilfsfreiwillige* and colloquially as *Hiwis*. Their usefulness and importance is reflected in the fact that wartime tables of organization and equipment (manpower authorizations) reflected their presence in a wide variety of duty positions.

Manytsch river line had been regained along the entire sector and was again firmly under German control.

Panzergrenadier-Regiment 128 assumed the sector Kassenowka — Tschabarnia — Hill 25.0.

But by 1500 hours, new enemy forces crossed the river unopposed southeast of Suprunowka and occupied Kirpitschnaja on the right wing of the division.

In the meantime, *Panzergruppe Behr* attacked the last enemy concentration in the division sector at Oktjabriskoje — Jushnaja. The remaining enemy there fled. The day turned out to be a very successful one for the division, especially for *Panzergruppe Behr*. The armored battle group had only eight tanks and two assault guns at its disposal. Despite that, and operating occasionally without infantry support, it defeated numerically greater Soviet forces, including the Soviet 302nd Rifle Division, and was able to clear the southern banks of the Manytsch.

Oberst Bachmann, who had been the commander of *PGR128* since its formation, was transferred back to Germany for a new assignment. *Major* von Einem, the commander of *PJA128*, assumed acting command of the regiment until the designated successor could arrive.

During the night of 19/20 January, the Soviets attempted in vain to take the bridge crossing point 14 kilometers east of Krassnyj Partisan. Despite the enemy bringing forward new forces at Kirpitschnaja, he likewise had little success in ejecting *Gruppe von Löw* from Suprunowka. At first light, the enemy attacked along the entire division sector. The weak combat outposts at Burgustinskij and Tschabarnia had to pull back. The infantry company composed of artillerymen distinguished itself through its bravery. The armored group advanced into an enemy attack conducted from the south and east and defeated it, even though the tanks were only conditionally operational due to the supply situation. A few of the tanks had only 5 main-gun rounds and 300 rounds of machine-gun ammunition. Tschabarnia was retaken in an immediate counterattack launched by the *I./PGR128*.

The Soviet main effort was concentrated at the bridge site. Despite extremely heavy artillery fire and continuous attacks, the defenders held their positions. Small enemy groups that had advanced across the river were wiped out. On the island in the river 4 kilometers west of Burgustinskij, the enemy initiated large-scale attempts to cross. In the evening dusk, tanks and infantry attacked the strongpoint of *Kampfgruppe von Einem* at Hill 25.0 and forced it to be evacuated. Strong enemy movements north of the river to the west led to the conclusion that new attempts were being made to bypass the German divisions south of Rostov and break through to the city.

An enemy attack launched at 2100 hours against Suprunowka made slow progress despite heavy enemy casualties. Since the German forces were too weak in the long run, *Oberstleutnant* Sander pulled back the brave men defending the village. Of its total trench strength of 60 men that morning, the force lost 10 dead, 20 badly wounded and 10 slightly wounded.

The enemy was turned back at Gorkaja after an immediate counterattack. He was attempting to bypass the bridge site.

Oberst von Vormann issued the following order-of-the-day after the recent successes of 20 January:

> At the beginning of December, the division was placed in this section of the front in order to close the gap that had come about among our allies as a result of attacks by superior enemy forces. It has always been the mission of the German soldier, who gives his full measure of duty and devotion, to restore order at endangered hot spots of the front.
>
> In the last few days it was paramount to protect the only bridge crossing over the Manytsch at Proletarskaja from enemy action. In recognition of the importance of this area, the enemy had chosen to throw four complete rifle divisions, the 6th, the 34th, the 91st and 126th, and the complete III Motorized Corps, with the 36th, 59th and 60th Motorized Rifle Brigades and two tank brigades (6th and 56th) against the *23. Panzer-Division*, which had already been weakened by earlier hard fighting.
>
> In these last few weeks, superhuman efforts have been demanded of you in the name of everyone against these numerically superior, determined and tough-fighting enemy forces. You have mastered this mission in the most difficult kind of defensive fighting with heroic devotion to duty. The intentions of the enemy can be viewed today as having failed. The high point has been crossed; the worst is behind us!
>
> Since 12 December 1942, the division has destroyed or captured: 3,000 Prisoners; 143 tanks; 36 artillery pieces; 43 antitank guns and antiaircraft guns; 108 antitank rifles; 37 mortars; and large quantities of machine guns, wheeled vehicles, small arms and automatic weapons of all types.
>
> For your bravery and your self-sacrificing and exemplary devotion to duty in the last few weeks, which has been cited numerous times in the *Wehrmacht* Daily Report, I would like to express my thanks and recognition to all of the soldiers of the *23. Panzer-Division* and all of the formations that were attached or in direct support.
>
> We bow our heads in respect for our fallen comrades. I wish a speedy recovery to all of our wounded.
>
> The fight continues!
>
> /signed/ von Vormann
> *Oberst* and Acting Division Commander

On 21 January, the division restricted its activities to the defense of the areas it had taken. An enemy attack near Manytschkaja collapsed. From the island in the river west of Burgustinskij, where the enemy was constructing a bridge, the enemy continued his preparations for bypassing to the northwest.

The enemy was being constantly reinforced in the area in front of the right wing of the division. At 1300 hours, two battalions attacked the weakened *Pionier-Lehr-Bataillon 1* at Gorkaja. Before tanks could come to the rescue, *Hauptmann* von Löw and his engineers turned back the attack. In the immediate counterattack that followed, the engineers and the tanks pushed the enemy back across the river.

At 1600 hours, the division started to disengage from the enemy, beginning on the right wing. *Sturmgeschütz-Abteilung 203* was attached to the division. *Kampfgruppe von Löw* marched to Chleborodnaja; *Kampfgruppe von* Einem to Shurawlewka — Melnikoff; Kampfgruppe *von Winning* to Wojensoweta; and *Eingreifgruppe Sander*[42] to Golowanowka — Olschanka. The friendly force to the left of the division was the *17. Panzer-Division*. The enemy was able to take the village of Wesselyj in its sector.

The divisional artillery assumed coverage of the trains of the *17. Panzer-Division*, which were screening near Werch. Chomutez. In addition, the artillery regiment relieved its former company composed of artillerymen who were employed as infantry with a new company formed for that purpose.

On 22 January, the enemy felt his way cautiously forward. By evening, he had occupied the abandoned villages of Blagodatnaja, Plodorotnaja, Trudowoj and Tschitscherin. The divisional antitank battalion formed an infantry company out of crewmembers who no longer had guns. What remained of the antitank and antiaircraft guns was consolidated into a second company.

During the morning hours of 23 January, the Soviets entered Puschkin, but an advance on Shurawlewka was turned back. Larger enemy formations struck Chleborodnaja and Plodorodnyj, which was occupied by *SS-Panzer-Grenadier-Regiment "Westland"*, several times without success. *Hauptmann* von Löw, acting on his own initiative, launched a counterattack with his engineers and assault guns, defeated the enemy forces and

42 Editor's Note: = (literally) "Intervention Group". This designation was usually applied to a reserve force.

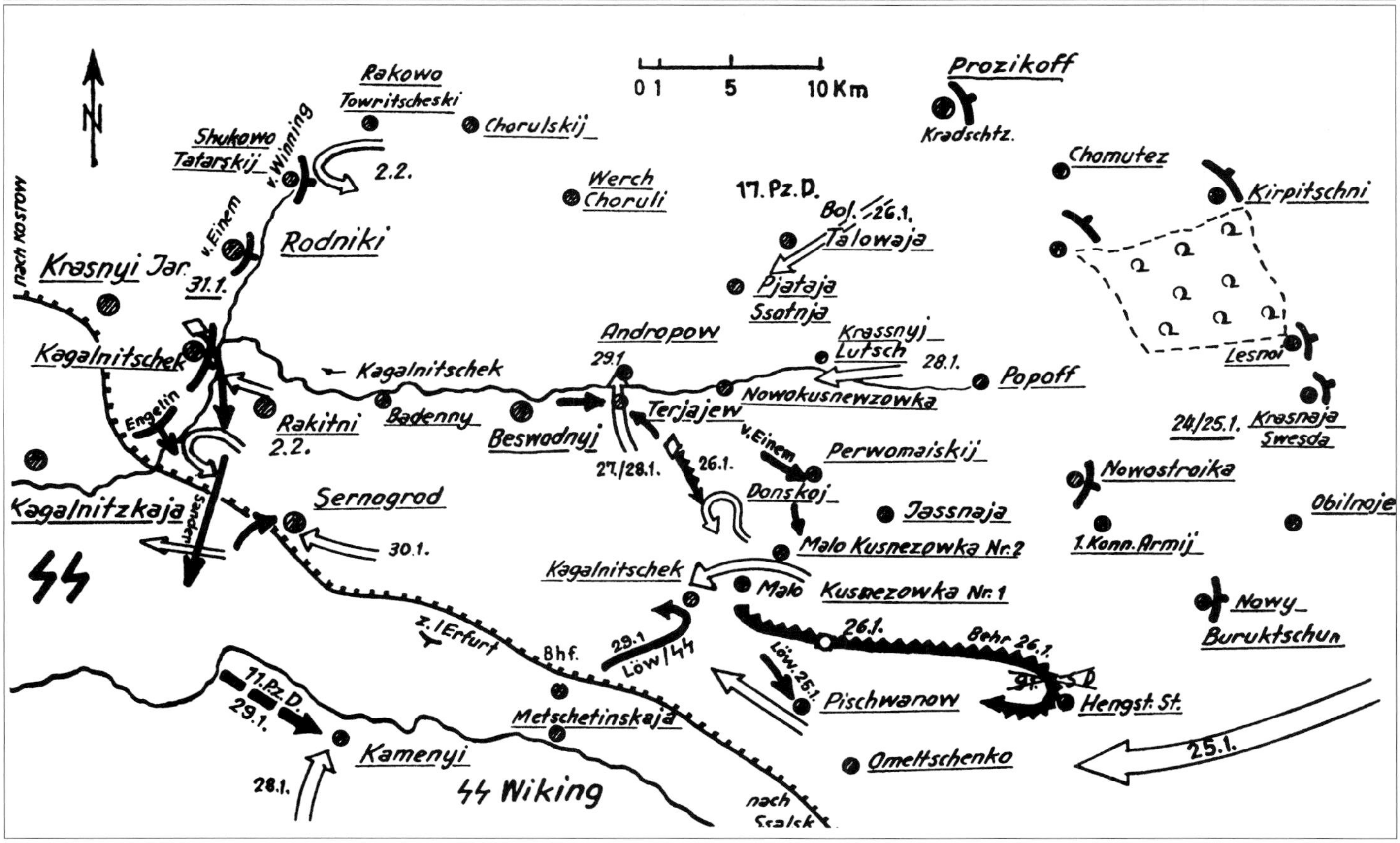

Map 30: Fighting Around Pischwanoff and Along the Kagalnitschek, 21 January to 2 February 1943.

captured three 12cm infantry guns, as well as four *panje* carts. The trench strength of *Kampfgruppe von Löw* was as follows: *Pionier-Lehr-Bataillon 1* — 11 men; the infantry company composed of artillerymen — 20; the rifle company composed of personnel from the trains of *PGR126* — 14. Besides the operational tanks, the division had the following armor-defeating weapons available: 1 7.5cm self-propelled antitank gun; one towed 7.5cm antitank gun; 2 towed 5cm antitank guns; 3 towed 2cm *Flak* (*PJA128*); 3 self-propelled 2cm *Flak* (*10./PGR128*); and 3 assault guns.

The Commanding General of the *LVII. Panzer-Korps*, *General der Panzertruppen* Kirchner, expressed his praise to the division commander for the performance of the division in the recent past.

The enemy advanced on Tolstowka. Moving from Trudowoj, an enemy column with artillery pieces attempted to bypass the German strongpoints and reach Lenina. *Panzergruppe Behr* was dispatched to interdict the enemy force. Advancing through Orshonikidse, Tschitscherin, the Puschkin Collective farm and Chleborodnaja, Behr's forces surprised several enemy groups on the march and destroyed 6 7.62cm antitank guns, 22 4.7cm antitank guns, 2 7.62 field cannon, 1 heavy infantry gun, 2 heavy machine guns, and 50 horse-drawn wagons. Fifty enemy dead were counted.

Despite all that, the enemy continued his efforts to bypass with freshly introduced forces and, at the same time, conducted preparations for attacking the strongpoints. The corps ordered a withdrawal at 2000 hours to the line Now. Buruktschun — Nowostroika — Krassnaja Swesda — Lesnoi — Chomutez. Later on, when the trains of the *17. Panzer-Division* were relieved, Prozikoff also had to be incorporated into the division sector. The *SPW* Battalion was attached to *Kampfgruppe Löw*.

At 1800 hours, *Kampfgruppe von Winning* was attacked in Wojensoweta. The enemy entered the village from the northwest and blocked the intended withdrawal route. While fighting, the battle group finally disengaged from the enemy and reached the new designated sectors, partly in vehicles, partly in sleds.

Six assault guns of *Sturmgeschütz-Abteilung 203* had to be detached and sent to *SS-Panzer-Grenadier-Division "Wiking"*. The motorcycle company relieved the trains of the *17. Panzer-Division* in Prozikoff; two 5cm antitank guns were attached to the motorcycle infantry.

On 24 January, the only contact with the enemy was through patrols. The enemy did not continue his advance until 25 January, when he moved against Nowostroika with a strong infantry force. A weak enemy group was turned back at Lesnoi. Soviet formations in front of *Kampfgruppe von Löw* attempted to bypass that force south of Nowostroika and Konnoj Armij (No. 1). Since the weak German forces did not suffice to screen the assigned terrain, *Kampfgruppe von Löw* moved out to conduct a local counterattack and turned back the enemy forces in Konnoj Armij (No. 1). The enemy left behind 20 dead, 21 prisoners, 1 7.62cm antitank gun and 2 antitank rifles.

In front of *Kampfgruppe von Winning*, the enemy entered the woods south of Werchne Chomutez. In accordance with received orders, the division pulled back at 2000 hours to the line Pischwanow — Malo Kusnezowka (No. 1) — Perwomaiskij — Krassnyj Lutsch — Pjataja Ssotnja. The friendly forces to the right was *SS-Panzer-Grenadier-Division "Wiking"* around Komuna; on the left, it was the *17. Panzer-Division* around Bol. Talowaja. The enemy did not interfere with the disengagements. When *Kampfgruppe von Löw* moved through Malo Kusnezowka and entered Pischwanow, it encountered Russian trains elements. According to prisoner statements, a regiment had already marched through the village to the west. The only resistance put up in the village came from an antitank gun and infantry armed with submachine guns.

Sturmgeschütz-Abteilung 243 was ordered to Donskoj. The headquarters of *Kampfgruppe von Einem* discovered enemy there as well. Due to a lack of forces, the headquarters element had to pull back to Nowo Kusnezowka initially.

At 0230 hours on 26 January, 200 Soviets attacked Malo Kusnezowka (No. 2) and pushed the German outposts back to Malo Kusnezowka (No. 1). Kagalnitschek, 4 kilometers to the south, was occupied by the enemy.

In Pischwanow, the enemy continuously received reinforcements. *Kampfgruppe von Löw* held out against a Soviet battalion; two artillery pieces were captured in fighting.

At 0600 hours, *Kampfgruppe Sander* moved out against Donskoj with the remaining five operational tanks of *PR201* and the motorcycle infantry company. At the same time, *Sturmgeschütz-Abteilung 203* entered Terjajew-Andropow with some of its elements. Donskoj was cleared of the enemy by 0800 hours; two antitank guns were captured and a few prisoners taken.

In the meantime, the enemy forces in Kagalnitschek, to the southeast of Malo Kusnezowka, were reinforced. Malo Kusnezowka (No. 2) and Jassnaja had a strong enemy presence. Advancing on Kagalnitschek, *Kampfgruppe Sander* destroyed the Soviet 613th Rifle Regiment and, moving through the village, continued its attack in the direction of Pischwanow. To the east of that village, 1,000 enemy infantry were preparing for operations; at the same time, enemy forces approached from the west. *Sturmgeschütz-Abteilung 203* was ordered to Donskoj.

It was quiet in the sector of *Kampfgruppe von Winning*.

The operational readiness of the infantry company formed from tank crews was reduced considerably by cases of frostbite.

Kampfgruppe von Löw succeeded in pushing the enemy out of Pischwanow. The battle group's strength did not suffice to occupy the entire village, however. At 1100 hours, *Hauptmann* Behr and his tanks and two assault guns (from *Sturmgeschütz-Abteilung 243*) attacked north of the village and advanced as far as the stud farm 7 kilometers further to the east. Densely massed Soviet formations were surprised there. According to prisoner statements, it was the main body of the 9th Rifle Division, with the 503rd and 561st Rifle regiments. Despite insufficient amounts of main-gun ammunition, 4 7.62cm antitank guns, 6 4.7cm antitank guns, a radio relay station, 50 horse-drawn wagons and 5 trucks were destroyed. Leaving behind 100 dead, the enemy fled to the east, south and north. Rallied by this success, *Kampfgruppe von Löw* moved out again in Pischwanow, took six reinforced field positions and destroyed 4 enemy infantry guns, 13 antitank rifles, 3 heavy machine guns and 50 horse-drawn wagons. The enemy left behind 80 dead; 150 prisoners were taken. It was only in the eastern-most part of the village that the Russians still held a strongpoint. Von Löw's forces were augmented by nine guns from *Sturmgeschütz-Abteilung 203*.

In the sector of the *17. Panzer-Division*, Bol. Talowaja was lost.

For the first time during these withdrawals, German soldiers saw long columns of fleeing civilians. Countless Caucasians preferred the loss of their homelands to a return of Soviet sovereignty, which would bring with it forced relocations and labor, as it had to a number of their fellow citizens.

The division received orders to hold its present positions on 27 January.

In the meantime, the enemy continued to reinforce his strongpoint at Pischwanow, retook Malo Kusnezowka (No. 2) in a counterattack and attacked the firing positions of the *4./PAR128* in Kagalnitschik with individual soldiers.

During the morning hours, the enemy forced his way into Malo Kusnezowka (No. 1). The Soviets were forced back out again by 0800 hours by the *II./PGR128* and *Sturmgeschütz-Abteilung 203*.

Soviet patrols were already feeling their way forward northwest of Donskoj. Large concentrations of forces were to be found around Pischwanow and outside of Perwomaiskij. *Kampfgruppe von Löw* was able to gain some breathing space by attacking, but it was concentrically attacked at 0900 hours.

A Soviet force took Kagalnitschek, southwest of Malo Kusnezowka; *Panzergruppe Sander* was employed against those forces. In Pischwanow, *Kampfgruppe von Löw* was subjected to heavy mortar and infantry gun fires. The assault guns could not be employed because of the presence of a massed antitank-gun belt. During the first hours of the morning, the battle group lost 32 men. Of the 250 men available for duty the previous day, only 116 were available to fight on this day.

At 1100 hours, *Panzergruppe Sander* cleared Kagalnitschek of the enemy, however, more and more fresh Soviet forces were appearing in front of the division's right wing. While some of those elements bypassed Pischwanow to the south and entered the defiles to the southwest of Donskoj, the enemy sacrificed large numbers of personnel at Pischwanow without being able to achieve any notable success.

In the meantime, *PR201* had formed yet another infantry company out of tank crews. *Oberleutnant* Stöcker was given command of this 3rd Company. It was ordered to Beswodnyj to secure the supply routes of the division, which were threatened again and again by enemy elements attempting to disrupt operations.

Kampfgruppe von Winning was able to scatter an enemy column marching south in front of its sector; later on, it had to fend off an enemy attack by weaker forces.

In the meantime, the fighting for Pischwanow and the two Malo Kusnezowkas continued. *Kampfgruppe Sander* caught an enemy force in the defiles southwest of Donskoj. Two antitank guns, a light infantry gun, a mortar and 13 trains vehicles were destroyed; 30 enemy dead were counted.

In Perwomaiskij and Malo Kusnezowka (No. 1), *Kampfgruppe von Einem* continued to hold out.

The onset of darkness on that day saw no interruption in the Soviet troop movements. An enemy force advancing on Kagalnitschek was well to the rear of *Kampfgruppe von Löw*.

At 1530 hours, reinforcements for the division arrived in the form of *Kampfbataillon Erfurt*[43] (*Hauptmann* Engelin) in Kasatschij. It was immediately dispatched to the front. *Eisenbahn-Pionier-Kompanie 52*[44], which was temporarily attached to the division, blew up the stretch of railway between Metschetinskaja and Ssernograd.

Despite being apprised of the worrisome situation on the right wing of the division, higher headquarters remained adamant about its orders to defend the area that was currently being held. The intent was to win time for establishing a defensive position around Rostov. Above and beyond that, higher headquarters also ordered Pischwanow being retaken once and for all and that the enemy on the right flank of the division be defeated. Promised were support from the *Luftwaffe*, a reinforcement of five tanks from the *17. Panzer-Division* and a concurrent attack by *SS-Panzer-Grenadier-Division "Wiking"*.

On this day, the division prevented a breakthrough through its positions and inflicted heavy casualties on the enemy, despite its weak battle groups scattered among widely separated strongpoints. Prisoners were brought in from the 91st and 126th Rifle Divisions.

Around 0100 hours during the night of 27/28 January, coming from the south, the enemy attacked the combat trains elements of the battle groups that had set up in Terjajew-Andropow. Losing the village and some

43 Editor's Note: = "Combat Battalion 'Erfurt'". This appears to have been some *ad hoc* type of formation that was hastily committed to the front in light of the German's precarious position.

44 Editor's Note: = 52nd Railway Engineer Company. This general headquarters asset was generally employed to fix, repair and build railways, not destroy them.

of their vehicles, the trains pulled back toward the front in the direction of *Kampfgruppe von Winning*.

A strong enemy infantry attack at Donskoj was turned back, but the enemy succeeded in establishing himself in the defiles west of the village.

Vehicles were lost over and over again along the supply routes of the division, despite the screening of the newly formed tanker infantry company, which also had to screen in the direction of Terjajew-Andropow at that point. The losses were caused by mines that the enemy placed on the roads at night. Soviet reconnaissance and combat patrols infiltrated everywhere.

In the morning, Soviet infantry advanced past Krassnyj Lutsch on both sides. The combat outposts of *Kampfgruppe von Winning* had to evacuate the village to avoid being encircled.

While *Kampfgruppe von Löw* moved out to attack the eastern portion of Pischwanow again, strong enemy forces marched past the village to the south, heading west. Further to the northwest, Malo Kusnezowka (No. 1) fell into Russian hands for the most part. Soon afterwards, the enemy also took Kagalnitschek again. *Panzergruppe Sander* shattered this enemy force in an immediate counterattack, destroying 2 armored cars, 5 trucks, 30 *panje* wagons, 4 3.7cm antitank guns, 2 7.62cm antitank guns, 3 7.62cm infantry guns, 9 antitank rifles, 3 heavy machine guns and untold amounts of small arms. Two hundred enemy dead were counted.

The enemy forces in Terjajew-Andropow remained quiet. The division only screened against those forces, since it did not have enough strength to be able to attack them.

The situation for *Kampfgruppe von Löw* appeared increasingly hopeless. Its combat power had sunk so low that it was no longer in a position to defend its positions for the coming night. The enemy was attacking continuously. A relief attack on the part of *SS-Panzer-Grenadier-Division "Wiking"* did not have the desired effect, since it ran into strong enemy forces far to the south of the village. At 1510 hours, shortly before receiving an order from the division to do so, *Hauptmann* von Löw gave up Pischwanow. The small group fought its way through to the west. It reached the rail station at Metschetinskaja, where it was immediately committed to a counterattack to the north on Kagalnitschek. Just south of the village, von Löw's forces ran into a Soviet regiment with a large amount of armor-defeating weapons. The battle group had to return to the rail station. As a result, the enemy was able to bring in additional forces through Pischwanow and into the area west of Donskoj without interruption.

Kampfgruppe von Winning was able to defeat an enemy group southeast of Pjataja Ssotnja in a surprise advance at night. Two antitank guns and one mortar were eliminated; 40 enemy dead were counted. However, the weak forces there were also insufficient to fix the numerically superior enemy and effectively engage him.

The divisional engineers were threatened from the rear.

It was intended by the corps for the division to clear Terjajew-Andropow on 29 January and then take Kagalnitschek with *Kampfgruppe Sander* and *Kampfgruppe von Löw*. At the same time, the recently introduced *11. Panzer-Division* was intended to attack Pischwanow. *SS-Panzer-Grenadier-Division "Wiking"* and five tanks from the *17. Panzer-Division* were supposed to support the attack of the *23. Panzer-Division*. *Kampfgruppe von Einem* was pulled back to Donskoj, while *Kampfgruppe von Winning* to Nowo-Kusnezowka.

Starting at 0530 hours, *Kampfgruppe Sander* cleared the eastern portion of the defiles west of Donskoj and forced an entrance into Terjajew-Andropow, fighting against mortars, antitank guns and antitank rifles. The weak 3rd Company of tankers attacked the village at the same time from Beswodnyj; it was supported by two tanks in its efforts. In a hard fight, the supply route of the division was cleared of the enemy. At 0855 hours, both groups linked up in Terjajew-Andropow, with *Kampfgruppe Sander* taking in 150 prisoners and destroying 7 antitank rifles, 3 antitank guns, 1 7.62cm infantry gun and 30 trains vehicles. The soldiers counted 40 enemy dead. The enemy had employed "mine dogs"[45] against the division for the first time, but they were ineffective, since they were killed before they could close on the vehicles.

In the sector of *SS-Panzer-Grenadier-Division "Wiking"* on the right, the enemy succeeded during the previous day and the night in getting into the rear of its formations and occupying Kamenyj with strong forces. To secure the deep flank of the *23. Panzer-Division*, the 2nd Company of *Kampfbataillon Erfurt* was employed south of the collective farm (Section 1) under the command of *Oberst Dr.* Born, the commander of the divisional artillery. The enemy attacked at 0830 hours and pushed the company back to the north. As a result of the immediate counterattack, however, the enemy was pushed back somewhat.

Kampfgruppe von Löw, which was reinforced by *Kampfbataillon Erfurt* (minus its 2nd Company), broke hard Soviet resistance 3 kilometers north of the rail station at Metschetinskaja. Von Löw and his men were joined in the attack by a battalion from *SS-Panzer-Grenadier-Regiment "Germania"*. The *11. Panzer-Division* entered Kamenyj at the same time. At 1100 hours, five tanks from *SS-Panzer-Abteilung "Wiking"* linked up with the 2nd Company of *Kampfbataillon Erfurt*, then attacked the enemy and completely shattered his forces. The young, combat-inexperienced company demonstrated magnificent *elan*. It took 79 Soviets prisoner and captured 8 heavy machine guns and several mortars and antitank rifles. The enemy dead numbered 80.

At 1215 hours, *Kampfgruppe Sander* cleared the defiles west of Terjajew-Andropow; *Kampfgruppe von Löw* was 1 kilometer west of Kagalnitschek. The enemy was soon ejected, in some cases by frontal assault, in other cases by enveloping movements. He fled to the north.

In the process of clearing the defiles around Donskoj, the enemy suffered extremely heavy casualties, since he was densely massed and unable to pull back. At that spot alone, he suffered more than 100 dead, He also lost 1 7.62cm antitank gun and 5 3.7cm antitank guns. The German forces suffered a severe blow, however, when the terrific commander of the motorcycle infantry company, *Oberleutnant Graf* Finkenstein, was killed at the head of his men.

The enemy continued to exert pressure from the area around Pischwanow and on both sides of Kagalnitschek. His tanks were employed on several occasions. The enemy attacked Beswodnyj from the defiles west of Donskoj, especially from the Kagalnik Defile. In the end, the 3rd Company, composed of tankers, had to evacuate most of the village.

At 1830 hours, a massed enemy attack ejected *Kampfgruppe von Löw* from Kagalnitschek. The group fought its way back in snow flurries, aggressively pursued by tanks. Soviet infantry followed.

At 1920 hours, Beswodnyj was lost once and for all to a battalion-sized enemy element. *Kompanie Stöcker* held the western side of Budennyj.

Kampfgruppe Sander eliminated the remnants of the Soviet 561st Rifle Regiment. It had also considerably battered and scattered the 152nd and 156th Rifle Brigades.

For 30 January, the corps ordered that Kagalnitschek be retaken in conjunction with *SS-Panzer-Grenadier-Division "Wiking"*. At the same time, the *11. Panzer-Division* was intended to undertake the attack on Pischwanow that was supposed to have taken place the previous day.

At 0430 hours on 30 January, a Soviet battle group of 1,000 men and 10 tanks entered Ssernograd, 18 kilometers west of Pischwanow, by surprise. The Soviets had most likely infiltrated through the gap west of

45 Editor's note: "Mine dogs" are exactly what the reader may imagine them to be: Dogs trained to approach and go underneath vehicles with mines strapped to their backs. Once the Germans recognized what was happening, they were able to eliminate the unfortunate animals in time. Another "lesson learned" for the Soviets was not to use their own vehicles in training, since the dogs tended to go to them when released for their missions.

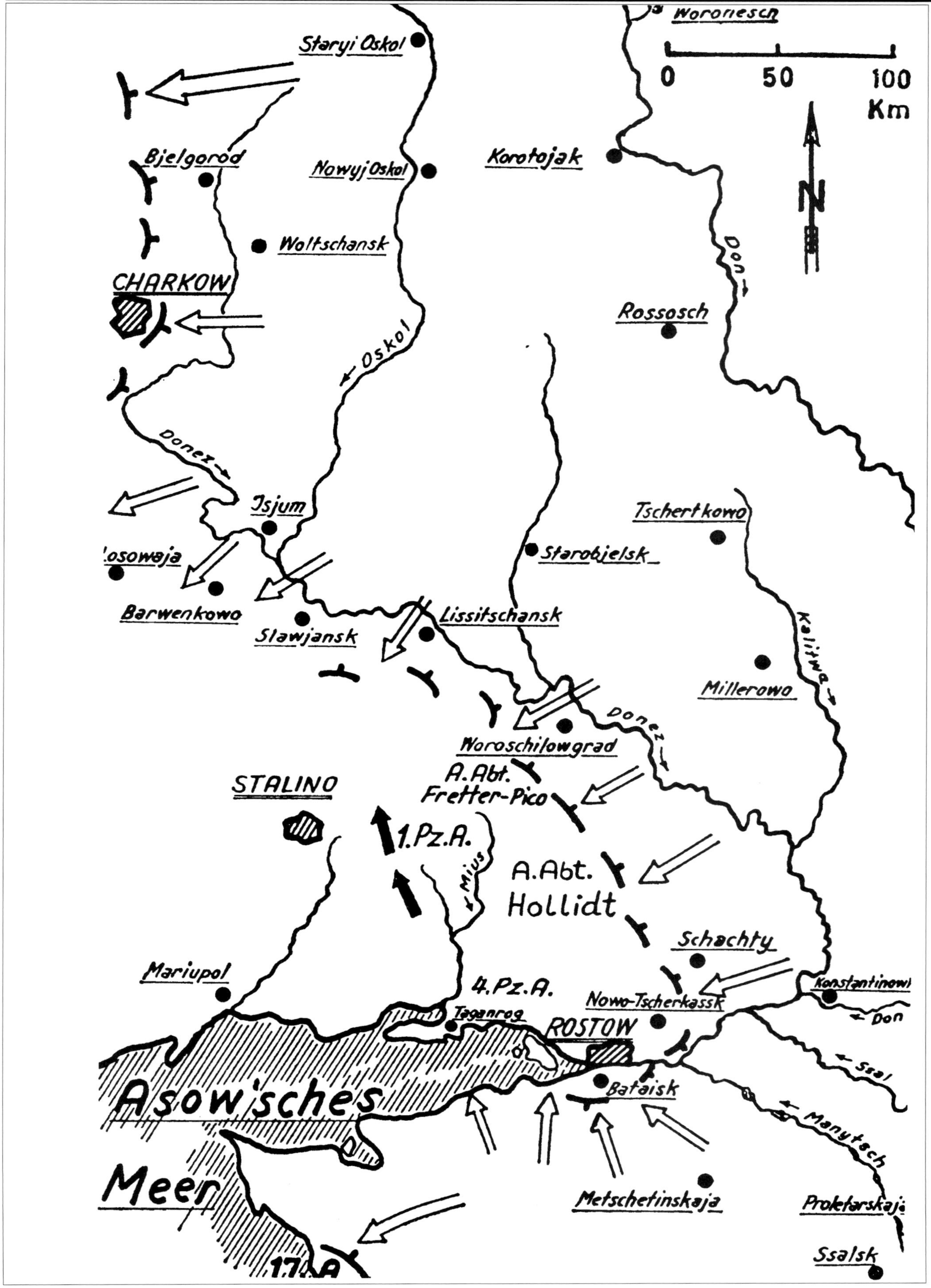

Map 31: The Over-All Situation on 31 January 1943 — Southern Sector.

Pischwanow. The staff of *Kampfgruppe Born* and weak trains elements had to evacuate the village as quickly as possible. Two assault guns that were positioned with the *2./Kampfbataillon Erfurt*, one *Panzer III* and three repaired tanks from *SS-Panzer-Abteilung "Wiking"* undertook an immediate counterattack, destroying four T-34's. The Soviet infantry remained quiet. The village was blocked off.

Without attacking either *Kampfgruppe von Einem* or *Kampfgruppe von Winning*, the enemy attempted on that day to gain ground to the northwest between Metschetinskaja and Beswodnyj. The planned counterattacks on Kagalnitschek and Pischwanow were not executed, because the *11. Panzer-Division* could not overcome the strong resistance at Kamenyj.

Kampfgruppe Sander cleared the defiles south of Beswodnyj, after the village itself had been retaken. Densely packed masses of Soviet forces in the defiles were shattered. *Kampfgruppe von Löw* attacked from the Metschetinskaja rail station to the north to prevent additional enemy forces from flowing into the Ssernograd area. *Kampfgruppe von Einem* was pulled back to Beswodnyj.

Panzergruppe Sander defeated large elements from both the 98th and 99th Rifle Brigades, as well as elements from the 152nd and 156th Rifle Brigades. Only a few prisoners were taken. In one defile alone, 400 enemy dead were counted. Several 7.62cm antitank guns, 8 heavy mortars, large numbers of antitank rifles, machine guns and small arms, as well as 40 trains vehicles, were destroyed.

Hauptmann Behr, the commander of the *I./PR201*, was awarded the Knight's Cross to the Iron Cross in recognition of the decisive role he played in operations conducted by his forces along the southern bank of the Manytsch.

At 1120 hours, the *LVII. Panzer-Korps* ordered the division to pull back to the line Ssernograd (exclusive) — Budennyj — collective farm 4 kilometers northeast of Budennyj — collective farm south of Rakowo Tawritscheskij. In order to effect that, *Kampfgruppe von Löw* was immediately ordered to Kagalnitschek, 18 kilometers east of Ssernograd. The assault guns were attached to *Kampfgruppe Sander*. *Kampfgruppe von Einem* went to Budennyj and the collective farm to the northeast; *Kampfgruppe von Winning* to the collective farm south of Rakowo Tawritscheskij. The enemy did not interfere with the movements; on the contrary, he started digging fortifications around Bol. Talowaja.

On 31 January, the Russians only felt their way forward hesitantly. The division made preparations for additional withdrawals and possibly being pulled out of the line.

Oberst von Vormann, the commander of the division, was promoted to *Generalmajor*.

The difficult fighting of the recent weeks, in which both command and soldiers accomplished the superhuman, then began to show fruit. The *1. Panzer-Armee* was able to pull back out of the Caucasus with the flank guard it was given through the *4. Panzer-Armee*. The divisions of the *17. Armee* had pulled back to the positions at the Kuban Bridgehead, which would be held for some time. The *1. Panzer-Armee* had been freed up for operations along the Donez, while the *4. Panzer-Armee* could then fight just south of Rostov. The obstinate stand of the *6. Armee*, which had been offered up for no operational value, was not without meaning when it came to the success of this withdrawal. There is no telling what would have happened had the Soviet divisions fixed in the fighting for the city along the Volga been freed up earlier to attack the weak and retreating German formations.

During the afternoon of 31 January, the enemy concentrated forces that stretched for kilometers on end around Beswodnyj. The Soviet Air Force flew several sorties against the evacuated village. Starting at 1700 hours, the division pulled back to the line Kagalnik rail station — Rodniki — Shuko Tatarskij —collective farm to the west of Shuko Tatarskij.

During the morning of 1 February, Russian armored cars in Shuko Tatarskij were turned back by *Kampfgruppe von Winning*.

Pionier-Lehr-Bataillon 1 was pulled out of the line by orders of the field army. *Hauptmann* von Löw reported out of the division with a trench strength of three officers, two noncommissioned officers and four enlisted men. The detachment of the battalion from the division signaled an end to a command and control relationship that had started in December. During the subsequent fighting, the battalion and its commander had performed magnificently. The division owed thanks to those extraordinary soldiers for many successes in both defense and offense. Assuming command of the former *Kampfgruppe von Löw* was *Hauptmann* Engelin, the commander of *Kampf-Bataillon Erfurt*.

At 1045 hours, *Kampfgruppe von Winning* was attacked by a Soviet battalion. Assault guns turned back the enemy, who subsequently prepared for additional operations with freshly introduced forces.

A corps order arrived at 1300 hours, according to which the division was to be detached from the corps on 3 February and to be placed at the disposal of the field army north of the Don at Rostov. A *Heeresgruppe*-planned operation by the division on the left wing of the field-army group did not come to pass when the division commander submitted a report on the deficient movement capability, supply situation and weaponry of the division.

At noon, using two assault guns, *Kampfgruppe Engelin* scattered two companies of Russians that were advancing.

Starting at 1530 hours, the enemy repeatedly attacked *Kampfgruppe von Winning* in Shuko-Tatarski. All of the attacks collapsed with high losses to the Soviets in the combined fires of the 1st and 2nd Infantry (Tanker) Companies.

In anticipation of the relief of the division, the commander ordered a reorganization of the troop elements for the expected reconstitution. To that end, *PR201* established the framework for all three of its battalions, but only made one battalion combat capable due to a lack of tanks. *Panzergrenadier-Regiment 126* was reformed. It received the *SPW* Battalion (the former *I./PGR126*), the *2.* and *5./KB23*, as well as the *II./PGR128* (which had formerly been the *II./PGR126*). To help fill up the two battalions, personnel were received from two companies and the headquarters of *Kampf-Bataillon Erfurt*.

Panzergrenadier-Regiment 128 consolidated its remaining elements into the *I./PGR128*. For its 2nd Battalion, it received the alert battalion of the *24. Panzer-Division*, which had been assigned to the division. Personnel were also received in the form of one company from *Kampf-Bataillon Erfurt*.

The armored car company and the motorcycle infantry company were joined together with the former headquarters and *Kradschützen-Bataillon 23* was reformed. The divisional artillery reorganized its elements. Using the guns available, it formed a firing battalion, while the remainder of the regiment assembled at the division base camp in Awdejewka (north of Stalino).

The antitank battalion remained unchanged, but *Hauptmann* Brünn assumed command in place of the departed *Major* von Einem.

On that day, the fate was also decided for the defenders of Stalingrad. After the *6. Armee* of *Generalfeldmarschall* von Paulus had to capitulate in the southern pocket on 31 January, the northern group, consisting of the remnants of the *XI. Armee-Korps* of *General der Artillerie* von Sedylitz, ceased combat operations. Of the 235,000 personnel who were in Stalingrad on the day of its encirclement, 95,000 became Soviet prisoners. More than 100,000 men had been killed or had died as a result of the various hardships endured there. Some 35,000 wounded and only a few non-wounded had been flown out of the pocket.

During the morning of 2 February, the division was ordered to pull out of the front lines during the night of 2/3 February. By noon on 3

February, a motorized reserve group was to be left behind in Mokri Batai in the rear of the sector of the *111. Infanterie-Division*.

During the day, the enemy attacked in the sectors of *Kampfgruppe von Winning* and *Kampfgruppe Engelin*. He was turned back at both locations but brought up fresh forces. The enemy lost 70 dead west of Rakowo Tawritscheskij, as well as eight antitank rifles and two machine guns. At 1030 hours, *Kampfgruppe Sander* pushed back the enemy on both sides of Kagalnitschek and then pursued him. Enemy dead numbered 150, while four 3.7cm antitank guns, two 7.62cm antitank guns, three heavy machine guns, four antitank rifles, two mortars and six trains vehicles were destroyed. An attack by *Kampfgruppe Engelin* from Kagalnitschek gained substantial ground to the east. Engelin's forces netted 150 prisoners and destroyed 15 antitank rifles, 7 heavy machine guns, 2 7.62cm antitank guns, 2 4.7cm antitank guns and 2 heavy infantry guns. In that attack, another 150 enemy dead were counted. Friendly losses: Two wounded.

Further to the south, *SS-Panzer-Grenadier-Division "Wiking"* was being hard pressed by vastly superior Soviet formations. *Kampfgruppe Sander* was sent south to assist. It ran into the enemy at Hill 75.4, forcing him to call off his attack and pull back to the east.

The enemy formed a new offensive main effort in front of the sector of *Kampfgruppe von Winning*. To the north of Shuko Tatarskij, assault guns and riflemen shattered a Russian assembly area. In the village proper, there was heavy fighting between the tankers-turned-infantrymen and the numerically greatly superior enemy. To the enemy's 70 killed, there were only 6 German losses.

The division started to disengage from the enemy at 1600 hours. *Kampfgruppe Engelin* was only able to do that by hard fighting and taking a lot of casualties. At 2225 hours, *Kampfgruppe Sander* was in position in Mokri Batai as the motorized corps reserve.

On 3 and 4 February, the division's troop elements occupied their quarters in Rostov, after *Eingreifgruppe Sander* was released from its mission by the *LVII. Panzer-Korps* at 1200 hours on 3 February. *Schwere Panzer-Abteilung 503*, under the command of *Oberstleutnant* Hoheisel, was attached to the division. Due to the shortage of fuel, only a portion of the trains could link up with the troop elements.

Between Rostov and the Mius 5-16 February 1943

While the formations of the *23. Panzer-Division* set up their quarters in Rostov and hoped for a bit of rest—even if only for a short while—after the heavy fighting of the last few months, the development of the situation soon demanded new operations elsewhere. To the south of the Don, on both sides of Rostov, a number of Soviet field armies were pressing against the German positions. In addition to the three field armies—the 2nd Guards and the 51st and 28th Armies—that had previously faced the *4. Panzer-Armee*, there were soon two more field armies—the 44th and 58th—that had arrived from the Northern Caucasian Front. *Armee-Abteilung Hollidt*, positioned east of Rostov on the Donez, not only faced heavy blows along its front, it was also threatened by an advance of several Soviet tank and mechanized corps that threatened an envelopment of the left wing of *Heeresgruppe Don* at Kamensk.

As early as 24 January, lead elements of Soviet cavalry formations appeared east of Woroschilowgrad on the south bank of the Donez. To the north of the Donez, the Russians soon made rapid gains west in the area that had been opened up by the collapse of the Italians and the Hungarians. The *19. Panzer-Division*, committed in the area around Starobelsk, was unable to decisively influence the situation. Portions of the Soviet forces swung to the southwest from this area and moved on a line running Lissitschansk — Slawjansk with some three or four tank corps and a rifle corps. The objective was also a large-scale envelopment maneuver intended to destroy the German forces fighting in the Donez area. The divisions of the *1. Panzer-Armee*, followed by those of the *4. Panzer-Armee*, that had been shunted through the Rostov bridgehead were intended by the field-army group to counter these enemy forces. They were still marching through the Donez area to the northwest, however.

The *23.Panzer-Division* sent reconnaissance parties to the area around Rostov-Nowotscherkassk. On 6 February, the division's engineers were employed in creating crossing points over the tank ditch east of the city and over the Tusloff. In addition, it was charged with taking prisoner all military-capable men between the ages of 15 and 45 years of age. At the same time, the division incorporated *Rittmeister* Fey's[46] alert battalion from the *24. Panzer-Division* into the division as the *II./PGR128*. In commemoration of the elements of the *24. Panzer-Division* that had been lost at Stalingrad, the company elements of the battalion continued to be referred to as *Schwadronen*.[47] What remained of the original *II./PGR128* was consolidated with the regiment's 1st Battalion, which was commanded by *Hauptmann* Ruge, who had been transferred into the division. *Hauptmann* Pauli, who had previously been assigned to *Pionier-Bataillon 26*, became the commander of the divisional engineers.

The enemy attacked without interruption in the bridgehead south of the Don. At noon on 6 February, he entered Bataisk. Despite a counterattack by both the *111. Infanterie-Division* and the *16. Infanterie-Division (mot.)*, he could not be ejected.

Countless spoils of war fell into Soviet hands in the expansive rail yards of Bataisk. More than 50 fully-loaded trains with rations, materiel and equipment, which had been earmarked for the *6. Armee* and *Heeresgruppe A*, were captured intact. The "harsh command environment" made it impossible for the forces that had still been able to pass by to at least supply themselves with the bare necessities. Hard words were often exchanged between the forces in the field and those entrusted with safeguarding the trains. Everyone saw only his argument as the correct one. But in the end, the trains remained where they were; there were no locomotives available to pull them across the bridge over the Don.

At 1500 hours, the *23. Panzer-Division* was reattached to the *LVII. Panzer-Korps*. It received the mission to establish a passage point for the *111. Infanterie-Division* on the north bank of the frozen-over Don. After the *111. Infanterie-Division* had passed, the division was then to assume the defense of the banks of the Don in the western part of the city and of the Don's delta east of the line Ssultan-Ssaly and Ust-Kuissug. The friendly forces to the right were the *444. Sicherungs-Division (Generalkommando z.b.V.)*.[48]

Panzergrenadier-Regiment 126 occupied the passage point with one battalion on both sides of the West Bridge and its other battalion on both sides of the crossing point to Ssolenoj Island. *Panzerjäger-Abteilung 128*, with its 2 7.5cm antitank guns, 3 5cm antitank guns and 100 riflemen, received orders to assume responsibility for the sector on the right wing between Ssmernikowo — Rostov railway bridge. This sector was intended to be manned later by *PGR128*. The mixed artillery battalion of *Hauptmann* Rodekurth was directed to support *PGR126*.

46 Editor's Note: = *Hauptmann* = captain. Personnel assigned to the *24. Panzer-Division* used cavalry ranks due to their close association with cavalry formations. The *24. Panzer-Division* was largely destroyed at Stalingrad. However, elements such as this battalion were caught outside the pocket when the Soviet completed their encirclement in late November. The division was later reformed and fought almost exclusively on the Eastern Front until the end of the war.

47 Editor's Note: In US Army usage, a *Schwadron* would be the equivalent of a "troop".

48 Editor's Note: = 444th Security Division (General Officer Command for Special Duty). These divisions were intended for object protection, had very limited mobility, little firepower and were manned by personnel who normally could not be assigned to forces in the field.

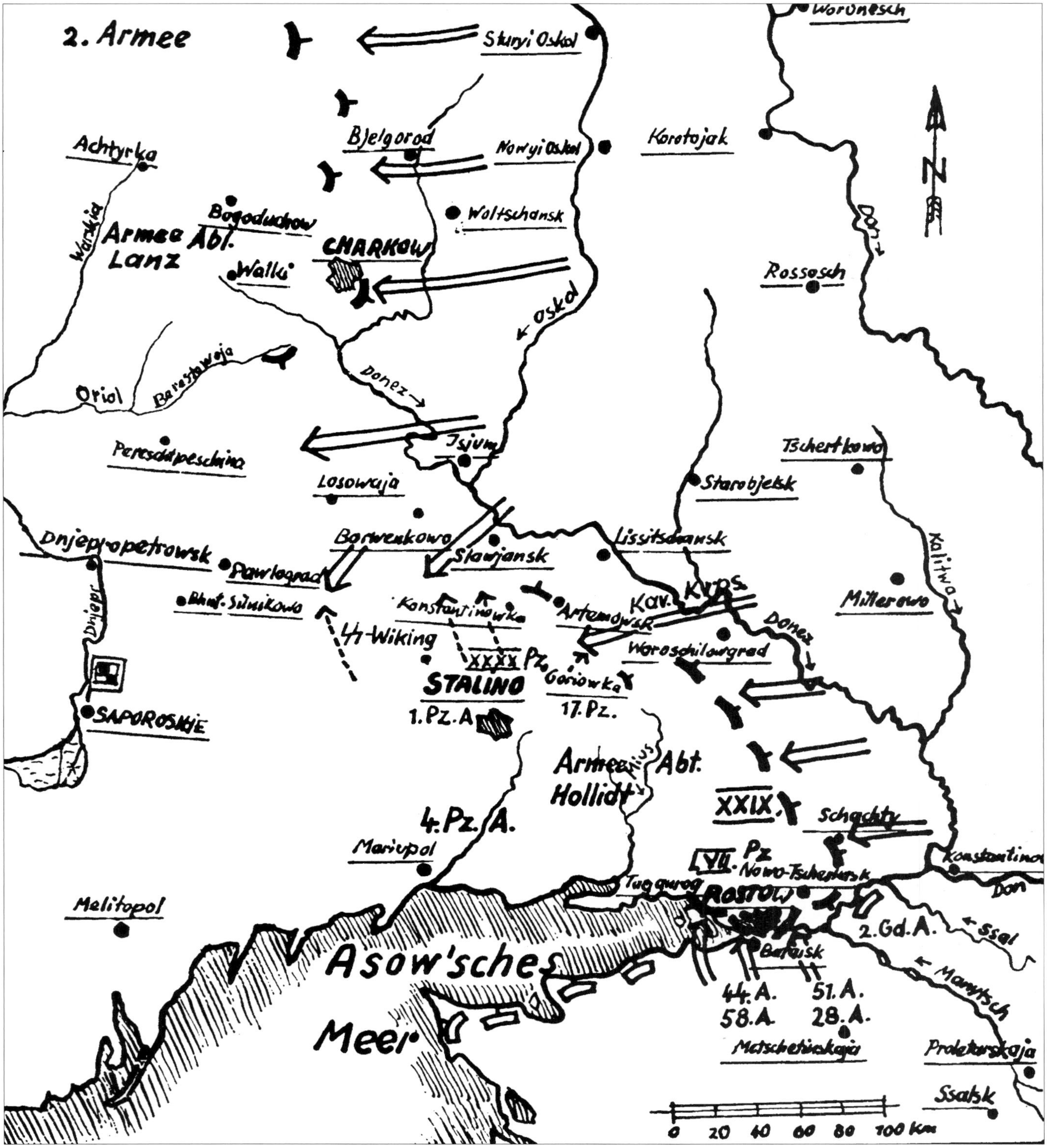

Map 32: The Over-All Situation on 10 February 1943.

During the morning of 7 February, the *111. Infanterie-Division* entered the passage point. The *I./PGR126* of *Hauptmann* Engelin departed for Saretschnaja and the *II./PGR126* for Nish. Gnilowskaja. The tank regiment, *PGR128* and *schwere Panzer-Abteilung 503*, which had been reattached, scouted the area designated for *PGR126*.

Delayed by extraordinarily difficult road conditions, *Hauptmann* Brünn's *PJA128* did not reach Ssemernikowo until 1400 hours. It occupied positions on Hill 37.5. *Sturmgeschütz-Abteilung 243* and *Aufklärungs-Abteilung 117*, the reconnaissance battalion of the *111. Infanterie-Division*, were attached to *Oberstleutnant* Winning's *PGR126*.

The divisional engineers closed out their operations along the Tusloff by taking 150 Russians prisoner.

With the onset of darkness, the enemy attacked along the rail line into the right wing of the *111. Infanterie-Division* on the left. The enemy succeeded in getting as far as the main train station of Rostov and causing considerable disruption to the German rearward lines of communications.

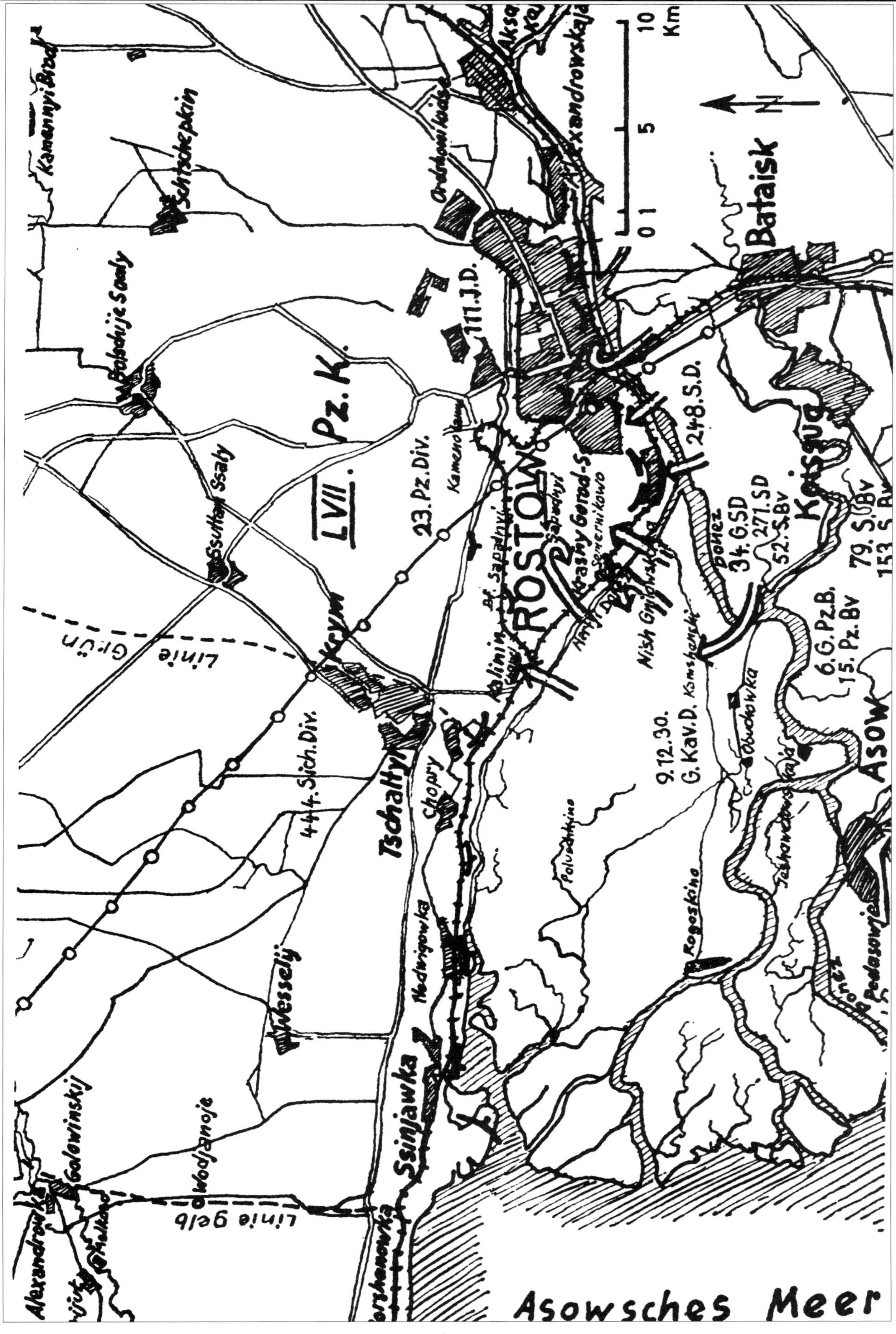

Map 33: Fighting in the Don Delta and the Lines of Resistance East of the Mius, 6-15 February 1943.

At the same time, *PJA128* reported heavy enemy movements on both sides of the Obuchowka — Poluschkino road. The enemy crossed over the iced-over Don between the *I.* and *II./PGR126* with a battalion. Despite the employment of four assault guns, it was impossible over time for the infantry battalions, which were barely half strength, to keep the broad sector free of the enemy. The enemy approached the north bank of the Don in widely dispersed formations again and again. Finally, a Soviet assault detachment was able to establish a foothold in the western part of Gnilowskaja.

Panzer-Pionier-Bataillon 51 was employed against the main train station from the northwest. Two 2cm *Flak* of the *IV./PAR128* were attached to it. At the same time, two companies from *Infanterie-Regiment 50* of the *111. Infanterie-Division* attacked from the east.

Aerial reconnaissance indicated expansive concentrations of Soviets—8,000 men, 1,500 cavalry and 2,000 vehicles—in the Kalinin — Poluschkino area on the right wing of the division. Two hundred forty vehicles were moving from Obuchowka to the north. According to a map captured by *PGR126*, the division was faced by several divisions that had orders to attack to the northeast.

The armored reserve, minus the motorcycle infantry company, was ordered to Sapadnyj.

During this period of withdrawals, the columns of the division logistics command were employed outside of the framework of the division on a recurring basis by order of the field army. Depots, motor pools and even civilian supply dumps had to be evacuated, in order to save them from the grasp of the enemy.

At 0820 hours on 8 February, Soviets appeared at the rail station in Sapadnyj; shortly thereafter, more were seen at the road and railway crossing 1.5 kilometers to the northwest. A *Flak* battery at Krassnyj Tschaltyr engaged enemy tanks in the tank ditches running parallel to the railway line. Contact with the *444. Sicherungs-Division* was lost. Protected by the broad delta of the Don, the enemy was able to infiltrate. The ice covering the Don and the Mertwyj Donez supported his tanks.

At 0940 hours, the enemy broke through the right wing of the antitank battalion. Further to the west, enemy armored cars and truck columns headed north. The enemy was also constantly increasing his presence in front of *PGR126*. The *I./Werfer-Regiment 54* was attached to the division and went into position 1.5 kilometers north of the eastern part of Nishne Gnilowskaja. *Panzergrenadier-Regiment 128* prepared for operations in Kamenolomni, while the motorcycle infantry company covered the Temernik crossings northwest of Rostov.

At 1130 hours, the tanks of *PR201* reached the rail station at Sapadnyj and safeguarded a fuel train that had been earmarked for the *LVII. Panzer-Korps*. Only two of the tankers had been damaged. In an advance against Ssemernikowo, a T-60 was trapped and destroyed. Following the report of an aerial observer concerning enemy tanks and infantry, *PR201* attacked along with the 7.5cm short-barreled main gun *Panzer III's* of the *Tiger* battalion toward the west along the railway line. The surprised enemy was scattered; 13 of his tanks were destroyed and only a few escaped to the west, where aerial reconnaissance had identified the main crossing point of the enemy over the Mertwyj Donez at Chapry.

The attack of *Hauptmann* Pauli's reinforced *PPB51* reached the bridge over the Temernik, just before the main train station, at 1230 hours. Contrary to reports that the *111. Infanterie-Division* had taken it, it was still held by a strong enemy contingent.

The situation on the right wing of the division continued to deteriorate. Around noon, 70 Russians entered the gap between *PJA128* and the *II./PGR126*. *Kradschützen-Bataillon 23* was sent to Krassnyj Tschaltyr to reinforce *Kampfgruppe Sander* (*PR201*). *Aufklärungs-Abteilung 117* was screening with a reinforced company along the Tschaltyrskaja Defile to the south and west. Another company of the battalion combed the terrain between Krassnyj Tschaltyr and the railway line.

Panzergrenadier-Regiment 128 (minus its 2nd Battalion) was sent forward to Sapadnyj in the afternoon.

The Soviets crossed the frozen Don on both sides of Hill 37.5, around which the antitank men had established a strongpoint on the north bank. The Soviets had advanced as far as the eastern portion of Nishne Gnilowskaja in the 1-kilometer gap that existed between them and the *II./PGR128*. *Hauptmann* Knebel's *II./PGR126* was also threatened at the same time from the east and was only holding the northern portion of the middle of the village. The 3-kilometer gap to the left was only weakly covered by a reconnaissance company around the area of the northern edge of Nishne Gnilowskaja.

In Werchne Gnilowskaja, the *I./PGR126* was positioned with a bent back left wing west of the railway bridge.

The situation for both the antitank personnel and the *II./PGR126* was particularly critical. Leaving them along the Don was condemning them to destruction. A recommendation by the division to pull its right wing back to Krassnyj Gorod-Ssad — Sapadnyj — Sapadnyj rail station — Krassnyj Tschaltyr was disapproved by the field army, which pointed out the seriousness of the over-all situation. The division received orders to take the northern bank of the Don at least as far as the defile west of Hill 37.5 and hold it. *Flak-Regiment 17*, located in Rostov, was directed to support the division by the *Luftwaffe*, however, the division was responsible for moving its guns and personnel. A 8.8cm *Flak* battery was attached to *Kampfgruppe Sander*.

That battle group, to which six *Tigers* and the *I./PGR128* were also attached, received the mission of ejecting the enemy from the eastern portion of Nish. Gnilowskaja during the night of 8/9 February and then advancing west as far as Ssemernikowo to clear the banks of the Don.

Kampfgruppe Hoheisel—schwere Panzer-Abteilung 503 (minus 6 *Tigers*), the *II./PGR128* and a battery of 8.8cm *Flak*—had the mission of keeping the western flank of the corps between the Tschaltyrskaja Defile and the Mertwyj Donez clear of the enemy through aggressive actions.

Hauptmann Pauli's *PPB51* cleared the area west and north of the main train station during the afternoon of 9 February. However, it was unable to make progress against the train station itself in the face of a well-concealed enemy in house-to-house fighting. *Oberleutnant* Noever's *3./PPB51* was positioned in front of the train station and a company to the right held a small bridgehead around a road bridge. Several advances on the part of Soviet assault detachments were bloodily repulsed by the engineers.

The enemy continued to assemble additional forces in front of *Kampfgruppe von Winning* and filtered them through the large gaps between the strongpoints. Effective artillery fires apparently had no effect on his activities.

At 0430 hours, *Kampfgruppe Sander* attacked Nishne Gnilowskaja from Krassnyj Gorod-Ssad. By 0840 hours, the western part of the village had been cleared of the enemy. Given covering fire by the tanks, the infantry continued westward. The *6./PGR126* reached the banks of the Don. At that location, the enemy fled across the ice to the southwest. The *I./PGR126* took up positions in the eastern half of Nishne Gnilowskaja. As soon as the German tanks turned their attention to other missions, the enemy attacked again. Taking considerable casualties, the *I./PGR126* had to pull back to the northern part of the village. As the result of an immediate counterattack conducted with the tanks, which had been summoned back, the infantry only partially succeeded in reaching the banks of the Don again. The losses suffered by the infantry were considerable. The *I./PGR126* alone lost 6 officers and 80 men killed or wounded. Several tanks were knocked out by antitank guns or antitank rifles. *Oberstleutnant* Sander broke off the attack, which offered little chance of success,

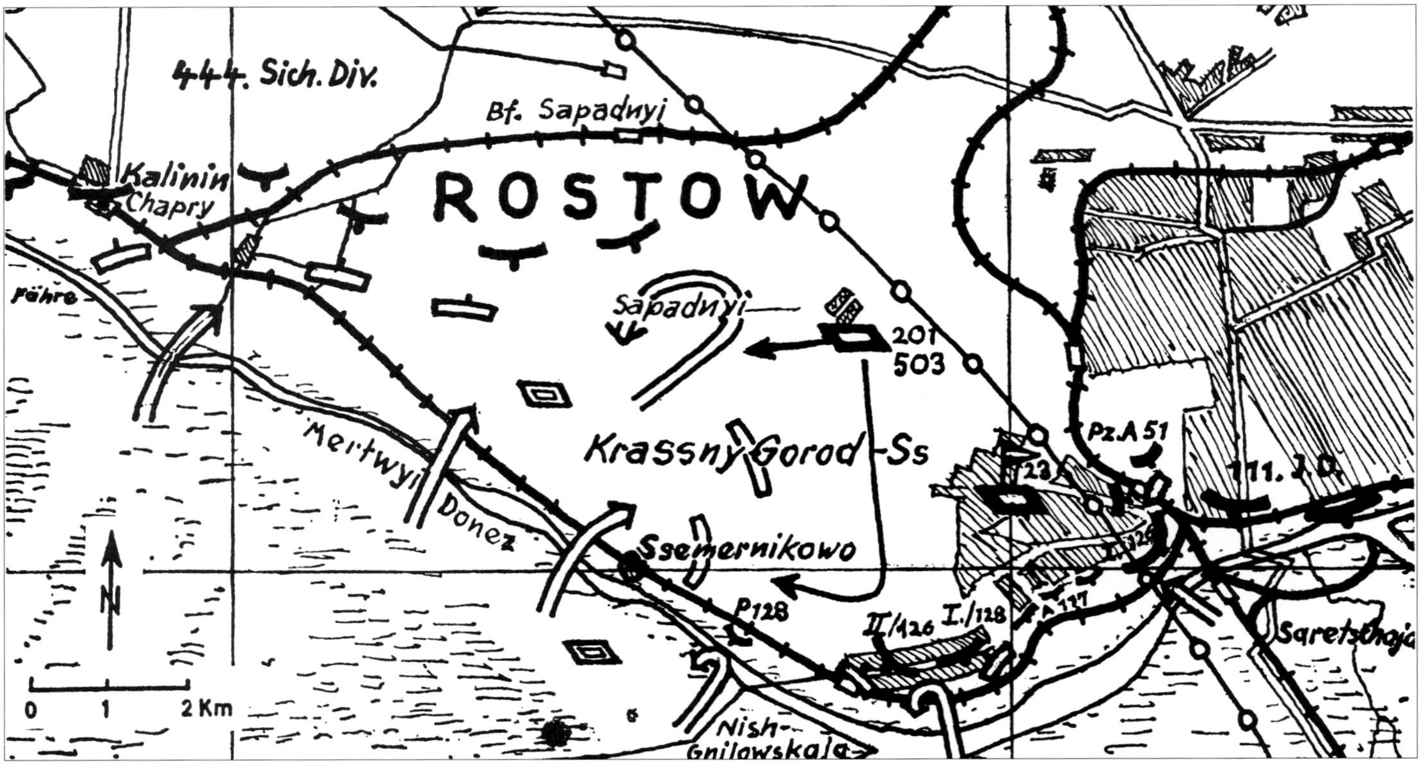

Map 34: Fighting Around Rostov on 10 February 1943.

and sent his tanks in the direction of Ssemernikowo, where he had been ordered to clear the area to the west. Prisoners taken in Nishne Gnilowskaja belonged to the 34th Guards Rifle Division. They had been ordered to take the village and then attack northeast toward Kamenolomni together with a tank brigade—25 T-34's and 25 KV-I's—which was located around Bataisk.

Kampfgruppe Hoheisel determined that the area north of the railway line, as well as the Rostov — Taganrog roadway, was clear of the enemy. At the road bridge 4 kilometers north of Chapry, it established contact with the *444. Sicherungs-Division*.

At 1130 hours, *Hauptmann* Pauli had the majority of his engineers move out to attack from the northwest, since frontal movement against the main train station barely made any progress. The attack carried to within 1 kilometer of the railway bridge. Contact was established to the right with the *I./PGR126*. However, success remained elusive in taking the blocks of houses around the railway property. Patrols established contact with *Infanterie-Regiment 50* of the *111. Infanterie-Division*, which was attacking east of the railway line.

Around noon, moving across the ice, Soviet motorcycle infantry and armored cars attacked the positions of the antitank battalion at Hill 37.5. One armored car was set alight. *Kampfgruppe Sander*, arriving from the west, put a final end to that Soviet attack. Several small groups of enemy forces and a 7.62cm antitank gun were eliminated in the defiles northeast of Ssemernikowo.

Three *Tigers* from *schwere Panzer-Abteilung 503* supported the attack of the *444. Sicherungs-Division* from Point 66.6 to the southeast.

On 10 February, the division once again was ordered to hold its positions along the Don or retake them. The infantry battalions remained in their previous positions and both armored battle groups—*Sander* and *Hoheisel*—were ordered to Sapadnyj. It was intended for them to attack the enemy south of Point 66.9 and the Sapadnyj stopping point or in Nishe Gnilowskaja.

During the course of 9 February, *Kampfgruppe Sander* had taken in more than 100 prisoners and destroyed 1 7.62cm antitank gun, 15 antitank rifles and 11 machine guns.

At 0200 hours on 10 February, strong enemy forces attacked the *II./PGR126* and the *I./PGR128* in Nishne Gnilowskaja. The battalions were able to hold their positions, however, the *I./PGR128* was bypassed. It was not until an immediate counterattack was launched that the enemy was finally ejected. The enemy was quiet in front of the sectors of *PJA128* and the *I./PGR126*; in contrast, he increased his forces to 400 in the sector in front of *PPB51*.

At 0600 hours, the engineers moved out to attack again. Tough resistance only allowed them slow progress.

The *I./PGR126* turned back an attack against it from the east.

The *Luftwaffe* attacked enemy concentrations off the division's right wing to good effect.

Supported by a heavy gun battery, *Panzergruppe Sander* reached Point 66.9 without encountering significant enemy resistance. In the continued advance on Point 44.6, strong enemy groups, which were outfitted with an unusually high number of armor-defeating weapons, were contained and destroyed. Ten antitank guns were overrun or blown to bits. Turning to the southeast, the tanks encountered superior enemy forces—tanks, antitank guns and antitank rifles—at the collective farm 800 meters northwest of Ssemernikowo. After destroying several antitank guns and antitank rifles, the enemy was compelled to flee, leaving behind numerous dead.

At the same time, *Panzergruppe Hoheisel* attacked along with infantry into Nishne Gnilowskaja. The *Tigers* either rammed the houses, which had been reinforced, or set them alight; the attack gradually gained ground. The losses of the infantry were once again so high, however, that they could not hold the area captured or prepare it for defense. An advance along the Don to roll up the enemy failed because the terrain was unsuitable for the *Tigers*. The enemy was able to recapture a portion of the housing blocks along the railway line that had been taken from him.

Supported by 2cm *Flak*, the engineers made good progress in the area around the train station, albeit with heavy losses. The attack had to be called off with the onset of darkness.

Both of the *Panzergruppen* assembled during the evening in Sapadnyj. *Panzergruppe Sander* was able to claim the following for the day: 6 tanks; 15 antitank gun (mostly 7.62cm); and numerous antitank rifles, mortars and machine guns. Six trains vehicles were captured for the *444. Sicherungs-Division*.

Using the concealment offered by the night, the Russians infiltrated through the left wing of the *I./PGR126* and attacked *PPB51* by surprise in the rear. *Panzergruppe Hoheisel*, supported by a troop from the *II./PGR128*, was ordered to attack and destroy those enemy forces during the morning of 11 February and then cut off the enemy in the area around the train station along with the engineers. Several attempts to break out during the night were turned back by the engineers while, at the same time, other enemy groups infiltrated into their rear.

During the morning of 11 February, several company-sized Soviet cavalry elements felt their way across the rail line west of Sapadnyj, but they were turned back.

The tanks attacking under the command of *Hauptmann* Wolf in *Panzergruppe Sander* encountered enemy tanks and antitank guns at Point +5.6. Wolf's tankers destroyed two tanks and several antitank guns, before the enemy pulled back to the southwest. At Point 66.9, contact was re-established with the *444. Sicherungs-Division*, whose infantry moved out for a combined attack south.

Panzergruppe Hoheisel cleared the housing blocks in the rear of *Oberleutnant* Noever's *2./PPB51* until 1030 hours. After being relieved by antitank personnel at the Temernik Bridge, the elements of the engineer battalion that were freed up closed the gap between *PPB51* and the *I./PGR126*.

In the meantime, the *111. Infanterie-Division* succeeded in clearing the final remaining enemy forces in the area of the train station. The only enemy forces left were on the 600-meter-wide penetration point on the railway bridge over the Don.

Seesaw fighting flared up around noon in Nishne Gnilowskaja. Attacking a numerically superior enemy force, the *I./PGR128* was unable to reach the banks of the Don. On the other hand, the *II./PGR126*, supported by assault guns, was able to clear up the area of a Soviet penetration in the western half of the village. Losses on both sides were high.

The enemy continuously brought up reinforcements across the ice of the Mertwyj Donez in front of the positions of *PJA128*. A Soviet battalion advanced north from Ssemernikowo.

The advance of the *Panzergruppe* led by *Hauptmann* Wolf, which worked closely with the *444. Sicherungs-Division*, reached the collective farm 800 meters north of Ssemernikowo at 1500 hours, after a strong blocking position of the Soviets that had been established to the north of it had been shattered. The enemy defended desperately to keep the collective farm. Three enemy tanks were set alight, but two German tanks were also knocked out and two *Tigers* damaged. The continued advance on Ssemernikowo proper was greeted with massed defensive fires coming from tanks, antitank guns and antitank rifles. Soviet artillery joined in the fight from firing positions on the south bank of the Don. *Hauptmann* Wolf broke off the attack. In the course of the withdrawal, a Russian company moving north was caught in the rear and scattered. Both division and field-army artillery supported the fighting the entire day by salvoes fired on Ssemernikowo and Nishne Gnilowskaja.

During the night, the artillery of both sides fired a large number of harassing fires. Aerial reconnaissance at daybreak reported rearward movements of the enemy from Ssemernikowo to the southwest. Since the enemy at the front did not appear any weaker, however, the aerial reconnaissance was probably reporting formations that had been relieved, which had been decimated in the fighting of the recent past.

At 0730 hours on 12 February, *schwere Panzer-Abteilung 503* moved out again against Ssemernikowo. The enemy had reoccupied the collective farm and only allowed himself to be pushed out after heavy fighting. Outside of the village, the Soviets clung to the railway embankment, which proved to be an impregnable tank obstacle, with the result that the attack had to be stopped.

At 0800 hours, with armor in support, the Soviets attacked the *II./PGR126* from the western portion of Nishne Gnilowskaja. The enemy was pushed back with high losses after *Sturmgeschütz-Abteilung 243* and *Panzergruppe Wolf* were committed.

At 0900 hours, the *LVII. Panzer-Korps* issued a warning order for moving back to the Mius Position on the evening of 13 February. According to the order, the *23. Panzer-Division* and the *16. Infanterie-Division (mot.)* had to cover the retrograde actions of the *111. Infanterie-Division* and the *15. Luftwaffen-Feld-Division*.[49] Following that, the *23. Panzer-Division* was to become the field-army reserve in an area 20 kilometers north of Taganrog.

During the morning of 13 February, the enemy assembled strong forces around Ssemernikowo. At noon, two tanks, accompanied by infantry, attacked the *II./PGR126*. However, the enemy attack collapsed.

The divisional engineers turned back Soviet assault detachments several times in house-to-house fighting.

The bridges at Ssultan-Ssaly, 15 kilometers northwest of Rostov, were prepared for demolition.

The withdrawal movements started at 2000 hours. The bridges in the city were blown up. *Panzergrenadier-Regiment 128* had to pull back from the city in the midst of advancing Russians. It took some time to get the regiment reorganized.

At midnight, the division's battle groups were in their new defensive positions: *PGR128* from Point +5.6 to the collective farm 2 kilometers northwest of the rail stop at Sapadnyj; *PGR126* from Leninawan to Trud; *Eingreifgruppe Sander* around Krassnyj Tschaltyr; and *PPB51* in Krym.

Generalmajor von Vormann issued the following order-of-the-day at the conclusion of the fighting for Rostov:

> In accordance with our orders, we held Rostov as long as required by our higher headquarters for the execution of their plans. The enemy's planned breakthrough west of the city, which would have threatened the greater Don Basin, was prevented by us. That placed especially high demands on the will to resist on the part of our grenadiers. You met those demands. You have my recognition.
>
> In attack after attack conducted by the tanks, enemy assembly areas and enemy forces that had broken through were shattered. My special thanks is extended to *schwere Panzer-Abteilung 503* for its devotion to duty and its willingness to assist.
>
> To force the breakthrough, the enemy employed the following:
>
> Starting on 8 February: The 271st Rifle Division; the 34th Guards Rifle Division; the 52nd, 79th and 159th Rifle Brigades; and rifle battalions of the 6th Guards Tank Brigade and the 15th Tank Brigade.
>
> Starting on 11 February: Elements of the IV Guards Cavalry Corps with the 9th, 12th and 30th Guards Cavalry Divisions and the 248th Rifle Division.
>
> In the course of five days, the division knocked out 31 tanks, including 2 T-34's, and 4 armored cars. Eliminated were 13 guns, 21 antitank guns, 58 antitank rifles, 2 infantry guns, 31 machine guns, numerous small arms and other equipment. The enemy lost 350 men taken prisoner; his losses were bloody and high.

49 Editor's Note: = 15th Air Force Field Division. These formations were composed of *Luftwaffe* personnel excess to the needs of the flying units. They were often well equipped but frequently poorly led, since the *Luftwaffe* initially insisted on using primarily air force officers to command the formations. Later on, Army officers were transferred into the divisions and many went on to have distinguished fighting records.

Onward to new deeds!

/signed/ von Vormann

On 14 February, the enemy only followed hesitantly. Sapadnyj was occupied by 400 men at 0530 hours. Reconnaissance efforts and small concentrations of enemy forces were shattered by artillery and rocket launchers. The attack by a Soviet battalion along the rail line around the area of Botanitsch Ssad collapsed. The deep right flank of the division was screened by the division's antitank forces and *Schwere Panzer-Abteilung 503* in Wesselyj.

At 1700 hours, the division, moving in conjunction with the *16. Infanterie-Division (mot.)* on the left, pulled back to the "Green" Line (Northern edge of Krym — Point 69.3 — Point 78.7 — Point 112.4). The reinforced *I./PGR126* had the mission of screening around Ssultan Ssaly as the rearguard until 0900 hours on 15 February. The division's motorcycle battalion held open the crossing point over the Tschaltyrskaja Defile and a company from *PGR126* guarded the road crossing 2 kilometers northwest of Krassnyj Krym.

During the morning of 15 February, the Russians felt their way forward against that road crossing, but they were turned back. At 09000 hours, the rearguard moved back in accordance with its orders; there was no enemy pressure. A standing patrol was left behind, but it did not have to pull back until the afternoon in the face of the advancing enemy.

Heavy enemy pressure against the corps on the left, the *XXIX. Armee-Korps*, forced an extension of the sector of the *LVII. Panzer-Korps*. The division had to include Popoff in its sector.

During the course of the afternoon, the antitank battalion and *schwere Panzer-Abteilung 503* were sent 20 kilometers northwest of Taganrog to their planned assembly areas. The *I./Werfer-Regiment 54* was detached from the division and sent to the *15. Luftwaffen-Feld-Division*. At the same time, the infantry was pulled back to the "Yellow" Line. It was to cover the *15. Luftwaffen-Feld-Division* in its occupation of the "Mole Position" (the Mius Position), while keeping the enemy at bay until the evening of 16 February. *Panzergrenadier-Regiment 128* had the sector Wodjanoje (exclusive) — Golowinskij (exclusive); *PGR126* had the sector Golowinskij (inclusive) — Popoff (inclusive). *Kampfgruppe Sander* was on standby in Kotranowskij and the divisional engineers in Melkosoff.

At 0430 hours on 16 February, *Sturmgeschütz-Abteilung 243* was hurriedly sent to the *16. Infanterie-Division (mot.)* in Nowo Sselje (4 kilometers northwest of Popoff), since it and the neighboring *79. Infanterie-Division* had been attacked by numerically superior Soviet armored forces.

At 0900 hours, an oral warning order from the *4. Panzer-Armee* arrived:

> Contrary to previous intent, *23. Panzer-Division* is to be allocated to the *XXIX. Armee-Korps* [*General der Infanterie* von Obstfelder] with the mission to hold open the bridgeheads at Denisowskij and Matwejew Kurgan with advanced forces and then screen the entire corps sector. Two infantry battalions are to be pulled out of the line immediately and sent to the new sector via Pokrowskoje. At 1700 hours, the remaining elements are to be pulled out of the "Yellow" Line and sent ahead [to the new sector] via Ssambek and Pokrowskoje.

That signaled the end of all hopes for a break in combat operations for the forces of the division. The two infantry regiments—*PGR126* (minus its 1st Battalion) and *PGR128* (minus its 2nd Battalion)—were pulled out of the line and set in march to Denisowskij and Matwejew Kurgan. The antitank battalion was ordered to Rjashenaja by radio. *Schwere Panzer-Abteilung 503* was detached from the division.

Rittmeister Fey's *II./PGR128* and the *I./PGR126* assumed the screening mission in the sector. Forward elements of the *I./PGR126* were still in Kusminskij. The divisional engineers started emplacing obstacles in the Ssambek bottom lands.

At 1230 hours, a Soviet attack group moved out on Kusminskij, taking advantage of the foggy thaw in the weather. The Soviets forced the *3./PGR126* back to Alexandrowka. An hour later, a strong enemy force attacked the *I./PGR126* and forced a penetration in close combat. *Hauptmann* Engelin as wounded. The battalion pulled back to the western slope of the Mokryj-Ssambek Defile.

The divisional engineers reinforced the *II./PGR128* with a company (1 officer and 20 men) in Golowinskij. The Russians put their main effort against the *I./PGR126*, however, and forced the battalion back to Prijut around 1600 hours.

At the onset of darkness, the infantry disengaged from the Soviet forces and moved into the new sector along with the other elements of the division that were still in the old sector.

The Destruction of the Soviet IV Guards Motorized/ Mechanized Corps (16 February to 19 March 1943)

Ever since the pincers attack on Stalingrad, the Red Army had dictated the course of events in southern Russia. Its efforts were directed at not allowing the initiative out of its hands again and destroying the German armies in the field before the upcoming mud period prohibited large-scale operations. In addition to the envelopment movements initiated in the area that had been broken through south of Kharkov, the Red Army gave its all in attempting to prevent the German divisions from occupying the old Mius Position. Its armored and motorized formations launched frontal attacks to that end. At Woroschilowgrad, a Soviet cavalry corps had advanced to Debalzewo, which was already west of the Mius Position. Large armored forces attacking against the center of the Mius Position on 16 February at Matwejew Kurgan attempted to eliminate the *79. Infanterie-Division* before it could reach the river and break through into the area south of Stalino.

Since there were no more reserves at all on the German side, the *23. Panzer-Division* was pulled out of its positions as quickly as possible in its former sector and sent to the area of operations of the *XXIX. Armee-Korps* around Denisowskij and Matwejew Kurgan. Later on, it was sent even further north as far as Alekssejewka.

The *79. Infanterie-Division* reported at noon that enemy tanks had reached the area 20 kilometers east of Matwejew Kurgan. At 1530 hours, the Soviets attacked Matwejew Kurgan itself with tanks. They were turned back for the time being by elements of the *79. Infanterie-Division* and *Flak*. The Russians occupied Staro Rotowka.

Genesenen-Bataillon 79[50], which was employed on both sides of Krinskij along the old Mius Position, was attached to the *23. Panzer-Division*. Two batteries of *PAR128* were brought up as expeditiously as possible.

Even before the *I./PGR128* could arrive from the south, a Soviet battle group, supported by tanks, attacked Alekssejewka and drove out the weak elements posted there from *Sicherungs-Regiment 177*. The corps ordered the division to throw the enemy back over the Mius on 17 February and retake Alekssejewka.

During the course of the evening of 16 February, the remaining elements of the division arrived in the new sector and southwest of Matwejew Kurgan after an 80-kilomter march.

Panzergrenadier-Regiment 128 was ordered to attack Alekssejewka from Alekssandrowka at 0900 hours on 17 February. At the same time, *PR201* was to advance from the southwest in support. The antitank battalion was attached to *PGR128* for commitment during an upcoming

50 Editor's Note: = 79th Convalescent Battalion. The battalion was composed of soldiers whose wounds allowed light duty but not a complete return to the rigors of the front. It was most likely an (unofficial) part of the *79. Infanterie-Division*.

Map 35: The Over-all Situation in the Area of the Donez, 15 February to 15 March 1943.

operation on the regiment's right flank. *Panzergrenadier-Regiment 126* had to release its 1st Battalion to the division; the battalion was sent to the Krynskij — Doropanoff area and remained on alert. The division engineers assembled around Wosykin.

The division pressed into its service all of the non-organic forces found in the sector of *PGR128*. These included: *Pionier-Bataillon 666*; elements of a battalion-sized cadre element from St. Pölten; the headquarters of *Sicherungs-Regiment 177*; *Bataillon Busch*; and *Genesenen-Bataillon 79*.

During the night, the screening group of the *79. Infanterie-Division* evacuated Matwejew Kurgan and pulled back to Stepanowskij.

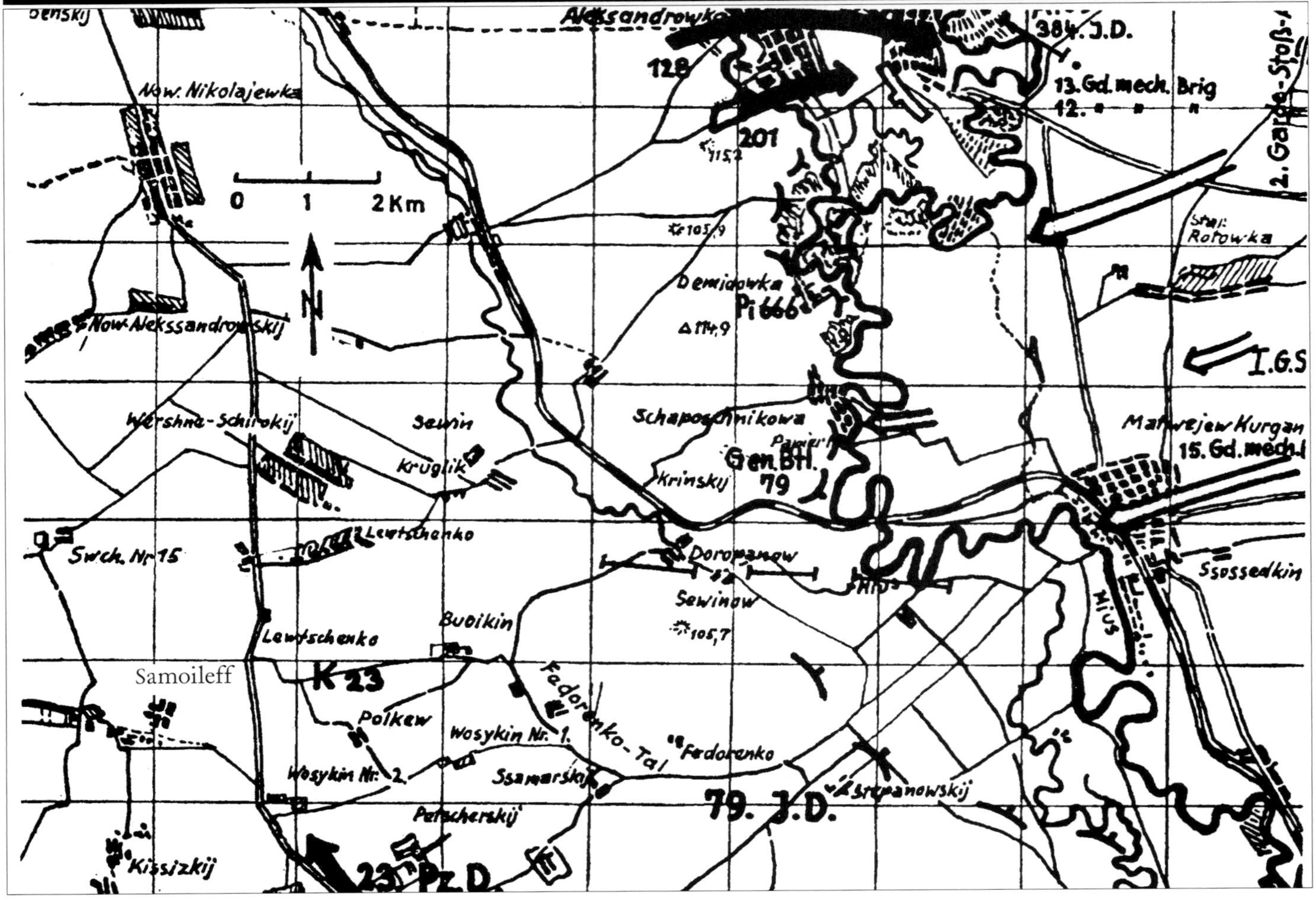

Map 36: Situation on 17 February 1943.

An attack by five enemy tanks against the *II./PGR126* in Denisowskij was turned back, with one T-34 being destroyed and another one damaged.

Panzergrenadier-Regiment 128, working with *PR201*, moved out during the morning of 17 February to attack. With little enemy resistance, it took Alekssejewka and cleared the surrounding area of the enemy. The bridge over the Mius, which was still intact, was blown up. Contact was established with the new friendly forces on the left, the *384. Infanterie-Division*, which was part of *Korps z.b.V. Mieth*[51], at Nowo Nadeshda. The *79. Infanterie-Division* was supposed to close up on the right at Sewinoff, 1 kilometer south of Krynskij. In Denisowskij, *PGR126* was temporarily attached to the *79. Infanterie-Division*. In exchange, the latter division's forces still positioned north of Sewinoff were attached to the *23. Panzer-Division*.

The tank regiment received five new *Panzer IV's*. In addition, five assault guns from *Sturmgeschütz-Abteilung 243* reported in to the division command post at Ssamoiloff. The motorcycle battalion remained in Polkew-Lewtschenko, since most of its motorcycles were inoperable due to the bad road conditions.

Artillery support for the division was provided by the mixed artillery battalion of *PAR128* and the *I./Werfer-Regiment 53*.

During the afternoon, the Russians marched in front of the left wing of the division and at Staro Rotowka.

51 Editor's Note: *z.b.V.* = *zur besonderen Verwendung* = special purpose. In this case, the "corps" was most likely a headquarters element with the capability to command and control a corps or corps equivalent, but did not have any of the normal corps troops assigned or attached to it, e.g., corps artillery. Some sources list this as having been the headquarters for the *IV. Armee-Korps*.

The divisional engineers blew up the bridge over the Mius near the paper factory (3 kilometers west of Matwejew Kurgan).

Toward evening, *PJA128* relieved *Pionier-Bataillon 666* at Demidowka, which then went to the *79. Infanterie-Division*. Platoon by platoon, *PGR128* relieved the remaining elements of *Sicherungs-Regiment 177*, *Bataillon Busch* and *Marsch-Bataillon St. Pölten*, which likewise were sent to support the *79. Infanterie-Division*. In return, the division was supposed to receive back the Headquarters and 2nd Battalion of *PGR126* from the *79. Infanterie-Division* on 18 February.

One hundred Soviets attacked the bridge site at Alekssejewka at first light on 18 February. They were turned back with heavy losses.

At 0830 hours, *Genesenen-Bataillon 79* was attacked in its sector north of the paper factory by a Soviet battalion. After defending for a short period, it gave up its positions and pulled back to the west. Elements of a battalion of the *79. Infanterie-Division*, which was on the right, also pulled back. The enemy immediately brought additional forces forward into the area of penetration and, using them, attacked Hill 114.9, southwest of Demidowka, from the southeast. Enemy tanks were reported in the area of Stepanowskij in front of the *79. Infanterie-Division*.

In order to clear up the threatening situation southwest of Demidowka, the division commander ordered a counterattack with the tanks and the assault guns that were located in the sector of the *I./PGR128*, as well as *PPB51* and the *I./PGR126*. Moving from Point 115.2, the self-propelled 2cm *Flak* of *PGR128* advanced to the south and brought some relief to the hard-pressed antitank personnel in Demidowka. The positions there were held. At the same time, elements of *Genesenen-Bataillon 79* were stopped at Kruglik and brought into position by a senior noncommissioned officer.

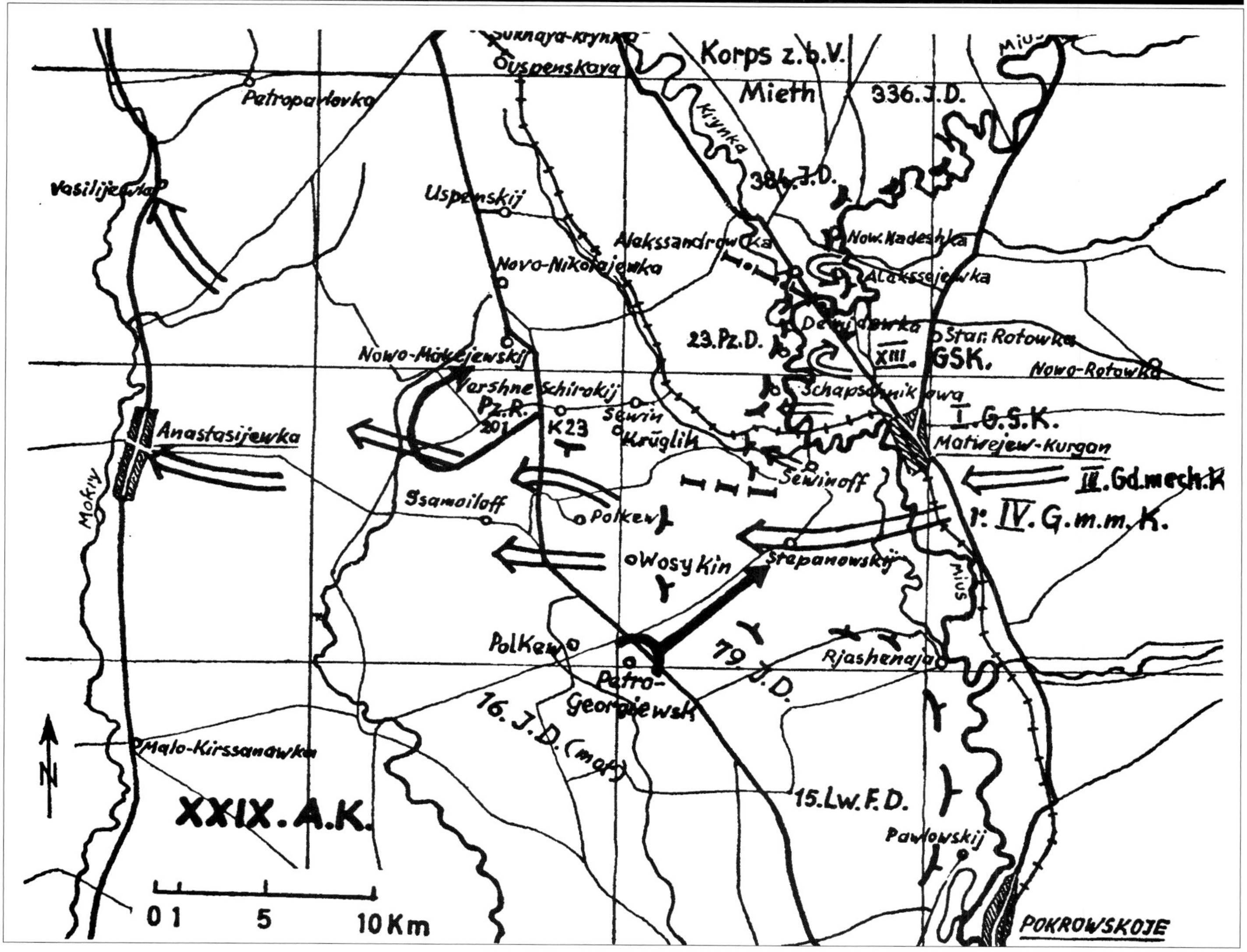

Map 37: Along the Mius on 19 February 1943.
The Breakthrough of the Soviet IV Guards Motorized/Mechanized Corps.

At 1220 hours, two Soviet battalions broke through the front lines of the neighboring *384. Infanterie-Division* on the left. They advanced as far as the area around Alekssejewka. The enemy also penetrated the lines in Nowo Nadeshda.

At 1250 hours, Sepanowskij, in the sector of the *79. Infanterie-Division*, fell to the Russians. Before assault guns urgently dispatched there by the *23. Panzer-Division* could intervene, enemy tanks were already advancing on both sides of the village to the southwest and the northwest. The front in that area had collapsed; the remnants of the *79. Infanterie-Division* assembled around Nowosselowskij, Nowomirowskij, Dobrizin, Garmasch and Polosoff. The Russians quickly made gains to the west.

In the division's sector, the counterattack west of Demidowka started at 1315 hours. Under the command of *Oberstleutnant* von Winning, the commander of *PGR126*, *Genesenen-Bataillon 79* took up positions in the line running along the edge of the hills 2 kilometers southwest of Doropanoff — paper factory (south of Schaposchnikowo). *Panzergruppe Sander* advanced across Point 105.9 (west of Demidowka) on Point 114.9 and brought the *I./PGR126* into position. A Soviet attack against the left wing of the antitank battalion was turned back by it without any outside assistance. At 1500 hours, the *II./PGR126,* attacking along with the *2./PPB51,* reached the area of the paper factory to the left of *Genesenen-Bataillon 79.* Following the attack, the combat engineers were withdrawn and reassembled around Doropanoff.

In the sector of the friendly forces to the right, a *Kampfgruppe* from the *16. Infanterie-Division (mot.)* was employed to clear up the situation, where it appeared a Soviet breakthrough was on the verge of happening. Advancing between Dobrizin and Wosykin No. 1, the Soviet tanks crossed the road to the west.

The two assault guns that had been dispatched by the *23. Panzer-Division* were unable to establish contact with elements of the *79. Infanterie-Division*. Acting on their own initiative, they advanced into Fedorenko Valley and knocked out five T-34's without suffering any losses.

In the neighboring sector on the left, the forces of the *23. Panzer-Division* employed there made good progress in their counterattack north of Alekssejewka. The enemy was unable to introduce more forces.

At the onset of darkness in the division's own sector, the *I./PGR126* was able to establish contact with the left wing of the antitank battalion. The effort to throw the Soviets back across the Mius did not succeed, however.

At 1700 hours, the Russians attacked Pokrowskij (3 kilometers west of Doropanoff) from the southeast and occupied it. At 1800 hours, strong motorized and armored forces of the enemy crossed the road 4 kilometers south of Werchne Schirrokij. The motorcycle infantry company, which had been employed in Lewtschenko to screen, was overrun by an armored enemy force and had to pull back to Werchne Scirokij, sustaining heavy casualties. Counterattacking with support from assault guns, the motorcycle infantry reentered Lewtschenko and took back the village in a fight lasting one and one-half hours.

On 19 February, the *16. Infanterie-Division (mot.)* intended to cut off the enemy from his rearward communications by attacking from Petro-Georgijewsk toward Stepanowskij. To support this attack, the *23. Panzer-Division* moved its ready-reaction force, *Eingreifgruppe Sander*, consisting of the division's tanks, the attached assault guns, motorcycle infantry and, later on, *PPB51*, forward to Werchne Schirokij and Lewtschenko.

While the tanks rolled toward their new assembly area during the darkness, the enemy once again attacked the antitank battalion at Demidowka and forced it to pull back to the eastern edge of hill 114.9 and Hill 105.9.

Oberstleutnant Sander, arriving in Werchne Schirokij, was informed that the enemy was continuously moving truck columns and tanks across the road to the west. On his own initiative, Sander moved with his tanks to the southwest and caught the enemy in the rear. Advancing via Collective Farm No. 15, one supply column after the other of the enemy was caught, with trucks loaded with fuel and ammunition going up in flames. The Russians counterattacked with their tanks; in a hard-fought engagement at close range, four T-34's were destroyed. Two German tanks were knocked out.

Panzergruppe Sander advanced as far as 3 kilometers east of Marfinskaja, eliminated additional enemy columns there and returned in the morning of 19 February at 0400 hours via Proletarskij to Werchne Schirokij. It was not until later that the importance of this night-time advance of the tanks became clear. The attack had shattered the supply columns of the Soviet IV Guards Motorized/Mechanized Corps, which had already reached Anastassijewka, 20 kilometers west of the Mius, with its lead elements. Sander's actions had made the continuation of the Soviet attack impossible.

Without realizing what had happened, the quartermaster section of the division had established itself in Marfinskaja. The next morning, it was determined that the supply soldiers had spent the night side by side in the buildings with the Russians. They quickly headed north, followed by main-gun rounds from the T-34's.

Additional enemy forces entered the breakthrough area to the south of the division sector. Using the concealment offered by darkness, an enemy group attacked Kruglik from the south and ejected the headquarters of *PGR126* from the village.

At the same time, the enemy continuously attacked at and south of Demidowka. *Hauptmann* Veigel's *I./PGR126* had to abandon Hill 114.9 to the enemy, but it was able to seal off a penetration into its lines. The *II./PGR126* was pushed out of a group of houses between Doropanoff and the paper factory. An attack launched on Doropanoff proper was turned back by *Genesenen-Bataillon 79*. Likewise, the enemy's numerous attacks at Schaposchnikowo brought him little in ground gained. In an immediate counterattack, the *I./PGR126* retook Schaposchnikowo and pushed the Soviets back to the Mius. The *II.PGR128* also reached the former main line of resistance along the rail line east of Doropanoff in a counterattack.

By first light, the *384. Infanterie-Division* had cleared up the enemy penetration north of Alekssejewka.

At 0500 hours on 19 February, the *16. Infanterie-Division (mot.)*, along with *Schwere Panzer-Abteilung 503*, moved out from Petro-Georgijewsk, 12 kilometers west of Rjashenaja, to attack.

Contact between the *23. Panzer-Division* and the *XXIX. Armee-Korps* was broken. The division thereupon requested that *Armee-Abteilung Hollidt* reattach it to the *General-Kommando z.b.V. Mieth*.

Panzergruppe Sander moved out at 0710 hours and attempted to take Kruglik in a surprise attack. Despite what earlier reconnaissance had indicated, the armored group encountered numerous antitank guns, so that the attack collapsed after the loss of two tanks and numerous casualties among *Oberleutnant* Schlingmann's engineers. It was not until the entire *Panzergruppe* attacked later on that the enemy was pushed back. Thanks to his numerically considerably superior forces, he was still able to hold the village proper, however. Combat outposts were manned north of the village and at Point 108.0. The main body of the battle group assembled in Werchne Schirokij.

At 0930 hours, the *16. Infanterie-Division (mot.)* took Stepanowskij, thus blocking the point of breakthrough by the Soviets. Moving through Ssamoiloff, Kisslitzkij and Krassnaja Step, the *4./KB23* established contact with the *16. Infanterie-Division (mot.)*. *Generalmajor* Vormann requested that division support his attack on Kruglik. It subsequently released the attached *schwere Panzer-Abteilung 503*, even though it had intended to use the *Tiger* battalion in its attack on Anastaassijewka. The *Tigers* arrived at Werchne Schorokij at 1400 hours.

In the meantime, radio contact was re-established with the *XXIX. Armee-Korps*. It announced its intention of retaking the former main line of resistance throughout the entire sector. The right boundary for the *23. Panzer-Division* was established at Hill 105.7, south of Doropanoff (exclusive).

At 1430 hours, the *Tigers* ejected the enemy once more from Kruglik and also from Ssewin. Once again, the combat engineers were too weak to hold the villages after the *Tigers* departed and the Soviets counterattacked. The enemy re-established himself in the buildings again.

At 1450 hours, surveillance patrols reported enemy movements from Anatassijewka to the east for the first time.

The *XXIX. Armee-Korps* continued to exercise command and control of the *23. Panzer-Division*, but it had *General-Kommando z.b.V. Mieth* be responsible for its logistics. Despite its shrunken combat strength, the division had to extend its frontage, which was not made much easier even after the arrival from the north of the *II./Grenadier-Regiment 610* with the *14.(Werfer)/Artillerie-Regiment 179*. The newly attached grenadier battalion was staged in Nowo Nikolajewka.

Schwere Panzer-Abteilung 503 was ordered back on 20 February to attack Kruglik again. The *16. Infanterie-Division (mot.)* intended on that day to clear Fedorenko Valley and then, together with the *Tiger* battalion, move on Anastassijewka.

During the night of 19/20 February, an enemy attack around Demidowka gained a little ground. Some weaker advances by enemy forces around Doropanoff were turned back by *Genesenen-Bataillon 79* during the morning hours. At 0630 hours on 20 February, the *Tigers* attacked Kruglik along with *PPB51* and the motorcycle infantry company. The enemy forces, numbering 500 men, were completely shattered. They left behind 140 dead and fled to the southwest. Numerous small arms and 10 7.62cm antitank guns were destroyed. While that fighting was going on, a Soviet column of battalion strength arriving from the east went around the right wing of *Genesenen-Bataillon 79*, advanced on Hill 105.7 and occupied it. In a concentric attack conducted by the *16. Infanterie-Division (mot.)* from Stepanowskij and the *Tiger* battalion from the northwest, the Soviet battle group was completely wiped out.

In front of the sector of the *23. Panzer-Division*, the enemy assembled new, strong forces, especially in the area around Matwejew Kurgan and Staro Rotowka. Sixty enemy tanks were identified. A large-scale attack was anticipated. Artillery support from the neighboring divisions was immediately requested and received. In addition, *Korps z.b.V. Mieth* also sent the *1./Flak-Regiment 38* with three 8.8cm *Flak*.

The enemy forces that had broken through toward Anastassijewka remained quiet. Only a few enemy tanks felt their way carefully forward to the east at Uspenskij. Elements of the *II./Grenadier-Regiment 610* were attached to *schwere Panzer-Abteilung 503* for infantry support in the planned attack on Anastassijewka and Marfinskaja on 21 February.

As part of the anticipated issuance of new equipment to the *II./PR201*, the personnel units that had been formed out of the *II.* and *III./PR201* and had been assembled with the trains at Karakuba, were sent to Saporoshe.

On 21 February, the *XXIX. Armee-Korps* placed five 8.8cm *Flak* at the division's disposal. The guns were sent to Uspenskij as the division reserve. *Panzer-Artillerie-Bataillon Rodekurth* of the division participated in the morning to good effect in shattering a strong enemy attack in the sector of the neighboring *Pionier-Bataillon 666* to the left. An enemy advance from Anastassijewka to the east was interdicted by *schwere Panzer-Abteilung 503* at Collective Farm No. 15.

At Schaposchnikow, the Russians succeeded in entering the northern part of the village, but the advance was eliminated by a counterattack conducted by the *I./PGR126* during the afternoon.

The counterattack of the *16. Infanterie-Division (mot.)* against the Soviet IV Guards Motorized/Mechanized Corps made good progress. The enemy was pushed back to the middle of Anastassijewka and Marfinskaja was cleared. When it turned dark, enemy artillery east of the Mius conducted heavy firing on the entire division sector and to the south. At the same time, the Red Air Force bombed and strafed the German positions. In total contrast were the German stocks of ammunition. For instance, for 11 light field howitzers, there were only 320 rounds.

At 0230 hours on 22 February, what remained of the Soviet IV Guards Motorized/Mechanized Corps moved out in its entirety from Anastassijewka to break out toward the east. At 0500 hours, the enemy's large-scale attack from the east started in the right-hand sector of the division between Sewinoff and Demidowka. Advancing with two battalions on the narrowest frontage possible, the Soviets forced an entry into the southern part of Demidowka and ejected the weak *PJA128* from the village to the northwest.

To the east of Anastassijewka, the enemy went around the elements of the *Tiger* battalion that were screening along the Ssamartskaja Defile and crossed the north-south road with the bulk of his forces. Four tanks and 35 trucks attempted to pull back through Werchne Schirokij. Thanks to the alertness of two cannoneers of the *IV./PAR128*, the enemy was unable to break out there. German tanks and assault guns that had moved out were able to completely eliminate that group. The majority of the trucks, among them many captured German ones, were captured intact. Two T-34's were destroyed and two captured.

The enemy attacking from the east forced a breakthrough through the positions of the *I./PGR126* on both sides of Schaposchnikowo at 0620 hours. The battalion pulled back to the west. The *II./PGR126*, on the right, turned back an enemy attack from the south, but then had to be pulled back to the slope northwest of Krynskij due to being threatened in the rear by the enemy that had broken through the sector of the 1st Battalion. In the process, the battalion suffered considerable casualties.

Before the Soviet corps could succeed in breaking out, it was pressed together in Fedorenko Valley by the *16. Infanterie-Division (mot.)*. Elements that attempted to break out to the west across Hill 105.7 were caught by the *I./Flak-Regiment 38*, positioned to the west, and completely destroyed. An armored car and 20 trucks went up in flames. The Commanding General of the Soviet corps, Major General Danatischin, was trapped during the clearing of the battlefield. Since he refused to be taken prisoner, he was shot.

The extent of the victory that the forces of the *XXIX. Armee-Korps* had wrought especially come to light in the synopsis offered by the division's intelligence officer, *Rittmeister Fürst* zu Sayn Wittgenstein, based on captured orders, reports and statements by prisoners:

The Destruction of the IV Guards Mechanized Corps

Lieutenant Colonel Anatol Winigradow, the commander of the 38th Guards Tank Regiment (13th Guards mechanized brigade), and his adjutant, 1st Lieutenant Demjan Badgora, both captured on 22 February 1943 west of Hill 1205.7, stated:

> The IV Guards Mechanized Corps moved out of Matwejew Kurgan during the evening of 18 February to the west with three guards mechanized brigades with a total strength of 1,000 riflemen and 45 tanks. The corps had the mission of breaking through as far as Anastassijewka in order to cut off the route back for the German forces. Since there was no resistance there, the [Commanding General], Major General Danastischin, wanted to advance further west. The final objective was announced as Mariupol. After the fuel columns were set alight by German tanks at Werchne Schirokij during the night of 18/19 February and the supply routes had been cut, the corps decided to remain in Anastassijewka.
>
> At 2100 hours on 21 February, a Russian aircraft landed southwest of Anastassijewka and presumably brought with it the order to break out to the east. At 2300 hours, the corresponding orders were issued. Around 0200 hours on 22 February, [the corps moved out in its entirety] from Anastassijewka. After heavy losses were sustained at Werchne Schirokij during an ambush by fire by German tanks and *Flak*, the column turned south so as to get out through Fedorenko Valley. To the east of Dubinin, strong elements were eliminated by German antiaircraft guns. The remnants of the IV Guards Mechanized Corps attempted to fight their way through to Matwejew Kurgan by moving east of Hill 105.7 through Doropanoff and along the railway line. They were wiped out south of Doropanoff.
>
> The attainment of the operational objective [of the corps] failed due to the loss of the fuel columns, the rapid closing of the German front, which prevented the bringing up of additional elements, as well as the result of the energetic actions of the tanks and antiaircraft guns during the breakout attempts of the encircled forces.

A captured statement by the head of a section of the NKVD in the 12th Guards Mechanized Brigade, Guards Lieutenant for Intelligence, Bacherew:

> The combat strength of my battalion before the attack on Matwejew Kurgan was 236 enlisted and 40 officers. In the course of the breakthrough through the enemy positions, only half of the soldiers performed their duty, while the other portion drove away in their vehicles. The battalion then found itself in a pocket. Starting on 19 February, the battalion commander was no longer up to his duties. Supplies of ammunition and fuel had been destroyed by enemy fires. At the time, there were 70 soldiers of the battalion in Anastassijewka; to that number must be added 25 who had already been captured by the Germans. Have rations for two days. Ammunition running out; completely missing hand grenades and tank grenades.

Interrogation record of Lieutenant Colonel Winogradow, Anatol Alexandrowitsch, born in 1905 in the Kasan area, commander of the 38th Guards Tank Regiment:

> Military career: 1925-28, infantry officer school at Ulianowsk; company commander in Leningrad until 1932. May to September 1932, training on tanks at the armor school; assistant battalion commander of a tank battalion until 1935. Following that, several months in the Far East conducting espionage activities. Garrison commander. 1941 commander of the reconnaissance battalion of the 58th Tank Division. First combat operations in November 1941 outside of Moscow, then Chief-of-Staff of the 35th Tank Brigade (30th Army). Since 15 October 1942, commander of the 44th Tank Regiment (62nd Motorized/Mechanized Brigade), which was redesignated as the 38th Guards Tank Regiment (13th Guards Mechanized Brigade) at the beginning of February 1943.
>
> Organization of the IV Guards Mechanized Corps: [The corps] belonged to the 51st Army, which was recently allocated to a shock army (5?). Commanding General: Major General Danastischin.
>
> Organization of the 13th Guards Mechanized Brigade: [three Guards Rifle Battalions, numbered 1-3]; 38th Guards Tank Regiment; 13th Guards Artillery Battalion; Antiaircraft Battalion; Mortar Battalion.
>
> Organization of the 12th Guards Mechanized Brigade and the 15th Guards Mechanized Brigade analogous. The tank regiments of those brigades had the numerical designators of 37 and 39. For some

time, the tank regiments were no longer organized in special tank brigades; instead, they have been attached to mechanized brigades.

Organization and equipment of the 38th Guards Tank Regiment: Headquarters with a command tank (T-34); 1st Company of 11 medium tanks (T-34); 2nd Company of 11 medium tanks (T-34); 3rd Company of 16 light tanks (T-70). Authorized strength: 39 tanks. Actual strength (20 February 1943): 16 tanks. Personnel authorized strength: 360 men.

Replacement situation: Personnel replacements from Swerdlowsk. Replacement detachment unknown. No shortage of replacements. However, length of training only short (three to four months).

Tank replacements also immediately upon request.

The steel [armor] appears to have become somewhat worse recently. Likewise, the construction has become cruder externally, but that can have little effect on combat power.

Logistics: Fuel for tanks was always available. His tanks never remained idle for a lack of fuel.

Rations were sufficient and better than before.

Operations: After being employed at Ssimownikij at the end of December 1942, in Pawlowka, near Ssimownikij, refitted.

No enemy contact during the approach through Schachtij, however, there were already mechanical losses of tanks.

First employment at Matwejew Kurgan. Mission: "Enemy withdrawing. Break through to Anastassijewka. Hold up the withdrawing enemy there and destroy him."

When the corps no longer encountered any resistance after breaking through, the Commanding General wanted to advance as far as Mariupol, however, could not do it due to the fuel columns not coming through.

The brigades of the corps were not up to full strength during the breakthrough: Each brigade had approximately 300 men. In all, a total of some 1000 men, in addition to 45 tanks, broke through.

While the corps was in Anastassijewka, the Commanding General had personally ordered the arming of the civilians in the occupied villages.

Interrogation record of 1st Lieutenant Badgora, Demjan, born 1922 in Kiev, chief-of-staff (adjutant) of the 38th Guards Tank Regiment:

Military career: 10 years of vocational-prep school; military academy at Kalinin from 1939-1941. Chief-of-Staff of a tank battalion (220th Tank regiment of the 110th Tank Division). Since 25 December 1942: Chief-of-Staff of the 38th Guards Tank Regiment. Special training on flamethrower tanks (T-26) and chemical agents (armor).

IV Guards Mechanized Corps: Corps allocated to the 51st Army until the beginning of February, then allocated to the 5th Shock Army. Neighboring corps unknown.

V Guards Mechanized Corps was supposed to follow, presumably to take the place of the IV Guards Mechanized Corps.

Since the tank divisions proved impractical and were split up, the main effort has been focused on the formation of mechanized corps, consisting of three mechanized brigades.

Organization of a mechanized brigade: Three rifle battalions; one tank regiment; one antiaircraft battalion; one artillery battalion, one mortar battalion, one antitank rifle company; and one signals company.

Efforts are being made to ensure that mechanized corps only have automatic weapons. Amount of weaponry considerably more than a normal rifle corps. The prisoner did not know the numbers.

Mission of the mechanized corps: Punch through, creating a pathway; break through deeply; and form pincers.

Operations: Mission of the regiment at Matwejew Kurgan was to break through to Anastassijewka and, from there, further to the west.

When the corps determined in Anastassijewka that the logistics columns had not followed and the supply route had been blocked, it was forced to remain [there]. When the rations and fuel ran out, the decision was made to break through back to the east.

The order to break through to the east was apparently brought by an aircraft, which landed near Anastassijewka during the evening of 21 February. The Commanding General went to the aircraft and issued orders for the breakout soon thereafter.

All of the combat elements of the [tank] regiment were to be found in Anastassijewka, albeit not at full strength.

General comments: Morale of the forces elevated, especially after they had been elevated to Guards status shortly before. This elevation had the following consequences: Double pay; better rations; Guards insignia (worn on the right breast); addition of the word Guard as part of the rank.

A new weapon—"Andruschka"—is apparently a "Stalin Organ" with less firing capacity. Some of the rounds with deep effect against bunkers; some with a greater explosive effect. Employment doctrine unknown.

There is supposed to be a German prisoner-of-war camp at Kalinin with about 400 prisoners, who are employed in road construction. It was stated there were separate camps for officers and enlisted.

Interrogation record of Red Army Private Ganiskow, Jakob, loader on a 4.5cm antitank gun in the antitank battery of the 15th Guards Mechanized Brigade:

The antitank gun remained behind in Matwejew Kurgan because a repair was needed and did not participate in the breakthrough of the corps to Anastassijewka. Five days ago (23 February) remnants of the IV Mechanized Corps arrived in Matwejew Kurgan. There were about 10 trucks and 2 light armored cars.

The rumor spread among the troops that the Commanding General, Major General Danastschin, was a prisoner of the Germans.

It was not known whether other elements of the IV Mechanized Corps had remained behind [and did not participate in the initial breakthrough].

***

The *Luftwaffe* attacked to good effect against the Russians advancing from the east. Unfortunately, 14 *Ju-87's* suddenly dove on Alekssekewka, which was being held by *Hauptmann* Ruge's *I./PGR128*, and destroyed numerous buildings that had been fortified into strongpoints.

The enemy position on Hill 114.9, west of Demidowka, which had been jutting into the German lines ever since 19 February, was attacked by *PPB51*, the *II./Grenadier-Regiment 610*, three assault guns and six 2cm *Flak* around noon. At 1300 hours, the hill was taken against tough enemy opposition, but the casualties were so high that the attack could not be continued further east. For a short period, *Oberleutnant* Noever's *3./PPB51* entered Schaposchnikowo with the assault guns; *Hauptmann* Veigel's *II./PGR126* reached the area around the paper factory in the course of the attack operation.

The losses sustained among battalion commanders and acting battalion commanders were exceptionally high. Wounded were *Hauptmann* Pauli (*PPB51*), *Hauptmann* Brünn (*PJA128*), the acting commander of the *I./PGR126* and *Oberleutnant* Noever (*3./PPB51*). The adjutant of *PGR126* was killed.

At 1430 hours, the *III./Grenadier-Regiment 535* arrived at Point 114.9. It had been made available through the comradely assistance of the *384. Infanterie-Division*. It went into position to the left of the *II./Grenadier-Regiment 610*. At the same time, the division artillery of the *384. Infanterie-Division*, *Artillerie-Regiment 384*, joined in the fight by supporting the operations around Demidowka.

Three hundred men from *Marschbataillon "Wöllersdorf"*[52] were sent to the division to cover the most urgent personnel shortages. The missing noncommissioned officers could not be replaced, however. The combat power of the infantry regiments continued to shrink.

That day saw the destruction of 8 tanks, 1 armored car and 80 motorized vehicles in the division sector alone. Only weak remnants of the IV Guards Motorized/Mechanized Corps succeeded in breaking through to Russian lines during the night in the sector of *Pionier-Bataillon 666* on the right. *Rittmeister* Fey's *II./PGR128* conducted a successful patrolling operation against Soviet bunker positions during the night in the area north of Demidowka.

At 0800 hours on 23 February, an enemy regiment attacked out of Schaposchnikowo. Despite extremely heavy casualties, the enemy continued to storm forward. In the end, weak elements reached the northern end of the defile north of Krynskij. The resumption of the German counterattack around noon in the area of Point 114.9 caught those enemy forces and ejected them to the east. Despite the support of the assault guns, the infantry and grenadiers were unable to drive the Soviets from the edge of the high ground. Once again, German losses were considerable. As it turned dark, the *1./Pionier-Bataillon 48* arrived to reinforce *PPB51*. It went into position on that battalion's right at Point 114.9.

The *II./PGR126* was attacked on three sides. Despite considerable losses, the battalion held its positions on both sides of the paper factory. In order to prevent its complete annihilation, the division commander finally ordered it to be pulled back as far as the bend in the railway line 1 kilometer west of the paper factory. Artillery, *Flak* and the *14.(Werfer)/Artillerie-Regiment 179* put a stop to every additional enemy attack. Besides massive artillery support, the enemy was also receiving additional help in the form of ruthless commitment of the Red Air Force.

The combat strengths of *PGR126* and *PJA128* had sunk to an absolute minimum. The ability of the division to fulfill its combat missions without being given more forces was in serious question. The *1./Pionier-Bataillon 48* had to be pulled out of the main line of resistance to assist in the urgent construction of positions. At 0400 hours on 24 February, the division received orders to retake the former main line of resistance running from the paper factory to Demidowka. To that end, it was reinforced with *Grenadier-Regiment (mot.) z.b.V. 287*, which was to arrive in Werchne Schirokij by 0600 hours. To the east and southeast of Alekssejewka, the enemy was assembling large numbers of infantry and rocket-launcher formations; otherwise, however, he remained quiet.

At 1130 hours, the *I./Grenadier-Regiment (mot.) z.b.V. 287* moved out from the area west of Alekssandrowka and moved south. At the same time, tanks and assault guns attacked south from Point 115.2. Even before reaching the German front lines there were losses sustained due to the heavy artillery fires from Soviet guns on the east bank of the Mius. The enemy defended desperately. An enemy immediate counterattack into the exposed open left flank of the *I./Grenadier-Regiment (mot.) z.b.V. 287* led to a difficult crisis, but it was mastered in the end. The battalion had fought all the way to the vicinity of the paper factory as it started to turn dark. The *II./Grenadier-Regiment (mot.) z.b.V. 287* had to call off its attack northwest of Demidowka due to the heavy losses sustained by flanking fires. The formations that had been committed there already were also unable to advance. The *II./Grenadier-Regiment (mot.) z.b.V. 287* was pulled back to its line of departure, and the regiment's 1st Battalion assumed the defense of the sector running from the east of Krynskij to the west of the paper factory. The *II./PGR126* was pulled out of the line and moved to Simowniki. The division engineers under *Leutnant* Sauthoff became the ready reserve in Proletarskij and Nowo-Alekssandrowskij, where they received orders to build fortifications along with the *1./Pionier-Bataillon 48* and *KB23*. The construction of the field fortifications was under the supervision of the commander of the *1./Pionier-Bataillon 48*, *Oberleutnant* Vogel.

The division intent then became to conduct an attack by sectors to regain the former main line of resistance along the Mius. To that end, the *I./Grenadier-Regiment (mot.) z.b.V. 287* moved out at 1130 hours on 25 February. After an hour, and encountering heavy resistance, it reached the area 800 meters west of the paper factory. At 1400 hours, the nose of the hill just west of the paper factory was firmly in German hands. The battalion then transitioned to the defense. *Genesenen-Bataillon 79* established contact with the right wing of that battalion.

The motorcycle infantry battalion was attached to *PGR126*. It maintained contact between the left wing of the *I./Grenadier-Regiment (mot.) z.b.V. 287* and the right wing of *Hauptmann* Aich's *III./Grenadier-Regiment 535* by means of a screening line.

The division was arranged in its sector from right to left as follows: *Genesenen-Bataillon 79*; *I./Grenadier-Regiment (mot.) z.b.V. 287*; *KB23*; *III./Grenadier-Regiment 535*; *I./PGR126*; *II./Grenadier-Regiment 610*; *PJA128*; *II./PGR128*; and *I./PGR128*. Available were: *II./PGR126*; *II./Grenadier-Regiment (mot.) z.b.V. 287*; *PPB51*; and the *1./Pionier-Bataillon 48*. From *Marsh-Bataillon "Don"*, the division received 140 replacements. Fifty soldiers who had been separated from the two infantry regiments reported back for duty.

The acting commander of *PGR128*, *Major* von Einem, and his adjutant were wounded by a salvo of rockets. The *II./PGR128* turned back a nighttime attack from the south on Alekssejewka. It was supported in its efforts by the divisional artillery of the *384. Infanterie-Division*.

Starting on the night of 25/26 February, the division transitioned to the defense, since it was no longer intended to retake the former main line of resistance in the face of the anticipated casualties. The *II./Grenadier-Regiment (mot.) z.b.V. 287* started to relive the motorcycle battalion and the *III./Grenadier-Regiment 535*. It was intended for the *I./PGR126* and the *II./Grenadier-Regiment 610* to be relieved by the *I./PGR128*, after that battalion had, in turn, been relieved by the fought-out *II./PGR126* at Alekssejewka.

The losses for the division from 16 to 26 February 1943 are listed below:

Formation	Officers			NCO's and Enlisted		
	KIA	WIA	MIA	KIA	WIA	MIA
PR201	—	—	—	7	9	—
PGR126	2	10	—	70	259	33
PGR128	—	2	—	5	38	3
PAR128	—	3	—	1	11	—
KB23	—	—	—	9	12	19
PPB51	—	5	—	6	51	8
PJA128	—	3	—	8	14	—
PNA128	—	—	—	—	1	—
Division logistics elements	—	—	—		5	—
Grenadier-Regiment z.b.V. (mot.) 287	1	6	—	24	139	3
General-Marsch-Bataillon XII/79	—	4	—	19	88	34

52 Editor's Note: = March Battalion "Wöllersdorf". March battalions (and companies) were generally *ad hoc* formations and units formed for the purposes of transporting replacements to the front. In this case, the battalion was diverted from its originally intended destination and pressed into the service of the *23. Panzer-Division*. Personnel thus gained usually stayed with their new formation.

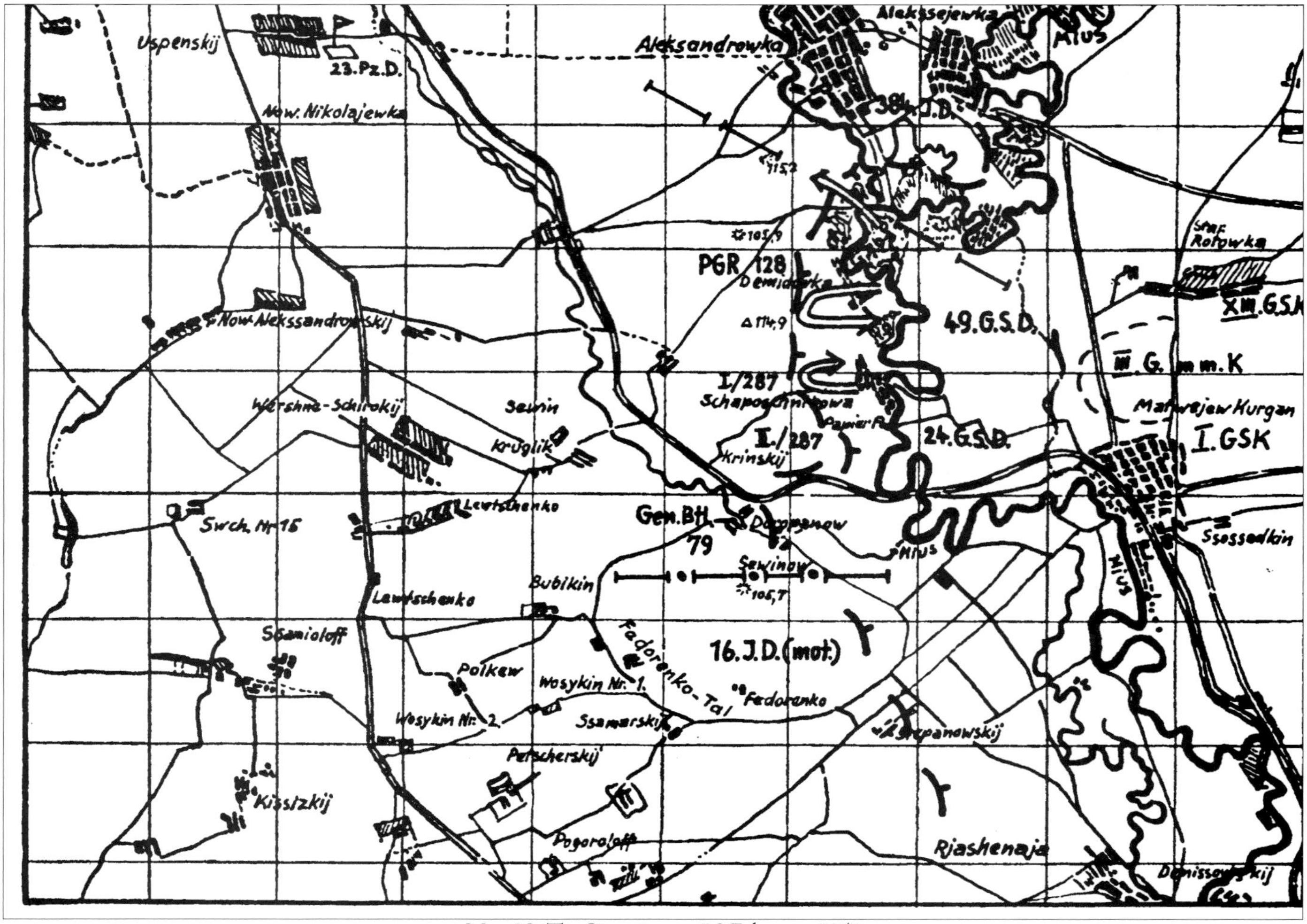

Map 38: The Situation on 28 February 1943.

Formation	Officers			NCO's and Enlisted		
III./Grenadier-Regiment 535	—	—		5	20	—
Totals	3	33	—	154	647	100

At 2400 hours on 27 February, the division moved from the command and control of the *XXIX. Armee-Korps* to that of *Korps z.b.V. Mieth*. On that occasion, the Commanding General of the *XXIX. Armee-Korps*, *General der Infanterie* von Obstfelder, issued the following order-of-the-day:

> The *23. Panzer-Division*, with its forces, *Sturmgeschütz-Abteilung 243* and the *I./Flak-Regiment 38* all made significant contributions to the destruction of the IV Motorized/Mechanized Corps, which was mentioned in the *Wehrmacht* Daily report on 24 February. Contributing to its destruction was, above all, due to cutting off the supply routes of the enemy that had penetrated, which then made it impossible for his continued advance west. By doing so, the prerequisites were created for the complete destruction of the IV Guards Motorized/Mechanized Corps. This meant not only the destruction of numerous tanks, vehicles and other articles of war, it also meant the elimination of a grave danger for our own front.
>
> I think of those killed during this fighting with gratitude and respect and wish the wounded a speedy recovery.
>
> I also wish to express my special recognition to the leaders and the troops for their proven offensive spirit and their brave commitment to duty. Once again, they have proven the superiority of the German soldier over the Bolshevik enemy.
>
> /signed/ von Obstfelder, *General der Infanterie*

***

The *II./Grenadier-Regiment 610* and the *II./Grenadier-Regiment 535*, which had been relieved by *PGR128*, assembled in Alekssandrowka.

At 1430 hours, densely massed forces of the enemy moved out to attack west of Schaposchnikowo. *Stuka* dive bombers, which happened to approach these forces by chance, identified and scattered them with high losses to the enemy. The *Luftwaffe* continuously attacked Soviet concentrations around Matwejew Kurgan during the day.

The 28th of February was ushered in with light frost and snowfall, as well as heavy artillery fires of all calibers and salvoes from Soviet heavy infantry weapons. At 0935 hours, three to four Soviet battalions attacked between the paper factory and the eastern slope of Hill 115.2. The German defensive fires brought the attack to a standstill. Four T-60's were also unable to rally the Soviet infantry forward. After a short while, three of those four were burning, victims of the assault guns. The fourth T-60 quickly turned away.

During the afternoon, two additional attacks conducted by freshly brought in forces also collapsed, despite strong support from Soviet artillery.

The construction of the German field fortifications made good progress.

According to a corps order, the division turned over the left-hand portion of its sector to the *384. Infanterie-Division* so that it could prepare a portion of its forces to become the ready reserve of the corps. The new left-hand boundary of the division was at Hill 115.2 (inclusive). The *II./PGR126* was relieved by the *384. Infanterie-Division* during the course of the night and moved to Anastassijewka, where the regimental headquarters and the 1st Battalion, as well as *PJA128*, were already located. Those two infantry battalions had been especially battered during the most recent fighting.

The *II./Grenadier-Regiment 610* was sent by truck to the *79. Infanterie-Division*; the *III./Grenadier-Regiment 535* returned to the *384. Infanterie-Division*, which, in turn, released the *II./PGR128*.

The following elements had assembled in Nowokarakuba, west of Wolnowacha: One of the division's maintenance companies; *Panzer-Werkstatt-Kompanie 201* (minus one platoon); cadre units of the *II.* and *III./PAR128*; what remained of the division's field-replacement battalion; the trains of the *II./PGR128*; the 2nd Medical Company; light engineer column. To the west of Saporoshe were cadre units from *PR201* (minus its 1st Battalion) and the *IV.(Flak)/PAR128*.

During the afternoon of 1 March, *Genesenen-Bataillon 79* was relieved by the *II./Grenadier-Regiment (mot.) z.b.V. 287* and sent to its parent division by truck. One battery from *Sturmgeschütz-Abteilung 243*—three guns—was sent to the *336. Infanterie-Division*.

Soviet battalion-sized attacks against Hill 105.9 and from Demidowka collapsed in front of the German lines. The mixed artillery battalion of the division shattered enemy concentrations near Matwejew Kurgan through its fires.

The main line of resistance was reinforced with continuously running line of wire obstacles and minefields.

During the morning of 2 March, an attack by two Soviet companies came to a standstill in front of the positions of the *I./PGR128*; weak elements were able to infiltrate in a narrow gap between the division's left wing and the right wing of the *384. Infanterie-Division*, which had not been closed due to a misunderstanding. The *23. Panzer-Division* received orders immediately to clear up the situation. The division declined the offer of making the *II./Grenadier-Regiment 535* on the left available for the operation; instead, the *4./KB23* was sent to the *I./PGR128* to reinforce it.

While preparations were underway to seal the penetration, 300 Soviets attacked the right wing of the battalion between Hills 114.9 and 105.9. Heavy artillery and mortar support enabled the enemy to make a small penetration. The *I./PGR128* lost seven light machine guns to shrapnel. An immediate counterattack was launched with the regimental reserve. Supported by three assault guns, the reserves turned back the enemy, although he had been able to bring up reinforcements to the area of the penetration in the meantime from Demidowka. Five Soviet antitank guns were eliminated.

The *4./KB23* moved out on the left wig of the *I./PGR128* in the afternoon and ejected the enemy forces that had infiltrated southeast of Hill 115.2 in close combat. The gap in the main line of resistance was closed. The *2.* and *3./Flak-Regiment 38* were sent to the sector of the *384. Infanterie-Division*.

In the days that followed, the enemy attempted several times to break into the German lines with large assault detachments. On two occasions, penetrations had to be eliminated with immediate counterattacks. The artillery battalion enjoyed good success in scattering enemy concentrations. Four more assault guns of *Sturmgeschütz-Abteilung 243* had to be sent to the sector of the *336. Infanterie-Division*, with the result that only five guns remained with the *23. Panzer-Division*. The assault gun battery of *Grenadier-Regiment (mot.) z.b.V. 287* returned to its regiment in Krynski; it had two guns operational.

On 5 March, an increased state of alert readiness was ordered across the entire front. Both *PGR126* and *PGR128* were ready to move, since Soviet deserters had reported an imminent Soviet offensive. The *Luftwaffe*, together with the artillery, engaged enemy concentrations throughout the corps sector. Widely dispersed around Matwejew Kurgan were 34 enemy tanks and numerous motorized vehicles. Late in the morning, the enemy started an artillery preparation. Soon thereafter, 400 Soviets attacked the sector between Hills 105.9 and 115.2. The enemy attack did not come to a standstill until just outside of the German lines. Two Soviet antitank guns were eliminated by *Flak*. The division's artillery battalion silenced three enemy batteries arrayed around the railway bridge across the Mius.

During the night of 5/6 March, 900 replacements arrived for the division.

The German Army High Command ordered that *PR201* be reorganized into only two battalions of four companies each.

Snowfall aided a surprise attack by 400 Soviets at first light on 6 March against the *I./PGR128* southeast of Hill 105.9. Despite heavy casualties, the enemy reached the wire obstacle. Individual Soviets climbed over it and entered the position. The German immediate counterattack ejected these forces, but it was unable to prevent the enemy from digging in 150 meters in front of the German positions. The construction of field fortifications by the enemy was identified on this day along the entire sector. The *16. Infanterie-Division (mot.)* and the *336. Infanterie-Division*, in addition to the *23. Panzer-Division*, reported larger-scale retrograde movements on the part of the enemy in the area around Matwejew Kurgan. To all appearances, the enemy was regrouping; large-scale rearward and little forward movement continued over the next few days. At night, Soviet harassment aircraft, such as the *U-2* "Sewing Machine," made continuous flights over the German front and unsettled the forces in the lines with their bombing runs.

On 8 March, the *I./Grenadier-Regiment (mot.) z.b.V. 287* succeeded in destroying a group of enemy soldiers numbering 70. The enemy group had approached the battalion's positions in the fog and was caught right in front of the wire when the fog lifted.

The *3./Heeres-Artillerie-Abteilung 585* went into position in the division's sector with its 21cm howitzers. The sound-ranging section of the division artillery regiment returned from its attachment to the *16. Infanterie-Division (mot.)*.

The division received additional replacements from Germany. The *II./PR201* was sent to the homeland for new equipment training on the *Panzer V "Panther"*. The *IV.(Flak)/PAR128* also returned to Germany to be reconstituted at the Wahn Training Area. The *1.(Panzerspäh)/KB23* was sent to Roshdestwensk.

During the evening of 12 March, a telephonic warning order arrived concerning the relief of the division and its movement to the Charzyssk — Makejewka area.

The re-establishment of the *II./PGR128* was started in Marfinskaja, which was to take the place of the elements that had been temporarily attached from the *24. Panzer-Division*.

A weak enemy advance west of Schaposchnikowo on 14 March was turned back. The heavy howitzers knocked out two enemy tanks around Matwejew Kurgan. Soviet deserters confirmed that the 24th Guards Rifle Division had been relieved in its positions around the paper factory by the 152nd Rifle Division.

The relief of the *23. Panzer-Division* started during the evening of 16 March. In the middle of these movements, which planned for only a partial assumption of the sector of *PGR128* by *Grenadier-Regiment (mot.) z.b.V. 287*, a strong enemy battalion attacked without any artillery preparation. The enemy pressed forward across the wire obstacle. Both grenadiers and infantrymen together brought the enemy force to a standstill and ejected it in a fight lasting 75 minutes. The divisional artillery prevented the enemy from bringing up reserves by firing final protective fires.

The *336. Infanterie-Division* assumed the division's sector incrementally. For the time being, *Grenadier-Regiment (mot.) z.b.V. 287* remained in its positions. The *1./Pionier-Bataillon 48* returned to the command and control of the *336. Infanterie-Division*. The mixed artillery battalion of the *23. Panzer-Division* was attached to the *336. Infanterie-Division*, remaining in its positions. *Sturmgeschütz-Abteilung 243* became the corps reserve. The relief-in-place was completed by 19 March.

The *23. Panzer-Division* then moved to its new assembly and battlefield reconstitution area. Billeting areas were drawn as follows: *PGR128* in Ilowaisk; *PPB51* in Sugress; *PJA128* in Kirowo; *KB23* in Chanshenkowo; *PGR128*, the majority of the division support command, *PNA128*, *Feld-Ersatz-Bataillon 128*, the 2nd Medical Company and the ambulance platoons in Makejewka; the 1st Medical Company in Ilowaisk (at the local military hospital); *PR201* (minus its 2nd Battalion) in Charzyssk; and the 2nd Maintenance Company in the Rembasa Works in Stalino. The cadre units of *PAR128* were still in the trains area at Karakuba. The alert battalion from the *24. Panzer-Division* was detached from *PGR128* and sent to France to rejoin that division for its reconstitution. Its equipment was transferred to *PGR128*.

Both *PR201* and *PGR126* were designated as a ready reserve by the headquarters of the *6. Armee*.

For the first time since 12 May 1942, the *23. Panzer-Division* was afforded the opportunity to conduct a battlefield reconstitution. It had a lot of heavy fighting behind it; on several occasions, it was on the verge of no longer existing. But the fighting spirit of its soldiers and the obstinacy it demonstrated saved it over and over again. The hard struggle for Stalingrad had demanded the utmost in the ability to resist on the part of every member of the division, regardless of whether he had been employed at the front, had been used to keep the logistics flowing or was responsible for the care of the wounded. It was during this winter that the division earned its place among the armored divisions of the Eastern Front, a status it would keep until the bitter days of May of 1945.

At the conclusion of the fighting along the Mius, the Commander-in-Chief of the *6. Armee*, *General der Infanterie* Hollidt, issued the following order-of-the-day on 9 March 1943:

> The *23. Panzer-Division* performed magnificently during the fighting from 16 to 26 February 1943 and inflicted extremely heavy casualties on the enemy in both the attack and the defense despite its numerical inferiority. The division was significantly involved in the successful defense of the Mius Position against enemy attacks and in the destruction of the Red IV Guards Motorized/Mechanized Corps, which had broken through the front.
>
> I would like to express my special recognition to all of the forces of the *23. Panzer-Division* involved, including the attached formations, and to the excellent leadership of *General* von Vormann.
>
> The Commander-in-Chief
> /signed/ Hollidt
> *General der Infanterie*

The Reconstitution of the 23. Panzer-Division in the Makejewka Area 20 March to 3 July 1943

March of 1943 allowed the German art of leadership, as well as the unbroken fighting spirit of the German soldier, which were recognized by both friend and foe alike in the early war years, to appear brilliantly one more time.

During those days, *Generalfeldmarschall* von Manstein and the forces of *Heeresgruppe Süd* succeeded in closing the front, which had been ripped apart everywhere after the catastrophe of Stalingrad and along the Don, and bringing the enemy to a standstill along the Mius and the Donez. Exploiting the last few days before the spring thaw, the *4. Panzer-Armee*, the *1. Panzer-Armee* and *Armee-Abteilung Kempf* closed the 100-kilometer-wide gap in the front from Grischino (west of Stalino) and the area south of Barwenkowo. At the same time, the *1. Panzer-Armee*, attacking north, had cleared the area of the Donez of the enemy and occupied the southern bank of the Donez between Lissitschansk and Isjum. On 14 March, Kharkov was retaken by *SS* formations and the area up to Belgorod cleared. Several Soviet field armies were destroyed; the Soviet offensive power had been broken.

But the German forces were also in dire need of reconstitution. The armored and motorized divisions became ready reserves behind the infantry divisions. Replacements in soldiers and materiel were conducted in a cycle established by the field-army group. In that process, the *23. Panzer-Division* was in sixth place.

Rittmeister Fey's alert battalion (from the *24. Panzer-Division*) and all of the personnel of other Stalingrad divisions were sent to Germany for the complete reconstitution and re-establishment of their formations. Those elements left their equipment behind for the *23. Panzer-Division*.

By order of the German Army High Command, the *22. Panzer-Division* was inactivated and its remaining elements consolidated with the *23. Panzer-Division*. That division had fought in a self-sacrificing way in the middle of the collapsing Rumanian 3rd Army against the onslaught of the Soviet formations and had lost the majority of its equipment. Its remnants were formed into *Kampfgruppe Burgstahler*, together with remnants of the *24. Panzer-Division*, and employed in the sectors of the *XVII. Armee-Korps* and the *384. Infanterie-Division*, where they contributed in no small manner to the success of the withdrawal to the Mius Position.

In the Malo-Tschistjakowo — Sneshnoje area on 6 April, the *23. Panzer-Division* received the following elements, all of them from the disbanded *22. Panzer-Division*:

- Remnants of *Kradschützen-Bataillon 24*
- *1.(Sfl.)/Panzerjäger-Abteilung 140* to *PJA128*
- One mixed company from *Panzer-Nachrichten-Abteilung 140* to *PNA128*
- One tank company from *Panzer-Regiment 204*, consisting of 10 *Panzer III's* with long 5cm main guns , 4 *Panzer III's* with 5cm main guns, and 2 *Panzer IV's* with long 7.5cm main guns to the *I./PR201*
- One armored group with three companies of *SPW's* to *PGR126*
- One maintenance company to the division maintenance services

The *I./PGR129* of *Hauptmann* Schägger followed later, which was to form the newly activated *Panzer-Feld-Lehr- und Ersatz-Bataillon 128*.[53] A *Sturm-Infanterie-Geschütz-Batterie* was also formed, which had seven 15cm heavy infantry guns mounted in an armored superstructure on a *Panzer IV chassis*. Led by *Oberleutnant* Götz von Schwanenflies, the battery was incorporated into the tank regiment as the *9.(StuIG)/PR201*.

During the first few days of April, the last element that had not reported back to the division—the *I./PAR128* in support of the *336. Infanterie-Division* along the Mius—returned.

Numerous officers, whose names would earn a good reputation in the *23. Panzer-Division*, joined the division as part of *Kampfgruppe Burgsthaler*. These included Hauptmann *Schägger, Hauptmann* Arnold, *Hauptmann* Bergmann, *Oberleutnant* Boulanger, *Oberleutnant* Zorell, *Oberleutnant* Götz von Schwanenflies, *Oberleutnant* von Berlepsch and *Oberleutnant* Grünwaldt.

Major Matzen, the commander of *Panzerjäger-Abteilung 140*, succeeded *Major* von Einem in command of *PJA128*. *Oberstleutnant* Sparre assumed command of *PGR128*. *Hauptmann* Holenia became the new commander of *PPB51*.

The convalescent and personnel battalion that arrived in quick succession were divided among the division's forces by the divisional adjutants.

53 Editor's Note: = 128th Armored Field Instructional and Replacement Battalion, which was a formation formed by the division itself.

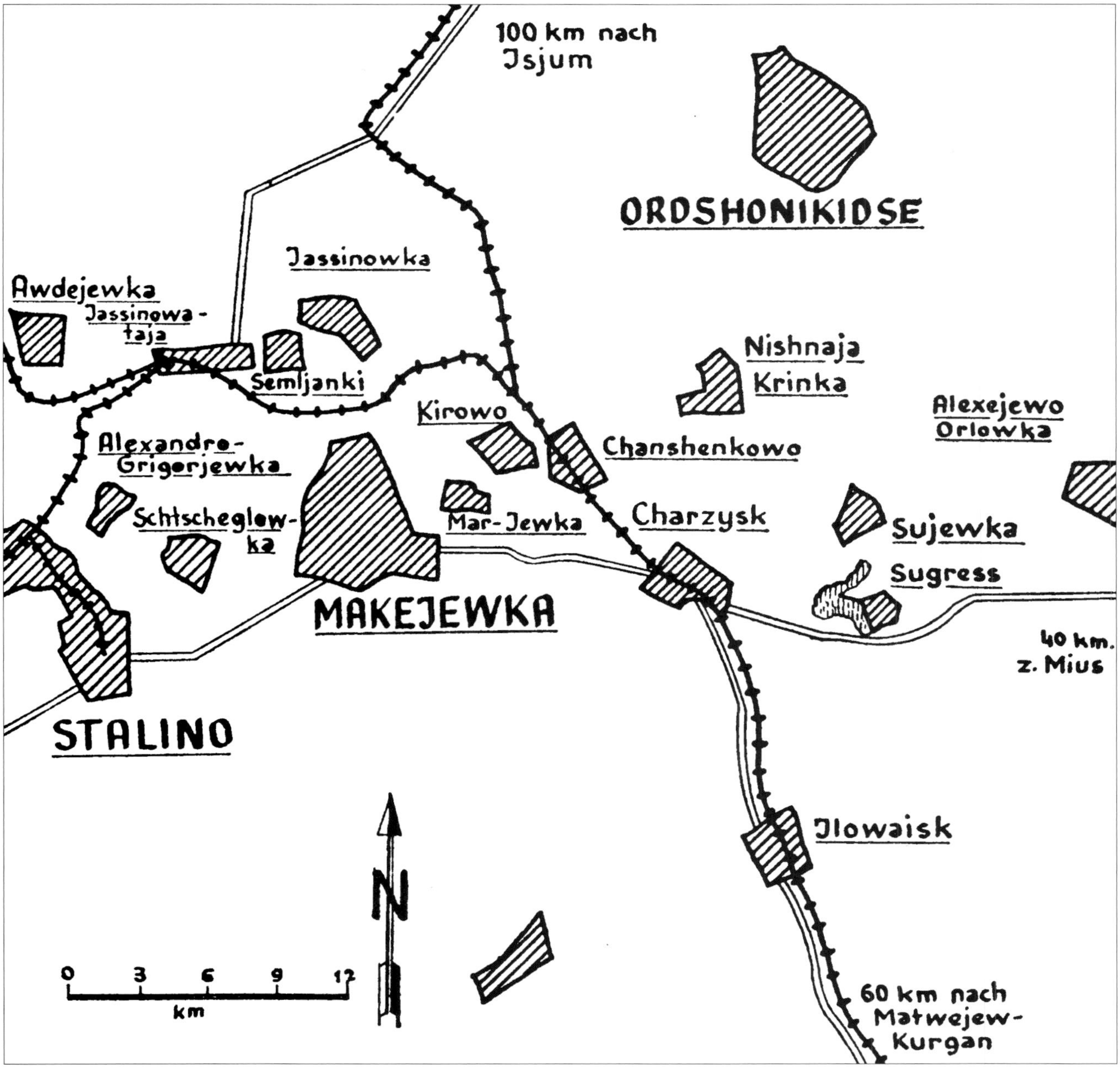

Map 39: Billeting Areas of the *23. Panzer-Division* Around Makejewka.

Personnel Replacements for the *23. Panzer-Division*
in the Timeframe from 18 March to 31 May 1943

Date	Unit/Formation	Officers	NCO's	Enlisted
31 March	*Genesenen-Marschkompanie*	—	—	185
3 April	*Marsch-Bataillon z.b.V. für schnelle Truppen 104*	—	17	460
11 April	*Flak-Marsch-Bataillon 5*		23	111
29 April	*Marsch-Bataillon 23/7 Panzer*	—	34	479
12 May	*General-Marsch-Kompanie 23/3 Panzer*	—	14	231
22 May	*General-Marsch-Kompanie 23/4 Panzer*	—	21	221
18 March to 31 May	Individual replacements	44	47	125
Totals		44	156	1839
10 April	*Kampfgruppe Burgsthaler*	42	404	1757
Aggregate		86	560	3596

Oberfeldwebel Wyrwa and *Gefreiter* Murauer of the division's operation's section.

April 1943: The division headquarters in Makejewka.

Personal hygine in the field.

The regimental band practises for the sports fest.

Oberst Burmeister, *Hauptmann* Stiewe and Rüdt von Collenberg.

Stiewe, the commander of the *III./PR 201*, with his adjutant.

General von Vormann attends the division's sportsfest. Next to him is *Oberstleutnant* von Winning, the commander of *PGR 126*.

The division enjoyed a short respite in April 1943, which allowed a battlefield reconstitution and a short break for the men.

Elements of PR 201 conduct a pass-in-review during the course of their battlefield reconstitution.

The regimental musicians appeared to get a work out during this period.

The Division Commander shares a lighter moment with the commander of *PR 201*, *Oberst* Sander. In the back is *Oberleutnant* Schulz, an Assistant Operations Officer in the division headquarters.

Oberst Sander appears to be a good sport as he is brought in to direct the band.

The Division Commander inspects his artillery. To his left is *Oberst* von Born, the commander of *PAR 128*. *Hauptamnn* Rebentisch accompanies von Vormann in his capacity as the Assistant Division Operations Officer.

The Division Command inspects *Major* Baran's *I./PAR 128*.

Members of the divisional artillery enjoy a short break on a nice day in Makejewka.

At Makejewka in May 1943, the division conducted an exercise during a lull in operations. Visiting the training were a number of dignitaries, including *General der Panzertruppen* Hube (*6. Armee*), here seen with the Division Commander, *Generalmajor* von Vormann.

General der Panzertruppen Hube.

On the far right is Hube, flaked by von Vormann. On the viewer's left are General Köhler, the commander of the 306. Infanterie-Division, and General Bork, the Chief-of-Staff of the 6. Armee.

Left: Oberleutnant H.-H. Grahn; right: Major Koch-Erpach.

Oberst Dr. Born, the Commander of PAR 128, and Oberleutnant Pollack, the divisional artillery adjutant, wait in the wings.

General von Vormann discusses the training with Oberst Sparre, the commander of PGR 128.

Soldiers take a break posing in and around one of the battery commander's staff cars ofPAR 128.

Supply personnel of PGR 126 receive orders at Makejewka.

Commanders and staff officers observe the training. In the first picture, Oberst Sander, the commander of PR 201, can be seen to the left. On the right is Hauptmann Rebentisch.

Observers at the training exercises.

The critique following the exercises.

An orthodox Soviet chuched misused by them for improper purposes.

An artillery forward observer's position.

Hotly contested Hill 277.9 along the Mius. A stream of prisoners starts to head to the rear.

The adjutant of *PAR 128*, *Oberleutnant* Pollack.

Gefreiter Lehmann, a motorcycle messenger for the headquarters of *PAR 128*. He was later killed in August 1943.

Hauptmann Behr (Knight's Cross), the commander of the *I./PR 201*, observes the sky while *Leutnant* Dern, the battalion adjutant, listens to radio traffic during the Second Battle along the Mius in July 1943.

The *15cm Sturm-Infanterie-Geschütz (sfl.)* of *PR 201*. These images were taken during the fighting along the Mius in July 1943.

The *sIG33B* was quite a rare vehicle. Only 24 were produced and the *23. Panzer-Division* was the only division equipped with it. An independent *StuG* company was sent to Stalingrad in November 1942. *9./PR 201* operated the vehicle. The 15cm weapon could demolish most houses and small buildings with 2 or 3 rounds.

In the foreground is a *Pz.Bef.Wg. III Ausf. F* medium command tank. Behind the line of prisoners is a *sIG33B*.

A Model 18 light field howizer of *PAR 128* at the moment of firing.

The divisonal battle staff in July 1943 along the Mius: *Oberst* Sparre (Commander, *PGR 128*), *Major i.G.* Litterscheidt (Operations Officer), *General* von Vormann, *Oberleutnant* Schubert and *Leutnant* Engel (Assistant operations Officer).

Leutnant Engel, *Oberstleutnant* von Winning (commander, *PGR 126*) and *Major i.G.* Litterscheid.

Leutnant Engel, *Major i.G.* Litterscheid, *Hauptmann* Rebentisch (Assistant Operations Officer) and *Leutnant* Dantzer (Liaison Officer).

New equipment; the ubiquitous *Kubelwagen* and a *Panzer IV Ausf, H.* Note the ever-present PK photographer.

July 1943: Final defensive measures are planned before a Soviet attack at the Secod Battle of Isjum.

Hauptmann Wolf, the commander of the *I./PR 201*, received the Knight's Cross in July 1943.

Hauptmann Rebentisch with the Division Commander, *Generalleutnant* von Vormann, during the fighting at Garanyj (Mius) in July 1943. On the right is *Leutnant* Engel, an assistant operations officer. in the division headquarters.

Von Vormann in his command and control *SPW*. Next to him is *Major* Hoffmann, the commander of *PNA 128*.

The command and control vehicles on the battlefield, heavily camouflaged against the resurgent Red Air Force.

Leutnant Heinrichs, the air-ground coordination officer, hard at work. Note that the *Leutnant* is a *Luftwaffe* officer.

A member of the division battle staff looks out onto the battlefield.

Hauptmann der Reserve Robert Alber, the commander of the *2./PR 201*, was awarded the Knight's Cross later on for his actions during the Second Battle Along the Mius.

Soviet prisoners and elements of the divisions military police detachment (recognizable by the gorgets they wore in the field).

The regimental headquarters and the *I./PR201* had 2 *Panzer II's*, 5 *Panzer III's* with short main guns, 12 *Panzer III's* with long main guns, 2 *Panzer III's* with short 7.5cm main guns and 26 *Panzer IV's* with long main guns.

Major Illig, the former commander of the *III./PR201*, was reassigned to the unassigned officer manpower pool of the German Army High Command after his battalion was inactivated.

On 14 April, *Major* Matzen reported his *PJA128* as operational with two companies of self-propelled antitank guns and one company of 2cm *Flak*.

The divisional engineers received new Type "K" bridging equipment.

A searchlight section was allocated to the *IV.(Flak)/PAR128*, whose heavy batteries had been sent to the Wahn Training Area near Cologne for reconstitution. The *Flak* battalion was also detached from the divisional artillery and redesignated as a separate battalion, *Heeres-Flak-Artillerie 278*.

The regiments and battalions conducted training from the individual level through the formation, with live fire exercises receiving emphasis. All engineers of the division were attached to *PPB51* for special training. At the same time, officers from the division headquarters and, later on, from all of the combat formations, conducted reconnaissance of the areas of operation within the sectors of the *XVII. Armee-Korps* and *General-Kommando z.b.V. Mieth*.

The recently formed *Panzer-Feld-Lehr- und Ersatz-Bataillon 128* of *Hauptmann* Schägger (Adjutant: *Oberleutnant* Grünwaldt) consisted of five companies: the 1st Company for *PGR126*; the 2nd Company for *PGR128*; the 3rd Company for engineers; the 4th Company for signals personnel; the 5th Heavy Company with a platoon of tanks (one *Panzer III* and two *Panzer IV's*), a section of artillery (one light field howitzer and one heavy field howitzer), one platoon of tank destroyers (one self-propelled antitank gun and one towed antitank gun), a section of *Flak* (one 8.8cm *Flak* and three 2cm towed and self-propelled *Flak*. A noncommissioned officer course was attached to each company. Attached to the battalion headquarters as well were *Pferdekolonne Lang*[54], the division band (*Musikmeister* Reiter) and the vehicle reserves of the division. The mission of the battalion was twofold: The training of noncommissioned officers and the in-processing of reserves for the combat forces.

The maintenance and repair services of the division and the regiment performed magnificently during these weeks. These elements, whose operations often stood in the shadows of the successes earned at the front, were given special recognition in Makejewka. *Oberfeldwebel* Schwarz, the maintenance section leader of the *6./PR201,* was awarded the Knight's Cross to the War Service Cross with Swords for his superb performance, frequently under enemy fire. He was the first and only soldier of the division to be so recognized during the war.

On 1 May, the division established *Waffen-Werkstatt-Kompanie 128*[55] from its own assets. Formed in Makejewka and under the command of *Oberleutnant* Mildenberger, the company was charged with the repair of all heavy weapons (except tank main guns), small arms, field messes etc. near the front. That responsibility formerly belonged to the division's two armament platoons.

On 8 May, the division reported it was completely ready for any type of offensive mission. The division was capable of moving 94% of its assets in one lift. It was only among the columns of the division support command that numerous trucks were still in need of overhauling.

The *3.(Fla)/PJA128* was redesignated and reassigned to the *Flak* battalion, where it was intended to become its 4th Battery. Until the heavy batteries returned from their reconstitution in Germany, however, the battery remained with the antitank battalion.

On 14 May, the ready reserve of the division—*PGR126*, the *3./PR201* and the *4./PAR128*—were placed on 2-hour alert standby. Enemy movements and increased artillery fires led to the conclusion that the enemy had offensive intentions along the Mius Front. The remaining elements of the division continued their training. The high point of that training was an exercise led by *Oberstleutnant* Sander, the commander of *PR201*, involving a *Kampfgruppe* with air support. The Commander-in-Chief of the *6. Armee*, *General der Infanterie* Hollidt, and numerous generals were on hand as observers. On 16 May, the alert status of the ready reserve was rescinded.

The infantry regiments each mounted rocket launchers on eight trucks in a weapons system of their own design. These launchers were then assigned to the heavy infantry gun companies as reinforcements.

The "K" type bridging column of *PPB51* was sent to Kharkov to help train *Pionier-Bataillon (mot.) 52*.

In the meantime, the final decision had been made in the *Führer* Headquarters concerning the operational intent for the summer of 1943 on the Eastern Front. By means of strong armored formations, the Soviet salient, which was 500-kilometers long and extended far to the west into the German front around Kursk, was to be eliminated by the *4. Panzer-Armee* advancing north from Belgorod and the *9. Armee* marching south from the area south of Orel. The strong Soviet formations positioned there were to be eliminated. The German Army High Command hoped to paralyze Soviet offensive power by that move. The original start date initially seen for the attack, 15 May, was postponed by Hitler, who was influenced by *Generaloberst* Model, even though the Chief of the General Staff of the Army, *General der Infanterie* Zeitzler, as well as the Commanders-in-Chief of *Heeresgruppe Süd* and *Heeresgruppe Mitte*, *Generalfeldmarschall* von Manstein and *Generalfeldmarschall* von Kluge, raised objections to doing so.

The enemy gained time and knowledge of the German plans. He finished reconstituting his forces in the field and pushed them forward toward the German front along the Mius and the Donez (near Isjum) in pursuit of his own offensive planning. Moreover, he considerably reinforced his forces positioned around Kursk and constructed a deeply echelonned defensive system.

The frontage of *Heeresgruppe Süd* was largely stripped of its reserves in favor of the German offensive grouping at Kursk. Only the *16. Panzergrenadier-Division* (as the former *16. Infanterie-Division (mot.)* was redesignated), the *23. Panzer-Division* and one infantry division remained behind as the ready reserves behind the frontages of the *6. Armee* and the *1. Panzer-Armee.*

Hitler ordered the start of the attack at Kursk for 5 July 1943

Ready Reserve Behind the 1. Panzer-Armee and the 6. Armee in July 1943 and Defensive Fighting at Dmitrijewka on the Mius 18 July to 2 August 194

On 3 July 1943, the division was ordered to be prepared to move on a moment's notice. In expectation of Soviet relief attacks after the start of *Operation "Zitadelle"* around Kursk, the division was to move to the boundary between the *6. Armee* and the *1. Panzer-Armee* in the Artemowsk area, 70 kilometers north of Makejewka.

The elements of the division had barely entered the area and started reconnaissance along the front, when new march orders were received. Starting 7 July, the division was allocated to the *XXIV. Panzer-Korps* of

54 Editor's Note: = Horse Column "Lang". Although armored divisions were not normally authorized horses, they were obviously being used within the *23. Panzer-Division*.

55 Editor's Note: = 128th Weapons Maintenance Company.

the *1. Panzer-Armee.* It was intended for the division to participate in a deception campaign by conducting day marches into the area around Sslawjansk, while *PR201* (minus the 1st Company, which was attached to *Kampfgruppe Sparre*), the division support command, the attached *Luftwaffe Flak* battalion and all of the combat trains were to remain in Artemowsk.

On 9 July, the division had to move further to the northwest as far as the area around Barwenkowo. The tracked and half-tracked vehicles were moved up by rail from Artemowsk and, in accordance with new orders, rolled into the Merefa area, south of Kharkov, through 11 July. By doing so, the division was back in the area of the great pocket battle of Kharkov of the spring of 1942. The division commander issued the following order-of-the-day on 13 July:

> Fourteen months ago, the division moved out of the same billets that you reoccupied today for the battles around Kharkov.
>
> A route of more than 5,000 kilometers has taken you as far as the Caucasus and across the Akssay back here again.
>
> The circle is closed.
>
> The names Kharkov — Oskol — Woronoesh — Nikolajewskaja on the Don — Bakssan — Terek — Alagir — Akssay — Manytsch — Rostov and Mius are mileposts for the deeds and fame of our division. Performance, reputation and honor obligate us. We stand ready and our fallen comrade are marching with us.
>
> Long live the *23. Panzer-Division*!
>
> /signed/ von Vormann

The remaining transport of the tanks had still not yet arrived when the division received movement orders to head 60 kilometers south into the area around Alexejewka. Soldiers were soon joking that they were on "streetcar line No. 23". But marching is what it did, even when cloudbursts sometimes turned the roads into seemingly bottomless pits of mud for hours on end and the main tank route—*Panzerstraße Ost*—had to be blocked to traffic by the military police for periods of time to keep the road from being destroyed.

It was intended for the division, together with the *17. Panzer-Division*, to prepare for operations southwest of Isjum as part of the *XXIV. Panzer-Korps.*

The forces of the division had no idea at the time of their extended marches that the last hopes of a victorious end to the war in Russia had been dashed. The offensive at Kursk had overburdened the combat power of the attack divisions. The success gained remained well behind those expected, because the enemy had had ample time to prepare for the German attack. On 12 July, the attack of *Generaloberst* Model's *9. Armee* bogged down, after the enemy had broken through the German front north of Orel on 11 July—a front stripped of all reserves—with strong forces. The enemy then threatened the rear of the *9. Armee.* On 15 July, the *4. Panzer-Armee*, which had enjoyed more success up to that point, had to return to its lines of departure, since victory was no longer obtainable.

On 16 July, the forces of the *23. Panzer-Division* conducted leaders' reconnaissance in the sectors of the *XXXX. Panzer-Korps* and the *LVII. Panzer-Korps*, especially to the south and southwest of Isjum. That evening, the division received new orders and a new sector: Artemowsk.

While Soviet attacks on both sides of Isjum were turned back by the divisions in position there, Soviet forces did succeed on 18 July in breaking through on the Mius on both sides of Kuibyschewo. Deep penetrations were obtained, especially west of Dmitrijewka. Counterattacks by the *16. Panzergrenadier-Division* were unable to eliminate the danger of a final Soviet breakthrough.

The *23. Panzer-Division* was alerted during the evening of 18 July. It was to move to the area east and south of Sneshoje, 25 kilometers northwest of Dmitrijewka, and attack southeast on 19 July.

Panzergruppe Sander—Headquarters and *I./PR201*, one company of self-propelled antitank guns from *PJA128*, the *3.(SPW)/PAA23*—moved out at 1930 hours and reached Sneshnoje at 0230 hours on 19 July after conducting a 170-kilometer night march. The infantry followed Sander's men.

At 0700 hours, *PGR126* moved out of the broken terrain northeast of Petrowskij, along with the attached *PJA128*. It crossed Point 214.3 and headed east. *Panzergrenadier-Regiment 128* moved through Perwomaisk and attacked south, toward Stepanowka. At 0830 hours, the armored group headed south, moving east of the Olchowtschik Defile. The *3./PPB51* was attached to it. The attack objectives were Stepanowka and Hill 213.9, 2 kilometers east of the village. The attack ran into enemy forces, which were themselves preparing to continue an attack to the northwest and west. Just outside of Stepanowka and north of Hill 213.9, the numerically vastly superior enemy offered stubborn resistance. From Olchowtschik Defile, the Soviets outflanked *PGR128.* At the same time, superior Soviet forces moved out to attack the right flank of the *I./PGR128* and overran the company of reserves that had been sent to block them.

It was not until *Oberleutnant* Lenberger's *4.(schwere)/PGR128* went into position that the onslaught of Russians could be turned back. They were engaged in close combat at pointblank range with heavy weapons. Strong antitank gun belts, reinforced by tanks, also flanked the armored group from the direction of Dmitrijewka. The attack came to a halt and sustained considerable casualties. All of the companies of the *I./PR201* lost their commanders and acting commanders; two were killed and two were badly wounded.

After artillery preparation and a *Stuka* attack, the division moved out again against Stepanowka at 1530 hours. But, once again, it made no progress. The positions of the *16. Panzergrenadier-Division* were broken through between Marinowka and Stepanowka. Twenty enemy tanks entered Garany.

As night fell, the results of the day's combat operation were tallied: 14 enemy tanks had been knocked out; 20 antitank guns, 45 light machine guns, 18 heavy machine guns, 7 infantry guns, 28 antitank rifles and numerous small arms were captured or destroyed. The losses sustained by the Soviets were bloody and high, especially those taken when the massed enemy forces in front of the armored group at Hill 213.9 fled.

But the friendly losses were extraordinarily high as well: 7 officers and 72 noncommissioned officers and enlisted personnel were killed; 13 officers and 244 noncommissioned officers and enlisted personnel wounded; and 33 noncommissioned officers and enlisted reported as missing in action. Eleven tanks had to be completely written off.

During the night of 19/20 July, the division transitioned to the defense with the engineer battalion on the right and *PGR128* on the left in a line running from Pont 230.9 (1 kilometers west of Stepanowka) to Point 214 (3 kilometers north/northeast of Stepanowka). The tank regiment, *PGR126*, *PAA23* and two battalions of the divisional artillery were positioned west of Hill 277.9 by field army orders, where they were to serve as a ready reserve.

The 20th of July was marked by constant enemy attacks with infantry and armor, supported by artillery and ground-attack aircraft. To the south of Point 214.3, the Soviets succeeded in breaking through the positions of *PPB51* and advancing to within 1.5 kilometers of the dominant terrain feature of Hill 277.9. The ready reserve, which was immediately employed in a counterattack, threw the enemy back to the road northwest of Point 230.9. At the same time, however, the *16. Panzergrenadier-Division* had to evacuate Ssaur-Mogilskij. Its reconnaissance battalion—*Panzer-Aufklärungs-Abteilung 116*—lost Hill 230.9. *Panzer-Aufklärungs-Abteilung 23*

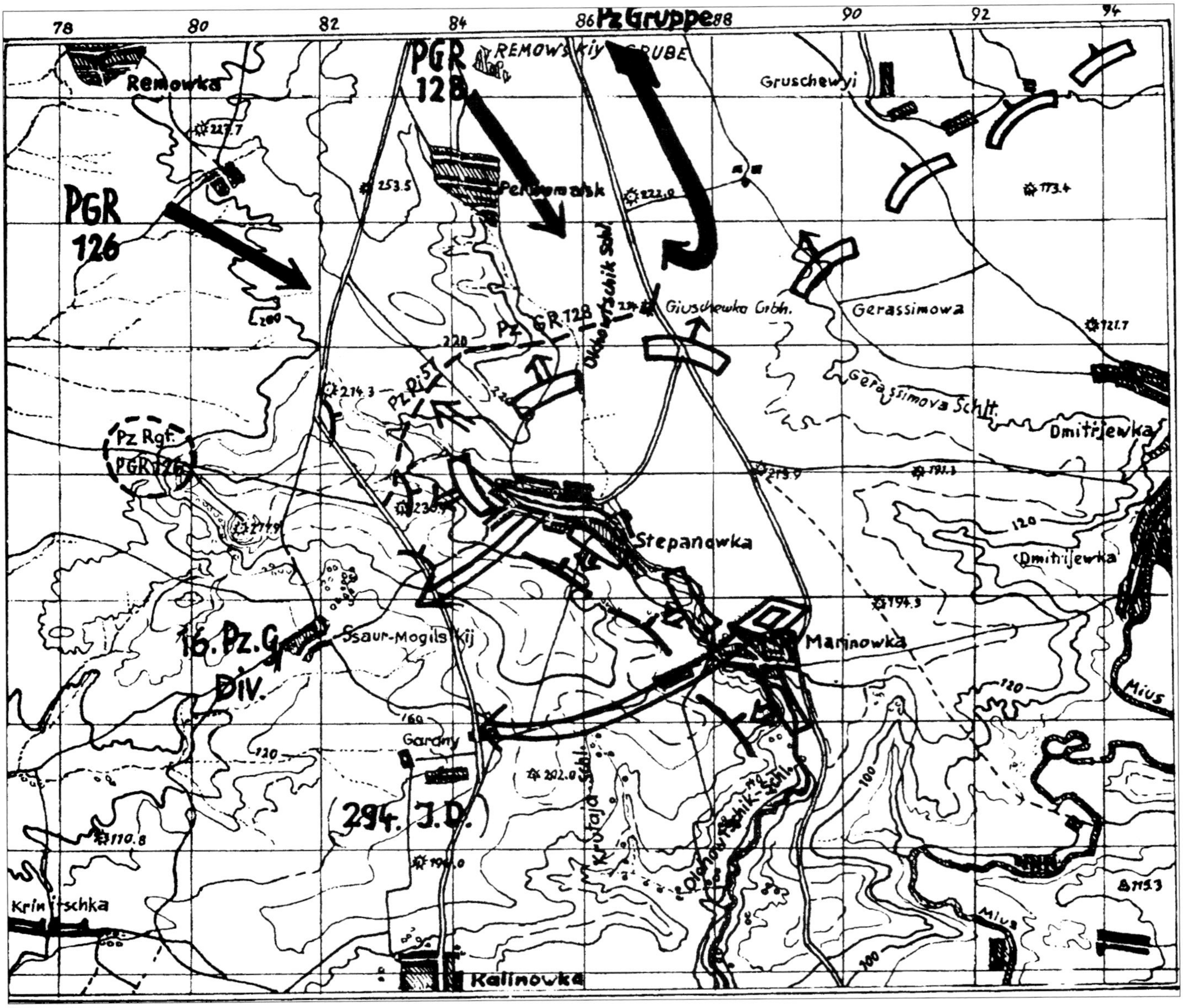

Map 41: Soviet Breakthrough Attempts Along the Mius, 17-19 July 1943.
(One grid line equals 2 kilometers)

was inserted into the line, where it occupied Hill 277.9 and the patch of woods on the hill's southeast slope (the latter by the *3./PAA23*). The battered *PPB51* had to be pulled out of the line.

On that day in that area of the division's sector, 24 Soviet attacks of regiment or battalion size were turned back between 0400 and 2300 hours. All had armor support. In front of the sector of *PGR128* alone there were 680 dead Soviets. Destroyed were 2 enemy tanks, 15 antitank guns and numerous antitank rifles and small arms.

The following enemy forces were arrayed before the division on that day: 40th Guards Rifle Division, 3rd Guards Rifle Division, 34th Guards Rifle Division, 96th Guards Rifle Division, 32nd Guards Tank Brigade, the 4th Motorized/Mechanized Brigade, the 5th Motorized/Mechanized Brigade, the 6th Motorized/Mechanized Brigade, the 21st Tank Regiment and the 22nd Tank Regiment.

Losses for the division included 41 dead, 218 wounded and 22 missing in action. The medical personnel of the division were busy day and night. Many of the wounded owed their lives to the ambulance platoons and the clearing stations at Sneshnoje and Stertikaja. Adjoining the 294th Field Hospital in Tschistjakowo, the 2nd Medical Company set up a field hospital for the slightly wounded as well as a medical collection point. Some 400-500 wounded transited this facility each day. A dental facility also took up work.

Enemy pressure increased on 21 July. Heavy artillery and rocket-launcher fires were placed on the division's sector at daylight. Soviet fighter-bombers attacked without interruption. Hill 277.9 became the hot spot of the defense. The enemy had to take it if he wanted to continue his breakthrough to the west. By 1200 hours, eight attacks had been beaten back, some of them in close combat. Elements of *Hauptmann* Schägger's *Panzer-Feld-Lehr- und Ersatz-Bataillon 128* were brought forward from Makejewka and employed on Hill 277.9 to reinforce the reconnaissance battalion. *Hauptmann* Schägger was designated as the commander of *PAA23*; his successor in the field replacement battalion was *Rittmeister Freiherr* Grote.

To the south of the hill, the enemy pressed forward against the *16. Panzergrenadier-Division*. That division's reconnaissance battalion, under *Major* Vogelsang, was attached to the *23. Panzer-Division*. Supported by *Panzergruppe Sander*, *Panzer-Aufklärungs-Abteilung 116* advanced on the hill 1.5 kilometers south of Ssaur-Mogilskij. It established contact on the right with the remnants of *Hauptmann* Henneberg's *Grenadier-Regiment 513* of the *294. Infanterie-Division*. Further to the right, *Panzergrenadier-Regiment 156* of the *16. Panzergrenadier-Division* closed up.

The enemy had 60 tanks ready for operations south of Ssaur-Mogilskij. All enemy attacks on that day were turned back through the combined efforts of all of the division's heavy weapons. On several occasions, the enemy was caught as he prepared to attack. German losses totaled 27 dead and 145 wounded.

On 22 July, the defenders of Hill 277.9 were once again in the hot spot of the fighting. With bitter determination, they clung to the small patch of woods, which had been ripped apart by artillery rounds and bombs, and the barren hilltop. The hill started to be referred to as "Schägger Hill". Divisional artillery, self-propelled antitank guns and tanks lent support. On that day, the enemy left behind 15 tanks in the German positions. The division suffered 19 dead and 145 wounded.

On 23 July, the division sector was extended by 17 kilometers to the point just north of Krinitschka. *Oberstleutnant* Sander, the commander of *PR201*, assumed responsibility for the sector west of Ssaur-Mogilskij as far as the right-hand division boundary. His other forces consisted of *PPB51*, *Gruppe Henneberg*, the *III./Grenadier-Regiment 50* of the *111. Infanterie-Division* and *Panzer-Aufklärungs-Abteilung 116*. In addition, the *I./PR201*, the *3./PAA23* and the *2./PJA128* were available to support the right wing. In the course of the day, the *7./PGR128* was also added to his *Panzergruppe* with the mission of preparing the eastern half of Krinitschka and the fruit orchards to the southeast for defense. Directed to provide support were the *2.(Lehr)/FAS I*[56], elements of *PAR128* and the *III./Artillerie-Regiment 146*.

At first light, *Hauptmann* Behr, the commander of the *I./PR201*, was radioed with the news that he had been promoted to *Major*. Just two hours later, he ran into a Soviet antitank ambush while attempting to establish contact with friendly forces to the right. *Major* Behr, his adjutant (*Leutnant* Ewerhard) and two men were killed. He had been the first Knight's Cross recipient of the regiment and had enjoyed great respect among both his subordinates and superiors due to both his human qualities and his professional virtues. The division's assistant operations officer, *Hauptmann* Rebentisch, assumed acting command of the orphaned battalion.

At 1315 hours, the enemy attacked with strong force from Garany to the west. The engineer battalion pulled back on its right wing, with the result that contact was lost with the *II./Panzergrenadier-Regiment 156* of the *16. Panzergrenadier-Division* on the right. The *I./PR201*, together with the *3./PAA23* advanced into the gap at 1645 hours. It was primarily thanks to the irresistible momentum of the *SPW* company that the enemy could be ejected in hard close combat. The enemy left 30 dead behind, as well as numerous infantry weapons. As a result, the point of penetration was back under German control. The engineers reorganized during the night and joined the *SPW* company on the right.

In the remaining sectors of the division, the primary emphasis was on the disruption of enemy concentrations and the engagement of enemy artillery through concentrated fires by the divisional artillery. On that day, the division destroyed 16 enemy tanks. The division's losses, not counting the attached forces, were 27 dead, 123 wounded and 3 missing.

At first light on 24 July, the *I./PR201* and the *3./PAA23* cleared out the point of penetration northeast of Krinitschka once and for all. One Soviet company was eliminated. The divisional engineers reoccupied the former main line of resistance. Toward noon, the engineers were relieved by *Gruppe Henneberg*, the remnants of *Grenadier-Regiment 513* of the *294. Infanterie-Division*. The engineers and the *7./PGR128* occupied positions in the second line of defense.

Enemy attacks against Hills 277.9 and 214.3 were shattered by *Stukas* and the artillery. Two T-34's were eliminated there, and the *2./PR201* on the right wing of the division blew apart three T-34's and two 7.62cm antitank guns. One German tank was lost. The forces of the division lost 8 dead, 60 wounded and 1 missing on that day.

During the morning of 25 July, the enemy brought fresh forces forward to Stepanowka. At 1200 hours, an infantry regiment and 26 tanks attacked to the northwest. The attack fell apart under concentrated artillery fires and a *Stuka* attack. One Soviet fighter-bomber was shot down by the *10.(Fla)/PGR126* west of Point 214.3.

At the onset of evening twilight, an enemy regiment, supported by tanks, attacked the positions of *PGR126* northwest of Hill 230.9. In an immediate counterattack, assault guns, armored cars from the reconnaissance battalion and the infantry drove back the enemy. At practically the same time, the Soviets attacked the positions of *PGR128* in three battalion-sized waves that were supported by tanks. Two enemy tanks were destroyed and the infantry was pushed back, suffering heavy losses.

The enemy was more successful on the right wing of *Kampfgruppe Sander*. He was able to achieve a small penetration and immediately set about digging in.

The rear areas of the division were constantly attacked day and night by Red Air Force flying formations. The phosphorous bombs were especially unpleasant due to their incendiary effect and the terrible wounds they caused. The dental clinic the 2nd Medical Company had established was destroyed by bombs. The 1st Medical Company also suffered at the hands of deliberate bombing attacks.

Hauptmann Alber, the commander of the *2./PR201*, who had just returned from home leave, was given command of the *I./PR201*. Toward evening, the battalion, minus its 1st Company but reinforced with a *SPW* platoon, was sent expeditiously to the sector of the *306. Infanterie-Division* of the *XVII. Armee-Korps*.

One company from *PGR126*, accompanied by armored cars from *PAA23*, advanced under the concealment offered by the night into enemy concentrations southeast of Hill 214.3 and inflicted considerable casualties on him. As a result, the enemy was no longer able to conduct a night attack.

Five T-34's, three 7.62cm antitank guns and five rocket launchers were destroyed; two enemy tanks were damaged. The division lost 21 dead and 116 wounded. On that day, the *23. Panzer-Division* claimed its 1,000th enemy tank since it started fighting on 12 May 1942.

On the right wing of the division, the enemy penetration from the previous evening was cleared up in an immediate counterattack. During the morning, the enemy was conspicuous in his movements, which indicated new attacks were not far away. The artillery engaged identified enemy batteries and also armor concentrations near Stepanowka.

Hauptmann Holenia left the division due to illness. His place as commander of *PPB51* was taken by *Hauptmann* Seyring.

At 1615 hours, a 10-minute artillery preparation from Soviet guns of all calibers was initiated in the right-hand sector of the division between the boundary and Hill 214.3. Then, the 23rd Guards Rifle Division, the 221st Guards Rifle Division, the 3rd Guards Rifle Division and the 96th Guards Rifle Division all attacked, with support from at least 120 IL-2 fighter-bombers that had fighter cover. In a struggle lasting 1 and 1/2 hours, the infantry, grenadiers and motorcycle infantry turned back the attack, all the while magnificently supported by antitank personnel, assault guns and 2cm *Flak* that set up in the open. Positions north of Hill 277.9 and on the right wing of the division that were temporarily lost were cleared of the enemy when the remaining tanks were employed. The troop elements of the division reported the following captured or destroyed on that day: 3 T-34's, 22 machine guns, 8 mortars, 4 rocket launchers

56 Editor's Note: Presumably *Feld-Artillerie-Schule I* (= 1st Field Artillery School).

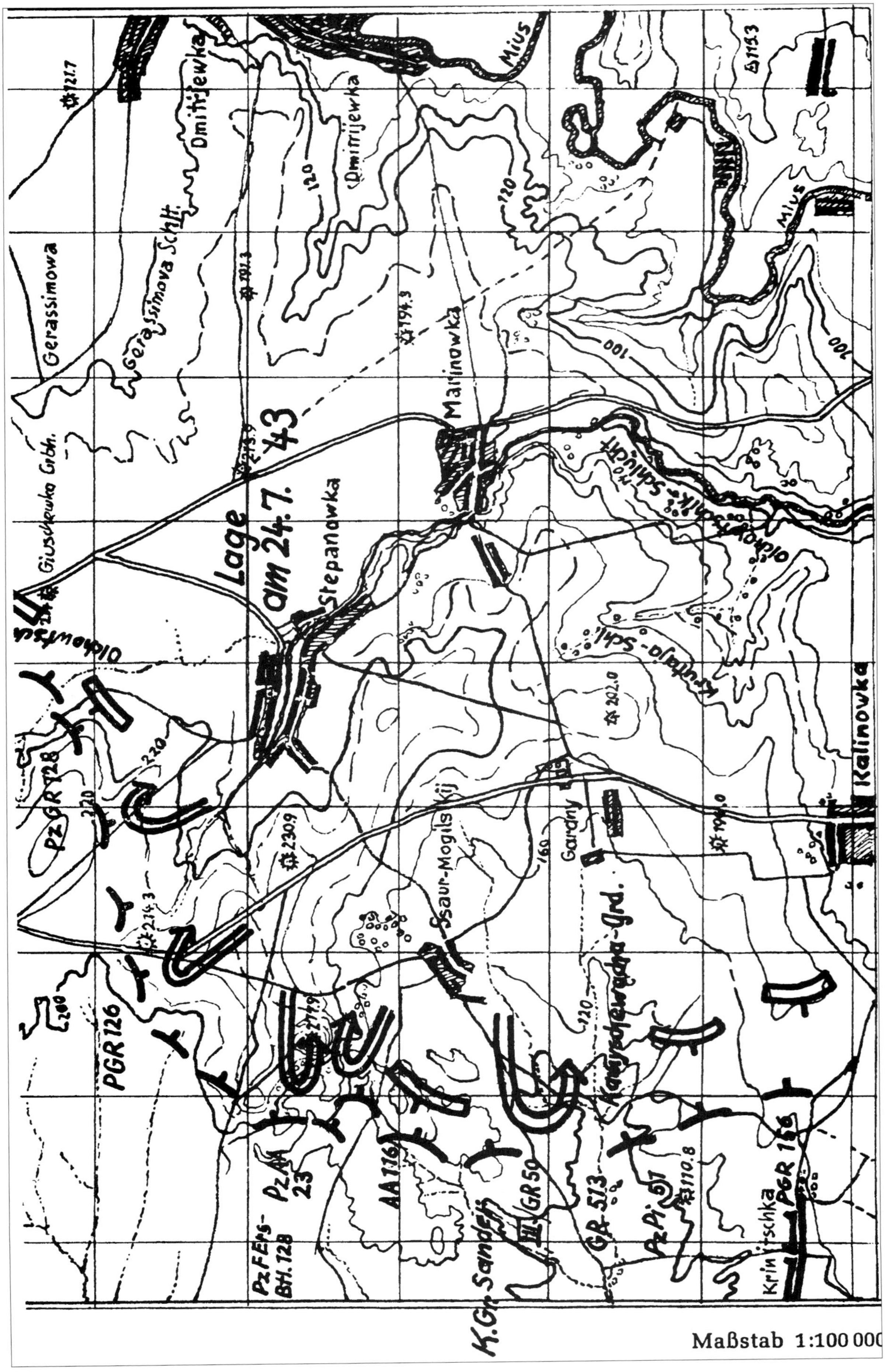

Map 42: Situation on 24 July 1943.

and 6 antitank rifles. More than 300 enemy dead were counted, but friendly losses were considerable as well.

On 24 July, *Rittmeister Freiherr* Grote was killed in a fatal accident while reconnoitering. His successor as the commander of the *Panzer-Feld-Lehr- und Ersatz-Bataillon 128* was *Oberleutnant* Grünwaldt.

The first phase of the fighting at Dmitrijewka drew to a close. The *23. Panzer-Division* had prevented the enemy from breaking through and sealed off the initial area of penetration. Eight Soviet rifle divisions of the II and IV Guards Motorized/Mechanized Corps had not been able to break the German resistance.

Generalmajor von Vormann was promoted to *Generalleutnant*.

On 27 July, signals intelligence of the *XXIV. Panzer-Korps* intercepted the following radio traffic:

After-action report (tactical time: 0745 hours)

The enemy defends stubbornly in the sectors 500 meters east of Hill 277.9 — west 200 meters Ssaur Mogilskij — 1 kilometers west of Hill 110.8 — 600 meters east of Krinitschka and further to the southeast. In the course of the second half of the day, stubborn attacks were launched again by our side. The enemy replied with stubborn defense. He conducted artillery and mortar fires on our infantry from the areas around the Kamyschewacha *Balka*, the Blochnizkaja *Balka* and Hill 277.9.

During the night, he conducted heavy machine-gun and riddle fire from the areas around Hills 172.3, 94.9 and 227.9. Observation indicated: Concentrations of enemy infantry in the area of the three hills that are located 1.5 kilometers northwest of Hill 230.9. Tanks and motorized vehicles observed on the Artemowka — Ssaur Mogilskij road ;up to 20 tanks and 50 motorized vehicles. A rocket launcher battery (six-barreled) conducted fires from the patch of woods 800 meters south of Hill 277.9. Enemy air forces bombed our assembly area. 50 approaching aircraft were observed. Summary: The enemy is defending stubbornly. He is bringing up personnel and equipment.

Gorbatschow

In the course of the day, the enemy placed heavy artillery and rocket fires on the area occupied by *Gruppe Henneberg*. After some 50 enemy fighter-bombers then attacked, enemy infantry moved out from both sides of the Kamyschewacha bottom land and attacked. In order to reinforce *Panzer-Aufklärungs-Abteilung 116*, *Leutnant* Herlitschka's tank company was brought forward. Before the enemy could reach the main line of resistance, his attack was blown to bits. The heavy infantry gun battery of *PR201* inflicted heavy losses on the enemy, with the result that he pulled back to his line of departure.

In exchange for the *III./Panzer-Artillerie-Regiment 146* of the *16. Panzergrenadier-Division*, the *23. Panzer-Division* received the *II./Artillerie-Regiment 40,* a general headquarters artillery formation.

During the night of 27/28 July, the *4./Heeres-Flak-Abteilung 278* shot down a Soviet R-5 aircraft.

In the days that followed, the enemy was quiet; he fortified his positions. On both sides, the artillery fired harassment fires. German artillery silenced two enemy batteries. Combat activities were largely absent on 29 July as well. Preparations for a German counterattack were concluded. The *II. SS-Panzer-Korps* of *SS-Obergruppenführer* Hausser prepared for its operations behind the left wing of the *23. Panzer-Division*.

The *23. Panzer-Division* received orders to move out on 30 July to serve as flank guard for the *SS* divisions and to fix the enemy at Ssaur-Mogilskij. After a short artillery preparation, *Kampfgruppe Schägger*, consisting of elements of *Panzer-Feld-Lehr- und Ersatz-Bataillon 128* and *PAA23*, moved out at 0810 hours. The battle group was then followed by the *II./PGR126* and the *I./PR201*.

The 315th Rifle Division, which the enemy had freshly introduced during the night of 29/30 July, defended stubbornly within his main battle area, which had numerous minefields, earthen bunkers and field fortifications. The presence of patches of woods and small villages also served to break up the terrain. Despite all that, *Kampfgruppe Schägger* overcame the initial difficult resistance and advanced to the western edge of the woods north of Ssaur-Mogilskij and to the northwest edge of the village proper. At the same time, the tanks, along with elements of the *II./PGR126*, had gone around the eastern part of the woods to the northeast and reached the *balka* 1.2 kilometers east of Ssaur-Mogilskij by 0930 hours.

Disregarding the fact that elements of *SS-Panzer-Grenadier-Division "Das Reich"* were still fighting back at Hill 230.9 and the open left flank of the *23. Panzer-Division* was becoming ever longer, *Hauptmann* Alber advanced on Garany on his own initiative with his tanks. His men took the village at 1130 hours and, 10 minutes later, Hill 196.0 1 kilometer to the south. Infantry from *PGR126* and scouts from the *SPW* company of *PAA23* then occupied the village. A deep wedge had been driven into the Soviet lines.

At the same time, the fighting for Ssaur-Mogilskij continued. The patch of woods was cleared in close-in fighting. Every single building in the village had to be wrested from the enemy. The enemy defended with extraordinary bravery. Final resistance was not broken until nine hours and fifty minutes had passed. All of *PGR128* was eventually committed incrementally in this struggle against snipers and magnificently camouflaged bunkers.

To the south of that combat sector, *Kampfgruppe Sander—Gruppe Henneberg, Panzer-Aufklärungs-Abteilung 116* and the *III./Grenadier-Regiment 50*—started its attack on a broad front at 1000 hours. The armored group of the *16. Panzergrenadier-Division* advanced from the southwest and was able to establish contact with *Hauptmann* Alber's tanks to the southwest of Point 196.0 at 1145 hours. That signaled the encirclement of the enemy in the area Ssaur-Mogilskij — Garany — Point 196.0 — Tyrlowatataja Defile. The pocket was reduced from the west by *Kampfgruppe Sander* and the *7./PGR128*. Two engineer companies had to be employed to clear extensive minefields.

The area to the west of Garany had been so secured by 1800 hours that *Panzergruppe Alber*, together with the *I./PGR126*, was able to attack Hill 202.2 east of Garany. In this, it worked closely with *SS-Panzer-Grenadier-Division "Das Reich"*, which had advanced as far as the lead elements of the *23. Panzer-Division* in the meantime. The enemy defended with great determination there, as well. Numerous antitank guns, antitank rifles and heavy weapons supported him in his defense. The hill was taken at 1915 hours. The tanks then immediately turned to the southwest and joined the fight of the infantry, who were encountering heavy resistance in the many defiles south and southwest of Garany. The tanks set up a "hedgehog" defense 1.5 kilometers southwest of Garany, while *PGR126* set up positions with its right wing on Point 262.6 and its left wing on the ridgeline north of Garany. It screened both to the west and the east at the same time. *Panzergrenadier-Regiment 128* was positioned around Ssaur-Mogilskij, oriented to the west and southwest.

The 30th day of July 1943 turned into one of special laurels for the *23. Panzer-Division*. Of the four attacking divisions—*23. Panzer-Division, SS-Panzer-Grenadier-Division "Das Reich", SS-Panzer-Grenadier-Division "Totenkopf"* and the *3. Panzer-Division*—it was the only one to reach its attack objectives. Not only that, it went significantly beyond them. *Kampfgruppe Schägger*, which had borne the main burden of the attack on Ssaur-Mogilskij, and *Panzergruppe Alber,* which forced the breakthrough to Garany, contributed in large part to that success. *Hauptmann* Schägger (*PAA23*), *Hauptmann* Alber (*I./PR201*) and *Unteroffizier* Baade (*5./PAA23*) were all later awarded the Knight's Cross. Receiving the German Cross in Gold was *Leutnant* Borbonus of the *1./PAA23*. *Unteroffizier* Bade was the gun commander of an antitank gun and, under his command, had knocked out numerous tanks at Hill 277.9 on the previous day, thus playing a decisive role in that defensive success.

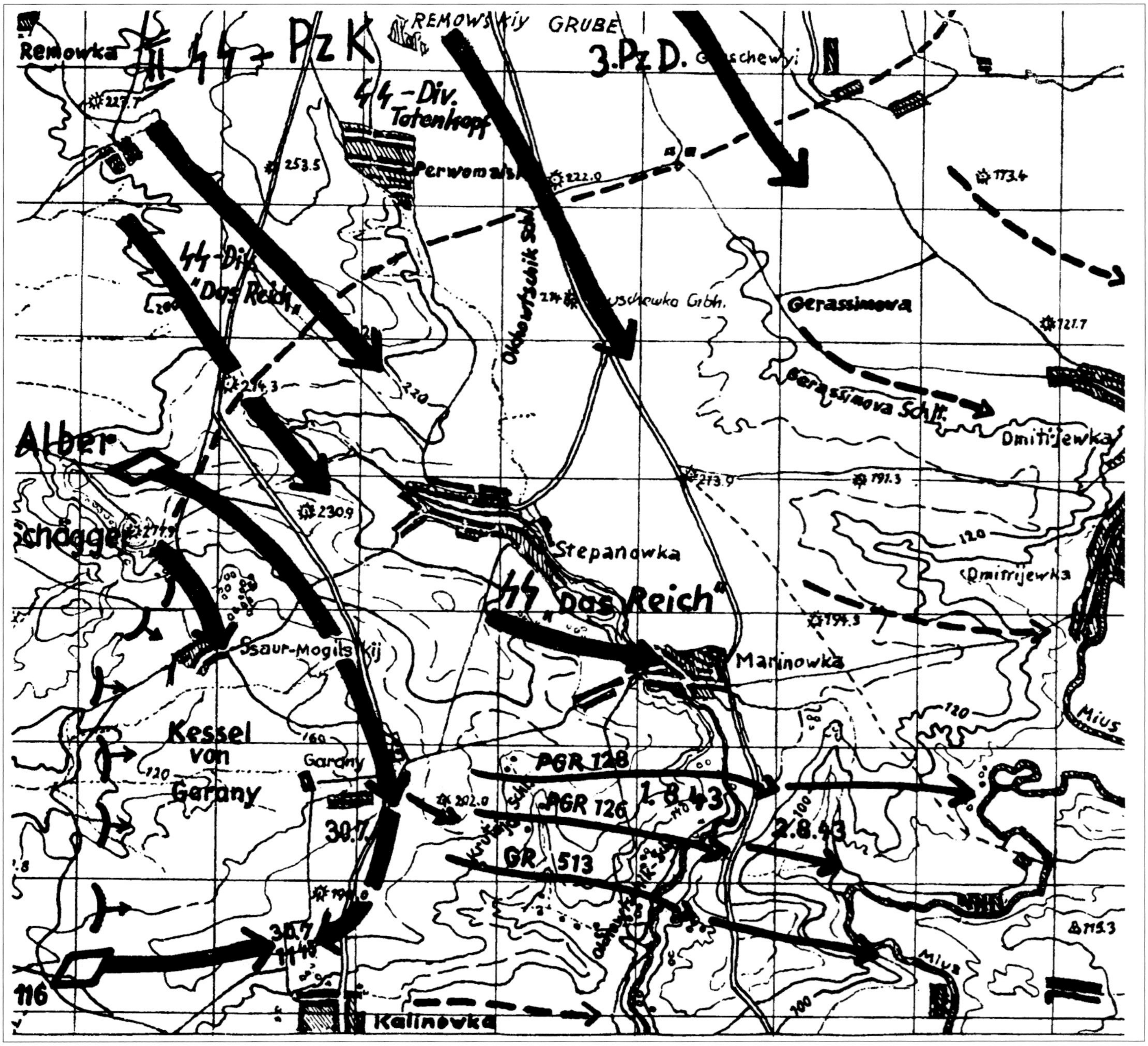

Map 43: The Counterattack of 30 July 1943.

On 31 July, the pocket west of Garany was cleared by the division. Only *PGR126* and *PJA128* screened to the east. Despite brave resistance on the part of the Soviets, the final resistance was broken after five hours. The battle groups then immediately reorganized between Garany and Ssaur-Mogilskij for continuing the attack east. By then, *PGR126* and *PJA128* had had to fend off several enemy attacks. The air forces of both sides also joined the fray. *Stukas* enjoyed particularly good results on enemy concentrations in the Krutaja Defile. *Panzer-Aufklärungs-Abteilung 116* returned to the command and control of its parent division.

The extent of the victory on 30 and 31 July over the enemy can be measured by the following: In all, 4,193 personnel of the Red Army—267 officers and 3,926 other ranks—were taken prisoner. The enemy suffered an even greater number in dead. Captured were 52 7.62cm antitank guns, 11 rocket launchers and 24 artillery pieces. Untold numbers of light weapons lay strewn over the battlefield.

The division's losses were 118 dead and 512 wounded.

At 0830 hours on 1 August, the attack on the Krutaja Defile started. Advancing frontally was *Gruppe Henneberg* (*Grenadier-Regiment 513*) on the right and *PGR126* on the left. Following behind was *PGR128* and *Panzergruppe Alber*, which had the mission of going around the Krutaja Defile to the north and taking Hill 203, 500 meters southwest of Marinowka. From there, they were then to advance on the Olchowtschik Defile.

The frontal attack made slow, but steady progress. *SS-Panzer-Grenadier-Division "Das Reich"* took Hill 203; *PGR128* reached the hedgerow 1 kilometer southeast of it at 1230 hours. *Panzergruppe Alber* was held up by several minefields between the Krutaja Defile and Hill 203.

At 1250 hours, *Gruppe Henneberg* and *PGR126* penetrated into the Krutaja defile and assaulted its eastern slope. The assault was immediately continued east toward the Olchowtschik Defile, which was reached at 1700 hours. At that time, *PGR128* was still fighting for the patch of woods 2 kilometers south of Marinowka. The enemy had extensively prepared

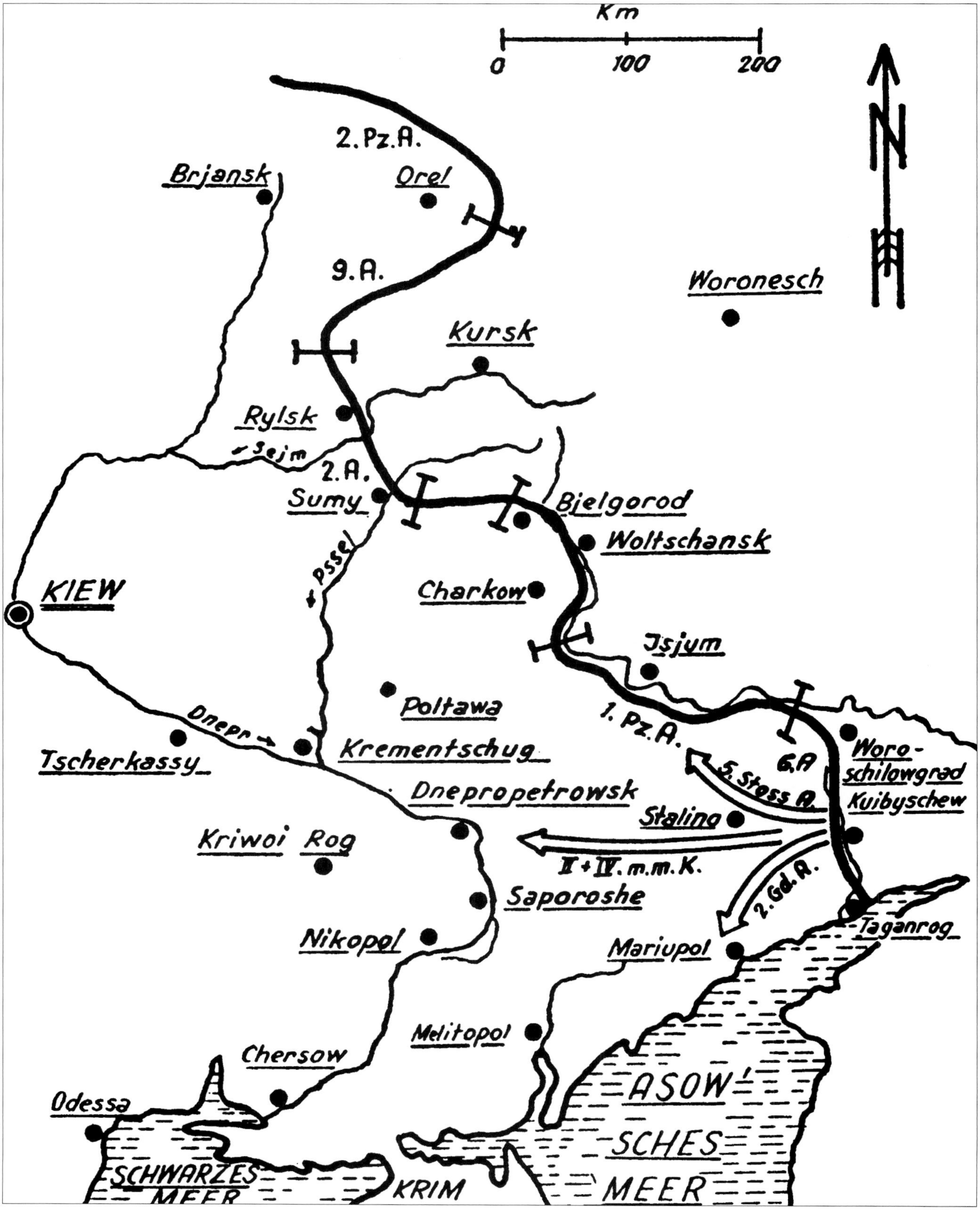

Map 44: Soviet Attack Plans Along the Mius (17 July 1943).

the patch of woods for defense and created a tough pocket of resistance, especially since a 24-ton bridge crossed the deep defile at this location. Soviet resistance was broken at 1745 hours, and the bridge was taken intact by the Germans. Bridgeheads were established and held against repeated enemy counterattacks.

The divisional artillery, which had been reinforced by the artillery of the *3. Panzer-Division* in the meantime, also contributed greatly to the over-all success of the attack. It engaged enemy pockets of resistance and concentrations and shattered them. The divisional artillery also effectively supported the attack of *SS-Panzer-Grenadier-Division "Das Reich"* on Marinowka.

SS-Panzer-Grenadier-Division" Totenkopf" took Hill 213.9 north of Marinowka.

The division suffered 38 dead and 138 wounded on this day, but the successful attacks kept the offensive spirit of the troops high.

On 2 August, all of the divisional artillery under *Oberst Dr.* Born initially supported the attack of the *SS* against the well-fortified and stubbornly defended high ground around Marinowka. Without the capture of that high ground, the continuation of the attack by the *23.Panzer-Division* was impossible. At 0900 hours, the high ground was in German hands. *Gruppe Henneberg* and *PGR128* moved out from their bridgeheads across the Olchowtschik Defile. The enemy pulled back. At 1130 hours, the former main line of resistance along the Mius was firmly back in German hands. Patrols and outposts moved out to the river line proper. The intervening area was cleared of scattered Russian forces.

Starting at 1600 hours, the division—in the form of *PGR128* and *Gruppe Henneberg*—was positioned along the bend of the Mius 1,200 meters north of Marinowskoje and the nose of the hill 500 meters west of the southern edge of Dmitrijewka. *Panzergrenadier-Regiment 126* assembled in the Krutaja Defile as the division reserve. The antitank battalion and the *I./PR201* were positioned around Garany.

The battle was over. The large-scale breakthrough attempt on the part of the enemy had ended with his destruction. Another 130 prisoners were brought in on 2 August. The following was destroyed on that day:

1 IL-2 fighter bomber
3 T-34's
1 armored car
7 antitank guns
2 artillery pieces
5 trucks
2 mortars
4 horse-drawn wagons
4 rocket launchers

The total losses suffered by the division from 19 July to 2 August:

Killed: 25 officers and 420 noncommissioned officers and enlisted personnel

Wounded: 99 officers and 1,909 noncommissioned officers and enlisted personnel

The intelligence officer of the division, *Rittmeister Fürst* zu Sayn-Wittgenstein, provided the following overview of the enemy situation:

> The enemy wanted to conduct the attack to relieve the pressure on the Belgorod area, since he was aware that strong German forces had been pulled out of the front elsewhere to be sent there. He considered the German front along the Mius to be weak. The objective of all enemy attacks was and is to drive the Germans out of the Ukraine and chase them away from the harvest of 1943. By doing so, it was hoped to hit the German basis for its foodstuff needs. It was not intended to alleviate the nutritional needs of the Soviets by doing so, since the importation of foodstuffs by means of American help (primarily canned meat) has already improved considerably.
>
> The Soviet attack on 17 July with the 5th Shock Army and the 2nd Guards Army was conducted as follows:
>
> Initially, the 5th Shock Army was to advance west, only then to turn north and roll up the German front in the direction of Kharkov.
>
> The 2nd Guards Army was given the same mission, only to the south and Mariupol.
>
> The II and IV Guards Motorized/Mechanized Corps were intended to advance deep to the west/southwest as far as the Dnjepr.
>
> The heavy losses of the motorized/mechanized corps in the first few days caused the command to relieve these formations with rifle divisions and then reinforce them with the addition of tanks until the hill and defile area, which was not good terrain for armor operations, was crossed. The eight rifle divisions [40th Guards, 34th Guards, 96th Guards, 3rd Guards, 49th Guards, 33rd Guards, 86th Guards and 221st Rifle Divisions] that appeared in front of the division during the first phase of the battle were followed on 27 and 28 July by the 315th Rifle Division and, on 29 July, by the 24th Guards Rifle Division, as well as the 127th Rifle Division.
>
> The divisions were at full strength and received additional replacements during the fighting.
>
> The German counterattack had hit the Soviet formations so hard that no organic formation of a larger size has been identified since 1 August. Only mixed formations were fighting, which were composed of personnel from all of the aforementioned Soviet divisions. To that must be added individual general headquarters forces of the 2nd Guards Army.
>
> Among the 4,495 prisoners taken during this battle, there are 275 officers, among which are 11 regimental commanders or acting regimental commanders. No prisoners were taken from division headquarters, since these immediately pulled back at the onset of the German attack. Troop elements of the *23. Panzer-Division* destroyed 62 Soviet tanks and 3 aircraft. The number of spoils of war initially reported were surpassed many fold. Their securing extended over the course of many days.

In the days that followed, the *23. Panzer-Division* set up for defense along the Mius Position with its two infantry regiments while relieving the two *SS* mechanized infantry divisions. An armored ready reserve was formed under the headquarters of *PR201* with the *I./PR201*, the heavy infantry gun battery of the tank regiment, the *3.(SPW)/PAA23* and the *3./Sturmgeschütz-Abteilung 203*. It was initially located in the Marinowka area but, since it was exposed to constant artillery fires and fighter-bomber attacks, it moved to Stepanowka.

On 3 August, since the regrouping of forces could not remain hidden from the enemy, he advanced on the recaptured positions with strong forces supported by fighter-bombers. The enemy attack was quickly beaten back, however.

On 4 August, *Hauptmann* Wolf arrived as the new commander of the *I./PR201*. In the days that followed, the armored ready reserve was reinforced by *PJA128* and the *4.(Flak)/Heeres-Flak-Abteilung 278*, as well as the *1.(PzSpäh)/PAA23*.

On 5 August, 15 T-34's broke through the main line of resistance and got as far as the combat trains around Stepanowka. Infantry from *PGR128* immediately launched a counterattack, destroying 10 tanks and forcing the others to rapidly pull back. One T-34 was captured intact and operational by *Oberleutnant* Schroeder of the *9./PGR128*. The resolve of the infantry during this attack was exemplary. Without any type of panic, they allowed the tanks to overrun them. Some of them did not even interrupt the lunch they had started, only to go after the tanks after they had finished. The big victory of the recent past had greatly boosted their self-confidence.

Five T-34's, which had crossed the main line of resistance further to the north, were destroyed by the *I./PR201* in short order. Weaker advances on the part of the enemy led to several penetrations in the defensive positions, but they were cleared up on the same day, one after the other.

After the conclusion of the fighting, it proved necessary for the first time since the division had started its combat operations for it to establish a detail for recovering and burying the dead in the division's sector. Up to then, the units themselves had recovered and buried their dead. That remained the case as far as the dead of the *23. Panzer-Division* were concerned. When the Soviet broke through in the middle of July, many soldiers from the formations fighting in the sector at the time were killed. The Soviets had not buried them and left them were they had fallen. Under the direction of the military police, the burial detail of the division canvassed the terrain in a deliberate fashion, recovered the dead, identified their personal effects and safeguarded what remained. Those dead were buried in four large mass graves before the division left the area of operations. The two chaplains of the division, who had been worked tirelessly with the forces in the field and especially the wounded in the recent past and who had provided much comfort, played a big role in the recovery operation.

An enemy attack on 6 August created a critical situation in the sector of the *I./PGR126,* but the enemy forces were turned back in an immediate counterattack launched by the tanks. Two attacks by division forces against small bridgeheads of the enemy did not have the desired success, since the enemy was well supported by heavy weapons and artillery from the east bank of the Mius.

On 10 August, *PR201* was redesignated as *Panzer-Regiment 23* by order of the German Army High Command. The regiment's 2nd Battalion was still undergoing new equipment training in Erlangen (Germany). No one at the front at the time knew how close the regiment was to losing its detached battalion. In the *Führer* Headquarters, Hitler occupied himself again and again with the outfitting of the armored divisions after the heavy losses sustained on all fronts. This pre-occupation extended all the way down to the last short-barreled *Panzer III*. Every issue of major equipment was sharply debated, especially when it concerned the newly equipped *Panther* battalions. For a while during the noon situation report at the *Führer* Headquarters on 26 July, the possibility existed of reassigning the battalion to the reformed *24. Panzer-Division*.

Oberstleutnant Freiherr von Wechmar assumed command of *PGR128* from the wounded *Oberstleutnant* Sparre.

Using internal assets, *PGR128* established its own dental clinic for a while, probably a unique occurrence in the annals of the German Armed Forces. Two dentists assigned to the 9th and 10th Companies set up shop in a bus and a truck. A Ukrainian assistant, a driver and a *Hiwi* rounded out the team. Well equipped, the enterprise was soon very popular. The main advantage was that the dental clinic could work near the forces in the field and eliminated the need for long waits.

The Second Defensive Battle at Isjum on the Donez 16 to 27 August 1943

By losing the battle to the west of Dmitrijewka on the Mius, the Soviets only had to give up the initiative for a short period and then only locally. For instance, this did not apply to the area around Isjum, where the enemy had moved out to attack several times since the end of spring 1943. Signs were mounting there of another offensive in the works. The formation of a bridgehead on the south bank of the Donez between Majaki (12 kilometers north of Sslawjansk) and Kamenka (8 kilometers south of Isjum) in fighting from 17 to 27 July belonged to the preparations for that offensive.

On 10 August 1943, the *23. Panzer-Division* was pulled out of its positions along the Mius and moved to Barwenkowo, partly by road, partly by rail. The division reported to the *XXXX. Panzer-Korps*, which was part of the *1. Panzer-Armee* of *Generaloberst* von Mackensen. A ready reserve was positioned in Dmitrijewka (30 kilometers south-southwest of Isjum), which consisted of an infantry battalion, a tank company and an antitank company. The divisional artillery was also employed to assist the divisions along the front. The 1st Battalion supported the *257. Infanterie-Division*, the 2nd Battalion the *46. Infanterie-Division* and the 3rd Battalion the *17. Panzer-Division*.

The division proper had three days in its new assembly area to perform maintenance on vehicles and weapons.

On 16 August, the enemy struck. After a heavy artillery preparation, masses of Soviet infantry and tanks attacked on a wide front on both sides of Dolgenkaja.

The *23. Panzer-Division* was alerted at 0840 hours and ordered to the Dmitrijewka — Wernopolje area. Even as the formations of the division were marching north, the enemy had advanced from the area around Passeka, made a deep penetration into the positions of the *17. Panzer-Division* and the *46. Infanterie-Division* and headed southwest. At 1100 hours, the *23. Panzer-Division* was directed against this enemy while still on the march and received the mission of taking back the former main line of resistance. By 1530 hours, the division succeeded in assembling elements around Dolgenkaja and to the east of it for launching an attack.

No artillery support was available, since the divisional artillery of both the *17. Panzer-Division* and the *46. Infanterie-Division* had more than their hands full with supporting their own forces. Of the battalions of *PAR128*, the 2nd Battalion, which had been in support of the *46. Infanterie-Division*, had been overrun by the enemy during the morning hours. The 1st Battalion, returning from the *257. Infanterie-Division*, arrived so late that it did not occupy firing positions north of Suligowka until 1740 hours. The 3rd Battalion was held by the *17. Panzer-Division* and was not ready to fire from positions northeast of Dubrowka until 1830 hours.

The *I./PR23* advanced into the attacking enemy and occupied Hill 204.0, a dominant terrain feature 2 kilometers northeast of Dolgenkaja, at 1600 hours. *Panzergrenadier-Regiment 126*, advancing in the face of continuous aerial attacks and heavy enemy fires, reached a line running Hill 204.0 — Hill 185.9 as it started to turn dark. There, it established contact with elements of the *46. Infanterie-Division* to the left. *Panzergrenadier-Regiment 128* (minus its 2nd Battalion) got bogged down in the extremely heavy flanking fires it was taking from the woods east of Ssisinki in the defile near Woltshij Schpil. On that day, 12 enemy tanks fell victim to the tanks of the division.

One tank company remained as the immediate ready reserve west of the Hill 204.0 — Hill 185.9 area. The rest of the battalion was positioned near Stepanowka, poised for operations.

Starting at 0800 hours on 17 August, the enemy attacked southwest and west of Ssisinki and at Hill 204.0 with strong forces. A penetration in the sector of the *I./PGR128* was quickly cleared up and two enemy tanks were knocked out. The enemy attacks collapsed in front of the main line of resistance at Hill 204.0. The enemy left behind 10 burned-out T-34's. Through 1330 hours, several repeated enemy advances with tanks and infantry at Ssisinki were shattered. An additional 12 enemy tanks were destroyed. The antitank guns of the *I./PGR128* knocked out four enemy tanks. The resoluteness of the infantry could not be surpassed to any greater degree.

While the frontally launched enemy attacks against the division, especially in the sector of *Hauptmann* Ruge's *I./PGR128*, remained unsuccessful in the morning, the situation did become threatening when the enemy attacked the same battalion from the flank after penetrating deeply into the sector of the friendly forces on the right. The Soviets also soon succeeded in penetrating the front at the boundary between the 1st and 2nd Battalions of *PGR128*. Finally, when the enemy who had penetrated to the right occupied the patch of woods to the east of Dolgenkaja and both battalions of *PGR128* were being attacked from the south, the situation became critical. The *I./PR23* joined the fray and, working closely together with the infantry, succeeded in restoring the old main line of resistance by the onset of darkness.

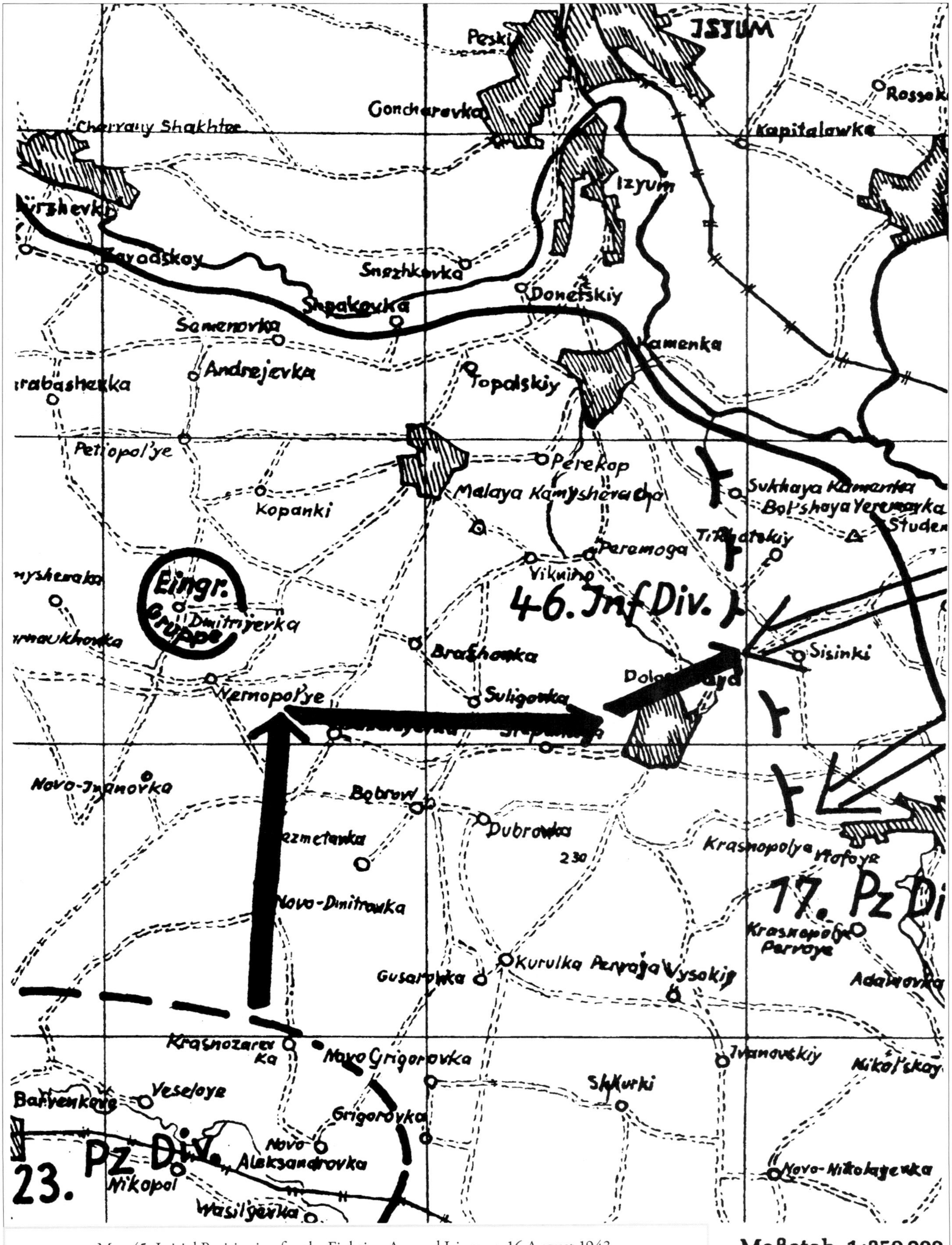

Map 45: Initial Positioning for the Fighting Around Isjum on 16 August 1943.

Maßstab 1:250 000

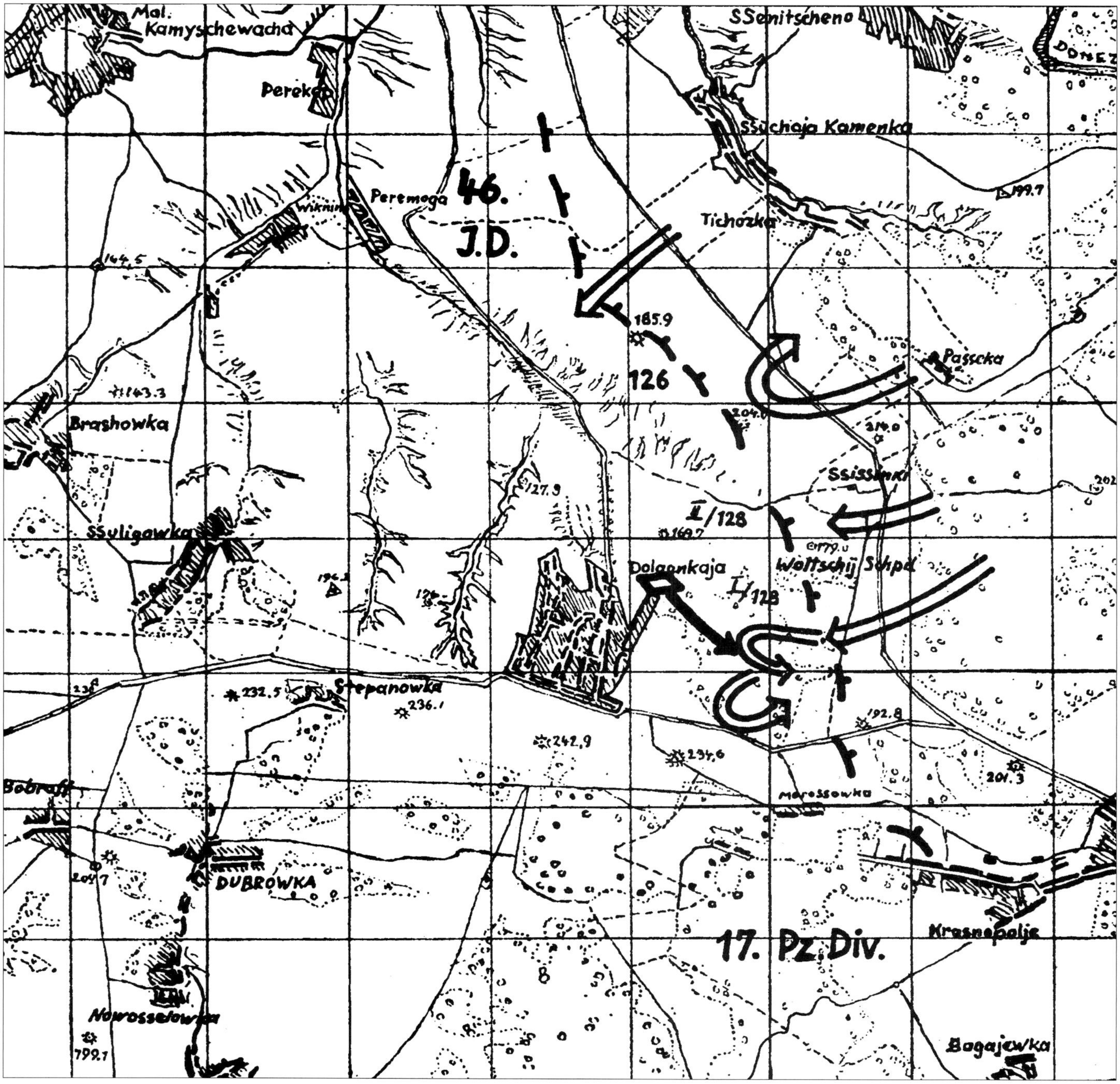

Map 46: Situation on 17 August 1943. (Grid lines at 2-kilometer intervals)

The tanks had barely moved out from the left wing to the right wing of the division, when 1 and 1/2 enemy infantry regiments, supported by tanks, attacked the left wing of *Oberstleutnant* von Winning's *PGR126*. Despite their defensive efforts, the infantry had to pull back their extreme left wing. The gap that had been torn open to the friendly forces on the left was blocked off during the night by the armored car company of *PAA23*.

The Russian air superiority that day was oppressive. Three IL-2's were destroyed by *Flak*, and 37 enemy tanks were left behind by the enemy in and in front of the German lines.

On 17 August, the division's 2nd Medical Company supported the main clearing station of the 2nd Medical Company of the *387. Infanterie-Division* with a group of surgeons.

The divisional engineers were brought forward during the night of 17/18 August. Moving out at first light, *PPB51* ejected the enemy forces that had penetrated on the left wing of the division and restored the previous day's main line of resistance. At 1000 hours, heavy artillery fires began impacting on Hills 204.0 and 185.9; Soviet fighter-bombers also joined the fray. Shortly thereafter, each hill was attacked by a separate infantry regiment, but the hills were held thanks to close coordination with the division's tanks. Seven enemy tanks were destroyed; the withdrawing enemy left a lot of dead behind.

While the defensive fighting was raging on the division's left wing, *PGR128* moved out to restore those parts of the main line of resistance that had been lost the previous day. *Hauptmann* Ruge, the commander of the 1st Battalion, assumed acting command of the regiment from *Oberstleutnant Freiherr* von Wechmar, who had only been with the division for a short time. Extremely stubborn enemy resistance west of Hill 179.0 had to be overcome. Working together with *PAA23* and the friendly forces to the right, ground was gradually regained and, by evening, the former main line of resistance and contact with the neighbors to the right had been reestablished.

Several weaker enemy advances against Hill 204.0 collapsed in front of the German lines. The divisional artillery, which once again supported with well-placed and concentrated fires, shattered Russian concentrations. The *Luftwaffe* also joined in supporting the fighting on the ground, despite the still-existing Soviet air superiority, and provided relief. In all, the enemy lost a total of nine tanks in the divisional sector on that day.

During the night of 18/19 August, there was noticeably heavy Soviet air activity over the Dolgenkaja area; more than 60 machines were counted between 0230 and 0310 hours alone.

Heeres-Flak-Artillerie-Abteilung 278, which had just completed reconstitution at the Wahn Training Area (Cologne) arrived by rail in Barwenkowo and assumed the air defense of the division sector right behind the main battle area. The battalion achieved a number of "kills", but it also suffered a few losses as the result of aerial attacks.

At first light, the enemy resumed his attacks with armor and infantry formations, which were given heavy artillery support. The enemy's main efforts were around Ssisinki and Hill 204.0. T-34's achieved a penetration in the valley to the west of Ssisinki. An antitank-gun platoon of *PGR126* that was hastily sent to the area knocked out all nine of the enemy tanks without suffering any losses of its own and helped stabilize the situation. The main line of resistance was held at Hill 204.0, with three T-34's being knocked out. The engineer platoon of the *8./PGR126* always seemed to be in the hot spots of the fighting for this hill.

The weak companies of *PGR128* had to hold out against greatly superior Soviet attacking forces. Overrun by enemy tanks over and over again, they threw back the enemy's infantry in close combat. In that sector, eight T-34's were knocked out by the antitank guns of the *I./PGR128*; one was knocked out by a rifle grenade. Despite being wounded four times, *Oberleutnant* Lenberger, the commander of the 4th Company (Heavy), remained with his antitank guns.

At 1300 hours, the *I./PR23* and *PAA323* moved out to close the gap between the two infantry regiments. At the same time, the tanks of the *17. Panzer-Division* and the *16. Panzergrenadier-Division* moved out of the patch of woods east of Dolgenkaja to the north to retake the former main line of resistance.

After accomplishing its attack mission, *PAA23* was inserted into the line on the right next to *PGR128*, where it established contact with the friendly forces to the right, the *17. Panzer-Division*. By evening of that day, the main line of resistance was completely back in the hands of the Germans, and the enemy had suffered heavy casualties. Based on intercepted radio traffic and the statements of prisoners, the majority of the enemy's armored formations had been wiped out and the rifle divisions had been badly battered. They were exhausted and completely disorganized.

In addition to antitank guns and antitank rifles, the division had knocked out the following on 19 August: 36 T-34's, 1 KV-I, 1 rocket launcher and 4 artillery pieces. Besides 4 deserters, 31 prisoners had been taken.

The exhausted remnants of *PGR128* were relieved during the night of 19/20 August by *PAA23*. They moved to the woods south of Dolgenkaja. The enemy was quiet the next day. To all appearances, he was assembling his forces and reorganizing. In four days of assaults, he had not succeeded in breaking through the defensive frontage of the *23. Panzer-Division*, despite the employment of six rifle divisions and three tank brigades.

On 21 August, there were signs of new Soviet offensive preparations. The divisional artillery, reinforced by a battery of 21cm howitzers and under the command and control of *Oberst Dr.* Born, engaged enemy concentrations in the woods around and south of Hill 218.1. Weaker enemy elements felt their way forward against the division's positions on several occasions; they were turned back. German patrols cleared the grain fields in front of and behind the main line of resistance.

An hour-long artillery barrage at 0400 hours initiated the start of combat operations on 22 August. At 0500 hours, 25 T-34's rolled toward the quarry west of Ssisinki. At the same time, other tanks, accompanied by infantry, attacked Hill 204.0. Both of the attacks collapsed in front of the main line of resistance, with numerous enemy tanks being destroyed.

The deluge of fire from the Soviet artillery and rocket launchers, as well as the fires from the infantry and tanks, during this time period was so intense that the German infantry could barely lift their heads out of their foxholes on the forward slope of the hills. For hours at a time, they did not know whether the man next to them in another foxhole was still alive.

In the sector of the friendly forces on the right, the enemy succeeded in achieving a deep penetration through the woods east and south of Dolgenkaja. *Generalleutnant* von Vormann ordered a counterattack by the *I./PR23* at Hill 234.6. This was then followed by a blocking mission along a line Hill 232.5 (1 kilometer south of Dolgenkaja) — Hill 242.9 — the eastern edge of Dolgenkaja — road bridge west of Ssisinki. The commander of *PR23*, *Oberstleutnant* Sander, organized a defense running along the line Hill 232.5 — Hill 242.9 (1 kilometer south of Dolgenkaja) and incorporated withdrawing elements of the *17. Panzer-Division* into his defense. The Russians concentrated their entire combat power in this area. Armored, mechanized and rifle formations attempted to force the decisive breakthrough in the area of penetration that had been taken. Thanks to the cooperation among all of the combat arms represented, the uninterruptedly assaulting enemy was turned back; 43 of his tanks were knocked out.

At the same time, *PGR126* and *PPB51* turned back repeated assaults of the enemy. The Soviet infantry was unable to advance as far as the main line of resistance. The T-34's, which continued their advance alone, were either eliminated in close combat or the infantry allowed themselves to be overrun, whereupon they were destroyed further to the rear by heavy weapons.

At 1500 hours, 70 Soviet tanks, along with a rifle division, moved in the direction of Dolgenkaja. Once again, the enemy was granted no success as a result of the defensive fires from *PR23* and the divisional artillery, as well as effective *Stuka* attacks.

Another gap started to yawn in the sector of the friendly forces to the right. A large threat developed, since the enemy identified the gap and funneled strong forces into the woods south of Dolgenkaja. A few of his tanks advanced from there in the afternoon toward the west. *Panzergrenadier-Regiment 128* and the divisional artillery eliminated five of the tanks around Stepanowka, and the rest fled. A difficult, but successful day drew to a close, with 90 Soviet tanks falling victim to the forces of the *23. Panzer-Division* on that 22 August.

Special laurels were achieved on that day by the *I./PR23,* which destroyed 65 enemy tanks in both immediate counterattacks and defensive actions. The battalion's 2nd Company alone accounted for 30 tanks. Of those 30, 12 were knocked out by the acting company commander, *Leutnant* Dern, and his crew.

The badly weakened infantry regiments of the divisions received some reinforcement in the form of the attachment of the *III./Grenadier-Regiment 466* and the *2.* and *3.(Fla)/Panzerjäger-Abteilung 257* of the *257. Infanterie-Division.* The attached battalion was inserted into the line along the east side of Dolgenkaja.

At 0500 hours on 23 August, the Russians resumed their attack on Dolgenkaja. The *III./Grenadier-Regiment 466* turned back the attack.

At 1100 hours, 40 tanks and supporting infantry suddenly stormed over Hill 242.9 and advanced on the southern edge of Dolgenkaja. The commander's tank of the *I./PR23* suddenly found itself inadvertently in the middle of five Soviet tanks. The battalion commander was not in the

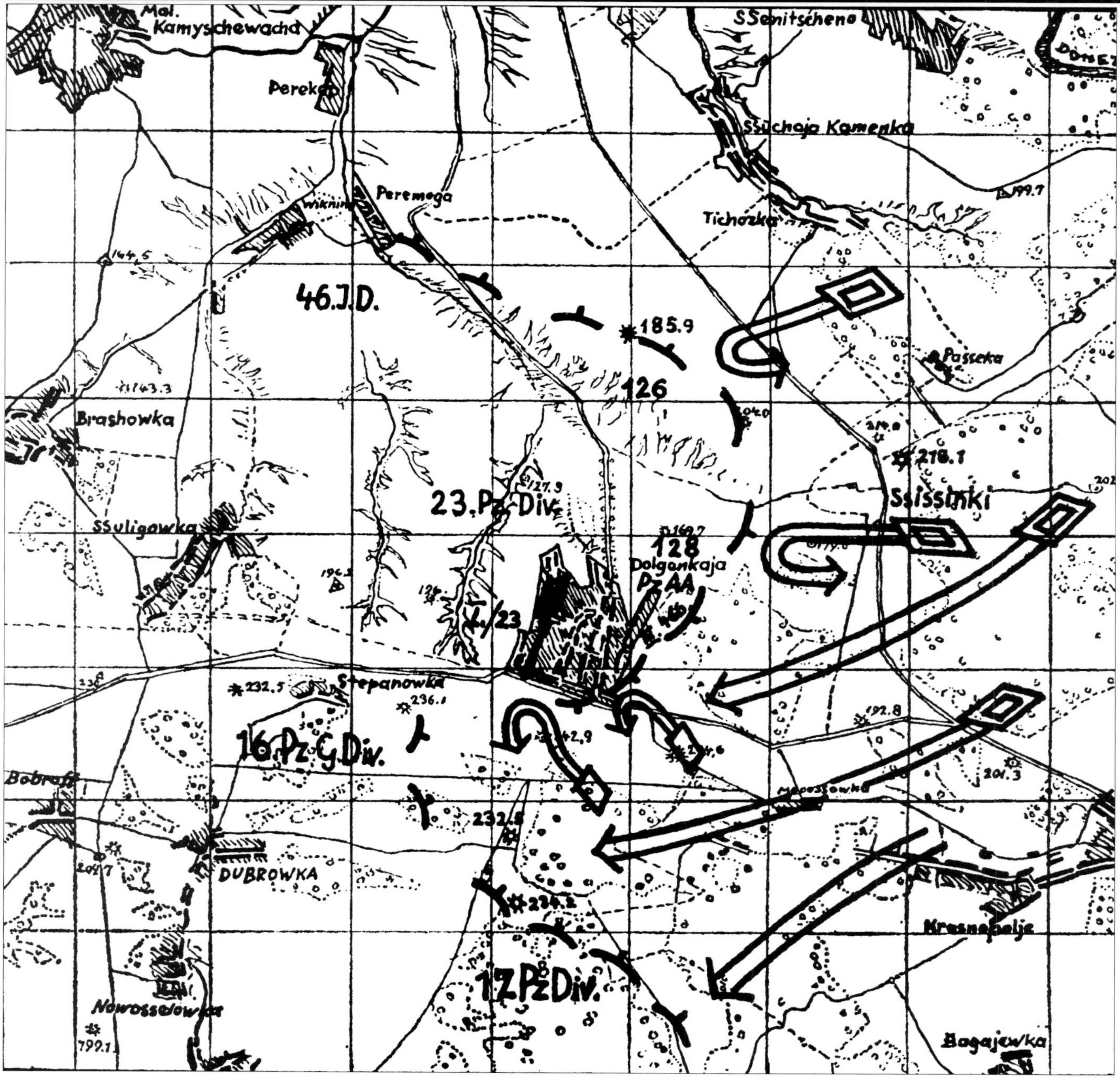

Map 47: Situation on 22 August 1943. (Grid lines at 2-kilometer intervals)

tank at the time; his experienced crew—*Unteroffizier* Baumann, *Unteroffizier* Zimmermann, *Funkmeister* Wiedemann and *Gefreiter* Eifler—kept its nerves and remained on board, setting all five T-34's alight. The remaining Soviet tanks were also knocked out for the most part; the Soviet attack collapsed.

Around noon, the enemy stopped his offensive measures. His infantry transitioned to the well-proven system of infiltration. The thin line of outposts manned by the infantry were powerless to prevent that. As a result, the terrain northeast of Dolgenkaja was lost.

Contact was temporarily established with the tanks of the *17. Panzer-Division* at Hill 242.9, but it could not be maintained. The *23. Panzer-Division*, which had held its positions despite the large-scale offensive operations of the enemy, found itself echeloned far forward into the enemy. The *16. Panzergrenadier-Division*, which was committed to a counterattack, fought in a line running Hill 236.1 — patch of woods west of Hill 232.9.

In order to address the situation of the *23. Panzer-Division* and allow it to shorten its lines, the *XXXX. Panzer-Korps* ordered it to pull back to a line running Hill 236.1 — Hill 196 — Hill 149.5 the following night.

On 23 August, the division knocked out 81 Soviet tanks. Of those, the *I./PR23* accounted for 56, without suffering any losses of its own.

Generalleutnant von Vormann was awarded the Knight's Cross. Every man of the division was happy to hear of that award for the deserving general. No one knew how to take care of soldiers, whether officer, noncommissioned officer or enlisted, like he did. The successes of the division were primarily due to his achievements.

It was exemplary how he knew how to issue orders to soldiers in the field, orders that were thoroughly steeped in the exacting practices of general-staff work and yet could rouse even the weakest soldier.

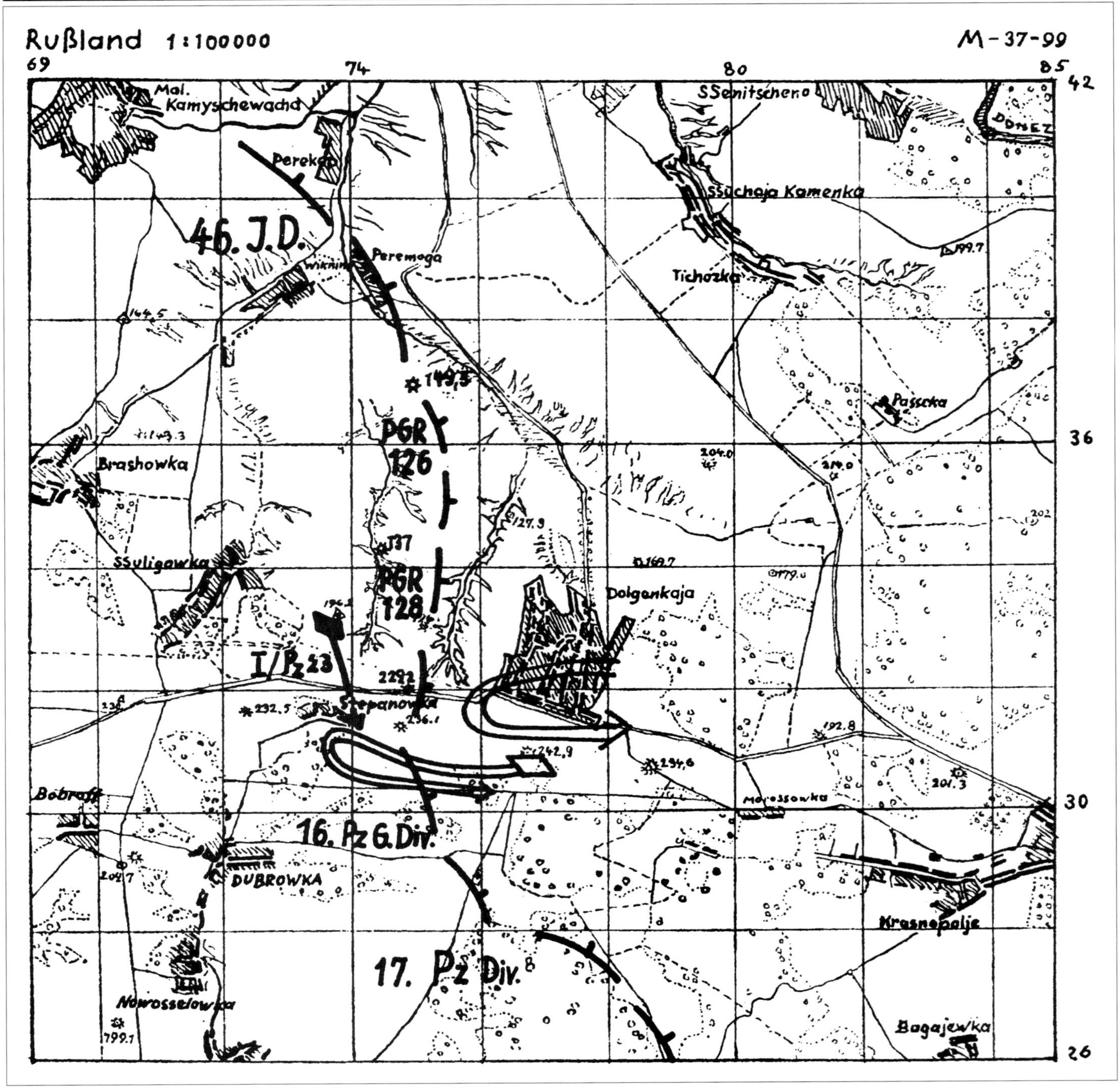

Map 48: Situation on 24 August 1943.

A small anecdote should suffice to reveal his sense of humor. During the first few months of 1943, it came into practice that officers of the division wore their tunic collars open with a tie underneath. *General* Hollidt had promptly forbidden that "breach of etiquette".[57] When the division went under the command and control of the *1. Panzer-Armee* in June, *General* von Vormann issued a laconic division order: "Ties may be worn again."

The withdrawal movements initiated during the night of 23/24 August were completed by 0300 hours. The enemy followed and attacked with increasing intensity during the morning hours, especially at Hill 236.1. Supported by the well-placed fires of the divisional artillery, the infantry were able to turn back all attacks.

At 1430 hours on 24 August, the enemy again placed barrage fires on the German positions with strong artillery and attacked Hill 236.1 from Dolgenkaja with 30 tanks and about a regiment of infantry. After many enemy tanks were knocked out, the attack collapsed. The enemy penetrated into the lines of the friendly forces on the right, however, and forced the terrain south of Hill 236.1 to be evacuated. Twelve enemy tanks advanced as far as Stepanowka. The *I./PR23* cleared up the situation in that sector, eliminated the enemy tanks and reestablished contact with the *16. Panzergrenadier-Division*.

57 Editor's Note: Officers wore a tunic closed at the neck with high collars. Obviously uncomfortable, especially in a combat situation, the officers opened the collar. Even though they still wore a tie with their shirt underneath, this was apparently unacceptable to Hollidt, the Commander-in-Chief at the time. Armor officers wore an open-necked tunic all the time, but they were also expected to wear a tie with their uniform shirt.

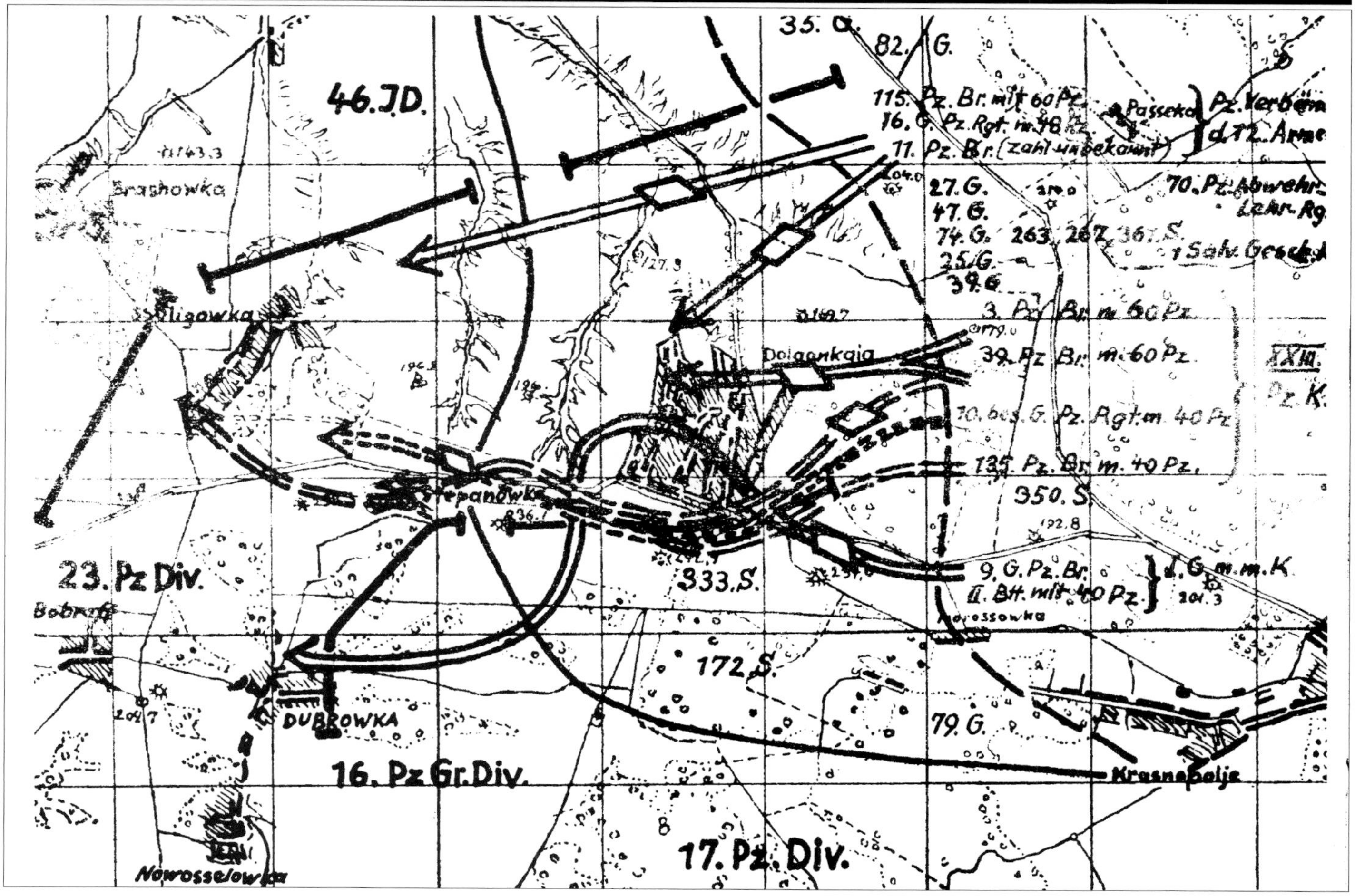

Map 49: Overview of the Fighting at Isjum.

Repeated attacks on the right wing of the division during the afternoon were turned back. Several enemy tanks were also knocked out there, with the result that a total of 35 enemy tanks could be reported as knocked out on that day.

On 24 August, the 2nd Medical Company, newly under the direction of *Stabsarzt Dr.* Gottschling, moved expeditiously from Kurulka to Nowo Dimitrowka, where it took over a clearing station that had been run by the *46. Infanterie-Division*. More than 200 patients cycled through in a span of 24 hours. Wounded were operated on day and night.

The 1st Medical Company, under *Stabsarzt Dr.* Weiß, was also busy at the same time in its clearing station in Losowaja. The field ambulances were constantly on the go in order to bring the wounded under a doctor's care.

On 24 August, due to the critical personnel situation, the *Panzer-Feld-Lehr- und Ersatz-Bataillon 128* of *Oberleutnant Grünwaldt* was reorganized as the *Divisions-Kampf-Schule 23. Panzer-Division*[58] on orders from higher headquarters. Its sole function was then to conduct noncommissioned officer training. By order of *Generalleutnant* von Vormann, however, the former organization of the battalion was essentially retained, with the result that the division continued to have a reserve of trained soldiers at its disposal.

58 Editor's Note: = Division-Level Combat School (*23. Panzer-Division*). This designation was somewhat misleading, as the reader will soon determine. According to the author, the division commander's intent was to form a "standing" reserve for the division, consisting of a core of noncommissioned officers and specialists from all of the combat arms, who would be available in an emergency for commitment. The decision to commit this force was not taken lightly, as the reader will see. In order to avoid confusion, the "school" will not be referred to as such. Instead, it will be referenced as the *DKS*, its German abbreviation.

During the night of 24/25 August, the division had to return the *III./Grenadier-Regiment 466*, along with the elements from *Panzerjäger-Abteilung 257*. The division's own infantry forces had become so weak in the meantime due to the many losses that the main line of resistance could only be held by a thin combat outpost line. It was only possible to defend the main line of resistance by placing 2cm *Flak* and tanks in the front lines.

On 25 August, the Soviets again attempted several times to decide the battle in their favor. They intended to shatter the few German defenders with a heavy artillery preparation, before two regiments attacked along a line running Hill 236.1 — 229.2. Taking heavy losses, the enemy fought his way to the main line of resistance, where he was finally turned back in close combat. Late in the afternoon, a Soviet attack of regimental size led to a penetration in the sector of *PGR126*, but it was quickly sealed off and cleared up in an immediate counterattack. During the night, the enemy penetrated at the same spot again. A tank company provisionally closed the gap at first light. There were no more infantry forces available to do that.

Hauptmann Seyring, the acting commander of *PPB51*, was wounded. *Hauptmann* Feldmann took his place.

The Soviets facing the division consisted primarily of soldiers from Uzbekistan. The enemy was exhausted. On 26 August, he only conducted individual weak advances against the right wing of the division and limited his activities primarily to artillery and mortar salvoes. On the following night, an attack by 200 men against *PGR128* was turned back after an hour of fighting.

The second round of defensive fighting south of Isjum, where the division had been at the hot spots since 16 August, was over. Despite desperate efforts and the employment of five Guards rifle divisions (the 25th, the 27th, the 39th, the 47th and the 82nd), four rifle divisions (the 263rd, the 267th, the 350th and the 361st), nine tank brigades (the 16th Guards, the 11th, the 115th, the 179th, the 212th, the 3rd, the 39th, the 135th and the 9th Guards), a Guards tank regiment (the 10th) and a motorized rifle brigade (the 56th), all of which belonged to the 12th Army, the XXIII Tank Corps and the I Guards Motorized/Mechanized Corps, the enemy had not succeeded in breaking through the German front in 12 days of fighting and reaching his far-ranging objectives.

During the period from 16-27 August, the *23. Panzer-Division* destroyed a total of

302 enemy tanks and 13 enemy aircraft.

In both offensive and defensive operations, it eliminated or captured a large number of guns, antitank guns and infantry weapons.

The losses of the division during the same period:

Killed: 17 officers and 280 noncommissioned officers and enlisted personnel

Wounded: 53 officers and 1282 noncommissioned officers and enlisted personnel

Missing: 1 officer and 184 noncommissioned officers and enlisted personnel

Hauptmann Ruge, the acting commander of *PGR128*, was awarded the Knight's Cross.

***

The Commander-in-Chief of the *1. Panzer-Armee*, *Generaloberst* von Mackensen, issued the following order-of-the-day on 25 August:

> TO: *23. Panzer-Division*
>
> In the second battle of defense conducted along the middle of the Donez, which has been raging since 16 August, the *23. Panzer-Division*, the *16. Panzergrenadier-Division* and the *17. Panzer-Division* have performed magnificently and heroically. The enemy was once again denied a decisive victory here in the main effort of the fighting. The performance of the forces in the field have earned my highest admiration. I recognize, without equivocation and with gratitude, the practically astonishing achievements made through your toughness and inner fortitude.
>
> /signed/ von Mackensen, *Generaloberst*

***

During the fighting around Isjum, the *DKS* continued its training. Soviet attacks along the Mius Front threatened to draw the *DKS* into them. In succeeded, however, in only having to participate in the local defense of Makejewka. It was not until the end of August, when the Soviets were only 20 kilometers east of Makejewka, that *Generalleutnant* von Vormann secured permission to move the *DKS* to Werchowzewo, west of Dnjepropetrowsk.

Oberst Dr. Born, who was reassigned as a corps artillery commander, was replaced by *Oberstleutnant* Vogl in command of *PAR128*.

Fighting with the XXX Armee-Korps and Blocking the Soviet Breakthrough at Sslawjanka 6-11 September 1943

The second round of defensive fighting around Isjum had come to a conclusion. The enemy had withdrawn his bled-white tank formations for battlefield reconstitution. A last effort to break through the positions of the *23. Panzer-Division* on 4 September brought no success with it, despite heavy artillery preparation and the frequent employment of fighter-bombers. The fighting, which lasted the entire day west and south of Dolgenkaja, only demanded additional heavy casualties from the Soviets. Ten T-34's penetrated into the main line of resistance of *PGR128*. The tough infantry allowed the tanks to overrun them. They then separated the tanks from their infantry, with the *I./PR23* and antitank guns knocking out six of them. The remaining four tanks saved themselves through flight. As a result, quiet returned to that sector of the front.

In contrast, the situation along the remaining frontage of *Heeresgruppe Süd* was considerably less sanguine, after *Generalfeldmarschall* von Manstein was unable to get his way against Hitler's views on how the war in the east was to be conducted. After *Operation "Zitadelle"* had been called off by the German command, the pursuing Soviets had been able to tear a gap in the German front 80 kilometers wide near Belgorod in a counterattack that was launched on 3 August. They had gained ground in the direction of Poltava. The attempt of the Soviets to encircle *Armee-Abteilung Kempf*—later redesignated as the *8. Armee*—at Kharkov was countered by the evacuation of the city on 22 August, in spite of Hitler's orders not to do so. The *4. Panzer-Armee*, fighting north of the area of penetration by the Soviets, was able to fend off the Soviet attacks. That was not the case along the Mius Front of the *6. Armee*, where Soviet divisions succeeded in penetrating into the contested area west of Dmitrijewka in the second half of July. Although a breakthrough was prevented, the lack of forces did not allow a complete restoration of the situation. On 23 August, the gap in the front to the east of Poltava was closed again through an attack.

On 27 August, after the repeated urgings of *Generalfeldmarschall* von Manstein, a briefing was held for Hitler with the Commanders-in-Chief of *Heeresgruppe Süd*, the *6. Armee*, the *1. Panzer-Armee*, the *8. Armee* and the *4. Panzer-Armee*. A Commanding General and *Generalleutnant* von Vormann, the commander of the *23. Panzer-Division*, were summoned there to report on conditions in the field. The considerable weakening of the German formations only allowed two solutions. Either the Donez area was to be abandoned—a solution Hitler did not want at all—or at least 12 divisions had to be sent to *Heeresgruppe Süd* to reinforce it. Hitler wanted to strive for the second solution, but he did nothing to see that it was carried out. Thus, the inevitable occurred.

On 29 August, the Russians attacked the *6. Armee* once again. They broke through its positions and advanced in the direction of Stalino and Mariupol. *Heeresgruppe Süd* ordered the *6. Armee* and the right wing of the *1. Panzer-Armee* to pull back to the "Turtle Position" on 31 August. Paralleling the Kriwoj Torez, the line ran eastern edge of Makejewka — eastern edge of Konstantinowka — eastern edge of Kramatorskaja — Sslawjansk and further to the northwest. Hitler agreed to this after the fact, but only to the extent that the absolute necessary be done. These repeated delays of a decision deprived the field-army group of the opportunity to conduct a deliberate withdrawal of its southern wing that would have spared forces. By then, it had become a matter of saving the German formations from destruction.

Meanwhile, the *17. Armee* of *Generaloberst* Ruoff became the only field army of *Generalfeldmarschall* von Kleist's *Heeresgruppe A* to be positioned in the Kuban Bridgehead and on the Crimea Peninsula. It was not until several futile recommendations had been made that *Generalfeldmarschall* von Manstein succeeded in convincing Hitler at a meeting on 8 September to evacuate the Kuban Bridgehead.

On 6 September, along the northern wing of the *6. Armee*, the enemy tore open a 45-kilometer-wide gap, in which only weak German forces were fighting. The Soviets crossed the "Turtle Position" between Kramatorskaja and Awdejewka, before the German divisions could occupy it.

It was in this situation that the *23. Panzer-Division* was pulled out of its positions during the night of 6/7 September and attached with the majority of its forces to *General der Artillerie* Fretter-Pico's *XXX. Armee-*

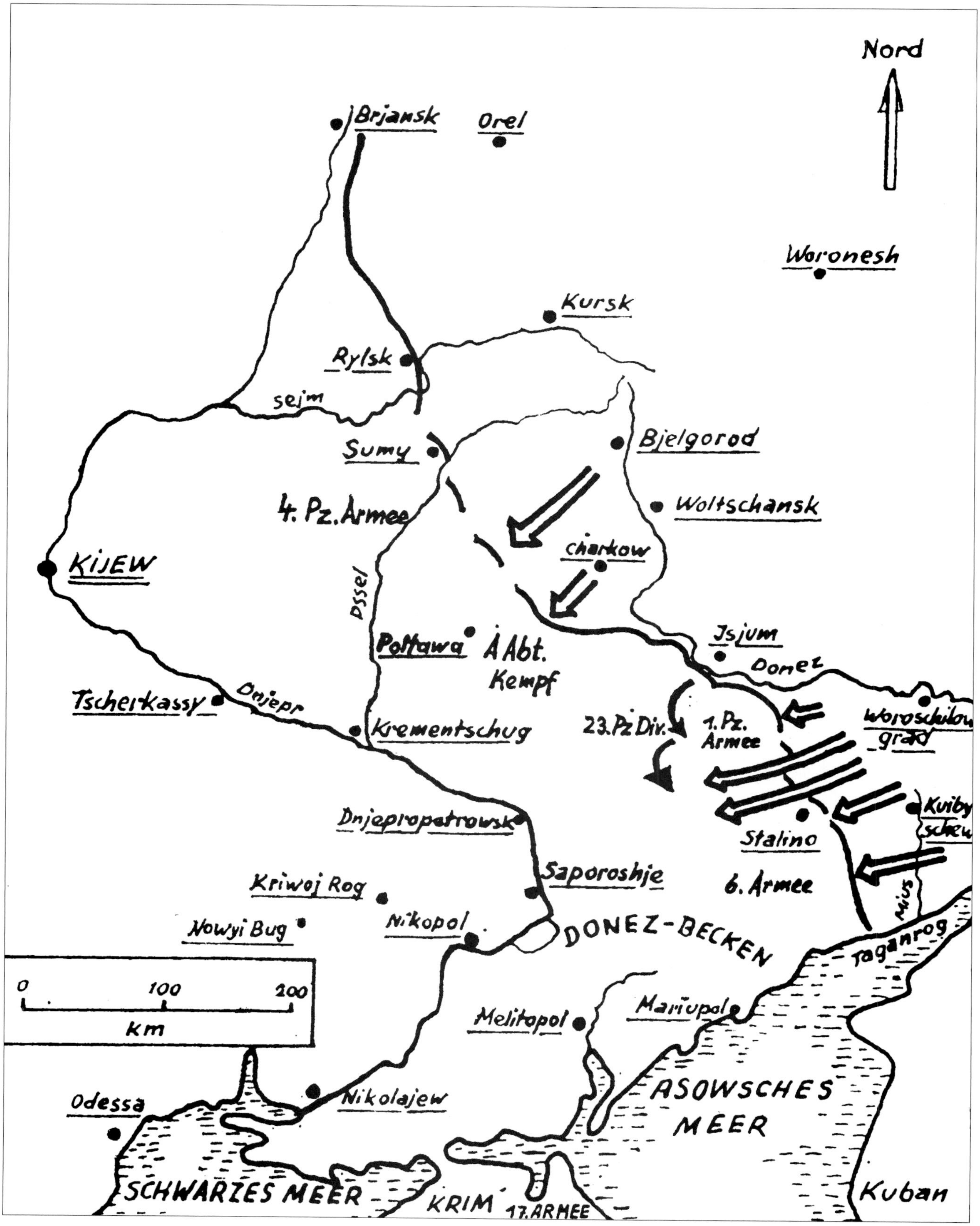

Map 50: Situation on 6 September 1943.

September 1943: The fighting along the Donez. Scenes from the division command post in the woods near Isjum. *Generalleutnant* von Vormann on the field telephone.

Sharing the table with the Division Commander is the division's head of administrative servcices, *Intendant* Dr. Gutschebauch. Waiting in the wings is the division's Logistics Officer, *Major* von Werneburg.

From the left: *Oberleutnant* Zirr, *Oberfeldwebel* Wyrwa, *Leutnant* Heinrichs (the air-ground coordination officer from the *Luftwaffe*), *Leutnant* Laux, *Leutnant* Engel, *Hauptman* Rebentisch and Rebentisch's brother, Heinz., an officer in the regiment. (Heinz was later killed in action.)

The brothers Rebentisch, Wyrwa, Engel, Heinrichs and Laux.

With the advent of autumn also came the transition to winter and the dreaded mud period.

September 1943: The massive dam at Saporoshe.

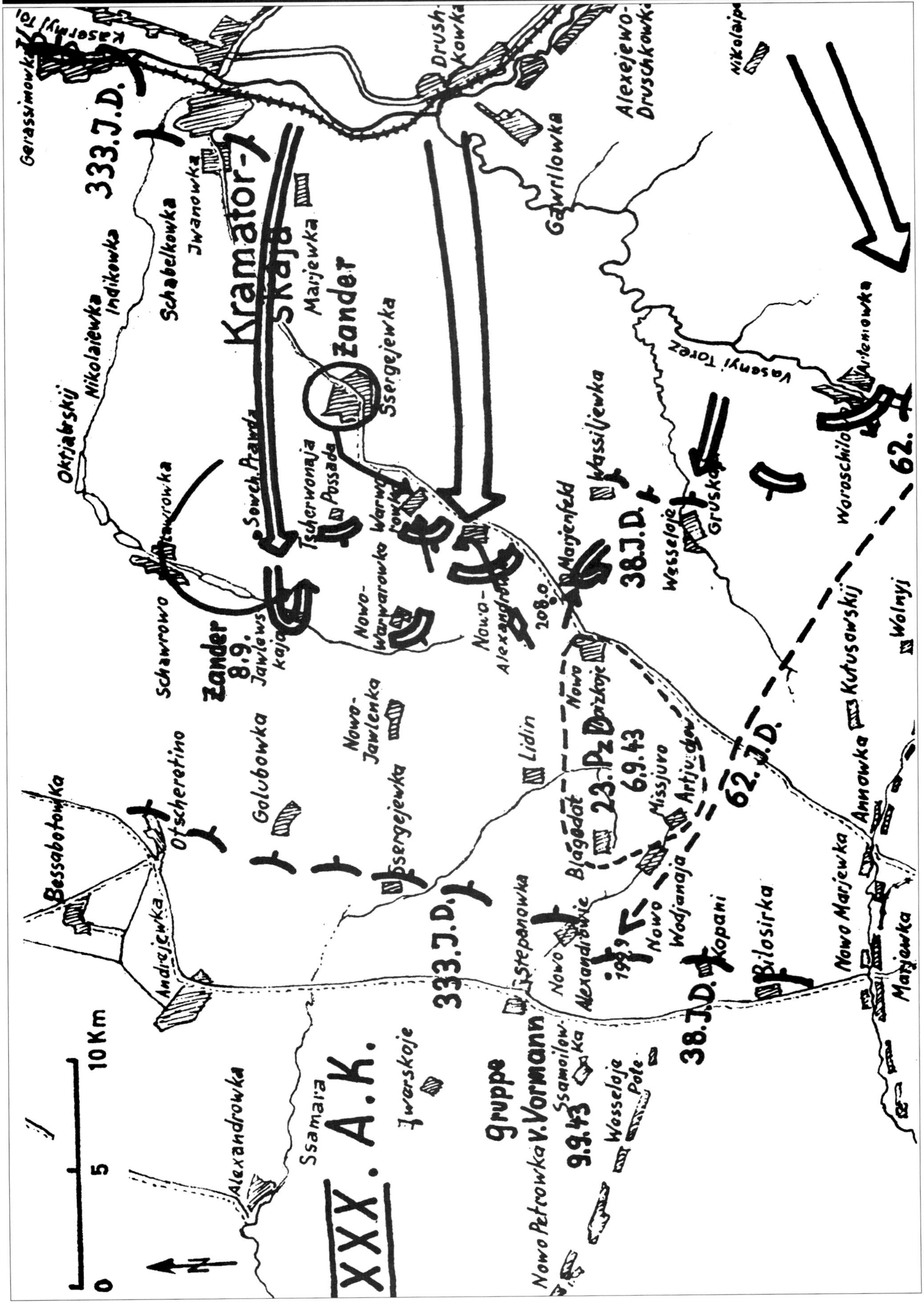

Map 51: Situation in the Sector of the XXX. *Armee-Korps*, 6-9 September 1943.

Korps. Remaining with the *XXXX. Panzer-Korps* as a ready reserve was *Oberstleutnant* von Winning's *Kampfgruppe*, consisting of *PGR128*, the *1./PR23*, the *4./Heeres-Flak-Abteilung 278*, a mixed battalion from the divisional artillery and the headquarters of the divisional reconnaissance battalion.[59] Although the *II./PR23*, which had recently been equipped and trained on the *Panther*, had sent advance parties to the division—a sight everyone enjoyed seeing—the battalion was diverted from the division. It was employed south of the breakthrough area as a result of the Soviet breakthrough in the area of operations of the *6. Armee*.

The *23. Panzer-Division* was tossed into a completely uncertain situation. Little was known by the division command of either the enemy or the friendly forces in the area. The *62. Infanterie-Division* held a bridgehead across the Kriwoi Torez at Oktjabrskoje along the northern edge of the Soviet breakthrough. It was reported that the *38. Infanterie-Division* was to the left of it, manning strongpoints along a line running Grusskaja — western edge of Wassiljewka. Until the right wing of the *333. Infanterie-Division* was reached in the area south of Iwanowka, there was a gap. In that gap, in the area between Ssergejewka — Marjewka, a ready reserve force under the command of *Oberst* Zander from the *16. Panzergrenadier-Division* operated, which consisted of the *II./Panzergrenadier-Regiment 60*, a tank company, an assault-gun battery, a mixed artillery battalion and a company from *Heeres-Panzer-Jäger-Abteilung 662*.[60]

The Soviet forces did not nearly so outnumber the German forces as they had at the recent fighting around Isjum, but the German infantry was completely exhausted. The enemy infiltrated through everywhere; generally, he avoided direct contact. Columns of refugees negatively affected the conduct of the fighting; it was attempted many times to evacuate the civilian populace.

In a night march, *PR23* (minus its 2nd Battalion), *PGR126*, *PAR128* (minus the *ad hoc* mixed battalion), *PJA128*, *PPB51* and *Heeres-Flak-Abteilung 278* reached the Missjuro Artjuchoff — Nowo Troizkoje — Blagodat area and prepared for operations there to the east, north or south.

The mission for 7 September called for catching the enemy armored forces that had crossed to the west over the Kasennyj Torez and eliminate them. Specific missions from the *XXX. Armee-Korps* also included attempting to establish contact first with the intact left wing of the *38. Infanterie-Division* east of Marjenfeld, then with the ready reserve group of *Oberst* Zander of the *16. Panzergrenadier-Division* in Ssergejewka and, finally, with the right wing of the *333. Infanterie-Division*. After completing that mission—and, if possible, on the same day—the division was to advance south in front of the sector of the *38. Infanterie-Division* and eliminate the enemy who had broken through at Artemowka. The ready reserve group of the *16. Panzergrenadier-Division* was attached to the *23. Panzer-Division*.

The Red Air Force dominated the air space. Fighter-bombers even attacked the well-marked vehicles of the medical elements, with the result that they could only move on an individual basis. The 1st Medical Company established a temporary clearing station in Nowo Alexandrowka. The 2nd Medical Company was sent to Werchowzewo across the Dnjepr, where it was to establish a rest area for the division. The quick turn of events did not allow that to happen, however.

After a short orders conference, *Panzergruppe Sander* and *PGR126* moved out to attack to the southeast. Nowo Alexandrowka was taken at 1030 hours after an engagement with enemy tanks and strong infantry. The divisional artillery supported the continued advance from positions west of Hill 208.2. *Heeres-Flak-Abteilung 278* provided area defense for the division from the Lidin area. While *PPB51, PJA128* and, later, *PGR126* screened and reconnoitered to the east, the armored battle group advanced northeast against Warwarowka. In an engagement with 35 enemy tanks, the *I./PR23* temporarily entered the village, but then had to pull back through Nowo Warwarowka in the face of superior enemy forces. At Nowo Warwarowka, it again ran into strong enemy forces and had to stop its attack.

At 1615 hours, *Gruppe Zander*, the reinforced *II./Panzergrenadier-Regiment 60*, attacked Warwarowka on its own initiative from the north, in an effort to establish contact with the *23. Panzer-Division*. At the same time, *PPB51*, along with the *1./PJA128*, both of which had moved out to envelop Warwarowka from the east, attacked the village and took it. The division succeeded on that day in intercepting the attack spearheads of the Soviets, which had been aiming for the deep left flank of the *XXX. Panzer-Korps* in Barwenkowo. A lot of German equipment, which had been abandoned in Nowo Alexandrowko, was recovered. In addition, the enemy lost one KV I, six T-34's, two armored cars and several 7.62cm antitank guns.

At 1900 hours, the following order was received from the *XXX. Armee-Korps*:

> *23. Panzer-Division* is to assemble during the night of 7/8 September in the Nowo Alexandrowka — Nowo Warwarowka area, in order to eliminate the enemy west of the Prawda Collective Farm and Tscherwonaja Possada by means of a rapid advance and push back the enemy who has advanced to Nowo Jawlewka to the area east and south of it. It is then to move out from the Marjenfeld — Nowo Alexandrowka area by the fastest means possible to advance south, in order to clarify the situation in front of the *38. Infanterie-Division* and further to the right as far as the *62. Infanterie-Division*. The intention is to prepare for operations the morning of the following day in the Ssuworowka area and hit the enemy, who has broken through between the *6. Armee* and the right wing of the *1. Panzer-Armee*, in the flank.

At the same time, however, the enemy entered Gruskaja with tanks and truck-mounted infantry, overran elements of the *38. Infanterie-Division* and advanced further to the northwest in the direction of Marjenfeld. He took that village and disrupted the communications between the elements of the *23. Panzer-Division* that were positioned in the areas around Nowo Troizkoje and Nowo Alexandrowka.

At that point, *Generalleutnant* von Vormann ordered the attack of those elements at first light on 8 September to the south.

During the night of 7/8 September, *Gruppe Zander* lost contact with *PR23*. It then swung out to the northwest in an effort to reestablish contact with the division by moving through Schawrowo to the south.

At first light on 8 September, *PPB51* assaulted Marjenfeld in a short, sharp fight. More than 100 enemy dead were counted and numerous infantry weapons were captured or destroyed.

The division reformed and screened along the line Missjuro Artjuchow — Nowo Wodjanaja — Lidin. *Kampfgruppe Zander*, attacking from the north, took Jawlenskaja at 1150 hours, while the defenders of Nowo Troizkoje had to fend off continuously conducted enemy attacks of battalion strength until noon.

The *XXX. Armee-Korps* ordered the formation of *Gruppe von Vormann* at 1115 hours, consisting of the *23. Panzer-Division* and the *38. Infanterie-Division*. For the night of 8/9 September, the division group and the *333. Infanterie-Division* were ordered to pull back to a line running Bilosirka — Kopani — Hill 199.9 (east of Nowo Alexandrowka) — Hill 199.2 (east of Ssergejewka) — western part of Golubowka — eastern part of Otscheretino.

At 1315 hours, the commander of the *I./Grenadier-Regiment 679* of the *333. Infanterie-Division*, reported that his battalion, together with elements of *Aufklärungs-Abteilung 333* of the same division, and

59 Editor's Note: Of interest here is the fact that the *Oberstleutnant* was not in command of his own regiment, *PGR126*, for the formation of the *Kampfgruppe*, but the sister regiment, *PGR128*.

60 Editor's Note: = 662nd Antitank Battalion (Separate), which was a general headquarters force. It had only been formed in July 1943 and was outfitted with 8.8cm antitank guns.

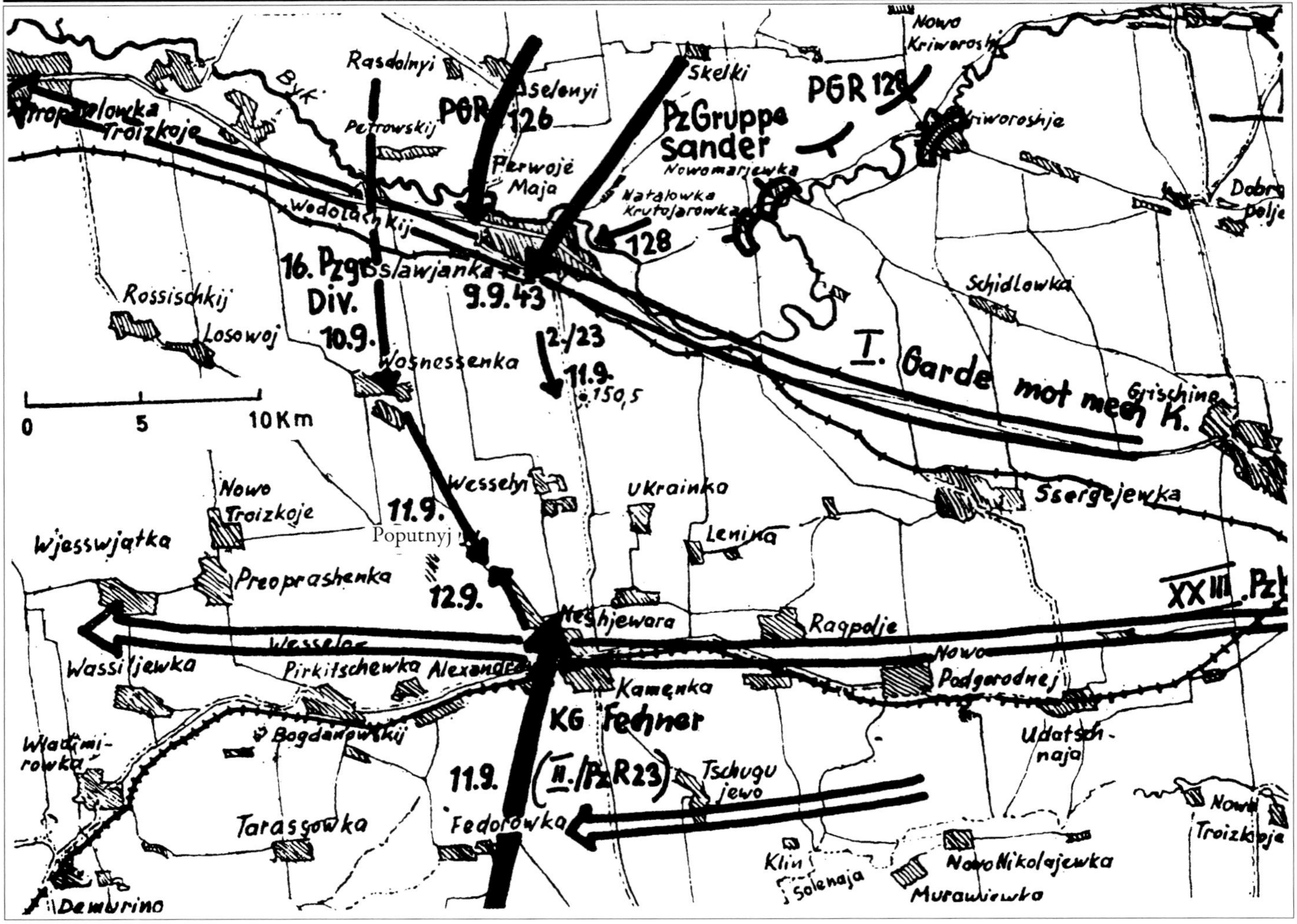

Map 52: The Operations of the *23. Panzer-Division* and its Attached Formations, as well as the *II./Panzer-Regiment 23*, in the Sslawjanka Area Around 12 September 1943.

four batteries of artillery were encircled in the area east of Jawlenskaja — Prawda Collective Farm. *Generalleutnant* von Vormann issued orders: "Break through to Nowo Jawlenka."

At the same time, the armored elements of *Gruppe Zander* moved out to conduct a relief attack on the Prawda Collective farm. The encircled battalion was able to break out under the cover offered by the armored vehicles; it assembled with *Gruppe Zander* east of Nowo Alexandrowka. The enemy only followed hesitantly.

At 1900 hours, the withdrawal movements of the division commenced, with the *38. Infanterie-Division* moving into a line running on both sides of Bilosirka —area 2 kilometers northeast of Kopani. An engineer squad from the *8./PGR128* was lost because it could not be informed of the withdrawal movement. Machine gun and rifle fire could be heard for a long time the next day, but then it turned quiet.

During the night, the *62. Infanterie-Division*, which had been bypassed on both sides in the area around Oktjabrskoje, was able to push its way through to the northwest, reaching the area around Stepanowka at first light.

On the morning of 9 September, the *333. Infanterie-Division* had its right wing in Nowo Alexandrowka. *Panzerkampfgruppe Sander* prepared for operations in Stepanowka. As a result of the recent actions, the entire *XXX. Armee-Korps* had been able to avoid encirclement by the enemy. At that point, it was massed together in a small area.

At 1300 hours on 9 September, the division was detached from the command and control of the *XXX. Armee-Korps* and went back to the *XXXX. Panzer-Korps*. At the same time, *Divisionsgruppe von Vormann* was dissolved and *Gruppe Zander* returned to the *16. Panzergrenadier-Division*. As a result of a shortening of the front to the left of the *XXX. Armee-Korps*, the *XXXX. Panzer-Korps* was released for other operations and was moved to the southwest with the mission of eliminating the enemy armored forces that had broken through and were headed for Dnjepropetrowsk with the main bodies of both the *23. Panzer-Division* and the *16. Panzergrenadier-Division*. The two Soviet corps that had already been encountered during the 2nd Battle of Isjum—the I Guards Motorized/Mechanized Corps and the XXIII Tanks Corps—had advanced from Konstantinowka through Gruschino. They had encountered little resistance in the rear areas of the divisions at the front and had already advanced to the area in front of Pawlograd. The rifle divisions that followed blocked the area of the penetration.

The *23. Panzer-Division* was to position itself north of Sslawjanka during the afternoon of 9 September so as to advance into the enemy's deep flank the following day.

Generalleutnant von Vormann decided to take Sslawjanka that same day, however. He intended to form a bridgehead south of the Byk and block the Soviet's supply route.

Panzergruppe Sander moved through Skelki at 1600 hours. The motorcycle scout platoon of the *I./PR23* advanced as far as the Byk and secured a crossing. Shortly thereafter, the tanks then crossed the small river on a weak bridge; after the bridge could no longer be used, they moved through a ford. The enemy was completely surprised. Numerous tanks, antitank guns, and infantry weapons were eliminated at pointblank range. As it started to get dark, the tanks were at the Sslawjanka rail station. The southern part of the village and its eastern outskirts were firmly in German hands. The enemy—it was primarily the 266th Rifle Division with attached tank and tank destroyer formations—was unable to collect himself for renewed resistance until the night had fallen. At 2315 hours, he also lost his contact with the I Guards Motorized/Mechanized Corps, which had remained intact up to that point, because *PGR126* had attacked south through Selenyj, shattered weak Soviet outposts, crossed the Byk at Perwoje Maja and, in nighttime house-to-house fighting, took the western part of Sslawjanka.

Panzergrenadier-Regiment 128, which had been returned to division control, screened the eastern flank of the division north of the Byk during the night of 9/10 September. During the morning of 10 September, it moved out through Natalowka to attack Sslawjanka, where it broke enemy resistance that had flared up, along with the light platoon of the regimental headquarters of *PR23*. Two German tanks were knocked out there early in the morning. Eight 7.52cm antitank guns fell into German hands.

During the course of 10 September, the enemy was pushed back further and further into the middle of Sslawjanka, since he no longer had the combat power to break out. Elements of the 266th Rifle Division, which were positioned to the east of Sslawjanka, attempted to relieve their cut-off forces again and again, but they were turned back with extremely heavy casualties. The Soviets only succeeded in disrupting the German supply lines to a considerable degree, with the result that a tank company finally had to be employed to protect them. The enemy that had been located along the deep left flank of the division in Krutojarowka, Nowo Marjewka and Kriworoshje remained quiet. To screen against them, *Heeres-Flak-Abteilung 278* went into position along the high ground east of Natalowka and Skelki.

Unpleasant for the infantry in Sslawjanka was the fact that the civilians, who had fled at the start of the fighting, were gradually starting to return and, because they could move about freely, showed the Soviets encircled in the village the German positions.

During the morning of 16 September, the *16. Panzergrenadier-Division* took Wodolashkij and then advanced further to the south on Wosnessenka.

At 0800 hours on the morning of 11 September, Sslawjenka was cleared of the last of the Soviets. Several relief attacks from the east and southeast collapsed, just as the one the previous day had. The *2./PR23* advanced south toward Wesselyj and eliminated a Bolshevik battalion and several antitank guns on Hill 150.5. Wesselyj was thick with enemy and could not be taken with the weak forces available.

In the course of the day, the *16. Panzergrenadier-Division* took Poputnyj, while the *9. Panzer-Division*—to which the *II.(Panther)/PR23* had been attached—took back Meshowaja and Kamenka. This closed the gap between the *6. Armee* and the *1. Panzer-Armee*. The two Soviet corps that had been cut off concentrated around Nikolajewka, 20 kilometers west of Sslawenka. It was anticipated that efforts would be made by the cut-off corps to break out and for relief attacks from the east to be conducted over the next few days.

Although the infantry and engineers had been greatly outnumbered by the enemy in Sslawjanka, they were able to destroy the following, in conjunction with the tanks:

The main body of the 266th Rifle Division

The 19th Guards Tank Regiment of the II Guards Motorized/Mechanized Corps (with 20 tanks)

The 179th Tank Destroyer Battalion (with 24 7.62cm antitank guns)

The 52nd Tank Destroyer Battalion (Separate)

The 575th Engineer Battalion (Separate)

Those enemy forces lost:

28 Tanks (24 T-34's and 4 T-60's)
26 7.62cm antitank guns
13 4.5cm antitank guns
4 7.62cm field pieces
35 antitank rifles
8 medium mortars
12 heavy machine guns
58 light machine guns
6 trucks
Several radio centers
50 horse-drawn vehicles
1 R-5 aircraft

5,000 rounds of light artillery ammunition and untold amounts of small arms and ammunition

In addition, the enemy lost 840 dead and 70 prisoners were taken.

Operations of the II./Panzer-Regiment 23 in the Donez Area 3-16 September 1943

The *II./PR23*, the former *II./PR201*, was equipped with the newly introduced *Panzer V "Panther"* from 20 March to 28 August 1943. As a result of an overburdening of the tank courses at Erlangen and the preferential issuance of equipment to the *Waffen-SS*, the conversion to the new equipment was delayed. After convalescing, *Hauptmann* Fechner reassumed command of his old battalion and relieved *Hauptmann* Behr, who was transferred to the 1st Battalion. Replacements were incorporated into the battalion, and personnel were reassigned to *Panzer-Abteilung 51* and *Panzer-Abteilung 52*, which departed earlier for the front. Final combat training at the Grafenwöhr Training Area was negatively influenced by the modifications and changes that were necessary for the new equipment, which was plagued with "teething problems".

On 28 August, the battalion headed back to the Eastern Front by rail. A return to the division, which was fighting south of Isjum, was prevented by the large-scale Soviet offensive against the heart of the Donez area. *Heeresgruppe Süd* directed the battalion to Makejewka, where it arrived on 3 September and was attached to the *XVII. Armee-Korps*.

The battalion was already being employed on the morning of 4 September. The *8./PR23* shattered enemy attacks on *Generalleutnant* Köhler's *306. Infanterie-Division* east of Kirowo. The main body of the battalion joined the fray in the sector of the *294. Infanterie-Division*, adjoining to the south. It shattered the lead Soviet attack elements that had penetrated in the area Artschadinskij settlement — Grussko Sarinskij — Greko Saizewo. For the most part, the enemy pulled back to Ilowaiskaja. He lost 12 antitank guns, 8 antitank rifles, 4 mortars and more than 100 dead. The German losses were limited to mechanical failures.

On 5 September, the *5./PR23* remained in Makejewka as the corps reserve. The rest of the battalion moved north to counterattack into the Krassnyj Jar area. It arrived in the nick of time to turn back an enemy attack on the German infantry, which was pulling back. While *Leutnant* Kuhn's platoon from the *7./PR23* supported *Grenadier-Regiment Gruber* of the *335. Infanterie-Division* east and north of Jassinowka, the battalion defeated strong enemy forces around Skotowaja, although it was unable to take the village itself. Four T-34's were destroyed. The number of operational tanks shrank to 37 as the result of numerous mechanical problems. *Oberleutnant* Hyprath's *6./PR23* was ordered to *Generalmajor* Weidemann's *335. Infanterie-Division*, while the rest of the battalion set up all-round defenses around Obuschek.

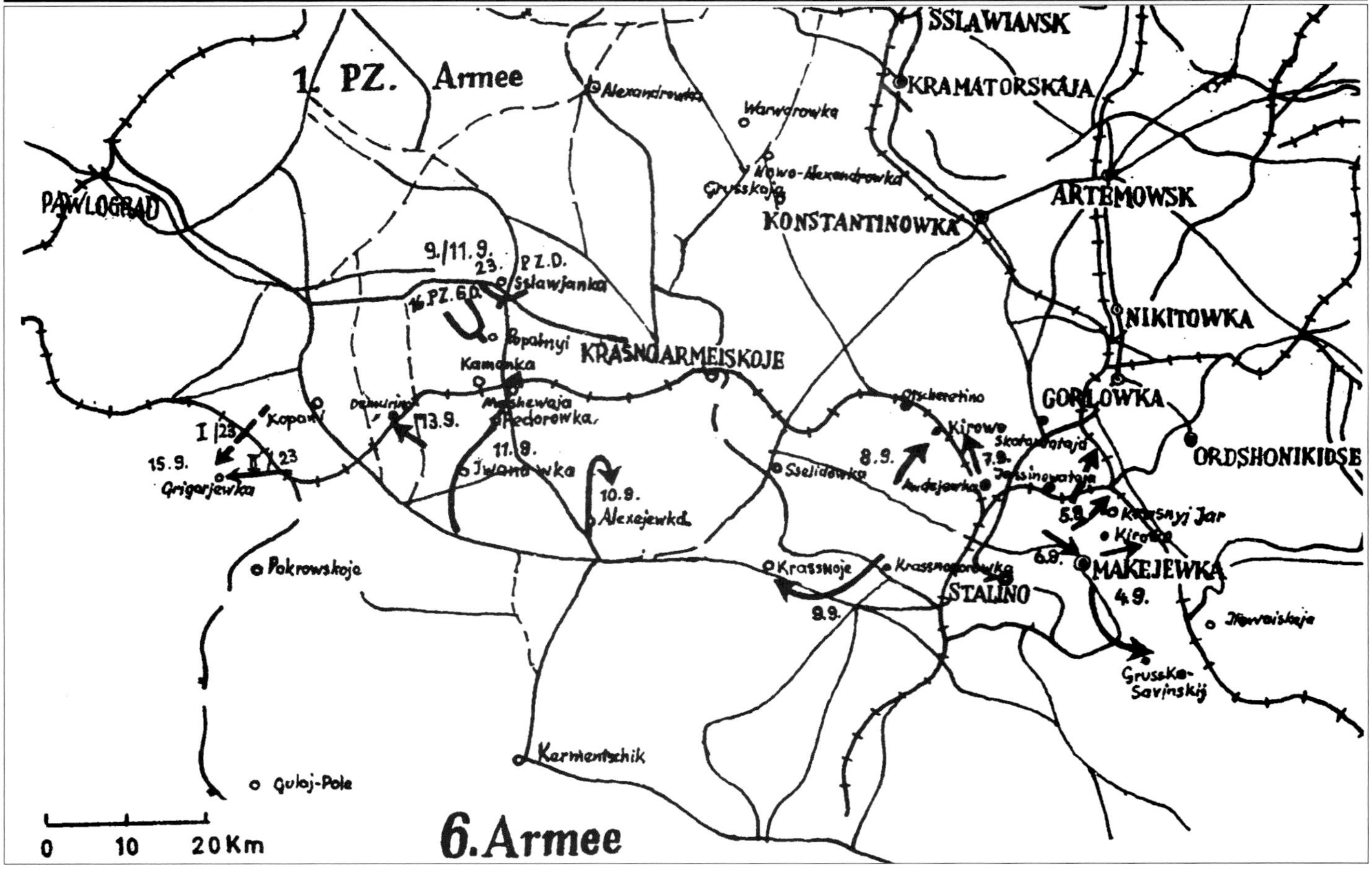

Map 53: Operations of the *II./PR23* from 4-15 September 1943

The *6./PR23* effectively supported *Grenadier-Regiment Stock* on 6 September. In the course of an immediate counterattack, a 10.5cm howitzer battery that had been lost to the enemy was recaptured. Ten enemy antitank guns and numerous weapons fell victim to the company, as well. The company was almost encircled by the Soviets, however, who were advancing practically everywhere. That evening, it cleared a path for the accompanying infantry back to Awdejewka. Three *Panthers* were lost, of which two had to be blown up due to mechanical problems.

The battalion joined the battle with the *306. Infanterie-Division* with its 7th and 8th Companies. In difficult fighting, it cleared up the penetration into the northern part of Makejewka. Destroyed were 16 enemy tanks, 9 antitank guns and numerous pieces of equipment. In the afternoon, the *7./PR23* intercepted German infantry pulling back south of Krassnyj and reestablished the front there.

Moving out of Awdejewka, the battalion supported the *335. Infanterie-Division* with *Oberleutnant* Fischer's 8th Company and the *306. Infanterie-Division* with its main body. Tanks from the *6./PR23* moving to the maintenance company suddenly found themselves facing enemy tanks west of Awdejewka. Without suffering any losses, six T-34's and one KV-1 were knocked out; what remained of the enemy moved back north. To the north, the enemy had advanced quite far to the west after a successful breakthrough. In the depths of the area of penetration, he also turned south. Tonenkij and Kirowo, 10 kilometers further to the south, were occupied by the enemy. In that area, the *II./PR23* knocked out four T-34's. While the main body of the battalion moved to Ismailowka to serve as the corps reserve, the *8./PR23* covered the withdrawal movements of the *335. Infanterie-Division* and conducted immediate counterattacks in the sectors of various battalions of the division. An addition four enemy tanks were destroyed by the battalion in a counterattack conducted south of Kirowo.

On 9 September, the battalion (minus its 8th Company) was attached to *Oberst* Jolasse's *9. Panzer-Division*. It attacked Krassnoje, 30 kilometers west of Krassnogorowka, with 12 *Panthers* and elements of the *9. Panzer-Division*. Eleven enemy tanks and nine antitank guns were destroyed; the village was cleared of the enemy.

The 10th of September, saw the *II./PR23* another 30 kilometers further to the west, attacking from Alexejewka to the north. Supported by the *II./Panzer-Artillerie-Regiment 102* of the *9. Panzer-Division*, additional enemy formations and trains elements were shattered. Nine artillery pieces, sixteen antitank guns and numerous major items of equipment were destroyed.

The *8./PR23* returned to the battalion after it had fought its way through enemy forces advancing southwest in the Krassnogorowka — Staro-Michailowka area.

Hauptmann Fechner enjoyed particular success with his newly formed *Kampfgruppe*—the *II./PR23*, elements of *Panzer-Regiment 33*, the *II./Panzer-Artillerie-Regiment 102*, the *3./Panzer-Pionier-Bataillon 86* and the *I./Panzergrenadier-Regiment 11*[61]—on 11 September. Advancing to the north through Iwanowka and Fedorowka from Podubnyj, the battle group took Kamenka and the Meshewaja rail station through quick, aggressive action that exploited a *Stuka* attack. By doing so, it blocked the supply route for the Soviet XXIII Tank Corps, which had broken through to the west. The *6./PR23* knocked out five enemy tanks, and numerous trains and communications vehicles were destroyed. In advancing on Poputnyj, the battle group nearly succeeded in closing the gap created by the breakthrough between the *6. Armee* and the *1. Panzer-Armee*. The *23. Panzer-Division* was only 15 kilometers away in Sslawjanka, and the *16. Panzergrenadier-Division* was to its southwest. Attacking from both east

61 Editor's Note: With the exception of Fechner's battalion, all of the remaining elements came from the *9. Panzer-Division*.

and west, the enemy attempted in vain to reopen the road at Kamenka. Without suffering any losses, 10 Soviet tanks and 2 antitank guns, in addition to other weapons and equipment, were destroyed.

On 12 September, *Kampfgruppe Fechner* established contact with the *16. Panzergrenadier-Division* at Poputnyj. Given the opportunity afforded, it could finally be resupplied there, after the supply route for the battle group had been interdicted by Russian elements pressing from both east and west at Fedorowka. Fighting continued at the blocking position established along the road, which was guarded by three *Panthers* and a platoon of engineers. The enemy suffered heavy casualties trying to take it. He lost 8 tanks, 1 antitank gun, 14 trucks, fuel and ammunition on that day.

In the course of the evening, Fedorowka was lost. Unfortunately, 14 *Panthers* of the battalion had to be blown up. They had been taken there for repair and could not be evacuated. After they had fired their last rounds and the infantry started to pull back, the explosive charges were armed.

All of the efforts by the Russians to bypass the blocking position on the road also failed on 13 September. At noon, *Kampfgruppe Fechner* was ordered to move to Demurino via Tarassowka. While *en route*, a strong enemy force was surprised and completely wiped out. The day's war spoils included 2 T-34's, 1 rocket launcher, 28 trucks and 11 horse-drawn vehicles.

On 14 September, *Kampfgruppe Fechner* marched west at the head of the *9. Panzer-Division*. The enemy took flight from Nowo Andrejewka and Selenyj Gaj when the Germans showed up in his rear. A large amount of equipment, four tanks, one assault gun, two armored cars and six artillery pieces, as well as large numbers of motorized vehicles, were either captured or destroyed.

On 15 September, Grigorjewka was reached without a fight. At noon, the reunion of the 2nd Battalion and the 1st Battalion, which marched in from the north, was celebrated. On 16 September, the 2nd Battalion was released from its attachment to the *9. Panzer-Division* and returned to its parent division. Five tanks out of the original eighty-five were still operational.

***

On the occasion of the return of the *II./PR23* to the *23. Panzer-Division*, *Oberst* Jolasse, the acting commander of the *9. Panzer-Division*, wrote the following order-of-the-day:

Division Command Post, 17 September 1943

TO: *Kampfgruppe Fechner*

I extend my special recognition to all of the forces of the *Kampfgruppe*, which, under the command of its brave and decisive commander, moved out of Iwanowka and entered Kamenka in an aggressively mounted attack on 11 September, took the Meshewaja rail station and cut off the enemy, who had broken through far to the west, from his supply lines by blocking the road and rail. By doing so, the battle group held its blocking position against all efforts to break through, even though it was entirely on its own and in the midst of the enemy without logistical support and supplies. It inflicted heavy, bloody losses on the enemy and his materiel and, above and beyond all that, contributed decisively to the destruction of the enemy.

To the departing *II./Panzer-Regiment 23*, under its exemplary commander, Major Fechner, I wish continued good fortunes of war, success and military laurels.

/signed/ Jolasse
Oberst and Acting Commander of the *9. Panzer-Division*

Retreat Across the Dnjepr and Defensive Fighting North of Pjatichatki 16 September to 18 October 1943

On the days that followed, the *23. Panzer-Division*, oriented east toward the ever-pressing enemy, pulled back to the Dnjepr as part of the front of *Generalfeldmarshall* von Manstein's *Heeresgruppe Süd*, which was once again cohesive. How difficult it was for the Soviets to gain ground and what kind of reputation the *23. Panzer-Division* had achieved can be gleaned from this radio message, which was intercepted at 0735 hours on 15 September:

> Everyone is advancing. The enemy has withdrawn from Poputnyj. At 0700 hours, Tschuchuwaj [the commander of the 1010th Rifle regiment] advanced. The enemy took prisoners. We suffered great losses. It was especially difficult at the hill. You are familiar, of course, with the *23. Panzer-Division*. Rengatsch [939th Rifle regiment] advanced due west.

The *II./PR23*, which had been badly weakened while serving with the *9. Panzer-Division*, was sent to Saporoshe to recover and repair its *Panzer V's*. The five *Panthers* that were still operational remained behind in the regiment under the command of *Oberleutnant* Hyprath. The lack of recovery means allowed *Major* Fechner to only retrieve a portion of his tanks, which almost exclusively had become non-operational due to mechanical failures. Twenty *Panthers* had to be blown up to avoid immediate capture by the Soviets. Although the new type of tank had proven itself admirably in combat, it was still susceptible to mechanical problems.

While the *II./PR23* was undergoing refitting in Saporoshe, the lead elements of Soviet attack formations broke through between the German bridgehead positions at Saporoshe and Dnjepropetrowsk and crossed the Dnjepr 40 kilometers north of Saporoshe. *Oberleutnant* Fischer and four *Panthers* were sent to support the *257. Infanterie-Division*, which had been directed against those enemy forces. They succeeded in pushing back the Soviets, but the enemy was still able to maintain a narrow bridgehead. Elements of *Panzer-Regiment 15* of the *11. Panzer-Division* relieved Fischer's group after a few days.

Major Ziegler, a recipient of the Oakleaves to the Knight's Cross, assumed command of *PGR128*.

In the midst of rainfall and knee-deep mud, the *23. Panzer-Division* moved in the direction of the bridgehead at Dnjepropetrowsk. The ruthless destruction of all infrastructure that was ordered by the *Führer* Headquarters—an action entitled "scorched earth" and based on the Soviet model of 1941—was only carried out by the division and its neighbors for a short period. From both a command and control standpoint, as well as from a tactical perspective, it proved to be completely unwise. Large portions of the populace had already been evacuated; likewise, large herds of cattle were already on their way to the Dnjepr.

The pressure exerted by the enemy against the German divisions that were being pressed ever tighter together there and also east of Saporoshe abated somewhat. To make up for that, he pressed on with determination—as was the case between the two large bridgeheads—against the Dnjepr at many other places as well. German forces along the west bank of the river were barely present. The heavy losses sustained during the difficult fighting, as well as the obstinacy of Hitler in trying to hold on to the Crimea, which led to an effort to establish a front between Saporoshe and Melitopol, delayed the ability of German formations to be employed in time for the defense of the river bank.

On 15 September, in an anticipatory move, *Generalleutnant* von Vormann issued orders by radio that the *DKS*, stationed in Werchowzewo, was to cover the banks of the river between Dnjeprodsershinsk and Krementschug with combat-capable patrols. It was to set up strongpoint-like outposts in conjunction with the *SS-Kavallerie-Division*.

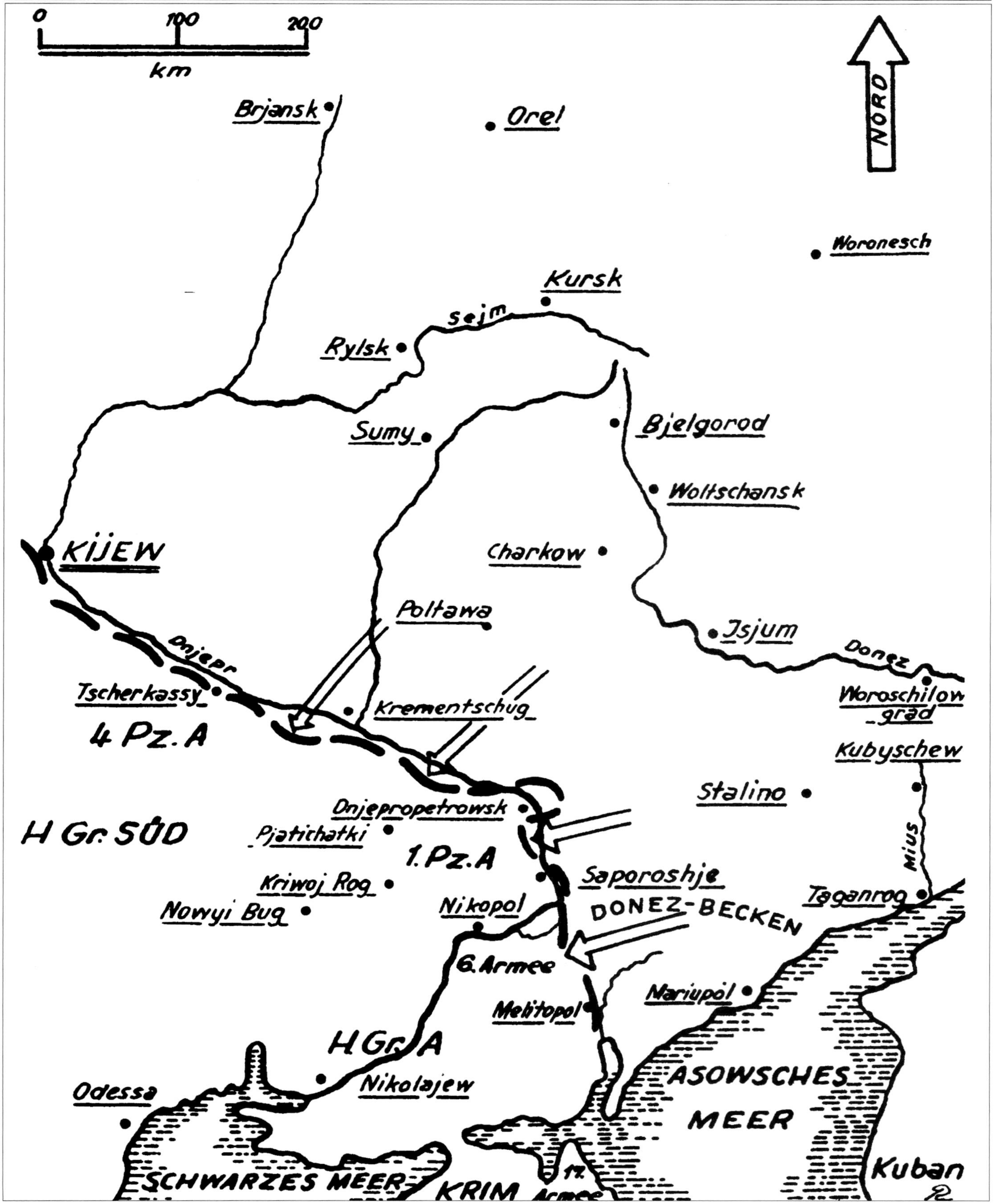

Map 54: Situation on 26 September 1943.

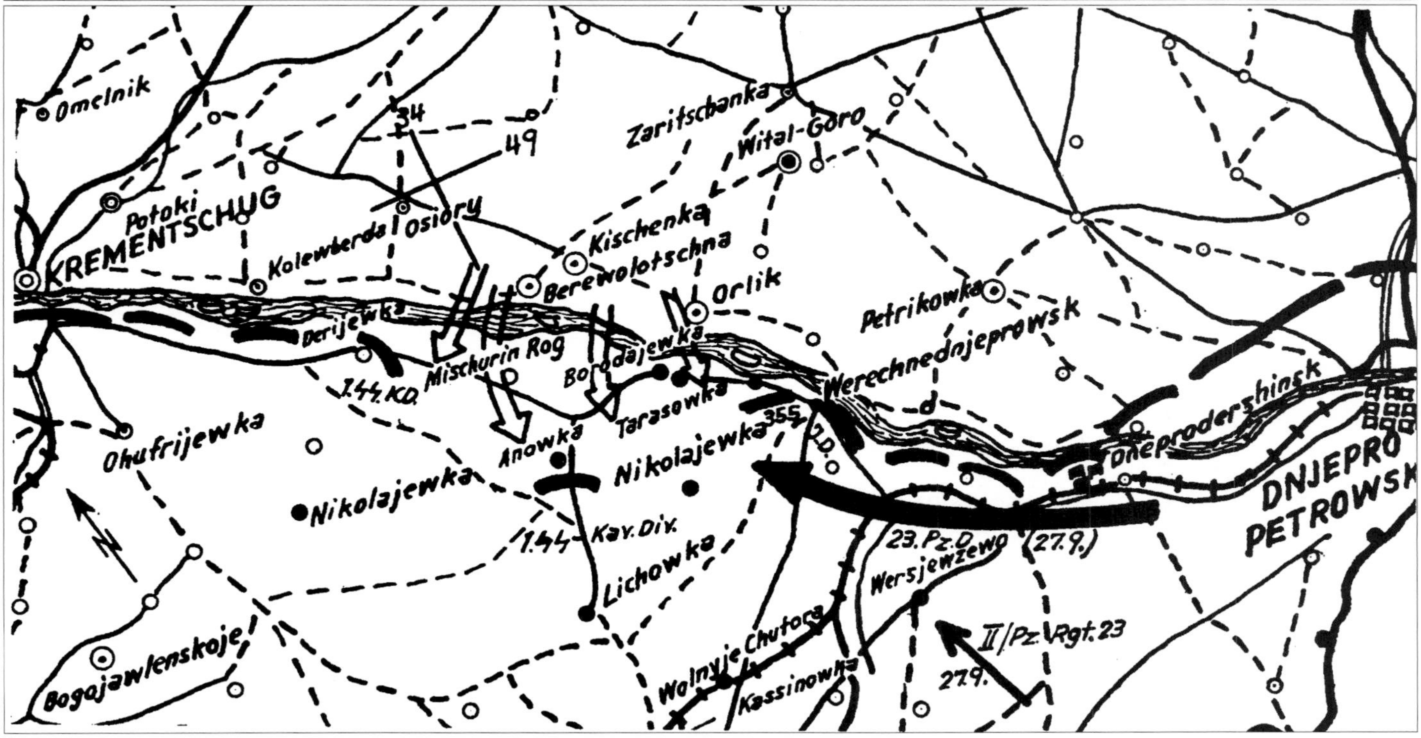

Map 55: Employment of the *23. Panzer-Division* on 27 September 1943.

In the process of carrying out that mission, every single one of the employed elements soon established contact with the enemy, who was crossing to the west bank of the river by boat, exploiting its many blind spots. The *DKS* lost four men killed and six wounded, before it was relieved on 26 September by the division's two infantry regiments.

The Soviets crossed the river at other points as well and established bridgeheads, in which they quickly brought forward more forces. They were thus able to establish good jumping-off points for their future operations.

Even before the *23. Panzer-Division* could move behind the bridgehead sector of the *125. Infanterie-Division* at Dnjepropetrowsk, the *Panther* Company had to move out from Michailowka toward Turgenjewskij and Slawgorod to advance against assaulting enemy armored forces. An engagement ensured, in which several enemy tanks were destroyed and a *Panther* burned out through enemy fire. The threat to the bridgehead position was eliminated.

With its heavy platoon, the 1st Medical Company took over the area of a field-army hospital in Dnjepropetrowsk, where hundreds of uncared-for wounded and sick personnel were found.

Traffic jams outside of Dnjepropetrowsk and the seemingly bottomless, sticky mud placed tremendous demands on the supply services and the trains. The wear and tear on the vehicles was enormous. Some vehicles dragged themselves from one mishap to the next—tire repairs; using "gravity fuel" (pouring fuel directly into the carburetor) whenever fuel pumps gave out; clutch problems that required driving without shifting—all of that became run-of-the-mill. The desire for self-preservation and loyalty to the vehicle spurred the personnel on to great deeds. Drivers were frequently separated from their units for days on end, only to suddenly reappear and take on their next assignment with resolve, even if cursing the "conditions in Russia." Winter chains were the last defense against the mud, until even they failed to perform.

On 19 September, the first elements of the division crossed the road bridge at Nowo Moskowsk and entered Dnjepropetrowsk, coming from Ssinelnikowo and the Ingres rail station. The *2./PAA23*, which was equipped with *Schwimmwagen*—amphibious scout cars—swam the river. The last elements of the division crossed the Dnjepr on 25 September. The city was already burning in numerous places. Acts of sabotage, aerial attacks, artillery fires and also panic on the part of German civil administration officials caused many buildings to catch on fire.

On 24 September, the enemy advanced to the Dnjepr in the vicinity of Dnjepropetrowsk. The clearing station of the 1st Medical Company had to be evacuated. All operational wheeled ambulances of the division were brought forward and took the wounded in relays to the waiting medical aircraft (*Ju-52's*) and hospital trains. On 25 September, Soviet artillery fired into the city. The last of the wounded were evacuated and then the 1st Medical Company also moved. On 29 September, it took over the buildings of the 40th Military Hospital in Lichowka.

On 27 September, the *II./PR23* arrived back at the division, moving from Saporoshe through Krinitschki. It took up billets in the area around the Werchowzewo rail station.

Nothing materialized out of the hoped-for short break in combat operations for the division. By 26 September, the division had already been attached to the *LII. Armee-Korps*. The next day, it moved 60 kilometers in a road march to the northwest, after the elements of the different divisions that were employed there were unable to eliminate the Soviet bridgeheads. While the *335. Infanterie-Division* was fighting around the bridgehead at Werchne-Dneprowsk, the *23. Panzer-Division* was initially charged with reducing the bridgehead at Tarasowka.

Oberst Sander, the commander of *PR23*, was awarded the Knight's Cross to the Iron Cross on 27 September for his success in combat during the fighting for Sslawjanka.

On 28 September, the division pushed the Soviets around Tarasowka into a small area. To completely clear the broken terrain, however, infantry forces were lacking. *Leutnant* Dantzer of the *1./PR23* was badly wounded during this fighting.

Major Ziegler, the acting commander of *PGR128*, left the division after only being with it a short while. Since *Hauptmann* Ruge was ill, *Hauptmann* von Wieluczki had to assume acting command of the regiment. He had just returned from Germany after having attended a battalion commander's course. He only had a few hour to prepare himself for his new duties. After losing numerous self-propelled antitank guns, the *PJA128* consolidated its remaining ones into a single company.

By 29 September, the badly weakened division, which really only had the combat power of a regimental group, was ordered to another hot spot and attached to *General der Panzertruppen* Kirchner's *LVII. Panzer-Korps* (Chief-of-Staff: *Oberst i.G.* Laegeler). In the area north of Lichowka, the division had to support *SS-Standartenführer* Streckenbach's *SS-Kavallerie-Division* against the Soviets, who were pressing out of their bridgehead along a broad front. Broken terrain, heavy vegetation and several islands in the Dnjepr facilitated the movements of the Soviets. In addition, the enemy was constantly bringing forward fresh forces.

At 1500 hours on 29 September, *Oberstleutnant* von Winning's *PGR126* and *Kampfgruppe Fechner*—consisting of elements of *PR23* and the *3.(SPW)/PAA23*—attacked through Annowka Nesamoshnik and overran weaker enemy forces. The infantry took Mischurin Rog and the high ground to the west. The attack was effectively supported by *Stuka* and fighter-bomber formations. The eight tanks of *Kampfgruppe Fechner* advanced almost to the river. Despite that, they were unsuccessful in stopping the river-crossing traffic south of Perewolotschnaja and south of Soloschino. The armored group prepared for upcoming operations that night at Michailowka, while the infantry and the remnants of the *SS* cavalry division had to content themselves with a thin outpost line along a frontage of 23 kilometers. The main line of resistance ran from north of Borodajewka — Kalushino — Nesamoshnik — Kommunar.

As the German divisions occupied their new positions along the south bank of the Dnjepr—positions that had had a great deal made of them—the command and the forces in the field experienced one disappointment after the other. On the one hand, the forces needed to stop the enemy from conducting river crossings were missing as a result of the deficient planning for the withdrawal. On the other hand, in the best of cases, the grenadiers and infantry often only found survey stakes for the construction of positions.

On 29 September, *PGR128* was still employed in support of the *335. Infanterie-Division. Hauptmann* von Wieluczki, who had only arrived a few days previously, was killed there. Once again, the regiment was without a commander.

Enemy forces that had infiltrated through the thinly held lines of the infantry showed up at night at the regimental command post. The enemy was chased away after close combat with pistols and hand grenades. Even the regimental physician, *Stabsarzt Dr.* Faderl, had to fight to defend himself against the Soviets, grabbing a shovel.

On 1 October, an armored group led by *Oberleutnant* Stöcker succeeded in moving from Kommunar across Hill 70.4 and into the Perzewa Defile, where it pushed back the enemy. Contact was established with a battle group from *Panzergrenadier-Division "Großdeutschland"* under the command of *Major* Gomille in Kommunar. Following that, the weak *Grenadier-Regiment 108* of the *38. Infanterie-Division*, which had approached the Nesamoshnik — Kommunar road south of Hill 156.9, was supported by the tanks and taken to the hill. While only taking minimal friendly losses, the armored group succeeded in destroying 10 antitank guns and numerous infantry weapons in two days. As a consequence of mechanical failures, however, only seven tanks, one assault infantry gun and nine *SPW's* were operational.

The *DKS*, under the direction of *Oberleutnant* Grünwaldt, was moved to Danilowka, 30 kilometers southwest of Pjatichatki. It sent replacements to the two infantry regiments, as well as releasing its entire 3rd Company (Engineer) and a third of its heavy company. From the assets of *Pferdekolonne Lang*, a horse-drawn trains element was established. Preparations were made to reorganize the *DKS* as a combat battalion. Despite that, training was continued.

The 2nd of October saw the loss of Mischurin Rog as the result of a concentric attack of fresh, numerically vastly superior Soviet infantry from the Dnjepr lowlands. Hill 122.7, which was also lost, was retaken by the tanks in a counterattack. Because it could not be held without also holding Mischurin Rog at the same time, it was eventually lost again. The main line of resistance—only occupied by means of strongpoints—ran along the Annowka — Nesamoshnik — Kommunar road. The tanks were positioned behind the line to be able to react at any time. The Soviets were constantly bringing fresh forces across the river, especially since they had succeeded in building bridges across the river south of Perewolotschnaja. The attacks by the *Luftwaffe* against the bridges and the ferry points achieved no lasting success.

To the right of the division, the situation was stabilized somewhat by the arrival of the *9. Panzer-Division*, *Panzergrenadier-Division "Großdeutschland"* and the *306. Infanterie-Division*. The dangerous overextension of the divisional sector remained, however, even after the *9. Panzer-Division* assumed the 8 kilometers of sector between Borodajewka — Annowka. The newly arrived divisions attacked the smaller bridgeheads in front of them the following day in an effort to reduce them. Although they succeeded in shrinking their size, they were unable to eliminate them completely. The same thing occurred to the left of the division's sector, where the *6. Panzer-Division* attempted in vain to reduce the enemy's bridgehead west of Kommunar.

In the division's sector, the enemy attacked again and again. Despite all their bravery, the weak infantry elements were not in a position to offer serious resistance. The few tanks available were divided up into groups and pounced on the enemy, wherever he appeared. These tactics were justified by their success; the main line of resistance remained in German hands. The increasing Soviet attacks on the crossroads south of Mischurin Rog and Hill 122.2, which was held by *PPB51*, led to the conclusion the Soviets were preparing for an attack. On 4 October, the engineers were thrown off the hill by an enemy attack. A few tanks and *SPW's* intercepted the engineers, took the hill in an immediate counterattack and pursued the enemy to the north. One *Panzer IV* was lost. *Leutnant* Adler (*PAA23*), *Leutnant* von Varchmin (*PR23*) and three men were killed. The enemy suffered numerous killed and the loss of many infantry weapons, including 10 antitank rifles.

The enemy air force joined the fight in great numbers. Several closed formations of Pe-2 bombers attacked the divisional sector. Soviet artillery and rocket launchers placed fires on the main line of resistance.

The majority of the aerial attacks, both day and night, were directed against the division's rear area. Popelnastoje, where the main clearing station of the 1st Medical Company was also located, was the most attacked locality. Soon not a single building was left undamaged. The division's engineer, *Oberbaurat* Biedermann[62], was killed in an air attack. Maintenance facilities and the trains of several divisions suffered losses, but it was not possible to pull back to other built-up areas.

During the night of 5/6 October, a Soviet battalion infiltrated through the German lines and established itself between the main line of resistance and the observation points of the heavy weapons. The next morning, most of the battalion was eliminated by the assault infantry guns of the *9./PR23*, which fired over open sights. What remained was captured and a large number of spoils were taken.

Some breathing room in the course of the constant massive enemy attacks was granted to the infantry by the rocket launchers mounted on the Opel *Blitz* trucks. *Generalleutnant* von Vormann had authorized

62 Editor's Note: An *Oberbaurat* was a uniformed civilian official, who was generally a structural or mechanical engineer and held a rank equivalent to that of a field-grade officer. He was charged with providing the division commander and his staff with advice of a technical nature. He should not be confused with the other officer of the division with the same title (in English), who was also the commander of the division's combat engineer battalion.

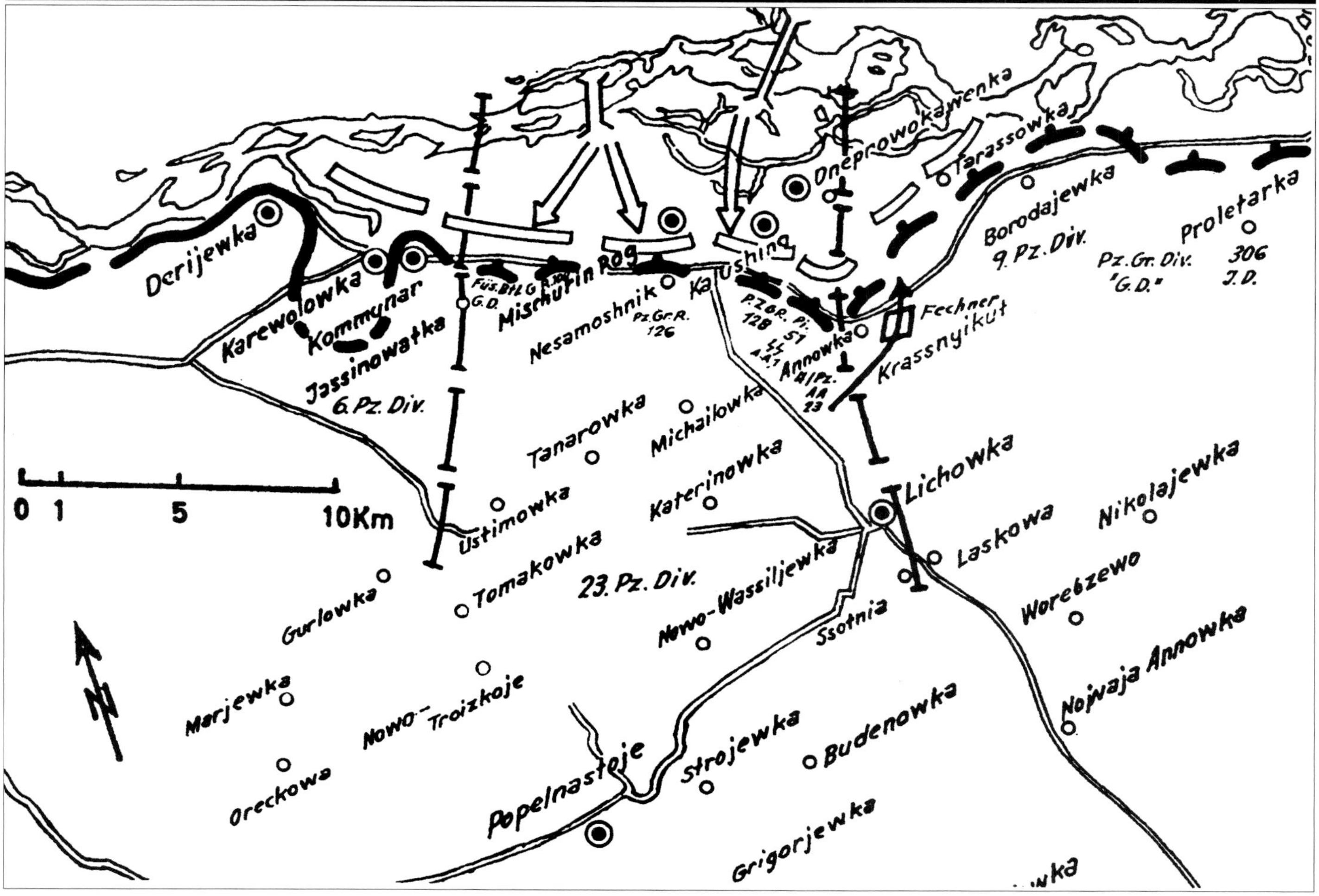

Map 56: Situation on 8 October 1943.

their mounting while the division was undergoing battlefield reconstitution in Makejewka. As a result of their devastating firepower from a distance of about a kilometer, they had proven themselves in all subsequent fighting.

On 6 October, the infantry cleared the rectangularly shaped woods south of Hill 85.2. At the same time, four tanks and five *SPW's* under the command of *Leutnant* Zander remained southwest of the crossroads. True to form—attack the enemy whenever his tanks went to another position—the Soviets attacked shortly thereafter with tanks and infantry from Kaluschino and Mischurin-Rog. *Panzergrenadier-Regiment 128* and *PPB51* evacuated their positions. The two armored groups then moved out in a concentric attack and reestablished the main line of resistance, in conjunction with the reconnaissance battalion from the *SS* cavalry division. The enemy took heavy losses.

On 7 October, 15 repaired tanks under the command of *Oberleutnant* Hyprath returned to the front. That same day, they were committed against Kaluschino and took down identified Soviet pockets of resistance in a systematic manner. One *Panzer IV* was lost; seven enemy antitank guns were eliminated.

The *23. Panzer-Division* was arrayed as follows in the main line of resistance on 8 October: The *4./PAA23* with 45 men at the Selenyj farmstead west of Annowka; *SS-Aufklärungs-Abteilung (SS-Kavallerie-Division)* with 110 men around the rectangular woods and southeast of Point 122.2; *PPB51* with 75 men around Hill 122.2; *PGR128* with 300 men on both sides of the crossroads south of Mischurin Rog; *PGR126* with 280 men on both sides of the northern part of Nesamoshnik; *Grenadier-Regiment 108* with 380 men along the road on both sides of Hill 177.3; *Füsilier-Bataillon "Großdeutschland"* with 130 men along the road southeast of Kommunar. The responsibility for Kommunar itself was assumed by the *6. Panzer-Division*, using remnants of *SS-Reiter-Regiment 1*. In all, the division had at its disposal on that day along 15 kilometers of frontage 1,100 infantry, 25 tanks and 8 *SPW's*. Influenced by the German defensive success of the past few days, Soviet offensive activities abated. Leaving its *Panzer III's* and *Panzer IV's* behind the main line of resistance, *Panzergruppe Fechner* was sent east to support the *9. Panzer-Division* in its fighting around the high ground south of Dnjeprowokamenka. *Panzergruppe Fechner* moved out to the north from the road crossing north of the Sapolitschki farmstead along with the elements of the *SS-Kavallerie-Division* that were screening there. In the terrain, which was criss-crossed by defiles, more than 120 Soviets were taken prisoner. Enemy infantry forces streaming back in massed groups were blown apart. Three T-34's were destroyed; eleven antitank guns and numerous infantry weapons were overrun. No German tanks were lost. *Leutnant* Kuhn and *Leutnant* Schroeder were killed; five men were wounded.

On 10 October, the new commander of *PGR128*, *Oberst* Bräuchle, arrived.

As a result of a renewed attack by *Panzergruppe Fechner*, together with the *Waffen-SS*, the main line of resistance just north of Annowka was pushed forward to the high ground. Without suffering any losses, 4 antitank guns, 10 antitank rifles and additional infantry weapons were destroyed.

The completely exhausted German infantry was not in a position, however, to hold the positions that had been attained. The infantry screened along the southern slope of the ridgeline and on both sides of the trail near Iwaschki on the morning of the following day. Despite being directed to follow the advancing tanks, the grenadiers could not be brought forward to occupy the old main line of resistance on the ridgeline.

At noon, 60 Soviets dug in on the hill 1 kilometer east of Hill 109.2, that is, to the south of the road crossing at the Sapolitschki farmstead. Before the armored group could race there from Annowka, an infantry company composed of artillerymen from *Panzergrenadier-Division "Großdeutschland"* drove the Soviets down from the hill. The tanks inflicted heavy losses on the withdrawing enemy force.

On that day, the commander of *PGR126*, *Oberstleutnant* von Winning, was killed outside of his command post by a direct hit from a mortar round. The division lost a reliable, experienced commander in him. For the time being, the regimental command was assumed by *Hauptmann* Stolle, the commander of the *II./PGR126*.

Major Fechner, the commander of the *II./PR23*, was awarded the Knight's Cross to the Iron Cross on 6 October for his decisive actions in the western part of the Donez area.

On 14 October, under the command of *Major* Fechner, armored groups from the *23. Panzer-Division*, the *9. Panzer-Division* and *Panzergrenadier-Division "Großdeutschland"* were formed. In hard fighting, they defeated a Soviet group of forces that had approached with the intentions of launching an offensive. Four T-34's and thirty antitank guns fell victims to the tanks on that day alone. As a result, the German frontage east of Omelnik Creek was secured.

A final attack was planned for 15 October in conjunction with the *9. Panzer-Division* to move the front forward in a position just south of Kalushino and close any existing gaps.

While these attack preparations were taking place, the Soviets launched an offensive with a main effort running along the line Hill 122.2 — crossroads south of Mischurin Rog — Nesamoshnik.

In just the sector of the *23. Panzer-Division* alone, the following formations were identified as part of the offensive:

- 1st Guards Airlanded Division, 9th Guards Airlanded Division, 10th Guards Airlanded Division, the 188th Rifle Division, the 6th Guards Airlanded Division, the 62nd Guards Rifle Division and the 110th Guards Rifle Division.
- The XXIX Tank Corps with the 25th Tank Brigade, the 277th Tank Battalion, the 53rd Mechanized Brigade, the 31st Tank Brigade and the 32nd Tank Battalion.
- The XVIII Tank Corps with the 110th Tank Brigade, the 181st Tank Brigade, the 171st Tank Brigade and the 32nd Motorized Rifle Battalion.
- The VII Motorized/Mechanized Corps with the 16th (62nd?) Motorized/Mechanized Brigade, the 63rd Motorized/Mechanized Brigade and the 64th Motorized/Mechanized Brigade.
- Elements of the I Motorized/Mechanized Corps.

The divisional engineers and *PGR128*, both fighting without armored support, were overrun by the enemy who attacked in wave after wave. The weak remnants of the battalions, which were 130 men strong prior to the attack, made it back to Hill 127.0 with 30 men. While still retaining its original mission to destroy the enemy forces south of Kalushino, the armored group was told to advance from its former attack sector to the northwest, in order to defeat the enemy south of the road and escort the infantry back to its former positions. Despite the shattering of numerous antitank-gun positions and infantry units, the armored group suffered heavy losses in the face of massed antitank weapons of all calibers—from the 15.2cm "Animal Hunter" tank destroyer (JSU 152) down to antitank rifles—the likes of which had never been seen before. These were especially formidable around the Nowaja Gromada collective farm and at Kalushino. By order of the division, the five remaining operational tanks disengaged from the enemy. Under the cover offered by them, a new front line was established with its right wing 2 kilometers north of the Selenyj farmstead. Three *Panzer V's* were total write-offs. The enemy lost 7 T-34's and 10 antitank guns.

During the afternoon, a freshly introduced enemy infantry formation with 40 tanks pushed back the German outposts on both sides of Nesamoshnik. Practically encircled, *PGR126* succeeded in withdrawing from the village through the only remaining narrow gap. The regiment went into position at Hill 139.1. *Grenadier-Regiment 108*, attacked on both sides of Hill 177.3, was able to retain its positions. The enemy was thrown back. Ten Soviet tanks, which had overrun the grenadiers, held out in the depressions west of Hill 177.3, without rejoining the fight.

Toward evening, it started to rain. The roads softened and the first difficulties for the motorized vehicles began to surface. The enemy, who advanced with tanks despite total darkness, took Hill 127.0 and tossed the completely exhausted men of *PGR128* back to Michailowka and the hills west of the Wassiljewka farmstead. Individual tanks and *SPW's* of *Major* Fechner held the high ground north of Michailowka in a nighttime engagement against enemy tanks and infantry. The enemy continued to advance in the depressions, however; he could not be engaged there by the German tanks and antitank guns.

Without a break, the enemy continued his offensive on 16 October. The armored group was taken over by *Hauptmann* Euler. It covered the withdrawal movements of the remnants of the infantry. At first light, enemy tanks and infantry advanced on the high ground north of Michailowka. They forced *PGR128* back south and wound up in the rear of the armored group, which was positioned along the northeastern slopes of the hills. Although the enemy was tossed back in an immediate counterattack launched by the tanks and the *SPW's*, there was soon a shortage of ammunition. The armored group moved back to the high ground around Belowtschina to screen and conduct resupply.

As a result of the capture of the high ground north of Michailowka by the enemy, there was a 10-kilometer gap in the lines as far as the positions of *Grenadier-Regiment 108*. Since there were also extensive enemy preparations for operations being conducted with 60 tanks there, that regiment and the battalion from *Füsilier-Regiment "Großdeutschland"*, adjoining on the left, were pulled back 5 kilometers to the southwest. In order to close the gap, which the division was no longer able to do with the forces at its disposal, the corps promised the addition of *Grenadier-Regiment 106* from the *15. Infanterie-Division*. Originally, it was intended for that regiment to arrive during the night of 15/16 October. The rain and the mud only allowed the regiment's 1st Battalion to arrive at Lichowka at 1000 hours on 16 October, however.

The trains of the division, some of which had already been sent on their way to Pjatichatki, had a difficult struggle as a result of the road conditions. The majority of them were able to pull back in the face of the pressing Soviet forces, however.

In the meantime, the enemy moved out from his assembly areas around Michailowka with 30 tanks. They surprised the *I./Heeres-Flak-Abteilung 278* in its positions and overran them, without the battery being in any position to offer serious resistance. The enemy tanks entered Werchne Kamenistaja and fell upon the command post of *Panzergrenadier-Division "Großdeutschland"*. For the time being, no German countermeasures were possible. That afternoon, the division's tank regiment had four *Panthers*, which had returned from the maintenance facilities, under the command of *Oberleutnant* Stöcker. They screened at Hill 151.9. There were also six tanks under the command of *Hauptmann* Euler—three *Panthers* and three *Panzer IV's* (with long main guns)—along the hilly terrain of Point 167.9. The non-operational tanks in the area around the Lipowyj farmstead were towed to positions to the north in order to ward off the expected enemy attack there. It was no longer possible to consider towing these tanks to repair facilities because of a lack of recovery means.

For inexplicable reasons, the enemy tanks that had entered Werchn. Kamenistaja left the village and headed north. The infantry did not re-

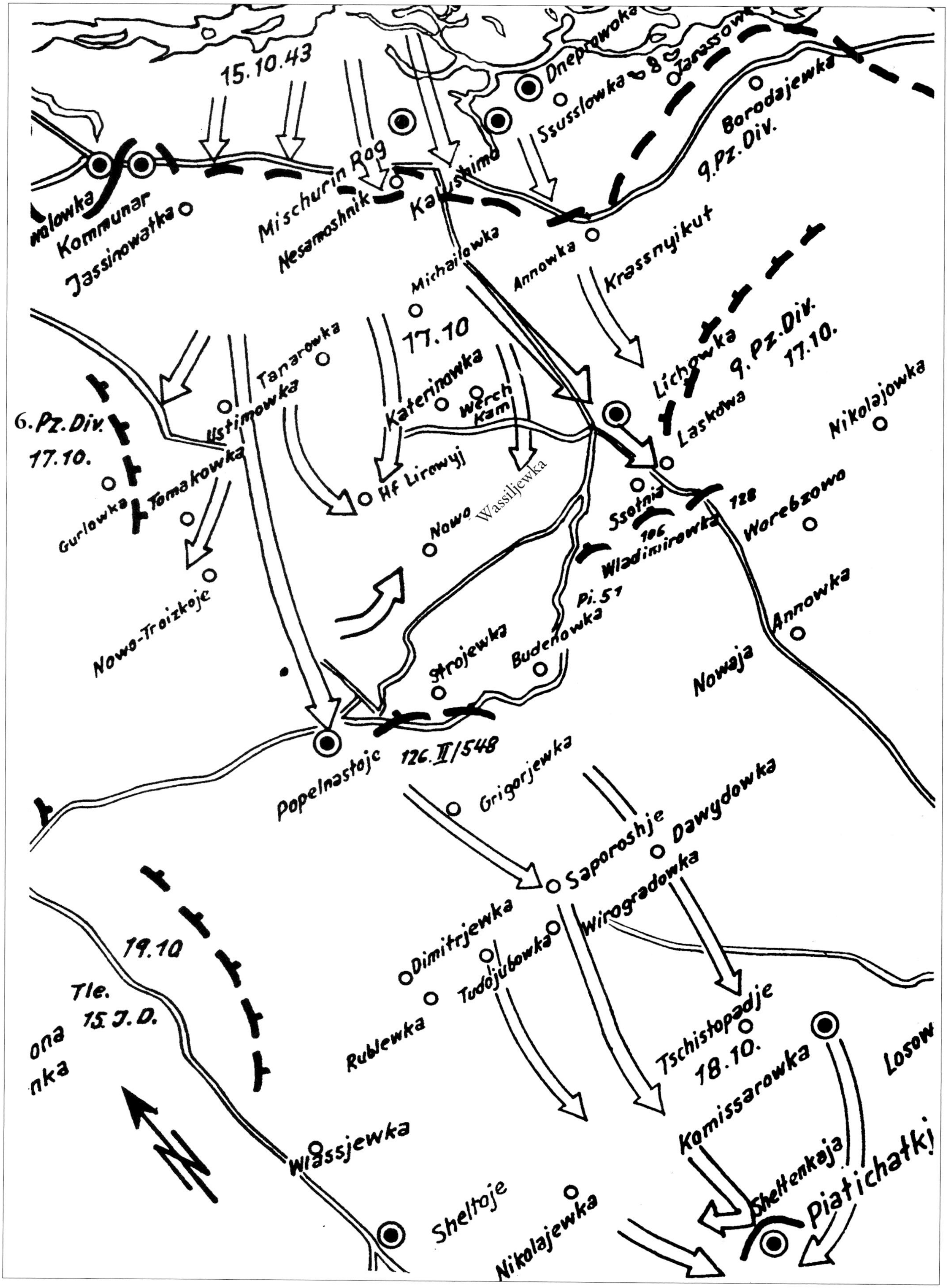

Map 57: The Soviet Attack from 15-18 October 1943.

main behind. At that point, the *I./Grenadier-Regiment 106* moved out, moved through the village and then advanced on Hill 151.9.

The enemy determined what was happening and committed infantry formations in division strength against Hill 151.9. Bitter fighting ensued. The five *Panthers* of *Oberleutnant* Stöcker decided the engagement. *Stukas* and artillery also joined in at the right moment and inflicted heavy casualties on the densely packed enemy. The Soviets fled the battlefield.

The two other battalions of *Grenadier-Regiment 106*, which had arrived in the meantime, cleared the southern slope of Hill 151.9 and set up defensive positions. In the meantime, however, *PGR126* saw itself threatened along its right flank, because portions of the enemy, who had advanced along the Grabowyj-Les Defile, had occupied the patches of woods along the eastern part of the village. The infantry was tossed back to the eastern part of the village. As a result, there was a 5-kilometer gap yawning to *Grenadier-Regiment 106*. As it turned dark, the *II./Grenadier-Regiment 548*, which had been expeditiously brought forward, was employed to bridge the gap.

According to their orders, *Grenadier-Regiment 108* and the fusilier battalion from *Panzergrenadier-Division "Großdeutschland"* (on the left) were supposed to establish contact with *PGR126* at Alexandro-Grigorjewka with their right wing. In advancing from Michailowka to the west, enemy tanks and infantry had already entered that village. Some of their elements were already to the west of it. Moving through Ustimowka, *Grenadier-Regiment 108* was able to establish contact with *PGR126* at Belowtschina. *Grenadier-Regiment 108* then lost contact with the fusiliers of *Panzergrenadier-Division "Großdeutschland"*, however. The *23. Panzer-Division* assigned command and control of that battalion to the *6. Panzer-Division*, since it no longer had the ability to do that itself.

When *Grenadier-Regiment 108* moved out at 1700 hours to occupy Belowtschina, an enemy armored attack, accompanied by mounted and following infantry, slammed right into the regiment. At the same time, *PGR128* was attacked from the north. Both regiments were ejected from their locations and pulled back toward Katerinowka. Three German tanks, which were covering the withdrawal movements to Belowtschina, knocked out four T-34's at short range. The tanks exploded immediately, and killed all of the infantry riding on board. A short while later, six additional T-34's were blown apart, one of them from a distance of 10 meters, after it had become lost among the German tanks! At the onset of darkness, a German counterattack moved the lines a kilometer back north. Despite that, there was a gap of 6 kilometers between Katerinowka and Ustimowka, which could not be closed.

Although the division had inflicted very heavy casualties on the enemy and had knocked out 44 enemy tanks on the first two days of his offensive, the heavy German losses had reduced the division's combat power to a minimum.

At first light on 17 October, the enemy moved out to attack with fresh forces. He had shifted his main effort to the left side of the sector, along the boundary between the *23. Panzer-Division* and the *6. Panzer-Division*. Five divisions, densely massed, streamed out of the defiles south of Michailowka toward the south and southwest.

Grenadier-Regiment 106, together with five *Panthers*, turned back four attacks on Hill 151.9. The enemy pulled back, but he attacked an hour later on a broad front with armor support. Twelve T-34's were knocked out, but the enemy finally succeeded in penetrating along the left wing of the regiment. The regiment's positions could not longer be held on the downward sloping, barren terrain. In a completely disciplined fashion, the regiment pulled back through Werchn. Kamenistaja and to the line of hills running from 111.8 to 148.2. Once there, it prepared to defend again. The divisional antitank battalion, the *SS-Aufklärungs-Abteilung*, *PPB51* and *PGR128* were threatened in their deep left flank at Hill 113.7 and had to pull back to the northern edge of the Werchn. Kamenistyj farmstead. The enemy, who was pursuing vigorously, was turned back.

The main effort of the enemy's attack was around the Lipowyj farmstead. After a Soviet armored attack with infantry early in the morning had been turned back by the grenadiers and the immobilized tanks that had been positioned behind them, the enemy tanks, which had advanced from Werchn. Kamenistaja, turned west toward Lipowyj. Attacked from the front, on both sides and then from the rear, the *II./Grenadier-Regiment 548*, *PGR126* and *Grenadier-Regiment 106* pulled back to the Lipowyj farmstead with their remnants, all the while having suffered heavy casualties. At the farmstead were some additional immobilized tanks, as well as a few *Flak*. The enemy attack started to waver; the batteries of the divisional artillery, the rocket launcher elements and the *Flak* south of Lipowyj changed positions. Under the direction of the division headquarters, the batteries were able to pull back, section by section, and were gradually able to cross the Omelnik to the east of Popelnastoje. There, *Oberstleutnant* Vogl, the division artillery commander, was able to employ them for operations once more.

The enemy assaulted Lipowyj again and again. At that point, it jutted far to the north as a strongpoint. During the morning, when the enemy swung out to the west in order to attack it from the southwest, and he also attacked at the same time from the north and the east, the village could no longer be held. One tank after the other fired off its last remaining ammunition and then had to be blown up. Several enemy tanks were destroyed. Even the personal intervention of the Chief-of-Staff of the *LVII. Panzer-Korps*, *Oberst i.G.* Laegeler, was unable to stabilize the untenable position. The last five operational tanks of *PR23* covered the withdrawal of the last wheeled vehicles and the infantry.

During that fighting for the Lipowyj farmstead, another Soviet assault group had identified the gap in the German front lines at Ustimowka. Not finding any resistance, the Soviets advanced south and entered Popelnastoje. *Generalleutnant* von Vormann and his battle staff found themselves right in front of the second Soviet attack wave when the infantry attempted to escape from the enemy tanks, which were already advancing east from out of Popelnastoje. Fortunately, the Soviets were not prepared for combat. They were sitting outside their tanks with the main guns fully elevated. As a result, *Gefreiter* Kohl was able to bring the general to safety in his staff car, despite the deeply muddied trails.

In Popelnastoje, the enemy tanks caused a near panic to break out among the trains. Unnecessary losses in men and materiel occurred, until five quasi-operational *Tigers* from *Panzergrenadier-Division "Großdeutschland"* left the maintenance facility there and joined the fray. Numerous T-34's were destroyed. Just one *Tiger* alone knocked out seven T-34's and then advanced to the north. The enemy left in a panic. As a result, it was possible to recover many vehicles from Popelnastoje. Unfortunately, the complete set-up for the divisional field post office was lost, once and for all, and could only be replaced in a field-expedient manner over time.

In addition, all of the equipment of the division's 1st Maintenance Company was lost, as well as numerous damaged vehicles and trains elements.

The small group of Soviet tanks, which was advancing east from Popelnastoje, blocked the route to Strojewka for elements of *Heeres-Flak-Abteilung 278* and wheeled vehicles. It was only possible to disengage from the enemy by taking casualties. *Oberleutnant* Bauer, the commander of the 1st Battery, was killed.

The German infantry fought its way back toward the south slope of the Omelik, east of Popelnastoje, between advancing enemy tanks, whose commanders often demonstrated terrific bravery, and enemy infantry.

Along the right wing of the division, the enemy infiltrated through the defile east of the Werchn. Kamenistyj farmstead and into the rear of *PGR128*. At the same time, he enveloped the right wing of *Grenadier-*

Regiment 106. While clearing Lichowka in close combat and house-to-house fighting, the regiments cleared a path toward the high ground south of the village. Once there, they set up for defense on both sides of the Lichowka — Ssakssagan road. By means of an immediate counterattack, they pushed the pursuing enemy back to Lichowka.

The remaining 15 men of *PPB51*, under their new battalion commander, *Hauptmann* Diestel, screened at Wladimirowka. It was the only infantry element employed between the left wing of *Grenadier-Regiment 106*, 5 kilometers northeast of Wladimirowka, and the *II./Luftwaffen-Flak-Regiment 241* in the Wladimirowka — Popelnastoje area.

The remnants of *PGR126*, along with seven tanks, were assembled on the hills southeast of Popelnastoje by the division and employed defensively there. The rain continued unabated; the roads, particularly in the depressions and hollows, became impassable. Innumerable trains vehicles from five divisions—the *6. Panzer-Division*, the *9. Panzer-Division*, the *23. Panzer-Division*, *Panzergrenadier-Division "Großdeutschland"* and the *SS-Kavallerie-Division*—blocked all of the routes and restricted the German conduct of the battle. Artillery, rocket launchers and *Flak* could not reach the positions they had been given. Pursuing enemy in the Grigorjewka Valley further increased the difficulties of command and control. The divisional headquarters went to Dawydowka. The enemy bypassed the screening group at Hill 155.0, southeast of Popelnastoje, and the force at Hill 173.7, which consisted of a few tanks and 25 infantry. Saporoshe and Winogradowka were prepared for defense. Three long-barreled *Panzer IV's* from the maintenance facility arrived in support. Artillery and *Flak* were positioned right in the front lines. Popelnastoje was finally lost during the course of the night. It had been held by a grenadier battalion that had been brought forward by the *336. Infanterie-Division*. On that day, 48 Soviet tanks were destroyed.

The *9.(sIG)/PGR128* encountered Russian tanks and infantry while pulling back in Grigorjewka. Despite heavy fires from all sides, it was possible to hold down the enemy long enough by means of the remaining heavy infantry guns and the launchers to enable all of the vehicles to continue the withdrawal.

The *LVII. Panzer-Korps* ordered the transfer of the left-hand portion of the division sector to *Generalleutnant* Buschenhagen's *15. Infanterie-Division*, which was entering the sector. All of the infantry forces of the *23. Panzer-Division* positioned west of the line running from the western edge of Budenowka (10 kilometers southeast of Popelnastoje) — middle of Sheltoje were attached to Buschenhagen's division. Those forces represented the remnants of the *II./Grenadier-Regiment 548*, *PGR126* and *Grenadier-Regiment 108*.

The armored force south of Popelnastoje was ordered to Saporoshe (via Rublewka) during the night of 17/18 October. To the west of Dmitrijewka, however, *Tigers* from *Panzergrenadier-Division "Großdeutschland"* that were screening opened fire on the group and knocked out two tanks, forcing the remaining ones to move back north. It was not until first light that the tanks were able to continue on to Saporoshe without interruption. When they arrived there, numerous T-34's with infantry were in the process of attacking it. Two of the enemy tanks were knocked out by the local defenses. Saporoshe was evacuated, because the enemy had bypassed it on both sides and there were not enough German forces. In Wassiljewka, the operational tanks of Stöker's, Hengerer's and Rohwedder's groups assembled.

In the meantime, enemy tanks entered Winogradowka, where the headquarters of the *LVII. Panzer-Korps* was just in the process of moving out. Eight tanks from *PR23*, which just happened to be returning to the front from the maintenance facility, attacked the enemy on their own initiative. They cleared the village of the enemy and screened the orderly withdrawal of all of the motorized vehicles and an artillery battalion.

Dawydowka was attacked a short while later. Tanks and infantry forced the *I./PAR128* and the remnants of *Heeres-Flak-Abteilung 278* to change positions. The *Flak* battalion was incorporated into the local defense of Losowatka — Komissarowka.

Along the right wing of the division, the enemy pressed against the hilltop positions of *PGR128* and *Grenadier-Regiment 106*. The enemy was thrown back in a counterattack. In the end, the enemy advanced past *Grenadier-Regiment 106* on the west side and headed south. The enemy then attacked the regiment in its deep left flank and, at the same time, along the front, forcing it to bend back its left wing toward Nowaja Annowka. The division was no longer in a position to command those forces, which were becoming more and more separated by the rapidly advancing Soviets. Consequently, they were attached to *Panzergrenadier-Division "Großdeutschland"*. In the sector of the *23. Panzer-Division*, which stretched for 20 kilometers, there were no more infantry forces to be found.

The enemy's main effort remained unchanged; it was within the division sector on both sides of the Popelnastoje — Pjatichatki road. The division decided to pull its tanks and the artillery, rocket launchers and *Flak* remaining to it into the area around and north of Pjatichatki. The tanks covered the withdrawal of all of the trains and the artillery by moving back, sector by sector, through Tschistopolje and Wassiljewka. There was no contact with friendly forces to either the right or left. The weak portions of the division were organized in such a manner that they were able to put up the greatest possible resistance to the pursuing enemy. *Oberst* Sander, the commander of *PR23* and the designated the local area commander for Pjatichatki, attempted to organize a local defense. Tanks from the regiment that were in the maintenance facility and could no longer be recovered or evacuated were set up as pockets of resistance along the outskirts of the locality. The local area commander, *Oberst* Bormann, who had been designated by the field army, attached all available infantry forces—mostly scattered elements—to *Oberst* Sander.

With a heavy heart, *Generalleutnant* von Vormann decided to bring the *DKS* to the front. At 1300 hours, it was ordered to report to Pjatichatki to assume responsibility for its defense.

The *DKS* moved out immediately, but it got caught up in the masses of fleeing trains elements and the logistics services of the infantry and armored divisions south of Pjatichatki. The soupy mud and the hopeless tangle of trucks, horse-drawn vehicles, damaged tanks, guns and personnel delayed the approach march; the commander was only able to force his way to Pjatichatki by threat of force. He arrived as it started to turn dark, when the enemy had already occupied large portions of the village. A new order was radioed from the division, ordering the *DKS* to be employed in the local defense of Danilowka.

During the afternoon, the 12 operational tanks of the regiment, under the command of *Hauptmann* Euler, turned back several enemy advances from the north and northwest. After recovering damaged tanks, the group pulled back to a sector 5 kilometers north of Pjatichatki. The enemy only followed hesitantly from the north. On the other hand, an enemy group consisting of tanks and infantry that had broken through at Kommissarowka advanced into the right flank of the German armored outposts. The fires from the T-34's and the accompanying infantry were already blocking the road and rail line east of Pjatichatki. Several of the motorized vehicles fleeing among the heavy traffic on the road were hit and burst into flames. Countless trains elements from other divisions, with trucks and horse-drawn vehicles, contributed to the confusion by moving among them. Scenes of panic ensued and, when the enemy tanks with weak mounted infantry advanced toward the village as it started to turn dark, the *ad hoc* groups of infantry collected from other divisions left their positions on the edge of the village without even thinking of defending against the Soviets. In a magnificent show of comradeship and

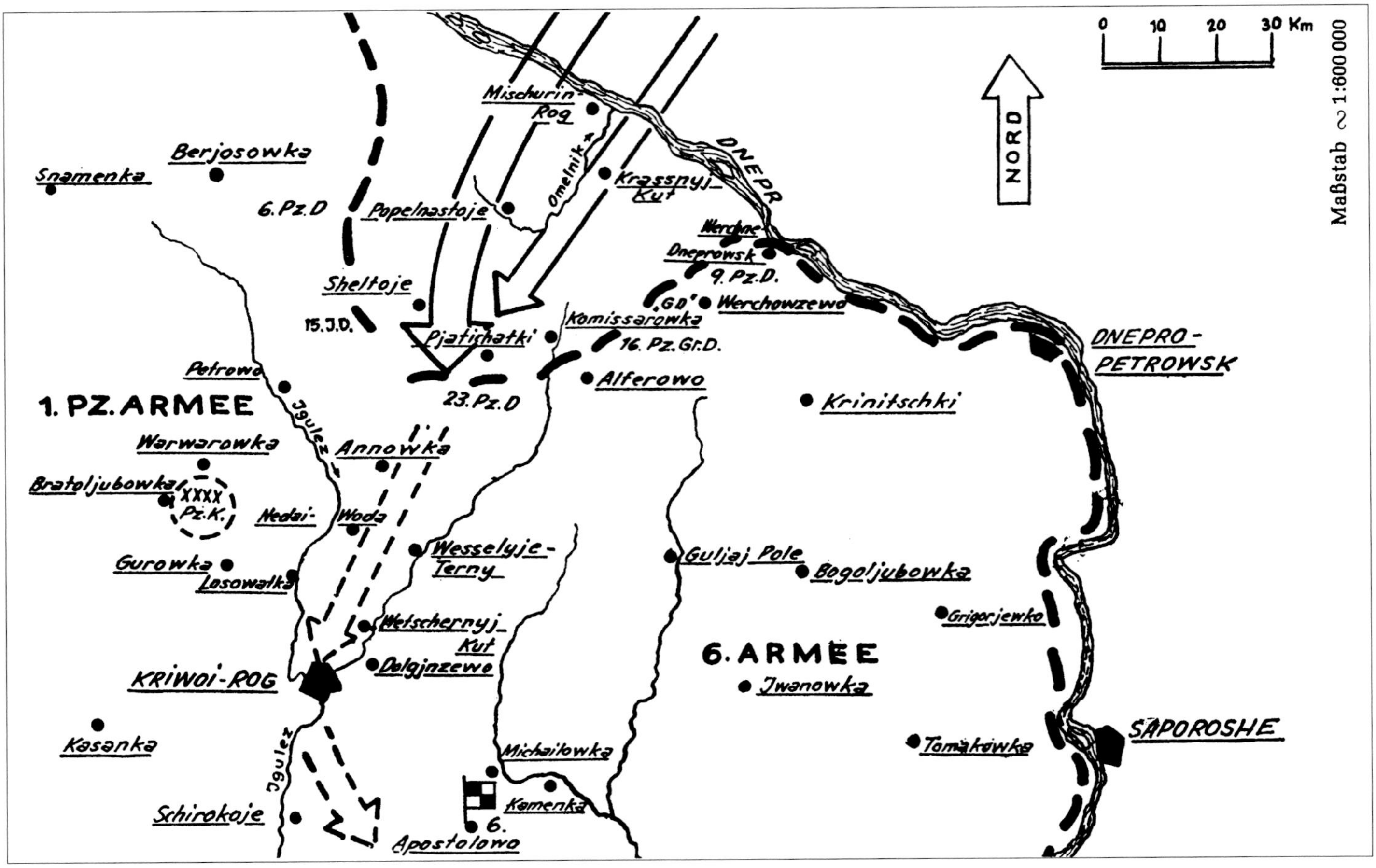

Map 58: Operational Objectives of the Soviets in the Dnjepr Bend in the Winter of 1943/1944.

bravery, however, the tank and *Flak* soldiers held their ground. Heavy attacks from the northeast were turned back with heavy losses to the enemy and the knocking out of many tanks, but when it turned dark, the enemy succeeded in approaching the village from the northwest. As a result of numerous immediate counterattacks to the northeast, north and northwest from the village, which was illuminated from innumerable fires, the enemy was turned back and additional enemy tanks destroyed. The German tanks employed on the edge of the village had to be blown up after they had expended all their ammunition. At the Pjatichatki train station were numerous trains, fully loaded with damaged and new equipment, as well as a hospital train full of wounded. For inexplicable reasons, the station management were unable to move the trains, despite numerous locomotives being on hand.

Around 2030 hours, the first elements of a weak enemy infantry force entered the eastern part of Pjatichatki. The German tanks screened the withdrawal of the *Flak* and pulled back, fighting, block by block. The seemingly endless columns of trains elements from other divisions continued to flee back. The enemy gradually occupied the entire village, but he did not pursue the German withdrawal movements. The tanks established a kill zone 2 kilometers south of Pjatichatki and covered the crossing of some 3,000 motorized vehicles over the deeply muddied bottom land at Ssachnowka. Most of *PAR128* went into position north of Kultura and turned back advances by weak Soviet infantry forces at pointblank range.

The First Battle of Kriwoi Rog 19 October to 4 November 1943

With the capture of Pjatichatki, the Soviet command believed it stood before the final breakthrough through the German front north of Kriwoi Rog. The important industrial center in the middle of the Dnjepr bend would then be exposed to the attacking field armies. At the same time, the opportunity would have been presented to encircle all of the German army corps on the Crimea and at Melitopol, Saporoshe and Dnjepropetrowsk by a further advance to the south to the lower Dnjepr.

As a result, the massive pressure of the enemy continued unabated like the point of a sword against the remnants of the *23. Panzer-Division*. The German divisions positioned on the ever-growing flanks of the deep penetration—divisions with which the infantry of the *23. Panzer-Division* were also fighting—only had to fend off weaker enemy attacks in the meantime.

Neither the *1. Panzer-Armee* nor *Heeresgruppe Süd* had reserves at their disposal that they could send to the *23. Panzer-Division*. The large-scale offensive initiated by the enemy at practically the same time along all sectors of the front also devoured any and all reserves within the other field-army groups.

The fact that *Generalleutnant* von Vormann had to commit the *DKS* to the fighting was a measure dictated by necessity, without which the division would have never been in the position to bring the Soviet advance to a halt. As a result, the division was risking its entire, laboriously assembled reserve of noncommissioned officers and specialists, such as radio operators, telephone operators, drivers and gun crews. But there was no other choice. By employing the *DKS* at Danilowka, it was blocking the Sheltoje Basin.

The *I.(Panther)/Panzer-Regiment 15* of the *11. Panzer-Division* was attached to the division with its 10 operational tanks on 19 October, when it blocked both sides of the Pjatichatki — Kriwoi Rog rail line in the vicinity of Krassnaja Wolja. The remaining 10 operational tanks of the *23. Panzer-Division* continued to screen on Hill 158.2 south of Pjatichatki,

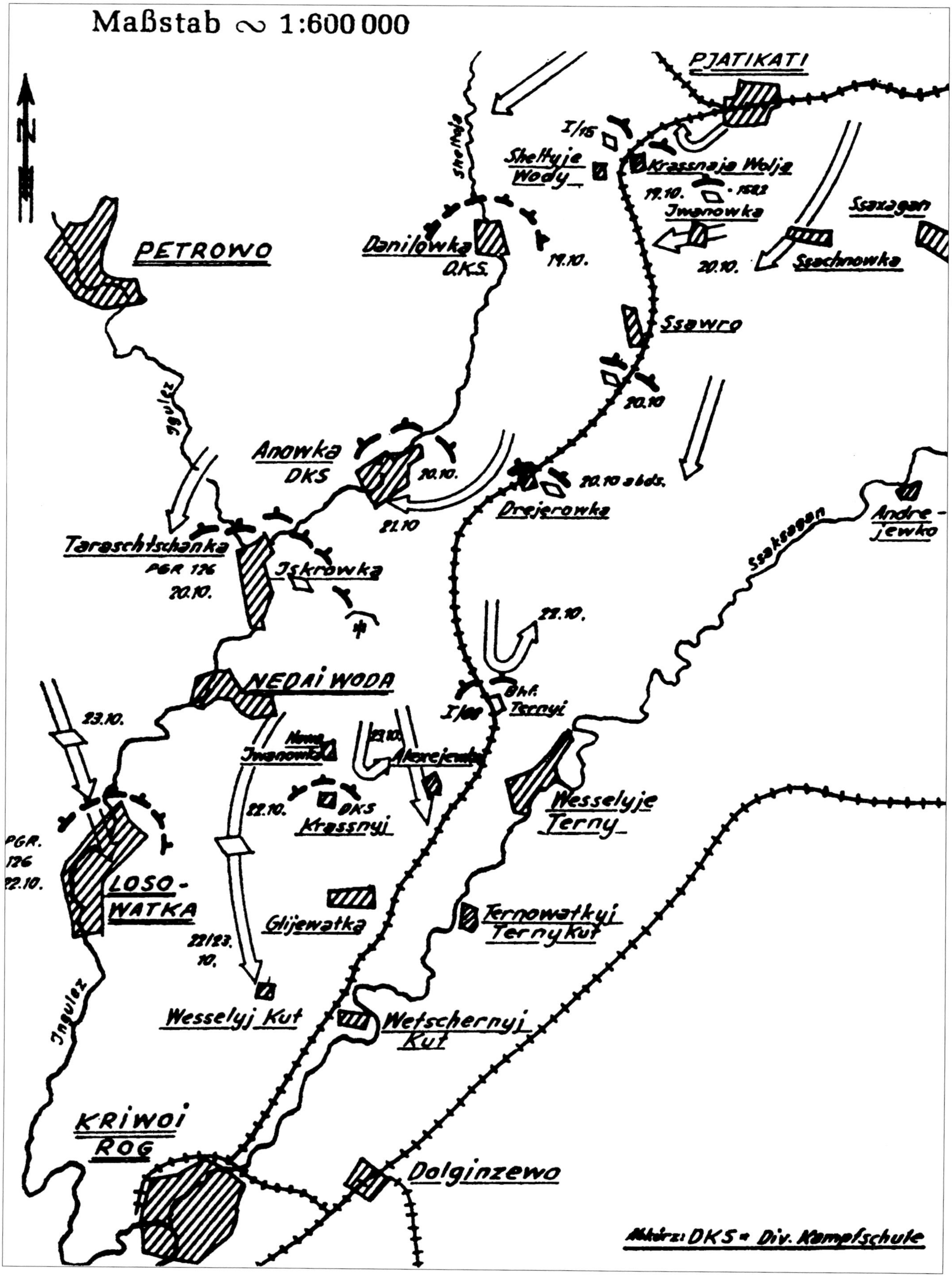

Map 59: Fighting North of Kriwoi Rog, 19-23 October 1943.

covering the continued withdrawal of German trains vehicles across the Ssachnowka Basin. Using two *Panzer IV's*, all of the vehicles were pulled through the deep mud by 1000 hours.

Hauptmann Euler advanced with the 10 *Panthers* from *Panzer-Regiment 15* against Pjatichatki to allow a locomotive to hook up to the hospital train and evacuate it. The enemy was completely surprised and did not realize the Germans' intentions until the locomotive signaled with its whistle to indicate it was ready to pull out. The pride in having accomplished the deed was suddenly and unexpectedly dampened by the discovery that only dead had been recovered, with the exception of two survivors. The completely drunk Russians had murdered the wounded the previous night with hand grenades and small arms.

During the afternoon of 19 October, combat reconnaissance efforts by Soviet tanks to the south were turned back and several T-34's knocked out. The divisional artillery was withdrawn from the area around Kultura, since the enemy had taken Sheltoje. The *DKS* was pulled back from its unfavorable positions around Danilowka to the area around Annowka. Its mission was to block the Sheltoje — Annowka and Petrowo — Annowka roads, along with five damaged tanks from *Panzergrenadier-Division "Großdeutschland"*.

The armored outposts of *Oberleutnant* Hyprath at Hill 158.2 and *Hauptmann* Koske (*Panzer-Regiment 15*) at the fork in the rail line at Sheltyje Wody remained intact during the night.

Reconnaissance determined considerable reinforcements of enemy formations in and around Pjatichatki. *Panzergruppe Hyprath* and *Panzergruppe Koske* were combined at Krassnaja Wolja.

During the morning of 20 October, the enemy occupied Ssachnowka, Iwanowka and, later on, Alexandrowka. An enemy advance along the railway line was repulsed. Around 1200 hours, the enemy attacked from Iwanowka to the west with strong infantry and armored forces. In accordance with its mission to delay the enemy advance along the Pjatichatki — Kriwoi Rog rail line, the division issued orders to the armored group to pull back to the hills south of the Ssawro rail stop. *Panzerzug 28*,[63] which had just been attached to the division, joined in the fighting and covered the withdrawal movements of the tanks. The enemy did not follow. Further to the west, however, where there were no more German formations, individual Soviet tanks were reported advancing toward Petrowo.

Panzergrenadier-Regiment 126 reported back to division command and control with a trench strength of 3 officers, 4 noncommissioned officers and 23 enlisted men. The only heavy weapon it had left was a 2cm *Flak*. The division was forced to commit this "second infantry formation" immediately. Mission: Block the Ingulez Valley at Taraschtschanka.

Three batteries of artillery and a battery of rocket launchers went into position at Annowka.

The *Panzergruppe*, under the command of *Oberst* Sander, was pulled back to Drejerowka during the evening of 20 October. The division reported destroying 25 T-34's since 18 October.

On 20 October, *Oberleutnant* von Berlepsch, the adjutant of the *DKS*, was caught in a tank attack by the Soviets. He was wounded and evacuated to a hospital train. He died 24 hours later on the train in an accident.

At first light on 21 October, three enemy tanks rolled into the southern portion of Annowka, after swinging around the village to the east. A short time later, they were followed by 20 T-34's and KV I's with mounted infantry. The *DKS* was faced with being attacked in its rear. The only weapon available against that enemy was a conditionally operational *Tiger* from *Panzergrenadier-Division "Großdeutschland"*. It immediately moved into the village and attacked the numerically vastly superior enemy. It set five of the enemy alight before a sixth enemy tank hit the *Tiger* in the commander's cupola, wounding the brave commander, *Feldwebel* Prenzler. An immobilized *Panther* from the same division also participated in the firefight from its position north of the village and knocked out two more T-34's, before it was knocked out. Enemy forces approaching from the north forced the *DKS* to fight on two sides. The antitank guns of the *DKS* knocked out two T-34's. Finally, the acting commander of the *DKS* ordered his men to pull back along the main line of resistance to the southwest and Iskrowka. That movement, which came as a surprise to the Soviets, succeeded with only a few casualties being taken.

The *DKS* arrived in Iskrowka, where it linked up with the *Panzergruppe*, which had been ordered there from Drejerowka. Together, they screened to the east, north and west.

Soviet combat reconnaissance, which attempted to feel its way forward to the south from Annowka, was engaged by the batteries positioned 2 kilometers south of it. In the end, the enemy pulled the majority of his tanks to the west across the Ingulez.

At Iskrowka, the *DKS* once again enjoyed contact with *PGR126* and screened north with that regiment. *Leutnant* Heinrichs, the air-ground coordination officer from the *Luftwaffe*, called in *Stuka* support on the enemy concentrations around Annowka. Within a half hour of the initial request, the *Stukas* were diving on the enemy and inflicting heavy casualties.

All replacements sent to the division had to be immediately committed to the fighting. The front was ablaze everywhere at the time.

The division directed a local defense of Losowatka with *ad hoc* forces from different formations under the command of *Hauptmann* Veigel of the *II./PGR126*. Artillery support was provided by two heavy self-propelled guns from *Panzergrenadier-Division "Großdeutschland"*. A few antitank guns, which had been fetched from out of the trains of differing divisions, were employed on the outskirts of the village for antitank defense. Leadership of the local defense was an acute problem, however, due to the lack of any communications equipment. The preparations for the defense were concluded in great haste, since the division expected armored formations, which had been identified to be of substantial size in the area 10 kilometers north of Losowatka, to attack that very night.

Outside of Taraschtschanka, the enemy only followed hesitantly. As soon as he discovered the weakness of the infantry forces screening there, however, his infantry infiltrated across the high ground west of the village to the south and southwest. The enemy then advanced at the same time against Iskrowka from the southeast, the east and the north. In order to avoid encirclement, the outposts pulled back under the cover of darkness. Under the acting commander, *Hauptmann* Stolle, *PGR126* reached Losowatka and assumed responsibility for the local defense. The *DKS*, attached to *Panzergruppe Sander*, occupied a new outpost line running Tscherwona Balka — Krasnyj — Road crossing south of Nedai Woda. It was joined there by *Panzergruppe Sander* and a *Flak* battery from the *Luftwaffe*.

The *I./Grenadier-Regiment 88* of the *15. Infanterie-Division*, which was newly attached to the division, defended the Perwomaiskij mines north of Wesselyje Terny.

At first light on 22 October, the antitank battalion of the Soviet 188th Rifle Division attempted to take the Terny train station in a *coup de main*. In spite of clever deception measures for the operations—sending out a German truck in advance that was manned by Soviet civilians—the grenadiers of the *I./Grenadier-Regiment 88* were not surprised. The assault detachment was shot to pieces. Two trucks, a prime mover, an antitank gun and numerous small arms were captured. Outside of Krassnyj, 15 enemy tanks approached the German outposts during the course of the day after patrols had preceded them. Two T-34's that had ventured too far forward were knocked out. Tank busters of the *Luftwaffe—Ju-87*

63 Editor's Note: = Armored Train Nr. 28. A number of armored trains were employed on both sides in the east. They usually had a locomotive with an armored cab and boiler, as well as a number of cars carrying a variety of armaments and defensive capabilities.

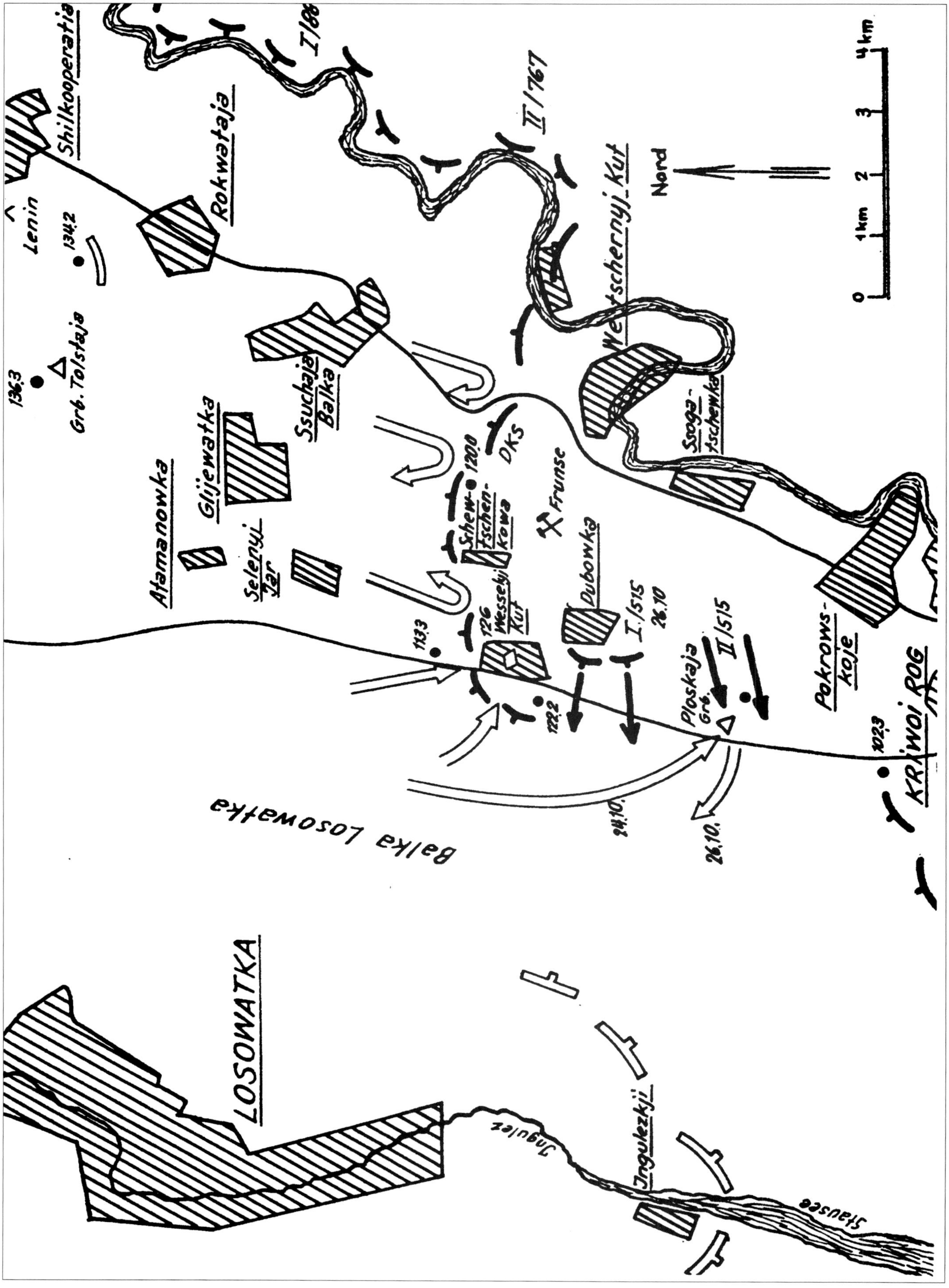

Map 60: The Situation from 24-26 October 1943.

G's with 3.7cm antitank cannon—attacked with great success and destroyed several enemy tanks.

Large gaps yawned between the three battle groups of the division north of Wesselyj Terny on both sides of Krassnyj and Losowatka. The enemy soon identified them and advanced west past Krassnyj during the night with 12 tanks with mounted infantry, moving deep into the division's rear. Without encountering a single German soldier, the Soviets occupied Wesselyj Kut.

Another enemy group of forces advanced in the vicinity of Alexejewka against the gap east of Krassnyj.

At 0500 hours on 23 October, the enemy attacked Krassnyj proper. An infantry regiment, supported by 10 tanks, forced a penetration west of the village. *Panzergruppe Fechner* moved out immediately and hit the enemy from the west. Fechner's battle group succeeded in blocking the escape route for a large portion of the enemy force and destroying it. Six enemy tanks were set alight, and 8 antitank guns 30 machine guns, several mortars and antitank rifles were captured or destroyed. Two officers and thirty-three men were taken prisoner; more than 100 enemy dead were counted.

While that fighting was taking place, 20 Soviet tanks and infantry attacked Losowatka from the northwest. The bravery of the infantry was in vain. Thick fog in the Ingulez Valley prevented observation for the artillery and the heavy weapons. *Panzergrenadier-Regiment 126* pulled back from the pursuing tanks to Wesselyj-Kut. The soldiers then ran into the enemy forces that had penetrated there the previous night. One antitank gun knocked out two T-34's; two more were destroyed by handheld weapons. The division's *Panzergruppe* raced in from Krassnyj to help. Two T-34's were knocked out at a range of 15 meters; they literally blew apart. In all, 12 enemy tanks were caught and destroyed. The weak remnants of the enemy's infantry pulled back to the north.

The enemy forces that had advanced as far as Alexejewka the previous day continued attacking south after the arrival of reinforcements. Without encountering any resistance, enemy elements occupied Hill 134.2, south of the Lenin mines, while other elements attempted to advance into the rear of the *DKS* south of Tscherwona Balka. The *DKS* pulled back its right wing and turned back the attack.

Fresh Soviet infantry forces marched into the gap in the front to the east of the *DKS* and continued south. *Generalleutnant* von Vormann felt compelled to pull the main line of resistance back to Ssokolowka — Hill 120.0 (north of the Frunse mines) — Schewtschenkowa. As a result of that measure, there was once again a cohesive line as far as Wesselyj Kut (*PGR126*). The *I./Grenadier-Regiment 88* and the newly attached *II./Grenadier-Regiment 767* from the *367. Infanterie-Division* screened from the hills southwest of Wesselyje Terny east of the Ssakssagan, where they had contact on the right with the *16. Panzergrenadier-Division*.

Weak combat outposts of those battalions turned back several attacks in platoon strength, until they were attacked late in the afternoon by 300-400 Soviets—mostly partisans, including women—and were practically encircled. They fought their way in close combat back to the German main line of resistance.

At the onset of darkness, the enemy started to push infantry and tanks forward all along the line, but especially in the Wesselyj Kut sector. An enemy battalion attacking with tank support was turned back. Shortly after midnight, the enemy moved out again. One tank entered the village, where it was destroyed in close-in fighting.

Early on 24 October, the enemy employed additional forces to attack, with Wesselyj Kut being his main effort. A Soviet battalion, supported by enemy tanks, overran the German positions at Schewtschenkowa and advanced to the outskirts of Wesselyj Kut. The German combat outposts at Hill 113.3 and at Weliki had to be pulled back. The lead company of *Panzer-Armee-Sturm-Bataillon 1*[64], which had just arrived in the sector, was employed by the commander of the *DKS* to guard the left flank at the Frunse mines.

Supported by six tanks, the German soldiers positioned at Wesselyj-Kut, attacked from both the east and the west, put up bitter resistance. The four enemy tanks attacking from the east were knocked, and the attack stalled. Additional tanks and a battalion-sized infantry force attempted to take the worker's settlement repeatedly. They only suffered heavy losses in both men and materiel, however. Two self-propelled 8.8cm antitank guns from *Heeres-Panzerjäger-Abteilung 662*, which arrived in Wesselyj Kut in the nick of time, contributed greatly to the success of the defense. The division's antitank battalion, which had had to be consolidated into a company as the result of a lack of guns, also supported the defensive efforts of the infantry. Artillery and rocket launchers shattered many Soviet concentrations. To the west of Wesselyj Kut, however, there were no more German forces, with the exception of weak outposts. They were not in the position to hold up the advancing enemy infantry. Ploskaja Grb was occupied and the road from Wesselyj Kut to Kriwoi Rog was blocked.

The Russians only advanced hesitantly in the sector of the *DKS*. As the result of a counterattack by the armored group and the field army's assault battalion, the enemy at the point of penetration at Schewtschenkowa was destroyed and the former main line of resistance was reoccupied.

That day saw the destruction of 14 T-34's, 1 assault gun, 10 antitank guns, 2 15cm artillery pieces, numerous mortars and 30 machine guns and antitank rifles.

At first light on 25 October, the enemy moved out against Wesselyj Kut again. The village had become a key position in the fighting for Kriwoi Rog. Five enemy tanks, accompanied by two companies of Soviet infantry, were turned back, with four of the tanks being knocked out in the process. Heartened by this success, the infantry pursued the withdrawing enemy and inflicted heavy losses on him in close combat. A short while later two more tanks were destroyed outside the village.

Around noon, the Russians concentrated their artillery, rocket-launcher and mortar fires on Wesselyj Kut, which soon was turned into a sea of rubble and ashes. At the same time, Soviet infantry advanced to the south, using the cover and concealment provided by Balka Losowatka, as far as the hedgerow around Ploskaja Grb. The division was faced with the decision of whether to pull back to the east bank of the Ssakssagan. By doing so, it would have given up the electric works at Wetschernyj Kut, located 1,000 meters behind the front, which continued to supply power for the manganese pits of Nikopol. At the eleventh hour, it was decided to bring *Grenadier-Regiment 515* of the *294. Infanterie-Division* forward on trucks to the division. It was intended for elements of this regiment to be employed that same night in the residential areas east of Ploskaja Grb., thus guarding the deep left flank of the division.

In the afternoon, the *DKS* reported heavy concentrations of enemy infantry in Balka Ssuchaja. As it started to turn dark, Soviet artillery and heavy weapons placed preparatory fires on the positions north of the Frunse mines. At 1700 hours, 3-4 battalions of infantry and numerous enemy tanks moved out to attack. Supported by the final protective fires of the artillery and the participation of a few friendly tanks, the *DKS* brought the enemy attack to a standstill. Contributing greatly to the success of the defensive effort was a section of *Flak*.

Major Draffehn's *Heeres-Flak-Abteilung 278* had suffered the loss of most of its 8.8cm and 2cm *Flak* in the fighting west of Popelnastoje and around Pjatichatki. Only one *Flak* section, under the command of *Leutnant Freiherr* von Steinaecker, could be employed to protect the infantry against enemy tanks. Steinaecker's men had already eliminated

64 Editor's Note: = 1st Armored Field Army Assault Battalion. This was a force assembled on a quasi-permanent basis to act as a standing ready reserve for the field army. It is not known how it was organized.

numerous enemy tanks while fighting as part of *Panzergruppe Sander* around and south of Pjatichatki. In the sector of the *DKS* on 25 October, one 8.8cm gun knocked out 12 enemy tanks and decided the engagement favorably for the Germans in the face of a strong attack. For his deeds, *Leutnant Freiherr* von Steinaecker was later awarded the Knight's Cross to the Iron Cross on 26 March 1944.

Along the Ssakssagan, the enemy restarted his activities to patrolling and the increased employment of partisans. At Wesselyje Terny, he attempted to repair the bridge over the Ssakssagan.

During the night of 25/26 October and the following day, the enemy brought forward considerable reinforcements in the form of armored and mechanized formations into the areas in front of the sectors of the *16. Panzergrenadier-Division* and the *23. Panzer-Division*. During the morning, 15 tanks and 130 trucks rolled to Rokowataja and Balka Ssuchaja. Twenty-two T-34's prepared for operations north of Hill 120.0 (2 kilometers north of the Frunse mines).

At the same time, Soviet infantry, supported by heavy weapons and artillery, attacked Wesselyj-Kut from the west. The enemy advanced as far as the middle of the worker's settlement, before the infantry could stop the attack. An immediate counterattack into the enemy's left flank ejected him for good. He left behind 45 dead, 6 machine guns, 5 antitank rifles and 9 prisoners. The village was firmly back in German hands. The combat power of *PGR126* was no longer sufficient, however, to recapture Hill 122.2, southwest of the village, which had been lost at the same time. Two antitank guns on the western side of Dubowka were the only weapons keeping the enemy from advancing east into the rear of the German positions. Around 1000 hours, the *I./Grenadier-Regiment 515*, which had been expected the previous night, arrived in Dubowka, just ahead of an enemy attack. Three Soviet self-propelled guns, accompanied by infantry, were turned back, with all three of the guns being destroyed.

An assault detachment from the *DKS* broke into an enemy concentration along the southern part of Balka Ssuchaja. It destroyed several trucks and a 7.62cm artillery piece. In addition to sustaining many dead, the enemy also had eight men captured. As a result of taking the prisoners, the division knew with certainty that the 64th Motorized/Mechanized brigade of the VII Motorized/Mechanized Corps had just been brought forward.

The *23. Panzer-Division* turned over the sector of the *I./Grenadier-Regiment 88* to the *16. Panzergrenadier-Division*, in order to be able to concentrate its forces more as part of the expected hot spot of the defensive fighting at Ssuchaja Balka and Wesselyj Kut. Toward noon, *Grenadier-Regiment 515*, along with four *Tigers* from the recently attached *schwere Panzer-Abteilung 506*, attacked and took Hill 122.2 and Ploskaja Grb. The *II./Grenadier-Regiment 515* inserted itself into a line running Ploskaja Grb. — Hill 102.3 and, as a result, established good contact with the local defenders of Kriwoi Rog.

Stukas and fighter-bombers attacked enemy concentrations in Rokowataja and Ssuchaja Balka. Prisoners stated that that one aerial attack had destroyed 27 trucks out of a group of 30.

The expected Soviet offensive did not materialize during the morning of 27 October. Six enemy tanks, which were feeling their way forward toward the German main line of resistance at Schewtschenkowka, encountered antitank-gun fire and turned back quickly after one of them was damaged.

Three attacks against the western part of Wesselyj-Kut were turned back. Additional enemy infantry forces marched through the Balka Losowatka and into the area west of Ploskaja Grb.

A combat patrol dispatched by the *DKS* destroyed two Soviet trucks and a field kitchen with its messing personnel; in addition, two Soviets were taken prisoner.

The trench strength of *PGR128* was reported as 4 officers, 7 noncommissioned officers and 18 enlisted after it returned from its attachment to *Panzergrenadier-Division "Großdeutschland"*. It had been with the latter division after being forced back into its sector in the course of the Soviet breakthrough northeast of Pjatichatki. The regiment was not capable of being employed for operations and went into the trains area for a battlefield reconstitution.

Most of *Heeres-Flak-Abteilung 278* was employed as infantry, since the division needed every rifle in the lines during this difficult period of great pressure.

While the 2nd Medical Company assembled initially in Kasanka and Nowy Bug, the 1st Medical Company accompanied the division in its retreat and treated the wounded by employing several smaller clearing stations. It was not until it reached Kriwoi Rog that it was able to establish a large clearing station in Schmakowo (east of Kriwoi Rog).

During the evening hours, Wesselyj-Kut was again the objective of several Soviet attacks. Three T-34's temporarily entered the village after they had been separated from their infantry, but they then pulled back.

After a few peaceful hours at night, enemy artillery placed barrage fires on the sector of the *DKS* at 0200 hours. Under the cover of continuous artillery fire and accompanied by a loud "Urrah" battle cry, superior Soviet infantry forces penetrated the German positions. They were only halted just outside the command post of the company on the right wing. At first light, the *DKS*, using its own forces, attacked the right flank of the enemy and completely wiped out the enemy forces that had penetrated. While the *DKS* only had two men wounded, the enemy lost 70 dead and 5 taken prisoner. Numerous infantry weapons were captured.

At the same time, a combat patrol from *PGR126* stormed an important hill in front of the main line of resistance and eliminated the enemy forces positioned there. A Soviet truck, which was approaching Wesselyj-Kut was destroyed and the personnel on board killed. As was determined later, the logistics officer of the Soviet 24th Rifle Division was among them.

The Soviet offensive forces in the area of Balka Ssuchaja appeared to be shifted to the west and into the area of Losowatka. The 28th of October passed more quietly than the previous day. The enemy attacked on along the right wing of the division with his main effort in the Ternowatkyj Kut area in the sector of the *I./Grenadier-Regiment 88*, which had been reattached to the division on the right. The attack, which was intended to roll up the *II./Grenadier-Regiment 767* in the Nowo-Iwanowka area from the north, was blocked. A penetration was sealed off and cleaned up in an immediate counterattack.

Replacements for the division—320 men—arrived, but there was not a single officer or noncommissioned officer among them. In light of the already existing shortage of leadership personnel, a meaningful employment of them did not seem possible.

Wesselyj-Kut remained the defensive focal point of the division on 29 October. The successful defensive effort on the part of *PGR126* had resulted in considerable gaps within the ranks of the regiment. A battalion-sized enemy attack from the west against Wesselyj-Kut ejected the brave infantrymen from the positions they had recaptured the previous day. The edge of the village was held, however, despite heavy rocket-launcher and artillery fires.

During the afternoon, new enemy concentrations were reported at Ingulestzkij (south of Losowatka) and, later on, at Glijewatka. The division was not attacked. During the night of 29/30 October, *Grenadier-Regiment 515* had to be released for commitment in the sector of the *XXX. Armee-Korps* in the area of Saporoshe. In order to conduct the relief in place, *Panzergrenadier-Regiment 156* of the *16. Panzergrenadier-Division* was attached to the *23. Panzer-Division*.

Looking at the over-all situation, the main focus of the fighting had shifted to the west, where the *XXXX. Panzer-Korps*, with the *14. Panzer-Division* and the *24. Panzer-Division*, moved out of the Alexandrija area and reached Gurowka and Wodjana. The first manifestations of those attacks showed in the abatement of pressure on the part of the enemy against the cleverly and successfully conducted defense of the blocking positions of the *11. Panzer-Division* west of Kriwoi Rog. Isolated rearward movements of the enemy were also determined in front of the *23. Panzer-Division* on the high ground east and northeast of Losowatka.

An attack by two Soviet companies at midnight against the positions of the *DKS* was the last offensive actions taken by the enemy in this phase of the fighting for Kriwoi Rog. The attack collapsed in front of the main line of resistance.

At first light on 30 October, the *11. Panzer-Division*, the *14. Panzer-Division* and the *24. Panzer-Division* moved out against Losowatka from the southwest, the west and the northwest. The enemy, who had become weak under this pressure, pulled back to the northeast from Losowatka in long columns.

Reinforced by *Panzer-Abteilung 116* and *Panzergrenadier-Regiment 156*—both of the *16. Panzergrenadier-Division*[65]—the *23. Panzer-Division* moved out around noon to destroy the Soviet blocking position south of Balka Losowatka. The enemy put up stiff resistance, which was reinforced in the end by the addition of a rifle regiment from the Soviet 24th Rifle Division. The tanks and infantry fought their way forward and against mines, antitank guns, artillery and infantry weapons.

Destroyed were 22 antitank and infantry guns, two tanks and untold amounts of machine guns and small arms; 300 enemy dead were counted and 25 prisoners taken. The Soviet artillery in Balka Losowatka was shot to pieces or forced to flee. The backbone of those forces, which had been assembled to attack and were still massed, had been broken.

Major Schägger took back command of *PGR126* after his convalescence. *Hauptmann* Stolle returned to command the 1st Battalion, but he was killed a short time later.

The divisional reconnaissance battalion, which had lost its commander, was taken over by *Hauptmann* Hoffmann. He commanded both the reconnaissance forces and *PNA128* until *Hauptmann* Koppe could arrive as the new commander of *PAA23*.

On 31 October, the fate of the Soviet forces northwest of Kriwoi Rog was sealed. The advance of the armored force had cut off all of the Soviet formations positioned south of Balka Losowatka. Desperate breakout attempts by the enemy, who charged the German positions repeatedly, were thwarted by the defensive fires of the infantry and the divisional artillery, which fired over open sights. The tanks completed the destruction of the enemy. The physical signs of success for the division on 30 and 31 October:

707 prisoners (including 26 officers)
6 tanks
1 fighter aircraft (Jak-1)
2 17.2cm cannon
1 12.2cm antitank gun
3 8.5cm antiaircraft guns
42 7.62cm antitank and infantry guns
17 mortars
Untold machine guns

***

The division, which was able to report the destruction of 193 enemy tanks since 15 October, saw its principal success in the fact that it succeeded in thwarting all enemy attacks on the key position at Wesselyj-Kut from 15-18 October with its exhausted elements. As a result, it had contributed significantly to the successful defense of Kriwoi Rog and the creation of the prerequisites for the successful attack of the *XXXX. Panzer-Korps*. On 1 November, the *23. Panzer-Division* moved out to the north along its entire sector and cleared the sector as far as the line Ternowatkyj Kut — south of Shilkooperazia — Hill 134.2 — Nowo Iwanowka of the enemy, who was putting up stiff resistance.

After absolutely every non-essential man was released from the trains of *PGR128*, that regiment was pushed forward for combat operations again. On 2 November, with the help of the division's armored group and the cover offered by both the *14. Panzer-Division* and the *24. Panzer-Division*, it occupied a defensive line running from Nowo-Iwanowka across the high ground north of Nedai-Woda and as far as the Ingulez. The elements that had been attached from the *16. Panzergrenadier-Division* returned to their parent division.

The attack of the *14. Panzer-Division* and the *24. Panzer-Division*, which were fighting in front of the new left wing of the division, bogged down at Sarja and the high ground to the west. The operation was called off; the divisions departed to the southwest. The enemy immediately exerted pressure and was already repeatedly attacking the positions north of Nedai Woda on 3 November.

During the afternoon of 3 November, *Panzergruppe Fechner*, together with *PGR128*, moved out to eliminate the enemy concentrations north of Nedai-Woda. The operation succeeded in inflicting heavy casualties on the enemy and temporarily taking Hill 134.5 (5 kilometers northeast of Nedai-Woda) from him. Most of the enemy pulled back, covered by heavy artillery fires and heavy weapons.

Further to the east, in the sector of *PGR126*, Soviet infantry attacked with tanks. They achieved a penetration that initially led to the loss of Tscherwona Balka and, later on, after bypassing the right wing of *Panzer-Armee-Sturm-Bataillon 1*, Nowo-Iwanowka.

The attack on *PGR126* was initiated by a heavy artillery barrage, which came as a complete surprise to the infantry. The majority of the soldiers had been using the opportunity afforded by the long-absent sun to dry themselves and their equipment out. It was at that moment that the combined artillery fires and enemy attack started. One soldier of the regiment, who suffered a wound in the attack, provided the following first-hand account:

> Despite rifle fire from the machine-gun nests that had not been put out of commission by fire, despite the support by friendly antitank guns and tanks, which fired over our heads, the steamroller got closer, the likes of which I had never seen before or after. Men, women, young people, almost children, in uniforms, in civilian clothes, with weapons and then again without them—all driven forward by Russian tanks and yelling men. They remained stacked in rows and yet the steamroller advanced and grew. From the background, new tanks with mounted infantry approached. Another 300 meters...200 meters...100 meters...then came orders to leave the positions. But it was too late for many of them; the mud in their foxholes wouldn't let them go. No one was able to help the wounded any more.

The weak remnants of the infantry pulled back to the south.

At the same time, superior enemy forces consisting of tanks and infantry penetrated into the positions of the *DKS* at Hill 134.5. They took the hill and advanced on Rokowataja.

Panzergruppe Fechner was immediately pulled back from Hill 134.5 and received the mission to take back the lost localities in conjunction with the infantry. Before it turned dark, it was possible to partially clear

Map 61: Counterattacks from 30 October to 3 November 1943.

65 Editor's Note: As opposed to a *Panzer-Division*, a *Panzergrenadier-Division* had only one tank battalion as part of its table of organization and equipment. The armored divisions had a regiment of three, later two, battalions. Generally speaking, however, the mechanized infantry divisions were authorized three regiments of *Panzergrenadiere*, as opposed to the two found in a *Panzer-Division*. Of course much of this is theoretical in terms of actual combat power and strength, as we have seen from the ongoing discussion in the book.

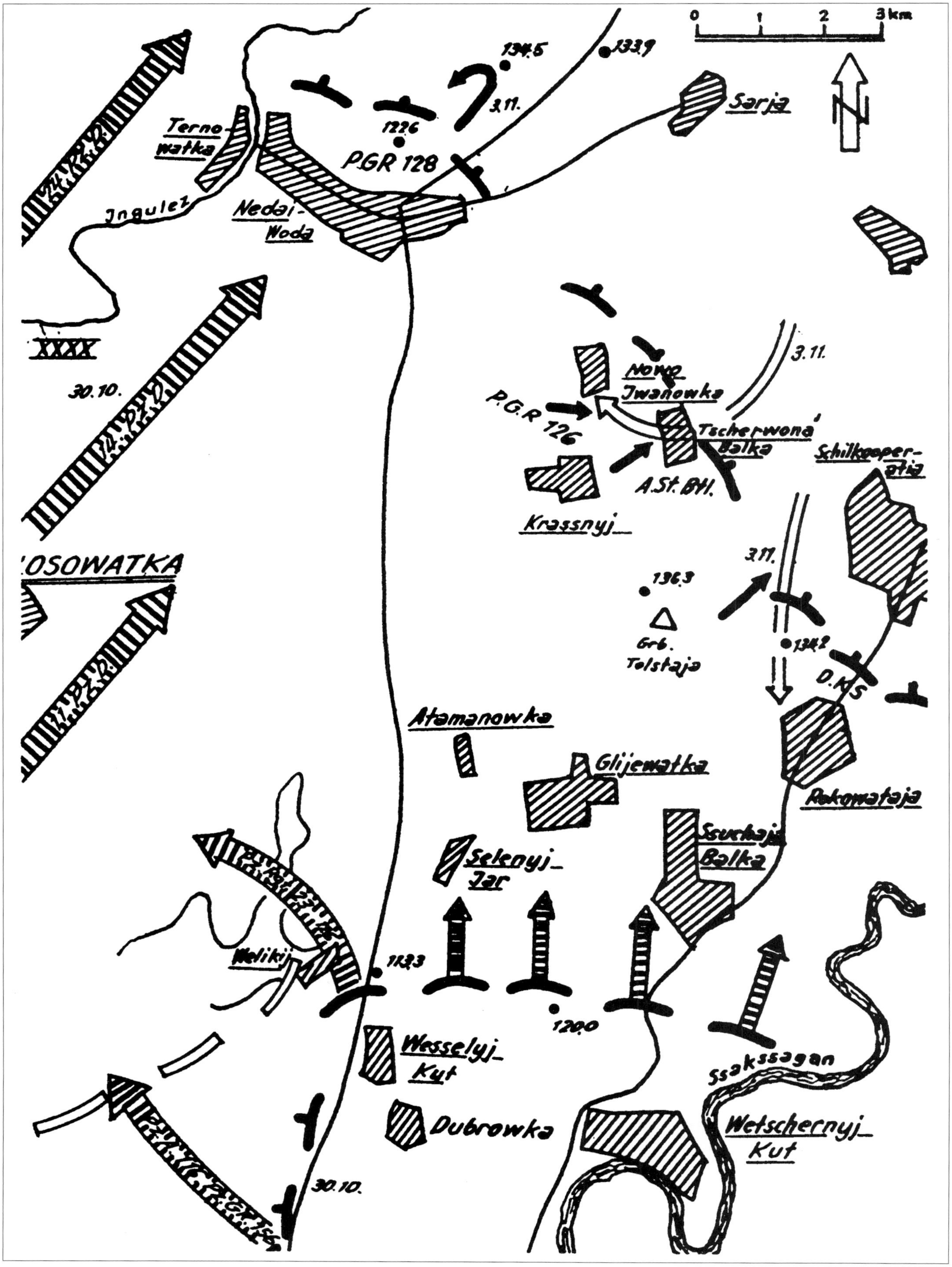
0 1 2 3 km
Sarja
Terno-watka
Ingulez
Nedai-Woda
PGR 128
3.11.
XXXX
30.10.
Nowo-Jwanowka
P.G.R 126
Tscherwona Balka
A.St. BYI.
Krassnyj
Schilkooper-atia
OSOWATKA
Grb. Tolstaja
D.K.S
Atamanowka
Glijewatka
Rokowataja
Ssuchaja Balka
Selenyj Jar
Weliki
Wesselyj Kut
Dubrowka
Ssakssagan
Wetschernyj Kut
30.10.

up the situation and the penetrations were sealed off. At first light on 4 November, *PGR126* and the *DKS* moved out with the tanks and retook the former main line of resistance by noon, with the exception of Hill 134.2. The considerable losses in personnel over the previous day necessitated the acceptance of a 1.5-kilometer-wide gap in the main line of resistance southeast of Tscherwona Balka.

On 3 and 4 November, 15 T-34's and 6 antitank guns, including an American "Anti-Tiger" gun (9cm), were destroyed. The Soviets suffered bloody and considerable losses.

The 2nd Medical Company, under the direction of *Stabsarzt Dr.* Kühner, was moved up to Kriwoi Rog in the meantime and established a forward clearing station at Losowatka.

The German Armed Forces Daily report of 4 November mentioned the achievements of the *23. Panzer-Division* as follows:

> In the difficult defensive fighting in the Dnjepr bend, the *23. Panzer-Division*, from southwest Germany, under the command of *Generalleutnant* von Vormann, has distinguished itself through its extraordinary bravery.

The division suffered a great loss at this time in the form of *Generalleutnant* von Vormann having to leave his command due to health reasons and being transferred to the German Army's unassigned officer manpower pool. During the 11 months of his command, von Vormann shaped the division through the strength of his character to such an extent that the division was able to master even the most difficult of critical situations.

Generalleutnant von Vormann's successor, *Oberst* Kraeber, arrived to assume command.

***

While the difficult fighting of the *23. Panzer-Division* north of Kriwoi Rog finally led to the reestablishment of a cohesive front in the great Dnjepr bend and led to a firm link-up between the *1. Panzer-Armee* and the *8. Armee*, thanks to the commitment of the *14. Panzer-Division* and the *24. Panzer-Division*, *Heeresgruppe Süd* had to master a number of difficult crises at other places along its frontage.

The *6. Armee*, which adjoined the *1. Panzer-Armee* on the right, had been allocated to *Heeresgruppe A* in the middle of October. It was intended for it to hold open the entrances to the Crimea, where the *17. Armee* continued to be positioned, from its Mariupol/Dnjepr Position. Strong enemy forces were pressing in that sector.

Although Hitler had ordered the bridgeheads of Saporoshe, Dnjepropetrowsk, Krementschug and Kiev to be held, they were gradually evacuated by the field-army group, whereby the bridgehead at Saporoshe was only allowed to be given up after heavy, casualty-intensive fighting. Hitler's orders kept the *XXXX. Panzer-Korps* in that bridgehead there for an unnecessarily long time. As a result, it was not available for clearing up the Mischurin Rog Bridgehead in October, where it could have been effectively employed.

By the end of September, the Soviets had already forced a bridgehead at Perejasslaw (north of Kanew). The Soviet attempt to expand the bridgehead by the employment of several airborne brigades failed in the face of the German resistance.[66]

At the extreme northern wing of the field-army group between the *4. Panzer-Armee* and the *2. Armee*, the enemy had advanced across the Desna. To the north of Kiev, the Soviets succeeded in crossing the Dnjepr in the middle of October. It was only through the employment of armored forces on the plateau on the west side of the river that they could be halted.

The wide gap torn open west of Pjatichatki between the *1. Panzer-Armee* and the *8. Armee* by the advance of five Soviet field armies could only be restored by *Generalfeldmarschall* von Manstein by taking all dispensable forces from the *XXX. Armee-Korps*. In the end, all of the *XXX. Armee-Korps* was pulled back to a line running from north of Saporoshe to north of Kriwoi Rog. Only a covering force was left behind on both sides of Dnjepropetrowsk along the Dnjepr. Any thought of attempting to restore the front along the Dnjepr as a result of the successful conclusion to the Battle of Kriwoi Rog at the beginning of November was not allowed as a result of the new crises developing elsewhere.

On 28 October, vastly superior enemy forces attacked the *6. Armee* between the Dnjepr and the coastline of the Asovian Sea and forced a breakthrough. The two corps of the field army in the north—the *IV. Armee-Korps* and the *XXIX. Armee-Korps*—swung back into a large bridgehead south of the Dnjepr, where they protected the deep flank of the *1. Panzer-Armee* and the city of Nikopol. The rest of the *6. Armee* pulled back to the west to the crossing points over the Bereslaw and the lower course of the river. The *17. Armee* was cut off on the Crimea and had to defend the narrow point of the peninsula, orienting to the north.

On 2 November, the Soviet command initiated a new offensive against the *4. Panzer-Armee*. It forced the evacuation of Kiev on 5 November and gained ground rapidly to the west in the direction of Fastow, Shitomir and Korosten, all of which were important rail nodal points for the logistics of the entire field army.

In the area of operations around Kriwoi Rog, the Red Army soon overcame the heavy losses sustained during the previous few weeks. Prisoner statements and intercepted radio messages confirmed the intention of the Soviets to break through between Ssakssagen and Ingulez, take Kriwoi Rog at all costs and cut off the *1. Panzer-Armee*. The following enemy formations were identified just in front of the sector of the *23. Panzer-Division* alone:

Elements of the 37th Army: 10th Guards Airlanded Division; 72nd Guards Rifle Division; 15th Guards Rifle Division; 62nd Guards Rifle Division (remnants); 1398th Antiaircraft Regiment; 188th Rifle Division; 92nd Rifle Division; and 213th Rifle Division.

Elements of the 5th Tank Army: I Guards Motorized/Mechanized Corps; V Guards Motorized/Mechanized Corps; VII Guards Motorized/Mechanized Corps; XVIII Tank Corps; XXIX Tank Corps; 7th Guards Motorized Rifle Brigade; 80th Motorized Rifle Brigade; 55th Assault Gun Brigade; 96th Motorcycle Battalion (Separate); 60th Motorized Artillery Regiment; 80th Tank Brigade; 155th Tank Brigade; 27th Armored Reconnaissance Battalion; 15th Mortar Battalion; 234th Field Army Howitzer regiment; and special-purpose armored elements.

Moreover, prisoner statements revealed that the Soviet XX Tank Corps (of the 5th Tank Army) was located in the Annowka area.

Any day could see the launching of the offensive by these formations. All measures needed for defending had been taken. The positions were fortified by bringing up all available forces and the employment of *Bau-Pionier-Bataillon 219*[67]. The artillery defensive fires of the division were reinforced by the attachment of *Werfergruppe Gardelegen* (the *II./Werfer-Regiment 54* and the *II./Werfer-Regiment 70*), *leichte Heeres-Artillerie-Abteilung 935* and *Mörser-Abteilung 736*[68].

Enemy assault detachments and individual tanks accompanied by infantry penetrated the thin combat outpost line of the division several times from 6-8 November. With assistance from the armored outposts, consisting of four *Panthers*, they were turned back again.

On 6 November, *Oberleutnant* Roltsch's antitank guns from the *8./PGR128* knocked out a T-34 from among the vehicles in a Soviet armored group that was in front of the northeast portion of Nedai Woda.

66 Editor's Note: Contributing to the Soviet's lack of success was the scattering of most of the forces dropped. The airborne forces suffered a early 50% casualty rate, and the Soviets did not attempt any more large-scale airborne operations during the remainder of the war.

67 Editor's Note: = 219th Engineer Battalion (Construction).

68 Editor's Note: = 736th Heavy Howitzer Battalion. Despite being a cognate, *Mörser* is not mortar; it is a howitzer of more than 20cm caliber. Usually, it was 21cm.

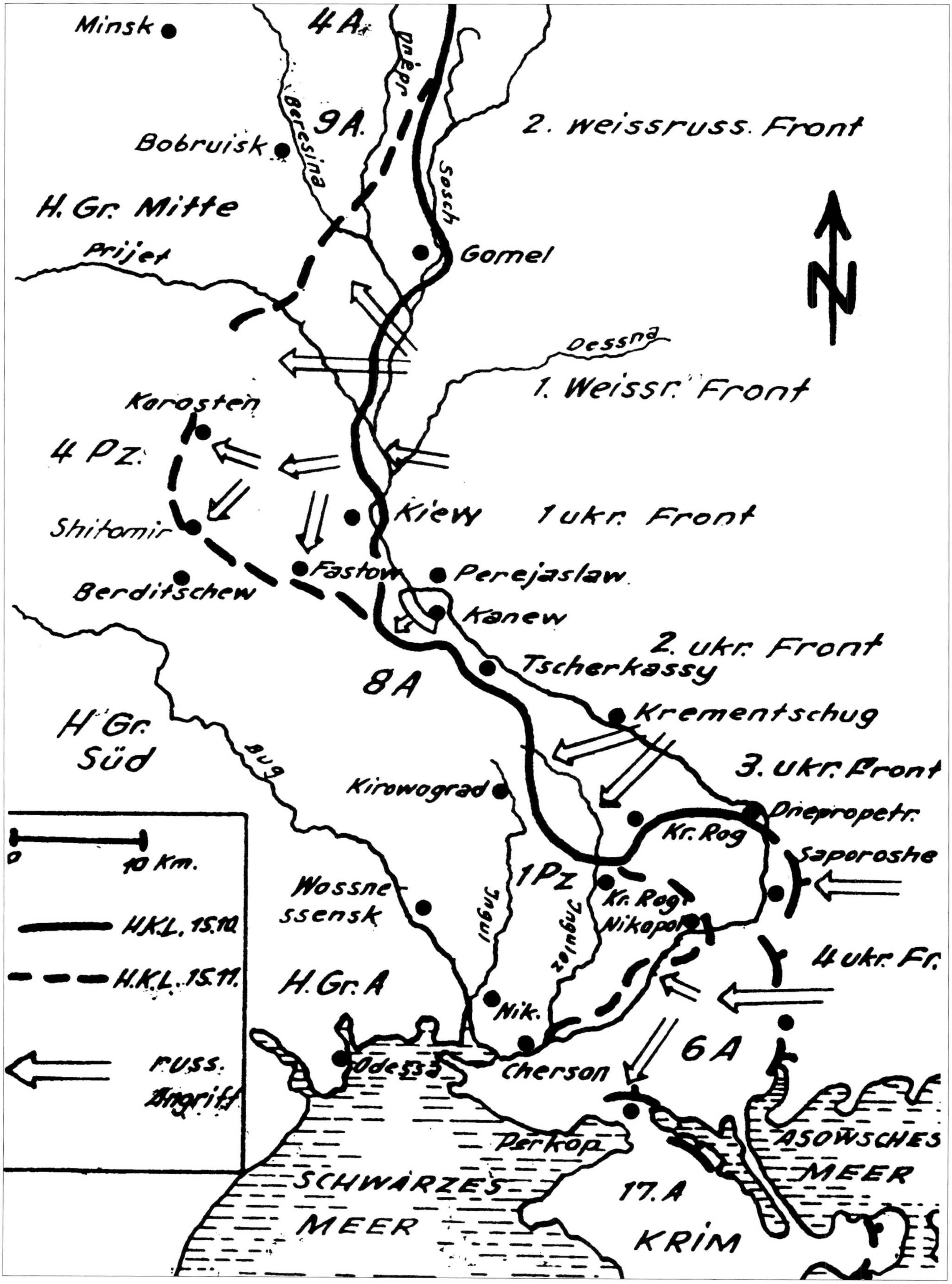

Map 62: The Over-All Situation in October and November 1943.

The gun commander of a 5cm antitank gun was deeply disappointed when the credit for the "kill" had to be given to the gun commander of a 7.5cm antitank gun.

At 0300 hours on 9 November, the enemy attacked across Hill 122.5 into the eastern portion of Nedai-Woda. He pushed back the few infantrymen there and followed them through the *balka* at Nedai Woda as far as Hill 120.3. In a counterattack launched at 0730 hours, three *Tigers* from *schwere Panzer-Abteilung 506* and three long-barreled *Panzer IV's*, in conjunction with the *3./PAA23*, attacked Hill 120.3, cleared the eastern portion of Nedai Woda of the enemy and enabled the infantry of *PGR128* to return to their positions along the northern portion of Nedai Woda by 1400 hours. Soviet attempts to attack along both sides of the Annowka —Nedai Woda road collapsed in the face of German artillery salvoes. According to prisoner statements, an entire regiment from the Soviet 228th Rifle Division had attacked with the mission of creating the prerequisites for a subsequent offensive by taking the entire village and establishing a good jump-off position.

Enemy concentrations north of Hill 122.5 were shattered by artillery fires. Assault detachments probing the thin outpost lines of the division were turned back by the employment of tanks.

In addition to a main clearing station, which would soon become very busy, the 2nd Medical Company, under the direction of *Stabsarzt Dr.* Schmid, established a bathing and delousing facility in Kriwoi Rog. Over the next few weeks, the personnel of the division could be shunted through these facilities, usually at night, after being pulled out of the line for a short period of time.

Through the employment of field-expedient means, the division's postal facility was able to resume work and provide the forces in the field with mail on a regular basis.

At first light on 10 November, the enemy again attacked Nedai Woda. Weak elements of *PGR128* were able to hold the southern part of the village, until the immediate counterattack by the division's tanks was able to eject most of the enemy. In the extreme northwest portion of the village, however, the Soviets were able to hold individual buildings, especially since the onset of darkness offered them additional concealment.

The battalions and companies of the infantry regiments had been bled white once again. While all of the *I./PGR126* consisted of a trench strength of exactly 70 men, including its heavy company, the *5./PGR128* had an end strength of only one noncommissioned officer and five enlisted!

Together with the infantry, five tanks and eight *SPW's* cleared the last remaining buildings of the enemy the following morning.

An immediate reaction force from the *11. Panzer-Division* assembled at Nedai Woda to help secure the boundary to the friendly division on the left, the *76. Infanterie-Division*. The enemy continued to bring up strong infantry forces in front of the division sector. He limited his activities in the next few days to probing the German main line of resistance in the form of assaults by anywhere from 100 to 200 men.

The division artillery was further reinforced by the attachment of *Arko 7*[69], *Werfer-Regiment 54* (with its 1st and 3rd Battalions), the *I./Artillerie-Abteilugng 628* (21cm howitzers), as well as the headquarters and the 1st Battalion of the divisional artillery of the *8. SS-Kavallerie-Division "Florian Geyer"*, as the division had been redesignated. At the time, the *I./PAR128* was in the Trikrati area (near Wossnessensk/Bug), where it was being restructured and organized as a self-propelled artillery battalion with two light and one heavy batteries. The battalion was being issued the *Wespe* self-propelled gun, with the 10.5cm Model 18 light field howitzer and the *Hummel*, with the 15cm Model 18 heavy field howitzer. Each of the batteries received six self-propelled guns.

At night, the divisional engineers emplaced mines and wire obstacles by sector in front of the main lines of resistance.

At 0500 hours on 14 November, an hour-long barrage-like preparatory artillery fire by heavy artillery and mortar elements was placed on the division sector between Ssakssagan and Ingulez. The expected offensive started at 0600 hours. Between 60 and 70 enemy tanks and strong infantry forces attacked, with the main effort between Nowo-Iwanowka and Nedai Woda. Additional strong forces advanced from Shilkooperazija to the southwest.

In the final protective fires of the artillery and rocket launchers, the enemy suffered high casualties, but nothing was initially able to stop this Russian attack steamroller. The infantry and the grenadiers of *Panzer-Armee-Sturm-Bataillon 1* were overrun in their foxholes, which had become mud pits after the continuous rainfall of the previous few days. Hills 138.5 and 123.4 were lost; at 0730 hours, the eastern portion of Nedai Woda was also lost. Nowo-Iwanowka fell and the enemy was located to the rear of the *DKS*.

Panzergruppe Fechner—consisting of *PR23*, *schwere Panzer-Abteilung 506* and the *3./PAA23*—moved out from the area around Hill 140.7 and initially pushed back the enemy who was advancing south of Nedai Woda. Two enemy tanks were eliminated. *Schwere Panzer-Abteilung 506*, which was employed against heavy concentrations of armor at Hill 138.5, knocked out 20 T-34's in the space of a few minutes. The effect of that on the Soviets was enormous. They fled back north, followed by the fires of the *Panthers* and the *Tigers*.

The field army assault battalion had reassembled defensively along the northern portion of Krassnyj in the meantime. The battalion was supported by three tanks. At 1330 hours, *Panzergruppe Fechner* arrived and moved out with the assault battalion to counterattack Nowo Iwanowka. Thanks to well-placed friendly fires and the knocking out of seven additional enemy tanks, the battle group made good progress. At 1500 hours, the village was again in German hands.

With the exception of its eastern part, Nedai Woda was firmly in the hands of *PGR128*, to which the *4.(Kradschütz.)/PAA23* had been attached for reinforcement, as well as two tanks under the command of *Leutnant* Peez. For short periods of time, the personnel manning Nedai Woda had to fight simultaneously to the east, south and north.

Three other tanks supported *PGR126* in its defense of the Tscherwona Balka; those tanks destroyed three T-34's.

As the result of a counterattack launched by all of the forces, most of the main line of resistance was reoccupied at 1600 hours. However, an enemy group of between 200 and 300 men held out behind the German lines between Nowo Iwanowka and Hill 140.7, however. Around Hill 138.5, the enemy was still on the northern slope.

Contributing greatly to the defensive success of the day was *Oberleutnant* Fischer, a company commander in *PR23*. As the leader of the *Panthers* within *Panzergruppe Fechner*, he had led the counterattack at Nowo Iwanowka to a complete success as a result of his clever leadership and personal bravery. He was later awarded the Knight's Cross to the Iron Cross, on 28 December 1943, for his performance in battle.

On that day, 31 enemy tanks were knocked out. An additional four were rendered immobile. Twelve antitank guns and 30 antitank rifles were eliminated; 217 prisoners were taken. Only two *Panthers* were lost to enemy fire.

Despite the strength of the divisional artillery and the effectiveness of *Panzergruppe Fechner* and the elements of *schwere Panzer-Abteilung 506*, the infantry combat power of the division was minimal. Part of the bargain was large gaps in the main line of resistance between the individual weak strongpoints. No reserves were available. At the urgent request

69 Editor's Note: = *Artillerie-Kommandeur 7* = Artillery Commander of the *VII. Armee-Korps*. The *Arko* was the senior artillery officer of a corps and had a staff for commanding and controlling corps-level artillery assets as well as directing the artillery fight of the divisions subordinated to the corps.

of the division, the field army sent *Regimentsgruppe Raatz* forward during the night of 14/15 November. It was intended for it to assume the sector of the field army's assault battalion, which had largely been shattered. The relief was only possible at Hill 138.5 and along the eastern slope of Hill 123.4 after overcoming considerable Soviet resistance.

Prisoners stated that the attack between Nowo Iwanowka and Nedai Woda had been conducted by four rifle divisions and a tank brigade. The division's successful defense had allowed the field army to employ its reserves at other hot spots, for instance, in the sector of the neighboring *76. Infanterie-Division* on the left. The enemy had succeeded in achieving a deep penetration there, that could only be sealed off after the employment of the *3. SS-Panzer-Division "Totenkopf"*. Seventy enemy tanks were knocked out in that sector.

The reaction force of the *11. Panzer-Division* at Losowatka was relieved by a battle group from the *14. Panzer-Division*. Rain without let up turned the roads into seemingly bottomless quagmires of mud and made any and all movement difficult.

A Soviet battalion, supported by tanks, attacked Nowo Iwanowka at 0815 hours on 15 November. However, it was turned back by the grenadiers and tanks there. Elements of *Regimentsgruppe Raatz* and tanks positioned south of Hill 140.7 attacked the 300 Russians who had been pressed together east of that hill the previous day. The enemy was completely eliminated, except for very small remnants that surrendered.

It was not possible to completely capture Hill 123.4 east of Nedai Woda. Two penetrations by the enemy could only be sealed off and cleared up by an immediate counterattack conducted by the *Tigers* and *Panthers*; seven T-34's were destroyed.

Continuous thrusts on the part of Soviet tanks and assault detachments ended without success and usually with the destruction of the attackers. It was only on the right wing of the *DKS* that the enemy succeeded in gaining a few hundred meters of terrain. In the course of the day, the following spoils of war were noted:

Destroyed: 23 tanks; 15 antitank guns; 1 artillery piece; 30 machine guns; 19 antitank rifles; and 1 truck.

329 prisoners were taken; 400 enemy dead were counted.

Generalfeldmarschall von Manstein, the Commander-in-Chief of *Heeresgruppe Süd*, recognized the achievements of the division in the following telegram to the division: "Bravo, *23. Panzer-Division*. You are damned good men!" (signed / von Manstein)

The acting commander of *PGR126*, *Major* Schägger, a recipient of the Knight's Cross, was killed by a direct hit from a mortar round while conducting reconnaissance in the regiment's sector.

The main line of resistance ran on 15 November from the northern edge of Rokowataja to Nowo-Iwanowka, where it turned west and then jumped sharply to the north at the eastern part of Nedai Woda. A 2-kilometer-gap between the area 1 kilometer west of Hill 138.5 and the eastern edge of Nedai Woda was only screened by *Panzergruppe Fechner*.

It was not until 18 November that the enemy had regained his strength enough to attack again. Thick fog prevented timely identification of the Russian attack positions. Toward 1330 hours, a battalion, supported by two T-34's, attacked just north of Hill 123.4. Artillery scattered that enemy force; both of the T-34's were destroyed. At 1345 hours, 500 Russians, supported by tanks, attempted to enter the northeastern part of Nedai Woda, advancing from the Nedai Woda defile. Artillery, rocket launchers and tanks inflicted heavy losses on the enemy, and four additional T-34's were destroyed. In addition, six antitank guns, including a 12.2cm one, were also destroyed.

During the night of 18/19 November and at first light, strong enemy forces attacked the sector of the *II./Grenadier-Regiment 767* on the extreme right wing of the division, east of the Ssakssagan. By means of immediate counterattacks, the battalion threw back the enemy forces that had penetrated several times. In the end, however, the Soviets claimed both sides of Hill 109.6. The battalion commander, *Hauptmann* König, was killed after he had remained with his men, despite having already been wounded twice.

During the afternoon, the former main line of resistance was partially recaptured with the help of a ready reserve force from *Panzergrenadier-Regiment 108* of the *14. Panzer-Division*.

The enemy brought up reinforcements in front of the western portion of the division's sector, particularly from the area around Sarja (headed toward Hill 134.5). At the same time, fortifications were observed being prepared in several successively echeloned lines. The enemy's artillery registered its fires.

During the morning of 20 November, Soviet artillery fired smoke in an effort to blind the tanks located 1 kilometers north of Hill 140.7 while, at the same time, an attack was launched at the boundary between *Regimentsgruppe Raatz* and *PGR128*. The grenadiers temporarily pulled back to the west, but they were soon brought back to their old positions by tanks advancing in an immediate counterattack.

The Soviets attacked 14 times on that day, anywhere from a company to a battalion in strength. The main efforts manifested themselves south of Shilkooperazia, north of Nowo-Iwanowka and both south and west of Hill 123.4. It was especially at Hill 123.4 that the numerically weak defenders suffered considerable casualties in the barren terrain. Ever larger gaps were torn in the main line of resistance. Tanks and *SPW's* had to be employed to overwatch them.

As it turned dark, the Soviets succeeded in making penetrations: Two into Tscherwona Balka and the other in the northern portion of Nedai Woda. Both of those penetrations were sealed off and eliminated by means of immediate counterattacks by midnight.

In the case of one of the penetrations at Tscherwona Balka and, a short while later, at Krassnyj, *Oberleutnant* Greiner-Bechert rallied the grenadiers and infantry who had been falling back. Together with the men of his *8.(schwere)/PGR126*, they conducted successful immediate counterattacks. Contributing greatly to all of the successes were the forward observers of the artillery and the rocket launchers. In the front lines themselves, they often had to pick up a rifle as well. Through the terrific fire direction of their batteries, they stopped many an enemy attack before it could penetrate into the main line of resistance. Whenever any opportunity was offered, the divisional and regimental engineers established field fortifications and wire and mine obstacles.

During the night of 20/21 November, the enemy entered the northeastern portion of Nedai Woda . Even after an immediate counterattack was launched, which caused considerable casualties to the infantry, he could not be dislodged. The following morning, 500 Soviets, supported by 10 T-34's, attacked Nowo Iwanowka and south of Hill 123.4. In addition, 13 more T-34's, escorted by infantry, advanced against the infantry still holding out in Nedai Woda. Well-placed artillery and rocket-launcher fires, as well as the employment of the tanks, prevented the enemy from succeeding. Five T-34's were destroyed.

The *DKS* turned back an attack by superior enemy forces on both sides of Hill 134.2. To the east of the Ssakssagan, the *II./Grenadier-Regiment 767* had retaken the former main line of resistance in its entire length. The battalion was so fought-out, however, that it had to be replaced by the newly attached *II./Grenadier-Regiment 336* of the *161. Infanterie-Division*. The *II./Grenadier-Regiment 767* was detached from its command and control relationship with the division.

In Nedai Woda, the enemy succeeded during the night of 22/23 November in pushing the weak outposts of *PGR128* back west to the church. The enemy brought strong forces forward across Hill 122.5 and from Balka Nedai Woda. He advanced with them via Hill 120.3 on Hill 140.2. Tanks and *SPW's* from *PAA23* threw the Russians back to Nedai

Woda, but they were unable to retake the village itself in the face of massive resistance from the enemy, who was supported by strong antitank defenses, artillery and rocket launchers.

Soviet fighter-bombers and tanks supported the Soviet attacks against Nowo Iwanowka. The village was held and five tanks were knocked out by *Major* Schwarz' *schwere Panzer-Jäger-Abteilung 662*. Tscherwona Balka also remained firmly in the hands of *PGR126*. Artillery and rocket-launcher fires of hitherto unseen dimensions were placed on the entire division sector.

As a result of the weak forces available—forces which allowed neither the expectation of retaking Nedai Woda or successfully defending it—the left wing of the division was pulled back to both sides of Hill 140.2 during the night. At first light, the enemy advanced on Hill 140.2 but was pushed back by a counterattack of the tanks on Nedai Woda. The enemy suffered heavy casualties during a renewed thrust along both sides of the Nedai Woda — Kriwoi Rog road; three T-34's were set alight. At 0900 hours on 23 November, 1,000 Soviets attacked Nowo Iwanowka, which was only defended by 40 grenadiers and three conditionally operational tanks. One building after the other had to be abandoned to the enemy, who was pressing on several sides at once. Soviet reinforcements forced the remaining defenders to pull back to Krassnyj. The weak forces of *Regimentsgruppe Raatz*, together with the attached remnants of the field army's assault battalion, were incapable of launching an immediate counterattack on the village. To the south of Nowo Iwanowka, the main line of resistance was occupied by weak strongpoints.

Tanks and *SPW's* overwatched the 1.5-kilometer-wide gap east of Hill 140.2 and covered the digging of fortifications 1 kilometer north of Hill 140.7, which was being conducted by *PPB51* and all of the trains of the division.

From the tank crews of *PR23* that no longer had vehicles, the regiment created a 3rd Battalion. Under the command of *Oberleutnant* Gauglitz, the *ad hoc* battalion received 45 new *SPW's* that had been issued, for which there were no infantry available to man. Only 10 operational tanks were left and fighting. The deep mud, the uninterrupted operations, which barely allowed anytime for maintenance, and the losses suffered in combat all played their part in shrinking their numbers.

At 0200 hours on 24 November, the enemy entered Tscherwona Balka from Nowo Iwanowka. He pushed the *II./PGR126* back to the southern part of the locality. One hour later, the *I./PGR128* had to pull back 1 kilometer to the south along the Nedai Woda — Kriwoi Rog road in the face of attacking enemy. The infantry were received by the tanks and incorporated into the hedgehog defensive position along with the trains and the combat engineers, who were preparing field fortifications. At first light, a counterattack by the tanks and the *SPW's* brought the infantry back to their old positions and 100 Soviets were taken prisoner. A counterattack that started promisingly against Tscherwona Balka bogged down after all of the attacking tanks were rendered non-operational.

The enemy also penetrated into the main line of resistance at Hill 136.3, south/southeast of Tscherwona Balka. There were no forces available for an immediate counterattack; it was only possible to provisionally block the penetration. Once again, the enemy's main efforts were directed against the completely exhausted and weak remnants of *Regimentsgruppe Raatz* and *PGR128*.

The soldiers, who were drenched to the bone from the rain that had fallen for days, were no longer able to offer resistance from their foxholes, which were filled knee-deep with mud. Penetrations in Krassnyj, the area northwest of it and both sides of Hill 140.2 were the consequence. Only the tireless efforts of the tanks and the tank destroyers, along with the concentrated fires of the artillery and the rocket launchers, prevented the worst from happening. With the exception of the main line of resistance north of Krassnyj, the former positions were retaken in the course of the day. Hill 136.3 was lost once and for all after an unsuccessful counterattack.

The physical and psychological strength of the infantry had reached its end point. Mud and the rain made their weapons unusable; efforts to construct positions drowned in mud. It was no longer possible to speak of a main line of resistance in view of the wide gaps that existed.

On 25 November, strong Soviet forces prepared for operations in front of the center and left-hand portions of the division sector. The 34 batteries available to the division—artillery, rocket launchers and *Flak*—tore great holes in the enemy ranks. But new forces were introduced to replace them. At 1100 hours, the enemy simultaneously attacked Hill 136.3, east of Tscherwona Balka, north of Krassnyj, northeast of Hill 140.7 and on both sides of Hill 140.2.

The Soviets attacked Krassnyj and the area west of it twice with some 800-1,000 men and tanks. The artillery and tanks tore great holes in the ranks of the advancing Soviets, who pulled back to the north after two T-34's were knocked out. In the pursuit that followed, one *Panzer IV* wound up in the middle of the Soviets and was knocked out by enemy tanks. It was only with difficulty that the crew managed to get back to German lines and save itself. A third Soviet attack finally led to the enemy entering Krassnyj.

The immediate counterattack of the weak reserves succeeded in taking back the village, with the exception of a few buildings, by the onset of darkness.

Hill 140.2 was temporarily lost but was retaken in conjunction with the ready reserve of the *II./Panzergrenadier-Regiment 108*.

During the night that followed, the enemy gained further ground in Krassnyj. In order to shorten the main line of resistance, *PGR126* was pulled back to the line running Hill 136.3 — eastern edge of Krassnyj. At the eleventh hour, *Grenadier-Regiment 513* of the *294. Infanterie-Division* was attached to the division for infantry reinforcement; it was brought into the sector by rail. The *II./Grenadier-Regiment 513* was employed the night of 25/26 November to counterattack Krassnyj.

The counterattack against Krassnyj proper started at 0600 hours on 26 November in thick fog. It was conducted by a company of *PPB51* and four *Panzer IV's*. After a short artillery preparation, the village was cleared, house by house, by the engineers, who maintained close contact with the tanks. The enemy put up bitter resistance. Suddenly, the fog lifted and exposed Soviet guns that had set up in the open north of Krassnyj. One 10cm howitzer and one 7.5cm cannon were blown to pieces, but two German tanks ran over mines. Krassnyj was once again firmly back in German hands.

A renewed counterattack against Hill 136.3, which was conducted by the *I./Grenadier-Regiment 513* with a heavy artillery preparation, was only a partial success.

From additional tank crews without vehicles, *PR23* established a "tanker" infantry company, which was sent to the *DKS*.

Once again since the start of the fighting, the division received reinforcements for the decimated infantry regiments: 450 replacements. The officers and noncommissioned officers, who had been lost, could not be replaced, however, with the result that the combat readiness could not be increased.

An effort by *PGR128* to re-establish contact with the friendly forces on the left failed in the face of heavy enemy resistance and flanking fires from the west bank of the Ingulez.

The 27th of November was again marked by enemy attacks, with the enemy's main effort being directed at the center of the division sector. The first attack, conducted by 200 men and 10 T-34's and launched from the direction of Hill 138.5, collapsed after 4 T-34's were knocked out by *Panzergruppe Quintel*. The Soviet artillery hammered Krassnyj uninterruptedly. The enemy assaulted the village 10 times that day; the only thing he

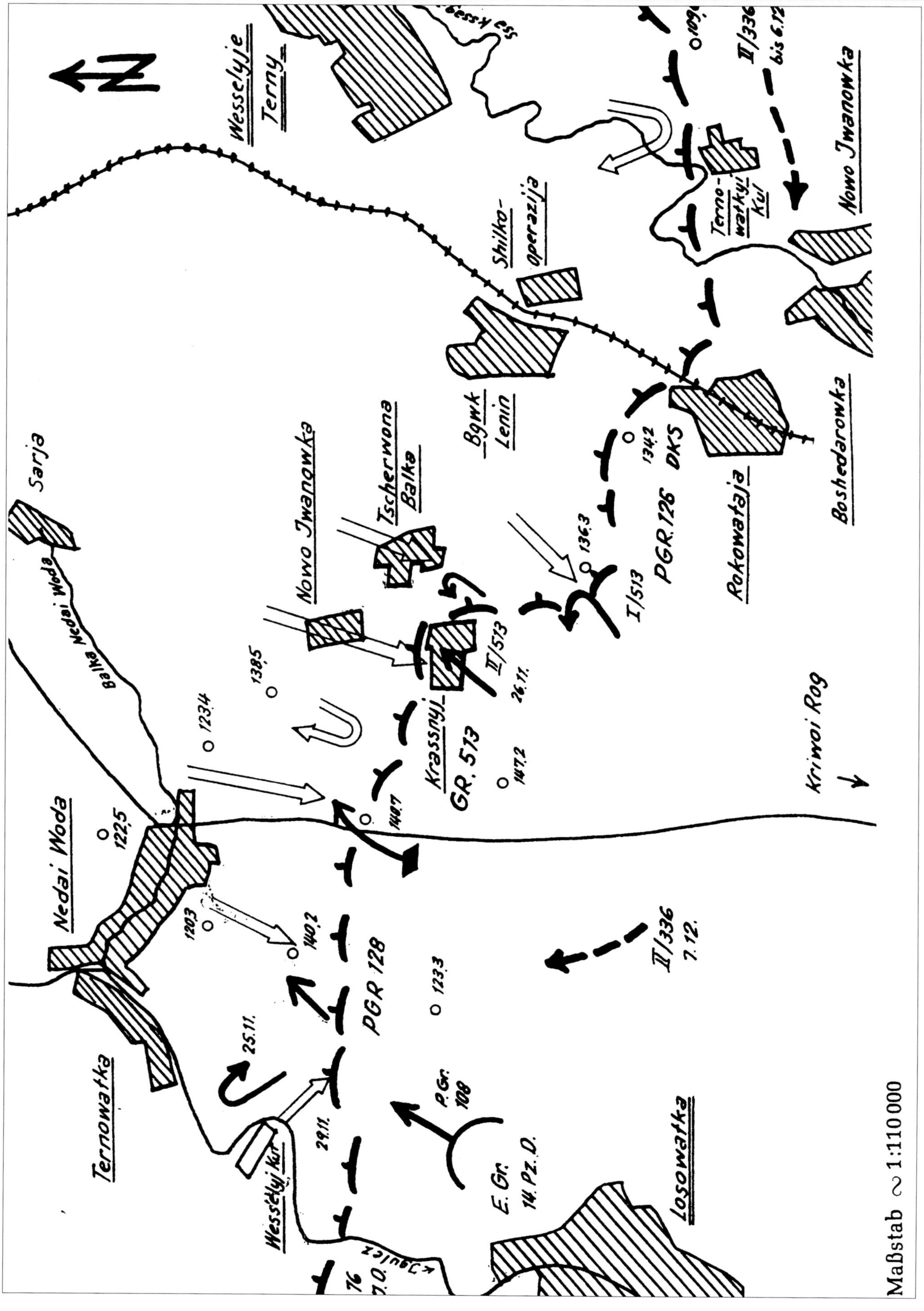

Map 63: The Fighting from 25 November to 31 December 1943.

November 1943: Personnel of *PGR 126* construct field positions at Glijewatka.

An effort is made to keep rain water from draining into the trench.

The future command post of *PGR 126*.

Captured Soviets await their fate as prisoners of war.

Prisoners form a bucket brigade to help drain the trenches.

The command post of the *I./PGR 126*.

An observation post.

Christmas Eve, 1943: Despite all the deprivations, Christmas was still celebrated.

Water and mud everywhere.

Sometimes draft animals were the best way to get "unstuck".

In the heavy mud wheeled vehicles were almost useless, even tracked vehicles had difficulties.

Oberleutnant Eichel (on the cart) and *Stabsarzt* Dr. Barczyk on the way to regimental headquarters.

was able to achieve, however, was infiltrating in the gap between Krassnyj and Hill 140.7 and establishing himself there.

Seven attacks were directed at the same time against Hill 140.2. All of them were shattered before they reached the German lines.

The enemy attacked repeatedly east of the Ssakssagan, in order to take Ternowatkij Kut. The *II./Grenadier-Regiment 336* was able to decide the day in defense and through immediate counterattacks.

In the sector of *PGR126*, the enemy reinforced his elements considerably on Hill 136.3. Six dug-in tanks were identified.

At 0100 hours on 28 November, the enemy attacked Hill 140.7 by surprise and without artillery preparation, taking it. The tanks, which had been alerted immediately, retook the hill in conjunction with the grenadiers and engineers. The hill was lost again at 0530 hours, however, only to be retaken an hour later. Additional attacks on the hill conducted the entire day were defeated, largely by artillery and rocket-launcher fires.

The *I./Grenadier-Regiment 513*, which had been pulled out of the line at Hill 136.3, was supposed to clear and close the gap between Krassnyj and Hill 140.7. The attack conducted during the day failed in the face of the enemy's defense, whereby five assault guns were lost. A *Panzergruppe* under the command of *Hauptmann* Bergmann of *PR23* was formed, consisting of *Panthers*, *Tigers* and 16 *SPW's* from the *ad hoc III./PR23*. Supported by the *I./Grenadier-Regiment 513* and the divisional artillery, *Panzergruppe Bergmann* overran the enemy. The enemy took flight from his positions. While only minimal friendly losses were suffered, the enemy took heavy casualties, losing many dead, and also losing more than 30 antitank guns and artillery pieces. One *SPW* was lost due to enemy action.

The enemy exploited the night once again at 0100 hours on 29 November to attack Krassnyj from Nowo Iwanowko. He occupied a few buildings but was quickly ejected in an immediate counterattack conducted by two tanks.

Heavy artillery fire initiated the Soviet attack that started at 0600 hours along the entire front between Krassnyj and the Ingulez. For the most part, the attacks were defeated. Weak enemy elements infiltrated east of Hill 140.2, while other elements crossed the Ingulez from Wesselyj-Kut and entered the defile running west of Hill 140.2. In the course of the defensive fighting, five *SPW's* of the *III./PR23* were temporarily lost. The crews, which had dismounted, ran south and right into the enemy forces in their rear. There were numerous wounded and three soldiers listed as missing, including *Oberleutnant* Beyerbach. The *SPW's* were recovered later.

In the Krassnyj area, the enemy took a few strongpoints west of the village. He was unable to hold them against a counterattack conducted at 2000 hours by *SPW's* and grenadiers. Numerous enemy dead and weapons were left behind in the retaken positions.

A short while later, Soviet tanks and infantry attacked Krassnyj from the east and advanced as far as the southern part. Together with grenadiers from the *I./Grenadier-Regiment 513*, tanks moved out for an immediate counterattack, destroyed two T-34's at 100 meters that had been illuminated by signal flares and threw the enemy infantry back with losses.

The 30th of November was quiet. A German operation, which was intended to clear up the situation around Hill 140.2 (under the command of *Hauptmann* Mahr), failed due to a misunderstanding. Two companies from *Panzergrenadier-Regiment 108* did not move out. The five tanks that were working with a company from *PGR128*—one *Tiger*, three *Panthers* and one *Panzer IV*—ran over mines and had to be blown up.

Generalleutnant Prinner's *Artillerie-Divisions-Stab z.b.V.*[70], which was directly attached to the *LVII. Panzer-Korps*, was directed to support the *LII. Armee-Korps*. To that end, it assumed command and control of all of the artillery assets within the division's sector. Soviet concentrations were shattered several times by the artillery. The infantry remained quiet as far as infantry operations were concerned, however, and he spent the time reorganizing his forces.

In the fighting between 21 October and 30 November 1943, the enemy lost the following in front of the division's sector:

20 artillery pieces
151 antitank guns
32 mortars
96 antitank rifles
13 motorized vehicles
117 machine guns
3 horse-drawn vehicles
10 infantry guns
4 assault guns
1 field kitchen and
168 tanks

In addition, 1,915 prisoners were taken and 3,835 enemy dead were counted.

During the days that followed, both sides improved the positions they had won. Assault detachments from *PGR126* blew up the German tanks that had been knocked out during the previous days during the attack on Hill 136.3, since Soviet snipers had been operating out of them. On 3 December, the northeastern portion of Krassnyj was lost as the result of an enemy infantry attack. After several unsuccessful immediate counterattacks, *Grenadier-Regiment 513* succeeded the following night in retaking the lost terrain.

The *DKS* was reinforced with a "tanker" infantry company, an infantry company composed of artillerymen and the issuance of heavy weapons and then designated as *"Kampfgruppe Grünwaldt"*. Replacements for the remaining companies of the battle group were gleaned by combing through the trains and from details provided by all of the rear-area services. In the process of doing so, it was realized that the remaining logistics personnel would be overburdened.

Fahrkolonne Lang had more than 269 horses and 59 vehicles at its disposal at the time, which were used constantly for logistics movements and, in addition, supported the *DKS*, *PAR128*, *PGR128* and the "tanker" infantry company.

At noon on 7 December, a battalion of the enemy attacked Hill 140.2 after an intensive mortar-fire preparation and drove off the few defending infantrymen there. In a deliberate counterattack conducted on 8 December by *Panzergrenadier-Regiment 108* and the *II./Grenadier-Regiment 336* the hill was retaken, but it was soon lost again. The friendly losses then prevented any additional counterattack.

Counterbattery fires and the engagement of enemy concentrations filled up the next few days.

On 12 December, the division's operations officer, *Major i.G.* Litterscheid, was transferred out of the division to be reassigned to the force structure branch of the Army General Staff. His successor was *Major i.G.* Weberstedt.

Using the concealment of darkness and a heavy artillery preparation, the Soviets attacked the sectors of *PGR126*, *Grenadier-Regiment 513* and the *II./Grenadier-Regiment 336* at 0330 hours on 14 December. The enemy was turned back at Krassnyj, but he was able to achieve a penetration at Hill 140.7. In seesaw fighting, *Grenadier-Regiment 513* temporarily lost the high ground, but it was able to retake it in the afternoon with tank and artillery support. Twenty-one Soviets were taken prisoner, all of whom belonged to penal companies. They had received the mission to move through the infantry in position and take Hills 136.3 and 140.7. These repeated attacks had the purpose of deceiving the Germans about

70 Editor's Note: = Special-Purpose Divisional Artillery Headquarters. This was an artillery command and control element that probably served essentially the same function of an *Arko*.

the weakness of the forces opposing them and also of preventing the withdrawal of forces to the new Soviet area of penetration near Kirowograd.

On 16 December, the nine operational *Tigers* of *schwere Panzer-Abteilung 506* were sent to the *13. Panzer-Division* at Kirowograd to support it. The heavy tank battalion continued to be attached to the *23. Panzer-Division*, but all of its remaining tanks were undergoing repairs.

On that same day, *PR23* had to form a detail of 250 men to be sent to Madgeburg (Germany) to pick up 50 new *Panthers*. The remaining elements of the *II./PR23* were pulled out of the front lines over the next few days and sent to Nikolskoje for a battlefield reconstitution. *Major* Wolf, the commander of the *I./PR23* replaced *Major* Fechner as the commander of the division's armored group. The *1./PR23* received all of the remaining *Panzer IV's* and the *4./PR23* transitioned to the *Panther*. The following armored vehicles were operational within *PR23* on 19 December 1943: 4 *Panzer V's*; 9 *Panzer IV's*; 2 *Panzer III's*; and 21 *SPW's*.

The year of 1943 drew to a close with counterbattery fires on both sides by artillery, rocket launchers and mortars. The year had brought a long string of difficult operations with it. Great success was achieved and the division earned the respect of both friend and foe under the command of *Generalleutnant* von Vormann. Heavy losses decimated it several times. It entered 1944 as a numerically weak but cohesive combat brotherhood.

The Final Fighting in the Dnjepr Bend 1 January to 29 March 1944

The start of the new year of 1944 was marked by a continuation of the Soviet intention to bring about the decision of the war in the east on the southern front between the Black Sea and the area around Kiev. The enemy ran against the German positions as he had in the autumn months of 1943, employing numerically considerably superior and fresh forces against the weak defensive lines that had been ordered by Hitler on the basis of economic and political considerations. Hitler continued to focus on the Crimea, Nikopol (with its manganese pits) and Saporoshe.

In the salient west of Kiev created by the Soviets during the previous eight weeks, five field armies—the 38th, the 1st Guards, the 1st Tank, the 18th and the 60th—were preparing for offensive operations to the west, south and northwest. Hitler was unable or unwilling to provide sufficient forces for the defense. *Generalfeldmarschall* von Manstein was also unable to secure permission to move the *1. Panzer-Armee*, with its six divisions, from the right wing of the field-army group to the left. Doing so would have meant abandoning the narrow shallow eastern-jutting salient that existed in the Dnjepr bend.

On 29 December, *Heeresgruppe Süd* decided to act on its own. The headquarters of the *1. Panzer-Armee* of *General der Panzertruppen* Hube, transferred its sector to the *6. Armee* of *Generaloberst* Hollidt and, by 3 January 1944, had assumed command and control of the sector from the Dnjepr to an area 45 kilometers southeast of Berditschew (the *XXIV. Panzer-Korps* and the *VII. Armee-Korps* and, later on, the *III. Panzer-Korps*). However, the front in the Dnjepr bend could not be pulled back in accordance with a *Führer* order. Just as these regroupings were taking place, the Soviets launched their offensive on 3 January against the *1. Panzer-Armee* and the *4. Panzer-Armee*, especially directed against the wide gap in the front that existed between these two field armies. At the same time, an offensive was launched in the Kirowograd area against the *8. Armee*. Attack after attack was launched against the frontage in the Dnjepr bend and the Nikopol bridgehead.

The *23. Panzer-Division* did not experience any heavy fighting at the start of 1944. Weaker attackers were turned back by the grenadiers.

The quiet time around the turn of the year was used by the forces of the division to keep on improving the main line of resistance. They constructed trenches, saps and bunkers. Extensive minefields and wire obstacles were emplaced in tireless work by the division engineers of *Hauptmann* Hellwig and the engineers of the regiments. A significant rise in front of the sector of *Kampfgruppe Ruge*, the so-called "Pritzel Hill", was tunneled under and leveled.

The replacements that had been culled from the rear-area services of the division performed well with all of the troop units to which they were attached. Although most of them were older and not experienced in the art of infantry fighting—many of them fathers—they found their way quickly in the unaccustomed environment and served as supports for the young soldiers who followed.

Kampfgruppe Ruge conducted several successful raids, which provided valuable documents concerning enemy intentions and operations. These results were praised several times in division orders-of-the-day. Radio intercept sections of the field army's signals regiment reported the Soviet intention of launching a larger-scale attack in the terrain around the mines. Concentrations of fires—artillery, the rocket-launcher battalion of *Hauptmann* Schiedel and all available heavy weapons—scattered the enemy's concentrations. The division's flash ranging battery determined the location of enemy firing positions, which were then engaged and destroyed by the artillery regiment's 2nd and 3rd Battalions.

After a few days, however, *Panzer-Beobachtungs-Batterie 128*[71] was reassigned from the division to *Beobachtungs-Abteilung 21*, a semi-mobile battalion being reconstituted in Perwomaisk (Ukraine). The light engineer column of *PPB51* was dissolved in accordance with orders received from the German Army High Command.

The acting division commander, *Oberst* Kraeber, was designated as the official commander after his promotion to *Generalmajor*.

On 1 January, *Oberst* Bräuchle left the division. His successor in command of *PGR128* was *Oberstleutnant* Eschenbach.

The *II./PR23* moved to Winniza on 4 January to be issued 70 *Panthers*. The crews that had been sent to Magdeburg were also there. Once again, the well-tested battalion was lost to the division for a considerable period of time. Based on the threatening development of the situation southwest of Kiev, it was allocated to the *1. Panzer-Armee* and forged into a heavy tank regiment under the command of *Oberstleutant* Bäke, along with *schwere Panzer-Abteilung 503* and another battalion of tanks.

On 6 January, the *6. Armee* ordered the formation of a ready-reaction force under the command of *Oberst* Sander. All of the operational tanks and *SPW's* of both the *23. Panzer-Division* and the *9. Panzer-Division* were attached to the battle group. On 8 January, the battle group, which had been attached to the *XXX. Armee-Korps*, assembled in Petrowo Dolina, 40 kilometers east/northeast of Kriwoi Rog. The *304. Infanterie-Division* was defending to the east.

On 10 January, *Hauptmann* Ruge assumed command of *Kampfgruppe Grünwaldt* for *Hauptmann* Grünwaldt, who had gone on home leave.

Hauptmann Neuhaus' *I.(Pz.Haub.)/PAR128* returned from its new equipment training on self-propelled artillery pieces and took up positions around the turn of the year in the area of Losowatka.

The personnel of the *4./PR23* were also dispatched to link up with the 2nd Battalion, where they were to be integrated. They left Kriwoi Rog on 12 January and arrived in Winniza on 18 January.

The enemy attempted repeatedly in front of the sector of the division to garner success through attacks, both with and without artillery preparation. All of the attacks collapsed in front of the main lines, thanks to the good coordination between the grenadiers and the artillery. On 13 January, divisional *Flak* shot down an IL-2.

On 10 January, *Kampfgruppe Sander* moved out to attack an enemy force that had penetrated just southeast of Petrowa Dolina. The enemy

71 The future would see this battery being moved to Poland, into the Tuchel Heath in Germany and then to West Prussia and Danzig. It was effectively destroyed in the fighting there, with its remnants moving to Schleswig-Holstein, where they were interned by the British.

was ejected, but the former main line of resistance was unable to be reoccupied due to a lack of infantry.

Using rolling air force sorties, the enemy continued his attacks against *General der Artillerie* Fretter-Pico's *XXX. Armee-Korps* on 11 January. The infantry of the *304. Infanterie-Division* was completely exhausted; *Grenadier-Regiment 88* of the *15. Infanterie-Division* was sent to their support. As a result of superior enemy defenses, *Panzergruppe Sander* was unable to achieve a convincing success and there were losses sustained among the *SPW's*. On 12 January, the armored group was able to completely destroy an enemy force that had entered Sheltyje by surprise. To the east, the enemy stubbornly resisted in Otrub. Although he was subjected to a deliberate attack, he could not be dislodged. *Kampfgruppe Sander* lost four tanks and there were numerous casualties among the soldiers of the *304. Infanterie-Division*. The following night, Nowo Kowno was lost. The tanks and *SPW's* established a security ring east of the farmsteads of Sheltyje in front of the main line of resistance, which was to be established. The grenadiers were completely exhausted. One enemy tank, a KV 85, was knocked out. On 15 January, only two tanks and six *SPW's* were operational. *Major* Wolf assumed command of this group and returned to the division in Glijewatka on 18 January.

In front of the *23. Panzer-Division*, the enemy conducted large-scale reliefs-in-place. Two raiding parties of *Kampfgruppe Ruge* suffered considerable casualties when they ran into enemy minefields. The *II./Artillerie-Regiment 38* of the *38. Infanterie-Division*, which was attached to the division on 14 January, formed *Artilleriegruppe Pohl* along with the divisional artillery's 3rd Battalion.

Heeres-Flak-Abteilung 278 was employed in area defense along the road to Kriwoi Rog with all of its remaining guns for the month of January.

The enemy in front of the division constructed field fortifications; he brought up materiel and used the railway from Pjatichatki as far as Ternyj to do so. The division's artillery destroyed railway cars, vehicles, antitank guns and observation posts. The Russians answered with their own salvoes, sometimes of heavy caliber. The enemy's artillery successes remained minimal, however. The *4./PAR128* was detached for a few days to the *LII. Armee-Korps*, neighboring on the left, in the Gurowka area. The battery returned to the division on 21 January.

On 22 January, *Hauptmann* Grünwaldt's *Kampfgruppe*, in coordination with *Artilleriegruppe Pohl*, conducted a raid against an enemy trench line that had been extended toward the German lines. The raid was a great success. More than 50 Soviets were killed and a prisoner taken as opposed to only 1 badly wounded casualty and two slightly wounded ones.

The division's *Flak* participated in the fighting, both on the ground and in the air.

Oberst Menton assumed command of *PGR126*.

On 30 January, the enemy moved out to attack the boundary between the *62. Infanterie-Division*, which had relieved the *16. Panzergrenadier-Division* in the meantime, and the *23. Panzer-Division*. The enemy's main effort was between Hill 118.7 (east of Wesselyje Terny) and Hill 109.6. The barrage fires that initiated the assault were placed along the entire sector of *Kampfgruppe Ruge*.

All of the armored elements of the division were collected together under *Oberst* Sander and dispatched by order of the *LVII. Panzer-Korps* to *Generalleutnant* von Hülsen's *62. Infanterie-Division*.

In that sector, the Russians had taken Hill 118.7 and reached Wesselo-Pole. At 0930, the enemy was at the northern edge of the Krutaja defile; further to the east, he had taken Nowo-Ssofijewka and Seleno Pole (Grünfeldt). The divisional artillery, especially *Artilleriegruppe Pohl*, engaged enemy attack movements, artillery positions and even an armored train, which attempted to join in the fighting from out of the area around Hill 109.4 (north of Kolatschewskoje). In the divisional sector proper, the enemy was quiet. Enemy concentrations at Kolomoizewo were shattered by artillery fires.

At 2035 hours, *Panzergruppe Sander* moved out from Nowo Pokrowka to attack. Against heavy resistance, it took Sinowjew. After the loss of two tanks, however, the continued attack on Seleno Pole collapsed.

At 0900 hours on 31 January, 200 Soviets entered the northern portion of Wodjanoje (5 kilometers east/southeast of Sseleno Pole) by surprise. Advancing through Iwanowka, the armored group eliminated the enemy. Ten prisoners were taken, and several antitank guns and mortars were captured. One IL-2 fighter-bomber was shot down.

In the division sector, the enemy was quiet, except for combat raids and harassing fires. Hill 109.6 was firmly under German control; it had become the pivotal point of the front, which ran to the southeast from there.

The originally planned combined attack of the *9. Panzer-Division* and the *23. Panzer-Division* to clear up the area the enemy had penetrated was called off since, in the meantime, the *9. Panzer-Division* was committed in the right-hand sector of the *XXX. Armee-Korps* due to a threatening penetration there.

During the afternoon, *Panzergruppe Sander*, together with the infantry, advanced over soft terrain to attack the Datschnyj settlement and Hill 110.6 to the north of it. Rolling attacks by the Red Air Force interfered with the attack preparations and thick snow squalls then interfered with the attack itself. Despite that, the attack objective was reached at 15.30 hours.

The spoils of war on that day: 29 prisoners; 300 enemy dead; 9 heavy machine guns; 2 mortars; 1 antitank gun; and a truck loaded with munitions.

In spite of the success, the front had to be pulled back during the evening due to the development of the situation in the sector of the *XXX. Armee-Korps*. *Panzergruppe Sander* prepared for further operations in the Krassnoje Pole — Trudoljubowka area.

The divisional artillery, together with the *I./Artillerie-Regiment 162* of the *62. Infanterie-Division*, also engaged Soviet concentrations and fire positions on 1 February. The enemy brought fresh forces, as well as large supply columns, forward without interruption and into the area of penetration in the sector of the friendly forces to the right. The Soviet armored train was driven out of Kolatschewskoje several times.

On 1 February, *PGR128* was relieved by forces from the *257. Infanterie-Division* and sent expeditiously to the sector of the *62. Infanterie-Division*. It turned back Soviet attacks south of Nowo Pokrowskoje and supported the grenadiers in the construction of a new defensive position.

On orders of the field army, *Panzergruppe Sander* was then sent to *Generalleutnant* Roepke's *46. Infanterie-Division* in Stalindorf ("Stalin" village). The armored group arrived at Marjewka on completely mud-bound roads at 1600 hours; it occupied Point +2.2 (four kilometers south of Nowyj Witebsk), turning to the north. The *I.(Pz.Haub.)/PAR128* was relieved from its sector north of Kriwoi Rog and marched to Marjewka to support *Panzergruppe Sander*. The enemy was feeling his way forward in that area against the 3-kilometer-wide gap in the lines. Although the original intent of the *XXX. Armee-Korps* had been to send the armored group, under *Major* Wolf, to Wossnessenskij and the *9. Panzer-Division*, the force remained at the "Progress" Collective farm at the behest of the *46. Infanterie-Division*.

On 2 February, the *6. Armee* came under the command of *Generalfeldmarschall* von Kleist's *Heeresgruppe A*, which previously only had command and control over the *17. Armee*.

On that same day, grenadiers from the *257. Infanterie-Division* relieved the *II./PGR126*, which was moved into the area southeast of Kriwoi Rog for new employment.

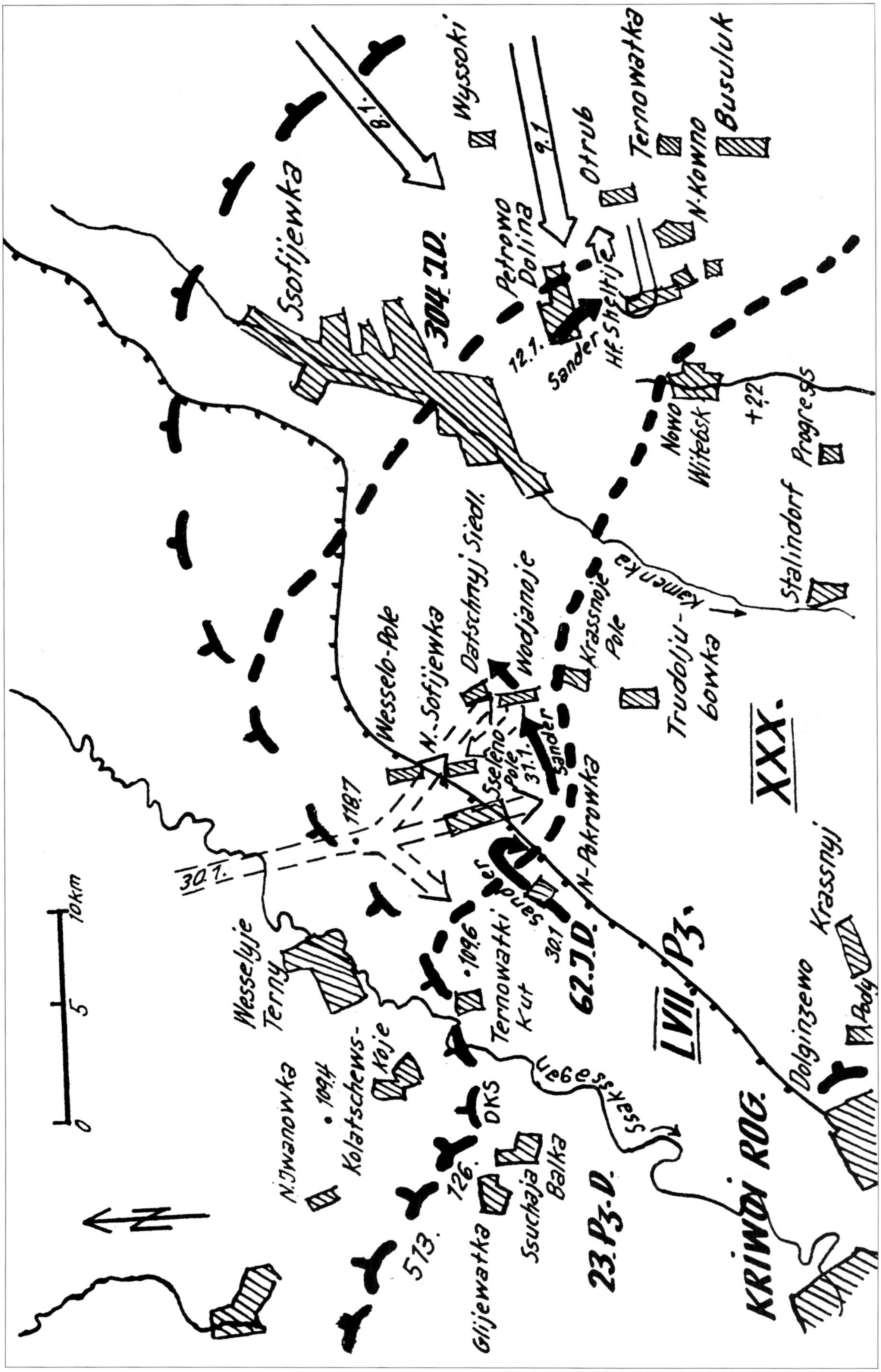

Map 64: Counterthrusts Conducted by *Panzergruppe Sander* within the Sector of the *XXX. Armee-Korps* from 8 to 31 January 1944.

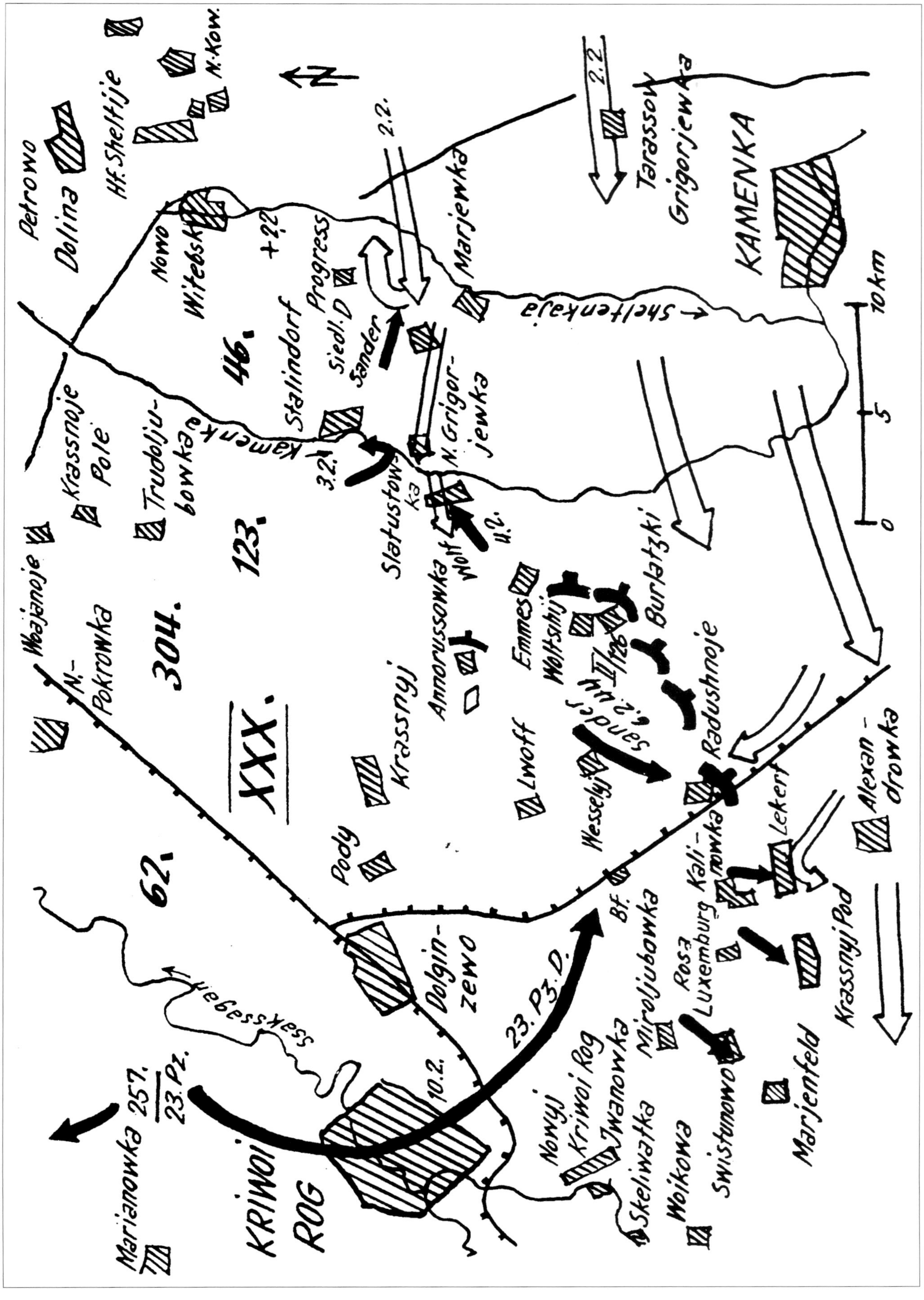

Map 65: Fighting Between 2 and 9 February Southeast of Kriwoi Rog.

The enemy did not attack in the division's sector. *Panzergruppe Sander* was fixed at Settlement "D" (8 kilometers south of Stalindorf) at noon on 2 February by the attack of two Soviet regiments, supported by 10 KV-85's. The launchers mounted on the *SPW's* inflicted heavy casualties on the enemy infantry; one tank was destroyed. During the effort to establish contact with the *9. Panzer-Division* at the Tarassowo — Grigorjewka settlement, *Major* Wolf ran into Soviets. During the night, both Settlement "D" and Nowo Grigorjewka to its west were lost, although heavy casualties were inflicted on the attackers.

The front bent increasingly more sharply to the south from the focal point of Hill 109.6, which continued to be held by the brave grenadiers of the *62. Infanterie-Division*. Every attempt to attack and every concentration of enemy forces north of Hill 109.6 was shattered by the artillery. The *7./PAR128* shot down an enemy aircraft, and the pilot was taken prisoner.

During the day, the localities of Nowo Pokrowka and Ternowatkyj were lost in the sector of the friendly forces on the right. The hills were held, however.

The armored group had shrunk to two tanks and seven *SPW's*. A counterattack on Nowo Grigorjewka, which was defended by 20 antitank guns and tanks, failed, with the result that the armored group had to pull back to Slatoustowka, where it covered the withdrawal movements of the *46. Infanterie-Division*. Toward noon, that locality was also lost in fighting with 35 enemy tanks and two to three regiments of infantry. Two German tanks were also lost. The infantry forces of the *46. Infanterie-Division*, which had been composed of alert units, were in no position to offer serious resistance.

The deep mud throughout the countryside caused even the movements of the enemy to slow down.

The *II./PGR126*, together with alert units from *PR23* and *PAR128*, arrived on 4 February at the location of the armored group, which was being led by *Major* Wolf. Together with those forces, the armored group retook Slatoustowka. Several assault guns and *SPW's* got stuck in the mud and could not be freed up again. When the area was abandoned in the afternoon, they had to be blown up.

The *II./PGR126* fought along the deep right flank of the armored group, where it conducted defensive and offensive operations around Burlatzki and Woltschij. Further to the south, enemy tanks had advanced as far as the Apostolowo — Kriwoi Rog road and rail line.

The armored group was ordered to Anorussowka at 1600 hours. Troop elements of the division moved wheeled vehicles back to the improved roads around Kriwoi Rog as a precaution against the "mud period". Among the artillery, the loss of numerous prime movers started to become a concern.

On 6 February, the armored group was ordered to move to the Radushnoje train station as quickly as possible, since enemy tanks were advancing along the rail line to Kriwoi Rog after a deep penetration. Three *Panzer IV's*, one command tank, four assault guns, one *SPW* and three self-propelled *Flak* arrived at the march objective shortly before midnight.

The *II./PGR126*, along with the attached alert units, successfully defended against several enemy attacks from its strongpoints in Burlatzki and Woltschij.

On 7 February, several Soviet raids penetrated into the main line of resistance of the division north of Kriwoi Rog. All of the penetrations were cleared up in short order, and the main line of resistance remained firmly in German hands. As on the previous days, the artillery engaged enemy movements.

In the area of *Panzergruppe Sander,* the Soviets were ejected from Krassnyj-Pod and the Lekert Colony. The enemy managed to hold Alexandrowka.

On 8 February, the *8./Panzer-Artillerie-Regiment 102* of the *9. Panzer-Division* took over the positions of the *4./PAR128*, which had been withdrawn to the south.

The enemy was assembling strong forces in front of *Panzergruppe Sander*, apparently with the intent to advance on Kriwoi Rog. Replacements for the *23. Panzer-Division*, which had arrived at the Radushnoje train station, were held up there by *Oberst* Sander due to the threat of an enemy attack. They were immediately employed as security.

On 9 February, the *8./PAR128* was withdrawn from its former positions.

Due to its minimal infantry forces, *Panzergruppe* Sander had to give up the "Rosa Luxemburg" Settlement and Kalinowka. *Major* Wolf was wounded. *Panzergruppe Sander* was ordered to Miroljubowka with the mission from the field army to screen the gap between Sswistunowo and the Ingulez in a mobile defense.

In the sector of the division north of the city, the attacking enemy infantry forced a penetration west of the Nedai Woda – Kriwoi Rog road. That same night, the former main line of resistance was restored in an immediate counterattack.

On 10 February, the headquarters of the division turned over command and control of the sector it had been successfully defending in heavy fighting since 22 October to the *257. Infanterie-Division*. The troop formations of the division were gradually withdrawn and moved to the area southeast of Kriwoi Rog, where the armored group, the *II./PGR126* and alert units were already fighting. The only formation of the division to remain in its formor sector was *Kampfgruppe Ruge*, forced to remain there due to its limited mobility.

As a result of the rain- and snowfall of the previous few days, the road network and the terrain had become a sea of mud. All movement took place at a snail's pace; one vehicle after the other became disabled, drowning in mud. Regardless of all of the difficulties that the enemy forces were also exposed to, the Soviet command drove forward its formations from the area around Apostolowo to the west and northwest. It hoped to cut off and take the city of Kriwoi Rog and its German defenders from the south.

Coming from the area northeast of Dolginzewo, *PGR128* arrived in the new sector of the division. Initially, only a few half-tracked and fully tacked vehicles arrived, because the seemingly bottomless mud had ripped all of the wheeled vehicles, whether motorized or horse-drawn, from every march serial and strewn them across the entire march route. The regimental headquarters initially remained just west of Dmitrijewka, which was still occupied by the trains elements of the infantry divisions. It was there that it was originally intended to occupy the established Kamenka Position, also known as the "Ursula" Position.

Panzergruppe Sander moved out at first light on 10 February from Sswistunowo to the southwest. It was supposed to establish contact with the *16. Panzergrenadier-Division*, which was located around Schirokoje. Strong enemy formations had already crossed the Schirokoje — Kriwoi Rog road and were positioned along the Ingulez. Under the concealment afforded by the morning fog, the armored group advanced west through the enemy-occupied "Marjen Field" Settlement. At 0630 hours, it encountered a Soviet antitank-gun belt at Point 99.3. The completely surprised enemy was overrun; 15 prisoners were taken. In a continued rapid advance, Nowo-Nikolajewka and Nowosselowka were cleared of the enemy. The infantry of the *16. Panzergrenadier-Division* succeeded in Ingulez of regaining the village and the hills to the east of it, by exploiting the southern advance of *Panzergruppe Sander*. Schirokoje remained in enemy hands. A shortage of fuel and ammunition forced the armored group to return to its original line of departure. Two assault guns and two tanks had to be abandoned east of Ingulez. The former due to a lack of fuel and the latter due to mechanical problems. While moving back,

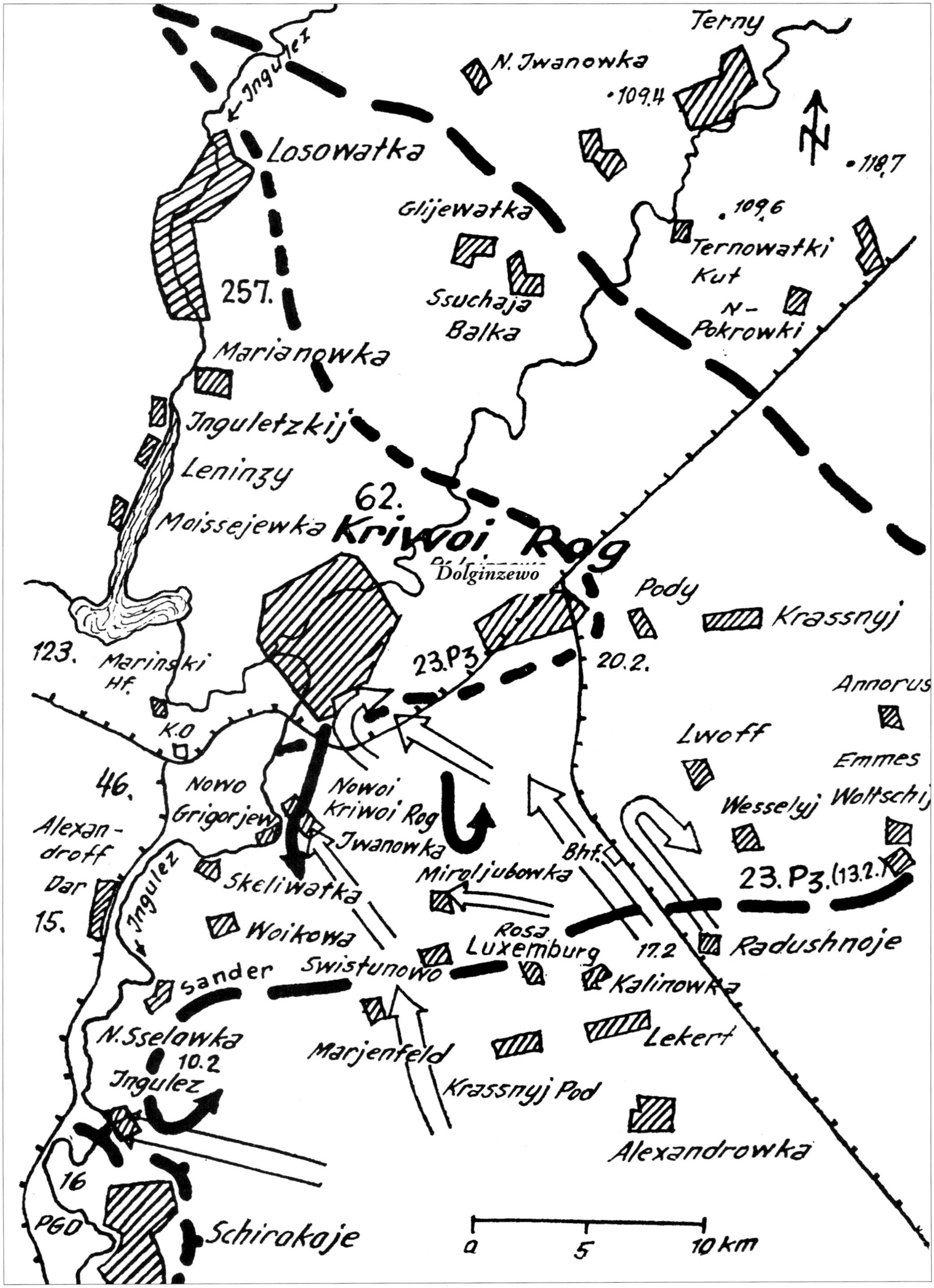
Terny
N. Jwanowka
109.4
118.7
109.6
Losowatka
Ingulez
Glijewatka
Ternowatki Kut
N-Pokrowki
257.
Ssuchaja Balka
Marianowka
Inguletzkij
Leninzy
62.
Moissejewka
Kriwoi Rog
Dolginzewo
Pody
Krassnyj
123.
Marinski Hf.
23.P3
20.2.
Annorus
K.O
Lwoff
Emmes
46.
Nowo Grigorjew
Nowoi Kriwoi Rog
Wesselyj
Woltschij
Alexandroff
Jwanowka
Bhf.
Dar
Skeliwatka
Miroljubowka
23.P3.(13.2.)
15.
Woikowa
Rosa Luxemburg
17.2
Radushnoje
Sander
Swistunowo
Kalinowka
N.Sselawka
Lekert
10.2
Marjenfeld
Ingulez
Krassnyj Pod
Alexandrowka
16
PGO
Schirokaje
0
5
10 km

new enemy infantry forces were attacked and scattered. In all, 12 antitank guns, 16 antitank rifles, 6 heavy machine guns and 8 trucks were captured or destroyed and 35 prisoners were taken. Two Soviet rifle regiments were considered to have been badly beaten and wiped out. As a result of this advance, valuable time was gained for setting up the defense along the Ingulez and around Kriwoi Rog.

The final elements of the divisional artillery north of Kriwoi Rog were relieved by *Panzer-Artillerie-Regiment 102* during the course of 11 February. The mud forced the employment of two prime movers for each gun, in order to pull it out of its position. Since one command vehicle after the other was lost to enemy action or mechanical problems, the artillery battalion commanders and forward observers increasingly switched to a proven means of transportation from earlier conflicts—the horse. The batteries went into positoin around the Wesselyj settlement.

Oberstleutnant i.G. Weberstedt assumed command of the armored group from *Oberst* Sander. From Sswistunowo, the armored group took and retook the "Marjenfeld" Settlement numerous times, after masses of enemy infantry continued to enter it.

Heeres-Flak-Abteilung 278, which was employed in the area defense of Kriwoi Rog, received its entire complement of weaponry during this time period.

The division defended, oriented to the south, along the line running Sswistunowo — Kalinowka — Radusnoje train station — Nowaja Sarja collective farm — Burlatzkij settlement — Woltschij settlement — Emmes. There were only small strongpoints along the overextended frontage; the artillery registered final protective fires to protect them. On the left wing of the division, the enemy stayed relatively quiet.

On 14 February, the armored group advanced into the rear of the enemy and enabled the main line of resistance to be moved forward to Hill 105.8 (4 kilometers west of Nowjy Ssad).

After the enemy's rapid thrust toward the Ingulez and Kriwoi Rog was thwarted primarily by the countermeasures of *Kampfgruppe Sander/ Weberstedt*, he attempted to go around the right wing of the division. At the same time, he brought forward fresh forces along the division's left wing. The counterattack of the *24. Panzer-Division* and the *3. Gebirgs-Division* in the area south of Apostolowo, which led to the sealing off and clearing up of a penetration to the south, did not appear to disrupt the Soviet preparations for an attack. The mud restricted every measure and countermeasure to the smallest of areas.

On that day, *Oberstleutnant* Eschenbach, the commander of *PGR128*, ran into a Soviet ambush, when he was riding horseback with two others on their way from Emmes to the area around Dmitrijewka and the "Ursula" Position, which was supposed to be there. He had wanted to conduct reconnaissance. He was wounded in the ambush and taken prisoner. Acting command of the regiment was passed to *Oberleutnant* Roltsch until *Major* Stetting could arrive.

During the night of 15/16 February, there was a sudden frost and heavy snow squalls. That meant new difficulties for the combat troops and the ever-decreasing numbers of vehicles.

On 17 February, Soviet infantry, supported by tanks, moved out to attack on both sides of the Apostolowo — Kriwoi Rog rail line. They broke through the weak defensive lines of the infantry between Kalinowka and the Radushnoje train station, occupied Nowo Wladimirowka and entered the "Meadows" collective farm, south of Kriwoi Rog, with weak advanced forces. While the fighting around Nowo Wladimirowka ended in a defensive success for the division after the two changed hands several times, the enemy was able to hold on to the area west of the railway line. In a counterattack, the armored group set seven armored vehicles, including two assault guns, alight in the area around Hill 101.5. There were not any infantry forces available to restore the situation, however. An *ad hoc* infantry platoon under the command of *Leutnant* Schreiber that was hastily assembled from knocked-out crews and trains personnel from *PR23* went into position south of the bridge at Miroljubowka. In a dismounted attack, the tankers stormed the bridge as it turned dark, thereby opening the connection between Miroljubowka and Kriwoi Rog that had been lost. The *4./PAR128* assumed responsibility for protecting the rear area for the main body of the division that was east of the railway line. It went into a firing position at the Lwoff settlement, with the guns oriented to the west.

Map 66: Fighting Around Kriwoi Rog from 10 to 21 February 1944.

On 18 February, the enemy moved out against the division along its entire frontage. The positions had to be pulled back, but the enemy did not continue to press.

Through a counterattack, the "Meadows" collective farm was cleared of the enemy in the morning by the infantry. The *III./PAR128* wet into position at the point on the map marked "Kas. Staw".

Miroljubowka was evacuated in the course of the morning by the infantry in the face of attacking enemy. An unsuccessful counterattack was launched by the tanks under *Leutnant* Herlitschka; his *Panther* was knocked out and he was reported as missing. The armored group was pulled back to the "Meadows" collective farm, since the Soviets had entered Nowyj Kriwoi Rog, 6 kilometers to the west, in the meantime.

Together with two tanks from the *9. Panzer-Division*, the armored group attacked Nowyj Kriwoi Rog, drove the enemy out and pursued him through Iwanowka to the south. A bridgehead was established around the two localities, against which the Soviets stormed incessantly, but without being able to take the key position.

On 19 February, the front was pulled back further to the southern edge of Kriwoi Rog — Dolginzewo. The artillery went into position around the Pody farmstead and the area to its south. The *23. Panzer-Division* received the mission to cover the withdrawal movements of the division that were still fighting east of the city. *Panzergrenadier-Regiment 126* was pulled out of its former positions in the line and went into position south of the Ingulez bridges. During the night of 19/20 February, the artillery started to change positions to the west bank of the Ingulez in the area around Krassnaja Poljana, which was only possible on a gun-by-gun basis due to a lack of prime movers. The 7th Battery had to blow up its last cannon, along with its non-operational prime mover, in the face of the attacking enemy.

Oberst Sander was given responsibility for the defense of the bridges over the Ingulez.

When the enemy crossed the Ingulez at Skeliwatka, 10 kilometers south/southwest of Kriwoi Rog, *Leutnant* von Oechelhaeuser attacked the enemy's bridgehead with a *Panther*, four *SPW's* and a few infantrymen and reduced it. The west bank of the Ingulez was cleared of the enemy. Sixty prisoners were taken and the positions were handed over to elements of the *15. Infanterie-Division*. Rocket launchers from *Werfer-Regiment 54* played a great role in the success of the operation, by eliminating several enemy antitank guns and artillery pieces on the east bank of the river.

In the iron works at Kriwoi Rog, *Hauptmann* Veigel's *II./PGR126* attacked an enemy force that had advanced as far as the regimental command post and drove it back. The 1st Battalion also had to fend off constant enemy advances. The village and rail station of Tscherwona, just east of the Ingulez, were taken in seesaw offensive and defensive fighting. The German losses were considerable. *Panzergrenadier-Regiment 128* went into position to the left of *PGR126* and defended the southeast portion of the city.

The infantry and divisional engineers had been in combat for three days without a break. They were unable to sleep or eat a warm meal. But they defended their positions in the broken-up terrain of the industrial part of the city with unshakeable resolve.

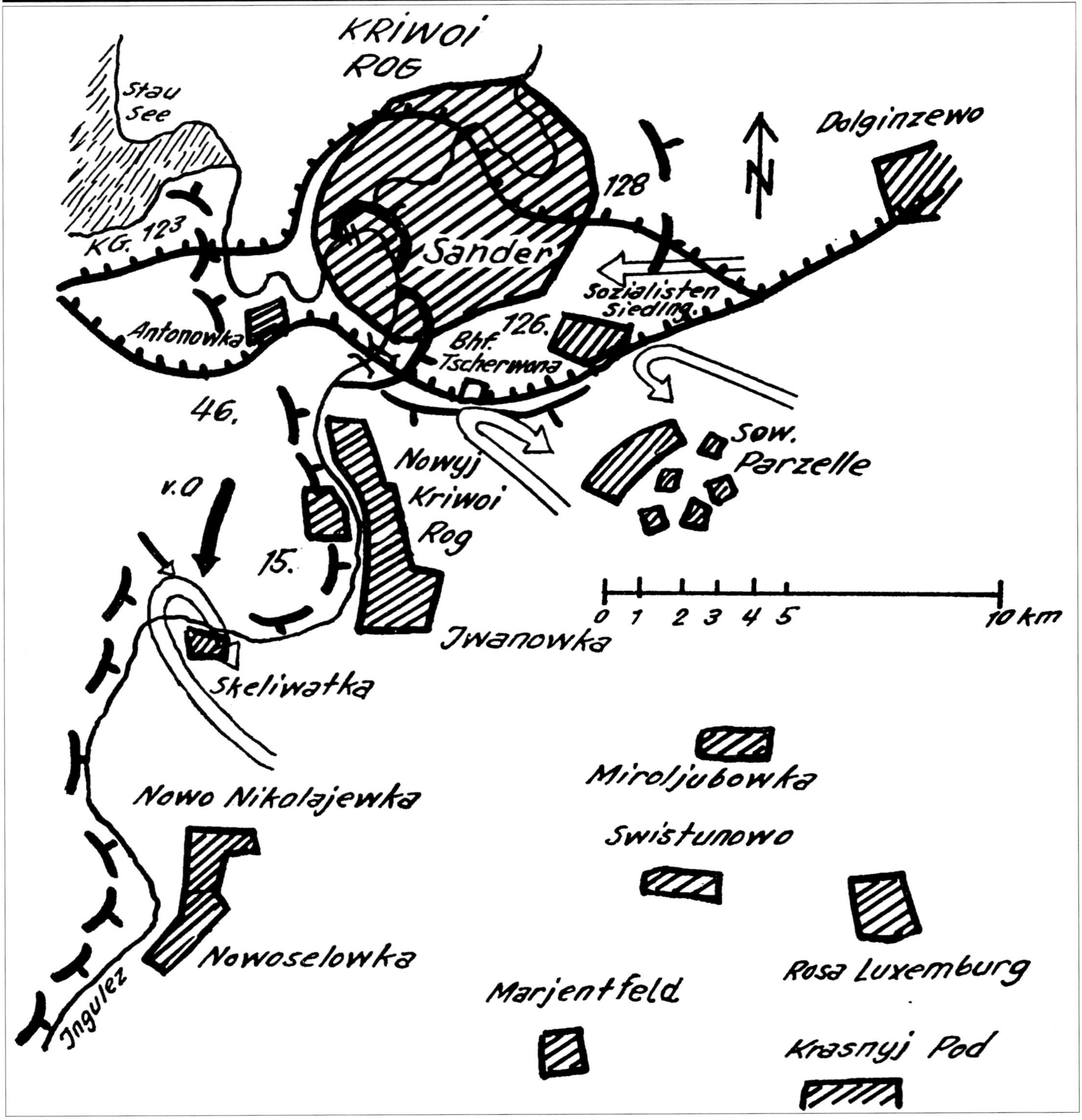

Map 67: The Evacuation of Kriwoi Rog on 22 February 1944.

In the city proper, demolitions of facilities important to the war effort had been ongoing for several days, including some facilities that had only come about after the Germans had occupied Kriwoi Rog. Civilian personnel and engineers from the field army were employed to do that.

The male population of Kriwoi Rog had already been moved to a processing camp west of the city as a precautionary measure to prevent any type of partisan activity. The women and children left behind were quiet.

The withdrawal of the divisions of the *XXX. Armee-Korps* from the sector east and north of Kriwoi Rog took place behind the positions of the *23. Panzer-Division*. In the course of those withdrawal movements, the former sector of the division north of the city between Ssuchaja Balka and the high ground north of Nedai Woda were also evacuated. *Kampfgruppe Ruge*, which was employed along the right wing of *Generalleutnant* von der Goltz' *257. Infanterie-Division*, also pulled back, step-by-step, along with *Oberstleutnant Freiherr* Grote's *Grenadier-Regiment 466*.

On 21 February, *Oberst* Sander assumed command for the entire defense of Kriwoi Rog along its southern and southeastern edges. The forces were placed at his disposal by the division: *PGR126*; *PGR128*; *PAA23*; *PJA128*; *schwere Panzerjäger-Abteilung 560*; *PPB51*; elements of *Grenadier-Regiment 88*; elements of *PR23*; the assault battalion of the *6. Armee*; and all of the forces belonging to the local area commander for Kriwoi Rog that were in the southern and eastern parts of the city.

Oberstleutnant Vogl, the commander of *PAR128*, assumed responsibility for the artillery battle of the main line of resistance, in coordination with *Oberst* Sander. The enemy tactic of infiltration could not be effectively countered with artillery, however. The enemy ceaselessly attempted to infiltrate through the thinly held line of strongpoints manned by the division. By doing so, he was able to occupy the "Socialist" settlement on the southeastern part of the city. An immediate counterattack launched by two tanks and two *SPW's*, along with a few infantrymen, failed in the face of the strong enemy superiority. The enemy employed an exceptional number of tank hunter/killer teams.

A Soviet attack against the Kriwoi Rog brickworks was turned back by the engineer platoon of the *8./PGR126* in close combat.

Durchgangsstraße IV[72] from Kriwoi Rog to the west was temporarily blocked by the enemy, with the result that *SPW's* had to fight their way through. Under the cover of *Kampfgruppe Sander*, the last trains of the division, as well as *46. Infanterie-Division* and the *123. Infanterie-Division*, which had still been fighting east of the city, crossed over the Ingulez and moved off to the west. Late in the afternoon, the first Soviets followed in their footsteps and entered the city from the east.

To the north of Kriwoi Rog, the *62. Infanterie-Division* and the *257. Infanterie-Division* had pulled back in the meantime to a half circle around the northeast and north of the city. During the withdrawal movements that continued during the night of 21/22 February, the enemy advanced into a gap that was not covered between the left wing of the *62. Infanterie-Division* and the right wing of *Kampfgruppe Ruge*. The battle group forces, under the command of *Hauptmann* Ruge, thwarted these enemy efforts and pushed them back to Ssuchaja Balka. At the same time, *Kampfgruppe Ruge* screened the orderly withdrawal of the two divisions along the northern edge of Kriwoi Rog to the west.

Kampfgruppe Sander was also able to hold its positions on 22 February. As a result, it was able to cover the establishment of a new line of defenses along the east bank of the Ingulez by the infantry divisions. Around 1500 hours, the individual elements of *Kampfgruppe Sander* were able to be withdrawn incrementally and pulled back to the bridges over the Ingulez. The enemy pressed hard and occupied the city. The last elements to fight in the city were the engineer platoon of the *8./PGR126* and *SPW*-mounted elements of the *10.(Fla.)/PGR126*. They pulled back to the high ground at Antonowka and then departed during the night for Wesselyj Gai.

Three tanks and six *SPW's* under the command of *Oberleutnant* Gauglitz advanced into the city from the bridges over the Ingulez one more time at 0500 hours on 23 February. They advanced against constant resistance in the direction of the slaughterhouse and inflicted heavy casualties on the thickly massed groups of advancing Soviets. After the Gauglitz' armored group returned at 0635 hours, the last bridge over the Ingulez was blown up. Later on, *Oberleutnant* Gauglitz was awarded the Knight's Cross to the Iron Cross for his exploits in Kriwoi Rog.

The *III./PAR128*, which had not only the regiment's 4th Battery attached to it, but also the *1.* and *2./Heeres-Flak-Abteilung 278*, participated in shattering enemy attacks and concentrations in front of the sector of the *15. Infanterie-Division* from its positions around Krassnaja Poljana. It was especially active in the area of Nowjy Kriwoi Rog. One IL-2 fighter-bomber was shot down. Heavy employment of Soviet artillery and air-force assets allowed no abatement of combat activity. However, the heavy snowfalls of the previous few days did let up.

The division was pulled out of the front to serve as the immediate counterattack reserve of the field army, but it was being torn apart more and more during this period. As much as the mud allowed, the trains were dispatched toward Wossnessensk, moving via Kasanka and Nowyj Bug. Most of the logistics facilities were in Nowyj Bug, with the quartermaster staff in Kasanka. With a great deal of difficulty, individually stranded vehicles were recovered.

The 2nd Medical Company of *Stabsarzt Dr.* Stenger established a clearing station in Nowo Sselowka, 10 kilometers east of Kasanka, under extraordinarily difficult conditions. It was constantly overfull. In addition, the mud made the transportation situation catastrophic.

On 24 February, the *III./PAR128* was ordered to Nowo Skelewatka, 30 kilometers northwest of Kriwoi Rog, to support the *79. Infanterie-Division*. It arrived there on 26 February with the headquarters battery and the one heavy howitzer of the 9th Battery. Through the seemingly bottomless mud, another heavy howitzer of the 8th Battery eventually followed. The rest of the battalion was not operational and assembled in Kasanka.

The *Panzergruppe* was dispatched at night on 24/25 February to Schwedowka, 20 kilometers southwest of Kriwoi Rog, to serve as a ready reserve. During the morning of 25 February, it was already being summoned to the sector of *Generalmajor Graf* Hülsen's *62. Infanterie-Division*. One *Panzer V*, one *Panzer IV*, one *Panzer III* and twelve *SPW's* were operational.

On 26 February, the armored group was sent to the sector of *Generalmajor* Röpke's *46. Infanterie-Division*. *Hauptmann* Koppe, the commander of *PAA23*, led the march, while *Oberst* Sander conducted a leader's reconnaissance of the tactical options for attack against the Marinskij farmstead and the limestone works. At 1100 hours, the battle group, under the command of *Hauptmann* Koppe, moved out to attack and rallied *Bataillon Fuchs* from the *46. Infanterie-Division* along with it. Stubborn enemy resistance was shattered, and the former main line of resistance west of the limestone works was restored. *Hauptmann* Koppe was wounded, and *Oberleutnant* Abel assumed acting command.

The division commander, *Generalmajor* Kraeber, issued the following order-of-the-day on 24 February:

> The difficult defensive fighting around Kriwoi Rog has come to a conclusion. For a quarter of a year, the division has been in the focal point of the fighting for this city. Its resistance at Wesselyj Kut, Nedai Woda and Krassnyj broke the strength of the attacking Russian forces in November and December.
>
> Drawn back into the fighting as a result of the Russian penetration in the area of operations of the *XXX. Armee-Korps*, the infantry protected the threatened southeast flank of Kriwoi Rog in three weeks of extremely heavy fighting under unimaginable weather conditions. At the same time, the armored group inflicted the heaviest of losses in men and materiel on the enemy over and over again in a mobile defense south of the city. Brought forward in forced marches, the division bore the main burden of defense in the fighting for the city. It is thanks to its fighting and the heroic devotion to duty of every man that our comrades in the neighboring divisions were able to pull back and reestablish themselves west of the city. The enemy took heavy casualties in the city in heavy street and house-to-house fighting. As a result of the deliberately planned demolitions, nothing of value fell into the hands of the Russians. I extend my greatest appreciation to the leaders and the forces in the field for their performance in marching and fighting. The division has proven itself worthy of its fallen comrades.
>
> Hail to the *Führer*!
>
> /signed/ Kraeber

Kampfgruppe Ruge pulled back to the west along with the *257. Infanterie-Division*. It was positioned behind that division as a ready reserve.

On 27 February, four tanks, one assault guns and six *SPW's* were operational. Soviet barrage fires led to the conclusion that they were

72 Editor's Note = Movement Route IV. This was essentially a main supply route that was intended to allow rapid movement into and out of Kriwoi Rog.

planning a new offensive west of Kriwoi Rog. The armored group scattered an enemy attack consisting of four tanks and infantry south of the Kriwoi Rog — Kasanka rail line. The Russians penetrated the lines of the *62. Infanterie-Division* on the left, however. The Russians crossed the Ingulez at Inguletzkij and advanced on Rodjonowka.

The enemy forced a penetration along the boundary between the *62. Infanterie-Division* and the *257. Infanterie-Division* and threatened the elements of the latter division in the flank along their bridgehead at Losowatka. *Hauptmann* Ruge's *DKS* personnel moved out to conduct a counterattack in the afternoon and threw the enemy back to the east along a line running Marjanowka — Losowatka. Te former main line of resistance was reoccupied. In addition to many dead and prisoners, the enemy lost numerous small arms and seven antitank guns.

Kampfgruppe Sander was brought forward through Christoforowka during the night and attacked from the south on 28 February with 12 *SPW's* from *PAA23* and infantry from the *62. Infanterie-Division*. At the same time, it attacked from the north with five tanks and escorting infantry. The attack had to be conducted twice before the enemy bridgehead was reduced and the main line of resistance was in friendly hands again. The tank and *SPW* crews only suffered three wounded. In contrast, 45 antitank guns, 8 7.62cm howitzers, 12 antitank rifles and 20 machine guns were destroyed. The enemy left behind some 300 to 400 dead in the area of penetration. *Leutnant* Engel of the *I./PR23* especially distinguished himself.

At 1130 hours on 26 February, *PGR126* was alerted and prepared to be employed as a ready reserve behind the sector of the *62. Infanterie-Division* in Krassnoje Utro.

Panzergrenadier-Regiment 128 was employed on the right wing of the *62. Infanterie-Division*, where it was drawn into heavy fighting east of Sselenyj Gai. The regiment, which basically only had its headquarters and a 30-man-strong battalion under *Hauptmann* von Kleist, once again took heavy losses.

During the night of 28/29 February, *PGR126* assumed the sector to the right of *PGR128* in the main line of resistance.

Kampfgruppe Ruge had to be employed again in order to throw back the enemy forces that had penetrated into the sector. The night attack failed, however, due to the attentiveness of the defending enemy. A Soviet counterattack was thrown back, and a firm line of resistance established from the southern tip of Losowatka to Hill 90.1.

On 29 February, one *Panzer III*, three *SPW's* outfitted with launchers and four *SPW's* were sent to Rodjonowka as a ready reserve. At noon, the headquarters of *PR23* was ordered to Nowyj Bug; the operational tanks and *SPW's* of the regiment were attached to *Oberleutnant* Abel's *PAA23*.

The enemy also moved out against the frontage of the infantry. Heavy fighting ensued. Thick fog made support by *PAR128* difficult. Nowo-Goonzowka was lost; the farmsteads at Marinskij were hotly contested. By means of immediate counterattacks, the penetrations of the Soviets were sealed off and cleared up by the *II./PGR126*.

Kampfgruppe Ruge, with its 46 men, was relieved from attachment to the *257. Infanterie-Division* and returned to the fold of the *23. Panzer-Division*. In order to reactivate the division's replacement battalion—*Panzer-Feldersatz-Bataillon 128*—the remaining personnel of the successful battle group were sent to the trains area west of the Bug and, later on, to Tecuci in Romania. The acting commander of the battalion was *Oberleutnant* Pritzel, who was previously the battalion adjutant.

On 1 March, the headquarters of the *23. Panzer-Division* assumed command of the defense of the sectors of the two infantry regiments. Soviet attacks on 3 March had as their intent the collapse of the entire German front west and southwest of Kriwoi Rog. While they succeeded in penetrating into the lines of the infantry division neighboring on the right, the infantry were able to successfully defend their sector. The *II./PGR126* was pulled out of the line in its sector and employed in guarding the right flank. The enemy attacked again on both 4 and 5 March. Small penetrations were cleared up by the infantry and the divisional engineers, who were reinforced by the antitank battalion and the armored group.

Hauptmann Rebentisch, formerly the assistant operations officer of the division, assumed command of the *I./PR23*.

The regimental staff of *PR23* arrived in Nowyj Bug on 2 March. The *III./PAR128* was relieved of its attachment to the *79. Infanterie-Division* and marched back in thick mud over the course of two days through Mitro-Belowka to Kasanka.

Despite the seemingly bottomless mud, the enemy continued to attack. The wide tracks on his armored vehicles prevented them from sinking too much. The light, tough steppe horses he employed also proved themselves to be considerably superior to their German counterparts. In the face of the Soviet infantry, who were driven forward in attacks in masses and without consideration of casualties, the thinly manned German lines were powerless. Heavy barrage fire was placed on the main line of resistance from 0830 to 0945 hours on 6 March. The enemy soon broke through the German lines at the Ingulez. The alert was sounded for Nowyj Bug, where the headquarters of the *6. Armee* was located, and for Kasanka. On his own initiative, *Oberst* Sander organized a local defense in Nowyj Bug with the dismounted elements of his regiment. In Kasanka, the local area commander, *Generalmajor* Beisswänger, incorporated the *III./PAR28* into his defenses. The battalion, which had the 4th and 9th Batteries and a field-army cannon battery, was unable to do much due to a shortage of ammunition.

On that day, the *23. Panzer-Division* was able to hold its portion of the main line of resistance against all attackers. The enemy continued to conduct constant thrusts during the night of 6/7 March as well.

On 7 March, the field army headquarters evacuated Nowyj Bug. Long rows of wheeled vehicles were stuck and helpless in the knee-deep mud on all of the roads in the area of operations.

Based on the deep penetration of the enemy in the direction of Nowyj Bug and the numerous other advances across the main line of resistance north and south of the division's sector, the front was pulled back. During the night of 7/8 March, the infantry were located in and around Makarowka. The enemy was already marching to the west, however, south of those positions.

The main clearing station in Nowo Sselowka was performing miracles. The main problem for the medical personnel was the evacuation of the wounded. During the evening of 7 March, there were still some 150 wounded there; the last of them were finally evacuated on the *Panje* carts of horse-drawn trains elements.

At 0330 hours on 8 March, enemy tanks and cavalry entered Nowyj Bug. Soviet cavalry advanced against the city from the north, east, south and southwest. Panic broke out among the withdrawing trains, which started to flee; vehicles were set on fire. As a result, the escape route was completely blocked. In the midst of the chaos, the local population started attacking the German forces.

The few combat forces in the city were incapable of offering any type of defense by the flood of fleeing trains elements from numerous divisions. *Oberst* Sander and *Oberleutnant* von Brandenstein of the *II./PR23*, who happened to go there by chance, rallied some 30 infantrymen, a long-barreled *Panzer IV* and six assault guns in order to keep at least the southern bridge over the creek that flowed through the city open. The enemy had already entered the city from all sides by then. At 1030 hours, *Oberst* Sander ordered a breakout to the west. Three assault guns were knocked out by strong antitank gun and antitank rifle belts, which had to be overrun, before the rest of the small battle group was able to assemble on the road to Olenowka 2 kilometers south of the city. Enemy horse patrols

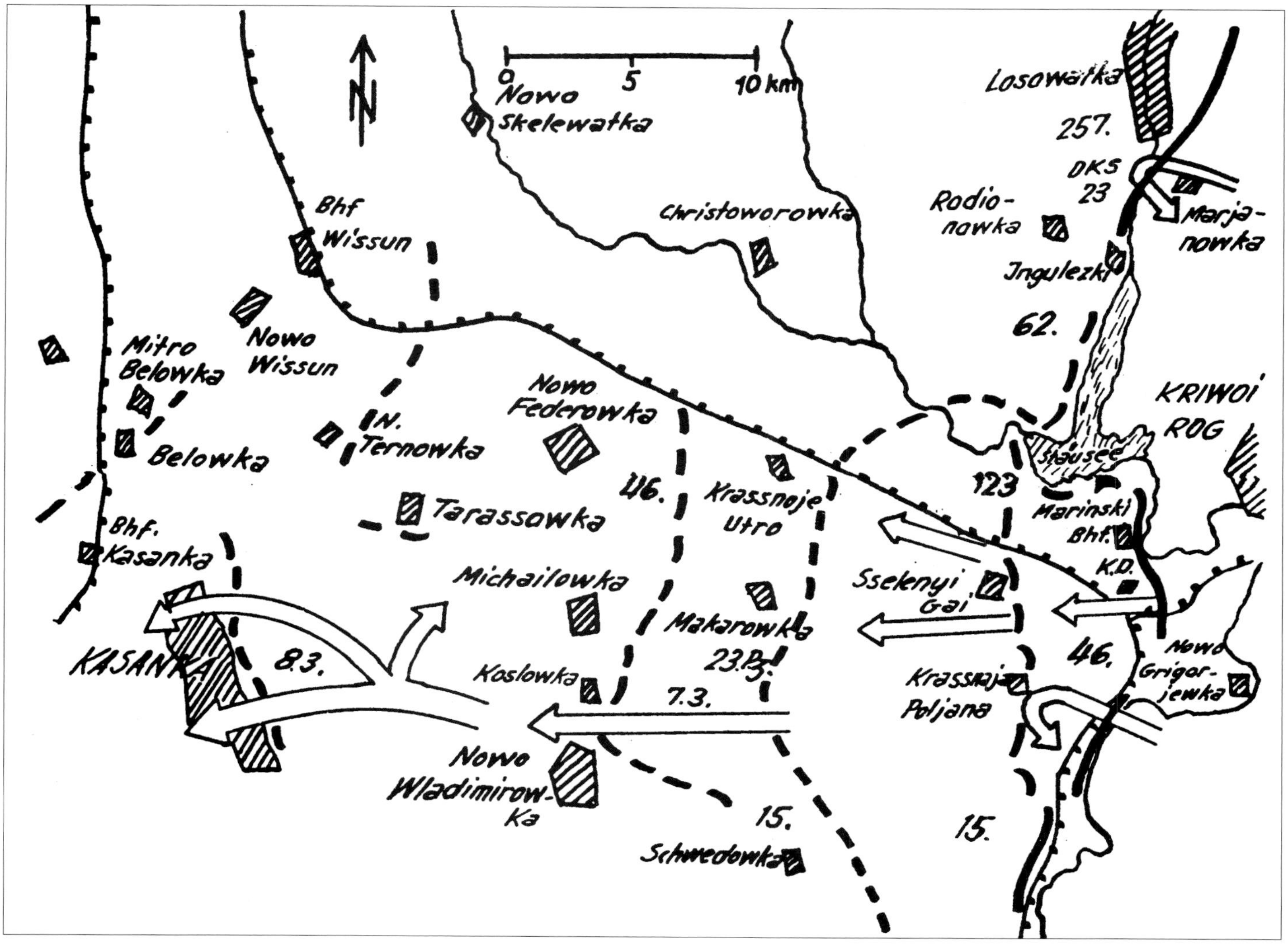

Map 68: Soviet Breakthrough to Kasanka, 7 and 8 March 1944.

were already feeling their way around that area and further to the west. A local defense was established around Olenowka and its bridge over the Ingulez. The headquarters of *PR23* went to Olgopol.

In the catastrophe associated with Nowyj Bug, the division lost its field post office for the second time. In addition, the maintenance company was lost, the 1st Medical Company (except for its 3rd Heavy Platoon), large portions of the division's logistics elements and the trains of all of the field forces. The mud made every attempt to escape to the west in a motorized vehicle a hopeless undertaking. The majority of the soldiers were able to save themselves on foot, but some of them later fell into the hands of the Soviet cavalry formations that had already advanced further west.

The forces in Kasanka set up a local defense during the morning. One tank, one assault gun, one *Hummel* self-propelled gun and three light howitzers from the *24. Panzer-Division* were employed along the southern edge of the locality, along with a 60-man-strong company from a security battalion. The main line of resistance north of the Soviet area of penetration was pulled back during the day to a line running Wesselyj Gai — Nowo-Wladimirowka — Michailowka — Nowo Fedorowka. In the evening, Soviet tanks entered Nowo-Wladimirowka.

The command post of the *23. Panzer-Division* was in the northern part of Kasanka. The city, especially the southern part, was completely filled. Troop elements, scattered units and trains from assorted divisions blocked the roads. The deeply muddy condition of the roads prevented leaving the city. Streets at a time were blocked by motorized vehicles that were massed, three-abreast, next to one another. No tank, no prime mover was able to get through there. Unclear command and control relationships did not allow for a cohesive defense of the city.

The armored group of the division (*PR23* and *PAA23*), which had shrunk to just two assault guns and a radio communications center from *PNA128* due to losses, was ordered to the northern part of the city during the morning of 9 March to defend there. The *2./PAA23*, which was under the command of *Oberleutnant* Schulz and was equipped with light *SPW's*, was to join the armored group. It had just arrived. Before those orders could be executed, however, enemy tanks broke through the German positions 5 kilometers east of Kasanka at first light. At 0700 hours, the first T-34's appeared in front of the two guns from the 4th Battery. One of the T-34's was destroyed. Moving across Hill 116.8 and to the north of it, 40 T-34's advanced and entered the city. Panic broke out, especially since the local area commander had ordered *Kanonenbatterie 711* to change positions to the western part of the city just before the attack. The guns of the *III./PAR128* were overrun or had to be blown up, since the infantry forces providing security immediately pulled back. The intended rail loading of non-operational weapons and vehicles at the Kasanka rail station had been rendered senseless by the capture of Nowyj Bug the previous day. One light field howitzer was evacuated by *Leutnant* Sommer, however.

The two assault guns of the *1./PR23* got bogged down without being able to gain a field of fire against the T-34's attacking somewhat to the south of them. Both had to be blown up. The radio vehicle was knocked out, killing two radio operators in the process. Radioed orders from the division that were received just before that happened dictated that *Hauptmann* Rebentisch was to take over the entire defense of the city. By then, however, the enemy had already penetrated deeply into Kasanka. The remaining forces set off to the west and northwest by foot. As a result of the gigantic spoils of war he had gained in Kasanka, the enemy did not follow. That was salvation for many soldiers, damaged weapons, tanks, self-propelled guns and assault guns.

In addition to what remained of *PAR128*, the division staff lost all of its equipment in Kamenka, as well as all of the 2nd Medical Company with its many ambulances and numerous trains elements.

South of Belowka, *Hauptmann* Rebentisch and his small band linked up with the *2./PAA23*, which had just arrived. The halftrack company represented the only intact combat organization of the division at the moment. Just west of Pischtschewewiza, it initially took over the mission of securing the road to Ustinowka. During the evening of 9 March, it established an outpost line along the Ssagaidak Defile.

The division headquarters moved through Beresowka to Bobrinez.

The infantry regiments—more accurately, their weak remnants—were positioned at the start of 9 March along a thin outpost line east of Koslowka and Michailowka. At 0300 hours, Soviet infantry and tanks entered Koslowka from the southwest and forced the infantry to pull back. *Panzergrenadier-Regiment 126* set up for the defense around Tarasowka, 10 kilometers northwest of Koslowka. Further to the south, the enemy was pressing west everywhere. At 1600 hours, the regiment pulled back to Taranowka. *Panzergrenadier-Regiment 128* was positioned immediately to the left of *PGR126*.

The following night, the *Panzergruppe* received orders to march southwest on 10 March and conduct a reconnaissance-in-force against the enemy who was advancing west from Nowyj Bug. The main body of the division, largely moving on foot, assembled south of Bobrinez in the area of Wassiljewka — Tarasowka. *Oberst* Sander and his regimental headquarters were ordered to Wossnessensk. The field trains of the division were directed to the area around Neikowa (also entered on the maps as Gnadenfeld or "Mercy Field"), 60 kilometers southwest of Wossnessensk as their objective.

Without encountering the enemy, the armored force felt its way east from Wesselyj Podol and Baselewo. On 11 March, it was attached to the *24. Panzer-Division*, where it continued to perform the same mission.

Panzergrenadier-Regiment 126 was attached to the *46. Infanterie-Division* and pulled back with that division along its right wing, moving through Ssoldatski and Maltschewskij. By 12 March, it reached the Korneitschenko area, where it returned to the fold of the division.

In the days that followed, the trains were scoured and cadre companies were formed from the division's troop elements, however, the *ad hoc* elements formed were not employed.

The armored group, which continued to be attached to *Generalmajor Freiherr* von Edelsheim's *24. Panzer-Division*, again monitored the area east of Olgopol on 12 March. On 13 March, the armored group had the remaining operational tanks of the *9. Panzer-Division* and the *24. Panzer-Division*—three *Panzer IV's* in all—attached to it. It observed the Soviet movements from outpost positions around Olgopol. The Soviets had shifted their main effort further to the south, in order to envelop the northern wing of the *6. Armee*.

The remnants of *PGR126* and *PGR128* were brought forward to Budenny on 13 March, since the *23. Panzer-Division* was tasked by the *LVII. Panzer-Korps* to hold open the retreat route to Wossnessensk, along with the *24. Panzer-Division* and those elements of the *384.Infanterie-Division* and the *257. Infanterie-Division* that were still capable of combat operations. In addition, they were to delay the Soviet advance.

At 1430 hours on 14 March, both of the regiments—whose combined strength was about that of a battalion—attacked Hill 105.9, east of Olgopol. The attack bogged down in the enemy's strong defensive fires. Mortar fires inflicted heavy casualties on the infantry, with *PGR126* suffering 25 wounded in addition to several dead.

The infantry were attached to the battle group of *Oberst* Péan, which consisted of elements of the *16. Panzergrenadier-Division*. On 15 March, they screened the area around and to the southwest of Olgopol, orienting south. The men were exposed to the wet and cold weather without any type of protection in the deeply muddied terrain. The requirement to screen the retreat of the division on the left, as well as maintaining some assistance for the corps of the *6. Armee* that had been enveloped by the Soviets further south, forced that kind of employment.

In the meantime, the armored group screened along the high ground south and southeast of Jelanez. The lead elements of the Soviet armored and cavalry forces were already west of the Gniloj Jelanez and had no more natural obstacles between them and Wossnessensk.

During the night of 15/16 March, the infantry pulled back to the west as part of four other divisions. During the morning, they reached Kolewka, marching via Ssakino, in an icy wind and the sudden onset of snow squalls. During the morning of 17 March, they were employed in screening in Schewtschenko, south of Jelanez. The enemy restricted his activities to mobile patrols.

After the armored group was released from attachment, the infantry were also released from their attachments at 1730 hours on 17 March and headed back to the division in Wossnessensk. They moved with great difficulty on foot. By the evening of 18 March, they passed the bridgehead position at Wossnessensk, which was manned by infantry. Almost all of the combat and field trains had been lost, since it was inconceivable of recovering them because of the horrific road conditions and the lack of recovery vehicles.

In the attempt to comb through its trains elements west of the Bug, there were a series of grotesque events as a result of the blocking of all Bug crossing points by the bridgehead commander of Wossnessensk, *Oberst* Weikinn, who had the command authority of a Commanding General. The commander of the *III./PAR128*, who had been empowered by his regiment to comb through the trains, was held up at the ferry point at Akmeschet so as to be presented to *Oberst* Weikinn. He had to flee in order to carry out his mission. But because every weapon and every man, regardless of his mission, was held up at the Bug crossings, whether going to or coming from the front, and incorporated into the bridgehead defense, the artillery commander's mission of combing through the trains proved to be a mission impossible.

After days of assembling and waiting for its future mission, the division received orders on 21 March to move into the Kischinew area. The movement took place partially by rail, partially by *Panje* cart and partially by foot. In expectation of difficulties in procuring rations, the forces in the field drove large herds of livestock to the west with them. The division headquarters and the headquarters of *PR23* moved to Odessa, right near the field-army headquarters.

While large portions of the division were held up at the Dnjepr crossings at Tighina and Tiraspol due to the congestion, the elements that had arrived in Kischinew were sent on to Jassy. Heavy snow squalls, which led to large drifts, and the complete traffic jams along the roads, often paralyzed all movement. When it reached its assigned area east of Jassy, the practically wiped-out division started a new chapter in its struggle against the Soviets.

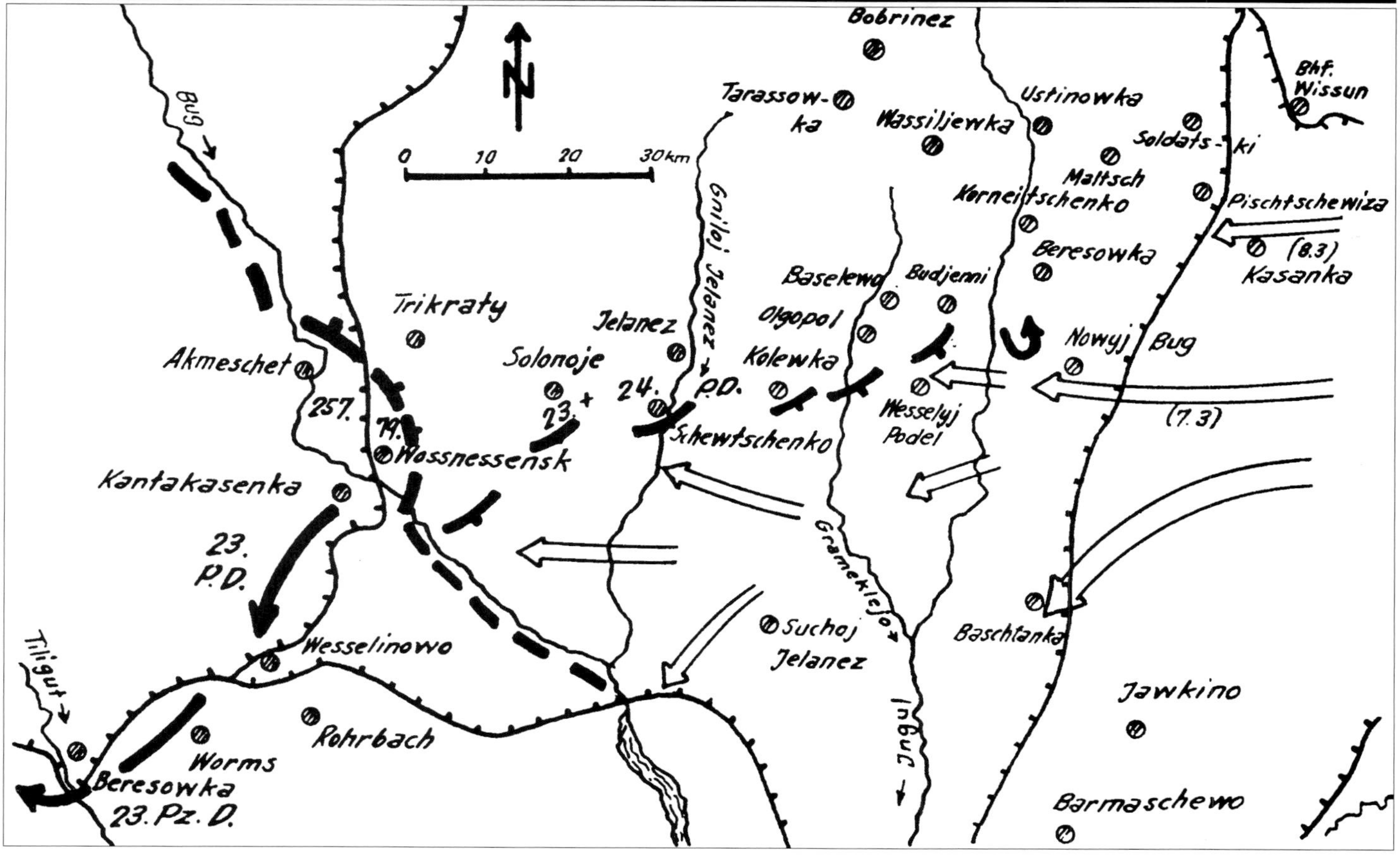

Map 69: Fighting Retreat to the Bug, 9-23 March 1944.

Through Transnistria[73] to the Pruth and the Fighting for Jassy 1 April to 25 July 1944

Ever since Kriwoi Rog had been retaken by the Soviets, the front along the sectors of *Heeresgruppe Süd* (*Generalfeldmarschall* von Kleist) and *Heeresgruppe A* (*Generalfeldmarschall* von Manstein) had no respite. Hitler increasingly intervened in the conduct of operations. He closed his eye to the arguments of his commanders-in-chief, only to agree to them at the last moment, when it was already practically too late. At the same time, he then attempted to shove off responsibility to those same commanders-in-chief. He did not keep his promises to introduce fresh forces; at the most, he released individual divisions, which then had to be tossed into the hot spots of the defensive fighting in the face of Soviet forces breaking through, where they were ruthlessly employed and exhausted. He could not be convinced to conduct a large-scale and militarily practical shortening or pulling back of the various fronts, which would have freed up forces. Usually he entrenched himself behind the argument of political necessity. For example, he clung to maintaining the Crimea, where the *17. Armee* of *Generaloberst* Ruoff, with its five German and seven Romanian divisions, as well as numerous coastal protection formations, were fixed. In the continental portion of the Soviet Union, Hitler also fixed strong forces in so-called "*feste Plätze*",[74] which he ordered defended to the last. It was his nonsensical hope that he would thus bring the Russian advance to a standstill by the blocking of important transportation nodal points. Severe sacrifices were the consequences. The divisions at the front received materiel only sparingly and, above all, no infantry replacements, with the result that their combat power sunk to a minimum.

The enemy quickly recognized his great opportunity. He tore broad and deep gaps in the German front with powerful thrusts of his formations, which had either been rapidly replenished or were completely new and fresh ones. His tanks advanced unimpeded across the frequently bottomless mud of the Ukraine.

The Soviet offensive of March 1944 had not only thrown the *6. Armee* out of a salient along the lower course of the Don that jutted out like a balcony. Above all, it had also pushed back the *1. Panzer-Armee*, along with the neighboring corps from the *8. Armee* on the right and the *4. Panzer-Armee* fighting on its left, in several operational chess moves. The German forces had been pushed back to Bessarabia, the Carpathian Mountains and the area around Lemberg (Lvov). The fronts had been ripped open, and the *1. Panzer-Armee* was encircled around Kamieniec-Podolski. The Dnjestr and Pruth Rivers had been crossed. Czernowitz (Cernauti) and Kolomea (Kolomya) were in Soviet hands. The attack spearheads of the enemy advanced into the Carpathians as far as the Jablunka Pass.

Despite the considerable loss of area, the *6. Armee* was still echeloned far to the east. As a result of a Soviet advance across the Dnjestr to

73 Editor's Note: According to Wikipedia, "Transnistria, during World War II, was a region of the USSR, occupied by Romania, during the maximum eastward expansion of the Axis Powers, from August 19, 1941 to January 29, 1944. Limited in the west by the Dniester river, in the east by the Southern Bug river, and in the south by the Black Sea, it comprised present-day Transnistria (which compared to the whole was only a small portion along the bank of the Dniester) and territories further east, including the Black Sea port of Odessa, which became the capital of Transnistria during WWII." (http://en.wikipedia.org/wiki/Transnistria_%28World_War_II%29)

74 Editor's note: = literally "firm places". These were akin to the modern military usage of the term "strongpoint", which was a position on the ground that was fortified to the point it was almost impregnable, the holding of which denied the enemy valuable terrain or bought time for other measures. That was the concept, however, the reality was often quite different and the *feste Plätze* often only served to eliminate even more vital German combat forces from areas where they could have been more usefully employed.

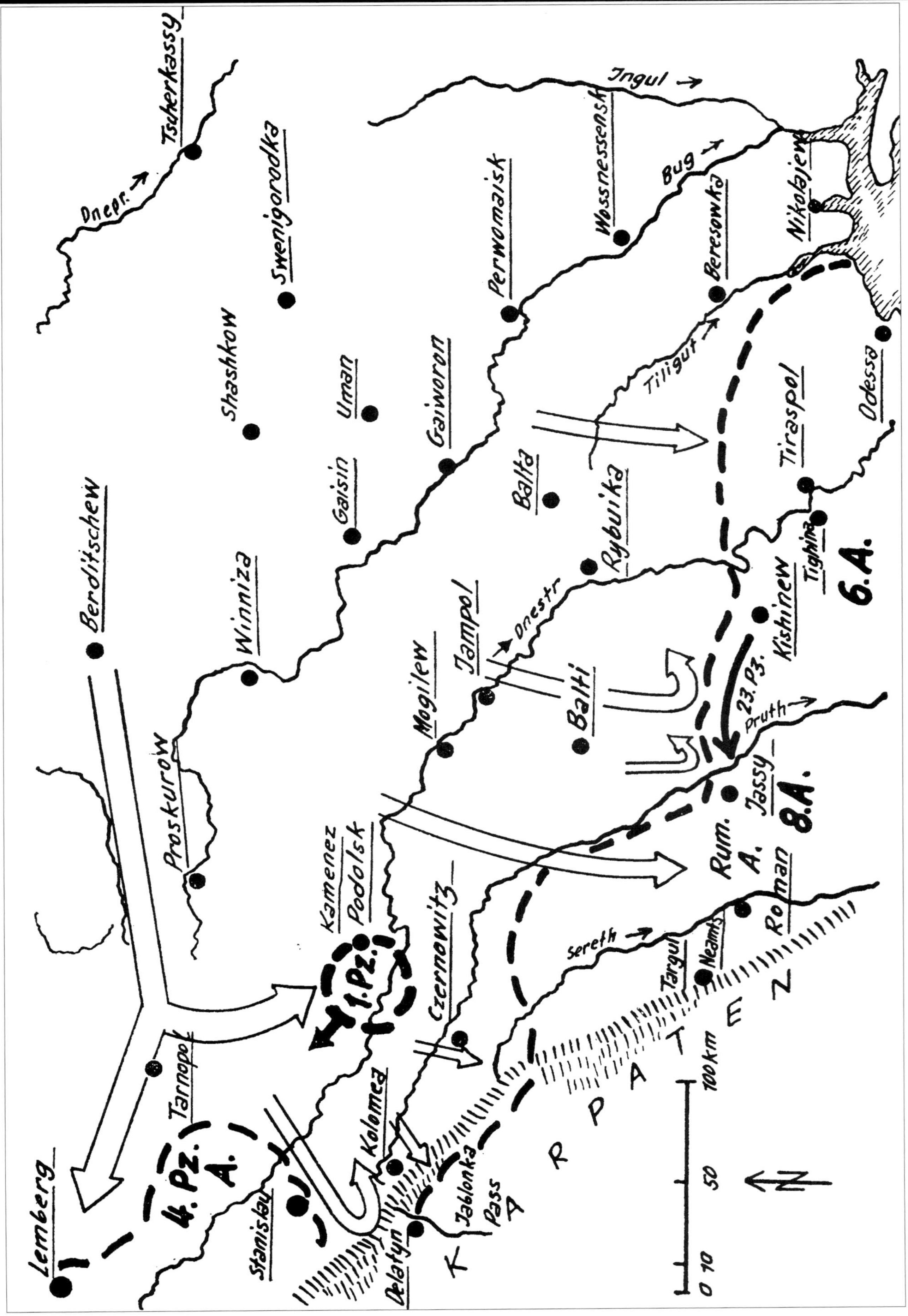

Map 70: The Situation at the beginning of April 1944.

the south, it, along with the main part of the *8. Armee*, was threatened with encirclement, if the effort did not succeed in moving powerful combat forces all the way through Bessarabia to throw against the enemy.

Initially, only *Panzergrenadier-Division "Großdeutschland"*, the greatly weakened *24. Panzer-Division* and the equally weak *79. Infanterie-Division* were available. They were rapidly moved through Kischinew (Chisinau) and thrown into the area around Jassy.

The *23. Panzer-Division* was no longer capable of combat operations after the loss of all of its tanks, the majority of its SPW's and wheeled vehicles, its artillery and *Flak*, and its infantry combat power. The logistics services of the division paid for the Soviet breakthrough at Nowyj Bug and Kasanka and the mud with roughly 75% of their materiel.

As much as possible, the troop elements of the division were transported by rail to Odessa from the Beresowka — Rohrbach area. Other troop elements marched by foot and rode on the few remaining motorized vehicles across the Tiligut at Beresowka to Tiraspol, where they crossed the Dnjestr under the walls of the old Turkish fortifications.

After four days of rest in Odessa, the two infantry regiments reached Kischinew by rail on 30 April. There they were consolidated into one regiment—*PGR126*—under *Oberst* Menton within 48 hours. Prior to the consolidation, neither "regiment" had more than a battalion's worth of men. *Panzergrenadier-Regiment 128* was dissolved. *Major* Stetting became the commander of what was left of *Kampfgruppe Ruge*, which was being reformed into the division's replacement battalion in Tecuci (Romania). The new *II./PGR126* under *Hauptmann* Veigel consisted of the two former battalions of the regiment. The *I./PGR126*, which consisted of the consolidated battalions of *PGR128*, was under the command of *Hauptmann* von Kleist. The *3./PPB51* was disbanded.

At the same time, *PR23* received orders to take over the training of the tank regiment of the Romanian 1st Imperial Tank Division "Romania Mare" in the Bacau area. To that end, it was to employ its personnel from its headquarters, the 1st Battalion and the Maintenance Company. In case of an alert, it was to use the German equipment that had been provided to the Romanians to go into battle, since they were not yet capable of operations. *Hauptmann* Rebentisch assumed acting command of the regiment, and the personnel were transported by aircraft of the Imperial Romanian Air Force from Kischinew to Bacau on 1 April. The motorized vehicles that were still on hand followed in a land march, while all non-essential remaining elements and trains were assembled in the division's designated area around Marasesti — Tecuci.

The *3./PAA23*, as well as the *SPW* battalion of the tank regiment, which had lost all of their vehicles, were attached to *PR23* for the training of the Romanian division.

Most of the divisional artillery was not capable of deployment. From all of the guns that remained, only three batteries could be formed, which were consolidated as an *ad hoc* 1st Battalion (mixed) and remained available for employment. All of the remaining elements of the regiment were sent to Tecuci for reconstitution.

The *2./PAA23*, which was still intact during the retreat to the Bug, arrived in Kischinew at the end of March after additional operations with its light *SPW's* in the Nikolajew area and north of Odessa. *Panzerjäger-Abteilung 128*, which had been reduced to a weak company with only a few guns, likewise assembled in Kischinew, along with the weak remnants of the division's engineers. *Heeres-Flak-Abteilung 278* had lost all of its guns and was only capable of being employed as infantry. Almost without exception, the logistics services were horse powered, after they had left their motorized vehicles behind in the mud. The division's medical services section once again had an operational heavy platoon in its 2nd Medical Company.

During that time of the almost complete destruction of the division, the reinforced *Grenadier-Regiment (mot.) 1031* was sent to Kischinew and assigned to it. In addition to his two line battalions, the regimental commander, *Major* Stichtenoth, had a heavy gun company (the 9th), an antiaircraft company (the 10th), an antitank company (the 11th) and an engineer company (the 12th).

Grenadier-Regiment (mot.) 1031 had been formed on 28 November 1943 by order of the Chief of Army Armament and Commander of the Replacement Army in the 2nd Wave of Replacement Forces in Bochum. It consisted primarily of convalescents from the *6. Panzer-Division* and the *16. Panzer-Division* and their replacement detachments. Most of the soldiers hailed from the Rhineland and Westphalia. The first regimental commander was *Oberstleutnant d.R.* Möller, with the commander of the 1st Battalion being *Hauptmann* Römbke. After a short formation period, the regiment trained at various training areas.

It was sent to the Odessa area in February 1944 (Altannenthal) to prepare for combat operations, and it received its baptism in the defensive fighting along the Dnjepr and the Ingulez between 23 February and 6 March 1944. From 7 to 26 March, it was involved in the defensive fighting north of Nikolajew and employed during the fighting retreat to the Bug. *Major* Stichtenoth assumed command of the regiment on 4 March.

Elements of the regiment—the regimental headquarters and the engineer company—had been employed with *Oberst* Schulz-Hein's *15. Luftwaffen-Feld-Division* with the mission of taking Barmaschewo. Under the command of *Major* Stichtenoth, the *II./Luftwaffen-Jäger-Regiment 9, Pionier-Bataillon 635, Pionier-Kompanie 1031*, the *III./Artillerie-Regiment 179*, the *2./Heeres-Kanonen-Abteilung 145*, a heavy field howitzer battery and two platoons of self-propelled antitank guns attacked and took the locality. By doing so, an important obstacle behind the withdrawing *6. Armee* had been eliminated.

Ever since 27 March, the regiment had fought north of Kischinew against Soviet lead elements that had advanced across the Dnjestr.

On 28 March, the *24. Panzer-Division*, which had assembled in Kischinew, moved out to attack through to Jassy and Targul Frumos and create the prerequisites for establishing a new front for the *8. Armee* in a line running Jassy — Targul Frumos — eastern edge of the Carpathians. Elements of *Panzergrenadier-Division "Großdeutschland"* followed it. Advanced Soviet elements had already established themselves along the road just east of the Pruth. They were driven back by the battle groups from the two divisions, which followed one another. Despite that, additional enemy forces infiltrated constantly.

The *23. Panzer-Division*, which had been attached to *General der Infanterie* Mieth's *IV. Armee-Korps*, received the mission on 31 March to reach the Jassy area behind *Panzergrenadier-Division "Großdeutschland"* as quickly as possible with advanced forces. *Kampfgruppe Stichtenoth* was formed from the following organic and attached forces: Headquarters of reinforced *Grenadier-Regiment (mot.) 1031*; the regimental signals platoon; elements of the regiment's antiaircraft company (one 2cm *Flak*); *PAA23* (minus two companies); *Heeres-Flak-Abteilung 278* (as infantry); the *2./PPB51*; the *1./Grenadier-Regiment 226* of the *79 Infanterie-Division* (elements attached outside of normal command and control mechanisms); the *II. (gemischte)/PAR128*[75]; and three guns from *Sturmgeschütz-Batterie 1017*.

The march, which took place in bitterly cold weather and considerable snow flurries, did not encounter major enemy forces. Ungheni Targ was reached after marching through Calarasi Targ. There, a Soviet battalion ambushed the elements of the divisional artillery and scattered them. It took some time to reassemble the battalion.

The battle group reached Jassy on 2 April and assumed responsibility for screening the city to the north. Armored reconnaissance patrols from *PAA23* reconnoitered north of Jassy and established contact with

75 Editor's Note: *gemischt* = mixed (Denoting an element that has subelements of differing weaponry. In this instance, light and heavy guns.)

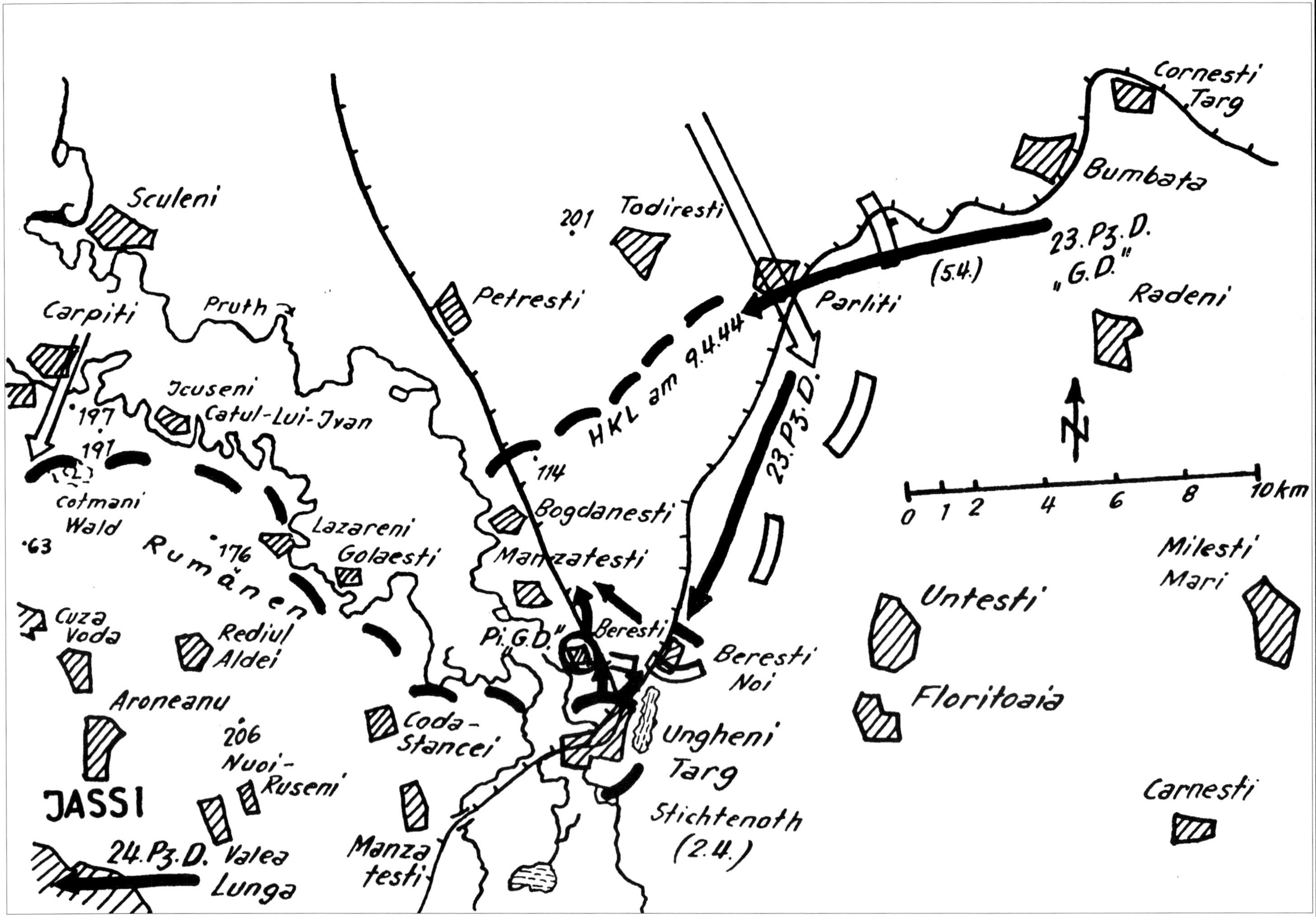

Map 71: The Fighting Around the Ungheni Targ Bridgehead from 2 to 9 April 1944.

weak outpost forces. Only Romanian forces were positioned there. That same day, a field-expedient armored train was fabricated, consisting of flat cars with *SPW's*, antitank guns and two squads of infantry. The train was given the mission of screening the rail line running from Kischinew —Calarasi — Ungheni Targ — Jassy and the road parallel to it. It was to be especially vigilant in the sector running from Parliti to Ungheni Targ and to keep the stretch open for the march of the *23. Panzer-Division*. The train had barely left Ungheni Targ for the east, when Soviet assault detachments blew up the rail line behind it. Demolished rail line was also reported in front of the train. Engineers were able to quickly repair the damage at Ungheni Targ, however.

Major Tiedemann, the commander of *PJA128*, received orders to bring a train full of munitions for *Panzergrenadier-Division "Großdeutschland"*, which was fighting at Parliti, from Kischinew to the west. The trains rolled forward through no-man's-land and in a snowstorm, at least until the Romanian train personnel fled. A noncommissioned officer of the battalion then served as the train's engineer and continued the movement. The antitank soldiers had to shovel the way clear for the train out of a deep snow bank, before they were able to deliver the munitions to *Panzergrenadier-Division "Großdeutschland"*, as ordered. The train was unloaded while under artillery fire.

The main body of the *23. Panzer-Division* moved out of Kischinew on 2 April, including the artillery-manned "infantry" company of Husemann. The intense storm and the deep snow drifts barely allowed any forward advance, with the result that only smaller, more mobile elements reached Calarasi. It had been directed that the division reach Jassy by 3 April. Strong snowfall that night with new, high snowdrifts tore the columns apart. It took 15 hours to cover a march distance of 18 kilometers. Even the soldiers of *Panzergrenadier-Division "Großdeutschland"*, who headed out in advance, were unable to make forward progress.

Kampfgruppe Stichtenoth was attached to *Generalmajor Freiherr* von Edelsheim's *24. Panzer-Division* in Jassy on 3 April. On 4 April, it was employed in the bridgehead at Ungheni Targ, which had previously been defended by two squadrons of the Romanian 5th Cavalry Division and two 7.5cm antitank guns. The *II./PAR128* was still not capable of combat operations, with the result that the battle group had to rely on its organic heavy infantry weapons.

The march serials of the division arrived in Calarasi in the meantime. *Panzergrenadier-Regiment 126* moved out at 1400 hours and reached Cornesti. Elements of *Panzergrenadier-Division "Großdeutschland"*, along with the division headquarters, were bogged down there. *Generalleutnant* von Manteuffel briefed the troop elements of the *23. Panzer-Division* that were arriving and discussed the planned attack on the Soviet forces, which were blocking the road at Parliti, on 5 April.

In the bridgehead at Ungheni Targ the report arrived at 1900 hours that *Panzer-Pionier-Bataillon "Großdeutschland"* had been encircled in Beresti, 3 kilometers to the north, and was in a critical situation. It had suffered considerable casualties while under heavy enemy fire. The battalion reported it would cross the Pruth to the west at night and pull back to the south.

At 0030 hours on 5 April, a detachment from the *"Großdeutschland"* engineers reported that the crossing attempt had failed and that help was urgently needed. At that point, *Hauptmann* Koppe's *PAA23* was funneled through the belt of mines around the bridgehead and set out to attack in the direction of Beresti with eight *SPW's*, two assault guns of *Sturmgeschütz-Batterie 1017*, one 7.5cm antitank gun and 62 grenadiers from the *5./Marsch-Bataillon Kothe*.

High snowdrifts forced *Hauptmann* Koppe to advance along the only road. The fighting started outside of Beresti. The enemy was overrun and a breakthrough into the village was effected with the *SPW's* and assault guns leading the way. The village, which was already partially occupied by the enemy, was cleared. At 0630 hours, the ring around *Panzer-Pionier-Bataillon "Großdeutschland"* had been broken open. The enemy pulled back. Following after him, the grenadiers of the march unit drove the enemy 1.5 kilometers further to the north. One assault gun and the 7.5cm antitank gun remained to support the engineers in Beresti, and the rest of the battle group returned to Ungheni Targ. Without suffering any losses, the following spoils of war were claimed: 1 7.62cm antitank gun and 1 medium mortar destroyed; 2 antitank rifles, 10 submachine guns, 10 light machine guns (with ammunition) and numerous semi-automatic rifles and rifles captured. The enemy lost 30 dead and 7 prisoners were taken. It was interesting to observe that the majority of the enemy soldiers were personnel who had just been conscripted from the retaken Ukrainian areas, many of whom had been employed by the German authorities.

During the day, the division occupied blocking positions in front of Parliti; in the afternoon, the village itself was occupied. *Kampfgruppe Stichtenoth* was notified by radio that the division intended to advance to Ungheni Targ on 6 April from Parliti.

On that same day, it was ordered that *Grenadier-Regiment (mot.) 1031* be assigned to the division and redesignated as *Panzergrenadier-Regiment 128*. The antitank company of the regiment was detached and reassigned to *PJA128*, and the regiment's engineer company was reassigned as the *3./PPB51*. At the same time, the battalion's 2nd Company was restructured as an armored engineer company.

Korpsgruppe Mieth, which had command and control of the Jassy — Pruth area of operations, directed that *Panzer-Pionier-Bataillon "Großdeutschland"* be pulled back from Beresti to the Ungheni Targ Bridgehead and be attached to *Kampfgruppe Stichtenoth*.

At 0230 hours on 6 April, after a 5-kilometer march, the *II./PGR126* prepared to attack Beresti Noi.

At 0445 hours, *Kampfgruppe Koppe* moved out of the bridgehead at Ungheni Targ and advanced along the rail line in the direction of Parliti. The field-expedient armored train accompanied the attack. Soviet tanks and infantry opened fire 1 kilometer south of Beresti. The elements that were attacking from Parliti the same time likewise broke enemy resistance. Ten T-34's were destroyed and heavy casualties inflicted on the Soviet infantry. The remnants of the enemy fled from the village to the north and suffered numerous casualties as they were pursued by artillery fires. Both of the battle groups linked up at 0640 hours, and Beresti Noi was cleared of the enemy.

Pursuing to the north, the grenadiers occupied the hill between Beresti Noi and Beresti, but they had to defend against attacking enemy tanks and infantry a short while later. Two Sherman tanks were knocked out by antitank guns and the assault guns; the Soviet infantry pulled back. A short while later, a T-34 was destroyed. Despite the heavy mortar and rocket-launcher fire, the German losses were slight.

While that fighting was taking place, another enemy group attempted to advance from Bogdanesti along the north/south rail line and enter Ungheni Targ in the rear of *Kampfgruppe Koppe*. A weak ready reserve from *Kampfgruppe Stichtenoth* attacked from out of the bridgehead, destroyed two T-34's and wiped out two enemy infantry companies.

At 1300 hours, *Kampfgruppe Koppe* returned to the bridgehead position. Screening on the right was *Heeres-Flak-Abteilung 278*, employed as infantry. The *Flak* soldiers also maintained contact with the *II./PGR126* employed on the hill north of Beresti Noi. The successes of the day included 15 destroyed enemy tanks, numerous machines guns, submachine guns, German small arms and a radio set. The enemy left behind eight prisoners and many dead, most of whom were carrying some sort of German equipment.

Kampfgruppe Stichtenoth returned to the command and control of the *23. Panzer-Division*. The division ordered an attack on Beresti and Bogdanesti in order to take Hill 114 northeast of the village at 0530 hours on 7 April. *Kampfgruppe Stichtenoth* was employed on the left; *PGR126* on the right. The division's mixed artillery battalion and a battery of Romanian artillery supported the operation. *Kampfgruppe Koppe*, in the lead, ran into a strong enemy defensive position along the southern edge of Beresti in addition to the sudden onset of fog. After an assault gun was lost, the attack was broken off at 0700 hours.

After a company of self-propelled antitank guns was brought forward, the attack was renewed. Beresti was taken in a concentric advance from the east and the south. *Oberleutnant* Jansen, the staff liaison officer of *PGR128*, assumed command of the regiment's 1st Battalion approaching from the east. He rallied his men forward through his exemplary bravery. A penetration was achieved; an enemy tank knocked out. Suffering heavy losses, the enemy pulled back to the north. Pursuing the enemy, the grenadiers took Hill 114 at 1500 hours and set up for defense. *Oberleutnant* Jansen was badly wounded. For his decisive actions on that day, he was later awarded the Knight's Cross to the Iron Cross on 15 May 1944.

The days that followed were quiet, with the exception of patrolling activity on both sides. *Panzergrenadier-Regiment 126* relieved *Kampfgruppe Stichtenoth*, which then prepared for further operations along the western side of the Pruth. The "armored train" was stripped of its weaponry and personnel. In the few days it had existed, it had more than proven its worth. It successfully participated in the fighting in the defense of the bridgehead position, as well as in the attack on Beresti Noi. In the course of its fighting, the men of the train destroyed a total of 11 enemy tanks, including 4 Shermans. Of the additional seven enemy tanks that were eliminated in front of the bridgehead position, the antitank guns of the Romanian cavalry accounted for three. The horsemen themselves fought very bravely.

The main clearing station of the division was set up in the women's clinic at Jassy. In the days that followed, it was transformed into a small hospital.

Soviet tanks attacked Ungheni Targ on 11 April; antitank guns eliminated five of them without suffering any losses.

The tank and *SPW* companies that had been sent to the Romanian 1st Armored Division had taken over the equipment in the meantime that they were supposed to in the event of an alert. These included 32 *Panzer IV's* (long barrels), 10 assault guns and 52 *SPW's*. The trains vehicles for the companies were provided by the Romanians. In the case of an alert, the Romanians were to remain with the German armored group. The Romanian personnel reported to Lieutenant Oltei, a young cavalry officer who had been awarded the Order of "Mihail Viteasu".

The Romanian 1st Armored Division was allocated to the headquarters of *General der Panzertruppen* Kirchner's *LVII. Panzer-Korps*, which was responsible for the Targul Frumos sector. The training activities that were directed by the Army Mission in Bucharest, which were necessary in every respect, suffered from strong misgivings on the part of the Romanians, who had the feeling that one wanted to take the German armored equipment away from them. *Oberst i.G.* Laegerler, the chief-of-staff of the *LVII. Panzer-Korps*, and *Oberst* Knabe, from the German liaison office, had to assist and intervene. The Romanian division commander, the Knight's Cross recipient, Major General Korne, was an excellent soldier and a true ally. That attitude was not widespread, however, especially since there were deep divisions within the Romanian officer corps and especially between officers, noncommissioned officers and enlisted personnel.

On 13 April, seven *Panzer IV's* arrived for the *23. Panzer-Division* at the Bacau rail station. They were transported on to Jassy and accepted there by elements of the *1./PR23* under *Leutnant* Rothe. On 16 April, *Oberst* Sander was transferred to the German Army's unassigned officer manpower pool, with his duties being assumed temporarily by *Hauptmann* Rebentisch.

On 22 April, the Romanian head of state, Marshall Antonescu, visited the Romanian 1st Armored Division and the training elements.

In the middle of April, *PAA23* was reorganized by order of the High Command, resulting in a headquarters company, four line companies and a supply company. The headquarters company was composed of the former armored car company and the signals platoon. The new *1./PAA23* was the former *2.(HalbkettenPzSpäh)/PAA23*; the new *2./PAA23* was formed from the former *3.(leSPW)/PAA23*; the new *3./PAA23* had two platoons of medium *SPW's* with light machine guns, one platoon with heavy machine guns and one platoon with heavy mortars; the new *4.(schwere)/PAA23*[76] had an antitank platoon with towed 7.5cm antitank guns, an engineer platoon, an antiaircraft platoon and a light infantry gun company.

Along the front at Jassy, the enemy had meanwhile taken Hill 162, northeast of Vulturul, during the night of 15/16 September after a strong artillery preparation. Weak enemy elements had advanced as far as the woods east of the village; the main body of the enemy's infantry and tanks advanced in the direction of Cuza Voda — Dorobantu. The Romanian forces pulled back to Sorogaru and Carligul without having put up any serious resistance.

Kampfgruppe Stichtenoth—consisting of *PGR128*, minus its 1st Battalion, *PPB51* and *PJA128*—was alerted during the morning of 16 April and advanced through Copou into the valley south of Vulturul.

The *I./PGR128* remained in Jassy as a ready reserve. Both battalions of *PGR126* were moved expeditiously out of their sectors east of the Pruth and moved forward to *Kampfgruppe Stichtenoth*. The headquarters of *PGR126* was given command and control of the formerly occupied sector, which was then occupied by *Heeres-Flak-Abteilung 278* and alert units.

Oberst Menton, the commander of *PGR126*, was sent to attend a division commander course; his successor was *Oberstleutnant* Fleck.

The *I./PGR126* occupied the northern edge of Vulturul and Hill 163.0 and screened to the north and east. The *II./PGR128* attacked east from the southern edge of Vulturul, cleared the woods of the enemy and took Hill 100, which was located to the east of the woods by 1350 hours. That battalion then transitioned to the defense.

At 1700 hours, the *II./PGR126*, together with Romanian elements, established contact with the *II./PGR128* on Hill 100, coming from the south after it had moved out from Cuza Voda. Strong enemy resistance, especially in front of the right wing of the *II./PGR126*, delayed the attack to retake Hill 162. Soviet fighter-bombers conducted continuous sorties the entire day against the attacking grenadiers and the firing positions of the heavy weapons. That night, the battalions transitioned to the defense along the line they had reached.

Toward noon, the *2./PGR128* was pushed forward to Vulturul to protect the open left flank. At the same time, six T-34's with mounted infantry attacked Vulturul, moving along the road from the north. The Romanian infantry in the village immediately pulled backing a panic. *Oberleutnant* Fils and his men quickly established a blocking position. One assault gun from *Sturmgeschütz-Batterie 1017* of the *17. Infanterie-Division* knocked out five of the T-34's; the sixth one was knocked out by a tank from *Gruppe Tiedemann* (*PJA128*). The rest of the *I./PGR128* was brought forward to Vulturul in the face of threatened continued enemy attacks, and it attacked at 1700 hours from the village to the north. With the support of three assault guns from *Sturmgeschütz-Batterie 1017* and two *Flak* from the *10.(Fla)/PGR128*, it broke through weaker enemy resistance and occupied Hills 152 and 154.

At 0530 hours on 17 April, three rapidly moving T-34's entered the northern portion of Vulturul. Grenadiers from the *1./PGR128* eliminat-

76 Editor's Note: *HalbkettenPzSpäh* = Halftracked Armmored reconnaissance; *leSPW* = *leichte SPW* = light armored personnal carrier (in this instance, halftracks); and *schwere* = heavy.

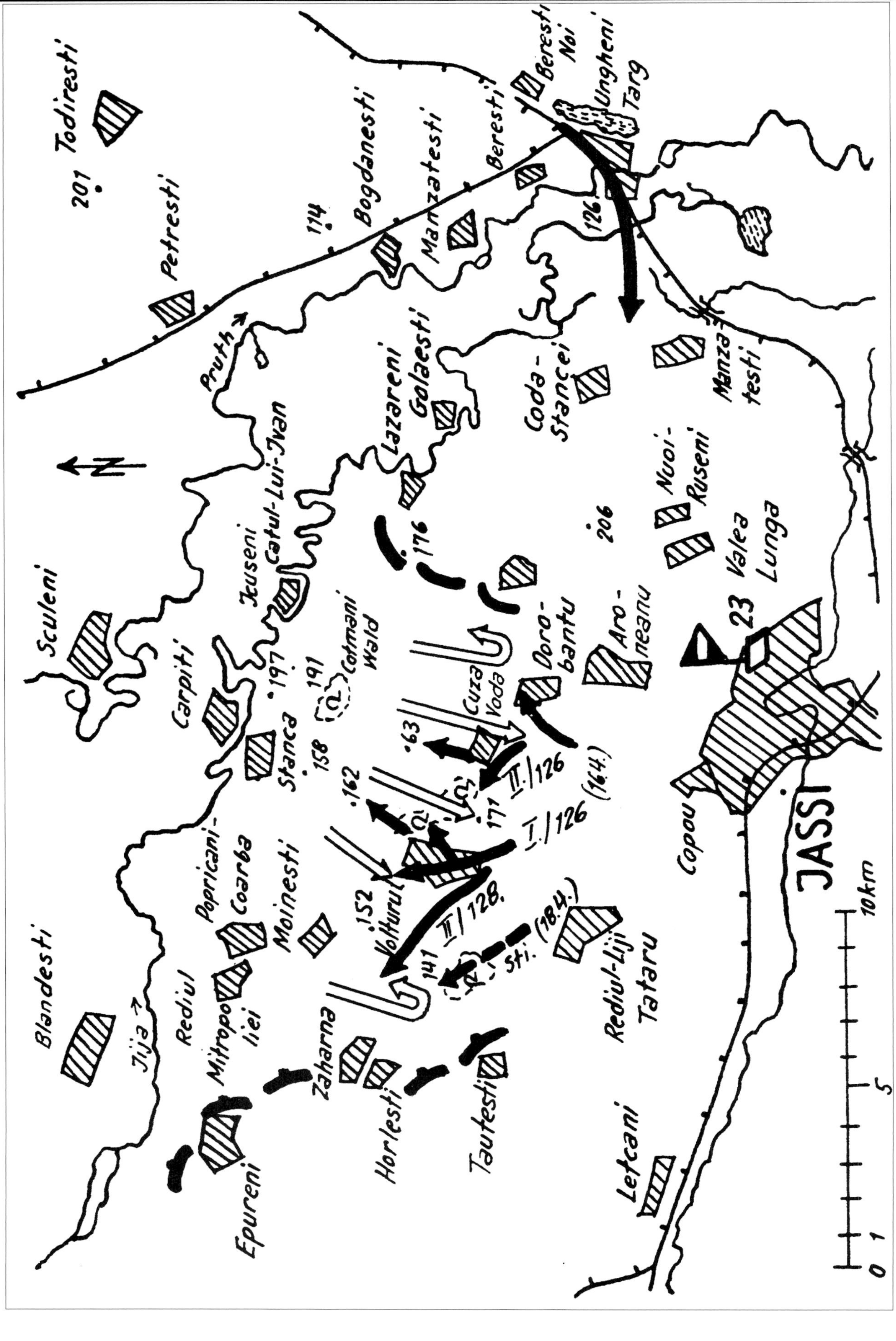

Map 72: Counterattack of the 23. *Panzer-Division* at Jassy from 16 to 21 April 1944.

ed two of them in close combat. The third one attempted to move back, but it broke through a bridge, where it was also set alight.

An enemy attack conducted by approximately two companies against the northeast corner of the woods was turned back by the *I./PGR126*. Heavy artillery and mortar fires on 17 April were also supported by rolling fighter-bomber attacks. During the afternoon, the enemy infiltrated through the Zaharna Valley to the southeast and through the main line of resistance. Romanian infantry pulled back to the south. At 1400 hours, *Leutnant* Kirch's *3./PGR128* was brought forward from Jassy. It moved out from Vulturul to the west and northwest. The company brought the Romanians back to their positions; it also remained at the front.

Most of the *I./PGR128* went into ready reserve status at the vineyards 2 kilometers south of Vulturul.

On 18 April, the *23. Panzer-Division* ordered an attack by *Gruppe Stichtenoth* to take back the former main line of resistance running from Grid Line 154 (northwest of Vulturul) — the northern tip of the woods west of Vulturul — Point 141. The attacking forces—the *I./PGR128*, a Romanian battalion, *PPB51* and *Panzer-Kompanie Rothe* of *PR23*—were supported by the *I./PAR128*.

The Romanian battalion arrived at 0730 hours, with the result that the attack could begin. By then, enemy artillery and mortar fire was falling on the assembly areas. The *3./PGR128* had already achieved a penetration into the Soviet positions earlier, at 0640 hours, along the edges of the valley northwest of Vulturul.

The headquarters of *PGR126* was relieved of its command and control duties east of the Pruth and reassumed command of its battalions north of Jassy.

At 1015 hours, the *I./PGR128* reached the former main line of resistance. At 1110 hours, the combat engineers, together with the Romanians, also cleared the patch of woods of the enemy. They had to reorganize, however, in order to continue their attack on to the former main line of resistance. *Oberleutnant* Münch's *4.(Kradsch.)/PAA23* supported the attack of *PGR128*.

At 1415 hours, the left-hand group moved out again. A strong Soviet fighter-bomber and artillery presence, as well as flanking fires from the high ground west of Zaharna, barely allowed the attack to advance. Considerable casualties forced the attack to be called off in the end. The Romanian battalions took up positions in the forward lines for the night, while the *I./PGR128* and *PPB51* were pulled back. Positioned behind the Romanians was the *7./PGR128*, which had been newly brought forward, and one platoon of the *I./PGR128*. The engineers took up quarters in a school 1 kilometer southeast of Rediul lui Tataru.

After a quiet night had passed, the enemy fired massive amounts of artillery at first light on the main line of resistance. The Romanian battalions employed there immediately pulled back. Even the use of force was unable to keep the Romanians in their blocking positions on the right. They even opened fire on the German infantry and pulled back further to the southeast, going around the blocking position there. Weak enemy forces that pursued occupied the main lines without finding any resistance. The *I./PGR126* turned back an enemy attack north of Vulturul.

Generalmajor Kraeber ordered an attack by *PGR128* to retake the former main line of resistance. The attack was to be launched after it turned dark on the night of 19/20 April. While the German battalions occupied attack positions, *Stukas* attacked Moinesti and the enemy-occupied hills at Stanca seven times during the day.

The *I./PGR128*, as well as the regiment's 6th and 7th Companies, moved out at 1830 hours on 19 April and were soon able to claim Grid Line 154 — northern edge of the patch of woods west of Vulturul — Hill 141.

After several artillery duels, a platoon of the *3./PGR128* entered the enemy-occupied trench of the former main line of resistance in the early-morning hours and rolled it up. A Soviet counterattack in battalion strength at first light was turned back by the *I./PGR128*.

Panzer-Kompanie Rothe was attached to *PAA23*.

At 0430 hours on 20 April, *Major* Stichtenoth's *PGR128* continued the German attack to regain the former main line of resistance. The attack only progressed slowly, due to the heavy enemy artillery and mortar fires. Friendly losses were high. At 0930 hours, the 1st Battalion reached the former main line of resistance in its entirety, where it had to fend off an immediate counterattack by a Soviet battalion. Despite heavy casualties inflicted by the heavy weapons of the *I./PGR128*, elements of the enemy force advanced as far as the trench line. It was only there that they could be thrown back. The German infantry observed time and again how their opposite numbers were threatened with weapons by their superiors and driven to attack.

At 1015 hours, the right wing of the 2nd Battalion established contact with the 1st Battalion. *Oberleutnant* Mathes' *6./PGR128* succeeded by 1130 hours in close combat in retaking the enemy's stubbornly defended positions on the hill north of the woods west of Vulturul. In so doing, the company suffered heavy losses. By 1300 hours, the former main line of resistance in that sector was firmly back under German control. The Soviets assaulted the positions several times in vain. In evening twilight, a penetration achieved by the enemy between the 1st and 3rd Companies was cleared up in an immediate counterattack conducted by a decisive noncommissioned officer of the 3rd Company, *Oberfeldwebel* Helmke.

During the night of 20/21 April, *Heeres-Flak-Abteilung 278*, which was employed as infantry and had been attached to *Kampfgruppe Stichtenoth*, relieved the *I./PGR128*. The latter battalion became a division reserve and was sent to Jassy. The *II./PGR128* was relieved by Romanians, however, the 6th Company remained in strongpoints in the main line of resistance and the 5th Company occupied a blocking position further to the rear. The 7th Company positioned itself in the woods at Breazu as a ready reserve.

With the exception of some artillery fires, the enemy remained quiet on 21 April. The reason for that may have been the high casualties he had suffered in the previous few days.

Panzergrenadier-Regiment 126 was relieved by elements of *Generalmajor* Weinknecht's *79. Infanterie-Division*. The battalions quartered in Jassy.

On 22 April, *Heeres-Flak-Abteilung 278* and the *II.*/PGR128 (with the exception of the 5th Company and two platoons of the 9th Company) were relieved by Romanian forces. The *Flak* battalion reported directly back to division command and control and went to Jassy. The infantry companies also went to Jassy, where the remaining elements that had remained in the front lines returned on 23 April after being relieved by Romanians.

As a result, the first phase of the battle for Jassy came to a close. The Soviet forces, for the most part, consisted of young soldiers, who had lived in the areas that had just been evacuated by the German forces and were then being rapidly committed to combat. Their tank crews had no experience whatsoever, with the result that the enemy was never able to exploit his oppressive numerical superiority. The T-34's were factory new, whereby the poor manufacturing techniques—for example, exposed weld lines—were noticeable.

During that period, *PGR128* lost the following personnel: Dead — 7 noncommissioned officers and 21 enlisted; wounded — 2 officers, 24 noncommissioned officers and 173 enlisted: and missing — 1 officer, 1 noncommissioned officer and 5 enlisted. The tangible success achieved by the regiment: 2 deserters; 28 prisoners; 9 destroyed enemy tanks; and 40 light and heavy machine guns.

After a few days of rest in Jassy, the division was alerted early in the morning of 26 April when a new offensive on the part of the Soviets was launched north of the city. Enemy tanks and infantry broke through at several places along the Romanian-occupied main line of resistance. The *79. Infanterie-Division* of *Generalmajor* Weinknecht maintained its positions and only had to pull back to the south for periods of time when its strongpoints were bypassed and it was attacked from the rear. Romanian artillery scattered fairly strong Soviet concentrations and attack groups through well-directed fires. The artillery was the best combat branch of the Romanian army; unfortunately, its firing methods leaned too much—and to its disadvantage—on the previously adapted French model of fire direction through wire lines. As a result, its command and control was prone to disruptions.

Major Tiedemann was designated as the local area commander for Jassy, along with his battalion headquarters. At the same time, he was directed as the antiarmor officer for the *IV. Armee-Korps*. As part of his inspections, he determined that the terrain north of Dorobantu was especially vulnerable, and he had a line of antitank defenses established there.

From that point on, the antitank forces became the corset stays for the Romanian infantry, where they proved themselves anew each day.

A clearing station for the 1st Medical Company was established in the former Jewish Hospital in Jassy. After being bombed several times, it was moved to the University Nerve Clinic at Buzau. The company's 4th Platoon (Decontamination) remained in Jassy to establish a delousing station.

The lead Soviet elements advanced to just outside the northern part of the city. All elements of the division were committed to the fighting; they sealed off points of penetration, conducted immediate counterattacks and pushed back the Soviet attackers—mostly infantry with heavy artillery support—to their jumping-off positions, together with the *79. Infanterie-Division* and the Romanians.

From 27 to 29 April, the surgeons of the 2nd Medical Company worked at three operating tables for 60 hours without a break. One medical operating section from the 1st medical Company provided assistance. The 2nd Medical Company established a soldier's home in Slanik, south of Jassy, along with a hospital for slightly wounded soldiers. Many soldiers were able to convalesce there and thus remained with the division.

Over time, the battalions of the *23. Panzer-Division* were pulled out of the front lines. Two companies each from the regiments remained behind the Romanian lines in strongpoints to act as "corset stays". In conducting a concentric attack on Dorobantu on 29 April, two battalions from the *79. Infanterie-Division* attacked from the south, while the *7./PGR128,* a company from *PPB51*, elements of *Panzergruppe Schulz* and a 2cm *Flak* approached from the northeast. Dorobantu was in German hands by 0725 hours, after German tanks knocked out two T-34's and an assault gun was captured. In all, the German forces were able to secure 21 enemy tanks in the village, of which the majority were even capable of being driven. *Panzerjäger-Abteilung 128* took 12 of them. The last remaining self-propelled 7.5cm tank destroyer of the battalion had been largely responsible for the fact that the Soviet tanks had not been able to leave the village to the north. *Major* Tiedemann established a company consisting of T-34's, T-43's and SU-85's under *Oberleutnant* Degener.

During the fighting for Dorobantu, the enemy attempted several times to break through the main line of resistance east of Hill 148 with battalion-sized infantry attacks, supported by tanks. Whenever the Romanians would abandon their positions, the German infantry would quickly rally them forward again.

The division had accomplished its mission of firmly retaking the former mainline of resistance. After detaching some immediate counterattack reserves, the troop elements established themselves for defending the positions. *Hauptmann* Bitter's *II./PGR128* had to bridge a gap to the friendly forces on the left by means of strongpoints until firm contact was established on the evening of 30 April. In addition to the infantry and the engineers, the *Flak* artillerymen also deserved special praise. They had attacked with only rifles and machine guns and had held the retaken main line of resistance against any and all enemy attacks.

The division suffered 47 dead, 430 wounded and 12 missing. The division destroyed or captured 25 enemy tanks, 31 artillery pieces, 40 machine guns, 3 mortars, 10 light infantry guns and untold amounts of small arms. In addition, 72 prisoners were taken. The enemy lost a considerably larger amount in dead and wounded.

The divisional logistics elements were able to regenerate themselves to a large extent. They were finally able to make up for the losses they had suffered at Kasanka and Nowyj Bug. They received materiel and personnel from vehicle columns that had newly arrived from Germany and which had arrived in Odessa in February. From 22 February to 10 March 1944, they drove convoys along the Odessa — Nikolajew road. They were based in Nikolajew on 13 March and, starting on 16 March, participated in the withdrawal through Beresowka, Odessa, Hancesti, Husi, Barlad, Tecuci and on to Jassy, where they arrived on 10 May. A portion of those elements were integrated into the 3rd Company of the Divisional Support Command.

Generaloberst Schörner, the Commander-in-Chief of the field-army group, visited the division several times. In contrast to the units and formations stationed in the "rear", the division had no bad experiences with the feared man. On the contrary, he proved to be accommodating and helpful, supporting every measure that contributed to the raising of combat readiness.

An *Obergefreiter* in the mess section of *PAA23* did not allow himself to be intimidated by the Commander-in-Chief. When the general visited the field kitchen of one of the companies, he found an opened carton of tea. He asked the *Obergefreiter*: "Don't you know that you lose 20% of your tea that way each day?" To which the *Obergefreiter* responded: "*Herr General*, well, then, there probably hasn't been anything there for a long time now, if that's the case." In the midst of resounding laughter, the general took his leave.

On 2 May, the enemy initiated a new offensive against the German front lines. The new offensive targeted the Targul Frumos area. In days of bitter fighting, *Panzergrenadier-Division "Großdeutschland"*, the *3. SS-Panzer-Division "Totenkopf"* and the *24. Panzer-Division* destroyed the majority of the attacking enemy tanks. The tanks and *SPW's* of the Romanian 1st Armored Division, which were put on alert by the *LVII. Panzer-Korps* as a precaution, were brought closer to the front, but they were not employed.

The training that had been started within all of the troop formations of the *23. Panzer-Division* continued. *Heeres-Flak-Abteilung 278* was issued new 8.8cm and 2cm *Flak*. *Panzergrenadier-Regiment 126* formed an 11th Company (Engineers) from the engineer platoons of its battalions and recent replacements. The first commander was *Hauptmann* Lenberger.

At the beginning of may, 10 assault guns arrived for the *I./PR23*, the first new equipment received in five weeks. In order to man the new equipment and, at the same time, establish the framework for rebuilding the tank regiment as part of the division, the personnel from the regimental headquarters and the *I./PR23*, who had been detailed to train the Romanian 1st Armored Division, were recalled. Command of the remaining training personnel was assumed by *Hauptmann* Bergmann.

During the course of May 1944, newly arrived personnel were incorporated into all of the troop elements of the division. Together with the experienced soldiers, they were trained for upcoming operations. Due to the lack of new equipment being issued, it proved impossible to completely reconstitute the division. Noncommissioned officers were schooled at various courses, and the specialists among the forces, especially the engineers, underwent numerous exercises under near-combat conditions. The

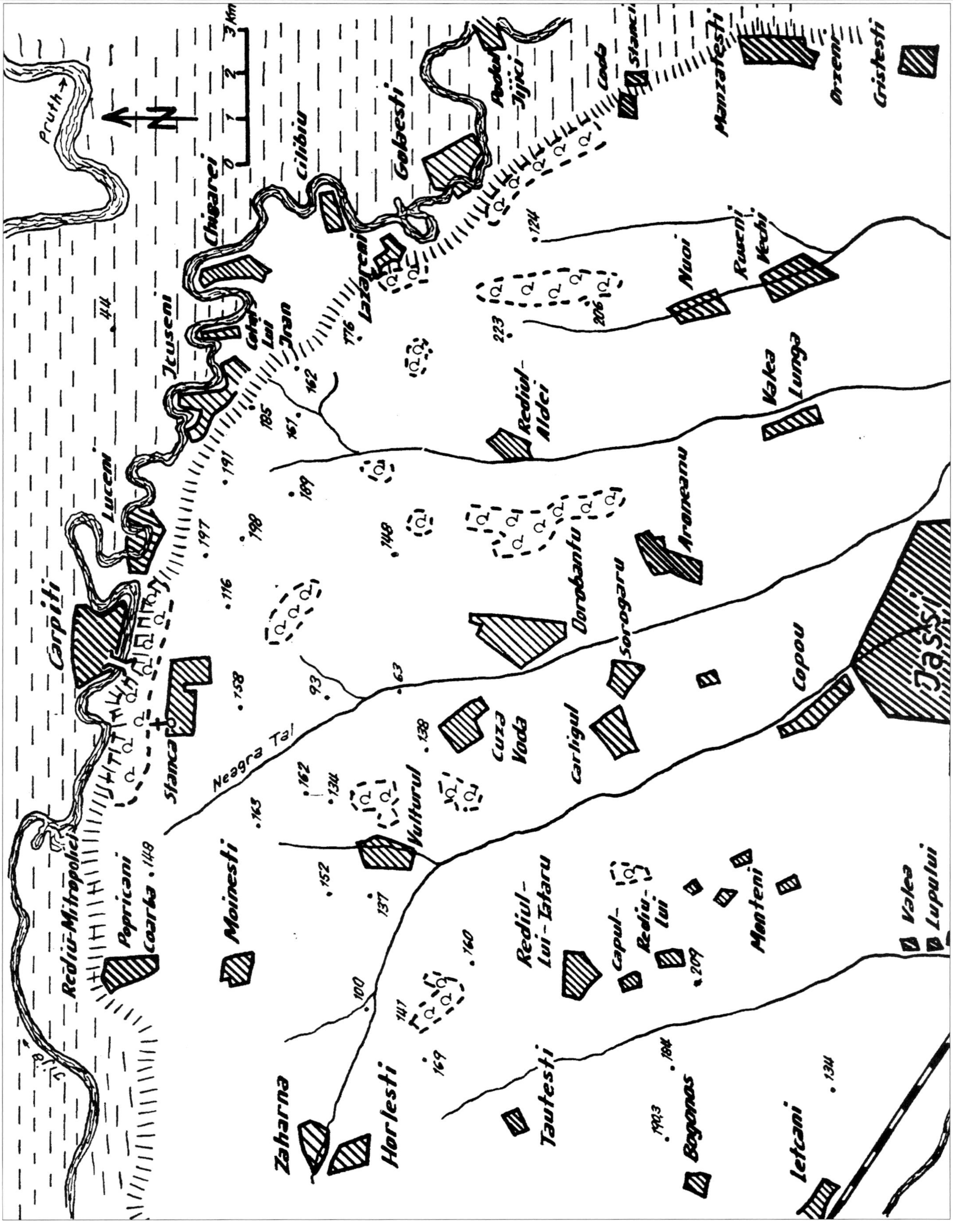

Map 73: The Area of Operations Around Jassy.

Soviet fighter-bombers, which suddenly attacked on a regular basis, gave the air-defense personnel training opportunities under "real" conditions. The batteries of the divisional artillery continued their training in firing positions supporting the *79. Infanterie-Division* and the Romanian divisions employed north of Jassy. Success was obtained on numerous occasions in the engagement of enemy artillery positions and in the support of combat patrols and raids.

Around 20 May, preparations were initiated for a German attack north of Jassy. It was intended to throw the Soviets on both sides of Stanca back over the steep banks of the Jija and the Pruth and into the level marshland so as to achieve some stability in that sector of the front.

Based on the way the enemy reacted, however, it was soon evident that he knew about these intentions. He brought up reinforcements in artillery and infantry and drove forward the establishment of an in-depth fortified position with all possible haste. The German soldier recognized and was full of respect for the abilities of his enemy in this area. Despite the recognition of the importance of a good position for defense, the digging of fortifications was and remains an area that had been neglected in training for the Germans.

The enemy also did not allow himself to be deceived when advance parties were sent to Kischinew (Chisinau) on 26 May to simulate a division move there.

Reconnaissance for the attack was conducted until 28 May. Advancing along the steep bank of the Pruth with the right wing, the *23. Panzer-Division* (on the right) and elements of the *79. Infanterie-Division* (on the left), supported by an armored group from the *24. Panzer-Division*, were supposed to gradually swing to the left and clear the high ground of the enemy. At the same time, Romanian divisions and the main body of the *79. Infanterie-Division* would attack the enemy from the front, advancing north.

Replacements that arrived just before the attack—350 men for *PGR126*—had to be incorporated into the ranks.

The *23. Panzer-Division* committed the reinforced *PGR126* with *PJA128* across Hill 194 against Hill 176 and the reinforced *PGR128* with *PPB51* to the left across Depression 89 to the north. *Panzergruppe Rebentisch*—the headquarters and *I./PR23*, elements of the *3.(SPW)/PAA23*, the engineer section of *PAA23* and the air-ground coordination officer and fire direction control officer of the *I./PAR128*—were intended to advance across the western slope of Hill 176 on Hills 161 and 185, rallying the attack of the infantry forward.

During the evening of 29 May, the division moved out of its billeting area in Jassy and into the designated assembly areas east of Rediul-Aldei. The tanks moved out in such a manner that they would not arrive at the line of departure until 10 minutes before the attack started, so as to deceive the enemy.

German and Romanian artillery fired a 20-minute preparatory fire on the enemy positions starting at 0345 hours on 30 May. At 0400 hours, the infantry moved out, followed by the tanks five minutes later. After breaking through the enemy's main line of resistance together, during which the infantry guided the tanks through a minefield, the heavy enemy resistance separated the infantry from the tanks. Even the *SPW's* could not follow the tanks, since they continuously got stuck in the enemy's trench system. Minefields caused losses; they could be bypassed, however, and also cleared by the regimental engineers, despite being taken under fire. At 0500 hours, the armored group was engaging infantry and antitank guns on the southwest slop of Hill 185. Three antitank guns were destroyed, but two German tanks were also knocked out, victims of an "ambush" antitank gun, which was position at Point 89, oriented to the north.[77]

77 Editor's Note: These ambush antitank guns were referred to in German as *Schweige-Pak* or "Silent" antitank guns, since they usually let the enemy roll past them before opening fire in an effort to catch them in the flanks and rear.

Additional casualties resulted from friendly fire from artillery and attacks by fighter-bombers (twice) on the armored group, which was well ahead of the lead elements of the armored group of the *24. Panzer-Division*. The air-ground coordination officer was unable to prevent those aerial attacks. *Leutnant* Rufer's tank crew showed exceptional pluck, as it repaired a shot-up track while disregarding enemy fire.

At the same time, the infantry took heavy losses in its fight in the enemy's system of positions, starting at Hill 176 and moving forward. *Oberleutnant* Sommer, the acting commander of the *II./PGR128*, was badly wounded; *Oberleutnant* Fils replaced him.

Since the division's attack had lost its cohesiveness, however, the armored group, which had been reduced to 12 tanks, pulled back, shattered enemy pockets of resistance at other parts of the main battle area and then attacked Hill 176 from the southwest, together with the *II./PGR128*. These forces broke through the deeply echeloned system of defenses, and two antitank guns were destroyed. At 1245 hours, Hill 176 was firmly in the hands of the two infantry regiments. The tank company of captured enemy tanks, which was established by *PJA128* after the first Battle of Jassy in April, destroyed several antitank guns.

Without waiting for the conclusion of the fighting on Hill 176, the armored group advanced north with two platoons from the *5./PGR128*, which mounted up on assault guns. One pocket of resistance after the other was cleared in an aggressively mounted attack. Several antitank guns, which were positioned oriented to the west so as to deliver flanking fires into the *24. Panzer-Division*, were overrun, and the western portion of Hill 185 was cleared of the enemy. The grenadiers from *PGR126*, who soon closed on the area, then assaulted the eastern half of Hill 185, together with the antitank battalion's "enemy" tank company. At the same time, the tanks, together with the *5./PGR128*, took Hill 191 from the southwest. An antitank-gun belt of the Soviets on the eastern edge of that hill was wiped out by the division's antitank forces and the grenadiers from Hill 185. The *11.(Pi.)/PGR126* rolled up Soviet positions on Hills 185 and 161. *Panzergrenadier-Regiment 128* established defensive positions, oriented to the northeast, on Hill 185 with its 1st Battalion and Hill 191 with its 2nd Battalion. In the meantime, the armored group had ejected the enemy from Hill 197and had established contact with the battle group from the *24. Panzer-Division* positioned at Hill 198. At 1900 ours, the armored group was attached to the *24. Panzer-Division* with the mission of supporting the firefight in the direction of Stanca and covering the right flank of the latter division's battle group. As a result of stubborn Soviet resistance, however, the attack did not progress well. Two assaults conducted by the weak battle groups of the two divisions against Stanca and the palace woodlands had to be broken off after casualties were sustained.

A Soviet immediate counterattack led to a breakthrough at Hill 85, which started to take on ominous dimensions. On his own initiative, *Oberleutnant* Henssler, the adjutant of *PGR126*, attacked with his men from the regimental headquarters and restored the situation. He was wounded three ties in the process. For his decisive actions, he was later awarded the Knight's Cross to the Iron Cross on 8 August 1944.

As it started to turn dark, the armored group prepared for further operations north of Hill 189. After being relieved by Romanian formations, which had been attached to the division, *PGR128* moved forward to the area of Hills 197 and 198 and prepared to attack Stanca. While the relief actions were taking place, the enemy entered the positions on Hill 191. The *2./PPB51* was able to restore the situation in an immediate counterattack.

The division's offensive brought the clearing stations 200 wounded. The lack of field ambulances, which still had not been replaced, led to considerable transportation difficulties.

At first light on 31 May, the armored group moved out from Hill 189 to the west as part of the *24. Panzer-Division*. The southern slope of Hill 158 was taken, but enemy tanks in the Neagra Valley advancing to the south overran the forward lines of the friendly forces to the left, the *79. Infanterie-Division*. The armored group pounced on this enemy force in the flank and destroyed 8 out of 12 enemy tanks without suffering any losses. The attack of the two armored groups did not make any progress against Stanca, however. *Panzergrenadier-Regiment 128*, which was attacking on the right, was able to enter the depression north of the Cotmai patch of woods during the morning, even though it faced increasing enemy defensive fires from heavy artillery and enemy fighter-bombers that joined in the attack on the ground. Supported by two assault guns, that battalion succeeded in entering Stanca around 1600 hours under the command of its exemplary acting commander, *Oberleutnant* Fils. The Stanca Palace, on the other hand, had been converted by the enemy into a fortress. While conducting a leader's reconnaissance to explore attack possibilities into that bulwark of the enemy's defenses, *Oberleutnant* Fils was mortally wounded.

At 1300 hours, *Panzergruppe Rebentisch*, followed by the armored group of the *24. Panzer-Division*, moved out to attack along the eastern edge of the marshy Neagra Valley to the north. At Depression 74, the tanks received extremely heavy fire from 12.2cm antitank guns from the area of Hill 148. The superior firepower of the guns, which were firing from a distance of 5 kilometers and could not be engaged by return German fires, forced the commander of the battle group to call off the attack. A direct hit on a *Panzer IV* bent a driver's hatch inward, tore off the drive sprocket and a final drive and badly wounded the driver.

The *II./PGR128* was employed at 1800 hours by *Oberstleutnant* Stichtenoth to support the regiment's 1st Battalion, which was already being supported by assault guns and divisional artillery in defending against an enemy counterattack by 12 tanks. The enemy was driven from the depression at Point 116 in tough, casualty-intensive fighting. Darkness then forced the attack to be called off.

On 1 June, the elements of the division that had established defensive positions along the steep banks of the Pruth and the Jija had to turn back numerous enemy counterattacks. At 0930 hours, *PGR128*, with *PPB51* on the right, moved out to attack the western slope of Hill 197, exploiting an attack by German fighter-bombers. Despite the fact that the attack that had been ordered for the *79. Infanterie-Division* on the right did not take place and the strong defensive efforts by the Soviets, the attack made good progress. At the moment the enemy's main line of resistance was entered, however, he counterattacked in regimental strength. Heavy fires by the German artillery forced the enemy to ground, but the German infantry was unable to hold its positions and was forced back to its line of departure. *Hauptmann* Schunk, the commander of the *II./PGR128*, was killed during that fighting.

At 1130 hours, 30 enemy tanks with infantry advanced to the south from east of the Stanca Palace. The enemy artillery supported the attack with massive fires. Thanks to the immediate commitment of German antitank guns and assault guns, the enemy tanks were shot to pieces in front of the main line of resistance. Heavy casualties were inflicted on the enemy infantry by German artillery fires.

The division's armored group was not available to support the infantry in this sector, because it had been attached to the *14. Panzer-Division* of the *IV. Armee-Korps*. It had occupied positions in the woods northwest of Cuza Woda, along with *Sturmgeschütz-Brigade 243*, which had been attached to it.

In the area of operations around the Stanca Palace the enemy continued to be reinforced. Recognizing the great importance of this bridgehead for his continued efforts to attack Jassy, he brought up tanks and infantry, with the latter digging in ad approaching ever closer to the German lines. At 1130 hours, after a half hour of artillery preparatory fires, the enemy attacked Hill 158 from the west with tanks and infantry. Tanks, assault guns and antitank guns eliminated the enemy tanks, and three of them fell victim to the *4./PGR128*. One of the enemy tanks was eliminated in close combat by means of a *Panzerschreck*[78].

While that fighting was taking place south of Stanca, *Panzergruppe Rebentisch* was employed as part of an attack operation of the*14. Panzer-Division* northwest of Vulturul. The objective was to reduce the enemy's front southwest of Stanca, thus realizing the original intention of the overall operations. Advancing across Depression134 and Hill 162, the armored group shattered tough enemy resistance on the road southwest of Hill 161. *Sturmgeschütz-Brigade 243*, moving on the right, suffered heavy casualties; its commander was killed and several officers and crews also fell. In the face of constant flanking fires from the east, the tanks fought their way forward to the north along the Cliffs 161 – 163. Without suffering any additional casualties, the ridgeline was cleared of the enemy, and contact was established with the armored groups of the *24. Panzer-Division* and *Panzergrenadier-Division "Großdeutschland"* attacking from the west 2 kilometers northwest of Hill 163. The combined attack to the east then encountered the antitank-gun and tank blocking positions of the Soviets, which had already proven impregnable on 1 June. In addition, the flanking fires from the area around Popricanii Coarba could not be eliminated. Despite the appearance of German fighter-bombers, including the "tank busters" of *Major* Rudel, who were armed with the *JU-87 G* with a 3.7cm antitank cannon and who had proven themselves numerous times the previous day, the enemy was not to be beaten. Even the *Tiger* battalion of *Panzergrenadier-Division "Großdeutschland"* was unable to make progress. An enemy immediate counterattack collapsed in the face of the main-gun fire of the German tanks, however.

Infantry did not arrive to hold the captured terrain until the night of 2/3 June. In accordance with its orders, *Panzergruppe Rebentisch* returned to Vulturul after being relieved. From there it prepared for further operations with the *14. Panzer-Division*; starting on 5 June, it was returned to the command and control of the *23. Panzer-Division*.

On 4 June, the German formations fighting in the area of Hills 161 and 162 attempted to push their positions forward to the north through attacks. The Soviet defenses, however, were too strong. In the division sector, patrolling activity then predominated. The *2.(schw.)/Heeres-Flak-Abteilung 278* was employed in the Roman area for area aerial defense.

On 5 June, German attack activities picked up again along the entire front. After extensive artillery and rocket-launcher preparatory fires, the *23. Panzer-Division*, the *79. Infanterie-Division* (with attached Romanian forces) and the four armored groups of the four armored and mechanized divisions (*23., 14., 24.* and *"Großdeutschland"*) moved out to attack. The enemy resistance was the greatest south and southeast of Stanca. Along the western slope of Hill 197, *PGR128* entered the enemy's forward positions along the edge of the Stanca Woods at 0400hours. *Panzergrenadier-Regiment 126* also entered the woods to the west of Stanca. An enemy immediate counterattack threw both of the regiments back. A second and third attack likewise did not bring the desired success, despite the support of the remaining four operational tanks of the armored group and a company from the *I./Grenadier-Regiment 672*.

Once again, the infantry had been too badly battered and was too exhausted to be able to throw back the numerically vastly superior enemy. They carried out two more assaults that day and were even able to penetrate the Soviet main battle area at several spots, but they were unable to maintain those gains in the face of the onset of the Soviet immediate counterattacks. During the course of a large-scale enemy infantry attack,

78 Editor's Note: The *Panzerschreck* was the German version of the US bazooka.

the grenadiers were finally forced to pull back to their lines of departure under the cover of darkness.

Oberst von Radowitz assumed acting command of the division from *Generalmajor* Kraeber, who was transferred to the German Army's general officer unassigned manpower pool.

The attack was renewed on the morning of 6 June after the night had passed without significant combat activity. Supported by tanks and self-propelled tank destroyers, the attack made slow progress, only to bog down again in front of the enemy positions. Extensive deliberate minefields, as well as hasty minefields constructed of scattered mines of both Soviet and Romanian origin, made the tanks have their work cut out for them. One company of 10 *Panzer IV's* reported a total of 13 incidents of battle damage due to mines within 9 days: Usually track damage, tears along weld lines and damage to the hulls.

The attacks were repeated at 1800 and 2000 hours, but, once again, they did not bring success. The infantry were pulled back to their lines of departure. On that day, the *I./PGR128* had lost its new acting battalion commander, *Oberleutnant* Pegel, when he was wounded. The trench strength of that battalion had been reduced to such an extent that *Oberstleutnant* Stichtenoth had all personnel of the 10th Company (*Flak*), the headquarters company and the trains who were not directly involved in operations put in the front lines.

The main clearing station of the division had treated 1,030 wounded since 30 May. The enemy attacked Jassy two times from the air—once by the Soviets and once by the Americans. Each time, a bomb landed in the main clearing station in the women's clinic. Casualties resulted. Two hundred wounded were evacuated in a field-expedient hospital train, and the clearing station was moved from the destroyed clinic to an estate south of the city.

While the enemy attacked Jassy and the rear area at night with heavy bomber formations, the combat activities at the front were limited to patrols and combat raids.

On 8 June, a raiding party from *PGR128* brought back 17 prisoners. The next day, a combat patrol from *PPB51* blew up four 12.2cm and two 17.6cm guns at Depression 116. During that time period, the enemy brought up considerable reinforcements, which were mostly inserted into his main battle area to the west of Stanca. The days were marked by artillery activity. The enemy's artillery was considerably stronger, but the better observation afforded to the Germans and the Romanians due to the elevated hill positions resulted in considerably greater success for them. A large number of batteries were destroyed, command posts eliminated through direct hits and the significant and overt traffic in the Soviet rear area was effectively disrupted.

The enemy succeeded in achieving a small penetration in the defile between Hills 185 and 191 in the sector of the Romanians to the right of *PGR128*. The penetration was sealed off and eliminated by the assault guns of the division.

On 13 June, an antitank-gun group consisting of 15 7.5cm antitank guns was attached to the division and placed under the command and control of the *III./PAR128*. Eight of the guns were brought into position within the sector of *PGR128*, six with *PGR126* and one with *PAA23*. A *Flak* section from *Panzergrenadier-Division "Großdeutschland"* was also temporarily attached to the *III./PAR128*.

It was quiet along the entire sector for the front during the last 10 days of June. On 21 June, the first elements of the *79. Infanterie-Division* arrived to relieve the division. They started on the left wing: First *PAA23*, then *PGR126* and, during the night of 21/22 June, *PGR128*. The only battalions remaining in operations at the front were the *II.* and *III./PAR128*. They were relived on 10 July and returned to the division.

The main body of the division occupied quarters in the Bolduresti — Bratuleni — Moreni area as the reserve force of the field army. Measures were undertaken there to restore the division's combat capabilities. The heavy fighting of the previous months had torn great gaps within the ranks of the infantry, the engineers and the reconnaissance soldiers. The division's tank regiment received considerable reinforcement by virtue of the fact that its 2nd Battalion was returned to its command and control on 5 June. With the *II./PR23* was also the *4./PR23*, which had been attached to the 2nd Battalion. On 26 June, the new regimental commander, *Oberstleutnant* Bernau, arrived. *Hauptmann* Rebentisch returned to the *I./PR23*.

On 5 July, *PGR128* was moved back into its old area of operations in order to conduct *Unternehmen "Eisenberg"* (Operation "Iron Mountain") with the *79. Infanterie-Division* north of Aroneanu. After an artillery preparation, *PGR128* attacked through the positions of *Grenadier-Regiment 212* on 9 July. Supported by *Stukas*, it broke into the Soviet's positions and brought the *Eisenberg* (Hill 185) back under German control by the onset of darkness. The fusilier battalion[79] of the *79. Infanterie-Division,* as well as six assault guns, provided valuable support. The new commander of the *I./PGR128*, *Hauptmann* Gabler, was wounded, but he remained with his troops.

After fending off several enemy attacks in the days that followed, during which the 1st Battalion joined up to the left of the 2nd Battalion in operations in the Stanca Defile, *PGR128* was pulled out of the line on 12 July and released back to the *23. Panzer-Division*. It bivouacked in the woods 2 kilometers east of Osoi Ligucari and moved along with the rest of the division on 16 July into the Radeni — Braesti — Sarca area.

At the conclusion of the fighting for the *Eisenberg*, the Commander-in-Chief of the *8. Armee*, *General der Infanterie* Wöhler, and the Commanding General of the *IV. Armee-Korps*, *General der Infanterie* Mieth, recognized the attack forces in special orders-of-the-day, to which the commander of the *79. Infanterie-Division*, *Generalleutnant* Weinknecht, joined in:

Corps Group Order-of-the-Day for 11 July 1944

> On 9 July 1944, the forces attached to *Generalleutnant* Weinknecht wrested an important piece of high ground from a bitterly defending enemy as part of a carefully prepared and powerfully executed attack operation. The enemy suffered heavy casualties; he lost at least 330 dead and 134 soldiers taken prisoner, as well as 2 artillery pieces, 10 antitank guns, 34 machine guns and numerous other weapons and munitions. Two aircraft were shot down. I extend my full recognition to the brave attack forces for their pluck and their offensive resolve; this also applies to all of the officers, noncommissioned officers and enlisted personnel of all branches who participated in the operation. We remember our comrades, who found a hero's death in accordance with their oath of fealty, in respect and proud grief. The spirit of death-defying fulfillment of duty shall live on in us; it will lead us to final victory. Long live the *Führer*!
>
> /signed/ Mieth, *General der Infanterie*
>
> With pride and great happiness, I pass on this recognition to my division. I would especially like to thank those formations that were directly involved in the attack for their exemplary sense of duty, their aggressiveness in the attack and their unshakeable fighting spirit.
>
> Those who especially distinguished themselves were *Panzergrenadier-Regiment 128*, under the leadership of its proven commander, *Oberstleutnant* Stichtenoth, the *6./Grenadier-Regiment 212*, under the command of *Leutnant* Spengler, who was killed in battle, the *3./Sturmgeschütz-Abteilung 228*, the *5./Grenadier-Regiment 208*, under the command of *Oberleutnant* Merkelbach, the *Divisions-Füsilier-Bataillon (Aufklärungs-Abteilung) 79*, with *Leutnant* Herrmann, who was killed at the head of his troop, and the *Flak* Company of *Panzerjäger-Abteilung 179*.

---

79 Editor's Note: By this stage of the war, the reconnaissance battalions of the infantry divisions had been redesignated as "fusilier" battalions. As such, they were the only true mobile force of the division, often receiving a complement of motor vehicles and, sometimes, armored vehicles as well.

I extend my special recognition to *Oberstleutnant* Plagemann, the commander of *Grenadier-Regiment 226*, who was decisively involved in the planning and execution of the attack, and *Major* Pöhl, currently the acting commander of *Grenadier-Regiment 212*.

Not least of all participating in the success of the day was the exceptional *Artillerie-Regiment 179*, reinforced by the *II./Artillerie-Regiment 70*, the *II. Artillerie-Regiment 40* and *schwere Heeres-Artillerie-Abteilung 809* (the 2nd and 3rd Batteries), under the leadership of the tried-and-true Commander, *Oberst* Wolf.

The preparation and direction of the artillery fight, conducted in an agile fashion, decisively supported the 16 hours of uninterrupted combat by the grenadiers, fusiliers and engineers.

Finally, we are thankful for the magnificent, aggressively conducted operations of the *Luftwaffe*, especially those of the *Stuka* attacks led by *Major* Rudel, who joined in the fray on the ground again and again and inflicted heavy losses on the enemy.

The division accomplished its mission.

/signed/ Weinknecht

Oberst von Radowitz was promoted to *Generalmajor* and also officially designated as the commander of the *23. Panzer-Division* at the same time.

New, large-scale offensives in the center sector of the German front led to deep penetrations and allowed the enemy to advance into the depths of Poland along a broad front. As a consequence of those events, which led to a direct threat to Germany, *Heeresgruppe Südukraine* had to give up the majority of its armored divisions, even though new offensive operations of the enemy in Romania were imminent.

For the *23. Panzer-Division*, this move meant a departure from Romania. Only cadre elements of two tank companies and a training detail from the *3./PAA23* remained with the Romanian 1st Imperial Armored Division as instructor personnel. They were replaced four weeks later by personnel from the *20. Panzer-Division*. As a result, they escaped in the nick of time the catastrophe unleashed on *Heeresgruppe Südukraine* by the treachery of the Romanians.

The "new" *PGR128* of *Oberstleutnant* Stichtenoth, which had been introduced to the division prior to the start of the fighting in Romania, had won a solid place within the framework of the division. The regiment had borne the main burden during all of the fighting around Jassy. The regiment's losses were substantial, but its successes were even greater.

From 29 May to 12 July 1944, the regiment lost the following:
130 dead
590 wounded
28 missing.
Its visible successes included:
90 prisoners
4 deserters
Numerous enemy dead
4 12.2cm artillery pieces
2 17.6cm artillery pieces
4 tanks
13 antitank guns
4 heavy machine guns
9 light machine guns
7 aircraft (IL-2's and Pe-2's)
Numerous small arms.

The II./Panzer-Regiment 23 in the Northern Ukraine 9 January to 4 June 1944

On 1 January 1944, the *II./PR23* was detached from the division and attached directly to the headquarters of *Heeresgruppe Süd*. The *Panthers* that were still operational were turned over to the 1st Battalion's 4th Company. In a road march lasting five days, the tank crews and trains of the battalion reached Shmerinka, where a detail under the command of *Hauptmann* Fischer was unloading 51 new *Panthers* and wheeled vehicles from trains.

Before the shortages in wheeled vehicles and, above all, in recovery means could be addressed, the battalion was already being alerted. The enemy had moved out to attack from his bridgeheads along the Dnjepr; he had reached the Bug north and northeast of Shmerinka and had already formed several bridgeheads. During the night of 9/10 January, the battalion was attached to the local area commander for Shmerinka for the purposes of defense. It was joined by *Hauptmann Graf* Kageneck's *schwere Panzer-Abteilung 503*, which was also located there for the purposes of reconstitution, as well as the *371. Infanterie-Division*. Their mission was to reduce the Russian bridgeheads along the Bug.

On 10 January, a *Tiger* company, which was supposed to attack the enemy bridgehead at Ssutiski, 20 kilometers east of Shmerinka, was already engaged by enemy tanks 3 kilometers southwest of Shmerinka. It succeeded in bringing elements of the *371. Infanterie-Division* into position for a local defense of Shukowzy.

The terrain had been softened up considerably in wet, cold weather consisting of snow, rain and frost at night. At 1130 hours on 10 January, *schwere Panzer-Abteilung 503* and elements of the *II./PR23* moved out to attack east. Contact was established with *Major* Herbst's *Panzerjäger-Abteilung 371* (*371. Infanterie-Division*) at Shukowzy. At 1400 hours, the *II./PR23* moved out along with a company of *Tigers*, a company of grenadiers and two platoons of engineers in order to advance to the Bug at Woroschilowka, moving through Nowo-Petrowsk. The *7./PR23* remained behind in Shuowzy to provide local security. After knocking out two enemy tanks, Nowo-Petrowsk was taken just before the onset of darkness and secured. The following morning, at 0730 hours, Majakiw was occupied. The *8./PR23* immediately advanced on Woroschilowka, along with a platoon of engineers. It destroyed an enemy antitank gun there and threw Soviet infantry back across the Bug. A bridge that was undergoing construction was blown up by the engineers. After establishing a defensive line along the Bug, the tank company returned to Majakiw, where the battalion moved out at 1030 hours with attached elements in the direction of Borskoff. Weak enemy elements were chased away, and Scherschni was brought back under German control.

On 12 January, the *7./PR23* supported the advance of *Kampfgruppe Herbst* of the *371. Infanterie-Division* on Swonicha and Koljuchow, while the main body of the battalion remained in Scherschni. The *6./PR23* and Herbst's battle group advanced on Nemiroff on 13 January, while the rest of the battalion forded the Bug to the north at Petschara. On 14 January, the battalion was attached to *General* Gollnick's *XXXXVI. Panzer-Korps*. It attacked Nemiroff in the morning at 0700 hours and took it after combating enemy infantry.

During the night of 14/15 January, the *II./PR23* was sent to the sector of *Generalmajor* Vogel's *101. Jäger-Division* to support the attack on Potoki and Ilinzy. Moving out from an assembly area north of Ruban at 0815 hours, the battalion occupied Potoki in conjunction with the light infantry division's *Aufklärungs-Abteilung 101*. Four T-34's were destroyed

Map 74: Operations of the *II./Panzer-Regiment 23* in the Northern Ukraine from January to June 1944.

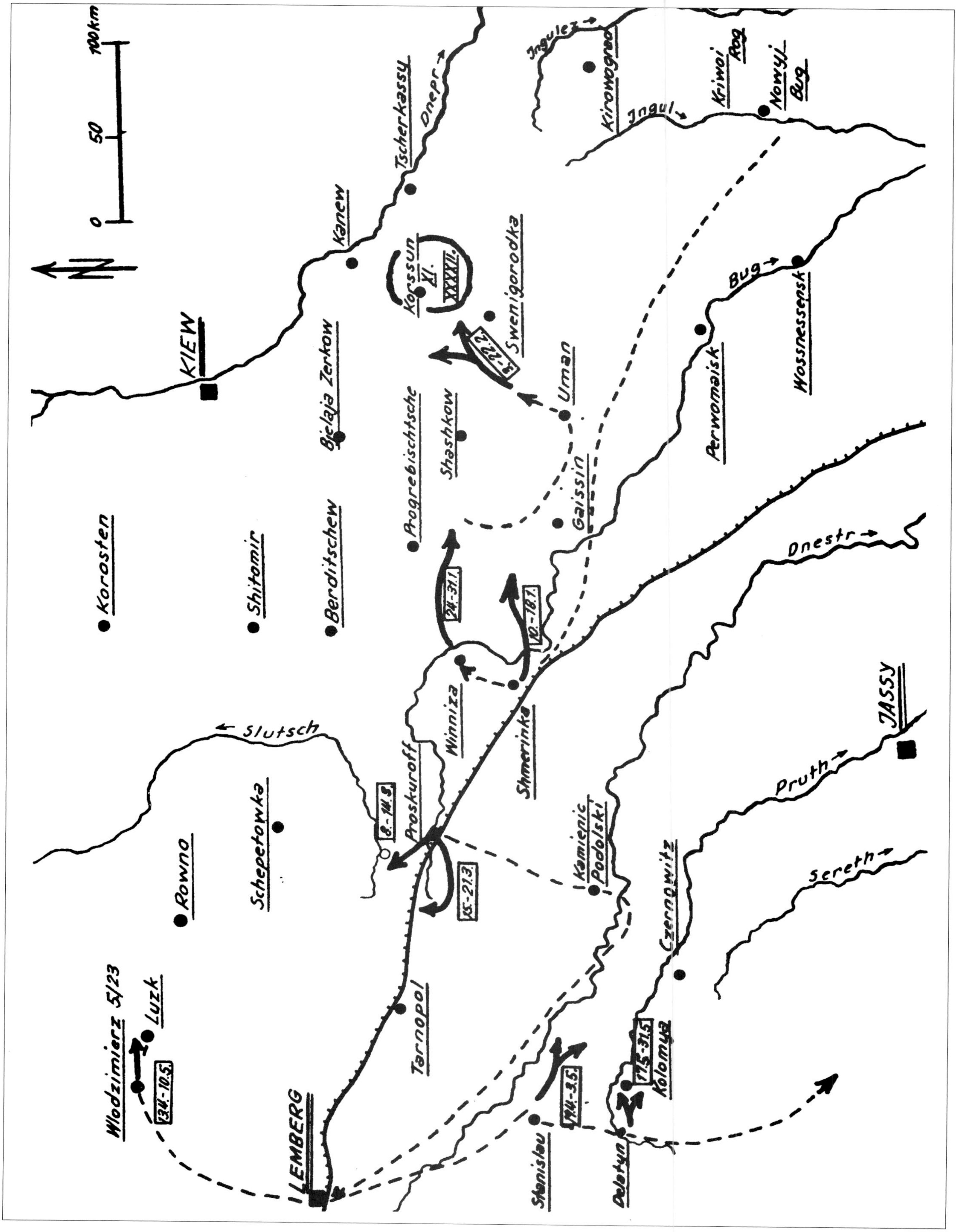
0
50
100km
N
KIEW
Kanew
Tscherkassy
Dnepr
Ingulez
Kirowograd
Ingul
Kriwoi Rog
Nowyj Bug
Korssun
XI.
XXXXII.
Swenigorodka
Bjelaja Zerkow
Pogrebischtsche
Shashkow
Uman
Gaissin
Perwomaisk
Wossnessensk
Bug
Koroston
Shitomir
Berditschew
Winniza
Shmerinka
Dnestr
JASSY
Pruth
Sereth
Slutsch
Rowno
Schepetowka
Proskuroff
Kamienic Podolski
Czernowitz
Tarnopol
Luzk
Wlodzimierz 5/23
LEMBERG
Stanislau
Delatyn
Kolomya
10.-18.1.
24.-31.1.
8.-14.3.
15.-21.3.
19.4.-3.5.
17.5.-31.5.
3.4.-10.5.

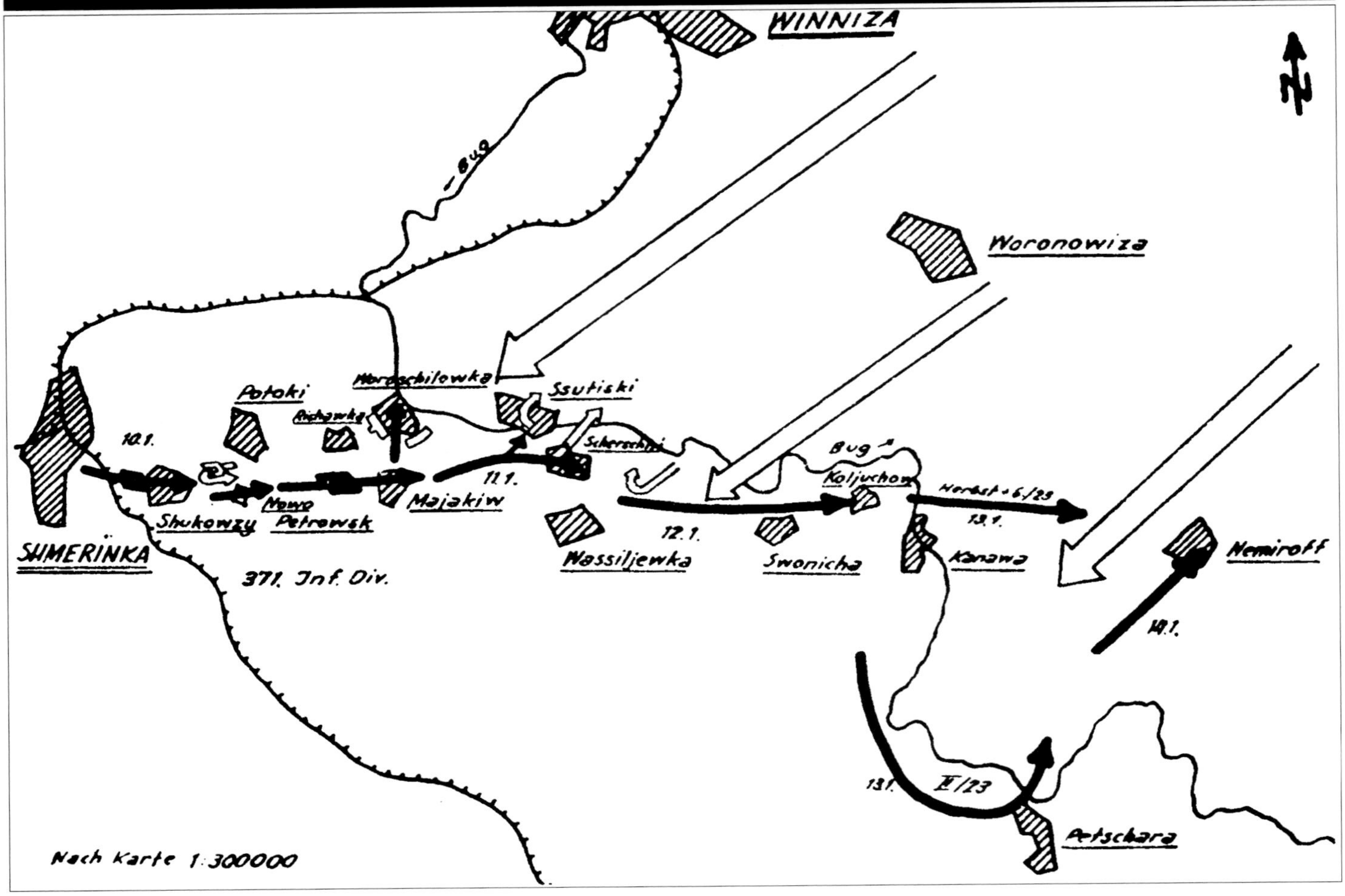

Map 75: Operations East of Shmerinka with the *371. Infanterie-Division.*

south of Shornitschtsche. The village was bypassed to the north in order to first eliminate a fortified and strong antitank-gun blocking position there. The antitank-gun belt, which was fixed in place by elements attacking from the front, was then overrun by the 7th and 8th Companies when they flanked the enemy on the left. Thirty antitank guns were eliminated or captured. While the *6./PR23* attacked the village proper along with the light infantry and cleared it by the onset of darkness, the rest of the battalion engaged and eliminated identified enemy tanks and antitank guns from firing positions north of the village. Two assault guns with 15.2cm main guns were eliminated in the village itself. An additional 5 T-34's, 8 trucks and 10 machine guns fell victim to the remaining companies.

The *6./PR23* attacked north on 16 January, together with *Jäger-Regiment 228*. The enemy put up stubborn resistance along the high ground west of Borissowka and in the patches of woods to the south. Swing far to the south, the German forces succeeded in entering Krassnenkoje. By evening, the gap in the front, which had existed that morning with *Panzer-Aufklärungs-Abteilung 17* of the *17. Panzer-Division* at Lojewzy, had been closing. As a result, the threatened breakthrough of the enemy to the south in that area was prevented. The *II./PR23* returned to Nemiroff; on 18 January, it moved back to Shmerinka. On 19 January, the battalion received its missing wheeled vehicles. In addition, the *4./PR23* also arrived to reinforce the battalion which, as a result, then had five line companies at its disposal. The following day the battalion was moved to Winniza, where additional *Panthers* had arrived from Germany.

On order from *Heeresgruppe Süd* on 23 January, *schweres Panzer-Regiment "Bäke"* was formed from *schwere Panzer-Abteilung 503* and the *II./PR23*. Its first mission was to eliminate the Soviet area of penetration east of Winniza by attacking to the east and also to eliminate the enemy forces that had advanced to the Bug to the south. During the night of 23/24 January, *Hauptmann* Euler's battalion, with its 37 *Panthers*, took up attack positions east of Priluka. In conjunction with *SS* formations, the Bila was crossed and Britzkoje taken. An immediate counterattack by four T-34's and an assault gun ended with the destruction of all five combat vehicles. In addition, 4 light field pieces, 12 mortars, 1 antitank rifle, 3 machine guns, 8 trucks and 2 staff cars were destroyed without any friendly losses.

On 25 January, the heavy tank regiment advanced further to the east. Three T-34's and a Sherman that attacked on the left flank were destroyed. Twenty enemy tanks that suddenly appeared in front of the German tanks proved to be decoys after the first round of fire. Strong enemy infantry forces then attempted to flee, but they were wiped out for the most part. Outside of Otscheretnja, the *7./PR23* overran an antiaircraft- and antitank-gun position. At the same time, together with the Tigers, a strong enemy position with numerous antitank guns north of the village was eliminated. In a continued advance to the north, the *7./PR23* ran into Soviet forces pulling back, and several trucks with limbered 4.7cm antitank guns were captured; two staff cars were crushed. One *Panther* and one command *Panther* were lost to enemy fires. While the *4./PR23* remained behind to screen to the north, the battalion attacked toward Sosoff to the southwest. Enemy tanks turned back after a short firefight and abandoned fleeing enemy infantry and trains elements to their fate, which was to be shot to pieces by the German tanks. At 1630 hours, the battalion entered the eastern portion of Sosoff; Soviet assault guns were still holding the western part of the village. German infantry arriving from the north fought for and cleared the rest of the village and then continued south. Destroyed that day were 23 enemy tanks, 27 antitank guns,

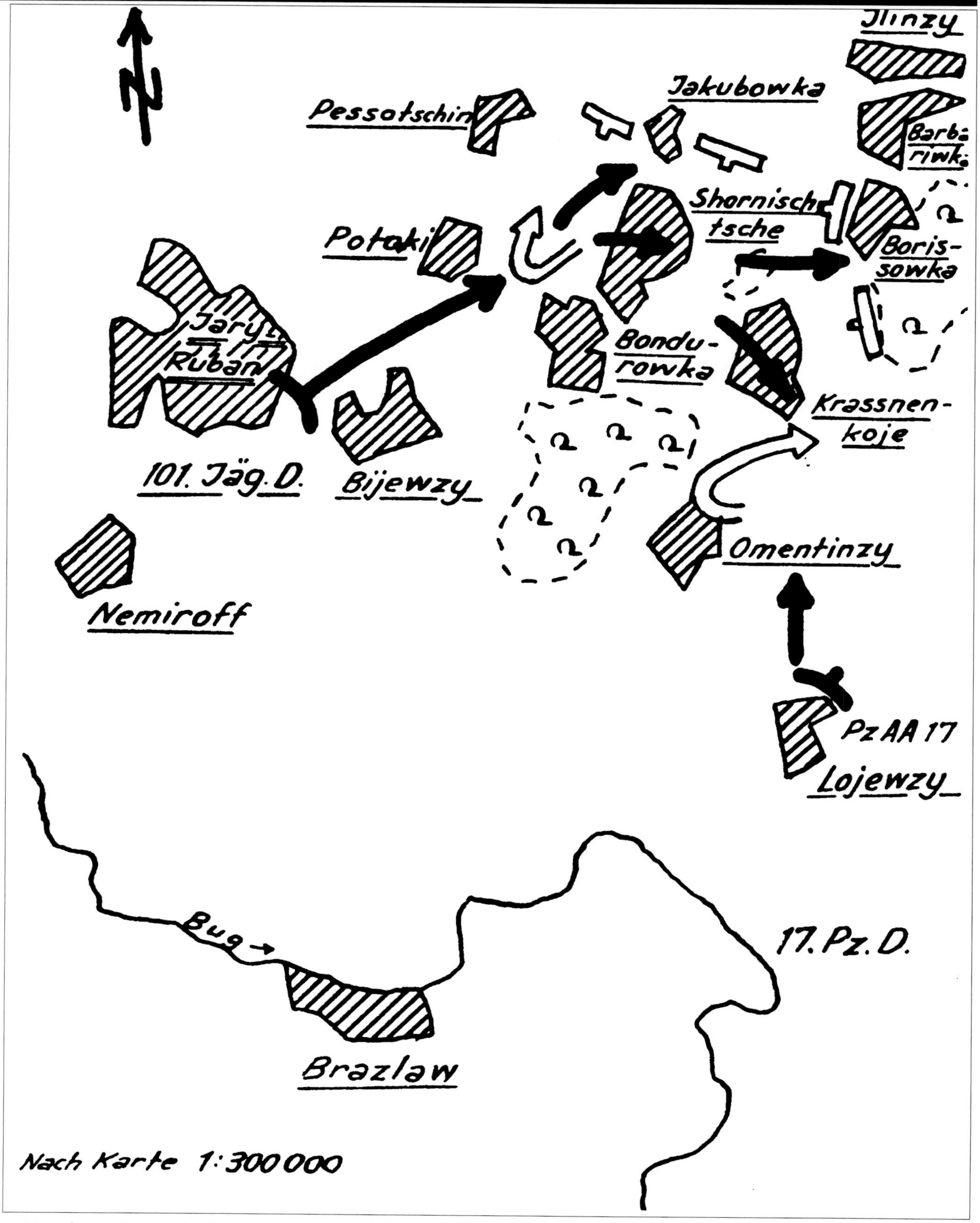

Map 76: Attacks of the *101. Jäger-Division* on 15 and 16 January 1944.

4 4.7cm antiaircraft guns, 1 antitank rifle, 2 machine guns and 15 trucks. In contrast, there were only two friendly losses.

On 26 January, the battalion initially had to deal with fuel supply problems. In the meantime, the *5./PR23*, as well as *Oberleutnant* Kujacinski's *4./PR23*, was ordered to support the attack of the infantry on Rotmistrowka, where the enemy had re-established himself with infantry and strong antitank defenses, and was blocking the road to Britzkoje. While the *5./PR23* destroyed 15 antitank guns and opened the supply route at Rotmistrowka, the *4./PR23*, together with the damaged tanks it was pro-

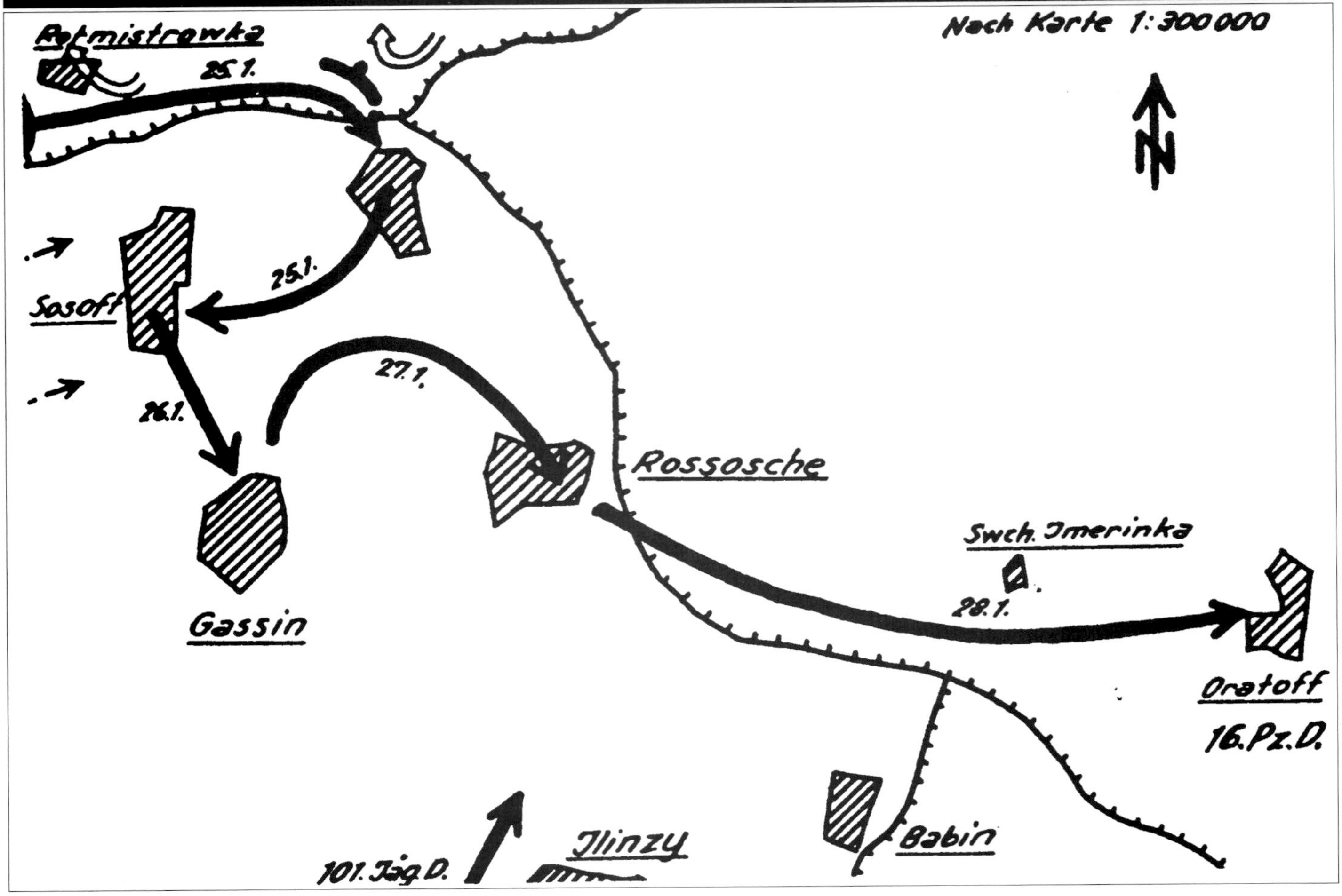

Map 77: Attacks of *schwere Panzer-Regiment Bäke* northeast of Winniza from 25-28 January 1944.

tecting, was attacked by Soviet tanks. Without the loss of any German tanks, 10 enemy tanks were destroyed.

At 1100 hours, *schweres Panzer-Regiment "Bäke"* moved out to the southeast, minus the *4.* and *5./PR23*. The Soviet infantry fled; enemy tanks and antitank guns that attempted to take up the fight were shot to pieces. The lead elements ran into hasty minefields as it turned dark. The engineer platoon of the *II./PR23* quickly cleared the mines so that the attack could be continued on another enemy position on the hill north of Gaissen. Two Soviet antitank guns were knocked out in the final twilight of the day. The battalion scored 15 enemy tanks and 22 antitank guns on that day. One *Panther* was a total loss due to enemy fires. The *SPW* of the battalion surgeon ran over a mine.

During the night, the enemy attempted to encircle the battle group in its hedgehog position by surrounding it with mines. In addition, he brought new antiarmor weaponry forward. Within a period of two hours at first light on 26 January, the engineer platoon cleared 140 mines. In the process of clearing them, the platoon leader and an engineer were killed. The battalion was ordered north to the hill east of Sosoff, but it had to engage and eliminate several enemy tanks and assault guns before it could move out. At noon, the battalion was re-supplied by the *1. SS-Panzer-Division "Leibstandarte SS Adolf Hitler"*, which was attacking on the left. As part of the entire battle group, it moved out at 1500 hours to the southeast in order to relieve elements of the *"Leibstandarte"* encircled in Rossosche. It arrived in Rossosche in the evening after overcoming considerable difficulties caused by the terrain that had been softened up by the thaw. There it established contact with *SS-Panzer-Grenadier-Regiment 1* of the *"Leibstandarte"*. On that day, the battalion succeeded in destroying or capturing 12 enemy tanks, 4 antitank guns, 3 machine guns and 4 trucks.

Contact was established with the *16. Panzer-Division* on 28 January by means of an advance on Oratoff. Efforts by the enemy forces that had advanced south to break out to the north were rendered naught several times during the course of the night. Despite that, they blocked the supply route again and again.

On 29 January, the *II./PR23* attacked to reopen the supply route to the west. At the Imerinka Collective Farm, well-camouflaged Soviet assault guns suddenly opened fire on the battalion. One *Panther* was a total loss; two other ones received hits. Three Soviet assault guns were knocked out. Bypassing the collective farm, the trains elements were brought forward to Oratoff.

In evening twilight Soviet infantry with tanks attacked Oratoff from the north. Four enemy tanks were destroyed; at that point, the enemy pulled back.

Oberleutnant Zirr's *7./PR23*, supported by four *Tigers*, was employed against a newly formed enemy defensive front north of Oratoff. in doing so, it ran into enemy forces in the Imerinka Collective Farm again. Ten enemy tanks, one assault gun and one antitank gun were destroyed. One *Tiger* was a complete loss. On 31 January, *schweres Panzer-Regiment Bäke* took the collective farm in a concentric attack. One enemy assault gun, one T-34 and three trucks were destroyed.

With this phase of the fighting, the counterattack of the *XXXXVI. Panzer-Korps* against the enemy forces that had penetrated the German front in the first few days of January drew to a close. The threat to the southern wing of *Heeresgruppe Süd* by the enemy breakthrough wedge had been eliminated. The front stabilized in this sector along a line running Pogrebischtsche — Shaschkoff.

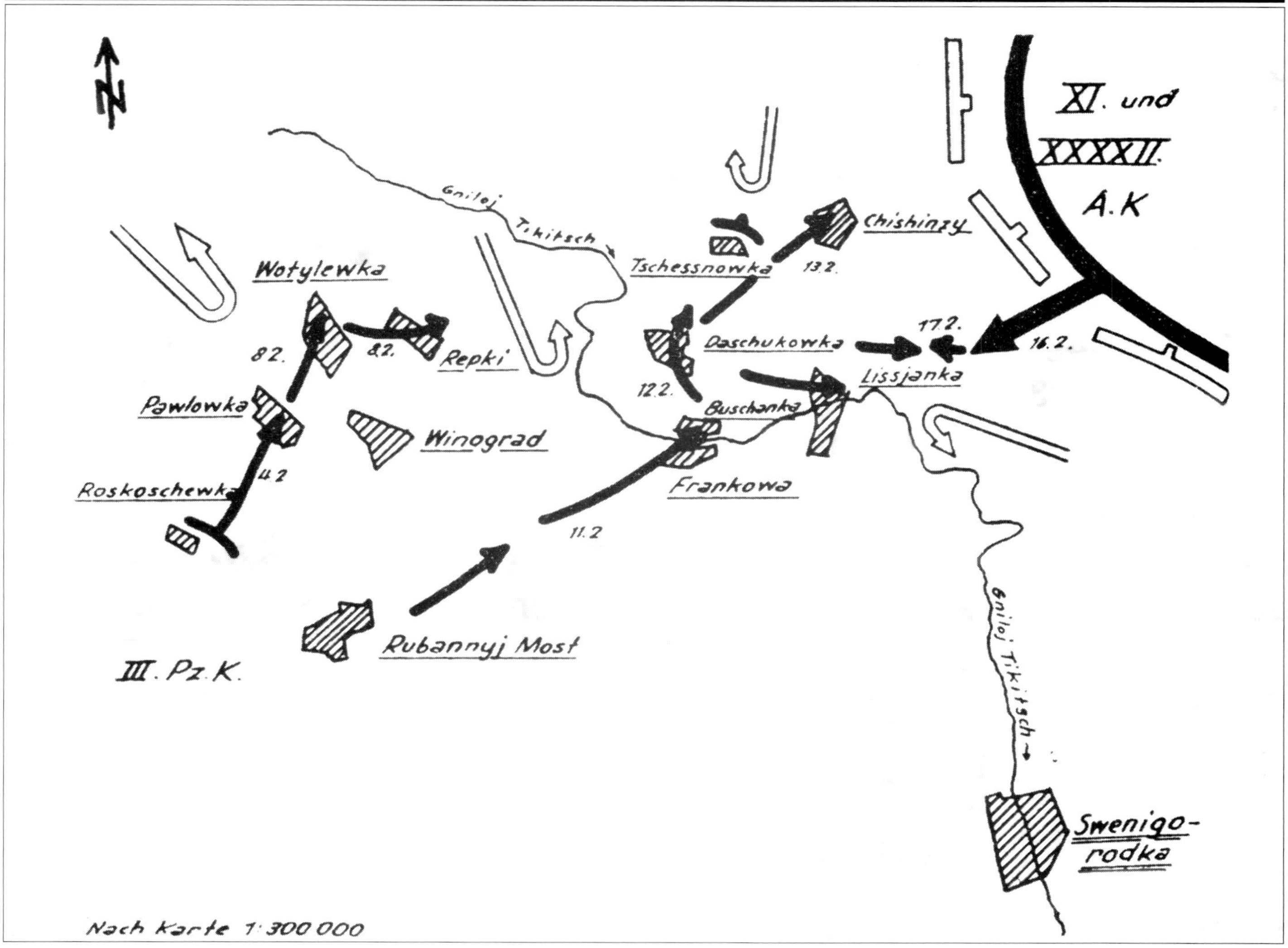

Map 78: Breaking the Encirclement of Tscherkassy from 4-17 February 1944.

Schweres Panzer-Regiment "Bäke" marched through Babin to Frantowka, where it was moved by rail to a new area of operations north of Uman. The regiment was attached to *General der Panzertruppen* Breith's *III. Panzer-Korps*, which was also new in the sector. Together with the *1. Panzer-Division*, the *16. Panzer-Division* and the *17. Panzer-Division*, it was intended for the corps to form an attack group to eliminate a difficult crisis in the area.

Despite the enemy's deep penetrations and the corresponding withdrawals of the German front at Kirowograd and in the greater Kiev area, the divisions in the center portion and southern wing of the *8. Armee* had had to hold their positions along the Dnjepr on both sides of Tscherkassy on the express orders of Hitler. The Soviets had continuously gained ground to the southwest and the west from the Kirowograd area, which had fallen on 9 January and, as a result, were positioned along the deep right flak of the *8. Armee*. Moving out from there and, at the same time, from the Bogusslaw — Korssun — Schewtschschenkowski area to the south, strong Soviet armored and infantry formations linked up at Swenigorodka in the rear of the *XI. Armee-Korps* and the *XXXXII. Armee-Korps*. Ten divisions, with more than 50,000 men, were encircled.

In order to relieve them, all available mechanized forces were quickly assembled. It was intended for four armored divisions to move out from the south (*8. Armee*) and for four more to move out from the west (*III. Panzer-Korps* of the *1. Panzer-Armee*) and break the ring while the encircled forces held their positions. From the sector of the *8. Armee*, the *3. Panzer-Division*, the *11. Panzer-Division*, the *13. Panzer-Division* and the *14. Panzer-Division* moved out under the command of the *XXXXVII. Panzer-Korps*, whose Commanding General was the former division commander, *General der Panzertruppen* Nikolaus von Vormann. The mud period of the early part of the year, together with the seemingly endless rainfall, turned the roads, trails and fields into seas of mud. Moving directly from their rail cars, the elements of *schweres Panzer-Regiment Bäke* advanced via Potasch, 30 kilometers north of Uman, and Buki into the assembly area at Roskoschewka. The regiment was attached to the *17. Panzer-Division*. Nine tanks of the *II./PR23* were operational.

At 0600 hours on 4 February, the *II./PR23*, reinforced by a company of *Tigers* from *schwere Panzer-Abteilung 503*, moved out to the north and broke through the Soviet positions after heavy fighting with enemy antitank guns and infantry. Together with the rest of the battle group, Pawlowka was taken and the road to its north blocked. A platoon of *Panthers* moved back to pick up the infantry. Two kilometers south of Pawlowka, the platoon encountered new enemy forces. Two Soviet assault guns and four antitank guns were destroyed to the loss of one *Panther*. The German infantry moved up. The successes for the battalion for the day: 2 assault guns; 11 antitank guns; 4 artillery pieces; 2 antitank rifles; 2 heavy machine guns; and 4 trucks. After securing the ground gained on 5 February, the *II./PR23* moved out again at 1900 hours in order to establish contact with the forward elements of the *16. Panzer-Division* in Wotylewka and enable them to be resupplied. At 0100 hours on 6 February, the mission was accomplished.

An attack by Soviet tanks and infantry ran into the attack of the *17. Panzer-Division* (on Repki from Wotylewka) during the morning of 7 February. The Soviets were turned back in a struggle that lasted the entire day.

Reinforced by 15 *Panthers* returning from the maintenance facilities, the *II./PR23* attacked Repki on 8 February with 18 *Panthers*. At the same time, *schwere Panzer-Abteilung 503*, swinging out to the left, blocked the retreat route for the withdrawing enemy. Repki was taken after a fight with enemy tanks, in the process of which one T-34, three assault guns and one truck were destroyed. One *Panther* was a total loss due to enemy fire. The Repki area was secured on 9 February. On that day, one assault gun and one truck with limbered antitank gun were destroyed by the *4./PR23*.

Schweres Panzer-Regiment Bäke was ordered to Rubany (via Winograd) on 10 February. In the evening, the long awaited resupply elements arrived, which had only been possible the previous few days by means of tracked vehicles. At 0700 hours on 11 February, after preparatory fires from the *18. Artillerie-Division* and the *1. Werfer-Brigade, Kampfgruppe Bäke*—the *II./PR23, Panzer-Regiment 2* (*16. Panzer-Division*) and the armored elements of the *16. Panzer-Division* (which had command and control of that sector)—moved out in the direction of Bushanka — Frankowka after preparatory fires from the *18. Artillerie-Division* and the *1. Werfer-Brigade*. It was there that they intended to break the ring of encirclement around the divisions in Tscherkassy. In an attack along a sector of 2-3 kilometers in width, the *Kampfgruppe* approached Frankowka after three hours. Enemy infantry with antitank guns and trains elements fled from the village. The *Panthers* pursued and formed a bridgehead on the far side of the Gniloj Tikitsch after an aggressive thrust. By doing that, large portions of the enemy forces had their retreat route ct off. Twelve "Stalin Organs" and many artillery pieces were captured. An enemy immediate counterattack conducted by 10 tanks ended with the destruction of 6 of them. The remaining tanks turned away. Even the enemy antitank guns that went into position along the left flank of the battle group were unable to change the situation. The antitank guns were destroyed. The adjutant of the *II./PR23*, *Leutnant* Mengel, conducted a reconnaissance thrust north and destroyed an aircraft that had landed in the fields in the process. A lack of fuel and munitions prevented the continued advance of the battle group.

The formation of a bridgehead across the Gniloj Tikitsch was the first decisive step in freeing the divisions encircled south of Tscherkassy. As the result of continuous enemy attacks, they had been pressed together into an ever-shrinking area.

At 0700 hours on 12 February, the battalion's four *Panthers*, three *Tigers* and *Panzer-Aufklärungs-Abteilung 16* (*16. Panzer-Division*) moved out against the high ground east of Daschukowka. The enemy attempted to disrupt German command and control by interfering with the radio traffic of the tanks. In the end, heavy defensive fires from tanks and antitank guns brought the attack to a standstill. Four *Panthers* were set alight; the enemy lost two T-34's, two assault guns and five antitank guns.

On 13 February, the remaining operational *Panthers* of the battalion attacked as part of *Panzer-Regiment 2*. Ten *Tigers* and *Panzer-Aufklärungs-Abteilung 16* attacked Daschukowka at the same time from the front, destroying numerous enemy tanks and antitank guns. The village was taken. In a further advance to the east, the crossroads north of Lissjanka was taken and the enemy supply traffic was interdicted. Three *Panthers*, under the command of *Hauptmann* Grüner of *Panzer-Regiment 2*, advanced against the village of Chishinzy, which was screened by numerous enemy tanks and antitank guns. In a night attack, *Panzer-Aufklärungs-Abteilung 16*, which had been committed there in the meantime, entered the village with the tanks. Before the last operational tank of the *II./PR23* would be lost through fighting there, the battalion was able to report the following successes for the day: seven tanks and assault guns; six antitank guns; and four trucks.

Two repaired *Panthers* reinforced the battle group in Chishinzy on 14 February. Despite that, it proved impossible to drive the enemy infantry from his stubbornly defended positions in and around the village. As a result, the battle group had to set up a hedgehog defense in the village again that evening.

On 15 February, the elements in Chishinzy returned to Tschesslowka. Due to a lack of recovery means, two *Panthers* had to be blown up. Together with *Panzer-Regiment 2*, three of the five operational *Panthers* assumed responsibility for screening Tschesslowka, while the other two joined in the attack of *Kampfgruppe Bäke* from Lissjanka to break open the ring of encirclement to the northeast. One T-34 was destroyed by the screening elements in Tschesslowka; others were forced away.

On 16 February, the greatly weakened relief forces were also unable to establish contact with the encircled corps. Correspondingly, the *XI. Armee-Korps* and the *XXXXII. Armee-Korps* received orders to break out to the southwest. Despite good preparations, they were also unable to gain but little ground in the direction of Lissjanka during the day. It was not until the night of 16/17 February that the breakout from the pocket succeeded for the desperate soldiers, who had to leave behind all of their heavy weapons and equipment in the race to get out. The Soviet blocking positions were simply overrun, with heavy, bloody losses on both sides. As a result of the thin corridor formed by the *16. Panzer-Division* and the *17. Panzer-Division*, 30,000 German soldiers were gradually able to escape capture. Of decisive importance in their escape were the outposts at Lissjanka, Tschesslowka and along the narrow corridor that stretched to Frankowka. Attacking enemy tanks were knocked out continuously. Gradually, however, the German tanks were also lost, either through enemy action or mechanical problems, and had to be blown up, since there was a lack of recovery means. All of the damaged tanks in the Frankowka area were employed in the local defenses.

In the afternoon of 18 February, enemy infantry and tanks blocked the road west of Frankowka. In a counterattack the next day, infantry and reconnaissance soldiers from the *16. Panzer-Division* reopened the single supply route to the southwest. A *Panther* of the *II./PR23* screening on the west side of the village knocked out four T-34's out of a group of Soviet tanks that attacked Frankowka from the west at first light; the remaining tanks turned away. German assault guns arriving from the west screened the supply route. The enemy fired artillery on Frankowka the entire day, but he was unable to impede the passage of the freed divisions.

The last elements of those divisions passed through Frankowka on the morning of 20 February; *Kampfgruppe Bäke* followed them. Three repaired tanks of the 2nd Battalion received the mission to tow damaged tanks out of Frankowka. Those tanks were suddenly attacked by 20 enemy tanks 3 kilometers west of the village. *Leutnant* Erb took up the firefight with his three *Panthers*, knocking out 13 enemy tanks without sustaining any friendly losses. His tanks also inflicted heavy casualties on the accompanying Soviet infantry. They were not successful in clearing the road, however. As the result of the mechanical problems on one of the towing tanks, neither of the damaged tanks could be recovered, and they had to be blown up in the face of enemy infantry working its way forward under cover of darkness. The crews fought their way through to Rubannyj Most.

On 21 February, the two remaining battle groups in Frankowka—*Kampfgruppe Bäke* and *Kampfgruppe Frank* (of the *16. Panzer-Division*)—moved out to break through to Rubannyj Most. The nine damaged tanks of the *II./PR23* in Frankowka could not be evacuated and were blown up. Heavy Soviet artillery fire continued to be placed on the village. Two Soviet infantry regiments were eliminated in the breakthrough to Rubannyj Most.

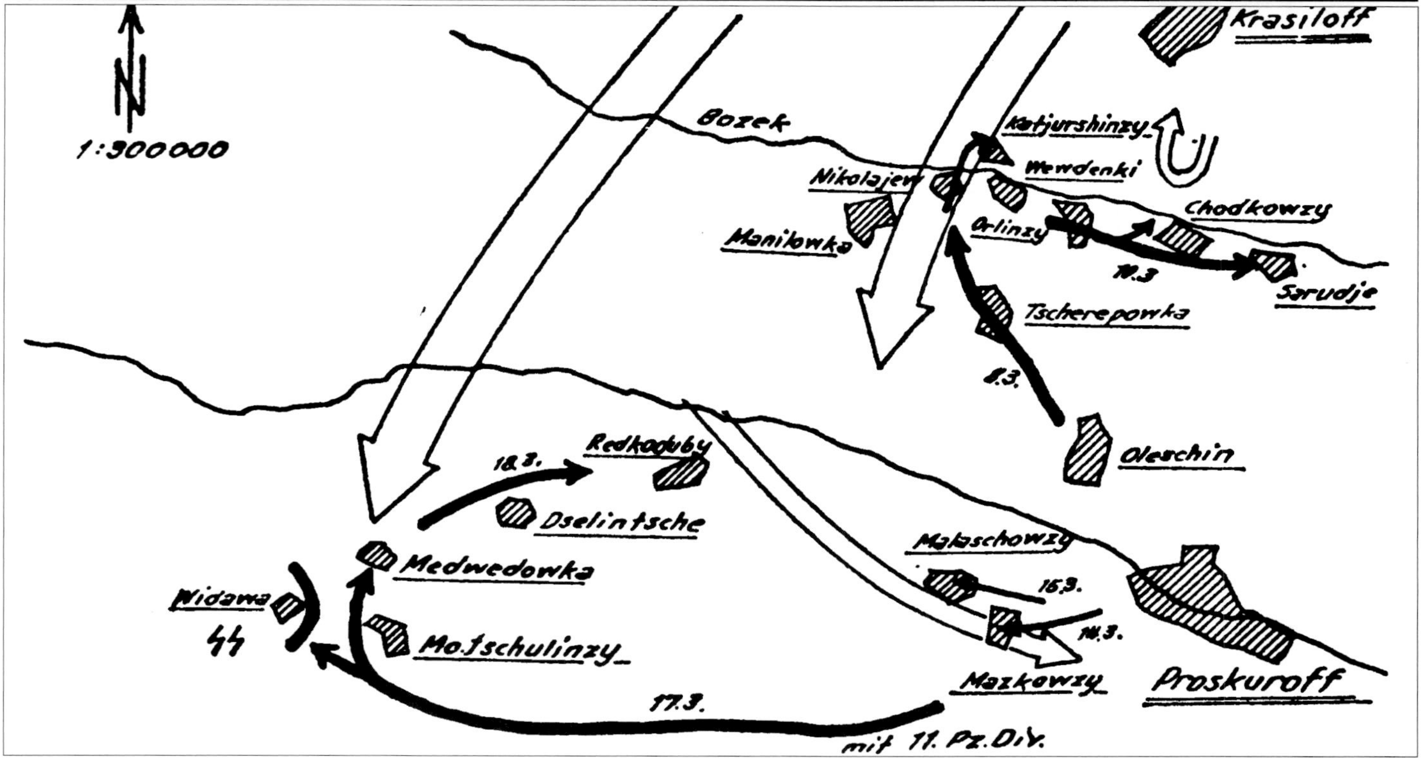

Map 79: Counterattacks North and West of Proskuroff from 8-18 March 1944.

The *II./PR23* was moved to Potasch on 23 February and began to repair the remaining *Panthers*. The wheeled elements of the battalion moved into the new reconstitution area of Winniza on 29 February. On 1 March, the last four remaining operational *Panthers* were transferred to *Panzer-Regiment 2*. *Hauptmann* Esser arrived as the new battalion commander, because *Major* Fechner was transferred to the gunnery school at Putlos as its new commander. *Hauptmann* Euler went to the division headquarters as the assistant division adjutant.

In the middle of the battalion movement to Winniza, the Soviets broke through as far as Potasch on 7 March. Five *Panthers*, which had been repaired in the meantime, under *Leutnant* Willscheid were unable to contain the attack. In the knee-deep mud they became mechanically disabled and had to be blown up. The other 18 damaged *Panthers* of the battalion, which were still located in Potasch, had to be blown up when the Russians took the village.

Schweres Panzer-Regiment Bäke was disbanded, effective 1 March. The commander, *Oberstleutnant* Bäke, was awarded the Swords to the Oak Leaves to the Knight's Cross of the Iron Cross for his great and decisive successes as commander of the regiment. He was the 49th member of the German Armed Forces to be so honored. The regiment had destroyed more than 500 enemy tanks and 400 artillery pieces of all types. Above all else, it had opened the way out of the Tscherkassy Pocket for 30,000 German soldiers.

In his farewell order, *Oberstleutnant* Bäke especially praised the logistics services of his two tank battalions under *Oberleutnant* Klemm and *Leutnant* Koppe, who created the prerequisites for the successful operations of the combat elements.

In Winniza, the *II./PR23* was directly subordinated to the headquarters of *General der Panzertruppen* Hube's *1. Panzer-Armee*. As early as 1545 hours on 6 March, the battalion was placed on an elevated alert status, even though it no longer had any *Panthers* and the maintenance services were busy with the repair of the wheeled vehicles.

The inflexible conduct of the war by Hitler had as a consequence that the front of the *1. Panzer-Armee* and the *4. Panzer-Armee* almost ran in an east-west direction after the difficult defensive fighting west of Kiev, while, at the same time, the right wing of the *6. Armee* of *Heeresgruppe Süd* was still echeloned far forward to the east, where it was fighting along the Ingulez. Consequently, the enemy centered his next offensive against the left wing of the field-army group in the area of Proskuroff. Attacking to the south, he attempted to throw the field-army group back to the Carpathians and destroy it by attacking against the entire front at the same time.

On 4 March, the formations of the 1st Ukrainian Front of Field Marshall Zhukov penetrated to the south through the frontage of the *4. Panzer-Armee* on both sides of Schepetowka. On 6 March, his lead elements were just 50 kilometers north of Proskuroff.

The *II./PR23* was ordered to Proskuroff to receive new *Panthers*, but it was only able to have 24 of them transferred from the *16. Panzer-Division*. The first time the vehicles moved out, two of them became total losses when they ignited on their own.

On 8 March, the enemy was 20 kilometers from Proskuroff. The battalion was alerted and attached to *Kampfgruppe Düwel* from the *17. Panzer-Division*. At 0900 hours on 9 March, it established contact with *Kampfgruppe Sievers*, which was already fighting outside of Nikolajew, after having moved from Olechin via Tscherepowka. The two battle groups then took Nikolajew in a fight against tanks, antitank guns and strong infantry. On his own initiative, *Leutnant* Hengerer and his *4./PR23* crossed a bridge over the Bozek bottomland and entered Katjurshinzy along with accompanying infantry. Nine T-34's and two antitank guns were destroyed, compared to a total loss of two German tanks.

The battle group of *Major* Düwel was given the mission of extending its sector by 12 kilometers to the east on 10 March. To that end, the attached *II./PR23*, along with an infantry battalion, was tasked with attacking Orlinzy, Chodkowzy and Sarudje. The *7./PR23*, which was the first company available, moved out ahead with a platoon of infantry. At 0625 hours, it moved through Wewdenki and Orlinzy. In thick fog, the company encountered enemy tanks outside of Chodkowzy, which were also attacking the village. The enemy was beaten back, losing one of his tanks. Chodkowzy was occupied and the bridge over Bozek Creek blown up. During the morning, the enemy attempted to cross the frozen-over creek and enter the village, but he was turned back, suffering considerable casualties. During the course of 11 and 12 March, the *Panthers* of the battalion eliminated enemy forces that had infiltrated to the high ground east of Chodkowzy and threw enemy forces that had infiltrated into Orlinzy back to the north. Two *Panthers* were total losses due to enemy fires. Twelve *Panthers* were still operational. On 13 March, the *4./PR23* set four T-34's on the north bank of Bozek Creek alight.

On 14 March, the *II./PR23* was attached to the *11. Panzer-Division* and moved to Proskuroff. *Oberfähnrich* Schulz[80] attacked west from Proskuroff with a few *Panthers* and pushed back advanced Soviet elements out of Mazkowzy (6 kilometers west of Proskuroff).

At 1000 hours on 15 March, the battalion moved out with nine *Panthers* from positions at Gretschany (10 kilometers west of Proskuroff) to attack Malaschowzy. Just outside the village, the enemy had established a strong antitank-gun belt, which was eliminated without delay. Marshland that was covered by additional antitank guns outside of the village was bypassed. The antitank guns were destroyed and entry into the village was forced. With the onset of darkness, however, the village could not be taken. During the night, the battalion was ordered back to Proskuroff with all of its operational *Panthers*. The battalion was able to claim 30 antitank guns destroyed that day.

After performing screening duties along the main supply route—*Durchgangstraße IV*—the battalion was attached to *Kampfgruppe Oberstleutnant Bäke*, with which it attacked on 17 March with 11 *Panthers*. After eliminating an antitank-gun belt, the battle group advanced rapidly and established contact with an *SS* division at Widawa, 40 kilometers west of Proskuroff. The battalion bivouacked in Motschulinzy and safeguarded the bridge at Medwedowka.

On 18 March, the battle group attacked north from Medwedowka and encountered strong enemy armor concentrations outside of Dselintsche. The village was taken after knocking out 10 enemy tanks. The attack was continued the following day. Under the command of *Oberfähnrich* Schulz, the six operational *Panthers* of the battalion participated in the attack. The attack objective of Redkoduby was not taken in the face of heavy enemy resistance, predominately from tanks and assault guns. Two *Panthers* were total losses due to enemy fires; four enemy tanks were set alight.

In the evening, the battalion was withdrawn from the front lines and turned over its remaining *Panthers* the next day to the *1. Panzer-Division*, the *11. Panzer-Division* and the *17. Panzer-Division*, since it was being sent to the Lemberg area to be reconstituted. The tank crews were sent there by truck in two march serials.

Six of the tanks left to the battalion, which were not operational, were supposed to be loaded by rail at the closest suitable train station. The large Soviet ground gains to the south made it necessary to take a long circuitous route through Kamieniec Podolski, Czernowicz and Stanislau. While the first truck convoy made it to Lemberg without problems, the second truck convoy was held up by enemy elements north of Kamieniec Podolski. The group of six *Panthers* was able to cross the Dnestr on 26 March and reach Chelmenti, 30 kilometers south-southeast of Kamieniec Podolski. There, however, it had already been bypassed to the west and south by the Russians. *Hauptmann* Esser and *Leutnant* Wassen attempted to find a way out, since the tanks were not operational. Neither officer returned from the reconnaissance; their fate was never determined. Since no routes could be found for the *Panthers*, they had to be blown up. The crews fought their way west, together with infantry, where they were able to continue the march west to Lemberg with the second truck convoy on 1 April. The truck convoy followed the *1. Infanterie-Division*, which was able to clear a path through the Russians north of the Dnestr. On 14 April, the last personnel of the battalion arrived in Lemberg, where they were ordered to report directly to *Heeresgruppe Nordukraine*[81]. In the meantime, 59 new *Panthers* had arrived. *Hauptmann* Fischer was directed by the field-army group to assume command of the battalion in place of the missing *Hauptmann* Esser.

By 13 April, the *5./PR23* made ready to march with its 12 *Panthers*. It was sent by rail to the headquarters of the *XXXXII. Armee-Korps* of the *4. Panzer-Armee* in Wlodzimierz. On 17 April, the company, along with two battalions of infantry, attacked from Zaturce as part of the *72. Infanterie-Division* in an effort to retake the village of Torczyn, which had been lost the previous day. After breaking through the forward enemy lines, the attack bogged down in front of a Soviet antitank-gun belt. Two *Panthers* were total losses; four crewmembers in all were killed.

At first light on 20 April, the *5./PR23* marched into the area around Jamki, in order to take Bujani with the *I./Grenadier-Regiment 124*. The attack did not achieve its objective in the face of strong Soviet antitank defenses, mines and difficult terrain. On 21 April, the tank company was attached to the *214. Infanterie-Division*. On 25 April, it supported the attack of the division's *Grenadier-Regiment 568* from Moczutki to the east with three *Panthers*. A dominant hill was taken, from which the attack was continued further to the north toward Swinarcin on 26 April. After fending off several immediate counterattacks on the part of the Soviets, the village was taken on 27 April and then held in the face of continued numerous counterattacks.

On 30 April, the company and supporting infantry attacked from Moczutki to the east with its five *Panthers*. In the course of the attack, four enemy antitank guns were eliminated.

Starting on 5 May, the *Panthers* supported the defensive efforts of the German infantry, along with five *Tigers*. On 10 May, they returned to the fold of the battalion. While the company was detached, it was able to book the following successes: 17 antitank guns; 1 heavy mortar; 7 antitank rifles; 3 heavy machine guns; and 1 tracked prime mover. Two *Panthers* were total losses during the period.

On 16 April, the *II./PR23*, minus the 5th Company which was in support of the *XXXXII. Armee-Korps*, was directed to Stanislau. There it was to be attached to the Hungarian 1st Army. By 19 April, the battalion had arrived in Stanislau by both road march and rail transport and was further attached to *Panzergruppe Knorr* of the *17. Panzer-Division*. In a road march conducted at night, the battalion moved through Tysmienica and reached a staging area in Jezierzany, 35 kilometers southeast of Stanislau.

There it was supposed to support the attack of *Kampfgruppe Bruxs* on the high ground south of Zywaczow with its 30 operational *Panthers*. The majority of the *6./PR23* ran into mines; the two other companies suffered heavy losses to the exceptionally strong Soviet antiarmor defenses. The battalion physician was mortally wounded. With his remaining operational tanks, *Hauptmann* Fischer attacked the village of Zywaczow from the south, took it and destroyed two enemy tanks. Without delay, the battalion advanced along the Zywaczow — Harasymow road to the east as far as the high ground to the west of the latter village. In the process, two heavy enemy tanks of a type unknown to that point were destroyed. In the course of that difficult fighting, the battalion lost 15 *Panthers*, while destroying a total of six enemy tanks and eight antitank guns.

During the morning of 21 April, 14 *Panthers* of the *II./PR23*, along with five attached *Tigers*, moved out of the area around the processing plant at Zielona to attack in the direction of Hill 302 northeast of Zabokruki. For the first time, the enemy employed his new 5.7cm antitank gun there. Several German tanks were lost, with two of them being total losses.

80 Editor's Note = officer candidate. The Germans used a different rank system to denote officer candidates.

81 Editor's Note: = Field-Army Group "Northern Ukraine".

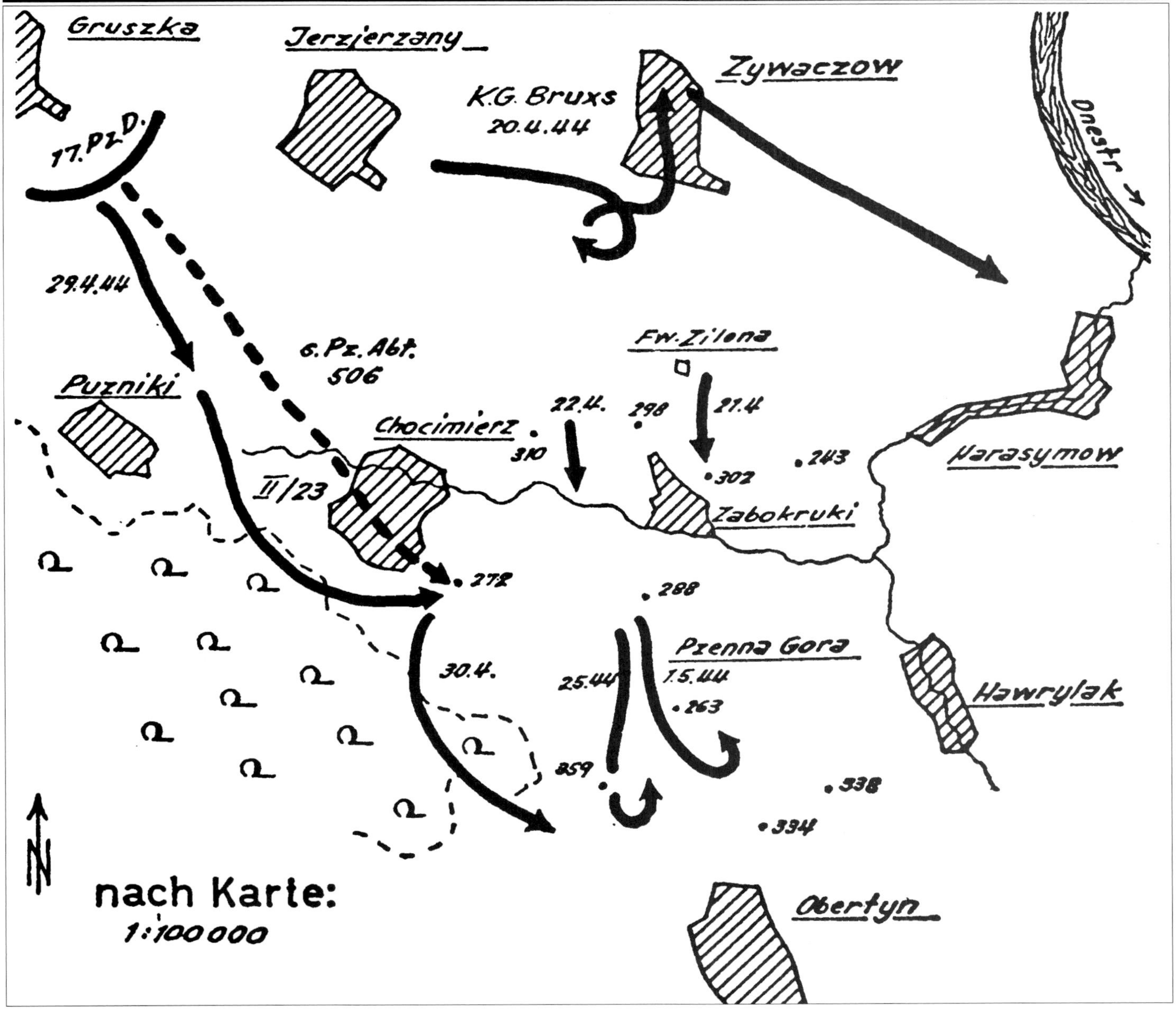

Map 80: Counterattacks with the *17. Panzer-Division* to the East of Stanislau from 20 April to 2 May 1944.

Leutnant Schiele was mortally wounded. Two enemy tanks and four antitank guns were destroyed. During the night, the battalion pulled back behind the infantry lines on Hill 298.

On 22 April, the nine *Panthers* that were still operational attacked south, east of Hill 301. The hill itself was heavily safeguarded by tanks and antitank guns. Two *Panthers* became total losses; despite several attempts, the attack yielded no success. Hill 298 was also lost temporarily, but it was later retaken.

On the evening of 25 April, the battalion marched to Gruszka and prepared for operations as part of the *17. Panzer-Division*. The attack was not ordered until 29 April. A wooded area west of Chocimierz was crossed when the elements headed south. At the same time, the *Tigers* of *schwere Panzer-Abteilung 506* took the village proper in a hard fight. The *II./PR23* assumed the lead in the attack and took Hill 272 along the road to Obertyn; an all-round defense was established there that night. The attack was continued on 30 April, but it was only able to gain little ground to the south, since the enemy had employed strong armored and assault-gun formations, against which the *Tigers*, attacking from the front, were unable to make progress. The *II./PR23*, together with a light infantry battalion from the *101. Jäger-Division*, swung out to the west, cleared a wooded area and was thus able to get the attack temporarily moving again. By evening, however, only five *Panthers* of the battalion were operational, after one had become a total loss and numerous other ones had suffered battle damage and mechanical problems.

On 1 May, the battle group moved out along a line running Hill 288 — Pszenna Gora to attack to the southeast in the direction of the Obertyn — Hawrylak road. Hill 263 was taken at 0730 hours after the enemy infantry positions had been overrun. The continued advance of the weak armored group failed, however, due to the numerous Soviet assault guns. Heavy artillery and rocket-launcher fires were placed on the battalion the entire day, but they did not cause any casualties.

On the following day, the battalion attacked with its six operational *Panthers* and two companies of *Tigers* from its hedgehog positions at Pszenna Gora to the south, in order to take Hill 359. Vastly superior numbers of enemy tanks prevented a success. Late in the afternoon of 2 May, repeated attacks conducted in conjunction with elements of *Panzer-Regiment 4* led to the temporary occupation of that hill. One more total loss

This photograph was taken after the fighting at Tscherkassy. *Hauptmann* Fischer, with the Knight's Cross, is surrounded by some of his officers. To the viewer's right front is *Oberleutnant* Hyprath, who was later killed in action. To the right rear is *Oberleutnant* Dittmann.

Tank crews without tanks prepare for employment as infantry.

Vehicles of *PJA 128* overcome the mud near Kriwoi Rog.

Infantry marching down a road with burning oil tanks in the background.

This Soviet assault gun, which was built using a captured *Panzer III*, was, in turn captured toward the end of December 1943 and put back into use by the *2./PJA 128*. The Soviets were quite impressed with the *StuG III* and their version obviously follows a similar layout. The gun and mantlet look to be taken directly from a T-34

Soldiers of PJA 128 outside of the German administrative command in Kriwoi Rog.

The 2./PJA 128 prior to a counterattack in Kriwoi Rog.

Replacing a track in the mud.

Looking for firing positions west of Kriwoi Rog.

On 4 April 1944, personnel prepare to be air lifted to Romania to assist in the training of the Romanian Imperial 1st Armored Division "Romania Mare". Seen here are *Leutnant* Dern and *Leutnant* Stopp.

The *1./PR 23*, equipped with assault guns instead of tanks, moves out to support a combined exercise with the Romanians.

General Korne, the Division Commander of the Romanian formation, in discussion with his tank regiment commander, Colonel von Benedikt. Note the later model *Panzer IV*, which had been issued to the allied forces, as well as the *Sd.Kfz. 251*.

Appearing at the rear of the Division Command is Colonel Canstantinesku. The German officer in the black *Panzer M43* field cap is *Hauptmann* Mielenhausen, an advisor detailed to assist the Romanian forces.

An exercise with the Romanians northwest of Roman. Despite assurances of solidarity, the Romanians were soon the conclude an agreement with the Soviets to turn against their former allies.

The *1./PR 23* returned to the command and control of the *23. Panzer-Division* in July 1944. *Generalmajor* Kraeber is on hand to welcome the company back.

Leutnant Mehler and *Leutnant* Blumenschein.

Hauptmann Gerd Fischer.

Leutnant Stopp at the regiment's command post.

Gerd Fischer and fellow officers. In the image on the right, *Oberleutnant* Stöcker wears a metal version of the division insignia on his black Panzer M43 field cap.

The movement to Poland in July 1944;the tanks have been loaded on the cars, and the crews await the moment to board and move out.

This *Panther* appears to have assumed the status of a "moving van" as well. It is well protected by spare track links but a hit from a strafing aircraft could have serious consequences.

Trucks were placed between the tanks to more evenly distribute the weight of the heavy armored vehicles.

From the left: *Stabsarzt Dr.* Amann, *Leutnant* Stopp, *Oberleutnant* Berndt, *Oberleutnant* Zirr, *Leutnant* Schreiber, *Inspekteur* ? and *Leutnant* Mehler.

From the left: *Oberleutnant* von Oechelhaeuser, *Major* Rebentisch, *Leutnant* Doncher, *Leutnant* Blumenschein and *Stabsarzt* Dr. Trautmann.

On 21 September 1944, Ernst Rebentisch was promoted to *Major*. These photos with the officer corps of the regiment were taken at the promotion ceremony.

The officer corps of the regiment.

This SU-85 was captured outside of Jassy and then employed by its new owners. Seen in these images are Leutnant Pross, Unteroffizier Seiffahrt, Sudholz, Heise and Schütze Würz. These tank destroyers/assault guns were a very effective use of the T-34 chassis.

Cleaning the ammunition on a captured T-34.

A rail-loaded *Panther* of the *II./PR 23*.

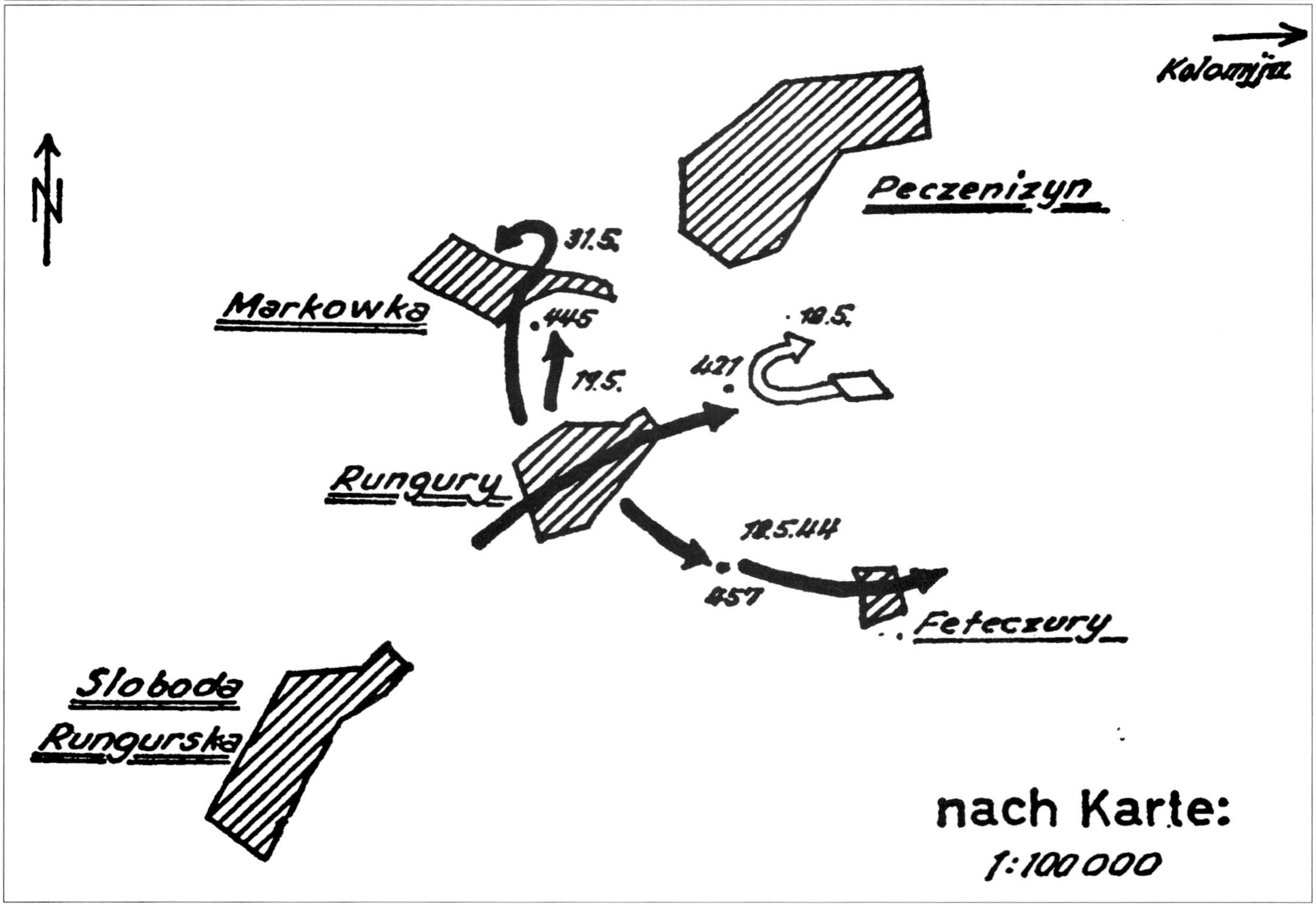

Map 81: Counterattack with the *16. Panzer-Division* West of Kolomya from 18-31 May 1944.

and numerous mechanical problems finally forced the battalion to be withdrawn from front-line operations.

In the days that followed, the damaged tanks were recovered, sometimes under enemy fire. Their repair was effected in Jezierzany.

On the evening of 5 May, the battalion was attached to the *16. Panzer-Division* in the Bratkowce area. Through 9 May, the combat elements moved to Chomiakow (10 kilometers south of Stanislau), and the trains moved to Stanislau proper, where they were joined by the *5./PR23*, which was returning from its operations with the *XXXXII. Armee-Korps*, on 10 May. Training and maintenance work closed the gaps that had formed. On 12 May, the battalion conducted a training demonstration exercise for *Generalfeldmarschall* Model, the Commander-in-Chief of *Heeresgruppe Nordukraine*, and Hungarian officers. Following the exercise, it moved to Drohomiercany. After a few days of training, telephonic orders arrived at 2400 hours on 17 May from *Oberstleutnant* Collin, the commander of *Panzer-Regiment 2*, that the battalion was to move out that same night into the Kolomya area, in order to conduct operations with the *16. Panzer-Division* as part of the *XI. Armee-Korps*. The battalion reached Sloboda Rungurska with 34 *Panthers* at 1400 hours on 17 May, after marching through Nadwirna, Delatyn and Luczki. Only two *Panthers* became disabled due to mechanical problems during the 80-kilometer-march in the Carpathian foothills.

In the previous few days, the enemy had succeeded in breaking through the Hungarian main line of resistance at several places west of Kolomya. The *16. Panzer-Division* received orders to restore the former main line of resistance. At 1600 hours, elements of the *II./PR23*, along with a mechanized infantry battalion, were given the task of bringing friendly grenadiers at, and south of Hill 421, back into the main line of resistance after advancing through Rungury. Enemy infantry was scattered and five antitank guns were destroyed. The mechanized infantry took prisoners. At 1830 hours, Hill 421 was in German hands and was secured by the *4./PR23* and the mechanized infantry.

On 18 May, the 4th Company was relieved by the 5th Company. At 0700 hours, the battalion headquarters and the 7th and 8th Companies moved out to attack Feteczury from Rungury. They took Hill 457 southeast of Rungury and continued the advance with infantry. One *Panther* was lost to a direct hit by artillery. Despite massive Soviet artillery fires, the battalion crossed two creek beds and reached the attack objective of Feteczury at 1000 hours. The friendly infantry was unable to maintain contact, however, and had to fight its way through terrain occupied by Soviet infantry, not reaching the hedgehog positions of the tanks until the onset of darkness.

At the same time, the *5./PR23*, defending on Hill 421 east of Rungury, had to fend off an enemy tank and infantry attack. It destroyed five T-34's and brought the Hungarian infantry, which had immediately fled, back into their positions. The day's tally saw the destruction of five T-34's, two antitank guns, four infantry guns and eight mortars. Fifteen prisoners were taken.

On 19 May, the enemy was ejected from his position on Hill 445, north of Rungury, by the *4./PR23* with four *Panthers*. The Hungarian infantry only followed the tanks hesitantly. They occupied the former main line of resistance and were reinforced that evening with antitank guns and additional infantry, with the result that the tanks could be pulled back to Rungury.

On 22 May, the *4./PR23* left the *II./PR23*, turned over its *Panthers* and returned to the regiment, which was conducting operations in Romania, after moving there by rail from Stanislau.

As a result of the continuous rainfall, the combat activities of the Soviets were limited to local advances, which could be turned back everywhere by the screening *Panthers*. In the process, 1 T-34, 1 antitank gun, 10 machine guns and 6 mortars were destroyed and bloody losses were inflicted on the enemy.

During the night of 30/31 May, the *II./PR23* prepared to attack Markowka. The attack started at first light on 31 May from the area of Hill 445. Together with the two infantry regiments of the *16. Panzer-Division*, they attempted to shorten and straighten the main line of resistance. While the right-hand attack wing made good progress despite difficult terrain, heavy resistance and heavy artillery fire, the left-hand wing suffered losses to mines and antitank guns. Engineers cleared lanes so that the attack could be continued forward. Soviet infantry was driven from a heavily fortified field position when taken under direct tank main-gun fires. The enemy brought up antitank guns on the right wing. Two Soviet 12.2cm antitank guns were destroyed. The German infantry fought its way forward to the tanks up front, but even more heavy minefields brought the attack on the right to a standstill.

The tangible successes of the day were measured by the destruction of 11 antitank guns, 1 infantry gun, 1 mortar, 2 heavy machine-gun bunkers, 8 additional heavy machine guns and numerous enemy dead. Together with the infantry, the positions that had been taken were secured. On the next day, the positions were maintained despite assaults from strong Soviet infantry forces. The enemy lost approximately 250 dead. The commander of the *16. Panzer-Division*, *Generalmajor* Back, commended the *II./PR23* for the successful attack.

On 4 June, the battalion was detached form the *16. Panzer-Division* in order to be transported by rail from Delatyn back to the division in Romania. Efforts to recover all of the damaged tanks by the departure of the last train were successful. They were towed to the loading ramps, with the result that valuable tanks remained under the control of the division. On 23 June, the last train arrived back at the division location in the Jassy area. The battalion initially took up quarters west of the city, while the division itself was still conducting operations north and northwest of the city. *Hauptmann* Fischer was designated as the official commander of the battalion by the division commander, *Generalmajor* Kraeber.

Fighting in Southern Poland and for the Bridgehead Over the Vistula at Sandomierz 29 July to 10 September 1944

On 22 June, the large Soviet offensive against *Generalfeldmarschall* Busch's *Heeresgruppe Mitte* was launched. From the very beginning, it succeeded in gaining deep penetrations into the sectors of the *4. Panzer-Armee*, the *9. Armee* and the *3. Panzer-Armee* in the areas around Bobruisk, Mogilew, Orscha and Vitebsk. In this instance, once again, Hitler's insistence on pre-ordained decisions prevented defensive countermeasures prior to the attack, which had been identified in time. His orders, which forbade any type of withdrawal for the forces in the field or the headquarters staffs, led to the loss of nearly 25 divisions in that area. It was a catastrophe that surpassed Stalingrad many fold, not only in numbers but also in its effect on the outcome of the war.

On 24 June 1944, the Commander-in-Chief of the *9. Armee, General* Jordan, was relieved of command and replaced by *General* von Vormann, the former commander of the *23. Panzer-Division*. Even he was unable to stop the encirclement of his field army around Bobruisk, which was completed on 29 June. On 28 June, *Generalfeldmarschall* Busch was replaced by *Generalfeldmarschall* Model, who also continued to remain in command of *Heeresgruppe Nordukraine*. A 300-kilomter-wide gap in the front had been torn open. Only 15,000 men of the *9. Armee* and small elements of the *3. Panzer-Armee* and the *4. Panzer-Armee* were able to pull back to the west, thanks to the decisiveness of their leaders, who acted in contravention of Hitler's orders.

On 4 July, *Heeresgruppe Mitte* had available eight formations of division strength in its 350-kilometer-wide sector to face four Soviets fronts with a total of 126 rifle divisions, 17 motorized brigades, 6 cavalry divisions, and 45 armored formations of brigade strength. On Hitler's orders, *Generaloberst* Lindemann's *Heeresgruppe Nord* had to hold its positions, although a withdrawal would have improved the over-all situation[82]. The consequence later on was its encirclement in Kurland.

By pulling out strong elements from both *Heeresgruppe Nord* and *Heeresgruppe Nordukraine*, the *4. Panzer-Armee*, the *2. Armee* and the *3. Panzer-Armee* were finally able to temporarily bring the enemy to a halt along a line running Brest-Litowsk — Grodno — Kowno. On 14 July, however, the 4th and 2nd Ukrainian Fronts moved out against the weakened *Heeresgruppe Nordukraine*, in order to take the middle portion of the Vistula and to advance to the south of it across the San to the west. The *1. Panzer-Armee* was broken through on both sides of Brody. On 16 July, the Soviets were positioned along the upper Bug north of Lemberg. The *4. Panzer-Armee* was broken through around Kowel. The lines could not be held along the Bug, either. On 22 July, the Soviets crossed the river at Cholm. While there was already fighting along the east side of Lemberg, the right wing of the *1. Panzer-Armee* was still holding at Stanislau so as to protect the passes through the Carpathians and prevent a Soviet penetration into Hungary. Lemberg was abandoned on 27 July. The Soviets pursued without let up, with the result that they were outside of Rzeszow on 3 August. On 6 August, they were making overtures for crossing the Wisloka and the Vistula (at Sandomierz).

It was during that phase of the fighting that the division was beginning to be transported out of Romania; starting on 23 July, it was loaded on trains at differing railheads around and west of Roman. The assembly area of the division was in the Krosno — Jaslo area for the time being. While some of the tracked elements were transported into the area around Jaslo, and other elements moved by train later on as far as Mielec, several elements of the division equipped with wheeled vehicles were detrained when they got to Slovakia.

On 27 July, the division headquarters and *PAA23* arrived in Jaslo. The reconnaissance battalion sent out its wheeled and half-tracked elements through Krosno to conduct reconnaissance to the east. Enemy forces were located 20 kilometers to the northeast of the city.

Due to the unclear situation in Poland, the division's reconnaissance battalion under *Hauptmann* Koppe proved to be an especially valuable asset. Moving ahead of the tanks and the infantry, it encountered concentrations of numerous enemy tanks and destroyed five of them with its two antitank guns. Following that, it turned back a battalion of Soviet infantry. In ceaseless fighting, it held up the enemy until an armored group could arrive to eliminate him. *Hauptmann* Koppe was later awarded the Knight's Cross to the Iron cross on 18 November 1944 for his exemplary performance of duty.

During the morning of 28 July, the combat elements of *PGR126* arrived; initially these were the regiment's troops and the 1st Battalion. As a precautionary measure, the combat and supply elements had already been separated while loading on the trains in Romania, since enemy contact was expected in the detraining area. In fact, the trains of the *I./PGR126* were engaged by antitank guns in the area northwest of Sanok.

82 Author's Note: Lindemann was later replaced by *General* Friessner.

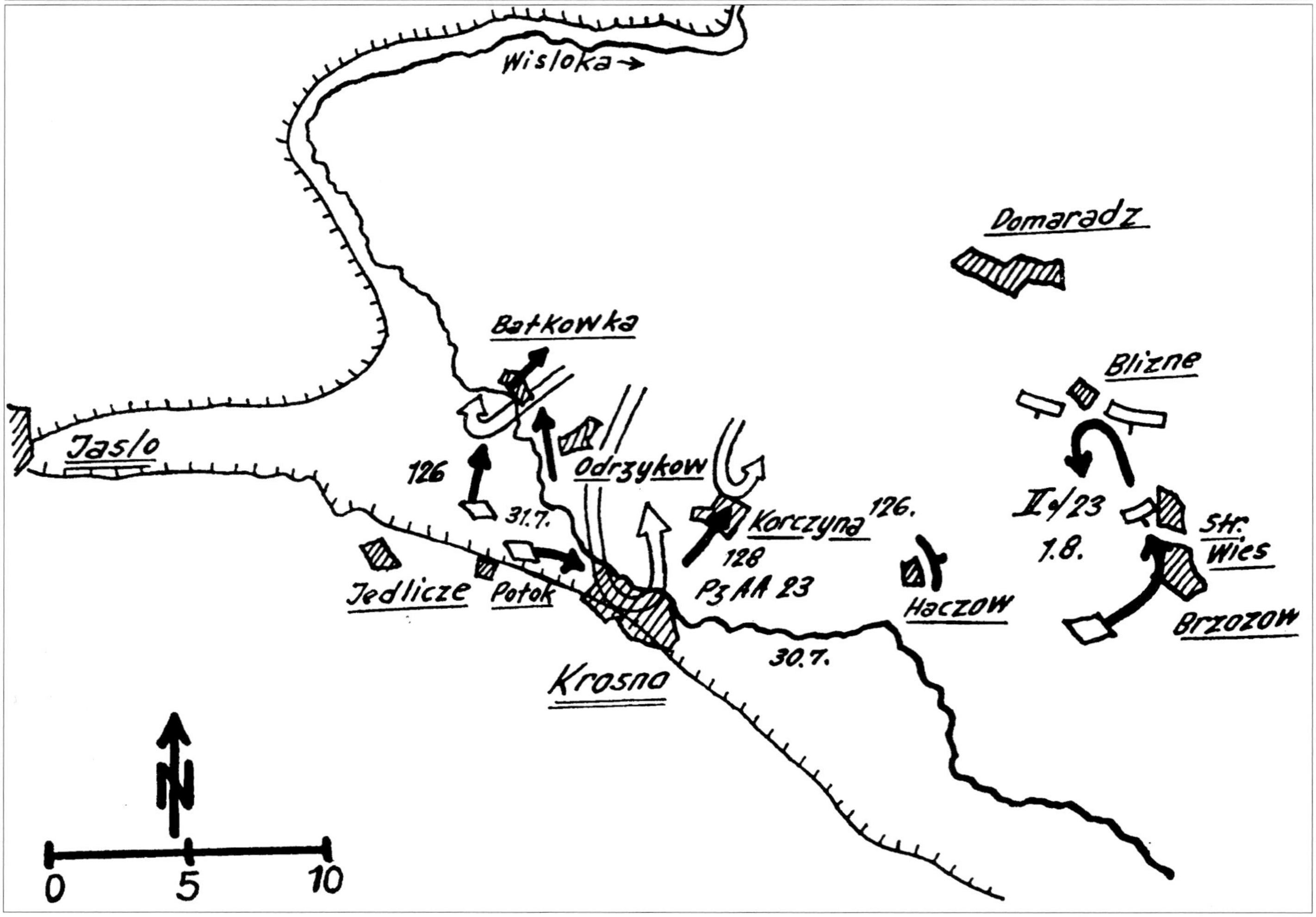

Map 82: Fighting in the Krosno — Blizne Area from 29 July to 1 August 1944.

The *I./PGR126* was given the mission of protecting the refinery at Jedlicze, which was still operating at full capacity. The regimental troops took up quarters in Potok.

The next troop element to arrive in Jaslo was *PGR128* at 0500 hours on 29 July. It was ordered to Krosno that afternoon.

The *23. Panzer-Division* received orders from the *III. Armee-Korps* to hold back the enemy as far as possible to the east of the Wisloka River and to screen the infantry formations that were newly arriving from the west as they established a main line of resistance along the river. *Panzergrenadier-Regiment 126* went into position along the east side of Haczow, 15 kilometers southeast of Krosno.

Hauptmann Gabler's *I./PGR128* was employed in an attack against enemy-occupied Korczyna, together with the *3.(SPW)/PAA23*. Dismounting just outside the village, the battalion, together with the *SPW's*, broke weak enemy resistance and started screening to the north and east from the village. At 0105 hours, the enemy attempted to retake the village with five tanks. One tank was destroyed by *Leutnant* Heinle of the 3rd Company and *Feldwebel* Steimer of the 4th Company with a *Panzerfaust*[83]; the other tanks then turned away. Heavy fog limited visibility to 20 meters.

Further to the east, in the area of Sanok, the *1. Panzer-Division* was fighting. At the same time, west of Reichshof (Rzeszow), the *24. Panzer-Division* was covering the withdrawals of the infantry divisions in the direction of Majdan and Mielec through a series of counterattacks and blocking positions.

At 0545 hours on 30 July, the *3./PGR128* turned back an attack on Korczyna by 150 infantry and cavalry. At 0700 hours, the enemy attacked Krosno in the rear of the battalion and blocked the road to Korczyna with 7 tanks and 250 infantry. Two additional attacks by tanks and infantry against the village were fended off by the *3./PGR128*.

In Krosno, the enemy tanks and infantry that had entered there were turned back by the *I./PGR128* in close coordination with the divisional escort company[84] of *Oberleutnant* Krichbaum. In an order-of-the day, *General* Radowitz singled out both elements for special praise.

In the meantime, the first elements of the *II./PR23* had also arrived in Krosno. The first company to arrive, the 5th Company of *Oberleutnant Freiherr* von Brandenstein, encountered enemy tanks just as it was entering the city. Five T-34's were destroyed, and the rest turned away hurriedly. Krosno was cleared of the enemy and the tank company screened on the east side.

Outside of Haczow, the enemy felt his way forward form the northeast. He occupied Debina and Hill 365. During the morning, a Soviet combat forces was turned away outside of Haczow. A short while later, the enemy placed harassing fires on the village with artillery and mortars.

In the meantime, *PAA23* attacked along the road to Korczyna. The battalion headquarters of the *I./PGR128* attacked along the road from

83 Editor's Note: The *Panzerfaust* was a handheld antitank rocket launcher, the precursor to the world-famous RPG-7.

84 Editor's Note: Escort companies were formed to protect the divisional command post but just as often as not were employed as a sort of additional standing reserve for situations such as the one described above.

Korczyna toward the reconnaissance battalion, an action that finally caused the enemy to retreat. Six prisoners were taken and one truck and a few heavy weapons were destroyed.

During the evening, the *I./PGR128* was pulled back from Korczyna to the south in order to occupy a new main line of resistance. *Panzergrenadier-Regiment 126* was pulled out of Haczow to occupy the new positions and positioned to the left of *PGR128* along the Wisloka in the Bratkowka area.

Enemy patrols feeling their way forward at 0830 hours on 31 July were followed by tanks with mounted infantry at 0945 hours. The weak combat outposts of *Hauptmann* Grünwaldt's *I./PGR126* were pushed back. The enemy advanced on Ustrobna through the middle of Bratkowka and across the bridge over the Wisloka. Four T-34's were destroyed by the antitank guns of the *4./PGR126*.

At 1300 hours, the *I./PGR126*, reinforced by *PAA23* and the *8./PR23*, moved out from the south to launch a counterattack on Bratkowka. The thrust, which was also initiated at the same time from the south out of Odrzykon and from the west, cleared the village of the enemy by 1515 hours. *Oberfähnrich* Klenke of the *8./PR23* scored the 500th "kill" for his battalion in the course of those operations. At 1800 hours, *Hauptmann* Grünwaldt's battalion attacked the high ground north of Bratkowka, in conjunction with the *8./PR23*, and took it.

The division received the mission on 1 August to interdict the logistics lines of communications of the strong enemy forces advancing west in the Blizne — Domaradz area by attacking to the northeast. In the course of the attack, the *I./PGR128* retook Korczyna and advanced further to the northeast. *Leutnant* Keese of the *4./PGR128* was killed; *Hauptmann* Gabler was wounded and replaced by *Hauptmann* Oechsle. *Panzergrenadier-Regiment 126* attacked with its 2nd Battalion, which had arrived in the meantime, against Odrzykon and with its 1st Battalion against Bratkowka. The regiment pushed the main line of resistance further to the north on the high ground. The losses were considerable, with the result that the 2nd Medical Company, employed in Jaslo, had plenty of work to do.

The *II./PR23* (minus its 5th Company) was forced to attack on the road due to the difficult and marshy terrain. Moving out from Brzozow, it encountered weaker enemy resistance at Str. Wies, overran an enemy artillery position south of Blizne and knocked out a Soviet armored car. At the outskirts of Blizne, the *Panthers*, moving behind one another, encountered an obstacle with 5.7cm antitank guns. In short order, two *Panthers* were complete losses and three suffered heavy battle damage. The antitank gun could only be knocked out after a while. The continued advance into the village encountered heavy resistance; in addition, the lead tank broke through a bridge. After the loss of another *Panther* to a Soviet assault gun, the battalion pulled back to the southwest. The battalion was ordered back to rejoin the division so that it could move to execute another mission. On that day, the *II./PR23* destroyed three T-34's (credited to the 5th Tank Company), seven antitank guns, four artillery pieces and an armored car.

During the night of 1/2 August, the division's infantry was relieved by *Grenadier-Regiment 1085*, while the tanks were already road marching through Jaslo, Pilzno and Debica to Mielec. Of six operational *Panthers*, four became mechanically disabled during the march. The *I.* and *III./PAR128*, as well as the *I./PR23*, arrived in Mielec on 1 August, where they established contact with *Major* Gebhardt's *Grenadier-Regiment 195* of the *78. Volkssturm-Division*. The batteries immediately went into position east and north of the city.

To the north of Mielec, the enemy had been able to advance west without noticeable resistance. He had reached the Vistula between Sandomierz and Baranow along a broad front and crossed it, while the *24. Panzer-Division* was still fixing the enemy to the east of Mielec. The *23. Panzer-Division* was attached to the *LIX. Armee-Korps* of *General der Infanterie* Schulz' *17. Armee*.

The mission of the *23. Panzer-Division* was to advance on Baranow from Mielec, destroy the Soviet ferry crossing points over the Vistula and destroy the basis for the bridgeheads on the west bank of the river.

Together with *Major* Stetting's *PGR126*, *Hauptmann* Rebentisch's *I./PR23* moved out to the north along the road at 1100 hours. Initially, the tank battalion only had eight assault guns and two *Panthers*. An enemy patrol consisting of motorcycles with sidecars was scattered at Tuszow-Narodowy; three motorcycles were destroyed. The infantry following the tanks captured a number of motorcycles and ejected about a company's worth of Soviets from the village to the east.

After 2 kilometers, the lead elements encountered a Russian antitank-gun belt, which was covering the crossroads west of Jaslany. The lead vehicle was set alight after numerous antitank-gun hits; the gun commander, *Oberfeldwebel* Lorisch and his entire crew was lost. Another assault gun, as well as the two *Panthers*, were knocked out after a short firefight; five tankers in all were killed. Numerous drainage ditches and the railway line, which had forced the advance to take place along the road up to that point, hindered cross country deployment. Two more assault guns were knocked out before they could reach a sufficient firing position for engaging the enemy antitank guns, which were largely concealed by the high grain in the fields. It was in that environment that one of the few disadvantages of the otherwise terrific German assault gun was revealed, especially since it had to be employed as a "tank" within a tank formation in contravention of its original purpose.

Around 1300 hours, reinforcements arrived in the form of the six *Panzer IV's* of *Oberleutnant* Donder's *3./PR23*, which had detrained in Mielec in the meantime, as well as five *Panthers* from the 2nd Battalion under the command of *Leutnant* Schönberger. At the same time, fighter-bombers that had been called on station by the Air-Ground Coordination Officer, arrived to join the ground fight. Together, the antitank-gun belt, consisting of nine 7.62cm antitank guns, was shattered in quick order. In addition, several 7.62cm infantry guns, as well as machine guns and antitank rifles, were destroyed. Covered by the divisional artillery, the tanks and assault guns advanced rapidly on Padew, entering the village at 1830 hours and eliminating weak enemy forces. The infantry cleared the ground that had been taken from the enemy.

The *2./Heeres-Flak-Abteilung 278* assumed responsibility for the defense of the air space over Mielec.

At 200 hours, the *I./PGR128*, which had been attached to *PGR126*, arrived in Padew and immediately advanced to the north. At 2355 hours, the *3./PGR128* took the road bridge over the canal at Bor intact, thus reaching its objective for the day.

On 3 August, the enemy, realizing the threat posed to his ferry crossing points and bridgeheads, attacked Padew from both the east and west. Despite constant fires from "Stalin Organs" and artillery, the infantry and tankers turned back all of the attacks. At 0430 hours, three T-34's attacked *Hauptmann* Böhme's *I./PGR126*; the antitank personnel eliminated two of them and the third one turned back, smoking. Three hours later, the *6./PGR126* turned back an enemy attack.

At 1100 hours, the *I./PGR128* moved out of the bridgehead at Bor and attacked in the direction of Dymitrow and Kolo. To its west, the regiment's 1st Battalion advanced to Domacyny, where it linked up with the *I./PGR126* on the left. The mission of the division was to destroy the ferries over the Vistula and capture the crossing points. The 1st and 2nd Battalions of the divisional artillery supported the attacks by firing on the villages.

In the midst of a pouring rain, *Panzergruppe Rebentisch* moved out at 1300 hours to support the attack. Domacyny and then Dymitroff were stormed in the face of strong enemy resistance. At 1900 hours, the

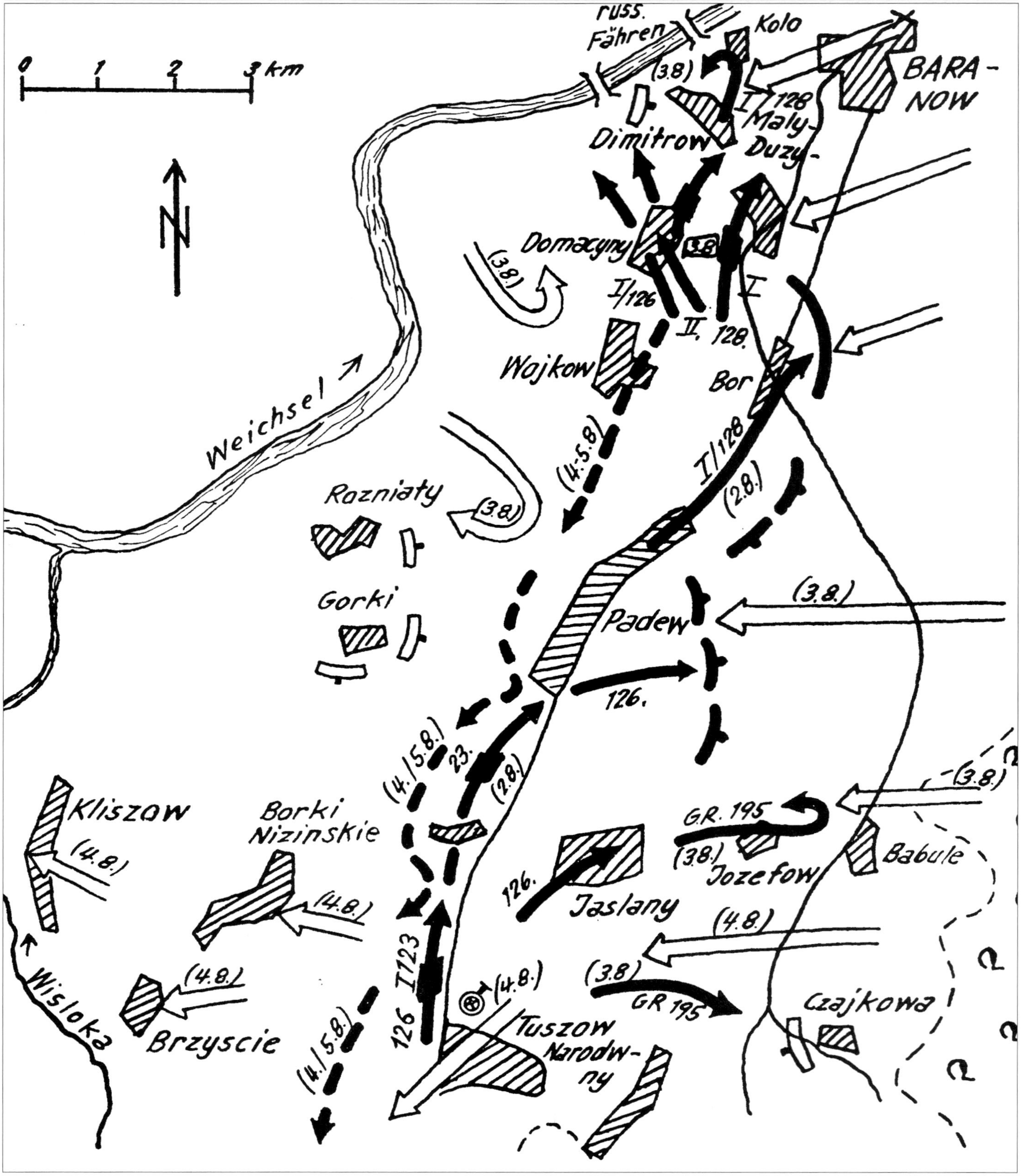

Map 83: Attack and Withdrawal North of Mielec from 2 to 5 August 1944.

I./PGR128 entered Kolo. It had to be taken in house-to-house fighting. *Leutnant* Lintl and *Leutnant* Wolfart were wounded. At 2100 hours, the southern portion of Kolo was in the battalion's hands. At the same time, the artillery and the tanks engaged the ferry crossing points north and west of Kolo. Despite all the casualties the enemy suffered in the process, he continuously attempted to resume ferry traffic. Undoubtedly, he had recognized the numerical inferiority of the German attackers and felt relatively secure against damaging blows.

In the course of the afternoon, the *II./PGR128*, with elements of *PGR126*, had to fend off several enemy attacks against the bridgehead position northeast of Padew. The enemy attacks were carried out with strong mortar and artillery support from Wola Baranowska.

After the onset of darkness, the tanks were pulled back to Dymitrow-Maly. *Hauptmann* Fischer assumed command of the armored group.

Along the east flank of the division, *Grenadier-Regiment 195*, which had been attached to the division, moved out to attack in the direction of Czajkowa and Babule in the afternoon. Supported by the *III./PAR128*, the regiment took the area just west and northwest of Czajkowa. The attack then broke down in the face of the enemy's defensive fires.

Southwest of Padew, several Soviet pockets of resistance were holding out. The *8./PAR128* was employed against them. Late in the afternoon, the enemy re-established himself in Padew. He brought up reinforcements from the east.

The division was directed to attack again on 4 August and break through to Baranow. *Oberstleutnant* Stichtenoth's *PGR128* and *Panzergruppe Fischer* moved out at 0700 hours. The terrain, which was criss-crossed by many ditches, made command and control of the attack difficult. Dymitrow-Maly was strongly manned by the enemy. It was not until that village was taken that an attack on Baranow proper was possible. The tanks crossed the embankment outside the village in sections and helped rally the grenadiers forward. Enemy tanks and antitank guns opened fire at short range. Three T-34's and several antitank guns had to be shot to pieces, before it was possible to move forward again. Superior numbers of Soviet artillery, some of it being fired from the west bank of the Vistula, inflicted heavy casualties on the infantry. Three *Panthers*, which had just made it to the edge of Dymitrow-Maly, were knocked out almost simultaneously by Soviet antitank guns in ambush positions. It was during that situation that enemy tanks and infantry advanced into the German forces from the northeast. As a result of changing positions, there was temporary confusion among the ranks of the German infantry, but the problem was quickly solved. The infantry moved back to Dymitrow-Duzy and then to the area to its west. *Leutnant* Schopfer and *Oberleutnant* Gutknecht (*I./PGR128*) were wounded.

While the enemy was still attacking along the front, he also attempted to envelop the German forces by launching another attack to the south of Dymitrow-Duzy. Those German forces pulled back, fighting, to Wojkow. When the German tanks launched immediate counterattacks, the enemy attack was finally brought to a standstill. During the afternoon, two Soviet companies attacked the railway bridge north of Padew. The enemy was turned back, suffering heavy losses. The division's antitank battalion made good use of the company of captured armored vehicles it had established. It fought with a small number of operational T-34s and SU 85s.

In the meantime, the situation along the east flank of the division had worsened considerably. While the enemy moved strong forces from out of the woods east of Jaslany to the north in the morning and only attacked with a company of infantry against Grochowo, he attacked in the afternoon across a broad front in increasing strength.

At 1300 hrs, the enemy was positioned outside the eastern side of the extended village of Padew. At 1400 hours, 600 Soviets attacked the road bridge at Bor and reduced the bridgehead. They were unable to succeed in taking the actual crossing, however. In a counterattack, the *II./PGR126* was able to restore the former main line of resistance east and northeast of Padew.

At 1830 hours, the enemy positioned himself anew to the east of Padew with strong forces. He then bypassed the strongpoints with tanks and infantry. After conducting that movement, he then attacked Padew simultaneously from the east, north and west, finally eliminating the bridgeheads along the railway line and the road bridge and forcing *PGR126* to rapidly pull back to the south, followed by *Grenadier-Regiment 195*. The German losses were considerable and the combat strengths sunk to an absolute minimum. Heavy weapons of the infantry and the divisional artillery were rushed into the front lines and shot the Soviet infantry to pieces in direct fire, before they changed positions.

Jaslany and, later on, Tuszow-Narodowy were lost. As a result, the Mielec — Baranow road was in enemy hands. The leading elements of the Soviet forces were soon entering the villages of Kliszow, Borki Nizinskie and Brzyszie on the Wisloka. Cut off were *PGR128*, the *I./PGR126*, the *5./PGR126* and *Panzergruppe Fischer*. In the effort to restore contact with them, the signals officer of *PR23*, *Oberleutnant* Hildebrandt, was killed. A short while later, the regimental commander, *Oberstleutnant* Bernau, was wounded.

Panzergrenadier-Regiment 128, minus its 1st Battalion, conducted a fighting withdrawal in the direction of Mielec and went into position again at Chorzelow.

At 2200 hours, after all of the lines of communication with the division had been cut, *Oberstleutnant* Stichtenoth decided to break through to the south with all of the elements fighting west of Padew and re-establish communications with the division. Leading the way was the *I./PGR128* with two tanks, followed by the main body of the grenadiers. The rearguard was the armored group with the *5./PGR126*. The breakout effort commenced at 0200 hours on 5 August. Not knowing how the situation had developed in the other sectors, the lead element initially attempted to get on the main road at Padew. In the moonlight, it came under heavy defensive fires from the Soviets 200 meters from the edge of the village and was forced back to the west. The same thing happened during the attempt to get on the main road at the crossroads at Jaslany. As a result, the movement was conducted cross-country over marshy terrain criss-crossed by ditches. Seven *Panthers* had to be towed the entire distance; only 6 tanks were conditionally operational. At 0400 hours, the lead element of *Gruppe Stichtenoth* reached the division outposts at Zlotniki; the battle group was then integrated into the line between the Chorzelow church and Zlotniki.

At 0900 hours, the rearguard, which had been cut off from the main body, reached Tuszow-Narodowy. It was greeted by heavy enemy fires there. One *Panther* and two assault guns became stuck and had to be abandoned by their crews. The rearguard assembled 3 kilometers northwest of Chorzelow, advanced against Tuszow-Narodowy one more time and retrieved the stuck vehicles.

The armored group assembled in the woods 4 kilometers southwest of Mielec and prepared for operations as the division reserve. *Hauptmann* Fischer assumed acting command of *PR23*.

For the execution of the breakthrough, *Oberstleutnant* Stichtenoth was later awarded the Knight's Cross to the Iron Cross on 5 September 1944. Through personal example and prudent leadership, he succeeded in leading the encircled battle group back to the division. While only suffering minimal losses, eight T-34's, two Joseph-Stalin's and two "Stalin Organs" were destroyed. In addition to the battle group commander, *Unteroffizier* Paul Stoll of the *6./PGR128* was also awarded the Knight's Cross to the Iron Cross on 2 September 1944 for exceptional bravery.

After the conclusion of the fighting in the area between Maidan and Mielec, the *23. Panzer-Division* pulled back to the west bank of the Wisloka through the Mielec Bridgehead.

Due to the constant pressure exerted by the enemy, the bridgehead at Mielec was evacuated during the night of 5/6 August. The division was directed to occupy a new defensive line on the west bank of the Wisloka, but the enemy had already been able to establish bridgeheads at several places.

The enemy immediately advanced into the withdrawal movements of the infantry. Although the bridge over the Wisloka could be effectively destroyed for some period of time, individual Soviet assault detachments

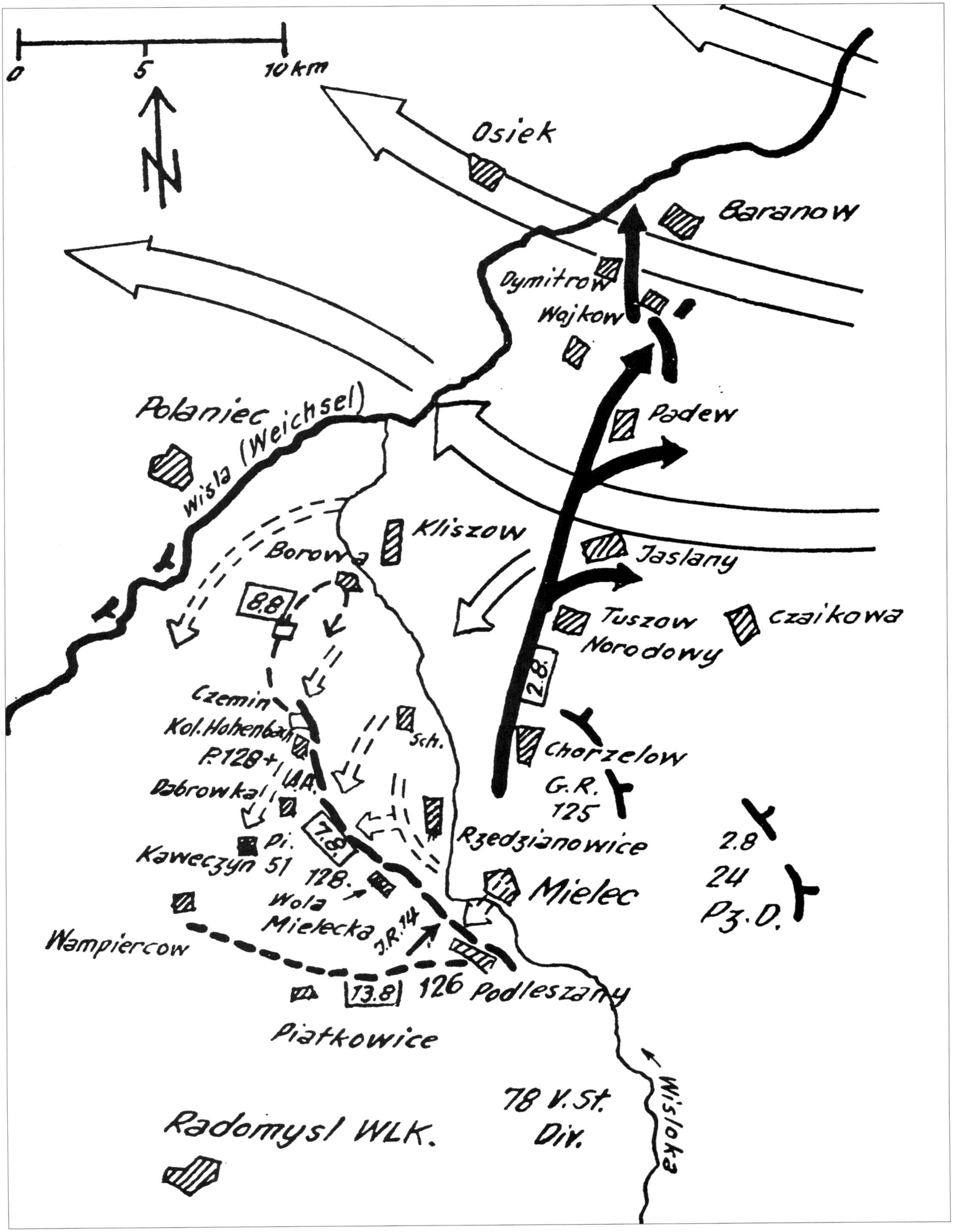
0
5
10 km
N
Osiek
Baranow
Dymitrow
Wajkow
Padew
Polaniec
Wisla (Weichsel)
Kliszow
Borowa
Jaslany
8.8
Tuszow
Norodowy
Czaikowa
2.8.
Czemin
Kol. Hohenbach
P. 128+
I.A.
Sch.
Chorzelow
G.R.
125
Dabrowka
Pi.
51
Kaweczyn
7.8.
128.
Rzedzianowice
2.8
24
Pz.D.
Mielec
Wola
Mielecka
J.R. 14
Wampiercow
13.8
126
Podleszany
Piatkowice
78 V.St.
Div.
Radomysl WLK.
Wisloka

were already crossing by boat before the infantry could establish their new main line of resistance.

The division's antitank battalion and reconnaissance battalion screened in a line running Czermin — Hohenbach Colony. The divisional engineers joined them on the right, followed by *PGR128* and *PGR126* later on. The tank regiment employed seven *Panthers* under *Oberleutnant* Hyprath with *PAA23* and five *Panthers* under *Oberleutnant Freiherr* von Brandenstein at Wola Mielecka.

During the day, the enemy continuously attacked form his bridgehead at Rzedzianowice, which he had been able to establish the previous day without a fight. The improved munitions situation for the artillery allowed effective support of the infantry, which was noticeably demonstrated outside of Rzedzianowice. The *8./PAR128* prevented crossing attempts by the enemy and scattered an enemy attack in the afternoon that had been directed against Wola Mielecka.

During the morning, additional Soviet groups forced a crossing over the river, exploiting the bridgehead in the vicinity of the bridge over the Wisloka. They soon attacked Podleszany and pushed back the main line of resistance of the *I./PGR126* on its left wing. An immediate counterattack forced the enemy back to 400 meters east of Podleszany, where it then bogged down in the beaten zone of the Soviet heavy weapons.

During a successful advance by *Gruppe Hyprath* and *PAA23* to the north, *Oberleutnant* Hyprath's tank was knocked out north of Hohenbach. He later died of his wounds. Two more *Panthers* were lost, after 11 Soviet antitank guns had been destroyed. The enemy was unable to gain any ground in that sector.

Together with *PPB51*, the *I./PGR128* attempted to take Rzedzianowice. The attack bogged down outside the village, however. Soviet attacks to the north and northwest initially forced the engineers from their positions, followed later by the infantry. A new outpost line was established in a line running Olszany — southern edge of the Hohenbach Colony (oriented to the northwest).

On 7 August, the *23. Panzer-Division* turned back all enemy attacks. A penetration at Wola Mielecka was cleaned up after *Panzergruppe von Brandenstein* was committed. Once again, the divisional artillery, with all of its battalions, played a significant role in the defensive success. *Hauptmann* Roltsch, who had been assigned to *PGR126*, was reassigned to the *I./PGR128* as its commander.

At 0500 hours on 8 August, *Panzergruppe Fischer* moved out to attack north and advanced as far as Borowa. From there, it turned southeast and joined in the fight against an enemy penetration in the area of the Hohenbach Colony. The enemy had formed his main effort between Sawada and Trzciana, but he was unable to advance against the German defenses, especially in the face of the well-placed artillery fires. On several occasions, he was scattered while still concentrating for the attack.

The enemy penetrated along the left wing of *PGR126* and advanced as far as Podleszany. In an immediate counterattack, the *I./PGR126* pushed the enemy back out of the village by 1230 hours. But then the enemy immediately assaulted the boundary between the two infantry regiments with fresh forces, entered the main line of resistance and threw the *I./PGR126* back to Podleszany and the western edge of Zawierzbie. *Hauptmann* Grünwaldt rallied his last remaining weak reserves; He then pulled his 2nd Company back out of its sector, which then remained open. Using those men, he attacked the enemy at 1400 hours and drove him back across the former main line of resistance to the east.

Later on, *Hauptmann* Grünwaldt was awarded the Knight's Cross to the Iron Cross for this deed on 17 September 1944. *Gefreiter* Karl Zierhofer, an assistant machine gunner from the *4.(schw.)/PGR126,* was awarded the Knight's Cross to the Iron Cross 4 October 1944 for his extraordinary bravery later on.

Map 84: Fighting Around Mielec from 2 to 13 August 1944.

Moving from the area around Czermin, the Soviets were able to succeed in penetrating the positions of the engineers and, later on, the adjoining *1./PGR128*. At the same time, the *2.* and *3./PGR128* were able to maintain their positions in the main line of resistance, despite considerable casualties. *Hauptmann* Oechsle, *Leutnant* Albrecht and *Leutnant* Ziller were wounded. *Gefreiter* Gruber of the *3./PGR128*, employed as a sniper, killed six enemy soldiers; *Gefreiter* Richter of the *1./PGR126*, who had been detailed to the battalion headquarters as a messenger, accounted for 16 opponents.

The armored group was alerted at 2100 hours. It was directed to move southwest from Dabrowka and establish contact with the left wing of *PGR128* (1st Company) and secure the gap between the left wing of that regiment and the northern edge of the woods. *Oberleutnant Freiherr* von Brandenstein, the commander of the *5./PR23,* was killed that day in an engagement with enemy tanks. *Oberstleutnant* Stichtenoth was badly wounded in a successful counterattack in the sector of the *1./PGR128*. *Major* Ruge assumed acting command of the regiment.

During the night of 8/9 August, the main line of resistance was pulled back to a line running Bren. Osuchowsky — east edge of Dabrowka — east edge of the large woods. The air forces of both sides were heavily involved in the fighting on the ground. On that day, 3 T-34's, 16 heavy antitank guns, 1 self-propelled artillery piece and 2 trucks fell victim to *PR23*.

On 9 August, the enemy resumed his attacks. The *1./PGR128*, which had been moved to the right wing of the battalion in the meantime, cleaned up an enemy penetration at Trzciana by means of an immediate counterattack. During the attack, however, the acting company commander, *Leutnant* von und zu Bodmann was killed.

Panzergruppe Marquardt, which was positioned along the eastern edge of the large patch of woods, continuously joined in the fray to assist *PGR128*. *Panzergruppe Fischer* supported the engineers and reconnaissance soldiers in their fight against numerically vastly superior Soviet infantry and tanks, which were attempting to break through in the Kaweczyn area. The enemy was ejected, suffering the loss of one KV-85, four T-34's, one 7.62cm antitank gun and six antitank rifles.

The Soviet attack in the center and right-hand portion of the division's sector was concentrated against the villages of Podleszany and Wola Mielecka. After numerous attempts, which caused the enemy many casualties, he finally succeeded in entering Wola Mielecka. The introduction of considerable reinforcements in this area led to the conclusion that further attacks were imminent.

The Soviet forces that had entered Wola Mielecka threatened the left flank of the *II./PGR126*. The acting regimental commander employed all of the 2cm *Flak* he had available to guard that flank.

Due to a lack of infantry forces, the strongpoints in the main line of resistance had to be reduced over and over again.

Toward evening, *PGR128*, supported by tanks, restored its former main line of resistance.

During the first hours of morning on 10 August, the enemy entered the lines of *PPB51* and concentrated his efforts against the gap between the engineers and the *I./PGR128*. The enemy was ejected in the course of a counterattack, which was supported by *Panzergruppe Fischer*. The fighting continued the entire day and saw the destruction of five T-34's, one 7.62cm antitank gun and one antitank rifle. Eight prisoners were taken and the enemy left behind some 200 dead.

The enemy concentrated strong forces in the morning around the crossroads south of Wola Mielecka. The artillery engaged the concentrations with all available tubes. However, the enemy moved out anyway, supported by his own numerically superior artillery. There were no German infantry formations in that sector to oppose him, with the result that the artillery outposts formed the only "front lines". The enemy suffered severe losses due to the well-placed artillery fires, with the result that he only got as far as the edge of the woods west of Wola Mielecka, where his attack bogged down.

The considerable losses suffered in the previous few days negatively affected the combat strength of the infantry. For instance, the *I./PGR128* had a trench strength of only 6 officers, 22 noncommissioned officers and 87 enlisted. The battalion had been directed to defend a sector of 2,600 meters with those forces and five light machine guns, three medium mortars and one 7.5cm antitank gun. The three rifle companies were consolidated into one company under the command of *Oberleutnant* Kunad.

At 2100 hours, *PGR126* pulled back its left wing as far as the woods at Rydzow.

In the area west of Wola Mielecka, a battalion from *Grenadier-Regiment 14* of the *78. Volkssturm-Division* was employed during the early morning hours of 11 August to counterattack along both sides of the Tarnow — Mielec road. It succeeded in pushing the enemy back to just east of the wood line.

At the same time, *PGR128* was involved in continuous defensive fighting against stubbornly attacking Soviet tanks and infantry. All of the enemy's attempts to break through were stymied, however, in close coordination with the division's tanks. Five T-34's and three 7.62cm antitank guns were knocked out. During the morning, the front between the left wing of *Grenadier-Regiment 14* and the right wing of *PGR128* was closed when both formations attacked at the same time.

The enemy resumed his offensive activities along the entire division sector on 12 August. Despite strong artillery support, he was unable to achieve a penetration anywhere. Three T-34's, six antitank guns and four mortars were destroyed.

The *4.(le.)/Heeres-Flak-Abteilung 278* was attached to the *I./PGR128*.

During the night of 12/13 August, the main line of resistance was pulled back to the area east of Podleszany — along the Mielec to Tarnow road — Piatkowice — 1 kilometer south of Wampierzow. The enemy did not disrupt the withdrawal movements, but started attacking again at first light. His attacks were weaker than in the previous days, however. He was unable to achieve success and lost a "Josef Stalin" tank, a T-34 and an antitank gun to the *Panthers* positioned as combat outposts.

On 13 August, the enemy placed barrage fires on the sector of *PGR168* from 0740 to 0810 hours. A Soviet battalion attacked the center of the regimental sector at 0815 hours and achieved small penetrations on both sides of the Podleszany — Tarnowice road. The *11.(Pi.)/PGR126* restored the situation in an immediate counterattack. The enemy suffered the loss of 4 officers and 60 men killed. At 0930 hours, divisional tanks, together with the *4./PAA23*, attacked and threw the enemy back to the east.

In the days that followed, combat activities increasingly abated. The enemy limited himself to minimal patrolling. German artillery engaged identified Soviet gun and battery positions. The *8./PAR128*, together with a 21cm heavy howitzer battery—the *1./Artillerie-Abteilung 777*—and a gun from the regiment's 5th Battery. placed deliberate fires on the airfield at Chorzelow.

On 15 August, *Heeres-Flak-Abteilung 278* provided air defense for the air space over Radomysl. *Oberleutnant* Polack, from the divisional artillery, assumed command of *PzFEB128*.

On 16 August, the *23. Panzer-Division* started to be relieved in its sector. *Panzergrenadier-Regiment 128* was relieved by *Grenadier-Regiment 671* of the *371. Infanterie-Division*. The relieved elements temporarily billeted in the area northeast of Tarnow. The arrival of replacements brought the battalion up to approximately 120 men each.

The tracked vehicles were loaded on trains at Czarna, east of Tarnow, on 17 August. The wheeled elements followed on the bad roads. The last elements of the division, including the *III./PAR128*, did not follow until they were relieved on 19 August. Moving through Kielce, Charzysko, Ostrowiec and Ozarow, *PGR128*, *PR23*, *PPB51*, *PAA23* and a portion of *PAR128* reached the area northwest of Wygoda-Bankowa by the evening of 18 August.

The *II./Grenadier-Regiment 14*, which had been attached to *PGR126*, was relieved on 16 August and replaced by *Füsilier-Bataillon 371* (*371. Infanterie-Division*). The relief took place after a successful immediate counterattack during the morning, in which three T-34's were destroyed. *Oberstleutnant* John resumed command of *PGR126* and *Major* Stetting was sent to a regimental command course. On 18 August, *PGR126* was relieved by elements of the *371. Infanterie-Division*.

The division was placed under the command and control of the *XXXXVIII. Panzer-Korps*. Together with the *1. Panzer-Division* and the *3. Panzer-Division*, the corps was directed to attack the large Soviet bridgehead over the Vistula on both sides of Sandomierz from the north and northwest. It was to seal off and reduce the bridgehead, as well as help out several German infantry divisions that had been encircled by breaking open the Soviet ring and relieving them.

In the course of attacking across the Vistula, the Soviets succeeded in encircling the *72. Infanterie-Division* north of Sandomierz. Since that division was unable to break out on its own, the *23. Panzer-Division* was moved into the area as expeditiously as possible.

On 19 August, the elements of the division that had arrived up to that point moved out to attack to the southwest. At 0615 hours, *Major* Ruge's *PGR128*, together with the attached *Füsilier-Bataillon 72* of the *72. Infanterie-Division,* departed their assembly areas. *Panzergruppe Fischer*—the *II./PR23* with 22 *Panthers*, the *3./PAA23* and the *2./PPB51*—followed at 0800 hours. The divisional artillery and a rocket-launcher brigade supported the attack.

The Sandomierz — Ostrowiec rail line was crossed to the south at 0900 hours without encountering strong enemy resistance. A Russian counterattack into the left flank of the *I./PGR128* was shattered by rocket launchers. The attack was then slowed down by increasing resistance, particularly from antiarmor defenses. One gun after the other had to be engaged and destroyed. The forward observers from the artillery and the rocket-launcher elements, who accompanied the attack, performed magnificently. At 1015 hours, the tanks entered Lukawa, together with *Füsilier-Bataillon 72*, and cleared the village. Half an hour later, *PGR128* conquered Kichary Stare, located 2 kilometers further to the east. Enemy tanks, approaching individually, were destroyed by the armored group.

At 1115 hours, the right wing of *Panzerkampfgruppe Fischer* established contact with *Grenadier-Regiment 184* of the *72. Infanterie-Division* at the trail out of Lukawa. The left wing of the armored group got hung up in poor terrain and had to move back so as to move forward again in the tracks of the elements on the right. In the process, two *Panthers* became total losses due to antitank-gun hits.

The attack by *PGR128* was flanked by enemy tanks coming out of Gory Wysoki. At 1500 hours, *Hauptmann* Roltsch employed his 2nd Company in attacking that village. The enemy was ejected. *Oberleutnant* Kunad was badly wounded. Suffering only 13 wounded, the *I./PGR128* took 5 prisoners, including 2 officers, and counted 30 enemy dead. It destroyed or captured five antitank guns, five trucks, two field kitchens, six machine guns and numerous small arms.

A planned attack by the battalion to the east and on Stupzca could not be carried out due to a shortage of heavy weapons. In the evening, four self-propelled antitank guns of *PJA128* arrived in P. Gory Wysoki to reinforce the battalion.

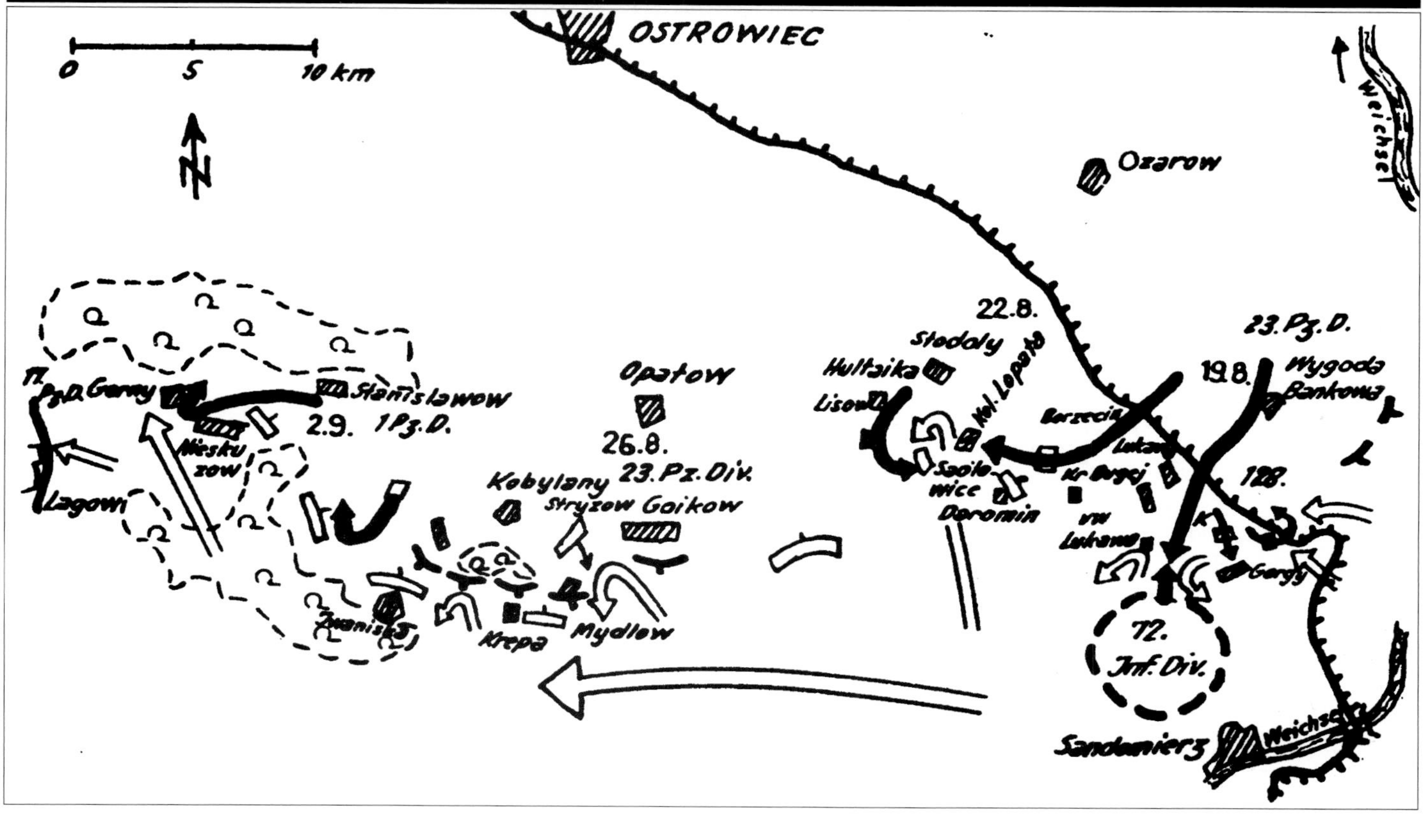

Map 85: Fighting Along the Northern Side of the Russian Bridgehead Along the Vistula to the East of Sandomierz-Baranow from 19 August to 2 September 1944.

On that day, the armored battle group destroyed: 17 T-34's, 3 assault guns, 20 antitank guns, 3 mortars, 8 trucks and 1 armored car. In addition, it inflicted heavy casualties on the enemy.

After the *I./PR23* arrived, 11 *Panzer V's*, 3 *Panzer IV's* and 6 assault guns were operational.

Heeres-Flak-Abteilung 278 provided area defense for the air space above Ostrowiec — Cmielow.

At 0300 hours on 20 August, the enemy attempted to advance north past the combat outposts of the armored group by attacking from the southwest and reducing the area of penetration. Elements of both tank battalions eliminated the enemy in a rapid riposte and continued to screen southwest from the positions reached the previous day.

At 0900 hours, the *I./PGR128* moved out from P. Gory Wysoki along with seven assault guns and four self-propelled antitank guns to attack east. The enemy placed flanking fires on the attack from heavy weapons in the village of Gory Wysoki.

The woods east of the village were cleared in the face of enemy resistance, and then the assault guns and self-propelled guns turned toward the village proper. In coordination with the mortar platoon of the battalion, which was being employed as infantry, they cleared the village of the enemy. Five prisoners were taken, two intact antitank guns were captured and five additional antitank guns were destroyed. The attempt by the battalion to carry the attack further east from the patch of woods failed in the face of Soviet tanks and antitank guns. In addition, the German attack elements ran into Soviet counterattacks conducted with superior forces on two occasions. The enemy was reinforced in the woods in front of the left wing of the battalion; he then attacked past the woods to the south with 10 T-34's and 150 infantry, reoccupying the village of Gory Wysoki. The assault guns and the self-propelled guns destroyed six of the T-34's, but the remaining ones opened fire into the rear of the battalion positioned in the woods. Since that position could not be held, *Hauptmann* Roltsch counterattacked Gory Wysoki with his battalion and cleared it of the enemy one more time. The battalion then set up for the defense. *Leutnant* Lintl was wounded.

The *Flak* companies of the division's two infantry regiments - the 10th Companies - were dissolved, and a *Flak* platoon was assigned to the heavy company of each of the battalions. The regimental engineer companies, previously the 11th Company of each Regiment, then became the 10th Company.

While fighting was taking place on the left wing, a counterattack had to be conducted on the right wing. During the night, the enemy had reoccupied Lukawa. *Panzergruppe Fischer* attacked at 1030 hours and, in conjunction with the fusiliers, cleared the village by 1200 hours.

At 1900 hours, enemy tanks and infantry attacked Lukawa-West from the west. Four *Panthers* of *Oberleutnant* Strohmeyer eliminated two T-34's in an immediate counterattack. At 2030 hours, tanks and fusiliers moved out to attack; one T-34 was knocked out at a distance of only two meters. The enemy was able to retain the northern part of the western portion of the village.

The 21st of August started with an attack of enemy tanks and infantry against the *SPW* company from *PAA23* screening at Fw. Lukawa. Two *Panthers* attacked together with the company and destroyed three T-34's.

Panzergrenadier-Regiment 126, which arrived during the night of 20/21 August, positioned its 2nd Battalion northwest of Pawlew and its 1st Battalion in Lukawa-West, reinforced by an armored group.

Moving out at 1045 hours, both battalions reached the former main line of resistance by 1145 hours. Lukawa was completely back in German hands. *Feldwebel* Förster of the *II./PR23* knocked out a "Josef Stalin" with five rounds.

At 1210 hours, the *I./PGR126* established contact on the right with *Grenadier-Regiment 505* of the *291. Infanterie-Division*.

At 1930 hours, the effort of a Soviet battalion to roll up the German main line of resistance by heading north between the forestry building for Lukawa and the village of Lukawa itself was nullified by two *Panthers* under *Oberleutnant* Strohmeyer and the *SPW* company of the reconnaissance battalion.

The *I./PGR128* was unable to establish contact with the friendly forces on the left, since the enemy had established strongpoints in the existing gap.

At 2030 hours, the armored group received orders to move out for a new mission. The tangible successes of the day: 1 "Josef Stalin" tank, 7 T-34's, 19 antitank guns and 4 ammunition trucks destroyed.

At night, the *II./PGR126* relieved *Grenadier-Regiment 505* and the *I./PGR126* relieved *Füsilier-Bataillon 72*.

The *I./PGR128* was relieved by an assault battalion at 2330 hours. The infantry initially went to Wygoda Bankowa and, at 0930 hours on 22 August, to Lukawa, in order to close the gap existing on the right of the regiment next to the 2nd Battalion with the *I./PGR126*.

The division's tank regiment was attached to the armored group of *Oberst* von Bernuth of the *3. Panzer-Division* on 22 August. In addition, elements of *schwere Panzer-Abteilung 501*, a *Tiger* battalion, was attached to Bernuth's armored group. It was directed that Borzecin be taken by the armored group, which consisted of 14 *Panthers*, 5 King Tigers, 8 *Panzer IV's* and 6 assault guns; it was to advance from Wygoda Bankowa, attacking to the southwest. After crossing Hill 231, which was occupied by the *I./PGR126* at 0600 hours, the armored group encountered stiff enemy resistance, especially antitank guns and artillery. After three hours, the enemy's batteries were silenced by a combined effort by all weapons. The tanks continued advancing in stifling heat, continuing artillery fires and rolling aerial attacks. By 1600 hours, Borzecin was firmly under German control. Leaving behind combat outposts, the armored group continued its advance to the Lopata farmstead. The tangible successes of the day: 1 "Josef Stalin" tank, 5 T-34's, 16 antitank guns and 4 trucks.

Hauptmann Böhme's *II./PGR126* went around the Bugzy agricultural facilities, since the enemy had established a strongpoint there that could not be taken with the available forces. The battalion went into position on the left next to the regiment's 1st Battalion.

At 1930 hours, the *II./PGR126*, together with the *I./PGR128*, moved out to attack the Bugzy agricultural facilities and took it in two hours of fighting.

During the night of 22/23 August, the infantry battalions were relived by *Grenadier-Regiment 505* of the *72. Infanterie-Division*, whereupon they initially billeted in Janowice, with the *II./PGR126* going to Grochocice.

The division received orders on 23 August to attack west and southwest from out of the area around Stodoly — Lopata Colony, eliminating the enemy at Hultajka and Sadlowice. At the same time, it was directed that contact be established with the *1. Panzer-Division*, which was attacking east from out of the Opatow area. The latter division had reached Lopata on 22 August, but then had to call off its attack in the face of overwhelming enemy numbers.

The *I./PGR126* was initially designated a division reserve in Janowice, but it was then attached to the *17. Panzer-Division*, which was also employed in the Opatow area in the effort to reduce the Soviet bridgehead.

Around noon, *Panzergruppe von Bernuth* moved out from Stodoly along the road and attacked west. It had been reinforced with the *3./PAA23* and the *II./PGR126*. German rocket launchers and artillery supported the attack. Hulttajka was defended by strong Soviet forces with dug-in tanks and antitank guns. Delivering deliberate fires, during which a Soviet assault gun and six tanks were destroyed in 20 minutes, the armored group approached the village. A penetration was achieved at 1400 hours, after which the village was cleared of the Soviet infantry in tough close combat conducted by the *3./PAA23*. Turning to the south, the armored group then fought its way toward the village of Lisow. Heavy artillery fire and constantly attacking enemy fighter-bombers, in some instances with up to 20 aircraft, made command and control of the attack considerably difficult.

The *Kampfgruppe* from the *1. Panzer-Division* was pulled back form the Lopata farmstead, and strong enemy forces immediately pursued, principally establishing themselves around Sadlowice.

In the meantime, *PGR128* also moved out against the Lopata Colony, which was still occupied in places by enemy infantry. Weak resistance was broken in the northern part of the residential area, while the infantry was unable to make forward progress in the western part. Several renewed attacks over the course of the entire day and in the night that followed only brought limited gains. *Oberleutnant* Jost of the *3./PGR128* was badly wounded.

The armored group knocked out three enemy tanks outside of Lisow and entered the village, which was then cleared by the infantry and reconnaissance elements. The *10.(Pi)/PGR126* cleared several minefields in the course of the attack and created lanes for the tanks. During the night, the battle groups set up hedgehog defenses around and southwest of Lisow.

On that day, *PR23* destroyed the following as part of *Kampfgruppe von Bernuth*: 11 T-34's, 2 assault guns, 11 antitank guns, 1 antitank/antiaircraft gun and 4 antitank rifles.

In the rear area, the trains and logistics vehicles were frequently fired at by Polish partisans. Losses in personnel and in materiel resulted.

The 2nd Medical Company established a rest and recovery center for the division's soldiers at Zakopane.

During the early-morning hours of 24 August, *PGR128* took the Lopata Colony. Superior numbers of enemy forces then prevented the planned attack on Sadlowice for the time being.

The division positioned 28 tanks just north of Lisow for additional operations. Around 0800 hours, the enemy surprised the German armored force and advanced against it with two KV-85's and four T-34's. An assault gun burned out after being hit; a short while later, however, all of the enemy tanks were destroyed.

The assembly area for the armored group was under constant artillery and mortar fire, as well as attacks from the air. Just before the start of the attack in the direction of Sadlowice, *Oberst* von Bernuth was badly wounded by artillery shrapnel. A few hours later, he died of his wounds. *Hauptmann* Fischer assumed acting command of the battle group.

Strong flanking fires made it impossible to directly attack Sadlowice from the west. As a result, the armored group moved out from the south at 1100 hours after the arrival of *schwere Panzer-Abteilung 509*. It then attacked Sadlowice after swinging 120 degrees and coming in from the south/southwest. Despite heavy flanking fires from the enemy west of Daromin, the armored group reached the southwestern portion of Sadlowice at 1630 hours without suffering any losses. Seven enemy tanks were destroyed in firefights conducted at pointblank range. The reconnaissance soldiers cleared the village, house by house, until *PGR126*, minus its 1st Battalion, arrived at 1945 hours. The infantry then completing clearing the village and set up for defense.

During the morning, the *II./PGR128* retook Borzecin, which had been lost the previous day. At 1300 hours, the *I./PGR128* moved out from the Lopata farmstead to the south, attacking the high ground northwest of Daromin and taking it after difficult fighting with Soviet infantry that resulted in heavy casualties. *Leutnant* Ohmstede was badly wounded in the process. The attempt to take Daromin proper in an attack starting at 1800 hours failed in the face of heavy Soviet weapons and tanks after taking 600 meters of ground. When the enemy moved out to launch a counterattack against both flanks of the battalion, it had to be pulled back to the high ground.

The *Panthers* of the *II./PR23* reported the destruction of 8 T-34's, 2 KV-85's, 1 assault gun, 12 antitank guns and 4 field pieces on 24 August.

The division had also successfully completed its mission in this sector. During the night, it was relieved by the *88. Infanterie-Division* in the Sadlowice area. *Panzergrenadier-Regiment 128* was relieved by *Panzergrenadier-Regiment 63* of *17. Panzer-Division* during the morning hours of 25 August.

The numbers of vehicles available to the infantry had been so thinned after the recent fighting that the battalions of the regiments could no longer move out at the same time in a motor march, despite the numerical weakness of those battalions. As a result, long-haul trucks had to be requested for temporary use fro the field army.

The new area of operations for the *23. Panzer-Division* was south of Opatow, where the Soviets had established strong defensive field fortifications along the northern flank of their area of penetration, which extended west as far as Lagow and beyond. The infantry regiments went into position south of Gojcow and Stryzowice, next to the *88. Infanterie-Division*. The divisional artillery provided cover from firing positions at Okalina. The arrival of replacements allowed the individual battalions to be brought up to about 200 men each.

The divisional artillery supported the attack of the neighboring *1. Panzer-Division* in the direction of Iwaniska by providing fire coordination parties. That division's attack bogged down outside of the bitterly contested Kobylany, however. The infantry of the *23. Panzer-Division* attacked south, well supported by artillery, and advanced the front toward Mydlowice. The oppressive Soviet air superiority seriously impeded every German attack. The *Luftwaffe* was not to be seen.

During the evening of 26 August, the *II./PGR126*, which was employed the furthest on the left, together with the *2./PGR128*, which was attached to it, closed the gap existing with the *88. Infanterie-Division*. The *3./PGR128* was charged with maintaining contact between the *1. Panzer-Division* and the *I./PGR126*, which was employed the furthest on the right in the division sector.

At 0500 hours on 27 August, *PGR126* and the *II./PGR128* moved out to attack Romanov and Krepa after an artillery and rocket-launcher preparation. The attack, which initially made good forward progress, bogged down in the face of increasing resistance on the part of the enemy, who was considerably supported by fighter-bombers.

At 1130 hours, the *I./PGR128* (minus its 2nd Company) was employed on the right wing of the division in order to enable a gap to be closed between the *I./PGR126* and the *II./PGR128*. In the attack, which was then resumed, Romanow and the woods to its west were taken. The *II./PGR126* was positioned along the southeast edge of the woods near Fw. Romanow at 1500 hours. The enemy lost numerous heavy weapons. Numerous prisoners were taken, and he suffered bloody losses. Contact was established with the *1. Panzer-Division* on the right.

The armored group screened southwest of Kobylany with four *Panzer V's* and an assault gun under *Oberleutnant* Marquardt. Eleven *Panthers* under *Oberleutnant* Kujacinski, which arrived during the morning, were attached to the *1. Panzer-Division* and sent to the area around the Planta government lands. The *Panthers* arrived just as the enemy attempted to take back the terrain that had been wrested from him. They contributed greatly to the successful defense of the area.

During the afternoon and evening, heavy fires from Soviet artillery, antitank guns and mortars were paced on the infantry positions.

On 28 August, *Hauptmann* Roltsch's *I./PGR128* improved its positions by attacking in the woods west of Romanow. Contact was lost with the *1. Panzer-Division* soon thereafter, however, since that division moved further to the west as part of its attack operations. The enemy immediately infiltrated into the gap that resulted and forced the infantry to pull back their positions. In the sector of the *II./PGR126*, Fw Romanow was lost at 1340 hours after a fight with a Soviet battalion. The enemy advanced close to the narrow-gauge railway south of Jozefow.

The attack of the *1. Panzer-Division*, reinforced by *Panzergruppe Kujacinski*, did not meet with success. In the effort to move out from the woods southwest of Iwaniska, six *Panthers* were lost—one a total loss—as well as an assault gun to enemy mines and fires. *Leutnant* Hilkert of the *4./PR23* was killed. *Oberleutnant* Marquardt and *Leutnant* Weber were wounded. Several renewed attacks by the armored group against the Planta government lands were fruitless.

During the night of 28/29 August, the *1. Panzer-Division*, committed on the right, was withdrawn from the lines. The *23. Panzer-Division* had to assume its sector. *Panzergruppe Kujacinski* returned to the division's command and control.

On 29 August, the enemy attacked the division's positions at several places with tanks and infantry. In a fight lasting several hours, the *I./PGR126* turned back a stubbornly conducted attack by the enemy on the battalion's left wing. The positions remained completely in the hands of the division. The *III./PAR128* provided effective support in the defensive fighting. It was able to immobilize a KV-85, while the tank regiment eliminated four T-34's, one KV-85, one "Josef Stalin" tank and six antitank guns. *Oberleutnant* Schley of the *III./PAR128* was killed; the battalion surgeon, *Stabsarzt Dr.* Albig, and *Leutnant* Herold of the *I./PGR128* were wounded.

Sturmgeschütz-Brigade 201 was attached to the division on 30 August. The enemy's activities in the division's sector were limited to a weak attack on Wymyslow, which was already scattered by barrage fires in front of the main line of resistance. The divisional artillery engaged targets in the areas of Haliszka and Toporow during the day.

The armored group, which was reattached to the *1. Panzer-Division*, participated in an attack on the Planta government lands, but the attack failed in the face of the superior Soviet defenses. Three German tanks were lost. One KV-85, six antitank guns and two enemy mortars were destroyed.

On 1 September, 13 *Panzer V's* of *Oberleutnant* Kujacinski were employed as part of *Kampfgruppe Oberst Friebe* of the *1. Panzer-Division*. They moved out from the area around Stanislawow, together with elements of *Panzer-Regiment 1* and two *Tiger II's* from *schwere Panzer-Abteilung 509*. They were given the mission of advancing west on both sides of the Opatow — Lagow road and establishing contact with the *17. Panzer-Division* of *Generalmajor* von der Meden. The lead elements, under the command of *Leutnant* Strecker of the *II./PR23*, fought their way forward through Olszownica and Nieskurzow toward Gorny in the face of heavy resistance from tanks, antitank guns and infantry, as well as barrage fires from Soviet artillery and rolling attacks by fighter-bombers. After the *Tigers* were lost due to mechanical reasons, the *Panthers* destroyed several antitank guns before friendly losses forced a temporary cessation of the attack. After three *Tigers* from *schwere Panzer-Abteilung 501* and three more *Panthers* arrived, additional ground was taken, but the attack objective could not be reached. At the cost of two total losses, one 12.2cm and five 7.62cm antitank guns were destroyed.

In the sector of the *23. Panzer-Division*, the enemy remained quiet, with the exception of patrolling. The divisional artillery engaged identified targets and strong enemy concentrations around and southeast of Iwaniska. During the night, the division's sector was shifted to the right as far as Bratkowszna. The relief took place incrementally, starting from the left wing.

During this period, the losses sustained to mines were quite noticeable. Tanks and motorized vehicles were lost; casualties were taken among the soldiers.

The 1st, 2nd and 3rd Ambulance Platoons were consolidated into *Krankenkraftwagen-Kompanie 128*.

On 2 September, the attack by *Kampfgruppe Friebe* to break through to Lagow was resumed. Five *Panzer V's* and five *Panzer IV's*, all under the command of *Leutnant* Strecker, moved out under the covering fires provided by 28 additional tanks. The entire company ran into mines in the depression outside of Gorny. Fortunately, the tanks could not be engaged by the Soviet antitank weapons, with the result that they could be recovered during the night. The attack operation was called off. Two 7.62cm antitank guns were destroyed.

The armored groups providing security among the infantry destroyed the following during the period from 30 August to 4 September 1944:

1 "Josef Stalin" heavy tank
1 KV-85
2 T-34's
4 antitank guns
2 mortars
3 machine guns
2 antitank rifles

Panzergruppe Strecker returned to the division's command and control.

On 2 September, the force-structure branch of the German Army high command ordered that all *Panzergrenadier* and *Panzer* battalions were to form supply companies.

The enemy in front of the division's sector transitioned to the defense. The divisional artillery had the extensive preparations of field fortifications and enemy artillery positions as its targets. The enemy's infantry remained quiet. The divisional sector was shifted further to the right again.

On 7 September, orders arrived to pull the division out of the line and move it a considerable distance. The division's antitank-gun battalion was threatened with disbandment after the loss of its antitank guns in the recent heavy fighting. *Major* Tiedemann succeeded in getting the force structure branch of the German Army high command to issue his battalion headquarters 2 of the new *Jagdpanzer IV* armed with the L70 7.5cm main gun, also used on the *Panther*. Two of his companies received 10 each of the vehicles. The battalion' 3rd Company remained with 7.5cm self-propelled antitank guns and with towed antitank guns of the same caliber. The new-equipment training was conducted at the Mielau Training Area within the space of one week. The battalion experienced several bombing attacks while there, where it lost its well-quipped maintenance platoon equipped with Skoda vehicles.

Starting on the night of 8/9 September, the division was relieved by the *17. Panzer-Division* in its sector. On 9 September, the tank regiment was the first formation to load out on trains at the Ostrowiec, Skarzysko-Kamienna and Starachowice railheads. The rest of the division followed incrementally. In some cases, the lack of transport means led to delays.

The elements were sent to the Budapest area, moving via Cracow, Moravian Ostrau and Preßburg (Bratislava), where the first elements detrained on 13 September.

Special meaning was ascribed to the detraining in Budapest, since the collapse of the regime was expected, as well as a subsequent withdrawal from the fight against the Soviet Union. Elements of the *23. Panzer-Division* were given the mission of putting on a show-of-force by moving through individual portions of the city. Nothing happened, however.

Panzergrenadier-Regiment 126 was relieved by *Panzergrenadier-Regiment 63* on 10 September.

The last train of the division departed Poland on 13 September with elements of the administrative sections and the medical battalion.

Hauptmann Rebentisch reassumed acting command of the regiment, with *Hauptmann* Kujacinski assuming command of the 1st Battalion and *Hauptmann* Fischer of the 2nd.

In the new assembly area, the training staff and its commander, *Hauptmann* Bergmann, which had been detailed to the Romanian 1st Armored Division ever since April 1944, returned to the regiment, after it had been able to fight its way back from out of the confused situation surrounding the Romanian treachery.

Since *Heeresgruppe Süd* had ordered all trains carrying armored vehicles, as well as all additional transports, to be diverted through Budapest, Debrecen and Großwardein into the area around and southeast of Klausenburg (Cluj), the elements of the division that had been assembled in Budapest moved into that area as well on 13 and 14 September. The division headquarters went to Klausenburg and *PR 23* to Kolozs (Cojozcna).

A portion of the trains and the rear-area services were directed to Stuhlweißenburg and detrained there. For the time being, they had no communications with the division. The residential section of the city of Stuhlweißenburg suffered its first air attack by western Allied aircraft shortly after the arrival of these elements of the *23. Panzer-Division*.

Generalmajor von Radowitz received the Knight's Cross to the Iron Cross on 17 September for his personal bravery and the proven bravery of the *23. Panzer-Division*.

The Fighting in Transylvania 22-26 September 1944

The collapse of *Heeresgruppe Südukraine* and the treacherous departure of Romania from the war preceded the movement of the *23. Panzer-Division* into the area of Transylvania. Only weak remnants of the *6. Armee* were able to fight their way back across the Sereth between Braila and Focsani, establish contact with the remnants of the *Flak* formations from the Ploesti area and pull back into Hungarian territory in the Szekler Tip. Elements of the *8. Armee* reached the Romanian and Hungarian borders between the Gyimes and Rodna Passes, where they were initially able to turn back every attack from the east.

The Soviet main effort was focused on advancing into the plains of the Danube. On 30 August, Bucharest, Ploesti and Constanza fell to them. The new Romanian government immediately declared war on Germany and raised an army of liberation to take back Transylvania. Bulgaria fell away from Germany, but it was occupied nonetheless by the Soviets, who did not declare war until 5 September 1944. On 6 September, the lead enemy attack elements were in Turnu Severin at the "Iron Gate" and linked up with Tito's partisans.

The Soviets took Kronstadt on 5 September. The German resistance, which had started to come back to life, was beginning to make itself noticeable. In the area south of Klausenburg, the kernel of a new *6. Armee* under *General der Artillerie* Fretter-Pico started to be formed, and it was combined with the Hungarian 2nd Army, composed of hastily formed replacement divisions. Initially, however, the gap between these two groups could not be closed. Advancing into this gap was the attack of the recently formed Romanian Liberation Army. The German command staked its fortune on one card: It had the Hungarian divisions attack south, throwing the surprised Romanians back to the Maros (Mures) River line before the Soviets realized the threat and detoured forces from their main thrust, which was headed west. For their part, the Soviets then had to attack north. By the middle of September, they had committed 25 rifle divisions and four mobile corps in attacking *Generaloberst* Friessner's *Heeresgruppe Süd*. They forced the evacuation of the Szeklet Tip and attacked the Eastern Carpathian passes with weaker forces, al the while maintaining their main effort in the area south of Klausenburg.

The *23. Panzer-Division* received orders on 21 September to employ elements of the divisional artillery the next day in support of the Hungarians fighting at Ludus. Just as measures to do that were being taken, new orders arrived for the employment of the entire division on 23 September to clean up a deep enemy penetration in the Hungarian positions at Thorenburg (Turda).

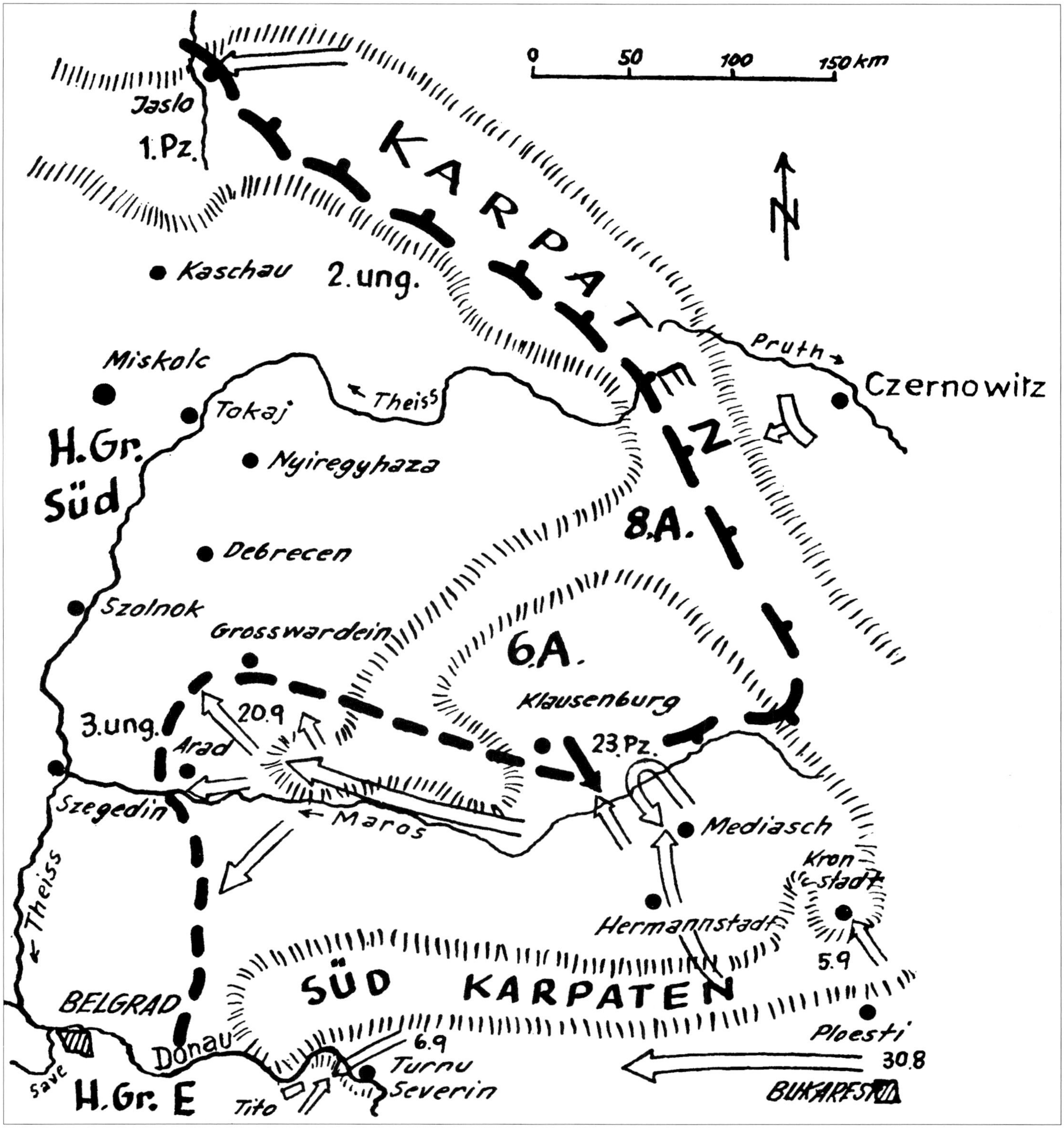

Map 86: Situation in Eastern Hungary on 20 September 1944.

During the night of 22/23 September, the division's forces occupied their assembly areas. The *I./PR23* was attached to *PGR126*; the *II./PR23* was attached to *PGR128*. With *PGR 128* on the left and *PGR126* on the right, the attack south was intended to throw the enemy out of the area around Thorenburg and to its east.

At 0700 hours, tanks with mounted infantry advanced across Hill 453. Strong antitank defenses on the part of the Soviets made a frontal attack impossible. *Hauptmann* Fischer advanced with most of his 2nd Battalion by swinging out to the left and along the rail line. His battalion eliminated enemy antitank guns in Vaskapu and overran an antitank-gun belt in the grain fields north of Hill 371 before it was able to get a good field of fire. Despite all that, the Soviet resistance was so strong that the infantry were unable to follow. Soviet fighter-bombers joined the fray on the ground incessantly and monitored every movement.

Panzergrenadier-Regiment 126 and the *I./PR23* made good progress in its first rush against slight enemy resistance. Hills 429 and 425 were

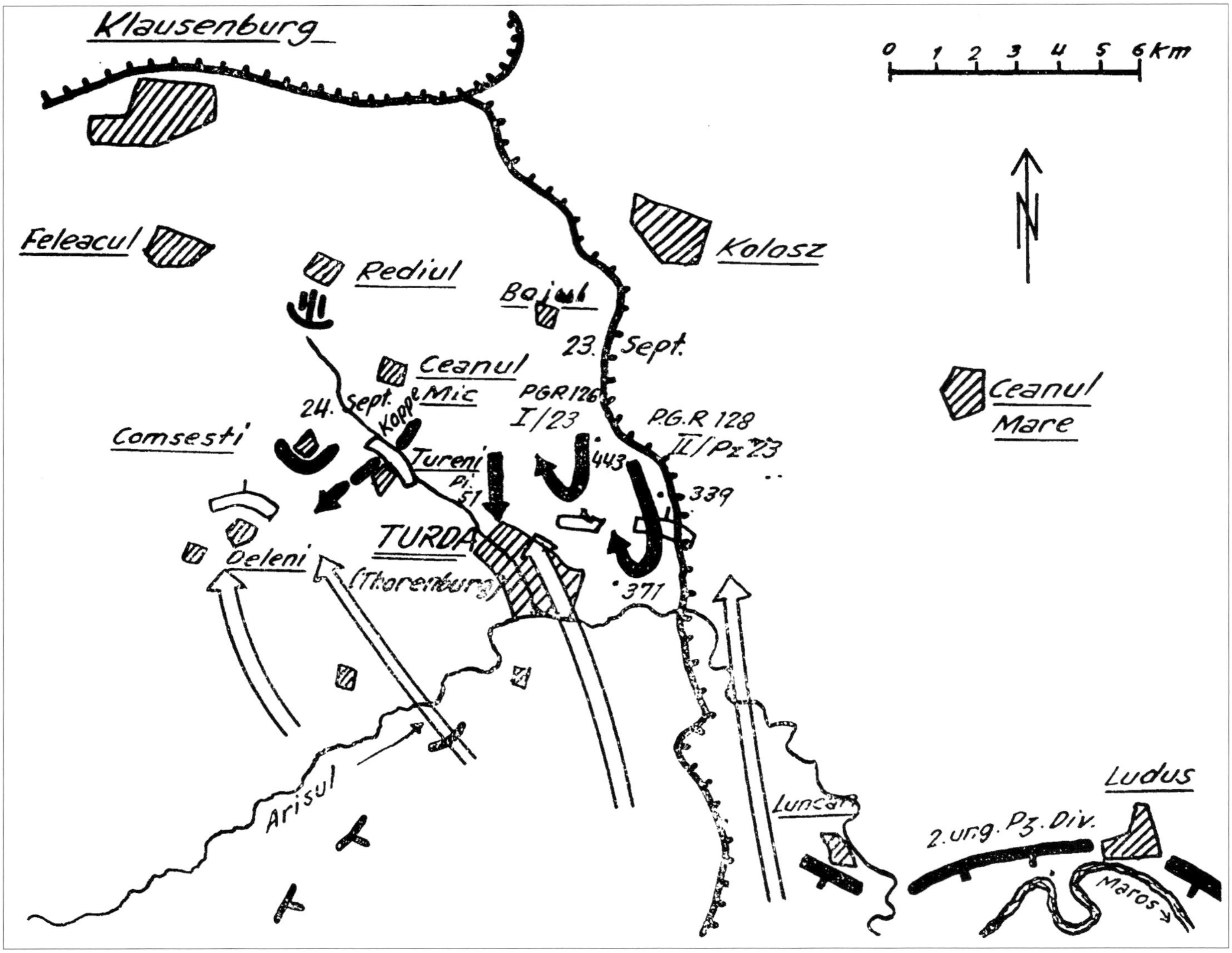

Map 87: Counterattacks at Thorenburg on 23 and 24 September 1944.

both taken. But then a Soviet antitank-gun belt oriented west and north blocked further progress. The attack bogged down with considerable losses. *Hauptmann* Grünwaldt, the commander of the *I./PGR126*, was wounded. *Oberleutnant* Donder of the *3./PR23* was killed along with his crew.

Advancing once again, *Hauptmann* Lenberger's *II./PGR126* was able to penetrate the enemy positions on Hill 424, northeast of Thorenburg, but there the attack bogged down. The medical clearing stations were overflowing. The medical armored vehicles of *PR23*, which accompanied the attack, were constantly on the go in order to transfer wounded to the field ambulances of the ambulance company. The main clearing station of the 1st Medical Company in the city was already more than filled to capacity in the early morning hours, especially since the Red Air Force was also constantly attacking Klausenburg and the main roads.

Evacuation of the wounded by the field-ambulance company generally could only take at night due to the Russian air superiority. The drivers of the company were almost constantly on the go on 23 and 24 September to take the wounded to the main clearing stations.

It was not until the afternoon of 23 September that the attack of the *II./PR23* and *PGR128* reached the foot of Hill 371. In the face of massive barrage fire on the part of the Soviets, it was possible to temporarily advance as far as the steep slope on the southern edge of the hill. The terrain could not be held, however, with the result that the main line of resistance had to be pulled back in the evening to a row of houses north of the hill.

Falling victim to *PR23* that day were 5 tanks, 1 assault gun, 37 heavy antitank guns, 4 prime movers and 3 trucks.

Hauptmann Noever's *PPB51* fought on the right wing of the division in Thorenburg. In the course of the heavy fighting, a few of the enemy's trains vehicles were captured, on which he crated around the results of his plunders. For the combat engineers, the bars of soap were of the highest quality and a highly welcome spoil of war, after they had only seen German wartime soap for a number of years.

On 24 September, *PR23*, minus its 4th Tank Company, was ordered to Ceanul Mic, in order to clear up a penetration into the Hungarian position west of Thorenburg. *Panzergrenadier-Regiment 126* conducted combat patrols in the "Horseshoe" Woods east of Thorenburg.

To the north of Thorenburg, there was only localized fighting, which allowed the infantry to improve their positions somewhat.

Heeres-Flak-Abteilung 278 assumed the mission of defending the air space over the Klausenburg area, especially around the rail station.

At 1730 hours, the division ordered the attack of *Gruppe Major Koppe—PAA23,* the *II./PR23* and the *II./PGR126*—on Tureni and Deleni. At 1830 hours, Tureni was cleared of the enemy. While continuing the advance against increasing enemy resistance, the terrain in front of Hill

627, which was criss-crossed by many defiles, was crossed and the hill was taken by the tanks under *Oberleutnant* Zirr. Divisional artillery supported the attack from positions southeast of Rediul (Röd). As it turned dark, elements of *PAA23* went into position on Hill 627; contact was established with the friendly forces on the right, *PGR126*, in the woods south of Comsesti.

During the night, the *II./PGR128* was employed on Hill 627. Two enemy infantry attacks were repulsed. The enemy started to concentrate stronger forces, especially tanks and antitank guns, in front of the sector. At first light, attacking enemy infantry were forced to turn back in the face of the defensive fires. One Soviet antitank gun was definitely destroyed; two other most likely destroyed. A short while later, three Soviet tanks were identified; their withering camouflage gave them away. At a distance of 70 meters, all three enemy tanks—a T-34, a T 43 and a "Josef Stalin"—were destroyed by one *Panther* within 30 seconds, with none of them returning more than one round.

At the same time, the *I./PR23* was positioned in the woods southeast of Feleacul, while the *II./PR23* (minus *Gruppe Leutnant Strecker*) was prepared for operations in Ceanul Mic. After being relieved by Hungarian forces, *PGR128*, minus its 2nd Battalion, quartered in Bojul.

Despite continuing heavy Soviet aerial activity and massed artillery fires on the main line of resistance and in the division's rear area, no significant casualties resulted.

In the meantime, strong Soviet forces penetrated through Mediasch and into the Maros Valley (Mures), where they advanced far to the west. They also advanced west further south. On 19 September, they occupied Temesvar and, on 20 September, Arad. They spread out in the area east of Gyula and Szalonta. Strong Soviet armored and cavalry formations started to concentrate south of Großwardein. German forces were not available. Only elements of the Hungarian 3rd Army were screening. They were directed to prevent the enemy from moving out of the mountain valleys to the northwest and west.

To the surprise of all, *Ju-87's* joined the fray on the ground. At the last moment, they were identified as being Romanian from their markings.

During the evening of 26 September, the *23. Panzer-Division* received orders to move to Großwardein. That same night, *Major* Koppe's *PAA23* started its road march. The rest followed the morning of 27 September, with the tracked elements being loaded on trains.

While the trains with the armored vehicles rolled on the stretch of rail from Klausenburg to Großwardein and were unloaded at small railheads east of the city, the wheeled elements reached the new area of operations using the Klausenburg — Großwardein road (movement: Klausenburg — Szilagysomly — Bihar — Großwardein).

The division reconnaissance battalion entered the eastern part of Großwardein, which was already occupied by Romanian and Soviet formations, on 27 September. Moving aggressively, the reconnaissance soldiers cleared block after block of the enemy. They established contact with the Hungarian forces that were still fighting in the middle of the city. That helped to rally the Hungarians and they joined in on the continued attack of *PAA23* on the south part of the city. As a result of its action, *PAA23* created the prerequisites for the rest of the division to move through the south part of the city and to the south.

The mission of the *23. Panzer-Division*, which was attached to *General der Panzertruppen* Breith's *III. Panzer-Korps*: Clear Großwardein and the area south of the city of the enemy as far as the old Romanian-Hungarian border. As part of that, the division was directed to establish contact with the Hungarian 3rd Army fighting in Nagy-Szalonta, 60 kilometers to the southwest. It was also directed to hold open the area for an approach march by German armored formations to launch an attack into the Soviet formations advancing in northwestern Romania.

At 0600 hours on 28 September, the division moved out of its assembly areas north and east of Großwardein. The tank regiment, minus its 2nd Tank Company, advanced through the eastern part of the city to the west and then turned south later. The division's reconnaissance battalion and Hungarian elements joined the *I./PR23*, which was leading the movement. They helped break the final, weak resistance.

Oberst John's *PGR126*, reinforced by the *2./PR23*, attacked south from out of the Fugyi area toward Pece Szt. Marton and Ronto where it encountered extremely heavy resistance. The acting commander of the *2./PR23*, *Leutnant* Peez was killed, as was *Leutnant* Bensemann. *Major* Ruge's *PGR128*, adjoining on the left, moved through Nagy Ker and took the dominant high ground of Hill 343 southeast of Hajo by 0730 hours with *Hauptmann* Roltsch's *I./PGR126*.

The tank regiment shattered enemy resistance in the open terrain west of Pece Szt. Marton by advancing rapidly to the south, and it crossed the rail line southwest of Ronto at Felixfürdo. An assault detachment of the *2./PGR128* ejected the enemy from Betfia (2 kilometers south of Point 343) at 1315 hours. It also prevented the enemy from pulling back out of Hajo to the south. In the meantime, Felker was taken by the *II./PGR128*.

Around 1800 hours, the four operations *Panthers* of the *II./PR23* entered Ronto along with grenadiers from *PGR126*. They linked up there with *PPB51*, which had been attacking from the north. Strong enemy elements in and south of the Ronto — Szt. Marton area were encircled. Without hesitation, the *Panthers* moved past Hajo to the west and headed south with the grenadiers. They took the area around Point 170, thus also encircling Hajo, which was then taken soon afterwards by the *I./PGR128*, advancing from the east.

A lack of fuel prevented an attack west by *PR23* that had been ordered for the evening. That evening, the division firmly held a line running Varadshehi — Point 170 — Hill 343 — Felker. *Panzer-Regiment 23* reported the following as destroyed: 4 tanks, 1 assault gun, 31 antitank guns, 5 mortars, 1 self-propelled antitank gun, 14 antitank rifles, 5 trucks and 10 heavy machine guns. The *I./PGR128* reported destroying one antitank gun, three heavy machine guns, four light machine guns, one antitank rifle and one truck. The losses suffered by the enemy were both bloody and extraordinarily high.

The German wounded were transported to Derecske and Debrecen, exploiting the initially good roads.

At first light on 29 September, *PR23*, along with the attached *3./PAA23*, moved west from Ronto in order to block the main road running from Großwardein to Nagy Szalonta and to cut off the retreat route of the remaining Soviets, who were holding out in the extreme southwestern portion of Großwardein. At the same time, an attack supported by the divisional artillery was launched by *PAA23* (minus its 3rd Company) and the Hungarians against the enemy forces in the city.

The armored group advanced southwest of Varadshehi into strong enemy infantry forces, mostly Romanians. After resisting a short while from groups of vegetation and blown-up bunkers left over from the former Romanian border fortifications, the enemy attempted to escape to the south. Only a few succeeded. More than 200 enemy dead were counted. The commander of the Romanian 11th Mountain Regiment went into German captivity with 40 men. Nagy Urögd was taken at 1130 hours and the road was blocked.

The blocking position on both sides of Nagy Urögd, which was manned by elements of *PGR126*, was attacked by the withdrawing enemy, who was retreating from north to south, around 1230 hours. After suffering considerable losses, the enemy forced a breakthrough to the south.

As the result of the German armored attack, the enemy along the southern edge of Großwardein broke off the fighting after his counterattack of regimental strength failed. He pulled back to the southwest.

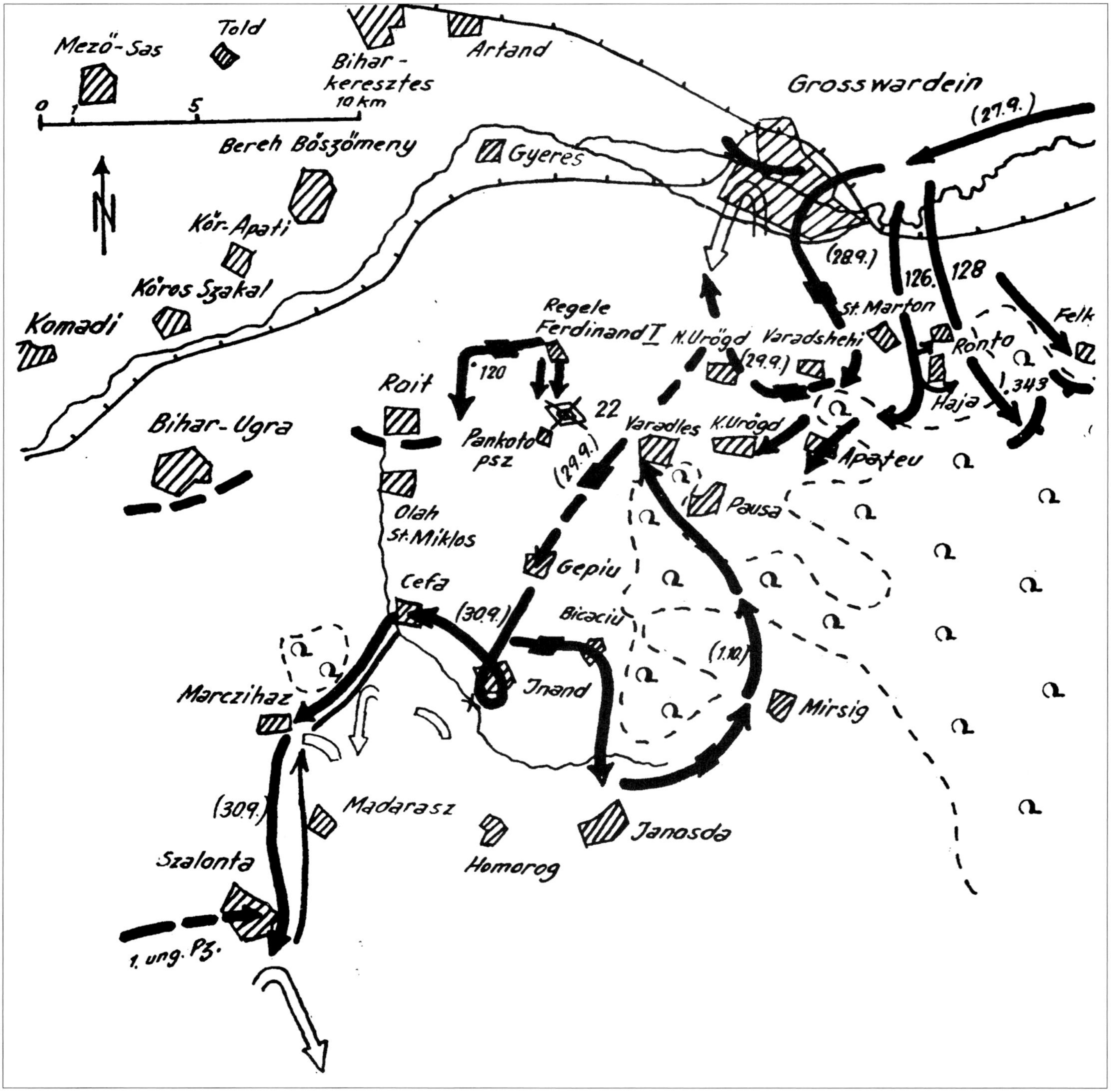

Map 88: Attacks of the *23. Panzer-Division* South of Großwardein from 28 September to 1 October 1944.

German and Hungarian formations, including elements of *PGR126*, followed the enemy along a broad front, taking the airstrip at 1330 hours, and closed up to the elements at evening. That evening, the main line of resistance ran from Olah-Apathi to Kis Urögd.

After taking a short break to resupply in Großwardein, where it was enthusiastically received by the local populace, the armored group moved out again at 1400 hours. Under covering fires from the *III./PAR128*, the armored group rolled through Nagy Urögd and soon thereafter cleared Varadles of weak enemy elements. The armored group resupplied in Gepiu, which the enemy had only vacated shortly before, according to the local populace, and screened during the night. A few scattered Romanians were gathered up from individual quarters. German artillery fired on villages south of the road. In addition to the personnel losses he had taken, the enemy suffered the loss of the following on that day: 24 antitank guns, 6 infantry guns (7.62cm), six artillery pieces (12.2cm), 20 mortars, 4 trucks, 32 machine guns and 15 prime movers.

Combat activity in front of the positions of *PGR128* and *PPB51* was restricted to artillery harassing fires and patrolling. *Panzergrenadier-Regiment 128* was attached to the Hungarian 12th Reserve Division, which had assumed that sector from the *23. Panzer-Division*.

The main clearing station of the 1st Medical Company in Bihar was full.

At 0700 hours on 30 September, the advance of the armored group along the road to Nagy Szalonta was continued. The village of Inand was evacuated in a panic by strong enemy formations in the face of the 15 attacking German tanks. The road bridge 10 kilometers northeast of Nagy Szalonta had been blown up; the canal proved to be an impregnable tank obstacle. An armored reconnaissance patrol from *PAA23* found an intact bridge 5 kilometers north of that point at Püspök-Radvany. Outposts from *PGR126* and *PJA128*, which were following the armored group, remained on the roadway. The main body of the battle group rolled through Inand to the bridge over the canal and deployed on the canal's far side for an attack on Madarasz, which was already being taken under fire by the *I.* and *III./PAR128*. The enemy put up heavy resistance. Eleven antitank guns and two trucks were destroyed, the village taken and then cleared by the following infantry. The eastern edge of Nagy Szalonta was reached at 1800 hours after further attacks. The roads heading northeast and east were blocked. The Hungarian 1st Armored Division, which had attacked Nagy Szalonta from the southwest, was already fighting in the city. The enemy, elements of the Romanian 1st Freedom Division, wound up in front of the guns of the armored group when they attempted to pull back to the east. Completely surprised, the Romanians attempted to escape to the south, tossed their weapons away or surrendered. Eighty prisoners were taken, and three 12.2cm guns were destroyed. With the onset of darkness, the main body of the enemy was able to get away to the south, however.

According to its orders, the armored group moved back to Cefa (Czeffa) when it turned dark. It resupplied there and prepared for new operations.

According to aerial reconnaissance and prisoner statements, strong Soviet forces were closing in on the area south and east of Nagy Szalonta. At the same time, the German armored formations still had not arrived from the middle of Hungary. A Soviet offensive would have been a severe threat to the entire front.

The *23. Panzer-Division* received orders to disrupt the Russian concentrations by means of armored thrusts. At 1000 hours on 1 October, *PR23*, supported by the attached *2.* and *3./PAA23*, the *10.(Pi.)/PGR126* and three self-propelled heavy infantry guns, moved out from Inand to attack. It was supported by the *I.* and *III./PAR128*. The battle group was comprised of 17 tanks and 30 *SPW's*.

The first attack objective, Bicaciu (Mezö Bikacs) was taken after destroying seven antitank guns. Turning to the south, the battle group reached Janosda (Janosd). Two enemy tanks were destroyed. The Russians and the Romanians pulled back in a panic. The rearward lines of communications of the enemy were blocked south of Miersig (Nyarszeg) and several motor vehicles were interdicted. A mortar position with 10 heavy and 6 medium mortars was overrun and crushed. Numerous prisoners, mostly Romanians, were taken. The battle group advanced through the wooded area along the road to the north and reached German lines again south of Veradles at 2000 hours. Despite the tireless efforts of the engineers in clearing obstacles and mines, the lead tank ran over a mine in the vicinity of the enemy's forward lines. There were no casualties. The tangible successes of the day: 2 enemy tanks, 7 antitank guns, 10 heavy mortars, 6 medium mortars, 2 trucks, 3 staff cars and 20 *Panje* wagons destroyed. There were 123 prisoners taken and numerous enemy dead were counted.

The mission of the armored group had been accomplished. Whether it had disrupted the enemy's large buildup in any appreciable manner would show itself in the next few days.

The enemy was quiet in front of the sectors of *PGR128* and the Hungarian 1st Reserve Division. Friendly patrols did not find any enemy until they were 5 kilometers south of Hill 343.

In expectation of an enemy attack, the armored group was moved to Regele Ferdinand I, north of Varadles, during the morning of 2 October. Inand, Mezö Bikacs and, shortly thereafter, Gepiu (Gyapju) were all occupied by the Soviets. Friendly forces were not employed there.

At noon, enemy tanks with infantry advanced from Gepiu on Varadles. The armored group was employed against the enemy's flank and forced him to turn back. Four T-34's were destroyed from coordinated fires from all weapons. Another four were destroyed in front of the sector of the *II./PGR126*. *Hauptmann* Schroeter, the commander of the *I./PGR126*, approached a T-34 and destroyed it with handheld weapons. The effort by the Hungarian forces adjoining *PGR126* on the left to retake Kis Urögd failed.

During the evening of 2 October, the enemy placed barrage fires on the front lines along Varadshehi — Hill 343 — Felker, as well as Hajo and Ronto. Later on, he continued placing heavy fires on the western sector as far as Varadles.

At 0300 hours on 3 October, the *II./PGR128*, employed south of Varadshehi, reported that the neighboring Hungarian formations were leaving their positions without offering resistance and that the enemy was penetrating between the strongpoints of the battalion. A platoon from the *3./PGR128*, reinforced with 2cm self-propelled *Flak*, cleared up the situation and escorted the Hungarians back to their positions.

At 0730 hours, Soviet and Romanian formations attacked the main line of resistance around and east of Varadles. By 0830 hours, all of the efforts to break through had been turned back by *Oberstleutnant* John's regiment.

At 0500 hours, the armored group moved out from Regele Ferdinand I with the mission of advancing on both sides of the rail line from Veradles to the southwest against the Pankota farmstead. Sixteen tanks were available. In Tanya, northwest of the Pankota farmstead, the right wing ran into enemy tanks. Five enemy tanks and three antitank guns were destroyed without any friendly losses. In the meantime, the *4./PR23* reached the farmstead and suddenly saw itself facing Soviet T-43's, T-34's, KV-85's and JS-122's. Sixteen enemy tanks and three antitank guns were knocked out, before the Soviets fled. *Hauptmann* Kujacinski, the commander of the *4./PR23*, and his crew knocked out five of them, obtaining his 51st "kill" in the process. For his performance of duty, he was later awarded the Knight's Cross to the Iron Cross on 18 November 1944. The *3./PR23* knocked out another tank and antitank gun on the left wing of the group, with the result that 11 T-34's, 8 T-43's, 3 JS-122's and 6 antitank guns were destroyed on that day without any German losses.

In the course of that successful fighting, *PR23* knocked out its 1,200th enemy tank. That record was praised in numerous articles in the press.

At 0715, Soviet infantry, supported by tanks, attacked across a broad front between Varadles and Varadshehi. Varadles was successfully defended by *PGR126* and the *III./PAR128*. Six enemy tanks were destroyed. The divisional engineers and the *9./PAR128* prevented a Russian entry into Nagy Urögd. There was constant close combat. The road between the two villages was occasionally crossed by the enemy. Although an immediate counterattack by the *2./PAA23* threw the enemy back, he continued to dominate the road with fire. The *2./Heeres-Flak-Abteilung 278* supported the fighting of the infantry regiments and successfully engaged ground targets and tanks.

To the west of Varadshehi, infiltrating enemy elements advanced as far as the city limits of Großwardein during the course of the day. It was not until the *3./PAA23* was employed, together with a Hungarian battalion, that the enemy group was eliminated. At the same time, the *5./PGR128* was temporarily encircled in Varadshehi.

Varadshehi changed hands three times that day; Varadles was lost for good. By evening of that hotly contested day, the main line of resistance was firmly in the hands of the *23. Panzer-Division* and the Hungarian formations attached to it. The Hungarians were motivated to fight through the example set by the Germans. The enemy was so impressed that he did not attempt any new offensive operations.

At 0945 hours on 4 October, the armored group received the mission to screen with some of its elements along the flat-topped high ground north of Barakony against reported enemy tanks. South of Point 120, the armored group crossed the Hungarian main line of resistance from the north. Not recognizing the German tanks, the Hungarians temporarily ran away, but they later returned to their positions. Just to the south of those positions, the small armored group encountered an advancing Romanian battalion. The Romanians marched right into a trap. Terrifically directed fires of the *II./PAR128* left only a little room for some Romanians to escape to the south. One hundred fifty Romanian dead remained on the battlefield, and 2 officers and 60 enlisted were taken as prisoners.

It was quiet along the division's main line of resistance.

Even on 5 October, the Russians only felt their way forward cautiously. As soon as German tanks appeared, they turned away. For instance, the village of Rojt, temporarily occupied by the Russians, was evacuated by the enemy when the German tanks approached.

During the morning of 6 October, a patrol conducted by the *2./PGR128* under *Leutnant* Heinle blew up a KV-85 chassis northwest of Point 269 and brought back as spoils a heavy machine gun, a submachine gun, a carbine and a few canisters of machine-gun ammunition. A patrol from the *4./PGR128* combed through Hajo and took two Soviets prisoner and captured an antitank rifle and a light machine gun.

The enemy pressed forward out of Barakony during the morning. *Panthers* of the *II./PR23* and elements of the *2./PAA23* threw him back. One *Panther* was a total loss from an antitank gun that fired on it from Olah-Szt. Mikos. Two other *Panthers* suffered slight damage. Seven Soviet antitank guns were destroyed.

That signaled the end of the fighting of the *23. Panzer-Division* around and south of Großwardein. By orders of the *6. Armee*, the division was relieved by *Generalleutnant* Abraham's *76. Infanterie-Division* during the night of 6/7 October.

The division's armored group—*PR23* and the *2./PAA23*—were already moving by 1730 hours to get to the new area of operations around Komadi on the Schnelle Kreisch. Due to a limited load-bearing capacity on the bridge at Gyires, the armored group had to march through Großwardein. It reached Köreszeg-Apati at 0600 hours on 7 October, where it resupplied.

Tank Battle On the Puszta[85] 6 to 28 October 1944

On 6 October 1944, fighting flared up in which the *23. Panzer-Division* would play a role for which it would win laurels. But when the battle broke out, neither the field-army group nor the German Army High Command had any conception of how it would grow like an avalanche. After half an hour of barrage fires, Soviet formations broke through the Hungarian positions between Mako and Nagy Szalonta. Without informing *Generaloberst* Frießner's *Heeresgruppe Süd,* the Commander-in-Chief of the Hungarian 3rd Army, Colonel General Heszleny, directed the retreat of his formations to the Theiß between Szegedin and Szolnok. The *Puszta* was thus open for the Soviets, who, contrary to initial expectations, placed their main effort heading north and not west under the concealment offered by the early-morning fog. At 1200 hours, neither German corps arrayed in the plain, the *LVII. Panzer-Korps* in Kondoros (northwest of Bekescsaba) and the *III. Panzer-Korps* in Derecske, had any idea of what the Hungarians had decided. The headquarters of the *LVII. Panzer-Korps* was literally shot out of its command post and temporarily scattered.

As was determined later, the enemy had moved out with his 46th Army, the 53rd Army, which had been beefed up with four motorized corps and the 6th Guards Tank Army. Headed for both sides of Komadi, which was the new area of operations ordered for the *23. Panzer-Division* during the afternoon of 6 October, was the attack wedge of the 6th Guards Tank Army with the V Guards Tank Corps and the V Motorized-Mechanized Corps.

During the night of 6/7 October, the division and the battle groups received their first intelligence concerning enemy movements, as well as the potential positions of the enemy along the Schnelle Kreisch. There was no reliable intelligence concerning the German formations that were caught up in the Hungarian retreat—the *22. SS-Freiwilligen-Kavallerie-Division*[86] in the area north of Nagy Szalonta.

At 0830 hours on 7 October, the armored group of the *23. Panzer-Division* entered Komadi and drove out weak Soviet motorized infantry elements. Together with *PGR128*, which arrived a short while later, the entire village was occupied and set up for defense, oriented to the south and southwest. At 0930 hours, the armored group and elements of *PGR128* moved out to the south to attack the bridge across the Schnelle Kreisch.

The mission was to open a route north across the Schnelle Kreisch for a battle group of the *22. SS-Freiwilligen-Kavallerie-Division* that was thought to be further south. The small village of Mihalytelep, half way to the canal, was found to be clear of the enemy, and it was occupied by the *I./PGR128*. In the densely vegetated terrain between a small canal moving past Mihalytelep from its northeastern outskirts to the southeast and the Schnelle Kreisch, which formed part of the canal channel and had eight-meter-tall embankments, the enemy had established a strong bridgehead.

The *Panther* moving in the lead was caught in concentric defensive fires 500 meters in front of the smaller canal and was a total loss. The German tanks that were following knocked out a T-43 and three T-34's, but they were unable to advance further into the Soviet bridgehead in the terrain that was partially marshy. The attack by the infantry also bogged down.

An intercepted enemy radio transmission indicated the commander of the bridgehead had been ordered to hold it under all circumstance or die trying. At 1530 hours, *Hauptmann* Roltsch's *I./PGR128* attacked from out of the southwestern portion of Komadi to the south. It advanced as far as the northern canal embankment, all the while magnificently supported by the self-propelled 2cm *Flak* of the *8./PGR128*. From there, the battalion turned to the east and advanced to within 30 meters of the bridge with its 2nd Company.

On the bridge proper were two enemy tanks that had been knocked out that morning by the armored group. The *II./PGR128*, with the attached *3./PGR128*, was employed to the left along the road leading to the bridge from Komadi.

The armored group screened the left wing of the *II./PGR128* with three assault guns from the *1./PR23*. The *3./PR23* supported *Hauptmann* Noever's *PPB51* to the west of Komadi. Together with Hungarian formations, *PGR126* screened along the Schnelle Kreisch at Körösszakali and to its east.

The 8th of October was inaugurated with a surprise advance by a few T-34's at first light about 2.5 kilometers southeast of Komadi. Soviet infantry immediately joined in the attack, including elements that had been able to make it to the north bank of the Schnelle Kreisch during the night in the sector of the *II./PGR128*. One of the infantry's antitank

85 Editor's Note: *Puszta* was the Hungarian word for its unique plains, which were located in an area approximately 100 x 1000 kilometers east of the Theiß River. The settlements there consisted of small villages and individual farmsteads. The latter, at least until the advent of the Communists were often owned by estate holders and noblemen. The actual work force there, the farmers, were often gypsies. The term *Puszta* was also used to indicate a single farmhouse and was abbreviated psz.

86 Editor's Note: Some sources indicate this *SS* division received the honorific of *"Maria Theresia"* in late 1944.

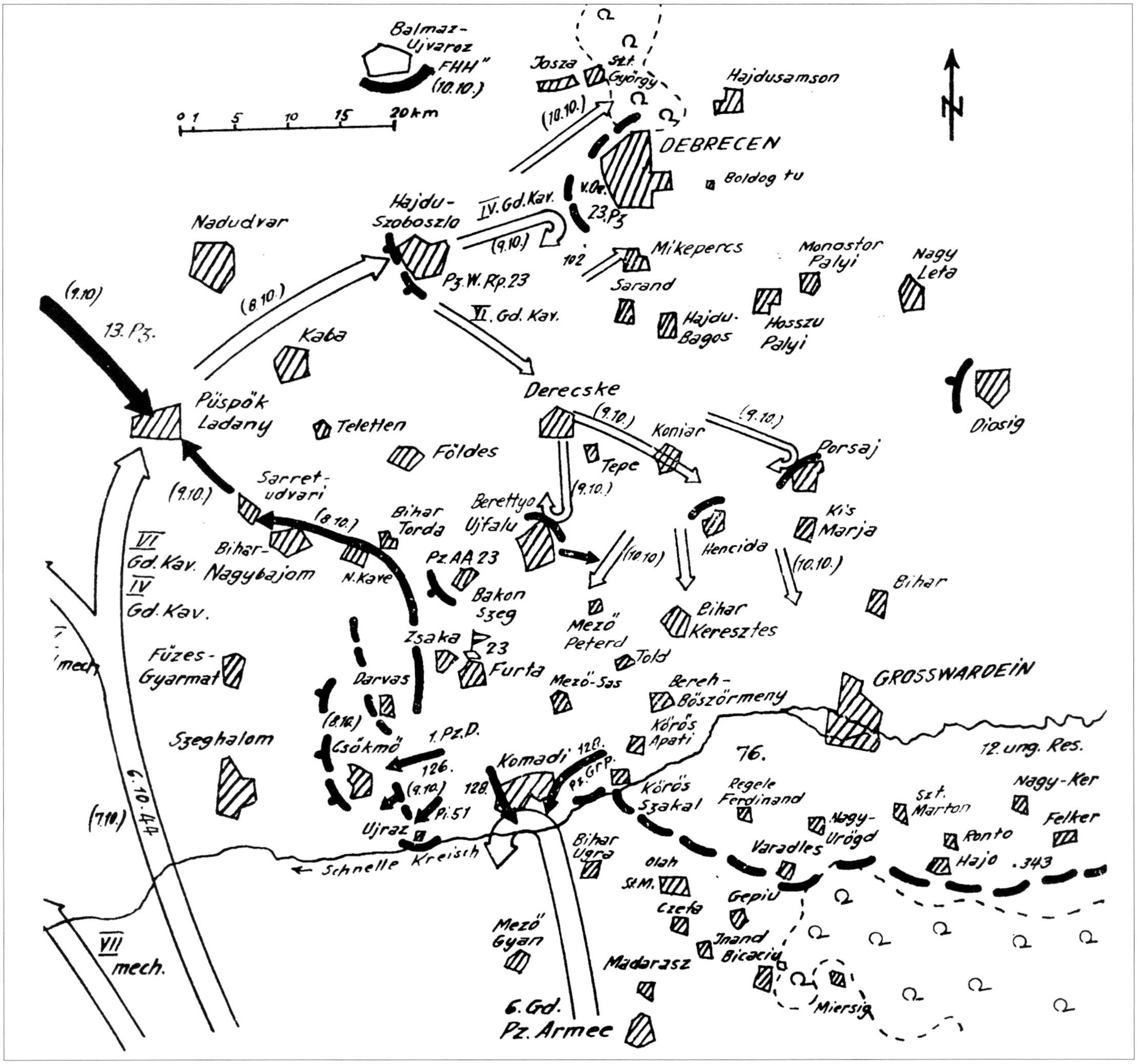

Armored Fighting in the Plains (1st Phase) from 8-10 October 1944.

guns was overrun, although the tank that did that pushed itself so far up onto the gun that its tracks began to freely rotate and the crew had to abandon the vehicle. The enemy advanced as far as the small ditch. After two T-34's were knocked out, the enemy's attack bogged down. A team from *PR23* recovered the stranded T-34 during the night and pulled it onto the road, whereupon it was then used in operations against its former owners. It did not last too long, however, and had to be blown up due to motor damage. But it and three of its contemporaries were able to perform good service for the Germans for a few days.

At 1130 hours, after a massive artillery preparation by the *I.* and *III./PAR128*, the infantry and tanks moved out to counterattack. Stiff resistance on the part of the enemy was broken. The German tanks and infantry made good progress, destroying five enemy tanks and six antitank guns. One *Panther* was a total loss due to hits from an antitank gun. The infantry captured large amounts of small arms and threw the enemy back across the northern canal embankment.

The Soviets fired at the church tower in Komadi, since they assumed there was an observation post there. A direct hit blew away the ladder to the bell tower, just as *Major* Ruge, *Hauptmann* Baran and other officers were there to get oriented. With some difficulty, a new way to descend had to be found.

Adjoining *PGR128* on the right, *PPB51* screened the north bank of the Schnelle Kreisch as far as just east of Ujiraz. There it had contact with infantry and reconnaissance soldiers form the *1. Panzer-Division*, which had been inserted along the eastern flank of the Soviet breakthrough area after having been concentrated in the Debrecen area.

During the fighting for Komadi, the tank regiment's maintenance company and the crews of its 2nd Tank Company were alerted by the local area commander in Hajdu-Szoboszlo (50 kilometers north of the Schnell Kreisch). Soviet armored formations had taken Püspök-Ladany, 20 kilometers to the southwest and were only 15 kilometers from Hajdu-Szoboszlo at that point. Protected by two damaged tanks, two assault guns and 44 personnel of the 2nd Tank Company under *Leutnant* Lindenmayer on the southwestern edge of the village and two additional damaged tanks and 25 men under *Leutnant* Häussler of the same company at the train station, the maintenance company departed for Nyiregyhaza. All 12 non-operational *Panthers* were loaded on rail cars and evacuated. Nineteen newly arrived damaged tanks were diverted to Debrecen. In addition, 50 tons of valuable tank replacement parts also made the train.

At 0430 hours on 9 October, Soviet cavalry pressed against the village of Hajdu-Szoboszlo. At a distance of 100 meters, the five German machine guns opened fire in the darkness and eliminated a troop. Soviet tanks escorting the cavalrymen remained stationary 1,000 meters outside of the village. When the German tanks that were screening opened fire at first light, the Soviet tanks immediately turned away.

The *2./PR23* suffered 4 dead and 10 badly wounded when its positions received mortar fire. Around noon, 70 German and 80 Hungarian police arrived and reinforced the screening group. During the afternoon, a *Flak* section under the command of *Hauptmann* Hinze arrived with two 8.8cm and three 2cm *Flak*.

A reconnaissance-in-force conducted in the direction of Püspök-Ladany resulted in an engagement with Soviet tanks and antitank guns. The tanks of *PR23* destroyed two enemy tanks and five antitank guns in the process; one 8.8cm and one 2cm *Flak* were damaged.

The division field-replacement battalion of *Oberleutnant* Polack, which had been located at Szalard, 30 kilometers north-northeast of Großwardein, since the middle of September had to discontinue its training activities. The Soviet breakthrough southwest of Debrecen forced *General* von Radowitz to move the battalion expeditiously into the area south of Debrecen to protect the rearward lines of communication of the division.

The depth of the enemy's breakthrough in the area between Karczag — Püspök-Ladany, coupled with the fact that its extent was still not readily discernible, made a shifting of the front to the west necessary. The *23. Panzer-Division* handed over its left sector as far as Körösszakal (inclusive) to the *76. Infanterie-Division* of *General* Abraham. The infantry division, which was operating under the command of the *LXXII. Armee-Korps z.b.V.* along with the Hungarian 12th Reserve Division, had continued to hold the positions it had wrested from the enemy south of Großwardein at the beginning of September without being subjected to any Russian attacks of significance. *Panzergrenadier-Regiment 126* and *PAA23* (minus its 2nd Company), which had been freed up by that action, relieved the elements of the *1. Panzer-Division*, which were screening in Ujiraz and Csökmö, in addition to establishing additional security at Darvas, Zsaka-Furta and south of Bakon-szeg. The division artillery went into position with its battalions northwest and north of Komadi.

Between Ujiraz and Komadi, 500-1000 Soviets were crossing the Schnelle Kreisch, whereby they could only be held in check for the time being. Eighteen men from a scattered *SS* unit arrived in the positions of the *I./PGR128* and used as reinforcements.

The Soviets, who had broken through at the bridge south of Komadi were ejected just before nightfall by tanks and *SPW's*. During the night, however, they infiltrated between the strongpoints again.

At first light on 9 October, the armored group moved out to attack again and brought the grenadiers back to the former main line of resistance. Individual advances by the enemy out of his bridgehead remained without success. *Unteroffizier* Böttle of the *2./PGR128* destroyed a T-34 with a *Panzerfaust*. Twenty enemy dead remained behind in the German lines.

In the area of Hajdu-Szoboszlo, Soviet infantry and cavalry, supported by four to six enemy tanks, pushed their way along the road leading from Püspök-Ladany and approached *Gruppe Lindenmayer*. At the same time, the police units screening to the north reported that strong enemy forces had bypassed the village to the north and were advancing east. The local area commander thereupon ordered the village to be evacuated. Despite the covering fires offered by *Gruppe Lindenmayer*, *Gruppe Häußler*, which was pulling back from the southern part of the village, had to clear a path through Soviet infantry, antitank guns and *panje* carts, sustaining bloody losses. Five antitank guns were overrun, but *Leutnant* Häußler was mortally wounded in the process. After blowing up two tanks that had become immobilized, the six screening tanks and their accompanying infantry back to a *Flak* position that had been established 6 kilometers southwest of Debrecen by the local area commander of that city. While conducting reconnaissance in the direction of Hajdu-Szoboszlo, *Leutnant* Lindenmayer determined that that a strong enemy column had already approached to within 5 kilometers of the blocking position. The enemy was driving civilians in front of it, mostly women and children.

Hauptmann Fischer, the commander of the *II./PR23*, ordered *Leutnant* Lindenmayer to move to Nyiregyhaza with the rest of the *2./PR23* and pick up repaired tanks there. Taking charge of the tanks remaining at the blocking position was *Oberleutnant* von Oechelhaeuser.

At 1400 hours, the Soviets appeared in front of the tanks, which were positioned in front of the *Flak*. With the first round fired, the civilians that were being driven forward in front of the Soviets sought cover in the roadside ditches. The lead enemy tank was knocked out. At that point, the enemy pulled back.

At 1545 hours, the enemy launched a deliberate attack with tanks, infantry and cavalry on both sides of the road. Seven enemy tanks were destroyed; four of them by the *Flak* and the remainder by the tanks. The Soviets then attempted to bypass the outposts on the right, which *Gruppe Oechelhaeuser* was able to prevent by successful immediate counterattacks. Two German tanks were damaged in the process.

On 10 October, the enemy prepared for delivering a great blow at Komadi. During the night, he brought up some 50 tanks. At first light, he attacked differing points of the bridge site with several packs of tanks and entered the front lines. About 800 Soviet infantry followed. The *2./PGR128* was encircled. Initially, only seven men were able to fight their way back to Komadi.

While the *3.* and *4./PGR128* established a blocking position in a swell in the ground just south of the village, the armored group, which had prepared for a counterattack, moved out from the southwestern edge of Komadi and, swinging west, then headed east. The armored group lost only two tanks to enemy-inflicted battle damage and one to a mechanical failure. At the same time, it destroyed 22 enemy armored vehicles—11 T-43's, 10 Shermans and an assault guns—while also knocking out a 12.2cm antitank gun and four 7.62cm antitank guns. The infantry retook Mihalytelep, reestablished contact with the 2nd Company and held a position running from the southern edge of Mihalytelep to Point 91 by noon.

During the course of the afternoon, enemy tanks felt their way forward on several occasions. Another six were knocked out, with one of the "kills" coming from an antitank gun of the *4./PGR128*. With those "kills" the total of enemy armored vehicles destroyed on that day in and around the German positions was 28. Komadi remained firmly under German control.

During the early morning hours, *PGR126* relieved *PPB51* in its positions east of Ujiraz and screened in a line running along the canal northwest of Darvas — the western edge of Moroszigete mjr. — the western and southern outskirts of Csökmö — Czirko mjr. — western side of Ujiraz. At 0800 hours, an attack by 10 enemy tanks was turned back. Antitank guns from *PJA128* and the regiment's heavy companies destroyed three tanks and an assault gun.

Despite additional defensive successes enjoyed by the regiment, Csölmö was lost shortly before noon in the course of a new attack by Soviet tanks and infantry. The new main line of resistance ran from Koroszigeti mjr. To the eas, along its deep western flank, the division screened from Bakon-szeg with *PAA23* and elements of *PPB51*.

The overall situation in the area of operations had become increasingly opaque by 10 October. The Soviet corps that had broken through and out of the area around Szeghalom through Püspök Ladany and to the north were at Debrecen — Mikepercs and Nagy Leta. They were deep in the rear of the German and Hungarian formations that were still fighting south of Großwardein and along the Schnelle Kreisch. While the IV Guards Cavalry Corps attacked Debrecen from the west and the south, the IX Motorized-Mechanized Corps and the VI Guards Cavalry Corps had crossed the Debrecen — Berettyo-Ujfalu road to the east and were attacking to the south from there. Their objective was to open the German front along the Schnelle Kreisch for the 6th Guards Tank Army, which had been battering itself there south of Komadi for days on end. The horse-mounted, motorized and mechanized formations of that field army were appearing in the entire area north of and between Berettyo-Ujfalu and Großwardein. Again and again, the command posts and trains elements found themselves subject to attack there, whereupon they either had to fight or withdraw. A number of brave deeds were performed during that period of which no one will ever know. Logistics, maintenance and replacement personnel suddenly became combat troops. Medics had to take arms against the enemy forces that appeared everywhere, so that they could protect their wounded, since the symbol of the Red Cross was not respected by the Soviets. Panic often broke out among the hastily assembled trains elements of differing divisions; in some cases, the trains personnel fled toward the front and the combat troops. The combat personnel, on the other hand, did not know about the tremendous threats posed in their rear. They only knew that munitions and fuel were delivered irregularly and in lesser quantities.

The main clearing stations of the two medical companies in Mezökeresztes and Biharkeresztes were attacked by enemy tanks that literally shot them out of their facilities. They had to pull back to Großwardein.

A short while earlier the logistics section of the division under *Major i.G.* Gilow had to pull out of Berettyo Ujfalu. It initially went to Mezö Keresztes. At that point, communications with the combat elements was completely interrupted. Nobody knew where the enemy was and what he would do next.

On 11 October, *Major i.G.* Gilow decided to move out of Großwardein, which was already being directly threatened, and head east (!), swinging out in a wide arc through Margitta, to reestablish contact with the division in the vicinity of Debrecen. That effort succeeded in a night march, which was joined by numerous trains elements, rear-area services and medical personnel with their patients.

During the night of 10/11 October, 80 noncommissioned officers and enlisted personnel from an *SS* regiment arrived to reinforce the infantry regiments. The enemy attacked at Komadi at 0600 hours with tanks and infantry. He was only partially able to enter the main line of resistance, heavily supported by mortars and artillery.

During the fighting conducted by *PPB51* around Bakon-szeg, which had been employed on the right wing of *PGR126*, *Oberfähnrich* Kleemann of the battalion's 2nd Company distinguished himself in sealing off and eliminating a penetration. During that round of fighting, Kleemann destroyed a JS-122 with a *Panzerfaust*.

In the area of operations around Debrecen, the enemy prepared to attack with some 40 to 50 tanks during the early morning hours of 10 October. Opposing them on the southwest edge of the city was *Gruppe Oechelhaeuser*, which had two *Panthers* and an assault gun. It was also supported by a section of *Flak* with two 8.8cm antiaircraft guns. In order to beat the Soviet to the punch—or at least slow them down—*Oberleutnant* Oechelhaeuser carefully advanced against the enemy tanks with his *Panther*. Opening fire at an effective range, he succeeded in destroying five of them by ambush. The remaining Soviets, who had been completely surprised, Soviets fled to the southwest.

Two hours then went by before the Soviets attacked again, this time with about 30 tanks and a battalion of infantry along both sides of the main road. The armored vehicles and the *Flak* did not open fire until the Soviets had approached to within 800 meters. Twelve enemy tanks were quickly set alight—five by the *Flak* and seven by the armored vehicles. The Soviets pulled back; their infantry dug in 2,000 meters in front of the blocking position.

Toward noon, six enemy tanks advanced far north of the German positions as far as the city limits of Debrecen. *Oberleutnant* Oechelhaeuser moved in that direction with his *Panther*, snuck up on the Soviets from the rear and set two of them alight. The remaining ones then took off to the north. That afternoon, only infantry continued to attempt to infiltrate in the direction of the city limits.

Because the *Flak* outposts positioned on the south side of Debrecen reported enemy concentrations, *Oberleutnant* Zirr of *PR23* was sent to reinforce the elements there with a *Panther*, an assault gun and the engineer platoon of the *II./PR23*. Soviet infantry assaulted at the onset of darkness and was thrown back after a short struggle. The sounds of armored vehicle tracks betrayed a new concentration, however.

Panzer-Regiment 23 is credited with the following "kills" for 10 October 1944: 19 T-34's, 12 KV-85's, 9 T-43's and 2 JS-122's.

The counterattack of the armored group, conducted as a pincers movement, enabled the infantry to regain their old positions around Komadi by 1000 hours. At the same time, four T-34's and a Sherman were eliminated without any friendly losses.

During the day, two *Panzer IV's* supported the infantry in their defense of the strongpoint of Milhalytelup and destroyed an additional four enemy tanks.

The *I./PGR126* was temporarily attached to *PGR128* in Komadi in order to cover a large-sized gap. The battalion's 2nd Company cleaned up an enemy penetration that had still remained by attacking from the northeast at 1715 hours.

Approaching from Czökmö, two Soviet tanks with mounted infantry attacked the weak outposts of the *II./PRG126* and the observation post of the *9./PAR128* at Czirko (Szöcsködi psz). They were forced to turn back by artillery fires. An enemy advance consisting of three armored cars, four tanks and 60 infantry that was launched from Czökmö to the northeast was later broken up by the fires of the 7th Battery. Armored cars and tanks were destroyed, in some cases by firing over open sites. The Soviet infantry pulled back.

To the north of *Gruppe von Oechelhaeuser*, the enemy infiltrated into the northern portion of Debrecen during the night of 10/11 October. *Hauptmann* Fischer, the commander of the *II./PR23*, attacked those enemy forces at 0630 hours with *Panthers* and the battalion's engineer platoon. Ground was slowly gained against hard resistance. Two *Panthers* got bogged down. After the arrival of two more *Panthers* from the outpost position on the southwest outskirts of the city, the enemy was finally thrown out of the city after almost five hours of fighting. That was just in the nick of time to send a *Panther* to the southern part of the city to the positions of *Gruppe Zirr*, which were then being attacked by Soviet tanks. The assault gun already positioned there was destroyed by enemy fires, however, all of the enemy's attacks were turned back.

At 1400 hours, the enemy was ejected from a brickworks located just in front of the southwestern blocking position by *Panzergruppe von Oechelhaeuser* and grenadiers. Four enemy tanks were destroyed in the process.

The troop elements of the division destroyed the following on that day: 15 T-34's, 5 KV-85's, 2 T-43's, 4 heavy machine guns, 6 mortars and 2 antitank guns.

The 12th of October started with an attack by all of the tanks in Debrecen—seven *Panthers* and an assault gun—a *Flak* platoon and a platoon of grenadiers. At 0700 hours, *Kampfgruppe Fischer* moved out to the south on orders of the local area commander for Debrecen in order to open up the road to the south and take Mikepercs. Mikepercs was reached through thick ground fog and cleared of weak enemy forces. But since the enemy dominated the Debrecen — Mikepercs road from the west with his fires, the tanks and the grenadiers attacked north after leaving behind outposts in Mikepercs. In a fight with enemy tanks, antitank guns and infantry, three Soviet tanks and five antitank guns were eliminated before the enemy was thrown across the railway line to the west. The latter action was done in conjunction with the division's field replacement battalion, especially its 2nd Company, which was also approaching from the east at the same time. In the process, the grenadiers captured a horse-drawn antitank gun. The 3rd Company (Artillery) of the replacement battalion delivered a high rate of fire from its single, horse-drawn Model 18 light field howitzer. The artillery observers were in the Mikepercs church tower and directed the artillery fires to just before the German main line of resistance.

The *III./PAR128* continued to provide covering fires in the area around Csökmö during 12 October. The 7th and 8th Batteries had to change position to the northwest during the day (closer to the enemy) in order to provide more effective fires as a result of not having sufficient charges for the guns.

In the area around Komadi, the enemy fired several salvoes into the main line of resistance, the Mihalytelep strongpoint and the village itself, before he started to attack at 1000 hours with tanks and infantry. Seven enemy tanks forced a temporary evacuation of the Mihalytelep strongpoint. When the armored group counterattacked, 12 enemy tanks out of the 18 were knocked out, most of them Shermans. Once again it was demonstrated that the enemy did not know the properties of the Sherman very well. The German main line of resistance was held until 1700 hours. Another enemy tank and infantry attack forced the evacuation of Mihalytelep. An immediate counterattack was not conducted, since a warning order for disengaging from the enemy had arrived in the meantime.

Hauptmann Noever, the commander of *PPB51*, was wounded that morning by shrapnel from an antitank gun round. Once again, the engineer battalion was without a commander.

At 1630 hours, six T-34's with mounted infantry suddenly attacked the firing positions of the *I./PAR128* northwest of Komadi. Before two alerted *Panthers* could arrive, the cannoneers, under the leadership of their commander, *Major* Baran, destroyed all of the enemy tanks and the accompanying infantry by firing over open sights.

At 1900 hours, the tanks and grenadiers pulled back from Komadi; at 2145 hours, the last rearguards of the *I./PGR128* left their positions. That signaled the end of one of the most successful engagements of the division. In six days of fighting, all combat arms of the division had prevented the crossing of the Schnelle Kreisch by the Soviet 6th Guards Tank Army when they defended Komadi. As a result, they decisively influenced the course of the fighting on the *puszta*. Large portions of the V Guards Tank Corps, the V Motorized-mechanized Corps and three rifle divisions were bled white in the fighting for the bridgehead. Ninety-four enemy tanks were destroyed. Snipers had 76 confirmed "kills". The German tank losses were almost non-existent. On the other hand, the personnel losses of the infantry were high but, in comparison to the Soviets, equally small.

The new main line of resistance for the *23. Panzer-Division* on 13 October extended from Darvas through Vekerd — Nagy Nyesta tn. — Körmösd psz to Told. The armored group was positioned next to the division command post in Furta. The divisional artillery was in firing positions north of the small Ölyvös Creek, which was ringed by embankments.

In the meantime, the enemy finally succeeded after two days of attacks against the front, rear and left flank of the *LXXII. Armee-Korps* to the left, that the Hungarian 12th reserve Division initially had to pull back, followed then by *General* Abraham's *76. Infanterie-Division*. Advancing from the north, the enemy stood in front of Artand on 13 October, after advanced elements had already entered the northern portion of Berettyo Ujfalu and Biharkeresztes on 10 and 11 October, only to be ejected. During the course of 13 October, pushed up to the positions of *PGR128* at the Körmösd psz and at Korhany hal. from the southeast. The enemy did not follow from the south yet, however.

At 1030 hours, two enemy tanks with motorized infantry advanced against the northeast corner of Korhany hal. Artillery, as well as a group of five *Panthers* and *SPW's* under *Oberleutnant* Marquardt, threw the enemy back. One T-43 was knocked out.

The combat trains of the division, which had pulled out of Csaka and Mezö on 12 October, found themselves engaged by Soviet artillery near Derecske and had to pull back further to Debrecen. On the other hand, *Panzergruppe Fischer* moved into Derecske and screened there on all sides. The Berettyo Ujfalu road had been interdicted, with the result that no supply operations were possible on that route. A shortage of ammunition was the consequence.

The 2nd Medical Company established its clearing station in Bagamer, 25 kilometers east-southeast of Debrecen.

By the morning of 14 October, the enemy had also started to follow the division from the south. At 0700 hours, strong enemy artillery salvoes were being placed on Mezö Sas. *Major* Ruge's *PGR128* set up outposts oriented south, east and northeast. The village of Told was held by elements of the *76. Infanterie-Division*. The enemy advanced against Mezö Sas from the southeast. He was turned back by the *2./PGR128*, supported by *Flak* elements. The regiment's 2nd Battalion was attacked from the south. *Panzergruppe Rebentisch* was dispatched from Furta against those enemy forces and ran into an enemy battalion, which then suffered heavy casualties, about 2 kilometers west of Mezö Sas. Soviet antitank guns southwest of Mezö Sas dominated the open *Puszta*, with the result that a continued advance by the tanks would have been senseless, especially since the enemy was attacking west from the area east of Mezö Peterd and was therefore aiming for the deep left flank of the division.

Artillery from the *III./PAR128* scattered an enemy attack coming from Vekerd, which consisted of five tanks, two personnel carriers and 100 infantry, that took place in front of the sectors of *PGR126* and *PPB51*. The enemy air force participated in the ground fighting to a large extent, with several bombing raids being conducted on Bakon-szeg. During the day, elements of the *76. Infanterie-Division* relieved engineers from *PPB51* there.

Attacking from the east, the enemy temporarily encircled *Oberst* Kissel's *Grenadier-Regiment 178* (*76. Infanterie-Division*) around noon in Told. A short while later, he took Mezö Peterd. *Oberleutnant* Quintel's *3./PR23* advanced in the direction of Told, established contact with the *76. Infanterie-Division* and made its withdrawal to the northwest easier by conducting an immediate counterattack with a limited objective.

At 1700 hours, the enemy succeeded in entering the southern portion of Mezö Sas, when he attacked from the south. The *3./PGR138* cleared up the situation in conjunction with two self-propelled *Flak*. *Panzergruppe Fischer*, which had been ordered to Berettyo Ujfalu by the regiment, was

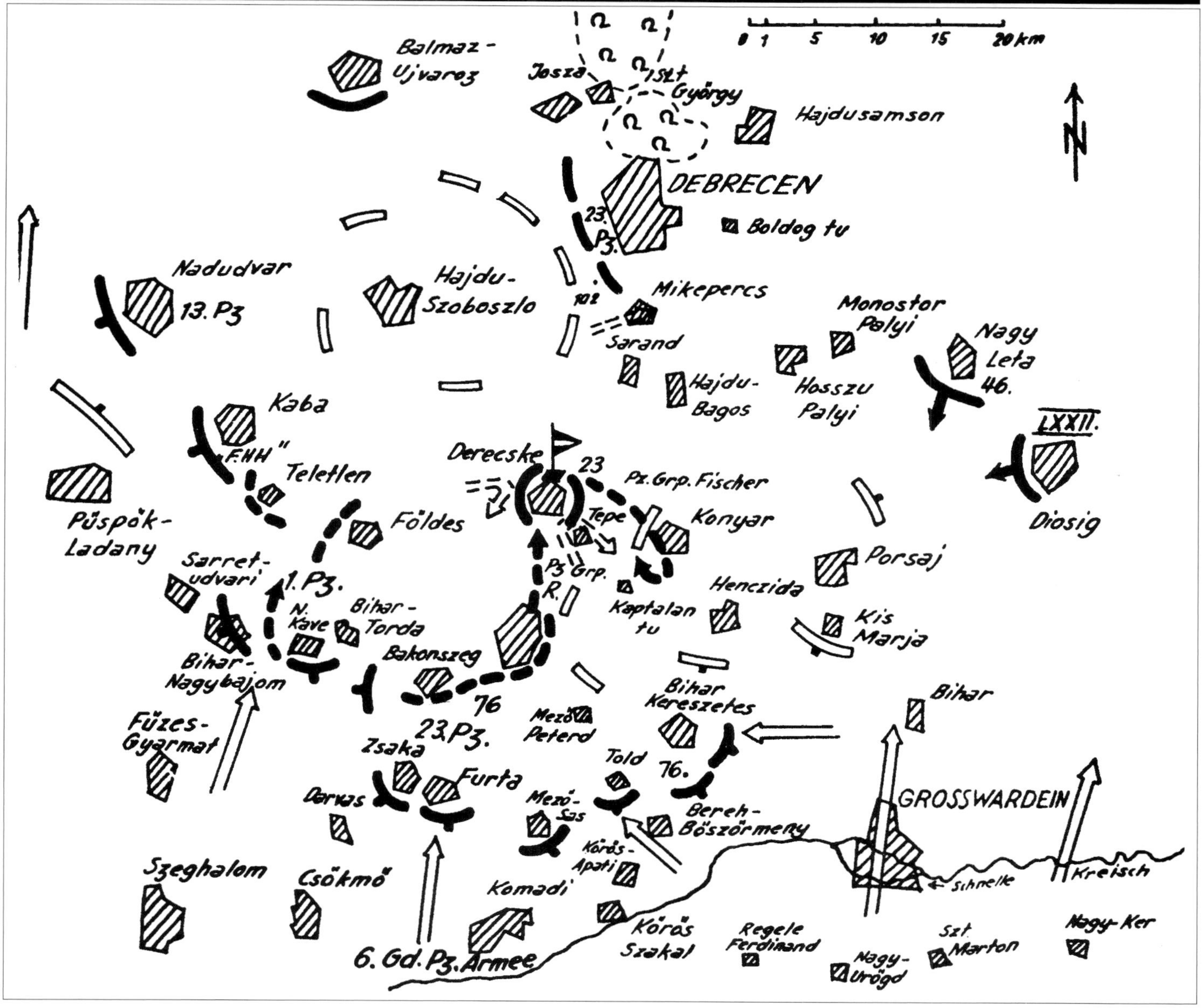

Map 90: Tank Fighting on the *Puszta*, 2nd Phase (13/14 October 1944).

detained in Derecske by the divisional commander, since the village had been attacked several times by Soviet formations.

Following the heavy Soviet attacks on Derecske, there were a lot of wounded there. Field ambulances were brought forward there during the night under cover of the tanks.

The main line of resistance of the *23. Panzer-Division* was ordered back to an area southwest, south and southeast of Berettyo Ujfalu during the evening of 14 October. The last remaining elements of the *76. Infanterie-Division*, which had been passed through the lines by the outposts of the *Kampfgruppe Rebentisch* at Berettyo Szt. Marton, took up quarters in Berettyo Ujfalu. The divisional artillery covered the main line of resistance from positions west of Berettyo Ujfalu, while the armored group prepared for operations in the widespread village, concurrently employing outposts along the northeastern portion of it. The elements of the *1. Panzer-Division*, which had been positioned there up to that point, moved to Földes.

The enemy was quiet in front of the right-hand side of the division sector on 15 October. Enemy infantry moved forward from the southeast across the embankment and toward the *I./PGR128*. Mortar and artillery salvoes were increasingly directed against the German positions. Toward noon, Soviet infantry, supported by three tanks, attacked Berettyo Ujfalu from the northeast. The Soviet infantry infiltrated into the village between the tanks that were screening. *Kampfgruppe Rebentisch* was unable to hold up the enemy in the buildings and gardens with the type of forces at its disposal. It was not until *Grenadier-Regiment 178* joined the fighting that the German counterattack produced successful results, whereby two of the three Soviet tanks were knocked out.

The main clearing station in Derecske had to be moved due to the impending threat.

A few damaged tanks from *PR23* ran into a group of Soviet forces west of Berettyo Ujfalu on their way to the maintenance facility. The enemy was attempting to penetrate to the north between Földes and Berettyo Ujfalu. The enemy forces had already been attacked from Földes by an engineer company from the *1. Panzer-Division*. Suddenly caught in a cross fire, the enemy force fell apart. The *1. Panzer-Division* reported 120 prisoners and 12 captured antitank guns.

On that 15 October, the Hungarian government under Admiral Horthy declared a ceasefire with the Soviets. Since the situation was not clear at the time, *Oberleutnant* Zirr received orders to secure the bridges over the Theiß at Tokay with two *Panthers* and 65 tankers employed as infantry, who came from the trains elements located in Nyiregyhaza.

As a result of the withdrawal of the *76. Infanterie-Division* as the left-hand neighbor of the *23. Panzer-Division*, an almost 25-kilometer-wide gap developed along the eastern flank of the division, in which the enemy was able to move about freely. It was not until he reached the Porsaj area that he encountered the *46. Infanterie-Division*, which had been fighting there since 12 October.

The*76. Infanterie-Division* was attached to the *23. Panzer-Division*. The infantry division was directed to relieve *PGR128* in Berettyo Ujfalu.

The *III. Panzer-Korps* ordered an attack east on 16 October by the armored group of *PR23* from the area around Berettyo Ujfalu — Derecske. To that end, the division received attached the operations elements of *Panzer-Abteilung 2109* of *Panzer-Brigade 109* and *Sturmgeschütz-Brigade 228*. The original intention—to have *Panzergruppe Rebentisch* establish contact with *Panzergruppe Fischer* at the canal bridge 4 kilometers south of Tepe—was not able to come about because *Panzergruppe Fischer* then received orders to attack south in the direction of Point 106 from Konyar (10 kilometers east of Derecske).

Panzergruppe Rebentisch moved north out of Berettyo Ujfalu at 0800 hours with six tanks—including three *Panthers* from *Panzer-Abteilung 2109*—and 12 *SPW's* from the *3./PAA23*. Enemy resistance was slight up to the bridge across the east-west canal 4 kilometers south of Tepe. Two tanks fell out with mechanical problems and returned to Berettyo Ujfalu. At the bridge over the canal, Soviet north-south movements consisting of vehicles and cavalry were observed. Just to the north of the bridge, hard fighting suddenly erupted with dismounted cavalry, antitank guns and antitank rifles. One *Panther* was hit and damaged and also had to move to the rear. The enemy suffered extremely heavy loses, since he was unable to disengage from the *SPW's*. The main weapons on both sides were hand grenades and submachine guns, while the tanks were busy engaging antitank guns and tanks that appeared.

At the same time, Derecske was attacked by strong enemy forces. Occasionally turning into close combat, the fighting was conducted by the division headquarters, *Heeres-Flak-Abteilung 278* and trains elements, to be joined later by elements of the division's replacement battalion. The enemy was turned back, and the *Flak* gunners knocked out seven enemy tanks.

In tireless efforts by the field ambulance company, the wounded were rescued from the advancing Soviets. As always, it was the objective of all of the division's medical personnel to see to it that no wounded fell into enemy hands.

Panzergruppe Rebentisch received orders to advance through to Derecske and create some breathing room against the enemy forces that had already entered the village. As the armored group advanced, it encountered enemy cavalry with numerous limbered antitank guns and vehicles coming from the direction of Derecske. The armored group was separated from the enemy forces by a canal that was five meters deep. Apparently, the enemy was pulling up stakes from the area in front of the southwestern portion of Derecske as a result of the pressure created by the armored group advancing in its rear. Racing at a full gallop, the cavalry attempted to get past the tanks and the *SPW's* to the south. The armored group inflicted extremely heavy casualties on the cavalry with its machine guns and main guns of all calibers. After the armored group enjoyed that success, a Soviet antitank-gun-belt on the western edge of Tepe put a temporary end to its continued advance. Two thousand meters of open fields that were flanked by Soviet antitank guns separated the armored group from the village. Nevertheless, the fighting ended in a defensive success as a result of the impression created by the approaching German armor.

At the same time, *Panzergruppe Fischer* had crossed the canal bridge south of Konyar, whereupon it entered into an engagement with Soviet tanks. Out of seven enemy tanks, four were destroyed. *Hauptmann* Fischer's command tank received several hits. With any grenadiers accompanying them, the armored group advanced south and, later on, west, in order to get to the road through the lake narrows at Kaptalan tn. Two more T-34's were knocked out and one German tank burned out after being hit. The lake barrows were guarded by an antitank-gun-belt. During the attempt to get through to the west just south of the canal, the armored group engaged in a firefight with enemy tanks on the southern edge of Tepe. The armored group, which consisted of only three *Panthers* and four assault guns, eliminated nine enemy tanks, including three JS-122's. Three German tanks were lost. While this fighting was going on, strong enemy forces attacked Konyar from the south. Before *Panzergruppe Fischer* could reach the bridge south of Konyar, the enemy was already there, as well as 2 kilometers west of it. The only option remaining for the breakout of the four remaining tanks, on which the crews of the knocked-out tanks were riding, was across the bridge and through a 1,000-meter-deep area occupied by the enemy to the south.

Hit several times, the *Panther* of the *Kampfgruppe* commander made it across the bridge. All of the remaining tanks got bogged down in the canal in their attempt to avoid enemy fires, with the result that the crews had to bail out in the middle of the Soviet infantry. A relief effort conducted by *Hauptmann* Fischer with weak forces that were still positioned in Konyar enabled the majority of the tankers to get to safety. The unfortunate outcome of the operation, with its loss of nine tanks, weighed heavily on the division, despite the numerical success achieved against a considerably stronger enemy, who lost 16 tanks.

After the return to Konyar, *Gruppe Fischer* was ordered to Hosszu-Palyi to screen there with the remaining *Panzer V's*, a tank destroyer and 25 men from the replacement battalion. That same night a first enemy attack had to be turned back.

The new main clearing station of the 2nd Medical Company in Sarand was driven from its location by fires from a "Stalin Organ" and aerial attacks. The 1st Medical Company operated a larger clearing station in Debrecen.

In the Berettyo Ujfalu area, the enemy was largely quiet on 16 October. By order of the division, the artillery and the infantry regiments moved through Földes and Derecske in a motor march to the area of Hajdu Bagos — Hosszu Palyi. The two regiments from the attached *76. Infanterie-Division—Füsilier-Regiment 230* and *Grenadier-Regiment 178*—temporarily relieved the division's infantry only to pull out of Brettyo Ujfalu themselves during the night of 16/17 October and march to Derecske through Tepe. At that point, it turned out to be fortuitous that *Panzergruppe Rebentisch* had not been able to move to Derecske during the day. From its hedgehog position west of Tepe, it held the road open for the two grenadier regiments and escorted them without enemy losses to Derecske by 0830 hours on 17 October. There they were attached to the *1. Panzer-Division*, after the *23. Panzer-Division* was once again given the mission of covering the east flank of the *III. Panzer-Korps*. By then, the *46. Infanterie-Division* had been brought closer to Debrecen. During the course of 16 October, the division destroyed a total of 29 tanks, 15 antitank guns, 20 antitank rifles and numerous additional weapons.

The fighting on 16 October led to the conclusion that the enemy would attempt to take Debrecen from the southeast after shifting his main effort further to the east. From there, he would thrust north to cut off the rearward lines of communications and avenues of withdrawal for the *8. Armee*, which was still fighting considerably further to the east. Despite all of their efforts, the enemy formations outside the southwest portion of Debrecen, which had been there since 10 October, had been unable to take the city. As a result, he then started to place his main offensive efforts on the city from the southeast. During the early morning hours of 17 October, the enemy entered Hosszu Palyi and advanced as far as the center of the village, before he was thrown back to his jumping-off points by an immediate counterattack launched by the tanks, engineers and scouts of *PR23*, as well as the division's replacement battalion.

The *II./PGR126* cleared the small patch of woods 2 kilometers southeast of Hajdu Bagos of the Russians.

Enemy concentrations south of Hajdu Bagos were scattered by the divisional artillery. An advance by the enemy ended with the knocking out of five tanks and a personnel carrier by troop elements of the division.

The 18th of October saw only weaker enemy attacks on the positions of the divisions south of the line running Sarand — Hajdu Bagos — Hosszu Palyi. Tanks of the *I./PR23*, as well as engineers from *PPB51* and division infantry, cleared up a penetration by Soviet tanks and infantry into Hajdu Bagos.

At 1300 hours, 27 Soviet tanks, including some JS-122's, as well as 300 infantry, concentrated in the woods southeast of Hajdu Bagos and, despite artillery fires by *PAR128* on that area, attacked at 1500 hours. The enemy had already been sapped of so much strength that both of the battalions of *PGR126* were able to turn him back.

Lead Soviet armored elements had already surfaced 30 kilometers northeast of Debrecen in Balkany and forced new decisions, especially since the enemy was feeling his way forward against Debrecen from the northeast as well. At 1800 hours, the division pulled back to a new screening position on both sides of Mikepercs, with *PGR128* on the right and *PGR126* on the left. The division's armored forces were positioned on stand-by in the woods 10 kilometers southeast of Debrecen.

During the early morning hours of 19 October, the *23. Panzer-Division* was ordered to the northern part of Debrecen, since the enemy had already occupied the "Apafa erdö" Woods 2 kilometers further to the north. The western, southern and southeastern edges of the city were defended by the *1. Panzer-Division* (along with the attached *76. Infanterie-Division*) and the *46. Infanterie-Division*, while the *13. Panzer-Division* and the *60. Panzergrenadier-Division "Feldherrnhalle"* screened west of the city on the *Puszta* south of Polgar. It was panicky in the city proper. During the morning, the Red Air Forces carpet bombed the city center.

While *PGR126* was employed around Pallag to screen to the east and north and *PGR128* (minus its 1st Battalion), together with the division's replacement battalion, established a screening line west of the city at Nemethy tn., the *I./PGR128* attacked along both side of the Debrecen — Hajdu samson road at 0530 hours. In the face of heavy resistance and strong flanking fires, only 600 meters of ground could be taken. A renewed attack, this time with the *II./PGR128* on the left, brought no gains on the ground.

At 1230 hours, the armored group attacked. It had been reinforced with 22 operational *SPW's* from *Panzergrenadier-Bataillon 2109* of *Panzer-Brigade 109*. Moving with *Panthers* and *SPW's* to the north from Boldog tn., the armored group hit the enemy advancing fro the east in the flank. Out of the group of 10 enemy tanks, 7 were knocked out. The attack bogged down, however, after covering 3 kilometers, when it ran into a strong antitank-gun-belt in broken-up terrain.

The assault guns of the tank regiment, which had been sent toward Nemethy tn. to support the infantry, bogged down in a marshy grain field, where they were immediately attacked by Soviet infantry. After employing two *Panthers* under *Feldwebel* Förster, all of the armored vehicles were freed up. The group then rejoined the rest of the *Kampfgruppe* after having had to move through the Russian forces, which had already advanced westward.

During the afternoon, the enemy succeeded in entering the outskirts and smaller settlements outside of Debrecen from the north. In doing so, they were able to bypass a number of German fighting formations, including the *46. Infanterie-Division*, the *1. Panzer-Division* and the *23. Panzer-Division*. The fighting forces knew nothing about the development of the situation in the city. Around 1600 hours, the two grenadier regiments of the *76. Infanterie-Division* moved past the ready positions of *Panzergruppe Rebentisch* while they were pulling back to the north while east of the city.

Around 1700 hours, a field ambulance from the division's ambulance company was fired at by a Russian/Romanian patrol, which disregarded the Red Cross. The driver, *Obergefreiter* Knödler, was wounded. The assistant driver, *Gefreiter* Dietmar, was killed by a round to the head. Knödler was able to make his way back to German lines.

A short while later, the division ordered a withdrawal to the area around Pallag. In the course of its withdrawal, *PGR128* made enemy contact around 1600 hours at the northern outskirts of Debrecen. The *I./PGR128* lost a few vehicles and its signals equipment. The armored group was unable to disengage from the enemy until it was almost night and was able to move through the enemy-occupied terrain without sustaining any casualties. Starting at 2200 hours, it was able to prepare for further operations from a concentration area at Pallag, 9 kilometers north of Debrecen.

The division's infantry occupied a screening line along the Debrecen — Pallag rail line during the night, oriented to the east.

The headquarters and line companies of *PJA128* arrived back at the division and supported both of the infantry regiments in their engagements against armored vehicles.

On 20 October, the enemy attempted to advance north from Debrecen. Seemingly uninterrupted strong enemy forces composed of infantry, tanks, antitank guns and *panje* carts marched northward along the Debrecen — Hajdusamson road, screened on the left flank by cavalry. At Molnar tn., those forces swung back on to the Debrecen — Hajdu -Hadhaz main road and continued north.

Panzergruppe Zirr, consisting of three *Panthers*, was employed against the enemy at Molnar tn. At 1000 hours. It knocked out an enemy tank east of the rail line and scattered enemy cavalry. The entire group then bogged down in marshy terrain. It was only able to free itself again after four hours of recovery work. No casualties were sustained.

At the same time, *PGR126*, on the right wing of the division, attacked the northeastern portion of Debrecen. It was supported in its attack by fires from the *II.* and *III./PAR128*, which concentrated on Point 129 and the Russian advance route. The enemy movements were temporarily impeded, but they were immediately continued on to the east. The enemy advanced north on both sides of the Debrecen — Hajdu-Hadhaz road and the rail line that ran parallel to it, all the while avoiding the *I./PGR128*, which was screening there.

The assault guns of the armored group advanced from Pallag to the east at noon. The interdicted the advance of the Soviets along the small road running 2 kilometers further to the east, chased away Soviet cavalry and interrupted traffic along the Debrecen — Hajdusamson road for two hours through their fires. Twenty Soviet trucks were destroyed, followed soon thereafter by three T-43's. An attack with nine enemy tanks that was launched against the assault guns failed.

Approaching from the northeast, a Soviet assault detachment succeeded in entering Pallag in the afternoon. The *10.(Pi.)/PGR126* prevented the Soviets from expanding their success and pushed the enemy forces back.

At 1700 hours, in accordance with its orders, the division pulled back to a new line of resistance running along the wood line and south of Szt. György mjr. *Panzergrenadier-Regiment 128* was designated as the division reserve. Pallag was evacuated at 1900 hours. The right-hand neighbor of the division was the *46. Infanterie-Division*. *Panzer-Brigade 109* was detached from its attachment to *Panzergruppe Rebentisch*.

The defensive fighting of the *III. Panzer-Korps*, whose main mission it was to hold up the enemy's advance to the north and allow the retreat of

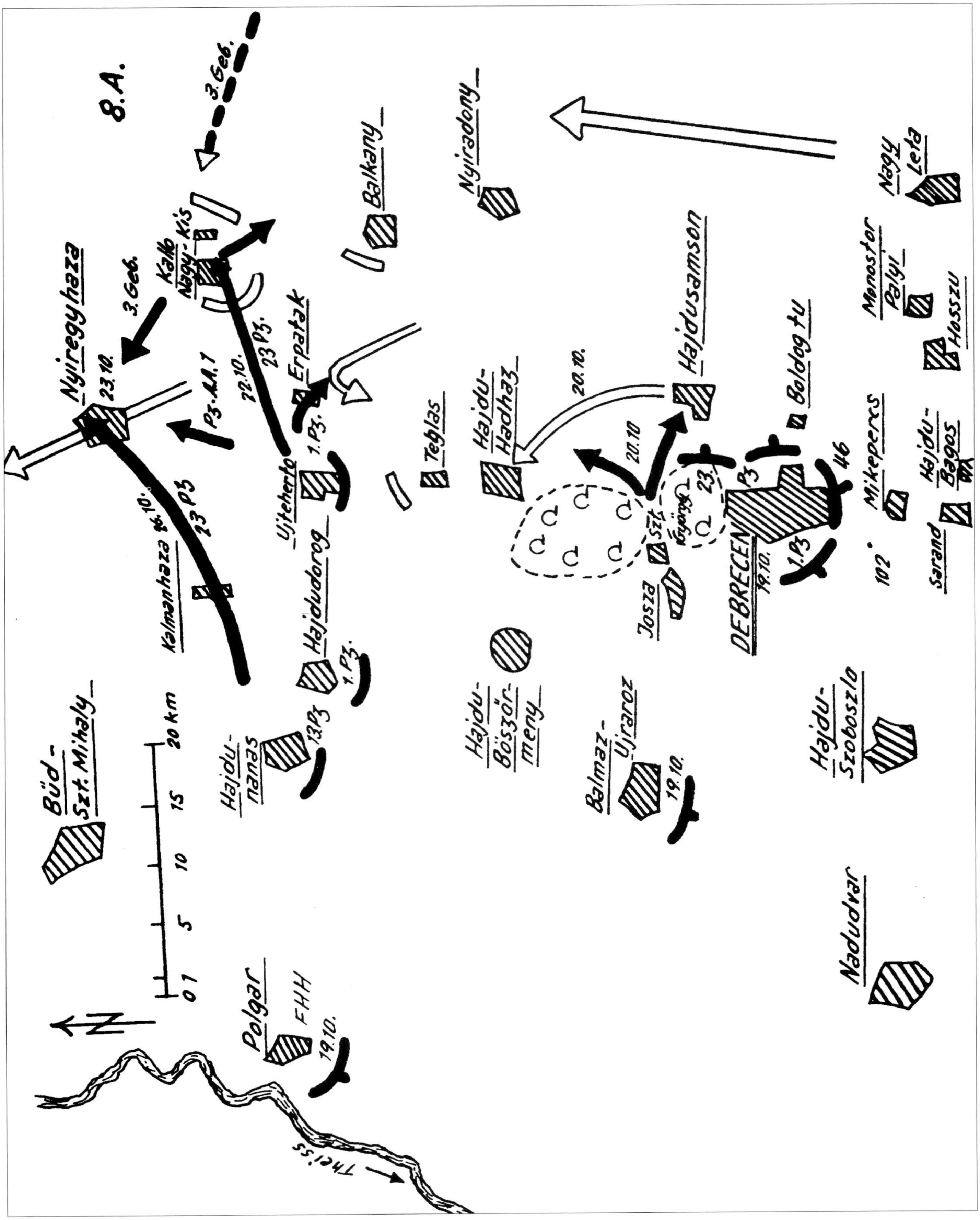

Map 91: Tank Fighting on the *Puszta*. Closing the Gap to the *8. Armee* at Kallo and Nyiregyhaza from 19-26 October 1944.

the *8. Armee* on the left to back behind the Theiß, experienced one crisis situation after the other. Although an attack by the *General der Panzertruppen* Kleemann's *IV. Panzer-Korps*—consisting of the *24. Panzer-Division* and the *4. SS-Polizei-Panzergrenadier-Division*—on 19 October and on the morning of 20 October from the bridgehead at Szolnok to the east was able to force the enemy to throw his 6th Guards Tank Army with its three mechanized formations from Debrecen to the west, it did little to influence the attack north by the Soviet 53rd Army west of Debrecen and the advance of five mobile formations under General Plijew to the east of the *III. Panzer-Korps*.

Panzergrenadier-Division "Feldherrnhalle" and the *13. Panzer-Division* were fighting around Balmuz-Ujvaros and south of Hajdu-Böszörmeny with their weak remnants. The *46. Infanterie-Division* was defending south of Josza; positioned behind it on 21 October was *PGR126* and rest of the operationally ready elements of the *23. Panzer-Division*. The *1. Panzer-Division* had already launched its attack east of Hajdu-Böszörrmeny on Hajdu-Hadhaz, which was occupied by the enemy, and was holding Teglas. At the same time, the Soviet lead attack elements were just outside of Nyiregyhaza, which was an important transportation nodal point 40 kilometers to the north. On 22 October, the Soviet took that city. As a result, the lines of communication of the *6. Armee* were cut to the *8. Armee*, which was still fighting 120 kilometers further east, as well as to the Hungarian 1st and 2nd Armies, which were to the left of the *8. Armee*.

The *23. Panzer-Division* was ordered to Uj-Feherto on 21 October, where it was to prepare to attack the deep flank of the enemy at Nagy Kallo.

The trains and the rear-area services of the division had to pull back rapidly across the Theiß to the northwest. A few tanks that were at the location of maintenance company of *PR23* and committed against the enemy were lost. *Hauptmann* Mittler was able to save the valuable maintenance equipment in the nick of time, however.

Hauptmann Fischer moved out to attack along the Uj-Feherto — Nagy-Kallo road with 10 tanks and elements of *PAA23*. Both of the infantry regiments followed. The weak outposts of the Soviets were overrun before they could fire a round. The same fate befell several antitank guns that attempted to go into position. The infantry and the tanks entered the village at the same time. The enemy's trains broke out in a panic. Despite that, the enemy put up stiff resistance. At 0900 hours, the train station was in German hands and, at 1100 hours, the eastern half of the village was in the hands of the infantry. Large amounts of spoils—weapons, vehicles and rations—fell into German hands. At 1330 hours, the *II./PGR126* reached the southern outskirts of Kallo, where the last remaining Soviets were cleared out by 1600 hours. After they were cleared, a large number of atrocities visited upon the Hungarian populace were discovered. Several women had been raped and then killed. The divisional artillery went into position just west of the retaken village, so as to better be able to supported the anticipated defensive fighting. That same evening, the enemy attempted to retake Nagy-Kallo, but he was turned back. Heavy enemy fires of all calibers and bombing runs by the Red Air Force inflicted a few casualties on the division.

The divisional engineers, along with the assault guns of the *1./P23*, screened to the north of Kallo.

The attack objective of the day—to block the logistics lines of communications of the enemy who had advanced on that day through Nyiregyhaza as far as the Theiß at Tokaj and Csap—had been completely achieved.

It was directed on 23 October to secure the position that had been reached and expand it in the face of anticipated breakout attempts from the north and relief attacks from the south. The position was to be held until the *3. Gebirgs-Division*, which was a part of the *8. Armee*, could establish contact from the east.

At 0530 hours, the armored group and the *II./PGR126* moved out to attack along both sides of the road to Biri. One *Panther* was lost in an engagement with well-camouflaged and stationary enemy tanks. Two T-43's were eliminated. The attack stalled after gaining 3 kilometers; the enemy then attempted to go around the attack group. The attack group was ordered back to Nagy-Kallo in the afternoon. Until then, the local defense turned back several infantry attacks from the north and south, with the divisional artillery providing valuable support. The first weak enemy elements, with individual tanks, infiltrated from north to south west of Nagy-Kallo. Greeted enthusiastically, the lead elements of the *3. Gebirgs-Division* arrived at the eastern part of the village just after midnight after putting in a long march. They relieved the troop elements of the *23. Panzer-Division* during the first few hours of 24 October. Those elements were immediately dispatched to block the way south for a group of Soviet forces southwest of Nyiregyhaza.

Patrols from *PAA23*, which kept the enemy around and north of Nyiregyhaza under observation, reported that a strong cavalry formation, supported by 20-30 tanks, was advancing from there toward Hajdu-Dorog.

The two infantry regiments and the divisional artillery prepared for the attack in Hajdu-Dorog, oriented to the north-northeast. At 1030 hours, the *III./PAR128* to the west of Hajdu-Dorog was ready to fire and immediately started engaging enemy forces 2,000 meters north of the village. Assault guns knocked out three tanks just outside the village. The armored group, reinforced by the *3.* and *4./PAA23* prepared for operations in Uj-Feherto. Around 1000 hours, it moved out to the northwest and engaged an enemy group 2 kilometers north of Kalmanhaza. In a fight lasting one and one-half hours, three enemy tanks were knocked out. Considerable casualties were inflicted on the Russian cavalry and several *panje* carts blown to pieces. The armored group then advanced further west and reached the crossroads 6 kilometers north of Hajdu-Dorog. In the meantime, both of the infantry regiments moved north out of the area in the vicinity of the crossroads at Csontos halom. They pushed back the enemy, who did not appear motivated for combat, at Point 125, where they were received by tanks and personnel carriers. The *II./PGR126* overran a Soviet antitank-gun-belt, captured the guns and inflicted considerable casualties on the enemy. The *I./PGR128* captured or destroyed 2 7.62cm antitank guns, 8 tripod-mounted heavy machine guns, 3 trucks, 10 *panje* wagons (with horses) and a heavy machine gun.

After the infantry arrived at the crossroads, the armored group moved out further to the west after leaving behind a tank outpost. The armored group pushed other enemy forces back north. The Soviet formation, the 30th Cavalry Division, was practically wiped out. The armored group reported the following as its spoils for the day: 5 enemy tanks; 24 antitank guns; 11 mortars; 5 antitank rifles; 1 heavy triple-barreled antiaircraft machine gun; 7 heavy machine guns; 3 light machine guns; 8 trucks (captured); 5 trucks (blown apart); 64 *panje* wagons (destroyed); and 7 prisoners.

During the night, *PGR126* secured the area that had been taken, while *PGR128* and the armored group billeted in Hajdunanas and provided the local security.

On 25 October, both the *1. Panzer-Division* (around Uj-Feherto and to its east) and the *3. Gebirgs-Division* (in Nagy Kallo) were involved in considerable defensive fighting, being subjected to constant relief attacks by the Soviets from the south. A local penetration at Uj-Feherto was cleared up in the afternoon by *Hauptmann* Böhmer's *II./PGR128* and *Panzer-Pionier-Bataillon 37* of the *1. Panzer-Division*. Three *Panthers* under the command of *Oberleutnant* Erb were sent from Hajdunanas to assist the *1. Panzer-Division*. They attacked south together with *Panzer-Pionier-Bataillon 37* and tanks from the latter division's *Panzer-Regiment 1* and took the group of buildings at Bot.

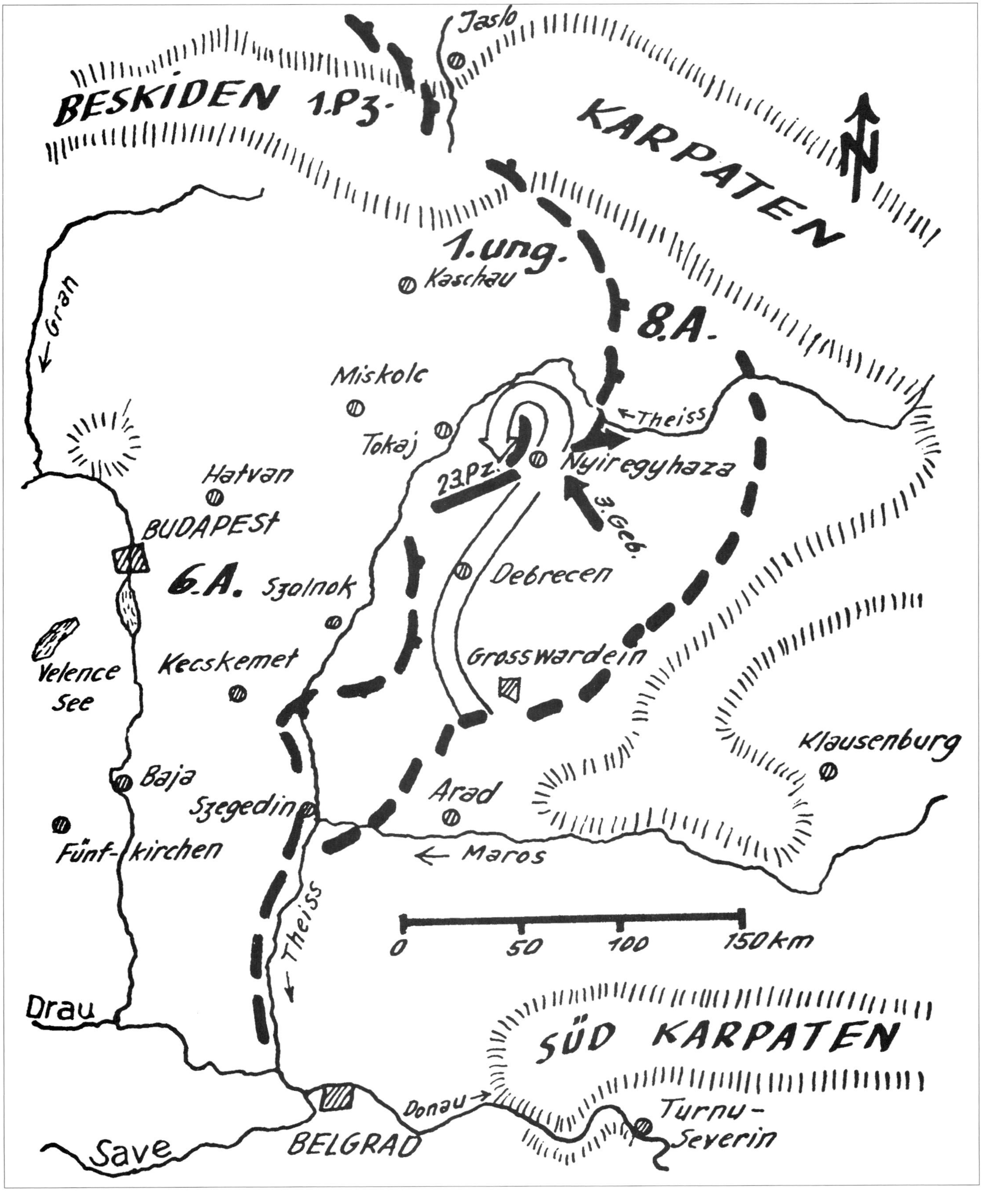

Map 92: The Over-all Situation on 26 October 1944. The Importance of the Victory at Nyireghaza.

The *I./PGR128*, which had also been attached to the *1. Panzer-Division* in the meantime, was sent to Uj-Feherto and employed during the evening in the main line of resistance between Uj-Feherto and Erpatak. In the morning, Nagymicske was occupied. Several enemy attacks were turned back through the evening of 26 October or were answered with counterattacks. That evening, the battalion was relieved from attachment to the *1. Panzer-Division* and returned with the regiment to division command and control.

Hauptmann Brehme's *III./PAR128* shattered several enemy attacks and immobilized three enemy tanks through fires.

At 1530 hours, *PGR126* marched through Uj-Feherto to Kallo and screened south between Kallo and Erpatak next to *Aufklärungs-Abteilung 8* of the *3. Gebirgs-Division*. At 0100 hours on 26 October, the regiment was relived by the mountain division's *Gebirgsjäger-Regiment 106* and went to Hajdu-Dorog. On 26 October, the *23. Panzer-Division* and the *3. Gebirgs-Division* received orders to eliminate the enemy around Nyiregyhaza. At 0900 hours, *Panzergruppe Fischer* moved out with eight tanks and the *2.* and *3./PAA23* (on *SPW's*) from the crossroads 6 kilometers north of Hajdu-Dorog to attack Nyiregyhaza. Following closely behind was the *I.(PzHaub.)/PAR128* and *Oberst* John's *PGR126* (mounted).

The enemy forces at Loci Bokor and in the area just to the west of Nyiregyhaza pulled back without offering significant resistance. After waiting a short while for the grenadiers of *PGR126* to arrive, the infantry of that regiment then attacked the southern part of the city, while the *Panthers* and the *2./PAA23* attacked the city from the south and the two assault guns from the *1./PR23* and the *3./PAA23* attacked the northern part of the city. The forces in the south succeeded in entering the city quickly; they fought block by block to the city center. From there they made it easier for the grenadiers of *PGR126* to enter the city.

The northern group initially overcame some antitank guns and then advanced into the city after blocking the road leading out of town to the northwest. One thousand prisoners, including ten Germans, were liberated from Soviet captivity and the enemy suffered heavy losses in both men and materiel. The enemy had also treated the local populace brutally there, and their liberators were enthusiastically greeted. During the afternoon, the battle group engaged the last remaining pockets of resistance in the southeastern portion of the city.

The *I./PAR128* provided terrific support, some of it coming from firing over open sights. Contact was established with the *3. Gebirgs-Division* 4 kilometers to the southeast after it started to turn dark. As a result, the boundary between the *6. Armee* and the *8. Armee* were firmed up anew and an additional step in the elimination of the Soviet corps north of Nyiregyhaza had been taken.

Practically located in the front lines, the division's 1st Medical Company tended to the wounded from its clearing station in Hajdunanas.

On 27 October, the division's field forces were pulled out of the front lines once again and concentrated at Hajdunanas. That signaled the end of the major fighting on the *Puszta* for the *23. Panzer-Division*.

***

During the period from 28 September to 28 October 1944, the division lost the following in dead: 9 Officers, 40 noncommissioned officers and 176 enlisted personnel. The wounded totaled 26 officers, 146 noncommissioned officers and 177 enlisted personnel. Reported missing in action were 11 noncommissioned officers and 33 enlisted personnel.

The total loses in major equipment and armored vehicles:

1 2cm *Flak 38* (towed)	2 8.8cm *Flak 37*
1 2cm *Flak 38* (self-propelled)	15 *Panzerkampfwagen V* (*Panther*)
3 7.5cm *Pak 40* (towed)	4 *Panzerkampfwagen IV*
1 8cm *Granatwerfer 34*	5 assault guns
1 *s.I.G. 38* (self-propelled)	2 Tank destroyers (self-propelled)
1 *l.F.H. 18* (towed)	1 armored car
1 *l.F.H. 18/2* (*Wespe*)	10 *SPW's*

The following were captured or destroyed in the same time period:

228 tanks	84 mortars
223 antitank guns	18 infantry guns
31 artillery pieces	95 antitank rifles
15 gun limbers	67 heavy machine guns
149 light machine guns	39 submachine guns
7 antiaircraft guns	164 trucks
Innumerable small arms	8 motorcycles
15 staff cars	Radio equipment of all types
360 horse-drawn wagons	Equipment for an engineer company
5 armored cars	

707 prisoners were taken; more than 3,500 enemy dead counted.

***

On 4 October 1944, the *23. Panzer-Division*, under the command of *Generalmajor* von Radowitz, was mentioned in the *Wehrmacht* Daily Report. On 22 October, *Major* Ruge, *Major* Rebentisch and *Oberleutnant* von Oechelhaeuser received a by-name mention.

Major Ruge, the commander of *PGR128*, was rewarded for his bravery and that of his regiment by becoming the 648th member of the German Armed Forces to receive the Oakleaves to the Knight's Cross of the Iron Cross on 16 November 1944.

Between the Theiß and the Danube 28 October to 29 November 1944

In the last days of October, the *8. Armee* pulled back in a deliberate manner into the positions won for it around Nyiregyhaza by *General der Panzertruppen* Breith's *III. Panzer-Korps*. The Soviet corps that had been encircled continued on to their inevitable ends. Only be leaving behind all of their equipment were portions of them able to escape south along byways.

On 28 October, the missions of the German armored divisions in that area of operations came to an end. The threat created by the Soviets in the wake of the Theiß being left exposed by German and Hungarian formations between Szolnok and Polgar made their employment in that area pressing, especially since the enemy broke through the front lines of the Hungarian 3rd Army on 29 October at Kecskemet and his lead tank elements had advanced as far as the outskirts of Budapest. The headquarters of the *6. Armee* assumed command and control of the forces of the Hungarian 3rd Army and was given responsibility for the entire area between the Danube and the Theiß.

The main body of the *23. Panzer-Division* followed the *1. Panzer-Division*, which moved out in advance on 29 October. After three days of marching through Polgar, Mezö-Kövesd and Jaszbereny, it reached the Czegled area.

The *23. Panzer-Division*, together with the *24. Panzer-Division*, was attached to the headquarters of the *LVII. Panzer-Korps*.

On 31 October, *PGR128* was located in Nagykörös. Following the heavy losses sustained during the fighting on the *puszta*, the two battalions were consolidated into one under the command and control of the headquarters of the 2nd Battalion. Two battalions of the divisional artillery were prepared to conduct fire missions. The divisional reconnaissance battalion scouted the entire area of operations. Based on reports that the enemy was advancing northwest from Kecskemet toward Lajosmisce, *PGR128* was employed west against that village. Without making enemy contact there, the regiment moved along the road to Kecskemet, followed by the *III./PAR128*. From firing positions at Somody, 6 kilometers northwest of Kecskemet, the artillery engaged concentrations of Russian infantry and tanks. There was no attack, however, since the enemy continued

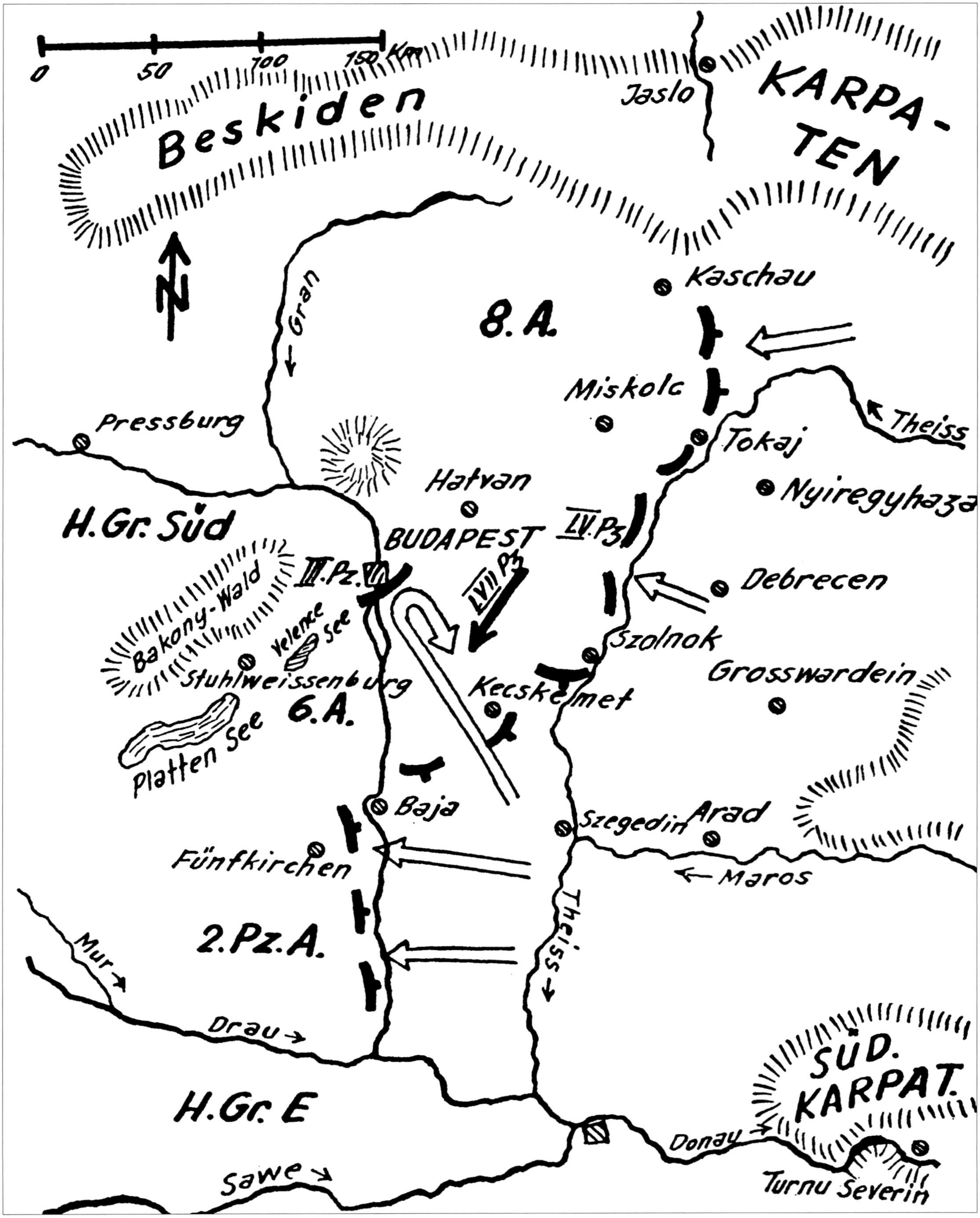

Map 93: Over-all Situation on 29 October 1944. The Soviet Advance on Budapest.

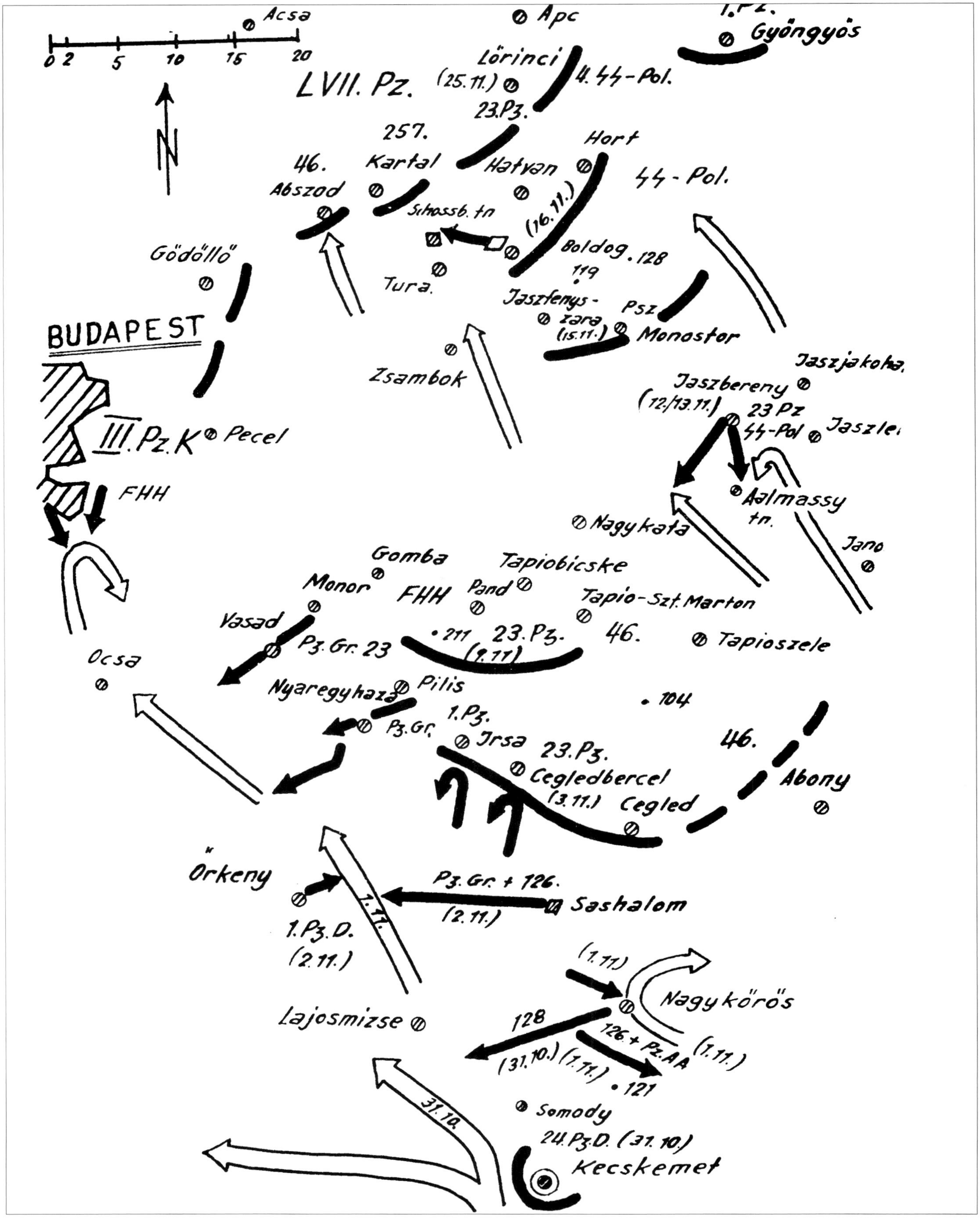

Map 94: Counterattacks and Withdrawal East of Budapest. 31 October to 25 November 1944.

to march west in the evening hours, moving south of the battle group. The battle group returned to Nagykörös, where *Kampfgruppe Fischer* had arrived with 10 tanks in the meantime, as well as *PGR126*.

As its first elements arrived, the division's 2nd Medical Company established its main clearing station, along with an ambulance stopping point, in Czegled. The 1st Medical Company also closed up soon thereafter, with the result that the two main clearing stations allowed faster treatment of the wounded in the case of larger-scale operations.

At 0800 hours on 1 November, a Russian-Romanian assault force entered Nagykörös. An immediate counterattack by *PAA23*, which had been reinforced with five tanks from the *I./PR23*, drove the enemy from the village, but not from the broken-up, densely vegetated terrain to the south.

Panzergrenadier-Regiment 126 attacked east from the area southwest of Nagykörös. Just before reaching the main road, an enemy antitank gun knocked out a *Tiger*, blocking the way for the remaining tanks. At 2200 hours, contact was established with the *24. Panzer-Division* by means of a patrol. Defenses were set up on Point 124 to the left of the *24. Panzer-Division*.

The armored elements—*PAA23* and the armored group—which were combined under the command of *Major* Koppe attacked south at 1330 hours. Despite strong flanking fires from the east, the group advanced as far as Point 121, 9 kilometers south of Nagykörös and established contact with *PGR126*. The divisional artillery engaged enemy concentrations. In the process, the *9./PAR128* destroyed two mortars and an antitank gun.

At 1700 hours, five *Panthers* had to be employed to relieve *Hauptmann* Arnold's *II./PAR128*, which was being attacked by Soviet infantry 6 kilometers south of Nagykörös. During the evening, the main line of resistance was pulled back to the southern edge of Nagykörös. *Schwere Panzer-Abteilung 509*, outfitted with the *Tiger II*, was attached to *PR23* under the command of *Oberstleutnant Prinz* zu Waldeck und Pyrmont. The heavy tank battalion was under the command of *Oberstleutnant Prinz* zu Waldeck und Pyrmont. During the course of this round of fighting, *Heeres-Flak-Abteilung 278* employed its 8.8cm *Flak* in both ground and air-defense roles, with its 2cm *Flak* being exclusively used against ground targets.

Because the enemy had broken through with armored forces on 1 November in the direction of Budapest and had bypassed the *24. Panzer-Division* on both sides of Kecskemet, the *23. Panzer-Division* was ordered to attack the enemy in his deep right flank. That same evening, the division was shifted 10 kilometers to the northwest. At 0940 hours on 2 November, the tank regiment, together with attached *Tigers*, five *Panzer IV's* from the *24. Panzer-Division* and *PGR126*, moved out to attack to the northwest from Sashalon (10 kilometers southwest of Czegled). The *II./PAR128* accompanied the attack with forward observers. At the same time, the *1. Panzer-Division* moved out to the northeast from Örkeny to cut off the enemy that had broken through.

There was soon fighting with enemy tanks and motorized infantry. Two enemy tanks were eliminated; three German assault guns were lost due to enemy action. Despite a downpour and poor visibility, not only the *Luftwaffe*, but also the Red Air Force joined in the fighting on the ground. After overrunning an antitank-gun belt and destroying additional enemy tanks, the group then moved rapidly into the enemy artillery and antitank guns, which attempted to escape but were overrun in some cases.

As soon as the attack threatened to stall, the infantry dismounted from the tanks and continued on foot against the enemy. Another assault gun was lost to enemy action. Toward 2200 hours, the attack groups were ordered back to Sashalom. Rain, darkness and difficult terrain made the withdrawal extraordinarily difficult, since several tanks had to be towed and the enemy followed close on the heels of the withdrawing force. Two *Königstiger* and a *Panther* had to be blown up, while all of the other tanks and assault guns had to be towed.

The battle group destroyed 7 enemy tanks, 13 antitank guns, 18 trucks, 1 2cm four-barreled antiaircraft gun and 8 horse-drawn wagons.

During 3 November, *PGR128* evacuated Nagykörös and occupied screening positions 10 kilometers southwest of Czegled, all the while covering the adjacent open areas with assault detachments. The *III./PAR128* formed an infantry company out of artillerymen and used it to screen east in the area around its firing positions at Darany tnj.

From a staging area at Alberti, *Kampfgruppe Fischer* attacked with seven tanks and the *4./PAA23* toward the southwest and occupied the Musik psz and Antomia mjr. To the south, Soviet infantry with heavy weapons was engaged and a Soviet assault gun destroyed. The *III./PAR128* covered the advance from positions at Czegledbercze1 (12 kilometers northwest of Czegled). In the meantime, the main line of resistance of the division had been pulled back to the Czegled — Alberti rail line. Elements from *PAA23* and *PJA128* relieved the armored group in the evening at the Musik psz, with the armored group thereupon preparing for further operations from an assembly area at Alberti.

On 4 November, the enemy attacked the rail line from the south. While he could be held in check in front of the division sector by means of artillery fires, he was able to block the road in the direction of Czegled and also to Pilis. Six tanks and four *SPW's* were employed to clear the road to Pilis; they were supported by the *I./PAR128*. One kilometer outside of Pilis, an assault gun was knocked out. Two enemy antitank guns were eliminated. The *I./PAR128* fired salvoes on enemy forces digging in along the edge of the woods 1.5 kilometers northwest of Alberti. The enemy suffered extremely heavy casualties from fused shells going off in the trees. Two more antitank guns were destroyed and more ground taken. At 1000 hours, the tanks established contact with elements of the *1. Panzer-Division* approaching from Pilis. Four more antitank guns were captured before the armored group returned to Alberti after completing its mission.

The enemy build-up in front of the division sector continued throughout the day. A penetration into Czegledbercze1 was cleared up by *PGR128*.

Moving from Pilis on 5 November, *Panzergruppe Fischer*, together with 14 tanks and *SPW's* from the *1. Panzer-Division*, occupied Nyaregyhaza. Three Soviet trucks were captured. At 1400 hours, the battle group continued its advance south and drove a completely surprised enemy force out of Weckerle mjr. It then occupied Ujhartyan, which was free of enemy forces, and blocked a Soviet supply route 4 kilometers further south. Numerous trucks and *panje* carts were surprised and shot to pieces. It was not until midnight that the battle group started its march back, whereby it eliminated another column of *panje* carts.

The two infantry regiments were subjected to increasing attacks by the enemy south and southwest of Irsa and Czegledbercze1. Despite final protective fires by the heavy weapons and artillery, the enemy penetrated the area between the two villages with tanks and infantry and crossed the railway embankment. One enemy tanks was destroyed by antitank guns of *PGR126*. The penetration could be partially cleared up by the *10.(Pi)/PGR126*. Czegledbercze1 was evacuated in the evening, and the main line of resistance pulled back to the southern outskirts of Irsa and the area to its east.

Hauptmann Fuhrmann's *PPB51*, which was employed on the left wing of the division between Hills 193 and 157 north of Czegledbercze1, was given the mission of screening the east flank of the division. Around noon, a large enemy force moved in front of the main line of resistance to the west and threatened *PGR128*, which was positioned to the right.

Map 95: Fighting in the Irsa — Alberti Area and Around Jaszbereny from 5-13 November 1944.

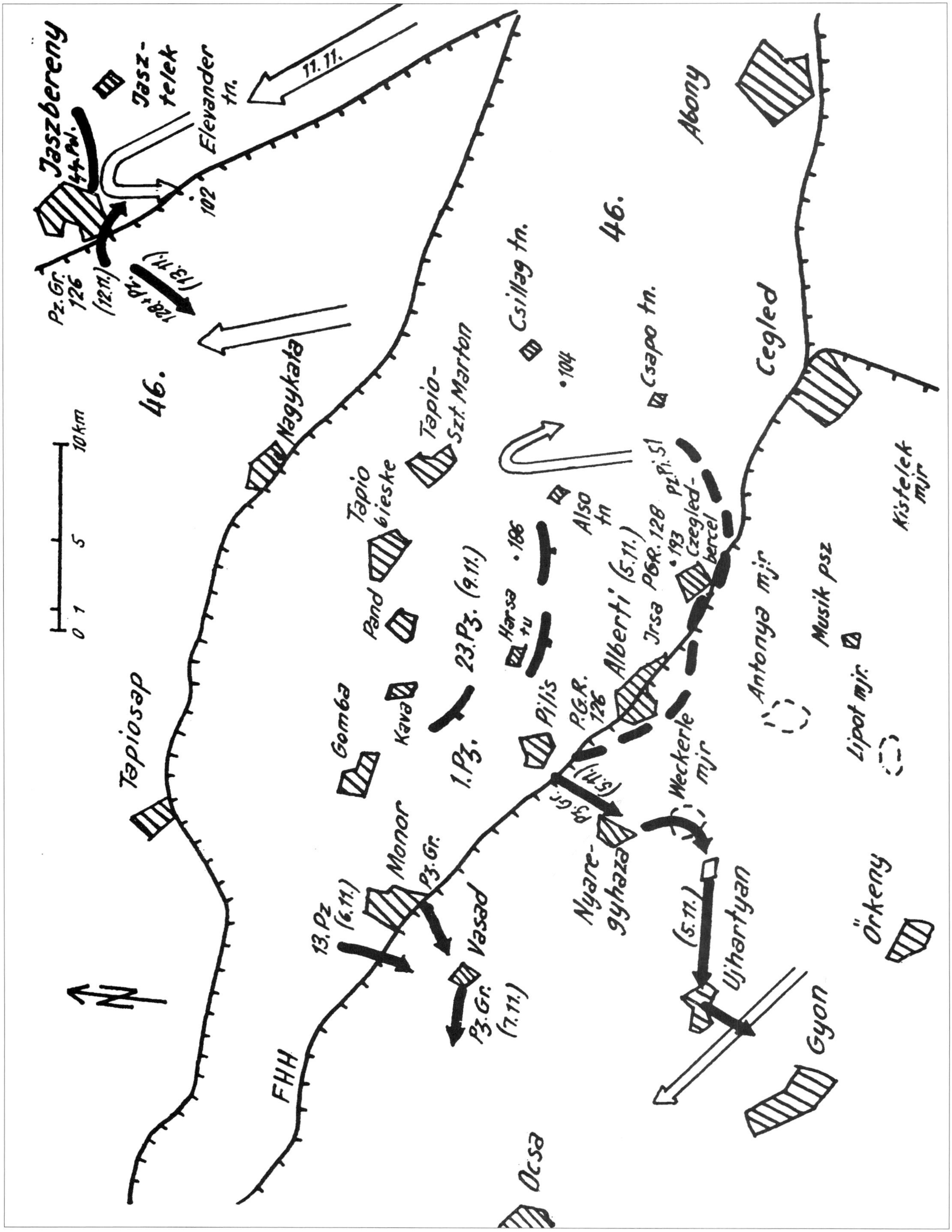
Jaszbereny
44.Pd.
Jasz-
telek
Elevander
tn.
11.11.
102
Pz.Gr.
126
(12.11.)
128.Pd.
(13.11.)
46.
Nagykata
Tapio-
Szt.Marton
Csillag tn.
104
Csapo tn.
46.
Abony
Cegled
Tapio
bicske
Pand
Also
tn
186
Harsa
tu
23.Pz. (9.11.)
Alberti (5.11.)
Jrsa
PGR. 128
Pz.Pi.51
193
Czegled-
bercel
Antonya mjr
Musik psz
Kistelek
mjr
Gomba
Kava
1.Pz.
Pilis
P.G.R.
126
Weckerle
mjr
Lipot mjr.
Tapiosap
0 1 5 10km
Monor
Pz.Gr.
13.Pz
(6.11.)
Vasad
Pz.Gr.
(7.11.)
Nyare-
gyhaza
(5.11.)
Ujhartyan
(5.11.)
Örkeny
Gyon
FHH
Ocsa

At that point, the *2./PPB51*, consisting of only nine men and under the leadership of *Oberfähnrich* Kleemann, attacked the enemy. With its two machine guns and a 2cm self-propelled *Flak*, the small force inflicted heavy casualties on the enemy and forced it to turn to attack the engineers. Once again, the enemy suffered heavy casualties and finally called off his advance in the afternoon. *Oberfähnrich* Kleemann was later rewarded for his bravery and the bravery of his men with the award of the Knight's Cross to the Iron Cross on 11 January 1945.

The enemy pursued only hesitantly on the morning of 6 November. In Irsa, 100 Soviet infantry forced back the wings of the *7./PGR126* and infiltrated into the southwestern block of buildings in Irsa. In an immediate counterattack, *Oberleutnant* Bergmann's *10.(Pi)/PGR126* restored the situation.

At 1315 hours, 300 enemy infantry advanced across the Irsa — Pilis road. The enemy was thrown back in a counterattack launched by the *I./PGR126* and *PAA23*. The enemy exerted strong pressure in Hill 199 in the afternoon. That evening, the main line of resistance had to be pulled back again. The divisional artillery went into position southwest of Tapio — Szt. Marton.

To support an attack by a battalion of the *13. Panzer-Division* that was launched from the northeast, five *Panthers* from *PR23* moved out during the afternoon of 6 November from Monor in the direction of Vasad. The force was only able to take about 800 meters of terrain in broken-up terrain, where the enemy was difficult to identify. The group eliminated five antitank guns, two mortars, eight heavy machine guns and five light machine guns, but it also lost a *Panzer V*.

The 7th of November passed quietly for the infantry. The enemy brought up new forces, which were engaged by the divisional artillery, which had been reinforced with a Hungarian light artillery battalion of 10 guns.

It was directed that the armored group repeat the attack that had failed yesterday, in conjunction with the *SPW* battalion of *Panzergrenadier-Division "Feldherrnhalle"*. Immediately after crossing the line of departure, the tanks received heavy antitank-gun fires and, at the same time, they were approached by Soviet tank hunter/killer teams. One tank was hit. Two antitank guns were eliminated, and the attack was then broken off. The armored group then moved to the mechanized infantry battalion from *Panzergrenadier-Division "Feldherrnhalle"*, which was attacking from the northeast, and cleared the village of Vasad with it. In addition, *Panzer-Artillerie-Regiment 73* of the *1. Panzer-Division* and German fighter-bombers also effectively participated in the fighting.

The tanks, together with an infantry battalion from the *1. Panzer-Division*, which had been brought forward to Vasad, moved out again as it started to turn dark to attack to the northwest and to screen south 2 kilometers northwest of the village. That evening, the front was pulled back. The armored group returned to Monor, where it was then moved to Tapiobicske on 8 October as the ready reserve.

On 8 November, the enemy attacked both of the infantry regiments several times. A penetration at 1300 hours in the sector of *Hauptmann* Schroeter's *I./PGR126* was sealed off at Hill 199 by the *3./PAA23* and the *10.(Pi.)/PGR126* and then cleared up in a nighttime immediate counterattack. Barrage fires by the artillery and salvoes on the enemy's areas of concentration inflicted heavy casualties. A penetration by a Soviet battalion into the main line of resistance at Point 104, and another one at Irsa, were cleared up by immediate counterattacks. Nine prisoners were taken.

At 0520 hours on 9 November, a Soviet infantry battalion attacked the left wing of the *II./PGR126*, but the enemy's attacked was turned back and he suffered heavy casualties. In the morning, the enemy entered the main line of resistance at Point 114 with 200-300 men. The counterattack then launched by *PAA23* was only able to retake ground slowly. To the south of Also-tanya, the enemy entered the mainline of resistance along 2 kilometers of frontage. The penetration was sealed off. Heavy weapons and the concentrated firs of *PAR128* then prevented any additional attempts to attack.

The main line of resistance was pulled back to the north 1.5 kilometers in the evening. The *46. Infanterie-Division* relieved the *23. Panzer-Division*, with the *23. Panzer-Division* then shifted to the right, where it was employed in the Kava area. *Panzergrenadier-Regiment 128* was on the left at Harsa tn.; *PGR128* on the right. The *I./PGR128* was reestablished after a Hungarian company of 3 officers, 7 noncommissioned officers and 110 enlisted personnel was added to it.

During the night of 10/11 November, the *I./PGR128* relieved *Panzer-Aufklärungs-Abteilung 1* and the *II./Panzergrenadier-Regiment 1*—both of the *1. Panzer-Division*—and established contact on the right with *Panzergrenadier-Division "Feldherrnhalle"*. The *II./PGR128* relieved the *I./Panzergrenadier-Regiment 1*.

During the morning of 11 November, the enemy attack along the entire front with strong infantry forces. After assaulting the lines several times in vain, he finally succeeded in making an penetration in the sector of the *I./PGR128*, whereupon a few Hungarians deserted. In an immediate counterattack supported by five *SPW's* of *PAA23* and three tank destroyers from *Panzerjäger-Abteilung 41* (*1. Panzer-Division*), the infantry reestablished the old main line of resistance after two hours of fighting. A Hungarian assault company arrived as reinforcements. In the sector of *PGR126* and its neighbor to the left south of Tapioszentmarton, the enemy's penetration was of greater proportions. Around Hill 199, the Soviets pushed the infantry back some 1.5 kilometers across a frontage of 1,200 meters. The armored group was alerted and attacked with 39 tanks, the *10.(Pi.)/PGR126* and a company from *PAA23*. The enemy was ejected from the area of penetration, and a group of farm buildings at Hill 208 was retaken. In the course of the attack, two light field howitzers, three prime movers and an antitank gun that had fallen into Soviet hands were recovered and evacuated. The attack was called off when it turned dark, especially since a warning order had been received announcing the movement of the entire division the coming night.

The enemy had succeeded in gaining considerable ground by advancing from the Szolnok area to the north and moving as far as just south of the road nodal point of Jaszbereny.

During the morning hours of 12 November, the infantry regiments disengaged from the enemy. *Panzergrenadier-Regiment 128* initially moved to Tapiobicske, where enemy tanks were already feeling their way forward at noon.

The armored group, which initially been ordered to Jasz-Jakohalma, was stopped in Jaszbereny at 1100 hours and employed, together with *PGR128*, against the enemy forces that were advancing along both sides of the Szolnok — Jaszbereny rail line. Just south of the city, the fight against enemy tanks and antitank guns had to been taken up. Destroying eight tanks and three heavy antitank guns, the armored group advanced as far as Point 102, 4 kilometers south of the city, and just northeast of the Z.S. switching station. A firefight against a strong enemy antitank-gun belt around Almassy tn. stopped the armored group from advancing further, especially since the enemy had already swung out to the west and reached the Nagykata — Jaszbereny road. The infantry were able to advance another 300 meters south, but they also bogged down. One *Panther* was lost, while additional enemy tanks, five antitank guns and five trucks were destroyed. The commander of the *7./PR23*, *Oberleutnant* Hillebrand, was mortally wounded.

After night fell, the main line of resistance was pulled back to the area south of Jaszbereny. The divisional artillery supported the defensive fighting from firing positions north of the city. *Panzergrenadier-Regiment 128* was positioned in Puszta-Monostor as a ready reserve.

On 13 November, Soviet attacks against Jaszbereny from the south were turned back. In the sector of the friendly forces to the right, however, the enemy attack succeeded in gaining ground to the north between Nagykata and Jaszbereny. At 1215 hours, the *II./PR23* supported an attack by the reconnaissance battalion of the *4. SS-Polizei-Panzer-Grenadier-Division* from Jaszbereny to the south. The attack objective was reached after an antitank gun was destroyed; the 20 *SS* soldiers who had attacked occupied the group of farm buildings 1,500 meters south of the city.

At 1330 hours, *PGR128*, which had been brought forward in the meantime, moved out to attack southwest from Jaszbereny, together with the *I./PR23*. The *III./PAR128* supported the defensive fighting of *Grenadier-Regiment 42* of the *46. Infanterie-Division* on the right. An armored group from *Panzergrenadier-Division "Feldherrnhalle"* attacked northeast from Nagykaty. These efforts were not successful in halting the Soviet attack, however. *Panzergrenadier-Regiment 128* reached its attack objective at the crossroads 5 kilometers south of Jaszbereny and established contact to both sides. Forty Soviets were taken prisoner; several machine guns and numerous small arms were captured.

On 13 November, *PGR126* was able to turn back weaker enemy attacks between the Nagykata — Jaszbereny road and the rail line, but 150 Soviets succeeded in penetrating the lines of *PGR126* at first light on 12 November as part of an overall attack against the entire division sector. One enemy tanks was knocked out by antitank personnel in front of the sector of the *3./PGR128*. In a counterattack, *PGR126*, together with a few *Panzer IV's*, was able to clear up the penetration into its lines. The Hungarians that had been attached attempted to pull back to the rear from the main line of resistance again and again, with the result that they placed an additional burden on the troops. Jaszbereny proper was defended by the *4. SS-Polizei-Panzer-grenadier-Division*, together with *Panzergruppe Fischer*. Fighter-bombers from both sides participated in the ground fighting during the entire day.

During the night of 14/15 November, the main line of resistance was pulled back to a line running south of Jasz-Fenyszaru — Puszta Monostor, with *PGR128* on the left and *PGR126* on the right. Around noon, the enemy again attacked along the entire divisional frontage. He was held in check in the right-hand sector by the artillery; in the left-hand sector, the armored group attacked to support *PGR126*. Smaller penetrations were cleared up by means of immediate counterattacks. The *6./PGR126* turned back an attack by 80 Soviets, even though they were supported to a striking degree by both artillery and fighter-bombers (IL-2's). Puszta Monostor was evacuated.

Several penetrations into the main line of resistance by the enemy on 16 November were sealed off and cleaned up by immediate counterattacks by the infantry and tanks. Of the five enemy tanks that overran the front lines in the course of the day, four were knocked out by antitank guns. The gun commander of a 2cm *Flak* of the *4./PGR128*, *Unteroffizier* Nobis, was promoted to *Feldwebel* for bravery on the battlefield. He had played a decisive role in defending against several enemy attacks. During the evening, the division moved back to the *"Karola"* Position, in the area south of Hatvan, as part of a continued withdrawal along the front Difficult terrain, some of it marshy, made all cross-country movements difficult. One *Panzer IV* and an armored artillery observer vehicle got stuck and had to be blown up. The right wing of the *I./PGR128*, moving into its positions along the new main line of resistance along the rail line 7 kilometers north of Boldog, found Soviets already there. An attack by 100 Russians ejected the *3./PGR128* from its positions, which could only be retaken after an immediate counterattack by the motorcycle platoon of the regiment and heavy weapons.

The enemy pressed strongly on both sides of the division's sector from the south and the east against the *46. Infanterie-Division* and the *4. SS-Polizei-Panzer-Grenadier-Division*. The divisional artillery, supported by an attached Hungarian heavy artillery battalion, helped the defensive efforts of those two divisions. During the afternoon, the enemy started to concentrate with some 36 tanks, 200 trucks with mounted infantry and strong artillery elements west of Hatvan around Puszta Sashalom. At 1700 hours, the combat outposts of the division were pulled back to the main line of resistance. Strong artillery. Mortar and tank main-gun fires were placed on the infantry positions the entire day. The battalion trench strengths had been reduced to about 100 men each, including the unreliable Hungarians. Many of those attached Hungarians, who had been sent as "reinforcements", were already scattered after a few hours. In spite of the continuous enemy pressure, an effort was made to turn the *Karola"* Position into a true main line of resistance and to reinforce it with mine obstacles.

At 2045 hours, the enemy attacked the right flank of *PGR126*, but he was turned back with losses. There was no contact with the *46. Infanterie-Division*.

On 18 November, the Soviets attacked the *7./PGR126* after an artillery preparation, but they were turned back. Tank destroyers from *PJA128* participated in the fighting. In the remaining sectors of the division, the enemy restricted himself to weaker advances. The mainline of resistance was pulled back in order to gain contact with the *46. Infanterie-Division*, although that proved impossible.

On 19 November, strong enemy forces infiltrated through the positions of the *I./PGR126* under cover of pitch-black night and heavy ground fog. In the morning, the *6./PGR126*, together with tanks and *SPW's*, attacked the enemy—600 men and heavy weapons—and reduced his positions to a small area, despite heavy resistance and inflicted heavy casualties on him. But the enemy forces could not be wiped out completely, since the main line of resistance if *PGR126* had to be pulled back once again.

The armored group supported the *46. Infanterie-Division* in its fight around Schloßberger tn. The main effort of the enemy's attacks in the division's sector was in the vicinity of Hill 128, 15 kilometers southeast of Hatvan. The Soviet attack to the west of the *23. Panzer-Division* slowly started to gain ground to the north.

The armored elements of the division were consolidated in Hatvan under *Major* Koppe, the commander of *PAA23*. A few *Panthers* under *Leutnant* Rebentisch were sent west from Hatvan on 21 November in order to engage enemy tanks with mounted infantry that had broken through north of Schloßberger tn. in the sector of the *II./PGR126*. The enemy tanks had overrun a *Flak* position. Two enemy tanks were knocked out by the *Panthers* and an additional three by the tank destroyers of *PJA128*. Three antitank guns, two mortars and thirty-five Soviets were eliminated in conjunction with an *SPW* company.

For the first time, personnel of a Hungarian "Freedom Division" appeared in front of the sector of the division. Under the Soviet leadership, they fought better than they had previously on the German side. The same applied to personnel of the Romanian "Freedom Divisions". Comparing them to the allies who fought on the German side is difficult, however, since the constant retreat, the loss of the homeland and the generally dire circumstances of the Germans often made it difficult for them to understand why and for whom they were still fighting. The personnel employed on the Russian side, on the other hand, were often fanatical personnel, who had been trained in Russia.

Another armored group from *PR23*, under the command of *Major* Fischer, was employed in the sector of the *4. SS-Polizei-Panzer-Grenadier-Division* east of Hatvan in thick fog to eliminate a Soviet concentration at Östreicher tn. As a consequence of the poor visibility, the battle group suddenly wound up right in front of Soviet antitank-gun belts and tanks, which knocked out two of the German tanks in the first firefight. The attack was called off.

The enemy pressure on both sides of the sector of the *23. Panzer-Division*, predominately to the east at that point, continued. A small penetration in the sector of *PGR126* at the Kerekharaszt psz was cleared up with tank support.

Panzergruppe Oberleutnant Quintel—seven *Panzer IV's* and one assault gun—was sent to the *1. Panzer-Division* in Gyöngyöspata during the morning of 22 November and directed to support *Panzer-Aufklärungs-Abteilung 1* at the Ferencz psz. On 23 November, an enemy attack was turned back and four tanks knocked out. In addition, *Panzergrenadier-Regiment 1* was supported in its successful counterattack to regain the main line of resistance at Rozna tnj.

In the sector of *PGR126*, the enemy infiltrated through the lines of the 5thCompany during the night of 23/24 November. The situation was restored the following morning by an attack by the *5./PGR126*, the headquarters of the 2nd Battalion, the *2./PAA23* and the *1./PJA128*. The enemy was pushed back, suffering considerable casualties.

On 24 November, the enemy attacked Hatvan from the east and placed the city under heavy artillery fires at the same time. Enemy tanks advancing to the north and east to the west of the city between the *46. Infanterie-Division* and the *23. Panzer-Division* late in the morning were attacked by *Panthers* from the division, which were eventually able to destroy four enemy tanks, two antitank guns, one personnel carrier and three trucks. One *Panther* was knocked out, and another one fell out due to mechanical problems. *Oberleutnant* Erb led recovery efforts in the evening dusk from his *Panther* and a *Bergepanther*[87], which succeeded in retrieving the knocked-out but not burned-out tank.

The positions of *PGR126*, especially those at Dohany mjr., were contested the entire day. Immediate counterattacks by the *10.(Pi.)/PGR126*, the *2./PAA23* and the *1./PJA128* cleared up all of the enemy penetrations in a short period. The *2./PJA128* was positioned to support *PGR128*.

Panzergruppe Quintel was sent to join *Divisionsgruppe Schmedes* at Lörinci, where it was directed to restore the former main line of resistance in a combined attack with *Grenadier-Bataillon Meyerhofer*. Despite eliminating three antitank guns, the attack objective was not reached.

During the night of 24/25 November, Hatvan was abandoned, when it appeared to be in imminent danger of being encircled by the enemy. The new main line of resistance ran past the southern outskirts of Hered to the northeast. The division's armored group was positioned in Apc (15 kilometers north of Hatvan) as the corps reserve.

The enemy did not advance to the new main line of resistance until 26 November, where it then pushed *PGR126* a small distance north. As he had the past few days, the enemy continued to attack on both sides of the division's sector with a great deal of tenacity.

A tank element of the division, under the command of *Oberleutnant* von Oechelhaeuser, was sent to the *357. Infanterie-Division*. It was directed to clear up an enemy penetration of infantry in the area of the Kis-Kartali psz by conducting a counterattack with 12 tanks. After sustaining a few casualties in the assembly area through Soviet artillery fires, the attack kicked off at 1600 hours, together with the infantry division's *Pionier-Bataillon 357*, some of which rode on the tanks. The Soviets were ejected from their positions. Three antitank guns were destroyed and the engineers taken to their new main line of resistance. *Leutnant* Rebentisch was killed. (Editor's note: This was the author's brother.)

Contact with the *357. Infanterie-Division*, which had only recently been inserted into the line to the right, was initially poor and was firmed up by *PGR126* on 27 November.

On 28 November, the *23. Panzer-Division* started to be pulled out of the line and moved to the right-bank of the Danube southwest of Budapest for new operations.

87 Editor's Note: The *Bergepanther* was an armored recovery vehicle based on the *Panther* chassis but with an open work compartment in lieu of a turret. It was generally considered an effective vehicle, albeit in perennial short supply.

The armored group moved via Szirak, Vanyarc and Bercel to Acsa Waitzen, where the tracked elements were loaded on trains. The wheeled elements road marched through Budapest with the march objective of the Simontornya area.

The infantry regiments, artillery, engineers and antitank personnel followed on 29 November after they were relieved by the *18. SS-Freiwilligen-Panzer-Grenadier-Division "Horst Wessel"* and the *I./Panzergrenadier-Regiment 93* of the *13. Panzer-Division*. Those elements marched through Acsa, Galgamacsa, Gödöllö and Budapest to a rest area around Martonvasar.

During the period from 31 October to 24 November 1944, the *23. Panzer-Division* had destroyed or captured the following in the area east of Budapest:

69 tanks	4 armored cars
5 aircraft	81 antitank guns
3 infantry guns	21 antitank rifles
7 mortars	50 light machine guns
1 2cm 4-barreled antiaircraft gun	33 heavy machine guns
15 submachine guns	45 trucks
17 horse-drawn wagons	8 horses

284 prisoners were counted, as well as 4 deserters. A considerable number more were casualties on the Soviet side.

The losses of the division during the same period:

Killed: 8 officers, 30 noncommissioned officers and 136 enlisted personnel

Wounded: 33 officers, 113 noncommissioned officers and 548 enlisted personnel

Missing: 1 noncommissioned officer and 43 enlisted personnel

Materiel losses (major items of equipment):

5 *Panzer IV's*	5 motorcycles
5 *Panzer V's*	10 staff cars
4 assault guns	6 trucks
3 recovery armored vehicles	3 prime movers
3 tank destroyers	2 *Maultiere* (half-tracked trucks)
1 captured tank	2 *SPW's*

The First Battle for Stuhlweißenburg 30 November 1944 – 2 January 1945

The casualty-intensive fighting east of Budapest had not delivered the desired breakthrough for the enemy nor had it brought the ordered conquest of Budapest by 7 November, the anniversary of the Red Revolution. In the last 10 days of November, the Soviet command regrouped its forces and shifted its offensive main effort to the 3rd Ukrainian front in front of the southern wing of *Heeresgruppe Süd* and the adjoining northern wing of *Generaloberst* Rendulic's *Heeresgruppe F*.

The Soviet has succeeded there in expanding their two bridgeheads over the Danube south of Mohacs and at Apatin and, finally, in uniting them. The Hungarian forces and individual German divisions under the command of the *2. Panzer-Armee* (*Heeresgruppe F*) and the Hungarian 3rd Army (*Heeresgruppe Süd*) were increasingly losing the combat power to prevent further ground gains by the Soviet field armies. Fanning out, the Soviet armor, motorized-mechanized and infantry formations advanced north and west. On 29 November, Fünfkirchen (Pecs) fell into enemy hands, after the Hungarian miners had fomented an uprising and started fighting the German and Hungarian formations as partisans. A few days later, the Soviets were in Szekszard and Zomba. On 1 December, their lead armored elements had already reached Dombovac and Ka-

Map 96: Operations South of Budapest, November and December 1944.

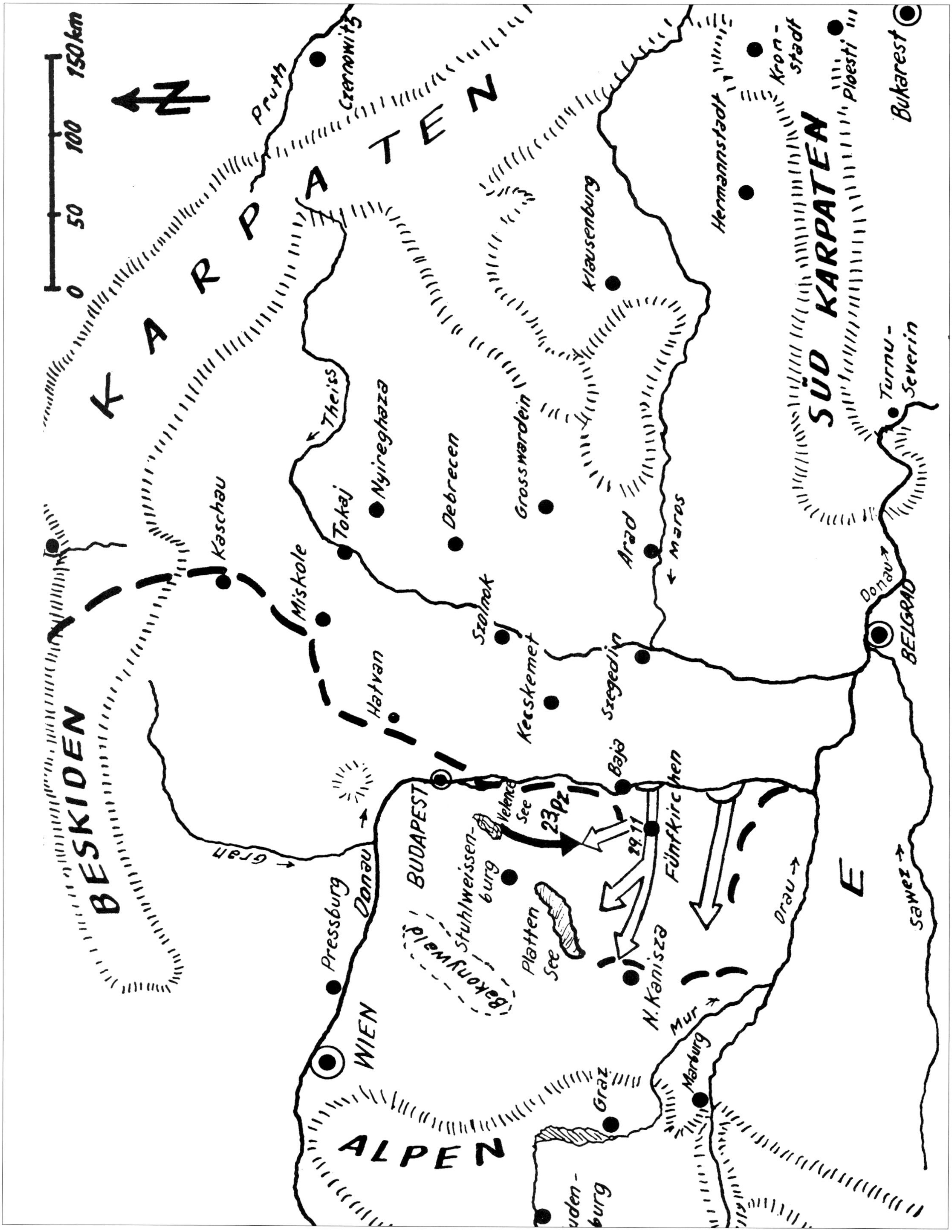

0
50
100
150 km
N
KARPATEN
BESKIDEN
SÜD KARPATEN
ALPEN
E
Pruth
Czernowitz
Theiss
Nyireghaza
Debrecen
Grosswardein
Klausenburg
Hermannstadt
Kron-
stadt
Ploesti
Bukarest
Turnu-
Severin
Maros
Arad
Kaschau
Miskole
Tokaj
Szolnok
Hatvan
Kecskemet
Szegedin
Baja
Donau
BELGRAD
BUDAPEST
Velence
See
23 Pz
29.11
Fünfkirchen
Stuhlweissen-
burg
Platten
See
Bakonywald
Gran
Donau
Pressburg
WIEN
N. Kanisza
Mur
Drau
Sawez
Marburg
Graz

posvar, 80 kilometers west of the Danube. They had thus left the Mecsek Mountains behind them and were aiming for the Hungarian oil-producing region, which was the last remaining relatively fruitful oil area left under German control. At the same time, the attack wedges of the 4th Guards Army that were advancing north were threatening the deep flank of *Armeegruppe Fretter-Pico*, consisting of the Hungarian 3rd Army and the *6. Armee*, southwest of Budapest.

As a result of the shortening of the front in the Hatvan area, the German command had freed up the *23. Panzer-Division* and the *1. Panzer-Division*, employing them under the command of *General der Panzertruppen* Kirchner's *LVII. Panzer-Korps* against these Soviet formations. Moving ahead of the corps, the *23. Panzer-Division* reached the Ozora — Simontornya area on 30 November. Motorized patrols from the infantry regiments and armored patrols of *PAA23* covered the area of Pecs — Pecsvarad — Batascek and the roads leading north from there. The mission of the *23. Panzer-Division* was to delay the Soviet advance as much as possible. *Sturmgeschütz-Brigade 325* and *schwere Panzer-Abteilung 503 (Tiger)* were attached to the division.

During the night of 30 November/1 December, troop elements of the division marched through Pincehely and into the area south of Högyesz. The *II./PGR126* occupied defensive positions south of Mucsi; held up by a lack of fuel, the rest of the regiment arrived by 1040 hours on 2 December. Just a short while later, there was enemy contact. During the morning, *PGR128* and elements of the armored group , supported by the *III./PAR128*, attacked from the march from Högyesz to the south. Hill 228, 6 kilometers south of the village, was cleared of the enemy and held against several attacks. The antitank guns and 2cm *Flak* of the *PGR128* contributed greatly to those successes. A Soviet self-propelled antitank gun was destroyed. To the east of the sector, the enemy continued to advance north through Kölesd, without encountering resistance from the Hungarians.

At noon, *PGR126* turned back an attack by 150 Soviets, but it had to pull its battalions back to Mucsi at 1430 hours, when it was attacked again, that time supported by five T-34's.

The *23. Panzer-Division*, which had no direct contact with neighboring formations to either the right or the left, was pulled back to a line running Pincehely — Racz-Egre during the night of 1/2 December, with *PGR126* and the armored group on the right and *PGR128* with *Sturmgeschütz-Brigade 325* on the left. During the afternoon, Hungarian outposts pulled back from the villages of Belecska (south of Pincehely) and Nagy-Szekely. The enemy immediately pursued and infiltrated under cover of dusk through the German outposts as far as the command post of the *I./PGR126*, until the battalion headquarters, the 4th Company and the 9th Company (Heavy Infantry Gun) brought him to a standstill.

In the sector of the *II./PGR126*, Soviets suddenly appeared, coming from the right flank, in the firing positions of the 8th Company. In an immediate counterattack, the armored group and the *10.(Pi)/PGR126* threw the enemy back and retook two infantry guns and a medium mortar that had been lost.

In the meantime, the enemy had pushed up to *PGR128* at Kis-Szekely and Racs-Egres. *Panzerjäger-Abteilung 128* reinforced the infantry. Late in the afternoon, Soviet infantry infiltrated into a gap between the two infantry regiments and advanced north west of Kis-Szekely. An infantry company composed of artillerymen from *PAR128* prevented the enemy's further advance in the direction of the gun firing positions around Csokas. The enemy forced a penetration into the main line of resistance at Racz-Egres.

The *3./PGR128*, reinforced by three tank destroyers and a 2cm *Flak*, moved out at 0200 hours on 3 December to retake the main line of resistance. The enemy lost 3 antitank guns, 1 heavy machine gun, 25 *panje* wagons and 30 dead (counted). The attack did not succeed, however, in taking all of the buildings of Racz-Egres from the enemy.

On 3 December, the enemy attacked all along the division's front. He fans his forces out—infantry, tanks and cavalry—from SarSzt.-Lörinc to the northwest, north and northeast. To the east of the division sector, Dunaföldvar fell into Soviet hands. At 1400 hours, an enemy battalion supported by two tanks attacked the *I./PGR126*, breaking through the main line of resistance between the 2nd and 3rd Companies and then advancing north. At 1700 hours, the regiment had to pull back to the high ground between Pincehely and Tolna-Nemedi. Pursuing enemy forces, some 150 men strong, split apart the 2nd Battalion and forced it further back. *Panzergruppe Dern*, consisting of four tanks, and the *10.(Pi.)/PGR126* threw the Soviets back in an immediate counterattack and took back a German antitank gun that had been captured by the enemy. Following that, *Panzergruppe Dern* and a battery from the *II./PAR128* were sent to Tolna-Nemedi to hold open the withdrawal route.

At 1700 hours, the bridge at Pincehely had to be blown up in the face of a pressing enemy. Under the cover offered by *Panzergruppe Fischer*, *PGR126* moved through Tolna-Nemedi to Simontornya, but the regiment's 2nd Battalion and *Panzergruppe Dern* remained in Tolna-Nemedi. *Panzergrenadier-Regiment 128* was pulled back to the high ground north of Simontornya.

While the Soviets attacked Tolna-Nemedi again and again on 4 December, they were unable to achieve any success until they were able to reach the first buildings in an attack from three sides, where they had concealment afforded to them from the east in a patch of woods outside of the village. A complete destruction of the bridges initially prevented any further advances in the marshy ground. Artillery and heavy infantry guns repeatedly scattered enemy concentrations in front of the defensive positions.

After darkness fell, *PGR126* was pulled back across the Sio to the high ground north of Ozora. The enemy already occupied that village and marched during the night in long columns along the south bank of the Sio Canal to the northwest.

Panzergruppe Fischer prepared for operations in Mezö-Szillas. At the same time, the enemy attacked the positions of *PGR128* at Simontornya several times in vain. The *III./PAR128* participated greatly in the defensive successes of the day. A small penetration in the sector of the *3./PGR128* could not be sealed off and cleaned up until after midnight and after several immediate counterattacks with *Tiger* support.

The division reconnaissance battalion, reinforced with four tanks, started fighting an enemy battle group that had entered Mezö-Komarom, 20 kilometers northwest of Simontornya, at 0800 hours. Supported by the *I./PAR128*, the reconnaissance force attacked the enemy from the north and east, destroyed a 7.62cm antitank gun and two antitank rifles and pushed the Soviets back to the village. The limit of advance was secured during the night.

The division field ambulance company, which had been overworked for weeks and months and suffering from a lack of vehicles, received 22 new Steyr and Phänomen ambulances.

Ever since first light on 5 December, the enemy continuously attacked Ozora and Simontornya. A lack off munitions for the artillery and the heavy weapons only allowed for an occasional response. While the *I./PGR128* was able to hold onto its positions, the 2nd Battalion and *PGR126* had to pull back north. The Soviets pursued vigorously and were already positioned just south of Igar at 0700 hours, where they forced some batteries to change positions.

Map 97: Delaying Actions of the *23. Panzer-Division* to the North of Fünfkirchen.

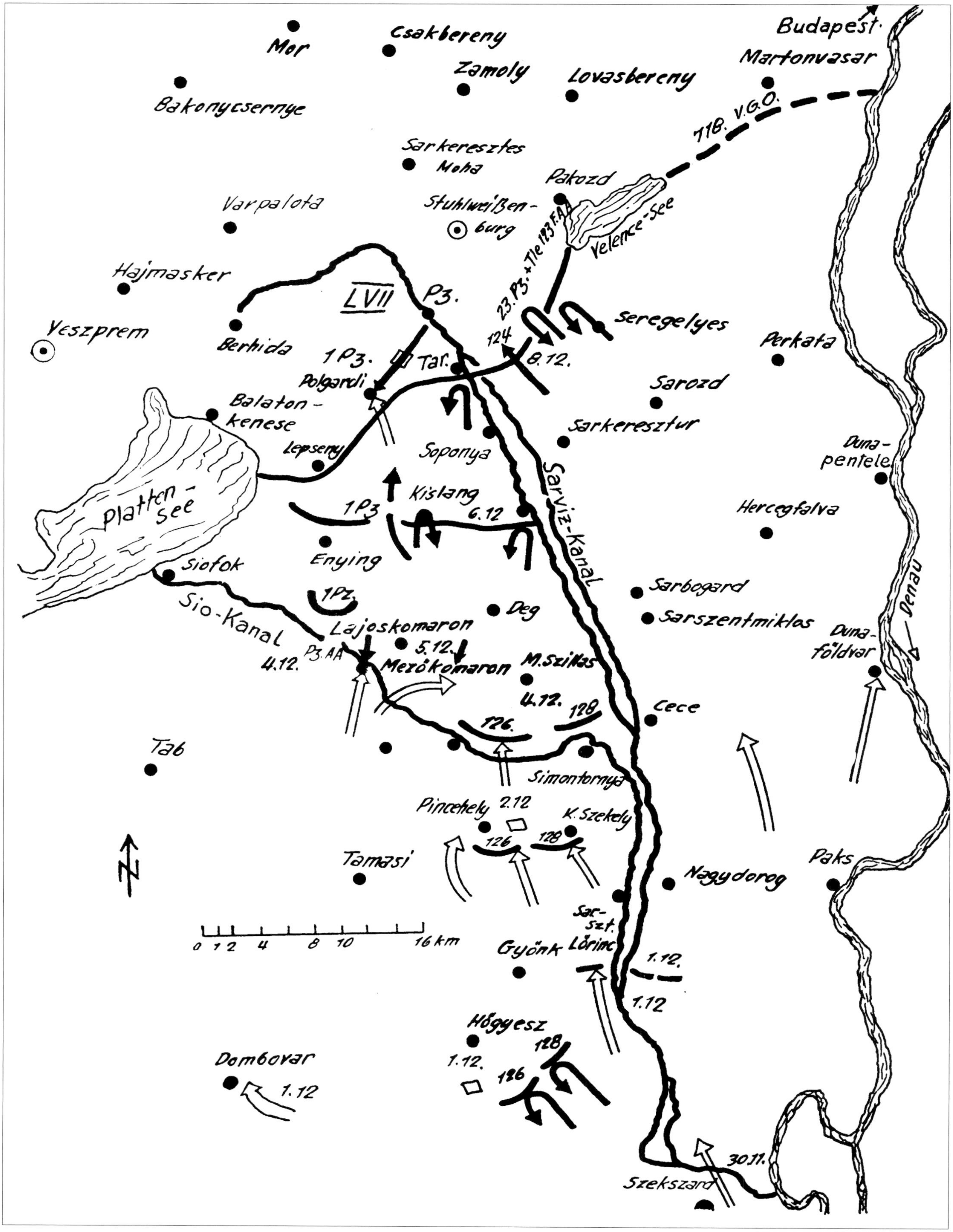
Mor
Csakbereny
Budapest
Martonvasar
Zamoly
Lovasbereny
Bakonycsernye
71B. V.G.O.
Sarkeresztes
Moha
Pakozd
Varpalota
Stuhlweißen-burg
Velence-See
23.Pz.+Tle 123 F.A.A.
Hajmasker
LVII
Pz.
Seregelyes
Veszprem
Berhida
124
8.12.
Perkata
1 Pz.
Tar.
Polgardi
Sarozd
Balaton-kenese
Sarkeresztur
Soponya
Lepseny
Duna-pentele
Sarviz-Kanal
Kislang
6.12
Platten-see
1 Pz
Hercegfalva
Enying
Siofok
Sarbogard
1 Pz.
Sio-Kanal
Deg
Lajoskomaron
Sarszentmiklos
Duna-földvar
Donau
5.12.
Pz.AA
4.12.
Mezökomaron
M.Szilas
4.12.
128
126.
Cece
Tab
Simontornya
Pincehely
2.12
K.Szekely
126
128
Tamasi
Paks
Nagydorog
Sar-Szt. Lörinc
0 1 2 4 8 10 16 km
Gyönk
1.12.
1.12
Högyesz
128
1.12.
126
Dombovar
1.12
30.11.
Szekszard
N

The *I./PGR128* cleared up an enemy penetration in the sector of its 3rd Company, whereby the enemy lost numerous light infantry weapons and suffered 28 killed. In accordance with its orders, the battalion pulled back to Sar-Egres at 1515 hours.

The attack directed against the *I./PGR126* by two Soviet battalions led to a small penetration, but it could be contained.

In the morning, the four tanks that had been sent to support *PAA23* ran into Soviets forces on their way back to Lajos-Komarom from being resupplied in Mezö-Szila (Szila-Balhas). The Soviets were engaging individual vehicles from the *1. Panzer-Division* and the *15. Flak-Division*, which were marching behind the *23. Panzer-Division*, in the village of Kp. Borgard. Together with 30 Hungarian and 15 German soldiers, the tanks cleared the village, safeguarded a fuel vehicle from the *Luftwaffe* and established contact with a *Flak* battery that was located 500 meters west of the village. Two tanks, two self-propelled *Flak* and the 30 Hungarians moved out to the south, completely clearing Kp. Borgard and then advancing in the direction of Hill 129. In the process, 300 Soviets on the march just in front of the hill were surprised and practically wiped out by the tanks. At the same time, the 2cm *Flak* opened fire on 120 *panje* wagons, which were moving from Ozora toward the Haraszt-Bogard psz. About half of all of the enemy vehicle were destroyed and 50 prisoners were taken. Another 200 Soviets were caught to the south of the Haraszt-Bogard psz, but they were being covered by several antitank guns. The two *Panzer IV's* eliminated 2 7.652cm antitank guns, 2 4.7cm antitank guns, 10 heavy machine guns and numerous antitank rifles, until they were forced to turn back by several antitank-gun and antitank rifle hits. The ground that had been softened by the constant rain of the past few days sealed the fate for the wounded tanks; both bogged down. A *Panther* ordered forward to recover them suffered the same fate. While the unsuccessful recovery efforts were underway, the Hungarian infantry withdrew in the face of the advancing Soviets and the tanks had to be blown up. The *Panther* was engaged at the same time by Soviet antitank guns. The last *Panzer IV* of that group pulled back from Lajos-Komarom that day with *PAA23* and screened from the crossroads west of Deg.

In the sector of *PGR126*, the enemy attacked the right wing of the 2nd Battalion from the northwest. The enemy forces were elements advancing from Mezö- and Lajos-Komarom. Toward noon, *PGR126* was pulled back to the "B" Line at Mezö-Szila (Szila-Balhas). Strong motorized patrols of the enemy pursued immediately. At 1700 hours, the entire division pulled back to the "B" Line south of Deg. At 2200 hours, the hard-pressing enemy forces achieved a penetration in the outpost line of *PGR126* on both sides of the Mezö-Szila — Deg road. There were no reserves available to launch an immediate counterattack.

The division pulled back again at 0300 hours on 6 December and established itself in a series of strongpoints along a line running Peterszallas (southwest of Kislang) — Point 129 — Ödönpsz — Point 150 — southern outskirts of Kalosz. In the afternoon, the Soviets pushed forward to the main line of resistance of both of the infantry regiments, using the thick fog as concealment. While *PGR128* on the left was initially able to turn back company-sized attacks, 150 Soviets broke through along the left wing of the *II./PGR126*. An attack that immediately followed on the open right flank of the battalion pushed it out of its positions. It moved back to the Ecsi psz; the enemy entered Kislang. The *I./PGR126*, which was then threatened in both the flank and rear, swung its right wing back to the north.

In a counterattack, the *10.(Pi.)/PGR126* and the *2./PAA23* forced the enemy partially out of Kislang. An immediate counterattack by the Soviets collapsed. At 1640 hours, *PGR126* was pulled back to the line 144 — 141 — Janos mjr. The armored group screened from Felsötarnoca toward the west , where armored patrols of *PAA23* were screening the area.

The combat power of the division had once again reached its nadir. Ten to twelve tanks were operational. The individual battalions of the infantry regiments had about 100 men each. There were only four light machine guns available to each of the companies. The *4.(schw.)/PGR128* only had a light machine gun, a self-propelled 2cm *Flak* and two medium mortars operational. Elements of the divisional artillery were no longer operational, because they lacked prime movers. On top of that, there was a constant shortage of munitions, so that even the guns that were being used never fired at their full potential. *Heeres-Flak-Abteilung 278* only had a few individual guns left; most of the battalion was employed as infantry on the left wing of *PGR128*.

Compared to the combat elements, the situation of the medical detachments of the division was good. Field Hospital 652 had been set up in Fehervarcsurgo behind the main clearing station of the 1st Medical Company in Szabadbattyan and the 2nd Medical Company in Stuhlweißenburg. There was a hospital train in Stuhlweißenburg; in Kisber, 40 kilometers northwest of Stuhlweißenburg, the field army had established the 511th Wounded Collection Point.

Toward 0200 hours and then again at 0330 hours on 7 December, the Soviets launched unsuccessful attacks against the *2./PGR128* along the southern outskirts of Kalosz. Between the canal and the road east of Kalosz, the enemy penetrated the lines of *Heeres-Flak-Abteilung 278*, but he was thrown back in an immediate counterattack launched by the tank destroyers of *PJA128*.

Panzergrenadier-Regiment 126 turned back an attack against its right wing at first light. The Soviets then bypassed the German strongpoints and, swinging out to the west, marched in the direction of Guras mjr, using the concealment afforded by the ground fog. *Panzergrenadier-Regiment 126* thereupon employed its wing company in screening to the northwest and west. The enemy continued to march; large enemy columns were identified marching across Point 147 (west of Felsötarnoca) in the direction of Polgardi.

At 1630 hours, the *LVII. Panzer-Korps* ordered the withdrawal to the *"Margarete"* Position. That position, located in the land narrows between Lakes Balaton and Velence, had been fortified in the meantime by the *153. Feld-Ausbildungs-Division*, Hungarian forces and details of volunteers. The division disengaged from the enemy at 1900 hours and, shortly after midnight, the division's troop elements established themselves in their new sectors, with *PGR126* on the right between Alsosomlyo —Tac and Pötölle and *PGR128* on the left from Pötölle through Belsöbarand to Külsöbarand, with *PPB51* and *Heeres-Flak-Abteilung 278* adjoining to the east as far as Dinnyes on Lake Valence. Hungarian formations and several companies from the *153. Feld-Ausbildungs-Division* were attached to the division's infantry. The *I.PGR128* received the *1./Feld-Ausbildungs-Regiment 716*, with its officer, 25 noncommissioned officers and 257 men, and a Hungarian battalion under the command of Captain Bartard. Coming under the command and control of the divisional artillery were several Hungarian light cannon batteries and two heavy field howitzers of the *1./SS-Artillerie-Abteilung 505*. The armored group was sent to Szabadbattyan to prepare for operations, but it was alerted at first light on 8 December and attached to the *1. Panzer-Division*, which, adjoining the *23. Panzer-Division* on the right, had been directed to defend the area from Lake Balaton to Polgardi. A strong enemy force had entered Polgardi, with the result that the *Margarethe* Position had already been torn open.

Supported by the *I./PAR128*, *Panzergruppe Fischer* moved out at 0630 hours on 8 December from the east against Polgardi with 13 tanks and the *3.(SPW)/PAA23*. At the same time, grenadiers from the *153. Feld-Ausbildungs-Division* and elements of the *1. Panzer-Division* had been directed to move against Polgardi from the north and west. Just outside the village, Soviet tank hunter/killer teams moved against the German tanks. The enemy was overrun. Entering Polgardi from the northeast, *Panzergruppe Fischer* advanced as far as the center of the village and established contact with the infantry force that had been encircled there the previous night. There was tough fighting for every building, but the enemy was gradually pushed back, until the attack group from the *1. Panzer-Division* arrived from the west and the enemy then fled in a panic to the south. Large amounts of weapons and equipment remained behind in German hands.

A strong enemy infantry attack conducted in the afternoon across the rail way line and in the direction of Polgardi collapsed in the face of combined fires from the tanks, *SPW's* and infantry. The armored group from the *23. Panzer-Division* reported its share of the successes that day: 13 7.62cm and 4.7cm antitank guns, 6 antitank rifles and 5 heavy and light machine guns destroyed. Captured were 10 rifles, 4 German medium mortars, 1 8.8cm *Flak*, 40 horse-drawn *panje* wagons and a German staff car. One hundred dead Soviets were counted. A German/Hungarian unit was relieved, and the main line of resistance in the *Margarethe* Position had been restored.

The commander of the *1. Panzer-Division* radioed the following: "Many thanks for the comradely support at Polgardi, especially *Major* Fischer and his brave men."

In the sector of the division's infantry, the enemy attacked several times without success from Seregelyes. Around 1000 hours, *PGR128* turned back an attack by 300 Soviets on both sides of the Soponya — Tac road. Artillery salvoes from the *II./PAR128* and the heavy weapons inflicted heavy casualties on the enemy. An advance by the tank destroyers and a few tanks drove the Soviets an additional 1,200 meters back in the direction of Soponya.

The strongpoint of Pötölle, along the west wing of *PGR126* was lost in the course of the afternoon against constantly repeated enemy attacks. All of the attacks at the railway bridge at Seregelyes and at Dinnyes were turned back, although Soviet infantry entered the positions of a Hungarian company next to the *I./PGR126*, which was employed on the right. Under the concealment afforded by the onset of darkness, the Soviets advanced through Selmyes psz. along the small canal in the direction of Belsöbarand, until an immediate counterattack by the infantry interdicted them.

Both infantry regiments received orders on 9 December to retake the terrain that had been lost the previous day. Before they could do that, however, the enemy attacked. At 0600 hours, he entered the positions of the *I./PGR126* southwest of Tac; the German immediate counterattack failed. A Soviet attack along both sides of the Soponya — Tac road also failed. At 1430 hours, Hill 142 west of Tac was lost.

Several renewed enemy attacks on the left wing of the division failed. Northwest of Seregelyes, the Soviets succeeded in penetrating the lines of the *II./PGR128*, but the penetration was sealed off.

Around 1400 hours, Soviet infantry ejected German forces from Belsöbarand and advanced toward the crossroads 2.5 kilometers to the east. The *I./PGR128*, attacked from three sides, pulled back to the embankment west and north of Belsöbarand. The village was occupied by the enemy. The artillery continuously engaged Soviet concentrations and scattered several attempted attacks. Aerial activity on both sides was slight.

At 1500 hours, *Major* von Plate's *II./PGR126*, supported by six tanks, launched a counterattack on Pötölle. An enemy attack that had just started, from which the German infantry in position were already withdrawing, was caught in the fires of the attack group and a *Flak* section from the *15. Flak-Division*. The enemy pulled back, pursued closed by the German attack group. Although three of the tanks got stuck in marshy terrain and the remaining ones were only able to move on roads, the enemy was ejected from Pötölle and the village was retaken. A Soviet counterattack from the sector of *PGR128* was unsuccessful. As a consequence of a significant Soviet penetration in a neighboring sector, however, the *6./PGR126* had to be pulled back to the vicinity of Point 124, since there was no longer any contact with friendly forces to the left.

Bottomless marshy terrain and roadways softened by rain made the employment of armored vehicles east of the Sarviz Canal problematic. Factored in had to be the constant danger of bottoming out, many hours of recovery work, mechanical problems and above-average consumption of fuel.

The losses sustained by the companies of the *156. Feld-Ausbildungs-Division* that had been incorporated into the ranks of the division were horrific. For instance, the *1./PGR128*—formerly the *1./Feld-Ausbildungs-Regiment 716*—lost 7 noncommissioned officers and 16 men dead on 8 and 9 December. An additional 9 noncommissioned officers and 56 enlisted personnel were wounded and 4 noncommissioned officers and 106 enlisted personnel could not be accounted for. The remaining companies of the *I./PGR126* lost a total of only 4 enlisted killed and 1 officer and 6 men wounded during the same period. Although a large portion of those who could not be accounted for returned to their company, the trench strength of the company had been reduced by 50% within the span of two days.

On 10 December, other elements of *Feld-Ausbildungs-Regiment 716* moved out together with *PGR128* to regain the fortified positions. The grenadiers were supported by *Panzergruppe Fischer*, which had eight tanks and the *3.(SPW)/PAA23* at the time. The *I./PGR128* was also reinforced with the *2./PJA128* and its eight tank destroyers. After just an hour, both Belsöbarand and Külsöbarand had been retaken and the main line of resistance reoccupied. The armored group destroyed 12 antitank guns, 7 antitank rifles and 3 heavy machine guns. The *I./PGR128*, together with the tank destroyers of *Oberleutnant* Mager, captured or destroyed: 2 light infantry guns, 4 antitank rifles, 6 heavy machine guns, 22 light machine guns, numerous small arms, signals equipment and several *panje* wagons. One hundred prisoners were taken, and 40 enemy dead were counted.

From Belsöbarand to the west there was a gap in the main line of resistance, because the Hungarians, who had been employed there, had not gone into position. The enemy was soon infiltrating there.

Starting at 1000 hours, *PGR126* had to defend against several fairly weak enemy attacks on both sides of the Soponya — Tac road. In the sector of the *II./PGR126*, the attack of a Soviet company on Pötölle collapsed. Strong enemy concentrations at Alsosomlyo were scattered by the divisional artillery and Hungarian mortars.

At 1600 hours, the enemy entered Pötölle in a sudden advance and could not be interdicted until he had reached the northern outskirts. There were no reserves to conduct an immediate counterattack.

Elements of *PR23* screened at Belsöbarand on 11 December and supported the infantry and grenadiers in their defense against Soviet advances. *Panzergruppe Schulz* attacked with three *Panthers* and *Oberleutnant* Meyer's *3./PAA23* in the sector of the *I./PGR126* with the mission of throwing back the enemy forces that had penetrated along the division's right-hand boundary at Alssomlyo. Even before the railway line was reached, the three *Panthers* got stuck in the marshy terrain. The attack was called off; one antitank gun and one T-34 were destroyed. After hours of fruitless efforts at recovery under enemy artillery fire, the three tanks had to be abandoned and blown up.

Heavy enemy fires were placed along the entire division sector. The enemy was reinforced at Alsosomlyo, Közep mjr. and Pötölle. Despite support from the tank destroyers of the *2./PJA128*, the attack of the *II./PGR128* northwest of Seregelyes to recapture the former main line of resistance was only able to advance 200 meters. The enemy defended desperately. For the first time, the Red Air Force also participated in the ground fighting. *Oberleutnant* Huifner of the *4./PGR128* was killed by a round to the head.

16 February 1944: The headquarters section of the *I./PGR 126* at Woltschj.

17 February 1944: Soldiers sleep whenever they can during short breaks in operations.

Headquarters vehicles of the *I./PGR 126* at Woltschj.

Retreat through the mud: March 1944 along the Ingulez. The casualties figures for the unfortunate horses were huge.

7 March 1944: The command post of the *I./PGR 126* at Selenyi Gaj. Camouflaged padded parkas are now available, reversible to white.

Where will the next train movement take us?

April 1944: The regimental headquarters of *PGR 126* changes positions in the Jassy area.

Knocked-out Soviet "Sherman". These tanks were quite popular with the Soviets due to their reliabilty, they were basically used for reconnaisance.

Snowdrifts block the road near Jassy.

The battalion headquarters of the *I./PGR 126* north of Jassy. Despite all the hardships, there is still something to smile about.

May 1944: The uniforms are turning threadbare and suffer from constant exposure to the elements and enemy fires.

Training the Romanians on the *Ofenrohr*, the German "Bazooka".

September 1944: *PGR 126* detrains at Tokaj.

November 1944: The defense of Stuhlweißenburg.

The building used by the corps' medical company as a field hospital.

German photographs taken near the very end of the war are hard to find for obvious reasons. Here we see *Oberleutnant* Schreiber of the *1./PR 23* with the battalion surgeon, *Stabsarzt* Dr. Trautmann, who was killed later.

Major Rebentisch on the way to the headquarters of the Romanian 1st Armored Division with *Oberleutnant Dittmann* - see below (shown wearing the adjutant's aiguilette).

The last wartime photo taken of Major Rebentisch.

A *Panther* of the *II./PR 23* is directed by a ground guide.

Gefreiter Heinz Fuchs was decorated with the Iron Cross, Second Class for his actions at the Baranow Bridgehead.

The author's brother, *Leutnant* Heinz Rebentisch, was killed in action on 22 November 1944. He was buried with full military honors at Gran (Danube).

The Hungarian plains in late 1944. *Oberleutnant* von Oechelhaeuser of the *3./PR 23* addresses crews.

The tank of *Leutnant* Krackow (viewer's left), who is seen talking to Bade, the Maintenance Officer of the *II./PR 23*, in the vicinity of Stuhlweißenburg. Both men seem well prepred for the elements, even if a bit "out of uniform"!

Oberleutnant Schreiber, the commander of the *1./PR 23*, along with the crew of his *Sturmgeschütz 101*.

Orders conference prio to the attack on Nyiregyhaza.

A *Schwerer Zugkraftwagen 18t FAMO* shelters from air attack next to a church.

The imposing main gun of the *Panther* is evident in this photo. The tank appears to be undergoing maintenance.

Quite possibly it is the weak final drive unit that is causing problems for this *Panther*.

For those units operating heavy tanks, such as the *Tiger* and *Panther* the *Bergepanther* was indespensible but always in short supply.

FAMO of the maintenance/recovery unit are in evidence. Two or three of these vehicles were needed to tow a Panther. In these conditions, probably 3.

Despatch riders catch a hurried meal.

Observing an attack through the scissors binoculars.

Although not strictly of this time period this is a good photo of *Panzergrenadiere* and their weapons .

On the following night, there was lots of Soviet patrolling activity. At 0200 hours on 12 December, 200 Soviets entered the right-hand sector of the *II./PGR126*. At 0400 hours, the enemy was working his way forward along both sides of the Soponya — Tac road. After an artillery preparation, he attacked at 0600 hours, entered Vilagos mjr. and advanced as far as Tac. Three *panthers* and the *3./PAA23*, along with the *I./PGR126* and the 10th Company of the regiment, moved out and pushed the enemy back to his line of departure in hard fighting that lasted until 1700 hours. Three antitank guns, two heavy machine guns and six antitank rifles were destroyed.

The positions of the *II./PGR126* at Pötölle were guarded by four tanks.

To the south of Belsöbarand, the enemy forced a crossing over the bottom land. One tank supported the immediate counterattack of the *2./PGR126*. It was knocked out by an enemy antitank gun, but the enemy was ejected and the main line of resistance reoccupied after a renewed Soviet attack was turned back. When several enemy patrols were discovered, several prisoners were taken.

Replacements for the infantry regiments raised the combat strengths of the battalions to approximately 250 men each. An additional Hungarian 7.5cm cannon battery was attached to the divisional artillery.

At first light on 13 December, the enemy entered Tac from the southwestern side. At 0700 hours, he also entered the village from the south in another attack, whereupon he advanced to the northern outskirts. Tanks and infantry moved out to launch an immediate counterattack, and the village was cleared of the enemy by 1130 hours. After regrouping, the counterattack force moved out again and threw the Soviets back to Vilagos mjr. by 1530 hours.

At 1630 hours, the Soviets once again entered the southern part of Tac. Mortars and heavy infantry guns prevented an advance beyond the middle of the village. The *1./PGR126*, fighting south of Tac, was pulled back to its southern outskirts.

At 0645 hours on 14 December, the *1.* and *2./PGR126*, together with nine tanks under *Oberleutnant* Schulz, as well as the *2.* and *3./PAA23*, moved out to counterattack in Tac. The village was taken in the face of strong resistance. The attack on Vilagos mjr. bogged down at 1130 hours at the cemetery; moving out once again, the *1./PGR126* entered the sugar factory in Vilagos mjr. at 1300 hours under the covering fires from the tanks and the *SPW's*. By 1600 hours, Vilagos mjr. had been cleared, but it was lost again three hours later after a massive counterattack by the Soviets. The enemy also entered the southwestern corner of Tac. Left behind the German lines were 9 enemy antitank guns, 2 light infantry guns and 50 enemy dead.

In the left-hand sector of the division, there were only artillery duels. The cemetery south of Tac was retaken by the armored group and the *I./PGR126* during the morning of 15 December. Two enemy antitank guns and a light infantry gun were destroyed.

After an artillery preparation, the Soviets attacked at 1445 hours between Point 124 (north of Pötölle) and Belsöbarand. The attack collapsed in front of the sectors of the *6./PGR126* at Point 124 and the *I./PGR128* at Belsöbarand, but the enemy made rapid advances against the Hungarians employed between the two regiments. Advancing to the east and west from that area of penetration, the enemy threatened both of the regiments in their deep flanks. The *2./PGR128*, together with tank destroyers, had to pull back to the north to the embankment. A temporary penetration from the left in the lines of the *6./PGR126* was cleared up by 2400 hours. *Major* von Plate, the commander of the *II./PGR126*, assumed acting command of the regiment.

The 16th of December started with Soviet attacks in the sector of the *II./PGR126*. He entered the lines of the 7thCompany west of the Pötölle — Fövenyi-psz road. At 0700 hours, 200 Soviets expanded the penetration as far as the road. Two counterattacks remained without success, despite the support of *SPW's*.

Further to the east, the *I./PGR128* moved out with *Oberleutnant* Schreiber's armored group to counterattack Belsöbarand. The village was taken in a fight against the Soviet's elite *Krassny drapani* division and the main line of resistance, which had previously been manned by Hungarians, was reoccupied. Destroyed or captured were 1 assault gun, 8 7.62cm antitank guns, 5 4.7cm antitank guns, 7 antitank rifles, 13 heavy machine guns, 8 light machine guns, 12 *panje* wagons and many small arms. Seven Soviets were taken prisoner and one hundred nineteen dead were counted.

At 0745 hours on 17 December, the penetration in the sector of the *7./PGR126* was cleaned up by two tanks and three *SPW's*. Tough enemy resistance made two attempts necessary before there was success, however.

Tac was lost in an attack from the southwest and south, but it was retaken on 18 December when the armored group was employed. The factory grounds around Vilagos mjr. were lost once and for all. The infantry had been weakened too much. Only some 30-35 men were available to defend a trench line 1 kilometer in length. Despite that, the Soviets did not succeed in shaking the resolve of the German soldiers by means of loudspeaker propaganda. Even the Hungarians, for the most part, remained loyal to their oath. Their completely insufficient armament, especially the lack of armor-defeating weapons, often allowed them to lose faith in their own strength.

The Soviet command brought reinforcements forward across the entire sector, with main efforts at Pötölle, Seregelyes and Dinnyes. Artillery salvoes by the reinforced divisional artillery scattered enemy columns and achieved observable success in Soviet antitank gun and artillery firing positions.

During this time period, the enemy had further reduced the Budapest Bridgehead and achieved several penetrations. The headquarters of the *III. Panzer-Korps* was relieved by the headquarters of the *IX. SS-Gebirgs-Korps* in Budapest.

North of the bend in the Danube, Soviet forces had penetrated west into the Hungarian lowlands at Ipolysag. The *8. Panzer-Division*, the only reserve of the field-army group, was moved there expeditiously from the Budapest area.

The *3. Panzer-Division* and the *6. Panzer-Division* which had brought up to conduct an attack ordered by the *Führer* Headquarters between Lakes Valence and Balaton, also had to be turned in the direction of Ipolysag on 18 December. However, the armored elements of both of those divisions had to remain as a ready reserve to the north of Stuhlweißenburg on express orders from the *Führer* Headquarters. As a result, both of those divisions were robbed of their real combat power. The headquarters of the *LVII. Panzer-Korps* also went to the Ipolysag area, whereby the *1. Panzer-Division* and the *23. Panzer-Division* were attached to *General der Panzertruppen* Breith's *III. Panzer-Korps*.

During the evening of 19 December, *PGR126* turned back an attack on Tac. During the nighttime hours, the *II./PGR126* and the *I./PGR128* were relieved by a Hungarian regiment, although the armored group and the artillery remained in their positions. The infantry and engineers who had been relieved immediately started work on building field fortifications and laying mines in a blocking position east of Szabadbattyan, even though they had been earmarked as ready reserves. The *II./PGR126* was sent to Föveny-psz, with its 6th Company being employed to reinforce the 1st Battalion in Tac.

At 0720 hours on 20 December, Soviet artillery started to place barrage fires on the sector from Tac to Lake Valence and the areas to the east. The barrage lasted 25 minutes on the main line of resistance and the

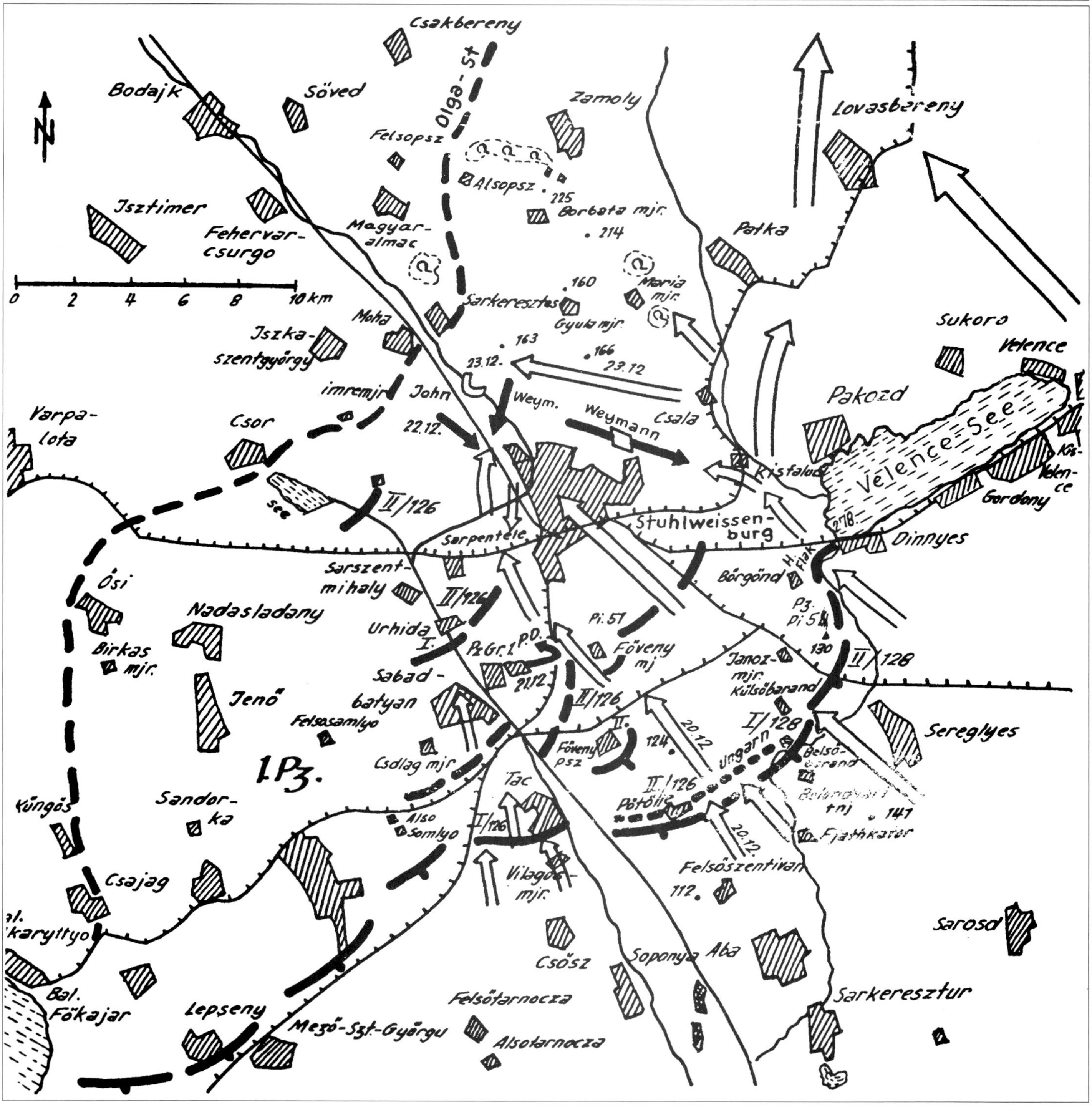

Map 98: Soviet Advance Against Stuhlweißenburg from 20 to 23 December 1944.

depths of the main battle area. Preparatory fires, not as massive as those in the eastern sector, were also placed in the area as far as Lake Balaton.

At 0740 hours, vastly superior infantry formations, supported by a few tanks, moved out. The Hungarian formations that had been brought up recently left their positions. *Hauptmann* Lenberger's *II./PGR126* positioned itself to defend Föveny-psz. The enemy did not attack it, however; he simply moved past it. The same thing happened to the *I./PGR128*. As a result of the pulling back of the Hungarians, individual elements of the infantry, *Heeres-Flak-Abteilung 278* (employed at Dinnyes) and elements of the *153. Feld-Ausbildungs-Division* were also affected. The divisional engineers went into position to the left of the *II./PGR126*.

At the same time, other Soviet formations moved out east of Lake Valence against the positions of the *271. Volks-Grenadier-Division* and broke through them.

Initially, there were no advances against Tac. The enemy went around the German strongpoints. The artillery fired protective fires, but it soon had to transition to firing over open sights at short distances so as to avoid falling into the hands of Soviet infantry. The *7./PAR128* was able to effect a change of position just in the nick of time in the face of assaulting Soviets charging with their battle cry of *Urräh*. Even so, one gun was lost in the process. The German and some Hungarian strongpoints defended stubbornly, all the while subjected to rolling fight-bomber attacks. Tac,

Föveny-psz. and the former main line of resistance from Janos mjr. to Börgönd were successfully defended for several hours.

The enemy was already crossing the railway line to the rear of the *II./PGR126*. *Panzergruppe Schreiber* destroyed two enemy assault guns. The struggle for Tac commenced at noon. It changed hands five times, before it had to be abandoned due to the over-all situation. *Panzergrenadier-Regiment 126* had to employ its 10th Company (Engineer) and its motorcycle scout platoon to close a gap between its battalions. Advanced enemy elements were thrown back. At 1400 hours, Föveny-psz was evacuated for good and the *II./PGR126* pulled back to a shortened line in the vicinity of Föveny tnj. The enemy continued to infiltrate the gap between *PGR126* and *PPB51* and move in the direction of Stuhlweißenburg.

A Soviet formation of about 2,000 men advanced through Dinnyes to the north and northwest. The grenadiers and *Flak* soldiers were unable to contain these numerically vastly superior forces. Kisfaludi mjr. and Pakozd were lost. The Soviets advanced into the area of high ground 5 kilometers east of Stuhlweißenburg.

As a result, the Soviet breakthrough through the land narrows and into the deep flank of the German and Hungarian forces still positioned further to the southwest had succeeded.

Gepanzerte Gruppe Weymann of the *3. Panzer-Division* was dispatched expeditiously to the division and attached with the express orders of the *6. Armee* to close the gap east of Stuhlweißenburg. By doing so, the prerequisites for the planned attack south of Lake Valence to the Danube would be retained. Attacking east of the city, the armored group destroyed numerous enemy tanks, antitank guns and infantry forces. It was not successful, however, in the broken-up terrain in overcoming the massed Soviet antiarmor defenses. *Panzergruppe Weymann* transitioned to the defense east of the city, where it had to fend off constant attacks from the east and the northeast. At the same time, the enemy continued to advance north of Lake Valence. He occupied Patka and joined up with the forces that had broken through that morning between Lake Valence and the Danube for a continued advance north and northwest. His objective was the encirclement of Budapest.

While the *1. Panzer-Division* was able to hold its lines—it was not in the sector of the main effort of the enemy's attack—the *23. Panzer-Division* was positioned in strongpoints along a line running from the embankment east of Alsosomlyo — Szabadbattyan rail station — Föveny tnj. — shortened lines[88] south of Stuhlweißenburg — high ground east of the city. As a precautionary measure, the trains occupied the *Olga* Position north of the city. Remnants of *PGR126*, with two tanks and three *SPW's*, were positioned around the Szabadbattyan rail station. The divisional engineers were around Föveny tnj, and *PGR128* had both of its battalions in the shortened position. During the night, portions of that position were lost; the infantry of *PGR128* had to temporarily pull back. At first light on 21 December, they retook the lost positions.

Kisfalud, which changed hands four times, was lost for good during the morning of 21 December, when almost all of the *Flak* soldiers defending there were lost.

The pressure of the Soviet attack did not let up that night or on 21 December. The enemy avoided any fighting for German strongpoints. He went around them and infiltrated deeply into the rear area. Five Hungarian artillery pieces fell into enemy hands, and one antitank gun from *PGR128* was lost after close-in fighting during an ambush.

During the morning of 21 December, the Soviets attacked the railway station and the southwestern edge of Szabadbattyan. In the sector of the *II./PGR126*, numerically superior enemy forces advanced northwest along the railway line. The battalion had to pull back to the woods northeast of Szabadbattyan. Strong enemy forces inserted themselves between the *I./PGR126* and the engineers in Föveny tnj.

An armored group and an *SPW* battalion from the *1. Panzer-Division* were attached to *PGR126* in order to reestablish contact with the 2nd Battalion and the engineers. The attack failed in the face of numerically superior enemy forces, however. In the meantime, five *Panthers* from *PR23* supported the defensive fighting of the *I./PGR126* and screened to the east.

At 1700 hours, the *II./PGR126* had to pull back along the Urhida — Stuhlweißenburg road. Two hours later, the Soviets placed barrage fires on Szabad- and Falu-Battyan. At the same time, the enemy attacked in an enveloping maneuver from the southeast and forced the remnants of the *I./PR126* back toward Urhida. At 2000 hours, the *II./PGR126* was again attacked by numerically vastly superior forces. It had to pull back to the area west of Sarpentele (canal — west of the canal — Sziget — Szeles domil — north of the canal).

The battalions of *PGR126*, which were only 60-70 men strong, were constantly being attacked from the front, while other enemy formations bypassed the strongpoints at the same time. The enemy had reached the railway line at Sarpentele and crossed it. Toward noon, enemy tanks and infantry entered the industrial area of Stuhlweißenburg on the northwest side of the city. The situation for the forces of the division still fighting on the south side of Stuhlweißenburg became increasingly precarious, since the Soviets were gaining ground on the east side of the city and were already near its outskirts.

At 1100 hours on 22 December, the *I./PGR126* was attached to *Kampfgruppe Huppert* (*Panzergrenadier-Regiment 1* of the *1. Panzer-Division*) The regimental headquarters of *PGR126* assumed command of a rapidly assembled battle group northwest of Stuhlweißenburg, which was intended to prevent the further advance of the Soviets along the city's western outskirts. The first elements to attack the industrial area were two command & control tanks and two radio *SPW's* of *PR23*, two engineer *SPW's* from *PAA23*, two *Wespen* from the *I./PAR128* and elements of *Division-Begleit-Kompanie 23*[89]. This small force pushed the enemy back south and inflicted heavy casualties on him; 42 Soviets were taken prisoner. When, in addition, an *SPW* battalion from *Gruppe Weymann* of the *3. Panzer-Division* forced the enemy back to within 1 kilometer of the railway line, the roads leading north and northwest out of Stuhlweißenburg were safeguarded. A few German fighter-bombers provided some relief by joining the fray on the ground. To the south of Gusztus psz., the motorcycle scout platoon of *PGR126*, along with a 2cm *Flak* and two *SPW's*, turned back an attack by 300 men. At 1600 hours, the *II./PGR126* was sent to Gusztus psz. to defend.

While strong artillery fires fell on Stuhlweißenburg without a letup, Soviet infantry prepared to attack the blocking position south of the city. At 1530 hours, the earth-brown masses advanced. Final protective fires from the artillery and heavy weapons tore apart the densely packed masses several times, but it proved impossible to holdback the enemy. The engineers and infantry had to abandon position after position. As it turned dark, the first building fell into the hands of the Soviets. Each city block was bitterly contested, while a large part of the local civilian populace believed it could survive the terror of the Soviet attack and the subsequent occupation of the city in its basements. Warning about atrocities, which the division had discovered first hand in eastern Hungary, were dismissed as so much *Nazi* propaganda. The civilians would soon learn differently!

Just before midnight, the last elements of the division evacuated Stuhlweißenburg. Around 0230 hours on 23 December, *PGR126* and

88 Editor's Note: The original German refers to this as a *Sehnenstellung*, for which there is no good English translation. Basically, a *Sehnenstellung* is a shortened, almost direct line between two points as opposed to a normal defensive line, which follows terrain features and may be concave or convex, depending on the situation.

89 Editor's Note = Division Escort Company. This company became a part of the tables of organization and equipment of divisions toward the end of the war in an effort to give the division headquarters "organic" protection and to have a quasi standing reserve for emergencies.

PPB51 had taken up positions along a line running Csor — Moha. *Panzergrenadier-Regiment 128* was still fighting north of Stuhlweißenburg. At 0330 hours, the enemy bypassed the elements of the *II./PGR126* that were still screening in Gusztus psz. The enemy entered the open area and forced the 2nd Battalion back to the north. The *I./PGR126* returned to the command and control of the regiment. To the south of Imre mjr., the *10.(Pi)/PGR126* turned back an enemy attack.

The Soviets were scarcely able to gain any more ground attacking from the front. They then attacked west with strong forces out of the area around Patka — Zamoly and to the north into the left flank and rear of the division. The enemy crossed the Stuhlweißenburg — Mor road with his lead elements and occupied Hill 153, southeast of Sarkeresztes. *Panzergrenadier-Regiment 128*, approaching from Stuhlweißenburg, was cut off from its contact with the division by those enemy forces, since the Gaja bottom land was marshy and impassable.

Together with *Panzergruppe Weymann*, the regiment moved out to attack. Working closely together, strong enemy forces on Hill 153 were shattered, whereby nearly 300 prisoners were taken there alone. The route to Sarkeresztes was then open. The regiment occupied its sector of the *Olga* Position. The enemy forces advancing rapidly into the deep flank of the division appeared again and again directly in front of the artillery firing positions. The *7./PAR128* was only able to escape from the enemy infantry, who had approached to within 100 meters, with the help of a *Panther*. The *SS* battery lost two of its guns when its prime movers were destroyed. A limbered gun from *Heeres-Artillerie-Abteilung 77* was destroyed when taken under direct fire.

The achievements of the artillery—*PAR128*, the *1./SS-Artillerie-Abteilung 505*, the *1./Heeres-Artillerie-Abteilung 77*, the *III./Heeres-Artillerie-Brigade 959* (21cm howitzers) and the Hungarian light battery—under *Oberstleutnant* Vogl were of great importance for the conduct of the defensive battle. Final protective fires, the engagement of individual targets, harassing fires and, in the end, even direct fires over open sights against attacking enemy tanks and infantry, as well as the changing of positions while under enemy infantry fires, placed the greatest of demands on every artilleryman.

During the afternoon of 23 December, the Soviets attacked constantly, supported by strong artillery and rocket-launcher formations. At 1500 hours, 400 Soviets bogged down in the defensive fires of the *II./PGR126*. The regiment's 1st Battalion went into position at Imre mjr., together with the engineer company. At 2300 hours, an attack by 150 Russians against Imre mjr. in front of the sector of the 10th Company failed.

Generalmajor Holste's *4. Kavallerie-Brigade*, which had just arrived in sector, engaged the enemy forces advancing on Mor from the east from west of Zamoly.

The majority of the enemy forces that had broken through in the sector of the *271. Volks-Grenadier-Division* between Lake Valence and the Danube were able to quickly gain ground to the north and northwest, despite German resistance that flared up again and again. Even the armored groups of the *13. Panzer-Division* and *Panzergrenadier-Division "Feldherrnhalle"* under the temporary command of *Generalmajor* Pape were unable to prevent the enemy from taking Bicske, Felsögalla and the areas west of Tata. On 24 December, the Soviets reached the bishop's residence of Esztergom (Gran) an der Donau, thus completing the encirclement of Budapest, where the main bodies of four German divisions, together with Hungarian formations, were fighting.

In the sector of the *23. Panzer-Division*, Sarkeresztes was lost to a numerically vastly superior enemy. *Major* von Plate, the acting commander of *PGR128*, was badly wounded when he was engaged by suddenly advancing Russians. Moha was also lost during the course of the day to an enemy who was assaulting without a break. Under the covering fires provided by the eight operational tanks of *PR23*, the "infantrymen" of the division—the remnants of the infantry regiments, the combat engineers, the *Flak* soldiers and the alert units of the divisional artillery and the tank regiment—moved back to the *Olga* Position. The position ran from out of Csor along the hill line to Iszkaszentgyörgy, Magyaralmas and further to the northeast. Before *PGR126* could pull back on the right wing of the division, it had to fend off several attacks, but it was unable to prevent the enemy from achieving penetrations into the positions of the 10th Company and the 1st Battalion. The regiment disengaged from the enemy at 1200 hours, but it was already turning back an attack of 200 Soviets at 1600 hours.

An alert unit, composed of trains elements from *PR23*, screened at Csakbereny, along with the division's escort company.

All available elements of the division were employed in the *Olga* Position. Reserves could not be formed due to the small trench strengths. To the west of the Gaja bottom land, *PGR126* and *PPB51* were defending; to the east, it was *PGR128* with its two battalions and the supply company. There was contact on the right with the *1. Panzer-Division*; on the left, it was with *Reiter-Regiment 41* of the *4. Kavallerie-Brigade,* although a gap had to be monitored by patrols.

Mörser-Abteilung 959 was released from its attachment to the divisional artillery. *Panzergruppe Weymann* returned to the *3. Panzer-Division*. It was thanks to its successful operations that the division was able to achieve numerous defensive successes.

At 0500 hours on the morning of 25 December, Soviets broke through the main line of resistance west and northwest of Imre mjr., exploiting the concealment offered by snowfall. The situation was restored at 0630 hours by *SPW's*.

An attack by five tanks and infantry from Imre mjr. to the northwest was turned back by *PGR126*, as was a new attack at 1330 hours. While the Soviets restricted their activities to patrolling along the left wing of the division, they continued to conduct offensive operations on the right wing. Assault detachments felt their forward from Moha. At 2100 hours, 400-500 Soviets, accompanied by two tanks, moved out of Imre mjr. and entered the main line of resistance, taking two strongpoints. *Panzergruppe Schulz'* tanks and *SPW's* moved out to launch an immediate counterattack and pushed the enemy back. Heavy infantry guns of the *9./PGR126* inflicted extensive casualties on the enemy. He left behind more than 80 dead along the main line of resistance.

The divisional artillery, reinforced by the *3./Heeres-Artillerie-Abteilung 809*, a 21cm howitzer battalion, shattered Soviet concentrations at Borbala psz., Margit psz. and Also psz. In addition, it provided artillery cover with its 1st Battalion for *Reiter-Regiment 41*, which was initially still operating south in front of the *Olga* Position.

There was heavy fog and snow flurries on 27 December. The *2./PAA23*, along with two tanks, was employed on the left wing of *PGR128* to clear up an enemy penetration, where the enemy had crossed the *Olga* Position in a place it was unoccupied. The mission was accomplished in a short period of time. One prisoner was taken, and the Soviets left behind thirty dead.

At 0900 hours, *PGR126*, receiving excellent support from artillery, turned back an attack by 120 Soviets, supported by two assault guns, along both sides of the Stuhlweißenburg — Csor road. Other advances at Moha and to its west also brought the Soviets no appreciable success.

The 28th of December was dominated by artillery duels. After an hour of barrage fires on the morning of 29 December, the Soviets moved out with tanks and infantry from Sarkeresztes to attack north. German antitank guns, tanks and tank destroyers destroyed 19 enemy tanks; in the final protective fires of the heavy weapons, the Soviet infantry suffered considerable casualties. Toward noon, the Soviets called off their attack.

In the sector of the *II./PGR126* southeast of Csor, an attack by 150 Soviets was turned back.

At 2300 hours, *PGR126* relieved *PPB51* so that the battalion could be freed up for engineer assignments, especially the emplacing of mines and wire obstacles.

During the last few days of 1944, preparations were made for the counterattack in the direction of Budapest. The division had to expand its sector to the east in order to relieve elements of the *4. Kavallerie-Brigade*. On 30 December, *PGR126* turned back an attack by 200 Soviets on its right wing.

On 31 December, the *I./PGR128* was relieved by *Panzergrenadier-Regiment 3* of the *3. Panzer-Division*.

By order of *Korpsgruppe Breith*, the division sent *Panzergruppe Rebentisch*, consisting of 18 tanks from *PR23* and three tank destroyers from *PJA128*, to the *1. Panzer-Division* in Berhida. The armored group was reinforced by three *Hetzer* tank destroyers of *Panzerjäger-Abteilung 37* of the *1. Panzer-Division*. The mission of the battle group, together with *Panzergrenadier-Regiment 113* of the *1. Panzer-Division*, was to clear a large vineyard east of the village that had been entered by the enemy and enable the establishment of a main line of resistance along the eastern edge of that area. The attack start time was set at 0010 hours on 1 January 1945. At the last minute, the attack was postponed, because the infantry were not yet ready to attack. The artillery preparatory fires could not be stopped, however, so that the planned 10 minutes of firing started promptly at midnight. It was some "fireworks" that introduced the New Year, and they symbolized the over-all situation of the war, especially the last few years of it. It was and remained in vain, despite all of the bravery, achievements and sacrifices of the German soldier.

The enemy east of Berhida had been warned. When the attack finally started at 0215 hours, after another short artillery salvo, the enemy responded with massive defensive fires against the attacking forces. The attack rolled along a width of 1.5 kilometers in the midst of biting cold and under snow-covered terrain that was well illuminated by a full moon. The enemy positions were somewhat more than 1.5 kilometers away. Within 15 minutes, the tanks were at the attack objective. Two *Panthers* and a tank destroyer were lost due to antitank guns and mines, but they could be recovered. The infantry, reinforced at the last minute by convalescent companies from the *Waffen-SS*, suffered considerable casualties and could only gradually be incorporated into the new main line of resistance. Heavy Soviet mortars fires were placed the entire time on the vineyard grounds.

The armored group was relieved at 0430 hours. The *Hetzer* tank destroyers remained behind to safeguard the infantry. The armored group marched through Berhida to Varpalota to serve as the corps reserve. From there, it returned to Fehervarcsurgo and the division during the night of 1/2 January. The first battle of Stuhlweißenburg had concluded with the stabilization of the defensive front.

During this phase of the fighting, the troop elements of the *23. Panzer-Division* once again performed magnificently. Especially noteworthy among the rear-area services was the performance of the division's ambulance company, which, in the four months of its existence, had transported 6,464 wounded to medical facilities and had covered 104,090 kilometers in the process.

Counterattacks to Relieve Budapest Second Battle of Stuhlweißenburg 7 January to 24 February 1945

While the fighting continued north of Stuhlweißenburg, *SS-Obergruppenführer und General der Waffen-SS* Gille's *IV. SS-Panzer-Korps*, with the *3. SS-Panzer-Division "Totenkopf"* and the *5. SS-Panzer-Division "Wiking"*, was pulled out of the sector of *Heeresgruppe Mitte* west of Warsaw on direct orders from Hitler and sent to the Komarom — Banhida — Tata area. It was joined there by the *96. Infanterie-Division*, which was pulled out of operations in southern Poland.

General der Infanterie Wöhler, former Commander-in-Chief of the *8. Armee*, had assumed command of *Heeresgruppe Süd*. The successor to *General der Artillerie* Fretter-Pico in command of the *6. Armee* was *General der Panzertuppe* Balck.

The *IV. SS-Panzer-Korps* moved out to the southeast on 1 January 1945 with the mission of breaking the ring of encirclement around Budapest and reestablishing contact with the defenders of the city. *Gruppe Pape*, which consisted of elements of the *3. Panzer-Division*, the *6. Panzer-Division*, the *8. Panzer-Division*, the Hungarian 1st Cavalry Division, the *271. Volks-Grenadier-Division* and non-encircled elements of the divisions in Budapest, was on the right of the *SS* corps and joined the attack. On 5 January, after overcoming bitter resistance on the part of the Soviets, the lead elements of the *SS* divisions were at Bicske and Zsambek, only 25 kilometers west of Budapest. Newly brought up enemy formations prevented any further advance, however.

At that point, the high command decided to conduct a rapid regrouping and movement of the offensive main effort to the are just south of the Danube, while *Gruppe Pape* relieved the *IV. SS-Panzer-Korps* at Bicske and Zsambek.

The forces attached to *General der Kavallerie* Harteneck's *Kavallerie-Korps*—the *1. Panzer-Division*, the *23. Panzer-Division* and the *4. Kavallerie-Brigade*—received orders to move out to the east on 7 January with a main effort on the left wing to advance on Zamoly and Csakvar. It was intended for the enemy to be deceived by this measure concerning the regrouping of the *SS* formations.

While *Generalmajor* Thunert's *1. Panzer-Division* conducted limited-objective attacks against Stuhlweißenburg and Gyula mjr., *Generalmajor* Holste's *4. Kavallerie-Brigade* moved out of its sector east of Söred on Zamoly.

The *23. Panzer-Division* was directed to cover the right flank of the cavalry brigade by attacking at the same time to the southeast and east.

At 0630 hours on 7 January 1945, a five-minute artillery preparation commenced on the Soviet positions by the divisional artillery, which had been reinforced by a *Volks-Werfer-Brigade*. The division's two infantry regiments, reinforced by *PJA128*, moved out of their positions north of Sarkeresztes —Also psz. to the southeast. *Panzergruppe Rebentisch*, with 19 tanks from *PR23*, *PAA23*, the *7./PGR126* and the *10.(Pi)/PGR126*, attacked east from Magyaralmas. The surprised enemy's lines were quickly penetrated; Also psz. soon fell into German hands in a concentric attack by tanks and infantry. Enemy infantry, which attempted to escape from the buildings, suffered considerable casualties. To the north of Also psz., Soviet infantry attempted in vain to hide in outbuildings and individual houses. They were smoked out and taken prisoner. The left wing of the armored group had to struggle against flanking fires from the left. One *Panzer IV* was lost, however, three 8.8cm *Flak*, which were being used by the enemy, were destroyed soon thereafter. *Oberleutnant* Schreiber and a battalion physician, *Stabsarzt Dr.* Amann, were wounded.

The right wing of the armored group advanced rapidly east, while *PGR126* took Borbala psz. further to the right. To the west of Borbala psz., Soviet antitank gun and artillery firing positions were overrun. Two antitank guns, three howitzers and several mortars were destroyed. After a short pause in a depression, the tanks attacked Borbala psz. from the southwest and northwest at the same time. The infantry and engineers followed and attacked on foot. Three Soviet assault guns and five T-43's were destroyed in a few minutes; two other T-43's and an American tank, a Sherman, were captured. Furthermore, numerous radio operating instructions fell into German hands along with the intact radio set of the one T-43.

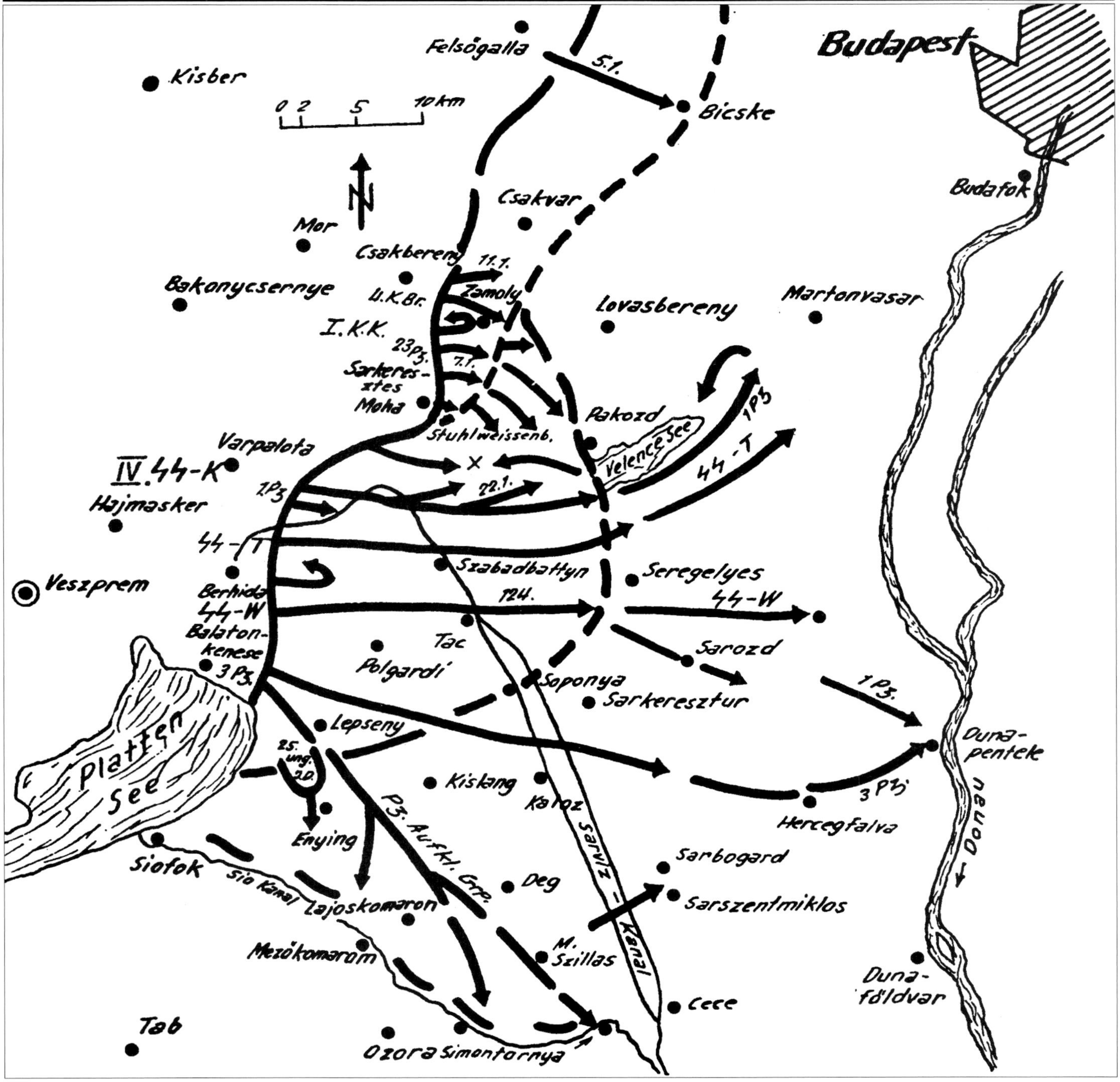

Map 99: Counterattack of *Kampfgruppe Breith* and the *IV. SS-Panzer-Korps* from 7 to 27 January 1945.

The attack was continued, but it ran into a fortified blocking position, guarded by antitank-guns and tanks, 500 meters east of Borbala psz. The position had been established in vineyards. While the Soviet 5.7cm antitank guns and well-camouflaged tanks were barely discernible, the German tanks approaching from more than 1 kilometer away across wide-open pasture land offered the enemy terrific targets. It was not possible to conduct the attack any other way. The onset of snow flurries and fog made matters worse for the gunners. Without being able to take on the enemy with aimed fires, two *Panzer IV's* and one *Panther* were lost.

The armored group returned to Borbala psz. and set up for an all-round defense, especially since there was no contact with the friendly forces on the left, which had hung back.

The infantry regiments gained ground in their attacks to the southeast. After overcoming tough enemy resistance, *PGR128* entered Sarkeresztes around noon and cleared the village of enemy. The German soldiers were greeted with a gruesome picture. Murdered men and raped, tortured and then murdered women and girls were found in many houses. The Soviets granted a few old people their lives, but they paid for them with the robbery of all of their possessions.

Soviet positions east of Sarkeresztes were cleared and the enemy driven to the southeast.

At 1500 hours, 6 *Königstiger* of *Schwere Panzer-Abteilung 503* and 10 assault guns with mounted riflemen from the *4. Kavallerie-Brigade* arrived at Borbala psz. In the middle of continued snow flurries, they moved out to attack the antitank-gun-belt south of Zamoly. One *Königstiger* was lost to an antitank-gun round; the remained returned to the line of departure soon thereafter.

A renewed attempt by *Panzergruppe Rebentisch* to hit the enemy blocking positioning the right flank and roll it up failed with the onset of darkness. For the night, the armored elements were ordered to Also psz., where they remained as a ready reserve on 8 January.

Nine tanks under the command of *Oberleutnant* Schreiber supported *PGR126* at noon on 8 January in defending against an enemy attack.

On 9 January, it was directed that the *23. Panzer-Division*, together with the attached *Panzergruppe Weymann* of the *3. Panzer-Division*, continue its attack southeast from the area east of Sarkeresztes. At the same time it formed up, a strong enemy attack with 80 Shermans and mounted infantry was launched from Zamoly in the direction of Gyula mjr. and Sarkeresztes. The *II./PGR126* was ejected from its positions and lost contact in the fog with its neighbors.

Panzergruppe Weymann immediately turned on the attacking enemy. It occupied an ambush position at Gyula mjr. and let the enemy approach. In a tank engagement lasting the entire day, it destroyed 57 Shermans, practically all of the tanks of the attacking Soviet 63rd Tank Brigade. The Soviet infantry also suffered considerable losses. During that fighting, *Major* Baran, the commander of the *I.(PzHaub)/PAR128*, was badly wounded by several rounds from a submachine gun during close-in fighting. He died a few days later, despite an immediate operation at the main clearing station at Acs-Teszer. The division had lost a magnificent artilleryman, who had been with it since it had been formed. *Hauptmann* Lenberger, the commander of the *II./PGR126*, was wounded; *Major* Grünwaldt assumed command of his battalion that evening. The armored group of the division, under the command of *Oberleutnant* Schulz, started fighting Soviet tanks that were attacking Borbala mjr. from the northwest at 0945 hours that morning. Out of a group of four tanks, two Shermans and a JS-122 were knocked out.

At 1530 hours, *Panzergruppe Schulz* moved out with the *2./PGR126* to attack south from east of Borbala psz. Its objective was to take back the main line of resistance at Hill 186 and open the supply route for *Panzergruppe Weymann*. In the process, another Sherman was knocked out, two 7.62cm antitank guns captures and 80 prisoners taken. A few men of the headquarters of the *II./PGR126*, under the command of *Oberleutnant* Schroeder, encountered a stronger enemy group in their advance on the former main line of resistance. The Soviets were already digging in along the area of penetration. Through the aggressive actions of the infantry, 78 surprised Soviets and a commissar were taken prisoner. More than 200 enemy dead and numerous infantry weapons remained behind in the German lines as tangible proof of success. By evening, the German lines ran approximately where the original main line of resistance had been.

The attack by the *IV. SS-Panzer-Korps* overran the enemy positions in the Eszterghom (Gran) area that day. Along the eastern face of the Vertes Mountains, the divisions gained ground in the direction of Szentendre, but then bogged down in the face of overwhelming enemy resistance 20 kilometers northwest of Budapest.

The attacks were not continued along the entire front on 10 January, since there was no prospect for a breakthrough to Budapest. In the situation briefings at the *Führer* Headquarters, the fighting north of Stuhlweißenburg and around the Vertes Mountains assumed special meaning. Hitler considered the employment of gliders to supply the defenders of Budapest. In the meantime, the defenders had been forced from the parts of the city east of the Danube to the west bank and its old fortress of Ofen. Their situation was becoming increasingly critical. Hitler pressed for a rapid regrouping of the *SS* and armored divisions for a renewed attack on Budapest, which was then directed to be launched from the area around Stuhlweißenburg to the east.

Panzergruppe Weymann returned to its parent division during the evening of 9 January, with the division being attached to the attack group of the *IV. SS-Panzer-Korps*.

On 11 January, *PJA128* advanced south of Borbola mjr. to the south and got as far as the high ground north of Stuhlweißenburg.

While the *4. Kavallerie-Brigade*, which had been reinforced with an armored group from the *1. Panzer-Division*, took Zamoly on 11 January, the *23. Panzer-Division* received orders to tie up and defeat as many enemy forces as possible through a limited-objective attack on Maria mjr.

To that end, *Panzergruppe Rebentisch*, consisting of 15 tanks, the *3.* and *4./PAA23* and 25 engineers from *PPB51*, moved out during the morning of 12 January. After sustaining a few losses through mechanical problems, the group moved through Gyula mjr., which was being screened by an armored car section. Enemy infantry in positions just to the east were driven back. Four hundred meters outside of Maia mjr., a *Panther* drove over a mine. It remained where it was and started covering the right flank of the battle group. The enemy had exploited a steeply arched slope in front of the depression that was home to the group of buildings known as Maria mjr. and did not open fire until the German group had approached to within 300 meters. The armored group fought its way forward—meter by meter—against some 8-10 heavy antitank guns and tanks. Enemy infantry in front of the buildings were shot to pieces.

At the same time, the *SPW's* of *PAA23* swung out far to the left and attacked Maria mjr. from the northwest. To the south of Tallian mjr., they swung toward the village and hit the enemy in the flank, supported by a *Panzer IV*. Exploiting the confusion among the Soviets, the tanks advanced and destroyed two Soviet assault guns, one at 30 meters, the other at 80. The enemy's resistance in the houses collapsed, and the enemy fled up the slope to the east of the buildings. The fires from the armored vehicles and especially those directed by the observers from *PAR128* tore great gaps in the ranks of the Soviet forces.

In the meantime, the enemy brought up reinforcements from the east and the south. In addition, he had additional defensive positions along the wood line on the high ground east of Maria mjr., from which he could overlook the village. In order to avoid unnecessary casualties, since the mission had been accomplished, the buildings of the village were not occupied. The *Panther* that had run over the mine initially and a *SPW* were recovered, so as to conduct an additional advance later to the south and southeast against Hill 180 and Hill 183 north of Csala.

While moving to the rear, one *Panther* ran over a mine and could not be recovered in the softened ground until four other *Panthers* were employed. Concentric fires were being placed on the group, but it did not prevent the recovery of the tank, despite a few casualties among the crews. After the recovery, however, all of the tanks of the group had been so damaged by hits that only a small thrust south by five *SPW's* could be conducted, instead of an attack.

At 1500 hours, a gun or howitzer of extremely large caliber took the group under directed fire. One round that impacted right next to a *Panzer IV* had the effect of tearing off the sideskirts, the right drive sprocket, four roadwheels and track and the superstructure above it. After darkness fell, however, the last tanks were recovered; impeded by mud and thawing ground, the armored group did not return to its line of departure until after midnight. On that day, the armored group destroyed two assault guns and at least 14 antitank guns of 5.7cm, 7.62cm and 12.2cm caliber.

An armored group from the *1. Panzer-Division* that was attached to the division on 11 and 12 January, returned to its parent division.

After a quiet 13 January, Soviet artillery and mortar fires returned to life in the division sector on 14 January. At 1630 hours, 15 enemy tanks and 200 men suddenly attacked the positions of *PGR126* west of Gyula mjr. and pushed the infantry back. The armored group immediately moved out from Borbala psz. and advanced into the enemy tanks that had approached to within 400 meters of the farmstead. The rapidly descending darkness prevented deliberate command and control measures; fire was returned on muzzle flashes. One T-34 was set alight; the remaining ones pulled back to the south. Together with *PAA23*, the path was cleared for the infantry back to the old main line of resistance. The Soviet infantry pulled back.

Heavy artillery and antitank-gun fires were placed on the assembly area of the armored group during the night in Borbala psz. *Major* Rebentisch and *Unteroffizier* Metzger were wounded. *Hauptmann* Kujacinski assumed command of the *I./PR23*.

On 16 January, most of the tanks were brought back to Magyaralmas, while two small groups remained behind the main line of resistance to support the infantry. In tireless efforts, *Panzer-Werkstatt-Kompanie 23* succeeded in getting several damaged tanks repaired.

At the same time, the approach march of the *IV. SS-Panzer-Korps* in the area between Lake Balaton and Berhida had been completed. The *3. Panzer-Division* (right) and the *1. Panzer-Division* (left) were attached to the corps. Later on, *Gruppe Pape*, consisting of German forces and the Hungarian 25th Division, as well as the *Kavallerie-Korps*, was brought up to cover the open right flank of the *SS* corps. The Headquarters of the *III. Panzer-Korps* reassumed command and control of the sector north of Stuhlweißenburg.

On 18 January, the *IV. SS-Panzer-Korps* moved out to attack east from south of Stuhlweißenburg. The Soviets were surprised by this attack; their front was torn open in many places.

The divisional reconnaissance battalion was attached to the *3. Panzer-Division* for this attack. Together with *Panzer-Aufklärungs-Abteilung 1* and *Panzer-Aufklärungs-Abteilung 3*, it formed a reconnaissance group for guarding the right flank of the *3. Panzer-Division*. On 18 January, it followed the lead attack elements from Balatonkenese. The reconnaissance group advanced to the Sio Canal on a broad front and screened the infiltration of Hungarian infantry formations into the main line of resistance on the north bank of the Sio Canal between Komarom and Simontornya. The Hungarians were fearful and lacked confidence, especially since they lacked armor-defeating weaponry in sufficient numbers.

Elements of *PPB51* supported the *5. SS-Panzer-Division "Wiking"* in crossing the Sarviz Canal. They were primarily employed to clear mines, but they were used to lay mines later on to protect the *SS* division against enemy flanking attacks.

The *23. Panzer-Division*, which was not directly involved in the attack, received orders to tie up Soviet forces by advances south and southeast and take the high ground north of Stuhlweißenburg.

Major Tiedemann's *PJA128*, along with a company of engineers from *PPB51*, threw back the enemy that had penetrated into Gyula mjr. during the previous few days and then advanced further south to Point 166. The divisional artillery fired on the tank destroyer personnel and the engineers by mistake, but no casualties were sustained.

At the same time, at 0645 hours on 18 January, *Panzergruppe Kujacinski*, consisting of 14 tanks from *PR23*, eight *Tigers* and four flamethrower tanks from *Panzer-Flamm-Kompanie 351*, advanced south from east of Sarkeresztes. An antitank-gun-belt was shattered, and engineers from *PGR128* cleared a lane through a minefield. The marshy bottomland west of Hill 153 was crossed over a narrow bridge. Soon thereafter, Soviet tanks and assault guns counterattacked. Without sustaining any friendly losses, two T-43's, one JS-122 and two assault guns were destroyed. The remaining Soviet armored vehicles turned away to the south. After destroying 14 antitank guns, the terrain was cleared of the enemy and the insertion of the infantry into a new defensive line northwest and north of Hill 153 was safeguarded.

There was no enemy contact on the left wing of the division.

The attack of the *IV. SS-Panzer-Korps* gained further ground on 19 January. The infantry built-up the positions that had been taken the previous day, while most of the armored group prepared for operations in Magyaralmas. Individual tanks screened right behind the main line of resistance.

The *1. Panzer-Division*, reinforced by a formation of Hungarian volunteers and the *I.(Panther)/PR24*, adjoined the *23. Panzer-Division* on the right. It blocked an important road at Börgönd and was positioned in a semi-circle around Stuhlweißenburg to the west, south and southeast. The other divisions crossed the Sarviz Canal to the east.

An operation planned by the *6. Armee* for the *23. Panzer-Division* to advance from the north against Stuhlweißenburg on 19 and 20 January was never realized, since the enemy brought up new forces into the Csakvar — Patka area. The attack divisions of the *IV. SS-Panzer-Korps* reached the Danube at Dunapentele and took Pusztasarozd and Nagy Perkayta. The lead elements of the *1. Panzer-Division* were at Dinnyes on Lake Valence.

On 20 January, the *6./PR23* was transferred 10 *Panzer V's* and a *Befehlspanzer V* from *Panzer-Abteilung 160* of the *60. Panzergrenadier-Division "Feldherrnhalle"*.

During the evening of 21 January, the *1. Panzer-Division* attacked Stuhlweißenburg and entered the city in a fight that lasted the entire night. The *23. Panzer-Division*, largely tied down in its sector, supported the attack by assault detachment operations conducted by *PPB51*, the infantry and the tank destroyer personnel against the northern outskirts of the city. The *1. Panzer-Division* expressed thanks via radio for the support.

The 22nd of January saw the division issued orders to attack south across the 153 — 166 line and then swing east north of Stuhlweißenburg to advance against Csala.

While *Oberstleutnant* Ruge's *PGR128* advanced south, drove the last remaining Soviets out of the area between 153 and Kis-Kecskemet and established contact with the elements of the *5. SS-Panzer-Division "Wiking"* advancing out of Stuhlweißenburg, *PGR126*, attacking further to the east, had to overcome stronger enemy resistance. The Soviets defended with exceptional determination, even after *Panzergruppe Kujacinski* was in their rear.

Panzergruppe Kujacinski had moved out with 10 tanks from *PR23* and 9 *Tigers* from *schwere Panzer-Abteilung 503* at 1100 hours. It retook Gyula mjr. and then advanced south as far as 1.5 kilometers north of the vineyards on the Stuhlweißenburg — Csala road. Numerous attacks by Soviet infantry and tanks were turned back with high losses for the enemy. At 1700 hours, the infantry regiments, supported in their fighting by *PJA128*, closed up to the armored group. The continued advance east of the armored group along the road to Csala encountered a strong defensive blocking position composed of antitank guns and tanks in the vicinity of Point 174, which could not be overcome. The tanks and the infantry transitioned to the defense for the night in their limit of advance. During this fighting, the armored group of the division accounted for 2 T-43's, 7 assault guns, 15 antitank guns and 3 trucks. Numerous small arms and enemy dead remained behind on the battlefield.

Until the evening of 22 January, armored reconnaissance patrols from *PAA23*, which had been employed along the right flank of the *3. Panzer-Division*, monitored the situation along the Sio Canal. They were then brought forward as part of their battalion to the east and across the Sarviz Canal.

At first light on 23 January, the division continued its attack on Csala. The armored group, reinforced during the night by a Hungarian tank company consisting of eight *Panzer IV's*, was directed to clear a path for the infantry. Despite excellent support from the divisional artillery, the armored group was not able to advance much beyond Hill 174. Swinging out to the northeast across Hill 183, it attacked the village from the north along the Panzeverö Defile. Against increasing enemy resistance, the tanks entered Csala at 1000 hours and cleared the village of the enemy, together with the infantry approaching from the west.

Massive artillery fires were placed the entire day on Csala. The effort by7 the armored group to advance further east failed in the face of the superior antiarmor defenses of the Soviets. The railway line could not be crossed. As a consequence of battle damage and mechanical failure, only seven regimental tanks, five *Tigers* and the eight Hungarian *Panzer IV's* were operational.

The two infantry regiments went into position around Csala and to its north. The main line of resistance of the division ran that evening from Csala through Points 183-204 to the area south of Tallian mjr.

The attack conducted by the *IV. SS-Panzer-Korps* that day reached beyond the southeast tip of Lake Valence to the area west of the Vali. The *5. SS-Panzer-Division "Wiking"* was south of Ercsi on the Danube. The armored reconnaissance group along the southern flank screened at Ozona, Simontornya and Cece. The enemy started to infiltrate between the attacking formations and the screening forces to an ever larger degree and conducted local counterattacks.

On 24 January, the *23. Panzer-Division* defended the positions it had taken the previous day. Heavy fires from Soviet artillery and tanks were placed on the sector of the division the entire day.

In the sector of the *3. Panzer-Division*, the *3./PAA23* was employed against the group of buildings at Sar melleki mjr., which were being held by the enemy as a strongpoint. Without support from heavy weapons and artillery, the attack bogged down in the face of position heavily reinforced with antitank guns and rifles. Three *SPW's* were lost; without being able to help the crews, the company had to break off the attack and attack further in the direction of Sarbogard.

On 25 January, a portion of the men arrived back at their company after they had hidden themselves right in front of the Soviets and worked their way back to the German positions at night. The *SPW* crew of *Unteroffizier* Pelzer had been discovered by the Soviets and shot, however.

On that day, the lead elements of the *5. SS-Panzer-Division "Wiking"* and the *1. Panzer-Division* were only 18 kilometers away from the encircling ring around the defenders of Budapest after they had crossed the Vali. Toward evening, however, the *IV. SS-Panzer-Korps* had to be halted and pulled back across the Vali, since the Soviets had moved out from the area around Bicske to the south with large armored formations.

The armored group of the *23. Panzer-Division*—six tanks from *PR23* and three tank destroyers from *PJA128*—attacked on 28 January along the boundary line to the *4. Kavallerie-Brigade*, so as to support the cavalry formation's attack east by launching an assault on Tallian mjr. Moving north from Gyula mjr. at 1350 hours, the armored group made rapid progress. One kilometer south of Tallian mjr., stronger enemy resistance had to be broken; five Soviet antitank guns were destroyed. The continued advance was made more difficult by not only the strong defenses to the front, but also the flanking fires being received from both sides. The battle group was forward echeloned to the right compared to the left-hand neighbors, who made no further progress. At that point, the armored group also had to pull back. In the concentric defensive fires of the Soviets, one *Panther* and one *Panzer IV* were compete losses. Five other tanks and tank destroyers were hit. That evening, the remainder of *Panzergruppe Kujacinski* returned to Gyula mjr.

In the *Führer* Headquarters on 27 January, the efforts to relieve Budapest were called off in view of the threatening situation developing southwest of Budapest and the onset of Soviet counterattacks further south. *Generaloberst* Guderian, the German Army Chief-of-Staff, reported the started withdrawal of the *23. Panzer-Division* to form a reserve.

Hitler hedged reservations, however, against that the withdrawal of the *23. Panzer-Division* by the *6. Armee* and the subsequent lengthening of the sector of the *4. Kavallerie-Brigade* to cover the vacated terrain. He was on the opinion that the enemy would immediately attack in that sector to take Stuhlweißenburg and cut off the formations to its south and east. As a minimum, the division should no be pulled out of the area, especially since it was the strongest of the armored divisions that were then employed around Stuhlweißenburg.

During the day, the German formations fighting east of Lake Valence had to yield to the overwhelming superiority of the enemy, despite having knocked out more than 200 tanks. They pulled back as far as the southeast corner of the lake. At the same time, the *3. Panzer-Division*, located south of Dunapentele, was threatened by a deep Soviet penetration into its left flank.

The third effort to relieve Budapest had also failed. Hitler clung to his plan, hatched in the course of January, of using the *6. SS-Panzer-Armee* of *SS-Oberstgruppenführer und Generaloberst der Waffen-SS* Dietrich, after it had been freed up from the Ardennes Offensive, to clear the west bank of the Danube of the Soviets and then have it attack to relieve Budapest.

In the meantime, the defenders of the city had been forced back into an ever-smaller area by the Soviets and their ammunition and rations became scarcer and scarcer. The calling off of the attack by the *IV. SS-Panzer-Korps*, with which they already had radio contact, weakened their ability to resist.

During the fighting from 6 December 1944 to 27 January 1945, the *23. Panzer-Division* had destroyed or captured the following:

280 tanks	104 antitank rifles
452 antitank guns	67 submachine guns
3 heavy guns	3 tractors
5 antiaircraft guns	220 *panje* wagons
15 mortars	4 self-propelled carriages
65 heavy machine guns	3 rocket launchers
2 staff cars	6 12.2cm guns
1 trailer	4 light infantry guns
25 assault guns	112 light machine guns
5 8.8cm *Flak* (German)	32 trucks
4 15.2cm guns	4 prime movers
12 heavy infantry guns	

1,507 mines had been removed. 949 prisoners and 13 deserters had been taken. *Panzergruppe Weymann* which had been temporarily attached from the *3. Panzer-Division*, had destroyed 147 tanks and assault guns and 220 antitank guns.

The division's losses during the same period:

a) Personnel:

Killed: 13 officers, 58 noncommissioned officers and 345 enlisted personnel

Wounded: 68 officers, 233 noncommissioned officers and 1,611 enlisted personnel

Missing: 2 officers, 19 noncommissioned officers and 330 enlisted personnel.

b) Materiel (total losses):

9 *Panzer V's*	10 prime movers
3 tank destroyers	18 staff cars
11 *SPW's*	4 assault guns
12 motorcycles	2 armored recovery vehicles
1 maintenance section	2 *Maultiere*
8 *Panzer IV's*	16 trucks
1 captured tank	

On 27 January, the *23. Panzer-Division* started to be relieved by the *4. Kavallerie-Brigade*. The original intent—to position the division as a ready reserve for the field army—was not realized. The development of the situation in the sector of the *IV. SS-Panzer-Korps*, especially that of the *3. Panzer-Division* at Dunapentele, made the expedited movement of

the division to the area around Aba, 20 kilometers south of Stuhlweißenburg, necessary. The Soviet attack north of Dunapentele to the west into the deep left flank of the *3. Panzer-Division*, as well as attacks from the south against the outposts in the line running Simontornya — Cece, interdicted the supply route for that division and threatened to encircle it.

As the troop elements of the division were freed up, they marched south through Stuhlweißenburg. By 0200 hours on 28 January, *PPB51, Panzerspähtrupp Hey* from *PAA23,* the *I./PAR128*, and *Panzergruppe Schulz* (the *8./PR23* with eight tanks) reached Aba. While another armored group remained temporarily with the *4. Kavallerie-Brigade*, the two infantry regiments and *PJA128* also moved into the Aba area after being relieved.

Toward noon on 28 January, an alert was sounded for the appearance of enemy tanks in the Közep mjr. area, 10 kilometers south-southeast of Sarkeresztur. *Panzergruppe Schulz* moved out, but it did not establish any contact with the enemy. Several Soviet trucks with limbered antitank guns advanced against the outposts of the division at Közep mjr. *Flak* eliminated seven of them; the remaining ones turned back to the southeast.

On 29 January, the division received orders from the *III. Panzer-Korps*, to which it had been reattached, to attack in the direction of Alsó Sismand psz., to the west of Hercegfalva. The divisional engineers and *PGR126* were employed together with *Panzergruppe Schulz*. The initial attack objective was the line running Garda mjr. — Hill 138. The start of the attack was delayed since the supporting artillery—*Artillerie-Regiment 277*—was not yet in position. At 0645 hours, the troop elements moved out in bitterly cold temperatures and heavy snow flurries. Hill 138 was crossed without encountering enemy resistance. In front of the *Hauptmann* Feige's *I./PGR126*, which was advancing on the left, the Soviet defenses started to respond. As a result, that battalion got held up behind the other elements. *Oberleutnant* Schulz attacked north with his tanks in order to clear the route for the infantry to Szilfa mjr. Just south of that group of buildings, a Soviet company with antitank guns, antitank rifles and machine guns was caught and destroyed. The armored group then turned back south again and supported *PPB51* in its taking of Garda mjr., where the Soviets defended bitterly.

Despite the assistance previously rendered, the *I./PGR126* was unable to advance in the face of new enemy resistance. The armored group was brought forward again to render support. With its help, it was possible to clear the farmstead of Szila mjr. of the enemy.

The Simontornya — Budapest rail line was crossed on a broad front. *Major* Grünwaldt's *II./PGR126* continued to advance as night fell. It took Hill 156 and ejected the enemy from Garda mjr. Because a loss of contact with friendly forces on the left appeared possible, the continued attack to the southeast was stopped at the point of it furthest advance. Joszef mjr., Hill 153 and Garda mjr. were occupied in strongpoint fashion.

At first light on 30 January, the battalion command post of the *II.PGR126* was attacked on three sides. *Obergefreiter* Schuster, a gunner on an antitank gun assigned to the *8./PGR126*, knocked out five T-34's out of a group of seven that had broken through, all in the space of less than 13 minutes. In addition, he also knocked out two trucks with limbered antitank guns. Later on, *Obergefreiter* Schuster was awarded the Knight's Cross to the Iron Cross on 5 February 1945 for his success and was mentioned by name in the German Armed Forces Daily Report of 2 February 1945.

With the mission of taking Nagy Lok, the *II./PGR126, PPB51* and the armored group moved out during the morning. The terrain, which was covered with deep snowdrifts, did not allow the attack group to approach the village from either the southwest nor the northeast. Around noon, the intention to attack had to be abandoned, since a strong Soviet infantry unit was moving along the rail line from the south and attacking Garda mjr. The armored group supported the defensive fighting and shattered the withdrawing enemy in an immediate counterattack.

At 1630 hours, the Soviets attacked the strongpoints in Joszef mjr. and Point 156 from the east and north. Again, with the employment of the armored group, they were driven away.

On that day, the *1. Panzer-Division*, relieved in its sector along Lake Valence by the *3. SS-Panzer-Division "Totenkopf"*, established contact with the *3. Panzer-Division* just north of Dunapentele and allowed it to withdraw to the northwest.

A shifting on the main line of resistance back to the Simontornya — Budapest rail line was ordered for the night of 30/31 January, with *PGR128* on the right, *PGR126* on the left and *PPB51* and a section of tanks positioned in Közep mjr. as a ready reserve. The divisional artillery had occupied firing positions with its batteries to the east of Sarkeresztur. The rear-area services of the division were brought forward to a line running Stuhlweißenburg — Hajmaker. The main clearing station reestablished itself in Stuhlweißenburg. In tireless efforts, all of the wounded of the divisions fighting in a semi-circle to the south of Stuhlweißenburg were treated, whenever they could not be transported to their respective medical personnel.

At first light on 1 February, a Soviet motorized battle group entered Sarszentagota from the south by surprise, driving back the outposts of *PGR128. Hauptmann* Kujacinski's armored group, which had been returned to division command and control in its entirety, joined the fighting with its nine tanks and drove the Soviets from the village. In a continued advance, the lead elements ran into heavy flanking fires from antitank guns. In the blink of an eye, one *Panther* was a complete loss. Two assault guns and a *Panzer IV* were hit and had to pull back. One enemy antitank gun was destroyed. On that day, a thaw set in and made the trails and roads in the marshy terrain very difficult to negotiate.

In the face of heavy enemy pressure, Közep mjr. had to be abandoned on 2 February. On 3 February, the enemy entered Sarkeresztur again. Five *Panthers* joined the fighting to support the infantry. The completely exhausted and numerically too weak infantry were separated from the tanks, however. Soviet tank hunter/killer teams and antitank guns made life difficult for the tankers; one of the tanks burned out after being hit by an antitank gun.

The main line of resistance was pulled back incrementally as part of a general withdrawal to the *Margarethe* Position. On 4 February, the front lines ran in front of Sarkeresztur. On 4 February, that village, as well as Aba, were abandoned, and a line running Felsöszentivan — Külsökajtor — Hill 143 (5 kilometers southwest of Seregelyes) was occupied. *Panzergruppe Kujacinski* was positioned for operations in Hehesvölgyi. The enemy was generally quiet, but he conducted considerable patrolling activity and fired occasional artillery salvoes.

The friendly forces to the left of the division was the *5. SS-Panzer-Division "Wiking"*, which defended the sector as far as Lake Valence and maintained contact with the *3. SS-Panzer-Division "Totenkopf"*. The *1. Panzer-Division* had been pulled out of the front lines, but it had to be employed almost immediately to the north of Stuhlweißenburg in the sector of the *4. Kavallerie-Brigade*, where the enemy had gained ground in the direction of Sarkeresztes with strong armored forces.

In the days that followed, the Soviets attacked the main line of resistance of the *23. Panzer-Division* with tanks and infantry again and again. During each attack, three or four assault guns or tanks accompanied each battalion. Three local penetrations on 6 February were cleared up by the infantry and the armored group. Four enemy tanks were destroyed in the fighting for Fiathkajtor, and heavy casualties were inflicted on the enemy.

On 7 February, all Soviet attacks in front of or in the main line of resistance were again turned back. There penetrations were cleared up in immediate counterattacks. Two Soviet assault guns, three tanks and five antitank guns were destroyed. During that round of fighting, the tank destroyers of *PJA128* again proved their value in an exceptional manner. Screening close to the main line of resistance, they were able to be committed to more distant hot spots thanks to their mobility.

In the area of Aba, a Soviet attack group succeeded in crossing the Sarviz Canal and Halom Creek and occupying the village of Csösz in the sector of the Hungarian division on the division's right. The leading elements of the enemy were already feeling their way toward Tac. *Major* Tiedemann, the commander of *PJA128*, formed a *Kampfgruppe* from his headquarters, the *3./PAA23*, a Hungarian rocket-launcher battery, a battery of 21cm howitzers, and two flamethrower tanks and four *Panthers* to clear up the situation. All of the Hungarian elements remaining in the sector were attached to him. During 8 February the area of penetration was sealed off and cleaned up.

On 9 February, *Hauptmann* Schulz' *PAA23* participated in the fighting with most of its forces. The enemy was tossed back across the canal with only minimal friendly losses. The mainline of resistance was restored along the Sarviz Canal. After receiving several antitank-gun hits, the *Panther* of the commander of the tank forces burned out. *Oberleutnant* Schulz, an experienced and well-proven tanker, and his driver were killed.

In a continuation of that attack, *Kampfgruppe Tiedemann* moved out between Halom Creek and the Sarviz Canal to attack south on 11 February. The battle group accompanied the attack of the *1. Panzer-Division*, which was advancing to restore the situation after Hungarian forces had pulled back from the area of Polgardi. Soponya and Nagylang were taken, and the bridges over Halom Creek and the Sarviz Canal were blown up.

In the division sector on that day, a Soviet attack with tanks and infantry threw elements of *PGR128* out of their positions along the southeast edge of Felsöszentivan (Hill115). In an immediate counterattack, together with the tank destroyers of the *2./PJA128*, the enemy was defeated and the mainline of resistance reoccupied to its former full extent.

On that day, the fighting for Budapest drew to a close. After the Hungarian and German defenders had run out of ammunition, the Commanding General of the *IX. SS-Gebirgs-Korps*, *SS-Obergruppenführer und General der Waffen-SS* von Pfeffer-Wildenbruch, gave permission to break out of the fortress. Only 2,000 men of the brave garrison would survive the attack conducted with cold steel and reach the German lines at Stuhlweißenburg over the next few days. Most of the Hungarian and German defenders had been killed or wound up in Soviet captivity.

Despite the fall of Budapest, Hitler remained committed to his plan to eliminate the enemy forces in the bend of the Danube and on the west bank of the river south, west and northwest of Budapest, to liberate Budapest and to hold the Soviets on the east bank of the Danube. This was to be done by the employment of the *6. SS-Panzer-Armee* and a simultaneous attack by the *2. Panzer-Armee* from the area around Nagy Kanisza and another attack by *Heeresgruppe E* across the Drau to the north.

For the immediate future, however, the *I. SS-Panzer-Korps* was pulled out of the area around Komarom and employed in the area of operations of the *8. Armee*, where it successfully participated in the destruction of Soviet forces west of the Gran and taking back the entire west bank of the river.

In the sector of the *23. Panzer-Division*, combat activities during the next few days were limited to artillery duels and individual combat patrols, in which isolated Soviet tanks participated. A female battalion was identified in front of the sector of *PGR126* on 12 February, but it was pulled out of the line a few days later.

On 12 February, both of the infantry regiments had to extend their frontages along the main line of resistance to the left, since elements of the *3. SS-Panzer-Division "Totenkopf"* had to be relieved between Point 143 and the area east of Bolondvari tnj. A T-43 suddenly appeared in front of the firing positions of the *9(s.IG.)/PGR126*, southeast of Belsöbarand. But before tank hunter/killer teams could approach, the tank got stuck. It then rotated its turret for minutes on end. Once it could be examined, it was determined that it was empty. The crew had bailed out. The tank was then blown up.

On 13 February, a combat patrol from the *10.(Pi)/PGR126* broke into the Soviet positions on Hill 133, east of Bolondvari tnj. and rolled them up. Soviet advances against Felsöszentivan, Point 112 (to the east of it), Bodakajtor, Fiathkajtor and Bolondvari tnj. were primarily broken up by well-directed fires from *PAR128*. The tank destroyers and the tanks had to help out the infantry on a few occasions.

Hauptmann Rompel assumed command of the *II./PGR126* from *Major* Grünwaldt, who was transferred into the German Army's unassigned officer manpower pool.

The Attack of the 6. SS-Panzer-Armee and the Retreat to the Borders of the Reich 25 February to 6 April 1945

At the end of February 1945, the struggle of the German Armed Forces centered around the fighting for the frontiers of the *Reich*. Advancing from France, Belgium and Holland, the Allies were driving on the Middle and Lower Rhine. In the east, the enemy had reached the Oder and cut off the formations fighting in East Pomerania and East Prussia. The front, ripped-apart in multiple places, was on fire. A shortage of personnel and materiel led to one improvisation after the other.

At the same time, the *6. SS-Panzer-Armee* marched into the area around Stuhlweißenburg to prepare for a local offensive, which made no sense to any one, whose objective was to take back the oil fields in the area around Fünfkirchen. In a conference with the Commanders-in-Chief, the Commanding Generals and the Division Commanders, all of the generals who had had recent experience in the Stuhlweißenburg area pointed out in no uncertain terms that the area south of Stuhlweißenburg and Lake Valence—which was already crisscrossed with marshy terrain, deep ditches and other natural obstacles—had become almost impassable as a result of the melting of the snow and the rain, which had fallen for days. They stated that any attack would bog down after a short while in the soupy mud and would sacrifice valuable materiel. Even the Hungarians shook their heads when they heard about the employment of the *6. SS-Panzer-Armee*. In peacetime during map exercises and war games conducted by the Hungarians, it had always been fundamentally assumed that an armored attack in the narrow area between Lakes Balaton and Velence would bog down. But even the most contentious of discussions and the courage of a few commanders in presenting their recommendations came to naught. The attack had been ordered.

On 25 February, the *1. Panzer-Division* assumed command and control of the sector of *PGR126*, relieving the regiment with its own *Panzergrenadier-Regiment 1*. The shortened main line of resistance of the *23. Panzer-Division* was then occupied by both of the infantry regiments, with reserves being formed at the same time. The *I.* and *II. SS-Panzer-Korps* closed up behind the *23. Panzer-Division* and the neighboring Hungarian formations on the right. To the left of the *1. Panzer-Division*, the recently introduced *356. Infanterie-Division* relieved the *3. SS-Panzer-Division "Totenkopf"*, which was to assume responsibility for the defense of the area north of Stuhlweißenburg, along with the *5. SS-Panzer-Division "Wiking"*. The *4. Kavallerie-Brigade*, which had been freed up on 9 March, moved to *General der Kavallerie* Harteneck's *I. Kavallerie-Korps*, which was employed on the right wing of the attack group.

After a thorough artillery preparation by all of the divisional artillery, a *Volks-Artillerie-Korps* and a rocket launcher corps, the offensive was launched along the entire front between Lakes Balaton and Velence at 0400 hours on 6 March. The *Schwerpunkt* of the offensive was in the

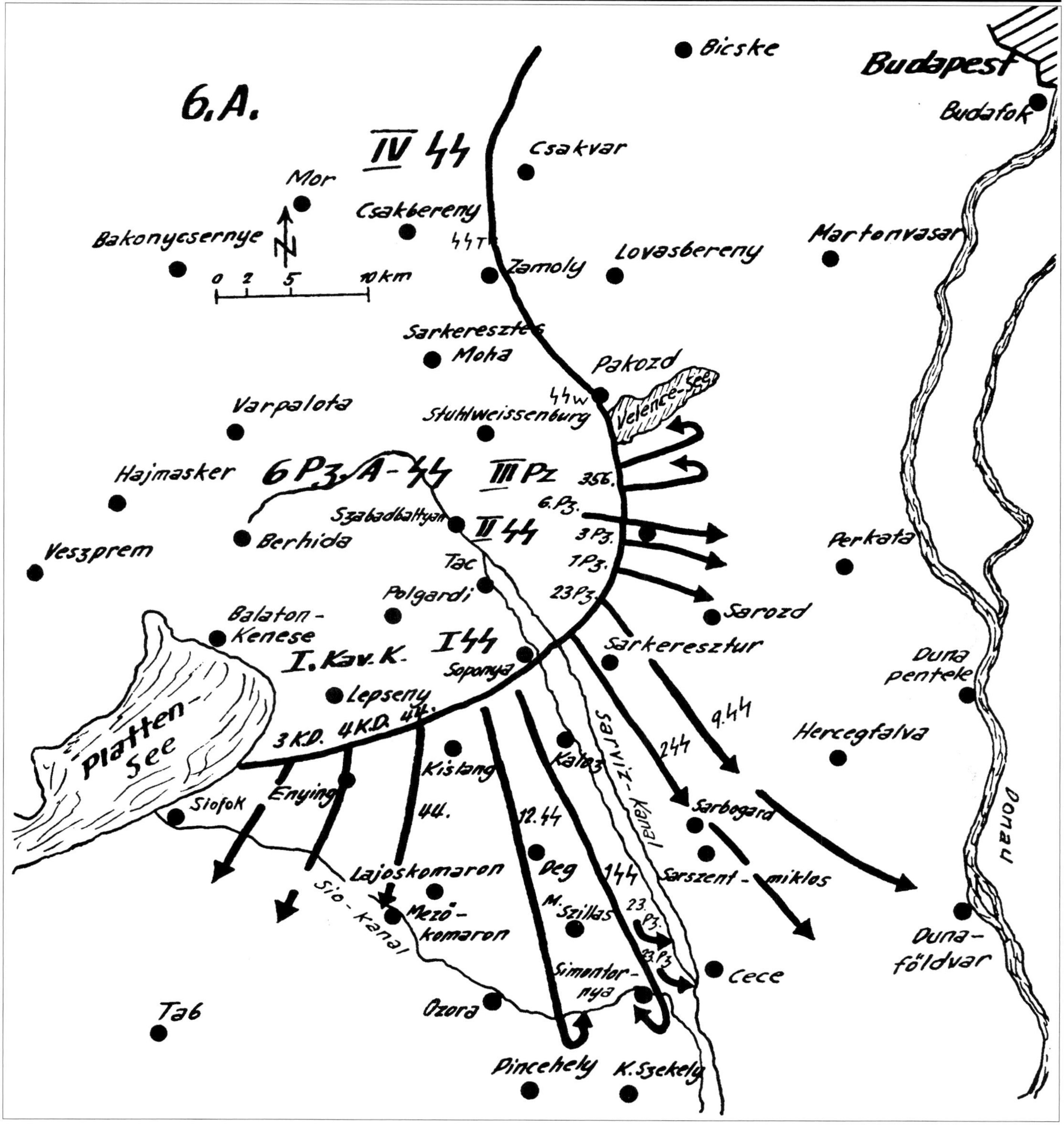

Map 100: Attack of the *6. SS-Panzer-Armee* on 6 March 1945.

sectors of the two *SS* armored corps. (The *I. SS-Panzer-Korps* was comprised of the *1. SS-Panzer-Division "Leibstandarte SS Adolf Hitler"* and the *12. SS-Panzer-Division "Hitlerjugend"* with the *II. SS-Panzer-Korps* composed of the *2. SS-Panzer-Division "Das Reich"* and the *9. SS-Panzer-Division "Hohenstaufen"*.) Both corps attacked on both sides of the Sarviz Canal to the south. Neighboring on the right was the *I. Kavallerie-Korps*, which was attacking to take the Sio Canal. To the east of the Sarviz Canal, the *III. Panzer-Korps* of *General der Panzertruppen* Breith attacked to the southeast. That corps, composed of the *1. Panzer-Division*, the *3. Panzer-Division* and the *356. Infanterie-Division*, moved out from a line running from Belsöbarand to Dinnyes.

The attack to the west of the Sarviz Canal made good progress, but the divisions of the *III. Panzer-Korps* were only able to make limited gains in the face of pouring rain and a stubbornly defending enemy. Considerable casualties thinned the ranks of the attacking formations, whose tanks were not able to deploy properly in the softened terrain.

The *SS* formations, which were to attack through the main line of resistance of the *23. Panzer-Division*, did not establish contact with

PGR126 and *PGR128* until the sound of the artillery fires had receded. At 0800 hours, the *SS* infantry crossed the front lines of the division. The Soviet's heavy weapons, especially the mortars and the artillery and, later on and despite the poor visibility, ground-attack aircraft, inflicted extremely heavy casualties on the *SS* companies that were advancing, sometimes in columns. Despite the participation of the tanks and tank destroyers of the *23. Panzer-Division*, which eliminated identified Soviet heavy weapons, the attack stalled initially.

In accordance with its orders, the *23. Panzer-Division* remained in its defensive positions so as to be available later on as the reserve for *Angriffgruppe Balck* in the Aba area.

Toward noon, the terrain gains effected by the friendly forces to both the left and right had their effect in this sector as well. The enemy pulled back to the area north of Aba. The *II. SS-Panzer-Korps* moved out again, advancing more rapidly this time. The conduct of the attack and the insufficiently prepared medical arrangements led to "horrific scenes", according to one eyewitness. The infantry of the division were occupied for a long time with "ripping open shirts and dressing wounded *SS* people." The main clearing stations in Stuhlweißenburg were overflowing after a short period. For everyone in the division with a sense of responsibility, it was depressing to see how brave and good soldiers were being sacrificed. The young men of the *SS*, who demonstrated extreme bravery in a deadly situation, could have formed a valuable noncommissioned officer corps in the Army, where they could have incomparably increased the combat power of the German Armed Forces, as opposed to being in the few elite *SS* divisions.

During the next two days, the attack to the southwest made more progress. The *I. Kavallerie-Korps*, with its Hungarian 20 Infantry Division and the *44. Infanterie-Division "Hoch- und Deutschmeister"*, reached the Sio Canal, the *I. SS-Panzer-Korps* took Simontornya and the *III. Panzer-Korps* was advancing on Agard and Gardony, south of Lake Velence.

The main clearing station of the 2nd Medical Company was subjected to a heavy bombing attack. One direct hit on the building housing the clearing station blew up in the attic.

On 9 March, the *23. Panzer-Division* was attached to the *6. SS-Panzer-Armee* and ordered to the Simontornya area. It looked as though the attack in that sector of the broadening front might come to a standstill in the face of superior enemy forces.

The division was inserted into the line to the left of the *1. SS-Panzer-Division "Leibstandarte SS Adolf Hitler"* and received orders to take the village of Sar Egres on 10 March in the face of a stubbornly defending enemy. Several attacks by the *SS* against the village up to that point had collapsed. While a few tanks remained in reserve under the command of *Hauptmann* Fischer, *Kampfgruppe Prinz zu Waldeck und Pyrmont* (*PR23*) was employed against the village, along with the *SPW's* of *PAA23* and both of the infantry regiments.

Moving out to the south at 1115 hours from Francs, *PGR126* (under the acting command of *Major* Hunk) and the armored group were directed to eject a strong enemy force consisting of tanks and antitank guns from the hill spur 2 kilometers north of Sar Egres. Moving aggressively, the hill was taken in less than 10 minutes, and the enemy was thrown back across the railway line to the village.

The tanks engaged identified enemy targets on the outskirts of Sar Egres and put several antitank guns and strongpoints out of action by the time the infantry arrived. Within the 90 minutes that the engagement took place, the German armor eliminated seven enemy tanks, seven antitank guns and one truck without suffering any friendly losses.

The infantry arrived at 1415 hours. They attacked the village from the front; at the same time, the tanks and the *SPW's* swung out to the right and attacked the village from the northwest. The enemy defended with great bravery. Even though another tank and two antitank guns were destroyed, and the heavy weapons of the infantry and the artillery of *PAR128* inflicted heavy casualties on the enemy, the attack did not achieve its objective. The Soviet defensive belt, consisting of more than 20 antitank guns and several heavy tanks, could not be overrun by the tanks attacking across a long, descending slope. The attack was called off, and the limit of advance was held.

During the attack, at the request of the *1. SS-Panzer-Division "Leibstandarte SS Adolf Hitler"*, the division employed the tank destroyer company of *PJA128* against a group of buildings southeast of Deg, which were supposedly occupied by the enemy and which also contained wounded *SS* men. The group of buildings turned out to be clear of the enemy, but it also did not contain any German wounded. Instead, tanks from the *12. SS-Panzer-Division "Hitlerjugend"* suddenly opened fire on the tank destroyers, and set three of them alight. All night long there was strikingly heavy artillery and searchlight activity on the part of the Soviets, even though the weather was stormy and rainy. An armored group from the division, along with the *2.* and *3./PAA23*, screened from the area of the hill spur north of Sar Egres.

On that day, the *3. Panzer-Division* was inserted into the front lines to the right of the *1. Panzer-Division* in the eastern half of the attack sector.

At 0500 hours on 11 March, *Panzergruppe Fischer*, consisting of *PR23* minus the tanks screening at the hill spur, attacked in the direction of Sar Egres from the northwest. That attack also failed in the face of the strong defense put up by the Soviets. It was unable to advance even after *Kampfgruppe Prinz zu Waldeck und Pyrmont* joined in the fighting from the north with all of its remaining tanks and the main body of *PAA23*. The enemy had built up the entire area between Sar Egres and Simontornya into an exceptionally strong antiarmor strongpoint. Soviet ground-attack formations (IL-2's) supported the Soviet forces on the ground in rolling attacks.

An attempt by the infantry to approach the village on their own also failed around 1100 hours.

At noon, *PR23*, along with the *2.* and *3./PAA23*, were employed to take Hill 133, 2 kilometers southwest of Sar Egres. At 1615 hours, the group under the command of *Hauptmann* Fischer moved out from the wooded defile 3 kilometers west of Sar Egres, took Hill 144 just to the east of the defile, but then bogged down in front of Hill 133. In an engagement against enemy tanks and antitank guns, three *Panthers* were lost.

As a result of the failure of the attacks up to that point to take Sar Egres, there was a violent disagreement between the division commander, *Generalleutnant* von Radowitz, and the Commander-in-Chief of the *6. SS-Panzer-Armee*, *SS-Oberstgruppenführer* Sepp Dietrich, who demanded the immediate taking of the village.

The division's two infantry regiments prepared to attack Sar Egres again. Supported by the *II.* and *III./PAR128*, as well as both of the companies of *PJA128*, the regiments moved out with a battalion each on 12 March. The remaining two battalions were directed to fix the enemy. The attack did not meet with success. A gap between the *II./PAR126* and the *I./PGR128* was covered by patrols.

At 1600 hours on the same afternoon, *Panzergruppe* Fischer moved out again from the wooded defile. With 17 tanks, it was able to force a breakthrough to the Simontornya — Cece road, despite heavy flanking fires from the right from the area around Simontornya and from the left from Hill 133. However, the railway embankment south of the road proved to be an insurmountable obstacle for armor. Swinging out to the east, an enemy infantry position was cleared before the Soviet antiarmor defenses at Sar Egres and Alsó mjr. were able to open up with fires against the German tanks. With the onset of darkness, the tanks were turned into gigantic targets by the Soviets firing signal flares and by illuminations rounds automatically fired when wires were disturbed in the barbed wire entanglements.

The *2./PJA128*, which had been directed to take a hill west of Sar Egres, along with a weak infantry company and a platoon of engineers, also had a similar experience. One tank destroyer wandered into a wire obstacle, whereupon illumination rounds went off everywhere and turned the entire area into daylight.

The *SS* divisions did not succeed in their assault on the high ground south of Simontornya. Their attacks collapsed again and again with heavy casualties.

The *6. Panzer-Division*, which had been pulled out of the line north of Stuhlweißenburg, was inserted into the eastern portion of the attack area. But its attack also proved unsuccessful in the face of the vastly superior enemy and the seemingly bottomless mud.

The struggle of the *23. Panzer-Division* for Sar Egres and the railway to he south of it continued on 13 March. At 0830 hours, both of the infantry regiments moved out with the battalions they had on their wings—the *I./PGR126* and the *II./PGR128*—while the battalions on the center of the sector conducted feints with combat patrols and assault detachments. The artillery fired a barrage on the cemetery at Sar Egres. Soviet fighter-bombers continuously joined in the fray; the *Luftwaffe* was barely noticeable.

The attack did not develop well; Soviet defenses were exceptionally strong. At 1500 hours, heavy weapons, especially heavy and light infantry guns, as well as the divisional artillery, fired another barrage on Sar Egres. At that point, all four of the infantry battalions moved out to attack. The *2./PGR128* reached the northern edge of Sar Egres at 1535 hours, but it had to pull back in the face of enemy defenses, which proved too strong. German fighter-bombers attacked Sar Egres and Cece. The attack, which recommenced to exploit the aerial attack, bogged down at 1630 hours, until the *SPW's* of the divisional reconnaissance and engineer battalions rallied it forward again.

At 1735 hours, the *I./PGR128* entered the northern part of Sar Egres and the *SPW's* forced a penetration into the cemetery. At 1830 hours, the entire northern part of Sar Egres was in German hands. The infantry immediately pursued the enemy forces, which were faltering, and cleared the center of the village and its southern portion of the enemy. Under the leadership of *Oberleutnant* Heinle and *Leutnant* Greiner, the *2./PGR128* continued advancing to the south and entered Egresi mjr. at 1930 hours. The company was forced to call off its attack 100 meters in front of the two bridges east of the farmstead by tank and machine-gun fires. *Hauptmann* Feige's *I./PGR126* relieved the 2nd Company of its sister regiment, which then returned to its parent battalion.

During the night *PGR126* set up defensively to the right of Sar Egres, while *PGR128* was on the left. Both regiments oriented east. The boundary between the two regiments was the center of the village. At the same time, the *Panzergruppe* continued to fight for the rail line 3 kilometers southwest of Sar Egres. During the afternoon, it destroyed one T-43 and three assault guns in its attack, but it was unable to gain any ground to the southeast. Once again, a shortage of ammunition made itself felt in an unpleasant way. Soviet fighter-bombers attacked ground targets continuously. One *Panther* of the *I./PR23* was completely destroyed by bombs.

After the onset of darkness, *Panzergruppe Fischer* renewed its attack along the Simontornya — Cece road. This time, the Soviet defenses were overrun, and Alsó mjr. was cleared of the enemy.

Including the tanks destroyed during the day, the armored group reported the following for its daily tally: 1 T43, 6 assault guns, 2 trucks, 7 antitank guns, 1 combination antitank/antiaircraft gun, 10 antitank rifles, 8 heavy machine guns and 1 light machine gun destroyed; 1 self-propelled 7.62cm antitank gun captured.

During the course of 14 March, heavy field-army artillery went into position in the area around Sar Egres and engaged targets in Dunaföldvar from there.

The attack of the *SS* divisions and that of the *III. Panzer-Korps* was continued, even though the *2. Panzer-Armee* at Kapsovar and elements of *Heeresgruppe F* had already called off their attacks after modest initial success. The combat power of the German armored divisions became increasingly weaker in the area of operations along the Sio Canal and south of Lake Velence. In the face of an oppressively superior and stubbornly defending enemy and the frequently impassable terrain, even the greatest of bravery and self-sacrifice were of little use.

To the north of Lake Velence, there were already signs of an impending offensive by the 2nd Ukrainian Front. The enemy was attacking the Hungarian formations in the western portion of the Vertes Mountains. Aerial reconnaissance indicated large concentrations of forces with tanks and motorized vehicles in the area of Lovasbereny.

In the division's sector, it was mostly quiet. *Oberstleutnant i.G.* Jahns arrived to replace *Major Prinz* zu Waldeck, who had been transferred to the unassigned officer manpower pool of the Army, as the commander of *PR23*. *Oberstleutnant* John retook command of *PGR126*.

Hauptmann Roltsch's *I./PGR128* was pulled out of the line along the railway line north of Sar Egres at 0400 hours on 15 March so that it could perform a special mission with engineers. After comprehensive scouting of the terrain around the village of Örs psz. and briefings from the forward observers of the *II./PAR128* and the *Waffen-SS*, the 1st Battalion prepared to attack during the night of 15/16 March. The battalion's mission was to establish a bridgehead on both sides of the bridge over the Sarviz Canal east of Örs psz. and to take Sar melleki mjr. Moving ahead of the battalion was *Stoßzug Kirch*[90] in assault boats, followed by the 1st and 3rd Companies. The 2nd Company was to follow later and advance southeast as far as Point 110. Heavy machine guns and mortars from the 4th Company were attached to the line companies.

The attack started at 0130 hours on 16 March. Soviet heavy weapons on the east embankment of the Sarviz Canal, primarily heavy machine guns, caused the first crossing attempt to be scuttled. A second attack at 0430 hours also failed. The German losses in personnel and assault craft were considerable. By 0830 hours, however, it was possible to bring 12 men of the 2nd Company into position on this side of the canal. Using the concealment provided by the morning fog, they crossed a 200-300 meter wide flood zone that was filled with water. A heavy machine gun was brought into position on an island in the middle of the flood zone and, later on, a few men were able to reach the west bank with the last remaining functional assault craft. The superior defenses of the Soviets, who also covered the depths of the area of operations with mortar and antitank-gun fires, led to a failure of that attack as well. The bridgehead could not be formed, and the *I./PGR128* moved back from the canal and established quarters in Ötvenkilencz psz.

The *6. SS-Panzer-Armee* had to recognize that it's attack to the south and to the Danube was condemned to failure.

The date of 16 March is also linked to the start of the most difficult crisis for the German and Hungarian formations between Lake Balaton and the Danube east of Komarom.

With a many-fold superiority in tank and infantry formations, the 2nd Ukrainian Front moved out to launch an offensive between Stuhlweißenburg and Mor, which soon expanded to the sectors of the front adjoining to the north. The Hungarian cavalry and infantry formations positioned there were broken through in the first rush; individual German "corset stays" composed of *Flak* and security units were unable to hold up the Soviets. The enemy entered the Bakony Woods south of Mor.

90 Editor's Note: = Assault Platoon "Kirch".

The left wing of the *IV. SS-Panzer-Korps*—the *3. SS-Panzer-Division "Totenkopf"*—was also pressed back.

The *12. SS-Panzer-Division "Hitlerjugend"*, which was pulled out of the sector west of Simontornya was directed to reinforce the *3. SS-Panzer-Division 'Totenkopf"* as expeditiously as possible, but it was also unable to prevent the Soviets from gaining further ground to the west. Varpolota, located on the main road from Stuhlweißenburg to the west, was threatened from the north and northeast. Almost all of the logistics elements, especially the maintenance companies and the rations entities for the divisions fighting south of Stuhlweißenburg, were located there.

Despite all that, the German command did not issue an order to pull the front back to the north. On the evening of 16 March, there was only a 15-kilometer-wide line-of-communications corridor to the west for the 12 German and 2 Hungarian divisions fighting in the arc of the front between Lakes Balaton and Velence. Stuhlweißenburg was declared a *fester Platz*.[91]

On 17 March, *Heeresgruppe Süd* withdrew all elements of the *6. SS-Panzer-Armee* from the front on both sides of the Sarviz Canal and pulled the front east of the canal back incrementally. Untold numbers of motorized vehicles became stuck in the soupy mud, and large amounts of materiel that had been newly issued to the *SS* divisions prior to the start of the offensive fell into Soviet hands, who, at that point, had also started their counteroffensive south.

During the course of 17 March, the *23. Panzer-Division* relieved the *1. SS-Panzer-Division "Leibstandarte SS Adolf Hitler"* on both sides of Simontornya. While it was still daylight, the operational tanks under the command of *Oberleutnant* Quintel rolled toward Simontornya. During the night of 17/18 March, the two infantry regiments incorporated new replacements into their ranks and relieved the *SS* infantry, with *PGR126* on the right and *PGR128* on the left. The divisional artillery went into position north of Simontornya with all of its battalions. Even before the tanks reached the village, they were subjected to heavy fires from the high ground to the south, as well as rolling attacks from ground-attack aircraft (IL-2's).

During the morning of 18 March, Soviet artillery and mortars fired heavy salvoes again and again on the main line of resistance, which ran south of Simontornya, and in the village proper. Supported by fighter-bombers, the Soviets attacked at 1200 hours and achieved penetrations in the sectors of *Hauptmann* Feige's *I./PGR126* and the *I./PGR128*. The main line of resistance had to be pulled back after an immediate counterattack by the armored group on Hill 220 did not achieve the desired effect. The enemy was positioned on dominant high ground and was able to identify every German measure, even in its preparatory stage. The artillery's forward observers were able to shatter additional advances of the Soviets and their areas of concentration with well-placed fires. The Red Air Force was also busy during the night bombing and strafing. The divisional engineers emplaced mines in threatened areas of terrain, mostly S mines. The regimental engineers of *PGR128* were employed alongside the divisional engineers of *Oberleutnant* Otto in the sector of the regiment's 1st Battalion, where a heavy demolitions charge was emplaced in front of the 3rd Company.

To the rear of the division, the enemy reached the area on both sides of Zircz on that day. The *III. Panzer-Korps*, to the south of Lake Velence, gradually pulled back in the face of a Soviet offensive along its frontage, with the result that its sector ran along the eastern side of the Sarviz Canal from Pötölle to the north to the eastern side of Stuhlweißenburg, connecting to the Hungarian 20th Infantry Division, which was securing along the west bank of the canal. At Stuhlweißenburg, the *1. Panzer-Division* had contact with the *5. SS-Panzer-Division "Wiking"*.

The *23. Panzer-Division*, which was the southern-most division fighting on 18 and 19 March, was attached to *General der Kavallerie* Harteneck's *I. Kavallerie-Korps* after the *6. SS-Panzer-Armee* pulled back. The corps was positioned along the Sio Canal with the *3. Kavallerie-Division* and the *4. Kavallerie-Division*.[92] The *44. Infanterie-Division "Hoch- und Deutschmeister"*, which had previously been attached to the corps, was reattached to the *III. Panzer-Korps* west of Polgardi and sent there.

During the evening of 19 March, *Panzergruppe Fischer*, consisting of 19 tanks from *PR23* and the *2./PAA23*, was dispatched to the Hungarian 20th Infantry Division in Deg. In that division's sector, Soviet forces had forced the Sarviz Canal 2 kilometers southeast of Kalosz in an attack from the east. They had formed a deep bridgehead at Kishörcsök psz.

The enemy made preparations to attack in front of the division sector on 19 March. At 0845 hours, the *2./PGR128* pre-empted a Soviet attack against the almost 150-meter-wide gap between it and the *2./PGR126*, throwing the enemy infantry back and closing the gap by 0945 hours. The Soviet response: Heavy mortar fires on the new positions.

Toward 1300 hours, Soviet tanks and infantry succeeded in gaining ground in the sector of *PGR126*. The regiment had to pull back gradually, starting on the right. It was able to hold its ground south of Simontornya, however. The *I./PGR128*, adjoining the regiment on the right, was able to restore the main line of resistance temporarily with a counterattack launched by its 2nd Company. No counterattacks were undertaken in the sector of *PGR126*, since a warning order had been received at 1600 hours for pulling back to the north.

Leaving behind rearguards, the infantry disengaged from the enemy at 2100 hours and crossed over to the north bank of the Sio Canal in assault boats. The rearguards followed at 2200 hours. Without being noticed by the enemy, the regiments mounted up on their combat vehicles and moved through Mezö-Szila (Szilas-Balhas) and into the main line of resistance east of Kp. Bogard — Angyad psz. — Ötvenkilencz. *Panzergruppe Fischer*, west of Kishörcsök, was reinforced by the *3./PPB51* and the *2./PJA128* (5 tank destroyers).

At 1115 hours on 20 March, five *Panthers* and the *3./PPB51* attacked Kishörcsök psz. They were temporarily able to enter the area of the group of buildings, but then they had to pull back to the western side of the settlement, since they did not have any infantry to be able to drive the Soviets out of the broken-up terrain. The *3./PPB51* had a 7.5cm towed antitank platoon, a 2cm towed *Flak* platoon and a platoon of medium *SPW's* with heavy rocket launchers at its disposal.

At 1230 hours, all of *Panzergruppe Fischer* was employed against the Soviet bridgehead. In the face of strong resistance from both sides of the canal, the attack made only slow progress in the marshy terrain. It bogged down once and for all 600 meters from the bridge. The *Panther* group and the combat engineers on the right wing of the battle group were unsuccessful in entering Kishörcsök psz. Concentric artillery and mortar fires forced the engineers to ground over and over again. Ten enemy tanks and five antitank guns were identified on the west bank of the canal; they received fire support from 13 Josef Stalins on the east bank. In a firefight lasting the entire afternoon, 13 enemy tanks were destroyed, and 1 *Panther* was lost due to antitank-gun fire. The constant reinforcement by fresh enemy forces made it impossible to reduce the bridgehead.

The enemy, pursuing from the south, did not approach the main line of resistance of the two infantry regiments until the afternoon. Artillery and mortar fires drove Soviets, who were feeling their way forward, out of Mezö-Szilas. At noon, the warning order was already on hand for another withdrawal during the evening of 20 March.

91 Editor's Note: = (roughly) "firm position". A *fester Platz* was intended as a strongpoint that was not to be given up under any circumstances.

92 Editor's Note: The cavalry "divisions" mentioned here were the cavalry brigades of the same number referenced earlier in the text and only redesignated as divisions with no substantial change in organization, manning or equipment.

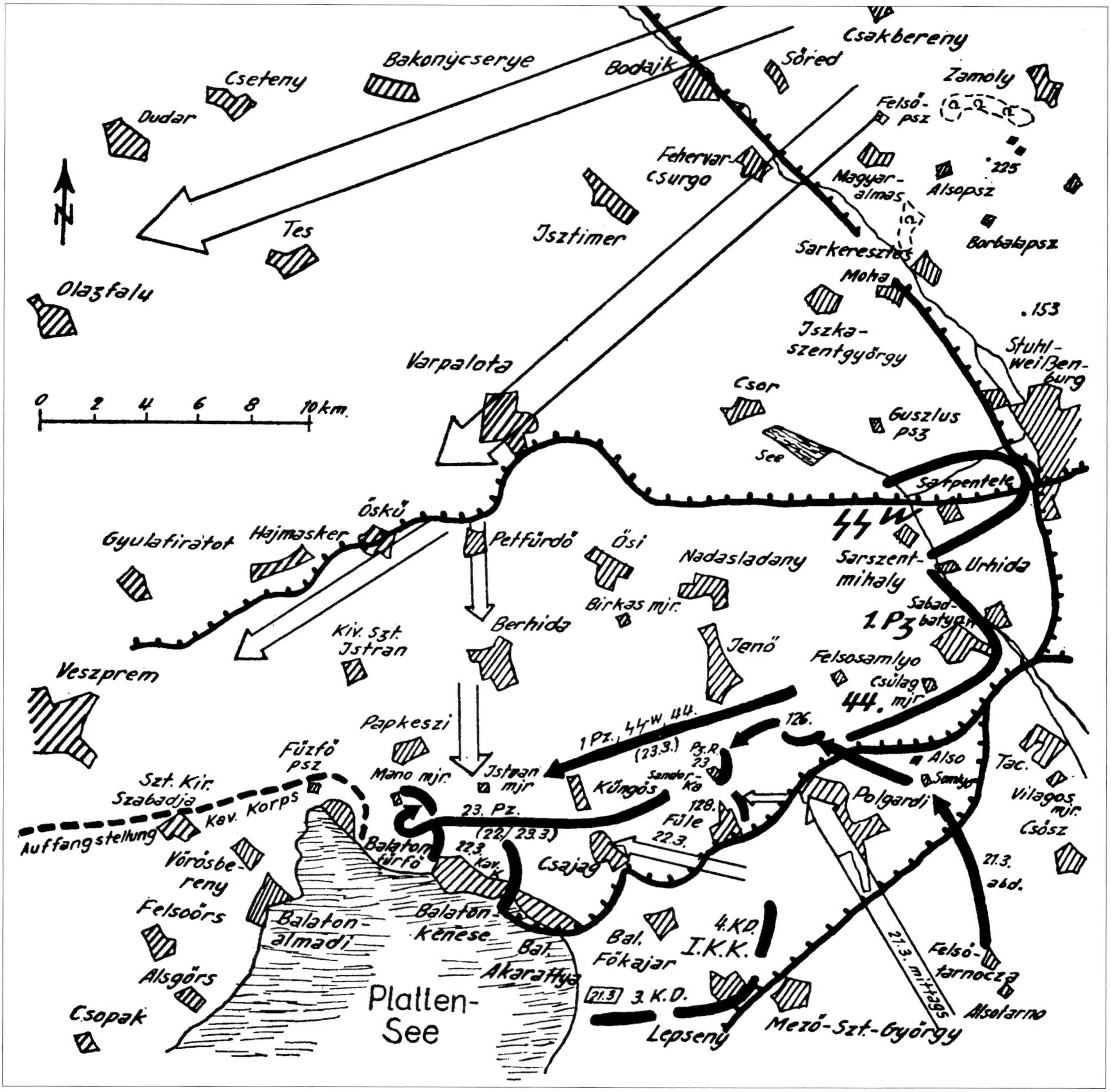

Map 101: The Soviet Breakthrough into the Bakony Woods, 20-23 March 1945.

During the night, almost all of the tanks of *Kampfgruppe Fischer* became stuck and had to be recovered in tiresome work that lasted for hours, in the course of which many mechanical problems developed.

The trains, which were located in the Hajmasker — Veszprem area, prepared to move. The Red Air Force systematically bombed all of the built-up areas days and night; as a result, the trains and the troop elements bivouacked in the woods.

During 20 March, Stuhlweißenburg was attacked on three sides. The *5. SS-Panzer-Division "Wiking"* fought to maintain the only road from the city that led southwest to Lake Balaton that was still in German hands. Soviet troop elements were already moving along the Varpalota — Veszprem road. The *1. Panzer-Division*, reinforced with the *I./Panzer-Regiment 24* of the *24. Panzer-Division*, fought its way back to the west bank of the Sarviz Canal on both sides of Szabadbattyan, along with the neighboring *44. Infanterie-Division "Hoch- und Deutschmeister"*. The *3. Panzer-Division* and the *356. Infanterie-Division*, which had been employed to the right of the aforementioned divisions, were pulled out of the line so as to be able to be employed in the Bakony Woods against the Soviet forces that continued to advance westward. During the day, the *3. Kavallerie-Division* and the *4. Kavallerie-Division* pulled back to Enying and Lepseny.

At 1830 hours, the *23. Panzer-Division*, in accordance with its orders, pulled back from its main line of resistance south of Deg and moved into position southwest, south and east of Kislang, along with the attached elements from the Hungarian 20th Infantry Division. The division had the mission of defending a line running from Kislang — Lobb mjr. The division's reconnaissance battalion, followed by *Panzergruppe Fischer* (three *Panzer V's*, four *Panzer IV's* and two *Panzer IVa's*), prepared for operations in Janos mjr.; three assault guns from the *I./PR23* screened in the sector of *PGR128* in Lobb mjr.

As *Panzergruppe Fischer* pulled back from Kishörcsök psz., enemy tanks pursued immediately and forced the armored group, which was already burdened with recovery efforts, to firefights. One *Panther* was lost to mechanical problems and another one to damage from a mine. Both of them had to be blown up.

While *PGR128* was able to identify long Soviet columns representing all branches of service advancing west of its sector to the north at first light on 21 March, it was also attacked at 0700 hours. An enemy advance on Peterszalla failed. However, concealed by thick fog, the enemy went around the strongpoints, and forced the regiment, as a result, to pull its right wing back to Ercsi psz.

At 0900 hours, enemy tanks and infantry entered Kislang from the south, without there having been any significant fighting on the part of the Hungarians employed to the south. In an immediate counterattack, the *I./PGR128* and the armored group threw the enemy back. Soon afterwards, however, 42 enemy tanks and infantry advanced on the village again. The order to withdraw was unable to be delivered to all of the companies in time. Elements of the infantry battalion were scattered and could only be reorganized when they got to the vicinity of Janos mjr. Ten enemy tanks immediately pursued to Janos mjr. In order to keep the Kislang — Polgardi road open, the *Panzer IV's* and the assault guns that had been brought up from Lobb mjr. screened just east and north of Kislang, where they destroyed four Shermans. The enemy tanks advanced into the infantry pulling back to the north, but they turned off after the aforementioned four had been knocked out. The majority of the enemy tanks and accompanying infantry departed Kislang to the northwest without engaging the division. Screening positions were occupied along Point 147 (northeast of Garas mjr.) — Alsotarnocsa — Point 155 (east of it). *Panthers* identified advancing enemy tanks in the vicinity of Alsotarnocsa around 1300 hours and knocked out two of them.

At 1500 hours, the armored group and the infantry received orders to prepare immediately for an attack to the north. Strong Soviet tank and infantry forces had advanced as far as the southern part of Polgardi from the southwest and had taken the first few buildings of the village. It was directed that the infantry and the armored group hit the enemy from the southeast by moving across the railway line south of Polgardi, supporting the counterattack of German forces from the north. The enemy was pressing hard on the screening line at Alsotarnocsa from the south. Just as both of the infantry regiments started to pull back toward Polgardi at 1600 hours, six enemy tanks and infantry appeared 300 meters in front of the rearguards. Under fire from the enemy's main guns and heavy weapons, the division pulled back. The bottomless mud became a deathtrap for many vehicles. Once again, many heavy demands were placed on the batteries of the divisional artillery.

In the meantime, Polgardi had fallen into enemy hands, which meant that any attack on the village did not make any sense. *Generalleutnant* von Radowitz thereupon ordered that Polgardi be bypassed to the west and the divisional elements occupy a blocking position as quickly as possible in the Füle — Sandorka — woods northeast of the Polgardi area. Together with the armored group, *PGR126* and *PPB51* fought their way through to the woods 1.5 kilometers west of Polgardi and set up outposts during the night. By 2300 hours, *PGR128*, *PJA128* and Hungarian elements moved around Polgardi via circuitous routes and made it to Füle, where they likewise set up screening positions.

Two *Panzer V's*, two *Panzer IV's* and an assault gun bogged down in the morass, as did two tank destroyers. As a result of a shortage of fuel and recovery means, they could not be recovered.

During the afternoon of 21 March, the *I./Panzer-Regiment 24*, with its few operational *Panthers*, was attached to the division. It was sent to the location of *PGR126*, while the division's armored group went to Sandorka, where it was resupplied.

During the course of that 21 March, Stuhlweißenburg was lost. Marching back with the rear-area services of the *1. Panzer-Division* and the *5. SS-Panzer-Division "Wiking"* was the division's field post office, which had unflappably continued working there despite all of the aerial attacks and artillery fires.

Two separately attacking groups of Soviet forces—with more than 200 tanks in all—advanced on Polgardi from the areas of Enying — Mezöszentgyörgy and Csösz — Tac — Kiscseri psz. These areas were deep in the rear of the division on both its right and left flanks. The cavalry divisions employed to the right of the division fought for Balatonfökajar during the evening of 21 March, while a gap existed to the left with the *44. Infanterie-Division "Hoch- und Deutschmeister"* as a result of the relief of the *3. Panzer-Division*. The *1. Panzer-Division* was employed along a line running Felsösomlyo — Falubattyan — Urhida. During the afternoon, the divisions fighting north of Polgardi were threatened with encirclement by the Soviets, whose simultaneous attacks from the north and south to the east of Küngös interrupted the German withdrawal movements.

At 1100 hour on 22 March, the last six operational armored vehicles of *PR23*—2 *Panzer V's*, two *Panzer IV's* and two assault guns—were in Sandorka. In the course of a Soviet aerial attack, the battalion physician of many years for the *I./PR23*, *Stabsarzt Dr.* Trautmann, was mortally wounded. He was well known far beyond the tank regiment for the quiet and sure way he treated the wounded and the sick.

Soviet tanks and infantry entered Csajag while fighting with the cavalry divisions. *Panzergruppe Fischer* was ordered into the area north of the village and given the mission of preventing a further Soviet advance to the north. The corps issued orders to unconditionally hold the current positions.

Before the armored group could reach the new positions, an armored reconnaissance patrol from *PAA23* reported: "10 enemy tanks attacking Istvan mjr." That meant that the enemy was already 10 kilometers northwest of Csajag, regardless of whether he had come from the north or the south! Two assault guns and one *Panzer IV* were sent to engage those tanks. The *Panzer IV* was knocked out by enemy tanks just north of Csajag. At that point, the two assault guns went over to the defense north of the village, along with elements from *PGR126*.

The enemy exerted pressure on the screening sector of *PGR128* east of Füle the entire day. *Oberleutnant* Heinle, the very competent commander of the *2./PGR128*, was wounded.

The Operations Officer of the division, *Major i.G.* Schumm, established contact with the *44. Infanterie-Division "Hoch- und Deutschmeister"*, the *1. Panzer-Division* and the *5. SS-Panzer-Division "Wiking"* to coordinate withdrawal movements. But it proved impossible to come to an agreement. Toward evening, the threatening catastrophe forced *Generalleutnant* von Radowitz to order the troop elements of the *23. Panzer-Division* to pull back to the north past Csajag during the night into the area of Mano mjr. The adjacent divisions were notified.

Contact to the right with the *4. Kavallerie-Division* only existed in the form of armored reconnaissance patrols. To the left, there was no contact at all with the *44. Infanterie-Division "Hoch- und Deutschmeister"* and the *1. Panzer-Division*. The division's elements disengaged from the enemy during the night and reached the area around Mano mjr. by bypassing Soviet positions. In the process, numerous personnel from other divisions linked up with the division.

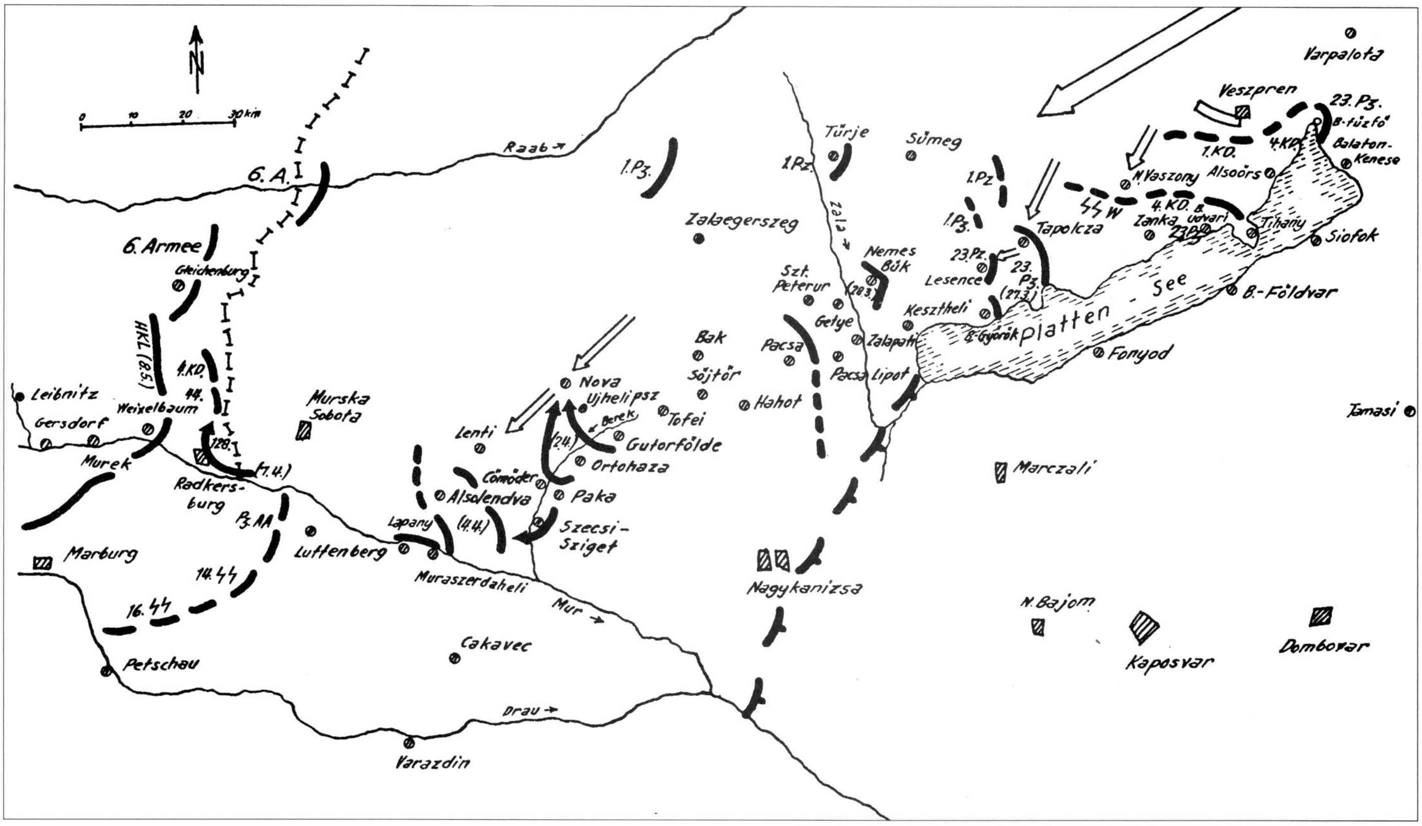

Map 102: Retreat from Lake Balaton to the Borders of the *Reich*, 24 March to 7 April 1945.

Tank destroyers from the *2./PJA128* screened the retreat routes of the division, in the process of which they destroyed 5 enemy tanks and a strong Soviet infantry unit in the course of a relief attack conducted together with units of the *5. SS-Panzer-Division "Wiking"*.

During those events, enemy tanks and infantry entered Varpalota during the course of 22 March. Two immobilized *Panthers* that were dug in there to provide local defense for the maintenance company of the tank regiment had to be blown up when they were unable to engage tanks that had entered the city to their rear. Seven additional *Panthers* just outside of Veszprem, which had been permitted to be evacuated by the *5. SS-Panzer-Division "Wiking"*, were unable to be moved because of insufficient recovery means and had to be blown up in the face of the advance of Soviet tanks that soon followed.

At first light on 23 March, Soviet tanks and infantry advanced against the strongpoints of the division and to both sides of Mano mjr. The last three operational armored vehicles of *PR23* supported the defensive fighting, and one T-34 was destroyed. The last *Panther* was knocked out; soon thereafter, one of the two assault guns was hit on the main gun and had to be sent to the rear. The last assault gun got stuck while changing positions and had to be blown up. The Soviet attack threw the division back to the high ground east of Balatonfüzfö, where all further assaults were turned back. In the meantime, the cavalry divisions had given up Balatonkenese and held open the rear of the *23. Panzer-Division* after passing the northeastern tip of Lake Balaton to the north of Vörösbereny and Szentkiralyszabadja. To assist them, the *I./Panzer-Regiment 24* was attached.

The troop elements of the division were able to evacuate a large number of wounded soldiers, predominantly *SS* personnel. During the night of 23/24 March, the *1. Panzer-Division*, together with a colorful mixture of elements from the *44. Infanterie-Division "Hoch- und Deutschmeister"* and the *5. SS-Panzer-Division "Wiking"*, broke out of the pocket at Jenö. Despite taking considerable losses, it fought its way through to Balatonfüzfö, where it passed through the lines of the *23. Panzer-Division* and elements of the *4. Kavallerie-Division*. They immediately marched through the outposts and into the Balatonfüred — Aszofö area.

The deep penetration of the Soviets into the Bakony Woods, which they had almost exited at Varoslöd, required an expansive withdrawal of the front. The *23. Panzer-Division*, along with the remnants of the *44. Infanterie-Division "Hoch- und Deutschmeister"*, as well as the *3. Kavallerie-Division* and the *4. Kavallerie-Division* remained attached to the *I. Kavallerie-Korps*.

A depressing picture of a rash retreat was to be seen along the roads paralleling Lake Balaton and 10 kilometers to the north. It became even more confusing as a result of the mixing up of all of the formations employed in that area. While individual divisions were expeditiously moved to the west in order to move further north to the Bakony Woods, where the divisions of the *6. SS-Panzer-Armee* were already fighting, and be integrated into the defensive effort, elements of their rear-area services were still located along Lake Balaton. It was the cumbersome maintenance companies and their recovery means that hindered the movements of the other divisions, which had to cover the retreat in the face of hard-pressing Soviet tanks and motorized infantry. Soviet ground-attack aircraft bombed and strafed this entanglement of vehicles, columns and horse-drawn trains, which often moved two to three abreast and with vehicles in tow due to a lack of fuel.

On 24 March, the division continued to screen east of Balatonalmadi and Vörösbereny and held open the bottleneck on the northeast tip of Lake Balaton for additional German soldiers, who had escaped from the Soviets. The cavalry divisions screened, adjoining to the left in a line running from east to west. They had contact with the *5. SS-Panzer-Division "Wiking"* of the *IV. SS-Panzer-Korps* at Kövesgyür, 12 kilometers southwest of Veszprem along the road to Tapolcza. The enemy felt his way forward against the main line of resistance with patrols and small groups of armored vehicles, but he was unable to achieve any significant penetrations. As a result, the retreat took on more discipline and order. During the evening of 24 March, the main line of resistance was moved back to the line running Balatonfüred — Hill 245 (3 kilometers to the north) without enemy pressure.

Hauptmann Schroeder assumed command of the *I./PGR126* from the wounded *Major* Feige. Assault craft from *PPB51* advanced across the lake until just outside of Siofok. German soldiers were observed on several occasions on the lake. They were trying to make contact with German forces by means of boats and improvised rafts. On 25 March, two groups from *PPB51* advanced in the direction of the peninsula near Aszofö that jutted into the lake and had the village of Tihany on it. A lot of refugees had burrowed holes in the ground on the peninsula to take shelter. The enemy, who had already occupied the entire south bank of the lake, had not yet advanced onto the peninsula.

The enemy started to exert stronger pressure against the screening line of the division, whereby he was offered protection by the numerous vineyards. At 1900 hours, the infantry left behind rearguards, consisting of the *10.(Pi)/PGR126*, and pulled back from the main line of resistance to reach a new line of resistance to the east of Balatonudvari and located at Örvenyes along the west bank of the creek that flowed into the lake.

At 1910 hours, four enemy tanks suddenly entered Balatonfüred by bypassing the obstacles that had been emplaced by the engineers. They scattered the *I./PGR128*, which was right in the process of reorganizing. The enemy advanced as far as Aszofö, pressing hard on the heels of the withdrawing infantry with tanks and infantry. At Aszofö, the enemy force ran into the combat engineers returning from the peninsula. After a short fight, the engineers succeeded in disengaging from the enemy and moved back to the German forces at Balatonudvari.

The new line of resistance to the east of Balatonudvari was occupied by 0200 hours. The *2./PJA128* screened in the sector of the infantry with its remaining operational tank destroyers. In addition to the daily task of screening the infantry occupying the new main lines of resistance every evening, *Hauptmann* Schulz' *PAA23* was given a special mission. His armored reconnaissance patrols constantly monitored the situation with the neighboring divisions so as to prevent unwelcome surprises for the forces of the *23. Panzer-Division* and, at the same time, constantly provide higher headquarters with information. The field army and the corps had little influence at the time. The division command bore the main burden those days of maintaining the combat power of the troops in the field, safeguarding their logistics under the most impossible of conditions and conducting the fight in such a manner that the retreat to the borders of the *Reich* was orderly and allowed the retention of as much materiel as possible.

A lack of fuel was the worst enemy of the division those days. Many vehicles had to be abandoned, since there was no more opportunities for the "convoys" of anywhere from four to six vehicles to tow any more.

Frequently, the division commander himself had to decide how to distribute the available and limited quantities of fuel. Only that which was combat ready would receive the allotment. As a result, tanks and tank destroyers had to be blown up again and again, even though only relatively small damage prevented them from being employed. But no fuel was available to safeguard them from the enemy.

With the help of an inventive engineer, *PAA23* was able to secure diesel fuel for some time from an improvised refinery in the southern part of the Bakony Woods.

On 26 March the enemy restricted his activities to occasional reconnaissance-in-force actions and mortar salvoes on the division's lines of resistance. The *SS* formations located along the Veszprem — Tapolcza road were pushed back by strong enemy attacks at Nagy Vaszony. Further to the north, the enemy advanced on Szöcz and Devecser.

At noon, a warning order for a significant withdrawal movement arrived. The situation of *General der Artillerie* de Angelis' *2. Panzer-Armee* between Lake Balaton and Drau made the relief of the *3. Kavallerie-Division* and the *4. Kavallerie-Division* north of Lake Balaton necessary and their immediate dispatch to the area of operations of the *2. Panzer-Armee*. The *23. Panzer-Division* had to assume the sectors to its left and leave the shore road at Zanka with the majority of its forces to reach the area around Tapolcza through Köveskal. The divisional reconnaissance battalion remained on the shore road. Covered by the *SPW* companies of *PAA23* and the *10.(Pi.)/PGR126*, the infantry, engineers and tank-destroyer crews pulled back from the line of resistance at Balatonudvari during the evening of 26 March and set up for the defense during the morning along the east side of Tapolcza. The reconnaissance battalion initially followed as a rearguard, turned off at Kapalantoti toward the southwest and, moving through Nemes-Tördemicz, reached Balatonederics to the west of a large marshy area.

The Red Air Force attacked Tapolcza around 0800 hours on 27 March in two waves. At 1020 hours, 40 enemy tanks with mounted infantry attacked Tapolcza from the north along both sides of the Zalahalap — Tapolcza road. The weak antitank weapons available were not enough to bring the attackers to a halt. At 1100 hours, the *I./PGR128*, employed on the left wing, disengaged from the enemy, who had already gained a foothold on the main road leading west to the battalion's rear.

Taking a circuitous route, the infantry reached the air strip west of the village and set up for the defense there at 1130 hours, so as to enable the jammed-up vehicles and columns in front of the bridges over Lesencze Creek to continue west. At 1700 hours, the division ordered the shifting of the main line of resistance to the west bank of Lesencze Creek with its extended marshland. *Panzergrenadier-Regiment 126* went to the east side of Lesencze-Tomaj and to the south; *PGR128* set up on the east side of Lesencze-Istvand. The bridges over the creek were blown up with the approach of the Soviet's lead attack elements.

The enemy approached the main line of resistance during the night. Mortars fired salvoes on the villages and the positions of the infantry.

At 0700 hours on 28 March, the enemy attacked *PGR126* at Lesencze-Tomaj and to the south. During the morning, the Soviets employed forces toward the south to cross the Lesencze east of Török psz. and threaten to block the retreat route for the division to Keszthely.

At that point, the division commander ordered the infantry regiments to disengage from their positions at 1100 hours and establish a new line of resistance from the railway bridge at Al.-Berki mjr. to the wood line west of Nemetfalu. The division engineers mined the bridge areas at and south of Lesencze-Tomaj. Marching on foot, the battalions reached the new main line of resistance by 1400 hours. The enemy only followed hesitantly; initially, his tanks were unable to cross through the marshland.

The *1. Panzer-Division* was the friendly force to the left, although contact was spotty. That division pulled back to the northwest from Zalaszanto on the afternoon of 28 March. As a result, the *23. Panzer-Division* lost contact with the *6. Armee*; it was attached to the *2. Panzer-Armee*.

At 1900 hours, the entire division moved back, leaving behind rearguards. It moved through Balatonederics, Balaton Györök and Keszthely to the area around Nemes Bük along the Zala. There the division had the mission of covering the rear and deep left flank of the *2. Panzer-Armee* in its continued withdrawal movements to the west.

The reduced personnel strengths of the infantry regiments were raised by combing through the trains, as well as establishing two companies out of excess armor personnel from *PR23*. One "tanker infantry" company each was attached to the two infantry regiments. Above and beyond that, the division employed *Major* Veigel's field replacement battalion and the field-replacement battalion of the *79. Infanterie-Division*, which had just been attached to the division.

The logistics services of the division moved back west incrementally along with the combat elements. This ensured that they would not be endangered, but it also ensured the resupplying of the troop elements would be guaranteed under all circumstances. The main clearing stations of the division were forced to displace frequently due to the rapid retreat.

During the night, the infantry regiments moved into the new main line of resistance, with *PGR126* on the right and *PGR128* on the left. The *I./PGR128* occupied a bridgehead position at Kustany, 3 kilometers northwest of Nemes Bük. The enemy only gradually approached the German main line of resistance.

The enemy attacked with strong infantry forces north of Egregy and forced a penetration in the sector of the *I./PGR126*. There was a danger that the Soviets would penetrate into the wooded area to the northwest. Lacking any other reserves, *Hauptmann* Schroeder attacked with his battalion headquarters, rallied the companies of his battalion back to the front and thus eliminated a pending danger. At 1630 hours, mortars of the *I./PGR128* destroyed a Soviet machine gun and a truck. At 1830 hours, Soviet cavalry attacked the *I./PGR128*, but the enemy force was shattered by fires from the divisional artillery and other heavy weapons.

The "tanker infantry" company attached to the *I./PGR128* was dissolved and its personnel distributed among the other companies of the battalion. At 2300 hours, the division pulled back from the main line of resistance without enemy pressure and motor marched to the new sector on both sides of Zalaapati — Bokahaza; the *I./PGR128* went to Getye.

The new main line of resistance was occupied until 0500 hours on 30 March. The two field-replacement battalions were inserted into the line next to the *I./PGR128*, with the division's field-replacement battalion on the right and the field-replacement battalion of the *79. Infanterie-Division* on the left. After a quiet morning, the enemy fired a few rounds from a mortar on the division's positions. Mortars and the divisional artillery shattered a Soviet concentration east of Kustany.

At 2200 hours, the division moved back again. It occupied positions on the high ground 2.5 kilometers east of Pasca. The enemy did not notice the withdrawal movement.

The *I./PGR128* was designated as the ready reserve behind the main line of resistance. For the first time since the loss of the assault guns at Mano mjr. on 23 March, an armored group of *PR23* was operational under *Major* Fischer. Working day and night, the maintenance company had made five *Panthers*, four *Panzer IV's* two *Jagdpanzer IV's* and one assault gun combat ready.

The division was unable to immediately make use of the armored group, however. It was attached to the *3. Kavallerie-Division*. Soviet motorized formations had advanced far to the west north of the left wing of the division and threatened to interdict the retreat route of the cavalry corps at Csömöder.

Scattered fires from Soviet artillery fell on the positions of the *23. Panzer-Division* in the afternoon. Enemy infantry only felt its way forward hesitantly against the divisional strongpoints.

During the night of 31 March/1 April, the armored group marched through Hahot, Söjtor and Tofej to Gutorfölde, from where it would attack Csömöder the next morning. The infantry disengaged from the main line of resistance at midnight and mounted their combat vehicles at Pacsa to get to the Gutorfölde area behind the armored group. The roads were jammed with trains, refugees and troop elements, so that it was only possible to move forward very slowly. The *I./PGR128* formed the rearguard. On that day, the trains and a portion of the rear-area services of the division crossed the borders of the *Reich*.

At 0800 hours on 1 April, the armored group moved out from Gutorfölde. At Kisiget, just after Ortohaza, two Soviet 7.62cm antitank guns opened fire from the north bank of the Berek into the right flanks of the armored vehicles. One *Panther* was hit. While the lead elements continued to move on, the *Panthers* engaged the antitank guns and silenced them.

In Paka, *Oberleutnant* Quintel, the leader of the armored group, established contact with a Hungarian headquarters. The Hungarians stated that Hungarian forces were in Csömöder. While approaching the village and the bridge over the Berek to its south, the tanks were suddenly engaged at 300 meters by Soviet light antitank guns. The firefight that then started drove numerous Soviets into the streets of Csömöder; there were no Hungarians to be seen far and wide. While numerous *panje* wagons fled to the north, the enemy infantry went into position after its first shock. The antitank guns were shot to pieces, but the two tanks were incapable of attacking the village itself. They placed it under fire with their main guns and machine guns, until an infantry "company" arrived with a *Leutnant* and seven men. The armored vehicles—a *Panzer IV* and an assault gun—moved out to attack with the infantry group, crossed the newly constructed wooden bridge and entered the village. The Soviet infantry positioned there did not show much determination without tank and antitank gun support and pulled back from Csömöder to the north.

At 1600 hours, *PGR128* closed up with the tanks, which were pursuing the Soviets, and advanced as far as the village of Hermyk, 8 kilometers north of Csömöder, where it transitioned to the defense. In the meantime, *PGR126* attacked Kissziget, supported by tank destroyers, and advanced north to the right of *PGR128*.

A patrol from the *3./PGR128* dispatched in the direction of Nova during the night of 1/2 April was turned back by the Soviets. The division received orders to take Nova so as to interdict the Soviet advance route to the southwest. At 0300 hours on 2 April, *PGR128*, reinforced by the two field replacement battalions and a battalion of alpine troops, moved out to attack. After taking Ujhely psz., 1,500 meters south of Nova, the attack bogged down in the face of extensive field fortifications constructed by the Soviets on Hills 238 and 235. The field-replacement battalion from the *79. Infanterie-Division* hung back somewhat, and the division's field-replacement battalion was pressed back somewhat by a Soviet immediate counterattack. Moving out once again, the *I./PGR128* reached the bend in the road 2 kilometers southwest of Nova at 1150 hours. Hill 235 proved impossible to take from the Soviets, who were supported by tanks. The attack also bogged down in front of Hill 238. The alpine troops and the *II./PGR128* moved out to attack again under the personal leadership of *Oberstleutnant* Ruge. Given excellent support by the *II.* and *III./PAR128* (*Major* Brehme), they stormed the hill.

The armored group attacked together with the *II./PGR128*, but it finally bogged down with its remaining five tanks in front of a Soviet blocking position formed by tanks and antitank guns north of Ujhely psz. Any further advance would have meant certain death without having the slightest chance of success.

An intercepted Soviet radio message indicated that the commander at Nova would pay with his head if the defense in that sector were not successful. The village of Nova remained in enemy hands.

The area that had been taken was held during the afternoon against several enemy counterattacks. The enemy fired numerous salvoes on the positions with mortars, antitank guns and tank main guns.

That day, trains elements of the division, particularly those of *PR23*, reached Hohenmauten (Muta), 10 kilometers east of Unterdrauburg.

Enemy forces that had advanced further west of Nova continued to threaten the rear and retreat routes of the division. During the evening of 2 April, it pulled back and occupied a new line of resistance on both sides of Bördöce, with *PGR128* and the field-replacement battalion of the *79. Infanterie-Division* and the division's field-replacement battalion on the left. The division engineers emplaced obstacles in front of the positions. The armored group and the tank destroyers were positioned right behind the main line of resistance as ready reserves.

During the morning of 3 April, the enemy attacked the *I./PGR128* after a heavy artillery preparation. He dislodged the 2nd Company, then the remaining companies from their positions. The penetration was sealed off in an immediate counterattack. However, it was not possible to regain the former main line of resistance against the enemy, who was supported by several tanks.

At 1400 hours, the division disengaged from the enemy and moved through Kerkaiklod and Szecsi-Sziget to the high ground just east of the former Yugoslavian-Hungarian border. The Soviets immediately pursued through Bördöce and engulfed the 15-man-strong *2./PGR128*, which formed the rearguard, in a casualty-intensive fight.

At 1800 hours, the new main line of resistance was occupied by the infantry and the men of the field-replacement battalions.

As part of the general withdrawal movements, the *23. Panzer-Division* was pulled back to a bridgehead position 10 kilometers north and northeast of Muraszerdahely (Mursko Sredisce) late in the morning of 4 April. From positions on the 300-meter-high hills which are in front of the channelized Lendava, the division screened the flow of German forces and refugees across the bridges over the Lendava at Alsolendva (Dolga Lendava) and the bridges over the Mur at Muraszerdahely. The *II./PGR128* was employed to the left of the 1st Battalion; further to the left was the field-replacement battalion from the *79. Infanterie-Division*, which had contact with the *4. Kavallerie-Division*.

The trains, which consisted mostly of *panje* wagons, had great difficulties to overcome in navigating the terrain and did not arrive behind the screening line until four hours later, around 1800 hours. The division pulled further back at 1930 hours after the last columns had crossed the bridges and headed south. The division's engineers blew up all of the canal bridges in the sector and, later on, the bridges over the Mur as well.

The new main line of resistance on the south bank of the Mur was occupied by the infantry around 0300 hours with the right wing positioned east of Muraszerdahely and the left wing at Lapany (Hlapicina).

During the morning of 5 April, the Soviets pushed forward from the north in the direction of the Mur. Other than slight mortar activity on both sides, there was no enemy contact. The armored elements of the division, elements of *PAR128* and *Heeres-Flak-Abteilung 278* marched from the area around Muraszerdahely to the south and, moving through Friedau (Ormoz), reached the area around Vitau, east of Luttenberg. This meant that those elements were in the portion of the *Reich* known as Südsteirmark after the Yugoslavian territory had been dissolved in 1941.

At 1200 hours on that day, the infantry disengaged from their positions on the south bank of the Mur, mounted up on their combat vehicles at Muraszerdahely and, moving via Mura Szt. Marton, reached Luttenberg, where they were resupplied and billeted until early on 6 April.

At 0600 hours on 6 April, *PGR128* moved out and, moving through Eichdorf and Bad Radein, reached Radkersburg. There it crossed the *Reich* borders of 1938 and continued marching in the direction of Dietzen.

Upon reaching the borders of the *Reich*, contact was reestablished between the *2. Panzer-Armee* and the *6. Armee*. Despite the shattering of the Hungarian-German front in the Bakony Woods, which made it possible for the Soviet field armies to advance far to the west, the Soviets did not succeed in catching up with, cutting off and destroying any larger-sized German formation before it reached the borders of the *Reich*.

Final Fighting on the Southeastern Border of the Reich and the Capitulation 7 April to 8 May 1945

While the *23. Panzer-Division* had previously served in foreign countries with the mission of holding territory conquered through offensive operations or defending the sovereignty of states allied with Germany against the Soviet Union, from that point forward it was concerned with the defense of German lands. In addition to defending the German-speaking population of Austria, which was again striving to be independent, there was also the responsibility for thousands of ethnic Germans, who had arrived in Steirmark, which had not been disturbed much by the war to that point, as bombed-out or evacuated refugees.

The enemy was positioned at Radkersburg, right in front of the borders of the *Reich,* with his lead elements. His direction of advance once again threatened the retreat route of the *23. Panzer-Division*. *Panzergrenadier-Regiment 128* prepared for a counterattack the next day. Attached to the regiment as reinforcements were a Hungarian infantry regiment and two repaired *Panthers* from *PR23*.

To the southeast of Radkersburg, *PAA23* covered the arrival of the division and its neighbors in the prepared positions in the vicinity of the *Reich* borders. The former commander of the division, *General der Panzertruppen* von Vormann, had played a considerable role in their expansion in his capacity as the Commander-in-Chief for the Defense of the *Reich* (Southeast).

In addition to the *23. Panzer-Division*, the *14. SS-Waffen-Grenadier-Division (ukrainische Nr. 1)*, the *16. SS-Panzer-Grenadier-Division "Reichsführer SS"* and *Kampfgruppe 44. Infanterie-Division "Hoch- und Deutschmeister"* were attached to the *I. Kavallerie-Korps*. The two *SS* divisions were employed to the right of the *23. Panzer-Division*. The divisional *Kampfgruppe* and the corps' own *3. Kavallerie-Division* and *4. Kavallerie-Division* were on the left or held back as the corps reserve.

Moving out on foot at 0200 hours on 7 April, the infantry reached the assembly area at Zelting. The attack started at 0600 hours. Initially, all went well and the bottom land along the *Reich* border was crossed. It was not until they were just outside of Kaltenbrunn (Vashidegkut) that the companies received strong defensive fires. Several officers were wounded; the losses in noncommissioned officers and enlisted personnel were considerable. The attack forces moved back temporarily and were then put into position just west of Kaltenbrunn.

The attack was called off at 1100 hours; the enemy did not follow. Elements of *Kampfgruppe 44. Infanterie-Division "Hoch- und Deutschmeister"* assumed the main line of resistance. *Panzergrenadier-Regiment 128* moved back to Halbenrain and established billets.

The *I./PGR128* was alerted in the evening that it was to be employed against an enemy penetration at Röhrl, 8 kilometers north of Halbenrain.

Oberst Froben assumed command of *PAR128* from *Oberst* Vogl.

At 0100 hours on 8 April, the *I./PGR128* moved out from Halbenrain on its combat vehicles. After a short while, the vehicles came to a standstill due to a lack of fuel. The men had to continue on foot, moving through Oberpurkla and Hurth to reach Röhrl. The sector given to the battalion was not occupied by the Russians, as had been assumed, but by the reconnaissance battalion of *Kampfgruppe 44. Infanterie-Division "Hoch- und Deutschmeister"*. The battalion assumed responsibility for a broad sector, which became narrower in the course of the day as the rest of the regiment was brought up. The Soviets attacked the positions at 1400 hours, 1545 hours and 2020 hours, but they were turned back each time by the infantry's heavy weapons and *PAR128*.

Panzergrenadier-Regiment 126 took up positions to the right of *PGR128* east of Hurth. At 2300 hours, the main line of resistance at Röhrl was pulled back to the west side of the valley floor. At 0300 hours on 9 April, contact was established to the left with *Aufklärungs-Abteilung 44* with contact on the right unchanged.

While the divisional infantry turned back several attacks north of Radkersburg on 9 April and cleared up penetrations by means of immediate counterattacks, the armored group arrived in Radkersburg as the last element of the division, coming from Unterhansdorf.

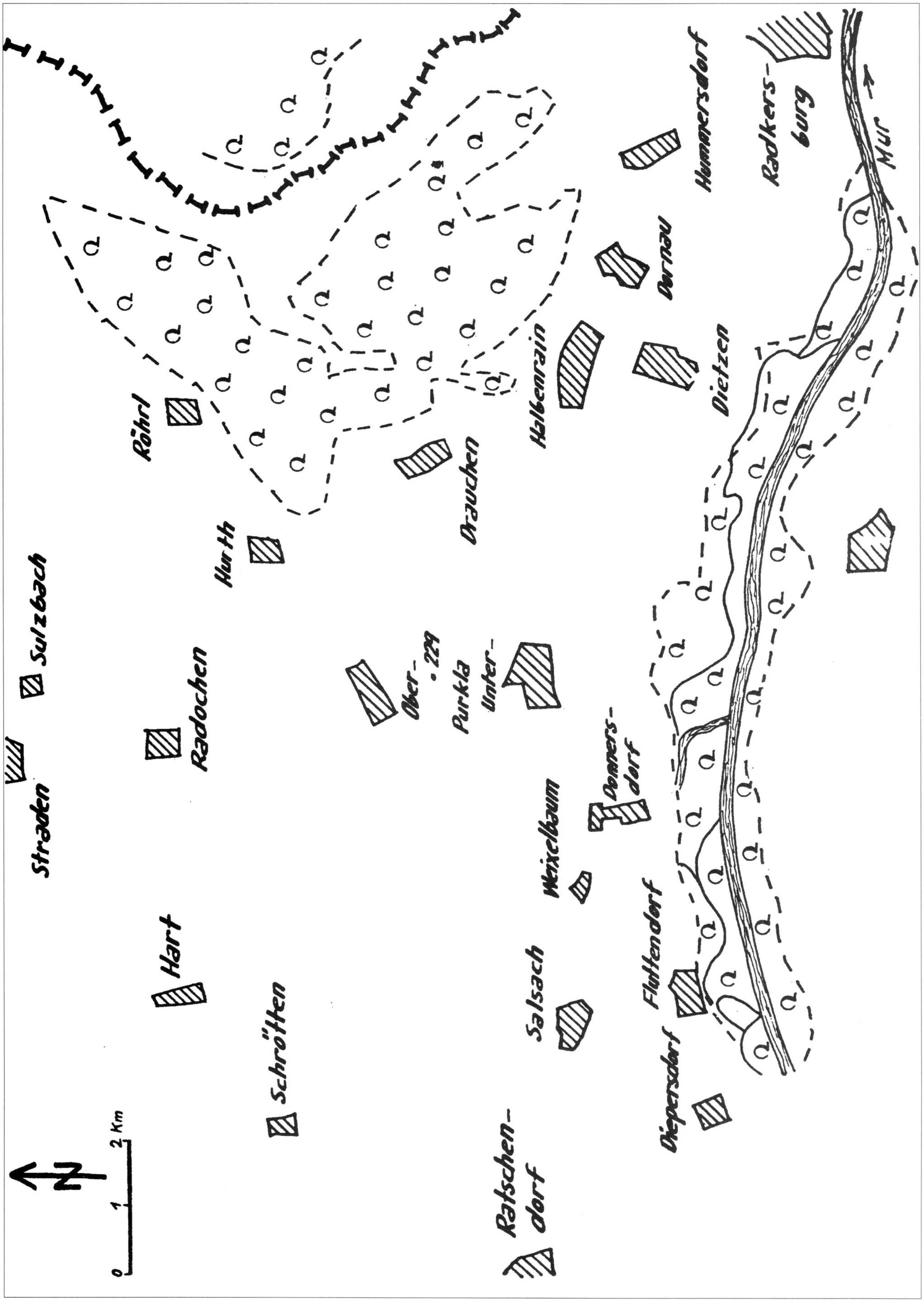

Map 103: The Last Area of Operations of the 23. *Panzer-Division* from 7 April to 8 May 1945.

After the evacuation of large numbers of the populace south of the Mur, including many bombed-out ethnic Germans, the evacuation of Radkersburg was almost complete. *Volkssturm* units[93] were sent to the division by the National Socialist party leadership of Steiermark in Graz. Those persons were either too old or too young, with the result that the division refused to use them at the front and sent the majority of them back home. One company of *Volkssturm* was employed behind each of the infantry regiments to assist in the construction of the second line of defense. A few members of the Hitler Youth were used as messengers but not in the main line of resistance.

The attitude of the local officials toward the division became increasingly unfriendly. The Austrian freedom movement, with its red-white-red banner, became more noticeable.

The enemy fired artillery salvoes on the main line of resistance on 10 April; he had numerous mortars and artillery pieces at his disposal. Soviet infantry penetrated the positions of the *3./PGR128* at 0740 hours. After taking considerable casualties, the trench strength of that company was down to six men. *Oberleutnant* Lintl was killed and two other company commanders were wounded. Any and all available personnel from the trains and the heavy companies were employed as infantry.

At 1045 hours, the enemy penetrated along the boundary on the left to *Aufklärungs-Abteilung 44*. Counterattacks conducted by the heavy companies did not have the desired effect. On the contrary, the enemy attacked from his area of penetration in an enveloping maneuver and forced the infantry to give up several hills during the day. The casualties continued to be high. *Unteroffizier* Meier assumed acting command of the *2./PGR128* after all of the officers were no longer available.

At 1600 hours, elements of the field-replacement battalion of the *79. Infanterie*-Division arrived to reinforce *PGR128*. The planned counterattack did not come to fruition, but the main line of resistance was held. The six men of the 3rd Company were reinforced by the battalion physician, his medical personnel and the battalion's messengers.

After being relieved by parts of the *4. Kavallerie-Division*, *PGR128* went to Drauchen, where the significantly shrunken battalions each consolidated several companies. During the evening of that day, the *2./PGR128* was praised in a division order for its defensive success and bravery.

On 11 April, the division prepared to move the front back to a line running Purkla — Radochen — east of Straden. *Panzergruppe Fischer* prepared for employment as the division's ready reserve at Fluttendorf. *Major* John, the commander of *PR23*, was named the local area commander for Mureck and supported by the regimental headquarters. The trains of the *23. Panzer-Division,* the *3. Kavallerie-Division* and the *4. Kavallerie-Division* were billeted there. His mission was initially to screen the right flank of the division along the banks of the Mur, oriented south. During the evening of 11 April, the infantry regiments, together with the battalions attached to them, occupied positions along the creek coming from Bad Gleichenberg. The right-hand neighbor of the division was the *14. SS-Waffen-Grenadier-Division (1. ukrainische)*, a division that was part of Vlassov's Army. It had elements north of the Mur, but its main body was south of it.

The numerous wounded soldiers of the previous few days were cared for at the main clearing station of the 1st Medical Company at the *Reichsarbeitdienst*[94] Treffling facility, located near Schönberg.

The following formations were employed in the main line of resistance of the division: *PGR126*, the division's field-replacement battalion and *PGR128*. The field-replacement battalion of the *79. Infanterie-Division* was the division reserve, as was *PPB51*. The division's antitank battalion employed tank destroyers in the sector of *PGR126*; towed antitank guns were employed in the sector of *PGR128*. Individual partisan activities began to spring up in the rear area of the division. For instance, a truck belonging to the infantry was engaged with hand grenades, probably thrown by so-called "Austrian Freedom Fighters". Three men were wounded in that attack. To the south of the Mur, in the former Yugoslavian territory, the partisans were considerably more active. Most of them were Yugoslavs who, together with deserters form the Croatian and other foreign forces, as well as Germans, ambushed individual soldiers and vehicles. Unfortunately, there were individual cases of desertion, predominately due to apprehension about being "sacrificed" in this last phase of the war. Whenever such a soldier was caught, there remained nothing left to do but a summary court-martial and execution by firing squad in accordance with military law.

Radkersburg was cleared after all the civilians had been evacuated.

On 12 April, the enemy attacked many times in company strength, with individual tanks in support. In most cases he was turned back, with the well-directed fires of *PAR128*, reinforced by a Hungarian artillery battalion, inflicting considerable casualties on him.

At 1900 hour, a Soviet force broke through *Kampfgruppe 44. Infanterie-Division "Hoch- und Deutschmeister"* on the left. With the exception of a company, which joined up with the *I./PGR128*, the friendly forces on the left were gone. The *3./PAA23* was brought forward to *PGR128* as soon as possible and used to screen the flank.

During the morning of 13 April, the *I./PGR128* occupied a new position south and southwest of Hill 336, which was occupied by *Kampfgruppe 44. Infanterie-Division "Hoch- und Deutschmeister"*. The main line of resistance of the *23. Panzer-Division* was pulled back to Weixelbaum — Oberpurkla — Radochen — Hill 332 — as far as south of Hill 336. The Ukrainian *SS* battalion that was employed to the right of *PGR126* was relieved by the *I./PGR126*, since the *SS* battalion was urgently needed to seal off a Soviet penetration further north.

The bled-white infantry regiments could no longer count on replacements from the home front. As a result, tankers without tanks and gunners without artillery pieces were used to reinforce the regiments.

During the days that followed, the fighting for Hill 336 in the sector of *Kampfgruppe 44. Infanterie-Division "Hoch- und Deutschmeister"* was in the foreground. The hill changed hands several times each day. Employing an assault battalion and cavalry battalions from the *4. Kavallerie-Division*, the hill was always retaken and then reoccupied by *Kampfgruppe 44. Infanterie-Division "Hoch- und Deutschmeister"*. The artillery of the *23. Panzer-Division* fired in general support of the fighting.

On 16 April, Hill 332 was temporarily lost. The enemy was ejected in an immediate counterattack by the *I./PGR128*. One enemy antitank gun, two heavy machine guns, several light machine guns and an antitank rifle were captured. The division's armored group, which was positioned behind the left wing of the division at Straden, did not need to be employed. *Oberleutnant* Quintel assumed command of the remaining operational tanks. *Hauptmann* Kujacinski came from the trains area around Znaim with cadre personnel from two companies and relieved *Major* Fischer, who then went to Unterdrauburg as the leader of the trains and the freed-up tank crews. A new-equipment detail form the regiment went to St. Valentin, near Linz, to pick up new *Panthers* from the factory.

At 1600 hours on 17 April, Hill 332 was lost one more time. In a counterattack, one battalion from the *4. Kavallerie-Division* threw the enemy back the following night. In order to screen the left flank of the division, a platoon from the field-replacement battalion of the *79. Infanterie-Division* was positioned west of Point 336.

93 Editor's Note: = People's Storm (literally). These were last-ditch units composed of otherwise militarily unqualified males (too young, too old, too infirm etc.)

94 Editor's Note: = *RAD* = *Reich* Labor Service, a paramilitary organization, which worked on infrastructure projects for the German government, using young men just prior to their induction to military service.

Soviet combat patrols attacked several times in the sector of *PGR126*, but they were turned back. Combat activity continued to wane in the days that followed. The situation was marked by patrolling to capture prisoners and by mortar salvoes. Every soldier knew the end of the war was not too far distant. The Soviets continued to reinforce their positions, emplacing wire obstacles and "Spanish Riders".

A sudden advance by Soviet infantry dislodged the right-wing company of the *I./PGR126* from its positions along the Mur marshes on 20 April. The main line of resistance was reoccupied after an immediate counterattack, without having to call upon the artillery or the armored group.

An assault-gun brigade under the command of *Major* Berg was attached to the division.

Two armored trains were employed along the railway line between Mureck and Weixelbaum during that period; they were attached to *PAR128*. They moved back and forth at a distance of 2 kilometers from one another. They played an important role in the firing plans of the divisional artillery.

After losing the last of its tank destroyers, the *1./PJA128* was equipped with bicycles and *Panzerfäuste* and reorganized as a *Panzer-Zerstörer-Kompanie,*[95] but it was never employed as such. The slowing down of combat activities along the front was used by the division to increase its combat power through the maintenance and overhaul of weapons and equipment. The maintenance companies played a significant role in these efforts. The division was also successful in incrementally pulling individual companies out of the lines for rest. The divisional military police section was employed in evacuating the civilian populace behind the front lines.

On 30 April, the *I./PGR128* relieved elements of *Reiter-Regiment 41* of the *4. Kavallerie-Division* at Point 336. Later on, the regiment's 2nd Battalion relieved the 1st Battalion. Combat activities continued to remain minor. Both sides succeeded in taking prisoners with patrols.

At the end of April, the Americans took Linz after advancing downstream along the Danube from Passau. Both *Heeresgruppe Süd* and the *6. Armee* attempted to find out from the Americans whether the defensive fighting against the Soviets could be continued until all the refugees and the armies in the field could be deliberately pulled back to the border of the *Reich* or a passage line. The contact with the Americans was intended to allow all of the logistics from the Munich area intended for the divisions fighting on the Eastern Front to continue to flow through the American lines.

The Chief-of-Staff of the *6. Armee*, *Generalmajor* Gaedke, was given that mission after the Americans had taken the Commander-in-Chief of *Heeresgruppe Süd, Generaloberst* Rendulic, and his staff prisoner. *Generalleutnant* von Radowitz was ordered to Gleisdorf, 24 kilometers east of Graz, to the headquarters of the *6. Armee*. The Americans turned down all separate negotiations with the Germans, however.

Based on the general situation, the field army issued the following orders:

1. During the afternoon of 8 May, capitulation negotiations were to be conducted with the enemy forces that the formation faced.

2. Any and all movements were forbidden starting at midnight 8 May.

While all of this was going on, the fighting at the front continued. Both sides employed snipers to a large extent. An assault-detachment operation conducted by the *I./PGR126* was successful and one Red Army soldier was taken prisoner.

The tankers and artillerymen employed within the ranks of the infantry regiments acquitted themselves well. The discipline among the forces in the field was good, despite the fact that everyone was aware of the impending end of the war and its conclusion. The attitude of the officers and noncommissioned officers remained unchanged, a sign of the tight bonds of comradeship that held all members of the division together.

In Unterdrauburg and Hohenmauten (Muta), *Major* Fischer and his cadre units of the *II./PR23* and the trains were alerted. He was initially given the mission of screening the corps rear area against partisans. After eight days of infantry training, the battalion formed three companies, which then wrested high ground south of Unterdrauburg and Hohenmauten from Yugoslavian partisans. At the same time, they screened in the Drau Valley against Soviet and Soviet-Bulgarian forces advancing from the east.

On 8 May, the news of the unconditional capitulation of the German Armed Forces on all fronts was announced on the radio. The Soviets in front of the division's sector fired jubilantly in the air with all of their weapons.

Knowing what was to be expected in the event the personnel of the division were taken prisoner by the Soviets, it was decided to pull back within the time allotted to try to lead the division's elements into British captivity.

While preparations were being made for the dispatching of parliamentarians within the division headquarters, the enemy attacked *PGR128*. He was turned back, in part, in front of the division sector, but he was able to penetrate along the boundary with the division's field-replacement battalion. The penetration was cleaned up by means of an immediate counterattack. It was vitally imperative at that point that the enemy be deceived with regard to the division's intention and that sufficient distance be maintained between friend and foe in the main line of resistance.

Major Fischer was designated by *Heeresgruppe E* (Commander-in-Chief Southeast) as the local area commander for Unterdrauburg. He was given the mission of screening a number of withdrawal movements: The *68. Infanterie-Division*, the *71. Infanterie-Division* and the *118. Jäger-Division* from the east along the Drau to Lavamünd; in addition, von Pannwitz' Cossack Division and the *13. SS-Gebirgs-Division "Handschar"* from the south through Unterdrauburg to Lavamünd. In Mureck, where the elements of the *PR23* that had been resting in Znaim had arrived in the meantime, a train arrived with 17 new *Panzer IV's* for the division. The tanks remained on the rail cars; the breechblocks and the gun optics were removed and tossed into the Mur. The engine oil was then drained and the motors run until the pistons froze.

Armored reconnaissance patrols from the *1./PAA23* moved out to the northwest with English-speaking officers on board. They scouted the possible departure routes designated by the division command and sought contact with the British, who were assumed to be approaching from upper Italy. No one knew where their lead elements were. No contact with anyone could be established, so the division was on its own in pulling back from the Soviets in the hope that it would not be handed over to them by the Western Allies later on.

Major Lenberger, who was assigned to *PGR126* and who had been with the division since it had been formed in 1941, received the mission of acting as a parliamentarian with the Soviets. He was directed to receive the capitulation conditions for the *23. Panzer-Division* from the headquarters of the Soviet 56th Army and arrange for a 10-hour ceasefire.

Nobody knew how the Soviets would react to the parliamentarian with the white flag. As a precautionary measure, the division ordered a barrage of artillery fire and an attack along the entire frontage, if *Major* Lenberger had not returned within a certain time.

Major Lenberger crossed the main line of resistance in the sector of the *2./PGR126*. Upon his crossing, the division issued orders not to fire. The parliamentarian was taken via Unterpurkla to the Soviet headquarters. Once there, he proposed a 10-hour ceasefire, which the Soviets accepted.

95 Editor's Note: = Tank Destroyer Company.

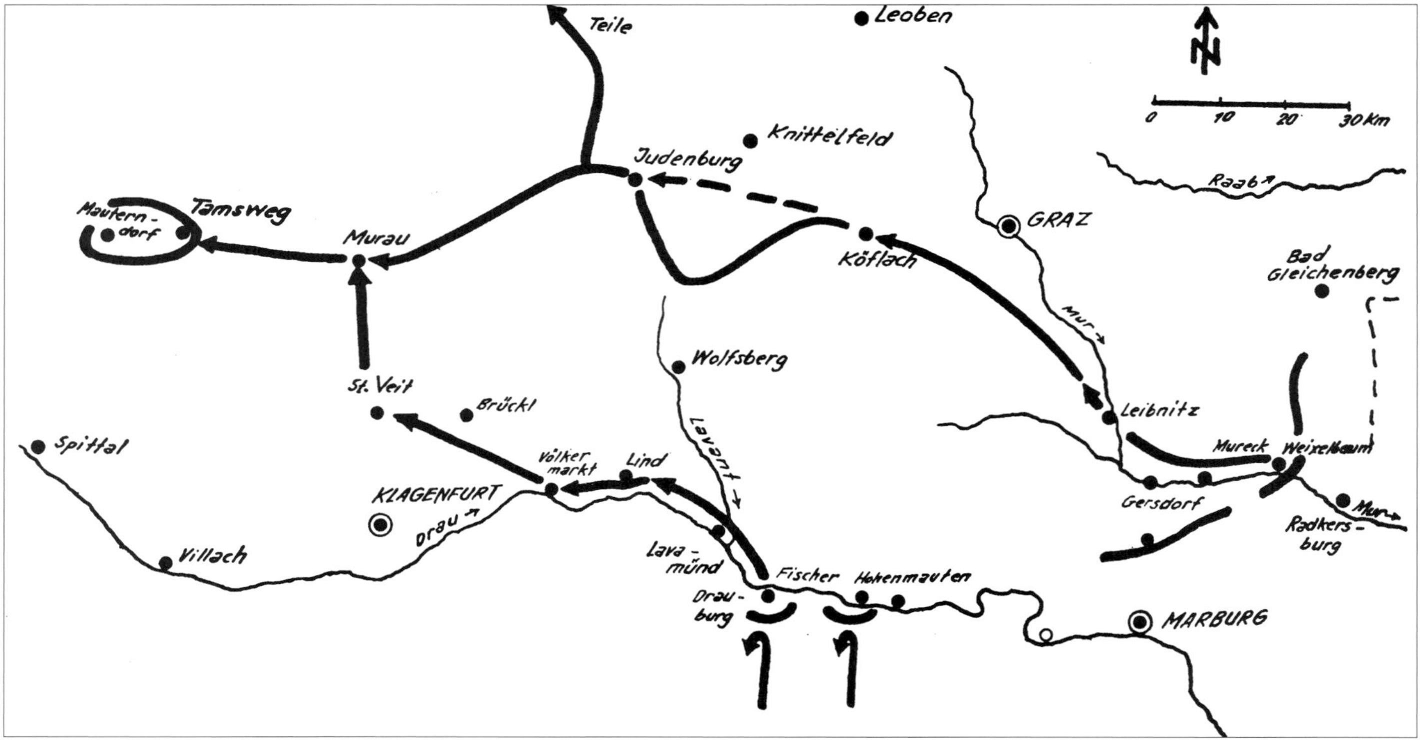

Map 104: The Route of the *23. Panzer-Division* Into British Captivity, 8-12 May 1945.

During the negotiations with *Major* Lenberger, there was a tragic event in the sector of the *2./PGR126*. Shortly after he had moved through the lines with a white flag, numerous Soviets came forward, some without weapons. They brought with them bottles of *schnapps* so as to celebrate the apparent end of the war by fraternizing with the German infantry. Due to the orders not to fire, they could not turn them back with weapons. Yelling and gesticulating with joy, they put their arms around the German soldiers and took about 20 of them with them to their trenches, whether they wanted to or not. Later on, those unfortunate men were taken to the Soviet command post in Unterpurkla and made prisoners. *Major* Lenberger saw them sitting there on his way back to the German lines without being able to help them.

In the meantime, the agreed-upon time limit for the return of *Major* Lenberger had almost passed. Everyone was waiting for his return with baited breath, and the last preparations for an attack were made. Tanks and *SPW's* of the ready reserve in Fluttendorf moved out and sent the Soviets running around in the sector of the *2./PGR128* scurrying back to their positions with short bursts of fire. The salvoes of the artillery and the heavy weapons started; at the same moment, however, *Major* Lenberger arrived in Weixelbaum.

He brought along the agreement to have a ceasefire go into effect starting at 2200 hours and the order that the division was to form up on the Unterpurkla — Oberpurkla road at 0800 hours on 9 May with a list of names of personnel. Separate collection points were designated for officers and noncommissioned officers. Finally, the Soviets guaranteed good treatment.

In the hours that followed, the division made preparations for its departure in as inconspicuous a manner as possible. Orders arrived from the *I. Kavallerie-Korps* that the division was not only to cover its own withdrawal, but that of the neighboring *Kampfgruppe 44. Infanterie-Division "Hoch- und Deutschmeister"* and the *4. Kavallerie-Division* to the north. Those two divisions could only pull back by first swinging south to get out of the mountainous terrain.

Only light weapons and rations for 14 days were allowed to be taken. Any and all baggage had to remain behind.

During the evening, all heavy weapons in the positions were rendered inoperable, with the gun optics and breechblocks being thrown into the Mur. Just before the ceasefire took effect, the remaining ammunition was fired off. In the case of the tanks and the self-propelled howitzers, the engines were destroyed by running them without oil and freezing the pistons. Only the divisional reconnaissance battalion retained all of its weapons and equipment. All of the remaining *SPW's*, observation vehicles, radio vehicles and field ambulances remained with their respective formations.

Just before 2200 hours, *PAA23* moved into the main line of resistance for the entire division with all of its *SPW's* and armored cars to cover the disengagement of the infantry. The divisional engineers placed demolition parties at all of the crossings in the division sector. While the remaining ammunition was fired off just prior to 2200 hours and the engines of the *SPW's* warmed up, the infantry pulled back under the curtain of noise and marched to their combat vehicles so as to reach the start points designated by the division at precisely the right minute. Preceding them were the crews of the heavy armored vehicles of the division and *PAR128*. Only the remaining three tank destroyers of *PJA128* remained in their sector so as to provide the reconnaissance personnel a back-up, if needed.

Everything was quiet in the enemy's sector, with the result that *PAA23* was also able to pull back at 2300 hours. The tank destroyers were driven together on the bridge over the Mur to form an obstacle; the vehicles were also rendered inoperable.

Kampfgruppe Fischer, after completing its mission, held its positions in Unterdrauburg until the evening of 8 May. An offer to be disarmed by the Yugoslavians was refused. During the evening of 8 May, Bulgarian forces attacked those positions from the east, but they were turned back. During the night, Fischer's battle group pulled back to Lavamünd, where it established contact with British forces. Continuing to march on via Lind, the battle group encountered an obstacle erected by Yugoslavian partisans in Völkermarkt. Employing two *SPW's* and a four-barreled 2cm *Flak*, the resistance was soon broken.

The main body of the division marched via Leitring, Wildon, Zwaring, Berndorf, Köflich and Twimberg to Judenburg. The horse-drawn columns marched via Salla to Judenburg. During the march, the division constantly received wild rumors about a Soviet breakthrough at Leoben which kept the soldiers uncertain as to whether the withdrawal would succeed. As a result of those rumors, valuable documents concerning the last phase of the division's fighting were destroyed. Most of the division moved through that city on 9 May. A panic ensued at Salla as the result of one of those rumors, which caused the loss of numerous horse-drawn wagons.

Hauptmann Schulz' *PAA23*, serving as the rearguard, moved back incrementally during the morning of 9 May. The *2.* and *3./PAA23* (*Oberleutnant* Keck and *Oberleutnant* Hain), as well as the last elements of *PPB51*, did not arrive in Wildon until 0300 hours. An assault-gun brigade and the *I./Flak-Regiment 8*, which joined up with the divisional elements there, were sent on ahead with the reconnaissance soldiers and combat engineers continuing to follow. The rearguard lost radio contact with the division and had to act on its own initiative. While that was happening, the *Freiheitssender Österreich*[96] was stirring up the populace and the Austrian militia to disarm the German Armed Forces.

At Twinberg, south of Judenburg, the lead elements of the division encountered the British approaching from the southwest. After somewhat lengthy negotiations, the division was allowed to continue its march. The soldiers of the division breathed easier for the first time.

The Soviets were surprised by the disengagements of the German divisions in most of the sectors. In the area of the *23. Panzer-Division*, they did not discover the division was gone until it had crossed the Kor mountain range, southwest of Graz.

On 9 and 10 May, ground-support aircraft (IL-2-s) attacked the German columns. Fortunately, there weren't any large losses. The rearguard was also attacked by them, after they had passed the British outposts on the pass between Unzmarkt and Scheifling. In the end, the Soviets were driven away by British fighters, which were flying intercept missions along the demarcation line. Between 10 and 12 May, the division marched via Murau and Tamsweg into the area designated by the British for its internment, which was located between Tamsweg and Mauterndorf. The remaining elements of the *I. Kavallerie-Korps* had reached the area ahead of the *23. Panzer-Division*.

Because of a mistake, the cadre units of the *I./PR23*, the divisional post office and the 1st Medical Company marched from Judenburg via the Tauern Pass and Trieben to Liezen/Enns. On the other hand, the *II./PR23* under *Major* Fischer reached the internment area of the division with all of the trains of the regiment. The elements that went to Liezen were able to cross the river there to the north ahead of the Soviets, who were advancing in the Enns Valley. They were then interned by the Americans. After a short halt on 9 May, they were directed via the Pyhrn Pass and Gmunden/Traunsee to Mauerkirchen, south of Braunau.

Scattered personnel of the division also joined this group, which grew to 2,000 men. Among them, for instance, was the new-equipment detail, which had picked up 10 new *Panzer V's* for *PR23* at the Nibelungenwerk in St. Valentin, 40 kilometers southeast of Linz. Road marching to the front, the detail was surprised by the news of the capitulation. It turned around and, moving through Knittelfeld and Zeltweg in the Mur Valley, reached the Judenburg area. The group marched along with the *I./PR23* to Liezen/Enns, where the new tanks were turned over to the Americans.

The horse-drawn trains of the 2nd Medical Company fell into Soviet hands. The company itself marched to Radstadt and Markt Pongau and was then moved to Bad Aibling on 25 May.

With all of its equipment, *PAA23* arrived at the bridge over the Mur at Tamsweg on 12 May. Its pass-in-review in front of *Generalleutnant* von Radowitz and the commanders of the troop elements signaled the completion of the assembly of the division in the Tamsweg — Mauterndorf area.

***

On that occasion, the division commander had the following order-of-the-day issued:

Comrades of the *23. Panzer-Division*!

> Never defeated on the battlefield, the division, in accordance with its orders, had to lay down its arms today, arms with which it honorably defended the fatherland to the very end. It is a pressing need for me in this difficult hour to express my thanks to you for the superhuman performance you have shown all times.
>
> My unshakeable decision not to let the division fall into the hands of the Russians has been achieved. We have turned ourselves over to the authority of the English. They have promised that a transfer to the Russians is out of the question.
>
> I have reason to believe that we will be demobilized in a proper manner after we have reached the homeland. To that end, I request of you that you—despite everything—complete the last portion of this difficult mission and continue to help out just as properly as you have fought this last war, with a proud demeanor and a clean conscience.
>
> Discharge notices, which had been made out to cover you in the case of Russian actions, are no longer valid. Whoever still feels he had been discharged no longer has the right to travel with my division and take food away from soldiers with a proper attitude.
>
> Whoever attempts to get home by himself more quickly than we do will land up in a prisoner-of-war camp as a deserter.
>
> If you demonstrate your old discipline, then you will receive honor and the respect of our people.

Long live Germany, our fatherland.

/signed/ von Radowitz

***

The British command had decided in the meantime not to turn over the divisions of the *I. Kavallerie-Korps* to the Soviets. Instead, it would send them as quickly as possible to Germany to be demobilized by the Americans.

In general, the British were quite friendly and accommodating. The disarming that occurred on 10 May by a Canadian armored reconnaissance battalion was done in a conspicuously proper manner, and the British commander of Mauterndorf, Major Mountjoy of the 5th Northampton Regiment, always proved to be ready to help.

Like the cavalry divisions and *Flak-Regiment 563*, which had entered the area in the same disciplined manner, the *23. Panzer-Division* had to ensure there was a distinct boundary around its area to separate it apart from the numerous soldiers from other troop units that were filtering through. The officers kept their pistols and every regiment was granted 20 rifles for guard and security duties. The personnel of the division, who had to be identifiable by their papers and the division's symbol—an arrow—worn on the upper left arm, were allowed to move freely within the internment area. This, many soldiers were able to take hikes to the nearby mountains. Some of the "flatlanders" were able to see the world from above for the first time. In addition to the maintenance of equipment and

96 Editor's Note: = "Freedom Station Austria". This was an underground radio station.

personal hygiene, the daily routine was enriched by presentations of a general educational nature, sports and riding tournaments.

An order issued by the British 78th Division protected the *I. Kavallerie-Korps* and *Flak-Regiment 563* from arbitrary confiscation of armed forces materiel by Britons and Americans. The troop elements were allowed to have a limited number of radios; all privately owned radios, all cameras and military watches, typewriters and mimeograph machines had to be turned in.

On 17 May, all of the roads over the passes to the north and west were completely jammed. A movement of the division proved to be out of the question at that time.

As early as 18 May, discharges were started by the Americans for the soldiers of the *I./PR23* and other members of the division who were interned at Mauerkirchen (Upper Austria). By 5 June, only 87 men were still interned of the original almost 2,000. By 9 June, the discharges were completed.

Portions of the 1st Medical Company went from Liezen via Radstadt to the St. Johann POW Camp in the Pon District. From there, they went to Klein-Elsterdorf near Tölz at the end of May. They set up a local clearing station at Weihen-Linden. At the beginning of June, they were discharged.

Starting on 21 May, the division sent clean-up details out along the Mauterndorf — Tamsweg road to clean up the agricultural areas, roads and trails of vehicular wrecks and rubble. *Panzer-Regiment 23* assumed responsibility for feeding and caring for a camp composed of civilians, mostly those who had been bombed out of their homes in Germany. The medical personnel set up a clearing station in Mauterndorf for the division.

The divisional engineers were employed in road work outside of the internment area and went to the work places daily by vehicle.

Contact with the local populace became increasingly friendly. The soldier's discipline and readiness to help garnered a great deal of respect.

By an order dated 25 May, soldiers who were no longer wanted in the units for disciplinary reasons could be transferred to the British administrative headquarters in Mauterndorf, where they would then be turned over to a POW camp, where they lost any privileges associated with being interned.

The departure of the divisions was delayed several times because of difficulties on the part of the US 7th Army. Austrians, Alsatians, Poles and soldiers of other nationalities were gradually pulled out of the internment camp and sent to a British discharge camp.

After direct negotiations with the Americans in Zell am See, the Americans declared they would allow the division to use its own vehicles to transport its soldiers to the designated discharge area around Aalen (Wuertemberg). That effort failed, however, after the British resisted, stating that the vehicles of the division were spoils of war.

By 14 June 1945, the negotiations had proceeded to the point where the division was at least allowed to use its vehicles to cross the Tauern Pass to Radstadt, where it would board trains. The vehicles had to return across the Tauern Pass, however. The drivers were soldiers the British had already enlisted as workers and therefore did not desire to be discharged at Aalen. Most of them were men who came from areas occupied by the Soviets or no longer had any immediate family. Many Austrians from the portion of their country that was occupied by the Soviets were also among them.

Formations were held to say farewell and joined the members of the regiments, divisional troop elements, battalions and companies together again one last time.

The Battalion Surgeon of the I./PR 23, Stabsarzt Dr. Amann, together with Oberleutnant Schreiber, the commander of the 1./PR 23, at the Fehervarcsurgo Palace.

In disciplined march columns, led by their officers and escorted by only a few Allied vehicles, the division rolled past the British general who had shown up for its departure on 15 June. The column moved from Mauterndorf through the Tauern Pass at Radstadt to Radstadt. On 16 June, the journey continued by train through Zell am See, Munich and Augsburg to Günzburg and Gundelfingen. Only the field kitchens and the motorcycles were allowed to accompany the trains. The trucks and staff cars returned to Mauterndorf.

On 17 June, trucks of the US Army picked up the personnel at the debarkation train stations and took them—packed like sardines in a can—to the discharge area of Aalen — Wasseralfingen, where they were enthusiastically greeted by the civilians with flowers and cigarettes. The discharges for the noncommissioned officers and enlisted personnel started immediately in the Swabian foundries and the former training facility for cavalry horses.

On 23 June, the officers and headquarters were discharged. Only *Generalleutnant* von Radowitz, *Major i.G.* Schumm and the division's military judge, *Dr.* Bornemann, were retained. At that point, trucks of the US Army took all of the discharged to places throughout the country, where each of the individual soldiers had indicated earlier that he wanted to go. Either by group or individually, the soldiers then went on home or—in the case of many, who came from areas that were in the Soviet Zone—initially to the house of an old comrade. Some of them, who returned home in the French Zone, were dealt the hard blow of captivity again, with transport to France and hard work for a long time. Years would go by before those comrades—and especially the ones in the Soviet Union—would return to their homeland. Difficult personal persecution would greet many in the first years of their return home, if they were ethnic Germans from Luxembourg, Alsace or Eupen-Malmédy, who had joined the division and even become noncommissioned officers and officers.

But nothing could let the shared experiences of the war years let them forget and destroy their pride in having done their duty in a good division as an honest, upright soldier.

May 1945, capitulation in Austria. Note the "divisional insignia" that the British had members of the division wear on their upper right sleeve is visible on some of the officers.

May 1945: Scenes from the period of internment in the Steiermark Area of Austria.

Hauptmann Rompel, *Hauptmann* Putrafki, *Leutnant* Maly.

Eichel joins the group.

The Kärnten region of Austria in May 1945.

The collection point in the Mauterndorf area.

Personal hygiene and maintenance of clothing and equipment fills the time.

Officers of *PGR 126*: *Oberst* John, the regimental commander (4th from the left), and *Hauptmann Rompel*, commander of the *II./PGR 126* (5th from left).

Four *Leutnante* of *PGR 126*: Gültig, Petereit, Manke and Höhner.

Hauptmann Röder, *Major* Veigel, *Leutnant* Knorr (Division Headquarters).

Major i.G. von Gilow, *Hauptmann* Röder, *Leutnant* Knorr.

The release camp at Aalenin June 1945: *Oberleutnant* Braun and *Hauptmann* Petrafki.

The capitulation in May 1945 in the Tamsweg — Mauterndorf area of Austria. The British mandated "divisional insignia" is even more evident in this photo.

Appendices

Appendix 1
The Formations of the 23. Panzer-Division
Headquarters, 23. Panzer-Division

During the first few days of October 1941 in Paris, the headquarters of *Panzer-Brigade 101*, which had been commanded by *Oberst* Elster and was composed of *Panzer-Regiment 203* and *Panzer-Regiment 204*, was redesignated and reorganized as Headquarters, *23. Panzer-Division*. Missing personnel were supplied through personnel levies from Military District V in Stuttgart.

Added to the division headquarters was a cartography section—*Divisions-Kartenstelle 128*—which was established by Military District III in Berlin on 10 December 1941 as per orders dated 22 November 1941 from the *OKH, Chef H Rüst und BdE*[97]. The personnel came from the *III.(Verm.Lehr- u. Ers)/Artillerie-Lehr-Regiment (mot.) 3*[98].

Headquarters, Schützen-Brigade 23 (later: Panzergrenadier-Brigade 23)

The formation of a Headquarters, *Schützen-Brigade 23* was directed by orders issued by the German Army High Command on 15 October 1941. Responsible for the execution of the order was Military District V in Stuttgart.[99]

The brigade headquarters was activated in Ludwigsburg and filled with personnel levies from *Schützen-Ersatz-Bataillon (mot.) 86*. *Oberst* von Heydebrand und der Lasa was designated as the brigade commander.

At the beginning of November 1941, the headquarters was moved to Paris and integrated into the *23. Panzer-Division*. The replacement detachment for the brigade headquarters was the aforementioned *Schützen-Ersatz-Bataillon (mot.) 86* in Ludwigsburg.

Panzer-Regiment 201 (later: Panzer-Regiment 23)

On 19 November 1940, the German Army High Command ordered the establishment of *Panzer-Regiment 201* (*OKH, Chef H Rüst und BdE*) to assume responsibility for the French armored vehicles captured in the French Campaign and make them capable of operational deployment for the German Armed Forces.

The activation of the regiment started on 1 December 1940 under the responsibility of Military District V in Stuttgart. After examining several possibilities for the home base for the new formation, the new regimental commander, *Oberstleutnant* Conze, decided in favor of the Mortier Garrison in Paris (Porte des Lilas).

Oberstleutnant Conze soon departed due to illness, and he was replaced by *Oberst* Werner-Ehrenfeucht. The commanders of the two battalions were *Major* von Heydebreck and *Hauptmann* Wolff. Cadres units from several tank regiments and replacement detachments from Military Districts IV, V, VI, VII and VIII arrived in December. They formed the regimental headquarters and two tank battalions, each of which had three line companies. On 11 December a regimental headquarters company and two battalion headquarters companies were established. The personnel for those entities came from Military Districts V and XIII.

On 13 December, the first French tanks—Type 35 Somuas and Type 38 Hotchkiss—were issued. Wheeled vehicles were taken from stocks of vehicles captured from the French, the Belgians and the British. Small arms were issued from captured French stocks. For logistical supply purposes, the regiment was attached to the *16. Infanterie-Division (mot.)* around the turn of the year.

At the time, the Armed Forces High Command was preparing for operations against Gibraltar. Since *Panzer-Regiment 201* could not be operationally ready for the planned timeline of the operation, the German Army High Command ordered the establishment of a *Panzer-Abteilung 301* on 15 January 1941. The battalion, under *Hauptmann* Mildebrath, consisted of a headquarters, a headquarters company and three line companies. To that end, the *3. Panzer-Division* provided one tank company from its *Panzer-Regiment 5*, two tank companies from its *Panzer-Regiment 6*. *Panzer-Regiment 201* was charged with establishing the headquarters company. In an extremely short period, the battalion, which was stationed at the former French Air Force Ministry in Paris—*Place Ballard*—was made operational, using equipment from *Panzer-Regiment 201*. The Commander-in-Chief of the German Army, *Generalfeldmarschall* von Brauchitsch, visited *Panzer-Abteilung 301* on 11 February 1941 and expressed great praise for the work it had done in getting activated.

For political reasons, the Gibraltar operation was not executed. *Panzer-Abteilung 301* remained under the administrative control of *Panzer-Regiment 201* in Paris.

In January 1941, the establishment of a second tank regiment using captured French tanks was started. Using *Panzer-Regiment 201* as a model, *Panzer-Regiment 202* was formed and, on 1 March 1941, both regiments were placed under the command and control of *Panzer-Brigade 100*. The new brigade was commanded by *Generalmajor* Haarde, using the headquarters from the former *8. Panzer-Brigade*.

On 7 March 1941, the German Army High Command ordered the establishment of *Panzer-Abteilung 211* for employment in Norway. The battalion was to be formed from *Panzer-Regiment 201*. To that end, the headquarters of the 2nd Battalion, along with the 4th and 6th Companies, were reassigned to the new formation. *Hauptmann* Wolff was designated the commander.

To replace the reassigned elements, *Panzer-Abteilung 301* was consolidated with *Panzer-Regiment 201* on 22 March 1941 and redesignated as its 2nd Battalion. The 5th Company of the former battalion was reassigned to the 1st Battalion.

For the time being, *Panzer-Abteilung 211* remained under the administrative control of *Panzer-Regiment 201* and sharpened its combat readiness with French equipment. On 25 April 1941, the battalion was

---

97 Editor's Note = *Chef Heeres-Rüstung und Befehlshaber des Ersatzheeres* = Chief of Army Armament and Commander of the Replacement Army. This was the umbrella organization that was responsible, among other things, for force-structure issues and determined tables of organization and equipment and issued orders for the activation, reorganization, consolidation and deactivation of the forces in the field and on the home front.

98 Editor's Note = *Vermischtes Lehr- und Ersatz-Bataillon* = Instructional and Replacement Battalion (Mixed).

99 Editor's Note: In the original German it is listed as *Wehrkreiskommando und Stellvertretendes General-Kommando V. Armee-Korps*. Corps were based geographically in the German Army. They were responsible for military affairs in the district they were stationed (*Wehrkreiskommando*) and also had a rear-area headquarters when the war-fighting corps headquarters was deployed in the field (*Stellvertretendes General-Kommando*). For simplicity, only the military district will be mentioned when reference is made to these entities.

allocated to the field army headquarters in Norway and left Paris by train. It later went to Salla, in Finland.

During the course of April and May 1941, the former 5th Tank Company, which had been redesignated as the 7th Tank Company, was issued the 32-ton French heavy tank, the B 2 (Renault). The company was detached from the regiment and, with another tank company that had the same equipment from *Panzer-Regiment 202*, was consolidated to form *Panzer-Abteilung (f) 102* on 4 June 1941. That battalion was later employed in the assault on Przemysl at the end of June 1941.

In May, the battalions established engineer platoons and light columns. The armored maintenance platoons that had been established in the meantime were consolidated to form an armored maintenance company.

Irrespective of the turmoil caused by the activations and reorganizations, *Panzer-Regiment 201* accomplished its mission. The French tanks were checked by means of extensive driving and firing tests, and were being tested for the effects of enemy fires upon them. Their weaponry was changed and they were modified. They received radio sets and were further modified to correspond to German tactical requirements. The regiment's companies conducted training at the Vincennes Training Area, located near the gates of Paris. Firing exercises were conducted up to platoon level at ranges at Mer du Sable. On 15 May 1941, *Panzer-Ersatz-Abteilung 100* was formed in Schwetzingen from personnel provided by both *Panzer-Regiment 201* and *Panzer-Regiment 202*. At the same time, the new replacement battalion was designated as the replacement detachment for the two regiments.

Over the course of several weeks during the summer, battalion, regiment and even brigade-level training was conducted at the large training area of Mailly le Camp, as well as at Suippes. Combined arms exercises with artillery and infantry, as well as *Luftwaffe* support, were conducted. At the same time, the cadres for the newly forming *Panzer-Regiment 203* and *Panzer-Regiment 204* were trained. *Panzer-Regiment 203* later became a general headquarters formation, which later provided a battalion to *Panzer-Regiment "Großdeutschland"* and to *Panzer-Regiment 1*. *Panzer-Regiment 204* was later part of the *22. Panzer-Division*. Rumanian armor officers were also trained.

Generalfeldmarschall von Witzleben and *Generaloberst* von Blaskowitz visited the regiment. The latter general officer especially emphasized formation training.

Having barely returned to Paris, the regiment had to be employed as a consequence of the activities of the resistance movements, which had flared up. The regimental headquarters and the 1st Battalion were sent to Belgium in the Mons — Charleroi area, while the 2nd Battalion went to the Bretage — Carhaix (east of Brest) area. Both groups were involved in security missions and anti-partisan warfare operations.

On 1 August 1941, the *7./PR23* was converted to an antitank company with self-propelled antitank guns. *Panzer-Regiment 201* provided 50% of the personnel with the rest coming from antitank elements of the *1. Armee*.

Starting in October the regiment began converting to the long-awaited German equipment, which was a harbinger of upcoming employment on the Eastern Front.

On 12 December 1941, *Generalmajor* von Boineburg-Lengsfeld accepted *Panzer-Regiment 201* into the framework of the *23. Panzer-Division* at a parade at the Polygon on *Avenue Viktor*.

On 23 December, the conversion to *Panzer II's, III's* and *IV's* by the regiment was completed. At the same time, the *7.(PzJäg)/Panzer-Regiment 201* was converted to a light tank company. The likewise converted sister company from *Panzer-Regiment 202* was incorporated into *Panzer-Regiment 201* as its 3rd Company. The light columns of the two battalions were reassigned to the division's logistics command to be a part of the division's supply columns. The regimental maintenance company received a third platoon.

The German Army High Command issued orders for the formation of a 3rd Battalion for the regiment on 2 February 1942. The *I./Panzer-Regiment 201* provided its 3rd Tank Company and the 2nd Battalion its 7th Tank Company. The headquarters company and the *12./Panzer-Regiment 201* were formed from personnel levies provided by *Panzer-Ersatz-Abteilung 100* in Schwetzingen and Military District IX in Kassel. The battalion, under the command of *Major* Illig, occupied billets in the Dupleix Barracks in Paris.

At the same time, the other elements of the regiment underwent winter and gunnery training with their new equipment at the La Valdahon Training Area in the French Jura region.

Starting on 1 March 1942, *Panzer-Ersatz-Abteilung 18* in Böblingen assumed responsibility for providing the regiment with replacements.

Schützen-Regiment 126 (later: Panzergrenadier-Regiment 126)

On 8 September 1941, Military District III in Berlin established the headquarters of *Schützen-Regiment 126* out of personnel levies from the *5. Panzer-Division*.

This was followed on 10 September, by the establishment of a headquarters for the 1st Battalion out of personnel levies from *Schützen-Ersatz-Bataillon 5* in Stettin, which was part of Military District II.

The Headquarters of the 2nd Battalion came into being on 15 September 1941 under the supervision of Military District III, with personnel provided by *Schützen-Regiment 13* of the *5. Panzer-Division*. On the same day, the regiment's 5th through 8th companies were formed.

The *5./Schützen-Regiment 126* was filled with personnel from the headquarters section of the *9./Schützen-Regiment 14* (*5. Panzer-Division*), one platoon from the *9./Schützen-Regiment 13*, one platoon from the *5./Infanterie-Gegiment 680* (*333. Infanterie-Division*) and one platoon from the *5./Infanterie-Regiment 577* (*305. Infanterie-Division*).

The *6./Schützen-Regiment 126* was filled with personnel from the *5./Infanterie-Regiment 57*, with the exception of one platoon, which went to the *5./Schützen-Regiment 126*.

The *7./Schützen-Regiment 126* was filled with personnel from the *5./Infanterie-Regiment 680,* with the exception of one platoon which went to the *5./Schützen-Regiment 126*.

The *8./Schützen-Regiment 126* was formed by the redesignation of the *9./Schützen-Regiment 13*.

The companies of the *I./Schützen-Regiment 126* were formed by Military Districts III, II and V on 17 and 18 September 1941.

The *1./Schützen-Regiment 126* was filled with personnel from the headquarters section and one platoon from the *4./Schützen-Regiment 13* (*5. Panzer-Division*), one platoon from the *5./Infanterie-Regiment 390* (*215. Infanterie-Division*) and one platoon from the *5./Infanterie-Regiment 571* (*302. Infanterie-Division*).

The *2./Schützen-Regiment 126* was filled with personnel from the *5./Infanterie-Regiment 571*, with the exception of one platoon, which went to the *1./Schützen-Regiment 126,* and a platoon from *Heeres-Wach-Bataillon 247*.

The *3./Schützen-Regiment 126* was filled with personnel from the *5./Infanterie-Regiment 390*, with the exception of one platoon, which went to the *1./Schützen-Regiment 126,* and one platoon from the *4./Schützen-Regiment 13*.

The *4./Schützen-Regiment 126* was filled with personnel from *Infanterie-Panzerjäger-Ersatz-Kompanie 25*, the *Geschütz-Ersatz-Kompanie für motorisierte Schützen-Einheiten 104* (Wiesbaden) and the *Ersatz-Kompanie für Pionierzüge (mot.) 104* (Saarburg).[100]

100 Editor's Note: = 25th Infantry Antitank Replacement Company, the 104th Gun Company for Motorized Rifle Units and the 104th Replacement

The companies that were incorporated into *Schützen-Regiment 126* for its formation were, without exception, from infantry regiments—the 571st, the 577th and the 680th—that had origins in divisions and regiments of long peacetime standing.

For instance, the *5./Infanterie-Regiment 571* derived from the *5./Infanterie-Regiment 94* of the *32. Infanterie-Division*, which was redesignated as the *1./Infanterie-Regiment 509* of the *292. Infanterie-Division* on 6 February 1940. On 15 November, it was redesignated as the *5./Infanterie-Regiment 571* before it was absorbed into *Schützen-Regiment 126*. Likewise, the *5./Infanterie-Regiment 577* was derived from the *7./Infanterie-Regiment 42* of the *46. Infanterie-Division*. That company became the *3.* and *9./Infanterie-Regiment 520* of the *296. Infanterie-Division*. In the end, the *9./Infanterie-Regiment 520* became the *7./Infanterie-Regiment 35* of the *25. Infanterie-Division* on 18 February 1940 which, in turn, became the *5./Infanterie-Regiment 680* on 15 November 1940.

At the beginning of October 1941, the elements of *Schützen-Regiment 126* began to assemble in Versailles, where they were billeted in the *Camp de Sartori*. The first steps to forming cohesiveness within the regiment were taken through individual, squad and platoon training; in addition, the men were introduced to the doctrines of operations of motorized rifle regiments, which the "leg" infantry were completely unaccustomed to. The weapons and vehicles gradually arrived. The 1st battalion received medium *SPW's*; the 2nd Battalion, as well as all of the trains, was issued French trucks and motorcycles. The first commander of the regiment was *Oberst* Kieler.

In December 1941, the regiment conducted battalion-sized combined exercises with tanks and artillery. That was followed by combined exercises at regiment and division level at the Sissonne Training Area near Laon, where formation training with live firing was conducted.

Schützen-Regiment 128 (later: Panzergrenadier-Regiment 128)

The first unit of the newly established regiment was the headquarters of the 1st Battalion, which was formed on 6 September 1940 by Military District IV in Dresden through personnel reassigned from the Replacement Army.

On 10 September, the *8(schw.)/Schützen-Regiment 128* was formed from the following elements: *3./Panzerjäger-Abteilung 53*; an antitank platoon and engineer platoon of *Schützen-Regiment 14*; an engineer platoon and some noncommissioned officers from *Panzer-Aufklärungs-Abteilung 8*; a light infantry gun platoon; and other replacement sources. On 1 December, another light infantry-gun platoon was added.

On 15 September 1941, the 2nd Battalion and its companies were established by Military District III in Liegnitz. The battalion headquarters was created out of personnel details from a number of replacement detachments, including Liegnitz, Sagan, Görlitz, Neiße, Hirschberg, Oppeln and Drachenbronn.

The *5./Schützen-Regiment 128* was filled with personnel from one platoon from the *9./Schützen-Regiment 14* (*5. Panzer-Division*), one platoon from the *5./Infanterie-Regiment 683* (*335. Infanterie-Division*) and one platoon from the *5./Infanterie-Regiment 686* (*336. Infanterie-Division*).

The *6./Schützen-Regiment 128* was filled with personnel from one platoon from the *9./Schützen-Regiment 14* (*5. Panzer-Division*), and two platoons from the *5./Infanterie-Regiment 683* (*335. Infanterie-Division*).

The *7./Schützen-Regiment 128* was filled with personnel from one platoon from the *9./Schützen-Regiment 14* (*5. Panzer-Division*), and two platoons from the *5./Infanterie-Regiment 686* (*336. Infanterie-Division*).

The companies of the 1st Battalion were formed on 17 September under the supervision of Military District III.

Company for Engineer Platoons (Motorized).

The *1./Schützen-Regiment 128* was filled with personnel from one platoon from the *4./Schützen-Regiment 14* (*5. Panzer-Division*), one platoon from the *5./Infanterie-Regiment 574* (*304. Infanterie-Division*) and one platoon from the *5./Infanterie-Regiment 593* (*323. Infanterie-Division*).

The *2./Schützen-Regiment 128* was filled with personnel from two platoons of the *5./Infanterie-Regiment 574* and one platoon from the *4./Schützen-Regiment 14* (*5. Panzer-Division*).

The *3./Schützen-Regiment 128* was filled with personnel from two platoons of the *5./Infanterie-Regiment 593* and one platoon from the *4./Schützen-Regiment 14* (*5. Panzer-Division*).

The regimental headquarters and the Headquarters Company—minus the antitank-gun platoon, the motorcycle platoon and the regimental band—were formed on 14 October by Military District V. On 20 October, the remainder of the company was formed (officially the 11th Company) by personnel details coming from within Military District V.

The *9.(s.IG.)/Schützen-Regiment 128* was formed on 25 November by Military District V in Pforzheim. Initially designated as *IG-Kompanie (mot.)*, it was redesignated as the former unit on 6 December.

During the first half of October, the units formed in Germany assembled at the new billeting area for the regiment in Vaucresson, St. Germain and Rueil-Malmaison.

On 20 October 1941, the regiment was formally activated and incorporated into the *23. Panzer-Division*, where it was made a part of *Oberst* von Heydebrand und der Lasa's *Schützen-Brigade 23*, along with *Schützen-Regiment 126*. The first regimental commander was *Oberstleutnant* Bachmann.

Weapons, equipment and vehicles were gradually issued to the regiment in the new billeting area. Both battalions were issued unarmored French trucks to make them mobile.

During the first few weeks, individual, squad and platoon training was conducted, which was followed by battalion-level exercises occasionally conducted together with the *III./Panzer-Regiment 201*, which afforded the opportunity for combined-arms training at the former French training area at *Mailly le Camp* near Chalons.

In January 1942, the regiment was moved to Sissonne, together with other elements, especially artillery, where division-level exercises and live firing took place for the first time.

Panzer-Artillerie-Regiment 128 Regimental Headquarters and Signals Platoon

The divisional artillery headquarters had its genesis on 26 August 1939, when the *Stab und Nachrichtenzug Artillerie-Regiment z.b.V. 606 (mot.)*[101] was formed. It was stationed along the *Westwall*[102] during the Polish Campaign and later employed during the Campaign in the West. It was a general headquarters artillery command and staff element responsible for directing the artillery fight of several artillery battalions consolidated for special missions.

Responsible for replacement personnel were *Artillerie-Regiment 12* and *leichte Artillerie-Ersatz-Abteilung 12* of Military District II. After the Campaign in the West, the headquarters participated in the planning for *Operation "Seelöwe"*. Later on, *Oberst* von Buch directed the artillery preparations and gunnery of four regiments during the planning phase for operations against Gibraltar, which never took place.

In April 1941, the headquarters was employed as a field-army artillery command and control headquarters during the Campaign in the Balkans in the areas between Marburg — Pettau and Agram. The rapid

101 Editor's Note: = 606th Motorized Artillery Regiment (Special Purpose) (Headquarters and Signals Platoon).

102 Editor's Note: The *Westwall* was more popularly referred to as the "Siegfried Line".

development of the campaign did not allow for the headquarters to be given any additional missions, with the result that it was moved to Gnesen in the General Government. It assumed responsibility for the command and control of several general-headquarters battalions.

The headquarters participated in the Summer Offensive against the Soviet Union in 1941, originally deploying from southern East Prussia. Moving through Bialystok, Minsk and Vitebsk, it got as far as Smolensk, all the time garnering praise for its superior performance in conducting the artillery battle. That was followed by employment at Welikie Luki within the framework of the *LVII. Panzer-Korps* and the *XXXX. Panzer-Korps*, at the Waldai Hills and at Staraja Russa. The headquarters participated in the Winter Offensive against Moscow with five attached artillery battalions. Moving through Juchno and Medyn, it got to within 70 kilometers of the Soviet capital, where it then experienced the bogging down of the offensive along the Narwa and the desperate defensive measures against the enemy, the mud and the cold. On 28 October, the headquarters was withdrawn from the front and moved as a regimental headquarters and Headquarters Battery to Maisons-Laffitte (near Paris), where it was to be redesignated and reorganized as *Artillerie-Regiment (mot.) 128*.

On 26 December 1941, the regiment was redesignated as *Panzer-Artillerie-Regiment 128*.

I./Panzer-Artillerie-Regiment 128

This battalion came from the *2./Artillerie-Regiment 187* of the *87. Infanterie-Division*. The division was formed in the fall of 1939 by Military District IV in Dresden. Employed during the Campaign in the West, it moved through the Ardennes, crossed the Meuse and the Somme and crowned its employment by the taking of Paris.

On 15 November 1940, the *2./Artillerie-Regiment 187* provided the cadre for the *III./Artillerie-Regiment 335* of the Baden-Wuertemberg *335. Infanterie-Division*, which was being established. The battalion consisted of a headquarters, a Headquarters Battery and two firing batteries. Its activation locations were Heidenheim, Mergelstetten and Bolheim.

After being employed in security duties along the demarcation line in France from May to October 1941, the battalion was reassigned from the *335. Infanterie-Division* and moved to Meaux, east of Paris, where it was reorganized and redesignated as a *leichte Artillerie-Abteilung (mot.)* under the command of *Major* Oswald. It received as its 3rd battery from the former *4./Artillerie-Regiment 215* of the Wuertemberg *215. Infanterie-Division*. Replacement personnel for all of the units of the battalion came from differing general headquarters motorized artillery battalions, especially from *schwere Artillerie-Abteilung 866* and *schwere Artillerie-Abteilung 865*. Under its new commander, *Oberstleutnant* Schlutius, the battalion was redesignated as the *I./Artillerie-Regiment 128 (mot.)* of the *23. Panzer-Division*.

In February 1942, it was moved to Argenteuil, with the replacement personnel initially coming from the *leichte Artillerie-Ersatz-Abteilung 90* in St. Dié (Military District V).

II./Panzer-Artillerie-Regiment 128

This battalion was originally activated as the *IV. (schw.)/Artillerie-Regiment 260* of the Wuertemberg *260. Infanterie-Division* on 26 August 1939 in Schwäbisch Gmünd. It was employed during the winter of 1939/1940 in securing the borders of the *Reich* in the area of the *Isteiner Klotz*, south of Freiburg.

Effective 2 May 1940, it was employed on the right wing and in the center of the forces employed in the west against France. It was fighting along the Loire when the French capitulated.

On 31 January 1941, the battalion was redesignated as *schwere Heeres-Artillerie-Abteilung 847*. It was employed in the front lines from the very first day of the Campaign in the East. It accompanied the attack initially from the Suwalki area. It participated in the fighting along the Desna, at Smolensk, at Wjasma and at Brjansk.

In October 1941, the battalion was pulled from the lines and sent to France. On 14 November 1941, it was redesignated and consolidated into the divisional artillery of the *23. Panzer-Division* as the *II./Artillerie-Regiment 128 (mot.)*. At the same time, it was also reorganized and issued light field howitzers. The commander at the time of the new-equipment training was *Hauptmann* Beck.

The light artillery column of the battalion, which had originally been formed in Vienna as a 48-ton *Kolonne Hermes* for *Artillerie-Regiment 603 (mot.),* was later integrated into the supply columns of the division's support command.

Leichte Artillerie-Ersatz-Abteilung (mot.) 90 in St. Dié was initially responsible for personnel replacement.

III. (schw.)/Panzer-Artillerie-Regiment 128

Formed under the supervision of Military District IX on 7 May 1941 as *schwere Heeres-Artillerie-Abteilung (mot.) 863*, the battalion entered combat for the first time in the invasion of the Soviet Union. It supported the attacking divisions in the southern portion of the Eastern Front. It was pulled out of the line on 24 December 1941 and sent to Mühlhausen in Thuringia. There, the battalion was reconstituted, a process lasting until 15 February 1942.

On 12 February, the battalion was reassigned to the *23. Panzer-Division* and redesignated as the *III./Panzer-Artillerie-Regiment 128*. Its 9th Battery was formed by the reassignment and redesignation of the *10.(s.FH.)/Artillerie-Regiment 205* of the Wuertemberg *205. Infanterie-Division*. The former *1./schwere Heeres-Artillerie-Abteilung 863 (mot.)* became the battalion's 7th Battery, and it received 10cm cannon. The remaining two battalions of the regiment kept their 15cm heavy field howitzers. The commander of the battalion was *Oberst* Büscher.

Schwere Artillerie-Ersatz-Abteilung 61 in Epinal (Military District V) was responsible for personnel replacements. The signals personnel replacements for the entire regiment came from *Nachrichten-Ersatz-Batterie 178* in Ulm.

IV. (Flak)/Panzer-Artillerie-Regiment 128 (see Heeres-Flak-Abteilung 278)

10. (Pz.Beob)/Panzer-Artillerie-Regiment 128 (later: Beobachtungs-Batterie (Pz.) 128)

The battery was formed from *Beobachtungs-Batterie 21* which, in turn, had been formed from *Beobachtungs-Abteilung 1* in Königsberg (renamed Kaliningrad by the Soviets, with the Russians continuing to occupy it as a naval base to this day). It participated in both the Campaign in Poland and in the Campaign in the West.

After being positioned in Poland, the battalion participated in the Campaign in the Soviet Union, mostly in support of the *71. Infanterie-Division*. It moved via Kiev and Poltava as far as Kharkov, where it was pulled out of the front during the winter of 1941/1942 and sent to Baumholder. The battalion was divided into three separate flash-ranging batteries (mechanized) for the *22. Panzer-Division*, the *23. Panzer-Division* and the *24. Panzer-Division*. Initially, *Beobachtungs-Ersatz-Abteilung 5* was responsible for personnel replacements. Later on, this responsibility was assumed by *Beobachtungs-Ersatz-Abteilung 44* in Olmütz.

The battery consisted of a headquarters section, a meteorological section, a survey platoon and a flash- and sound-ranging section. The latter had four surveying and evaluation sections.

In April 1942, the trains headed east once again, this time to Kharkov, where the *23. Panzer-Division* had also arrived in the meantime. The battery was incorporated into the divisional artillery.

Heeres-Flak-Abteilung (mot.) 278

During the spring of 1941, *Heeres-Flak-Abteilung 278* was activated in St. Wendel (Saar). The batteries were formed through personnel details from a *Luftwaffe* antiaircraft battery from *Flak-Ersatz-Abteilung 64* (Kassel-Hasenhecke) and personnel from an artillery battalion.

Shortly after it was established, the battalion was moved to the General Government of Poland. From there, it participated in the Campaign in the Soviet Union on 22 June 1941, advancing across the frontier at Samoshja Sokal. During the winter of 1941/1942, most of the battalion was located in the Sumy — Rowno area, with other elements in Shitomir.

In February 1942, the battalion was reconstituted at the Wahn Training Area near Cologne. The battalion consisted of a headquarters, a Headquarters Battery, two heavy batteries, each with four 8.8cm *Flak* and three 2cm *Flak 38*, and a light battery with twelve 2cm *Flak 38*.

At the end of April, the battalion started entraining for the Eastern Front, where it arrived in Kharkov on 12 May. It was initially assigned to the divisional artillery, where it became the 4th Battalion and its batteries renumbered from 10 to 12. Later on, it became a separate battalion again. Its commander was *Major* Draffehn; the replacement detachment was *Heeres-Flak-Ersatz- und Ausbildungs-Abteilung 278* in Mannheim-Käfertal.

Panzer-Pionier-Bataillon 51

The divisional engineer battalion has the honor of having the longest and most distinguished military lineage of any formation before joining the *23. Panzer-Division*.

The battalion was formed in Dessau-Roßlau on 1 October 1937 as *Pioneer-Bataillon 52*. To form the battalion, it received a company each from *Pionier-Bataillon 16* in Höxter, *Pionier-Bataillon 19* in Holzminden and *Pionier-Bataillon 13* in Magdeburg. It also received some personnel from the engineer battalion in Riesa.

In March 1938, the fully motorized battalion, under the command of *Oberstleutnant* Mikosch, left its billeting area in the barracks of the Dessau-Roßlau Training Area and participated in the march into Austria. During the following summer, it spent three months along the Saar in building up the fortifications of the *Westwall*. It then moved back to its new barracks at Rinteln an der Weser. As a corps troop, it reported to the headquarters of the *XI. Armee-Korps* in Hannover.

On 5 November 1938, the battalion's 3rd Company was detached and redesignated as the *4./Pionier-Lehr-Bataillon 1*. On 26 August 1939, however, the company returned to its parent battalion as part of the general mobilization of the German Army.

Before the war started, the battalion was moved up to the eastern frontier. It built a military bridge over the Oder at Kosel and accompanied the attacking divisions through Tschenstochau to Warsaw, starting on 1 September 1939. At Annapol, the battalion erected a bridge across the Vistula, before it was employed in an attack against the west side of Warsaw on 27 September. Together with the infantry, within two hours it took two forts stubbornly defended by the Poles. The capitulation of Warsaw at 1000 hours on 27 September ended its combat employment in the Polish Campaign. The battalion went to Demblin-Irena, and then to Posen to perform some engineer missions. From there it was sent back to the western part of the *Reich*.

The 12th of May 1940 was a singular day in the history of *Pionier-Bataillon 51*. In accordance with previously practiced plans, which were laid out in exacting detail, the engineers crossed the Albert Canal in assault boats and, together with glider-borne paratroopers, stormed Fort Eben-Emael, a fort complex located north of Lüttich (Liége), which had previously been considered impregnable. By doing so, the prerequisites were created for an unimpeded march by the army into Belgium. *Oberstleutnant* Mikosch and *Oberfeldwebel* Portsteffen were both awarded the Knight's Cross to the Iron Cross for performance of duty, which decisively influenced the outcome of the engagement.

After the Campaign in the West, *Pionier-Bataillon 51* was involved in the preparations for *Unternehmen "Seelöwe"*, the planned invasion of Great Britain, and, later on, the attack preparations for the invasion of Gibraltar. Had the invasion taken place, it would have been the third formation that later belonged to the *23. Panzer-Division* to be so involved. Together with *Flak*, the intent had been for the engineers to launch the final assault on the cliff fortress. After the Gibraltar operation was abandoned, the battalion, which had been redesignated as *Sturm-Pionier-Bataillon 51*, participated in the Russian Campaign from the very first day. It advanced in the center sector of the front against Kaluga.

In January 1942, the greatly weakened battalion was moved to Camp Pieske (near Meseritz in the Neumark district). It was there that the battalion headquarters and the 2nd and 3d Companies were reconstituted. Through personnel levies from *Pionier-Ersatz-Bataillon 19* in Holzminden—the replacement detachment for the battalion—*Brüko K 151*[103] was established on 7 January 1942 and the armored engineer company of the *23. Panzer-Division* on 24 February of the same year.

While the training of the battalion was still in progress in Meseritz, the two new units from Holzminden under *Hauptmann* Senftleben and *Oberleutnant* Diestel were moved to Pontoise at the end of February 1942. The armored engineer company was outfitted with medium *SPW's*; command of it was assumed in March by *Oberleutnant* Schäfer.

Brüko K 151 was initially issued *B-Gerät* and *C-Gerät*. Its new K-type bridging equipment was received just before the unit departed for Kharkov. The transportation means for this equipment was the ill-suited 4.5-ton Matford truck, which could only be employed in the Soviet Union through the use of extensive improvisation; all of the British trucks were soon mechanically disabled. The bridging column and the armored engineer company arrived in Kharkov at the same time as the rest of the division. It was not until 12 May that the battalion headquarters, the 2nd and 3rd Companies and the light engineer column followed. On 21 May, the battalion was restructured and redesignated as *Panzer-Pionier-Bataillon 51*. The armored engineer company was assigned to the battalion as its 3rd Company. The former 3rd Company was redesignated as the 1st Company. The first commander of the redesignated battalion was *Major* Zeydlick. *Panzer-Pionier-Ersatz-Bataillon 5* in Ulm was designated the replacement detachment for *PPB51* once the latter was reintegrated into the *23. Panzer-Division*.

Kradschützen-Bataillon 23 (later: Panzer-Aufklärungs-Abteilung 23)

The lineage of the motorcycle battalion can be traced to *Reiter-Regiment 4* of Potsdam. *Kraftfahrabteilung 3* was formed from one of its squadrons in 1933 remaining stationed in Potsdam. (At the time there were several battalions with the same number.) In 1937, *Aufklärungs-*

103 Editor's Note = Bridging Column (K 151). The "K" refers to the type of bridging equipment, as do the "B" and "G" mentioned below.

Abteilung 8 (mot.) was created from it. For a while, the battalion was part of *Aufklärungs-Regiment 6*, which was later assimilated into first the *1. leichte* and then the *5. Panzer-Division*.

As part of the *5. Panzer-Division*, both *Aufklärungs-Abteilung 8 (mot.)* and *Kradschützen-Battalion 55* participated in the Campaign against Yugoslavia and Greece. After those operations, the division was equipped for fighting in Africa. Despite that, it went to the Eastern front. Just before that happened, however, *Panzer-Aufklärungs-Abteilung 8* was detached from the division, along with elements of *Kradschützen-Bataillon 55*, and sent to Rambouillet and Labosé. A few elements of *Panzer-Aufklärungs-Abteilung 8* remained with the *5. Panzer-Division* to be used in other troop elements, especially in *Kradschützen-Bataillon 55*.

On 13 September 1941, the battalion was redesignated as *Kradschützen-Bataillon 23*. Military District III was responsible for the reorganization and re-equipping of the formation. Replacing the *Ersatz-Abteilung für motorisierte Aufklärungs-Einheiten 3* in Stahndsorf was *Kradschützen-Ersatz-Bataillon 2* in Vienna.

The battalion was formed as follows: The battalion staff came from the former *Panzer-Aufklärungs-Abteilung 8*; the *1. (Pz.Späh) Kompanie* was formed from elements coming from all of the companies of *Kradschützen-Ersatz-Bataillon 6*; the *2. (leichte SPW) Kompanie* from elements of the *3./Panzer-Aufklärungs-Abteilung 8* and the *4./Kradschützen-Bataillon 55*; the *3. (Kradschützen) Kompanie* from elements of the *3./Panzer-Aufklärungs-Abteilung 8* and the *4./Kradschützen-Bataillon 55*; the *4. (Kradschützen) Kompanie* from elements of the *3./Panzer-Aufklärungs-Abteilung 8* and the *4./Kradschützen-Bataillon 55*; and the *5. (schwere) Kompanie* from the *4. (schwere)/Panzer-Aufklärungs-Abteilung 8*. The light supply columns of the battalion came from the light supply columns of *Panzer-Aufklärungs-Abteilung 8*.

The battalion was moved to Versailles in January 1942 and incorporated into the *23. Panzer-Division*. The cadre of long-serving noncommissioned officers ensured the new battalion had a good framework within which to work and guaranteed a high level of training and good performance in combat.

Panzerjäger-Abteilung 128

In accordance with orders from the German Army High Command dated 26 January 1942, the battalion was activated under the supervision of Military District XIII in Nuremberg. The cadre elements, primarily from convalescents from *Panzerjäger-Abteilung 10* and *Panzerjäger-Abteilung 52*, were formed in Straubing (Danube) by *Panzerjäger-Ersatz-Abteilung 10* on 13 February 1942. The battalion consisted of a headquarters, a signals section and two line companies. The first commander of the battalion was *Major Dr.* Maus.

It had been directed that the battalion be ready for combat deployment by 15 February 1942, but that goal proved impossible to reach. The battalion conducted gunnery exercises for the companies from 28 February to 8 March 1942 at the Sissone Training Area in France. In addition, battalion exercises were conducted there, before the formation was moved to Paris on 11 March and incorporated into *Generalmajor* von Boineburg's *23. Panzer-Division*.

Flak-Kompanie (mot.) 633, which had been directed to be consolidated with the battalion, had already been formed by Military District XIII on 8 January 1942, using personnel from *Flak-Ersatz-Bataillon (mot.) 47*.

The battalion had only 10 days to get accustomed to its new division. On 21 March 1942, the trains started rolling from Versailles-Matelots to the east.

Panzer-Nachrichten-Abteilung 128

Based on a directive of Military District XI in Hanover, the *1. (Fernsprech- und Funk-) Kompanie 128* was initially formed on 2 October 1941. The establishment of the battalion then followed, starting on 22 January 1942. It consisted of a headquarters and a *1.(Fernsprech-) Kompanie* and a *2. (Funk-) Kompanie*. It was initially lodged in the *Gasthaus Hofjäger* in Magdeburg. The initial company that had been formed was consolidated with the newly formed companies. Most of the battalion was composed of personnel originally from *Panzer-Nachrichten-Ersatz-Abteilung 82* in Magdeburg, including a number of convalescents from *Panzer-Nachrichten-Abteilung 82*. There were also newly trained soldiers, however, and a few men came from *Nachrichten-Ersatz-Abteilung 19* in Hanover.

After a few days, the battalion was moved and billeted in the Magdeburg suburb of Groß-Ottersleben. Once there, the battalion's light supply column was established.

The battalion was equipped with German vehicles: *Kfz. 17's*, *Kfz. 61's*, 4-wheeled radio vehicles, 8-wheeled radio vehicles and radio *SPW's*.

On 25 January 1942, the battalion was moved to the division's activation area and was billeted in the Legionnaires' Barracks in Versailles. The battalion's replacement detachment remained *Panzer-Nachrichten-Ersatz-Abteilung 82* in Magdeburg.

Feld-Ersatz-Bataillon 128

The battalion was formed in the spring of 1942 from personnel details and cadre elements from differing replacement detachments of Military District V in Eßlingen. Given its largest mission, most of the personnel came from mechanized infantry replacement detachments. The first command of the battalion was *Hauptmann* Thurm.

In April 1942, the battalion was moved by rail to Kharkov, where the division had arrived in the meantime. It arrived there on 12 May, after the fighting northeast of the city had already flared up.

Sanitäts-Truppen 128

Two motorized medical companies and three separate field-ambulance platoons formed *Sanitätstruppen 128*. In September 1944, the three ambulance platoons were consolidated into *Krankenkraftwagen-Kompanie 128*.

Sanitäts-Kompanie b (mot.) 1/128

The acting headquarters of the *XI. Armee-Korps* in Hanover directed the establishment of this company for the *23. Panzer-Division*, based on orders from the German Army High Command, on 20 January 1942. On 29 January, the company was formed in Vehlen (near Bückeburg) under the supervision of *Sanitäts-Ersatz-Abteilung 11* (same location). The replacement detachment provided the medical personnel, while *Kraftfahr-Ersatz-Abteilung 3* in Burg bei Magdeburg provided the vehicle drivers. *Oberstabsarzt Dr.* Ostmann assumed command of the company.

At the beginning of March 1942, the personnel of the company were moved to Versailles, where it was billeted in the *Ecole militaire*. It was there that the company was issued its equipment and vehicles, which came predominately from captured French stocks.

On 14 May 1943, a 4th Platoon (Decontamination) was formed by *Sanitäts-Ersatz- und Ausbildungs-Abteilung 4* in Eilenburg and added to the company.

Sanitäts-Kompanie b (mot.) 2/128

On 9 February 1942, *Sanitäts-Abteilung 7* in Miesbach (Upper Bavaria) started to form this company on orders from the acting headquarters of the *VII. Armee-Korps* in Munich. The medical detachment provided the medical personnel, and *Kraftfahr-Ersatz-Abteilung 7* in Munich provided the vehicle drivers.

At the end of February 1942, the personnel of the company arrived in Versailles under the command of *Oberstabsarzt Dr.* Luther and incorporated into the division. Like its sister company, it was issued equipment for one heavy and two light clearing station platoons. It was issued French vehicles, mostly Peugeots and Renaults, to make it mobile. In addition to the clearing station platoons, both of the companies had a dental section and an apothecary.

Krankenkraftwagen-Züge 1, 2 and *3/128*

Kraftfahr-Ersatz-Abteilung 5 in Villingen (Black Forest) started to form *Krankenkraftwagen-Zug 1* on 22 October 1941, after receiving activation orders from the acting command of the *V. Armee-Korps* in Stuttgart. That replacement detachment, along with *Sanitäts-Ersatz-Abteilung 5* in Ulm, provided the necessary personnel.

The establishment of the remaining two platoons started on 18 and 27 December 1941 by the same replacement detachment. There was not much time available, since the initial elements of the platoons were moved to the division's activation area on 31 December 1941. They were assigned billets at Cheville la Rue near Paris.

The complement of vehicles gradually arrived in January 1942. Only some of the vehicles were French; the field ambulances themselves were of German origin—*Phänomen* vehicles designed for four lying or six sitting wounded.

The three platoon leaders were *Oberleutnant* Gieth, *Oberleutnant* Raetz and *Leutnant* Müller.

During the time available to them in France, the medical units conducted training, emphasizing coordination between the main clearing stations and the ambulance platoons, as well as the technical aspects of operating a clearing station.

Divisions-Nachschub-Truppen 128 (later: Panzer-Divisions-Nachschubtruppen 128)

The first element of the division support command to be established was its headquarters, which was formed on 8 October 1941 by *Kraftfahr-Ersatz-Abteilung 5* in Villingen (Black Forest). After a short time, it was moved to Paris as *Aufstellungs-Stab Dinafü 128*.[104] At the same time, various supply elements were established in Germany from differing replacement detachments. In the area around Paris, the light supply columns of the *I.* and *II./Panzer-Regiment 201* and the *II./Artillerie-Regiment (mot.) 128* were incorporated into the structure of the division support command.

The following elements were established by the Replacement Army:

1. (kleine) Kraftwagen-Kolonne[105]: 22 October 1941 by *Kraftfahr-Ersatz-Abteilung 5* in Villingen (Military District V).

2. (kleine) Kraftwagen-Kolonne: 16 October 1941 by *Kraftfahr-Ersatz-Abteilung 5* in Villingen (Military District V).

5. (große) Kraftwagen-Kolonne: 22 October 1941 by *Kraftfahr-Ersatz-Abteilung 5* in Villingen (Military District V).

6. (große) Kraftwagen-Kolonne: 6 October 1941 by *Kraftfahr-Ersatz-Abteilung 5* in Villingen (Military District V).

7. (große) Kraftwagen-Kolonne für Betriebstoff: 9 October 1941 by *Kraftfahr-Ersatz-Abteilung 27* in Augsburg (Military District VII).[106]

8. (große) Kraftwagen-Kolonne für Betriebstoff: 5 October 1941 by *Kraftfahr-Ersatz-Abteilung 13* in Nuremburg (Military District XIII).

10. (große) Kraftwagen-Kolonne für Betriebstoff: 22 December 1941 by *Kraftfahr-Ersatz-Abteilung 10* in Nuremburg (Military District X).

11. (kleine) Kraftwagen-Kolonne: 29 December 1941 by *Kraftfahr-Ersatz-Abteilung 27* in Augsburg (Military District VII).

In January 1942, 14 supply columns, as well as the supply company, for the 128th Division Support Command were assembled at Choisy le Roi, near Paris. The commander was *Major* Vollberg.

The vehicles were issued in the division's activation area. With the exception of a few specialized vehicles, they were all of French or British origin. In addition to the Peugeot trucks and Gnome-Rhone motorcycles, there were trucks to be found from the following manufacturers: Renault, Panhard, Matford and Bedford.

Werkstattkompanie 128 (later: Kraftfahr-Parktrupp 128)

During December 1941, three maintenance companies were established for the *23. Panzer-Division* in Germany. The 1st Company was formed in Hanover (Military District XI), the 2nd Company in Königshütte (Upper Silesia) (Military District VIII) (20 December) and the 3rd Company in Vienna (Military District XVII).

In January 1942, the cadre units of the three companies arrived in Versailles. The respective company commanders were *Oberleutnant* Ermich, *Oberleutnant* Schmiedel and *Hauptmann* David.

The authorized vehicles were gradually issued. With the exception of a few special-purpose vehicles, they were all of French manufacture and the men had to get used to them through constant practice and training. Logistically and administratively, the companies initially reported to the division support command, but they then reported directly to the Division Engineer, starting in 1943.

Waffen-Werkstatt-Kompanie 128

This company was a special entity within the *23. Panzer-Division*. It was first formed in 1943 and only later officially made a part of the division's table of organization and equipment. It was formed by combining the armaments platoons of the 1st and 2nd Maintenance Companies. The company commander was *Oberleutnant* Mildenberger.

Verwaltungstruppen 128

Verwaltungstruppen 128 was initially just a collective term for the division's rations section, its bakery company and its butcher's company. The units were separate entities, however, and received their orders from staff officers reporting to the division logistics officer. Later on, they reported directly to the staff officer directly for command and control purposes.

Divisions-Verpflegungsamt (mot) 128 (abbreviation: *DVA 128*)[107]

The rations section was formed in November 1941 under the control of *Stabszahlmeister*[108] Dabringhausen from *Armee-Verpflegungs-Amt 590* of the *1. Armee* in France. The civilian officials and soldiers assigned to the section almost all came from the Kassel area.

The rations section initially billeted in Versailles. At the end of December 1941, its equipment arrived, with the result that it was ready to

104 Editor's Note: = Activation Headquarters for the 128th Division Supported Command.

105 Editor's Note: = 1st Supply Column (Light). Subsequent elements listed are analogous, with *"große"* = (Heavy)

106 Editor's Note: These were long-haul lift capacity for fuel, being able to carry 50 cubic meters in a single lift.

107 Editor's Note: = 128th Division Rations Section (motorized)

108 Editor's Note: = Rank for a uniformed civilian official.

perform its mission effective 1 January 1942. On 12 April 1944, the section was restructured and redesignated as *Verwaltungs-Kompanie 128*.[109]

Bäckerei-Kompanie (mot.) 128

The personnel for the company were identified in Vienna in December 1941 under the supervision of Military District XVII. During the first few days of January 1942, the personnel were transported to the Paris area and, like many other elements, billeted in Versailles.

Most of the personnel assigned to the company were Austrians, mostly from Vienna. The replacement detachment was *Verwaltungstruppen-Ersatz-Abteilung 3* in Vienna. The equipment for the company arrived between 1 and 15 February 1942, with the result that the personnel of the company under *Oberleutnant* Modasky could be trained for their future duties.

Schlächterei-Kompanie (mot.) 128

The company was formed on 24 October 1941 by the Headquarters of the *1. Armee*, using a personnel detail from *Schlächterei-Kompanie 204*. In addition to the 2 veterinarians, 2 paymasters and 56 butchers from that element, other personnel arrived from *Kraftfahr-Ersatz-Abteilung 10* in Hamburg and the *3./Verwaltungstruppen-Ersatz-Abteilung 1* in Berlin. The majority of the personnel from the original butcher company came from Hessia and Wurttemberg. The company commander was *Oberveterinär Dr.* Volz.

After the company was integrated into the division, *Kraftfahr-Ersatz-Abteilung 5* in Villingen and *Verwaltungstruppen-Ersatz-Abteilung 3* in Vienna were designated as the replacement detachments.

***

After completing their respective initial training and familiarization with their equipment, the three units conducted a logistics exercise for *Generalmajor* von Boineburg in February 1942.

Feldpostamt (mot.) 128

The division's post office was established on 13 October 1941 under *Feldpostmeister* Weiß in Düsseldorf under the direction of Military District VI. It had an initial strength of 18 men. That same month, the post office was sent to Paris (Bessières Barracks) and integrated into the division. By November of that year, it had received responsibility from *Armeepostamt 1* the responsibility for providing postal services to the elements joining the *23. Panzer-Division*.

In addition to it daily postal work, the personnel of the unit were trained on light infantry weapons in order to be able to conduct self-defense.

109 Editor's Note: = 128th Administrative Company. Whether this represents an expansion of its previous mission or merely an acknowledgement of all of its duties is unknown.

Appendix 2
Replacement Formations and Elements for the 23. Panzer-Division

This listing is intended to provide an overview of the troop elements of the Replacement Army that were responsible for providing personnel replacements for the regiments, battalions and troop elements of the *23. Panzer-Division*. They were responsible for providing personnel replacements, even if replacements were provided by other elements.

The responsible replacement detachments changed several times in the course of the war. It will be attempted to reflect this in the order of presentation in the listing.[110]

110 Editor's Note: The replacement detachments are only listed in their original German.

Troop Element	Replacement Detachment and Location	Date / Year
Stab, 23. Panzer-Division, and *Division-Begleit-Kompanie*	*Stellvertretendes General-Kommando V. Armee-Korps* (Stuttgart) (*Panzer-Ersatz-Abteilung 7* [Böblingen], *Panzergrenadier-Ersatz-Bataillon 86* and *Panzergrenadier-Ersatz-Bataillon 215* [Reutlingen])	
Divisions-Kartenstelle (mot.) 128	*III. (Vermischtes Lehr- und Ersatz.)/Artillerie-Lehr-Regiment (mot.) 3* (Jüterbog)	10 December 1941
Panzer-Regiment 201 (*Panzer-Regiment 23*)	*Panzer-Ersatz-Abteilung 7* (Böblingen), *Panzer-Ersatz-Abteilung 100* (Schwetzingen) and *Panzer-Ersatz-Abteilung 18* (Böblingen)	1 December 1940 15 May 1941 and 1 March 1942
9. (Sturm-Infanterie-Geschütz) Batterie	*Sturmgeschütz-Ersatz-Abteilung 200* (Schweinfurt)	May 1943
Stab, Schützen-Brigade 23 (*Panzergrenadier-Brigade 23*)	*Schützen-Ersatz-Bataillon 86* (Ludwigsburg) *Nachrichten-Ersatz-Kompanie für motorisierte Schützen-Einheiten 86* (Stuttgart-Zuffenhausen)	

Troop Element	Replacement Detachment and Location	Date / Year
Schützen-Regiment 126 (*Panzergrenadier-Regiment 126*)	*Schützen-Ersatz-Bataillon* 86 (Ludwigsburg)	10 September 1941
	Kradschützen-Ersatz-Bataillon 9 (Sondershausen)	
	Kompanie-Ersatz-Kompanie für motorisierte Schützen-Einheiten 86 (Stuttgart-Zuffenhausen)	
	Infanterie-Panzerjäger-Ersatz-Kompanie 25 (Ludwigsburg)	
	Ersatz-Kompanie für Pionier-Züge (mot.) 104 (Mainz-Castell; later, Heidelberg)	
	Geschütz-Ersatz-Kompanie für motorisierte Schützen-Einheiten 104 (Wiesbaden)	
	Panzergrenadier-Ersatz-Bataillon 215 (Reutlingen)	21 November 1942
	Panzer-Aufklärungs-Ersatz-Kompanie 9 (Sondershausen)	
	Panzergrenadier-Nachrichten-Ersatz-Kompanie 86 (Stuttgart-Zuffenhausen	
	Infanterie-Panzerjäger-Ersatz-Kompanie 25 (Ludwigsburg)	
	Infanterie-Geschütz-Ersatz- und Ausbildungs-Kompanie (mot.) 104 (Darmstadt)	
	Panzergrenadier-Pionier-Ersatz- und Ausbildungs-Kompanie 25 (Ulm)	June 1944
Schützen-Regiment 128 (*Panzergrenadier-Regiment 128*)	*Schützen-Ersatz-Bataillon* 86 (Ludwigsburg)	10 September 1941
	Kradschützen-Ersatz-Bataillon 9 (Sondershausen)	
	Nachricten-Ersatz-Kompanie für motorisierte Schützen-Einheiten 86 (Stuttgart-Zuffenhausen)	
	Infanterie-Panzerjäger-Ersatz-Kompanie 25 (Ludwigsburg)	
	Ersatz-Kompanie für Pionier-Züge (mot.) 104 (Mainz-Castell; later, Saarburg)	25 November 1941
	Geschütz-Ersatz-Kompanie für motorisierte Schützen-Einheiten 104 (Wiesbaden and Landau)	
	Panzergrenadier-Ersatz-Bataillon 215 (Reutlingen)	17 July 1942
	Panzer-Aufklärungs-Ersatz-Kompanie 9 (Sondershausen)	
	Panzergrenadier-Nachrichten-Ersatz-Kompanie 86 (Stuttgart-Zuffenhausen	
	Infanterie-Panzerjäger-Ersatz-Kompanie 25 (Ludwigsburg)	22 April 1943
	Infanterie-Geschütz-Ersatz- und Ausbildungs-Kompanie (mot.) 104 (Darmstadt)	21 July 1942
	Panzergrenadier-Pionier-Ersatz- und Ausbildungs-Kompanie 25 (Ulm)	
	Kraftfahr-Park-Ersatz- und Ausbildungs-Kompanie 25 (Neckarsulm)	21 July 1942
	Fla-Ersatz-Bataillon (mot.) 52 (Delmenhorst)	
Panzer-Artillerie-Regiment 128	*Leichte Artillerie-Ersatz-Abteilung (mot.) 90* (St. Dié)	13 November 1941
	Nachrichten-Ersatz-Batterie 178 (Ulm)	
	Schwere Artillerie-Ersatz-Abteilung 260 (mot.) (Epinal)	12 February 1942
	Beobachtungs-Ersatz-Abteilung 7 (Munich)	
	Leichte Artillerie-Ersatz-Abteilung (mot.) 260 (Ludwigsburg)	20 November 1942
	Beobachtungs-Ersatz- und Ausbildungs-Abteilung 44 (Olmütz)	Middle of 1943
	Panzer-Haubitz-Ersatz- und Ausbildungs-Abteilung 201 (Groß Born)	November 1943
Heeres-Flak-Abteilung 278 (also *IV./ Panzer-Artillerie-Regiment 128*)	*Heeres-Flak-Artillerie-Ersatz-Abteilung 278* (Mannheim-Käfertal)	February 1942
Panzer-Pionier-Bataillon 51	*Panzer-Pionier-Ersatz-Bataillon 5* (Ulm) *Panzer-Pioneer-Ersatz-Bataillon 19* (Holzminden)	February 1942
Panzerjäger-Abteilung 128	*Panzerjäger-Ersatz-Abteilung 10* (Straubing)	13 February 1942
	Panzerjäger-Ersatz-Abteilung 5 (Karlsruhe)	April 1942

Troop Element	Replacement Detachment and Location	Date / Year
Flug-Abwehr-Kompanie 633 (later, *4./Heeres-Flak-Abteilung 278*)	*Flug-Abwehr-Ersatz-Bataillon (mot.) 47*	
Panzer-Nachrichten-Abteilung 128	*Panzer-Nachrichten-Ersatz-Abteilung 82* (Magdeburg)	14 October 1941
Kradschützen-Bataillon 23 (*Panzer-Aufklärungs-Abteilung 23*)	*Kradschützen-Ersatz-Bataillon 2* (Vienna)	19 September 1941
	Infanterie-Panzerjäger-Ersatz-Kompanie 25 (Ludwigsburg)	
	Geschütz-Ersatz-Kompanie für motorisierte Schützen-Einheiten 104 (Wiesbaden)	
	Ersatz-Kompanie für Pionier-Züge (mot.) 104 (Mainz-Castell)	
	Kradschützen-Ersatz-Bataillon 9 (Sondershausen)	4 September 1942
	Panzer-Aufklärungs-Ersatz-Abteilung 9 (Sondershausen)	22 April 1943
	Infanterie-Panzerjäger-Ersatz-Kompanie 25 (Ludwigsburg)	
	Infanterie-Geschütz-Ersatz- und Ausbildungs-Kompanie (mot.) 104 (Darmstadt)	
	Ersatz-Kompanie für Pionier-Züge (mot.) 104 (Heidelberg)	
	Panzer-Aufklärungs-Ersatz-Abteilung 55 (Hirschberg)	November 1943
Sanitätstruppen 128	*Sanitäts-Ersatz- und Ausbildungs-Abteilung 5* (Ulm)	December 1941
	Kraftfahr-Ersatz-Abteilung 5 (Villingen/Black Forest)	
Verwaltungstruppen 128	*Infanterie-Ersatz-Bataillon 34* (Hagenau)	November 1943
	Kraftfahr-Ersatz- und Ausbildungs-Abteilung 5 (Villingen/ Black Forest; later, Mühlheim/Baden)	
Kraftfahrparktruppen 128	*Kraftfahrparktruppen-Ersatz- und Ausbildungs-Abteilung 5* (Neckarsulm)	
Feldgendarmerie-Trupp 128	*Feldgendarmerie-Ersatz-Abteilung* (Litzmannstadt)	
Feldpostamt 128	*Feldpost-Ersatz- und Ausbildungs-Abteilung* (Meierhöfen)	

Appendix 3
Command and Control Relationships of the 23. Panzer-Division
Excerpt from the Schematic Wartime Organization of the German Army

Date	*23. PD*	Corps	Field Army	Field-Army Group	Neighboring Divisions[1]
2 October 1941	Activation	—	*1. Armee*	*Oberbefehlshaber West*	—
10 March 1942	Activation	—	*1. Armee*	*Oberbefehlshaber West*	—
17 March 1942	In transit to Kharkov	—	—	—	—
5 April 1942	Main body in Kharkov	—	—	*Heeresgruppe Süd*	—
22 April 1942	Kharkov	—	—	*Heeresgruppe Süd*	—
11 May 1942	Kharkov	—	—	*Heeresgruppe Süd*	—
12 May 1942	Kharkov (North)	*LI. AK*[2]	*6. Armee*	*Heeresgruppe Süd*	1/3 of *44., 297., 71.*
14 May 1942	Kharkov (North)	*Korps-Gruppe Breith*	*6. Armee*	*Heeresgruppe Süd*	1/3 of *44.*, 1/3 of *71.*, elements of *3. PD*
19 May 1942	Kharkov (North)	*LI. AK*	*6. Armee*	*Heeresgruppe Süd*	Elements of *3. PD*
23 May 1942	Kharkov (South)	*Korps-Gruppe Breith*	*6. Armee*	*Heeresgruppe Süd*	*3.* and *16. PD, 44.*
8 June 1942	Reconstitution	*XXXX. PzK.*	*6. Armee*	*Heeresgruppe Süd*	*3. PD*
30 June 1942	Woltschansk	*XXXX. PzK.*	*6. Armee*	*Heeresgruppe Süd*	*3. PD, 29. (mot.)*
4 July 1942	Krugloje	*XXXX. PzK.*	*6. Armee*	*Heeresgruppe Süd*	*3. PD, 29. (mot.), 336., 100. JD*

Date	*23. PD*	Corps	Field Army	Field-Army Group	Neighboring Divisions[1]
5 July 1942	Repjewka	*XXXXVIII. PzK.*	*2. Armee*	*Heeresgruppe Süd*	*24. PD, 16. (mot.), GD*
6 July 1942	Don (east of Repjewka)	*XXXX. PzK.*	*6. Armee*	*Heeresgruppe Süd*	*3. PD, 29. (mot.), 336., 100. JD*
9 July 1942	Rossosch	*XXXX. PzK.*	*6. Armee*	*Heeresgruppe B*	As above, plus *389., 75.*
15 July 1942	Millerowo	*XXXX. PzK.*	*4. Pz-Armee*	*Heeresgruppe A*	*3. PD*
22 July 1942	Tazinskaja	—	*4. Pz-Armee*	*Heeresgruppe A*	—
28 July 1942	Martinowka	*XXXX. PzK.*	*4. Pz-Armee*	*Heeresgruppe A*	*3. PD*
2 August 1942	Baschanta	*XXXX. PzK.*	*1. Pz-Armee*	*Heeresgruppe A*	*3. PD*
10 August 1942	Mineralnyje Wody	*XXXX. PzK.*	*1. Pz-Armee*	*Heeresgruppe A*	*3. PD*
20 August 1942	Bakssan	*XXXX. PzK.*	*1. Pz-Armee*	*Heeresgruppe A*	*3. PD, 2. rum. GebDiv, I./GJR 99*
27 August 1942	Bakssan (elements)	*III. PzK.*	*1. Pz-Armee*	*Heeresgruppe A*	*2. rum. GebDiv, I./GJR 99*
27 August 1942	Prochladnyj (elements)	*XXXX. PzK.*	*1. Pz-Armee*	*Heeresgruppe A*	*3.* and *13. PD*
2 September 1942	Bakssan (elements)	*III. PzK.*	*1. Pz-Armee*	*Heeresgruppe A*	*2. rum. GebDiv, I./GJR 99*
2 September 1942	Mosdok (elements)	*LII. AK*	*1. Pz-Armee*	*Heeresgruppe A*	*111., 370.*
2 September 1942	Stary Jurt (elements)	*XXXX. PzK.*	*1. Pz-Armee*	*Heeresgruppe A*	*3.* and *13. PD*
13 September 1942	Bakssan (elements)	*III. PzK.*	*1. Pz-Armee*	*Heeresgruppe A*	*2. rum. GebDiv, I./GJR 99*
13 September 1942	Naurskaja (elements)	*XXXX. PzK.*	*1. Pz-Armee*	*Heeresgruppe A*	*3. PD*
17 September 1942	Bakssan (elements)	*III. PzK.*	*1. Pz-Armee*	*Heeresgruppe A*	*2. rum. GebDiv, I./GJR 99*
17 September 1942	Ischerskaja (elements)	*XXXX. PzK.*	*1. Pz-Armee*	*Heeresgruppe A*	*3. PD*
20 September 1942	Bakssan (elements)	*III. PzK.*	*1. Pz-Armee*	*Heeresgruppe A*	*2. rum. GebDiv, I./GJR 99*
20 September 1942	Mosdok Bridgehead (elements)	*LII. AK*	*1. Pz-Armee*	*Heeresgruppe A*	*111., 370., 13. PD*
20 September 1942	Konsowod (elements)	*XXXX. PzK.*	*1. Pz-Armee*	*Heeresgruppe A*	*3. PD, Kosaken-Regiment von Jungschultz*
26 September 1942	Bakssan (main body)	*III. PzK.*	*1. Pz-Armee*	*Heeresgruppe A*	*2. rum. GebDiv, I./GJR 99, 13. PD, 370.*
26 September 1942	Mosdok (elements)	*XXXX. PzK.*	*1. Pz-Armee*	*Heeresgruppe A*	*3. PD, Kosaken-Regiment von Jungschultz*
10 October 1942	Bakssan-Maisskij	*III. PzK.*	*1. Pz-Armee*	*Heeresgruppe A*	*2. rum. GebDiv, I./GJR 99, 13. PD, 370.*
26 October 1942	Argudan	*III. PzK.*	*1. Pz-Armee*	*Heeresgruppe A*	*2. rum. GebDiv, I./GJR 99, 13. PD, 370.*
3 November 1942	Mairamadag	*III. PzK.*	*1. Pz-Armee*	*Heeresgruppe A*	*2. rum. GebDiv, I./GJR 99, 13. PD*
10 November 1942	Mairamadag	*III. PzK.*	*1. Pz-Armee*	*Heeresgruppe A*	*2. rum. GebDiv, I./GJR 99, 13. PD, SS-W*
24 November 1942	Dsuarikau	*III. PzK.*	*1. Pz-Armee*	*Heeresgruppe A*	*2. rum. GebDiv, I./GJR 99, 13. PD, SS-W*
1 December 1942	Transport	—	—	*Heeresgruppe Don*	—
3 December 1942	Remontnaja	*LVII. PzK.*	*4. Pz-Armee*	*Heeresgruppe Don*	*6. PD., 15. Flak., 5. rum. KD, 8. rum. KD*
12 December 1942	Pimentscherni	*LVII. PzK.*	*4. Pz-Armee*	*Heeresgruppe Don*	*6. PD., 15. Flak., 5. rum. KD, 8. rum. KD*
17 December 1942	Akssaj	*LVII. PzK.*	*4. Pz-Armee*	*Heeresgruppe Don*	*6. PD., 17. PD, 15. Flak., 5. rum. KD, 8. rum. KD*
23 December 1942	Akssaj	*LVII. PzK.*	*4. Pz-Armee*	*Heeresgruppe Don*	*17. PD, 15. Flak., 5. rum. KD, 8. rum. KD*
31 December 1942	Remontnaja	*LVII. PzK.*	*4. Pz-Armee*	*Heeresgruppe Don*	*17. PD, SS-W,* elements of *16. (mot.)*
2 January 1943	Orlowskaja	*LVII. PzK.*	*4. Pz-Armee*	*Heeresgruppe Don*	*17. PD, SS-W*
8 January 1943	Krassnyj Skotowod	*LVII. PzK.*	*4. Pz-Armee*	*Heeresgruppe Don*	*17. PD, SS-W*

Date	*23. PD*	Corps	Field Army	Field-Army Group	Neighboring Divisions[1]
12 January 1943	Krassnyj Skotowod	*LVII. PzK.*	*4. Pz-Armee*	*Heeresgruppe Don*	*17. PD, SS-W, 16. (mot.)*
18 January 1943	South of Manytsch	*LVII. PzK.*	*4. Pz-Armee*	*Heeresgruppe Don*	*17. PD, SS-W*
23 January 1943	South of Manytsch	*LVII. PzK.*	*4. Pz-Armee*	*Heeresgruppe Don*	*SS-W*
29 January 1943	Kagelnitschek	*LVII. PzK.*	*4. Pz-Armee*	*Heeresgruppe Don*	*SS-W, 17. PD, 11. PD*
3 February 1943	Bataisk Bridgehead	*LVII. PzK.*	*4. Pz-Armee*	*Heeresgruppe Don*	*111., 16. (mot.), 17. PD*
11 February 1943	Rostow	Commander of Don Bridgehead *LVII. PzK.*	*4. Pz-Armee*	*Heeresgruppe Don*	*16. (mot.), 15. LwFD, 111.*
15 February 1943	West of Rostow	*LVII. PzK.*	*4. Pz-Armee*	*Heeresgruppe Süd*	*16. (mot.), 15. LwFD*
16 February 1943	Mius	*XXIX. AK*	*4. Pz-Armee*	*Heeresgruppe Süd*	*79., 15. LwFD, 16. (mot.)*
20 February 1943	Mius	*XXIX. AK*	*Armee-Abt. Hollidt*	*Heeresgruppe Süd*	*79., 16. (mot.)*
24 February 1943	Mius	*XXIX. AK*	*Armee-Abt. Hollidt*	*Heeresgruppe Süd*	*79., 16. (mot.), 15. LwFD, mot. Reg 287*
27 February 1943	Mius	*Korps z.b.V. Mieth*	*Armee-Abt. Hollidt*	*Heeresgruppe Süd*	*384., 336.*
4 March 1943	Mius	*Korps z.b.V. Mieth*	*Armee-Abt. Hollidt*	*Heeresgruppe Süd*	*384., 336.*
16 March 1943	Mius	*Korps z.b.V. Mieth*	*Armee-Abt. Hollidt*	*Heeresgruppe Süd*	*Gruppe Oberst Salengre, 336.*
18 March 1943	Makejewka	—	*6. Armee*	*Heeresgruppe Süd*	—
29 March 1943	Makejewka	—	*6. Armee*	*Heeresgruppe Süd*	—
18 April 1943	Makejewka	*XXIV. PzK.*	*6. Armee*	*Heeresgruppe Süd*	*16. (mot.)*
1 May 1943	Makejewka	—	*6. Armee*	*Heeresgruppe Süd*	—
14 May 1943	Makejewka	—	*6. Armee*	*Heeresgruppe Süd*	—
1 June 1943	Makejewka	—	*6. Armee*	*Heeresgruppe Süd*	—
21 June 1943	Makejewka	—	*6. Armee*	*Heeresgruppe Süd*	—
7 July 1943	Artemowsk	*XXIV. PzK.*	*1. Pz-Armee*	*Heeresgruppe Süd*	—
14 July 1943	South of Isjum	*XXIV. PzK.*	*1. Pz-Armee*	*Heeresgruppe Süd*	*17. PD*
19 July 1943	Sneshnoje	*XXIV. PzK.*	*6. Armee*	*Heeresgruppe Süd*	*16. PGD*
25 July 1943	Dmitrijewka/Mius	*XXIV. PzK.*	*6. Armee*	*Heeresgruppe Süd*	*16. PGD* and 1/3 of *111.*
5 August 1943	Dmitrijewka/Mius	*XXIV. PzK.*	*6. Armee*	*Heeresgruppe Süd*	*16. PGD*
11 August 1943	Movement	—	*1. Pz-Armee*	*Heeresgruppe Süd*	—
13 August 1943	South of Isjum	*XXXX. PzK.*	*1. Pz-Armee*	*Heeresgruppe Süd*	*387., 17. PD, 46., 257.*
17 August 1943	Dolgenkaja	*XXXX. PzK.*	*1. Pz-Armee*	*Heeresgruppe Süd*	*387., 17. PD, 46., 257.*
19 August 1943	Dolgenkaja	*XXXX. PzK.*	*1. Pz-Armee*	*Heeresgruppe Süd*	*387., 17. PD, 16. PGD, 46., 257.*
25 August 1943	Dolgenkaja	*XXXX. PzK.*	*1. Pz-Armee*	*Heeresgruppe Süd*	*387., 17. PD, 16. PGD, 46., 257.*
4 September 1943	South of Dolgenkaja	*XXXX. PzK.*	*1. Pz-Armee*	*Heeresgruppe Süd*	*387., 17. PD, 16. PGD, 46., 257.*
7 September 1943	West of Kramatorskaja	*XXXX. PzK.*	*1. Pz-Armee*	*Heeresgruppe Süd*	*62., 38.,* elements of *16. PGD, 333.*
9 September 1943	Slawjanka	*XXXX. PzK.*	*1. Pz-Armee*	*Heeresgruppe Süd*	*16. PGD*
15 September 1943	Grigorjewka	*XXXX. PzK.*	*1. Pz-Armee*	*Heeresgruppe Süd*	*KG 9. PD, 16. PGD, 125.*
20 September 1943	Dnjepropetrowsk	*LVII. PzK.*	*1. Pz-Armee*	*Heeresgruppe Süd*	*KG 62., KG 38., 387., 46., 15.*
26 September 1943	Tarasowka	*LII. AK*	*1. Pz-Armee*	*Heeresgruppe Süd*	*355.*
29 September 1943	Mischurin Rog	*LVII. PzK.*	*1. Pz-Armee*	*Heeresgruppe Süd*	*SS-KD*

Date	*23. PD*	Corps	Field Army	Field-Army Group	Neighboring Divisions[1]
1 October 1943	Mischurin Rog	*LVII. PzK.*	*1. Pz-Armee*	*Heeresgruppe Süd*	Elements of *GD*, elements of *38., SS-KD*
10 October 1943	Mischurin Rog	*LII. AK*	*1. Pz-Armee*	*Heeresgruppe Süd*	*9. PD, 355.*, elements of *SS-KD*
15 October 1943	Mischurin Rog	*LVII. PzK.*	*1. Pz-Armee*	*Heeresgruppe Süd*	Elements of *62.*, elements of *38., 306., GD*, elements of *6. PD*, elements of *SS-KD*
21 October 1943	North of Kriwoi Rog	*LVII. PzK.*	*1. Pz-Armee*	*Heeresgruppe Süd*	Elements of *62.*, elements of *38., 15., 306.*, elements of *SS-KD*
28 October 1943	North of Kriwoi Rog	*LVII. PzK.*	*1. Pz-Armee*	*Heeresgruppe Süd*	*15.*, elements of *17. PD*, elements of *SS-T*
8 November 1943	North of Kriwoi Rog	*LVII. PzK.*	*1. Pz-Armee*	*Heeresgruppe Süd*	*Gruppe Schwerin (16. PD), GD, Gruppe Sperl (9. PD* and *1. SS-KD), 62., KG 38.*
20 November 1943	North of Kriwoi Rog	*LVII. PzK.*	*1. Pz-Armee*	*Heeresgruppe Süd*	*16. PGD, 9. PD, 15., 62., GD*
3 December 1943	North of Kriwoi Rog	*LVII. PzK.*	*1. Pz-Armee*	*Heeresgruppe Süd*	*16. PGD, 9. PD, 15., 62., GD*, 1/3 of *294.*
14 December 1943	North of Kriwoi Rog	*LVII. PzK.*	*1. Pz-Armee*	*Heeresgruppe Süd*	*9. PD, 15., 62.*, 1/3 of *294.*, 1/3 of *14. PD*
26 December 1943	North of Kriwoi Rog	*LVII. PzK.*	*1. Pz-Armee*	*Heeresgruppe Süd*	*9. PD, 15., 62.*, 1/3 of *294.*, elements of *SS-T*
29 December 1943	North of Kriwoi Rog	*LVII. PzK.*	*6. Armee*	*Heeresgruppe Süd*	*9. PD, 15., 62.*, 1/3 of *294.*, elements of *SS-T*
1 January 1944	North of Kriwoi Rog	*LVII. PzK.*	*6. Armee*	*Heeresgruppe Süd*	*62.*, 1/3 of *294., SS-T*
6 January 1944	East of Kriwoi Rog (armored elements)	*XXX. AK*	*6. Armee*	*Heeresgruppe Süd*	*304., 123., 46., 9. PD, 257.*
6 January 1944	North of Kriwoi Rog (main body)	*LVII. PzK.*	*6. Armee*	*Heeresgruppe Süd*	*62.*, 1/3 of *294., SS-T*
18 January 1944	North of Kriwoi Rog (main body)	*LVII. PzK.*	*6. Armee*	*Heeresgruppe Süd*	*62.*, 1/3 of *294., SS-T*
30 January 1944	North of Kriwoi Rog (main body)	*LVII. PzK.*	*6. Armee*	*Heeresgruppe Süd*	*62.*, 1/3 of *294., SS-T, 9. PD*
1 February 1944	East of Kriwoi Rog (armored elements)	*XXX. AK*	*6. Armee*	*Heeresgruppe Süd*	*304., 123., 46., 9. PD, 257.*
1 February 1944	North of Kriwoi Rog (main body)	*LVII. PzK.*	*6. Armee*	*Heeresgruppe Süd*	*62.*, 1/3 of *294., SS-T*
5 February 1944	Southeast of Kriwoi Rog (1/3)	*XXX. AK*	*6. Armee*	*Heeresgruppe Süd*	*304., 123., 46., 9. PD, 257.*
5 February 1944	North of Kriwoi Rog (2/3)	*LVII. PzK.*	*6. Armee*	*Heeresgruppe Süd*	*62.*, 1/3 of *294.*
10 February 1944	Southeast of Kriwoi Rog	*XXX. AK*	*6. Armee*	*Heeresgruppe Süd*	*304., 123., 46.*
20 February 1944	Kriwoi Rog	*XXX. AK*	*6. Armee*	*Heeresgruppe Süd*	*15., 304., 123., 46.*
1 March 1944	West of Kriwoi Rog	*LVII. PzK.*	*6. Armee*	*Heeresgruppe Süd*	*16. PGD, 15., KG 123., 257.* (with elements of *294., 62.* and *9. PD*), *46.*
13 March 1944	Jenalez	*LVII. PzK.*	*6. Armee*	*Heeresgruppe Süd*	*24. PD* (and *16. PGD*), *KG 384., KG 257., 46.*
21 March 1944	Wossnessensk	—	*6. Armee*	*Heeresgruppe Süd*	—
26 March 1944	Odessa	—	*6. Armee*	*Heeresgruppe Südukraine*	—
2 April 1944	Kischinew	*IV. AK*	*8. Armee*	*Heeresgruppe Südukraine*	*24. PD, GD, 79.*
15 April 1944	Jassy	*IV. AK*	*8. Armee*	*Heeresgruppe Südukraine*	*79., KG 376., 5. rum. KD, 7. rum. KD*
1 May 1944	Jassy	*Korpsgruppe Mieth (IV. AK)*	*8. Armee*	*Heeresgruppe Südukraine*	*79., 376., 5. rum. KD, 7. rum. KD, 3. rum.*
28 May 1944	Jassy	*Korpsgruppe Mieth (IV. AK)*	*8. Armee*	*Heeresgruppe Südukraine*	*79., 376., 3. rum., 11. rum.*

Date	*23. PD*	Corps	Field Army	Field-Army Group	Neighboring Divisions[1]
28 May 1944	Jassy	*Korpsgruppe Mieth (IV. AK)*	*8. Armee*	*Heeresgruppe Südukraine*	*79., 376., 24. PD, 14. PD, 3. rum., 11. rum.*
5 June 1944	Jassy	*Korpsgruppe Mieth* (main body)	*8. Armee*	*Heeresgruppe Südukraine*	*79., 376., 3. rum., 11. rum.*
15 June 1944	Jassy	*LVII. PzK* (elements)	*8. Armee*	*Heeresgruppe Südukraine*	*24. PD, 14. PD, GD*
22 June 1944	Jassy	*Korpsgruppe Mieth (IV. AK)*	*8. Armee*	*Heeresgruppe Südukraine*	*79., 376., 3. rum., 11. rum.*
15 July 1944	Jassy	—	*8. Armee*	*Heeresgruppe Südukraine*	—
29 July 1944	Movement Mielec (main body)	—	—	—	—
29 July 1944	Movement Jaslo (elements)	*III. PzK*	*17. Armee*	*Heeresgruppe Mitte*	*1. PD*
2 August 1944	Mielec	*LIX. AK*	*17. Armee*	*Heeresgruppe Mitte*	*78. VST, 24. PD*
15 August 1944	West of Mielec	*LIX. AK*	*17. Armee*	*Heeresgruppe Mitte*	*78. VST, 371.*
19 August 1944	East of Opatow	*XXXXVIII. PzK*	*4. Pz-Armee*	*Heeresgruppe Mitte*	*72., 1. PD, 291., 3. PD*
26 August 1944	East of Opatow	*XXXXVIII. PzK*	*4. Pz-Armee*	*Heeresgruppe Mitte*	*88., 1.PD, 17.PD*
31 August1944	Southwest of Opatow	*XXXXVIII. PzK*	*4. Pz-Armee*	*Heeresgruppe Mitte*	*1. PD, 3. PD,* remnants of *213. SD*
9 September 1944	Movement from Poland	—	—	—	—
12 September 1944	Budapest	—	—	*Heeresgruppe Südukraine*	—
21 September 1944	Thorenburg	—	*6. Armee*	*Heeresgruppe Südukraine*	Hungarian 2nd Armored Division, *KG 20. PD*
27 September 1944	Großwardein	*III. PzK*	*6. Armee*	*Heeresgruppe Süd*	—
28 September 1944	Großwardein	*Korpsgruppe Breith (III. PzK* and Hungarian VII Corps*)*	*Armee-Gruppe Fretter-Pico* (Hungarian 6th and 2nd Armies)	*Heeresgruppe Süd*	Hungarian 12th and 8th Reserve Divisions
6 October 1944	Southwest of Großwardein	*Korpsgruppe Breith (III. PzK* and Hungarian VII Corps*)*	*Armee-Gruppe Fretter-Pico* (Hungarian 6th and 2nd Armies)	*Heeresgruppe Süd*	*1. PD, 76.,* Hungarian 12th and 8th Reserve Divisions
12 October 1944	Komadi	*III. PzK*	*6. Armee*	*Heeresgruppe Süd*	*13. PD, 1. PD, 46., KG 22. SS-KD, KG "FHH"*
14 October 1944	Berettyo-Ujfalu	*III. PzK*	*6. Armee*	*Heeresgruppe Süd*	*13. PD, 1. PD, 76., KG 22. SS-KD, KG "FHH", PB 109*
20 October 1944	Debrecen	*III. PzK*	*6. Armee*	*Heeresgruppe Süd*	*13. PD, 1. PD, 46., 76., KG 22. SS-KD, KG "FHH", PB 109*
26 October 1944	Nyiregyhaza	*III. PzK*	*6. Armee*	*Heeresgruppe Süd*	*13. PD, 1. PD, KG "FHH", 3. GebDiv, 15.*

Date	*23. PD*	Corps	Field Army	Field-Army Group	Neighboring Divisions[1]
29 October 1944	Cegled	*LVII. PzK*	*Armee-Gruppe Fretter-Pico*	*Heeresgruppe Süd*	*1. PD, 24. PD*
5 November 1944	Irsa-Pilis	*LVII. PzK*	*Armee-Gruppe Fretter-Pico*	*Heeresgruppe Süd*	*1. PD, 24. PD, 13. PD, KG "FHH"*
10 November 1944	Southwest of Jaszbereny	*LVII. PzK*	*Armee-Gruppe Fretter-Pico*	*Heeresgruppe Süd*	*1. PD, KG "FHH", 46.*
18 November 1944	South of Hatvan	*LVII. PzK*	*Armee-Gruppe Fretter-Pico*	*Heeresgruppe Süd*	*46., 4. SS-PGD*
26 November 1944	Hatvan	*LVII. PzK*	*Armee-Gruppe Fretter-Pico*	*Heeresgruppe Süd*	*KG 357., 4. SS-PGD, 18. SS-PGD, 46.*
29 November 1944	Simontornya	*LVII. PzK*	*Armee-Gruppe Fretter-Pico*	*Heeresgruppe Süd*	*1. PD*
7 December 1944	"Margarethe" Position	*LVII. PzK*	*Armee-Gruppe Fretter-Pico*	*Heeresgruppe Süd*	*1. PD, 153. Feld-Artillerie-Division*
18 December 1944	"Margarethe" Position	*III. PzK*	*6. Armee*	*Heeresgruppe Süd*	*1. PD*
20 December 1944	Stuhlweißenburg	*III. PzK*	*6. Armee*	*Heeresgruppe Süd*	*1. PD*, armored elements of *3. PD*
23 December 1944	"Olga" Position (north of Stuhlweißenburg)	*I. KavKorps / Kampfgruppe Breith*	*Armeegruppe Balck*	*Heeresgruppe Süd*	*1. PD, 4. KavBrig*
7 January 1945	"Olga" Position	*I. KavKorps / Kampfgruppe Breith*	*Armeegruppe Balck*	*Heeresgruppe Süd*	*4. KavBrig*
16 January 1945	"Olga" Position	*I. KavKorps / Kampfgruppe Breith*	*Armeegruppe Balck*	*Heeresgruppe Süd*	*4. KavBrig*
29 January 1945	Aba	*III. PzK*	*Armeegruppe Balck*	*Heeresgruppe Süd*	*3. PD, 1. PD, 25. ung.*
19 February 1945	North of Aba	*III. PzK*	*Armeegruppe Balck*	*Heeresgruppe Süd*	*3. PD, 1. PD, 25. ung.*
1 March 1945	North of Aba	*III. PzK*	*Armeegruppe Balck*	*Heeresgruppe Süd*	*3. PD, 1. PD, 356., 25. ung.*
6 March 1945	North of Aba	*III. PzK*	*Armeegruppe Balck*	*Heeresgruppe Süd*	—
9 March 1945	Sar Egres	*I. SS-PzK*	*6. SS-Pz-Armee*	*Heeresgruppe Süd*	*20. ung., 3. KD, 4. KD*
17 March 1945	Simontornya	*I. KavKorps*	*6. Armee*	*Heeresgruppe Süd*	*20. ung., 3. KD, 4. KD*
23 March 1945	Lake Balaton	*I. KavKorps*	*6. Armee*	*Heeresgruppe Süd*	*KG 44., 3. KD, 4. KD*
26 March 1945	Lake Balaton	*I. KavKorps*	*6. Armee*	*Heeresgruppe Süd*	*KG 44.*
28 March 1945	Keszthely	*I. KavKorps*	*2. Pz-Armee*	*Heeresgruppe Süd*	*KG 44.*
12 April 1945	North of Radkersburg	*I. KavKorps*	*2. Pz-Armee*	*Heeresgruppe Süd*	*4. KD, KG 44., 3. KD, 16. SS-PGD, 14. SS*

Date	*23. PD*	Corps	Field Army	Field-Army Group	Neighboring Divisions[1]
7 May 1945	East of Mureck	*I. KavKorps*	*2. Pz-Armee*	*Heeresgruppe Südost*	*4. KD, 3. KD, KG 44., 16. SS-PGD*

1 Editor's Note: Unless specified otherwise, the references are to infantry divisions. *PD = Panzer-Division; rum. = rumänisch* (Romanian); *GebDiv = Gebirgs-Division; GJR = Gebirgsjäger-Regiment; LwFD = Luftwaffen-Feld-Division; JD = Jäger-Division; GD = Panzergrenadier-Division "Großdeutschland"; SS-W = 5. SS-Panzer-Division "Wiking"; KD = Kavallerie-Division; 287 = motorisiertes Regiment z.b.V. 287; PGD = Panzergrenadier-Division; KG = Kampfgruppe; SS-T = 3. SS-Panzer-Division "Totenkopf"; SD = Sicherungs-Division; ung. = ungarisch* (Hungarian); *FHH = Feldherrnhalle; PB = Panzer-Brigade; KavKorps = Kavallerie-Korps; KavBrig = Kavallerie-Brigade*

2 Editor's Note: *AK= Armee-Korps; PzK = Panzer-Korps*

3 Editor's Note: It is not known what section this was.

4 Editor's Note: Rank listed is at the time of the award.

Appendix 4
Engagement Days of the 23. Panzer-Division

Date / Year	Type of Engagement	Senior Command (Field Army)
1941/1942		
15 October 1941 – 20 March 1942	Participation in the occupation of France	
21 March 1942 – 11 May 1942	Preparations for operations and defensive operations in the Kharkov area	*6. Armee*
12-21 May 1942	Defensive fighting northeast of Kharkov	*6. Armee*
22 – 27 May 1942	Pocket battle southwest of Kharkov	*6. Armee*
28 May 1942 – 27 June 1942	Defensive operations and preparations for operations east of Kharkov	*6. Armee*
28 June 1942 – 7 July 1942	Breakthrough and pursuit in the direction of the Upper Don; capture of Woronesch	*2.* and *6. Armee*
8 – 19 July 1942	Breakthrough and pursuit to the Middle Don	*6. Armee*
20 July 1942 – 13 August 1942	Pursuit across the Lower Don	*4. Panzer-Armee*
19 August 1942 – 18 November 1942	Fighting in the Terek area	*1. Panzer-Armee*
19-24 November 1942	Fighting in the Terek area	*1. Panzer-Armee*
12-24 December 1942	Relief Attack (Stalingrad)	*4. Panzer-Armee*
1943		
15 December 1942 – 11 February 1943	Defensive fighting east of the Lower Don and along the Manytsch	*4. Panzer-Armee*
14 February 1943 – 4 March 1943	Defensive fighting in the Donez area	*6. Armee*
5 – 31 March 1943	Defensive fighting along the Mius/Donez Position	*6. Armee*
1 April 1943 – 3 July 1943	Employment in the area of operations of the *6. Armee*	*6. Armee*
4 July 1943 – 17 August 1943	Defensive fighting along the Mius and the Middle Don, including:	
17 July 1943 – 2 August 1943	Defensive fighting along the Mius	*6. Armee*
18 August 1943 – 27 September 1943	Defensive fighting in southern Russia and withdrawal to the Dnjepr, including:	*1. Panzer-Armee*
18 – 26 August 1943	The 2nd Defensive Battle at Isjum	*1. Panzer-Armee*
27 August 1943 – 16 September 1943	Defensive fighting along the Mius and the Donez Basin	*1. Panzer-Armee*
28 September 1943 – 31 December 1943	Defensive fighting along the Dnjepr, including:	
15 October 1943 – 9 December 1943	Defensive fighting in the Dnjepropetrowsk — Kriwoi Rog area	*1. Panzer-Armee* and *6. Armee*

Date / Year	Type of Engagement	Senior Command (Field Army)
1944		
1 – 19 January 1944	Defensive fighting in the southern Ukraine and west of Kiev, including:	*6. Armee*
1 – 19 January 1944	3rd Defensive Battle in the Nikopol Bridgehead and north of Kriwoi Rog	*6. Armee*
30 January 1944 – 2 February 1944	Defensive fighting for Kriwoi Rog and withdrawal from the Nikopol area	*6. Armee*
20 January 1944 – 12 May 1944	Defensive fighting on the Crimea peninsula and in the southern Ukraine, including:	*6. Armee*
3 – 22 February 1944	Defensive fighting for Kriwoi Rog and withdrawal from the Nikopol area	*6. Armee*
23 February 1944 – 6 March 1944	Defensive fighting along the Dnjepr and the Ingulez	*6. Armee*
7 – 26 March 1944	Defensive fighting north of Nikolajew and fighting withdrawal to the Bug	*6. Armee*
27 March 1944 – 12 May 1944	Defensive fighting in northern Bessarabia and in the foothills of the Carpathians	*8. Armee*
26 April 1944 – 12 May 1944	Defensive fighting along the Upper Moldau	*8. Armee*
13 May 1944 – 22 July 1944	Positional warfare in the area of operations of *Heeresgruppe Südukraine*, including:	*8. Armee*
30 May 1944 – 6 June 1944	Offensive operations north of Jassy	*8. Armee*
30 July 1944 – 1 August 1944	Fighting in the Krosno area	*17. Armee*
2 – 18 August 1944	Offensive and defensive operations in the Mielec area	*17. Armee*
19 August 1944 – 8 September 1944	Offensive operations against the Soviet bridgehead on the Vistula northwest of Sandomierz	*4. Panzer-Armee*
22 – 25 September 1944	Defensive fighting north of Thorenburg	*6. Armee*
26 September 1944 – 5 October 1944	Offensive and defensive operations at Großwardein and to the north	*6. Armee*
6 – 27 October 1944	Defensive fighting on the Hungarian plains (*puszta*)	*6. Armee*
30 October 1944 – 28 November 1944	Defensive fighting between the Middle Theiß and the Danube	*6. Armee*
1945		
30 November 1944 – 4 February 1945	Defensive and offensive operations south and north of Stuhlweißenburg	*6. Armee*
5 February – 4 March 1945	Defensive fighting south of Stuhlweißenburg and in the "Margarethe" Position	*6. Armee*
5 – 18 March 1945	Offensive operations south of Stuhlweißenburg and advance to the Sio River	*6. SS-Panzer-Armee*
19 – 28 March 1945	Withdrawal movements and defensive fighting along the north bank of Lake Balaton	*6. Armee*
29 March 1945 – 4 April 1945	Fighting withdrawal to the Mur River at Muraszerdaheli	*2. Panzer-Armee*
4 April 1945 – 8 May 1945	Defensive fighting along the German/Hungarian frontier	*2.Panzer-Armee*

Appendix 5

Total Losses of the 23. Panzer-Division (based on German Red Cross Records)

7,476 Dead	2,883 Missing

Losses Sustained by the Individual Troop Elements

The numbers listed below come from the German government agency responsible for notifying the next-of-kin of those killed during the war as part of the German Armed Forces[111]. That agency has based those figures on the original loss reports it has at its disposal.

111 Editor's Note: This agency has the rather unwieldy title in German of *"Dienststelle für die Benachrichtigung der nächsten Angehörigen von Gefallenen der ehemaligen deutschen Wehrmacht (WASt)"* (roughly: Agency for the Notification of Next-of-Kin of the Dead of the Former German Armed Forces").

The information provided should not necessarily be considered complete. Difficulties with the entries and the incompleteness of the documents available do not allow reconciliation. The different goals in capturing the numbers of losses also lead to differences in the numbers provided by the German Red Cross and the government.

Despite these issues, it is important to include the numbers of losses, because they provide a good overview of the make-up of the overall casualties by the individual troop elements of the division. The *Divisions-Kampfschule* is included in the tallies for the divisional headquarters and the escort company. Likewise regrettable is the fact that some troop elements are missing entirely. In the case of *Heeres-Flak-Abteilung 278* and *Panzer-Pionier-Bataillon 51*, losses are also included for the period before those formations joined the division.

Division Headquarters, Escort Company and *Kampfschule*

Losses	Rank Category	1939	1940	1941	1942	1943	1944	1945
Dead	Officers	—	—	—	5	5	3	—
	NCO's	—	—	—	4	11	5	—
	Enlisted	—	—	—	5	37	17	2
Missing	Officers	—	—	—	—	1	—	—
	NCO's	—	—	—	—	1	—	—
	Enlisted	—	—	—	3	14	4	—
Wounded	Officers	—	—	—	2	3	3	—
	NCO's	—	—	—	1	33	7	—
	Enlisted	—	—	—	2	186	38	—

Feld-Ersatz-Bataillon 128

Losses	Rank Category	1939	1940	1941	1942	1943	1944	1945
Dead	Officers	—	—	—	—	3	—	—
	NCO's	—	—	—	—	5	2	3
	Enlisted	—	—	—	4	14	4	16
Missing	Officers	—	—	—	—	—	—	—
	NCO's	—	—	—	—	—	1	—
	Enlisted	—	—	—	1	2	3	—
Wounded	Officers	—	—	—	—	2	3	—
	NCO's	—	—	—	—	6	27	—
	Enlisted	—	—	—	2	49	47	1

Headquarters, *Schützen-Brigade 23* (*Panzergrenadier-Brigade 23*)

Losses	Rank Category	1939	1940	1941	1942	1943	1944	1945
Dead	Officers	—	—	—	4	—	—	—
	NCO's	—	—	—	2	—	—	—
	Enlisted	—	—	—	3	—	—	—
Missing	Officers	—	—	—	—	—	—	—
	NCO's	—	—	—	—	—	—	—
	Enlisted	—	—	—	2	—	—	—
Wounded	Officers	—	—	—	4	—	—	—
	NCO's	—	—	—	—	—	—	—
	Enlisted	—	—	—	15	—	—	—

Panzer-Regiment 201 (Panzer-Regiment 23)

Losses	Rank Category	1939	1940	1941	1942	1943	1944	1945
Dead	Officers	—	—	—	31	20	14	5
	NCO's	—	—	—	83	51	63	8
	Enlisted	—	—	—	196	122	76	8
Missing	Officers	—	—	—	1	—	2	—
	NCO's	—	—	—	2	6	5	—
	Enlisted	—	—	—	18	33	22	—
Wounded	Officers	—	—	—	67	27	21	—
	NCO's	—	—	—	157	141	148	1
	Enlisted	—	—	—	552	484	331	—

Schützen-Regiment 126 (Panzergrenadier-Regiment 126)

Losses	Rank Category	1939	1940	1941	1942	1943	1944	1945
Dead	Officers	—	—	—	9	15	14	4
	NCO's	—	—	—	41	95	75	12
	Enlisted	—	—	—	284	508	387	78
Missing	Officers	—	—	—	1	1	4	—
	NCO's	—	—	—	3	16	25	—
	Enlisted	—	—	—	71	229	182	9
Wounded	Officers	—	—	—	46	78	57	3
	NCO's	—	—	—	172	343	245	21
	Enlisted	—	—	—	882	2,223	1,376	152

Schützen-Regiment 128 (Panzergrenadier-Regiment 128)

Losses	Rank Category	1939	1940	1941	1942	1943	1944	1945
Dead	Officers	—	—	—	9	19	10	15
	NCO's	—	—	—	80	74	97	30
	Enlisted	—	—	—	329	447	542	185
Missing	Officers	—	—	—	2	1	4	—
	NCO's	—	—	—	7	9	21	1
	Enlisted	—	—	—	38	116	223	61
Wounded	Officers	—	—	—	28	39	64	7
	NCO's	—	—	—	149	208	319	35
	Enlisted	—	—	—	929	1,551	2,037	298

Panzer-Artillerie-Regiment 128

Losses	Rank Category	1939	1940	1941	1942	1943	1944	1945
Dead	Officers	—	—	—	17	10	5	1
	NCO's	—	—	—	30	37	18	4
	Enlisted	—	—	2	162	101	55	7
Missing	Officers	—	—	—	—	4	1	—
	NCO's	—	—	—	1	4	9	—
	Enlisted	—	—	—	13	21	31	—
Wounded	Officers	—	—	—	38	48	22	2
	NCO's	—	—	—	83	92	67	3
	Enlisted	—	—	—	454	351	212	8

Kradschützen-Bataillon 23 (Panzer-Aufklärungs-Abteilung 23)

Losses	Rank Category	1939	1940	1941	1942	1943	1944	1945
Dead	Officers	—	—	—	12	15	4	—
	NCO's	—	—	—	45	28	17	8
	Enlisted	—	—	—	272	160	50	10
Missing	Officers	—	—	—	—	—	—	—
	NCO's	—	—	—	5	8	3	—
	Enlisted	—	—	—	64	48	17	—
Wounded	Officers	—	—	—	42	37	22	—
	NCO's	—	—	—	159	172	106	—
	Enlisted	—	—	—	706	795	337	—

Panzerjäger-Abteilung 128

Losses	Rank Category	1939	1940	1941	1942	1943	1944	1945
Dead	Officers	—	—	—	3	3	4	1
	NCO's	—	—	—	9	14	7	5
	Enlisted	—	—	—	60	66	25	8
Missing	Officers	—	—	—	—	1	—	—
	NCO's	—	—	—	—	1	4	—
	Enlisted	—	—	—	5	5	9	—
Wounded	Officers	—	—	—	4	22	17	1
	NCO's	—	—	—	59	87	65	7
	Enlisted	—	—	—	267	314	164	12

Pionier-Bataillon 51, Sturm-Pionier-Bataillon 51,Panzer-Pionier-Bataillon 51

Losses	Rank Category	1939	1940	1941	1942	1943	1944	1945
Dead	Officers	2	2	4	3	6	7	2
	NCO's	9	3	8	9	23	20	12
	Enlisted	16	29	63	91	148	124	48
Missing	Officers	—	—	—	—	—	—	—
	NCO's		—	—	—	6	5	1
	Enlisted	1	—	15	7	62	75	11
Wounded	Officers		1	18	31	34	34	2
	NCO's	3	17	23	50	130	112	21
	Enlisted	15	67	259	305	655	800	117

Panzer-Nachrichten-Abteilung 128

Losses	Rank Category	1939	1940	1941	1942	1943	1944	1945
Dead	Officers	—	—	—	—	1	1	—
	NCO's	—	—	—	6	5	6	1
	Enlisted	—	—	—	20	23	29	4
Missing	Officers	—	—	—	—	—	—	—
	NCO's	—	—	—	—	1	4	—
	Enlisted	—	—	—	3	6	15	—
Wounded	Officers	—	—	—	1	—	1	—
	NCO's	—	—	—	5	3	8	—
	Enlisted	—	—	—	27	38	51	—

Heeres-Flak-Abteilung 278

Losses	Rank Category	1939	1940	1941	1942	1943	1944	1945
Dead	Officers	—	—	—	—	5	4	—
	NCO's	—	—	—	1	17	16	2
	Enlisted	—	—	—	2	66	78	4
Missing	Officers	—	—	—	—	—	1	—
	NCO's	—	—	—	—	4	4	—
	Enlisted	—	—	—	—	22	31	—
Wounded	Officers	—	—	—	—	9	4	—
	NCO's	—	—	4	—	19	34	—
	Enlisted	—	—	9	—	143	215	—

Divisions-Nachschubtruppen128, Panzer-Divisions-Nachschubtruppen 128, Verwaltungstruppen 128, Kraftfahrpark-Truppen 128

Losses	Rank Category	1939	1940	1941	1942	1943	1944	1945
Dead	Officers	—	—	—	—	1	—	1
	NCO's	—	—	—	6	—	2	—
	Enlisted	—	—	—	12	13	18	4
Missing	Officers	—	—	—	—	—	—	—
	NCO's	—	—	—	—	1	2	—
	Enlisted	—	—	—	1	1	8	2
Wounded	Officers	—	—	—	—	1	—	—
	NCO's	—	—	—	1	12	2	—
	Enlisted	—	—	—	6	32	19	5

Sanitäts-Einheiten 128

Losses	Rank Category	1939	1940	1941	1942	1943	1944	1945
Dead	Officers	—	—	—	—	—	—	1
	NCO's	—	—	—	4	—	—	1
	Enlisted	—	—	—	9	5	3	2
Missing	Officers	—	—	—	—	1	—	—
	NCO's	—	—	—	—	—	—	—
	Enlisted	—	—	—	—	4	2	—
Wounded	Officers	—	—	—	—	—	—	—
	NCO's	—	—	—	2	1	2	—
	Enlisted	—	—	—	18	11	8	2

Feldgendarmerie-Trupp 128

Losses	Rank Category	1939	1940	1941	1942	1943	1944	1945
Dead	Officers	—	—	—	—	—	—	—
	NCO's	—	—	—	2	—	—	—
	Enlisted	—	—	—	2	—	—	—
Missing	Officers	—	—	—	—	—	—	—
	NCO's	—	—	—	—	—	1	—
	Enlisted	—	—	—	—	—	—	—
Wounded	Officers	—	—	—	—	—	—	—
	NCO's	—	—	—	—	5	—	—
	Enlisted	—	—	—	—	1	1	—

A **Officers**

Element	Officers			Civilians		
	Authorized	On Hand	Shortfall	Authorized	On Hand	Shortfall
Division Headquarters	19	19	—	12	12	—
PR23 w/ *StuG-Batterie*	61	63	—	14	14	—
PGR 126	54	18	36	9	4	5
PGR 128	54	37	17	9	8	1
PAR 128	64	49	15	12	12	—
PAA 23	24	22	2	5	5	—
PJA 128	11	9	2	4	4	—
PNA 128	13	11	2	3	3	—

Noncommissioned Officers and Enlisted

Element	NCO's			Enlisted		
	Auth	On Hand	Shortfall	Auth	On Hand	Shortfall
Division Headquarters	42	42	—	115	51	64
PR23 w/ *StuG-Batterie*	906	890	16	1,381	1,381	—
PGR 126	436	215	221	1,818	1,106	712
PGR 128	436	263	173	1,818	1,458	360
PAR 128	358	300	58	1,498	1,404	94
HFA 278	137	113	24	696	889	—
PAA 23	216	152	64	958	726	232
PJA 128	108	45	63	229	160	69
PPB 51	111	85	26	688	533	155
PNA128	99	87	12	359	347	12
Division Support Command	136	136	—	644	582	62
Division Admin Personnel	38	35	3	171	177	—
Division Medical Personnel	74	62	12	411	412	—
Division Section V[4]	39	43	4	219	269	—
Division Armaments Personnel	11	9	2	50	51	—
Military Police	58	40	—	3	15	6
Post Office	200	45		1,200	294	—
Topography Section	1	1	—	6	5	1
Division Security Platoon	—	10	—	—	55	—
Totals	3,221	2,588	678	11,064	9921	1,703

Weapons Status

Type of Weapon	Authorized	On Hand	Shortfall
Pistole 08/38	4,380	2,170	1,670
Other types of pistols	—	540	—
Karabiner 98k	8,864	8,463	401
Karabiner 98k w/ telescope	531	50	481
Gewehr 41	531	28	503
Rifle Grenade Launcher	387	388	
Maschinenpistole 38/40	999	882	117
Armored vehicle machine guns	426	185	241
Leichte MG 34/42	702	423	241
Schwere MG 34/42	78	34	44
Other machine guns	—	38	—
Heavy mortar (8cm)	40	24	16
Light mortar (5cm)	—	3	—
3.7cm Pak (SPW)	6	2	4
5cm Pak 38	21	22	—
7.5cm Pak 40 (towed)	9	10	
7.5cm Pak 40 (self-propelled)	26	9 7.5cm 1 5cm	—
7.62cm Pak (self-propelled)	—	—	—
7.5cm Pak (SPW)	—	2	—
Heavy antitank rifle (carried)	14	7	7
Heavy antitank rifle (*SPW*)	1	3	—
Light infantry gun (towed)	20	15	5
Heavy infantry gun (Model 33) (towed)	8	6	2
Heavy infantry gun (self-propelled)	7	5	2
2cm Flak 30 (trailer mounted)	57	5	—
2cm Flak 30 (self-propelled)	57	—	—
2cm Flak 38 (trailer mounted)	57	20	—
2cm Flak 38 (self-propelled)	57	25	—
2cm Flak (4 barreled, trailer mounted and self-propelled)	4	6	—
Light field howitzer (Model 18) (towed)	20	20	—
Heavy field howitzer (Model 18) (towed)	8	8	—
10cm schwere Kanone (Model 18)	4	4	—
Schweres Wurfgerät 40	14	5	9
8.8cm Flak 36/37	8	10	—
Heavy field howitzer (Model 18/1) (self-propelled) (*Hummel*)	6	6	—
7.5cm KwK. l/70 "Panther"	96	6	90

Armored Vehicle Status

	Pz V (7,5cm)	*Pz III (5cm)*	*Pz III (7,5cm)*	*IV (7,5cm)*	*IV (Hummel)*	*Befehlspanzer 267*	*Befehlspanzer 268*
Authorized	96	11	—	93	6	4	1
On Hand	6	20	2	28	6	4	—
Operational	6	14	2	21	6	3	—
Shortfall	90	—	—	65	—	—	1

	Self-propelled (German and Czech)	Heavy infantry gun on *Pz III*	Armored Car	Armored signals vehicle	*SPW*	Armored artillery observation vehicle	*Pz III* observation tank
Authorized	26	5	24	6	201	13	2
On Hand	10	5	23	15	68	12	2
Operational	6	4	14	11	52	5	2
Shortfall	16	—	—	—	133	1	—

Wheeled Vehicle Status

Status	Motorcycles		Staff Cars		Trucks	
	No sidecar	With sidecar	—	Cross-country	—	Cross-country
Authorized	524	369	225	663	837	737
On Hand	162	322	328	563	1,555	285
Operational	147	305	302	511	1,416	224
Shortfall	362	47	—	100	—	452
Excess	—	—	103	—	720	—

Status	Prime Movers						
	1-ton	3-ton	5-ton	8-ton	12-ton	18-ton	7/1
Authorized	161	31	—	32	1	7	4
On Hand	114	40	26	27	19	7	2
Operational	107	39	22	21	18	7	2
Shortfall	47	—	—	5	—	—	2
Excess	—	9	26	—	18	—	—

Overview of Vehicular Status by Formation

	Motorcycles		Staff cars		Trucks		Prime Movers 1-5 ton		Prime Movers 5-18 ton	
Div HQs	19	19	35	39	35	33	2	2	—	—
PR23	41	41	49	53	135	126	10	10	14	14
PGR 126	65	54	94	88	250	245	53	44	—	—
PGR 128	61	53	95	119	308	348	57	43	1	1
PAR 128	46	42	200	196	242	225	35	33	15	15
HFA 278		42		77		88		7		12
PJA128	23	13	40	30	58	35	25	15	4	3
PPB 51	41	41	31	34	148	145	2	2	1	1
PAA23	131	103	67	66	92	80	11	9	1	1
PNA128	13	13	88	88	35	35	1	1	—	—

	Motorcycles		Staff cars		Trucks		Prime Movers 1-5 ton		Prime Movers 5-18 ton	
Div Spt Cmd	26	26	34	34	294	291	—	—	—	—
Admin Sec	6	11	6	6	35	38	1	1	—	—
Med Sec	11	11	17	17	101	101	—	—	—	—
Maint Sec	9	9	12	12	66	75	5	6	7	10
Field Training Bat.	3	5	9	9	21	47	6	7	—	—
Weapons Co	1	1	2	2	14	17	—	—	—	—
MP Sec	—	—	23	23	8	8	—	—	—	—
Post Off	—	—	1	1	4	4				

Appendix 7

Knight's Cross Recipients of the Division

Oakleaves to the Knight's Cross of the Iron Cross

Date	Name	Rank	Duty Position / Formation	Comments
16 November 1944	Ruge, Gerd	*Major*	Acting commander, *PGR 128*	648th member of the German Armed Forces to be so honored

Knight's Cross of the Iron Cross[112]

Date	Name	Rank[5]	Duty Position / Formation	Comments
4 October 1942	Zejdlik, Franz	*Major*	Commander, *PPB 51*	Last rank held: *Oberstleutnant*
25 January 1943	Behr, Rudolf	*Hauptmann*	Commander, *III./PR 201*	Killed 23 July 1943. Promoted to *Major* posthumously
26 August 1943	Bade, Kurt	*Unteroffizier*	Platoon leader, *4./PAA23*	Last rank held: *Oberfeldwebel*
22 August 1943	Von Vormann, Nikolaus	*Generalleutnant*	Commander, *23. Panzer-Division*	Last rank held: *General der Panzertruppen*
7 September 1943	Alber, Robert	*Hauptmann der Reserve*	Acting Commander, *I./PR 201*	
7 September 1943	Ruge, Gerd	*Hauptmann*	Commander, *I./PGR 128*	Oak Leaves (See above.)
16 September 1943	Schägger, Peter	*Major der Reserve*	Commander, *PAA 23*	Honor Roll Clasp (14 August 1942)
19 September 1943	Sander, Joachim	*Oberstleutnant*	Commander, *PR 23*	729th recipient of the Oakleaves to the Knight's Cross on 5 February 1945 (posthumously) as an *Oberst* and commander of *Panzer-Regiment 31*
6 October 1943	Fechner, Fritz	*Major*	Commander, *III./PR 23*	Last rank held: *Oberstleutnant*
28 December 1943	Fischer, Gerhard	*Oberleutnant*	Commander, *8./PR 23*	Last rank held: *Major*
15 April 1944	Wolf, Alfred	*Major*	Commander, *I./PR 23*	

112 Editor's Note: Information contained in this table differs on occasion to what was published in the original German edition published in 1963. The differing data come from the latest research contained in Veit Scherzer's *Ritterkreuzträger, 1939-1945* (Jena (Germany): Scherzers Militaire Verlag, 2005).

Date	Name	Rank[5]	Duty Position / Formation	Comments
15 May 1944	Jansen, Willi	*Oberleutnant der Reserve*	Liaison Officer in *PGR 128*	Last rank held: *Hauptmann der Reserve*
8 August 1944	Henssler, Walter	*Oberleutnant der Reserve*	Adjutant in *PGR 126*	Last rank held: *Hauptmann der Reserve*
2 September 1944	Stoll, Paul	*Unteroffizier*	Section leader in the *7./ PGR 128*	
5 September 1944	Stichtenoth, Friedrich	*Oberstleutnant*	Commander, *PGR 128*	Honor Roll Clasp on 17 May 1944. Last rank held: *Oberst*
17 September 1944	Von Radowitz, Joseph	*Oberst*	Acting Commander of the *23. Panzer-Division*	Last rank held: *Generalleutnant*
17 September 1944	Grünwaldt, Wilhelm	*Hauptmann der Reserve*	Commander, *I./PGR 126*	Honor Roll Clasp on 17 August 1944. Last rank held: *Major der Reserve*
4 October 1944	Zierhofer, Karl	*Gefreiter*	Machine Gunner in the *1./PGR 126*	Died of wounds 28 April 1945
18 November 1944	Koppe, Rudolf	*Hauptmann*	Commander, *PAA 23*	Honor Roll Clasp on 15 May 1944. Last rank held: *Major*
18 November 1944	Kujacinski, Norbert	*Hauptmann der Reserve*	Commander, *4./PR 23*	Last rank held: *Major der Reserve*
9 December 1944	Eisermann, Erich	*Feldwebel*	Reconnaissance Section Leader in the *1./PAA 23*	Last rank held: *Oberfeldwebel*
11 January 1945	Kleemann, Willy	*Oberfähnrich*	Acting Commander of the *2./PPB 51*	Last rank held: *Leutnant der Reserve*
5 February1945	Schuster, Karl	*Obergefreiter*	Gunner in the *8./PGR 126*	Apparently killed in Hungary that same month
18 February 1945	Keck, Johannes	*Leutnant der Reserve*	Acting Commander of the *2./PAA 23*	
28 March 1945	Hain, Horst	*Oberleutnant*	Commander, *3./PAA 23*	Last rank held: *Hauptmann (Bundeswehr)*

Knight's Cross of the War Service Cross with Swords

28 April 1945	Schwarz, Friedrich	*Oberfeldwebel*	Maintenance Section Leader in the *6./PR 23*

Appendix 8

Recognition in the Supplements to the Wehrmacht Daily Report

26 May 1942	Battle of Kharkov: Closing the southern pocket by the *23. Panzer-Division* of *Generalmajor* von Boineburg.
29 July 1942	Recognition of the *23. Panzer-Division* of *Generalmajor* Mack for the destruction of a Russian motorized/mechanized corps.
2 August 1942	*Oberleutnant* Fechner, *Panzer-Regiment 201*, for his decisive participation in the destruction of a Russian motorized/ mechanized corps in Martinowka.
4 February 1943	*LVII. Panzer-Korps* (*6. Panzer-Division*, *17. Panzer-Division* and the *23. Panzer-Division*) for the fighting northeast of the Manytsch.
August 1943	*23. Panzer-Division*, under the command of *Generalmajor* von Vormann, for the reduction of the Soviet bridgehead west of Dmitrijewka.
28 August 1943	*23. Panzer-Division*, under the command of *Generalleutnant* von Vormann, for the defensive success at Isjum.
4 November 1943	"During the difficult fighting in the Dnjepr Bend, the southwest German *23. Panzer-Division*, under the command of *Generalleutnant* von Vormann, distinguished itself through its exceptional bravery"

6 March 1943	Recognition of the *23. Panzer-Division* of *Oberst* Kraeber for the fighting in the area of Kriwoi Rog.
May 1944	*23. Panzer-Division*, under *Generalmajor* Kraeber, for the defensive fighting north of Jassy.
2 August 1944	*Hauptmann* Rebentisch, *I./Panzer-Regiment 23*, and *Leutnant* Ohmstede, *I./Panzergrenadier-Regiment 128*, for the reduction of the Soviet bridgehead at Baranow.
4 October 1944	"During the fighting in Transylvania, the *23. Panzer-Division*, from Baden-Wuertemberg and under the command of *Generalmajor* von Radowitz, has especially distinguished itself in both offense and defense."
22 October 1944	"In the large armored battle for Debrecen, *Major* Ruge, the commander of *Panzergrenadier-Regiment 128*, *Major* Rebentisch, the commander of *Panzer-Regiment 23*, *Oberleutnant* von Oechelhaueser in *Panzer-Regiment 23*, and *Leutnant* Mobis, the leader of a *Flak* section, especially distinguished themselves."
25 October 1944	"In the fighting around Debrecen, our armored formations destroyed the main body of the Soviet 30th Cavalry Division, which had been cut off from its rearward lines of communications, and the Soviet 30th Tank Brigade." (The text refers to the elements cut off in Kallo and Nyiregyhaza.)
2 February 1945	Recognition of *Obergefreiter* Schuster of the *8./Panzergrenadier-Regiment 126*, who destroyed numerous Soviet tanks.

Appendix 9

Commanders and Acting Commanders of the 23. Panzer-Division and Its Subordinate Troop Elements

Division Command

Generalmajor Freiherr von Boineburg-Lengsfeld (C)[113]; *Generalmajor* Mack (C); *Oberst* von Buch (Commander, *PAR 128*) (AC); *Oberst* Brückner (Commander, *Schützen-Regiment 126*)(AC); *Generalleutnant Freiherr* von Boineburg-Lengsfeld (C); *Oberst d.G.* Rossmann (*Arko 7*)(AC); *Oberst* (*Generalmajor, Generalleutnant, General der Panzertruppen*) von Vormann (C); *Oberst* (*Generalmajor*) Kraeber (C); *Oberst* (*Generalmajor, Generalleutnant*) von Radowitz (C).

1st General Staff Officer (Operations Officer)

Major i.G. Reichel; *Major i.G.* Freyer; *Major i.G.* Liese (Acting operations Officer); *Major i.G. Graf* Bernsdorff (Acting operations Officer); *Hauptmann i.G.* (*Major i.G.*) Litterscheid; *Major i.G.* (*Oberstleutnant i.G.*) Weberstedt; *Major i.G.* Schumm.

2nd General Staff Officer (Logistics Officer)

Hauptmann i.G. (*Major i.G.*) Keyl; *Hauptmann i.G.* Braun; *Hauptmann i.G.* (*Major i.G.*) Koch-Erpach; *Hauptmann i.G.* von Werneburg; *Hauptmann* Hinrichs; *Hauptmann* Ruge (Acting Logistics officer); *Major i.G.* Siebel; *Major i.G.* Müller; *Major i.G.* Gilow.

3rd General Staff Officer (Intelligence Officer)

Rittmeister Hey; *Rittmeister* Furst zu Sayn-Wittgenstein; *Oberleutnant* Lorke.

Divisional Adjutant (Officer Personnel)

Hauptmann Michelle; *Hauptmann* (*Major*) von Kunow; *Hauptmann* Euler; *Major* Schätz; *Major* Rebentisch (Acting Divisional Adjutant)(Commander, *I./PR 23*); *Major* Grünwaldt (Acting Divisional Adjutant)(Commander, *II./PGR 126*); *Major Freiherr* von Crossing.

Panzer-Regiment 201 (*Panzer-Regiment 23*)

Oberstleutnant Conze (C); *Oberst* Werner-Ehrenfeucht (C); *Oberstleutnant* Soltmann (Commander, *II./PR 201*)(AC); *Oberst* Pochat (C); *Oberstleutnant* von Heydebreck (Commander, *I./PR 201*) (AC); *Oberstleutnant* Soltmann (Commander, *II./PR 201*)(AC); *Oberst* Burmeister; *Oberst* Werner-Ehrenfeucht (C); *Major* Illig (Commander, *III./PR 201*)(AC); *Oberstleutnant* von Heydebreck (C); *Oberstleutnant* (*Oberst*) Sander (C); *Hauptmann* Rebentisch (Commander, *I./PR 23*) (AC); *Oberstleutnant* Bernau; *Hauptmann* Fischer (Commander, *II./PR 23*)(AC); *Major* Rebentisch (Commander, *I./PR 23*)(AC); *Oberstleutnant Prinz* zu Wedlock und Pyrmont (C); *Major i.G.* Johns (C).

I./Panzer-Regiment 201 (*I./Panzer-Regiment 23*)

Major (*Oberstleutnant*) von Heydebreck (C); *Oberleutnant* Rebentisch (Commander, *1./PR 201*)(AC); *Oberleutnant* Alber (Commander, *2./PR 201*)(AC); *Hauptmann* von Bülow (C); *Hauptmann* Stiewe (C); *Hauptmann (Major)* Behr (C); *Hauptmann* Rebentisch (Division Adjutant)(AC); *Hauptmann* Alber (Commander, *2./PR 201*) (AC); *Hauptmann (Major)* Wolf (C); *Hauptmann (Major)* Rebentisch (C); *Hauptmann (Major)* Kujacinski (C).

II./Panzer-Regiment 201 (*II./Panzer-Regiment 23*)

Major Mildebrath (C); *Oberstleutnant* Kelpe (C); *Oberstleutnant* Soltmann (C); *Hauptmann* Alber (Commander, *5./PR 201*)(AC); *Hauptmann (Major)* Fechner (C); *Hauptmann* Tilemann (C); *Major* Fechner (C); *Hauptmann* Euler (AC); *Hauptmann* Esser (C); *Hauptmann (Major)* Fischer (C).

III./Panzer-Regiment 201

Major Illig (C); *Hauptmann* Stiewe (Commander, *6./PR 201*)(AC); *Major* Illig (C).

Schützen-Brigade 23 (*Panzergrenadier-Brigade 23*)

Oberst von Heydebrand und der Lasa (C); *Oberstleutnant* Bachmann (Commander, *SR 128*) (AC); *Oberst* von Bodenhausen (C); *Oberst* Burmeister (AC); *Oberst* von Brückner (Commander, *PGR 126*)(AC).

Schützen-Regiment 126 (*Panzergrenadier-Regiment 126*)[114]

Oberst Kieler (C); *Oberst Dr.* Müller (C); *Major* Zeydlick (Commander, *PPB 51*)(AC); *Oberstleutnant* Wellmann (Commander, *Schützen-Regiment 3, 3. Panzer-Division*)(AC); *Oberst* von Brückner (C); *Hauptmann* Stolle (Commander, *I./PGR 126*)(AC); *Major* Schägger

113 Editor's Note: (C) equals Commander; (AC) = Acting Commander. Command authority remained the same, but an Acting Commander was intended to be a temporary position until the officially designated Commander arrived.

114 Author's Note: In the case of the *Schützen-Regimenter* and the *Panzergrenadier-Regimenter* is was not possible to determine the names of all of the commanders or acting commanders nor to list them chronologically. As a result, this listing cannot purport to be anything more than a listing of the known names. Several of the officers were assigned to both regiments or more than one battalion.

(Commander, *PAA 23*)(AC); *Oberst* Menton (C); *Oberstleutnant* Fleck (C); *Oberstleutnant* (*Oberst*) John (C); *Major* Stetting (Commander, *PzFEB 128*)(AC); *Major* Huck (AC); *Oberstleutnant* (*Oberst*) John (C).

Schützen-Regiment 128 (*Panzergrenadier-Regiment 128*)

Oberstleutnant (*Oberst*) Bachmann (C); *Major* von Unger (Commander, *II./SR 126*)(AC); *Oberstleutnant* Stegmann (Commander, *II./SR 126*)(AC); *Major* von Einem (Commander, *PJA 128*)(AC); *Oberst* Bachmann (C); *Oberstleutnant* Sparre (C); *Oberstleutnant* (*Oberst*) *Freiherr* von Wechmar (C); *Hauptmann* Ruge (Commander, *I./PG 128*)(AC); *Major* Ziegler (detailed to the *23. Panzer-Division*)(AC); *Hauptmann* von Wieluczky (Commander, *II./PG 128*)(AC); *Oberst* Bräuchle (C); *Oberstleutnant* Eschenbach (C); *Major* Stetting (Commander, *DKS*)(AC).

Grenadier-Regiment (mot.) 1031 (new *Panzergrenadier-Regiment 128*)

Oberstleutnant der Reserve Möller (not with the *23. Panzer-Division*) (C); *Major* (*Oberstleutnant*) Stichtenoth (C); *Major* (*Oberstleutnant*) Ruge (C); *major* von Plate (Commander, *II./PGR 126*)(AC); *Oberstleutnant* (*Oberst*) Ruge (C)

I./Schützen-Regiment 126 (*I./Panzergrenadier-Regiment 126*)

Hauptmann Neubeck; *Hauptmann* Enneper; *Hauptmann* Liehr; *Hauptmann* Bucher; *Oberleutnant* Kappauf; *Hauptmann* Engelin; *Hauptmann* Feichtinger; *Hauptmann* Stolle; *Hauptmann* Franke; *Hauptmann* Roltsch; *Hauptmann* Grünwaldt; *Hauptmann* Schröter; *Major* Veigel; *Hauptmann* Feige; *Hauptmann* Schroeder.

II./Schützen-Regiment 126 (*II./Panzergrenadier-Regiment 126*)

Major Cunze; *Hauptmann* Werner; *Hauptmann* (*Major*) von Eisenhardt-Rothe; *Oberstleutnant* Stegmann; *Major* (*Oberstleutnant*) König; *Hauptmann* Knebel; *Hauptmann* Veigel; *Hauptmann* Böhme; *Hauptmann* Schunk; *Hauptmann* Pinkert; *Major* von Plate; *Hauptmann* Lenberger; *Major* Grünwaldt; *Hauptmann* Rompel.

I./Schützen-Regiment 128 (*I./Panzergrenadier-Regiment 128*)(old and new)

Oberstleutnant Reimann; *Rittmeister* Borchardt; *Hauptmann* Fanselau (also Commander of the 2nd Battalion at the same time); *Hauptmann* Richter; *Hauptmann* Döring; *Hauptmann* Claussen; *Major* Stetting; *Hauptmann* Ruge; *Hauptmann* Kirsch; *Hauptmann* Mahr; *Hauptmann* Berlin; *Oberleutnant* Pegel; *Hauptmann* Gabler; *Hauptmann* Oechsle; *Hauptmann* Roltsch.

II./Schützen-Regiment 128 (*II./Panzergrenadier-Regiment 128*)(old and new)

Major von Unger; *Hauptmann Dr.* Dreschler; *Hauptmann* Fanselau (also Commander of the 1st Battalion at the same time); *Hauptmann* Stetting; *Rittmeister* Fey (Alert Battalion of the *24. Panzer-Division*); *Hauptmann* Bittermann; *Hauptmann* von Wieluczky; *Hauptmann* von Kleist; *Hauptmann* Bitter; *Oberleutnant* Sommer; *Hauptmann* Fils; *Hauptmann* von Oehmichen; *Major* Veigel; *Hauptmann* Halverscheid; *Hauptmann* Böhmer.

Panzer-Artillerie-Regiment 128

Oberst von Buch (C); *Oberstleutnant* Schlutius (C); *Oberst* von Buch (C); *Major* Hamann (Commander, *III./PAR 128*)(AC); *Oberst Dr.* Born (C); *Oberstleutnant* (*Oberst*) Vogl (C); *Oberst* Froben (C).

I./Panzer-Artillerie-Regiment 128

Oberstleutnant Oswald (C); *Oberstleutnant* Schlutius (C); *Hauptmann* Pickard (C); *Hauptmann* Rodekurth (C); *Hauptmann* von Bünau (C); *Hauptmann* Neuhaus (C); *Hauptmann* Baran (C); *Hauptmann* Luiz (C); *Hauptmann* Haile (C).

II./Panzer-Artillerie-Regiment 128

Hauptmann Beck (C); *Major* Sänger (C); *Major* Bickel (C); *Oberstleutnant* Köbius (C); *Hauptmann* Wieder (C); *Hauptmann* Arnold (C); *Hauptmann Zorell (C).*

III./Panzer-Artillerie-Regiment 128

Oberst Büscher (C); *Major* Hamann (C); *Hauptmann Dr.* Nehm (AC); *Major* Pohl (C); *Major* Scherer (C); *Hauptmann* Brehme; *Hauptmann* Münnich (C).

Beobachtungs-Batterie (Pz) 128 (Initially: *10. (Pz.Beob.)/PAR 128*)

Hauptmann Mitschies; *Oberleutnant* Baran; *Oberleutnant* Gross.

Heeres-Flak-Artillerie-Abteilung 278 (Initially: *IV./PAR 128*)

Major Draffehn (C); *Major* Bruck (C).

Kradschützen-Bataillon 23 (*Panzer-Aufklärungs-Abteilung 23*)

Hauptmann von Kunow (AC); *Major* von Görne (C); *Major* von Haagen (C); *Major* Richter (C); *Hauptmann* Rohrbach (C); *Hauptmann* von Kunow (C); *Oberleutnant* von Süsskind (AC); *Rittmeister* Weißbach (C); *Major* von Einem (simultaneously also Commander of *PJA 128*) (AC); *Hauptmann* (*Major*) Schägger (C); *Hauptmann* Hoffmann (simultaneously also Commander of *PNA 128*)(AC); *Hauptmann* (*Major*) Koppe (C); *Oberleutnant* Abel (AC); *Hauptmann* (*Major*) Schulz (C).

Panzerjäger-Abteilung 128

Major Dr. Maus (C); *Hauptmann* von Eisenhardt-Rothe (C); *Major* von Einem (C); *Hauptmann* Brünn (AC); *Major* Matzen (C); *Hauptmann* (*Major*) Tiedemann (C).

Panzer-Pionier-Bataillon 51

Oberst Mikosch (not with the *23. Panzer-Division*)(C); *Major* Zeydlick (C); *Hauptmann* Hesse (C); *Hauptmann* Seyring (AC); *Hauptmann* Pauli (C); *Leutnant* Sauthoff (AC); *Hauptmann* Holenia (C); *Hauptmann* Seyring (AC); *Hauptmann* Feldmann (C); *Hauptmann* Schlingmann (AC); *Hauptmann* Hellwig (AC); *Oberleutnant* Eichhorn (AC); *Hauptmann* Diestel (C); *Hauptmann* Noever (C); *Oberleutnant* Brandes (AC); *Hauptmann* Fuhrmann (C).

Panzernachrichten-Abteilung 128

Major Freiherr von Peckenzell (C); *Hauptmann* (*Major*) Hoffmann (C); *Hauptmann* Beck (C); *Hauptmann* Meyer (Vitus)(C).

Feld-Ersatz-Bataillon 128 (later: *Feld-Lehr- und Ersatz-Bataillon 128, Divisionskampfschule 23. Panzer-Division* and *Panzer-Feldersatz-Bataillon 128*)

Hauptmann Thurm (C); *Oberstleutnant* Stegmann (C); *Hauptmann* Schägger (C); *Rittmeister Freiherr* Grote (AC/C); *Hauptmann* Ruge (AC); *Oberleutnant* Pritzel (AC); *Major* Stetting (C); *Hauptmann* Wanner (C); *Oberleutnant* Polack (AC); *Major* Veigel (C).

Divisions-Nachschubtruppen 128 (*Dinafü 128, Kodina 128*)

Major Vollberg (C); *Major der Reserve* Wiese (C); *Major der Reserve* Stenger (C).

Sanitätstruppen 128

Oberfeldarzt (Oberstarzt) Dr. Hilstein; *Oberstabsarzt Dr.* Becker.

Divisionsverwaltungstruppen 128

Intendanturrat-Assistant Dr. Riemenschneider; *Intendanturrat* (*Oberstabsintendant*) Kroll; *Stabszahlmeister* (*Stabsintendant*) Lehmann (Acting Administrative Chief); *Intendanturrat* (*Oberstabsintendant*) *Dr.* Gutzschebauch.

Kraftfahrparktruppen 128

Major Dr. Schütte; *Baurat* Biedermann; *Major* Gerlach.

Waffenwerkstatt-Kompanie

Oberleutnant Mildenberger.

Feldpostamt 128

Feldpostmeister Weiß.

Feldgendarmerietrupp 128

Major Görlach; *Hauptmann* Naumann

Appendix 10

Commanders and Senior Staff of the 23. Panzer-Division and Its Subordinate Troop Elements (as of 15 April 1945)

Division Commander: *Generalleutnant* von Radowitz
1st General Staff Officer (Operations Officer): *Major i.G.* Schumm
Assistant Operations Officer: *Hauptmann* Dittmann
2nd General Staff officer (Logistics Officer): *Major i.G.* Gilow
3rd General Staff Officer (Intelligence Officer): *Oberleutnant* Lorke
Division Adjutant (Officer Personnel): *Major Freiherr* von Rössing
Panzer-Regiment 23: *Major d.G.* Jahns
Panzergrenadier-Regiment 126: *Oberst* John
Panzergrenadier-Regiment 128: *Oberst* Ruge
Panzer-Artillerie-Regiment 128: *Oberst* Froben
Heeres-Flak-Artillerie-Abteilung 278: *Major* Bruck
Panzer-Aufklärungs-Abteilung 23: *Hauptmann* Schulz
Panzerjäger-Abteilung 128: *Major* Tiedemann
Panzer-Pionier-Bataillon 51: *Hauptmann* Fuhrmann
Panzer-Nachrichten-Abteilung 128: *Hauptmann* Maier
Panzer-Feld-Ersatz-Bataillon 128: *Major* Veigel
Panzer-Nachschubtruppen 128: *Major* Stenger
Sanitätstruppen 128: *Oberstabsarzt Dr.* Becker
Verwaltungstruppen 128: *Stabsintendant Dr.* Gutzschebauch
Kraftfahrparktruppen 128: *Major* Gerlach
Divisions-Waffen-Offizier: *Hauptmann* Kaufmann
Divisions-Veterinär-Offizier: *Stabsveterinär Dr.* Siegler

Appendix 11

Listing of Armored vehicles Knocked Out by the 23. Panzer-Division

1. Battle of Kharkov (Northern Sector) from 13 – 22 May 1942:

Date	Enemy AFV's Knocked Out	Date	Enemy AFV's Knocked Out
13 May	11	18 May	20
14 May	10	19 May	9
15 May	24	20 May	21
16 May	5	21 May	19
17 May	10	22 May	7
		Total:	136

While attached to the *VIII. Armee-Korps* from 12 – 22 May 1942, *Panzerjäger-Abteilung 128* knocked out 58 enemy armored fighting vehicles and the *I./Panzer-Regiment 201* knocked out 28 for a total of 86 enemy vehicles.

2. Pocket battle southwest of Kharkov from 23 – 29 May 1942

Date	Enemy AFV's Knocked Out
23 May	0
24 – 25 May	13
26 May	42
27 May	40
Total:	95

3. Advance to the Caucasus from 28 June to 21 November 1942

Date	Enemy AFV's Knocked Out	Date	Enemy AFV's Knocked Out
28 June	5	29 July	61
30 June	25	1 – 10 August	69
1 July	10	26 – 28 October	16
3 July	3	31 October to 2 November	22
6 July	16	3 November	1
7 July	16	7 November	6
8 July	0	8 November	5
9 July	8	9 November	3
11 July	7	10 November	2
12 July	27	13 November	5
14 July	8	16 November	5
15 July	3	17 November	13
16 July	3	21 November	2
28 July	4		
		Total:	349

4. Relief Attack on Stalingrad and Retreat to the Mius Position from 14 December 1942 to 17 March 1943

Date	Enemy AFV's Knocked Out	Date	Enemy AFV's Knocked Out
14 December	7	11 January	4
15 December	19	15 January	6
16 December	18	18 January	2
17 December	22	30 January	4
18 December	14	8 February	6
19 December	9	9 February	12
20 December	7	10 February	6
21 December	8	11 February	7
27 December	8	12 February	12
28 December	19	17 February	1
30 December	10	19 February	8
31 December	19	22 February	13
2 January	2	27 February	1
6 January	19	28 February	3
8 January	5	4 March	2
10 January	9		
		Total:	282

5. Battle for Stepanowka from 19 – 25 July 1943:

Date	Enemy AFV's Knocked Out	Date	Enemy AFV's Knocked Out
19 July	14	24 July	2
20 July	2	25 July	5
22 July	15	26 July	3
23 July	16		
		Total:	57

6. Counterattack Along the Mius and Defensive Fighting West of Dmitrijewka from 31 July to 10 August 1943:

Date	Enemy AFV's Knocked Out		Enemy AFV's Knocked Out
2 August	3		24
			27

7. Second Battle at Isjum from 16 August to 6 September 1943:

Date	Enemy AFV's Knocked Out	Date	Enemy AFV's Knocked Out
16 August	22	25 August	1
17 August	47	26 August	1
18 August	24	28 August	3
19 August	51	29 August	4
22 August	90	30 August	3
23 August	81	2 September	7
24 August	35	3 September	3
		Total:	372

8. Defensive fighting west of Kramatorskaja and defensive movement to the Dnjepr from 7 – 24 September 1943:

Date	Enemy AFV's Knocked Out	Date	Enemy AFV's Knocked Out
7 September	7	11 September	13
10 September	15	20 September	9
		Total:	44

9. Counterattack Against the Bridgehead at Mischurin Rog and Defensive Fighting at Mischurin Rog from 30 September to 14 October 1943:

Date	Enemy AFV's Knocked Out	Date	Enemy AFV's Knocked Out
3 October	2	8 October	3
4 October	8	9 October	3
6 October	2	14 October	3
		Total:	21

10. Fighting Withdrawal to Kriwoi Rog from 15 to 31 October 1943:

Date	Enemy AFV's Knocked Out	Date	Enemy AFV's Knocked Out
15 October	16	23 October	22
16 October	38	24 October	12
17 October	32	25 October	6
18 October	26	26 October	3
20 October	15	30 October	2
21 October	10	31 October	4
22 October	2		
		Total:	188

11. Counterattack and Defensive Fighting North of Kriwoi Rog from 1 November to 31 December 1943:

Date	Enemy AFV's Knocked Out	Date	Enemy AFV's Knocked Out
3 – 4 November	15	21 November	5
14 November	34	22 November	5
15 November	16	23 November	3
16 November	7	25 November	2
18 November	6	27 November	4
		29 November	2
		Total:	99

12. Fighting East, Southeast and West of Kriwoi Rog and Retreat to the Bug from 1 January to 29 March 1944 (Numbers should be considered minimums due to a lack of insufficient reports and summaries.):

Date	Enemy AFV's Knocked Out	Date	Enemy AFV's Knocked Out
12 January	1	17 February	7
2 February	1	9 March	1
1		Total:	10

13. Fighting in the Jassy Area East and West of the Pruth from 1 April 1944 to 25 July 1944:

Date	Enemy AFV's Knocked Out	Date	Enemy AFV's Knocked Out
1 – 5 April	3	17 April	3
6 April	15	29 April	25
7 April	1	31 May	12
11 April	5	1 June	4
16 April	6		
		Total:	74

14. Counterattacks of the *II./Panzer-Regiment 23* in the North and West Ukraine from 9 January to 4 June 1944:

Date	Enemy AFV's Knocked Out	Date	Enemy AFV's Knocked Out
15 January	11	12 February	4
24 January	5	13 February	7
25 January	23	15 February	1
26 January	15	18 February	4
27 January	12	20 February	13
29 January	7	8 March	9
30 January	11	13 March	4
31 January	2	18 March	4
4 February	2	16 April	6
8 February	2	21 April	2
10 February	1	15 May	5
11 February	6	22 May	1
		Total:	157

15. Defensive fighting and Counterattacks in Southern Poland and at the Baranow bridgehead from 28 July to 10 September 1944:

Date	Enemy AFV's Knocked Out	Date	Enemy AFV's Knocked Out
28 July	5	19 August	20
29 July	1	20 August	11
30 July	5	21 August	8
31 July	5	22 August	6
1 August	4	23 August	13
3 August	2	24 August	11
4 August	8	29 August	7
8 August	3	30 August	1
9 August	5	1 – 4 September	4
12 August	3		
		Total:	122

16. Fighting in Transylvania and Armored Engagements on the Hungarian Plains from 22 September to 27 October 1944:

Date	Enemy AFV's Knocked Out	Date	Enemy AFV's Knocked Out
23 September	6	12 October	18
25 September	3	13 October	1
28 September	5	15 October	2
1 October	2	16 October	29
2 October	8	17 October	5
3 October	22	18 October	4
6 October	1	19 October	7
7 October	4	20 October	4
8 October	2	23 October	2
9 October	3	24 October	5
10 October	47	25 October	3
11 October	22		
		Total:	205

17. Defensive Fighting North of Kecskemet and East of Budapest from 28 October to 29 November 1944:

Date	Enemy AFV's Knocked Out	Date	Enemy AFV's Knocked Out
2 November	7	16 November	4
3 November	1	19 November	5
5 November	1	22 November	4
8 November	12	24 November	4
14 November	1		
		Total:	39

18. Defensive Fighting and Counterattacks South and North of Stuhlweißenburg from 30 November 1944 to 24 February 1945:

Date	Enemy AFV's Knocked Out	Date	Enemy AFV's Knocked Out
1 December	1	14 January	1
16 December	1	18 January	5
20 December	2	19-25 January	173
7 January	11	30 January	5
9 January	61	6 February	4
11 January	2	7 February	5
		Total:	271

19. Offensive operations of the *6. SS-Panzer-Armee* South of Stuhlweißenburg, Retreat to the Borders of the *Reich* and Period Until the Capitulation from 25 February to 8 May 1945:

Date	Enemy AFV's Knocked Out	Date	Enemy AFV's Knocked Out
9 March	8	21 March	4
13 March	7	22 March	5
20 March	13	23 March	1
		Total:	38

In all, the troop elements of the *23. Panzer-Division* knocked out 2,672 Soviet tanks and assault guns.

Appendix 12

Fate of the Tank Destroyers of Panzerjäger-Abteilung 128 in Hungary

Of the 20 *Jagdpanzer IV* tank destroyers,

- 3 were knocked out by Soviet antitank guns or tanks
- 3 were destroyed by friendly fire from the *12. SS-Panzer-Division "Hitlerjugend"*
- 11 were blown up due to mechanical problems or lack of fuel and
- 3 were rendered inoperable by their own crews on 8 May 1945 when the division pulled back at Mureck.

Appendix 13

Tables of Organization and Equipment of the 23. Panzer-Division

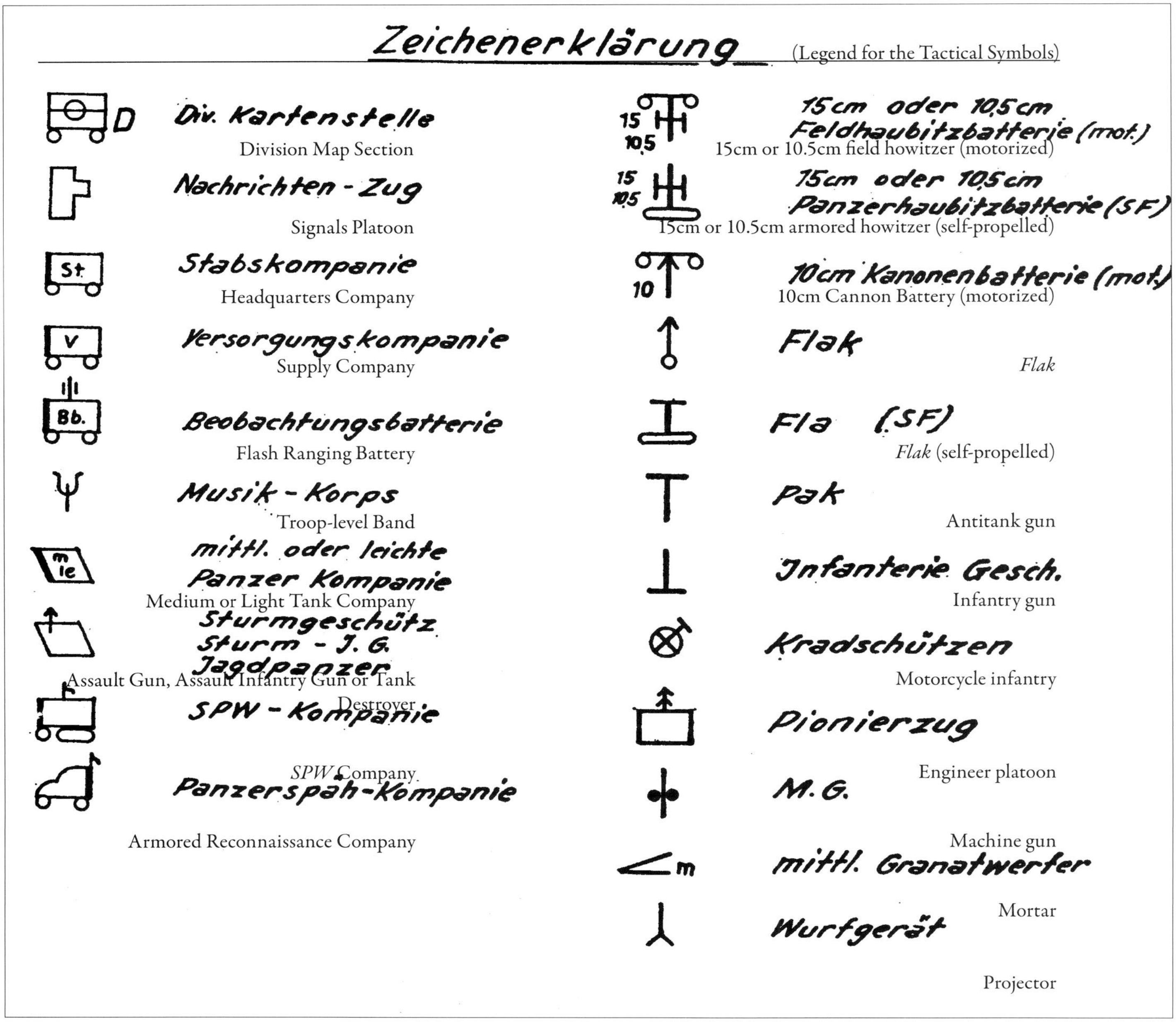

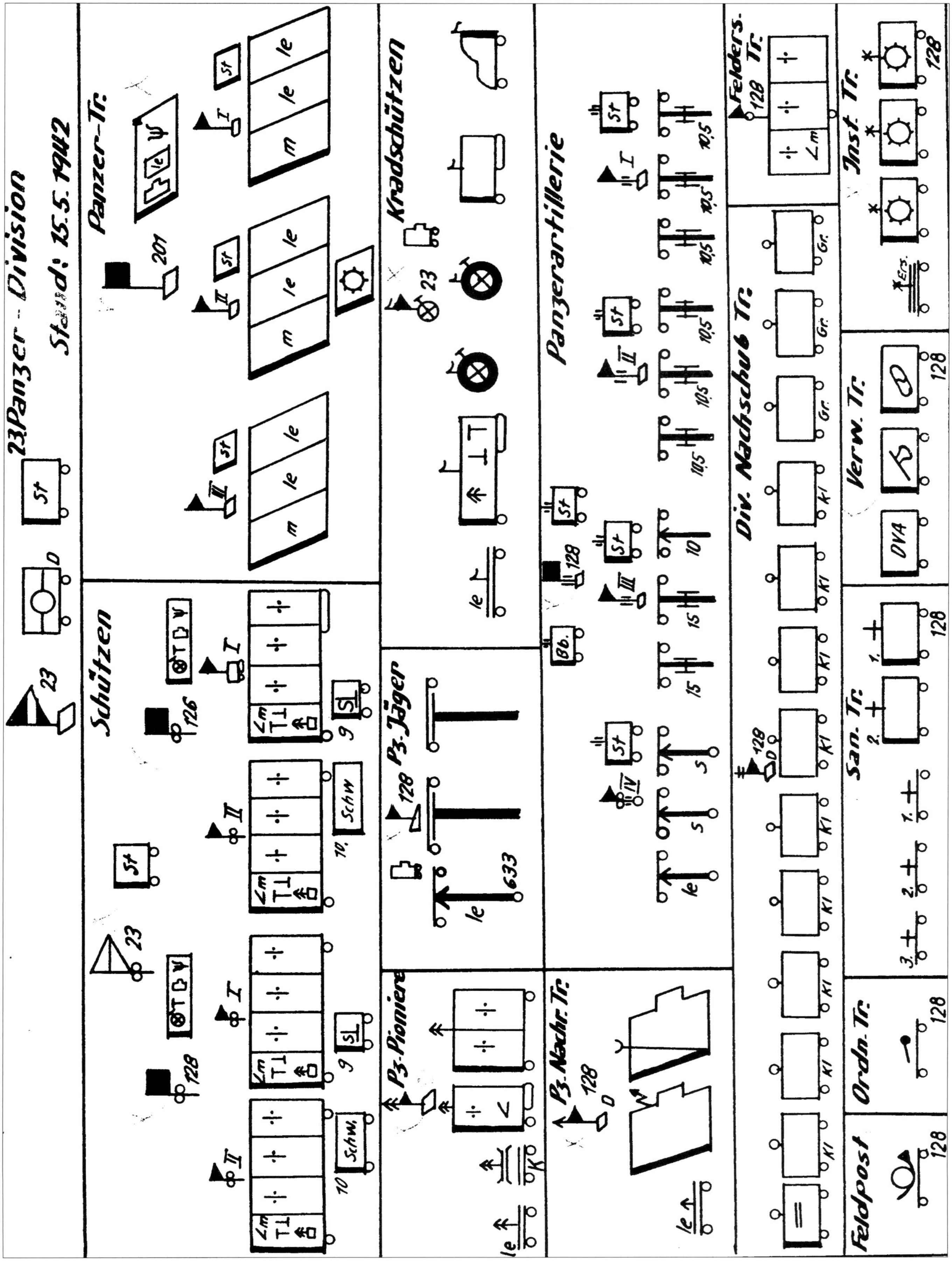
23 Panzer - Division
15.5.1942
Panzer-Tr.
Schützen
Kradschützen
Pz. Jäger
Pz.-Pioniere
Panzerartillerie
Pz. Nachr. Tr.
Div. Nachschub Tr.
Felders. Tr.
Inst. Tr.
Verw. Tr.
San. Tr.
Ordn. Tr.
Feldpost

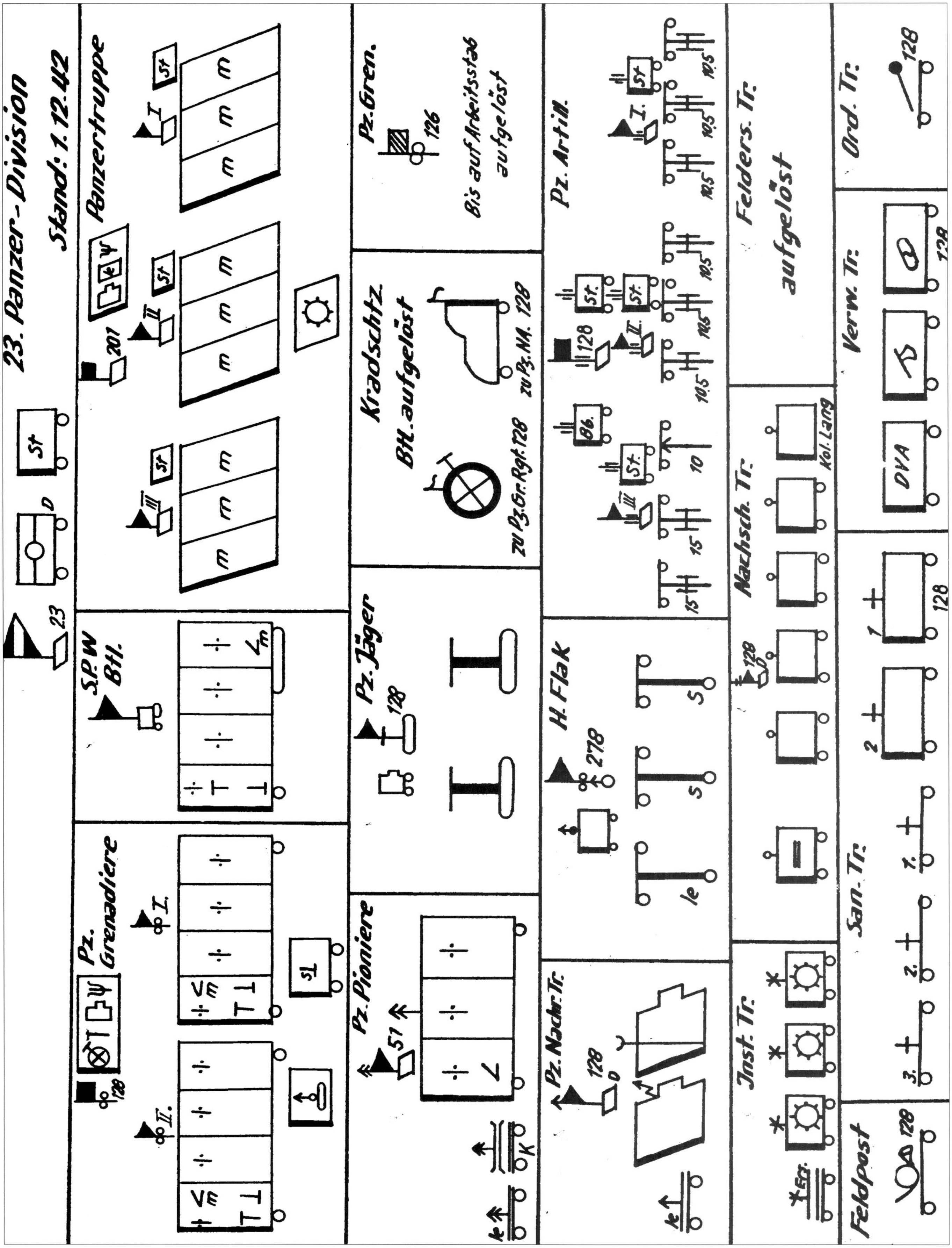
23. Panzer-Division
Stand: 1.12.42
Panzertruppe
Pz. Grenadiere
S.P.W Btl.
Pz. Pioniere
Pz. Jäger
Kradschtz Btl. aufgelöst
zu Pz.Gr.Rgt. 128
zu Pz.N.A. 128
Pz. Gren.
Bis auf Arbeitsstab aufgelöst
Pz. Nachr. Tr.
H. Flak
Pz. Artill.
Inst. Tr.
Nachsch. Tr.
Kol. Lang
Felders. Tr.
aufgelöst
Feldpost
San. Tr.
Verw. Tr.
DVA
Ord. Tr.

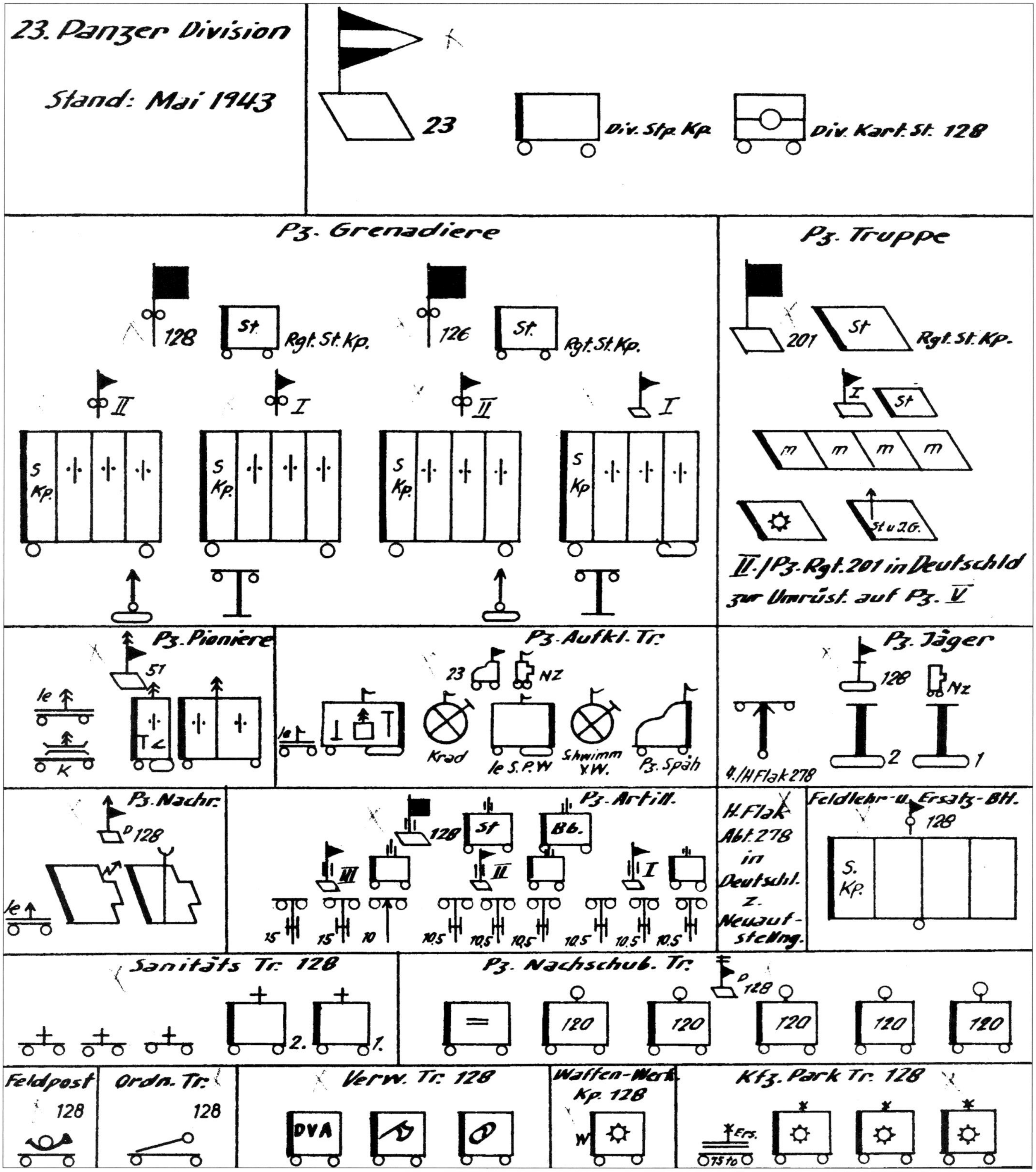
23. Panzer Division
Stand: Mai 1943
23
Div. Stp. Kp.
Div. Kart. St. 128
Pz. Grenadiere
128
St
Rgt. St. Kp.
126
St.
Rgt. St. Kp.
II
I
II
I
S Kp.
S Kp.
S Kp.
S Kp.
Pz. Truppe
201
St
Rgt. St. Kp.
I
St
m
m
m
m
Stu. G.
II./Pz. Rgt. 201 in Deutschld
zur Umrüst. auf Pz. V
Pz. Pioniere
51
le
K
Pz. Aufkl. Tr.
23
NZ
le
Krad
le S.P.W
Schwimm K.W.
Pz. Späh
Pz. Jäger
128
Nz
4./H Flak 278
2
1
Pz. Nachr.
D 128
le
Pz. Artill.
128
St
Bb.
III
II
I
15
15
10
10,5
10,5
10,5
10,5
10,5
10,5
H. Flak Abt. 278 in Deutschl. z. Neuaufstellng.
Feldlehr-u. Ersatz-BH.
128
S. Kp.
Sanitäts Tr. 128
2.
1.
Pz. Nachschub. Tr.
D 128
=
120
120
120
120
120
Feldpost
128
Ordn. Tr.
128
Verw. Tr. 128
DVA
Waffen-Werk. Kp. 128
W
Kfz. Park Tr. 128
Ers.
75 to

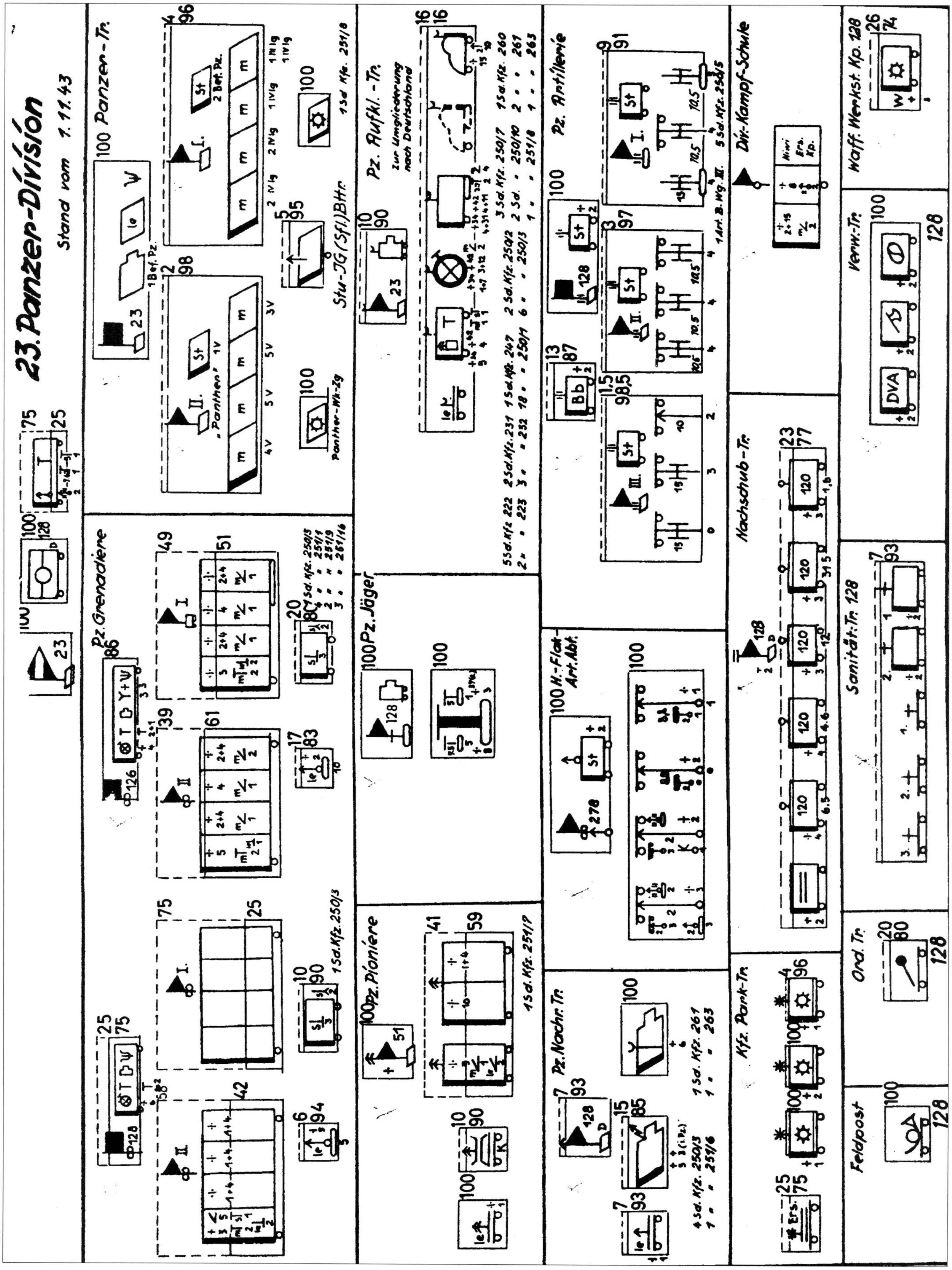
23. Panzer-Division
Stand vom 1.11.43
100 Panzer-Tr.
Pz Grenadiere
Pz. Pioniere
100 Pz. Jäger
Pz. Aufkl.-Tr.
zur Umgliederung nach Deutschland
Stu-JG (Sfl.) Bttr.
Panther-Wk-Zg
Pz. Artillerie
100 H.-Flak-Art.Abt.
Pz. Nachr. Tr.
Kfz. Park-Tr.
Nachschub-Tr.
Div.-Kampf-Schule
Sanität.-Tr. 128
Feldpost
Ord. Tr.
Verw.-Tr.
Waff. Werkst. Kp. 128

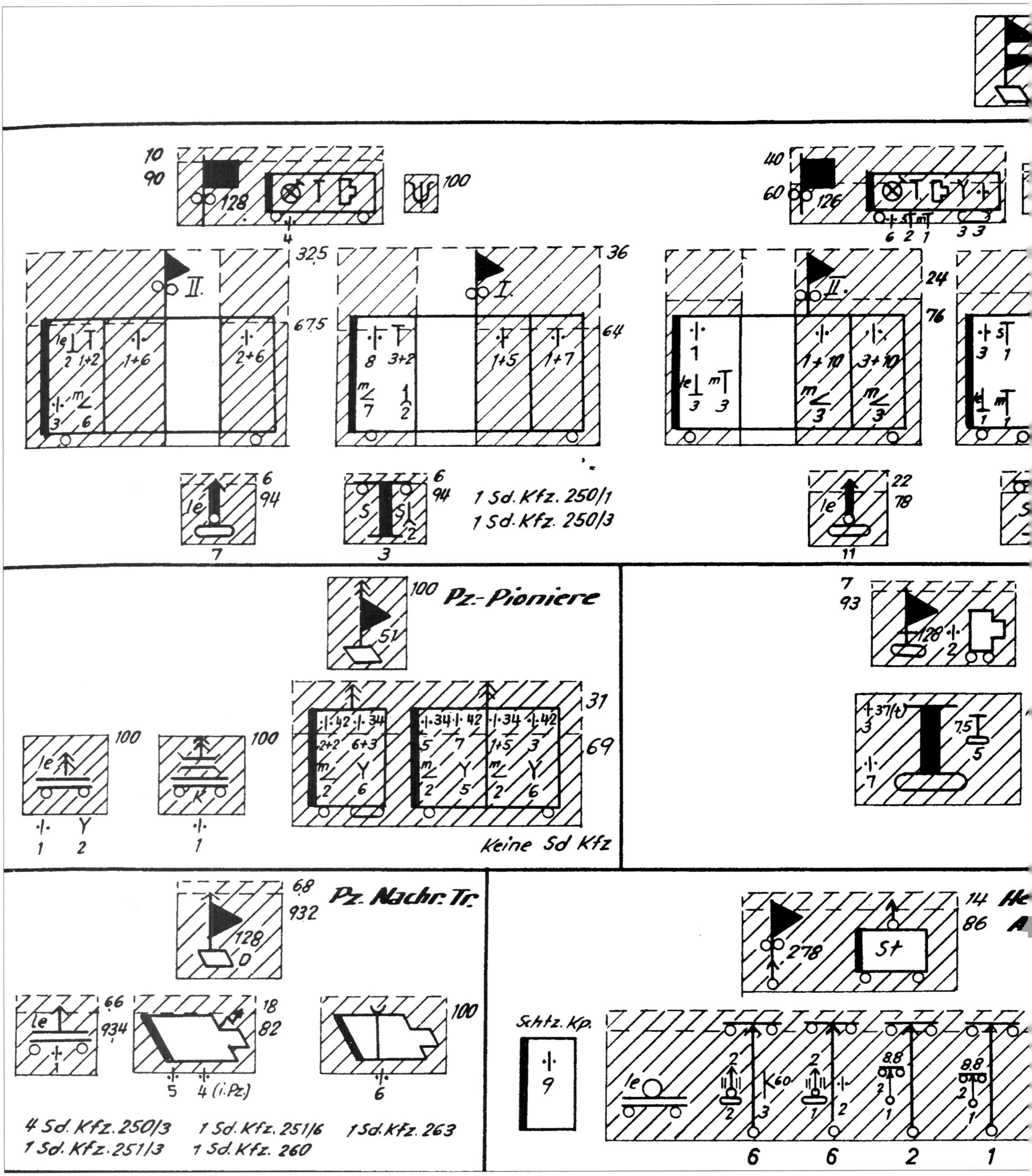
1 Sd. Kfz. 250/1
1 Sd. Kfz. 250/3
Pz.-Pioniere
Keine Sd Kfz
Pz. Nachr. Tr.
4 Sd. Kfz. 250/3
1 Sd. Kfz. 251/3
1 Sd. Kfz. 251/6
1 Sd. Kfz. 260
1 Sd. Kfz. 263
Schtz. Kp.

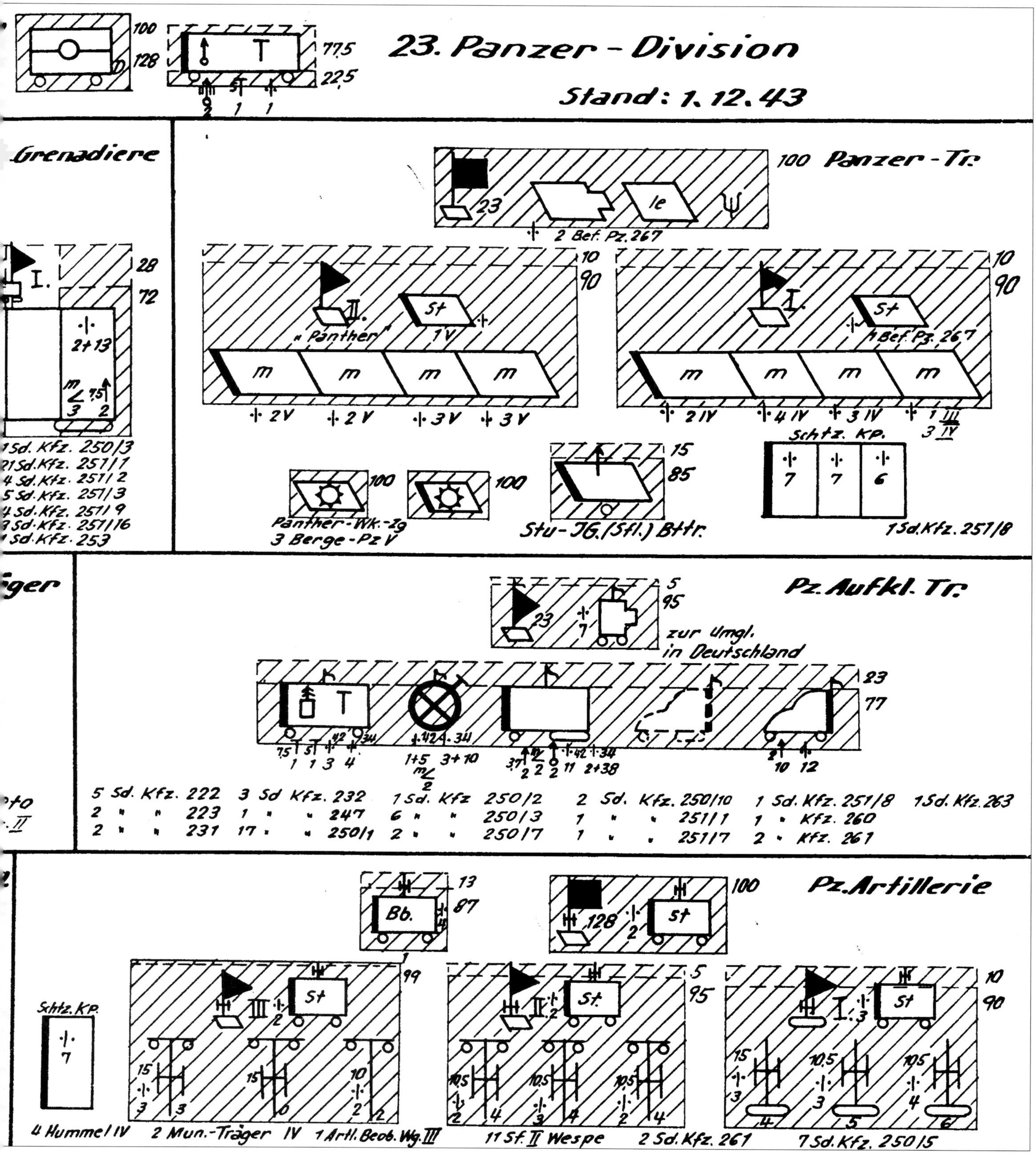

Continued next page

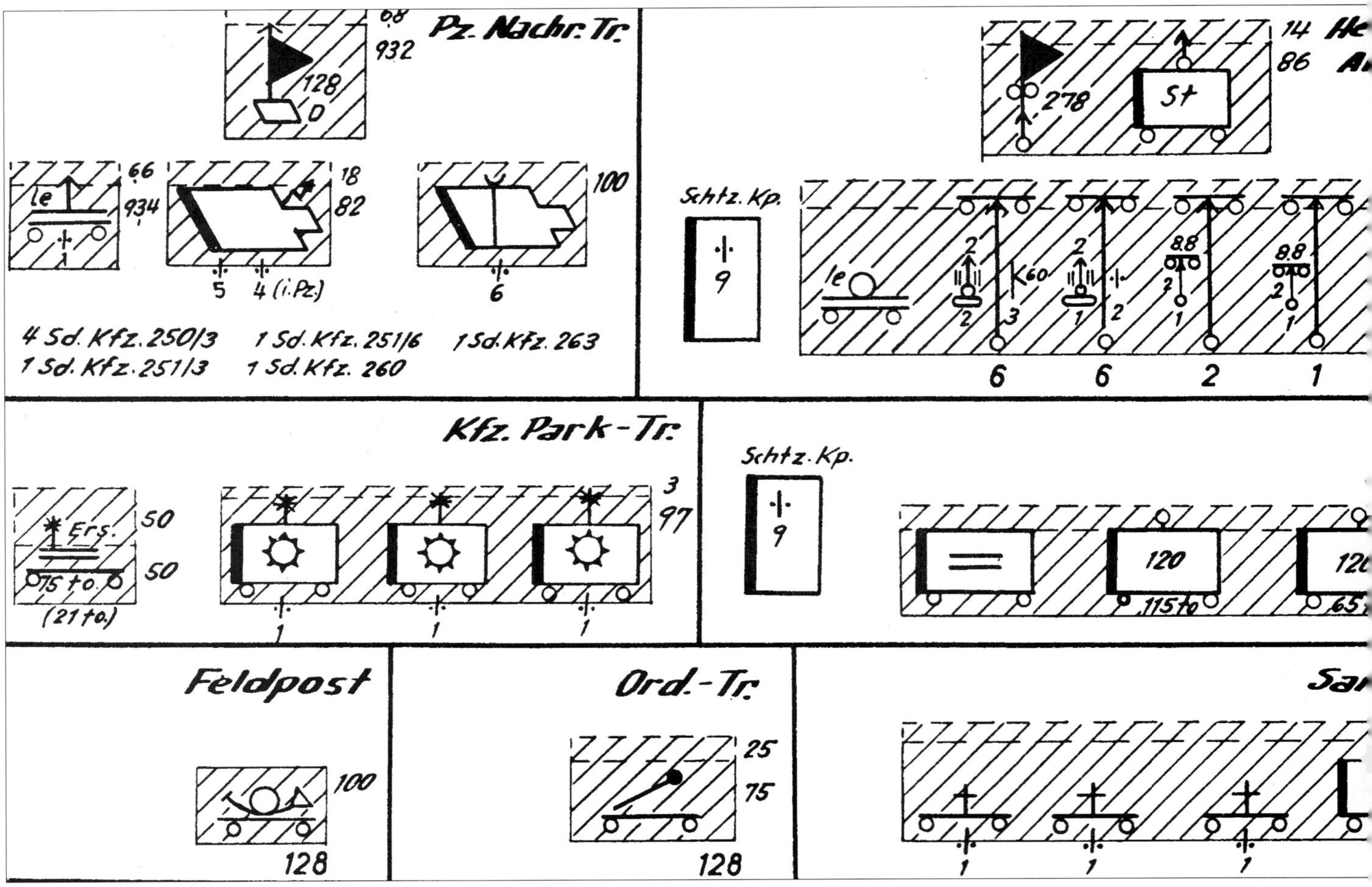
Pz. Nachr. Tr.
4 Sd. Kfz. 250/3
1 Sd. Kfz. 251/3
1 Sd. Kfz. 251/6
1 Sd. Kfz. 260
1 Sd. Kfz. 263
Schtz. Kp.
Kfz. Park-Tr.
Ers.
15 to.
(21 to.)
Feldpost
Ord.-Tr.

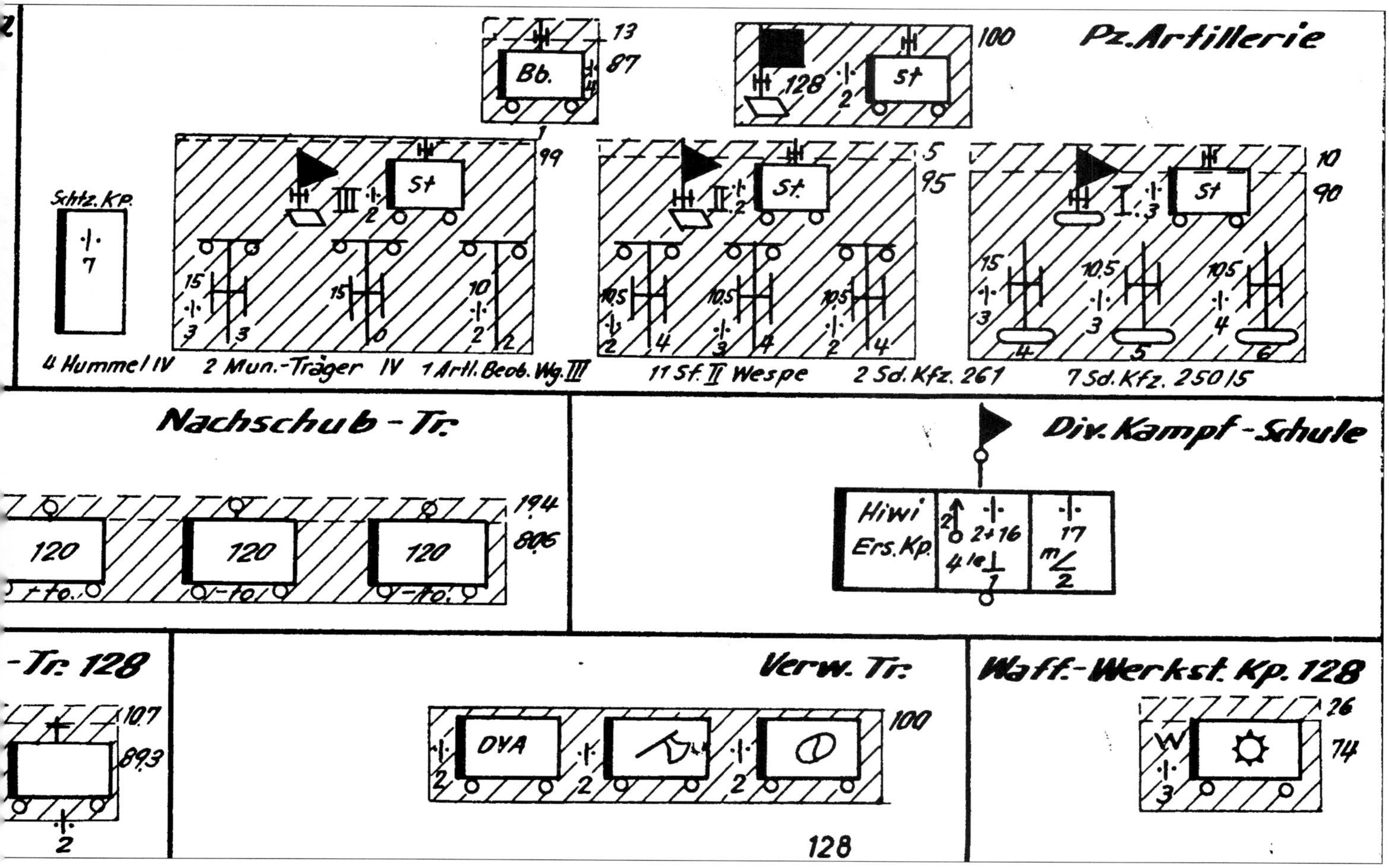
Pz. Artillerie
Bb.
13
87
100
128
St
99
Schtz. Kp.
5
95
10
90
15
10
10.5
4 Hummel IV
2 Mun.-Träger IV
1 Artl. Beob. Wg. III
11 Sf. II Wespe
2 Sd. Kfz. 261
7 Sd. Kfz. 250/5
Nachschub-Tr.
194
806
120
Div. Kampf-Schule
Hiwi
Ers. Kp.
2+16
17
-Tr. 128
107
893
Verw. Tr.
100
DVA
128
Waff.-Werkst. Kp. 128
26
74

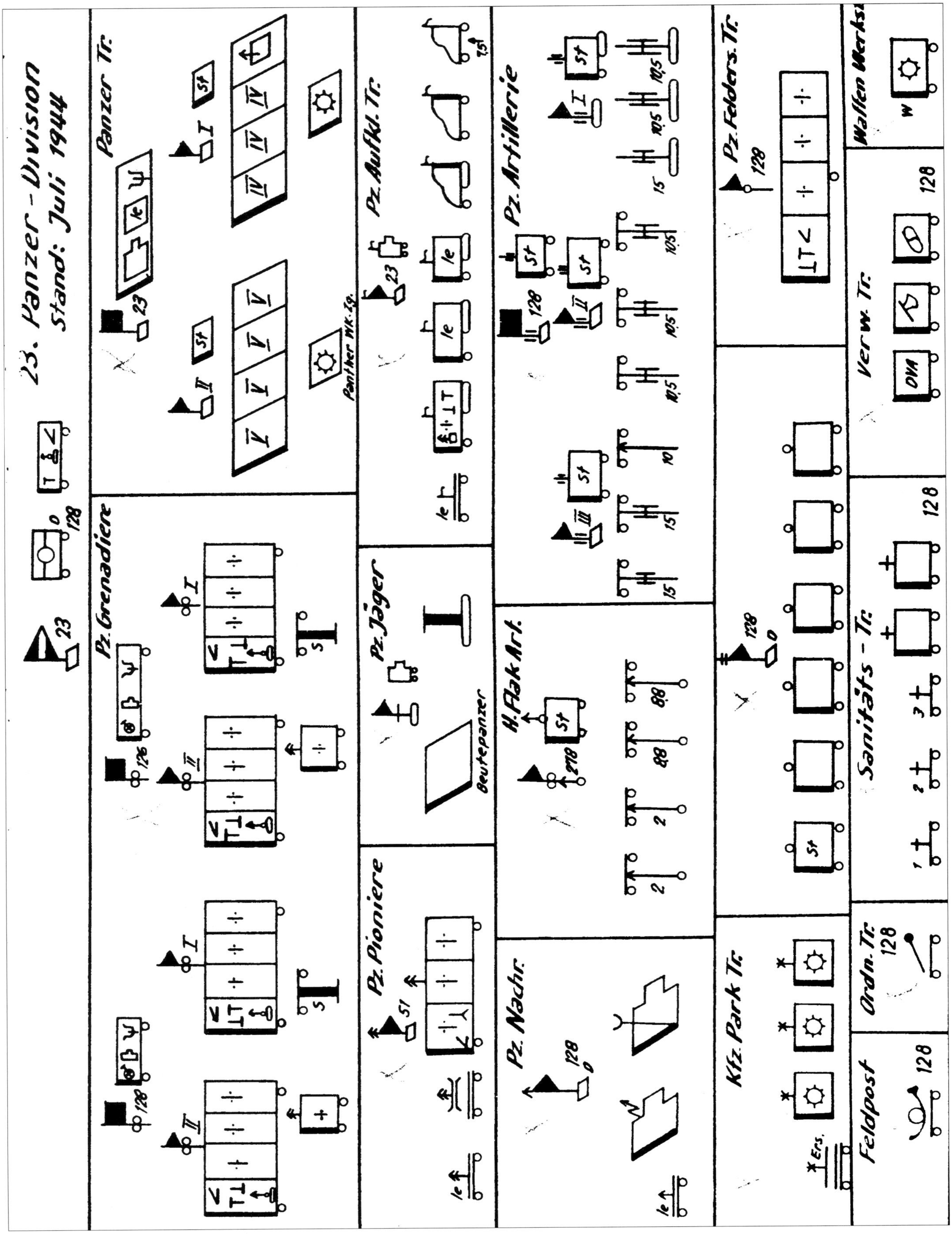
23. Panzer-Division
Stand: Juli 1944
Panzer Tr.
Panther Wk. Zg.
Pz. Grenadiere
Pz. Aufkl. Tr.
Pz. Jäger
Beutepanzer
Pz. Pioniere
Pz. Artillerie
H. Flak Art.
Pz. Nachr.
Pz. Felders. Tr.
Kfz. Park Tr.
Sanitäts - Tr.
Verw. Tr.
Waffen Werkst
Ordn. Tr.
Feldpost

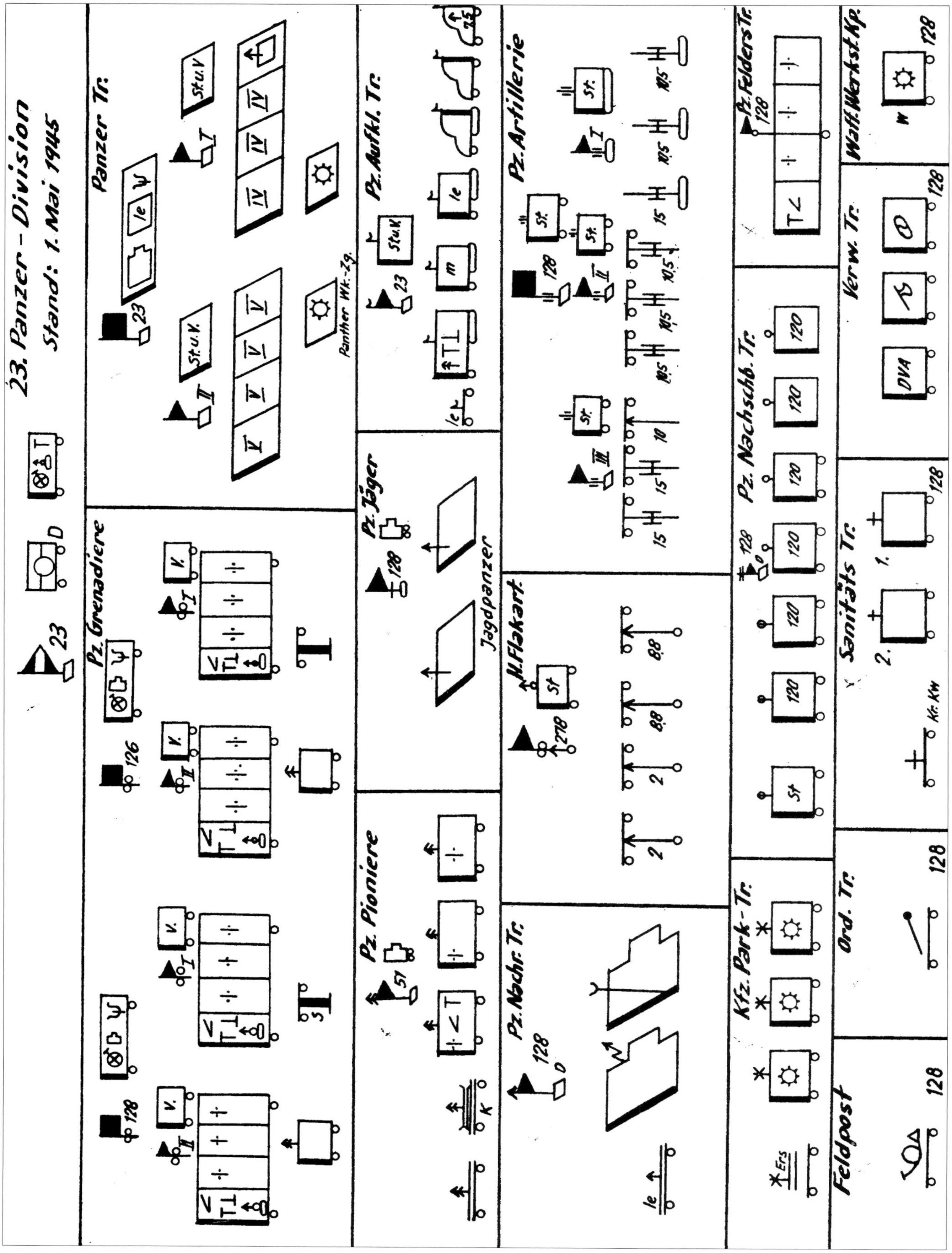
23. Panzer-Division
Stand: 1. Mai 1945
Panzer Tr.
Panther Wk.-Zg.
Pz. Grenadiere
Pz. Aufkl. Tr.
Pz. Jäger
Jagdpanzer
Pz. Pioniere
Pz. Artillerie
H. Flakart.
Pz. Nachr. Tr.
Pz. FeldErs. Tr.
Pz. Nachschb. Tr.
Kfz. Park-Tr.
Sanitäts Tr.
Ord. Tr.
Verw. Tr.
Feldpost
Waff. Werkst. Kp.

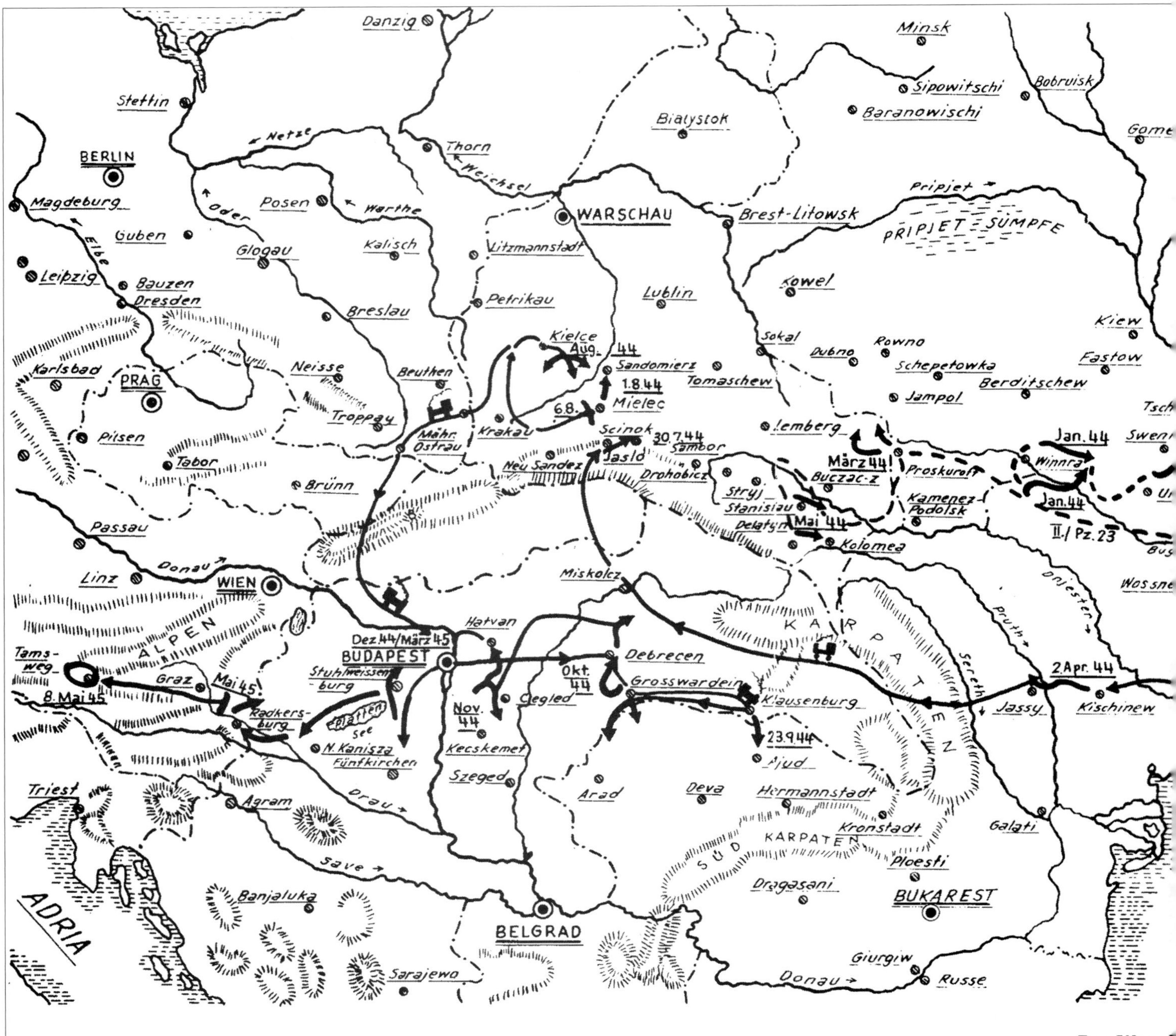
Danzig
Minsk
Stettin
Sipowitschi
Bobruisk
Baranowischi
Bialystok
Netze
Gomel
BERLIN
Thorn
Weichsel
Pripjet
Magdeburg
Posen
Warthe
Oder
WARSCHAU
Brest-Litowsk
PRIPJET-SÜMPFE
Elbe
Guben
Glogau
Kalisch
Litzmannstadt
Leipzig
Bauzen
Dresden
Kowel
Lublin
Breslau
Petrikau
Kiew
Kielce
Aug. 44
Sokal
Rowno
Dubno
Fastow
Karlsbad
PRAG
Neisse
Beuthen
Sandomierz
Tomaschew
Schepetowka
Berditschew
1.8.44
Mielec
Jampol
Troppau
6.8.
Pilsen
Mähr. Ostrau
Krakau
Scinok
30.7.44
Sambor
Lemberg
Jan. 44
Tabor
Neu Sandez
Jaslo
Drohobicz
März 44
Winnra
Proskuroff
Brünn
Buczacz
Stryj
Stanislau
Kamenez-Podolsk
Jan. 44
Delatyn
Mai 44
Passau
Kolomea
II./Pz.23
Donau
Linz
WIEN
Miskolcz
Dnjester
Wossne
Pruth
ALPEN
Hatvan
KARPATEN
Dez 44/März 45
BUDAPEST
Tamsweg
Debrecen
Sereth
2.Apr. 44
Graz
Mai 45
Stuhlweissenburg
Okt. 44
Grosswardein
8. Mai 45
Radkersburg
Platten See
Cegled
Klausenburg
Jassy
Kischinew
Nov. 44
N. Kanisza
Kecskemet
23.9.44
Fünfkirchen
Ajud
Szeged
Triest
Arad
Deva
Hermannstadt
Agram
Drau
Kronstadt
Galati
SÜD KARPATEN
Save
Ploesti
Dragasani
ADRIA
Banjaluka
BUKAREST
BELGRAD
Giurgiw
Sarajewo
Donau
Russe

Der Weg d

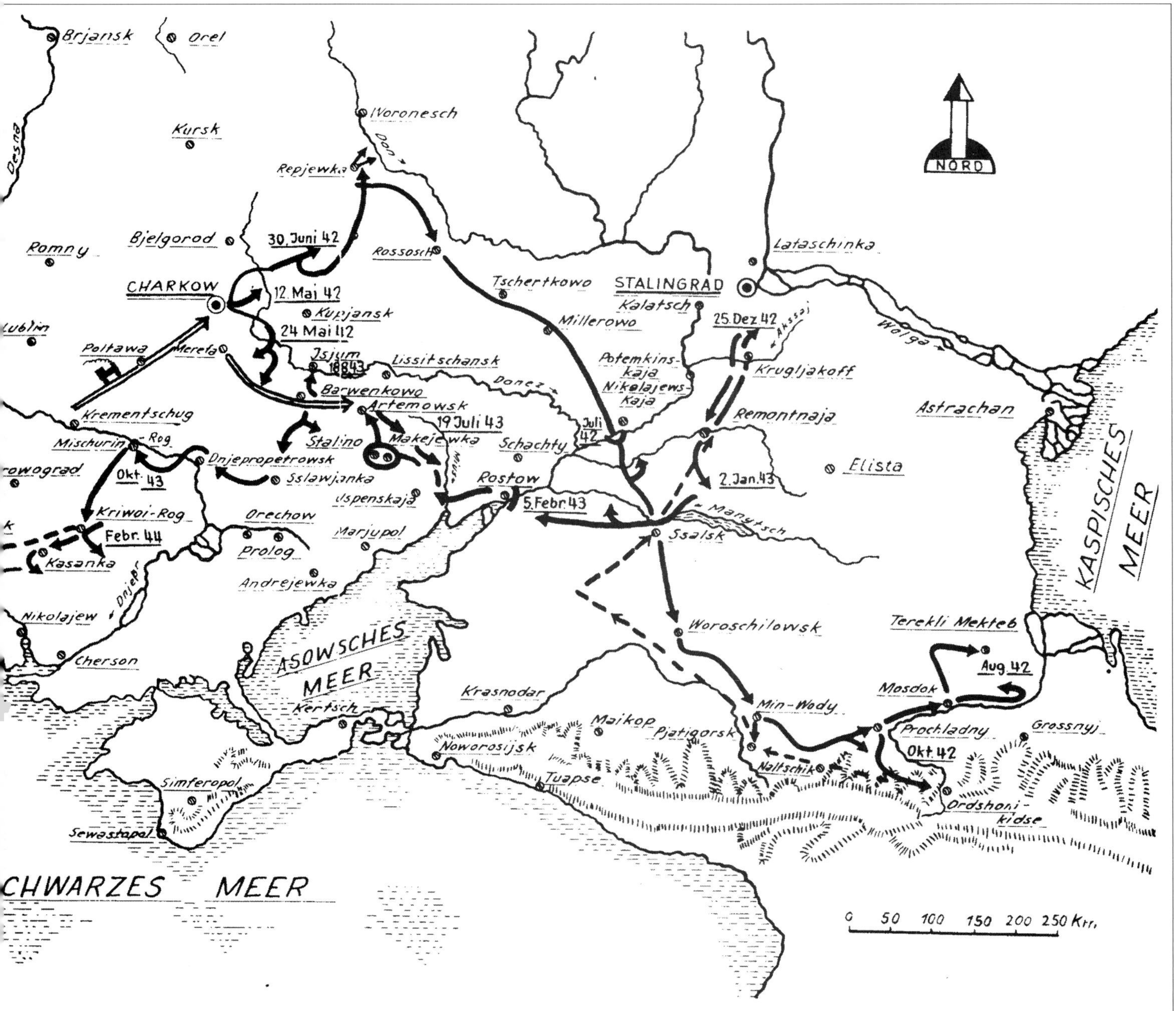

zer-Division

Appendix 14

Field Post Numbers of the Troop Elements of the 23. Panzer-Division

Headquarters, *23. Panzer-Division*	37 641
Headquarters, *Schützen-Brigade 23*	47 790
Panzer-Regiment 201 (*23*), Headquarters	11 206
I./PR 201 (*23*) (1st to 4th Companies)	08 403
II./PR 201 (*23*) (5th to 8th Companies)	40 345
III./PR 201 (*23*) (9th to 12th Companies)	32 377
9.(StuG) Kompanie	01 650
Panzer-Werkstatt-Kompanie (Maintenance Company (Armor))	56 778
Schützen-Regiment 126 (*PGR 126*), Headquarters	00 352
Headquarters Company	45 323
I./SR 126 (*PGR 126*) (1st to 4th Companies)	32 377
II./SR 126 (*PGR 126*) (5th to 8th Companies)	32 811
9. (sIG) Kompanie	44 045
Schwere Kompanie (Heavy Company)	03 310
10. (Fla) Kompanie	27 491
11 (Pi.) Kompanie (later, the 10th Company)	35 690
Schützen-Regiment 128 (*PGR 128*), Headquarters	40 446
Headquarters Company	47 155
I./SR 128 (*PGR 128*) (1st to 4th Companies)	33 878
II./SR 128 (*PGR 128*) (5th to 8th Companies)	34 262
9. (sIG) Kompanie	46 806
Schwere Kompanie (Heavy Company)	34 361
10. (Fla) Kompanie	32 302
Panzergrenadier-Regiment 128 (formerly *Grenadier-Regiment mot. 1031*), Headquarters	56 057
I./PGR 128) (1st to 4th Companies)	57 323
II./PGR 128) (5th to 8th Companies)	58 189
9. (sIG) Kompanie	56 451
10. (Fla) Kompanie	32 301
Kradschützen-Bataillon 23 (*Panzer-Aufklärungs-Abteilung 23*)	20 150
Panzerjäger-Abteilung 128	45 426
Panzer-Artillerie-Regiment 128, Headquarters	17 831
Headquarters Battery	47 919
I./PAR 128 (1st to 3rd Batteries)	23 535
II./PAR 128 (4th to 6th Batteries)	28 834
III./PAR 128 (7th to 9th Batteries)	32 747
10. (PzBeob) Batterie	14 640
Panzernachrichten-Abteilung 128	43 353
Heeres-Flak-Artillerie-Abteilung 278 (*IV./PAR 128*)	44 211
Panzer-Pionier-Kompanie der 23. Panzer-Division	21 920
Panzer-Pionier-Bataillon 51	21 920

Feld-Ersatz-Bataillon 128	34 820
Divisions-Nachschub-Führer, Headquarters	34 886
1st to 4th Small Motorized Columns	44 795
5th to 6th Large Motorized Columns	46 815
7th to 12th Large Motorized Columns	39 986
1. Werkstatt-Kompanie 128	40 356
2. Werkstatt-Kompanie 128	37 641
2. Werkstatt-Kompanie 128	
1. Sanitäts-Kompanie 128	
2. Sanitäts-Kompanie 128	34 942
1. Krankenkraftwagenzug	42 248
2. Krankenkraftwagenzug	24 313
3. Krankenkraftwagenzug	26 964
Krankenkraftwagen-Kompanie 128	42 248
Divisions-Verpflegungs-Amt 128	41 684
Schlächterei-Kompanie 128	41 376
Bäckerei-Kompanie 128	
Waffen-Werkstatt-Kompanie 128	
Feldpostamt 128	
Feldgendarmerie-Trupp 128	

Primary Sources

Daily logs of the *23. Panzer-Division*, *Panzer-Regiment 201* (*23*), the *I./Panzergrenadier-Regiment 128*, *Panzergrenadier-Regiment 126* and the *III./Panzer-Artillerie-Regiment 128*.

After-action reports of the *23. Panzer-Division* (Operations) concerning individual battles and engagements.

Summary reports by individual elements of the *23. Panzer-Division*.

"Schematische Kriegsgliederung des deutschen Heeres" ("Schematic Overview of the German Army"), from documents available at the German Federal Archives in Koblenz.

Lineage charts of the elements of the *23. Panzer-Division*, from documents available at the German Federal Archives in Koblenz.

Casualty lists maintained by the Deutsche Dienststelle für die Benachrichtigung der nächsten Angehörigen von Gefallenen der ehemaligen deutschen Wehrmacht (WASt).

Personal diaries of former members of the *23. Panzer-Division*.

First-hand accounts and responses to inquiries from former members of the *23. Panzer-Division*.

Secondary Sources

Tippelskirch, Kurt von, General a.D., *Geschichte des Zweiten Weltkriegs (History of the 2nd World War)*. Bonn: Athenäum-Verlag, 1956.

Fretter-Pico, Maximilian, General der Artillerie a.D., *Mißbrauchte Infanterie (Misused Infantry)*. Frankfurt a.M.: Verlag Bernard und Graefe, 1957.

Frießner, Hans, Generaloberst a.D., *Verratenne, Schlachten*. Holsten-Verlag: Hamburg, 1956.

Manstein, Erich von, Generalfeldmarschall a.D., *Verratene Siege (Betrayed Victories)*. Bonn: Athenaeum-Verlag, 1956.

Kissel, Hans, General a.D., *Die Panzerschlachten an der Puszta (The Armored Engagements on the Puszta)*. Neckargemünd: Kurt-Vowinckel-Verlag, 1960.

Heiber, ?, Hitlers Lagebesprechungen 1942-1945 (Hitler's Situation Briefings). Stuttgart: Deutsche Verlagsanstalt, 1962.